ACTA CONVENTUS NEO-LATINI TORONTONENSIS

medieval & renaissance
texts & studies

Volume 86

ACTA CONVENTUS NEO-LATINI TORONTONENSIS

Proceedings of the Seventh International Congress of Neo-Latin Studies

Toronto 8 August to 13 August 1988

EDITED BY

ALEXANDER DALZELL
CHARLES FANTAZZI
RICHARD J. SCHOECK

medieval & renaissance texts & studies
Binghamton, New York
1991

A generous grant from Pegasus Limited for the Advancement
of Neo-Latin Studies has helped meet publication costs of this book.

Library of Congress Cataloging-in-Publication Data

International Congress of Neo-Latin Studies (7th : 1988 : Toronto, Ont.)
Acta Conventus Neo-Latini Torontonensis : proceedings of the seventh International Congress of Neo-Latin Studies : Toronto, 8 August to 13 August, 1988 / edited by Alexander Dalzell, Charles Fantazzi, Richard J. Schoeck.
p. cm. — (Medieval & Renaissance texts & studies ; v. 86)
Includes index.
ISBN 0-86698-098-9
1. Latin literature, Medieval and modern—History and criticism—Congresses. 2. Latin philology, Medieval and modern—Congresses. 3. Learning and scholarship—History—Congresses. 4. Civilization, Medieval—Congresses. 5. Renaissance—Congresses. 6. Classicism—Congresses. 7. Humanists—Congresses. I. Dalzell, Alexander. II. Fantazzi, Charles. III. Schoeck, Richard J. IV. Title. V. Series.
PA8002.I57 1988
470—dc20 91-15986
CIP

This book is made to last.
It is set in Baskerville, smythe-sewn
and printed on acid-free paper
to library specifications

Printed in the United States of America

ACTA CONVENTUS NEO-LATINI TORONTONENSIS

PLENARY PAPERS

SEMINARS

THOMAS MORE AND BIOGRAPHY

Organizer: Elizabeth McCutcheon

Participants:

ERASMUS AND LITERARY CRITICISM

Organizers: Robert Sider and Erika Rummel

Participants:

PLENARY PAPERS

Le concept de l'encyclopaedia dans l'oeuvre de Guillaume Budé

MAURICE LEBEL

Mon propos porte sur le concept de l'*encyclopaedia* dans l'oeuvre de Budé. Voici comment je vais le traiter. Avant d'entrer dans le vif du sujet, je vais essayer de situer les écrits de Guillaume Budé dans leur milieu et dans leur temps, car on se doit de situer tous les textes qu'on étudie, quels qu'ils soient, dans leur contexte social. C'est qu'ils appartiennent à l'histoire, comme nous tous nous lui appartenons. De même qu'on ne peut comprendre n'importe quelle période sans connaître la période antérieure, de même on ne peut imposer aujourd'hui à un monde révolu un concept qu'il ignorait. Après cette entrée en matière en guise d'introduction, j'essaierai de répondre aux quatre questions suivantes, si hasardeuses soient-elles: 1° Où Budé exprime-t-il son concept de l'*encyclopaedia*? 2° Quel en est le contenu? 3° Dans quelle mesure est-il original? 4° Sa pensée a-t-elle évolué sur le sujet? Je terminerai en me demandant ce qu'il en reste.

I

C'est durant le premier humanisme français, sous Louis XII (1492-1515) et François 1er (1515-1547), que Guillaume Budé a publié ses *Opera Omnia* en grec et en latin, soit de 1505 à 1535. Il nous reste aussi de lui trois livres posthumes: *Forensia, De l'Institution du Prince, Apophtegmes,* parus respectivement en 1544, en 1547 et en 1548, mais composés entre 1515 et 1527. *L'Institution du Prince* est l'unique volume que Budé ait jamais écrit en français. On n'a peut-être pas suffisamment remarqué qu'il a débuté dans sa carrière par la traduction du grec en latin et qu'il a continué à se livrer à cet exercice en pleine production intellectuelle. Témoin sa traduction, en 1505, de quatre opuscules moraux et philosophiques de Plutarque, dont le choix seul est très révélateur de son esprit. Ce sont les: *De Tranquillitate et Securitate Animi, De Placitis Philosophorum Naturalibus, De Fortuna Romanorum, De Fortuna vel Virtute Alexandri.* Témoin aussi, en 1526, sa traduction du *De Mundo* d'Aristote, du *De Mundo* de Philon d'Alexandrie, puis d'une lettre de Basile le Grand à Grégoire de Nazianze, *De Vita in Solitudine Agenda.* Est aussi révélateur de son esprit méditatif et philosophique son traité personnel de sagesse en trois livres, paru en 1520, *De Contemptu Rerum Fortuitarum*, où il médite sur la chance et sur les obligations du chrétien face à la bonne et à la mauvaise fortune. Bref, à l'instar des grands humanistes de son temps, tels que Lefèvre d'Etaples, Erasme, Josse Bade, son éditeur, il s'est livré à la traduction de textes grecs en latin, comme il a écrit en latin et en grec. Boccace, à 40 ans, se met à écrire en latin. Au XVIe siècle, on compte jusqu'à 700 poètes latins. De nombreux humanistes feront comme Leonardo Bruni, Erasme et Budé, ils écriront en latin. Mais Michel-Ange, Léonard de Vinci et François 1er ignoraient le latin.

Il va sans dire que la réputation de Budé ne repose pas sur les écrits que je viens de mentionner. Tout au plus révèlent-ils une constante chez lui, qui est celle du philosophe, non pas à la manière de Platon, penseur, mais à la manière d'Isocrate qui aimait se donner le titre de philosophe; Budé fera de même, comme il l'écrit en grec à Germain de Brie le 19 décembre 1520, le mot philosophe étant pris dans l'acception isocratique du terme, c'est-à-dire d'esprit curieux toujours en éveil, avide de culture, d'idées générales et de savoir désintéressé.

Ce qui a fait la gloire de Budé, ce sont plutôt ses trois gros ouvrages savants, pétris d'érudition, que sont: les *Annotationes in Pandectas*, de 1508 et de 1526, complétées par les *Forensia* de 1544, le *De Asse* de 1515 et les *Commentarii linguae graecae* de 1529. A peine eurent-ils paru en librarie qu'il fut salué comme le premier et le plus grand philologue français de son temps. Sa vaste correspondance avec les plus grands humanistes de sa génération, ses *Epistolae latinae et graecae*, qui comprennent entre autres 56 lettres grecques, publiées en 1531, ne manquèrent point d'entretenir et de répandre sa renommée parmi les érudits et les lettrés d'alors aussi bien en France qu'à l'étranger; elles furent même étudiées dans les col-lèges au XVIe siècle. Son *De Philologia* en deux livres, qui parut la même année, en 1532, que son *De studio literarum recte et commode instituendo*, et son *De transitu hellenismi ad christianismum* en trois livres, qu'il publia trois ans plus tard, en 1535, révélèrent tout ensemble l'étendue de son savoir et la richesse de ses idées, la profonde connaissance qu'il avait de son milieu et de son temps, sans oublier le vif désir qui l'animait de le transformer.

Tous ses ouvrages, Guillaume Budé les a traduits ou composés en trois décennies, de 1505 à 1535, durant le période du premier humanisme français. Celle-ci est caractérisée par une effervescence sans précédent dans tous les domaines de l'activitié créatrice, intellectuelle et sociale, par un bouleversement des formes artistiques et des modes de vie, par une transformation de l'enseignement secondaire et supérieur, par des découvertes et des inventions. Le terme de "nouveauté" domine alors partout et exerce une fascination singulière sur les humanistes, les lettrés et le grand public. Ceux-ci éprouvent le sentiment que quelque chose de noveau se produit; ils ont conscience d'être modernes, d'apporter du neuf à leur milieu et à leur temps. L'adjectif nouveau—*novus, novae litterae*, Nouveau Monde, songeons à Jacques Cartier et à Rabelais qui l'emploient aussi souvent que Budé—loin d'impliquer un jugement sur la qualité, signifie seulement une constatation, un état de fait. Mais à force d'être répété il acquiert une valeur en soi, sans savoir au juste pourquoi, dans quelle mesure celle-ci se distingue de ce qui existait déjà. Ce qui compte à tout prix, c'est la nouveauté. Or, qu'y a-t-il de plus éphémère quc la nouveauté? Ainsi ccux qu'on appelle aujourd'hui les nouveaux philosophes ne sont-ils pas déjà dépassés, voire anciens? La nouveauté n'est pas non plus nécessairement synonyme de qualité. Elle ne l'était pas à la Renaissance. Pas davantage ne l'est-elle aujourd'hui.

Cette vision des choses était d'autant plus répandue que l'imprimerie, introduite à Paris, en 1470, en multipliant les livres dans le monde savant aussi bien que dans le peuple, était alors considérée comme la Xe Muse et redoutée des théologiens de la Sorbonne. Les humanistes, eux, conscients qu'ils étaient de faire du nouveau en remontant à l'étude de l' Antiquité, eurent tôt fait de tirer le meilleur parti de la récente invention de Gutenberg. Ils avaient, il est vrai, une connaissance fort imparfaite de l'Antiquité, comme du Moyen Age d'ailleurs; mais ils brûlaient de la mieux connaître et de la faire revivre. Faute de véritable perspective historique, ils n'avaient pas idée qu'elle avait duré environ 1300 ans, soit d'Homère à Boèce et Cassiodore. Ce qui les intéressait le plus, c'étaient l'époque hellénistique, les deux derniers siècles de la république romaine et l'Empire d'Occident; ils connaissaient beaucoups moins bien les siècles de Périclès et de Démosthène. De toute façon, ils tenaient le retour aux sources antiques, non comme une évasion fallacieuse dans le passé ou une sorte de retraite idéale en Arcadie, mais plutôt comme un moyen de progrès en réaction contre les siècles antérieurs, voire comme une véritable révolution intellectuelle, comme une renaissance, une seconde naissance, que Budé rend par ces mots: *restitutio*, *instauratio*, *interpolatio*, *reperititio*, *redivivatio*, *reditio*, *resurrectio*, *reditus*, *rediviva*.

Cette révolution intellectuelle, car c'en fut une, possède plusieurs traits caractéristiques, dont l'un des principaux, au niveau de l'enseignement, est la querelle de l'encyclopédisme. La première du genre éclata à Athènes vers 425 du temps d'Aristophane et sous l'influence des sophistes qui enseignaient l'art de parler et d'argumenter, puis dispensaient à leurs disciples une culture générale s'adressant à l'homme tout entier, c'est-à-dire une formation générale, des virtualités, des qualités de l'esprit par l'étude de l'éloquence, de la philosophie et des mathématiques. Le premier à définir cette culture générale est nul autre qu'Isocrate, mort presque centenaire, qui enseigna la rhétorique, face à l'Académie de Platon, pendant plus de 60 ans. Il suffit, en effet, de lire, par exemple, les *Nuées* et la *Paix* d'Aristophane, puis les discours-essais littéraires d'Isocrate, comme l'*Aréopagitique*, l'*Échange*, le *Panégyrique* et le *Panathénaïque*, pour constater que l'enseignement des gymnases et de l'éphébie subissait alors une crise, soit de 425 à 350 av. J.C. une crise profonde, la première querelle de l'encyclopédisme en Europe. C'est à Athènes, et non à Rome du temps de Sénèque et de Quintilien, comme on l'a trop souvent écrit, qu'elle éclata d'abord et se prolongea même à l'epoque hellénistique. Celle de Rome vint en second lieu. Quant à la troisième, elle dé-buta en Italie au XIVe siècle, se répandit ensuite en France, en Allemagne, en Angleterre, dans les Pays-Bas et dura jusqu'à la fin du XVIe siècle.

Pétrarque, l'initiateur de la révolution intellectuelle et le restaurateur des *studia humanitatis*, s'appelait déjà moderne, bien avant Rimbaud. Comme lui, les humanistes du temps de Louis XII et de François Ier admiraient passionnément le passé d'Athènes et de Rome; beacoup d'entre eux, mais pas tous loin de là, tenaient aussi pour barbares, obscurs, ténébreux, les siècles postérieurs à la conversion de Constantin. Si le terme de Renaissance possède une résonance à la fois esthétique, littéraire, philosophique et scientifique, c'est aux artistes, aux humanistes et aux savants d'Italie, qu'il le doit. Si la Grèce vaincue a conquis ses vainqueurs, l'Italie, à son tour, a réussi à imposer au reste de l'Europe sa vision de l'Antiquité revue, corrigée, modifiée et enrichie de sa vision du Moyen Age. Il existe un synchronisme étonnant entre la résurrection des lettres de l'Antiquité et celle de l'architecture, de la peinture et de la sculpture. Voilà ce qui poussa peut-être Marsile Ficin, néo-platonicien, à proclamer avec chauvinisme et enthousiasme: "C'est indubitablement un âge d'or qui a ramené à la lumière les arts libéraux auparavant presque détruits: grammaire, éloquence, peinture, architecture, sculpture, musique. Et le tout à Florence." Tout de même! Il fait fi un peu trop cavalièrement de l'art roman et de l'art gothique; il parle comme si le Moyen Age avait perdu contact avec l'Antiquité, alors qu'il n'en est rien, comme le prouvent la conservation et la copie de nombreux manuscrits anciens ordonnées par Charlemagne et l'Anglais Alcuin, le retour aux études classiques aux XIe et XIIe siècles, le succès extraordinaire du *Roman de Thèbes*, du *Roman de Troie*, du *Roman d'Enée*, l'étude d'Aristote par Thomas d'Aquin qui, dans sa *Somme théologique*, essaie de concilier l'hellénisme et le christianisme, la grande épopée latine de Pétrarque, *Africa*, laquelle n'aurait jamais vu le jour sans l'emploi par le poète du fameux dictionnaire mythologique, *Liber ymaginum deorum*. En fait, c'est en Italie que, durant le Moyen Age, les souvenirs de l'Antiquité s'étaient le mieux conservés en plus grand nombre et de façon plus vivace qu'ailleurs. En 1518, le célèbre humaniste allemand, Ulrich von Hutten, va jusqu'à s'écrier: "O siècle, ô études, c'est une joie de vivre!" En 1532, Rabelais, avec qui Budé a correspondu en grec, écrit dans son *Pantagruel* cette phrase fort instructive: "Je voy les brigans, les bourreaulx, les aventuriers, les palefreniers de maintenant plus doctes que les docteurs et prescheurs de mon temps."

Pas de rupture brutale et complète entre ce qu'il est convenu d'appeler le Moyen Age et la Renaissance. Le premier humanisme français, avec son renouveau des arts, des lettres et des sciences, ne s'oppose pas plus au Moyen Age qu'il ne se relie d'entrée de jeu à la redécouverte de l'Antiquité païenne gréco-romaine. Il est aussi beaucoup plus qu'un retour exclusif au passé. C'est que, de 1500 à 1550, parallèlement à l'étude enthousiaste des Anciens, se déroulent des faits qui n'ont rien à voir avec l'Antiquité, par exemple, l'imprimerie et la vulgarisation de la culture à laquelle se convertissent nouveaux riches et nobles, la hausse générale du niveau de vie, l'accroissement extraordinaire de la population, le souci de restaurer l'Eglise primitive sous l'influence de Luther et de Calvin, l'aventure maritime et la conquête des océans, les anticipations de Léonard de Vinci, architecte, ingénieur et peintre, une série d'inventions remarquables: l'horloge mécanique, le haut fourneau, la caravelle, la lettre de change, l'assurance maritime, le perfectionnement de l'artillerie et de la comptabilitié, l'emploi des armes à feu, des cryptogrammes, des emblèmes et des symboles. Les gens de la Renaissance ont tellement conscience de la modernité de leur époque qu'ils prétendent même faire mieux que l'Antiquité. Guillaume Budé appartenait, bien sûr, à cette catégorie d'esprits, avides de nouveau et de savoir.

II

Innombrables sont les mots nouveaux dans les *Opera Omnia* de Guillaume Budé. Ce sont des néologismes de bon aloi, composés qu'ils sont, aussi bien en grec qu'en latin, par le premier grand philologue classique de

France. A noter que Budé est beaucoup plus grec que latin d'esprit. Ainsi le vocable *encyclopaedia* est forgé sur le grec ἐγκύκλιος παιδεία, la culture circulaire. Le mot implique la métaphore géométrique des connaissances et frappe ainsi l'imagination. Il ne possède, je me hâte de le dire, aucune connotation avec le terme courant d'encyclopédie en usage depuis l'*Encyclopédie ou le Dictionnaire raisonné des sciences, des arts et des métiers* de Diderot et d'Alembert, pas plus d'ailleurs que le mot *philologia* signifie pour Budé la même chose que pour nous. Loin de là! Voilà pourquoi il vaut mieux employer les mots latins *encyclopedia* et *philologia* pour éviter toute équivoque. A dire vrai, le mot encyclopédie, dans le sens qu'on lui donne aujourd'hui, c'est-à-dire d'ouvrage traitant de toutes les connaissances humaines, remonte au temps de Varron, de Caton l'Ancien et de Pline l'Ancien; il etait même d'usage courant au VIIe siècle de notre ère, puisque deux Espagnols, Isidore de Séville (560–636) et Ildephonse (607–669), archevêque de Tolède, l'emploient alors dans l'acception moderne du terme. Le Moyen Age compte un nombre considérable d'encyclopédies sous les noms de *Specula*, de *Tableaux*, de *Trésors*, de *Summae*. Ainsi, pour me limiter à quelques noms, Suidas (Xe siècle), Vincent de Beauvais (XIIe), Thomas d'Aquin (XIIIe) et Georges Valla (XVe) sont bien connus pour leurs ouvrages respectifs où ils traitent soit de toutes les connaissances dans un ordre alphabétique ou méthodique, soit de toutes les connaissances d'une science donnée.

Mais Guillaume Budé, bien qu'il ne soit ni un professeur ni un théoricien de l'education–il est avant tout un chercheur, un érudit, un philologue, un savant, un moraliste, un philosophe–s'en sert, lui, presque toujours dans l'acception éducative, entendant par là la formation générale des qualités de l'esprit des jeunes de niveau secondaire par l'étude d'un cycle de connaissances. Tel est le sens que lui donnaient les Anciens tels que: Polybe, Strabon, Denys d'Halicarnasse, Plutarque, Lucien, Athénée, Grégoire de Nazianze (ἐγκύκλιος παίδευσις), sans parler des Latins tels que Cicéron, Vitruve, Quintilien, Appien, Tite-Live, Pline l'Ancien, Aulu-Gelle, Eutrope, Orose et Cassiodore.

L'annaliste latin Fabius Pictor (L.1.) qui nous a laissé 43 fragments—Tite-Live le qualifie de *longe antiquissimus scriptor* (2.40.10), contemporain de la bataille de Trasimène–est probablement le premier à avoir employé le mot latin *encyclopaedia*, quand il écrit: "Ut efficiatur orbis ille doctrinae quem Graeci encyclopaediam vocant," comme Budé est probablement le premier à l'avoir employé en France en 1508 dans ses *Annotations aux Pandectes*. Vitruve écrit ce qui suit dans la Préface et le livre 1 (ch. 1) de son traité *De Architectura*: "Encyclios enim disciplina, ut corpus unum, ex his membris composita. Quum autem animadverterint omnes disciplinae inter se conjunctionem rerum et communicationem habere, fieri posse facile credent.... Encyclios doctrinarum omnium disciplina." Pline l'Ancien parle de l'*encyclia disciplina* dans son *Histoire naturelle* (10.124), tandis que Quintilien écrit dans son *Institution Oratoire* (L.1, ch. 10): "Disciplinarum series ostendens omnium artium inter se connexionem.... Orbis ille doctrinae quem Graeci ἐγκυκλοαπαιδείαν vocant." Sous la plume de Denys d'Halicarnasse, de Polybe et de Plutarque, c'est ἐγκύκλιος παιδεία que l'on relève. Les mots *encyclopaedia* ἐγκύκλιος παιδεία, ἐγκυκλοπαιδεία, figurent au moins une trentaine de fois dans les oeuvres de Budé depuis ses *Annotations aux Pandectes* (1508), jusqu'au *De Transitu hellenismi ad christianismum* (1535); il va même jusqu'à les définir et à les expliquer de nouveau, mais en français, cette fois, dans son ouvrage posthume, *L'Institution du Prince* (1547). Pour Budé, comme pour Rabelais et Du Bellay, le mot était plus grec que français.

Quoi qu'il en soit, ce constat révèle la permanence de la pensée de Budé. Il est question de l'*encyclopaedia* aussi bien dans son *De Asse*, dans ses *Commentaires de la langue grecque*, dans sa Correspondance grecque et latine, dans ses deux plaidoyers *pro domo* que sont le *De Philologia* et le *De studio literarum recte*, parus la même année, en 1532, puis le *De transitu* en 1535. Ce n'est donc pas seulement dans ses trois derniers ouvrages, publiés à son déclin en 1532 et en 1535, que figure son concept de l'*encyclopaedia*; il fait jour, pour ainsi dire, un peu partout dans l'ensemble de son oeuvre, le *terminus a quo* étant les *Annotationes ad Pandectes* (1508) et le *terminus ad quem*, *L'Institution du Prince* (1547).

La façon dont il se sert du mot *encyclopaedia* est aussi révélatrice que sa constance à s'en servir. En effet, il parle d'*encyclopaedia* à brûle-pourpoint, au moment où l'on y pense le moins, car Budé, loin d'être un modèle de composition logique et ordonnée, est plutôt passé maître dans l'art d'introduire des digressions ou des réflexions marginales. Par exemple, seulement dans le second livre du *De Philologia*—je viens de traduire les deux livres du *De Philologia*, ma traduction paraîtra en librairie l'an prochain—où il consacre environ 20 pages sur 35 à un *Traité de la vénerie*, traduit du latin en français par le grand érudit Louis Le Roy dit Regius, en 1547, mais publié pour la première fois en 1861, soit plus de trois siècles plus tard, dans le second livre du *De Philologia*, il est question cinq fois d'*encyclopaedia* même à l'intérieur de ce dit *Traité*. Tantôt il emploie le mot même, tantôt il a recours à des périphrases, à des synonymes, à des circonlocutions, à des définitions, à des commentaires, à des explications, ce qui revient au même pour lui, son esprit bouillonnant devant tourner en rond dans tous les azimuts. Cette façon de procéder est pour le moins surprenante, pour ne pas dire déroutante, de la part d'un grand érudit, qui était pourtant nourri des auteurs classiques grecs et latins, férus de composition et familiers avec l'art du paragraphe. On ne trouve donc pas chez lui d'exposé suivi sur le sujet; ce qui ne simplifie pas pour autant le travail du chercheur, désireux de cerner le concept de l'*encyclopaedia* chez Budé. Fait singulier, ni Erasme ni Rabelais n'emploient le mot *encyclopaedia*, dans le même sens que Budé; mais Josse Bade, le célèbre éditeur humaniste des oeuvres de Guillaume Budé qui a publié tant de traités d'éducation, ne lui donne pas d'autre signification que celle de Budé.

III

Comment Budé conçoit-il l'*encyclopaedia*? Son concept, il le doit à l'Antiquité, au Moyen Age et au début de la Renaissance dont il est nourri. Isocrate, Polybe et Denys d'Halicarnasse tiennent la grammaire, la rhétorique, la philosophie, les sciences et les mathématiques pour les éléments constitutifs de l'ἐγκύκλιος παιδεία ou pour le cycle des connaissances indispensables à la formation générale des virtualités, des qualités de l'esprit des jeunes de 12 à 19 ans, du gymnase à l'éphébie inclusivement; ces connaissances servent de base à des études spécialisées. Varron ajoute aux arts libéraux: l'architecture, l'astrologie, la musique et la médecine. Pline l'Ancien, lui, insiste sur la médecine dérivée du règne végétal, sur l'anthropologie, la botanique, la cosmographie et la géographie, la minéralogie et la zoologie, voire l'art figuratif. Quant aux grammairiens grecs du Moyen Age, Jena Zonar (XIe) et Jean Tzetzès (XIIe), ils s'en tiennent au *trivium* et au *quadrivium*, c'est-à-dire, d'une part, à la grammaire, à la rhétorique et à la dialectique, d'autre part, à l'arithmétique, à la musique, à la géométrie et à l'astronomie, suivant en cela Martianus Capella qui, dans ses *Noces de Mercure et de la Philologie*, traite de ces sept arts libéraux. A noter que le *quadrivium* est fondé sur les mathématiques qui en sont comme le dénominateur commun. Budé a personnellement annoté son exemplaire du texte de Capella, comme je l'ai moi-même constaté, à Paris, á la Bibliothèque Nationale (Réserve Z 3), en le lisant: il est criblé de notes manuscrites de Guillaume Budé. Boèce adopte le plan de l'ouvrage allégorique de Capella, lequel, soit dit en passant, n'a pas encore été traduit en français, dans sa *Consolatio Philosophiae*, qui devint comme le bréviaire des enseignants au Moyen Age. Fait digne de remarque, chez tous ces auteurs anciens et médiévaux, il n'est nullement question de l'histoire. Or, Budé y ajoute l'histoire, et ce n'est pas sa moindre contribution.

Dans son concept de l'*encyclopaedia*, entrent, bien sûr, les arts libéraux, les lettres grecques et latines, la philologie ou l'étude des textes anciens, surtout des historiens, des poètes et des orateurs. Par rhétorique il entend les belles lettres, les bonnes lettres, qu'il appelle aussi les humanités. Dans le même livre 2 de *De Philologia*, il parle de la recherche et des chercheurs, comme il parle des disciplines libérales, comme il y est question de l'éloquence juridique, politique, épidictique et militaire. Non content de faire l'éloge des inventions récentes de son époque, qui dépassent de beaucoup celles de l'Antiquité, il y consacre dix pages à l'histoire, dont la connaissance, selon lui, permet de conjecturer l'avenir d'après le passé.

Budé était trop nourri des historiens grecs et latins qu'il lisait *aperto liberto*, et qu'il cite même souvent, il était trop familier avec Cicéron, qui attachait une grande importance à l'histoire dans la formation des orateurs, bien plus, il était trop critique de son milieu, de son temps, des siècles antérieurs, comme de l'antiquité gréco-romaine, pour ne pas faire entrer l'histoire dans son concept de l'*encyclopaedia*, dans son cycle de conaissances indispensables aux jeunes, avides de servir leur pays par la parole et par la plume. Il va même jusqu'à regretter amèrement, au livre 2 du *De Philologia*, que les historiens français n'aient pu réussir jusqu'ici à rivaliser avec les meilleurs de la Grèce et de Rome pour écrire avec art, en un style agréable et persuasif, l'histoire de France, le passé glorieux des Gaulois au Moyen Age. Mais il nourrit le ferme espoir que, grâce à l'enseignement efficace de la philologie, de l'étude des historiens et des orateurs de l'Antiquité païenne, que l'on verra un jour en France des historiens capables d'écrire sur leur pays des ouvrages comparables à ceux d'Hérodote et de Thucydide, de Xénophon et de Polybe, de Strabon, de Flavius Josèphe et de Plutarque, qu'il nomme d'ailleurs en toutes lettres, sans parler des historiens latins. Il s'en prend tout particulièrement à Tite-Live qui ne cache pas sa haine injuste à l'endroit des Gaulois, tandis que Flavius Josèphe rétablit la vérité en affirmant que partout les Gaulois se montrent courageux et invincibles; ce qui ne déplaît ni à Budé, ni à François 1er qui aiment beaucoup l'histoire, comme on peut le lire au livre 2 du *De Philologia*.

Outre l'histoire, Budé ajoute la mythologie gréco-romaine au concept traditionnel de l'*encyclopaedia*. Il l'aime passionnément, autant, sinon plus que Platon lui-même, son maître, qu'il cite souvent. En effet, à l'instar de Platon, il emploie sans cesse, partout dans son oeuvre, les mythes anciens tantôt pour illustrer sa pensée, tantôt pour agrémenter son style, ici pour distraire ou reposer le lecteur d'un exposé trop abstrait ou didactique, là pour le pur plaisir de plaire. Son esprit est nourri des légendes et des mythes de l'Antiquité classique. Il est même familier avec les récits fabuleux les plus rares, les moins bien connus du grand public cultivé. S'il juge bon de les rappeler, il ne les confond point, cependant, avec l'histoire, laquelle s'appuie sur des faits authentiques, sur des textes, des documents, et non sur l'imagination fantaisiste des poètes et du peuple, comme c'est le cas pour les mythes, qui ont connu cinq phases de développement d'Homère à Lucien, des premiers aux derniers mythographes païens. Chrétien convaincu, Budé ne manque pas, cela va sans dire, de faire une critique sévère des mythes, de s'inscrire en faux et de protester contre tout ce qu'ils renferment d'immoral. Car il est parfaitement conscient que la Renaissance en cours peut conduire et a même en fait déjà conduit plus d'un esprit de son temps à un certain néo-paganisme, peut-être plus apparent que réel; il met donc le lecteur en garde contre tout aveuglement à cet égard; il tenait les mythes païens pour révolus, dépassés, depuis l'avènement du christianisme. Il s'en prend tout particulièrement aux poètes néo-latins et aux Italiens auxquels il reproche de se complaire dans les mythes païens et de corrompre ainsi l'esprit de leurs lecteurs. Cela dit, les mythes, employés à bon escient, peuvent stimuler les orateurs et les poètes en herbe sur les bancs du collège et de l'université, comme ils peuvent les inspirer plus tard dans la vie; musiciens, peintres et sculpteurs peuvent aussi y avoir recours, ce qu'ils ne manquaient pas de faire d'ailleurs, même du temps de Budé. En effet, l'emploi de la mythologie s'accentuera même avec le progrès de son siècle, car elle était alors considérée comme un trésor d'images, d'allégories, de fables, de symboles, d'expériences, de visions.

Avec l'introduction par Budé de l'histoire et de la mythologie dans l'*encyclopaedia*, on est loin du *trivium* et du *quadrivium* qui avaient régné en maîtres jusque-là. Budé apporte du nouveau: il est original. Il fait éclater la sclérose des traditions scolastiques; du même coup, il secoue la pesanteur des structures de l'enseignement traditionnel. Il a beau user encore d'un langage qui lui vient du passé, en grande partie du moins, il crée un nombre considérable de néologismes pour exprimer adéquatement sa pensée; il a le sens du moderne, de l'histoire vécue; il prend conscience de ce qui se passe autour de lui, parce qu'il connaît le passé qui est, comme la vie, mouvement, évolution, création, transformation. Il sait que son siècle, bien qu'il critique assez sévèrement, possède plus de connaissances et de science que les siècles antérieurs, révèle une plus grande maîtrise de la nature, exprime un plus vif amour du corps, du paysage et du cosmos, nourrit même un culte plus ardent pour l'homme et la famille.

Il sait aussi que son siècle, qui parle tant de l'homme nouveau, tient l'homme pour la merveille des merveilles, comme l'avaient fait antérieurement la Genèse et l'Evangile, l'Arabie et la Perse, l'Egypte et la Grèce ancienne, Philon d'Alexandrie et Jean Pic de la Mirandole pour qui l'homme est: "Magnum miraculum et admirandum." Au XVe siècle même, Marsile Ficin était allé jusqu'à s'écrier dans sa *Theologia platonica*: "L'homme pourvoit à la totalité des êtres vivants et non vivants; vraiment c'est un Dieu." *Est quidem Deus*. Terme ambigu, il est vrai, mais prudent. Car Marsile Ficin ne sacralise pas l'homme. Mais les Anciens, qui croyaient que l'homme peut arriver par lui-même à la sagesse, étaient portés à faire un dieu de l'homme. Voilà pourquoi Budé déteste la mythologie de l'Antiquité païenne et s'en prend aux poètes néo-latins, comme à la Renaissance italienne, de la véhiculer sans discernement, sans esprit critique; pour lui, elle est dépassée, révolue, depuis la Révélation et l'avènement du christianisme. Sans rechercher le contenu métaphysique des mythes, il y voit cependant un certain contenu religieux; tout en reconnaissant que les mythes ne nous renseignent guère sur l'origine de l'homme et sa destinée, sur le cosmos et son ordre, il aime toutefois les grands mythes païens qu'il trouve fondamentaux parce qu'ils révèlent un peu partout les modes permanents d'opération de l'esprit humain. De ces mythes, il se sert abondamment comme d'outils pour appuyer sa réflexion théologique et pour illustrer sa pensée sur la subordination de la culture profane au christianisme. Et cela notamment dans son dernier ouvrage, le *De Transitu hellenismi ad christianismum* (1535). En bref, chez lui, le christianisme et les grands mythes païens fondamentaux font bon ménage dans le *De Transitu*.

Outre l'histoire et la mythologie des grands mythes, Budé ajoute l'éloquence et la philosophie; pour lui, les deux sont inséparables l'une de l'autre, la philosophie étant la mère, la nourrice de l'éloquence, avec la connaissance, bien sûr, des bonnes lettres grecques et latines, les deux ornières du savoir. Rabelais complète ce point de vue en y ajoutant avec raison les sciences de la nature. Il ne se contente pas de faire l'éloge de l'éloquence, qui a tiré son art d'Esculape et dont le pouvoir infini est symbolisé par Mercure allant du ciel aux enfers; il cite même Hésiode qui tient l'éloquence pour la maîtresse des enfers et du ciel. Il est convaincu, comme Isocrate et Cicéron, qu'il n'existe point de véritable savoir sans l'art de la parole et de l'écriture, les deux moyens par excellence de communication. C'est par l'étude, la connaissance et l'effet des bonnes lettres gréco-latines et de la philosophie que l'éloquence doit être adéquate, efficace et utile. Il en profite pour pester, en passant, contre l'asservissement de l'éloquence en France. Il parle abondamment de ce sujet dans son *De Philologia*, où il distingue cinq types d'éloquence: juridique, militaire, pédagogique, poétique et religieuse.

Je dis bien l'éloquence poétique. Comme la fusion entre la rhétorique et la poésie s'est produite au Moyen Age, il n'est pas du tout surprenant de voir Budé attacher autant d'importance à la poésie comme on le voit dans le *De Studio literarum*, le *De Philologia*, et le *De Transitu hellenismi*. D'ailleurs, il aimait trop Homère et Hésiode, les tragiques grecs et Platon, Virgile et Horace pour ne pas aimer la poésie. Et puis lui-même pense un peu comme un poète par images, par métaphores, par comparaisons, par allégories, par allusions, par symboles. Bien plus, sous le seul règne de Francois 1er, on voit plus de poètes en France qu'il n'y en avait jamais eu depuis la naissance de la poésie en ce pays. En bref, pour Budé, la maîtrise de l'éloquence, de la prose en général, est inséparable de l'étude des bonnes lettres; elle reste le but premier des hommes avides de culture générale. Elle fait partie du cycle des disciplines libérales, de l'*encyclopaedia*, de l'ordre de la culture, du *cursus studiorum*. C'est qu'elle circonscrit et limite la zone consacrée à l'*encyclopaedia*, c'est qu'elle tend de tous les points du cercle au centre lui-même. Elle doit traiter de sujets dignes d'admiration et se soumettre à l'art fort important du commentaire et de la critique.

Budé n'a que faire de la dialectique et de la rhétorique du *trivium*, qui s'occupent uniquement des mécaniques et des techniques de l'argumentation et de l'expression. Ce qui doit nourrir l'éloquence, c'est l'histoire ou la connaissance du passé; c'est aussi la connaissance du présent, l'observation du milieu et des moeurs. L'orateur doit connaître son temps. Budé est un fin observateur moraliste beaucoup plus qu'un philosophe politique et social. Il fait penser plutôt à Isocrate et à Plutarque qu'à Platon et à Aristote, véritables penseurs et théoriciens. Comme Isocrate et Plutarque, il observe et censure souvent l'état de la société, les lois et les institutions de son temps. Comme eux, il possède des idées générales, morales et politiques, il se livre à des réflexions et à des commentaires de son cru; il ne cesse de dire ce qu'il pense dans ses oeuvres, depuis les *Annotations aux Pandectes* jusqu'au *De Transitu hellenismi* inclusivement. Il se pose sans cesse des questions sur lui-même, comme sur l'avenir de la première civilisation du livre, du livre de poche, c'est-à-dire du livre de masse, sur la société, le christianisme, le salut du chrétien, sur la fin de la culture profane dans la vie, sur les rapports entre le profane et le sacré, sur le monde, car il n'a pas traduit en vain le *De Mundo* d'Aristote et le *De Mundo* de Philon le juif, comme il n'a pas traduit en vain quatre essais moraux et philosophiques de Plutarque. Fort versé en architecture qu'il a étudiée sous Giacondo, en mathématiques, voire en la mystique des nombres, il revient souvent sur ces sujets. Quant à la philosophie antique, il est loin de l'ignorer; il en a fait le tour depuis Homère et les pré-socratiques jusqu'à Epicure et Lucrèce; mais il déteste l'athéisme oule polythéisme, le matérialisme ou le scepticisme qu'elle enseigne. En revanche, il aime Platon pour qui la philosophie est une méditation de la mort, Aristote pour qui la philosophie est la science qui contemple la vérité, Cicéron pour qui la philosophie est l'art de vivre. Ces trois penseurs et leurs oeuvres forment comme le piédestal de sa conception de la philosophie. L'étude de cette philosophie antique et l'étude des lettres gréco-latines sont pour Budé des exercices propédeutiques ou préparatoires à l'étude de la philosophie théologique, de la *philotheoria*, de la *theurgia*, de la philosophie sacro-sainte qui seule mérite le nom de contemplation. Tous ces thèmes, Budé les aborde dans le *De Asse*, le *De contemptu rerum*, le *De Studio literarum*, le *De Philologia*, le *De Transitu hellenismi*.

La philosophie sacro-sainte, fondée sur l'étude de la Bible et des commentaires des Pères de l'Eglise grecque et latine, est, dans l'esprit de Budé, le *terminus ad quem* de l'*encyclopaedia*. En d'autres termes, la culture générale prépare à la philosophie théologique dont elle est la couronnement; en subordonnant l'*encyclopaedia* à cette dernière, Budé se révèle un produit authentique du Moyen Age chrétien qui subordonnait toute connaissance à la science suprême, la théologie; il a le sens chrétien de l'histoire. Il a beau être fier d'appartenir à la Renaissance et d'y travailler à sa façon, il reste marqué par le Moyen Age chrétien. A l'instar de la plupart des humanistes et des lettrés des années 1500–1540, il est nourri à la fois de l'Antiquité païenne et de l'Antiquité chrétienne, ce qui ne l'empêche pas de connaître aussi des écrivains nationaux tels que Rabelais, Marguerite de Navarre et Clément Marot. Les Pères de l'Eglise grecque et latine, les grandes esprits du Moyen Age, comme saint Bonaventure, saint Bruno, saint Bernard et saint Thomas d'Aquin, constituent avec leurs oeuvres et leurs commentaires de la Bible une part fort importante de la culture de la Renaissance. Ils sont des maîtres, non pas à penser, mais à faire penser, ce qui vaut beaucoup mieux.

On ne doit pas oublier non plus que les lettrés de la Renaissance s'intéressaient beaucoup plus que nous aux problèmes religieux. C'est que la Renaissance est aussi un retour à l'Antiquité chrétienne, aux sources primitives du christianisme. Il n'existait pas alors, comme aujourd'hui, de dichotomie entre la culture laïque ou profane et la culture religieuse. Parallèlement à la Renaissance d'ordre culturel se développe la Renaissance d'ordre religieux. Budé est parfaitement au courant des deux renouveaux, d'une part, des arts, des lettres et des sciences de l'Antiquité païenne, d'autre part, de la pensée et de la vie de l'Antiquité chrétienne. Double retour à deux sources distinctes, l'une païenne, l'autre chrétienne.

La culture nouvelle ou l'éducation nouvelle qui résulte de cette vision de la réalité cherche à abolir la notion de temps, de discontinuité ou de rupture entre le passé païen et le passé chrétien, entre l'Antiquité, le Moyen Age et la Renaissance. La clef de cette culture est l'amour, la passion du texte, de l'écrit, la *philologia*; c'est la lecture, la traduction, l'exégèse des mots, des textes; c'est la science des textes. Au fond, c'est une pratique, et une pratique sans trop de discernement, sans choix, car on étudie alors aussi bien Claudien, Apulée et Aulu-Gelle que Virgile, Ovide et Horace. Les bonnes lettres embrassent tous les textes grecs et latins; pas de choix comme aujourd'hui dans les Collèges et les Facultés; l'avidité des humanistes ne conaissait point de bornes, et leur goût était éclectique. L'important pour eux est de lire, de traduire, d'analyser et d'assimiler des textes. Les textes deviennent objets de science, même les textes bibliques et les écrits théologiques. Tout en reconnaissant la théologie comme la science suprême, ils la voient alors de façon différente, c'est-à-dire pas du tout comme au Moyen Age; pleins de mépris pour la scolastique abstraite et sclérosée, ils insistent de préférence sur l'étude de la Bible et de la patristique grecque et latine. La nouvelle culture, fondée sur l'étude des textes, possède désormais deux pôles: le profane et le sacré. Elle poursuit deux objectifs: former l'*homo doctissimus* et *humanissimus*, l'*homo christianus* et *philosophico-theologus*. Elle est divisée, partagée, sceptique quant à sa finalité. D'autant plus que les philologues étaient souvent traités par leurs adversaires d'hérétiques ou d'incroyants, et que l'incroyance faisait déjà ses ravages dans la société. De là l'évolution du concept d'*encyclopaedia* chez Budé.

IV

En 30 ans, de 1505 à 1535, son attitude évolue considérablement à l'égard de l'Antiquité païenne et de l'*encyclopaedia*. A mesure qu'il avance dans sa carrière et que celle-ci approche de son déclin, il passe de la culture profane à la culture religieuse. Il s'intéresse d'abord profondément aux études anciennes, notamment à l'histoire, à la littérature et à la philosophie, comme le prouvent sa traduction de quatre essais philosophiques de Plutarque (1505) et sa traduction du *De Mundo* d'Aristote et du *De Mundo* de Philon le Juif (1526), puis la publication de ses trois grands ouvrages philologiques, les *Annotations aux Pandectes* (1508), le *De Asse* (1515) et les *Commentarii linguae graecae* (1529), qui portent sur le monde antique et sa société. De 1520 à 1535, il publie quatre ouvrages strictement personnels: le *De contemptu rerum fortuitarum* (1520), le *De Philologia* (1532), le *De Studio literarum* (1532) et le *De Transitu hellenismi ad christianismum* (1535), où il est toujours question, bien sûr, de mythologie et de *philologia*, mais davantage de philosophie et de philosophie sacro-sainte, de religion, des saintes Ecritures et des Pères de l'Eglise. La même observation s'applique à ses *Epistolae latinae et graecae* (1531).

Les *Commentarii linguae graecae* sont un immense inventaire de la langue grecque. Ils comprennent, outre 7000 articles grecs, d'innombrables remarques sur la langue latine; ils fourmillent aussi de notes de toutes sortes, quelque peu désordonnées, rédigées au fil de la plume, semble-t-il, l'oeil contre la montre; on a le sentiment que l'auteur brûle de vider son carquois. Les *Annotations aux Pandectes* traitent en profondeur du droit romain, du fait juridique et de la restauration du *Digeste*. Le *De Asse*, l'ouvrage le plus fini et le plus célèbre de Budé, est un traité méticuleux et nouveau d'économie comparée, de la conversion des unités de poids, de mesures et de monnaies des Grecs et des Romains, des Egyptiens et des Hébreux. Ces deux grands ouvrages philologiques se complètent l'un l'autre par la description de différents aspects de la société antique, comme ils se ressemblent par leurs préfaces, leurs débuts, la longueur et l'importance de leurs digressions. Chacune d'elles, en effet, comprend environ une dizaine de pages, l'une portant, par exemple, sur Homère ou le théâtre ou la rhétorique, l'autre sur les jeux ou le luxe ou les institutions juridiques, celle-ci sur la corruption des moeurs à la afin du règne de Louis XI, celle-là sur le rapport des lettres profanes et du christianisme. Digressions d'ordre culturel, historique, moral et politique.

Mais le *De Asse* diffère énormément des *Annotations aux Pandectes* par la conclusion aussi inattendue que disproportionnée par rapport à l'ensemble du traité. Elle révèle déjà un esprit nouveau chez Budé. Apparemment, c'est un hors d'oeuvre de 100 pages. Toutefois, à y regarder de plus près, il n'est pas sans relation avec le sujet. C'est que Budé emploie ici le mot *as* romain de façon métaphorique ou symbolique, comme il fait d'ailleurs de la mythologie classique; les richesses matérielles que l'*as* représente démontrent la vanité des choses périssables du monde au prix des valeurs spirituelles, de la sagesse divine. Au fond, dans cet épilogue, Budé résume en chrétien la pensée maîtresse exprimée par Plutarque dans ses quatre essais moraux et philosophiques que Budé avait traduits et publiés en 1505: le mépris des richesses matérielles et des choses fortuites, la sérénité en face de la mort, la méfiance des sens, la domination sur les passions, l'aspiration à l'immortalité de la partie spirituelle de notre être, l'utilité morale des lettres profanes. Budé élargit donc son concept de l'*encyclopaedia* à la fin du *De Asse*. Pour lui, l'*encyclopaedia* est double, laïque et profane, morale et religieuse. Sans rompre avec la *philologia* qu'il appelle, métaphoriquement, tantôt sa fiancée, tantôt sa maîtresse, il commence alors à se tourner vers la culture morale et religieuse.

Il fait un pas de plus, en 1520, dans son essai fort personnel, le *De contemptu rerum fortuitarum*, où les digressions ne font point défaut, comme à l'accoutumée. Il y est question, bien sûr, de *Philologia*, de *mea Philologia* qu'il répète, des Grecs et des Romains mais beaucoup plus des Grecs, d'Homère à Marc-Antoine et Cléopâtre, tous les deux pétris de culture grecque. Il parle aussi des *artes liberales*, de l'*encyclopaedia*, voire de *philosophia* et de *theologia*. Ce livre se lit comme une longue méditation sur la chance, sur le hasard, sur les obligations du chrétien qui pense en face de la bonne et de la mauvaise fortune, sur le bonheur et le malheur qui sont le lot de la condition humaine. Cet essai, strictement personnel, est divisé en trois livres. Pessimiste et sombre, il est l'oeuvre d'un chrétien puritain, révolté contre les adoucissements qu'on donnait alors à l'Evangile; on dirait, à le lire, que Budé est un pré-réformiste. Il écrit entre autres:

> Je ne regrette pas d'avoir opté pour la *philologia*, princesse et source de la pensée et de la philosophie, ce qui me vaudra la reconnaissance de la postérité et une satisfaction personnelle, du moins jusqu'à ma retraite....Quant à nous, nous sommes mis à l'oeuvre avec ardeur et si, avec la grâce de Dieu, nous le menons à bien, rien ne sera plus magnifique que cette *Encyclopaedia*, qui ne pourra ni rire de nous ni nous mépriser....

Budé termine ainsi son *De Contemptu*: "Cet ouvrage a été écrit à la lumière des enseignements sacrés de Salomon plutôt que sous l'inspiration de Zénon, de Chrysippe ou de quelque autre philosophe de ce genre."

Budé publie coup sur coup, en 1532, deux autres ouvrages encore plus personnels que son *De contemptu rerum fortuitarum*, en ce sens qu'ils sont deux plaidoyers *pro domo*, soit son *De studio literarum* et son *De Philologia*. Dans ces deux livres il insiste tout particulièrement sur la subordination de l'*encyclopaedia* dont le grec et le latin sont les deux clefs principales, à la recherche de la sagesse divine et aux études sacro-saintes des Ecritures. Il y cite en exemple Grégoire de Nazianze qui renonça aux lettres profanes pour s'adonner à l'Ecriture Sainte. Il fait ressortir les beautés de l'*Ancien* et du *Nouveau Testament*, exhorte les lecteurs à en faire la lecture et à se familiariser avec les commentaires des Pères. Il s'élève contre la philosophie antique, dangereuse, impuissante, mensongère, païenne, lui préférant de beaucoup la philosophie authentique se dégageant de la Bible, qui est la parole de Dieu et la parole sur Dieu. Il montre par là les limites des lettres anciennes, si utiles soient-elles pour la formation des esprits: elles n'enseignent ni la vraie connaissance de soi, ni l'humilité, ni la vraie sagesse.

Dans le *De studio literarum*, Budé prend la défense de la tête bien faite plutôt que bien remplie, multiplie ses souvenirs personnels sur les difficultés que rencontre l'autodidacte et souligne l'unité foncière des études littéraires qui ont pour fondement l'exercice du jugement critique à partir de l'histoire et de la philosophie. Bien plus, il y prend la défense de la théologie qu'il tient pour la science suprême, la reine des sciences; par cette attitude, il révèle son appartenance au Moyen Age. Il en veut, cependant, à la vieille théologie qui sent, écrit-il, "le rance, le ranci." Il n'empêche qu'il se porte à la défense de la théologie authentique, étant donné qu'elle risquait de demeurer à l'écart du renouveau des études philologiques. D'autant plus que les théologiens eux-mêmes étaient pétris d'animosité contre les philologues; ces derniers considéraient la théologie comme une science nouvelle à l'étude de laquelle ils appliquaient l'analyse serrée des texts, l'exégèse, la méthode philologique, sans oublier l'étude des commentaires des Pères de l'Eglise et la méditation profonde des Saintes Ecritures.

Les théologiens se méfiaient aussi, non sans raison, de la rhétorique creuse et vide, cultivée pour elle-même en vase clos. Désireux de les désarmer, Budé part alors en guerre contre tous ceux qui imitent aveuglément Cicéron; il les stigmatise, même sans merci. Aussi son *De studio literarum* se lit-il comme un éloquent manifeste de modernisme et d'opposition aux cicéroniens de tout acabit. Il va même jusqu'à avouer ce qui suit; "Il n'est certes pas facile à tout le monde de passer (d'émigrer, *migrare*, verbe favori de Budé) des lettres profanes des Grecs aux Saintes Ecritures des Hébreux, après s'être abondamment et longuement versé dans les lettres profanes, d'opérer un brusque passage à la philosophie plus sainte, dont le but unique est la contemplation des vérités divines." Budé affirme aussi qu'on peut apprendre des Anciens la composition, la correction et l'élégance de style, puis s'éloigner d'eux pour exprimer la pensée moderne, qui est la pensée chrétienne. Puis il se pose la question suivante: "Pourquoi le grec ou le latin serait-il, dans le domaine du sacré, des rites, des cérémonies du culte, incapable de cette renaissance? Quant à moi, j'estime qu'il faut revêtir l'éloquence d'un manteau nouveau dont le tissu s'accorde à la métamorphose des lois, des institutions civiles et des rites religieux." Dans le *De studio literarum*, Budé invite le chrétien à passer de l'éloquence latine aux études théologiques, à faire servir la culture ancienne à l'interprétation de la Bible, à méditer les mystères du christianisme, à conduire peu à peu son esprit à la contemplation divine. En bref, la culture ancienne profane est pour lui comme une préparation ou une propédeutique à l'étude des textes de la Bible et de ses commentateurs. Par contraste, Martianus Capella présentait, au Ve siècle de notre ère, les sept arts libéraux comme les esclaves oú les servantes de Mercure et de la *Philologia*, comme si le christianisme n'était jamais venu sur terre.

Dans le *De Philologia*, qui est aussi un témoignage personnel, voire un véritable plaidoyer *pro domo*, où Budé se complaît un peu trop dans les digressions–le lecteur peut en relever quatre dans le premier livre, au moins cinq dans le second–l'auteur avoue sentir l'aiguillon de la *philologia* le pénétrer de plus en plus. Il reconnaît aussi qu'elle a encore mauvaise presse, au moment où il écrit, en 1532, accusé qu'elle est par les théologiens de la Sorbonne de saper le christianisme établi depuis des siècles et de répandre des erreurs dans le pays. Budé y répond à toutes les attaques dont elle est l'objet; son amour pour elle est toujours indéfectible; elle l'enserre même encore comme du gui ou du lierre. Ici, comme dans le *De Studio literarum*, son concept de l'*encyclopaedia*, de la culture des lettres profanes, n'est jamais dissocié de la conscience et de l'expérience. Il y parle abondamment du grec et du latin, de l'histoire et de la philosophie, de la sacro-sainte philosophie qui fait partie de l'*encyclopaedia* au même titre que la théologie nouvelle, l'exégèse, la méthode philologique. Il tient pour peu sages et superficiels tout ensemble ceux qui cultivent l'éloquence d'apparat creuse et vide et ceux qui refusent d'embrasser la sacro-sainte philosophie.

En 1532, dans son *De Studio literarum* et son *De Philologia*, Budé révèle un changement net d'attitude à l'endroit de la culture profane. Il y est toujours divisé et partagé; il n'a pas encore franchi le Rubicon, c'est-à-dire effectué le passage de l'hellénisme ou du paganisme au christianisme proprement dit. Il fera le bond final de 1500 ans dans son *De Transitu hellenismi ad christianismum* en 1535, soit cinq ans avant sa mort. Il aime employer ces mots: *transferre*, *transire*, *transitus*, *migrare*, *migratio*, car il n'y a rien d'immobile dans sa tournure d'esprit; il a même en horreur et l'immobilisme de la vieille théologie et celui de la mythologie périmée des Anciens.

Je tiens le *De Transitu*, que j'ai traduit, non sans sueur et avec un succès relatif, car le latin de la Renaissance est beaucoup plus complexe et plus difficile à rendre que le latin médiéval, pour le testament spirituel de Budé, pour une oeuvre poétique, pour une profonde méditation religieuse, quelque peu incohérente, où la littérature et la mythologie, la philosophie et la théologie jouent un rôle prépondérant; il est aussi un grand hymne chrétien, où l'auteur pose comme un Père de l'Eglise, nouvelle vague. En ce gros ouvrage de fin de carrière, divisé en trois livres de longueur et de valeur différentes, il mobilise tout, met tout en oeuvre, tous azimuts: la culture païenne de la Renaissance, les mythes de l'Antiquité, les poètes, les orateurs et les philosophes de l'Antiquité, la Bible elle-même et les Pères de l'Eglise grecque et latine. C'est un livre à la fois mythologique, philosophique et théologique, poétique et symbolique, en partie obscur, difficile et rébarbatif, mais vraiment grandiose, sur les rapports des lettres anciennes et du christianisme.

Dans le premier livre, le lecteur moderne trouve, entre autres, un vibrant appel au réveil de la foi, un tableau haut en couleurs de la société française du temps de Budé et une longue description des beautés et des richesses de l'Ecriture sainte; cette description complète celle qui figure dans le *De Studio*. Le deuxième livre, de beaucoup le plus dur et le plus long, décrit de long en large la crise religieuse contemporaine, où l'incroyance et l'indifférence étaient monnaie courante, célèbre de nouveau les beautés et les richesses de la Bible, traite du libre arbitre, de théologie, de théurgie et de philosophie. Le mythe d'Ulysse, qui occupe le tiers du livre, est chargé d'images marines et odysséennes. Tel Ulysse attaché au mât de son radeau, *homo navigator*, le chrétien est attaché aux bras de la croix; comme Ulysse, il doit être vigilant et veiller aux écueils et aux tentations. Budé décrit ici un duel entre la mythologie et le christianisme, entre la Bible et le paganisme mythologique. Il est aussi familier avec l'Ecriture Sainte qu'avec l'*Imitation de Jésus-Christ* de Thomas à Kempis. On dirait qu'il a cherché à écrire un essai de christologie. Si le deuxième livre ressemble fort à une tragédie sur la chute et la déchéance de l'homme, le troisième, tout en reprenant quelques thèmes des deux livres antérieurs, est un hymne à la lumière, une remontée vers la clarté, un chant d'espérance, l'homme déchu par le péché, ayant été depuis la Révélation et la venue du Messie régénéré et associé au plan divin.

On le voit, le *De Transitu* est le prolongement et l'application du *De Studio*. Budé a fait le plongeon final. A l'instar de Grégoire de Nazianze, il retourne définitivement à l'Ecriture Sainte, non sans jeter un dernier regard mélancolique sur l'hellénisme et la mythologie. La mythologie occupe, soit dit en passant, une place si importante chez lui qu'on pourrait écrire un essai fort substantiel intitulé: *La mythologie antique dans l'oeuvre de Guillaume Budé*, car il est fort attentif aux débats de son temps sur la valeur allégorique et symbolique des mythes; mais il n'a que faire de Babylone et de l'Egypte, qu'il emploie souvent comme symboles métaphoriques de l'hellénisme, qui signifie désormais pour lui lettres profanes, athéisme, idolâtrie, matérialisme, paganisme, polythéisme, scepticisme. Il considère son traité comme un appel à la conversion intérieure. De sorte que les divers éléments de l'*encyclopaedia*: l'histoire et la philosophie, l'éloquence et la poésie, l'exégèse et la philologie, sont désormais pour lui des disciplines préparatoires ou propédeutiques à la philosophie théologique, qui seule mérite le nom de contemplation.

Conclusion

On le voit par ce qui précède, Guillaume Budé a contribué énormément à la renaissance de l'*encyclopaedia*, des lettres antiques, des *humaniores literae*, des *disciplinae humaniores*, des *artes liberales*, des *studia humanitatis*, des lettres d'humanité. Il a accompli sa tâche, il est vrai, aux dépens, pour ne pas dire au mépris, de la langue française. C'est qu'il appartenait, forcément comme nous tous appartenons au nôtre, à son temps, à son époque, à son milieu, où les érudits employaient le latin comme langue internationale de communication. Chez lui est visible aussi l'absence de plan à tiroirs ou à compartiments; il pèche énormément par manque de composition ordonnée, serrée et suivie, ce qui ne simplifie pas la tâche des chercheurs contemporains qui lisent ses ouvrages. Il pratique à outrance, comme c'était l'usage de son temps, les digressions, la comparaison et la métaphore, l'allégorie et le symbole, la circonlocution et la périphrase, les allusions et les souvenirs. On rejette aujour'hui toutes ces pratiques discursives dans le monde du savoir, l'érudition contemporaine formant un singulier contraste avec l'érudition de la Renaissance. Même des mots, tels que *encyclopaedia* et *philologia* ne signifiaient pas du tout la même chose pour les esprits de la Renaissance que les mots courants aujourd'hui d'encyclopédie et de philologie. Ce qui différencie aussi notre époque de celle de la Renaissance, c'est le masque des sources, la pratique pour le moins étrange des citations et des références, le choix des modèles, l'esprit fragmentaire, hétérogène, instable ou mobile à l'extrême, ce qui déconcerte le lecteur d'aujourd'hui.

Tout cela dit au chapitre des défauts de l'érudition à l'époque de la Renaissance, Budé ne demeure pas moins l'un des premiers en France à avoir compris et démontré l'importance des manuscrits pour l'exégèse des livres antiques, à pratiquer une recension très scrupuleuse des manuscrits, à confronter entre eux les textes des Anciens, comme il fut le premier à prouver que la *philologia* enchaîne et entraîne dans son choeur les autres disciplines et qu'elle débouche éventuellement sur la science encyclopédique, la *doctrina orbicularis*. Philologue et polyglotte plutôt que philosophe versé dans les abstractions, il peut être considéré comme le précurseur de la méthode comparative, comme on peut le voir dans son chef-d'oeuvre, le *De Asse*.

Budé a élargi le concept classique, traditionnel et médiéval de l'*encyclopaedia*, en faisant éclater les sept arts libéraux et en y ajoutant d'autres disciplines telles que: l'histoire et le sens chrétien qu'il en a, l'analyse critique des textes, l'exégège, les commentaires, la philosophie première et la sacro-sainte philosophie, fondée sur l'étude de la Bible et de ses commentateurs. Bien avant Victor Hugo, il a fait la guerre à la rhétorique et a prôné l'éloquence pragmatique et utile, consciencieuse et effective. Il a exprimé son concept qui atteindra dorénavant les élèves du cours secondaire et les étudiants d'université, non pas d'une façon méthodique ou systématique en un ou deux volumes, mais plutôt de façon éparpillée, sporadique, presque dans tous ses ouvrages, ce qui prouve qu'il y pensait toujours. Il ne pouvait le faire autrement, car il n'était ni professeur ni théoricien de l'éducation, ce qui ne l'a pas empêché d'exprimer çà et là ses idées pédagogiques; on pourrait même les rassembler en forme de gerbe et montrer que Montaigne en a fait son miel. Voilà pourquoi, étant donné la façon d'écrire de Budé, il n'est pas facile de préciser, avec certitude et preuves à l'appui, l'impact de son concept de l'*encyclopaedia* au XVIe siècle.

Toutefois, il n'est pas présompueux de penser qu'il n'est pas passé inaperçu, pour ainsi dire, comme une lettre à la poste, vu les nombreuses réimpressions de la plupart de ses ouvrages au XVIe siècle. Ainsi l'éloge qu'il fait régulièrement du grec et du latin, des humanités classiques, de l'histoire, son plaidoyer en faveur de l'étude des textes et de l'éloquence pratique et réfléchie, son amour évident des mythes, parce qu'ils sont exprimés par des poètes en des oeuvres littéraires de valeur durable et parce que les poètes anciens, interprètes des mythes, ressemblent aux théologiens, aux spécialistes du discours sacré: voilà autant d'idées qui ont probablement retenu l'attention de quelques esprits sérieux dans le domaine de l'enseignement et des lettres. Son plaidoyer constant et nourri pour la philosophie et la sacro-sainte philosophie, pour les Saintes Ecritures et les commentaires des Pères de l'Eglise grecque et latine, a peut-être aussi influé sur le *Ratio studiorum* des Jésuites qui était alors en germination à l'époque de la Réforme.

Chez les Anciens, l'*encyclopaedia* ou l'ἐγκύκλιος παιδεία signifiait un ensemble de connaissances générales que tout homme instruit se devait d'acquérir et de se former l'esprit par leur acquisition avant de se consacrer à une étude spéciale et d'aborder la vie pratique. Telle était leur conception de la culture générale de l'esprit. Budé, qui a poursuivi ses recherches et publié ses ouvrages pendant environ 35 ans, soit de 1500 à 1535, emploie le mot *encyclopaedia* une trentaine de fois dans son oeuvre. Mais pas toujours, loin de là, dans l'acception des Anciens. Et cela grâce à sa connaissance, en plus de l'Antiquité, du Moyen Age et de la Renaissance.

Il a repensé leur concept, il l'a élargi et complété en y insérant des disciplines qui n'y figuraient point depuis des siècles, comme l'histoire, la philologie et la sacro-sainte philosophie. Bien plus, il a modifié son concept de l'*encyclopaedia*, surtout de 1525 à 1535, dans les dernières années de sa carrière, comme le révèlent ses *Commentarii linguae graecae* (1529), ses *Epistolae latinae et graecae* (1531), son *De Studio literarum recte et commode instituendo* (1532), son *De Philologia* (1532) et son *De Transitu hellenismi ad christianismum* (1535). Pendant cette décennie, il devint de plus en plus un penseur, un philosophe chrétien. Il entend alors par *encyclopaedia* la formation complète, susceptible de préparer et de produire un esprit complet, habilité à étudier la philosophie, à faire des réflexions et des recherches philosophiques, voire à aborder la philosophie supérieure ou sacrée, c'est-à-dire les Saintes Ecritures et les Pères de l'Eglise en vue du Bien et du bien commun, selon les idées de Platon et du *Nouveau Testament.*

De même que la religion de Budé n'est pas celle de Rabelais, de même son concept de l'*encyclopaedia* n'est pas celui de Rabelais qui y introduit les sciences naturelles, voire les sciences physiques et mathématiques, ce à quoi Budé n'a point pensé, bien qu'il fût fort versé en mathématiques et dans la valeur pythagoricienne des nombres. Erasme ne conçoit pas non plus l'*encyclopaedia* tout à fait comme Budé, car il y introduit beaucoup plus de grammaire, de poésie, et de prose que ne le fait Budé. Ce qui est certain aussi, c'est que le mot *encyclopaedia*, bien qu'employé, entre autres, par Fabius Pictor et Quintilien, Vitruve et Pline l'Ancien, ne figure dans aucun dictionnaire latin, par exemple, ni dans les dictionnaires Gaffiot et Quicherat, ni dans l'*Oxford Latin Dictionary* et dans le *A Latin Dictionary* de Lewis et Short, pas davantage dans le *Lexicon Totius Latinitatis* de Forcellini et le *Lexicon minus mediae Latinitatis* de Niermeyer. On ne relève même aucune référence à Guillaume Budé dans le *Thesaurus linguae latinae* (1531, 1532), Henri Estienne se contentant d'y citer Fabius Pictor et Vitruve en cinq lignes. Le mot grec ἐγκυκλιοπαιδεία, si souvent employé par Budé, qui le doit à Quintilien, ne figure ni dans le Bailly ni dans le Liddell and Scott. Robert Estienne accorde une large place à ce mot dans son *Thesaurus graecae linguae* (1572), sans mentionner cependant le nom de Guillaume Budé une seule fois. Reconnaissons qu'il aurait pu être mieux traité à cet égard par les lexicographes. Par bonheur, il l'est beaucoup mieux aujourd'hui, surtout depuis quelques décennies, la France et le Canada conjuguant leurs efforts pour traduire et réinterpréter l'oeuvre du plus grand humaniste et philologue français de la Renaissance. Le présent est garant de l'avenir.

Université Laval, Québec

Das Diarium in Mittelalter und Renaissance

PAUL GERHARD SCHMIDT

Der eine oder andere aus unserem Kreis hat wohl zu irgendeiner Phase seines Lebens ein Tagebuch geführt, entweder während des Studiums, auf Reisen oder in besonderen Situationen. Mancher führt es kontinuierlich das ganze Leben hindurch und hat die Gewohnheit, täglich eine Eintragung vorzunehmen. Der kontinuierliche Diarist—wenn ich einmal diesen Ausdruck verwenden darf—stellt mitunter die Tätigkeit des Tagebuchschreibens über den Inhalt des Tagebuchs. Er vermerkt auch, wenn er an einem Tag nichts getan und gedacht hat, wenn er mit der Welt haderte oder krank war; indem er seine Inaktivität am Ende des Tages im Tagebuch festhält, beweist er sich, daß er doch noch aktiv ist und sein Leben in Ordnung hält. Das Führen eines Tagebuches, wohl weiter verbreitet als in der Öffentlichkeit eingestanden, ist für manchen eine tägliche Lebensgewohnheit und sogar—notwendigkeit, gewissermaßen ein Akt seelischer Hygiene, der mit der gleichen Regelmäßigkeit erfolgt wie etwa der Griff zur Zahnbürste. Das Tagebuchschreiben ist vielfach als moralisch hochstehende Tätigkeit angesehen, empfohlen und angestrebt worden.[1] Am 1. Januar 1753 trug der Lexikograph Dr. Johnson folgende Neujahrsvorsätze in sein Tagebuch ein:[2]

1. To rise early,
2. To lose no time,
3. To keep a Journal.

---

[1] G. R. Hocke, *Das europäische Tagebuch* (Wiesbaden ²1978); P. Boerner, *Tagebuch* Realienbücher für Germanisten (Stuttgart, 1969).

[2] *Samuel Johnson, Diaries, Prayers, and Annals*, ed. E. L. McAdam, Jr., with Donald and Mary Hyde (New Haven, 1958), 50.

Wie schwer ihm die Erfüllung dieser Vorsätze fiel, kann man einem acht Jahre später erfolgten Eintrag entnehmen. Zu Ostern 1761, am Datum eines kirchlichen Festes, trug er als Vorsätze ein:[3]

1. To avoid Idleness.
2. To regulate my sleep as to length and choice of hours.
3. To set down every day what shall be done the day following.
4. To keep a Journal.
5. To worship God more diligently.
6. To go to Church every Sunday.
7. To study the Scriptures.
8. To read a certain portion every week.

Das 18. und 19. Jahrhundert hat viele solcher Bekenntnistagebücher und intime Journale hervorgebracht, in denen Eingeständnisse eigenen Versagens eine große Rolle spielen. Im August 1738, vor fast genau 250 Jahren, notierte Albrecht von Haller: "wieder eine Woche, da ich im Guten mehr ab als zugenommen."[4] Das Tagebuch ist Ort der Selbstbeichte, in dem Gedanken und Gefühle festgehalten, zugleich aber auch Fortschritte registriert werden. Durch die Beobachtung der eigenen Handlungen sollte in dieser Epoche die Entwicklung der Persönlichkeit gefördert werden. Im Tagebuch hielt der Diarist Erkenntnisse fest, die er gewonnen hatte, und skizzierte Pläne für seine künftigen Arbeiten. Herder entwickelte in seinem Tagebuch den Gedanken, "ein Tagebuch der zu bildenden Menschheit" und damit ein Buch über die menschliche Seele zu verfassen. Ein solches Werk, dessen war er sich sicher, "das wird bleiben."[5]

Es sind viele Tagebücher geblieben–sowohl solche, die im Blick auf eine spätere Publikation niedergeschrieben wurden als vor allem auch die vielen anderen, deren Verfasser nur für sich selbst schrieben und deshalb darauf achteten, daß ihre Aufzeichnungen nicht von anderen gelesen werden konnten. Deshalb chiffrierten sie, verwendeten sie Buchstaben aus anderen Alphabeten oder führten das Diarium in einer Sprache, die ihrer häuslichen Umgebung nicht vertraut war, gebrauchten für mehrfach wiederkehrende Begriffe selbsterfundene Abkürzungen und Symbole, die in der Regel nicht so leicht auflösbar sind wie der gezeichnete Pokal des Ernst Theodor Amadeus Hoffmann, der im Tagebuch seine Zechereien

[3] Johnson (wie Anm. 2) 73.

[4] Zitat nach Hocke (wie Anm. 1) 623.

[5] Zitat nach Hocke 645–47.

mit diesem Piktogramm und dem Zusatz "un poco" oder "Champagner" versah und seine erotischen Eskapaden mit der Skizze eines Schmetterlings andeutete.[6]

Obwohl wir zu wissen glauben, was ein Tagebuch ist, bereitet seine Definition Schwierigkeiten. Denn die Grenze zu anderen Textformen und Inhalten ist fließend. Ein diaristisch geführter Reisebericht—etwa das Tagebuch einer Badereise oder einer italienischen Reise—läßt sich mit gleicher Berechtigung beiden im Titel genannten Genera zuordnen. Ähnliches gilt für die Autobiographie in Tagebuchform, die Memoiren, den Briefroman, in dem sich die Korrespondenten wechselseitig ihre Tagebuchaufzeichnungen zusenden. Das Tagebuch muß ferner nicht notwendig von nur einer Person verfaßt sein. Es ist in diesem Zusammenhang auf das Kriegstagebuch zu verweisen, auf das Wetterjournal, die Krankengeschichte mit kontinuierlichen Befundserhebungen, die täglichen Messungen bei einem Experiment oder andere regelmäßig geführte Aufzeichnungen, für die es unerheblich ist, ob sie von einer bestimmten Person oder einer Vielzahl beliebiger Personen niedergeschrieben werden.

Hinsichtlich der Inhalte gibt es kaum eine feste Regel oder Begrenzung. Im Tagebuch kann fast jedes Thema und jede Sache zur Sprache kommen. Detaillierte Hinrichtungsszenen enthält etwa das Tagebuch des Nachrichters. Nicht wenige Henker haben Tagebücher hinterlassen, die vermutlich in erster Linie als Geschäfts—und Rechnungsbücher angelegt waren, mit denen Lohn—und Materialkosten abgerechnet wurden.[7] Über das Hinrichtungsdatum, Zahl und Namen der Delinquenten hinaus enthalten sie oft Schilderungen der begangenen Untaten und sie beschreiben den Seelenzustand und die Gemütsverfassung der verstockten oder reumütigen Verurteilten bei ihrem letzten Gang; es ist eine für die Kriminal—und Kulturgeschichte aufschlußreiche, farbige Quellengattung. Um die Palette der Themenbereiche abzurunden, sei noch eine weitere Form von Aufzeichnungen angeführt, die schon in der Antike gefordert wurde. Der Name Tagebuch, Diarium bzw. Ephemeris, gab Raum zu der Überlegung, ob man nicht auch Nachtbücher, Epinyktides, anlegen solle, in denen man die Träume aufzeichne.[8] Träume und Visionen sind denn auch häufig

---

[6] Vgl. Hocke 682–87.

[7] *Maister Franntzn Schmidts Nachrichters inn Nürmberg all sein Richten.* Nach der Handschrift hrsg. u. eingel. von Albrecht Keller (Leipzig, 1913); P. Putzer, *Das Salzburger Scharfrichtertagebuch*, (Schriften des Instituts für Historische Kriminologie 1) (St. Johann/Wien, 1985) (mit weiteren Literaturangaben).

[8] Boerner (wie Anm. 1) 38.

festgehalten worden. Sie lassen sich einem bestimmten Datum zuordnen und sie enthalten oft eine persönliche Botschaft für den Träumer. Das berühmteste und vielleicht bekannteste Beispiel aus der Renaissance ist Dürers Traumgesicht vom 7./8. Juni 1525, als ihm träumte "wy fill grosser wassern van himell fillen," was ihn so heftig erschreckte, daß er stundenlang nach seinem Traum zitterte. Er hat ihn in Worten und in einer Farbskizze zu Papier gebracht.[9]

Das Traumbuch des Artemidor aus Ephesos hat sich aus der Antike erhalten, ein Tagebuch m. W. nicht. Die am Hofe Alexanders des Großen geführten Ephemerides, Berichte über das Fortschreiten seiner tödlichen Krankheit, sind aus der späteren Alexanderhistoriographie zu erschließen.[10] Aus dem klassischen Altertum hat sich also kein Diarium erhalten; der Renaissance stand kein einziges antikes Werk als Imitationsmodell zur Verfügung.

Die Frage, welches das älteste Tagebuch ist, läßt sich nicht beantworten. In der Forschung über Diarien wird entweder auf babylonische Gestirnbeobachtungen, auf die verlorenen Alexander-Ephemerides oder auf die Meditationen des Kartäusers Guigo verwiesen. Guigo, im Jahre 1110 zum Prior der Grande Chartreuse gewählt, gilt als der einzige Tagebuchautor des Mittelalters. Denn einhellig geht man davon aus, daß das Tagebuchführen zögernd im 15. Jahrhundert, in großer Breite erst im 16. Jahrhundert einsetzte und daß die ersten europäischen Tagebuchschreiber Bürger and Gelehrte in Paris und in den italienischen Stadtstaaten waren. Das Tagebuch scheint schlechthin die für die Renaissance mit ihrer Entdeckung des Individuums charakteristische literarische Form zu sein.

Soweit diese Feststellung die Renaissance betrifft, will ich sie keineswegs in Frage stellen oder entkräften, für das Mittelalter aber muß sie revidiert werden. Es gibt mehrere mittelalterliche Texte, die ich als Tagebücher bezeichnen möchte; Guigos Werk gehört jedoch nicht dazu. Wer seine sehr lesenswerten Meditationen zu den Tagebüchern zählt, tut dies ohnehin nur mit Zögern und Bedenken. Guigo war kein kontinuierlicher Diarist. Er hat über einen größeren Zeitraum hin seine Gedanken in einer ausgefeilten sprachlichen Fassung notiert. Seine etwa 500 Aphorismen und Maximen sind ausnahmslos undatiert. Der direkte Tagesbezug ist nicht

---

[9] *Dürer, Schriftlicher Nachlaß.* Erster Band: Autobiographische Schriften ... hrsg. von Hans Rupprich, (Berlin 1956), 214f. (146–202: Tagebuch der Reise in die Niederlande).

[10] Pauly-Wissowa, *Real-Encyclopädie der classischen Altertumswissenschaft,* (Stuttgart, 1905), 10. Halbband, Sp. 2749–53 s. v. Ephemerides.

mehr erkennbar. Es handelt sich um für jedermann gültige Reflexionen über die Wahrheit, über die Liebe, über Gott und den Nächsten, die man zu Recht mit Marc Aurels Betrachtungen "An sich selbst" verglichen hat.[11] Typisch für Guigo ist ein Satz wie der folgende: "Wenn du dich selbst in deiner Unreinheit ertragen kannst, warum erträgst du dann nicht auch jeden anderen Menschen?" ("Si te ipsum tam immundum toleras, cur non quemlibet alium?"[12]). Häufig finden sich Selbstanklagen bei ihm und er wirft sich vor, daß er der Welt mehr diene als Gott. Einmal beschuldigt er sich, daß er zu sehr auf die Mehrung des Klostergutes bedacht sei und darüber die wichtigeren spirituellen Aufgaben vernachlässige. Guigo steht unverkennbar in der von der Regula Benedicti begründeten Tradition, die ihrerseits schon auf stoischem Gedankengut fußt. Benedikt forderte im 4. Kapitel seiner Regel, der Mönch solle "mala sua praeterita cum lacrimis vel gemitu cotidie in oratione Deo confiteri,"[13] also täglich sein Gewissen erforschen und die Sünden und Verfehlungen des Tages im Gebet zu Gott beichten. Dieser Forderung ist das mittelalterliche Mönchtum in seinen besten Vertretern mit großem Ernst nachgekommen. Die tägliche Gewissenserforschung lenkt den Blick in das Innere des Menschen und auf Gott. Guigos Meditationen, aus monastischer Lebensform erwachsen, stehen im Grenzbereich von Diaristik und geistlicher Autobiographie. Georg Misch hat sie denn auch in seiner großen Darstellung der Geschichte der Autobiographie behandelt.

Der Mitte des 13. Jahrhunderts gehört ein Werk an, das bisher nicht zu den Diarien gezählt wurde, weil sein Titel und seine Gebrauchsfunktion es einer anderen Gattung zuordnen. Es ist das Registrum visitationum des Odo Rigaud, der von 1248 bis 1275 Erzbischof von Rouen war. Der Franziskaner Odo, Freund und Beichtvater des später kanonisierten Ludwig IX. von Frankreich, ist seinen Pflichten als Bischof mit großer Gewissenhaftigkeit nachgekommen. Eine seiner wichtigsten Aufgaben sah er in der Aufsicht über den Klerus seiner Diözese. Wie auch heute noch Bischof oder Kirchenleitung in regelmäßigen Abständen die ihnen unterstellten Gemeinden visitieren und sich dabei ein Bild von der Amtsführung der Ortsgeistlichen machen und auf die Abstellung von Mängeln drängen, kontrollierte der mittelalterliche Bischof Klöster und Pfarreien,

---

[11] G. Misch, *Geschichte der Autobiographie.* Frankfurt 1959, 3. Band, 2. Teil: *Das Hochmittelalter im Anfang* (über Guigo 397–433, hier: 399).

[12] *Guigues Ier, Prieur de Chartreuse, Les Méditations* (Sources Chrétiennes 308), (Paris, 1983), 140 (Nr. 122).

[13] *Benedicti Regula,* ed. R. Hanslik (CSEL 75), (Wien, 1960), 32.

prüfte ihre geistliche, sittliche und finanzielle Ordnung, verhängte Disziplinarstrafen und führte notwendige Reformen durch. Aus dem Spätmittelalter sind zahlreiche Visitationsprotokolle erhalten;[14] aus dem 13. Jahrhundert gibt es kein zweites, das sich mit Odos Registrum visitationum vergleichen ließe, das im Druck über 800 stattliche Quartseiten umfaßt.[15] Das Werk ist viel beachtet worden, weil es Aufschluß über den Bildungsstand und die Lebensführung des normannischen Klerus im 13. Jahrhundert bietet. Odo durchreiste unablässig seine Diözese und prüfte die Geistlichen. Diese Prüfungen darf man sich durchaus als Prüfungen im eigentlichen Wortsinn vorstellen. Er ließ seine Kleriker das Pater Noster aufsagen, einen Satz aus der Bibel ins Französische übersetzen und lateinische Wörter konjugieren und deklinieren. Er scheute sich nicht, nach der Deklination von "deus" zu fragen und vermerkte am 16. März 1260, daß Nikolaus Quesnel unsicher war, ob der Akkusativ Plural "deos" oder "dos" laute.[16] Bei den Dorfbewohnern und anderen Gewährsleuten erkundigte er sich nach dem sittlichen Lebenswandel und dem Leumund seiner Geistlichen. Das Registrum visitationum listet häufig wiederkehrende Standardverfehlungen der einfachen Kleriker auf: Der Ortspfarrer lebt mit einer zu jungen Köchin oder einer Konkubine zusammen, er unterhält ein offenes Verhältnis zu einer Ehefrau, er versorgt seine Kinder mit dem Gut der Kirche, besucht regelmäßig die Tabernen, betrinkt sich und vernachlässigt den Gottesdienst, weil er lieber auf seinen Feldern arbeitet; er trägt kein geistliches Gewand, geht zur Jagd, ist oft in Waffen zu sehen, verwickelt sich in Raufereien und Zweikämpfe, behandelt seine alten Eltern schlecht.... Die Reihe ließe sich fortsetzen, es gibt kaum ein Vergehen gegen die Standesvorschriften und die Regeln des menschlichen Zusammenlebens, das nicht im Registrum erschiene. Was für den Pfarrklerus gilt, trifft auch für die Ordensangehörigen zu.

In den von ihm kontrollierten Klöstern und Prioraten fand Odo ähnliche Mißstände. Nur selten konnte er den Eintrag vornehmen: Invenimus omnia in bono statu. In der Regel mußte er feststellen, daß die Mönche die Ordensvorschriften nicht einhielten. Sie brechen das Schweigegebot, schlafen in weichen Betten mit Kopfkissen, sie essen Fleisch und

[14] N. Coulet, *Les visites pastorales* (Turnhout, 1977).

[15] *Regestrum visitationum archiepiscopi Rothomagensis. Journal des visites pastorales d'Eude Rigaud, archevêque de Rouen MCCXLVIII–MCCLXIX*, publ. par. Th. Bonnin. Rouen 1847. Vgl. außerdem P. Andrieu-Guitrancourt, *L'archevêque Eudes Rigaud et la vie de l'église au XIIIe siècle d'après le "Regestrum visitationum"* (Paris, 1938).

[16] Regestrum (wie Anm. 15) 395; wiederabgedruckt von Ch. H. Beeson, *A Primer of Medieval Latin*, 1925; reprint, 1973, 297.

feiern Gelage, sie erhalten Besuch von Laien, und Frauen gehen im Kloster ungehindert ein und aus. Der einzelne Mönch verfügt über Eigentum und bewahrt seinen Privatbesitz in einer verschließbaren Truhe oder einem Spind auf, das Kloster selbst aber ist verschuldet, notwendige Reparaturen der Klostergebäude werden nicht ausgeführt, der Abt legt keine Abrechnungen vor. Kelche und andere für den Gottesdienst erforderliche Geräte fehlen, ebenso mangelt es an liturgischen Büchern. Die Stimmung im Kloster ist durch Feindseligkeit vergiftet, bestimmte Mönche reden nicht miteinander, der Abt hält sich vom gemeinsamen Klosterleben fern und gibt den anderen ein schlechtes Vorbild, indem er über die Matutin hinaus in den Tag schläft.

Odos Registrum ist nach einem festen Schema gegliedert. Es beginnt mit dem Datum und dem Ort der Visitation, dann gibt es an, ob der Erzbischof auf eigene Kosten reiste oder ob er Gast der visitierten Institution war—es ist damit gleichzeitig ein Rechnungs—und Haushaltungsbuch, denn es verzeichnet die Ausgaben des Erzbischofs. Dann folgt die Bestandsaufnahme nach dem festen Schema eines Fragebogens. Das Registrum listet die Mängel und Beanstandungen auf und schließt mit Auflagen und der Ankündigung von Sanktionen. Wer bis zur nächsten Visitation nicht die monierten Mängel abstellt, soll wissen, welche Konsequenzen das für ihn haben wird. Wer sich etwa auch nach der zweiten Verwarnung nicht von seiner Konkubine trennt, läuft Gefahr, dann seine Pfarrei zu verlieren. Es ist bezeichnend für die im 13. Jahrhundert zunehmende Verrechtlichung der Kirche, daß in das Registrum sofort vollziehbare Vollstreckungsurkunden aufgenommen werden, die die vermahnten Ortsgeistlichen ihrem Erzbischof ausstellen mußten, so daß er sie gegebenenfalls ohne Einschaltung des lästigen Rechtsweges sofort des Amtes entheben konnte, wenn sie ihm erneut als rückfällig gemeldet wurden oder Anlaß zu Klagen über ihr sittliches Verhalten boten.

Weil das Registrum es gestattete, die Visitation mit dem Blick auf die Resultate der vorangegangenen Jahre durchzuführen, war es ein unentbehrliches Arbeitsinstrument für den Visitator, der sein Amt mit Konsequenz ausüben wollte. Darüber hinaus ist es m. E. auch ein echtes Diarium, was man bisher nicht beachtet hat. Denn Odo hat für jeden Tag des Jahres einen Eintrag vorgenommen, auch für die Tage, an denen er nicht visitierte. Er führte das Register als Itinerar. Manche Einträge enthalten nur das Tagesdatum und den Namen des Ortes, an dem er sich gerade aufhielt. Gelegentlich finden sich Angaben über seine Gesundheit. Odo litt an der Gicht. Um Linderung seiner Schmerzen und um Heilung zu finden, unternahm er mehrere Pilgerreisen, die ihn über die Grenzen seiner Diözese führten. Auch die Romreise des Jahres 1253 ist Tag für Tag im Registrum visitationum dokumentiert. Odo verstand sich nicht als Tourist und er hat keine Beschreibung der Sehenswürdigkeiten der Heiligen Stadt hinterlassen. Er hat keinen Sinn für die Ruinensentimentalität, die Hildebert im 12. Jahrhundert in Rom empfand. Zur Heiligen Stadt vermerkt Odo im Register nur, daß er dem Papst den Fußkuß leistete, daß er die Reliquien der Apostel verehrt und die Messe gelesen habe. Sein Registrum–oder soll ich Diarium sagen?–gibt stets an, wann er eine Predigt hielt und wann er "in pontificalibus" zelebrierte. Es hält seine Amtshandlungen und seine Werke der Frömmigkeit fest, so als wollte er das Register wie einen Tätigkeitsnachweis beim Jüngsten Gericht präsentieren. Seine Krankheiten registriert er deshalb nicht aus Freude an hypochondrischer Selbstbeobachtung, sondern er führt sie an, wenn sie ihn bei seinen Aufgaben hindern. Sehr ausführlich schildert er, wie er einmal trotz seiner eigenen Krankheit eine Reise unternahm, weil der erkrankte König ihn brieflich dazu aufforderte. Als Beichvater fühlte er sich verpflichtet, dem kranken Herrscher beizustehen.[17]

Odos Person tritt in den Hintergrund, aber das Tagebuch gestattet es dennoch, seine Persönlichkeit zu charakterisieren. Er hat sich einige Male auch persönliche Bermerkungen über das Fehlverhalten anderer nicht versagt; er kommentiert es mit der trockenen Wendung "quod nobis valde displicuit."[18] Das nimmt gleichsam die Mißfallensäußerung der Queen Victoria vorweg, ihr indigniertes "We are not amused."

Charisma und eine geheimnisvolle Aura passen nicht zu Odo. Sein Registrum zeichnet die Tätigkeit eines von Reformeifer und Verantwortungsbewußtsein erfüllten Bischofs auf, eines Mannes, der sich nicht selbst bespiegelt, der seinen Lesern nicht neue Einsichten und Erkenntnisse vermitteln, aber für jeden Tag seines Lebens beweisen will, daß er seinen Pflichten nachgekommen ist. Mit seinem Tagebuch-Rechenschaftsbericht hat sich der bescheidene und energische Franziskaner ein bleibendes Monument geschaffen.

Anfechtungen und Zweifel kannte Odo nicht, zumindest vertraute er sie nicht dem Registrum an.Einige Jahre vor ihm entstand das Tagebuch eines deutschen Zisterziensers, das gleichfalls Sorge um das Heil der ihm anvertrauten Seelen erkennen läßt, in erster Linie aber Zeugnis von den Ängsten seines Verfassers ablegt. Ich spreche von dem Prior und späteren Abt Richalm von Schöntal. Es gibt mehrere Klöster dieses Namens. Richalm lebte und amtierte in Schöntal an der Jagst. Das Geschlecht der

[17] Regestrum (wie Anm. 15) 335.
[18] Regestrum 307, 324 u. ö.

Berlichingen hat dort seine Grablege und der bekannteste Berlichingen, Götz mit der eisernen Faust, ist in Richalms Kloster beigesetzt worden. Über Richalm gibt es bisher keine Untersuchung, er ist wie viele lateinische Autoren des 13. Jahrhunderts praktisch unbekannt.[19] Richalm hat nicht selbst Tagebuch geführt.

Ein junger Novize, gleichsam sein Eckermann, notierte Aussprüche des Abtes auf einer Wachstafel, legte sie Richalm vor und übertrug den von ihm gebilligten Wortlaut auf Pergament. Da der Sekretär den Abt möglichst wörtlich zitierte und der Abt die Aufzeichnungen kontrollierte und autorisierte, können wir das Werk Richalm selbst zuschreiben und den Anteil des Sekretärs vernachlässigen. Richalm muß von düsterer Gemütsart gewesen sein; zudem litt er unter mehreren Krankheiten. Er fühlte sich oft unwohl, vertrug keinen Widerspruch und steigerte sich in eine Art Verfolgungswahn. So glaubte er, überall von Teufeln umgeben und von ihnen überwacht zu sein. Ging er durch das Kloster, vernahm er ihre Stimmen, die deutlich hörbar riefen: "Richalm kommt." Schlief ein Mönch während der Matutin ein, so sah Richalm den oder die Teufel, die den Schlaf herbeigeführt hatten. Wollte ein Mönch heimlich das Kloster für immer verlassen, so wußte Richalm, wer ihn dazu antrieb und ihm die bösen Gedanken ins Ohr blies. Kurzum–Richalm sah überall den alten bösen Feind oder eine ganze Legion Teufel am Werk. Seine Aufzeichnungen haben missionarischen Charakter. Er will seine Leser auf diese Entdeckung und ihre ständige Bedrohung aufmerksam machen. Man mag über Richalms Wahrnehmungen lächeln oder ihn bemitleiden. Sieht man aber von seiner Idée fixe ab, wird man feststellen, daß er das Leben im Kloster sehr genau beobachtet hat. Bei wohl keinem anderen Autor des Mittelalters dürfte man den Satz lesen, den Richalm einmal ausspricht. Er stellt fest, daß sich selbst in großen Klöstern bestenfalls ein oder zwei Mönche finden lassen, die sich freiwillig und gern im Kloster aufhalten. Er schreibt das dem unheilvollen Wirken der Dämonen zu, seine Beobachtung selbst aber wird durch diesen Erklärungsversuch in ihrer Bedeutung nicht beeinträchtigt. Der Leidensdruck im Kloster, von dem wir sonst wenig wissen, muß groß gewesen sein. Zu Richalms Aufgaben gehörte es, den Mönchen ihre Arbeit zuzuteilen und sie zu beaufsichtigen. Er berichtet mehrfach von Widerworten und Arbeitsverweigerung. Für seine eigene Person hat er sich geradezu in die Arbeit hineingeflüchtet. Er lobt

[19] *Richalms Liber revelationum* ist von Bernhard Pez im Anecdotorum thesaurus novissimus, Augsburg 1721, 1, 2, Sp. 373–472 ediert. Eine Neuausgabe wird von mir vorbereitet.

begeistert das Ablenkungspotential der körperlichen Arbeit, die vorübergehend alle Sorgen vergessen läßt. Seine herausgehobene Stellung, der er sich vielleicht nicht gewachsen fühlte, brachte ihn in immer neue Konflikte mit seiner Umgebung. Er geriet in einen Grenzbereich zwischen Realität und Wahn. Sein Tagebuch registriert auch dies; es wird zum Nachtbuch. Es hält seine Traumgesichte, seine Auditionen und Televisionen, seine Begegnungen mit Verstorbenen fest. Richalms Visionen ereigneten sich vor allem zu hohen kirchlichen Feiertagen. Das ist eine aus der Visionsliteratur vertraute Erscheinung, wonach herausgehobene Kirchenfeste die Erlebnisfähigkeit steigern und die Wahrnehmung von Traumgesichten begünstigen. Zwei Visionärinnen, Elisabeth von Schönau im 12. und Gertrud von Helfta im 13. Jahrhundert, haben ihre Visionen in ähnlicher, am Kalender orientierter Folge aufzeichnen lassen. Sie gehören mit Richalm in die Gruppe der tage- bzw. nachtbuchführenden Visionäre.

Die beiden mittelalterlichen Diarien, das sei zugegeben, entsprechen nicht unseren Vorstellungen von einem Tagebuch. Sie sind nicht zu dem Zweck angelegt, Einblick in die Gedanken eines Individuums zu geben. Odo hat sein Journal als Kontrolleur und Aufseher seiner Diözese geführt, als Episcopus; er gibt Rechenschaft über seine Amtsführung und seine Aufwendungen, über seine Reisen und er nutzt die Gelegenheit, von seiner Gesundheit zu berichten. Er hat ein Amtsregister mit privaten Bemerkungen geführt; es ist aber auffällig, daß er es sich zur Regel gemacht hat, zu jedem Tag eine Eintragung vorzunehmen, selbst wenn dieser Eintrag nur aus dem Namen des Ortes besteht, an dem sich der Erzbischof aufhielt.

Richalms Aufzeichnungen stehen nicht unter dieser Diktatur des Kalenders. Als er der Niederschrift seiner Visionen zustimmte, wollte er nicht Rechenschaft über sein Klosteramt ablegen, sondern die Mönche mahnen und erbauen. Seine unsystematische Art der Aufzeichnung kehrt in den Tagebüchern der Bürger und Ratsschreiber des 15. und 16. Jahrhunderts wieder, deren Diarien zugleich Stadtchroniken und Sammlungen von Memorabilia sind.[20] Die nationalsprachlichen Tagebücher, die Kunstreisen Albrecht Dürers und das Bordbuch des Christoph Kolumbus müssen hier unberücksichtigt bleiben. Aus den lateinischen Tagebüchern der Renaissance wähle ich zwei aus, die in besonderer Weise den Vergleich mit den Diarien des 13. Jahrhunderts ermöglichen: das Diarium eines Ordensangehörigen und das eines Bischofs.

Bischof Ulrich Putsch von Brixen stellt sich anders dar als Erzbischof

[20] Magdalena Buchholz, *Die Anfänge der deutschen Tagebuchschreibung* (Diss. Königsberg, 1942; Münster, 1983).

Odo von Rouen. Während Odo das Bischofsamt sicher nicht angestrebt hat und der alten Tradition des "nolo episcopari" verpflichtet war, wollte Ulrich II. unbedingt Bischof werden. Der erste Eintrag im Tagebuch[21] teilt seine Wahl mit, weist auf die Widerstände, auf die Konkurrenten um das Amt und auf die intensiven Auseinandersetzungen während der Wahl hin. Der nächste Eintrag vermerkt, daß die Bestätigung des Papstes nur 'cum maxima difficultate' erlangt wurde. Seine Gegner hätten unzutreffende Gerüchte lanciert und ihn mit Schmutz überschüttet. Hier schreibt der typische Karrierist, der ein Amt zur Steigerung seines Selbstwertgefühls benötigt. Das noch keineswegs humanistische Latein Ulrichs macht das überdeutlich. "Ego ivi personaliter": ich selbst in höchsteigener Person. Diese Egozentrik eines Ehrgeizigen tritt überall zutage.

Auch der Bischof von Brixen mußte seine Diözese visitieren und er stieß dabei auf Mißstände und Vernachlässigung. Ulrich wußte, was man von ihm erwartete, und er drängte auf Reformen. Aber Ungehorsam gegen die von ihm getroffenen Verfügungen sah er als eine gegen seine Person gerichtete Beleidigung an. Wo er Not lindert, wo er einer Kirche ein fehlendes liturgisches Buch stiftet, stellt er sich als Geber ungebührlich in den Vordergrund. Letzten Endes will auch er sich durch Wohltaten den Himmel verdienen, wichtiger war ihm aber doch wohl, die Bewunderung seiner Umgebung zu erlangen.

Wie Odo verzeichnete er, wann er predigte und die Messe zelebrierte, aber er vergißt selten dabei anzugeben, wie groß sein Gefolge war und wie viele Menschen ihm zuhörten. Fast zwanghaft tut er alles, um seinen Ruhm zu mehren. Jede von ihm veranlaßte Reparatur—sein Lieblingswort ist "feci fieri"—wurde unverzüglich schriftlich festgehalten. Das Tagebuch dient ihm—wie das auch bei Odo zu beobachten war—zugleich als Rechnungsbuch. Auffällig ist nun, daß er bei mehreren Posten keine Zahlen nennt, sondern vage und prahlerisch von magnae expensae spricht. Diese großen Kosten und hohen Aufwendungen entstanden bei öffentlichen Auftritten und bei dem Ausbau von Burgen. Wie ein Landesherr versuchte er ja, seine Macht und seinen Einfluß zu vergrößern; Konflikte mit dem einheimischen Adel, mit den "terrigenae," waren unvermeidlich. Die ausführlichste Schilderung seines Diariums handelt von einer heftigen Auseinandersetzung mit mehreren Adeligen. Die Anlässe des Streits werden nicht deutlich, der Konflikt eskaliert und es kommt dazu, daß der

[21] V. Schaller, Ulrich II. Putsch, Bischof von Brixen, und sein Tagebuch, 1427–1437, in *Zeitschrift des Ferdinandeums für Tirol und Vorarlberg, 3. Folge, 36. Heft*, 1892, 225–322 u. 568–72.

Dichter Oswald von Wolkenstein seinem Bischof eine heftige Ohrfeige versetzt.[22] Dieser Abschnitt des Tagebuchs fällt aus dem Rahmen der übrigen Aufzeichnungen, so daß es den Anschein hat, als sei diese sorgfältig stilisierte Partie dazu bestimmt gewesen als Brief oder Denkschrift über den Vorfall zu kursieren. Unter geschickter Anspielung auf Christi Gefangennahme in Gethsemane wird geschildert, wie sich ein zweiter Judas dem Bischof nähert und wie sich an ihm der Satz des Evangeliums erfüllte, daß er "in die Hände der Sünder überantwortet wurde" (Matth. 26, 45).

Es gibt nicht nur den christusgleich leidenden Bischof Ulrich, sondern auch den strafenden. Wer unbefugt in seinen Gewässern fischt, dem sollen Hände und Füße abgehackt werden; wer beleidigende Schriften gegen ihn in Umlauf setzt, dem kündigt er drohend den gebührenden Lohn an. Man tut Ulrich wohl kein Unrecht, wenn man feststellt, daß das Bischofsamt für ihn Mittel der Selbstdarstellung war, daß seine Geschenke und magnae expensae Eindruck in der Öffentlichkeit machen und seine Position verbessern sollten, und daß er Gegner und Konkurrenten rücksichtslos bekämpfte. Ulrich II. von Brixen ist gewiß kein bedeutender Kirchenfürst der Renaissance gewesen. Seine Bildung ist unerheblich, sein Einfluß war geringer als er dachte. Wenn man aber die Eigenheiten und die Schwächen einer Epoche studieren will, bietet sich dieses Tagebuch als Studienobjekt an. Zu den unhumanistischen sprachlichen Formen Ulrichs gehören das mehrfach verwendete arbitravimus oder gar das concilium Basiliensem (wenn es sich dabei nicht um einen Fehler des Herausgebers handelt); quod wird nach mittelalterlichem Usus konsekutiv verwendet–z.B. "tantus frigor quod" oder "ita ruinosum quod"–und wenn Ulrich auf zu erwartende hohe Ausgaben hinweist, sagt er: "et erit me constare infinitam summam pecuniarum."[23]

Unter sprachlichem Aspekt ist auch das 2.Tagebuch des 15. Jahrhunderts, von dem ich hier sprechen will, noch nicht als humanistisch zu bezeichnen. Sein Autor ist Johannes Busch, der als Mitarbeiter des Nikolaus von Kues Klöster in Nord- und Mitteldeutschland visitierte. Der gebürtige Niederländer Johannes Busch, der bei den Windesheimer Kanonikern ausgebildet war, hat seine Erfahrungen und Reisen in Deutschland in behäbiger Breite in seinem Liber de reformatione monasteriorum[24] festgehalten. Das Bild, das er von den sittlichen Zuständen

[22] D. Kühn, *Ich Wolkenstein*. Eine Biographie, (Frankfurt, 1980), 470 f.

[23] Schaller (wie Anm. 21) 317.

[24] *Des Augustinerpropstes Johannes Busch Chronicon Windeshemense und Liber de reformatione monasteriorum,* hrsg. von Karl Grube, Geschichtsquellen der Provinz

in den Klöstern der Jahrhundertmitte entwirft, ist niederschmetternd; auch er fand nur selten die Klöster in bono statu. Gelegentlich wußte er sich nicht anders zu helfen, als daß er alle Insassen eines Klosters einzeln strafversetzte und an ihre Stelle reformaufgeschlossene Mönche in die verlassenen Gebäude brachte. Hier geht es mir aber nicht um sein Reformwerk, sondern um seinen Bericht. Er dokumentiert seine Tätigkeit als Visitator; den größten Raum nehmen aber Lebensschicksale ein. Johannes Busch mußte häufig lange Reisen unternehmen. Er reiste selten allein, vielleicht suchte er auch Reisegesellschaft. Er muß die Gabe besessen haben, zuhören zu können und seinen Mitreisenden die Zunge zu lösen. So hörte er Geschichten von Unglücksfällen, von Verbrechen, von merkwürdigen Begebenheiten—und dies alles nicht in seiner Eigenschaft als Visitator oder Geistlicher, sondern als Reisender. Er hat diese Geschichten, die nur von Menschen, nicht von Dingen oder Naturereignissen handeln, in seinem Liber de reformatione monasteriorum festgehalten. Trieb ihn Kuriosität oder was veranlaßte ihn zu seinen Aufzeichnungen? Denn es geht nicht um Abrechnungen oder Leistungsnachweise, die Geschichten handeln nicht von ihm, sondern von fremden Personen. Wollte er Wechselfälle menschlichen Glückes oder menschliche Bosheit und Niedertracht als Exempla sammeln und sie in seinen Predigten verwenden? Ich vermag es nicht anzugeben.

Spätere Tagebücher von Geistlichen bis in die Zeit des 30jährigen Krieges registrieren weiterhin die gelesenen Messen, das Mitwirken bei Hochzeiten und Beerdigungen und sie enthalten Aufzeichnungen über Prozessionsriten—sind also fast immer mit dem Blick auf den intendierten Nutzen geschrieen.[25] Johannes Busch hat sein Tagebuch von diesen Zeilen emanzipiert.

Er war offensichtlich mit sich und der Welt so im Einklang, daß er das Tagebuch nicht als Klagemauer, als Hilfe bei der Lebenswältigung oder als Tempel des eigenen Ruhmes benötigte. In der Tradition der Gattung läßt sein Tagebuch einen neuen Typ von Diarium erkennen. Sein Autor ist der in sich selbst ruhende, dem Diesseits zugewandte Mensch, der selbständig seinen Weg geht.

Es bleibt uns ein Blick auf die Diaristik des 16. bis 18. Jahrhunderts. Die

---

Sachsen 19 (Halle, 1886).

[25] Franz Falk, *Die pfarramtlichen Aufzeichnungen (Liber consuetudinum) des Florentius Diel zu St. Christoph in Mainz (1491–1518)*, (Erläuterungen und Ergänzungen zu Janssens Geschichte des deutschen Volkes IV, 3), (Freiburg, 1904); Benedikt Pitschmann, Aus dem Tagebuch eines Flüchtlings des Dreißigjährigen Krieges. Abt Karl Stengel von Anhausen in Kremsmünster, in *Studien und Mitteilungen zur Geschichte des Benediktinerordens und seiner Zweige* 88 (1977): 53–145.

geistlichen Beweggründe treten in dieser Epoche in den Hintergrund. Es geht nicht mehr darum, vor Gott Rechenschaft über ein anvertrautes Amt abzulegen, die Diarien handeln fast ausschließlich vom Menschen, sie werden säkularisiert und trivialisiert. Um 1600 notiert der Tübinger Professor für klassische Philologie Martin Crusius für jeden Tag des Jahres das Wetter, zählt seine Tischgenossen auf und skizziert die Sitzordnung, nennt die Weinsorten und die Zahl der Gänge bei einem Essen.[26] Selbst die Speisen führt er wie auf einer Menükarte jeweils an, dies oft in deutschen Einschüben; er springt zwischen Deutsch, Latein und Griechisch emsig hin und her, nicht als Stilmittel, sondern aus Bequemlichkeit. Seine glanzlosen Aufzeichnungen spiegeln eine kleine provinzielle Welt, in der ein erhaltener Brief, das Holz für den Ofen, ein Unfall oder die Apfelernte Erwähnung finden. Crusius hielt in seinen Aufzeichnungen fest, wie viele Seiten er täglich aus den klassischen Sprachen übersetzte, wie viele Vorlesungsstunden er hielt. Wegen einer Disputation in der Theologischen Fakultät fielen die Lehrveranstaltungen auch der Philosophen aus. So konnte er notieren: "Liberi eramus propter Disputationem hanc a docendo. Ego domi manens, sex paginas ... verti." Wer die Alltagswirklichkeit einer Universität um 1600, die bescheidenen Lebensumstände der Gelehrten und ihren Umgang mit der lateinischen Sprache kennenlernen will, dem sei die Lektüre dieses Diariums empfohlen.

Crusius machte auch Aufzeichnungen über seine Gesundheit. In den Diarien der Neuzeit gilt diesem Punkt eine besondere Aufmerksamkeit. Das körperliche Wohlbefinden bzw. die mancherlei Epidemien, Krankheiten und Gebresten scheinen mitunter das Hauptmotiv für das Führen eines Tagebuchs gewesen zu sein–ich nenne Montaigne, Samuel Pepys, Daniel Defoe und den eingangs erwähnten Dr. Johnson. Johnson war im Laufe seines Lebens dazu übergegangen, sein Tagebuch teils englisch, teils lateinisch zu führen. Der lateinischen Sprache als der Sprache der Wissenschaft bediente er sich zu Aufzeichnungen über die eingenommenen Medikamente und ihre Wirkungen. Diese medizinischen Eintragungen variieren nur wenig. Bald heißt es: "nox insomnis et tristis, nox misera, nox placida sed sine somno, tota nocte mente turbatissima vigilavi, somnus fere nullus, anhelitus molestus, crura et femora tument."[27] Das Tagebuch ist hier zum Klagebuch geworden, zu einem Dokument, das den körperlichen Verfall registriert. Wer nach dem Lebensgefühl vergangener Epochen, nach dem pursuit of happiness fragt, findet in den

---

[26] *Diarium Martini Crusii, 1596–1605*, Bd. 1–3, (Tübingen, 1927–1958).

[27] S. Johnson (wie Anm. 2) 386–416.

vielen, oft noch ungedruckten lateinischen Diarien der Neuzeit ein reiches Anschauungsmaterial.[28]

Freiburg

[28] Nachtrag: Hinweise auf weitere Tagebücher verdanke ich Bernhard Kytzler, Jean-Claude Margolin, Leo Miller, Edwin Rabbie und Mine Skafte Jensen. Da lateinisch geführte Tagebücher m.W. bibliographisch bisher nicht erfaßt sind, lasse ich einige Titel folgen (sie fehlen z.B. in der verdienstvollen Bibliographie von William Matthews, *British Diaries. An Annotated Bibliography of British Diaries written between 1442 and 1942.* (London, 1950). *Johannis Burckardi Liber Notarum ab anno MCCCLXXXIII usque ad annum MDVI* a cura di Enrico Celani, Città di Castello 1906; Hieronymus Cardanus, Opera omnia, (Stuttgart, 1966); *Diarium van Arend van Buchell,* hg. von G. Brom und L. A. van Langeraad, (Amsterdam, 1907); A. Wolters, *Konrad von Heresbach und der Clevische Hof zu seiner Zeit,* (Elberfeld, 1867), V; *Journal autobiographique du cardinal Jérôme Aléandre (1480–1530)* par H. Omont (Paris, 1895); *Diarium Everardi Bronchorstii sive Adversaria omnium quae gesta sunt in Academia Leydensi (1591–1627),* hg. von J. C. van Slee ('s Gravenhage, 1898); Peder Hegelunds Almanokoptegnelser 1565–1613, hg. von Bue Kaae (Ribe, 1976); Leo Miller, *John Milton and the Oldenburg Safeguard: New Light on Milton and his Friends in the Commonwealth from the Diaries and Letters of Hermann Mylius, Agonist in the Early History of Modern Diplomacy* (New York, 1985); Das Tagebuch Placidus Bacheberles, letzten Abts von Schuttern, aus dem Jahr 1794, hg. von Hermann Schmid, in *Freiburger Diözesanarchiv 105* (1985) 297–338; *Mathematisches Tagebuch 1796–1814 von Carl Friedrich Gauss* mit deutscher Übersetzung von E. Schuhmann (Leipzig, 1976).

The Language of Eternity: The Role of Latin in 16th-Century Danish Culture

MINNA SKAFTE JENSEN

International movements have certain recognizable characteristics wherever they occur. Even so, they never remain quite the same under new conditions. When the Renaissance reached Denmark during the sixteenth century, it kept its general features: the revival of ancient learning, the interest in the individual and the decisive role played by the printing press. On its way through Germany it had been deeply coloured by religious controversies, and its first manifestations in Denmark were closely linked with the discussions for and against Lutheran Protestantism. Its final Danish breakthrough came in the wake of the Reformation in 1536. During the following decades, it was formed in special ways by factors such as nationalism, the feeling among the intellectuals of belonging to the periphery of Europe, the growing economic and political power of the nobility and especially of the kings, their ambitions of regaining the dominant position among the Nordic countries and a period of relative economic prosperity. Parallels can probably be drawn from elsewhere to each and all of these factors, but even so the Danish compound bore its own stamp. The poem presented below is unusual in being bilingual, but in other ways it is typical. Since most of the central issues of Danish cultural discourse towards the end of the sixteenth century are represented in it, it may serve as a point of departure for this introduction to Danish culture at that time and the place occupied by the Latin language within that culture.

A Nobleman's Epitaph

The inscription in figure 1 commemorates one of the most prominent Danish noblemen of the time, Jørgen Rosenkrantz. He was for decades a member of the King's Council, and when in 1588 Frederic II died, leaving an heir who was still a minor, Jørgen Rosenkrantz became one of the four members of the regency. At his own death in 1596 he was the most powerful man in the country. The poem was probably composed almost twenty years earlier. It is painted on a wooden board and hangs on the wall of a chapel in the church of Hornslet in Jutland. It is written in two columns with Roman letters for the Latin version and Gothic letters for the Danish. The poem is encircled by sixteen coats of arms belonging to Jørgen Rosenkrantz' ancestors. At the bottom there is a black area framed by two figures, *Pietas* and *Justitia*.

Fig. 1. Jørgen Rosenkrantz' memorial poem in the church of Hornslet. Photo by Kirsten Nijkamp.

On the opposite wall of the small chapel is a painting of the Resurrection (figure 2). It has the form of a three-panelled altar-piece, with the male and female members of the family kneeling on the left and right wing respectively. It is inscribed with quotations from the Bible, all concerned with the Resurrection. Following the curved top line of the central painting are the words, *Johannis XI: Ego sum resurrectio et vita. Qui credit in me, etiam si mortuus fuerit, vivet; et omnis qui vivit et credit in me, non morietur in æternum. Credis hoc?* Above the head of Jørgen Rosenkrantz the text is: *Scio enim quod redemptor meus vivit, et in novissimo die de terra surrecturus sum. Et rursum circumdabor pelle mea et in carne mea videbo Deum meum. Quem visurus sum ego ipse, et oculi mei conspecturi sunt, et non alius. Reposita est hæc spes in sinu meo.* Above his wife, Dorthe Lange, there are two quotations: *Johannis XI: Utique Domine ego credidi, quod tu es Christus, filius dei vivi, qui in hunc mundum venisti,* and *Marci IX: Credo Domine, succurre incredulitati meæ.*

The painting is thought to be the work of an unidentified Netherlandic artist. Nor is it known who composed the poem.[1] Stranger, perhaps, is the fact that nowhere on this monumental epitaph does the name of the deceased occur. The church is full of epitaphs of various members of the Rosenkrantz family, all duly named. Jørgen Rosenkrantz took over a small mediaeval parish church in 1560 and started rebuilding and transforming it into something like a family sepulchre, to which he had the relics of his

---

I am grateful to John D. Kendal for editing my English.

[1] C. A. Jensen: *Danske adelige Gravsten fra Sengotikens og Renaissancens Tid. Studier over Værksteder og Kunstnere* 2 (Copenhagen: Høst 1953), p. 10, mentions Tobias Gemperlin as the painter. H.Honnens de Lichtenberg: *Motiver og budskaber i kirkelige og verdslige vaerker i Danmark i tiden fra reformationen til år 1600* (Copenhagen: Museum Tusculanum, forthcoming) has a detailed discussion of the epitaph as no. C 14. She ascribes the painting to a "Netherlandic mannerist" with Italian connections and mentions Pieter Pourbus' circle perhaps one of his sons as well as pupils of Frans Floris as artists to be considered in this connection. She takes 1577–78 as the probable date of the painting. The poem has not, to my knowledge, been seriously studied before. C. A. Jensen suggests that Jørgen Rosenkrantz himself might be the author (*Rosenholm og Rosenkrantzerne*, ed. by Hans Rosenkrantz, Copenhagen: Koppel 1924, p. 148). In my opinion the quality of the double poem makes it unlikely that it should be the work of an amateur. Also, I doubt that composition of poetry would have appealed to the noble Jørgen Rosenkrantz as a suitable enterprise, cf. Peter Zeeberg's contribution to the present volume. I think the poem was written already in 1575, but lack space to argue for this view here. For Jørgen Rosenkrantz' life, see A. Heise: *Bidrag til Familien Rosenkrantz's Historie i det 16. Aarhundredes sidste Halvdel* (Copenhagen: Bianco Luno 1885–87), 327–417. J. R. left a handwritten autobiography, edited in *Danske Magazin* 4 (1750): 193–204.

Fig. 2. Triptych painting with resurrection scene and donors' portraits.
Photo by Kirsten Nijkamp.

ancestors transposed from various places in the country, and where he planned to be buried himself in due course. Perhaps his name was to have been inscribed in the black area at the bottom of the text board, but for some reason it was never filled in. Alternatively, the anonymity of his epitaph may be seen as a mark of pride: the whole church is his monument, and he can take for granted that all who see it will know whose epitaph they are regarding.

Tandem hunc, curarum nexu vitaque solutus,
  Quo conderer mihi ipse condidi locum:
Extructo ut cernis, secreta in parte sacello,
  ut svaviter mea hac qviescam in cellula.
Vox SALVATORIS donec lætissima letho 5
  Cev blandulo fusum sopore me excitet.
Ipse Animam providens ipsum hoc ex pulvere corpus
  Prodire splendidum iubebit et novum.
Hunc in Carne mea spectabo Hominemque Deumque
  Alius havt oculis, sed his ipsis meis. 10

Nunc oblita mihi tot cultæ iugera terræ,
  Nemora, lacus, arces, opes, regum domus:
Et gesti in patria, non infima munia, honores
  Hev umbratilis felicitas, hev vanitas,
Non oblita tamen patriae mea nomina: si qvid 15
  (Scit) profui: prodesse certe usque volui.
Non oblita Deo mea nomina: namque notavit
  Jam olim inter Electos suo vitæ in libro.
Justifico aspersum quia GRATIS sangvine christi,
  in filio fecit, FIDE me filium. 20

Tu quicumque loco post me dominaberis isti:
  Ne obrue meum, neve inqvietes, pulverem.
Lingva animaque favens potius dic: ossa quiescant
  Huic molliter, qvi nemini vixit gravis.
Qvisqvis es ad metam mecum properabis eandem 25
  Legem hanc is attulit, qui edens pomum abstulit.
Mature vitam et mores Componito morti:
  Improvidum, ni feceris, mors opprimet.
Jamque mori dum vivis adhuc, meditabere Mihi qvod
  Hodie est, Tibi erit cras: Bene mori magnæ artis est.

Dette Sted haffuer ieg dertil uduold
  Jeg her vild' haffue min sidste tilhold

Oc dette Capel til den end' oc act
  Her bygt at Soffue der Rolig og Sact
Indtil min Frelser mig wecker igien 5
  Paa yderste Dag Foruden all meen
Min Siel haffuer hand hos sig foruart
  Mit Legom igien opstaar nyt oc klart:
Ia, siunlig da omgiffues med min Hud,
  Oc Ieg i mit kiød selff skue min Gud. 10

Ald Werdsens handel haffuer ieg forlat
  Skoffu' oc March med godz, husz og anden skat
Befalning oc ære, sampt meere Sligt
  Ach huad er det ganske Forgengeligt,
Mit Naffn, dis haffuer ieg et ret godt mod 15
  Skall bliff' i ærlig Amindelse oc god,
Mit Naffn er ey heller hos Gud forgett
  vdi Liffsens Bog haffuer han det sett
Fordi hand haffuer mine Synder aftoed
  aff Naaden ved Troen i Christi Blod. 20

Nu Beder Jeg alle, Som faa i wold'
  Dette sted', i lader mig Behold'
Mit huile Kammer oc ynske mig Fred
  Ia, tencke oc paa eder Selff herved
huor snart forløber eders dag' oc Tid 25
  At i kunde lære saa med ald Flid
Eders leffnet at Bedre oc vell end'
  Beder Gud eder dertil Naaden send'
Thi huad som mig monn' wederforet vær'
  Det vil wist hend' eder all' oc en Huer.[2] 30

(Translation of the Danish version):

This place have I chosen with the purpose
here to have my final resort,
and built this chapel with the end and design
here to sleep peacefully and quietly
until my Saviour wakes me again 5
on the last day free from all harm.

[2] Copied from the original, with abbreviations solved and verse-counting added.

My soul he has kept in his guardianship;
my body will rise again new and bright,
yea, be covered visibly in my skin,
and in my own flesh I shall behold my God. 10

All turmoil of the world have I left,
forest and field, with property, estate, and other riches,
command and honour and more of that kind.
Alas, how very transitory it is!
My name, I have firm confidence, 15
will remain of honourable and good memory;
nor has my name been forgotten by God,
who has written it in the Book of Life,
since he has washed away my sins
in grace, by faith, in Christ's blood. 20

Now I ask all who may be given charge
of this place that you let me keep
my resting room and wish me peace,
yea, think also of yourselves in so doing,
how soon your days and time will pass, 25
so that you might learn with all diligence
to improve your lives and end them well.
Pray to God to send you his grace to that end,
for what has happened to me
is certain to befall you each and everyone. 30

Both versions of the poem contain three 10-line stanzas. The deceased is speaking. In the first stanza he declares that he has built the chapel for his own tomb where he will rest until his Saviour wakes him up: risen from the dead he shall see Christ with his own eyes. It is closely modelled on the Biblical quotation above Jørgen Rosenkrantz' portrait. The theme of the second stanza is the vanity of worldly honour and riches; his name, however, will endure, for God has written it into his Book of Life. The third stanza is addressed to his descendants, who are asked not to disturb his peace, but to contemplate their own deaths and prepare in time. The combination of paintings, biblical quotations and verse inscription might be interpreted as a huge emblem with its characteristic triad structure of picture, title and epigram.

The text and its setting exemplify what Philippe Ariès has called "tamed death": "A ritual organized by the dying person himself, who presided over it and knew its protocol".[3] Long before death was at hand, Jørgen Rosenkrantz prepared for the event; this is underlined in the first verses of the poem, and the theme recurs as the moral at the end of it. Ariès has commented on the way in which the Book of Life changed during the Middle Ages; from being God's register of those selected to join him in Paradise, as it is in Revelations, it developed into an account book in which each individual's good and bad deeds were written for the final account to be made up on the Day of Judgement. In the mediaeval *Dies Irae* such a Book of Life is the basis for the judgement, and Ariès also gives examples where the book contains not the names of the redeemed but those of the damned.[4] In the present twin poem, however, the Book of Life is referred to with philological correctness as containing the names of God's chosen. Compare the way the painting is inscribed with quotations from the Bible, correctly copied and with references to chapters and books for the viewer to control.[5] The epitaph is made by and for people who know their Bible. The Job passage has acquired a new meaning in its new context. In a sense, the deceased's eagerness to see Christ with his own eyes is truly humanist: with the distribution of reliable Bibles in print, it had become possible to learn God's words by personal experience. A further step towards its source would be to face Him.

Latin and Danish

The two versions adhere to poetical conventions from Latin and Danish traditions respectively. The Latin poem consists of distichs, alternating hexameters and iambic senars as in Horace's sixteenth epode. This metre is more ambitious than the much more common hexameter-pentameter distichs, and still a suitable form for an inscription. The Danish version is made up of ten-syllable rhyming couplets with four stresses in each line. Since hexameters and senars have from twelve to seventeen syllables, the Latin version is slightly longer than the Danish. That is surprising, considering that Latin normally needs fewer words than the vernaculars to

[3] Philippe Ariès: *Western Attitudes Toward Death: From the Middle Ages to the Present* (Baltimore, London: Johns Hopkins 1974), 11.

[4] Philippe Ariès: *L'homme devant la mort* (Paris: du Seuil 1977), 106-9.

[5] The quotations are Job 19.25–27, Mark. 9.24, John. 11.25–27. For the Old Testament the text follows the Vulgate, for the New Testament the first edition by Erasmus (Basel: Frobenius 1516). The subsequent editions of Erasmus differ slightly in the John passage.

express a given idea. Add to this that the Danish version abounds in pleonasms, and the question poses itself: what has the Latin version got that is lacking in the Danish one? A series of stylistic refinements, elements that belong to *ornatus* in rhetorical handbooks, but also quite a few matters of content that are either just alluded to in the Danish version or completely absent.

In the first stanza, there is the elegant ambiguity in the opening word, *tandem*. Introducing a funeral text and leading up to an expression of *taedium vitae*, it suggests that finally the speaker has reached his goal, death. However, both the position of the pronoun *hunc* and the punctuation make it clear that what he has finally achieved is the building of his funeral chapel. The notion of death as a liberation from the toils of life is not expressed in the Danish poem. The pun on the two senses of *condere* is special to the Latin poem, too. The following lines are rich in alliteration and assonance, the s's in 3-4, *lætissima letho* in 5, which is also an oxymoron, and especially the i's and s's of line 10: *Alius haut oculis, sed his ipsis meis.* The "I" of the poem is given prominence by the frequent use of the first person pronoun, often reinforced with *ipse*. And the anaphora in line 7 of *ipse* for the Saviour and *ipsum* for the resurrected "I" suggests a meeting of two parties that are to a certain degree equal: as Christ is both man and God, *Hominemque Deumque*, the deceased will be able to see him with his human but no longer mortal eyes. The Danish version is more vague. The dead body comes to life again—there is nothing corresponding to *iubebit*—and it becomes visible to others, whereas in the Latin version the whole emphasis is on the resurrected man's active looking at God.

The second stanza of the Latin poem is structured by the anaphora from line 11 to 15 and 17: *nunc oblita—non oblita*, which creates a tension between the first four lines and their description of vanity and the last six lines, which dwell upon what does after all remain. The Danish poem also has anaphora between lines 15 and 17, but nothing to stress the fundamental opposition between the two parts of the stanza. And then the Latin poem is much more explicit concerning the mortal deeds of the speaker than is the Danish one, the first two distichs of which might apply to any rich and influential man. What the Latin lines say fits precisely the individual Jørgen Rosenkrantz. As the youngest of three brothers he had not inherited a manor house with adjoining land, but scattered property, from which he had managed, through a lifetime's exchanges and bargains, to create a great estate with fields, forests and lakes, and where he had built Rosenholm, one of the most splendid castles of the period: *jugera terræ, nemora, lacus, arces. Opes* are riches in general, whereas the words *regum domus* refer specifically to the fact that during his career he was in charge of three of the king's castles, Koldinghus, Dronningborg, and Kalø. Line 13 mentions that he has had important duties: belonging to the inner circle of the king, he had been entrusted with diplomatic missions such as negotiations with possible allies against Sweden during the Nordic Seven Years' war, and he had been a member of the peace commission at the end of that war. He is certain that his native country will not forget his name–*patria* is mentioned twice in the Latin poem, but plays no role in the Danish one. The two versions agree in asserting that God has written his name in the Book of Life, and in underscoring the orthodox Lutheran doctrine that this has happened by the pure grace of Christ's blood. The literary models of the stanza are biblical; besides Revelations there is the vanity motif of Ecclesiastes.

This second stanza of the Latin poem is a small masterpiece of ideological rhetoric.[6] On the surface it deals with the vanity of all mortal pursuits and with salvation by the grace of God. But just below the surface it is about Jørgen Rosenkrantz' very personal merits. The introductory phrase, *nunc oblita mihi*, is equivalent to the classical orator's declaration of the items he is not going to mention, leading to a rather detailed catalogue of what Jørgen Rosenkrantz could pride himself on. And there is a refined use of the figure *climax* through the first four of the stanza's five distichs: the first step consists of the deceased's material property, the second of his deeds in the service of his native country; third comes the fame that he has earned by them, and finally we hear of the reward that awaits him in Paradise. On the face of it, this is simply an enumeration ascending step by step, but in reality it functions as a logical argumentation: Jørgen Rosenkrantz' riches, power, and meritorious deeds lead naturally to immortal renown not only on earth but also in heaven. It is not said that he himself has deserved to have his name written in the Book of Life; on the contrary, it is explicitly stated that this is solely due to Christ, underlined in the elegant verse 20 with its alliteration and assonance and its use of *filius* in two senses. But the deceased's merits resound through all the assertions that human endeavour is vanity and grace unconditional.

The last Latin stanza is formed as an ancient funeral inscription of the *siste viator* type; the pattern of the genre explains the slightly awkward *quicumque*: Jørgen Rosenkrantz could expect his descendants to take over, but the ancient model required an unspecified addressee, the incidental passer-by. The stanza is a compact example of *imitatio* of ancient pagan

[6] By "ideology" I mean: a world-view, appealing to emotions rather than logic, and often expressed implicitly under a different surface message.

models, except for line 26 where the Fall of Man is mentioned, but in decent classical attire. Line 23 contains a formula from Roman religion, well-known from Horace's third Roman ode, and lines 23–24 use a topos from Hellenistic funeral epigrams as we know them from the 7th book of the Greek Anthology. Line 25 has taken its metaphor from the Roman circus, and lines 27–29 are pure Stoicism; especially verse 29 suggests phrases from Seneca on the topic of *cotidie mori.*[7] Prepare your death, let it not overtake you unexpectedly, is the message. Christian notions of sin, repentance and redemption do not occur at all in this last stanza, except that they might be said to be included in the final allusion to the *artes moriendi*, handbooks on how to die piously.[8] The stanza's fusion of pagan and Christian lets classical antiquity prevail—not only in the form, but also very much in the content. Notice how elegantly the rhythm moves towards the end: throughout the poem there has been a quiet, dignified movement with each distich as a well-rounded whole, properly divided into two halves. But in the very last distich the twofold pattern is cut into three, giving a staccato effect and a feeling of a compact mass of ideas being squeezed into a minimum of space, making the three dogmas stand out sharply.

The corresponding Danish stanza contains the prayer that the tomb may remain undisturbed, and the stress on death as a general condition, common to all human beings. There is no Greek Anthology, no Roman circus, no Stoicism, no handbook on dying, nor any Adam biting the fatal apple. Instead, there is an appeal that the readers may mend their ways in time and pray God for mercy. This is the only point where the Danish version has something that the Latin one lacks. The stanza is hymn-like, close in tone to many of the poems in the new Danish hymnal by Hans Thommisøn, published 1569.

As a whole, the Danish version is no uninteresting poem either, only very different from the Latin one. It is not as compact as its counterpart and it makes no efforts to cram all the topics of the Latin poem into its more limited space. On the contrary, it takes its time, leaves out what does not find room, and has a simple and natural flow. It is much more pious, but by no means self-effacing; apart from its affinities to hymns, I think it

---

[7] Seneca *Ad Luc.* 1.2.3.

[8] *Ars moriendi.* Holztafeldruck von c. 1470. Hrsg. und eing. von Otto Clemen (Zwickau: F.Ullmann 1910). Rainer Rudolf: *Ars moriendi. Von der Kunst des heilsamen Lebens und Sterbens.* Forschungen zur Volkskunde Bd. 39 (Cologne, Graz: Böhlau 1957).

has as its model the mediaeval *Rhymed Chronicle*, which was published in 1495 as the first Danish-language book in print and was well known in the sixteenth century, when it had several reprints. In this poem the Danish kings step forward one by one and render account of their lives and deeds. Not a bad model for an ambitious nobleman.

To sum up: even though the two poems convey a common message, they do so in very different ways. Latin provides more than just the language; with the phrases go metaphors, connotations, and ways of argumentation that make the Lutheran message look like a natural heir to ancient philosophy. Such a fusion of ancient and Christian, which is very typical of Danish Neo-Latin poetry, is often so dominant as to make the religious disputes against Catholicism disappear. This element, and with it the general impression of enthusiasm for learning, is reserved for the Latin version. If the Danish poem had been transmitted alone we should not have thought of antiquity in this connection, and the text would by no means have struck us as an example of classical revival. Half a century later things had changed: the Danish poets of the Baroque age strove to transplant the ancient models into their mother tongue. Not so here: Danish poetry is one thing, Latin another.

Both poems are elegant; but the Latin one has a variety of subtle techniques of rhetoric and rhythm to play on that the Danish one lacks. In both poems there is a basic tension between the dignified,self-confident nobleman and his humble Lutheran message. But the Latin form offers the poet opportunity to let the individual merits of the deceased shine forth, whereas his dignity is of a much more general kind in the Danish version.

The Choice of Language

For whom were the two poems written? As a rule, Latin texts were meant to reach an international audience; but since these texts did not appear in print but stayed on their wall in Hornslet, international readability cannot have been of first importance here. They must have been primarily addressed to the deceased's own family, and I would suggest that the Latin and Danish versions were meant for the male and female members respectively. By 1575, Latin had almost regained its mediaeval status as the normal written language in Denmark, but only for men. If women were taught to read and write, they learned Danish. To what degree Latin had become the normal choice can be deduced from the fact that there are occasions where an author explains why he writes Danish, whereas I know of no examples where a poet explains why he has chosen Latin. A case in many respects parallel to our poem is a verse-chronicle from c.1580 celebrating a noble family. It was written by a commoner, the poet Claus Christophersen Lyschander, and as it was meant only for the noble family itself, it was therefore not printed. Lyschander writes that he has chosen Danish in order that the ladies of the family should not be excluded from reading his poem. When you look at the painting for Jørgen Rosenkrantz with the members of his family so neatly divided up according to sex and consider that it is hanging just opposite the bilingual verse-inscription, you can almost see them reading: the men, Latin; and the women, Danish.[9]

The choice of language was by no means simple. Different considerations intersected in a complex of inconsistent criteria: Latin for an international audience, Danish for a national one. Latin for the educated, Danish for the uneducated. Latin for the commoners, Danish or German for the aristocracy. Latin for men, Danish for women. Latin for personal messages, Danish for general ones. Shortly afterwards, King Frederic II had a similar choice to make for the texts of a magnificent series of tapestries, woven to decorate his new castle of Kronborg in Elsinore. The motif was highly representative: the complete list of Danish kings. Even though he had both Latin and Danish poems at his disposal, he finally chose German.[10]

The balance among the various possible languages shifted somewhat during the century. Fifty years earlier, the first generation of Danish humanists had been guided by their enthusiasm for learning, their nationalism, and their concern for popular education, and they were very much aware of the possibilities offered by the printing press. Thus Christian Pedersen had had the great Latin history of Denmark by the mediaeval scholar Saxo Grammaticus printed in Paris in 1514.[11] It had an obvious message for an international as well as for a national audience, that of

---

[9] Besides Lyschander, I refer to Rasmus Hansen Reravius' introduction to *Frederik II's og Dronning Sophies Kronings og Bryllups Historie* (Copenhagen: Lor. Benedicht 1576). When in 1560 the German poet Hieronymus Osius described a war fought by the Danish King, he dedicated a Latin version to the King and a German one to Electress Anna of Sachsen (Karen Skovgaard-Petersen has drawn my attention to this). It fits into this pattern that Anders Sørensen Vedel dedicated his collection of Danish ballads to Queen Sophie (1591).

[10] M. Mackeprang & Sigrid Flamand Christensen: *Kronborgtapeterne*. Avec un resumé en français (Copenhagen: Selskabet til Udgivelse af Skrifter om danske Mindesmærker 1950).

[11] Cf. Karsten Friis-Jensen's paper in this volume.

Denmark's long history and powerful status in former times. Christian Pedersen had also made the first translation of the New Testament into Danish, published a Latin-Danish vocabulary, and argued—in print and in Danish—for Latin as the teaching language of the schools in order that the young students should be able to participate in the international scholarly discussions on a par with others.[12] In the decades leading up to the Lutheran Reformation, Danish had been in frequent use as the written language for the discussions carried on between Catholics and Protestants while at the same time appealing to a much broader audience. But when after the Reformation a ramified and centralized system of schools was instituted, it was decided to use Latin as the teaching language for the same reason as that put forward by Christian Pedersen: young Danes should not be handicapped in their careers in the world of learning. Thus for nationalistic reasons, Danish lost ground to Latin. Books were still published in Danish, but mainly such in which well-educated authors talked down to their readers. When they wrote for their equals, in Denmark or abroad, they wrote Latin.[13]

A comprehensive study of Danish wedding poetry from the sixteenth century has recently been made. The total list is of 79 items, all after 1540. There are 72 in Latin, 5 in Danish, and 2 in Greek. Here no doubt there was more prestige attached to Latin—or even Greek—than to Danish, and it was therefore more honourable to receive an epithalamium in Latin than in Danish. Even so, the dominance of Latin is remarkable.[14]

Texts from the last decades of the sixteenth century often give the impression that the authors find it easier to express themselves in Latin than in Danish. Latin was the language in which they had been trained, from the very moment when they had started to learn their letters; they had had its orthography and grammar inculcated and been taught the

---

[12] Chr. Pedersen: *Om børn ath holde till Scole och Studium Och ath skicke gode Scolemestere till dem* (Antwerp: Willem Vorsterman 1531).

[13] Erik Dal has made a statistical study of the choice of languages in Danish books: "Bücher in dänischer Sprache vor 1600," *Gutenberg-Jahrbuch* 62 (1987): 37–46, showing that Danish was in fact the language of the majority of printed books. The investigation does not, however, show the varying importance of the books concerned, nor the ups and downs during the century. It is interesting to compare the situation in 1580 to that in 1530: Lauritz Nielsen's bibliography has 12 titles from 1530 with 10 in Danish and 2 in Latin, whereas for 1580 it has 29, 14 in Danish and 15 in Latin.

[14] Pernille Harsting: *Latinske bryllupsdigte i Danmark i det 16. århundrede* (Copenhagen: Muesum Tusculanum, forthcoming).

basic rules of verse-making. To compose in Danish demanded more innovative energy.[15]

A Multilingual Almanac

The mix-up of languages, the dominant position of Latin, and the development over half a century are documented in interesting detail by the calendar notes of Peder Hegelund. He was born in Ribe in Jutland of a rich and influential burgher family, went to the local Latin school, studied in Leipzig and Wittenberg and held posts as a teacher, vicar and finally bishop in his native town. He was also a poet and is nowadays best known as the author of the first school drama in Danish, *Susanna* (Cph. 1578). From his hand an almost unbroken series of annotated calendars from 1565 to 1613 has been preserved. Their main language is Latin, with an occasional use of Greek, German, Danish, Hebrew, and small drawings, e.g., a pair of legs to illustrate that a letter has been sent off with a friend. His notes concern both personal and public affairs. As a young student in Germany he writes in some detail whenever news come in of events in the Swedish-Danish war, but otherwise his notes are brief, telling of the students' lives, courses he attends, magisterial promotions, visits from home, letters sent and received. Later in his life, he continues to comment on his work, mentions visitors and letters, the texts he teaches, the dramas he has his pupils perform. Thus he notes for June 4th 1571 that his pupils have performed Buchanan's *Jephta*. Events in his own life, his marriages and children, bargains, reading and publications are noted. There are details of everyday life in Ribe, who has married whom, who has died, who has been fighting, who has been condemned for witchcraft and, of course, of disasters like fire, flood and pestilence.[16]

During his student years Latin is almost universal, with Greek as the second choice. German is used mostly for practical matters such as noting purchases and doing accounts. The first note in Danish, and the only one

[15] Hieronymus Osius: *Beschreibung des Kriegs . . . wider die Ditmarsen*, 1560 p. A. v.r explains that since the author is less trained in writing German than Latin, his Latin poem is longer and more precise than his German one (cf. note 8). L. Forster: "Europäischer Petrarkismus als Vorschule der Dichtung," in *Petrarca*, ed. A. Buck. Wege der Forschung, vol. 353 (Darmstadt 1976): 424–43, has a survey (p. 432) of reasons why poets preferred Latin to the vernaculars, including the explanation that the ready-made models facilitated Latin composition.

[16] *Peder Hegelunds almanakoptegnelser 1565–1613*. Udg. ved Bue Kaae. I–II (Ribe: Historisk Samfund for Ribe Amt, 1976).

the whole first year, comes on September 8th and says: "Market day is held in Ribe." Over the years, Danish spreads more and more so as to become the normal language of the notes, with Latin as number two; German disappears, while Greek and even Hebrew remain for casual use. This is, of course, the development of an individual, and the initial dominance of Latin is connected with the fact that the author lived in a university milieu and spoke the language regularly. But it is noteworthy how well Latin keeps its position long after Peder Hegelund had established himself in Ribe. And the pattern fits well enough into the general picture offered by other sources.

Languages used by Peder Hegelund in his calendar notes, 1565-1613:

	Latin	*Greek*	*Danish*	*Germ.*	*Hebr.*	*Draw.*	*G&L*	*L&D*	*G&D*	*Total*
1565	127	14	1	3	0	8	11	0	0	164
	77.4	8.5	0.6	1.8		4.9	6.7			
1575	65	5	25	0	2	0	6	10	1	114
	57.0	4.4	21.9		1.8		5.3	8.8	0.9	
1585	30	1	41	0	0	2	4	9	1	88
	34.1	1.1	46.6			2.3	4.5	10.2	1.1	
1595	74	3	193	1	0	10	1	26	6	314
	23.6	1.0	61.5	0.3		3.2	0.3	8.3	1.9	
1605	28	0	275	2	0	3	1	15	1	325
	8.6		84.6	0.6		0.9	0.3	4.6	0.3	
1613	88	11	333	0	0	5	7	25	11	480
	18.3	2.3	69.4			1.0	1.5	5.2	2.3	

Hegelund made his calendar notes for his own use, so here the choices of language were not made with readers in mind, except for the few notes in Hebrew. They occur at stages in the author's life when he considered marrying and mentioned the women he had in mind. The idea was probably to safeguard such notes against unwanted readers.[17] In some

---

[17] This is what the editor, Bue Kaae, suggests p. XVI; a further possibility is that Hegelund found the exotic Hebrew form more romantic than Latin or Danish.

cases there is an obvious link between the content of the note and the language used. The Danish words concerning the market in Ribe are an example; also from the student period, notes about Greek studies tend to be written in Greek. Notes about university affairs and learned life in general are in Latin right up to the end of the almanac. In Ribe, household affairs are in Danish—cattle breeding, hay-harvest, brewing of beer, etc.—whereas Latin and Danish seem to be equally well-suited for notes concerning school and church.

Often the choice of language seems more arbitrary. A note on an execution of two criminals begins in Latin and shifts into Greek when it comes to details, as if the exotic language gives added intensity. Similarly, Hegelund drops an occasional Greek phrase at dramatic points in his otherwise Latin notes concerning war events. Drinking parties are regularly mentioned not in words but with a drawing of a cup—as a kind of euphemism perhaps? When Latin is no longer his normal choice, it is still used on certain solemn occasions, such as the deaths of important persons, or the disaster when the tower of the church collapsed during a storm. And, finally, Latin continues to be preferred for personal affairs. Notes of his official travels are in Danish, while the private trips tend to be in Latin. The same is true for comments on letter-writing and the composition of books. At one point, he has had an unpleasant dream of losing some of his teeth—which he mentions in Latin. And when he grows old, notes on coughs, fevers and rheumatism are in Latin, while the weather, another subject that comes in latish in the notes and gradually grows more and more important, is invariably mentioned in Danish.

Orality, Literacy and Print

This variety of written languages had no direct counterpart in speaking. There was no competition to Danish as the normal spoken language of the country,[18] but it existed in a variety of dialects, of which no single one had as yet acquired the status of *the* national tongue. However, in some parts of the population German was important too, mainly among the highest nobility and artisans. And then there was the spoken Latin of the learned milieus.

The great majority of the population was illiterate and most "literature"

---

[18] By "Denmark" I here mean the mother country excluding the colonies and the duchies of Schleswig-Holstein.

therefore oral. Writing had, of course, been known for centuries and everybody was aware of its existence—people had been surrounded by writing since time immemorial: they were familiar with inscriptions on buildings, church walls and tombstones; they knew that the laws were written, and that God's words existed in a book. But the advent of printing had given writing a much more important place in people's lives. Even without being able to read you were affected by the centralized religious teaching that the Protestant church expounded, book in hand, and in church you learned by heart the hymns that those who could read sang from their new Danish-language hymnals. And publishers tried to influence existing oral traditions by imitating them in printed books, either with the wish to educate, or in order to gain a profit by selling entertaining works.

For those who could read, printing had done more than just making knowledge far more accessible. It had also, as emphasized by Elizabeth Eisenstein,[19] brought a new awareness of certain matters even if they had been known all along. I shall mention only a few main points.

There was a new awareness that things had to be written in order to be preserved. Thus it became a fashion among the nobility to collect oral ballads. A selection of a hundred such ballads was edited in print by Anders Sørensen Vedel in 1591, with the purpose among other things of stimulating the repertoire of songs in use. But he also had a nationalistic-historical purpose: he asserts that these ballads are very old and well worth comparing with the oral traditions of other nations, and he hopes that they will provide useful material for the study of Danish grammar, which has yet to be started.

There was a vivid interest in history with a clear concern for the present. Noble ladies compiled genealogies to confirm the age and importance of their houses, and poets were paid by noble patrons for celebrating their ancestry in suitable genres. The kings established the office of royal historiographer in order to have the nation's history described, and they gave generous rewards to poets who made their or the nation's history the subject of their poetry.

The existence of many languages and different systems of writing became a recognized fact. Greek and Hebrew had their special letters. With musical notation, melodies could be written. Roman type was used for the

---

[19] Elizabeth L. Eisenstein: *The Printing Press as an Agent of Change. Communications and Cultural Transformations in Early-Modern Europe*, 2 vols. (Cambridge Univ. Press, 1979).

Latin language and blackletter for Danish and German. There was a feeling that certain alphabets suited certain languages, just as certain messages came through better in one language than in another. All this fitted into the overall world view that God had written his wisdom into the Book of Nature in a special code, for the wise and patient reader to decipher—as if written "in a glass, in a riddle".[20] And the flood of classical authors in print must have added to the feeling that all knowledge was already there; what was needed was careful reading and interpretation rather than the breaking of new ground.

The interest in national history and in arcane writing systems combined into a fascination with the runes. As yet, no serious research was being done, but the runes were useful all the same as national monuments. In a pastoral from 1560, Erasmus Laetus has a scene where a shepherd finds and deciphers a runic inscription.[21] The ancient model for the passage is Calpurnius Siculus' first eclogue where shepherds find a message from the god Faunus written on the trunk of a tree. But whereas Calpurnius' shepherds simply read their message, the Danish poet surrounds the event with all kinds of solemn mystification: the shepherd has been abroad to seek wisdom, only to learn that he must find it in his own native country; he is guided in this pursuit by a prophetic bird, and before finally reading the inscription he has to clear it of the symbolic moss with which less pious ages have let it be overgrown.

In all this the general message was that Denmark was no barbarian country. Even if Danes lived on the outskirts of the civilized world, they had their part to play in the culture of Europe. The Latin language was very important in this connection, not only for the rational reason that you had to argue in Latin in order to be understood abroad, but also because the language itself was the most important mark of civilization. It is an overall implicit message in Danish Neo-Latin poetry, whatever its explicit topic, that Denmark is part of the civilized world. The poetic phrase for it is the international topos of inviting the Muses, and they are duly invited to Denmark in poem after poem from the 1550's onwards.[22]

---

[20] 1 Ep.Cor. 13.12; the English translation "through a glass, darkly" is less precise than both the Vulgate and Erasmus: "per speculum in ænigmate."

[21] Erasmus Lætus: "Ecloga V, Myrmix" in *Bucolica*, cum dedicatoria Philippi Melanthonis præfatione (Wittenberg: Jørgen Rhaw's heirs 1560).

[22] E.g., Johannes Franciscus Ripensis: *Elegiarum liber primus* (Wittenberg: Jürgen Rhaw's heirs 1554), elegy 3; Lætus' 7th eclogue and Melanchthon's preface to the volume; Johannes Pratensis: *Daphnis* (Copenhagen: Lorentz Benedicht 1563); Tycho

At the end of the preceding century Conrad Celtis had declared that the centre of the world had moved northwards to Germany, and now the Danish poets were trying, if not to move the centre, then at least to expand the boundaries of civilisation further northwards.

The Language of Eternity

The ideological status of Latin was not only linked with its being the international language, but also with its function as the language common to all epochs. In Latin you could read the wisdom of classical antiquity, and you could speak to coming generations.[23] Since Latin is the language of eternity, by describing persons, events, or localities in Latin poems you render them immortal. Not least in areas peripheral to the mainstreams of culture, this consideration carried enormous weight. Through their Latin poems, Danish poets struggled to gain a place for their nation's history and geography not only on the map of Europe, but on that of eternity.

This also applies to Jørgen Rosenkrantz' epitaph. The poem's main theme is immortality as against transience. Everything human is transitory, but belief in the resurrection of the flesh brings with it the prospect of individual eternity. In the meantime, however, earthly glory should not be disregarded either. While the passport to heavenly immortality was Christ's book, enrolling for worldly eternity might seem a more complicated affair. How did you make sure that you were properly registered?

Just as in more mundane matters poets and patrons had to consider various media before making their choice, there were many ways in which to register for glory. Jørgen Rosenkrantz chose to have his name written in various languages and more than one system of writing. He had his poem composed in both Latin and Danish, written in Roman and Gothic letters. He had the text surrounded with his ancestral coats of arms, a "language" that guaranteed the kind of immortality that goes with the lineage. He had his and his family's portraits painted, thus preserving their

---

Brahe: "Elegy to Urania" in *De nova stella* (Copenhagen: Lorentz Benedicht 1573). Cf. Fred J. Nichols: *An Anthology of Neo-Latin Poetry* (New Haven, London: Yale Univ. Press 1979), 5–6.

[23] Walther Ludwig in his edition of Tito Strozzi's *Borsias* (Munich: Fink 1977), 26–27.

individual features. He had the relics of his ancestors collected around him as a kind of physical genealogy. And all these treasures were preserved in the church he had built as a great monument to himself, clearly readable in the landscape. In short, he had had his name written into all available books.

University of Copenhagen

Le armi e le lettere: per la storia di un tópos *umanistico*

FRANCESCO TATEO

Alla fine del sec. XVI Alessandro Tassoni, il più grande critico italiano dell'epoca, riflettendo fra l'altro sulla utilità dei letterati e degli uomini d'arme, diceva senza ombra di esitazione: "Considerisi Roma senza Cicerone, senza Sallustio, senza Varrone, senza Lucrezio e senza gli altri suoi letterati, che sarà la medesima; ma considerisi senza Camillo, senza Fabbio, senza Marcello, senza Scipione, senza Mario, senza Pompeo e senza gli altri di questa schiera, che furono uomini bellicosi, e vedrassi ch'ella non avanza Tivoli né Montefiascone."[1] E' il più netto capovolgimento dell'ottica umanistica non solo per la sostanziale irriverenza verso i modelli allora più accreditati dell'oratoria, della storiografia, dell'erudizione e della poesia, per opera dei quali Roma non avrebbe potuto superare i limiti della provincia (Tivoli, Montefiascone), ma perché si intaccava profondamente il principio del classicismo sancito nel proemio del Valla alle *Elegantiae*: Roma sconfitta nelle armi era vittoriosa nelle lettere e conservava il suo impero grazie alla lingua e in special modo a quella di Cicerone. L'inconsueto *tópos*, impertinente, del Tassoni illumina la struttura topica dell'argomento del Valla (la lingua può ben sostituire le armi), che ha un perfetto corrispettivo nell'uso che a sua volta Landino avrebbe fatto di un famoso luogo dell'*Iliade*, in cui le lettere, nella figura del consigliere colto, Nestore, più che essere contrapposte alle armi, le sostituivano perfettamente. Infatti Agamennone, in Omero, era sicuro che se avesse avuto altri dieci Nestori, altro che i suoi eroi, avrebbe conqui-

[1] A. Tassoni, *Pensieri diversi*, in *Prose politiche e morali*, a cura di G. Rossi, voll. 2 (1930; reprint a cura di P. Puliatti, Bari: Laterza, 1978), 1:196–97.

stato Troia in men che non si dica,[2] mentre l'umanista fiorentino, mantenendo il senso della superiorità delle lettere, ma trasformandone la forma, sosteneva che se ci fossero stati soltanto due Federico di Urbino l'Italia sarebbe divenuta un'altra Atene. Dove è da notare che le parti si invertono e la conquista, che questa volta è una conquista culturale, si ritiene possibile ad opera non di un Nestore, ma di Federico, un uomo d'arme come Agamennone (ammiratore delle lettere anche lui). Il critico modenese, che aveva in mente il contemporaneo duca di Savoia Carlo Emanuele I, condottiero più assai che letterato, ma non insensibile al mecenatismo, anzi non lontano dalla figura dei principi umanisti, sembra sostanzialmente seguire lo schema usato dal Landino nella scelta di Federico, un condottiero convertitosi alle lettere ma rimasto un valoroso uomo d'armi, garanzia di solidità per il ducato. Quel che scompare dell'umanista quattrocentesco è il tentativo sottile di far passare il duca di Urbino come direttamente impegnato nelle lettere e quindi come esempio della possibilità e opportunità che le due arti s'incontrino e si fondino, addirittura nella stessa persona.[3]

Tassoni rifiutava del principe proprio la presunzione di congiungere nella stessa persona la spada e il libro. Il tema della minore utilità delle lettere per la grandezza e la potenza dello Stato è in effetti diverso da quello della impossibile congiunzione delle lettere e delle armi nella stessa persona; ma come il primo, nella linea—per così dire—civile dell'umanesimo italiano, era stato confutato proprio attraverso l'esempio tipico del principe letterato e guerriero, così il secondo torna a riproporsi in funzione antiumanistica ancora attraverso l'esemplare condizione del principe guerriero e non letterato. "Le lettere—dice infatti il critico cinquecentesco

---

[2] C. Landino, *Disputationes Camaldulenses*, ed. crit. a cura di P. Lohe (Firenze: Sansoni editore, 1980), p. 116. Cf. *Iliade*, 2.370–74.

[3] "Habemus nostra tempestate Federicum Feretranum Urbinatum principem, quem ego maximis superiorum aetatum imperatorum comparandum non dubito. Plurimae sunt ac omnino admirandae in viro excellentissimo virtutes, ingenium acerrimum et ad omnia vehemens, tantum autem litterarum studium, ut nulla unquam a negotiis cessatio detur, quin otium illud ad litteras non transferat; effecitque multa legendo, multa audiendo, plurima disputando, ut inter litteratissimos iure censeatur. Sed fac ipsum ita se totum huiuscemodi speculationibus tradidisse, ut imperium quod pacatissimum florentissimumque administrat penitus neglexerit, remque militarem, in qua et suae aetatis duces sine controversia superat, et cum omni antiquitate contendit, nunquam attigerit; ex tanto viro ad quem hominem redibit?," Landino, *Disput.*, 1, op. cit., 32. Ma il passo appartiene all'intervento di Lorenzo, ed è interessante ritrovarvi la medesima argomentazione che il Tassoni svolgerà in maniera paradossale: Federico non sarebbe stato nulla senza l'arte militare.

—possono fare un uomo più degno degli altri, in quanto che gli altri ammireranno il suo sapere, non però signoreggiante agli altri, ma l'armi lo fanno non solo più degno degli altri, quanto alla privata opinione, ma signore degli altri; perciocché la virtù dell'armi è dominante e signoreggiante. E questa sola stimavano i Lacedemoni, i Macedoni, i Persi, i Parti, i Germani e i Romani, popoli dominatori degli altri. E perciò fu detto che le lettere erano da uomo privato, e l'armi da re."[4] Perché si potesse dir tutto questo era necessario che la scienza politica avallasse l'idea del dominio in sé come fine, e che i Romani ed i Macedoni potessero esser citati assieme ai Parti e ai Germani (Tassoni citerà insieme finanche Spagnoli e Turchi), ma era anche necessario che si potesse distinguere con tanta nettezza la sfera del privato da quella del pubblico, il ruolo del suddito da quello del signore, e vederli persino in contrasto, sino a poter dire non solo che al principe non è necessario, per perfezionarsi e per ben fondare la sua propria attività, essere impegnato direttamente nelle lettere, ma che egli non deve esserlo, perché ciò nuocerebbe alla sua preparazione militare, lo distoglierebbe dal suo impegno più vero, gli farebbe presumere di poter fare quello che non sa con conseguenti errori, renderebbe perfino peggiore l'uso della potenza (la dottrina aggiunge veleno alla ferocia del leone).[5]

Questa serie di ragioni, che s'inseriscono in un dibattito assai vario riaccesosi a fine Cinquecento, corrisponde ad una tematica già dibattuta sia pure con esito generalmente diverso nell'età umanistica, e rimanda ai più importanti filoni della trattatistica del Quattrocento, dal problema del rapporto fra vita attiva e contemplativa, alla riflessione etica sul Principe, al sistema delle arti e dei rapporti fra arti liberali e meccaniche, alla definizione della vita civile e alla speculazione sulla duplice natura dell'uomo e la sua composizione che implica un ambito fisico e una prospettiva metafisica. La vitalità della topica umanistica relativa al tema delle armi e delle lettere si dimostra dunque proprio nello sforzo di confutare e demistificare le convinzioni umanistiche. Ma la dipendenza dalla tradizione umanistica non è tanto in questo, quanto nel metodo di spingere certi argomenti discutibili al loro limite paradossale. Si pensi all'affermazione della vanità delle dottrine e delle scienze "perché quelle—dice Tassoni sposando dichiaratamente lo scetticismo assoluto di Sesto Empirico—che alcune sette di filosofi hanno chiamate scienze, non sono che mere opinioni da diversi diversamente intese." Si pensi alla svalutazione

[4] Tassoni, op. cit., 1:197.

[5] Ibid., 1:177.

dei "pensieri dell'intelletto," che opera di terza mano, peggio che il senso il quale pur s'inganna; si pensi all'idea che la logica, la fisica e la metafisica siano accomunate con "altri simili perdimenti di tempo," al fatto che venga citata positivamente l'esortazione di Paolo II ai Romani–tratta nientedimeno che dal racconto pieno di riserve del Platina–di non lasciar "occupare i figliuoli e consumar la gioventù loro in cosiffatti perdimenti di tempo,"[6] cui si aggiunge una citazione da Marziale, quando il poeta si lamenta di essere stato instradato alle lettere.

Certo, quando tutta un'argomentazione rivolta a dimostrare come i letterati non abbiano mai avuta preminenza nei ranghi dello stato, se non lì dove s'identificavano col potere sacerdotale o con quello civile, si conclude con un esempio espresso in forma comica ("Anzi Solone stesso, che diede le leggi ad Atene, vide la patria occupata dalle armi di Pisistrato, e la si bevve in pace"),[7] sorgerebbe il sospetto che la superiorità delle armi costituisca piuttosto la constatazione di un fatto riprovato, dal momento che anche chi doveva contrastarla non lo ha fatto. Ma tutto il discorso ha una portata realistica che pare il rovescio della riflessione umanistica, ed anzi il miglior commento ad essa, perché ne dipende totalmente. E innanzi tutto il rifiuto di dedicare l'opera ad un principe (che espressamente richiama per contrasto il trattato di Vegezio sulla milizia,[8] ma forse l'analoga scelta bizzarra di un famoso trattatista del duello rilanciato nel Cinquecento, Paride dal Pozzo)[9] ci fa pensare per contrasto ancora al Landino e alla sua congiunzione di vita attiva e contemplativa, laddove per Tassoni la contemplazione, né congiunta né separata non "non pure, è necessaria, ma né anche utile per chi governa."[10]

In effetti il Landino era stato uno dei maggiori responsabili del connubio fra vita attiva e vita contemplativa, che comportava non solo la confusione dei ruoli dell'uomo di lettere e dell'uomo d'azione, ma anche lo stravolgimento dei significati specifici che certe parole avevano in relazione con specifiche funzioni sociali e col senso comune. La contemplazione monastica confluita nelle lettere, e le lettere riportate alla loro funzione pubblica dissolvono i connotati professionali al di là della stessa

[6] Ibid., 1:181, cf. B. Platina, *Liber de vita Christi ac omnium Pontificum.*

[7] Tassoni, op. cit., 1:189.

[8] La polemica contro l'idea di Vegezio che l'occupazione del principe debba riguardare i "bonarum artium studia," se per tali non s'intende soltanto tutto quello "che all'arte del governare s'appartiene," è esplicita nel *Quisito VI*, op. cit., 1:178–79.

[9] P. Puteo, *De duello* (Napoli: Sixtus Riessenger, 1476–77). Cf. F. Tateo, *Chierici e fuedatari del Mezzogiorno* (Bari: Laterza, 1984), 93.

[10] Tassoni, op. cit., 173.

suggestione ciceroniana che è alla base del sofisma. Perché Cicerone, che è all'origine del gioco verbale per cui–si direbbe–*otium* e *negotium* 'convertuntur,'[11] aveva avvertito drammaticamente, nella sua esistenza, il contrasto fra l'ozio della riflessione e il negozio del governo politico e militare, e se aveva idealizzato l'accordo fra difesa della patria, azione militare e gloria celeste in un condottiero sapiente, Scipione, lo aveva fatto, appunto, nella prospettiva mitica del *somnium*, ribadita poi in senso mistico-platonico da Macrobio,[12] mentre Landino disegna una realtà politica in cui nell'*otium* della lettura, divenuto in effetti *negotium* civile, si dissolvono indistintamente la contemplazione e l'azione. Si tratta di una conclusione assai prevedibile, il solito compromesso accademico-ciceroniano che esaurisce il contenuto filosofico del trattato del Landino, ma non il senso della sua operazione letteraria: "Chi, tenendo un giusto conto della vita attiva e della vita contemplativa–dice Battista recependo la blanda obiezione di Lorenzo–affida all'azione quel che richiedono l'umanità, il vincolo sociale, l'amore della patria, io lo considero un uomo. Ma costui si rivolgerà alla speculazione in modo da non dimenticare che è nato per quella, fino a che lo permetta la nostra umana debolezza."[13]

Nell'azione, nel *negotium* inteso come limite della contemplazione, ma ad essa strettamente collegata per la stessa nozione di uomo, è implicito l'uso delle armi, ma nella misura in cui l'etica civile tollera l'uso della forza per la difesa della patria ("patriae amor"); molto più interessante però è il modo in cui per tutto il trattato landiniano proprio le armi rappresentano, semplicemente, una ricercata e ricorrente metafora del superamento delle armi e della forza. Lorenzo, al di là del richiamo alla ineludibilità della vita attiva, e anzi all'opinione comune della sua superiorità ("cum constantissimo omnium nationum consensu negotiosos semper otiosis praelatos videamus"),[14] ricorre allo specifico tema delle armi per caratterizzare la vita complessiva dell'uomo in lotta contro il *dolor* e la *voluptas*, cioè tesa al superamento della guerra delle passioni e alla conquista della pace dell'anima: Dio ci ha inviati sulla terra "ut adversus plurimas difficultates viriliter *pugnando* duos *saevissimos hostes*, dolorem et voluptatem, superaremus, quibus *profligatis* perpetua pace frueremur." E' la premessa per subordinare la virtù guerriera alle virtù della pace. Un gioco topico che si ripercuote sulla metafora iniziale del discorso di Lorenzo, dalla quale appren-

---

[11] *De officiis*, 3.1; Cfr. Landino, *Disput.*, 1, op. cit., 34.
[12] Macrobio, *Comm.*, 1:8:8.
[13] Landino, *Disput.*, 1, op. cit., 47.
[14] Ibid., 34.

diamo il carattere strumentale della sua obiezione e la disponibilità a darla sostanzialmente vinta a Battista: Lorenzo dichiara di intervenire polemicamente nella discussione per permettere alla speculazione, difesa da Battista, di uscir vittoriosa come da uno scontro e celebrare il trionfo.[15]

Il dialogo è concepito come uno scontro armato dove la speculazione "oziosa" si tramuta in virtù attiva e come tale riesce vittoriosa dello stesso *negotium*, anzi supera le avversità del mondo per la pace suprema. Così nello stesso proemio Landino aveva opposto alle fatiche belliche, alle veglie, ai pericoli affrontati per guadagnare beni nocivi, la lotta contro la fortuna che si può condurre solo armandosi di quelle armi che attingono il vero bene, ed aveva espressamente ricordato a Federico d'Urbino la distinzione fra "pacis ac belli studia," fra la pace che va cercata per sé e la guerra che è solo strumento di pace.

La metafora non poteva trovare sbocco più significativo che nel mito storico di Numa Pompilio, richiamato a proposito di Federico,[16] in quello pagano di Ercole che sconfigge i mostri,[17] nella storia cristiana di Paolo,[18] l'apostolo armato la cui conquista del mondo viene ricondotta alle armi della parola, le lettere, ma soprattutto nel mito di Enea che abbandona Troia, cui è dedicata la metà delle *Disputationes* sotto forma di un commento ai primi sei libri del poema virgiliano. L'allegoria dell'*Eneide*, a parte le implicazioni dantesche e platoniche, non è che la parte esemplificativa del trattato, dove l'eroe è visto non come guerriero alla conquista della sede laziale (è significativo che al Landino non interessino i sei libri di guerra, considerati evidentemente come narrazione storica), ma come colui che si spoglia via via dell'abito di guerriero per assumere quello di viaggiatore verso gli Elisi (pari allo Scipione del *Somnium*). Basterà citare la curiosa simbologia di Troia, la cui difesa da parte di Enea rappresenterebbe la difesa del corpo (Troia è l'origine del corpo "quae necesse est ut pereat"): "Pugnat Aeneas pro vita voluptuosa illaque demersus deos videre nequit."[19] Le armi di Enea in

---

[15] "ad huius vestrae speculationis gloriam pertinere puto, ut omnes intelligant illam ex eo certamine victricem evasisse de eoque adversario triumphasse, qui illi non incruentam victoriam reliquerit," ibid., 26.

[16] Ibid., 5.

[17] Ibid., 32.

[18] "quanti tu Paulum apostolum facis? . . . Intuere genus eius dicendi, quo quid aut planius aut ad docendum acutius aut ad commovendum efficacius cogitari possit non reperio . . . Hic ergo vir itane in sua se cellula obcludens meditari perrexit, ut ceterorum salutem penitus negligeret . . . quot profectiones, quot navigationes adversus valitudinem suscepit, in quot pericula, in quot calamitates incidit. . . ." ibid., 33.

[19] Ibid., 130.

difesa di Troia sono dunque segno di attaccamento alla carne, alla Venere terrena, laddove contro Troia lottano Pallade, la dea armata di sapienza, e Giunone che rappresenta la lotta dell'uomo contro le passioni per giungere al dominio. Nelle figure divine la guerra si metaforizza e si annulla come tale divenendo anzi simbolo di sapienza e spirituale potenza.

Quello del Landino non è un trattato sulle armi e le lettere nel senso specifico, cioè una disputa sulla supremazia fra gli *status* professionali; anzi, ignorando lo *status* autonomo del guerriero, rispecchia la scarsa considerazione che Firenze faceva degli eserciti, puntando piuttosto sugli strumenti politici e sulle opere di difesa.[20] La più schietta, forse ingenua versione umanistica della disputa si può invece rintracciare nelle *Vite* di Vespasiano da Bisticci che insistono, a proposito di principi notoriamente conosciuti come uomini d'arme, sulla disposizione alle lettere che completava la loro figura umana. Le pagine su Federico d'Urbino hanno per secoli conformato l'immagine del Rinascimento, ma esse sviluppano uno degli argomenti connessi con il *tópos* delle lettere e delle armi, perché l'arte delle armi e quella delle lettere sono viste come altrettante professioni miracolosamente congiunte in una sola persona. Si direbbe che lo scrittore segnali il fatto eccezionale e semmai si compiaccia della possibilità di tale congiunzione, ma proprio perché si tratta di attività tanto disparate e difficilmente armonizzabili.[21] E tuttavia egli decide con molta semplicità una questione che non era stata, non era e non sarà pacifica, se cioè le lettere giovino, o siano indiffe-

---

[20] Ibid., 133. Il simbolo della guerra per il turbamento dell'anima era stato sviluppato da Petrarca nel trattato *De vita solitaria*, che prende spunto anch'esso dalla massima di Scipione sulla solitudine che è colloquio con se stesso: "Alii regant urbem populi, alii militum exercitum, et nobis urbs animi nostri est, nostrarum exercitus curarum: bellis civilibus et externis quatimur. An putamus ullam inquietiorem esse rempublicam quam humani status animi est? an credimus leviores nobis hic hostes esse quam apud Numantiam Scipioni? Ille unam urbem et unum populum oppugnabat; nos adversus mundum, carnem et demonia certamus," F. Petrarca, *Prose*, (Milano-Napoli: Ricciardi, 1955), 402. L'identificazione della città con la sede delle passioni ha in Petrarca un'ascendenza biblica ed evoca ovviamente il *tópos* della città piena di noie contro la campagna distensiva, ma l'esempio di Numanzia come il nemico da superare coincide in certo qual senso con il simbolo di Troia, città "barbara," da abbandonare. Si aggiunga che nel caso petrarchesco si ha l'implicito confronto fra la guerra che lo spirito ingaggia per debellare il nemico e conquistare la pace, e la guerra come ostilità, resistenza alla giustizia, offesa. La prima è rappresentata dall'impresa di Scipione, la seconda dalla ribellione della città spagnola. D'altro canto la guerra, identificandosi nella figura di un uomo colto, si distingue dalla guerra nel senso puramente militare del termine.

[21] Cf. J. R. Hale, *Renaissance War Studies* (London: The Hambledon Press, 1983), 381.

renti, o nuocciano all'arte militare e in genere alla formazione di un principe: "che difficile è a uno capitano singulare potere far bene e' fatti dell'arme, s'egli non ha la peritia delle lettere, come ebe il Duca d'Urbino."[22] Eppure una vera congiunzione di armi e lettere si sarebbe avuta soltanto in due casi eccezionali, con Federico di Urbino e Alessandro Sforza, a proposito del quale Vespasiano notava che "grandissima differenzia è d'avere congiunte l'arme colle lettere o nolle avere."[23]

L'ottica della *humanitas*, fondamentalmente conciliativa, funziona insomma sul piano ideale, eccezionale, eliminando gli aspetti contrastanti dei due punti di vista del letterato e del guerriero; così nell'ottica politica della vita civile la guerra conserva il suo posto in armonia con le virtù del governo, proprie dell'*orator* e del *prudens*, inserendosi nel disegno della città ideale come difesa della patria. Nella *Vita civile* di Matteo Palmieri, dove la dipendenza dal *Somnium Scipionis* è perfino ostentata nell'immaginosa conclusione che celebra il glorioso campione di Campaldino, [24] non emerge alcuna diffidenza da parte del letterato nei confronti dell'uomo d'armi, se non fosse per l'insistenza sulle regole morali e religiose che dovrebbero essere, come lo furono anticamente, alla base dell'azione bellica, a cominciare dall'opportunità di ricorrere alla forza militare, strumento bestiale, quando è vano ogni tentativo di far valere la ragione con la forza della parola.[25] Anzi non manca di affiorare, e in termini polemici, l' idea che la guerra apporti maggior gloria che tutti gli altri "esercizi"; una constatazione che era già parsa discutibile ad Ilicino nel suo commento ad un famoso passo dei *Trionfi* del Petrarca.[26] La visione cavalleresca della guerra, fondata su un valore morale e quasi estetico come la manifestazione della virtù e la gloria, era proiettata nell'antichità romana: "ogni loro gloria era posta in più eccellentemente fare et sopra agli altri apparere in virtù. Per questo ciascuno appetiva

---

[22] Vespasiano da Bisticci, *Vite degli uomini illustri*, a cura di A. Greco, voll. 2 (Firenze: Istit. Nazionale di studi sul Rinascimento, 1976), 1:379.

[23] Ibid., 426.

[24] M. Palmieri, *La vita civile*, ed. crit. a cura di G. Belloni (Firenze: Sansoni editore, 1982), 199–208.

[25] L'affermazione del diritto e la gloria erano le due ragioni che avrebbero anticamente giustificato le guerre: "Dua modi sono in questione, l'uno per disputazione, quando legittimamente si cerca il dovere di ciascuno, l'altro per forza, quando con armi si combatte quale sia la potenzia maggiore," ibid., 115. Ambedue i modi ricordano il costume cavalleresco, nonostante l'esemplificazione classica: ibid., 116–29.

[26] In effetti il *Trionfo della Fama* dedicava due capitoli ad esaltare i grandi condottieri, mentre il terzo capitolo, destinato ad esaltare la cultura letteraria in largo senso, comprendente cioè filosofi e storici, si conclude con i pericoli cui induce l'arte della parola.

assaltare i nemici, quegli animosamente ferire, salire alle mura e vincere i luoghi forti et essere veduto mentre che tali fatti operava."[27] Sotto il vezzo umanistico di attribuire agli antichi ogni modello di virtù, si cela il dubbio sulla giustizia delle guerre attuali, che spiega anche l'insistenza sui precetti etici, etico-cavallereschi, dovremmo dire (la bellezza dei gesti, o le norme giuridiche, la dichiarazione di guerra ecc.), che rendono umana la ferocia, santificano la guerra e la rendono pari alle attività dello spirito. Proprio l'istituto cavalleresco aveva trasferito le armi nel campo della virtù, accostandole al governo civile e quindi al vero e proprio campo d'azione delle lettere, mediante le regole e le finalità ideali.

Pochi anni prima il Bruni, che pur intendeva offrire, col *De militia*, un trattato formativo dell'uomo d'arme, non taceva la sostanziale disumanità della vita militare, impressa perfino nel nome (malizia o *mollitia* per il contrario 'durezza'),[28] ma cercava di ricollegare il moderno *miles* al senso nobile e perfino religioso che aveva anticamente la condizione militare.[29] La stessa dipendenza dal mondo antico, fondata sulla storia, implicava l'altra questione, anch'essa inerente al nostro *tópos*, se cioè a monte della più brutale delle azioni umane dovesse esserci la consapevolezza, proveniente dalla cultura, del ruolo antico del militare, oltre l'abilità proveniente dall'esperienza diretta e dal mestiere.

Quando Machiavelli riprenderà la questione molte cose erano frattanto accadute sul piano reale (l'invasione straniera ad esempio) e sul piano culturale (la ricostruzione della trattatistica politica ed etica), perché un'opera sull'arte della guerra potesse incentrarsi sulla tradizione cavalleresca e gingillarsi su una controverisa accademica circa la superiorità delle arti. Ma tanto più colpisce il fatto che il segretario fiorentino, il quale intendeva

---

[27] Palmieri, op. cit., 127. Sulla concezione della guerra come manifestazione della virtù cf. Hale 374–75.

[28] L. Bruni, *De militia*, in M. Maccioni, *Osservazioni e dissertazioni varie sopra il Diritto Feudale* (Livorno: 1764), 87.

[29] La *militia* degli antichi comprendeva *pedites* ed *equites*, ed era in sommo onore se Romolo la raccomandò al culto dei Romani e se il genere equestre rappresentò un titolo di nobiltà. L'accezione dispregiativa assunta talora dalla parola *miles* non toglie che l'attuale *militia* corrisponda all'antica ("Militia igitur nostra sic primaevae vetustaeque institutioni congruit," *De militia*, op. cit., 94) come dimostrerebbe l'onore cavalleresco collegato con un compito civile e religioso: "est enim miles nihil aliud quam custos civium et propulsator belli, legitime ad hoc sacramento adactus," ibid., 92 (il tema è sviluppato in seguito, quando si parla espressamente dell'ordine cavalleresco, 101–6). Cf. C. C. Bayley, *War and Society in Renaissance Florence: The De Militia of L. Bruni* (Toronto, 1961) e la recensione di P. O. Kristeller in *The Canadian Historical Review* (Toronto: University of Toronto Press, 1962).

raccogliere sistematici insegnamenti d'ordine pratico per sopperire alla decadenza della preparazione bellica degli Italiani, muovesse dal *tópos* della battaglia della arti. Difatti l'impianto del suo discorso, giusto o non giusto che fosse a livello tecnico-politico, mirava innanzi tutto, umanisticamente, a distruggere i fondamenti dell'arte militare come professione specifica, a condannare gli uomini che "usavano lo esercizio del soldo per loro propria arte,"[30] in quanto diventano fomentatori di guerra, e a puntare sulla formazione di uomini buoni i quali non usano la guerra come mestiere, ma nell'ambito di una più complessiva funzione umana (*homo bonus belli peritus*—oseremmo dire). La matrice umanistica e la prospettiva della vita civile emergono chiaramente nel concepimento della milizia come scienza e nel dissolvimento della corporazione dei militari intesi come artisti nel senso medievale del termine. Il difficile proposito del Machiavelli di fare del militare soprattutto un uomo che conosca le arti della pace e che in occasione della guerra sia convenientemente preparato sembrerebbe contraddire alla sua stessa intenzione di costituire un'arte della guerra con sue tecniche e ragioni specifiche. Infatti, mentre la pratica militare non dovrebbe distinguersi dalla funzione politica del Principe, la specificità della guerra gli fa ipotizzare un principe che in pace non faccia nulla senza il conforto e la guida del consigliere e che in guerra, per ragioni specificamente militari, si comporti come un tiranno.

Che il Machiavelli si facesse condizionare dalla questione delle armi e delle lettere è indubbio, laddove si pensi che il dialogo è strutturato mediante un intreccio di opinioni alla maniera albertiana. L'uomo d'arme, Fabrizio Colonna, polemizza contro la professione militare e difende il ruolo di consigliere su quello di generale,[31] come risulterebbe in tempo di pace quando affianca il re nel governo, mentre Cosimo Rucellai, un poeta molto giovane e inesperto della guerra, sostiene inizialmete la tesi improbabile della superiorità dell'arte militare: "io me l'aveva presupposta la piú eccellente e la piú onorevole che si facesse."[32] C'e inoltre, in Machiavelli, il sotteso riferimento al gioco antitetico dell'etimologia di *militia* da *mollitia*: la durezza del servizio militare (in senso positivo ovviamente: la cose forti e aspre degli antichi)[33] è contrapposta alla mollezza del piacere (le cose delicate e molli

[30] N. Machiavelli, *L'arte della guerra*, in *Tutte le opere di N. M.*, a cura di F. Flora e C. Cordiè, 2 voll. (Milano: Mondadori, 1949), 1:456.

[31] Ibid., 458–63. Il concetto era già in Guarino, che dedicava a Francesco Barbaro la traduzione del *Focione* di Plutarco segnalando il personaggio greco come "sapientem pacis atque belli consiliarium ": *Epistole* di Guarino Veronese a cura di R. Sabbadini, 3 voll. (Venezia: R. Deputazione veneta di Storia patria, 1915), 2:195.

[32] Machiavelli, op. cit., 1:456.

[33] "Quanto meglio arebbono fatto quelli (sia detto con pace di tutti) a cercare di

dei moderni), mentre la durezza come ferocia bellica si contrappone alla civiltà (mollezza in senso positivo) come cultura della pace.

Da un intento di conciliazione in senso umanistico era sorta in effetti l'*Arte della Guerra* di Machiavelli (basta leggere le prime battute del proemio),[34] dall'intento cioè di superare l'opinione di un fondamentale contrasto fra vita civile e vita militare, su cui si basa la distinzione delle rispettive arti, fino a proporre l'incontro del politico e del guerriero nella stessa persona. Sarebbe facile a questo punto individuare, in un confronto con l'analogo e pur diverso ragionamento del *Cortegiano* di Baldassar Castiglione, i motivi di fondo che differenziano la cultura fiorentina legata alla tradizione della vita civile, segnata principalmente dall'esercizio delle lettere, dalla cultura cortigiana ancorata all'instituzione cavalleresca. Machiavelli proponeva anche lui un cortigiano guerriero che fosse anzitutto un "conoscitore" dell'arte delle armi, cioè esperto nelle armi ma in quanto anche lettore di storia, e rifiutava. non la durezza della milizia che va affrontata all'interno delle sue regole, ma la bestialità della angusta pratica militare, identificandola con la brutalità della ineducazione all'arte militare. Gli uomini dediti esclusivamente alle armi si rivelano all'occorrenza inetti: a Roma, come nell'Italia moderna, la nascita della specifica professione militare avrebbe segnato l'inizio della rovina, ricondotta a Cesare e Pompeo.[35] La creazione dell'arte della guerra dissolve in effetti la controversia della dignità maggiore delle lettere o delle armi, ma non smarrisce il tema della supremazia della cultura in quanto fondamento dell'azione.

Sembrerebbe che l'epicureo Machiavelli utilizzi, sia pure trasfigurandolo realisticamente, proprio il *tópos* dell'anima, sede dell'*ars*, quale elemento più

---

somigliare gli antichi nelle cose forti e aspre, non nelle delicate e molli . . . ," ibid., 451.

[34] "Hanno, Lorenzo, molti tenuto e tengono questa opinione: che e' non sia cosa alcuna che minore convenienza abbia con un'altra, ne che sia tanto dissimile, quanto la vita civile dalla militare," ibid., 447.

[35] "E dico che Pompeo e Cesare, e quasi tutti quegli capitani che furono a Roma dopo l'ultima guerra cartaginese, acquistarono fama come valenti uomini, non come buoni; e quegli che erano vivuti avanti a loro acquistarono gloria come valenti e buoni. Il che nacque perché questi non presero lo esercizio della guerra per loro arte, e quegli che io nominai prima, come loro arte la usarono. . . . Perché Ottaviano prima e poi Tiberio, pensando più alla potenza propria che all'utile publico, cominciarono a disarmare il popolo romano per poterlo più facilmente comandare, e a tenere continuamente quegli medesimi eserciti alle frontiere dello Imperio. E perché ancora non giudicarono bastassero a tenere in freno il popolo e senato romano, ordinarono uno esercito chiamato Pretoriano. . . . Dalle quali cose procedé prima la divisione dello imperio e in ultimo la rovina di quello," ibid., 457–60.

nobile del corpo, che forniva il modello metafisico al principio della superiorità delle lettere sulle armi. Ora, proprio questo principio viene prospettato criticamente attraverso la posizione del Bembo, il quale nel dialogo del *Cortegiano* definisce le lettere come nutrimento dell'anima, e le armi come operazione del corpo secondo un'accezione platonica in senso stretto (le lettere "senza altra compagnia, tanto son di dignità all'arme superiori quanto l'animo al corpo, per appartenere propriamente la operazion d'esse all'animo, così come quella delle arme al corpo").[36] La confutazione è affidata dall'autore al Conte di Canossa, il quale enuncia una tesi analoga a quella machiavelliana della connessione fra le due arti, ma riservando la preminenza alle armi che costituirebbero il primo e più comprensivo compito del cortegiano ("Anzi all'animo e al corpo appartiene la operazion dell'arme"). Anche lui dissolve però—sia pure con una facezia—la disputa scolastica proponendo un duello fra un operatore delle lettere e un operatore delle armi, ciascuno con i suoi strumenti, per vedere chi riesce vincitore. Al tentativo di far delle armi l'ornamento delle lettere (corrispettivo mondano e cortigiano della proposta di Machiavelli) si sostituisce nel Castiglione quello di far delle lettere l'ornamento delle armi. Una chiara esemplificazione può essere il raffronto fra le *Stanze* del Poliziano e l'*Orlando innamorato* di Boiardo, che negli stessi anni mitizzano rispettivamente la tradizione civile toscana e quella cavalleresca della corte estense, le *Stanze* facendo abbandonare Marte nelle braccia di Venere e celebrando il trionfo della dea delle arti belle, l'*Orlando* facendo difendere al paladino contro il barbaro Agricane il pregio del sapere che come un fiore adorna l'uomo il cui primo onore sono però sempre le armi.[37]

Nel *Cortegiano* incontriamo dunque ad un estremo la posizione del Bembo (le lettere anzitutto). All'altro estremo, quella dei Francesi per i quali le lettere sarebbero perfino nocive alle armi.[38] La *medietas* della corte opera un compromesso in funzione della nobiltà cavalleresca del cortigiano, dove il corpo gioca ormai un ruolo positivo estraneo al più schietto platonismo.

---

[36] B. Castiglione, *Il libro del Cortegiano*, 1:45.

[37] Mi sembra riduttivo riferirsi a questo famoso passo del Boiardo (*Orlando Innamorato*, 1:18:43–44; cf. Hale, op. cit., 364) per mostrare come le lettere siano, per il paladino a differenza che per il barbaro, armonizzate con la nobiltà del guerriero ("Rispose Orlando: –Io tiro teco a un segno / Che l'arme son de l'omo il primo onore; / Ma non già che il saper faccia men degno, / Anci lo adorna come un prato il fiore."). Al fondo dei versi boiardeschi c'è l'altra questione del rapporto fra armi e lettere, risolta dal Boiardo in termini "cortigiani": le lettere non danneggiano, ma "adornano" più che essere fondamentale supporto della formazione dell'uomo d'armi.

[38] *Il Libro del Cortegiano*, 1:42.

In quegli anni tuttavia la questione teologico-scolastica dell'anima e del corpo non era tramontata, anzi emergeva nelle forme più rigorosamente dialettiche in una disputa fra Agostino Nifo,[39] napoletano di origine ma trapiantato a Padova, e Luca Prassicio, studioso di vecchia tempra averroistica, che dedicava il suo libro, per confutare la dissertazione del Nifo in favore delle armi,[40] ad un nobile feudatario dell'Accademia pontaniana, Andrea Matteo Acquaviva, duca d'Atri, principe guerriero e letterato egli stesso, ma difensore del pregio delle lettere come attività dell'anima, necessaria funzione dell'uomo superiore, complemento e anzi fondamento dell'uomo d'armi.[41] I ruoli sociali e le ideologie sembrano confondersi: l'uomo d'arme e il suo ammiratore danno in sostanza la palma alle lettere, mentre il filosofo dà la palma alle armi.

La chiave di questa aporia risiede ovviamente nei sottesi referenti dottrinari, cioè nella questione teologica dell'anima. Il senso sostanziale della disputa, che altrove esaminerò dettagliatamente, si può cogliere nell'uso diverso che Prassicio fa del mito di Marte e di Venere ignorando la simbologia umanistico-platonica della dea delle arti belle, capace di trasformare la guerra in virtù di pace, la metaforica giostra gloriosa di Giuliano dei Medici. Marte non può essere per Prassicio che la ferocia militare: il mito esprimerebbe un significato psicologico-sociale, realistico, non etico-metafisico, cioè l'attutimento dell'efferatezza militare ad opera della vita uxoria e in genere del contatto con le donne, senza il quale il *miles* si abbandonerebbe all'estrema violenza. Il concetto della convergenza fra le lettere e le armi, fra la funzione dell'intelletto e la vita delle passioni, è lontano dalla mentalità dell'aristotelico meridionale, impegnato a far quadrare con Averroè Aristotele e s. Tommaso.

Meno rigorosamente il signore feudale cui era dedicata la dissertazione, il quale—come si è detto—era un pontaniano, si preoccupava di respingere l'idea che le lettere indebolissero le armi (era l'interpretazione data al mito dai sostenitori della superiorità della vita militare), mostrando come anzi esse, le lettere, la corroborano insegnando il disprezzo del pericolo e indirizzando le passioni verso l'esito positivo delle virtù. Non è un caso che Pontano avesse dedicato a lui il trattato *De magnanimitate*, esaltando

---

[39] Autore del *De armorum leterarumque comparatione* (Napoli: Sigismondo Mayr, 1526), su cui cf. G. Paparelli, *Feritas, Humanitas, Divinitas, l'essenza umanistica del Rinascimento* (Napoli: Guida editori, 1973), 57–65.

[40] *Illustri Hadrie Duci omni scientia omnique disciplina pollenti ac decorato Lucas Prassicius Aversanus* (Aversa: per Antonium de Frizis, 1520).

[41] F. Tateo, op. cit., 69–96.

nel proemio il modello di educazione letteraria e militare scelto da suo padre Giulio Antonio per i figli.[42] Ma nel Pontano il *tópos* umanistico dell'armonica congiunzione era più evidente. Per il feudatario, come per il suo suddito, i valori delle lettere erano rappresentati da Mercurio, non da Venere, Mercurio che libera Marte dalle catene della necessità,[43] ossia della natura inferiore, non lo ostacola, lo favorisce anzi rimanendone sostanzialmente distinto. Per l'Acquaviva, come per Prassicio, la scienza non è in funzione del fare o fusa con esso, non è insomma un *agere*, come nella tradizione fiorentina, ma è un riscatto dal *facere*, un *cognoscere*, in cui l'uomo si libera dalla materia e si realizza perfettamente. Il feudatario avverte la vita militare come un *servitium*, un duro *servitium*, e non in essa sente di realizzarsi, ma nell'*otium* della vita intellettiva che è liberazione dalle catene, poiché quella che entra in contatto con le passioni non è la parte superiore dell'anima, ma quella preposta all'incontro con la natura inferiore, cui appartiene l'operazione delle armi.

Queste ragioni filosofico-teologiche di fondo sono più evidenti nella dissertazione scolastica di Luca Prassicio, nella quale un'ampia sezione è rivolta a confutare l'assemblaggio dell'arte militare e delle altre arti, meccaniche e liberali insieme, che era stato il forte argomento del Nifo. Ogni arte, aveva detto il Nifo, dall'oratoria alla medicina, è condizionata dalla fortuna nel senso che la riuscita dipende dall'eventuale superamento di ostacoli quali il pubblico, la malattia o le insidie del nemico, ostacoli che rientrano nel campo del variabile, della fortuna, e costituiscono forze negative da dominare. L'argomento riflette in termini scolastici una posizione simile a quella del Machiavelli, per il quale l'arte della guerra mirava appunto a superare, quasi a trasformare, la fortuna, e con essa la bestialità della violenza e dell'inesperienza, allineandosi alle altre scienze. La risposta di Prassicio, fedele alla tradizione astrologica e aristotelica della scuola meridionale, non disponibile a interpretare l'azione dell'uomo

---

[42] "Pater vero tuus, cum ipse quidem minime assequi posset quod maxime utique cupiebat, ut militaribus ornamentis, laudes eas adiungeret, quae e literarum comparantur studiis atque cognitione, illud tamen summa cura, singulari etiam diligentia praestitit et opera, quo tuque fratresque item tui, quamdiu aetas cuiusque tulit, optimis sub praeceptoribus instituti, ita erudiremini ut, cum aetas ipsa firmior iam magisque robusta ad tubam vocasset et gladium, ipsis e ludis literarum atque historiarum de lectionibus, animi magnitudinem cumque ea pariter maximorum vobiscum ducum atque imperatorum exempla in aciem afferretis," I. I. Pontani *De Magnanimitate*, ed. crit. a cura di F. Tateo (Firenze: Istituto nazionale di studi sul Rinascimento, 1969), 1–2.

[43] A. M. Acquaviva, *Commentarium in translationem libelli Plutarchi de virtute morali* (Napoli: per Antonium De Frizis, 1526), praefatio.

in termini di trasformazione della natura, ribadisce appunto il ruolo dell'arte partendo dalla più evidente esemplificazione della scienza medica, la quale cura - o dovrebbe curare - non forzando la natura, ma conoscendone le leggi e favorendone i processi, giacché la natura solo apparentemente è disordine, irrazionalità, fortuna.

Ciò implica la potenziale "sanità" della natura e la sua disposizione entro un sistema astrologico ordinato verso il superamento del male della materia. Ma l'arte è soprattutto scienza, operazione dell'intelletto, e si qualifica per la sua indipendenza dalla natura; essa quindi è perfetta indipendentemente dagli esiti dell'azione. Le sconfitte dell'Acquaviva guerriero ricevono così una piena giustificazione attraverso la difesa delle lettere come non nocive alla milizia, ma valide di per se stesse, per il loro specifico fine. Forse la dedica all'Acquaviva "omni scientia omnique militari disciplina pollenti ac decorato" rifletteva la netta distinzione che non concepiva la milizia se non come pratica bellica, disciplina, impropriamente fatta oggetto di scienza. E comunque l'accoppiamento dei due meriti ricalca, sia pure con sfumature diverse, il modello landiniano di Federico d'Urbino. Non sorge il dubbio, al Prassicio, che se le due qualità fossero così distinte com'egli sostiene, e l'una si riferisse all'anima nel suo principio divino, l'altra al corpo nel suo principio materiale, l'accostamento nella stessa persona, per non dire la fusione, sarebbe per lo meno problematico. Ma in una prospettiva averroistica questo era possibile.

Il dubbio venne al Galateo, un umanista della cerchia stessa cui apparteneva l'Acquaviva, ma un po' atipico—come altra volta ho detto.[44] La sua testimonianza culturale è oltremodo importante perché vi troviamo affermata proprio l'opportunità di distinguere la persona del principe da quella del letterato, che nel Tassoni ritroveremo ribadita con motivazioni e finalità diverse, ma forse con la stessa disposizione di ordine aristotelico a distinguere i ruoli e le professioni. Nella più nota epistola sulla "dignità delle scienze e delle discipline" le armi sono incluse, secondo un criterio diffuso, nella categoria dell'*agere*, della vita attiva, e come tali abbassate rispetto alla vita contemplativa. Ma dell'*agere* esse rappresentano la manifestazione bestiale, l'istinto brutale che accomuna personaggi come Cesare e Catilina e si rivela al fondo della conquista imperiale romana. Il fondo è agostiniano. Ma in una più tarda epistola, riconoscendo inutili le lettere al miglioramento della società, anzi riconoscendole dannose come indicherebbe il mito di Venere e Marte, singolarmente stravolto nel significato

[44] F. Tateo, "Diagnosi del potere nell'oratoria di un medico," in *Chierici e feudatari*, op. cit., 3–19.

per farne un segno dell'influsso nefasto delle lettere, lamentando lo scarso vantaggio che i letterati ricevono dalla loro professione, e confutando perfino il valore educativo delle lettere, fa l'elogio dei principi che si sono limitati ad "amare", piuttosto che dedicarsi a coltivare le lettere, e quasi paradossalmente riscopre la superiorità delle armi (che almeno sono più utili).[45]

Emerge in questa serie di contraddizioni, sui cui risvolti storici e biografici non è ora il caso di soffermarsi, il metodo retorico di dibattere pro e contro il valore delle arti concorrenti. L'umanista, assumendo alternativamente le armi e le lettere nella loro estrema manifestazione negativa, finisce con l'annullare gli argomenti di ambo le parti in una direzione soprattutto etico-religiosa. Non è un caso che egli denunci un fenomeno che si stava attuando sotto i suoi occhi, il recupero della trattatistica militare che legittimava lo scontro armato e sanciva l'autonomia e la legittimità delle norme che lo regolano. In effetti il *De duello* di Paride Del Pozzo, al quale allude polemicamente, e che stava per uscire in lingua volgare nel 1518, era divenuto il classico di un genere che risaliva al trecentesco trattatello di Giovanni da Legnano e sarebbe stato incrementato per tutto il Cinque e Seicento nel contesto dell'istituzione nobiliare e cortigiana.

Non si trattava della linea scientifica e politica del trattato machiavelliano, ma di una linea giuridico-formale che dava spazio alle norme del comportamento e quindi agli aspetti etici della professione militare e concepiva le lettere e le armi come strumenti di professioni diverse. Il modello non è più, ovviamente, il trattato etico-filosofico ciceroniano, che anzi favoriva l'accostamento, ma l'operetta *De re militari* di Vegezio, che non solo forniva la materia per buona parte degli argomenti tecnici, ma sembrava prospettare nel pur breve proemio, modesta dedica al Principe, una particolare soluzione del tormentato *tópos* attraverso l'omaggio fatto da un conoscitore di cose militari, ma letterato, all'autorità suprema.

Vegezio aveva dedicato al principe il suo libro *De re militari* perché il principe ha il compito di conoscere ogni cosa per riversarne l'insegnamento o l'esempio sui sudditi. Il letterato riconosceva la sua funzione subalterna. Questo libro è presente agli scrittori *de re militari* fra Quattro

[45] Antonio De Ferrariis Galateo, *Epistole*, ed. crit. a cura di A. Altamura (Lecce: Centro di Studi salentini, 1959): "Qui arma litteris anteponunt, quamvis non recte, ut duo antistites sapientiae Plato et Aristoteles existimant, utiliora tamen suadent et quae vitare et liberatati magis conducere videntur. Haec enim mihi videtur esse ars principum: donare primum et parcere, strenuos esse et peritos rei bellicae, opprimere malos ne aliis noceant, iuvare bonos ut aliis prosint," Epist. XXXIII, 208–9 (ho corretto "existiment" in "existimant" sulla base dell'autografo, Vat. Lat. 7584).

e Cinquecento. Battista della Valle, che scrisse un fortunatissimo trattato in volgare di natura tutta tecnica sull'arte della guerra curando l'aspetto strategico, lui che era un uomo di guerra, quasi si scusava di presentarsi al suo signore nel ruolo di maestro in cose delle quali il principe per esperienza è conoscitore e inventore.

Il trattato *De duello* di Paride Del Pozzo, che originariamente (erano i tempi di Alfonso di Aragona) fu concepito con una dedica spiritosa a Marte per evitare i guai provocati dall'antico Paride quando offrì il pomo a Venere incorrendo nell'ira delle altre dee, fu ristampato e diffuso nel Cinquecento, ma con una dedica sostitutiva di Minuziano ad un nobile milanese, nella quale l'umanista respingeva l'eventuale accusa di aver voluto dare ad un principe insegnamenti in materia di guerra, quando invece è lui, il principe, il maggiore esperto, tecnico e pratico, di queste cose.[46] Si riconoscono in questi ricalchi di Vegezio lo schema che oppone l'esperienza diretta alla funzione didascalica e conoscitiva delle lettere, e l'imbarazzo nel segnare i limiti fra consigliere colto e principe esperto. Minore scrupolo e maggiore coerenza aveva mostrato Machiavelli quando aveva offerto ad un principe un libro sull'arte di governare e ad un consigliere un'opera sull'arte della guerra. Si trattava di trasferire nell'arte militare il principio del ritorno agli antichi come riscatto dalla decadenza, e il letterato non rinunciava alla sua parte e alla sua dignità. Era un tacito rifiuto del modello francese dell'uomo d'arme non compromesso con lo studio delle lettere—e quindi anche della guerra come pratica di fierezza, barbarie insomma, nonostante la critica rivolta d'altra parte alle mollezze cui era approdata certa imitazione degli antichi.

Il *tópos* della opposizione e relazione fra lettere ed armi funziona anche nella disputa che in vario modo si apre fra Quattro e Cinquecento sul fallimento degli stati italiani. La mollezza di un'arte senza impegno pratico, che poteva confondersi col mero godimento, e la durezza di una guerra senz'arte, che poteva confondersi con la pura ferocia, sono i

[46] "non veritus sum alicuius calumniam, quod in hac editione, dum meum erga te animum demonstro, nullam neque rei, neque persone rationem habuerim, qui de militaribus preliis opus tui nominis presidio communiverim, quando is tu existis, qui in hac materia quid iura divina humanaque permittant atque decernant, quid ipsa natura, quid armorum usus et maiorum exempla suadeant, cum assiduo studio variaque lectione tum ingenii acrimonia ac morum observatione planissime intelligas": cf. la roccolta citata alla n. 48, f. 123v. La dedica del Minuziano ("Tractatus elegans et copiosus de re militari undecim libris distinctus in quibus singularis certaminis materia luculenter descripta ac tradita est auctore Paride a Puteo iuriscons. clariss. Amplissimo integerrimoque viro Jafredo Caroli Regis Senatus Mediolanensis Presidi ac moderatori sapientissimo") porta la data del 1509.

termini estremi entro i quali la mentalità umanistica cerca di trovare lo spazio per una virtù bellica non estranea all'*humanitas*. Un testo estremamente significativo a riguardo è quello offertoci ancora dal Galateo con l'epistola al Summonte sull'episodio della disfida di Barletta, il cruento torneo giocato da tredici italiani e tredici francesi nel 1503 per una questione d'onore e divenuto nella storia italiana un segno di gloria nazionale nel momento in cui proprio la difesa bellica della considdetta libertà veniva meno.[47]

I Francesi avevano accusato gli Italiani di essere imbelli e infidi, due attributi negativi riferibili ad una civiltà matura in decadenza, cui si opponeva la fierezza bellicosa dei barbari. Al centro figuravano le virtù antiche della magnanimità, della *libertas*, della *fortitudo*, che l'autore cerca di rivendicare agli italiani attraverso il discorso di un condottiero spagnolo il quale difendeva la tradizione italiana, in quanto anche romana, riportando i vizi degli Italiani, come l'indisciplina, alla caratteristica virtù della *civilitas*, ossia all'odio verso i tiranni. Così Galateo poteva pur approvare lo scontro armato, motivato dall'onore e dalla gloria, nella prospettiva delle antiche virtù, lui che altrove rifiutava come segno, sempre, di violenza e di barbarie il duello, condannando, forse proprio in occasione della ristampa e traduzione del *De duello* di Paride Del Pozzo, il *revival* di un genere che andava riprendendo quota nel generale rilancio dell'interesse giuridico per la normativa cavalleresca sostenuta dalla riscossa della nobiltà guerriera. Ne è segno la imponente riedizione dei trattati sulle norme del duello e sulla preminenza del *doctor* o del *miles* uscita a Lione nel 1549 in un momento significativo di *revanche* della monarchia e della nobiltà francese ed europea, con l'intenzione di illustrare e documentare il libro XII del codice di Giustiano[48] (due anni prima era salito al trono Enrico II).

In effetti la prospettiva religiosa non compromessa con il potere mirava a contrapporre le lettere e le armi come vizi estremi della virtuosa *humanitas*, piuttosto che a ravvicinarle attraverso il recupero delle lettere alla virtù attiva e della guerra all'etica, anzi a denunciare l'eccesso di mollezza da una parte e di violenza dall'altra. E' la posizione rappresentata nella maniera più eloquente da Erasmo, che denunciò nel ciceronianismo un aspetto della decadente *voluptas* e nell'opuscolo *Dulce bellum inexpertis* la

---

[47] Galateo, op. cit., 173–79 (Epist. XXIX, Ad Chrisostomum, *De pugna tredecim equitum*).

[48] *Duodecimum volumen Tractatuum e variis iuris interpretibus collectorum*. Habet eos tractatus qui ad duodecimum librum Codicis Iustinianei pertinent (Lugduni: Tomas Bartellus, 1549).

disumanità incondizionata della guerra. Nell'esaltazione della pace e nella denigrazione della guerra, nell'elogio degli *honestissimarum disciplinarum studia* e nella rappresentazione degli orrori della guerra vengono ripresi e discussi molti argomenti della tradizione disposti in una requisitoria secondo una sottile linea dimostrativa che svela il rischio di un ennesimo tentativo di risolvere il *tópos* della opposizione fra lettere ed armi con un impiego–si direbbe–sofistico del principio dell'armonia degli opposti: la guerra nata per l'utilità e cresciuta per avidità selvaggia, quantunque santificata dal diritto e dalla morale attraverso la bontà delle norme e dei fini, non è diventata per questo più accettabile, ma semplicemente più insidiosa e più immorale.

Università di Bari

SEMINAR

Thomas More and Biography

Thomas Stapleton's Use of More's English Works *(1557) in his* Vita Thomae Mori *(1588)*

GERMAIN MARC'HADOUR

In his preface to *Vita et illustre martyrium Thomae Mori,*[1] Stapleton tells us that he was born in July 1535, the very month of More's birth into eternal light. Writing in 1588, he is exactly the age at which More lost his father (1530): as More on that occasion suddenly felt old, Stapleton too senses the onset of old age: "me senio jam appetente." In the three decades since he left England rather than accept Elizabeth as supreme head of the English church, he had published as enormous amount: first a million words of English while a theology student at Louvain, and several millions in Latin after losing hope of England's foreseeable return to the Roman unity of the church.

---

[1] The third panel of Stapleton's *Tres Thomae,* the other Thomases being the Apostle and Becket. The book was published at Douai in 1588 and was often reprinted by itself or in Stapleton's *Opera omnia.* The Frankfurt edition of 1689, retitled *Vita et obitus Thomae Mori* (no doubt to avoid prejudging More's martyrdom) is available in a Minerva reprint of 1964. The first English translation, by Msgr. Phillip E. Hallett, published as *The Life and Illustrious Martyrdom of Sir Thomas More* (London, 1928) was edited by E. E. Reynolds with annotations and an excellent introduction (London, 1966). This edition is available in the reprint by Fordham University Press (New York and London, 1984).

The only book-length monograph on Stapleton is Marvin R. O'Connell's *Thomas Stapleton and the Counter Reformation* (New Haven: Yale University Press, 1964). I know of only one unpublished Ph.D. dissertation on his life of More: that of Sr. Mary Celestine Cepress intitled "Thomas Stapleton's *Vita Mori*: A Critical Analysis and History" (Catholic University of America, Washington DC, 1952). Other relevant material can be found in my article "Tres Thomas" in *Proceedings of the PMR Conference* (1985), vol. 10 (Villanova, 1987), 23–40.

Ordained a priest during the reign of Mary (1558) with a B.A. from New College, Oxford (1556), he received his D.D. in 1571 from the University of Douai, where he also taught until Philip II appointed him (1590) Regius Professor of Sacred Scripture at Louvain, where he died on 12 October 1598. He was in great demand as a preacher, and the lives of his first two Thomases had their nuclei in panegyrics he had delivered on their feastdays, 21 and 29 December 1586. His spiritual fervor included a brave attempt at becoming a Jesuit (1585–1586). He never advanced to profession but retained an admiring envy toward such confessors of the faith as Edmund Campion, and not a few Douai students of his who crossed the channel into danger right after their ordination. The leitmotiv of his hagiographic trilogy is the three Thomases' shared glory of martyrdom.

As a controversialist, Stapleton is hardly inferior to his better known contemporary, St. Robert Bellarmine, and there is a polemical edge to all his works, even his biographies. It is especially perceptible in his rehabilitation of the vilified St. Thomas Becket. In the *Vita Mori* the apologetic concern never comes obtrusively to the fore. Of course, a confident tone and a belligerent stance were not considered at all indecorous in an aging professor during the early post-Tridentine era, when the Catholic Church was, if ever it was, "ecclesia in terris militans." And a similar spirit pervades the works of Protestant controversialists and martyrologists in the same generation, such as John Foxe's *Acts and Monuments.*

Yet More's multi-faceted greatness prevents Stapleton from being haunted by the bloody end of his hero. Though "the glory of God and the edification of the reader" are the motives of his work, "pleasure" is also an aim added in the very first sentence of the proemium ("voluptatem singularem"). More's own "elegantia et suavitas" are ideals Stapleton wishes to pursue in conjuring up the full man. *Utopia* is the first book he quotes from, and More's witty sayings and merry tales claim all of chapter 13 ("Acute et facete dicta vel responsa").

Stapleton's sources for *Vita Mori* were many and manifold: Roper's memoir via Harpsfield's unpublished biography, Erasmus' correspondence, Pole's *Pro unitate,* Sander's influential account of the Anglican schism, and other "docti viri" (Cochlaeus, Giovio and others, even the Lutheran Rivius), whose testimonies fill the last chapter of *Vita Mori.* Stapleton's major set of documents are some thirty letters which came into his hands from More's secretary John Harris. These might well have been lost forever if Stapleton had not incorporated them into his biography. They were written by Colet, Fisher, Tunstal, Gunnell, Bishop Veysey, and other friends and colleagues of More's. But for the sake of a closer look at Stapleton's *Vita Mori,* the scope of this essay will be limited to the use he made of More's own writings; and since he himself, taking for granted his readers' acquaintance with the fairly recent edition of More's Opera (Louvain, 1565; reissued 1566), quotes and translates more extensively from *The workes of Sir Thomas More ... wrytten by him in the Englysh tonge* (London, 1557), I too will concentrate on that volume, his ubiquitous English source.[2]

Stapleton was 22 and still at Oxford when the sturdy folio of More's *English Works,* dedicated to Queen Mary by More's nephew William Rastell, was published on 30 April 1557. Via the English Jesuit College at Liège, Stapleton's copy made its way to the Bibliothèque Nationale in Paris. It carries his signature in Latin, as well as the later location "Collegij Anglicani Soc. Iesu Leod." Several hands have marked the copy in several inks, but Stapleton's marginalia and markings are the most numerous and obvious.[3]

In Pico's letter to his nephew Gianfrancesco, Stapleton seems to have compared More's English with the Latin original, for he completes the meaningless sentence "that lest thei should begin to do yuel" (p. 15G) by inserting after "thei" the parenthesis: (leue to speak euyll, we sh.).*The Life of John Picus* bears no other mark; yet this one is witness enough of attentive perusal.

In *The History of King Richard the Third,* Stapleton marks the sentence about Hastings (55G, lines 7–10); "when he most feared, he was in good suerty: when he rekened him self surest, he lost his life, & that within two howres after." Opposite 57E, lines 9–11, he writes "Sapienter dic[tum]," so that we can expect to find this in the special chapter devoted to More's "wise sayings" and indeed we do. More's English is: "men vse if they haue an euil turne, to write it in marble: & whoso doth vs a good tourne, we write it in duste." Stapleton seems to have consulted More's own Latin, which he reproduces, only inverting the order of 'siquid' and 'mali': "Beneficia pulveri, si quid mali patimur marmori insculpimus." It is the aptness of More's comparison that he admires here, and the marginal gloss "Simile" also punctuates his reading of More's *Four Last Things.* It marks, among others, a passage concerning the depravation of man's "infected taste" (74C): "Like as a sick man feleth no swetenes in sugar, &

[2] Available in the facsimile published by the Scolar Press (London, 1978) with an introduction by K. J. Wilson.

[3] I shall ignore such details as the insertion of the preposition "of" after "maner" in More's "no maner thyng" (sig. C2, E1) precisely because the modernization this implies seems to me posterior to Stapleton: "no maner thyng" was acceptable throughout the Tudor period.

some women with child haue such fond lust that thei had leuer eate terre [that is, tar] than tryacle, & rather pitch than marmelade, and some whole people loue talow better than butter...." "Simile" recurs in the same column against 74D.

Horizontal underlining is very frequent. A vertical line draws attention to longer passages: for instance, the fifteen present participles on 77F which detail "The paines of death"[4] and the illusion denounced at 79E (and at greater length in *A Dialogue of Comfort*): "as a man maye see a thing so far of, that he woteth not whither it be a bushe or a beast."

Pending a fuller, ideally exhaustive examination of Stapleton's marginalia and markings in *English Works*, I shall turn the pages with you and pause at representative samples. At 84G, arguing that all the world is a prison, More reckons pride in one's forbears "as worshipful, as if a gentleman thefe when he should goe to Tyburne, wold leue for a memoriall, tharmes of his auncesters painted on a post in Newgate." Stapleton marks this, as he also does the startling anecdote of a cutpurse who practises his craft at the very bar of the tribunal on the eve of hanging from the gallows (column 93CD).

The unsightly fruits of gluttony (column 99BC) inspire More, whose enumeration twice includes three nouns ("face," "skin" and "body") with a triple set of verbs in the present indicative and of epithets, then three past participles and six present participles (More is a pioneer in the relentless advance of the *-ing* form) until we reach, as a climax, the roll of "diseases," some with popular names, others with Greek labels which smell of the physician's manual: "the dropsy, the colike, the stone, the strangury, the gout, the cramp, the paulesy, the pocks, the pestilence, and the apoplexy."

Like the two Newgate anecdotes, the next cascade of brief Tacitean clauses to catch Stapleton's eye derives from More experience as advocate and undersheriff. It describes, with eight strokes, what happened in early Tudor England when a slain body was found: "the coroner sitteth, the queste is charged, the verdict geuen, the felony founden, the doer endited, the proces sued, the felon arrained, and dyeth for the dead" (column 100H).

In More's polemical works, Stapleton is less attentive to style; he reacts as a professional divine to the layman's arguments. Thus, on page 141 (*A Dialogue concerning Heresies*, book 1, chapter 18), the chapter heading

---

[4] The whole passage, with a Latin specimen of the "genre," is quoted in my "Thomas More et les Chartreux," *Moreana* nos. 95-96 (November 1987): 195.

begins: "The author differreth the answer...." Above this Stapleton has written: "He aunswereth in the viij[th] chapter of the seconde boke"—which seems to indicate that he has turned the ensuing leaves all the way to page 147. In the bottom margin of page 159, an even longer entry about "the refutatyon of Tyndall" directs the reader to "the thyrde booke" of More's *Confutation*, "fol. 487 D." The sixteenth and last chapter of book 3, in which "the author sheweth his mind, that it wer conuenient to haue the byble in englishe" contains an unusual wealth of response from Stapleton: no fewer than seven passages are underlined on page 241 alone. The margin bears an X and a large O; the numbers 1, 2, 3, 4 mark the clergy's arguments against allowing the bible to fall into the hands of the laity, and the refutations of these specious reasons. The last number, 5, occurs on page 242, and the markings continue to be frequent to the end of that beautifully balanced chapter (including a reference to the *Confutation*: "Vide authorem fo 849 H").

Where More surveys "the bookes of Tindall and hys felowes" in his preface to the *Confutation*, the folio pages 341–43 are one solid continuum with no physical guide to individual titles—a mere "Then" introduces each new item. To provide signposts along this path Stapleton numbers the works in the margin, from 1 to 16, and underlines such key terms or names as "newe testament ... booke of obedience ... saynt Iohn ... beggars ... George Iaye" and so on. Further on in the same important preface, he draws a square to frame the end of a paragraph (351C), puts a "nota" at 351G, and adds a few further glosses: "obedience that heretyques teacheth" (above 353A); "Bookes of deuotion" (at the bottom of page 356, where More recommends Hilton, Gerson, and Bonaventure); "Sim" (356G) to mark the poison/treacle image which Stapleton himself later used in the title of one of his biblical works: *Antidota*, that is, a "treacle" against the poison of Calvin and Beza.

Stapleton's captions can be quite revealing of his own leanings and emphases. In book 7 of the *Confutation*, after More (for the eleventh time, at least, in his polemical career) has quoted James 2:20 ("Faith without good works is dead," 711D), one might expect a post-Tridentine professor to write "fides sine operibus" as the Vulgate has it, but the actual gloss is "fides sine charitate," as if in echo of More's own formulation in the letter to Bugenhagen: "caritatis opera, sine quibus fides mortua est."[5]

The unfinished ninth book of the *Confutation* first appeared in *The*

[5] Elizabeth F. Rogers, *The Correspondence of Sir Thomas More* (Princeton, NJ, 1947), 344, line 702.

English Works; in the words of the running head, it represents "the sum of the books before concerning the Church." As a recapitulation should, it lines up all the points in an orderly way. More himself uses "first ... Secondlye ... Thirdly ... Fourthly" and again "For the fyrst proofe ..." (p. 816). Stapleton adds the welcome aid of arabic numbers, one row running up to 9 between page 817 and page 823, and another going from 1 to 14 over the four pages 824–27. When he discovers that argument 14 ("the church of Christ is a company mixed of good and badde," 826D) repeats argument 10 (825H), he strikes off 14, writes 10, and then resumes numbering 11, 12, 13, reaching 14 at 827C.

Stapleton seems to have found More's works in defence of the real presence less relevant to his own day: he puts only a single mark on the *Letter against Frith* (835A), and his only gloss on the much longer *Answer to a Poisoned Book* merely repeats what More says in the text: "Tindal capt of ye englissh heretikes" (1037G), while in the *Treatise to receive the blessed Body of Our Lord* his only remark is a correction of "Math." to "Luke" (marginal gloss at 1268F).

The Apology of Sir Thomas More, rich in autobiographical details, mobilizes Stapleton's pen with far greater frequency. At 849D he spotted fourteen lines which he had bypassed at 224A in book 3, chapter 10, of the *Dialogue Concerning Heresies*. In *The Apology* More refers us to his earlier book and repeats the passage verbatim. Stapleton adds a vertical bar to the printer's quotation signs. The passage is famous, the more so no doubt because it occurs in the two most read of More's English works of controversy: to emend Tyndale's New Testament would mean, says More, to sew up every hole in a net and to eat, after scraping it, the bread poisoned by your enemy. But in Stapleton's notes on *The Apology* the theologian is not swallowed by the biographer: in a six-line note beginning with "Yet" (863G) and partly illegible because a later binding has eaten off part of the margin, Stapleton enlists the authority of St. Thomas, of St. Denys, and "of all the divines now" in favor of an opinion not shared by More, namely "that the dampned spyrites haue all theyr naturall gyftes as whole and as parfytte, as they hadde before theyr fall." The printed gloss "In my Lorde Cardinal wolses daies" (892B) may have prompted Stapleton to write the more specific remark: "Wolse cause of pompous apparell in the clergy." More's text merely alludes to Wolsey's "yeares not longe paste," marred by "the pryde and ouer sight of some few" priests. At 901D, coming across the name of George Iay (Joye), which he had already singled out in the preface to the *Confutation*, Stapleton underlines "now for all that wedded in Antwarpe." In the last chapter, where More justifies his "fansies and sportes & mery tales" through Horace's dictum "a man may sometime saye full soth in game," Stapleton adds the Latin original: "Ridentem dicere verum quid vetat" (927F).

In *A Dialogue of Comfort* Stapleton underlines a grim vignette of a gamester who plays cards till "the pure panges of death" (1162E), which he also translates as a "wise saying" in chapter 12 of *Vita Mori*. At 1171A he writes "eutrapelia" in Greek letters, perhaps to correct the "sutrapelia" of the printed text. Twenty lines further on, he underlines Antony's oft quoted confession: "myselfe am of nature euen halfe a gigglot and more" (1171C). His interest in similes continues to be attested by the word "Sim." at 1171F. The 1557 glossator also pointed out some of them, such as "The similitude of the bridge" (1197G). Here Stapleton adds a vertical bar, and this is one of the longest stretches he incorporates into his *Vita Mori*. More directly biographic is the remark "So did Sir Tho. More himselfe" at 1201E, where Antony says: "Lette hym also choose hymselfe some secrete solitary place in his owne house." This gloss recurs opposite the profile of the rich man who "hath vnto rychesse no loue" (1209H). It is clear to Stapleton that in More's *A Dialogue of Comfort* the Turks in Hungary were a screen for the church's enemies in England. Where Antony speaks of this fifth column of apostates, Stapleton refers to "The heretikes . . . in england" (1214B).

That the two treatises upon the passion (pp. 1270–1404) are untouched might cause some suprise. Yet one should remember that the first is a book More never finished or revised, and that the second is Mary Basset's translation of a Tower work which was printed in the Louvain edition of More's Opera (1565).

The letters which fill the last 37 pages of *The English Works* provide plenty of grist for Stapleton's mill. He lists in the margin the virtues they demonstrate: "Pietas, Charitas, Mediocritas" (1447A). Immediately following is the gloss "cur causas tacuit." At 1454E Stapleton emends "damno" to "Domino" (Rom. 14:4), and he uses the fly-leaf at the end of the volume to index 38 "merry tales" and "proper comparisons."

Two of Stapleton's central chapters are anthologies from More's *English Works*: "Apophthegmata, sapienter & pie dicta Thomae Mori" (chapter 12) and "Acute & facete dicta vel responsa" (chapter 13). Chapter 13, however, begins with five quotations from More's *Epistola adversus Pomeranum*, probably because this unpublished work was not known to the readers of More's Opera (1565).[6]

---

[6] The first page of chapter 13 of Stapleton *Vita Mori* is reproduced in *Moreana* 26 (June 1970): 14, as an appendix to an essay in which Charles Crawford shows that the

More's *English Works* also yielded information for Stapleton's life of Thomas Becket. He learned from More, he says, that Becket bore the first brunt of Protestant iconoclasm: the destruction of the statue of Becket on London Bridge was an omen of the wholesale assault which was to take place in 1538 by royal edict.[7]

Thus Stapleton's glosses, underlinings, and vertical lines in More's *English Works* show how carefully and thoroughly he read that folio volume in preparation for his *Vita Mori*. A comparison of his Latin with the passages he translated from More's English would also reveal his skill and accuracy as a translator.

Université Catholique de l'Ouest, Angers

handwritten comments on the Oscott College copy of the *Epistola adversus Pomeranum* "are by Stapleton and should throw light on his *Life of More*."

[7] In his *Debellation of Salem and Bizance* More wrote: "some . . . pulled downe of late vpon London bridge the image of the blessed martyr sayne [sic] Thomas" (935F). See my note "On Stapleton's Second Thomas," *Moreana* 27–28 (November 1970): 137–39.

Puns, Paradoxes, and Heuristic Inquiry: The "De Servis" Section of More's Utopia

ELIZABETH MCCUTCHEON

The "De Servis" section in Book II of the *Utopia* can seem like little more than a hodge-podge of disparate, albeit striking, social practices, especially when read mimetically, as the text itself encourages us to do. Admittedly, some of the customs harmonize or neutralize incongruities in sixteenth-century Europe, portraying a more congruent image of social life that could be thought of as "eutopian." The Utopians neither overvalue nor undervalue natural beauty, for example, and they honor those who have served their country well with statues in the market place, hoping to incite others to virtue. We hear, too, of the relationship between ruler and ruled, whether husband and wife or magistrate and people. "*Con*uiuunt amabiliter," says Hythlodaeus (192/30; my emphasis), emphasizing a reciprocal balance between complementary opposites that parallels the views expressed by sixteenth-century humanists (see Erasmus's *Education of a Christian Prince*, for example) and translates contractual into human relationships.[1] But humanist commonplaces like these are easily detached and they are overshadowed by the very strange customs that Hythlodaeus otherwise describes—customs that seem designed to

---

[1] Conveniently at hand in *The Collected Works of Erasmus*, vol. 27, ed. A. H. T. Levi, trans. Neil M. Cheshire and Michael J. Heath (Toronto: University of Toronto Press, 1986). Consider this description of the good prince: "The good prince must have the same attitude towards his subjects as a good paterfamilias has towards his household; for what else is a kingdom but a large family, and what is a king but the father of very many people?" (229). Cf. the following: "There is a mutual interchange between the prince and the people" (236).

provoke and startle, if not estrange, the reader and have led to dystopian interpretations of the text.[2]

This curious mix of the eutopian, utopian, and dystopian, presented in an apparently random order, has driven translators (like readers generally) to a variety of expedients: the Yale edition, for instance, turns "De Servis" into "Slavery, [Etc.],"[3] while Robert Adams breaks the section into five separate parts, highlighting the major issues, all perplexing: "Slaves," "Care of the Sick and Dying," "Marriage Customs," "Punishments, Legal Procedures, and Customs," and "Foreign Relations."[4] Even Ralph Robynson (who shared some part of More's milieu) obviously struggled before settling for "Of Bondemen, sicke persons, wedlocke, and dyuers other matters."[5]

I do not want to impose an artificial order upon this material. The subject matter is heterogeneous, the breaks and shifts in thought crucial. Exaggerating an authorial strategy and replicating the inherently paradoxical structure of the larger *Utopia*, "De Servis" depends upon pivot points that are signalled by sharp shifts in thought.[6] Moreover, the major segments are themselves unstable, breaking apart or otherwise contradicting themselves internally and requiring us to shift our point of view and reinterpret a text that is never univocal. There is, too, an oblique self-referentiality about the discourse, made wholly visible when Hythlodaeus explains how Utopians treat fools, that allows the authorial More to signal his consciousness of the text and reinforces the joco-serious perspective

---

[2] For two different but interesting discussions of the way that utopias can be read both as "eutopian" and dystopian, see Gary Saul Morson, *The Boundaries of Genre: Dostoevsky's "Diary of a Writer" and the Traditions of Literary Utopia* (Austin: University of Text Press, 1981); and Peter Ruppert, *Reader in a Strange Land: The Activity of Reading Literary Utopias* (Athens and London: The University of Georgia Press, 1986). Also relevant is Shlomo Avineri, "War and Slavery in More's *Utopia*," *International Review of Social History* 7 (1962): 260–90. Sixteenth-century readers often were aware of these tensions, sometimes characterizing *Utopia* as an ideal pattern, sometimes dismissing it as a poetical (and useless) fiction, its claims both implausible and absurd.

[3] *Utopia, The Complete Works of St. Thomas More*, vol. 4, ed. Edward Surtz, S.J., and J. H. Hexter (New Haven: Yale University Press, 1965), 185/15. Citations from the Latin text of the *Utopia* and related material will be taken from this edition and included parenthetically in the text.

[4] In Sir Thomas More, *Utopia: A New Translation, Backgrounds, Criticism*, trans. and ed. Robert M. Adams (New York: Norton, 1975), 64–71.

[5] *The Utopia of Sir Thomas More*, trans. Ralph Robynson, ed. J. H. Lupton (Oxford: Clarendon Press, 1895), 221.

[6] For more on this strategy and the workings of paradox in general, see Elizabeth McCutcheon, *My Dear Peter: The "Ars Poetica" and Hermeneutics for More's "Utopia"* (Angers: *Moreana*, 1983).

that grounds it and invites a multi-faceted response from the reader.

"De Servis" never wholly falls apart, however. Indeed, as a whole, it functions as a metaphoric bridge, letting us move, by zigs and zags, from the preceding section, "De Peregrinatione," in some sense the ethical core of Utopia's commonwealth,[7] to the subsequent section on warfare. More specifically, the initial topic, servitude or bondage, turns us back to issues central to "De Peregrinatione" and beyond that to the dialogue about crime and punishment in Book I, while the discourse on treaties, at the end of "De Servis" (the Utopians never make them, although they are endemic in early modern Europe) frames the problematic discourse on military matters. Less obvious, and more interesting, are the many internal links, partly etymological, partly associative, and partly conceptual, that hold this section together or (more accurately) keep it from falling apart altogether. Implicit in and created by the puns and paradoxes, these links adumbrate large concerns about bonding and binding and initiate the heuristic inquiry in which readers are invited to participate.

The first and all-important word-play involves *seruus* itself. There is no private property in Utopia, one person cannot own another, and no one is born into servitude. So Utopia's *serui* are not slaves in our sense of the word, and the usual translations are misleading in this and other ways. What we need, instead, is some sense of service shading into servitude, as in the exchange between Hythlodaeus and Peter Giles over *seruias* and *inseruias* early in Book I (54/27–28) or in the double translation of *seruus* as "a seruant, a bondeman," in Cooper's *Thesaurus Linguae*.[8] These translations, like Robynson's "Bondemen," usefully focus on critical concerns for all of "De Servis"—and for the larger *Utopia*. Those who are *serui* in Utopia are bound (or bind themselves) and *de facto* serve the whole social order. But almost all of the customs treated in this section are concrete manifestations of bonds or ties that connect parts of the self, one person with another, or people with a larger social or cosmic order. At times such bonds are overtly treated as contracts. They often *are* contracts,

---

[7] See, in particular, George M. Logan, *The Meaning of More's "Utopia"* (Princeton: Princeton Univ. Press, 1983), 144–81, and Elizabeth McCutcheon, "More's *Utopia* and Cicero's *Paradoxa Stoicorum*," *Moreana* 86 (July, 1985): 3–22.

[8] In Thomas Cooper, *Thesaurus Linguae Romanae & Britannicae* (London, 1565). See, too, the seminal discussion by Andre Prevost in his edition of More's *Utopia* (Paris: Mame, 1978), 699, n. 119. On the importance of the "bond of service" in Tudor England, see David Starkey, "The Age of the Household: Politics, Society and the Arts c. 1350–c. 1550," in *The Later Middle Ages*, ed. Stephen Medcalf (Methuen: London, 1981), 225–90.

in fact, in Western Europe. And the nature of these bonds repeatedly invites questions about justice and equity, the very issues that connect Books I and II of the *Utopia* and are essential to the Utopian form as More has created it.

Suicide (or quasi-suicide), for instance, leads to a reflection upon the relationship between the body and soul and self and other before and after death, while marriage, the primary social relationship in Utopia, even etymologically is a *conjugium* or yoking. Similarly, a number of Utopian practices reflect that country's belief that public officials are (or should be) the servants of their country, in the service of their fellow citizens, elsewhere often just a pious hope. Like marriage, laws bind, and Hythlodaeus's discourse invites a consideration of fairness and plays etymologically upon the root for tying while it advances Utopia's attack upon Western European laws: "They themselves think it most unfair [*iniquissimum*] that any group of men should be bound [*obligari*] by laws which are either too numerous to be read through or too obscure to be understood by anyone" (195/11–14). Finally, the discussion of treaties invites reflection upon those things that bind one country to another and how and why those bonds (really contracts) are broken, matters of immediate relevance to More, other humanists, and all of Europe in and around 1516.[9] Thus Raphael Hythlodaeus's almost invariably dead-pan commentary opens up some of the most serious issues any society faces, even when it answers (or purports to answer) them. And it indirectly reveals the degree to which we could see Hythlodaeus as a gymnosophist and Thomas More, himself, as a Socratic gadfly who amuses, perplexes, and disquiets by turn, but never lets us forget the fundamental question he is putting before us: justice and injustice in the commonwealth.

No longer can we read the text simply mimetically, then. Rather, we find a series of joco-serious case studies that we are invited to deconstruct and reconstruct, often simultaneously. Obviously I cannot treat all these cases here. Let me focus, then, on the problem of the *serui*, since this is a patent crux and Hythlodaeus's point of departure. He starts boldly, naming four very different groups that constitute the *serui* or bondspersons of Utopia: prisoners of war, limited to those who were captured in wars that the Utopians themselves fought;[10] Utopian inhabitants who

[9] Cf. the treatment in *Utopia* with Erasmus's commentary on treaties in his *Education of a Christian Prince*, 275–77.

[10] This invites a contrast with the rules for prisoners of war in Henry VIII's war statutes (London, 1513); even children could be taken for ransom and sold, if their

have, in effect, enslaved or imprisoned themselves by committing some heinous crime; persons from other countries who have been condemned to death there for some offense and are either purchased cheaply by Utopian merchants or (more frequently) acquired gratis; and "hard-working and poverty-stricken drudge[s] of another country" who voluntarily choose servitude or service in Utopia, where they are treated more humanely than they were in their own country, to which they are, in any case, free to return—but rarely do (185/31–33).

We are free to search for explanations; in fact, the initial marginal gloss encourages us to compare and contrast practices and policies elsewhere (185/16–17). We can appeal to other texts, too; the servitude of persons in the second group, in particular, seems to reflect Augustine's idea of the origin of bondage: "Sinne therefore is the mother of seruitude, and first cause of man subiection to man."[11] Failing to internalize and act upon Utopia's calculus of pleasure and virtue, these people have made themselves what Augustine would have called the servants of sin,[12] and their external situation—they are loaded with chains, albeit ones made of gold (in almost all other countries a source of pride) and dealt with most severely—literalizes their internal condition, from Utopia's perspective, and punishes what Hythlodaeus sometimes calls crime, sometimes an offense or sin (190/14, 29). Moreover, the insistent link between crime/sin and hard work suggests another Augustinian and biblical echo and reflects a certain rough justice: servitude may bring about reformation. If the *serui* work hard enough, that is, and are sorrier for their offense than for their punishment, their servitude may be lightened or remitted.

Yet Raphael's discourse subverts some part of this subtext. Augustine concluded his discussion of bondage by charging servants to obey their masters, no matter how unjust their situation seemed, urging them to accept a *status quo* until "iniquity be ouerpassed, and all mans power and principality disannuled, and God onely be all in all."[13] By contrast, Utopia offers the poor a paradoxical alternative that implicitly challenges part of Augustine's compromise and sharpens our sense of the gross injustice in Europe, while mischievously confusing our sense of service and

---

fathers were noble or rich enough, that is.

[11] *Saint Augustine, of the Citie of God*, ed. J. L. Vives, trans. J. H. (London, 1620), 725.

[12] Cf. Erasmus, *Education of a Christian Prince*: "All slavery is pitiable and dishonourable, but the most pitiable and dishonourable form of slavery is to be a slave to vice and shameful desires" (221).

[13] *Of the Citie of God*, 725.

freedom. There are even more obvious problems. According to Hythlodaeus, the largest group of *serui* consists of criminals from other countries who would otherwise have been killed. What do we make of the constant flow of criminals into Utopia, though: criminals acquired, for the most part, gratis? Or of the Utopian merchants who fetch them? This resembles what Gary Larson's comic strip calls humor "On the Far Side"; we have a black comedy that illuminates conditions in the actual world, where people become fodder. The point is a serious one, signalling a recurrent Morean preoccupation with the relation between money or property and life (compare marriage in Utopia and elsewhere) and asking us to recall conditions for the death penalty in England. We could argue, too, that the Utopians put to good use, that is, in the service of their commonwealth, what other countries throw away or waste, simultaneously saving the lives of these *serui* and contributing to their reformation. Yet, we could also argue that the Utopians have found a very cheap solution to their servant problem; they don't like hard work and the *serui* do a lot of the hard physical labor. This may sound flippant, even cynical. But long ago Lupton pointed out how Utopia's treatment of these criminals suggests that a "humane policy is also the most profitable,"[14] underscoring the strange but inseparable mix of humanity and self-interest that characterizes so many practices in this section and generates other, more discomfiting paradoxes.

Here, as so frequently, the mix of humor (often sardonic), cynicism, irony, and seriousness is a sign of unresolved and unresolvable incongruities and tensions in Utopia, in sixteenth-century Europe, and in the world as we know it. By preferring servitude to capital punishment (up to a point, at least), the Utopians have refashioned punishment as it existed in early modern Europe. No longer is it a manifestation of royal power, in other words (as it was in Tudor England and other monarchal governments), but an expression of the social order and values of the commonweal, punishing violations of the social bonds between and among people and establishing a punishment that fits the crime.[15] Moreover, Utopian practices anticipate changes in the criminal system in eighteenth-century Europe, and we can better understand why the Utopians rely so much upon shaming mechanisms.[16] But quite different causes—war, sin, crime,

---

[14] In the introduction to his edition of the *Utopia*, li.

[15] For more on punishment and its revelation of social values, see Michel Foucault, *Discipline and Punish: The Birth of the Prison*, trans. Alan Sheridan (New York: Pantheon, 1977).

[16] Stephen Greenblatt, *Renaissance Self-Fashioning: From More to Shakespeare* (Chica-

poverty—connected because they are all manifestations of injustice on either a personal or societal level, lead to the same general result, albeit with differences in degree that let us make a fine discrimination between poverty and other causes: the poverty-stricken *serui* wear no chains. Being a *seruus* in Utopia may ameliorate injustice, then, benefitting both the *seruus* and the social order as a whole. But it hardly solves all the problems the text raises (the *serui*-war link is particularly problematic), nor does it bring about complete justice. Indeed it generates injustices of its own, or would do if Utopia were not a fantasy world.

In this connection we can remember More's second letter to Peter Giles (appearing only in the 1517 edition), in which he answered the objections of some "sharp-sighted" reader who had detected "some little absurdities" in the institutions of Utopia: "What should he be so minded as if there were nothing absurd elsewhere in the world or as if any of all the philosophers had ever ordered the commonwealth, the ruler, or even the private home without instituting some feature that had better be changed" (249/28, 29, 31–34)? Thus we are encouraged to reopen questions that Hythlodaeus often presents as if they were solutions, despite his disclaimers. We do so, though, with a fuller sense of the social, ethical, and political issues involved, a sharper sense of how unjust extant institutions and customs may be, and a deeper sense of how complex the question of community is.

As so frequently happens in the *Utopia*, "De Servis" articulates these concerns inductively and deviously; we need to play with each of the customs imagined and described in such extraordinary detail, detecting the incongruities in Hythlodaeus's densely realized discourse and juxtaposing one with another in Utopia and elsewhere. Marriage, for instance, is the most fully developed segment in "De Servis." Its extended treatment of bonds entered into and kept or broken (at once intensely comic and intensely serious and worthy of the lawyer its author is) invites comparison with the long segment on treaties, which are always broken in that part of the world—though never in Europe, according to Hythlodaeus—as well as with European marriage practices. And it also reopens questions about what keeping one's word means, bringing us face to face with the idea of community.

Behind all these customs, moreover, is the still larger question of equity and justice. "Aequitas"—"Equitee: iustice: euennesse: likenes of facion," according to Cooper's *Thesaurus*—is part of the first marginal comment in

---

go: The Univ. of Chicago Press, 1980), 47–58, tellingly explores the place of shame in the communal ethos that constitutes Utopia and its social and psychological significance for More himself.

the "De Servis" section. Whether we read that remark straightforwardly (the gloss asks us to admire Utopia's "aequitas"), take it as an ironic aside with respect to the problem of prisoners of war or the larger war problem, or read it both ways, its presence is striking. And it signals a recurrent concern that reappears in the segments on marriage and the law and becomes wholly overt in the discourse on treaty-making and breaking. Finally Raphael Hythlodaeus falls into diatribe as he concludes that "all justice" [*iustitia tota*] seems to be "a plebeian and low virtue which is far below the majesty of kings" (199/10–11). Or else there are at least two forms of it: one fit for the common people, "bound by many chains," the other for kings, and so free that "every thing is permissible to it—except what it finds disagreeable" (199/16–17). Thanks, in part, to the litotic negations that open the text and intensify a dilemma that Erasmus also addressed in his *Education of a Christian Prince*, the Latin is stronger still: "cui nihil non liceat nisi quod non libeat" (198/13–14)—that is, to which nothing is not permitted except what does not please.[17] The instruments of justice are made the instruments of injustice, and Hythlodaeus, albeit speaking as an iconoclast, is, from our perspective, prophetic about the powers of the king as these developed in the course of the 1520s and 30s in England and elsewhere.

It is easy to characterize Hythlodaeus's position and feel his moral outrage. Here, proleptically, is the voice of the revolutionary. It is harder, however, to characterize the point of view of the author, who will subsequently find himself challenging monarchal power at the cost of his life while using every legal means to try to preserve it. Like Plato, Augustine, and Erasmus, More *is* preoccupied with justice and equity, and he is extraordinarily sensitive to the abuses, aberrations, and misuses of justice in Western Europe in 1516. But he writes as the lawyer he is as well as a philosopher, politician, and creative writer; hence the preoccupation, at once serious and playful, with contracts and bonds and his preference for concrete cases that problematize the text and let him open up questions about values, in general, and justice, equity, and the meaning of community, in particular.[18] Moreover, Raphael Hythlodaeus's final diatribe is, from one point of view, a too-easy generalization of justice/injustice that

[17] Cf. Erasmus: "Do not think you may do anything you please. . . . Train yourself in such a way that nothing pleases you which is not permissible . . ." (218).

[18] See too John Rastell's prologue to his *Le Liver des Assises & Plees del Corone*, addressing questions about the definition of the commonwealth and relationships between laws and the commonweal. Rastell (More's brother-in-law) first published this work c. 1514; I have consulted the London, 1561 edition; see sig. Aii–Aiii.

calls for reflection and refinement. In this and other ways, More's text tacitly acknowledges the realities of power and the profit motive that Raphael Hythlodaeus and Utopia as place challenge at the same time that it underscores the tragic gaps between principles and practices and principle and principle. Finally, perhaps, we are left with a heightened awareness of *injustice* and its effects, and a series of questions–never to be fully answered in this world–about just what is just and fair and how equity can be established in and for the commonweal.

University of Hawaii

Neo-Latin Resources for Biography: A Preliminary View

R. J. SCHOECK

Rosalie Colie has called our attention to a dominant aspect of Renaissance thought and letters: "Rhetorical education, always a model-following enterprise, increasingly stressed *structures* as well as styles to be imitated in the humane letters–epistles, orations, discourses, dialogues, histories, poems–always discoverable to the enthusiastic new man of letters by kind."[1] To Colie's list we must add biography, for biography emerged from the shadows of history and was nurtured by new historical perspectives which gave greater attention to the individual, as Peter G. Bietenholz has shown in his monograph on *History and Biography in the Work of Erasmus of Rotterdam.*[2]

The writing of biography is a mimetic art, and in any period the writer is guided, often indeed inspired, sometimes constrained, by accepted models, although in biography a writer must work within an understood

---

[1] Rosalie Colie, *The Resources of Kind–Genre-Theory in the Renaissance* (Berkeley: Univ. of California Press, 1973), 4. See my extended comment on *imitatio* in " 'Lighting a Candle to the Place': On the Dimensions and Implications of *Imitatio* in the Renaissance," *Italian Culture* 4 (1983): 123–43.

On biography as genre, still useful is Donald A. Stauffer, *English Biography before 1700* (Cambridge: Harvard Univ. Press, 1930; repr. New York, 1964); and there is a useful collection of documents on biography available at the end of the seventeenth century in James L. Clifford, ed., *Biography as an Art* (New York: Oxford Univ. Press, 1962). Too little known to English Renaissance students are Sem Dresden, *De structuur van de biographie* (Den Haag: Daamen, 1956), and T. A. Dorey, ed., *Latin Biography* (London: Routledge & K. Paul, 1967).

[2] Peter G. Bietenholz, *History and Biography in the Work of Erasmus of Rotterdam*, Travaux d' Humanisme et Renaissance, vol. 87 (Genève: Librairie Droz, 1966).

theory of history. But what is involved in mimesis is of course the concept of *imitatio*, which I have attempted to discuss in rather enlarged terms in "'Lighting a Candle to That Place....'"[3] In this paper I shall offer a sketch, necessarily provisional, of the potentials for our study of Renaissance biography that are to be found in the prefaces and commentaries upon classical and patristic authors. For the concern of this program is to examine the writing of lives of Thomas More done in the sixteenth century. These Renaissance biographies were written by humanists, that is to say, by men—and what a pity that we do not have a biography by one of the women of More's family or school: what would we not give for a life of More by Margaret Roper.

To be sure, there were also patristic and medieval models—of which only a small proportion of the later medieval writings were not in Latin—and all of these shared, with differences, the conventions of rhetorical development of subject and *topoi*. Thus, notably, the tradition of the saint's life—the legends of the saints that were intended to be read individually as well as communally for instruction and following[4]—and this tradition was still a powerful influence in both religious life and literature in the sixteenth century. With the early lives of the founders of the Brethren of the Common Life, for example, one finds lives that are molded in the tradition of the saint's life. Some of us have argued for the influence of this saint's life tradition in the shaping of Roper's *Life of More*, for the work is constructed around the holding forth as the virtue iconified More's superlative virtue of conscience, his "cleere unspotted conscience."[5] Even here as well, there is the as yet not fully studied question of how much the classical rhetorical tradition provided techniques and models for the late-medieval saints' lives, like those in the tradition of the Brethren of the Common Life and the congregation of the Canons of St. Augustine.[6] This question is the more important because of the customs

[3] "'Lighting a Candle'": cited in n. 1 above.

[4] See H. Delehaye, *The Legends of the Saints*, ed. R. J. Schoeck (Notre Dame: Univ. of Notre Dame Press, 1961), Introduction.

[5] In "On the Spiritual Life of St. Thomas More," *Thought* 52 (1977); 324–27, I have touched very briefly on this question; see further "Tommaso Moro," in *Bibliotheca Sanctorum* (Rome, 1969) 12: 601–4. We know that Erasmus was schooled in a tradition that emphasized oral reading, as I have summarized in a chapter on Erasmus' spirituality in *Erasmus Grandescens* (Nieuwkoop: B. DeGraaf, 1988). The *Imitation of Christ* cuts across several of the lines that I have been developing, with its vigorously emphasized concept of imitating or following Christ, in a work to be read individually and communally. See also *The Achievement of Thomas More* (Victoria, B.C.: English Literary Studies, 1976), 40–41.

[6] See the discussion of Augustinian spirituality and of the Brethren of the Com-

of reading saints' lives aloud at certain meals, both in religious communities and in households like those of Thomas More.

We need to return to the full resources of rhetoric, which provided techniques and reader expectations for the delineation of character. In his individual portraitures in the General Prologue to *The Canterbury Tales*—so much like the miniature portraits in late medieval art—Chaucer (as Coghill has made clear) was being his most rhetorical even as he achieved his memorably individualized portraits that now strike us as so original:

> Me thynketh it acordaunt to resoun
> To telle yow al the condicioun
> Of ech of hem, so as it semed me,
> And which they weren, and of what degree,
> And eek in what array that they were inne
> (*GP* 37–41)

Here Chaucer expresses explicitly the interest in *array* and in the *degree* of each of the pilgrims, and he follows the Ciceronian prescriptions for detailing the character of a man or woman by beginning with the parentage and proceeding through the attributes. *Resoun* (a technical term in rhetoric) announces the sense of rhetorical order or suitable arrangement; and *condicioun* calls into question the whole state of the individual being, both inner and outer. I am not arguing that Chaucer was necessarily a model for the sixteenth-century biographers of More, although surely they would all have read him. Rather, I am indicating that little more than a century earlier than they wrote, the great Middle English poet found rhetorical techniques and models more than adequate for his kind of biographical writing.[7] To sum up my emphasis on the several traditions of biographical writing: in addition to the classical models provided by such a range as Plutarch's presentation of comparative biography; of the studies of individuals by Suetonius, Sallust, and others; and of the studies by Thucydides and Livy of individuals in civic contexts, there were patristic and medieval traditions of biographical writings as well. Nor can we neglect the nascent Neo-Latin biographical tradition of the fifteenth century, and I remind you of C. W. T. Blackwell's most informative paper on "Humanism and Politics in English Royal Biography," in the *Acta Conventus Neo-Latini Sanctandreani*, which studies the use of Cicero by

---

mon Life in *Erasmus Grandescens* (1988).

[7] See R. C. Goffin, "Chaucer and 'Reason'," *MLR* 21 (1926): 13–18; and Nevill Coghill, *Chaucer* (London: Oxford Univ. Press, 1960).

Titus Livius Frulovisi and the uses of Plutarch and Sallust by Bernard André in their lives of Henry V (1438) and of Henry VII (1500–1503).[8] All of these several traditions of biographical writing were available to the generation of More and Erasmus, and increasingly we are being made aware of the richness of the rhetorical tradition itself as well as of the strategies and techniques available to biographers.[9]

To this wealth that is to be found in the classical tradition as continued and modified by patristic, medieval and humanistic rhetorical teaching, we must now add the profusion of enlargements or applications of classical thought in the form of notes, *adnotationes, castigationes*, prefaces, commentaries, and such[10]—not excluding the marginal manuscript glosses and notes which often circulated or were at least read by others than the scholars themselves.[11] The force of the commentaries especially is to document the use of the texts in teaching, and to provide clues as to how those texts were being interpreted. One central author has been studied in detail in the studies by John O. Ward of medieval and Renaissance commentaries on Cicero. The continuity of such a master-author cannot

---

[8] C. W. T. Blackwell, "Humanism and Politics in English Royal Biography: The Use of Cicero, Plutarch, and Sallust in the *Vita Henrici Quinti* (1438) by Titus Livius de Frulovisi and the *Vita Henrici Septimi* (1500–1503) by Bernard André," in *Acta Conventus Neo-Latini Sanctandreani*, ed. I. D. McFarlane, Medieval & Renaissance Texts & Studies, vol. 38 (Binghamton, NY, 1986), 431–40.

[9] This richness is manifested in the collection of Newberry Conference essays edited by J. J. Murphy in *Renaissance Eloquence* (Berkeley: Univ. of California Press, 1983). Quite simply, the role of rhetoric was deepened and enlarged by a number of Renaissance humanists who did more than merely receive: see Wesley Trimpi, "The Quality of Fiction: the Rhetorical Transmission of Literary Theory," *Traditio* 30 (1974), enlarged in his *Muses of One Mind* (Princeton: Princeton Univ. Press, 1983). In this context it is appropriate to cite two works which indicate the broadening: Charles Trinkaus, *In Our Image and Likeness: Humanity and Divinity in Italian Humanist Thought*, 2 vols. (Chicago: Univ. of Chicago Press, 1970), and Ernesto Grassi, *Rhetoric as Philosophy* (University Station, PA: State Univ. of Pennsylvania Press, 1980).

[10] For commentaries there is a most useful collection of studies in the volume edited by August Buck, *Der Kommentar in der Renaissance* (Boppard: Boldt, 1974). For a larger view, see the very useful study by Tore Janson of classical and medieval *Latin Prose Prefaces* (Stockholm: 1964), and the studies by O. Schottenloher (1955) and Gualdo Rosa (1973). – The general techniques of classical scholarship are surveyed in J. E. Sandys, *A History of Classical Scholarship*, 3rd ed., 3 vols. (Cambridge: Cambridge Univ. Press, 1908); E. J. Kenney, *The Classical Text* (Berkeley: Univ. of California Press, 1974), provides a keen analysis of various aspects of editing during this period, especially emendation.

[11] Cf. the numerous interesting examples provided by Anthony Grafton in volume 1 of his Scaliger biography: *J. J. Scaliger* (London: Warburg Institute, 1984).

be questioned, and one must be impressed by the increasing openness during the Renaissance of the text to interpretation and use.[12] Thus, to take a single example, but one fundamental to the history of biography, Thomas More's *Life of Richard III*: Richard Sylvester has analysed More's use of Sallust, Suetonius and Tacitus for the understanding and presenting of character, and I need not remind this group of the brilliant demonstration in his introduction to More's *Life* of the many-sidedness of the work. For Sylvester penetratingly commented on the numerous borrowings and imitations, analogues and allusions, and he succeeds in making it possible for the twentieth-century student to understand the process of fusing the disparate elements into a single biography.

The full story of the classical tradition of biography during the Renaissance has yet to be written, although Bietenholz has written well on Erasmus and biography; but the reading and teaching of biography during the Renaissance must include not only the basic texts of Plutarch, Suetonius, Sallust, Tacitus, and others, it must also study commentaries on those texts. We know what was read; we need to know more about how it was read, and taught, and imitated.

Here, there is time to take up only one classical example and to sketch the availability of some of the resources of which I have been speaking, and I propose to take Plutarch's *Lives* and to suggest some of the prefaces and commentaries that were available to sixteenth-century writers of biography. Many of More's friends and acquaintances were in fact engaged in translating Plutarch,[13] including Erasmus, whose *Opuscula Plutarchi nuper traducta. Erasmo interprete*, was printed in 1512 and frequently reprinted. Other Plutarchan works followed.

Early in the fifteenth century Leonardo Bruni had translated a number of the lives, and shortly afterwards Guarino da Verona added Latin translations of fifteen more. Later in the century Francesco Filelfo published four Latin translations, and then in a Rome edition of 1470 Campano presented a Latin translation of all of the lives. Just as Plato—at much

---

[12] See John O. Ward, "Glosses and Commentaries on Cicero's *Rhetoric*," in *Medieval Eloquence: Studies in the Theory and Practice of Medieval Rhetoric*, ed. J. J. Murphy (Berkeley: Univ. of California Press, 1978), and "Commentators on Ciceronian Rhetoric," in *Renaissance Eloquence: Studies in the Theory and Practice of Renaissance Rhetoric*, ed. J. J. Murphy (Berkeley: Univ. of California Press, 1983). See also n. 30 below.

[13] On this point: "More, Plutarch, and King Agis: Spartan History and the Meaning of *Utopia*," reprinted from *Philological Quarterly* in *Essential Articles for the Study of Thomas More*, ed. R. S. Sylvester and G. Marc'hadour (Hamden: Archon, 1977), 174 ff.

the same time—was now available in a complete Latin translation by Ficino, so the *Lives* of Plutarch were now accessible in a complete Latin translation. Interest naturally continued and deepened.[14]

In 1509 Michael Hummelberg, who was associated in editing classical texts with Lefèvre d'Etaples and Josse Bade, and who became a close associate and friend of Beatus Rhenanus, wrote about the writing and teaching of Girolamo Aleandro; for Aleandro had been working on the Aldine edition of Plutarch's *Moralia* in 1507, and in Paris in 1509 Aleandro was lecturing on Greek and publishing three treatises by Plutarch with Gourmont. In the ambitious preface to this Plutarchan work, Aleandro spoke to students of the true philosophy (that is, not scholasticism) and promised to edit and explain all the Greek authors—poets, orators, historians, philosophers, theologians, and Fathers of the Church—a breathtakingly ambitious proposal, even for a twenty-nine year old. In the preface to this work he spoke of Plutarch: "Quod hactenus feci in tribus hisce, quos Latine expositiuri sumus, gravissimi scriptoris Plutarchi commentariis, facturus itidem. . . ."[15] Clearly a sense of the importance of commentaries is underscored here.

In 1514 Josse Bade (who, as we know, published much of Erasmus and More), re-edited the *Lives* of Plutarch, with the help of a student of Aleandro's, Gérard de Verceil.[16] The preface by Bade is addressed to Aleandro and is dated 1 December 1514. In the text (which is provided by Renouard, volume III), we can see the new emphases of humanists in the reading and teaching of biography.[17]

---

[14] One sees an interest in Plutarch as a moral philosopher, of course, as with Guillaume Budé's translation of four treatises of Plutarch: *De placitis philosophorum*, *De fortuna Romanorum* (1503), and *De tranquillitate et securitate animi* and *De fortuna vel virtute Alexandri* (1505). Thus Plutarch was thought to be "juge équitable des sectes et maître délicat de morale pratique": A. Renaudet, *Préréforme et Humanisme à Paris pendant les premières guerres d'Italie (1494–1517)*, 2 ed. (Paris: Librairie d'Argences, 1953), 282.

[15] Renaudet, *Préréforme*, p. 513 & n. 5. Cf. *Contemporaries of Erasmus*, ed. P. G. Bietenholz et al., vol. 1 (Toronto: Univ. of Toronto Press, 1985), 29, on Aleandro. Aleandro had a spurt of enormous productivity from 1509 to 1514, and this led to his becoming principal of the Collège des Lombards from 1511 and being appointed rector of the university in March 1513.

[16] See A. Renaudet, *Préréforme*, p. 661 & note.

[17] Bietenholz discusses the question of history and biography with respect to Erasmus, but without considering the question of how biography might be taught. For a general discussion of the impact of all of the classical heritage upon education see R. R. Bolgar, *The Classical Heritage and Its Beneficiaries* (Cambridge: Cambridge Univ. Press, 1954); one of the best general treatments of Renaissance education is Eugenio

We can now look to Erasmus and Thomas More for further illustration of the Renaissance use of classics in the writing of biography. Erasmus has been studied intensively by Bietenholz, who emphasizes, quite rightly, aspects of biography as history—although I believe, as I have tried to make clear, that biography must be considered under the aegis of rhetoric as well. In the view of Bietenholz, Erasmus "expressed a profound concern with the truth of all historical knowledge acquired by man, a concern that advanced the humanistic spirit of inquiry and forecast many facets of the complex historical thought of the modern age."[18]

Erasmus wrote several lives himself, and they differ considerably. In his *Hieronymi vita* he wrote a life that was history (in the terms of Bietenholz), and it was written to accompany his great edition of Jerome in 1516, on which Professor John Olin has been working.[19] The edition and the *Vita Hieronymi* measure Erasmus' lifelong dedication to the study of Jerome and his work, which mattered in two principal ways to Erasmus. First, because Jerome was the great translator of and commentator upon the Bible, and because Jerome's fusion of classical studies and Scripture was a fountain of inspiration for Erasmus and his concept of *philosophia Christi*: *ex purissimis fontibus, Christi philosophiam hauriebat*, Erasmus wrote in his *Vita*.[20] There Erasmus first criticized the use of fictitious stories and vindicated the "Saint in the face of medieval and incompetent biographers."[21] Then follows a detailed biographical account from birth to death, proceeding to opinions on Jerome's virginity and on the merits of

---

Garin, *L'educazione in Europa, 1400–1600* (Bari, 1957). For a history of the scholarship involved in study of the classics (to be adjusted by more recent studies at a number of points), J. E. Sandys, *A History of Classical Scholarship from the Sixth Century B.C. to the End of the Middle Ages*, 3 vols. (Cambridge: Cambridge Univ. Press, 1903–8).

[18] Bietenholz, *History and Biography*, 12. For any humanist in the sixteenth century there were serious problems in the meaning of history and in the ways of writing history, and biography may well be considered, at least in part, under the aegis of history. But it needs to be studied as rhetoric, and in other ways as well.

[19] John C. Olin has stressed the *Vita*'s mode as an encomium and also a plea: "*Eloquentia, Erudio, Fides*: Erasmus's *Life of Jerome*," *Acta Conventus Neo-Latini Sanctandreani*, ed. I. D. McFarlane, Medieval & Renaissance Texts & Studies, vol. 38 (Binghamton, NY, 1986), 269–74. See further Joseph Coppens, "Le portrait de Saint Jérôme d'après Erasme," *Colloquia Erasmiana Turonensia*, ed. J.-C. Margolin, 2 vols. (Toronto: Univ. of Toronto Press, 1972), 821–28.

[20] *Erasmi opuscula*: *A Supplement to the Opera omnia*, ed. W. K. Ferguson (The Hague: Nijhoff, 1933; repr. Hildesheim, 1978), 151/493. There are obvious Ciceronian echoes as well as those from the Roman poets and historians.

[21] Bietenholz, *History and Biography*, p. 91.

his literary style, as well as on his theology.[22] There were other editions of the Church Fathers which Erasmus completed at Basel, but in none of them did he write a biography, perhaps, as Bietenholz suggests, because he felt himself growing old (as he began to do in the early 1520s) and because his time was now too precious for the kind of research that he had lavished on Jerome.[23]

Two other Erasmian biographies need to be mentioned: the one letter in which he portrayed Thomas More, and the other which gave a double portrait of John Colet and Jean Vitrier. More's portrait is in the letter to Ulrich von Hutten of July 1519.[24] It is familiar to all of you, and Germain Marc'hadour has commented on it in loving detail. There, clearly, one finds skillful employment of all of the resources of rhetoric of which I have been speaking. The double portrait of Colet and Vitrier is contained in a letter to Jodocus Jonas, dated June 1521, and it invites comparison with the double portrait of Erasmus and Peter Gilles by Quentin Metsys. It too is well-known enough to all of you. These are available to us today; they were also familiar to contemporaries and followers of More and Erasmus. In Erasmus' letter-portraits are to be found something very like Dutch genre-paintings of family life in simple and charming detail. One feels (Bietenholz comments) that with More's family

> Erasmus here beheld a practical application of *philosophia Christi* with which his own nature was incompatible—that he admired in More not so much his own disciple as rather a congenial spirit endowed with many qualities that Erasmus himself lacked. It is on this basis that he envisaged a Plutarch-like comparison between the lives of More and Budé, but regrettably did not go beyond a mere hint.[25]

Let me extend this use of Bietenholz by drawing upon his comment that

> there is some evidence of a favourable response from among his contemporaries. Moringus, who himself wrote several biographies, including one of Augustine, expressed his admiration for *Hieronymi vita.* [Allen VII, 393] Allen notes an English translation, in 1533 [by Tyndale], of the letter addressed to Jonas containing the portraits of Vitrier and Colet. [IV, 507 n.] ... in the subsequent life of More by

---

[22] Ibid., 91–92.

[23] Ibid., 95.

[24] Allen 4, 12 ff. Marc'hadour has spoken on "Erasmus: First and Best Biographer of Thomas More," *Erasmus of Rotterdam Society Yearbook Seven* (1987), 1 ff.

[25] Bietenholz, *History and Biography*, 93.

Harpsfield Erasmus' letter is used as an obvious source. . . .[26]

As for More: about 1506—or as Sylvester reckons, 1510—More wrote his *Life of Pico*, which, Richard Sylvester wrote, "indirectly inherits the Suetonius method, which had been followed by Paulinus in his *Life of Ambrose* and by Einhardus in his *Life of Charlemagne*."[27] Further, More adapted one of Suetonius' tales about Tiberius in his 1509 coronation poems to Henry VIII. *Richard III*, Sylvester argues most convincingly, follows or adapts Suetonius, Sallust, and Tacitus.[28] But let us pick up the clue in Erasmus' 1519 letter to Hutten where he tells us that More worked hard in his middle years to polish his prose: *per omne scripti genus stilum exercens*.[29] The classical models were there to be followed for the writing of the lives of Pico and Richard—Plutarch, Sallust, Suetonius, Tacitus—but we cannot say what editions he used, or what commentaries he knew. But we can echo Sylvester's words: "he borrowed from everyone," and "his Latin words are tesselated with words or phrases from a variety of authors."[30]

To conclude: it is premature to offer a firm conclusion to what is avowedly a provisional study. I intend to spend some of my time in Europe during the next two or three years reading more prefaces (a number of which I intend to collect and put together), and above all to look more closely at the commentaries on the classical writers of biography that have been cited. In writing on *Medieval Aspects of Renaissance Learning*, Paul O. Kristeller has spoken of the central importance of the commentary among the literary genres for scholarly literature of the late Middle Ages: textbook, commentary, quaestio, and treatise. "The commentary," he concludes, "should probably be considered as the most important form of scholarly literature of the Middle Ages."[31] That evalu-

---

[26] Ibid., 97.

[27] Richard S. Sylvester, introduction to *The History of King Richard III*, volume 2 in The Yale Edition of the Complete Works of St. Thomas More (New Haven: Yale Univ. Press, 1963), p. lxxxviii n.

[28] See "Genesis and Models" section in the Introduction cited, pp. lxxx ff.

[29] Allen 4, 21/249—*CWE* 7:23/271, "by practising his pen in every sort of writing."

[30] Sylvester, loc. cit., p. lxxxiii. *Tesselated* was one of Dick Sylvester's favorite words, and he would have relished the fact that one of the citations in the *Oxford Latin Dictionary* (1982) is from Suetonius' *Julius*, 46: *tesellata pauimenta*—that is, constructed from or adorned with mosaic work.

[31] Paul O. Kristeller, *Medieval Aspects of Renaissance Learning*, ed. Edward P. Mahoney (Durham, N.C.: Duke Univ. Press, 1974), 6. The commentary on Sallust by Lorenzo Valla is an outstanding example of the importance of commentaries, and Blackwell has conjectured that André may have read Valla's commentary, for both

ation can be carried forward with the valuable work of August Buck on the commentary in the Renaissance.[32]

What is manifest, I trust, is that sixteenth-century biographers of Thomas More had a rich thesaurus of models, *topoi*, and lore from which to draw: rhetorical conventions of description, new developments in the writing of lives of religious men and women and now the writing of the lives of devoted lay men and women, new efforts to see literary works in historical context, and, perhaps most of all, a new urgency that derived from the tensions and challenges of the Reformation and Counter-Reformation. At some future date we shall want to compare lives of Luther and other reformers, or Foxe's *Book of Martyrs*, more intensively with Roman Catholic biographical writings—and the new vernacular with the more traditional Latin. But that must remain a rather distant task. What is necessary first is to examine to what extent the very nature of tradition and the viability of old conventions came into question, not unlike the challenging of tradition in our own post-modernist world.[33]

Universität Trier

---

saw Sallust's prooemium as a locus for historical style, they described the prooemium in rhetorical terms which focused on the orator-historian, they emphasized Sallust's 'brevitas' and they both were interested in the correct stylistic use of digressions.

I quote from Blackwell, "Humanism and Politics," 435. See Sallust, *Bellum Catalinum, cum commento L. Valli* (Venice, 1492), sig. a. ii.

[32] August Buck, ed. *Der Kommentar in der Renaissance.* Mitteilung. Kommission für Humanismusforschung, 1 (Boppard: Boldt, 1975).

[33] I am aware that the assertion of a continuum, or the affirmation of tradition, is itself a critical (and even a political and theological) statement: see my "Erasmus in England, 1499–1517: *Translatio studii* and the *Studia humanitatis*," *Classical and Modern Literature* 7 (1987); 269–83—repr. in *Erasmus Grandescens* (Nieuwkoop: DeGraaf, 1988).

Perhaps in a post-modernist world what will be needed will be contrastive, rather than comparative, approaches.

SEMINAR

Erasmus and Literary Criticism

Erasmus on the Use and Abuse of Metaphor

LAUREL CARRINGTON

Although my paper's title points to Erasmus's concerns about metaphor, my actual subject draws on a series of issues of which this is only a part. To begin with, the place of metaphor in the classical discipline of rhetoric is extremely important, as is Erasmus's complex relationship to that tradition. Erasmus's use of metaphor in his own writing, as well as his explicit statements about metaphor, likewise bear upon my immediate concern. Above all, however, I am interested in showing how the question of metaphor can throw light on Erasmus's work and on the many areas in which Erasmus was involved with using and writing about language.

For when we look at Erasmus, we see a man who wore many hats: educator, biblical scholar, writer, and religious reformer. All of his roles reveal him as deeply concerned with the use and power of language, yet because the tasks that occupied him were so varied, often the attitudes he professed toward language seem to be at odds with one another. Erasmus the writer embraced an approach to prose writing that can only be described as that of the virtuoso practitioner, as we detect in his opening to the *De Copia*: "Ut non est aliud vel admirabilius, vel magnificentius quam oratio, divite quadam sententiarum verborumque copia, aurei fluminis instar, exuberans. . . ."[1] Works such as *De Copia*, *Parabolae*, and *De Conscribendis Epistolis* combine a lively admiration for fine writing with a workmanlike concern for the tools needed to write well. As a biblical scholar, Erasmus showed another kind of concern with language, focusing on the priority of purifying the text of Scripture in order to base interpretation on biblical language that was accurate and capable of being read in its

[1] Desiderius Erasmus, *Opera omnia*, ed. J. Clericus (Leiden, 1703–1706, henceforth cited as *LB*), vol. 1, 3A.

own linguistic context. Thus, understanding the Greek of the time of the New Testament became for him the key to solving problems of biblical exegesis, along with a painstaking attention to detail in comparing manuscripts.

In contrast with these concerns, however, we find Erasmus as a religious reformer embracing the *philosophia Christi*, an inner sense of Christ's message that depends on personal piety and a pure and humble spirit. Language is important here in the form of good preaching, for as Erasmus writes in his paraphrase on Romans 10:17,

> Porro fides concipitur in animo, non per experimenta, sed per Apostolorum praedicationem, hoc est, non per oculos concipitur, sed per aures, per quas in animum obedientem transfunditur Evangelium Christi.[2]

Yet the success of good preaching depends not on its being a commanding verbal performance, nor on the listener's ability to understand in detail the meaning of each word, but rather on the hearer having an appropriate frame of mind, represented in this passage by the "obedient soul."

Thus Erasmus shows in three of his roles three varying levels of concern with language. It is my belief that the question of metaphor as it appears in Erasmus's work can bring new perspectives to a study of his different approaches. My plan is first to show how Erasmus's definition of the term "metaphor" is consistent with the classical tradition, then to speak more of the position of metaphor within that tradition, and finally to explore the ways in which Erasmus responds to these aspects of the tradition in his own writing and commentary.

Let me first of all define "metaphor" itself. In its technical sense, metaphor is a rhetorical figure in which a term is used to designate something other than its literal meaning. Erasmus in *De Copia* defines it this way:

> Alia vero varietatis ratio ex Metaphora nascitur, quae Latine Translatio dicitur. Propterea quod vocem a genuina ac propria significatione, ad non propriam transfert.[3]

A broader use of the term refers to the extended metaphor, in which a comparison between two phenomena is drawn out over one or more

---

[2] *LB* VII, 812B–C.

[3] *LB* I, 17D–E.

sentences. Erasmus refers specifically to these kinds of statements in his *Parabolae*, a work offered for the express purpose of providing writers with a comprehensive list of such comparisons drawn from ancient authors:

> Cur enim non sic appellem has "ὁμοιώσεις," ex opulentissimo summorum authorum mundo selectas?... non nitorem modo, sed universam prope sermonis dignitatem a metaphoris proficisci. Nihil autem aliud est παραβολή, quam Cicero collationem vocat, quam explicata metaphora.[4]

Although my interest is in both levels of metaphor, it is at the level of the word that I would like to focus primarily.

Quintilian mentions that the Stoic rhetoricians of Greece looked upon metaphor with some suspicion: "Quid enim, inquiunt, attinet circuitu res ostendere et translationibus, ... cum sua cuique sint adsignata nomina?"[5] The Stoics had adopted two premises about language: that words are signs for things, and that language, like a proper mirror, should reflect the world in a one-to-one correspondence between words and things. Although such a view might seem extreme in its inflexibility, the first of the two premises became a commonplace of all rhetoric. Cicero's Crassus in *De Oratore* shows his agreement when in reference to literal names he writes, "quae propria sunt et certa quasi vocabula rerum, paene una nata cum rebus ipsis...."[6] Crassus goes on to say that Latin, unlike Greek, suffers from a deficiency of vocabulary, so that not all things had names from the very beginning. Metaphor was adopted to remedy this lack:

> Nam ut vestis frigoris depellendi causa reperta primo, post adhiberi coepta est ad ornatum etiam corporis et dignitatem, sic verbi translatio instituta est inopiae causa, frequentata delectationis.[7]

Out of necessity came the added advantage of delight. Part of metaphor's effectiveness, Crassus maintains, comes from its ability to call to mind the resemblances among different things: "illustrat id quod intellegi volumus

---

[4] Desiderius Erasmus of Rotterdam, *Opera omnia* (Amsterdam: North Holland, 1971–), vol. 1-5, 88–90.

[5] *The Institutio Oratoria of Quintilian*, with an English translation by H. E. Butler (London: William Heinemann Ltd., 1936), 12.10.41.

[6] Marcus Tullius Cicero, *De Oratore*, ed. A. S. Wilkins (Oxford: Clarendon Press, 1963), 3.37.149.

[7] Ibid. 3.38.155.

eius rei quam alieno verbo posuimus similitudo."[8] Yet the metaphor, relying on similitude, is nonetheless *alienum*, out of its proper place. There is a one-to-one correspondence between word and thing that metaphor supplements and temporarily disrupts.

Since, then, metaphor was seen as a kind of disruption even by an author like Cicero, who championed its use, it was important for writers and rhetoricians to determine exactly what level of disruption was tolerable in order to protect the representational function of language. Derrida's *White Mythology* describes this task first of all in terms of a mapping out of linguistic territory for the discipline of philosophy. Pure philosophy, which seeks the truth, can use language only in a way that leaves no room for metaphor or word play: nouns in their proper sense name things, and this is the foundation of all philosophy.

> A noun is proper when it has but a single sense. Better, it is only in this case that it is properly a noun. Univocity is the essence, or better, the *telos* of language. No philosophy as such has ever renounced this Aristotelian ideal. This ideal is philosophy.[9]

What univocity accomplishes is a doubling so perfect that the language is ultimately self-cancelling. Aristotle's careful distinctions between rhetoric and philosophy on the one hand and rhetoric and poetics on the other are an attempt to control, through the separation of disciplines by linguistic practices, the disruption of all tropes in language-use. Good rhetoric is designated as the art of persuasion; or, more specifically, "the faculty of discovering in the particular case what are the available means of persuasion."[10] Unlike philosophy, it must deal with signs and names. It shares with philosophy the recognition that language is purely conventional, not natural,[11] yet it must avoid becoming false rhetoric by refraining from any exploitation of the contingency of signifiers, concerning itself rigorously with the truth. In cases where the truth is not determined, rhetoric

---

[8] Ibid. 3.38.155.

[9] Jacques Derrida, *White Mythology: Metaphor in the Text of Philosophy*, from *Margins of Philosophy*, trans. Alan Bass (Chicago: Univ. of Chicago Press, 1982), 247.

[10] *The Rhetoric of Aristotle*, trans. Lane Cooper (New York: D. Appleton and Company, 1932), 1.1.2. Aristotle's refinement of this definition is intended to avoid the undesirable conclusion that rhetoric could participate in persuading someone to believe a falsehood; thus in the case of a falsehood, there would be *no* proper means of persuasion available to the art of rhetoric.

[11] Aristotle, *Categories and De Interpretatione*, trans. E. M. Edgehill (Oxford: Oxford Univ. Press, 1928), 16a20.

must soberly negotiate among the levels of probability applying to competing propositions. In the course of these duties, the use of ornament is introduced to decorate and to delight.

It is as an ornament that Erasmus describes metaphor in *Parabolae*. In so doing, he is speaking along lines established by the ancient rhetoricians, who classify metaphor as a trope or figure of speech, all of which are described as ornaments. Thus it should be our task at this point to understand something about the role of ornament in classical rhetoric. Both Cicero and Quintilian see it as something added on to plain speech: as Cicero's Crassus specifies,

> tantum significabo brevi, neque verborum ornatum inveniri posse non partis expressisque sententiis neque esse ullam sententiam illustrem sine luce verborum.[12]

According to this passage, one should first determine in basic form what one wishes to say, and then afterward embellish one's speech. In other words, ornament does not enter into the first stages of putting an idea into speech. Neither should it seem detached from the language in which it appears: for example, in speaking of metaphor, Quintilian writes,

> Quae quidem cum ita est ab ipsa nobis concessa natura, ut indocti quoque ac non sentientes ea frequenter utantur, tum ita iucunda atque nitida, ut in oratione quamlibet clara proprio lumine eluceat.[13]

The ornament of metaphor is rooted here in a concept of speech that is "natural." What Quintilian appears to mean by "natural" in this passage is something along the lines of "spontaneous" or "unstudied," in spite of the fact that elsewhere he recommends a careful, three-step approach to ornamentation.[14] Metaphor has the peculiar advantage that it is at the same time distinguished, and yet natural–it is an ornament that does not seem to be.

This rather contradictory desire that speech be at the same time distinguished and natural haunts the imagination of writers long after Quintilian. Erasmus picks up on Quintilian's ideal of "natural" speech when he writes a letter to Anthony of Luxembourg, praising his style:

---

[12] Cicero, *De Oratore* 3.6.24.

[13] Quintilian, *Institutio Oratoria* 8.6.4.

[14] Ibid. 8.3.61: "Ornatum est, quod perspicuo ac probabili plus est. Eius primi sunt gradus in eo quod velis [concipiendo et] exprimendo, tertius, qui haec nitidiora faciat, quod proprie dixeris cultum."

> maiorem in modum delectavit stilus ille simplex et naturalis; verba non ascita sed una cum ipsis sententiis cohaerentia; sensus sani ac solidi, nihil neque in verbis neque in sententiis aut portentosum aut distortum aut coactum aut imminutum denique aut redundans.[15]

According to Erasmus, there is a neat conformity between word and thing evident in Anthony's writing. Like the classical rhetoricians, Erasmus holds that words are signs for things, and that language mirrors the world, although he does not examine systematically the relationship between words and things, and at times is quite casual in his allusions to that relationship.[16] In saying here that the words altogether cohere with the *sententiae*, Erasmus is assuming that he can entirely discern his friend's thoughts from the words he has chosen. Such a judgment rests on an assumption of common understanding of words, a community of discourse. The mirror reflects well, with the use of natural and simple language; in the case of a distorting mirror, language could be monstrous, unnatural, misshapen, twisted, forced, or strained.

Let us for a point of contrast turn to Erasmus's evaluation of another correspondent, Guillaume Budé. In answering Budé's request for a judgment of his book, *De Asse*, Erasmus writes:

> Iam animadverto te metaphoris ac parabolis impendio delectari, quas habes plaerasque mire raras et insigniter argutas; sed quam semel amplexus sis, ab ea vix unquam divelli potes: unde fit ut cum totus sermo gemmeus sit potius quam gemmis distinctus, nonnihil videatur a naturali simplicitate recedere.[17]

It is on the basis of metaphor that Erasmus criticizes Budé. Metaphor is a gem, but when the *sermo* becomes *gemmeus*, completely covered with gems, it ceases to be simple and natural—the virtues Erasmus has attributed to Luxembourg's writing. The boundaries between what is *proprium* and what is *alienum* have been violated. Thus, metaphor as a distinctive ornament is permissible only if the sense of propriety—what is each word's "proper" place—remains.

---

[15] *Erasmi Epistolae*, ed. P. S. Allen (Oxford: Clarendon Press, 1906–1958, henceforth cited as *EE*), 1:354, lines 4 ff.

[16] For example, in *De Copia Verborum ac Rerum*, where one would most expect to find such a discussion, he merely refers to the fact that although *verbum* and *res* are so intimately connected that it would seem impossible to separate them, he has elected to treat them separately here for pedagogical purposes. See *LB* I, 6A.

[17] *EE* 2:369, lines 243 ff.

Erasmus elaborates further on what it is about nature that is so attractive, using here the adjective *nativum* to contrast with *artificium*:

> Utque cum in iis quae constant artificio alios alia capiant, quod nativum sit, id occulta quadam vi tangit et allicit omnes, nec paulo iucundius irrepit et illabitur in animos hominum veluti cognatum.[18]

Here Erasmus hints at a relationship between language and man, the creature who uses it, yet he backs away from pure identification of the two when he writes *veluti cognatum*, "as if related," implying, of course, that they actually are not. This subtlety points to the problem involved in speaking of language, agreed by all to be a convention, as a product of nature. Obviously, words like *natura* and *nativum* are themselves being used metaphorically—language that is "natural" *resembles* the simplicity of nature, which should serve as a model for good speech. Man, a creature of nature himself, should look inside his own soul to find that model, which is perhaps what Erasmus has in mind when he writes in another letter to Budé, "sermo praecipua mentis imago est."[19]

What, then, is Erasmus's concept of the role of metaphor in speech that is natural? We can see that unlike the Stoics, Erasmus does not reject metaphor, yet his definition in *De Copia* and critique of Budé rest on a clear understanding of metaphor as a transgression of a direct word-to-thing correspondence. Like all writers, he must confront the question of what level of disruption is tolerable. We can turn to the German philosopher Heidegger, who in an early work explains what he thinks is behind the drive to keep the "proper" distance between metaphor and literal speech, thus keeping metaphor carefully in its place:

> The notions of transposition and of metaphor rest on the distinction, not to say the separation, of the sensory and the non-sensory as two domains each subsisting for itself. This kind of separation between the sensory and the non-sensory is a fundamental characteristic of what is called metaphysics, which confers upon Western thought its essential characteristics. . . . The metaphorical exists only within the borders of metaphysics.[20]

Heidegger asserts here that metaphysics strives to eliminate the concrete from its language; thus, what metaphor does is apply concrete terminology

---

[18] Ibid., 369, lines 247 ff.

[19] Ibid., 467, line 323.

[20] Martin Heidegger, *Der Satz vom Grund*, quoted from Derrida, op. cit., 226, n.29.

in an abstract sense. In other words, remembering Cicero's contention that Latin lacked vocabulary, we can imagine that those terms that are missing from the language are terms that could render abstract meanings literally. Somehow, the universe of concrete experience needed first to be recruited into the cause of metaphysics, and then to be expunged from metaphysics. Metaphysics thus blanches out the concrete associations that linger on and appropriates terminology that is in effect no longer evocative of the sensory world. It is such a step that allows Erasmus to refer to language as "natural" without its having anything to do with physical nature.

This, according to Derrida, is the "Aristotelian ideal," to which philosophy aspires. I suggest that this ideal plays a paradoxical role in Erasmus's writing. We can gain insight into the matter by looking at Erasmus's portrayal of two stages in the evolution of language. The first occurs as a result of catastrophe, or falling from grace. That perfect emblem of fallenness, Folly, puts the case as follows:

> Siquidem simplex illa aurei seculi gens, nullis armata disciplinis, solo naturae ductu, instinctuque vivebat. Quorsum enim opus erat Grammatica, cum eadem esset omnibus lingua, nec aliud sermone petebatur, nisi ut alius alium intelligeret? Quis usus Dialectices, ubi nulla erat pugnantium inter se sententiarum dimicatio? Quis Rhetoricae locus, cum nullus alteri negotium facesseret?. . . At labente paulatim aetatis aureae puritate, primum a malis, ut dixi, geniis inventae sunt artes. . . .[21]

We see that the sciences of which she speaks are those of the trivium, imposed on mankind by evil forces who saw and exploited man's falling away from a community of understanding and transparent use of language. Fighting and troublemaking were the cause and the result of the fall, which is charted in the language that prevails before and after. Of course, Folly's voice is deliberately intended to be suspect—the very least one can say about this passage is that it shows Erasmus poking fun at his own immediate areas of concern, and thus that the passage is a playful attempt at self-denigration. Yet behind the exaggeration there is an ideal of language asserting itself that has more than a hint of Stoicism to it. There is no need for sciences of language in the Golden Age because language already does exactly what it ought to do: communicate meaning. At the same time, people also do what they ought: live in harmonious community, understanding and reflecting one another's best interests, so that no persuasion is necessary.

---

[21] *LB* 4:433D–434A.

Fantasies of a golden age are commonplaces of both Renaissance and classical writers, although what is striking about this one is the extent to which it focuses on language as the sign of an early state of health and the symptom of subsequent decay. Another example of such a fantasy appears in Cicero's *De Oratore*, which mourns a similar loss of innocence, also attributable to a corruption in the use of language. Here, Cicero holds Socrates responsible for the decline:

> hoc commune nomen eripuit, sapienterque sentiendi, et ornate dicendi scientiam, re cohaerentis, disputationibus suis separavit.... Hinc discidium illud exstitit quasi linguae atque cordis, absurdum sane et inutile et reprehendendum, ut alii nos sapere, alii dicere docerent.[22]

In this passage, the sciences of language are not seen as evil; rather a misuse of such science of right speaking, in detachment from right thought and right action, is seen as dangerous. What is consistent is that both Folly and Cicero's Crassus assert an ideal of integrity—between man and man in community, or between heart and voice in speaking one's soul. The fall is a falling apart, a disintegration.

In Cicero's complaint, metaphor occupies a curious position. First, in looking especially at the case of Socrates, one can see that Socrates' distrust of language in the *Cratylus*, his admonition to look for truth not in words, but in things themselves,[23] is analogous to his distrust of the physical world and the senses that reveal it, and his seeking of a truth beyond the sensory. Metaphysics was born when Socrates took the step of looking elsewhere for truth than in sensory reality, or when he separated truth from appearance. A language fashioned to communicate things about the sensory world would not do to explore the domain of truth, and so metaphor in turn was born from metaphysics; resemblances were exploited to fill in where literal language could not go. Language, expressing one meaning through its resemblance to another, became not the communicator of meaning but the veil over meaning, that had to be lifted in order to see the truth. In this scheme of things metaphor is not a remedy so much as a stop-gap, which could cause mischief if the displacement were to turn into a usurpation.

Cicero, even though he criticizes Socrates for bringing about this state of affairs, still lives in a world where metaphor and literal speech are kept

---

[22] Cicero, op. cit., 3.16.60–61.

[23] *The Collected Dialogues of Plato*, ed. Edith Hamilton and Huntington Cairns (Princeton: Princeton Univ. Press, 1983), *Cratylus* 439b.

carefully distinct. The same is true of Erasmus who, although he indirectly criticizes the Stoicism of his own creation Folly in works such as *De Copia*, yet accepts the divisions and distinctions upon which Folly's vision is based: that is, that a perfect language would reflect perfectly the meaning it communicated. In fact, *De Copia* itself may be seen as a rule-book for how to survive well linguistically in a post-lapsarian world.

As a kind of summary, I would like to turn briefly to Erasmus's biblical exegesis, where he holds to the view that God's word can be understood only through the *departure* from literal meaning. In thinking thus he stands well within a tradition established by the ancient Greek theologians, whom he greatly admired. The spiritual sense, looking beyond the literal, gives insight into that which is beyond language to express. Scriptural language is thus a sign not directly of divine things, but of itself, the covering that must be bypassed in order to view divine things. Erasmus bids Christians to think in these terms when he writes in the *Enchiridion*,

> Ex interpretibus divinae scripturae eos potissimum dilige, qui a littera quammaxime recedunt. Cuiusmodi sunt in primis post Paulum Origenes, Ambrosius, Hieronymus, Augustinus. Video enim neotericos theologos litterae nimium libenter inhaerere et captiosis quibusdam argutiis magis quam eruendis mysteriis operam dare, quasi vero non vere dixerit Paulus legem nostram spiritualem esse.[24]

Here we have the opposite extreme to Folly's vision of a pure form of communication that can be accepted at face value. It also represents what I see as the second turn in Erasmus's vision of the evolution of language. As we have seen, Folly describes the first as a fall from an early state of moral and linguistic innocence. But corresponding to Folly's description of the fall is Erasmus's construction in *Enchiridion* and other pietistic works of the path to redemption, through a right understanding of scriptural language. Proper understanding occurs when language that is not purely transparent miraculously becomes so to the divinely inspired, *or* to him whose education in the right use of figurative language enables him to read it. Thus, if metaphor is one of the marks of fallenness, it is also through an educated reading of metaphor that man must work out his redemption.

St. Olaf College

[24] Desiderius Erasmus, *Ausgewählte Werke*, ed. Hajo and Annemarie Holborn (Munich: C. H. Beck, 1964), 33–34.

Probati autores *as Models of the Biblical Translator**

E. RUMMEL

Discussing the qualities of the professional theologian in his *Dialogus de tribus linguis*, the Louvain theologian Jacques Masson lashed out against certain unnamed pedants and their excessive concern for language and style. "They combine rhetoric with theology," he wrote. "Without rhetoric, they say, [theology] is unpolished, insipid, feeble, ineffectual, and unworthy of man. They claim that it was rhetoric or poetry that gave us the distinguished theologians of old." These men, he continued, approved of a book only when it was *purus, castus, elegans* and rejected all others as barbarous: *rejicitur liber si barbarus, id est, si non pure Latinus*.[1] Many readers saw in Masson's acerbic remarks an attack on Erasmus,[2] whose edition

---

*The following abbreviations will be used in references to Erasmian texts: Allen: *Opus Epistolarum Des. Erasmi Roterodami*, ed. P. S. Allen (Oxford, 1906–58); ASD: *Opera Omnia Desiderii Erasmi Roterodami* (Amsterdam, 1969–); CWE: The Colledcted Works of Erasmus (Toronto, 1974–; Holborn: H. and A. Holborn, *Desiderius Erasmus. Ausgewählte Werke* (Munich, 1974); LB: *Desiderii Erasmi Roterodami Opera Omnia*, ed. J. Leclerc (Leiden, 1703–6).

[1] F. Pijper, *Disputationes contra Lutherum* (The Hague, 1905) 81. On Masson and his controversy with Erasmus see most recently J. Bentley, "New Testament Scholarship at Louvain in the Early Sixteenth Century," *Studies in Medieval and Renaissance History* n.s. 2 (1979): 51–79. For biographical information on Masson see the article by J. E. Vercruysse in *Katholische Theologen der Reformationszeit*, ed. E. Iserloh, vol. 2 (Münster, 1985), 7–26.

[2] Erasmus himself denied this supposition: *Non assentior autem suspicioni quorundam qui totam imaginem qua . . . depingit crassae theologiae sophistam existimant in me tendere* (LB IX 104A). There is no doubt, however, that the *Dialogus* as a whole was aimed at Erasmus since Masson himself admitted as much in a tract published after his death (*Opera omnia*, Louvain: Gravius, 1550, fol. 169 verso).

of the New Testament with its prolegomena recommending language studies had aroused a great deal of indignation among conservative theologians. Erasmus had boldly revised the text of the Vulgate, correcting not only textual corruptions and mistranslations but also grammar and style.[3] Defending such emendations, he argued that "many people recoiled from the holy books because of their unpolished, not to say, unkempt style" (LB VI fol. **3 verso).* He pleaded the case of scholarly readers: "If we simplify our language for the benefit of ignorant and simple folk, should we not help educated readers too by purifying the language?" (CWE Ep. 843:38–40). The time was ripe, he said, to render the New Testament *puro castoque sermone*. This phrase obviously piqued Masson who mimicked Erasmus' concern for stylistic purity in his description of the pedant. In the prolegomena to the New Testament edition—especially in the *Methodus* later enlarged and published separately under the title *Ratio verae theologiae*—Erasmus encouraged students of theology to study languages. Like the pedant criticized by Masson, he claimed that "language studies . . . gave us the distinguished theologians of old" (Holborn *Ratio* 190:17). Borrowing a metaphor from Jerome, he called philology the handmaid of Queen Theology. This *pedissequa* was lowly, but indispensable.[4]

Conservative theologians, however, rejected Erasmus' notions of a *theologia rhetorica*. Noël Beda, one of Erasmus' most relentless critics at the faculty of theology in Paris, saw Erasmus as nothing but a meddling humanist. The *humanistae theologizantes*, as he called them contemptuously, wished to subject Holy Writ to the same criteria as secular writings, but Scripture was above literary criticism.[5] Many conservative theologians shared Beda's opinion. Erasmus' effort to improve the style of the Vulgate was accordingly met by a chorus of protest: The word of God must not be subjected to the rules of Donatus; elegance must not become an issue in sacred writings; "God was not offended by solecisms."[6] As the Spanish

---

[3] For a synopsis of the controversies generated by the publication of Erasmus' New Testament see E. Rummel, *Erasmus' Annotations on the New Testament* (Toronto, 1986), 123–27.

[4] Allen Ep. 182:134.

[5] For Beda's controversy with Erasmus see J. Farge, *Orthodoxy and Reform in Early Reformation France: The Faculty of Theology of Paris 1500–1543* (Leiden, 1985). Beda's expression *humanistae theologizantes* is quoted by Erasmus at LB IX 520 A.

[6] *In divinis literis non esse recipiendam sermonis elegantiam* is quoted as a commonplace by Erasmus at LB IX 777c; for the other expressions see LB VI fol. **3 verso. On the dispute concerning biblical style see E. Rummel, "God and Solecism: Erasmus

theologian Sancho Carranza put it summarily: "Scriptural studies do not inquire into mode of expression, neatness, charm, or fluency of speech, but rather into the content and meaning of speech."[7]

Erasmus, in turn, insisted that philologists could play a useful role in scriptural studies. Indeed, "the whole business of translating the Holy Scriptures is manifestly a grammarian's function," he wrote (CWE Ep. 182:144–45). In revising the Vulgate his aim had been to render the words of the evangelists and apostles in simple, yet correct Latin: *ut totus Novi Testamenti sermo simplex quidem, sed tamen Latinus esset* (LB VI fol. **3 verso). The question remained, however, whose standards of correctness were to apply. Certainly they were not the standards of scholastic writers whose style Erasmus frequently ridiculed. Nor was Erasmus ready to embrace the other extreme and rewrite the New Testament in Ciceronian style. Rather he trod a middle course between "Scotuses and the Ciceronian apes."[8] To begin with, he was willing to take into consideration *recepta Christianis vocabula*, "established Christian vocabulary" (CWE 28, p. 389). To ignore the Christian tradition would be absurd, he wrote, and illustrated the point by recalling a sermon preached by a purist at the papal court in Rome. Rigorously observing classical idiom, he had addressed the pope as Jupiter Optimus Maximus, likened the suffering of Christ to the death of Socrates, his resurrection to the apotheosis of Roman emperors, and his divine glory to the triumphs of Julius Caesar (ibidem, pp. 384–86). Common sense dictated that the principle of *aptum et decorum* be observed by a speaker. A speaker who applied incongruous pagan terms to Christian subjects was absurd, he concluded (ibidem, p. 447). Erasmus, then, recognized the existence of a biblical idiom. Dialecticians, philosophers, orators, grammarians, physicians, and mathematicians all used *peculiares voces*, he wrote.[9] It would be unfair to deny this privilege to theologians and translators of scriptural texts. Among Christian "technical terms" he listed words like *fides, fidelis, benedictus, in nomine Jesu*, and *gratia.*[10] In his *Annotations on the New Testament* he commented accordingly. Remarking,

as Literary Critic of the Bible," *Erasmus of Rotterdam Yearbook* 7 (1987): 54–72.

[7] Sanctius Carranza, *Apologia de tribus locis* (Basel: Froben, 1520) sig. o3 verso.

[8] CWE 28, p. 390; Erasmus notes that the expression "Ciceronian apes" was coined by Poliziano in his dispute with Scala (CWE 28, p. 444). For Erasmus' verdict on scholastic writers see C. R. Thompson "Better Teachers than Scotus or Aquinas," *Medieval and Renaissance Studies* 2 (1968): 114–45.

[9] LB VI fol. **3 verso, similarly *Annotationes*, ibidem, 58E and *Ciceronianus* CWE 28, p. 391.

[10] LB VI fol. **3 verso.

for example, on the translation of *eulogemene* by *benedicta,* he noted that "*benedictus* and *maledictus* are not found in Latin authors in the sense of praiseworthy and blameworthy, yet we must wink at some things of this kind, whether we want to or not, because they are too well established and cannot be changed without creating a stir."[11] Of course the translator ought to be consistent in the use of scriptural idiom: "If it is Christian to disregard Latin usage in these cases, to adopt a foreign idiom and to create a special new Christian idiom, why is it not done in all other cases as well? For what is correct and done judiciously must be done in each case" (LB VI 108E).

Similarly Erasmus commented on the peculiar use of *infidelis*: "*Infidelis* is not Latin, but in Scripture it is used to denote someone who does not believe" (LB VI 562F). Elsewhere he notes that *collectis* in the sense of *collatione* was not classical Latin but "firmly established" in church usage (LB VI 744E). *Sacramentum* was another word that had taken on a special meaning in scriptural texts. As Erasmus explained, it had not always had the same meaning of "sacrament." "In antiquity *sacramentum* was an oath or a religious obligation" (LB VI 855B). A similar case was the word *honorare,* which meant "to honour" in classical Latin, but "according to scriptural usage pertains more to sustenance than to honour" (LB VI 81E). In these cases, then, Erasmus was willing to make concessions to the biblical idiom. In many others, however, he saw no mitigating circumstances to justify the Vulgate translator's solecisms and deviations from the classical norm. In such cases he did not hesitate to correct the text and refer readers to the usage of what he termed *probi* or *probati autores.* Unfortunately Erasmus does not oblige us with a definition or list of whom he considered standard authors, but in *De ratione studii* he enumerated authors that might serve as models to young students. Among the Greeks he assigned "first place to Lucian, second to Demosthenes, and third to Herodotus; again, among the poets, first place to Aristophanes, second to Homer, third to Euripides.... Among Latin writers who is more valuable as a standard of language than Terence? ... Should someone think that a few, selected comedies of Plautus, free from impropriety should be added to the above, I would personally not demur. Second place will go to Virgil, third to Horace, fourth to Cicero, and fifth to Caesar. If someone thinks that Sallust should be included, I would not offer much objection" (CWE 24, p. 669:5–16). This provides the reader

[11] LB VI 223F; note, however, that at 565D–E (Rom. 1:25) Erasmus changes the Vulgate's *benedictus* (translating *eulogetos*) to *laudandus,* commenting apologetically: *Adeo passim receptum est in Sacris Litteris ut vix liceat mutare.*

with a general idea of Erasmus' stylistic preferences but does not supply him with a definitive list of *probati autores* to be used as a standard for revising the Vulgate. In fact, we shall see that in this task Erasmus restricted himself to a rather narrower circle of authors, since he did not want the meaning of the text obscured by poetic or archaic usage.

Some examples of revisions justified by reference to *probati/probi autores* will illustrate this practice: In the first edition of his New Testament (1516) Erasmus changed *poenitentiam agite*—the Vulgate version of Matt. 3:2—to *poeniteat vos*, explaining the revision in the corresponding annotation: "I would not want to label *poenitentiam agere* (in the sense of 'being moved by regrets') barbarous or unidiomatic, but I do not recall reading the phrase in *probos autores*" (LB VI 17F). Since the revision was severely criticized because of its perceived doctrinal implications—that is, an implied denial of the sacrament of penance—Erasmus modified his translation in later editions to placate his critics. The final version read *poenitentiam agite vitae prioris*.

Elsewhere Erasmus changed *genimina* (the Vulgate at Matt. 23:33) to *progenies*, explaining the emendation by reference to the usage of classical authors: "I do not think that *genimina* has ever been found in *probatos autores*. For *geno*, which Varro and Lucretius used for *gigno* (but in a poetic composition), is too archaic to be used today by anyone" (LB VI 20C).

At Matt. 13:23 he replaced *centesimum* by *centuplum*, arguing in his note ad locum that the former was unidiomatic. "It is not yet clear to me whether *centesimum* can be found in *probos autores* in the sense of *centenum* or *centuplum*." Eventually he discovered a relevant passage in Pliny and emended the note accordingly. In spite of the classical precedent, however, he retained *centuplum* in the text, perhaps for the sake of clarity.

Erasmus also used arguments based on the usage of *probati autores* in his polemic with Jacobus Stunica, a collaborator on the Complutensian Polygot who turned into an obstinate critic of Erasmus' New Testament edition.[12] In half a dozen tracts published between 1520 and 1524 Stunica attacked Erasmus' emendations on both theological and philological grounds. Two of his publications dealt more specifically with matters of idiom and style: *Annotationes contra Erasmum Roterodamum* (Alcalá, 1520) and *Assertio ecclesiasticae translationis* (Rome, 1524). In his replies Erasmus refused to admit Stunica's criticisms, arguing that they were not supported by evidence from classical authors: "I am not interested in what *can* be said," he wrote. "Let Stunica proffer what he has found in *probatos autor-*

[12] For Erasmus' controversy with Stunica see H. J. de Jonge's introduction to the text of Erasmus' apologia in ASD IX-2 and E. Rummel, *Erasmus and His Catholic Critics: 1515–1522* (Nieuwkoop, 1989), 145–78.

es" (ASD IX-2, p. 86:560-61). Discussing the correct use of the prepositions *ex* and *de*, he rejected Stunica's position on similar grounds: "So far he has found no standard Latin author [*autorem probatum*] to prove what he asserts" (ibidem, p. 78:352).

In the second edition of the New Testament (1519) Erasmus provided an *Index solecismorum*, a list of unidiomatic expressions in the Vulgate. To each item he added a brief comment, noting that the traditional wording deviated from standard usage. "*Venit ministrare* ... is not Latin"; "What Latin speaker ever said *ad invicem*?" "What Latin speaker ever said *auditum* for 'words spoken'?" (LB VI fol. *5 verso). Stunica reacted angrily to what he considered irreverent criticism of a text endorsed by a long tradition. The Vulgate version, he insisted, was both correct and elegant.[13] He was hard pressed, however, to verify this statement and advance cogent arguments against Erasmus. In his apologia, the latter staunchly maintained his position, insisting that Stunica document the use of disputed phrases in standard authors. An unusual expression could only be excused "if that form of speech can be found in *probatos autores*" (LB IX 393C). "Let Stunica show that *probatos autores* spoke thus," he demanded (ibidem, 395F). In a few cases Stunica was successful in finding a classical precedent. Erasmus responded by raising his standards and rejecting the testimony of Plautus, Terence, and Suetonius. Plautus was an "obsolete" author, he claimed, who indulged in "poetic licence". One could not use him as a norm for prose composition (ibidem, 393E). Nor did Suetonius meet the standards of the more exacting judges of the Latin language.[14] The translator must use discretion in following the usage of Roman writers, "or else one might say *scibo* instead of *sciam*, because Terence spoke thus" (ibidem, 398E). As for later Christian writers—they did not count at all. "The fact that Ambrose spoke thus, does not make it Latin" (ibidem, 395B).

Even if Erasmus does not explicitly refer the reader to *probati autores*, it is clear that he emended the Vulgate on the basis of classical usage. His annotations on Paul's Epistle to the Colossians furnish representative examples: At 1:9 he replaced *non desinimus pro vobis orantes et postulantes* with *non desinimus ... orare et postulare* since in classical usage *desinere* demands a complementary infinitive. At 1:13 he replaced *filii dilectionis* by

---

[13] Jacobus Stunica, *Assertio ecclesiasticae translationis* (Rome: [Bladus] 1524) sig. A ii verso.

[14] LB IX 395B. One reason why Erasmus had reservations about accepting Suetonius as a model was his predilection for Graecisms. Cf LB VI 218B: *Suetonius suo more Graecam loquutionem referens....*

filii sibi dilecti, explaining that the phrase found in the Vulgate reproduced a Hebrew idiom (LB VI 884D). At 1:20 he replaced a dangling participle with an ablative absolute, "or else the phrase will not be free of solecism; for one cannot speak in Latin ... as the Greeks do" (ibidem, 886C). In chapter 2 he queried the phrase *triumphans illos* (the Vulgate version at Col. 2:15). Normally a different construction was used with the verb *triumphare*. "There are some people who are bothered by the phrase *triumphans illos* because it is not quite Latin; to be sure, Virgil said *triumphatas gentes*, nor is this mode of expression rare in historiographers. *Triumphare foeminam* is rather unusual, however, although it can be found in Trebellius Pollio" (ibidem, 890E). Similarly he replaced the phrase *nolite mentiri invicem* by *ne mentiamini alius adversus alium* at Col. 3:9, correcting the unidiomatic expression.

It would appear from these examples that Erasmus adopted the grammatical rules and vocabulary commonly found in classical prose authors, shying away from idiosyncrasies and poetic licence. Moreover, he seems to limit *probati autores* to the golden period of Latin literature, rejecting both archaic and Christian authors, and giving a reluctant hearing to authors like Pliny and Suetonius. No doubt his governing principle was *claritas*. This was best served by following the common usage of mainstream authors whose expressions were familiar to readers and would therefore be readily understood.

To return to Masson's description of the pedant: the Louvain theologian exaggerated Erasmus' predilections in the tradition of polemic literature. His portrait of the pedant is a caricature. The real Erasmus was more flexible than Masson's doctrinaire arbiter of style. He did advocate a return to classical usage wherever feasible, but was prepared to concede to theologians their idiom proper. Thus he accepted certain expressions that had become entrenched by tradition as biblical *termini technici*. There was no reason, however, to absolve the biblical translator from all obligation to observe classical norms of speech, thereby forcing scholarly readers to lower their standards. It was better for others to raise their sights and learn correct Latin. Of course there was reluctance among established theologians to admit "that they must give up as old men what they had learned as smooth-cheeked youngsters," but such reluctance must be overcome. It was better to learn late than never: *An praestat nescire quod cognitu necessarium est, quam serius discere?*[15]

---

[15] LB VI fol. ***1 verso, ***2 verso.

Erasmus on the Epistle to the Romans: A "Literary" Reading

ROBERT SIDER

In both the *Methodus* (1516) and the *Ratio* (1518, 1519) Erasmus stressed the importance of reading the Bible with an appreciation of its "literary" qualities. In the *Methodus* he asserted that the Bible has a closer affinity with poetry than with philosophy (Holborn, 155).[1] A proper reading of the Bible should transform the reader (Holborn, 151); but it is from literary artistry that one derives a pleasure which helps to make the written word effective. Thus in a 1520 addition to the *Ratio* Erasmus notes that as a result of figures the scriptures enter our minds with greater delight and force (Holborn, 272). It is one of the tasks of the interpreter, therefore, to bring out the force of the figures. It is my purpose in this essay to consider how, in the Annotations, Erasmus himself read the Biblical text as a literary artifact.

For his own exposition of the literary art of scripture Erasmus began from the perspectives of grammar and rhetoric, and relied upon the techniques and the vocabulary appropriate to these disciplines. Though Jacques Chomarat has in a general way shown the presence of these grammatical and rhetorical terms in Erasmus' Annotations,[2] a more precise assessment of Erasmus' efforts towards a literary reading of the Bible can emerge only if we are attentive to two features of his exposition

---

[1] References to the *Methodus* and *Ratio* are from Annemarie and Hajo Holborn, *Desiderius Erasmus Roterodamus. Ausgewählte Werke* (Munich, C. H. Beck'sche Verlagsbuchhandlung, 1933).

[2] Jacques Chomarat, *Grammaire et rhétorique chez Erasme* (Paris: Société d' Edition "Les Belles lettres" 1:541–86).

in the Annotations: (1) the Annotations reflect an appreciation of the particularity of each author and book within the Bible as a whole; for Erasmus, therefore, a "literary reading" included not only stylistic analysis but also a study of the relation between the human author and his audience;[3] (2) the Annotations grew enormously over the five editions from 1516 to 1535, and reflect growth in Erasmus' appreciation of the literary qualities of the Biblical text. Because of Erasmus' appreciation of the particularity of author and book, it will be fruitful to limit our discussion here to a single book—the Epistle to the Romans; because of the growth of the editions, it will be essential to trace developments in Erasmus' literary analysis from 1516 to 1535. I shall consider first Erasmus' elucidation of the artistry of the Biblical author in relating to his audience, then turn to Erasmus' analysis of style.

I. The Author and his Audience

From classical times, rhetoricians had taken account of the manner in which a speaker might win the good will of his audience, and establish his authority. Erasmus, too, in his *Annotations* on Romans, undertook to reveal the art of Paul in establishing his authority, winning the confidence of his readers and maintaining their good will. He sees the Apostle's skill particularly in the way in which he works out the tension between his own Apostolic authority and personal distinction on the one hand, and, on the other, his readers' sense of dignity, perhaps even their arrogance as Romans. Already in the first two editions, Erasmus established the central terms of his analysis. He points almost immediately, at the very beginning of the book, to elements of *ethos*, and notes how in Rom. 1:1 Paul commended himself and his authority: "At once in the very beginning ... he wins trust and gains authority" ("*vocatus*," 553D [1516]).[4] The next note explicated further the artistry of personal commendation: "He commends his office with a fine sense of climax, for [he says that] he had not only been called to perform the service of an Apostle, but had been set apart

---

[3] The Annotations also include observations on the author's argument, the *logos* of classical rhetorical theory. Since, in the Annotations on Romans, these observations are relatively few, and for the most part seek to clarify the course of the argument rather than to describe the artistry of the argumentation, I omit further discussion of them here.

[4] References are to Vol. 6 of the Leiden edition (LB). The dates, in square brackets, refer to the words quoted, not to the entire annotation.

and separated for the task of preaching the gospel" ("*segregatus*" 554B [1516]). Erasmus returns to the artifice of *ethos* in an annotation near the end of the Epistle. He sees Rom. 15:18 as a "little preface" to Paul's narrative of his exploits in the proclamation of the gospel from Jerusalem to Illyrium. This "preface" is added, he notes, to win the reader's confidence, and to obviate the charge of arrogance otherwise invited by the bold account of Paul's deeds in 15:18–19 ("*non enim*" 647F [1516]).

Erasmus seems well aware of the subtle assessments made by the author of a letter about both himself and his addressee, and repeatedly shows how Paul artfully modifies his language to accommodate Roman self-esteem and to avoid a sense of hauteur. Rom. 1:11–12 is a case in point. Paul had said that he wished to impart a spiritual gift to the Romans to strengthen them, but he immediately adds a mitigating qualification: he meant rather that they should find comfort among themselves, or, if one prefers a stronger reading, that he and they should be mutually comforted. "The Apostle feared that he might offend the Romans with their somewhat arrogant disposition if they appeared to need strengthening, as though they were vacillating or wavering. Thus he explains this strengthening as 'mutual comfort,' speaking, as usual, with the greatest modesty" ("*simul*" 560F–61B [1516]). In the 1519 edition Erasmus shows how Paul again, near the end of the epistle, carefully shapes his language in a way that reveals his sensitivity to Roman self-perception. The pronoun αὐτοί of Rom. 15:14, he argues, is artfully included, creating an emphasis which reflects Paul's recognition that the Romans did not need his admonition, for they were able to admonish themselves ("*ita ut*" 647D).[5]

The examples above come for the first two editions, and belong to the "frame," so to speak, of the epistle. In the last two editions Erasmus' observations on the literary artifice by which *ethos* is established are significantly more pervasive and emphatic. In 1527 he developed the annotation just considered by appealing to Chrysostom, who had, he says, "noted the steps by which the Apostle had softened and modified his expression: First he said 'strengthen,' then, fearing the proud Romans would say, 'What! are we weak?' . . . he softened the expression and [spoke of] comfort. . . . Finally he added the notion of a 'common' faith laying aside the mask of teacher and assuming that of a fellow disciple" ("*simul*"

[5] Cf. Peter Abelard's *Commentary on Romans* (PL 178.787C–88D, 793B–C, 798B, 966C) where the elements of *ethos* in these verses are noted; also the *Glossa ordinaria* (Paris, 1590, vol. 6). Erasmus' notes, however, are striking for the manner in which they reveal his sense of the conscious artistry in the text.

561C on Rom. 1:12). Erasmus comments on the artfulness: "This is pious cunning and, so to speak, holy flattery" (561D). Again in 1527 Erasmus supports a reading (adopted in 1516) of Rom. 8:9 by observing that Paul would address his readers with gentleness; harsher remarks would be directed to others ("*si tamen*" 601E). In 1535 he defends the indicative in Rom. 5:1 ("We have peace") noting that the indicative offers a form of admonition that suits Paul's modesty and civility. This, too, is a familiar "figure"—to use the indicative to express what we wish to be done. The *modestia* of the Apostle is a matter of considerable concern for Erasmus, particularly in 1535. On the one hand his *modestia*, clearly defined, might well serve as a model for contemporary bishops; on the other hand it had relevance to the tone of Paul's letter, to the authority of the writer and the response of the reader. Consequently, in this edition, Erasmus added to his comments on Rom. 15:17–23 what is perhaps his most striking statement of the Apostle's *modestia*. Once more recalling Chrysostom, he notes that the Apostle established his authority not by episcopal insignia but by a telling account of the great deeds performed through the Spirit: "Of these he arrogates none to himself, but gives all the glory to God, a man boasting with the greatest modesty, and modest in his vaunting, proud in Christ, humble in himself" ("*prodigiorum*" 648E). Thus one observes through the five editions of the Annotations a steadily growing emphasis upon the Apostle's literary skill in attempting to control the response of his audience.

II. The Analysis of Style

Erasmus' sensitivity to the literary qualities of the Greek text of Romans finds expression in persistent efforts to call attention to style in the Epistle. I wish here to consider primarily (1) the chief forms his stylistic criticism took and (2) the changing character of his criticism from the early (1516, 1519) to the late (1527, 1535) editions.

In the first two editions, Erasmus' most persistent interest in Paul's style arises from the pleasure he believes it brings. He is, moreover, primarily interested in the pleasant effect of similar sounds in associated words. "There is a delightful relationship [*festiva affinitas*] in ἐδοκίμασαν and ἀδόκιμον" ("*in reprobrum*" 566D [1516] on Rom. 1:28); "To those who read Greek there is a not unpleasing relationship [*non ingrata affinitas*] in πορνεία and πονηρία" ("*nequitia*" 566F [1519] on Rom. 1:29); "It is true that in *decus-dedecus* the pleasure [*iucunditas*] of the figure [i.e., in the Greek τιμὴν καὶ ἀτιμίαν is rendered" ("*aliud*" 614F [1516] on Rom.

9:21); "there is a pleasant play [*iucunda allusio*] in the Greek ...ὑπερφρονεῖν, φρονεῖν, εἰς τὸ σωφρονεῖν"("*sapere*" 630D [1516] on Rom. 12:3). In Rom. 4:18 Erasmus notes the *iucunda relatio* of the apparently contradictory "beyond hope, he believed through hope" ("*in spem*" 581C [1519]); and in Rom. 13:8 he recalls Augustine to observe the *gratia* of the "pairs," "tribute to whom tribute," "tax to whom tax, ..." ("*nemini*" 636D [1519]).

Apart from several passages of elaborate stylistic analysis which we shall presently observe, the 1527 edition adds relatively little to an appreciation of the pleasure to be derived from the language of Paul. When we do meet observations of this kind in the 1527 edition, we generally find them in the context of a more technical rhetorical vocabulary. Thus to the annotation just cited on Rom. 4:8, Erasmus added in 1527 the word "*traductio*." Already in 1516 he had found the repetition of δικαιοσύνην in Rom. 10:3 *festivior*, but in 1527 corrected the technical term from *conduplicatio* to *traductio* ("*et suam*" 617E).[6] Similarly in 1527 he explained further the pleasure he had found in 1516 in the words ἀπειθοῦσι–πειθομένοις of Rom. 2:8, by adding a clause noting that these words exemplify ἐναντίωσις. Or again, he identifies for the first time in 1527 the δίλημμα of Rom. 4:10 as a rhetorical figure and speaks of the *gratia* it brings ("*in circumcisione*," 578F).

The last two editions do, however, show a much more lively interest in the "forcefulness" of Paul's language and thought than did the first two. It is true that Erasmus had recognized in 1516 and 1519 some features in the Pauline text that intensified the expression. But the editions of 1527 and 1535 contain approximately twice as many observations on the "force" of Pauline expression as those of 1516 and 1519.[7] In 1527 he expresses repeated interest in the effect of the "question" (*interrogatio* and *percontatio*) in Romans. He comments on the question of Rom. 3:27 ("Where now is boasting?"), that "questions" (*percontationes*) of this sort greatly add to the sharpness of a passage ("*ubi est*" 577B). One finds similar observations in the annotations on Rom. 4:10 ("*in circumcisione*" 578F) and Rom. 11:1 ("*dico*" 621C). Further, he defends readings of the Greek text in part on the basis of the effectiveness of expression, apparently with the assumption that Paul strove for force, sharpness, and dignity of language. In 1535 he added to a note begun in 1516 and

[6] On *conduplicatio* see *Ecclesiastes* 3 (LB V 990F–91A and 999E–1000C).

[7] I count 12 such observations in the last two editions as opposed to 6 in the first two.

continued in 1519, that ἔχθρα was better read as a noun than an adjective because it is "more effective and more in keeping with the style of Paul" ("*inimica*" 6010E).

The annotations on five passages, Rom. 5:3-5, 8:29-39, 12:6-21, 13:8-9, and 13:12-14, became in the 1527 edition a *tour de force* of stylistic analysis. All of them have counterparts in Augustine's *De doctrina christiana*,[8] and it is clear from Erasmus' specific reference to the *Doctrina* that they all have their genesis in that great work. Already in 1519 Erasmus had cited the *Doctrina* in a brief discussion of the two passages from Romans 13. The 1527 edition, however, marks a major development not only in the extension of the analysis to the other passages in Romans which Augustine had cited to illustrate style, but also in the nature of the analysis, particularly in chapters 8, 12 and 13.

Augustine had cited these passages primarily to illustrate the middle and the high styles, the passages from chapters 12 and 13 illustrating the former, that from chapter 8 the latter. Augustine for the most part simply quoted the passages, though he occasionally noted in passing the graceful arrangement of cola and commata in the rhythm, and in 4.20.42 he observes briefly that in the grand style force of expression is not dependent for its effect upon the various adornments of style, though in fact they are usually present.

Erasmus takes up the pen at the point where Augustine had put it down. He accepts, for example, Augustine's characterization of Rom. 8:29-39 as a passage in the grand style where force and pleasure are combined. He proceeds, however, to show precisely where the force, where the pleasure lies; and he employs the technical language of rhetoric to do so—a feature we have already observed especially characteristic of the 1527 edition. He notes the pleasure (*iucunditas*) in the *gradatio* of verses 29-30: foreknew, foreordained, called, justified, glorified; in the sound effects of words (*cadentia, desinentia*); in repetition (*traductio*); in opposites such as life-death, things present-things to come. He finds the force (δείνωσις) of the passage in the phrasing (*comparia*), the *asyndeta*, and, above all, in the questions (*interrogatio* and *percontatio*—identified elsewhere, as we have seen, in the 1527 edition as contributing to *acrimonia* and *vehementia*) (608C-D). Likewise in commenting on Rom. 12:6-21 he accepts Augustine's judgment that the passage illustrates the middle style, but Erasmus goes on to reveal its beauties. "Scarcely any

[8] Respectively in 4.7.11, 4.20.43, and the final three in sequential order, in 4.20.40 (PL 34.93-4, 110, and for the final three 107-108).

other passage in Paul," he says, "is bettered ordered and, so to speak, *picturatior*" (637C–D), and he proceeds to identify phrase and period, repetition, contrasts, the sound effects of words, and concludes that no song could be *jucundior*. Analysis in this mode is not reserved only for the passages Augustine had cited in the *De doctrina christiana*: by 1527 it had apparently become an established technique for the reading of this Epistle, as a 1527 addition to an annotation on Rom. 2:12 witnesses, where Erasmus notes that the entire verse has become *picturatus* by the repetition of words and by the set of opposites, and *modulatus* by the rhythm of the phrases ("*sine lege peccaverunt*" 571D).

From the first edition of the New Testament, Erasmus endeavored to demonstrate that Paul's letter to the Romans, in the original Greek, was a work of considerable artistry. His annotations attempt to reveal, on the one hand, the author of the letter shaping his work to win the approval of his readers and, on the other, the literary qualities that convey pleasure in the reading of scripture, and generate a sense of forcefulness in the text. So much we might expect from the humanist and philologian. It is, perhaps, more surprising to discover that as Erasmus became embattled in theological controversy subsequent to his first edition, his commitment to a literary reading of the Bible did not fade; on the contrary, the evidence of this study indicates that the fourth edition of the Annotations in 1527 was a landmark in the articulation of the nature of the stylistic power—as well as the beauty—of the epistle to the Romans, and that the final edition offered some of his most pungent comments on the Apostle's effort to control the response of his audience.

Dickinson College

SEMINAR

Epistolography

The Present State of Scholarship in Renaissance Epistolography

EMIL J. POLAK

There has been significant growth in the interest and study of Renaissance epistolography in recent years. This talk dealt with the expanding research and increasing number of studies on the historical and literary aspects of the art of letter writing from the fourteenth through the seventeenth century. The appearance of two international scholarly organizations, the IANLS and the ISHR, has facilitated the expanding interest in a generally neglected subject. Some university courses now include the study of the *ars dictaminis*; Ph.D. dissertations are presenting the results of original research on various aspects of epistolary composition. Monographs, chapters in books on rhetoric, and encyclopedia entries on this field of discourse have been appearing in increasing number. A variety of journals has contained the results of investigations on the subject.

Attention was also given to the enormous amount of exploration, examination, and analysis that remains to be done. Most of the epistolographers and their works have not been studied. The relationship of the Medieval dictaminal tradition and Renaissance Humanism requires study. The letters in the formularies and model letter collections merit examination for various purposes. The practice of letter writing in relation to the theory and doctrines is itself worthy of examination. In sum, an important part of the intellectual life extending from England to Poland and Czechoslovakia over a span of four hundred years deserves systematic and careful study.

The Epistolae Ad Exercitationem Accommodatae *of Gasparino Barzizza*

CHARLES FANTAZZI

Both Erasmus and Vives have commendatory words for Gasparino Barzizza in their discussions of Latin style. Vives is rather niggardly in his praise, as he rehearses the epistolary style of Latin writers from antiquity to his own age at the end of his *De conscribendis epistolis:* "qui aetate avorum primus coepit in Italia Latine balbutire, Gasparinus; cuius epistolae vel hac de causa merentur laudem quia in saeculo doctorum primae,"[1] i.e., the first to be written in the age of the new learning. The credit for having been the first to revive Latin from semi-barbarism is also accorded him by other writers of the period, Bartolomeo Fazio and Marcantonio Sabellico. Fazio said of him in his *De viris illustribus*: "Gasparinus Bergomensis unus est ex iis vel in primis fuit qui consopitam diu eloquentiam excitaverunt,"[2] and Sabellico thought of him as one who harked back to a period of elegance before the Gothic storm had swept over Italy.[3]

In an early letter[4] to his friend Cornelis Gerard of Gouda in which he defends the stylistic precepts of Valla, Erasmus also acknowledges the eloquence of other Italian writers, naming Aeneas Silvius, Agostino Dati,

---

[1] *Ioannis Lodovici Vivis Valentini Opera*, ed. Greg. Maiansius, 8 vols. (Valencia, 1782–90), 1:313.

[2] Bartolomeo Fazio, *De viris illustribus* (Florence, 1745), 28.

[3] Marcantonio Sabellico, *De linguae latinae reparatione* (Venice, 1502), fol. 110.

[4] CWE 1, Ep 23. 76–79.

Guarino, Poggio and Gasparino. In the *De conscribendis* he is less complimentary since in the context he is emphasizing that only the best models should be studied, and consequently Pliny and Cicero are to be preferred to any other later writers who, despite their merits, must necessarily be considered less worthy of imitation.[5]

Barzizza was known to his contemporaries as a true disciple of Cicero,[6] which indeed he was, but, as is clear from a cursory examination of the style of the *Epistolae ad exercitationem accommodatae,* said to be his most Ciceronian work, he cannot be ranked among the abject followers of Ciceronianism. His reputation was based largely on these fictitious letters set for the most part in Republican Rome. They immediately became popular as school exercises and were circulated widely in manuscript, first in Italy and then north of the Alps. The first known printed edition was published by Jean Lapierre (Johannes de Lapide) at the Sorbonne in 1470, which seems to be the first work to have been printed there. This was followed by twenty more editions before 1505, all printed in the North: Paris, Basel, Strasburg, Reutlingen, Louvain and Deventer.[7] They were later included in the edition of Barzizza's works published by Cardinal Giuseppe Alessandro Furietti in 1723 in homage to his fellow Bergamasque, reprinted in Bologna in 1969. I cite from this edition.[8]

There has been no thorough study of this important experiment in the history of epistolography, which signalled a breaking away from the arid formalism of the *dictamen* tradition to the more eloquent models of Cicero's correspondence. After Petrarch's momentous discovery of the letters to Atticus, Quintus and Brutus in 1345 and Salutati's recovery through his friend Pasquino de'Capelli of the *Ad familiares* found in the

---

[5] Erasmus, *De conscribendis epistolis* CWE 25, 44.

[6] In his inaugural lecture after assuming the chair of rhetoric left vacant by Barzizza, Antonio da Rho had this to say of his predecessor: "Gasparinum Pergamensem, qui, ut aiunt, Ciceronem ipsum ita menti, ita memoriae commendarat, ut vel exstinctum ipse ex integro illum suscitare et in lucem afferre quidem potuisset." K. Muellner, *Reden und Briefe italienischer Humanisten* (Vienna: A. Hölder, 1899), 166.

[7] For a complete list of early editions see *Gesamtkatalog der Wiegendrucke* (Leipzig, 1928), vol. 3, columns 552–58. It is thought that the book was not printed in Italy in the fifteenth century because its inculcating of the principles of a civic sense was politically dangerous. Cf. Gilles Gerard Meersseman, "Il De arte epistolandi di G. De Veris," *Italia medioevale e umanistica* 15 (1972): 215.

[8] There are many more letters in codex 519 of the Jagellonian Library in Cracow, 83v–170r, which represent an earlier version of the collection. Cf. *Catalogus codicum manuscriptorum medii aevi Latinorum, qui in Bibliotheca Jagellonica Cracoviae asservantur,* vol. 3 (Bratislava, 1984): 197–241.

Cathedral Library of Vercelli, great impetus was given to the classical style in letter-writing. As early as 1419 the letters of Cicero became part of the school curriculum in the school of Guarino Guarini in Verona. They must certainly have been included among the texts of Cicero that Barzizza taught in Padua.

I should like first to give a general description of the format and themes of the letters and then examine cursorily their stylistic qualities. Barzizza employs a clever didactic device in arranging the imaginary letters in the form of an epistolary exchange. In this way he provides the student with various ways of expressing the same thought, since the respondent, especially at the beginning of the letter, will make reference to matters broached by his correspondent. A similar method is found in a scholastic exercise written under his direction in 1410 by Nicola Contarini and Francesco Barbaro, in which there is free discussion between pupil and teacher.[9]

The central theme of the letters is that of friendship in all its ramifications, with particular emphasis on the conflict between personal interests and the state, the protection of a friend's reputation against calumny and slander, and the duties of loyalty. Such sentiments are to be found frequently in the letters of Cicero, as, for example, in the well-known correspondence with Gaius Matius, the friend of Caesar, and in Petrarch. The very first exchange concerns the casting aside of an old acquaintance, who is given the generic name of Sempronius. The writer implores that his action will be interpreted in the correct light, confident that his friend will defend him. The respondent promises his fidelity but cautions that it is hard to eradicate an opinion once it has taken root. In the first five sets of letters that aspect of the duties of friendship which involves the conflict between private loyalties and the interests of the state is a dominant theme. In one exchange of letters the subject is the abandonment of a friend's legal defense in deference to the prestige of the republic. Law and equity, a dichotomy much debated in the Roman schools of declamation, prevail over private concerns. In another pair of letters the discussion rises to the more politically dangerous subject of the loss of the freedom of speech that existed in the old days of the republic, since there is now no leader who really has the concerns of the state at heart. Once again it is the fear of personal loss (*discrimen rerum suarum*, Furietti, p. 229) that is pitted against the higher interests of the state.

A conspicuous portion of the letters has to do with the friend's keeping

[9] Cf. Guido Martellotti, "Gasparino Barzizza," *Dizionario biografico degli Italiani*, vol. 7:36.

faith even in the face of adverse criticism directed at the corespondent in his absence. Concerning this aspect of friendship Barzizza inserts a dictum in one of his letters, which may well be of his own composition, that it is the mark of a good man that he does not easily believe of another what he himself would not have admitted in his own conduct, "Maxime enim puto boni hominis esse non facile de alio credere quod ipse non admisisset" (Furietti, p. 231). In matters of friendship it is important not to emphasize unduly one's own services. This is well illustrated in one exchange, in which the first writer protests that there was never any personal advantage that he would not neglect in deference to his friend's good or any inconvenience that he would not undergo in order to be of benefit to his friend. His respondent chides him for protesting too much and once again Barzizza provides a fitting comment, that nothing is less characteristic of those who love than that they should remember their own good offices but forget those of another ("nihil enim mihi videtur minus amantium esse quam sui officii meminisse et alieni oblivisci." Furietti, p. 243). In all of these discussions, however, friendship is always made subordinate to right conduct, *honestum*. One must be prepared to prosecute even a friend's friend when necessary.

Of interest are samples of admonitory letters sent from concerned friends or relatives to students who have slackened in their studies. Such examples were later imitated by Carolus Virulus in his very popular *Epistolarum formulae*. In one letter the admonisher in rather severe language warns his correspondent that if he continues in the direction he has now taken (*perseveraveris pergere*, Furietti, p. 292, is the alliterative phrase used) all his friends will cease to look after his interests, and he will return to his city in great disgrace. The answer is a lively defense of student escapades, in which the writer says he is no different from others; "nihil facio praeter morem aliorum" (Furietti, p. 293). He pleads for more temperate chastisement while acknowledging that it was paternal. His last sentence is a good show of bravado: "me talem efficiam, cui inimici mei invideant et amici congratulentur."

Other letters are concerned with public events, the internal strife of the republic, troubles in the East, preparations for war, the conduct of military campaigns. Most of these events are represented against the implicit background of ancient Rome, but in one exchange the scene is suddenly transferred to the contemporary scene in Northern Italy, the political fortunes of Cremona, Brescia, and Bergamo (Furietti, p. 263). Other letters may contain allusions to contemporary events also, such as one that tells of a prince who had formerly suppressed liberty by force of arms but now openly shared his powers with the common people (Furietti, p. 267).

In another missive we learn of a very young man elected to leadership in his republic against the *mos maiorum* because of his outstanding courage (Furietti, p. 271). There are very few strictly anecdotal letters, notably one that tells of highwaymen in Tuscany who captured a traveler but then let him go with provisions for the road because of his wit and good character, illustrating that sometimes thieves are more honorable than law-abiding citizens (Furietti, p. 270).

The subject turns to the praise of religion in four pairs of letters, its importance for ensuring the greatness of ancient Rome and its necessity together with philosophy and letters to achieve a tranquil and full life, but, the writer counsels, better no religion than an inert, apathetic kind, which is more equivalent to sacrilege. Another letter draws its inspiration from a reading of St. Basil on divine worship (Furietti, p. 286).

The theme of personal integrity pervades many of the letters, such as the inability to suffer infringement of one's honour with equanimity, or to reap hatred in return for good deeds. Mixed in with these discussions of lofty sentiments are other more practical reports on financial matters, the conduct of court cases and the management of estates, as one finds also in Cicero and Pliny.

A series of letters towards the end of the collection treat of the respect owed to aging parents and of the bitterness of old age. Many of the latter type are very despondent in tone, which elicit in the answers an attempt at epistolary consolation. In one the writer laments that he has been reduced to a worse state than his enemies could ever have imagined or hoped for. Another is ready to offer his throat to the executioner. Advice of various kinds is given. In one instance the respondent urges that the aggrieved man leave the company of men and withdraw from material things so that he will return lightened of his burdens. Another counsellor quotes a phrase from a letter of Cicero to Atticus (11.12.4): "stabis animo erecto et perferendo vinces fortunam" (Furietti, p. 326). The very last letter of the collection, as we have it, refers once again to the sacredness of friendship, which must rise above all personal advantage and pleasure. The writer in this case—and perhaps Barzizza purposely closes on this note—does not claim to be numbered among his correspondent's friends and yet promises his help, prepared to come to his defense, which his friends have villainously abandoned.

With this general idea of the content of the model letters we may attempt some cursory description of the Latin style used in them. Barzizza was known to his contemporaries as a champion and apostle of Ciceronian style. It was to him that Bishop Gerardo Landriani had entrusted the transcription of the manuscripts of the *De oratore*, the *Orator* and the

Brutus, which he had discovered in the cathedral of Lodi in 1421.[10] Before this discovery the first two works were known only in a mutilated version, and indeed it was Barzizza who had attempted to fill in many of the lacunae. Guarino wrote of him that it was through his efforts that Cicero was loved and read in all the Italian schools: "cuius ductu et auspiciis Cicero amatur, legitur et per Italorum gymnasia summa cum gloria volitat."[11] Yet, as Sabbadini long ago pointed out,[12] he was not always Ciceronian either in vocabulary or syntax. In his private letters, in particular, he ignores grammatical canons and achieves a greater naturalness of style. In the *Exercitationes* he is more formal, since they were meant as models, but it must be emphasized that the style of these letters is a far cry from that of Cicero's. His was a spontaneous, elegant yet colloquial language, difficult to emulate by any other writer of Latin. As Erasmus remarked in his *De conscribendis epistolis,* you may write on the spur of the moment if you wish, write whatever comes to your head (*quidquid in buccam venerit*, a well-known phrase of Cicero's), as long as it is the way Cicero wrote to Atticus.[13] Cicero employs many more diminutives used in everyday language like *perbelle, misellus, pulchellus, mi vetule, meliuscule, rumusculi,* even such coinages as *subturpicula.* He often dispenses with the more formal rhythms of the clausulae, especially in his letters to Atticus and prefers to write *more Romano,* in a good straightforward language without artifice, as he noted in a letter to Julius Caesar, apologizing that he was *putidusculi*, "in rather poor taste," in that letter, since he was intent on recommending his friend Trebatius (*Ad fam.* 7.5.3).

The letters composed by Barzizza resemble the more formal type of letter used by Cicero in his *commendaticiae* (*Ad fam.* 13), and in certain carefully written letters, as that to Cato, in which he seeks his support in the Senate for a *supplicatio* honoring his victory over the Parthians during his governorship of Cilicia (*Ad fam.* 15.4), the first letter to his brother Quintus, which was more of an open letter meant for a wider audience, or the very ornate letter to Lucceius (*Ad fam.* 5.12) *valde bella*, as Cicero himself calls it (*Ad Att.* 4.6.4).

In matters of vocabulary, the *Exercitationes* certainly exhibit a generally

---

[10] Barzizza, in turn, assigned the task to Cosma Raimondi da Cremona. Cf. Eugenio Garin, *Storia di Milano* vol 6 (Rome: 1955): 575.

[11] *Epistolario di Guarino Veronese*, ed. R. Sabbadini (Venice: 1915–19, rep. Turin: Bottega d'Erasmo, 1967), 1:345.

[12] R. Sabbadini, *Storia del Ciceronianismo* (Turin: Loescher, 1885), 13.

[13] *Ad Att.* 12.1.2; 14.7.1, cited in Erasmus, *De conscribendis epistolis* CWE 25, 15.

Ciceronian character, but Barzizza does not hesitate to use unfamiliar words from the comic writers and later Latin usage. In substantiation of what Sabbadini remarked only en *passant*, I shall give a list, which does not at all pretend to be exhaustive, of some of the non-Ciceronian words found in these model letters. From Plautus and Terence Barzizza takes such words and expressions as *animo otioso, integrascit, percunctator, interminatus sum*. He is not averse to using vocabulary from Seneca, Tacitus and Quintilian not to be found in Cicero, such as *captivitas, praeoccupare, profectus* in the sense of profit, *pollicitatio*, common enough in other writers, but found only once in Cicero, *in antecessum accipere*. At other times he introduces words from late Latin writers, terms from the jurists, *fideiussio, sarcinulas componere* ("pack up your belongings") from Ulpian, ultimately from Varro; *principans*, found in Sidonius Apollinaris; *machinamenta* in a transferred sense, witnessed only by Apuleius; and non-classical words such as *defloratam, funerarer, pecuniola, caritudo, detractione*, in its modern connotation; or expressions that are not found in classical writers, such as *oculi dolere* or *crepare*, in the sense of envy, and the phrases *ab inexpectato* and *in praesentia*.

In matters of syntax I should characterize Barzizza's style as cautious, avoiding longer periods and seeming to favour constructions such as concessive clauses, comparative noun clauses, indirect questions and the like. From Cicero Barzizza derives a predilection for balanced antithesis, which he uses to good effect, as "periculum factum est, unde praesidium expectabamus," (Furietti, p. 226); or "odium pro benevolentia consequi et quos nostro devinctos beneficio speramus, eosdem nobis inimicos reddere" (Furietti, p.309); "nullam rem tam arduam esse quam non putem esse levissimam" (Furietti, p. 324). Alliteration is another rhetorical device frequently exploited in the prose of the letters, sometimes enhanced by a kind of emulation in the use of this figure by the two fictitious correspondents. One letter ends: "speramus clementiam suam mutaturam esse in melius mala, quibus conflictamur ac pene conficimur"(Furietti, p. 253); the next one begins: "literae tuae tantam attulerunt animo meo molestiam ut nullo tempore majori in maerore fuerim."

The didactic method of the pairing of letters allows for the teaching of the use of synonyms and similar expressions, as the respondent comments on the contents of the letter he has received. This is illustrated in the very first exchange. In referring to the rejection of a former friend, the verb *rejiciebam* is varied to *destituissem* in the second letter, and the sentiment "tamen cum ad incredibilem animi tui sapientiam judicium meum referebam, nihil erat, quare id a te improbari putarem" (Furietti, p. 220) is reechoed in different words, "tamen cum haberem animum tuum multis iudiciis perspectum, nullo pacto induci poteram ut in ea re temere quicquam te factum putarem." Or again one letter ends in a rather elegant contrast: "ne cuius vita improbata fit eius orationi fidem habeas" (Furietti, p. 231), reaffirmed by the respondent in the more emphatic indicative mood: "Horum hominum ut vitam semper improbavi, ita numquam orationi eorum fidem habui"(p. 231).

The prose rhythms of Barzizza in these exercises, especially at the end of letters, are vaguely reminiscent of Ciceronian cadences but they do not adhere to the rules of quantity nor are they confined to the usual combinations of cretics and trochees found in Cicero. It must be remembered also in this regard that even Cicero used a freer, more natural rhythm in his letters than in his orations. In the *Exercitationes* Barzizza seems to favor double trochees and double cretics rather than the cretic plus spondee. On September 9, 1441 Guineforte Barzizza, Gasparino's son, wrote a letter to Gianlucido Gonzaga, student at the school of Guarino, which he sent to accompany a copy of his father's model letters. He confers rather fulsome praise on them: "tantam suavitatem in se habent, ut magnam delectationem earum lectio afferre possit, tantum sucum, ut nemo tam ieiunus atque inops in dicendo sit, qui non brevi se refectum, si avide hauserit, atque ditatum sentiat, etc."[14] These words may betray an exaggerated filial devotion, but the *Exercitationes* were indeed an interesting pedagogical experiment in the history of the art of letter writing.

University of Windsor

[14] Ludwig Bertalot, "Die älteste Briefsammlung des Gasparinus Barzizza," *Beiträge zur Forschung* n.s. 2 (1939): 39.

The Composition of Erasmus' Opus de conscribendis epistolis *Evidence for the Growth of a Mind*

JUDITH RICE HENDERSON

In an address to the Second International Congress of Neo-Latin Studies (Amsterdam, 19–24 August 1973), published in the *Acta*, Alain Jolidon describes the composition history of Erasmus' *Opus de conscribendis epistolis* as "un témoin particulièrement précieux pour qui s'intéresse à l'évolution psychologique et littéraire d'Erasme."[1] As he notes, it spans thirty-six years, from the first draft composed in Paris for Robert Fisher in 1498 to Erasmus' final revisions in 1534, two years before his death. Moreover, evidence about the process of composition can be found in 1) Erasmus' correspondence; 2) citations of an early manuscript in Johannes Despauterius' *Syntaxis* (Paris: J. Badius, 1509); 3) independent editions of the *Encomium matrimonii* (first published Louvain: T. Martens, 1518), which was also included in the treatise as a sample letter of persuasion; 4) the pirated *Brevissima maximeque compendiaria conficiendarum epistolarum formula* (Basel? A. Petri? 1519–20?); 5) the pirated *Libellus de conscribendis epistolis* (Cambridge: J. Siberch, 1521); 6) the first authorized edition (Basel: J. Froben, 1522); and 7) the revised *Opus de conscribendis epistolis* (Basel: H. Froben and N. Episcopius, 1534). Jolidon is surely right. Tracing the evolution of a treatise which Erasmus revised throughout his adult life must enlarge our understanding of the growth of his mind.

---

[1] "L'évolution psychologique et littéraire d'Erasme d'après les variantes du 'De conscribendis epistolis,' " in *Acta Conventus Neo-Latini Amstelodamensis*, ed. P. Tuynman, G. C. Kuiper, and E. Kessler, Humanistische Bibliothek, I, 26 (Munich, 1979), 566–87. Hereafter cited as 1973 *Acta*.

Jolidon compares the authorized edition of 1522 with the pirated *Libellus* written, he argues, in 1499. Focusing especially on style, he concludes that in revising his early draft, Erasmus shows himself more sober and circumspect as a result of controversy, purifies his style of medievalisms, and enriches his expression. Jolidon's argument that Siberch published the *Encomium matrimonii* in the *Libellus* from Erasmus' early draft of his treatise on letter-writing, not from Martens' 1518 *Declamationes aliquot Erasmi Roterodami*, has convinced Jean-Claude Margolin.[2] In an important note, Jolidon dates the composition of the pirated *Formula* after the *Libellus*, "de 1500 environ, en raison d'une allusion à l'incredibilis nitor' des lettres de Politien (cf. la dédicace des 'Adagiorum collectanea' à Mountjoy, lettre n° 126 de juin 1500, l. 133), de l'absence complète de la locution NEC ... QUIDEM, si fréquente dans 'l'édition Siberch, et plus généralement de la totale indépendance de cette dernière édition (qui ignore Politien) par rapport à la 'Formula' " (p. 583 n. 1). These suggestions challenge the conclusions of James D. Tracy, Jolidon's predecessor in the study of Erasmus' intellectual development.[3]

In a subsequent presentation to the Fifth International Congress of Neo-Latin Studies (St. Andrews, 24 August to 1 September 1982), also published in the *Acta*, Jolidon reviews internal and external evidence in an effort to solve certain problems concerning the composition, contents, and publication history of the *Formula*, "un des textes les plus énigmatiques de l'illustre Rotterdamois."[4] Here he abandons his suggestion that the *Formula* postdates the *Libellus* for the more common view that it stems from the first draft of Erasmus' treatise. Jolidon notes that Erasmus cites the *Epistolimaioi charaktéres* attributed to Libanius but will not admit that this reference establishes a *terminus post quem* for the composition of the *Formula*, proposing instead that Erasmus saw it in manuscript (p. 240 n. 8). The *editio princeps* of pseudo-Libanius was published not, as Jolidon

---

[2] See his introduction to the *Encomium matrimonii* in *Opera omnia Desiderii Erasmi Roterodami* (Amsterdam, 1975), I-5:335-82. Margolin thus corrects his introduction to the *Opus de conscribendis epistolis* in the *Opera omnia* (Amsterdam, 1971), I-2:170. The Amsterdam edition of Erasmus' works is hereafter cited as *ASD*.

[3] "On the Composition Dates of Seven of Erasmus' Writings," *Bibliothèque d'Humanisme et Renaissance* 31 (1969): 355-64. Cf. Tracy's *Erasmus: The Growth of a Mind*, Travaux d'Humanisme et Renaissance 126 (Geneva, 1972).

[4] "Histoire d'un opuscule d'Erasme: La *Brevissima maximeque compendiaria conficiendarum epistolarum formula*," in *Acta Conventus Neo-Latini Sanctandreani*, ed. I. D. McFarlane, Medieval & Renaissance Texts & Studies, vol. 38 (Binghamton, NY, 1986), 229-43. Hereafter cited as 1982 *Acta*.

says, on 29 March 1499 but in July 1501.[5] I suggest that Erasmus composed the *Formula* no earlier than the second half of 1501. Jolidon's argument in the 1982 *Acta* that Matthes Maler first pirated the *Formula* at Erfurt in 1520 is also questionable. R. A. B. Mynors has argued convincingly that Adam Petri published a lost first edition at Basel in late 1519 or early 1520.[6] Jolidon's chronology of the three extant 1520 editions, supplemented by a bibliography of later editions to 1602, remains an important contribution to the publication history of the treatise. His careful analysis of the contents of the work shows in particular Erasmus' reliance on Quintilian and other authorities.

The definitive composition history of the *Opus de conscribendis epistolis* has yet to be written, especially since an important document, although long known, has not been studied: the citations of Erasmus in Despauterius' *Syntaxis*. Having recently edited and analyzed these citations, I have been stimulated to continue the task proposed by Jolidon. Here I shall draw upon two forthcoming articles—"Despauterius' *Syntaxis* (1509): The Earliest Publication of Erasmus' *De conscribendis epistolis*" and "The Enigma of Erasmus' *Conficiendarum epistolarum formula*"—to revise the composition history of the *Opus de conscribendis epistolis* and to explore its implications for Erasmus' intellectual development.[7]

The authorized edition of Erasmus' treatise falls into four sections of unequal lengths. Neither Erasmus nor his publisher has marked these divisions, which I shall call A, B, C, and D, but the chapters in each section are closely related in content. In A, Erasmus defines the letter as a genre and discusses its variations of style (*ASD* I-2:209–27). In B, he discusses methods of teaching letter-writing (*ASD* I-2:227–66). In C, he

[5] See *Libanii Opera*, ed. Richard Förster (Leipzig, 1927), 9:21–22. The description in the *Gesamtkatalog der Wiegendrucke*, 8.2 (Stuttgart-Berlin, 1973), cols. 65–69, no. 9367, of the 1499 Aldine edition of Greek epistolographers edited by Marcus Musurus does not mention the *Epistolimaioi charaktêres* attributed to Libanius. John Monfasani, who has seen a copy of this edition, assures me that it contains the *editio princeps* of the *Typoi epistolikoi* of pseudo-Demetrius but not the work attributed to Libanius. Cf. Monfasani, "Three Notes on Renaissance Rhetoric," *Rhetorica* 5 (1987): 107–18.

[6] In *Collected Works of Erasmus* (Toronto, 1985), 25:256–57. The English translation of Erasmus' works will be cited hereafter as *CWE*.

[7] *Humanistica Lovaniensia* 37 (1988): 175–210, and *Renaissance and Reformation* n.s. 13 (1989): 313–30, respectively. The second paper was circulated to participants in the seminar on epistolography at the 1988 Congress of Neo-Latin Studies. Both studies are products of research on Renaissance letter-writing theory and practice funded by the Social Sciences and Humanities Research Council of Canada. Please see my forthcoming articles for documentation of the argument that follows.

treats the etiquette of epistolary formulas, especially of salutation and valediction (*ASD* I-2:266–300). In D, he classifies letters according to their varied functions and offers both rules and examples for the argument and organization of his types (*ASD* I-2:301–579). Thus Erasmus provides a complete textbook of epistolary rhetoric, covering *inventio* and *dispositio* (D) and *elocutio* (A, C) and incorporating an instructor's manual (B). He omits only the two divisions of rhetoric, *actio* and *memoria*, inapplicable to a written genre.

If we assume that the first draft of the treatise, composed for Robert Fisher in 1498, is lost, the earliest version extant seems to be the *Libellus de conscribendis epistolis* (composed 1499), a draft of Section D of the finished treatise. Erasmus will later replace its brief introductory remarks on style with Sections A–C of the *Opus*. The *Libellus* begins with the classical distinction between the intimate, conversational style of the letter (*sermo*) and the public, declamatory style of the oration (*contentio*). Erasmus inveighs against medieval conventions of salutation and encourages imitation of classical formulas, but he accepts innovation as long as the writer avoids barbarism and parasitic flattery. Borrowing from Francesco Negro's *Opusculum scribendi epistolas* (Venice: H. Lichtenstein, 1488) a classification of letters as "mixed" and "unmixed," he nevertheless takes his Quattrocento predecessor to task for insisting that every letter include an introduction. Erasmus then further classifies "unmixed" letters as deliberative, demonstrative, and judicial, dividing these again into species, as in the *Opus*. Letters that do not fall into these *causae orationis* he labels "extraordinary." He describes the topics the writer will use to develop each species of argument, their order, and the best means of making the argument persuasive. For each species he provides illustrations.

The author of the *Libellus* has completely assimilated Italian humanism. He feels free to criticize Quattrocento handbooks of letter-writing, but he writes in the tradition they established, an uneasy synthesis between medieval art (*ars dictaminis*) and classical imitation.[8] The *ars dictaminis* adapted rhetoric to written composition, especially letter-writing. The letter, like the oration, was divided into parts, usually five: *salutatio, exordium, narratio, petitio, conclusio*. Its style was formal, its purpose persua-

---

[8] On this tradition, see my earlier studies, "Erasmus on the Art of Letter-Writing," in *Renaissance Eloquence: Studies in the Theory and Practice of Renaissance Rhetoric*, ed. James J. Murphy (Berkeley, 1983), 331–55, and "Defining the Genre of the Letter: Juan Luis Vives' *De conscribendis epistolis*," *Renaissance and Reformation* n.s. 7 (1983): 89–105.

sion, its use often public. In any case, medieval theorists did not distinguish the formal, public letter from the familiar, private letter. Even the familiar letter followed the rules of art. The Quattrocento humanists paid lip service to the classical definition of the letter as a conversation between absent friends on their personal affairs, and they tried to purify epistolary style of medieval barbarism, but they continued to teach letter-writing as an art of persuasion. Nothing about the *Libellus* is remarkable except its thoroughness. Only an imagination of Erasmian fecundity could have described methods of inventing and amplifying epistolary arguments in such copious detail.

The *Formula* may provide clues to the next stage in revision. Here Erasmus praises the letters of Angelo Poliziano. Poliziano's correspondence was first published posthumously in his *Omnia opera* (Venice: *in aedibus Aldi Romani*, July 1498), but Erasmus seems not to have seen it for some two years. He does not mention it in the *Libellus*, as he certainly would have done had he known it. In the *Formula*, as Jolidon has observed, Erasmus admires the *incredibilis nitor* of Poliziano's letters, echoing the phrase he used to describe Poliziano's style in the dedication to Mountjoy of the *Adagiorum collectanea* (Paris: J. Philippi, 1500). In the *Opus*, Poliziano is Erasmus' favorite contemporary letter-writer. He warmly recommends him as a model, and he expands the examples of invective he had cited in the *Libellus* by adding Poliziano's debate with the Ciceronian Bartolomeo Scala (*ASD* I-2:536–37).

The relationship of the tiny, disjointed *Formula* to Erasmus' work-in-progress on letter-writing is enigmatic. It cannot be an epitome of the *Libellus*. Although it touches the same topics (style and the threefold classification of letters as demonstrative, deliberative, and judicial), it ignores important material (formulas for greeting and farewell, epithets, the "mixed" letter, "extraordinary" letters, and the detailed description and illustration of the argument and organization of each type of "unmixed" letter). Moreover, as Jolidon observes, much of the work is not original but mere paraphrase. I have argued that the *Formula* is Erasmus' notes for revision rather than a new draft. Reading Poliziano's correspondence had alerted Erasmus to current issues in Italian humanism. Poliziano's dedicatory letter to Piero de' Medici and his exchanges with Bartolomeo Scala and Paolo Cortesi advocate eclectic reading and imitation of classical models in opposition to a narrow, exclusive Ciceronianism.

Although the *Formula* opens by quoting "Libanius," Erasmus has begun to question the classical distinction between the letter and the oration. There are some, he argues, "who maintain that there should be no use of artificial rules in personal, everyday letters, but that they should be made up of common sense and ordinary language."[9] Erasmus admits that the rigid medieval division of letters into salutation, exordium, narration, and conclusion seems ridiculous, but he insists that the letter-writer, like the orator, can benefit from the "sure methods and principles" of rhetoric (p. 262). Classical models only seem artless, he suggests, citing the example of Pliny, whose "style is controlled and elaborated with great ingenuity and refinement, yet it gives the appearance of being effortless, improvised, and extemporaneous" (p. 258). Erasmus seeks support in the literature, especially Quintilian, in defense of his thesis that letter-writing is an art. The letter is an all-purpose genre, even more versatile than the oration. If the writer is to treat many subjects under many circumstances, he must develop his skills by reading widely in diverse authors and diverse genres. He must learn rules, but he must exercise good judgment in using them, considering the purpose he is trying to achieve. He must practice diligently, but he must not be too self-conscious. Ultimately, he will become a good writer only if he follows his own genius. Erasmus is moving toward the balance of nature, art, and exercise, coupled with eclectic reading and imitation, that characterizes his mature pedagogy. The *Formula* contains the seeds of the *De ratione studii, De copia, Opus de conscribendis epistolis,* and *Ciceronianus.*

Erasmus mentions revising his treatise on letter-writing in letters written from 2 May 1499 to 27 January 1501.[10] In 1502, he lost his patrons through the deaths of the Bishop of Cambrai and Jacob Batt and the remarriage of Anna van Borssele, Lady of Veere, for whose son Adolph of Burgundy the treatise was intended. A preface to a revised version, addressed to William Blount, Baron Mountjoy, might have been written in either 1499 or 1509 (ep. 117). Erasmus then makes no further reference to the work until November 1511 (ep. 241), the period when he was advising Dean John Colet on the curriculum of St. Paul's School in London and composing textbooks for that new foundation, but we know that he had continued to revise and expand it after 1501, perhaps for Mountjoy. By 11 November 1508, when Despauterius completed his *Syntaxis*, the Flemish grammarian had seen a draft of the *Opus de conscribendis epistolis*. Despauterius quotes extensively from Section A on the nature and style of the letter and Section C on formulas of salutation and valediction, and he alludes to Section B on teaching methods and Section

[9] Trans. Charles Fantazzi, in *CWE* 25:261.

[10] *Opus epistolarum Des. Erasmi Roterodami*, ed. P. S. Allen et al., 12 vols. (Oxford, 1906–58), epp. 95, 130, 138, 145.

D on the classification and arguments of letters. In these citations, Erasmus' description of his friend Jacobus Tutor as *Handwerpiae agens*, that is, pensionary of Antwerp, establishes a *terminus post quem* of late 1505 for the manuscript Despauterius saw, and other internal evidence suggests that Erasmus completed this stage of the revision by August 1506, perhaps when he stopped in Paris that summer *en route* from England to Italy. Despauterius, who had known Erasmus at Louvain from 1502 to 1504, might have obtained the manuscript from his publisher Badius, with whom Erasmus had left other papers, or from another mutual friend. In late 1508, Erasmus was working at the Aldine press in Venice, and there is no evidence to suggest that he sent the manuscript back to Paris or Louvain from Italy.

In any event, Erasmus must have written this version of the treatise before 6 April 1509, when he heard the Good Friday sermon addressed to the Pope in Rome that he criticized in the *Ciceronianus* (*ASD* I-2: 637–39). Scholars have assumed that his anti-Ciceronianism began in reaction to this and other experiences in Italy, but Erasmus was already seeking a practical *via media* between barbaric medieval formulas and an equally legalistic neo-classical purism. Despauterius quotes Erasmus' amusing parody of the medieval salutation and his attack on the pretentious titles assumed by theologians and other clerics (*ASD* I-2: 282–83, 293–95). He also quotes from seven of the first eight chapters of the *Opus*. In these chapters, I have argued, Erasmus answers the Ciceronians.[11] He asserts that letter-writing cannot be limited to a simple, artless, conversational style. Letters can treat any subject. They are written to an individual, not to a general audience. Therefore, the writer must observe decorum, varying his style to suit his matter and the circumstances and personality of his correspondent. The letter "is by nature diverse and capable of almost infinite variation"; "it should be flexible, and, as the polyp adapts itself to every condition of its surroundings, so a letter should adapt itself to every kind of subject and circumstance."[12] Erasmus' argument echoes Poliziano, as Despauterius observes in his note on the opening chapter of the *Opus* in *Annotationes ad Syntaxim* ([Paris]: J. Badius, [1510]).

Although in 1515 and 1517 Beatus Rhenanus urged Erasmus to prepare his treatise for Froben's press (epp. 330, 581), he completed it only when the pirating of his early manuscripts from 1519 to 1521 forced him to do so. Committed now to theology and embroiled in religious controversy, he

---

[11] See "Erasmus on the Art of Letter-Writing."

[12] Trans. Charles Fantazzi, *CWE* 25:12, 19.

returned to the work reluctantly. How extensively he revised at this time we cannot be certain because Despauterius' selections offer no firm basis for comparison. Erasmus may well have expanded Section B as he worked with Colet on the curriculum of St. Paul's in 1511. If we compare the *Opus de conscribendis epistolis* with the *Libellus*, we can see that by 1522 he had greatly expanded Section D, adding a classification of letters taken from the *Typoi epistolikoi* of pseudo-Demetrius, enlarging his advice on developing arguments, and citing scores of new illustrations. Probably this material, like such collections as the *Adagia*, was accumulated over many years. As Jolidon (1973 *Acta*) and Charles Fantazzi (*CWE* 25:2–9) have shown, in revising the *Libellus*, Erasmus removed personal references and replaced model letters that may have seemed too frivolous or outspoken. He developed this circumspection after 1506, probably after his own New Testament of 1516 and Luther's Ninety-Five Theses of 1517 had heated the intellectual climate. From the earlier version that Despauterius had seen, Erasmus removed an excessively virulent address to theologians who insist on the title *magister noster*. Nevertheless, he retained the *Encomium matrimonii* in the authorized edition even though it had come under attack at Louvain. Margolin has shown that in his final revisions of 1534, which focused on this sample letter of persuasion, Erasmus qualified his criticisms of monasticism and celibacy while otherwise strengthening his argument (*ASD* I-2:196–97).

In revising the *Opus de conscribendis epistolis* in 1522 and 1534, Erasmus perhaps expanded his argument, improved his style, chastened his wit, objectified his tone, and tempered his satire, but he did not fundamentally change his thought. Examination of the pirated *Libellus* and *Formula* and of Despauterius' citations in his *Syntaxis* suggests that by 1499 Erasmus had thoroughly assimilated Italian humanism. Reading the correspondence of Angelo Poliziano about 1500, he became alarmed by the development of humanism toward extreme neo-classicism. He found Poliziano a congenial model, approving his eclecticism and his distaste for Ciceronianism, and was spurred by his influence to a critical reassessment of his Italian contemporaries. Before he crossed the Alps in 1506, this process of reassessment had led Erasmus to that complex but common sense balance of nature, art, and imitation that characterizes his mature thought. His experiences in Italy only confirmed his conviction that the humanist too intent on imitating the classical world would be unable to contribute to his own.

University of Saskatchewan

SEMINAR

Bilingualism: Latin and the Vernacular at the End of the Middle Ages

Le bilinguisme latin-français à la fin du Moyen Age

SERGE LUSIGNAN ET GILBERT OUY

Au moment où Serge Lusignan publiait son ouvrage *Parler vulgairement*,[1] Gilbert Ouy avait, de son côté, entrepris depuis quelque temps déjà des recherches sur le phénomène du bilinguisme latin-français, s'intéressant particulièrement à des auteurs de la fin du XIVe ou du début du XVe siècle, comme Jean Gerson ou Jean de Montreuil, dont on a la chance de posséder certains textes en deux versions, l'une latine, l'autre française.[2]

Ayant lu attentivement le livre, Gilbert Ouy n'a pu relever qu'un seul point de désaccord avec son collègue canadien: celui-ci estime en effet que—à la différence de l'Angleterre, où le français n'était pas la langue maternelle—la langue vulgaire n'a pas dû faire en France l'objet d'un enseignement écrit; en d'autres termes, il n'a sans doute jamais existé, pense-t-il, de livres de grammaire française comme il y en avait pour l'enseignement du latin: assimilable, dans la pensée des hommes de cette époque, à un art mécanique un peu au même titre que, par exemple, la sculpture ou la métallurgie, la pratique de la langue vulgaire n'était pas, bien sûr, dépourvue de normes, mais elle ne devait être enseignée qu'oralement.[3]

---

[1] Serge Lusignan, *Parler vulgairement: les intellectuels et la langue française aux XIIIe et XIVe siècles* (Montréal-Paris, 1987), 204 pp.

[2] Gilbert Ouy, *Un exemple de bilinguisme au début du XVe siècle: les versions originales latine et française de quelques oeuvres de Gerson*, dans *Le Moyen Français*, Actes du Ve Colloque International sur le Moyen Français, Milan, 6–8 mai 1985, vol. II (Milan, 1986), 33–66.—Id., *Bilinguisme ou trilinguisme? Latin commun, latin savant et français aux XIVe et XVe siècles*, dans *Etat et Eglise dans la genèse de l'Etat moderne*, Actes du Colloque international de Madrid, décembre 1986 (Paris: C.N.R.S., 1987), 85–101.

[3] v. notamment S. Lusignan, o. c., 126: "En étant assimilée à un art mécanique, la

G. Ouy, quant à lui, imagine qu'il a dû exister des manuels d'enseignement du français, sans doute même à deux niveaux: un niveau élémentaire, celui des petites écoles, et un niveau supérieur, correspondant à la Faculté des Arts, ou encore à la formation donnée aux jeunes notaires de la chancellerie royale où, dès le début du XIVe siècle, une bonne partie des actes était rédigée en français.

Certes, la différence entre le nombre de livres médiévaux d'enseignement du français retrouvés en Angleterre—une bonne trentaine—et en France—aucun jusqu'ici—est sans nul doute statistiquement significative. Mais a-t-on vraiment le droit d'en conclure que de tels ouvrages n'ont jamais existé en France? S'il y en a eu, leur disparition pourrait s'expliquer par deux facteurs au moins: d'une part, la très faible valeur marchande des manuels de l'enseignement élémentaire et le peu de soin qu'en prenaient les enfants; d'autre part—et ce facteur aurait joué bien davantage en France qu'en Angleterre—la rapide évolution de la langue au cours de cette période, qui aurait rendu de tels ouvrages très vite caducs, donc peu dignes d'être conservés. Si l'on devait en retrouver un jour quelques vestiges, ce serait plus vraisemblablement parmi les vieux papiers qui servaient à faire les plus anciens cartons de reliure[4] que sur les rayons d'une bibliothèque. En pareil cas, il n'y aurait là qu'un nouvel exemple parmi tant d'autres de la loi, récemment mise en évidence par les recherches de codicologie quantitative de Carla Bozzolo et Ezio Ornato, selon laquelle les livres les moins bien représentés dans les collections modernes sont précisément ceux qui étaient les moins rares—et avaient donc le moins de valeur—au Moyen Age.[5] Ainsi, combien subsiste-t-il aujourd'hui de ces petites brochures de nouvelles qui n'avaient pas attendu pour circuler l'invention de l'imprimerie? ou encore de ces

---

langue française demeure dans l'antichambre du savoir universitaire. La réflexion qui accompagne sa pratique ne peut accéder au niveau de l'écrit théorique."

[4] v. à ce sujet G. Ouy, dans *L'Histoire et ses méthodes* ("Encyclopédie de la Pléiade", vol. XI), (Paris, 1961), 1079-84.

[5] Carla Bozzolo et Ezio Ornato, *Pour une histoire du livre manuscrit au Moyen Age: trois essais de codicologie quantitative* (Paris: C.N.R.S., 1980), 361 pp. V. notamment p. 75: "L'intensité de l'effort de conservation des livres dépend de leur *prix* et de leur *valeur d'usage*"; et (p. 76) ce fait significatif: pour les volumes de la *parva libraria* du Collège de Sorbonne inventoriés et prisés en 1338, le taux de conservation varie en fonction du prix et, "pour les valeurs les plus basses, le pourcentage des pertes est de 95% environ." Encore s'agit-il là d'ouvrages conservés dans une bibliothèque, dont les chances de survie étaient donc particulièrement grandes. A plus forte raison, sauf hasard exceptionnel, auraient été voués à la disparition des petits manuels élémentaires en langue vulgaire, indignes de figurer dans une bibliothèque.

feuilles de propagande politique ou religieuse que l'on diffusait en grandes quantités, notamment dans les milieux universitaires?[6]

Une autre objection de G. Ouy—mais mieux vaudrait parler d'une interrogation—porte sur le concept de *langue maternelle*: certes, il est indiscutable que, pour un Anglais des années 1400, le français n'était pas la langue maternelle. Mais n'en allait-il pas un peu de même, par exemple, pour un jeune paysan de Picardie qui, à la maison, n'avait jamais entendu parler que le patois de son village et qui, lorsqu'il se rendait à la ville la plus proche, s'entretenait avec les gens qu'il rencontrait dans le dialecte de la région?

Il subsistait d'ailleurs en France, jusqu'à une époque toute récente, des vestiges d'une telle situation linguistique: ceux des Parisiens qui ont gardé des souvenirs précis de la période qui a précédé la dernière guerre n'ont pas oublié comment, même dans des campagnes relativement proches de la capitale, comme par exemple la région de Laon, ou, à plus forte raison, en Gascogne ou dans le Périgord, ils entendaient les paysans converser entre eux en une langue qui leur était totalement incompréhensible, et dont seul un linguiste eût été capable de déceler qu'elle était très proche du français. La seule différence avec le Moyen Age—mais elle est de taille—c'est que, vers les années 1930, il existait, depuis longtemps déjà, dans toute la France des écoles dont la fréquentation était obligatoire, et où l'on enseignait à tous les enfants une langue française unifiée, normalisée que tous, en principe, savaient non seulement parler—avec, bien sûr, des accents caractéristiques des divers terroirs—mais encore lire et écrire. En outre, la population se déplaçait bien davantage dans le pays, le service militaire mettait en contact des jeunes gens originaires de diverses régions, et la presse, la radio, le cinéma diffusaient toujours plus largement la langue nationale.

Comment les choses se passaient-elles vers 1400? Prenons un exemple concret et, semble-t-il, tout à fait représentatif: celui du jeune Jean Gerson.

Il était né en 1363 dans un hameau des Ardennes proche de Rethel, où son père exerçait le métier de charron. Même si ce dernier était capable de s'exprimer assez correctement en français commun; même si—comme,

[6] Les distributions de "tracts" existaient déjà—évidemment à une moindre échelle que de nos jours—bien avant l'invention de l'imprimerie: ainsi, dans les mois qui suivirent le déclenchement du Schisme en 1378, les partisans d'Urbain VI diffusèrent parmi les universitaires parisiens un libelle de Giovanni da Legnano afin de les dissuader de se rallier à Clément VII. Trois exemplaires identiques de ce texte de propagande nous ont été par hasard conservés dans un gros recueil (Paris, B.N. lat. 14643).

semble-t-il, une proportion non négligeable des villageois de Champagne à cette époque—il avait reçu la tonsure de clerc; et en admettant, de surplus, que—comme une partie seulement des clercs—il ait su lire et écrire, nous pouvons cependant avoir la quasi-certitude que la langue que le futur chancelier de l'Université entendait et parlait au foyer paternel n'était pas le français, mais bien le patois du Réthelois, une variante fortement teintée de picard du dialecte champenois.

Comment, dans ces conditions, l'enfant avait-il fait l'apprentissage du français? Ici, nous en sommes réduits à une accumulation d'hypothèses. On sait, par le témoignage de Gerson lui-même, que le père attachait beaucoup d'importance à l'instruction de ses nombreux enfants. Il n'est donc pas impossible que l'humble artisan leur ait lui-même enseigné un peu de français commun, langue véhiculaire dont la connaissance était évidemment indispensable pour se faire comprendre des habitants d'autres provinces du royaume. Il se peut aussi que, dans la mesure de ses modestes compétences, le curé du village voisin ait dispensé à ses jeunes paroissiens, outre quelques notions de catéchisme, certaines connaissances de base, avant d'expédier les plus studieux d'entre eux vers quelque école monastique de la région. Il est probable, en effet, que le petit Jean fut confié de bonne heure à l'écolâtre de l'abbaye bénédictine de Saint-Rémi de Reims, puisque le hameau de Gerson faisait partie de son domaine. Dans ce cas, qu'y apprit-il? Sans nul doute, une bonne pratique de l'écriture, et probablement une solide base de grammaire latine. Mais avait-il beaucoup approfondi sa connaissance du français lorsque, en 1377, ayant reçu la "couronne"—la tonsure de clerc—des mains mêmes de l'archevêque de Reims (ce qui justifiait un jeu de mots, et Gerson n'a pas manqué de le faire), il fut expédié, âgé d'un peu plus de treize ans, au Collège de Navarre, dont les bourses étaient en principe réservées aux "pauvres écoliers" originaires de Champagne.

Devenu pensionnaire du prestigieux établissement de la Montagne Sainte-Geneviève, non seulement il n'allait vraisemblablement pas s'y perfectionner en français, mais l'usage de cette langue lui devenait sévèrement interdit par le réglement (au reste, Gerson lui-même ne formulera-t-il pas cette même interdiction[7] lorsque, bien plus tard, il rédigera le réglement des études pour les enfants de choeur de Notre Dame de Paris?). Où, quand, comment, dans ces conditions, l'auteur que

[7] "Item accuset quilibet socium suum super sequentibus, videlicet: *si audierit eum loqui gallicum*, si iuraverit, si mentitus fuerit . . ." (ms. Paris, B.N., nouv. acq. lat. 3043, fol. 48r).

l'on considère généralement, à juste titre, comme le meilleur prosateur français de la fin du Moyen Age a-t-il appris la langue qu'il maniait avec tant de maîtrise?

Bien que le terme soit quelque peu galvaudé, il est permis de dire qu'il y a là un mystère. Mais—et c'est fort heureux—les historiens ont commencé, depuis quelque temps, à prendre conscience de leur ignorance, et s'attendent à déboucher sur l'inconnu pour peu qu'ils entreprennent d'approfondir sérieusement un problème jusqu'alors considéré comme résolu.

L'exemple de Gerson, s'il est particulièrement intéressant, n'a rien d'exceptionnel: la question se pose en termes analogues pour tous les grands auteurs de la période considérée qui ont écrit en langue vulgaire. Faut-il admettre qu'un simple enseignement oral reçu pendant l'enfance leur ait suffi pour accéder à une telle maîtrise? Doit-on supposer, au contraire, qu'il a existé des livres et une technique d'apprentissage assez élaborée dont—pour la France, tout au moins—aucune trace n'a survécu? Encore une fois, il paraît un peu risqué de tirer argument de l'absence de tout manuel d'origine française dans nos bibliothèques pour affirmer que des manuscrits d'enseignement de la langue vulgaire n'ont jamais existé en France; mais il serait évidemment encore plus imprudent, et d'ailleurs fort paradoxal, de voir là une présomption en faveur de leur existence!

Ce qui, en revanche, n'est pas du domaine de l'hypothèse, c'est la remarquable conscience de la langue manifestée par les grands lettrés tels qu'Evrard de Conty, Pierre d'Ailly, Jean Gerson, Jean de Montreuil, Laurent de Premierfait ou Christine de Pizan, dont des manuscrits autographes ou originaux sont parvenus jusqu'à nous.[8]

Dans des documents autographes retrouvés dans les Archives du Nord, on voit Pierre d'Ailly (1351-1420) user de façon quasi-systématique de deux types d'orthographe:[9] l'une, que l'on pourrait qualifier de "courante", lui sert pour ses brouillons; l'autre, une orthographe "d'apparat", est utilisée pour la mise au net d'une lettre destinée au duc de Bourgogne: là, le prélat s'emploie à éliminer la plupart des y qui apparaissaient dans

---

[8] v. G. Ouy, *Les orthographes de divers auteurs français des XIVe et XVe siècles: présentation et étude de quelques manuscrits autographes*, dans *Le Moyen Français* (Actes du VIe Colloque International sur le Moyen Français, Milan, mai 1988), sous presse.—G. Ouy et Christine M. Reno, *Les hésitations de Christine: étude des variantes de graphies dans trois manuscrits autographes de Christine de Pizan*, dans "Revue des langues romanes" 92.2 (1988): 265–86.

[9] v. Nina Catach et G. Ouy, *De Pierre d'Ailly à Jean Antoine de Baïf: un exemple de double orthographe à la fin du XIVe siècle*, dans "Romania" 97 (1976): 218–48.

le brouillon; il accorde tous les participes passés employés avec l'auxiliaire avoir (*ay ja administrés plusieurs sacremens et fais plusieurs offices episcopauls*), alors qu'il écrivait tout naturellement au brouillon *administré* et *fait*; il rétablit presque toujours le e caduc final, que nous remplaçons aujourd'hui par une apostrophe (*je estoye, de innobedience*), tandisqu'il pratique l'apocope (*jestoye*) au brouillon, etc. Il s'agit là du phénomène de la "double orthographe", qui a été bien étudié pour le XVIe siècle, mais dont l'existence dès la fin du XIVe siècle (le document est de 1397) n'a été que récemment mise en évidence.

Il est à peu près certain que la "double orthographe" était habituelle à l'époque. Ainsi, les divergences assez considérables que l'on relève entre les copies d'oeuvres en français de Gerson exécutées par son jeune frère, le célestin Jean—qui travaillait très probablement d'après des brouillons—et l'unique autographe en langue vulgaire actuellement identifié,[10] calligraphié par le chancelier, doivent trouver là leur explication. Dans ce dernier manuscrit, qui contient des textes catéchétiques destinés aux "simples gens", on voit que Gerson use à dessein d'une orthographe aussi simple que possible, éliminant la plupart des lettres "étymologiques", des redoublements de consonnes inutiles , réservant l'usage de l'y à quelques emplois bien précis, etc. Ceci implique évidemment une réflexion sur la langue. Tout à l'inverse, Laurent de Premierfait qui, à la même époque, destine ses traductions françaises à un public bien différent, celui de l'aristocratie, invente une orthographe "savante", inutilement compliquée, et décide de rétablir en français un gérondif nettement distinct du participe présent, dont la forme varie d'ailleurs selon le type du verbe latin qui a donné naissance au verbe français: *en chantand, en fuyend*, etc. Il prélude ainsi aux extravagances pédantesques qui marqueront l'orthographe du XVIe siècle, et dont maints vestiges ont, hélas, survécu jusqu'à notre époque.

Ce dernier exemple, en raison même, peut-être, de son caractère un peu caricatural, est révélateur. On imagine fort mal, en effet, une telle attitude face aux problèmes grammaticaux ou orthographiques, chez des auteurs des générations antérieures. Nous sommes là en présence, non pas d'une *évolution*, mais d'une véritable *mutation*. On pourrait exprimer cela de façon, certes, simpliste, mais commode, en disant que la Renaissance vient de commencer. Quelques décennies après les Florentins, les Français ont découvert la philologie[11] et, en même temps qu'ils cher-

---

[10] v. G. Ouy, *Un exemple . . .* , (reproduction d'une page de ce ms. p. 41, et extraits pp. 54 et 56).

[11] v. S. Lusignan, o. c., 125: "L'âge de la philologie n'est pas encore arrivé. Il

chent dans les oeuvres de Cicéron ou de Quintilien les moyens de ressusciter le latin antique, ils devinent déjà dans le français le futur substitut d'une langue qui, elle, était encore vivante: ce latin scolastique que, bien avant Rabelais, Pétrarque et ses disciples avaient condamné à mort.

Serge Lusignan, qui s'intéresse principalement aux XIIIe et XIVe siècles, et Gilbert Ouy, qui étudie les humanistes de la période qui suit immédiatement, sont donc situés, en quelque sorte, sur deux versants opposés de la montagne: il n'est guère surprenant, dans ces conditions, qu'ils ne décrivent pas le même paysage.

(G.O.)

Gilbert Ouy souligne avec raison l'importance qu'il faut accorder à l'expérience linguistique du locuteur quant à la distance entre sa langue vernaculaire maternelle et l'utilisation qu'il fait de celle-ci dans des modes scripturaires. L'écriture implique un processus de réflexivité sur la langue[12] dont l'existence est d'ailleurs confirmée par les recherches de Gilbert Ouy sur les manuscrits autographes et les phénomènes (notamment la double orthographe) qu'ils mettent en évidence. Mais encore faut-il déterminer la nature de la réflexivité qui accompagne le geste d'écrire en langue vernaculaire au Moyen Age et les modalité de son expression. La constatation d'une norme de l'écriture justifie implicitement pour nous la recherche du "Petit Robert" ou du "Grévisse" qui l'a inspirée; mais peut-être s'agit-il d'un mode particulier de notre propre rationalité linguistique. Et si pour des expériences linguistiques extérieurement semblables aux nôtres la culture médiévale avait développé des modes de rationalité différents? C'est l'hypothèse que fait Serge Lusignan lorsqu'il avance l'idée que les pratiques de la langue vernaculaire relèvent au Moyen Age du même type de rationalité que celui qui sous-tend l'exercice des métiers ou arts mécaniques. Il s'agirait d'une rationalité qui ne se traduit jamais dans un discours théorique écrit. Cette hypothèse philosophique, qui exclut par principe la possibilité de l'existence de grammaires écrites du français en pays d'oïl aux XIVe et XVe siècles, ne doit toutefois pas se transformer en hypothèse de recherche historique qui détournerait l'historien de fouiller les fonds de manuscrits ou d'archives et de sonder les cartons des vieilles reliures.

---

faudra, pour que cela se produise, que l'attitude change radicalement face à la langue non seulement vernaculaire, mais surtout latine." C'est là en effet tout le problème: l'attitude face à la langue change avec l'apparition de l'Humanisme.

[12] v. S. Lusignan, o. c., 120 sqq.

Stimulé par ces discussions, Serge Lusignan a exploré un autre domaine de l'expérience linguistique médiévale où se manifeste cette tension entre la langue vernaculaire maternelle et son utilisation écrite réfléchie, soit le discours juridique et administratif. Indéniablement, celui-ci provoque le développement d'un registre nouveau de l'expression vernaculaire. Qu'on nous permette de citer pour preuve ce long texte de Philippe de Beaumanoir, datant des années 1280, remarquable par sa clarté tout autant que par sa précocité:

> Li clerc ont une maniere de parler mout bele selonc le latin. Mes li lai qui ont a pledier contre aus en court laie n'entendent pas bien les mos meismes qu'il dient en françois, tout soient il bel et convenable au plet. Et pour ce, de ce qui plus souvent est dit en la court laie et dont plus grans mestiers est, nous traiterons en cest chapitre en tel maniere que li lai le puissent entendre. C'est assavoir des *demandes* qui sont fetes et que l'en puet et doit fere en court laie, lesqueus demandes li clerc apelent *libelles*; et autant vaut "demande" comme "libelle". Et aprés nous traiterons des *defenses* que li defenderes doit metre avant contre celi qui demande, lesqueus defenses li clerc apelent *excepcions*. Et aprés nous traiterons des defenses que cil qui demande met avant pour destruire les defenses que li defenderes met contre sa demande, lesqueus defenses li clerc apelent *replicacions*.[13]

Ce texte rappelle les réflexions sur la nature propre du vocabulaire technique d'une langue, que vont faire, au siècle suivant, les traducteurs d'ouvrages latins savants en français.[14]

Interroger la langue juridique pouvait s'avérer fructueux puisque sa pratique a laissé énormément de traces documentaires. Parmi celles-ci, nous avons examiné un petit corpus de recueils qui se présentent comme des aide-mémoire des notaires de la chancellerie royale ou du Parlement. Ils dérivent d'un modèle latin qui nous est mieux connu puisque son principal représentant, le *Stilus curiae Parlamenti* de Guillaume Du Breuil, existe en édition critique.[15] Ces petits manuscrits, écrits sur papier et visiblement compilés pour un usage personnel, sont en français et datent souvent de la seconde moitié du XVe siècle. De formes très variables, ils peuvent contenir des rappels de points de droit ou de procédure, des

---

[13] Philippe de Beaumanoir, *Coutumes de Beauvaisis*, éd. A. Salmon, t. I (Paris, 1899; réimpr. 1970), ch. 6, par. 196, 98.

[14] v. S. Lusignan, o. c., 151.

[15] Guillaume Du Breuil, *Stilus Curie Parlamenti*, éd. F. Aubert (Paris, 1909).

modèles de lettres administratives, des glossaires bilingues de noms d'évêchés, des styles de Parlement proprement dits, etc. A notre connaissance, ils n'ont jamais fait l'objet d'éditions ni d'études systématiques.[16] Etant donnée la nature de ces recueils, on pourrait penser qu'ils aient contenu des notions d'orthographe ou de grammaire qui rappelaient aux notaires les normes du français qu'ils écrivaient.

Indéniablement, ces recueils attestent que la langue des notaires obéit à une norme:

> Et premierement, le secretaire du roy, quelque autre science qu'il ait, doit avoir et estre principalement fort fondé en grammaire, car s'il n'est bon grammarien, difficile est qu'il sache bien faire et orthographier lettres; et ne doit point signer une lettre que il ne l'ait vue au long et corrigee, si il y a a corriger, tant en langaige que en l'orthographe.[17]

Un autre souligne pour sa part:

> Et doit bien prendre garde le notaire qui les signe que elles soient bien orthographiees car souventes fois on les trouve mal escriptes et mal poinctees.[18]

On sait qu'à partir du XIVe siècle se manifeste le souci de s'assurer d'une façon ou d'une autre de la compétence linguistique des secrétaires et notaires du roi.[19] Un peu plus tard, on voit Nicolas de Clamanges refuser de se joindre à la chancellerie parisienne en invoquant entre autres raisons (ou peut-être comme prétexte) le fait qu'il ne sait pas écrire correctement le français.[20] Il existe assurément un savoir qui régit l'utilisation du français écrit par les notaires royaux.

---

[16] Avec l'aide précieuse d'Alain Nadeau, nous avons dépouillé à la Bibliothèque nationale de Paris les mss. suivants du fonds français: 1937, 2840, 2841, 5277, 5279, 5727, 10814, 14030, 14031, 14032, 14370, 14371, 18110, 18114, 21810, 23051 et Nouv. Acq. fr. 2468.

[17] Paris, B.N. fr. 5727, fol. 19r.

[18] Paris, B.N. fr. 14370, fol. 34r.

[19] v. Octave Morel, *La grande chancellerie royale et l'expédition des lettres royaux* (Paris, 1900), 76 sqq.

[20] ép. XIV (à Jean de Montreuil), ms. original de Montpellier, B.U. H 87, fol. 31: "... dic, si placet, quo sim ydiomate scripurus: latinone an vulgari? Non latino—te puto dicturum—quod a nostris iam gallicis curiis repudiatum est. Si vulgari dixeris, quomodo in eo scribendi genere me dices edoctum, quod necdum attigi?" (cité par Ezio Ornato, *Jean Muret et ses amis Nicolas de Clamanges et Jean de Montreuil* (Genève-Paris, 1969), 68.

Les aide-mémoire des notaires rendent-ils compte de ce savoir? A ce niveau, l'enquête s'avère très décevante. Les manuscrits que nous avons consultés ne contiennent rien qui s'apparente à la littérature didactique du français utilisée en Angleterre à la fin du XIVe et au début du XVe siècles pour la formation des administrateurs.[21] Ils se limitent tous à enseigner l'écriture par des modèles de lettres ou de formulaires: ce sont essentiellement des *artes dictaminis*. Dans quelques cas, très rares, on trouvera une remarque de nature grammaticale; nous reproduisons ici les deux plus intéressantes que nous ayons trouvées:

> Item a huissiers, sergens, prevos, excepté celluy de Paris (...) et a autres telz menuz officiers, [le roy] parle en ses lettres par *tu*. Et a gens conseillers ou de son conseil, a clers d'offices notables, a baillis, senechaulx et *maxime* quant ilz sont chevaliers, le roy parle par vous; et aussi quant la lettre s'adresse a plusieurs....[22]

> Item nota bien que ce mot *faites*, quant il vient du verbe qui se diroit en latin *facite* ou *faciatis*, se doit escripre sans c; mais quant il vient du participe que l'on dit ou latin *factus*, *facta* ou *factum*, l'on y doit mectre ct. Et ainsi de ce mot: *dites*.[23]

Bien évidemment, la présente discussion est loin de clore le débat. Elle nous incite plutôt à poursuivre la confrontation des pratiques manuscrites médiévales dont témoignent d'une part les manuscrits et, d'autre part, les réflexions sur la langue qui émergent çà et là dans les traités les plus divers. Nul doute qu'en s'attachant patiemment à démêler les liens ténus entre la théorie et la pratique de la langue, on devrait parvenir à mieux comprendre comment naquit entre le XIVe et le XVe siècle le français comme langue de savoir et de culture.

(S.L.)

G.O.
C.N.R.S. (Paris)
Equipe de recherche sur la culture écrite du Moyen Age tardif

S.L.
Université de Montréal
Institut d'Etudes médiévales

[21] v. S. Lusignan, o. c., 94 sqq.
[22] Paris, B.N. fr. 1937, fol. 17r.
[23] Paris, B.N. fr. 14370, fol. 7v.

COMMUNICATIONS

A Spinozistic Perspective on the Jephthah Tragedies by George Buchanan (c.1643) and Joost van den Vondel (1659)

FOKKE AKKERMAN

It would appear that of the many dramatic treatments of the Jephthah theme in the sixteenth and seventeenth centuries only Vondel's "treurspel" *Jeptha of offerbelofte* is to all intents an *imitatio* of Buchanan's "tragoedia" *Iephthes sive votum*. That Vondel wanted it to be just that, appears from the title of his drama, which is a literal translation of Buchanan's, from Vondel's praise and criticism of Buchanan's play immediately in the opening section of his theoretical preface, from dozens of lines that have been translated directly by Vondel from the Scotsman's text, and from the whole structure of the play. Vondel borrowed all his main characters from Buchanan; both poets concentrated on the vow and the sacrifice; neither of them has included the negotations between Jephthah and his brothers, or those between Jephthah and the Ammonites, in the dramatic action; neither poet has introduced a lover for the daughter, or thought fit to insert comic scenes to amuse the audience. Both poets had the firm intention to bring an ideal tragedy in the Greek manner on the stage.[1]

I wish to thank my colleague Dr. A. J. Vanderjagt for his kind help in shaping the English of this article.

For more literature than I could give here, see my article "Jefta bij Buchanan en Vondel," *Tijdschrift voor Nederlandse Taal- en Letterkunde* 103, 4 (1987): 270–89; for recent literature on Vondel see Marijke Spies, "Vondel in veelvoud. Het Vondelonderzoek sinds de jaren vijftig," ibid., 235–69; cf. also James A. Parente, *Religious*

In the following I shall try to concentrate on the texts and, consequently, to abstain from remarks on dramatic theory, from theological speculations upon the Jephthah story in the Bible, and from historical observations about the religious beliefs of Buchanan, Vondel and their audiences or readers. It may be useful, however, to point out in advance that there are firmly established biblical keynotes from which no poet in the sixteenth and seventeenth centuries could afford to deviate.
I call attention to four of these:

1. There is no doubt that the Bible looks upon human sacrifice with the greatest revulsion.
2. It is a grave obligation to carry out what has been promised to God.
3. To pronounce a "rash vow" is a sin: a biblical form of *hybris*.
4. Jephthah is one of the great Judges, a saviour of Israël, and must so be regarded as a noble hero.

As a consequence, the tragic tension is already part of the biblical story itself; the poets did not have to invent it.[2] I shall now first characterize Buchanan's tragedy, then Vondel's and, finally, a Spinozistic perspective on both dramas will be outlined.

In Buchanan's *Iephthes* we admire an ingenious balance of language, structure and ideas. Yet this piece of literature is a mixture of highly heterogeneous traditions: a biblical story and a biblical message as Buchanan saw it, a Greek conception of tragedy, a Latin rhetorical-poetical text incorporating a great variety of literary erudition.

The prologue functions in much the same way as in some Euripidean dramas, which offers the poet the opportunity to state the biblical view on the story, i.e., the tenor of the book of Judges, right at the beginning of the play. Thus he can develop its actions and events against this biblical background without admitting any intervention from outside into the actions and decisions of the human characters. More specifically: Jephthah takes his vow and decides to sacrifice his daughter without any divine

Drama and the Humanist Tradition (Leiden, New York, Copenhagen, Cologne, 1987).

[1] The *imitatio*-character of Vondel's *Jeptha* has been argued convincingly by W. A. P. Smit, *Van Pascha tot Noah . . .*, 3 vols. (Zwolle, 1956–62), 2: 240–379. Smit has also shown (2, 248–50) that Vondel was well acquainted with G. J. Vossius, *De imitatione* (1647).

[2] On human sacrifice: Deut. 18:9–10; 12:31; 2 Kings 16:3 etc.; on the obligation to fulfil a vow: Deut. 23:21–33; on rash vows: Eccles. 5:1–6; on Jephthah: 1 Sam. 12:11; Heb. 11:32.

intervention, approval or disapproval. When after the ἀναγνώρισις he tries to justify his vow by referring to the victory that God has accorded him (v. 1164), he gives a personal account of the events, just as the daughter's point of view, *viz.*, that she dies as an expiatory offering for her people, is a noble but strictly human belief.

The mother, Storge, like the other main characters, does not have a consistent, psychologically developed personality. She expresses a limited range of ideas and emotions. Her rôle is very important: she pronounces the first words of the play, after the prologue, and the last ones. In the first and final episodes it is her part to express her love for her daughter and the sorrow caused by the latter's horrible death. In the closing episode the lines regarding her allude to the mother of Christ at the foot of the cross, when the people consecrate her in the words: "feminam unam beatam maxime et miserrimam" (vv. 1441–42): the poet is clearly alluding to the "mater pia, fons amoris." No doubt he chose her Greek name *Storge* deliberately, as a translation of *Pietas*.

The character of the daughter Iphis, too, presents some fluctuations, but towards the end of the play she assumes the traits of the suffering Christ, as later poets, theologians and modern critics have not failed to observe. I presume that Buchanan took her name from the story in Ovid's *Metamorphoses* (11.669–797), in which a girl Iphis is brought up by her mother disguised as a boy; but when her father is about to marry her off to a girl, she is changed into a boy by the goddess Isis in the nick of time. I take it that Buchanan wanted to refer to this story precisely on this account. Twice Iphis's "animus virilis" (vv. 1333, 1410) is praised; she is called a "virago" (v. 1395); in connection with Iphis, the last choral ode makes an allusion to Joan of Arc, who, as Walsh has observed, put on men's clothing before being put to the stake.[3] Before and after Buchanan, scholars and poets liked to view the story of Jephthah and his daughter as a prefiguration of the expiatory sacrifice of Christ (Jephthah [= Christ] offering his earthly life [= his daughter]),[4] but in Buchanan's play, so it

[3] P. G. Walsh, "Buchanan and Classical Drama," in *Acta Conventus Neo-Latini Sanctandreani*, ed. I. D. McFarlane. Medieval & Renaissance Text & Studies, vol. 38 (Binghamton, NY, 1986), 109. For other points of reference of the name *Iphis*, see Walsh, 104.

[4] See J. H. McGregor, "The sense of tragedy in George Buchanan's Jephthes," *Humanistica Lovaniensia* 31 (1982): 120–40, esp. 132, 134. From a poetical point of view it makes a great difference whether the poet alludes to the Sacrifice of Christ within the drama itself, making it thus in some degree allegorical, as Buchanan has done, or in a dedicatory poem only, as is the case in Vondel's *Jeptha*.

seems, we witness a kind of disconnection between father and daughter. In his drama these two characters are human beings in their own right, one of whom, Iphis, finds herself eventually playing the part of the Redeemer, whereas the other, Jephthah, must fulfil the rôle of the tragic hero in the Greek sense of the term. To realize this cast, the poet deemed it necessary for Iphis to undergo first, as it were, a transsexual metamorphosis.

Jephthah is a noble hero, who has made an error by taking the vow, his ἁμαρτία, who then clings obstinately to his conviction that he must carry out what he has promised, i.e., his ἄτη, and so goes to ruin. Jephthah's ἄτη, his blindness, comes out clearest in the longest and central episode of the play: the debate with the *sacerdos*. Like the rest, this piece is very well organized: Jephthah speaks the first and the final words, but it is the priest who holds the floor: 158 lines against 56 for Jephthah. The episode has five parts, each of which contains a specific argument. In the first we are confronted with the problem of man's freedom to refrain from sinning, or rather with the lack of freedom to commit gruesome deeds such as Jephthah is about to commit, deeds forbidden by natural law, by true piety and by God the Father. The second part contains an *altercatio* between the priest and Jephthah on the question whether vows and sacrifices are permitted, or even obligatory. Jephthah upholds an ethics based on intentions: good intentions are to express themselves in a strict observation of the letter of biblical precepts and examples. In the third section the *sacerdos* unfolds a view of the Bible as a moral law which serves as a guideline for our decisions ("a lamp to my feet", Psalms 119:105). But it is a law that will on no account grant a licence for cruelty, stupidity and error, which may come in the wake of human ordinances. In the fourth division Jephthah's attitude and problem are placed in the socio-political context of ignorant people that flatter tyrants and extol their crimes. One feature of this ignorance is to cling blindly to a dogma once it has been adopted. The fifth part is a peroration, in which both points of view are summed up. The priest contends: "You [he employs the plural *vos*!] close your eyes to the light of truth [lumen veritatis] and try to win a reputation from your crimes with resounding slogans; moral laws are of the same kind as natural laws; they cannot be changed by men." And Jephthah "prefers the absurd and simple truth to specious but godless wisdom."

I venture to suggest that we should regard the viewpoint and arguments presented by the priest as those of Buchanan himself. They contain in a nutshell a modern biblical-humanistic ethics with strong Erasmian accents, which also has much in common with protestant views then in vogue.[5] In

[5] By Erasmian accents I mean a strong aversion to formalistic dogmatism and

this way Jephthah becomes a tragic hero, who adopts a wrong attitude prompted by foolish emotions,[6] which are ultimately determined by the religious fanaticism of the age, and who is eventually ready for his ghastly deed. This attitude and this political context represent, as it were, the necessity, the ἀνάγκη, that often fetters heroes of Greek tragedy. In the debate with the priest the rôle of Jephthah is not unlike that of Creon in Sophocles' *Antigone*. And the tragedy of Jephthah's fate is transcended by the sadness implied in Buchanan's message: the sadness of a more rationalistic biblical-humanistic ethics, which is aware of it's own weak position in sixteenth century society.

The drama as a whole, then, is not built up from the units of individual characters confronted with realistic situations or problems. It is rather an ongoing debate between emotions and ideas, each of which is embodied in a particular character or the chorus, in a particular episode or an ode.[7]

§ § §

When we turn from the neo-classical Latin schooldrama of Buchanan to Vondel's Dutch play for the public theater, the transition is almost a cultural shock. A simple enumeration of the most important differences in the treatment of the subject matter may be of some help for a better understanding of both tragedies:

1. Vondel's drama does not consist of episodes and choral odes but of

---

ritualism ("not the letter but the spirit"), and a line of reasoning by means of rhetorical commonplaces. It has been a persistent misapprehension to regard the position of the priest as one that has to be judged negatively, e.g., as a kind of caricature of the shallow scholasticism of the Sorbonne, and to recognize true religious depth in the stand of Jephthah; so for example R. Lebègue, *La tragédie religieuse en France* (Paris, 1929), 232 and Smit, op. cit., 2:269. Prof. Walsh agreed with me (orally at the Toronto congress; cf. also his article cited in n. 3, 107–8) that Buchanan stands behind the words of the priest, but as his sources he gives St. Thomas Aquinas, St. Jerome and the Old Testament. Cf. also P. Sharrat in *George Buchanan Tragedies*, eds. P. Sharrat and P. G. Walsh (Edinburgh, 1983), Introduction, pp. 10–20). Prof. W. Nijenhuis (University of Groningen) at my request kindly read the debate of Jephthah and the priest in Buchanan. His comment on my suggestion of Erasmianism was: "The words of the priest, though rather flat, fit in the climate of Erasmian humanism. Jephthah, too, is superficial. The debate is a skirmish of two moralists lacking real depth."

[6] Perhaps the *adfectibus stultis* of vv. 931–32 as opposed to the *adfectos sacros* of v. 872 is an echo of the then modern doctrine of good and bad emotions, as put forward by Vives (*De anima et vita*, 1538) and Melanchthon (*De anima*, 1540).

[7] I found particularly useful R. Griffiths, *The Dramatic Technique of Antoine de Montchrestien: Rhetoric and Style in French Renaissance Tragedy* (Oxford, 1970).

five acts, each concluded by a lyric sung by a *rey*. This change has great consequences, as it diminishes the number of structural units from the 14 of Buchanan's *Iephthes* (prologue, 7 episodes and 6 choral odes) to 5 in Vondel (for the *reyen* are more closely linked to the preceding acts than the odes in Buchanan to the preceding episodes). In this way the attention shifts from the thoughts, emotions and narratives which form the contents of Buchanan's episodes and odes to the characters and their mental states which are central in Vondel's acts. To illustrate this shift one instance may suffice: in the first act of Vondel's *Jeptha*, the "Slotvoogd," a kind of *major domus* intimately connected with Jephthah and his wife, arrives as a messenger from the Judge to report to his wife the victory gained by her husband. The spouse reacts to the report and so remains the central figure of the act. Buchanan had the victory reported to the *chorus* by an abstract *nuntius*. In his treatment the narrative coincides with the episode.

2. Vondel's *Jeptha* has no prologue, which means that the external biblical perspective on the dramatic events is lacking. In this way the play loses the nature of a biblical message, which, on the other hand, it certainly had in Buchanan's concept. One can even doubt whether the *Jeptha* is a biblical drama at all. Vondel, at any rate, in this case took his subject matter not from the Bible but from the Scots humanist's text.

3. The sparing commonplace character of Buchanan's text,–i.e., its typical Latin style, is in Vondel dissolved into a profuse, rich poetry that in transformation loses a great deal of its dialectical force.

4. Vondel's narrative of events is crammed with realistic details unthinkable in Buchanan. Owing to these last two distinctions Vondel's *Jeptha* is much longer than Buchanan's *Iephthes*: 1978 against 1450 verses.

5. Vondel's characters have ceased to function as allegorical references and have lost their inconsistency; in Buchanan's play these aspects were created by the varying affects and thoughts of the cast. In Vondel, however, they are no longer pieces on the rhetorical-allegorical chessboard. His drama is centred *in* the characters themselves.

6. The ethical and religious thesis of Buchanan's play,–i.e., its topical political meaning–is missing altogether. Vondel's drama is about individual men and their acts.

7. The most striking change Buchanan's play underwent in Vondel's *imitatio* appears in the plot. Vondel has restored the two-months' delay of the biblical story, which had been requested by the daughter and granted her to bewail her virginity in the mountains. The play commences just before dawn as this period draws to its close. In these two months Jephthah has fought and won a second battle, this time against the Ephraimites (Judges 12:1–6). The mother fills up the entire first act. She is awaiting the

return of her daughter and her husband, but she is unaware of the sacrifice arranged for by Jephthah and Iphis. Towards the end of the act she goes offstage to return only in the final act, when the sacrifice has been carried out and Jephthah has departed to Silo to reconcile himself with God and the archpriest. Thus there is in the entire play not a single encounter of husband and wife nor of mother and daughter.

In his preface Vondel has circumstantially justified this modification of the intrigue. He blames Buchanan mostly for leaving the two-months' delay of the sacrifice out of his *Iephthes*. He does so expressly on the authority of the poetics of Heinsius and Vossius. This somewhat formalistic objection to Buchanan's treatment of the biblical story is of course inspired by the unity of time at stake here.[8] Yet Vondel gladly adopted the other poetic licences Buchanan had allowed himself; in many respects he himself went much further. I think we should not let ourselves be misled by these poetical or rather theological explanations on Vondel's part. What he has changed in comparison with Buchanan's concept, he cannot account for himself in terms of contemporary poetics or theology. His characters are the bearers of an emotionality that differs vastly from that of Buchanan's *dramatis personae*. Besides, he has filled in Buchanan's abstract scheme with so many details that he creates a realistic context in which a confrontation between husband and wife to discuss the sacrifice of their daughter becomes downright inconceivable.[9] Elsewhere in his preface Vondel betrays the emotional changes that are at the back of his reshuffling of the intrigue. He writes: "This history also offers the true nature of tragedy; the difficulty and floundering do not take place simply between ordinary or distant relatives, but between next of kin, between father, mother and daughter (an only daughter) and husband and wife." Vondel had strong opinions about matrimonial love, which he sees as the terrestrial reflection of a cosmic force.[10] His characters in *Jeptha* have

---

[8] D. Heinsius, *De tragoediae constitutione liber* (ed. Lugd. Bat., 1643), chap. 17, p. 204: "In periodo autem Dramatis nos ipse [Buchanan] ludit. ad minimum enim mensium duorum est. Duos enim deplorandam fuisse virginitatem, quis nescit?" The same objection in G. J. Vossius, *Poeticarum institutionum libri tres* (ed. Amsterdam, 1647) I, II, III, 2, p. 13.

[9] Because of the foreseeable reaction of the mother any encounter between her and Jephthah or Iphis is avoided at great pains by the environment; see vv. 785–98; 1290–1326; 1897–1908. The actual reaction in vv. 1833–1882 is of a "cutting explosive force and primitivism" in the words of J.G. Bomhoff as quoted by Smit, op. cit. 2: 352.

[10] Cf. K. Langvik Johannessen, "Het huwelijk in Vondels drama," in *Visies op Vondel na 300 jaar*, eds. S. F. Witstein and E. K. Grootes (Den Haag, 1979), 289–305.

drifted far apart; they embody totally different attitudes in life. His Jephthah is a haughty, high-handed zealot, who "suffered from an Abraham complex," as Parente has put it aptly.[11] But this may well be a modern reaction to the character. Vondel may have meant him to be a man of unflinching fidelity to his beliefs, who might even deserve some admiration, though he goes to ruin through his blind one-sidedness. Nevertheless, he is a man of quickly changing emotions: determination alternates with despair, self-pity, self-accusation, sheer arrogance, stupidity, remorse. Ultimately he becomes reconciled with God. Buchanan's hero was still in some way protected by the traditional dogmas and opinions of his society. Vondel's Jephthah acts solely from his own conscience.[12] The *sacerdos* in the fifth episode of Buchanan's play is a humanist of Erasmian stamp, who makes a lonely stand against the superstitions of his age. The two priests in the third act of Vondel's drama represent the common sense of ecclesiastical authority. Their main argument is: "Thou shalt not kill." The mother—her name in Vondel's play is Filopaie, a pseudo-Greek word that he coined himself[13]—embodies the strong maternal love of an independent, rich Amsterdam matron rather than being a rhetorical abstraction of love and sorrow. Iphis hardly participates in the action. From her first radiant appearance in the lyric concluding the first act she is and remains angelically pure, innocent and obedient, rejoicing in the coming sacrifice. There is a marked sexist atmosphere around her and no question of any change in her attitude as there was in the models of Buchanan and Euripides.

Vondel's *Jeptha* was a succesful play.[14] It centers around a real dilemma, it shows characters rich in contrast and of diverse emotions; the plot is ingeniously built, the whole story thrilling, the poetry splendid. Of all the Jephthah plays in the sixteenth and seventeenth centuries it is by far the most lively piece of literature. But I think that too much has been made of its religious or moral depth. Of course, there is no denying the moral lesson as voiced by the "Hofpriester" in the play (vv. 1956–1978): the conflict between individual conscience and church authority was certainly of real significance to Vondel and his audience or readers. But to the extent that the theme (the vow and the sacrifice) is losing its obvious-

---

[11] Parente, op. cit., 150.

[12] On "conscience" ("geweten") see vv. 948; 1087–88; 1121–31; 1319; cf. n. 19.

[13] No doubt because of Heinsius's criticism of the name Storge (op. cit., 205). Heinsius did not see through Buchanan's significant names.

[14] From its first staging on November 24th, 1659, the *Jeptha* saw eleven performances in the years 1659–63; see E. Oey-De Vita and M. Geesink, *Academie en Schouwburg, Amsterdams Toneelrepertoire 1617–1665* (Amsterdam, 1983), 136–45.

ness as a suitable subject for rhetorical drama, Vondel's tragedy assumes melodramatic features. The dilemma of its hero may be real, but Jephthah fails to win our sympathetic understanding, perhaps because we have too much sympathy for the reactions of his environment (Filopaie, Iphis, the priests). And, on the other hand, the poet does not allow us to take sides against his protagonist for other reasons than the sacrifice, as we do in the case of Euripides' *Iphigenia in Aulis* against Agamemnon, or, at least in the fifth episode, against Buchanan's Jephthah. The natural coincidence of subject matter and topical meaning as it is seen in Buchanan's *Iephthes*, has gone lost in Vondel. Neither in his preface, which is entirely devoted to the writing of tragedy, nor in the play itself do any original religious or philosophical insights appear. Above all Vondel was ambitiously intent on constructing an ideal tragedy according to all poetical precepts he could lay hands on.[15] He wanted the play to serve as a model for future generations of poets. In this respect too he was trying to supplant Buchanan's *Iephthes*. But in the actual result of his efforts there is also much of the popular drama: emotional outbursts, sensation, sex and violence. For the lasting succes of his art Vondel depended on large and mixed audiences. As a newspaper critic phrases it: "Vondel certainly wanted to edify the people, but at the same time mother needed her due share of crying."[16]

---

[15] In his preface Vondel mentions first Aristotle, then Vossius, quoting an oral communication concerning Buchanan's trespassing upon the Bible, Aristotle again, next Ronsard on the use of "vers commun" (*Préface de Franciade*, 1587). Finally, he enumerates the authors on poetics he has read and reread: Aristotle, Horace and their interpreters and commentators: Robertellus (Francesco Robortello, 1516–67: *In librum Aristotelis de arte poetica explicationes*, 1548); Madius, Lombardus (Vincenzo Maggi, died probably in 1564, and Bartolommeo Lombardi: *In Aristotelis librum de poetica communes explicationes*, containing also an *in Horatii librum de arte poetica interpretatio*, 1550); Scaliger (Julius Caesar Scaliger, 1484–1558: *Poetices libri septem*, 1561); Heinsius (Daniel Heinsius, 1580–1655: *De tragoediae constitutione*, 1611); Huigh de Groot (Hugo Grotius, 1583–1645: Preface to his translation of Euripides' *Phoenissae*, 1630); Castelvetro (Ludovico Castelvetro, 1505–71: *Poetica d'Aristotele vulgarizzata et sposta*, 1570); Delrius (Martinus Antonius Delrio, 1551–1608: *Syntagma tragoediae latinae*, 1593–94); Strada (Famiano Strada, 1572–1649: *Prolusiones Academicae*, 1627); Vossius (Gerardus Joannes Vossius, 1577–1649: *Poeticae Institutiones*, 1647); Menardieres (Hippolyte-Jules Pilet de la Mesnardières, 1610–63: *Poétique*, 1639). Vondel also mentions the composer Orlando di Lasso (1532–94) to indicate the level of competence needed for the director of choir and musicians.

[16] Jac Heijer in NRC-Handelsblad of 23. Dec. 1988.

Spinoza (1632–1677) was a contemporary and fellow townsman of Vondel (1587–1679). They must have known each other. We know that Spinoza took a keen interest in the theater. Studying the Bible was one of his main intellectual occupations during the 50s and 60s. It is hardly conceivable that he should never have attended the performance of one of Vondel's biblical plays. But could he connect them with his own philosophy? Spinoza was a rationalist; in his understanding of man he was heir to the Aristotelian-Stoic doctrine of the emotions. With their neat oppositions of *affectus*, *mores* and *conditiones* the comedies of Terence appealed to his taste. He quotes often from them. Spinoza's doctrine of the emotions in Parts III and IV of his *Ethics* looks like a philosophical counterpart to the tragedies of Racine, who in this respect certainly continued the conception of drama that was inaugurated in France by Buchanan. The baroque and popular breakthrough of Vondel's drama must have remained alien to the philosopher. In the last resort Spinoza was a political thinker, Vondel was not. Vondel translated his humanist models and the Bible directly into sentiment and grandiose religious and moral concepts, into fine poetry and great drama. Spinoza devoted himself to painstaking historical and philological research in the sacred texts in order to retrieve their "true sense." For these reasons I think that Vondel and Spinoza remained intellectually foreign to each other. In their time and work a dissociation has taken place between dramatic conceptualization and dramatic characterization on the one hand and rational philosophy on the other, a cleft not yet there in the work of Buchanan.

In the viewpoint of Buchanan's *sacerdos* as opposed to that of Jephthah we observe fundamentally the same difference of opinion that exists between Spinoza and the theologians of his days. The doctrine that obedience to simple moral law is the essential message of the Bible, and that this moral law has the same status as the law of nature, occurs in both. The political context in which this law operates is of crucial importance for both the poet's and the philosopher's point of view. They also share the conviction that man's actions and beliefs are ultimately psychologically determined, directly or through the community in which they live.

One might ask whether a concept of tragedy is at all conceivable in the rigid deterministic system of Spinoza. He does not acknowledge a personal God as the ultimate foundation of morality, he does not believe in fate or chance. Everything that is or happens results from causes with inevitable necessity. "He who goes mad from the bite of a dog is, indeed, to be excused, and yet is rightly suffocated."[17] The lives of individuals and communities are determined just as irreversibly as is the weather. But this is a scientific truth, not a moral one. We have but a very incomplete insight into causes and consequences, so that every step we take hovers between hope and fear; morally this is freedom. From Spinoza's point of view Jephthah has said too much in fright and fear: he was unable to check his tongue, he was guided by wrong emotions. In taking the vow he was the victim of his passions, in fulfilling it of superstition. He has to tackle the dilemma whether or not to sacrifice his daughter. But is he really free in his choice? Jephthah had been taught that it is essential to carry out wat one has promised God, so he is unwavering in his loyalty. The priest in Buchanan's play confronts him with a wiser point of view: he has committed a sin and he cannot undo it by perpetrating a crime. So, we could add, he has to remain in a state of sin from which only God can save him.[18] But this thought Jephthah cannot endure.

The man bitten by a mad dog suffers innocently but he is not in a tragic situation. In Spinoza's way of thinking it could be called tragedy, when a man is steered by emotions, which are partly anchored in collective beliefs and superstitions, and then, by adhering to his principles with fidelity and tenacity, causes his own and other people's ruin. The concept of an individual conscience as an incentive to action is conspicuously absent from Spinoza's philosophy; he knows only a guilty conscience (remorse, *conscientiae morsus*) which he condemns as "animi impotentis ... signum."[19] Tragic man rouses pity and sympathy, even if we reject his deeds and beliefs. In this sense Vondel's Jephthah is hardly a good tragic hero. But in this sense there is, I believe, a Spinozistic conception of tragedy. It is represented, for example, in the story of Juda el Fido, the Spanish nobleman who went over to the Jewish faith as a consequence of his Hebrew studies. Condemned to death by the Inquisition, he was burned at the stake at Valladolid in 1644. In the midst of the flames he began to sing the hymn of Psalm 31: "To thee, O God, I commit my

---

[17] Spinoza in *Ep.* 78, trans. A. Wolf, 1966.

[18] This last consequence is not drawn by Buchanan; it is of course wholly outside Spinoza's doctrine. But it is in Vondel, cf. v. 1031.

[19] Spinoza, *Ethica* IV, prop. 47, schol. For various meanings of "conscience" in the Renaissance, see Peggy Muñoz Simonds, "Some Images of the Conscience in Emblem Literature" in *Acta conventus Neo-Latini Guelpherbytani.* Proceedings of the Sixth International Congress of Neo-Latin Studies, eds. Stella P. Revard, Fidel Rädle, Mario A. Di Cesare. Medieval & Renaissance Texts & Studies, vol. 53 (Binghamton, NY, 1988), 315–30.

soul," and died in the middle of the hymn.[20] Spinoza had come to reject as *superstitio* the faith Juda el Fido had newly embraced, but at the same time he felt admiration and pity for the victim of this faith and also for the collective fate of the Jewish people.[21] I think that something like this is at the back of Buchanan's ideas. If so, this illustrates that Spinoza's thinking is not the philosopher's stone suddenly fallen from heaven in the seventeenth century. It is a link in a long chain of moral and religious thought. The Greek conception of tragedy has given this thought a new dimension.

Allow me in conclusion to quote a passage from Spinoza expressing some disdain for scenic plays: "Anyone who has read the stories of Holy Writ, but has not paid attention to the lesson they are consigned to convey or mended his ways, might as well have read the Koran or the poetic dramas (poetarum fabulas scenicas)."[22] Was Vondel here in Spinoza's mind? Vondel is a post-humanist poet, who in breaking away from the neo-classical drama which he imitates stands almost at the threshold of the romantic age. Spinoza holds political and religious beliefs which are far ahead of his times. Both are deeply indebted to the long traditions of antiquity and humanism. But they are irrevocably separated from each other in thinking and writing.

University of Groningen

[20] Spinoza, *Ep.* 76, trans. A. Wolf.

[21] Spinoza, *Tract. theol.-pol.*, chap. 17 (ed. C. Gebhardt, 1925, vol. 3, p. 215, lines 16–31).

[22] Spinoza, op. cit., chap. 5 (ed. Gebh., p. 79, lines 16–21), trans. A. G. Wernham, 1958.

Learned Scandinavian Women in the 17th and 18th Centuries

MARIANNE ALENIUS

Sources

Learned women are a borderline phenomenon between Latin and the vernacular. We know them from two sources. Partly from texts about them, and partly from their own works. The texts about them are primarily in Latin, but their own works are, for the most part, written in the vernacular. In order to study them, it is consistently necessary to alternate between Neo-Latin texts and texts in the modern national languages.

In European scholarship outside Scandinavia there is a wealth of literature which can provide inspiration as to the material which exists on learned women.[1] In Scandinavia very little research has been undertaken on learned women, primarily published in the Scandinavian languages.

Thus, the purpose of this paper is first of all to point out that this

---

[1] Interesting examples from the European Renaissance in Northern Italy are found in: *Beyond Their Sex. Learned Women of the European Past*, ed. Patricia Labalme (New York, 1980). Mid- and Western Europe are well documented in *Female Scholars. A Tradition of Learned Women before 1800*, ed. J. R. Brink (Montreal: Eden Press, Women's Publications, 1980), whereas in Jean M. Woods and Maria Fürstenwald's *Schriftstellerinnen, Künstlerinnen und Gelehrte Frauen des Deutschen Barock* (Stuttgart, 1984), and *Res Publica Litteraria. Die Institution der Gelehrsamkeit in der frühen Neuzeit*, ed. Neumeister, S. and C. Wiedemann (Teil II, 6: "Die gelehrte Frau im 17. Jahrhundert"), Wolfenbüttler Arbeiten zur Barockforschung, Band 14. (Wiesbaden, 1987), we find an overview of the situation regarding our immediate neighbors in Germany. More disappointing from our point of view is Roland H. Bainton, *Women of the Reformation*, vol. 3 (Minneapolis, 1977), "From Spain to Scandinavia," in which only 5 Scandinavian women are mentioned, of whom none were particularly learned.

cultural phenomenon of the European Renaissance, learned women, existed and was known and described, also in Scandinavia, during the period up to around 1800, secondly to have a look at what the learned women of Scandinavia accomplished, and finally, to present examples from a discussion carried out in Latin, from the beginning of the 18th century, concerning the way in which a learned woman was to be defined.

Within Scandinavia we have knowledge of about 150 learned women. The majority of these, about 110, are Danish; about 20 Norwegian; and about 25 Swedish; none as yet from Iceland and Finland. For the most part, men were the ones who wrote about these women. This is true both in Scandinavia and in the rest of Europe. Perhaps this has something to do with the fact that women were clearly expected to conduct themselves in a humble and modest fashion.

A "gynæceum" is a literary genre within the history of learning: a rational panegyric catalog of women and their intellectual pursuits. Where Denmark is concerned, I am familiar with seven works in this genre, written during the period from around 1650 to 1800. Four of them are written in Danish, whereas three are in Latin.[2] One of the Danish works, "Hæltinners Pryd" (The Adornment of Heroines), is written by a woman, Leonora Christine Ulfeldt (the daughter of King Christian IV), who is to be numbered among the learned women herself. To my knowledge, her gynæceum is the only one in Europe written by a woman.[3]

The largest printed Latin gynæceum we have is Albert Thura's "Gynæceum Daniæ litteratum," which was published in Altona in 1732. Albert Thura has collected a total of 100 women, a number he is extremely proud of. He has placed several surplus women in an appendix, among others a few medieval Icelandic women, and in his preface he provides a separate catalog of female patrons of the arts. Their gifts are often very modest, but it is the thought that counts when a woman, for example, sets

---

[2] The Latin gynæcea are: a) Otto Sperling the younger (1634–1715), *De foeminis doctis*. MS in The Royal Library, Copenhagen (Gl. kgl. Saml. 2110 a–b in quarto); b) Matthias Henriksen Schacht (1660–1700), "Schediasma, exhibens specimen de Eruditis Mulieribus Daniae," in *Nova Literaria Maris Balthici et Septentrionis* (Lübeck, 1700), 209–19; c) Albert Thura (1700–40), *Gynaeceum Daniae Litteratum*, Altona 1732. Cf. M. Alenius, "Skrifter om lærde danske kvinder," in *Litteratur og lærdom*. Renæssancestudier bind 1 (Copenhagen: Museum Tusculanum Press, 1987), 35–48.

[3] Leonora Christina, *Hæltinners Pryd*, ed. Christopher Maaløe (Copenhagen: Det Danske Sprog- og Litteraturselskab, 1977). Only a fourth of the original work has been preserved. A portion of it was written while Leonora Christina Ulfeldt (1621–98) was serving a 22-year prison sentence in Copenhagen. Here she was in contact with the gynæceum author Otto Sperling.

up a fund for the yearly distribution of paper and pens to a needy pupil.

After Thura there were two simliar works in the Danish language. The first of these, by Frederik Christian Schønau, is by far the most interesting within the history of scholarship. It appeared in 1753.[4] Like Thura, Schønau has 100 women. In order to make room for twenty-three new entries, he must sacrifice some of Thura's. His preface provides a thorough introduction to the European gynæceum genre.

The last gynæceum also appeared in Danish, in 1793–1795.[5] The author, H. J. Birch, only provides nine new Danes, reducing the remaining corpus drastically, not because those who are rejected are not learned, but because he is more interested in faithful wives than in unmarried female scholars.

From Sweden we have an academic dissertation on philosophical women: Johan Esberg's "Exercitium Academicum Mulieres Philosophantes adumbrans," defended in Upsala in 1699. "Mulieres philosophantes" is not a gynæceum, but a Latin treatise which takes it point of departure in women who were interested in philosophy in Greco-Roman antiquity. No Latin gynæcea are extant, but we know the title of a single work which may have been written in Latin, parts of which seem to be preserved in an article in "Stockholms Magasin för 1780" where 23 learned Swedish women are listed.[6]

Influence from Southern Europe on the Scandinavian gynæcea is extremely obvious. The prefaces to these works clearly show that the authors are aware of the fact that they are writing within an existing tradition. Competition also belongs to this tradition. The national pride found in the Danish works is no less than that found in the remaining European works. What counts is having as great a number of learned women as possible.

The fact that we have relatively numerous and detailed works on the

---

[4] Frederik Christian Schønau (1728–72), *Lærde danske Fruentimmer* (Copenhagen, 1753).

[5] Hans Jørgen Birch (1750–95), *Billedgallerie for Fruentimmer indeholdende Levnetsbeskrivelser over berømte og lærde danske, norske og udenlandske Fruentimmere* (Copenhagen, 1793–95).

[6] The article in Stockholms Magasin, edited by Magnus Swederus, April 1780, pp. 207–22, and May 1780, pp. 247–54, is anonymous. In a short preface the author refers to an unpublished work "Gynæceum Sveciæ Litteratum, eller Afhandling om lärda Swenska Fruentimmer" which may have been in Latin. The original manuscript is now lost. Dr. Eva Haettner Olafsson and Mag. Valborg Lindgärde have drawn my attention to this article referring also to another Swedish Gynæceum listing women from the whole world: "Försök til en Historia öfwer Namnkunniga, Men i synnerhet Lärda Fruentimmer, författad af Carl P. Westrin," Stockholm 1793.

learned women–as well as so many learned women!–is no doubt due primarily to Otto Sperling (1634–1715). His work is from the decades around 1700. It was in Latin, and even though it was never published, it became known in wide circles both inside Denmark and abroad.

Otto Sperling The Younger's "De foeminis doctis" is found today in a manuscript in The Royal Library in Copenhagen. Sperling began as a lawyer but was far more interested in humanistic studies, which he cultivated with emphasis on ancient literature, history, and numismatics.[7] During the years between 1681 and 1683 Sperling was associated with Colbert's library in Paris and later lived in Hamburg for several years. One of Sperling's goals in life was to collect information on the learned women of the entire world. At his death his collection consisted of 1399 biographies of women written in Latin.

His collection of information on learned women extended over several decades, and his plan was to complete the work for publication around 1700. The lack of a publisher and resources–and perhaps the lack of ability to turn a collection into a finished work–most probably explains why he did not succeed in preparing his work for publication prior to his death. But the inspiration derived from Otto Sperling is clearly that which gave rise to most of the remaining Danish gynæcea.

In Sperling's Latin correspondence we find a number of letters to and from men which deal with the learned woman and which reveal the method he used to establish his collection. In addition he had an extremely unusual talent and desire for encouraging the women he was in contact with to write. This is also evident in his correspondence, where there are more letters to and from women than I have found with any other person from the seventeenth and eighteenth centuries in Scandinavia.[8] Several autobiographical accounts in Latin by Scandinavian women are of particular interest. The finest example of such correspondence is that between Otto Sperling and the learned Swedish woman, Sophia Elisabeth Brenner. It consists of a little over 25 letters in Latin.

In addition to the gynæcea, we have the women's own works. The material is extensive, but rarely in Latin. From the women in the seventeenth century we have in particular: literature on Christian upbringing,

---

[7] M. Alenius, "Love at first [W]ink. A Fragment of Otto Sperling's Neolatin correspondence," in *A Litterary Miscellany Presented to Eric Jacobsen*, ed. Graham D. Caie and Holger Nørgaard (Copenhagen, Publications of the Department of English, University of Copenhagen, vol. 16, 1988), 164–84.

[8] Sperling's letters to women are listed op. cit. pp. 168–69. Letters from women pp. 170–72.

psalms, translations of theological tracts, moral treatises and prayer books from German and French into Danish. Outside the Christian literature we find occasional poetry and genealogies. And finally, there are rarities like a novel, an autobiography, a polyglot collection of poetry, a tragedy, and a treatise on moral philosophy. From the eighteenth century the number of genres becomes more varied and less bound to religion, and we find comedies, letters, epistolary novels, diaries, autobiographies, cookbooks, and experiments with small poems in new reworkings of the European genres: Anacreontic poetry, heroids, etc.

The women whom we know were familiar with Latin seem to have shown very little interest in writing in Latin. They used their knowledge to read and learn and to teach. In their own poems, several of them have also drawn inspiration and motifs from the classical authors. In two instances we know that they used them for translations. In the 1670s, Anna Margrethe Quitzow translated the first three books of Caesar's Gallic Wars. Her translation was never published, however. And from the hand of our most learned woman, Birgitte Thott, we have a translation of Seneca.

Birgitte Thott

Instead of listing the names of a number of our most famous women, I will single out one individual, not a typical one, but a worthy representative of the Scandinavian learned women—the Danish noblewoman, Birgitte Thott, who lived from 1610 to 1662.[9] Her major work stems from her period as a childless widow: a translation of Seneca's *Philosophus*, printed in 1658. Already at the time of her youth she was referred to as a budding Danish Anna Maria van Schurman. The first of the book's introductory Latin panegyric poems is, in fact, written by Anna Maria van Schurman. Here she refers to her Danish colleague as the tenth Muse of the North. Birgitte Thott's Seneca translation was the first complete translation of a classical author into Danish and aroused great interest, not least because it was a work of literary prose written in the vernacular.[10] Prose literature was almost non-existent in Danish at this time, and if authors of

[9] Cf. M. Alenius, "Seneca-oversætteren Birgitte Thott—et fagligt portræt," in *Danske Studier* 1983, ed. I. Kjær and Fl. Lundgreen-Nielsen, (Copenhagen, Akademisk Forlag, 1983), 5-46. In this there is a bibliography of Birgitte Thott's works.

[10] The translation does not include Seneca's Tragedies and *Apocolocynthosis*.

literature or esthetics expressed themselves in the vernacular it was in the form of poetic texts.

Birgitte Thott's huge manuscript "Om et lyksaligt liv" ("On a Blissful Life"), comprising 200 folio leaves, is unique.[11] It is written in Danish, with 50 chapters. The work is filled to the brim with references to the founding fathers of the church, the moral philosophers and not least the antique philosophers. Birgitte Thott harvests from the classical literature while simultaneously weaving in local material. In this respect it is a typical piece of Renaissance literature and could easily have been written in Latin. Seen from the point of view of Danish national literatur, however, it is atypical. Denmark has a wealth of small educational works based on the Bible, but a "De vita beata," which unites Christianity and stoicism as this one does, as if it were written by Justus Lipsius, is not known otherwise.

Birgitte Thott's intention is to educate the individual person with regard to moral responsibility in relation to one's self and to others. But it is not only the individual as such that is to be educated and to be given support by Cicero and Aristotle. Birgitte Thott has a particular social group in mind: the women. To this end she draws support from Plutarch and Seneca. Under the protection of these two knights she marches forward as the first advocate of women's rights in Scandinavia. Quite unexpectedly, amidst the regular basic questions of a philosophical nature, she smuggles in two chapters (chapters 45 and 46) "on the use of studies" and on "how correct utilization of studies is beneficial and by no means detrimental to women." She agitates for the woman's right to study and for the good influence of studies on the individual who desires to attain to virtue. Like the Spanish humanist Juan Luis Vives and like Schurman, she stresses the fact that studies cannot be detrimental to women, and like them, she does not demand political rights for women. She is interested in the woman's right to have access to knowledge. She rejects arguments to the effect that women are not good at learning and shows how the two sexes are treated differently already in their upbringing as children. She points out that while the girls were kept to their household chores and advised against wasting their time on books, the boys were dragged off to instruction, whether they wanted to be or not. The preface to her Seneca translation is even dedicated to women. Here she points out that it is

[11] The work is unpublished. The original has been lost, presumably burned in the Sorø Academy fire in 1832 together with other works and her correspondence. Two extant copies, almost contemporary, are found in Karen Brahes Bibliotek in Landsarkivet for Fyn, Denmark (A VI, 19 and A VI, 20).

characteristic that the literature that can teach you something and that helps you to become a better person is written in Latin. But precisely Latin lies outside the scope of the majority of women. Thus, she notes that it is not least in order to get women to see what they are missing out on without Latin that she translates such a morally instructive author as Seneca. She herself writes freely in Latin when she is writing to men.[12] For Birgitte Thott, Latin was useful when it came to important correspondence with men, but more than that it was a means of gaining access to the knowledge which they possessed. After that she regarded it as her duty to pass on what she had learned to other women in Danish.

Not all learned women published anything. Quite frequently the gynæcea provide no more information about a given woman than her name, possibly her marital status and a remark to the effect that she was considered to be very learned during her lifetime. It is difficult to determine what sort of learning lay hidden behind such remarks. In one single instance remarks on such learnedness have been preserved. These concern the now totally forgotten Martha Lous who had studied during her entire youth and at the age of seventeen was given the offer of being examined by a professor. At the examination she received a written recommendation in German which she translated into Latin herself. In it we find a record of her accomplishments in Latin, Greek, Hebrew, theology, history, geography, philosophy, etc.

About Martha Lous, Schönau tells us (p. 979) that

> sie einen guten Lateinischen Stilum schreibet, in Theologia Cathetica, und Acroamatica, wie auch Historia Biblia wohl bewandert ist, Autores Latinos sehr wohl verstehet, das ganze neue Testament in Griechischer Sprache gelesen, auch in der Grundsprache des alten Testaments sich etwas geübt hat, und gute Wissenschaft in der Hebräischen Grammatic besitzt, ferner die Fragen aus einem Compendio Historiæ Universalis und der Geographie sehr wohl beantworten kan, ja auch mehr weiss, als in einem Compendio stehet; Dann auch . . .

–and it continues here concerning her philosophical studies. Just how many Martha Lous's are hidden behind the long list of names in general we do not know.

---

[12] Only two letters in Latin from Birgitte Thott have been preserved (cf. note 11). Her Latin correspondence, however, was still known at the close of the 18th century.

How Learned Were the Learned Women?

Roughly, we have the names of around 130 Dano-Norwegian so-called "learned women" and around 25 Swedish. They were, of course, not all equally learned, and in this connection it could be interesting to have a look at the way in which they regarded Latin.

In the year 1700 Matthias Henriksen Schacht published an article in Latin in which 36 Dano-Norwegian women were mentioned, the first printed Dano-Norwegian gynæceum.[13] This article gave rise to a debate. A well-known bishop in Jutland, Jens Bircherod (1658–1708), initiated a discussion about it with the leading expert on learned women, Otto Sperling. In many ways, Bircherod symbolizes the traditional learned Latin humanist. He was worried by the threat of inflation in the notion of learning. Anybody at all, or rather any old woman, could call herself learned if there were no fixed guidelines to indicate what actually comprised learning.

> Indeed, if merely knowledge of the French language or of some other foreign language is enough to be praised for being a learned woman, then your "learned chamber of women" will no doubt grow tremendously

he wrote to Sperling in 1702.[14]

Bircherod stipulates knowledge of Latin as the minimum requirement for bearing the title of learned: On this basis he can quickly shorten Schacht's list. His first task was to separate the women into groups according to their so-called learning. The first group was made up of the authors of prayer books. This group had nine members. "They can be counted as national authors, but they cannot rise to the heights of those women who have absorbed 'laudable scholarship' " in his opinion. Group two consisted of women who had published, or had intended to publish, various didactic treatises. Eight in all. Group three comprised women who were familiar with French, German, English, or other foreign languages, which he termed "linguas exoticas," but not Latin. Thus he got rid of another five. Group four had only two members, Anne Gjøe and Karen Brahe. They

---

[13] Cf. note 2

[14] "Et vero, si sola lingvæ Gallicæ aut alius peregrinæ notitia eruditarum encomio fæminarum sufficiat, literatum Tuum Gynæceum absque dubio in immensum excrescat." Bircherod's letter of November 27, 1702 is unpublished. Pp. 5–15 deal with the learned women. (The Royal Library in Copenhagen. Gl. kgl. Saml. 3092 VI.1 in quarto).

are known for having established a library and for the founding of a home for unmarried ladies of rank where eight women at a time could live and study. Men could visit the library as guests, a privilege which was utilized by Albert Thura, among others, when he was writing his Gynæceum.

Bircherod's group five contained poets, i.e., poets who did not attain to the level of the Norwegian Dorothea Engelbretsdatter. This group had five members. Of the remaining seven women, he allows four to assume a place among the learned, among these Birgitte Thott. And of his own accord he adds two that were not found in Matthias Schacht's list: Leonora Christine Ulfeldt and Marie Below.

According to Bircherod, it was the case that all six of these could be shown to have knowledge of Latin. In comparison we can mention that the German Paullinus, in his gynæceum from 1695,[15] divides his women into very learned and less learned, "hoch-gelahrte und wohl-gelahrte." All four of his very learned women knew Latin.

A reply in Latin from Otto Sperling to Jens Bircherod has been preserved. The former writes:

> As to that which you point out concerning our learned women, it is indeed completely true that they have not been in contact with all forms of learning, but that some are more learned than others. But even those whom you consider to be learned: Below, Thott, Quitzow, Bredal, and Engelbrecht are in fact not learned beyond Latin. For I cannot see that they have done anything about Greek and Hebrew, and in this way there are at least some aspects of learning they apparently have not acquired.[16]

Thus, Sperling recognizes the fact that "their" women are not qualified to receive the title of learned from a formalistic point of view. On the other hand, he continues:

> But we can also establish learning solely within the Danish language, or within one foreign language or another; to the extent that it is

---

[15] Christian Franz Paullinus: Hoch- und Wohlgelahrtes Teutsches Frauenzimmer (Frankfurt und Leipzig 1706).

[16] "Quæ de feminis nostris doctis monuisti, vera sunt omnino, non illas partes omnes solidæ eruditionis attigisse, sed alias aliis doctiores fuisse. Nam et illæ, quas tu doctas censuisti, Beloviam, Tottiam, Qvitzoviam, Bredalinam, Engelbrechtiam, non ultra latinam lingvam doctæ fuerunt; Græca enim et Hebræa nec illas video attigisse, atque sic partem saltem aliquam eruditionis acqvisivisse sibi videntur." (The Royal Library in Copenhagen, MS. Ny kgl. Saml. 1986c, vol. 41 in quarto). Date of the letter, 29 Dec. 1702.

> unreasonable to exclude completely from any kind of learning those who have taken it upon themselves to translate and rework books in their own native language, or have written their own independent commentaries to something in Danish. They are, in fact, all famous for their writings, even though they have not acquired the basic learning which you require. Therefore, their persistency, to the extent that it is connected with even just a little education, should definitely be pointed out to posterity, since it is no little praise that is due them who lend support as second and third in line.[17]

Thus, Sperling knows what is normally understood to be a learned woman, and that he himself is extending the notion of learning. It was logical to do this if one looked at the possibilities available to women for stimulating the intellect at all. It was also in the spirit of the time to recognize the value of cultural transmission in the mother tongue in the form of translations, poetry, and scholarship.

In the subsequent gynæcea Otto Sperling's view was the one to prevail. Albert Thura went through similar considerations. He expresses a certain degree of concern regarding the organization of his material. He writes in the preface that he has considered separating the women in his gynæceum into two chambers, one for the very learned and one for the less learned. He does not mention which criteria he would employ in order to undertake such a division, but points out the risk involved in placing someone incorrectly, i.e., placing a learned person together with the half-learned or the reverse. The lack of information about them and the modesty of the learned involves a risk he does not dare to run. He chooses the diplomatic solution and lets them occupy the same room.

In the work itself, sixteen are mentioned of whom he maintains that they know Latin. Four more are described without use of the word Latin, in wording that indicates that he thought they knew this language. Concerning eight of those who were familiar with Latin he notes that they also knew Greek, or had tried to learn it. And one also knew Hebrew, we are told. From another source we know that at least one more knew Hebrew.

---

[17] "Iam vero et in Danica lingva sola eruditionem præstare possumus, et in quavis lingva: ita ut illas (illis ms.), quæ vertendis et in suam lingvam transferendis libris operatæ, aut suo ingenio aliqvid commentatæ sunt, in Danica lingva, ab eruditione omni penitus excludere nequaquam liceat. Sunt enim scriptis claræ omnes, licet solidam eruditionem illam, qvam tu postulas, non assecuta sint: ideoque illarum industria, utpote cum eruditione aliqva conjuncta, maxime est laudanda posteris, et magni facienda; cum in secundis et tertiis etiam subsistere laus non minima sit." (ibid.)

Among the 23 new learned women in Frederik Christian Schönau, there are only three who are familiar with Latin. Of these, Martha Lous, as already mentioned, also knew Greek and Hebrew. In the last Danish gynæceum, H. J. Birch's, Latin is no longer the criterion. However, it is clearly characteristic that the most learned among them, Charlotta Dorothea Biehl, recalls in her old age how she dreamed, as a five-year-old, of being able to learn Latin.

Conclusion

Thus, we can conclude the following: In Scandinavia 150 learned women were known from the period between 1500 and 1800. The majority of these were Danish. A few were Norwegian and Swedish. We know none from Iceland or Finland.

The notion of learning according to which they were evaluated was not unambiguous. According to the most narrow definition, knowledge of Latin was required. If we adhere to such a definition, there can hardly have been more than 25 or 30 out of the 160 who could be called learned. The men who collected information on them and described them, however, seem to have thought that there were other qualities than Latin that should count. Literature in the vernacular, for example, was gradually becoming more and more esteemed during this period. The attitude of the women themselves to Latin seems to have been that they would like to learn it, but were rarely given the opportunity.

However, if they did know Latin, there was a greater demand for them to utilize this knowledge for the purpose of enlightenment in the national language than there was for writing their own works in Latin, even though it is clear, where most of them are concerned, that they were quite competent when it came to writing Neo-Latin.

University of Copenhagen

Florens Wilson and the Politics of Irenicism

DOMINIC BAKER-SMITH

Jacopo Sadoleto died in Rome on 18 October, 1547. The ageing cardinal had been failing for some months, but shortly before his death it appears that he was well enough to receive a visitor, a *littérateur* with reformist sympathies. Since this visitor, Orgetorix Sphinter, has not left a fiery trail across history it is difficult to discover much about him: he may have been Hungarian by birth, he was certainly familiar with Aonio Paleario (himself a figure of marked ambivalence in matters of religious loyalty), and he had some dealings with the important Basle printer Johannes Oporinus.[1] It was Oporinus, an irenical entrepreneur who handled publications from both sides of the religious divide which was still far from sharply defined, that printed a collection of Latin poems on religious themes under the title *Pii, graves, atque elegantes poetae aliquot*. It is undated but certainly from the period 1548–1550, and it contains a prefatory letter addressed by Sphinter to Oporinus in which he describes his recent meeting with Sadoleto.[2] In a sense Sadoleto is given credit for the concept behind the volume.

According to Sphinter the old man had lamented the way in which

---

[1] M. Young, *The Life and Times of Aonio Paleario* (London, 1860), 1:152 and 2:182–83; F. Buisson, *Sébastien Castellion: sa vie et son oeuvre* (Paris, 1892), 2:289. For Oporinus and his contacts see Peter G. Bietenholz, *Basle and France in the Sixteenth Century* (Geneva, 1971).

[2] The fact that Sphinter's letter is addressed "Romae" suggests that he wrote it soon after the meeting with Sadoleto since he is reported in Strasbourg by January 1548 (Mann, *Paleario*, 2:182); the reference to "Helvetiis nostris" sounds odd from an Hungarian, though it may be a courtesy to Oporinus.

religion, which ought to have been a principle of harmony, now served to divide the intellectual community. Personal contact was inhibited and even the free exchange of writings was problematic: "for what can now be received in Italy from the Germans or the Swiss without grave distrust? And what Italian work does not find detractors ready among the Germans and Swiss?" When Sadoleto touches on the greater brilliance of the Italian poets Sphinter counters that "nostri homines"—here one senses that the reference is as much confessional as ethnic—were too sensitive to theological matters to approve the mingling of pagan and Christian elements within the same volume. This, he concludes, is the reason for the lower status of poetry "apud nostros."

Sadoleto's response was to recall a proposal which he had first aired some years before in a letter to a printer for a volume that would bring together outstanding poems which combined classical literary elegance with religious inspiration. While he was ready to acknowledge the achievement of non-Italians, both in scholarship and literary studies, it was to his own countrymen that he turned in the first place for the reconciliation of Christian teaching with classical forms, and the names that are put forward are those of Sannazaro, Paleario, Vida and Marcantonio Flaminio.[3] What Sadoleto is recalling here is a letter he had sent to the Lyonnais printer Sebastian Gryphius in September 1535; this is of some interest since it was written in his excitement after an initial reading of Paleario's *De immortalitate animorum*. Gryphius, to whom we shall return later, was another example of a printer who exploited the shifting boundary between orthodoxy and reform and Sadoleto, as bishop of Carpentras, had frequent dealings with him. The letter about Paleario's poem recommends its publication and suggests the suitability of printing it with works by Sannazaro and Vida. What excites Sadoleto's enthusiasm is Paleario's clarity of expression in handling a complex topic, combined with the classical propriety of his verse. But he is careful to emphasise that his response is not confined to the literary or even the intellectual level: the most important quality of the work is its subjective force which takes the reader beyond the level of didactic utility to inflame the soul with love of true religion.[4]

---

[3] "Nam neque nos, ut quidem truncos, aut stipites putabat: sed nostris hominibus eruditionem, nonnunquam etiam eloquentiam concedebat: Italos vero affirmabat imitationis studiossisimus, novis in rebus effinxisse, atque expressisse imaginem antiquitatis" (a2v–a3r). Sadoleto places the issue of religious poetry at the centre of the dispute over imitation.

[4] Sadoleto, *Opera omnia* (Verona, 1737), 1:116 ("et, quod ego pluris quam reliqua

The proposal which Sadoleto aired in his letter to Gryphius is tacitly accepted as the model for Oporinus's volume and its very title, *Pii, graves, elegantes poetae aliquot*, echoes his ideal of Christian eloquence. The greater part of the contents follows his prescription and is Italian in origin: Sannazaro's *De Partu Virginis* and *De morte Christi lamentatio* are there, so are Vida's *Christiad*, Paleario's *De Immortalitate animorum* and a number of verse psalm translations by Marcantonio Flaminio. But then some transalpine items are added: Flaminio's twenty-six psalms are supplemented by Sebastian Castellio's *Odae in Psalmos XL* and included with them is an ode by Florentius Volusenus, the Florens Wilson of my title, which is modelled on Horace's "Sic te diva potens Cypri" (*Carminum*, I.3) and treats the familiar humanist theme of "tranquillitas animi" in a resolutely evangelical manner. Castellio is the junior contributor: born in Savoy in 1515 he is best known as Calvin's opponent over freedom of conscience in the Servetus affair of 1553–1554. After leaving Geneva for Basle in 1545 he worked in Oporinus's printing house and the inclusion of so much of his recent work in the volume suggests some degree of personal involvement. He may also have been responsible for the inclusion of Wilson's ode since he must certainly have encountered him during his stay in Lyons in the late 1530's when Wilson was associated with the Collège de la Trinité and was a friend of Gryphius. But Wilson was in any case known to Sadoleto, with whom he corresponded as late as 1546 on the delicate topic of confessional affiliation, and his name was not unknown in Switzerland. His *Commentatio Theologica*, first printed by Gryphius in 1539, had been reprinted in Basle by Hieronymous Curio in 1544, very probably at the prompting of Conrad Gesner who had met Wilson in Lyons and clearly admired his writings.[5]

Now I have gone into these details about the genesis of Oporinus's anthology for a purpose: it provides an apt illustration of the network of contacts and of shared aspirations which marks the Neo-Latin community in the early decades of the Reformation period. Sadoleto, like his friend Reginald Pole, was suspect as being too familiar with heretics, if not actually heterodox himself, and his earnest support of Paleario when the latter was under suspicion in 1542 did his posthumous reputation little

omnia facio, Christiani mens, integra, castaque religio erga Deum ipsum honos, pietas, studium, in eo libro vel maxime, non solum docere mentes errantium, sed etiam animos incendere ad amorem purae religionis possunt.")

[5] Gesner, *Bibliotheca Universalis* (Zurich, 1545), fol. 245v. For Gesner's influence on Curio see his *Pandectarum sive partitionum universalium . . . libri xxi* (Zurich, 1548), fol. 87; I owe this reference to Professor H. R. Guggisberg.

good when Paleario was eventually executed for heresy in 1570. Did Sadoleto know something, or was he naive? Of other contributors to the volume Flaminio died in his bed in 1550, ironically enough attended by Cardinal Caraffa, the chief Inquisitor, who happened to be passing when the viaticum was borne in; as Pope Paul IV Caraffa would later declare that he wished he could dig up Flaminio's body and burn it.[6] There is no evidence that Flaminio was a deliberate heretic or Nicodemite (in Calvin's term) but recent opinion strongly supports his role as the dominant voice behind the notorious *Beneficio di Giesu Cristo* which was condemned in the mid-1540's. So, even if we disregard Oporinus's transalpine additions—Castellio and Wilson—the Italians of Sadoleto's choice represent enough ambivalence to set a few pyres smouldering. Which brings me back to the question: was Sadoleto naive or conniving? Surely the answer must be neither. Both the letters that I have mentioned, that of Sadoleto to Gryphius and its echo in that of Sphinter to Oporinus, alert us to a series of related concerns. At their centre is the ideal of Christian eloquence or what we can term *theologia rhetorica*; this had been a feature of humanist activity since Petrarch, adapting the classical arts of persuasion to the urgent pastoral needs of a church in decline. Sadoleto would surely endorse Horace's claim,

> Non satis est pulchra esse poemata; dulci sunto
> et quocumque volent animum auditoris agunto.
>
> 'Tis not enough, th'elaborate Muse affords
> Her poems beautie, but a sweet delight
> To worke the hearers minds, still, to their plight.[7]

If there is a single defining feature of humanism it is that rhetorical concern with the affective rather than the definitive function of language; hence the desire for an authentic *imitatio*, one that might recapture the force of classical Latinity and utilise it in the service of Christian spirituality. But a further point follows: the association of this *theologia rhetorica* with a tendency to minimise the problems of confessional difference. Language which is apt, in Sadoleto's phrase, "animos incendere" is not easily reconciled with scholastic precision. The consequences of this can be traced in the scattered irenical episodes characteristic of humanism

---

[6] Carol Maddison, *Marcantonio Flaminio: Poet, Humanist and Reformer* (London, 1965), p. 201-2.

[7] Horace, *De Arte Poetica*, 99-100; the translation is that of Ben Jonson (1640 version).

from Poggio to Grotius, which reflect its sense of language as a social medium rather than a container for abstract truths.[8] A closer look at the career of Florens Wilson may clarify this point.

A striking feature of that career is the way in which Wilson's movements provide a series of links between religious episodes or factions usually treated in isolation. After his education in Scotland, where he had been born around 1504, Wilson appears as tutor to Wolsey's son, Thomas Wynter, in 1528. This brought him into some intimacy with the architects of the Henrician schism, in particular Cromwell, Gardiner and that other apologist for royal supremacy Thomas Starkey. At the same time, since Wynter was resident in Paris, Wilson gained the notice of the French supporters of moderate reform such as Guillaume and Jean de Bellay, while his *Psalmi quintidecimi enarratio* of 1531 was dedicated to the Cardinal of Lorraine.[9] Such associations may seem primarily political, but the display of Hebrew in this book and in the *In Psalmum quinquaginta enarratio*, dedicated to Gardiner in the following year, can be taken as a gesture of alignment in the fierce dispute over the foundation of the trilingual Collège Royale. In 1535 Wilson spent some time with Sadoleto in Carpentras (following the recommendation of Starkey) and by 1538 he was settled in Lyons where he taught at the Collège de la Trinité, an institution with marked evangelical tendencies.[10] He also worked for Gryphius, the most extensive printer of Erasmus's works in France, and was part of a remarkable group of Neo-Latin poets which included Gilbert Ducher, Bourbon (by this time another "Cromwellian"), Vulteius, Macrin and Dolet.[11] This Lyons circle was highly ambivalent in its confessional

[8] On Poggio and Jerome of Prague see Nancy S. Struever, *The Language of History in the Renaissance* (Princeton, 1970), 189.

[9] *Florentii Voluseni Britanni ad illustrissimum Dominum Cardinalem Lotharingum Psalmi quintidecimi enarratio* (Paris: L. Cynaeus, 1531). Wilson reveals in the dedication that he had been introduced to Lorraine by Guillaume du Bellay and Sir Francis Bryan, the English ambassador.

[10] On the Collège de la Trinité see G. Brasart de Groër, "Le Collège, agent d'infiltration de la Réforme" in *Aspects de la Propagande Religieuse*, H. Meylan, ed. (Geneva, 1957), 167–75, with Meylan's balancing comments on pp. vii–xv.

[11]

Ad Florentium Volusenum
Auxilii cupiens, erecta mente levavi
  In montes oculos terque, quaterque meos.
Sed solum a Domino auxilium, Volusene, videbam,
  Qui nulla solus cuncta creavit ope.
Sedulos hic custos nunquam dormitet, ut errans
  Huc illuc pedibus commoveare tuis.

loyalties, but most of its members were there precisely because it was still possible to keep options open and one suspects that for most of them such a condition of dialectical poise was an essential element of religious vitality. Yet Wilson was also known in the Italian community, a possible consequence of his earlier friendship with Antonio Bonvisi in London,[12] and there are signs that he was in touch with the *spirituali* gathered in Lucca around the figure of Peter Martyr Vermigli. Certainly the dedications of the two major works which he completed in Lyons, the *Commentatio Theologica* (1539) and the *De Animi Tranquillitate* (1543), both printed by Gryphius, point to links with Vermigli's circle.

Yet analysis of these two works suggests that Wilson held to a basically Catholic formulation of faith (Purgatory and the Papacy excepted) but responded to the nuances of reform. The *De Animi Tranquillitate* in particular can be seen as an attempt to reconcile orthodoxy, taken in a residual sense,[13] with aspects of the reformers' teaching precisely through a stress on the subjective and persuasive function of language: it is the subjective impact of an idea rather than its objective validity which is emphasised. Above all it is the professional theologians, the "recentiores" who are criticized, "Siquando illis sacra tractantur, nullae sunt flammae, nullus impetus orationis, quo incendatur ad rerum amorem lector."[14] Wilson's writings in his Lyons phase seek with growing urgency

---

Non dormitabit, neque dormiet optimus ille
  Pastor, Idumaei cura, salusque gregis.
Custodit Dominus tua te protectio, ne unquam
  Luce ve sol urat, luna ve nocte sua.
Quantum hic mortalis vives, custodiet omni
  Exitum, et egressum dulitate tuum.
(G. Ducherius, *Epigrammaton libri duo*) Lyons, S. Gryphius, 1538, 50.)

Bourbon congratulates Cromwell on his appointment as vicar-general in the 1538 version of his *Nugae* (also printed by Gryphius), p. 286; see also p. 251. For an account of the group see J. C. Margolin, "Le Cercle Humaniste Lyonnais d'après l'edition des *Epigrammata* (1537) de Jean Visagier," *Actes du Colloque sur l'Humanisme Lyonnais au XVIe siècle* (Grenoble, 1974), 151–83.

[12] On this friendship see *Letters and Papers of Henry VIII,* 8:856, 43; also Wilson's letter to Starkey, "Lugduni, in aedibus A. Bonnisii," of December 1535 (British Library, Cotton MS. Nero B.VI.20) and his poem "Dum totam erraret," in *De Animi Tranquillitate* (Lyons: S. Gryphius, 1543), 229.

[13] Cf. "Iam & Ecclesiae, hoc est, tot praestantium in omni sapientiae genere virorum, summus de Christiano dogmate consensus, iam inde ab eius exordio in hunc usque diem non parum hic obtinere debet momenti." *De Animi Tranquillitate,* 313.

[14] *De Animi Tranquillitate,* 343.

to invest piety with this *impetus orationis* so as to give it personal force: in the *De Animi Tranquillitate*, written as it is after the crisis year of 1542 and addressed to a refugee from the Inquisition in Lucca, he appropriates the Reformers' dynamic conception of faith in an effort to satisfy the need for personal assurance of salvation. Such an attempt to have it both ways appears highly typical of other conciliatory (or ambivalent) figures like Sadoleto or Flaminio who bring a classicizing sensibility to religious discourse. In fact it is tempting to see some affinity with the formula of double justification agreed by Contarini and Melanchthon at the Diet of Regensburg in 1540. It was the collapse of that proposal which marked the beginning of the end for *theologia rhetorica*.

But that was in the future: for the moment I want to focus on the *Commentatio Theologica*. It is difficult to separate the work from its reception, recorded in the confident list of friends who had approved it, Sir John Borthwick, Panagius Hoccedius, Stephen Gardiner and his nephew Germain. Borthwick, *enseigne* of the Scottish Archers, would be condemned as a heretic *in absentia* by a Scottish court in 1540; Germain Gardiner, secretary as well as nephew to Stephen Gardiner and author of a tract against John Frith, would be hung and disembowelled at Tyburn as a papist four years later; his uncle, like Lorraine's secretary Hoccedius, followed a more circumspect path, yet he too would be in the Tower by 1548. It seems very likely that the *Commentatio* was circulated in manuscript when the court visited Lyons in 1538 and Stephen Gardiner was present as English ambassador; in that case there was still little sign of the grim future which awaited its readers. In this respect it stands as a paradigm for the disintegration of humanist reform.

The book, which Wilson also refers to as a *precatio*, is made up of some three hundred and forty-five prose verses or aphorisms, comparable to a psalm structure: each verse contains matter for reflection but forms part of a wider discourse, addressed to the soul and to God. Very much in the spirit of Erasmus's *Modus orandi Deum*, Wilson employs a reflexive rhetoric which is aimed at the suppliant rather than the recipient; in fact, the reader is actively an *orator* in two senses of that word, defining the role he must enact.[15] Given the density of scriptural quotation and allusion in

[15] "Ita nobis expedit orare frequenter, non ut Deus discat a nobis, quid sit opus, sed ut assuescamus ea quibus egemus ab illo sperare, utque desyderium aeternae vitae magis ac magis ascendatur in nobis, dum frequenter hic animum intendimus, ac ardenter petamus ab eo, qui solus dare potest." *Modus Orandi Deum* (Lyons: T. Paganus, 1542), sig.b6v–7. Cf. Charles Trinkaus, *In Our Image and Likeness* (London, 1970), 1:12, where he discusses Petrarch's practice of meditation.

the text the *Commentatio* offers an appropriation of the biblical encounter which the reader must seize into his personal circumstances. But what marks this book and separates it from any Erasmian concept of decorum is its syncretising vocabulary. It is this which makes it so obviously a product of its time and place, adopting in its extended discourse the features already familiar in the Lyonnais poets and defended by Dolet in the *Erasmianus*: "what was elegant and beautiful in Cicero's day is still beautiful. It is absurd to think of painting God as Jove, but the painter will use the same colours whether he paints Jove or Christ."[16]

As an illustration of Wilson's syncretistic use of such *colores* we can take two consecutive verses which provide a direct encounter between the biblical and the classical:

> Si ascendero in coelum, tu illic es: si ad inferos demigrem, ades. Si sumptis diliculo pennis ad extremum usque mare deferar, manus tua est, quae et ducit, et detinet.
>
> Tu unus ille hominumque deumque pater, summus Iupiter, cuius numine omnia sunt plena. Tu spiritus, qui coelum, terram, camposque liquentes intus alit. Tu mens illa, quae per magni huius corporis artus infusa totam molem agitat.[17]

The first verse is a straight rendering of that most awesome of Psalms, 139:8–10. ("If I ascend up into heaven, thou art there; if I make my bed in hell, behold thou art there. If I take the wings of the morning and dwell in the uttermost parts of the sea: even there shall thy hand lead me, and thy right hand shall hold me.") Then, in the second verse, this cosmic sense of God is presented in classical form, that of "summus Jupiter" whose power is expressed in an adaptation of Anchises' words in the *Aeneid* 6.724–27,

> Principio coelum, ac terras, camposque liquentes,
> Lucentemque globum Lunae, Titaniaque astra
> Spiritus intus alit, totamque infusa per artus.
> Mens agitat molem, et magno se corpore miscet.
>
> Now, first. The sky and the lands, the watery plains, the moon's gleam-

---

[16] "Sane quae elegantia erant & venusta tempore Ciceronis verba, dicendique modus pulcher, nostra aetate nihilominus elegans est, & venustus, & pulcher." *L'Erasmianus sive Ciceronianus d'Etienne Dolet* (1535), ed. Emile V. Telle (Geneva, 1974), 174; I. Scott, *Controversies over the Imitation of Cicero* (New York, 1910), 176.

[17] In Gryphius's edition (1539) the passage is on p. 51; in Curio's (1544) on p. 93.

ing face, the Titanic Sun and the stars are all strengthened by Spirit working within them, and by Mind, which is blended into all the vast universe and pervades every part of it, enlivening the whole mass.[18]

The creative functions of Virgil's *Spiritus* and *Mens* are thus reclaimed for the God of Abraham, Isaac and Jacob. There are many other such transformations: the sun is Phoebus, the ocean Amphritite, and Satan becomes "Tartareus tyrannus." This is typical of the way Wilson sets the two inheritances in a dynamic relation, the scriptural core of the *Commentatio* set off and heightened by classical resources of diction, mythology and literary allusion.

Discussions of the *imitatio* debate, particularly with reference to the *Ciceronianus*, tend to assume too sharp a dichotomy between the diachronic Erasmians and the synchronic purists. It is important to note that Wilson's aim is reconciliation: at the conclusion of the *De Animi Tranquillitate* he attacks those who are displeased "si desint Thespiades, Ioves, Veneres, Ledae, & fabulosa id genus Graecorum commenta" (p. 392). His ode, modelled on Horace but focussed on Christ crucified, is sung to the lyre as a Christian replacement. Erasmus might deplore his confusion of God and Jupiter but Wilson in turn criticises Erasmus for his neglect of "puritas Romani sermonis" (that "Romani" is a revealing emphasis). In fact Wilson's classicizing habit and his preferred themes–awe before creation, the dignity of man, the cross of Christ–are what one would expect in the Lyonnais circle. The one constant influence for them in Paris and then later in Lyons had been Guillaume Budé and it is in the *De Asse* and, in particular, the *De Transitu* that we can find a precedent for just this kind of syncretism.

In a recent discussion of the Ciceronianus debate Thomas M. Greene picks on what he terms "the classical synchronism" of Bembo, Vida and Scaliger as an evasion of a painful present, the Italy of foreign invasions.[19] In the case of the Lyonnais group it is the religious situation that seems definitive: their syncretism handles devotional themes in a linguistic code which evades not only scholastic associations but even scholastic precision. That a work such as the *De Animi Tranquillitate*, which opens with the news of Ochino's and Vermigli's flight from the Inquisition, should end with the singing of a Christian-Horatian ode on peace of mind

---

[18] The translation is that of W. F. Jackson Knight, *The Aeneid* (Harmondsworth, 1956), 169.

[19] *The Light in Troy* (New Haven/London, 1982), 188.

has a clear logic. It seems equally fitting that such an ode should find an afterlife, side-by-side with Castellio, in Oporinus' irenical anthology. As the later attacks on Sadoleto and Flaminio, and on the Lyonnais circle, make clear, ambiguity could no longer be countenanced in the context of counter-Reformation.

University of Amsterdam

Richard Mulcaster's Positions *and Girolamo Mercuriale's* De arte gymnastica

WILLIAM BARKER

In 1581 Richard Mulcaster, the Elizabethan schoolmaster, saw published the first of his two important treatises which together attempt, but fail, to do what Quintilian did for Roman education—to sum up conventional practice and to lay down a foundation (he calls it a "plat" or platform) for the future structure of English education. This book is called, in the full manner of the age, *Positions Wherin those Primitive Circumstances Be Examined, Which Are Necessarie for the Training Up of Children, either for Skill in their Booke, or Health in their Bodie.*[1] These "positions" are theses or points for debate and the "primitive circumstances" are the basic rhetorical divisions he uses to structure his lengthy deliberative argument. Mulcaster is concerned with the intellectual development of children from about four or five, when they might begin to read, through grammar school, until they are ready to move on to the university. Most of *Positions* is a detailed defence of a program for children's "skill in their booke." The author dwells on education in the elementary and grammar schools (whose

---

[1] London: Thomas Chare [=Chard] for Thomas Vautrollier, 1581; cited by page number below. There is a variant title page which simply lists Vautrollier as publisher. The series was continued with *The First Part of the Elementarie* (London: Thomas Vautrollier, 1582), principally on English orthography, though the first few chapters and the peroration cover material directly relevant to Mulcaster's program. A biography is by Richard L. DeMolen,"Richard Mulcaster: An Elizabethan Savant," *Shakespeare Studies* 8 (1975): 29–82. Further material on Mulcaster, including a detailed analysis of his use of Mercuriale's *De arte gymnastica* may be found in my Ph.D. dissertation, "Richard Mulcaster's *Positions*: A Critical Old-Spelling Edition with Commentary" (University of Toronto, 1981).

programs he promises to outline in subsequent volumes), reform of the training of teachers, instruction for girls, and so on. All of this is presented as deliberative advice to the Queen and her ministers, and throughout Mulcaster emphasizes the political significance of his reforms, which are all directed to uniformity in religion and politics. A good third of the book is, however, given over to the other topic announced in the title—"health in their bodie." This is the matter that I shall here examine—what Mulcaster wrote about sports and how he depended on the Latin treatise of a near contemporary Italian physician named Girolamo Mercuriale for the great bulk of what he had to say.

Positions is divided into three parts—first, a short series of preliminary chapters that summarize what is to come and that propose and defend a rhetorical division of the matter; next, a long series of chapters on physical education, and finally chapters on the general shape of institutional reform for English education. In his discussion of education, Mulcaster is determined to recuperate from the writings of Plato, Aristotle, and Xenophon the program of the Greeks and to situate this program within a specifically English framework. Although he refers often to Quintilian, he is actually shifting the basis of education away from the Roman model of the professionally skilled rhetor or lawyer implicit in much of humanist theory to a broader Greek model of the complete citizen. Thus, he spends the largest section of *Positions* discussing a subject that neither Cicero nor Quintilian mentions in relation to rhetoric—sports.

His section on sports begins with a general defence of physical education, then goes on to what he calls indoor and outdoor sports, and ends with his suggestions for the "training master" or coach. In some ways the first part of his program—indoor sports—must have seemed odd or even absurd to his contemporaries. Such exercises as loud speaking, holding your breath, and even laughing he presents as seriously as he does dancing or fencing. Yet these unusual exercises were well known to Antiquity and are entirely defensible within the categories of Galenic medicine. His program for outdoor sports would however have seemed more familiar to his English contemporaries. Swimming, running, riding, shooting the longbow, and hunting were the traditional sports of a feudal warrior class that had by the early part of the sixteenth century been transformed into the gentry.[2] Mulcaster wishes to see all the traditional sports as part of a

---

[2] Sir Thomas Elyot's *The Boke Named the Governour* (1531) describes the nostalgic ideal of the sixteenth-century knight, embodied in the 1570s and 1580s by an exemplar like Sir Philip Sidney, skilled in "wrestling ... r[u]nning ... shooting ... swim-

regular school program, under the supervision of his "training master." As he progresses sport by sport he carefully analyses each one for its benefits and drawbacks, and subjects each to the scrutiny of the Galenic catagories. Everyone knows a child is hot and moist in his physical complexion, but if a child sits for long hours in study, his body will suffer. Will the sport sufficiently excite the natural heat of the body in order to overcome the coldness brought on by too many hours in the classroom and the library? Or will it too suddenly dry out the body that by its nature must retain a great deal of this youthful moisture? Will the sport improve the appetite? Or will it cause the student to feel unwell and to fall off his food? Every aspect of the sport is considered in the light of the humoral balance of the child or scholar practising it.

Now and then it is sometimes all too clear, from his limited enthusiasm and information, that Mulcaster has never practised some of the sports he describes. Furthermore, it is clear that although he speaks about a sport within the context of schools and education, he has not a clue how to bring that sport into the general curriculum of a school, certainly not into the understaffed schools of Elizabethan England. It is all quite theoretical. And yet he is able to admit that he is describing a theoretical ideal, not a standard for regular day-to-day practice. His reform is not to be absolute, but to be set within the "circumstances" of the time, place, habits, and so on of his fellow Englishmen (here he uses the word "circumstances" in a more modern sense although it is related, via the Aristotelian categories, to the "circumstances" of rhetoric). By his application of "circumstances" he tries to set his theoretical program within a contemporary context.

Nevertheless, despite this attention to circumstances, there seems something remarkably bookish about Mulcaster's discussion of sports for English schools. He talks about the English situation and tries to orient his suggestions to the English scene, and yet most of his authorities are

---

ming ... hunting" (Edmund Spenser, "Astrophel: A Pastoral Elegy," in *Minor Poems*, ed. E. de Sélincourt [Oxford: Clarendon Press, 1910], 339–40). Surveys of sixteenth-century sports include Lilly C. Stone, "English Sports and Recreations," in *Life and Letters in Tudor and Stuart England*, ed. L. B. Wright and V. A. LaMar (Ithaca, NY: Cornell University Press for the Folger Shakespeare Library, 1962), 427–79; Dennis Brailsford, *Sport and Society: Elizabeth to Anne* (Toronto: University of Toronto Press, 1969); the essays on various sports in vol. 2 of *Shakespeare's England*, ed. Sidney Lee (Oxford: Clarendon Press, 1916); Joseph Strutt, *The Sports and Pastimes of the People of England from the Earliest Period*, new ed. much enlarged by J. C. Cox (London: Methuen, 1903). The only separate study of Mulcaster on sports is Selvio and Alda P. dal Piaz, *Un ginnasiarca dell'età elisabettiana "Richard Mulcaster"* (Arezzo: D. Badiali, 1967), a short survey of his ideas with minimal reference to context.

classical. Despite the remarkable attempt to argue for sports and the principle of "a wise minde, and a healthfull bodie" (p. 42), the chapters seem curiously second-hand. An exception is the lively and anecdotal chapter called "Of Shooting"; Mulcaster, like Roger Ascham, was a known enthusiast, a member of the famous knights of Prince Arthur who annually gathered in patriotic tribute to celebrate the traditional English long bow.[3] Yet he does little justice to other sports, and his arguments for them seem pale.

There is an explanation for the thinness of his arguments, and he provides it himself near the end of the section on physical education. In chapter 35 of *Positions*, almost in an aside, he says:

> For the professed argument of the whole booke, I know not any comparable to *Hieronymus Mercurialis*, a verie learned *Italian Physician* now in our time, which hath taken great paines to sift out of all writers, what so ever concerneth the whole *Gymnasticall* and exercising argument, whose advice in this question I have my selfe much used, where he did fit my purpose. (p. 128)

It turns out that most of his many pages on physical education are borrowed, adapted from, or sometimes directly translated from the *De arte gymnastica libri sex* by the Italian physician Girolamo Mercuriale. The extent of Mulcaster's debt was first analysed almost a hundred years ago by Georg Schmid.[4] Even so, few subsequent readers of *Positions* seem to know that what they are reading is a digest and reorganization of a treatise first published in Venice in 1569.

Girolamo Mercuriale was an almost exact contemporary of Mulcaster.[5]

---

[3] See Roger Ascham's *Toxophilus* of 1545 and chapter 26 of *Positions.*

[4] Georg Schmid, "Richard Mulcaster," in Karl Adolf Schmid, ed., *Geschichte der Erziehung vom Anfang an bis auf unsere Zeit,* 5 vols. in 7 (Stuttgart: J. G. Cotta, 1884–1902), (1892) 3: 373–76.

[5] I have been unable to find any thorough modern study of Mercuriale. What follows is based on Vincenzo Busacchi, "Girolamo Mercuriale nel 350° anniversario della morte," *Romagna Medica* 8 (1956): 417–30; the translator's introduction to Girolamo Mercuriale, *Arte ginnastica,* tr. Ippolito Galante (Rome: Banco di San Spirito, 1960), xix–xxvi; the entry on Mercuriale in J.-F. Michaud, *Biographie universelle,* 2nd rev. ed., 45 vols. (Paris: Delagrave et Cie., n.d.); P. Paoletti, *Gerolamo Mercuriale e il suo tempo: Studio eseguito su 62 lettere* (Lanciano: Cooperativa Editoriale Tipografica, 1963). On the contents of *De arte gymnastica* there are the two not entirely satisfactory articles by W. Brunoni and by M. Terzi and W. Ronchi in the volume of *Romagna Medica* above. There are also two curious attempts to turn Mercuriale into a precursor of the Fascist doctrine of physical culture; see Giuseppe Mazzini, *Jeronimo Mercuriale (1530–1606) y su "De Arte Gymnastica"* (Santiago, Chile: Imprento "Cultura," 1940) and René Suaudeau and C. Suaudeau-Deterne, *La Renaissance de la gymnastique*

He was born in Forlì in 1530, studied at Bologna and Padua, and worked as a physician and teacher. He wrote many books—on the nursing of children, skin diseases, diseases of women, and so on—as well as commentaries and lectures. He was a successful practitioner. From 1562 to 1569 he was physician to Cardinal Alessandro Farnese, to whom he dedicated the first edition of the *De arte gymnastica*. He became very famous in 1573 when he cured Maximilian II from a deadly illness. That same year he also rededicated the *De arte gymnastica*, now in a second illustrated edition, to the emperor. In later years he taught in Bologna and in Pisa; he died in 1606, a celebrated practitioner and an important humanist scholar of medicine.

Mercuriale's treatise is almost entirely concerned with ancient sport, "exercitationum omnium vetustarum genera" as the title page emphasizes, and is an extraordinarily well-documented survey of the Greek and Latin sources for the study of physical exercise. The first book treats of definitions and of the early history of gymnastics, goes on to discuss the various locations where ancient sports were practised (*palaestra*, *gymnasium*, baths, and so on) and finally establishes the matter of the rest of the volume—medical gymnastics, as opposed to martial exercise and athletics or the professional sports of the gladiator. Books 2 and 3 are a detailed analysis of the history and practice of the many sports the author classifies under "gymnastica medica"—leaping, various forms of ball games, dancing, wrestling, throwing of the discus, walking, running, riding, swimming, hunting, and the like. Included among these are a few of the less well-known sports, however famous among the ancients, such as pancreatic wrestling, the use of the *halterus*, and a few activities which we today would call exercise of a kind if not sport as such—holding the breath, loud speaking, and drills for the voice. Books 4 through 6 are more specifically medical than those preceding. Book 4 presents the effect of exercise on different physical types (chap. 7 wonders, for instance, "An corpora aegra ullo pacto exerceri conveniat"). Books 5 and 6, following the same order as books 2 and 3 re-examine each of the sports, this time analysing their benefits and harms from a medical point of view. The chapter "De cursus natura" at book 5, chapter 7, for instance, completes the discussion of running begun in "De cursu" at book 2, chapter 10. Together these two chapters provide a history and analysis of running as a sport of "gymnastica medica," including all the benefits and harms that the sport induces.

---

médicale du XVe au XVIIe siècle et le "De Arte Gymnastica" de Mercurialis (Clermont-Ferrand: Librairie Queyriaux, 1943).

As one may well imagine, the author's double approach to each of his sports does not provide the book with much continuity. As Jacques Ulmann, the historian of sports, says, "préoccupations médicales et historiques interfèrent."[6] Yet the work is immensely learned with references to at least 122 ancient authorities–principally Hippocrates, Galen, Aristotle, Celsus, Oribasius, Aetius, as well as the Arabs Avicenna, Averroes, and Rhazes. Mercuriale reads these sources critically, and often places differing opinions side by side to allow the reader to see how sound medical advice may be obtained through the weighing of apparently contradictory authority.

We don't know how Mulcaster came across Mercuriale's *De arte gymnastica*, although we do know that for every topic in his *Positions*, not just for sports, he wished to support his arguments by reference to up-to-date as well as classical authority. For instance, in preparation for a never written section of his *Elementarie* on drawing and penmanship he wrote to the celebrated cartographer Abraham Ortelius to ask him about books on drawing and mentions that he had himself already looked at Pliny, Vitruvius, and Dürer.[7] No doubt he cast about in the same way for material on sports. Yet how he got to the book is unknown, indeed even which edition he followed.[8]

To get a precise idea of how Mulcaster used Mercuriale's treatise, one should set the two books side by side and read them together, and this is what I shall now do for one part of the texts. Mulcaster's chapter 21 "Of Running" is based on those chapters "De cursu" (2.10) and "De cursus natura" (5.7) mentioned above. Mulcaster begins his little essay on run-

---

[6] Jacques Ulmann, *De la Gymnastique aux sports modernes*, 3rd ed. (Paris: J. Vrin, 1977), 99; 97–114 on *De arte gymnastica.* Ulmann does not seem entirely sympathetic to the historical project implicit in much of humanist thought, including its science.

[7] On microfilm in the British Library (Department of Manuscripts, M/457); transcribed in *Ecclesiae Londino-Batavorum Archivum*, ed. J. H. Hessels, 3 vols. in 4 (Cambridge: University Press, 1887–97), 1: 249–52.

[8] After a fairly close comparison of the texts (runs of the editions are found in the British Library and the Osler and Rare Book libraries of McGill University) I cannot specify which of three possible editions he read. Besides the first edition of Venice 1569 there is a slightly revised and now illustrated edition of Venice 1573 also published by the Giunta family and a reprint of Paris, 1577, published by Du Puys; there is also an edition of 1601 (rpt. Rome: Banco di San Spirito, 1960; for the accompanying translation, see note 5 above). On the woodcuts in 1573 and later editions, see Harvard College Library Department of Printing and Graphic Arts, *Catalogue of Books and Manuscripts Part II: Italian 16th Century Books*, comp. Ruth Mortimer (Cambridge, MA: Harvard Univ. Press, 1974), no. 302.

ning by proving its utility. The first paragraph is an extended paralipsis, in which he tells the reader that "To polissh out this point with those effectuall reasons [regarding the necessity of running] ... were to me nothing needefull." As part of this circumlocutory device he maintains that it is not necessary to tell "what *Alexander* the *Macedonian*, nor what *Papyrius* the *Romain* did by swift foote, nor that *Homere* gave *Achilles* his epithete of his footmanship"; he need only state "that *running* is an exercise for health, which if reason cannot winne, whereof every man can judge, sure historie will not." In many other chapters, the historical proof is often taken from the early chapters of *De arte*; this time however Mulcaster has gone elsewhere, to Sir Thomas Elyot who refers to Alexander, Papirius, and "swifte foote Achilles" in his observations on the benefits of running in book 1, chapter 16, of his *Boke Named the Governour*. Mulcaster then proceeds from his preliminary historical proof to a division of running by type: two kinds "vehement swift" and "gentle and moderate" he analyses at some length, and he concludes his chapter with the "other kindes of running," namely "long outright," "streight backward," "round about," "uphill," "downhill," "in ... clothes," "out of ... clothes," "in winter," "in sommer." All this is from Mercuriale, and is a condensation of five pages of *De arte* in which running is divided into "uelocius, atque uehementius," "remissius & placidius," "in rectum," "in retro," "circulariter," "per accliuia," "per decliuia," "tecto corpore," "nudi corporis," "in hyeme," and "in aestate," in the same order followed by Mulcaster. The English follows the Latin closely, although a great deal has been omitted. Most of the references to ancient authorities, for instance, have been passed over—"sapienter Theodorus Priscianus scriptum reliquit," "ab Aretaeo," "a Celso," "credidit Rufus Ephesius," "secundum Antyllum," and similar formulae are dropped. Also left out are debates on the harms of running to those with what Mulcaster translates as "an ill heade, or a weake bulke, or burning and hoat urine" and on running in and out of clothes. Throughout this chapter Mulcaster is intent on providing sure opinion, not debate. To argue points pro and con would vitiate his deliberative style which must be strong and positive; moreover he would lose the avowed central train of his topic, which is education, not medicine. The only debate he gives in the chapter is at the very end, where he mentions contrasting views on running in summer and winter, and provides a simple resolution. In the second half of the chapter there is only one observation added to the material from Mercuriale, and that is the image of a "chafed [i.e., vexed, irritated] deare" who must run from the hunter but who would keenly like the hunter to "give him leave to pisse"—a fanciful image to show the danger of running with a full bladder, and quite in keeping with Mulcaster's style which throughout *Positions* now and then plays with intentionally amusing digressions to give relief to purely technical discussion. Likewise, his alliterations continue sound-patterns used all the way through *Positions*: examples are "defluxions and distillings" (combining definition and alliteration for Mercuriale's simple "defluxiones"), "cooleth the flesh & furthereth not the feeding" (for "carnem refrigerat, nec alimenti reddit capaciorem," itself a chiastic alliteration), and "as the fore warning of some forreine disease" (for "quibus morbus forinsecus immineat").

Overall, as this analysis of chapter 21 of *Positions* shows, and as a close reading of other chapters would also demonstrate, Mulcaster condenses his source by omitting debate and authorities. He adds to Mercuriale a few historical examples and images, and he transforms the fairly straightforward medical jargon of the *De arte gymnastica* into his own "close" style of writing. These chapters on sports may be the least successful in *Positions*—the most heavily studded with authorities most of whom are borrowed directly from Mercuriale, the least concerned with students and parents, the most lacking in personal observation and experience. Yet they do show us Mulcaster attempting to work in as full a manner as he could with a subject seemingly unfamiliar to him, and the chapters on dancing, archery, ball games, and the training master do show a concern with contemporary practice which is not found in the *De arte gymnastica* of Girolamo Mercuriale.

The fact that Mulcaster relied on Mercuriale as he does and the manner in which he modifies his source are directly related to the ideological direction of his argument. Richard Mulcaster is one of the three most important writers in sixteenth-century English pedagogy; the other two are Sir Thomas Elyot and Roger Ascham. Unlike his two predecessors, however, Mulcaster is not specifically concerned with the education of the gentleman. His program considers all social groups. In a sense, his recommendations reflect an important shift in late sixteenth-century schooling. By the 1580s the schools of England had been rapidly expanding in both size and social composition. The education of the gentleman, formerly undertaken under the guidance of a tutor in a great house, was still in practice, but had begun to break down—Philip Sidney and Fulke Greville, for instance, both very well born, studied under Thomas Ashton at Shrewsbury. By the 1580s, the programs of Elyot and Ascham had become obsolete. Not that they disappeared as nostalgic ideals, but they corresponded hardly at all with contemporary practice in the schools. Mulcaster, for instance, taught 250 boys with the help of only three ushers or assistant masters. Ashton taught 450 with as little manpower. It was a hectic environment. Yet Mulcaster is resolutely in favour of this public education, and brings forth all the ancient authorities to attack the notion of private instruction. He is a supporter of a strong central state that retains hierarchy but that does not give undue worth to any degree except for the monarchy itself. In his mind *everyone* is to go to the state schools. Even women, in his tortured and ambivalent chapter on the education of girls, must have some contact with the classrooms of the state.

The whole program of sports fits into his more general claims. The schools will retain the best of the older education of the gentleman, but they will not be just for the gentlemen or the wealthy. Yet how can he present his argument? He cannot argue that horseback riding and fencing must be taught because these are *socially* correct. This would undercut his argument that they should be open to all. So he has undertaken a different approach. These sports will be practised, along with many others, because they are *medically* sound. The whole social aspect of sports is obscured by an apparently scientific argument in their favour. Yet this scientific—or perhaps one should say pseudo-scientific—argument for sports is really part of Mulcaster's rhetorical method. What is accepted method for one end in Mercuriale becomes reused but entirely redirected in Mulcaster. In other words, everything the medical humanist Mercuriale says about a sport is intended to disseminate and increase medical knowledge; everything the educational propagandist Mulcaster says—no matter how scientific or how well supported by authorities—is used as part of a defence of a uniform system of public education. In the shift of emphasis we see one way Neo-Latin scholarship is adapted for vernacular needs in sixteenth-century England.

Memorial University of Newfoundland

The Problem of Faction Versus Fiction in Early Renaissance Art Theory

LISE BEK

The Terminological Puzzle in Alberti's Treatise on Painting

Some people, with a gift for serendipity, stumble upon bright new ideas without being aware of their novelty. The *princeps* of the Italian humanists of the early Renaissance, Leon Battista Alberti, however, was not that kind of man; on the contrary, if we take a look at his writings on art theory, at least, he always seems keenly aware of his innovations, judging from his open or disguised criticism and polemics against his predecessors or contemporaries of a more conservative observation. It is the more surprising, therefore, that in his treatise on painting, written in his–and the century's–thirties, he appears to have made a backward step in his thinking from its first Italian version, *Della Pittura*, which I am inclined to date to 1436, to the Latin version, *De Pictura*, dating presumably from about 1440.[1] But it may be possible to find a plausible explanation for this. A suggestion would be that the humanist literary tradition as well as the Latin writers on the visual arts, offering themselves as the

---

[1] The true versions of the texts are given simultaneously in Leon Battista Alberti *Opere Volgari* vol. 1, ed. Cecil Grayson (Bari, 1973). There has been some discussion as to the dating of the two versions. But to me it seems likely that the Italian one was inspired by his fresh encounter with the marvels of Florentine art in the years immediately after his first visit to the city in 1428, whereas the Latin version would be nicely accounted for by his wish to leave the city in the late thirties.

proper models for his topic, imposed on Alberti certain limits that, for some reason, he did not want to transgress.

The matter under discussion in this paper is a curious, but as far as I am informed, hitherto unnoticed discrepancy of terminology between the two versions of the Albertian text. It is the more curious since elsewhere one text follows the other quite closely, except for a few interpolations of a typically humanistic or scholarly kind, made in the Latin version.[2]

The passage in question is to be found at the very beginning of the treatise, in paragraph two of its first book, using Cecil Grayson's paragraphing.[3] Here the author sets out to define the basic formal elements of the picture: the point, the line, and the surface. But immediately before this he gives his definition of the art of painting as such, stating that things invisible are no concern of the painter. In its literal sense it sounds like a prompt refutation of the opinion expressed by Alberti's elder colleague, Cennino Cennini, in his *Libro dell' arte*, written, according to its concluding note, in 1437.[4] In the first chapter of the book Cennini claims that the painter is able, through his art, to reveal the true things, covered normally under the shadow of the visible word. It must be noticed in this connexion that Cennini was a representative of the more traditional trend in Florentine art and art theory, reaching back to Giotto and Dante.[5] Alberti for his part, then, continues to remind the painter that he should confine himself to representing solely what can be seen, objects and phenomena of the visible world, in other words. In paraphrasing the Italian as well as the Latin text, the word "represent" seems to be fairly appropriate. It is, in fact, the one given in the two English translations of recent date, John R. Spencer's from 1956 and Cecil Grayson's from about 20 years later.[6] Alberti, however, uses two different words in the two texts, namely, *fingere* in the Italian version and *imitare* in the Latin. As both words were equally known and usable in either of the two languages, he

[2] In the English edition of Leon Battista Alberti *On Painting*, ed. John R. Spencer (London, 1956), the interpolations are easily traceable, inserted as they are in italics in the text.

[3] The paragraphing system represented in the edition mentioned in note 1.

[4] Cf. Cennino Cennini *Il Libro dell'arte*, ed. Franco Ronelle (Florence, 1971).

[5] In my article "Voti Frateschi, Virtu di huminista e regole del pittore; Cennino Cennini sub specie Albertiane" in *Analecta Romana Instituti Danici* 6 (1973): 63–106, I have opposed Cennini's medievalism of a markedly Franciscan observation with the humanism of Alberti.

[6] Cf. Spencer's edition mentioned in note 2 as well as Leon Battista Alberti *On Painting and On Sculpture*, ed. Cecil Grayson (London, 1972).

must have had a particular reason for doing so. But before we embark on an investigation of this question, it will be useful to find out what, precisely, Alberti intended to say.

Later in the first book of his treatise, Alberti tries, by means of common-sense philosophy and mathematical optics, to convince the reader of the possibility of reducing the whole world, including man, to a smaller scale without anybody noticing any difference, provided the diminution be made proportionately for all objects. The reason is, so he says, that the human being will always tend to judge his surroundings by measurement, using his own body as his yardstick. At the end of the first book, furthermore, Alberti instructs the painter about how to produce in his picture that kind of mini-world, by using the linear perspective construction.

The method of linear perspective had been practised by the Florentine artists throughout the early decades of the century. It had been proved valid, moreover, especially for the rendering of architectonic prospects of real buildings, thanks to the experiment made as early as 1420 by the architect Filippo Brunelleschi, to whom Alberti was, eventually, to dedicate the Italian version of his treaties.[7] At this point it is worth noticing that what Alberti had in mind with his perspective construction was neither such an architectural device nor the kind of illusionism for which linear perspective was so widely explored in the following centuries. The mini-world to be made by the artist was not to be simply a reorganization or extension of the world proper of the beholder. Far more, it had to be another world to be observed by him behind the frame of the picture, as if looked at through an open window, as Alberti himself puts it in paragraph 19. In other words, a sharp boundary between the world of the beholder and that of the picture had to be drawn in order to safeguard the moral implications of the latter as representing a higher state of value compared to that of the beholder and not to be rivalled by him, but to impress, instead, itself upon his mind.

To describe the process of construction in question, Alberti, in his Italian text, naturally turned to a term current in the actual discussion of the humanist circle to which he belonged. In Florence a literary debate on the nature of poetic creation had been going on for a long time. Whereas at the threshold of the fourteenth century, Dante in his *Divine Comedy* had maintained that poetry was what he called a *bella menzogna*, Giovanni Bocaccio, half a century later, had been of a slightly different opinion. And so was, decidedly, Coluccio Salutati. In his *De Laboribus Herculis*,

[7] Cf. the dedicatory letter to the Italian version.

finished in 1405, he points out that through poetry a new sort of reality is created, which is *ficta*, as opposed to existing reality, i.e., *facta*.[8]

Alberti, to be true, after having laid down, in the first book of his treatise, the rules for the technical execution of the picture, was mostly concerned in the remaining two books with the transfer of the poetic and rhetorical standards and models of Antiquity into his chosen field of painting. Nothing would have occurred more easily to him than to draw for his terminology also upon the writing on literature of his own day, to use it for his own specific purpose, translating it at the same time into the vernacular.

But let us turn, then, to the Latin text and to the term *imitare*. As is evidenced through every page of his treatise, Alberti was well versed in the ancient writers on the visual arts and made extensive use of his knowledge. So he often exemplifies his own views by referring to artists or works of art mentioned by Pliny the Elder in the *Historia Naturalis*.[9] Likewise, he rephrases one of the Vitruvian passages, in the *De Architectura*, on the formation of pictorial depth illusion to suit the description of his own linear perspective construction.[10]

In Vitruvius the word *imitare* is used about the rendering of stone incrustation in the pictorial wall decoration of the I Pompeiianic Style, it being an imitation of nature. Pliny, however, uses the term variously to signify both the imitation of nature and of the works of other artists. In these two, as in other Roman authors, the quality of a piece of art is duly praised on behalf of its life likeness, *vivum similis,* or its truthfulness to nature, *similitudo veritatis*. It was, indeed, this kind of imitative skill which the Ancients admired in the two Greek painters, Zeoxis and Parhasios, as shown in the anecdote told by Pliny about their painting, one a basket of grapes, the other a curtain seemingly drawn before the picture, to see whose rendering of nature was the more deceiving.[11] The idea of imita-

---

[8] On the Florentine poetics of the 14th century and especially on that of Salutati, cf. J. Lindhardt, *Rhetor, Poeta, Historicus: Studien uber rhetorische Erkenntnis und Lebensanschauung im Italienischen Renaissance–Humanismus* (Leyden, 1979), 2:93–151.

[9] Most of the editions and translations of the treatise comment on this fact. It is typical for Alberti, however, that he more often than not cautiously conceals his sources.

[10] I hope, on a later occasion, to be able to return to the problem of Alberti's extremely sophisticated re-use of the Vitruvian text.

[11] The anecdote is told in *Nat. Hist.* (IX, XXXV, 65). It describes the wager commonly dealt with by later authors on the arts. The fact that it does not seem to have attracted Alberti's attention may support the point made in this paper.

tion was, in fact, quite in accordance with the ancient concept of the visual art as *mimesis*. What was expected from the artist in ancient Greece or Rome was precisely his creation of a sense-deceiving illusion of that illusion to the senses which made up the world of things in contrast to the geometrical order of higher reality. Through the imitation of existing things, "things that are or could be," as Vitruvius has it, the work of art came into existence itself, but as an imitative object rather than an artistic creation. Hence the artist was regarded as a craftsman who made artifacts. In the Middle Ages the view upon the arts and artists, broadly speaking, remained the same. The work of art was considered to be, more or less, an enlargement or a supplement to divine creation, and the artist to be working as the obedient tool of its creator, God.

At the end of the fourteenth century, finally, the word *imitare* reoccurs in connexion with the visual arts, this time in a strictly humanistic text. In his lives of Giotto and his pupils, Alberti's elder fellow-townsman, Filippo Villani, relates about one of these that he was called the monkey of nature, *natura simia*, from his cleverness at imitation.[12] And from the following passage we learn that this meant a detailed rendering of the human figure in its outward appearance, its skin, hair, and so on. It should be interposed, incidentally, that in his biographies of the Florentine painters Villani lent heavily upon Pliny the Elder in structure and style as well as in content.

But it was certainly not that kind of surface illusion Alberti wanted the artist to produce. When his painter was enjoined only to occupy himself with things seen, it was not in order to bewilder the senses of the beholder by confronting him with a mere shadow of the shadowy reality of the world of things; his task was instead to challenge the rational judgment of his counterpart, disclosing to his alert eyes, in the perspective picture, the geometric order of true reality. Neither did Alberti intend his artist to add some tiny detail to the world created by God, but rather to create a new world of his own, similar in structure, but not necessarily in terms of surface appearance, to the God-created one. Alberti, consequently, was able to qualify the artist with the role and power of another God, *Deus alter*.

To describe the realization of the work of art thus detached from the reality which Salutati had termed the factual one, Alberti could afford, without interfering with any established literary tradition, to use in his

---

[12] Vilani's text has been rendered in Latin as well as in translation and is commented upon in Michael Baxandall: *Giotto and the Orators, Humanist Observers of Painting in Italy and the Discovery of a Pictorial Composition* (Oxford, 1971).

vernacular text the term *fingere*. But in the case of the Latin version the situation was more complicated. In the ancient writers on the visual arts he would find no justification whatsoever for using the same term. So he made his choice, a little deliberately, so it seems, from the stock of ancient vocabulary, already familiar to the new audience that he intended to reach, no doubt, by the Latin version of his treatise: mainly the humanistically educated courtiers and scholars outside Florence, to whose delight also the above-mentioned interpolations were made, accordingly. *De Pictura* was dedicated, in fact, to the Duke of Mantua, Gian Francesco Gonzago.[13]

Yet, Alberti must have realized that the idea of imitation was not fully consistent with his new concept of pictorial art. In his treatise he repeatedly reminds the reader that what he sets down on its pages is not parroting the teachings of the Ancients, but his own genuine discoveries. At the end of the first book, in particular in paragraph 21, he is eager to stress that as far as the composition of the picture is concerned, to which belongs, not least, its perspective construction, it was a field totally unknown in Antiquity.[14]

But perhaps Alberti was right, all the same, in moderating his radicalism, trying instead to follow the literary standards and terminological precepts of the authors preferred by his fellow-humanists. The following observation may provide an indication in this direction.

When, shortly after the middle of the century, the non-Florentine humanists, such as Cyriacus of Ancona and Bartholomeo Fazio, were searching among the works of art produced by their contemporaries to find some suitable pretence for their own exercise of the ancient rhetorical genre of *ekphrasis* or art description, their eyes fell, characteristically enough, not on the multitude of Italian pictures, but on the few ones brought into the peninsula from Flanders. In the detail-realism or genre-paintings, executed in the magic oil technique by the two Netherlandish masters, Jan van Eyck and Roger van der Weyden, the humanists seem to have recognised the kind of surface illusion described to them by the Roman authors, for which reason they could, conveniently, use them as their models. And they did so, without questioning how far the reality, represented in the altar-pieces and the devotional pictures of transalpine provenance, was identical with that depicted for instance in the still-life of the Roman wall decoration.[15] Consequently, in their descriptions, they

[13] Cf. the dedication of the Latin edition.

[14] Cf. Baxandall, *Giotto and the Orators*, 121 ff.

[15] The most prominent texts by the two humanists are given in note 2 of Irwin

manage to catch only the formal aspects of the new Netherlandish art, without grasping, however, its intrinsic meaning or content. Thus, no mention is made of its hallmark, according to Irwin Panofsky, the all-pervading Christian symbolism in disguise.[16] And yet these humanists did the best they could. In their defence it must be admitted that their Roman models must have been even more unfit for the description of the works of the Italian Renaissance. In them they would find no words to characterize the hard-cut, crystalline stereometry of form or the empty extension of space in a Masaccio or a Piero de la Francesca.

From this we may conclude that either his humanist colleagues did not fully understand the Albertian innovation as regards the concept of art, announced in his treatise on painting, or they were more intent on the renewal of their own branch of art, that of rhetoric, than on a revolution of the visual arts. In the long run, however, it was the Albertian concept of art that triumphed as the concept on which Western pictorial tradition was built, until, at the end of the previous century, the decomposition of the continuity of perspective space began with the Expressionists and other early Modernists.[17]

In spite of this, art critics throughout the whole of this period, from the father of Raphael, Giovanni Santi, to the so-called father of modern art criticism, Denis Diderot, continued to derive profit from the Roman authors, preferably Pliny the Elder, so as to flavour with their eloquence their own observations on contemporary artistic production.[18] But when judging these borrowings, it must constantly be born in mind that they were brought into function in quite a new context, involving quite a different idea of reality as well as a different concept of the visual arts, not as an imitation of the factual world of things, but as an artistic creation, through re-construction, of a new fictitious reality.

Århus

Panofsky's *Early Netherlandish Painting, its Origin and Character* (Princeton, 1958), whereas Baxandall op. cit. has a complete transcription of Fazio's artists' biographies.

[16] Cf. Panofsky, op. cit.

[17] Cf. Pierre Francastel *Vers une Sociologie de L'Art* (Paris, 1974).

[18] Santi's text from his rhymed chronicle to Federico da Montefeltro has been transcribed by me from the manuscript (Cod. Vat. Ottob. Lat. 1305) and is commented upon in "Giovanni Santi's 'Disputa de la Pictura,' " a polemical treatise, in *Analecta Romana Instituti Danici*, 5 (1969): 75–106. For Diderot's paraphrasing of Pliny's text one might especially turn to this description in the *Salon*, 1763, of one of Jardin's still-lives, in which reference is made to the anecdote mentioned above.

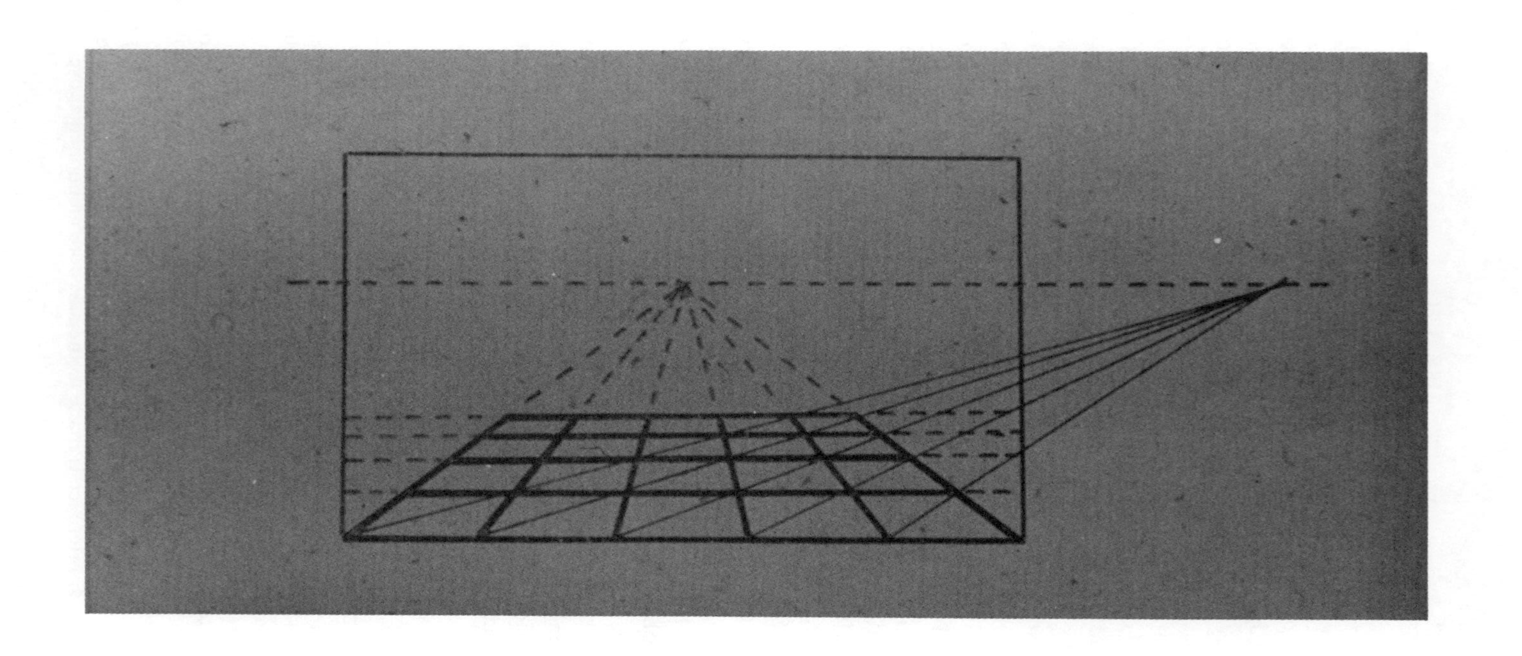

Fig. 1. Tracing the Albertian way of perspective construction, from the description of his treatise, paragraph 19.

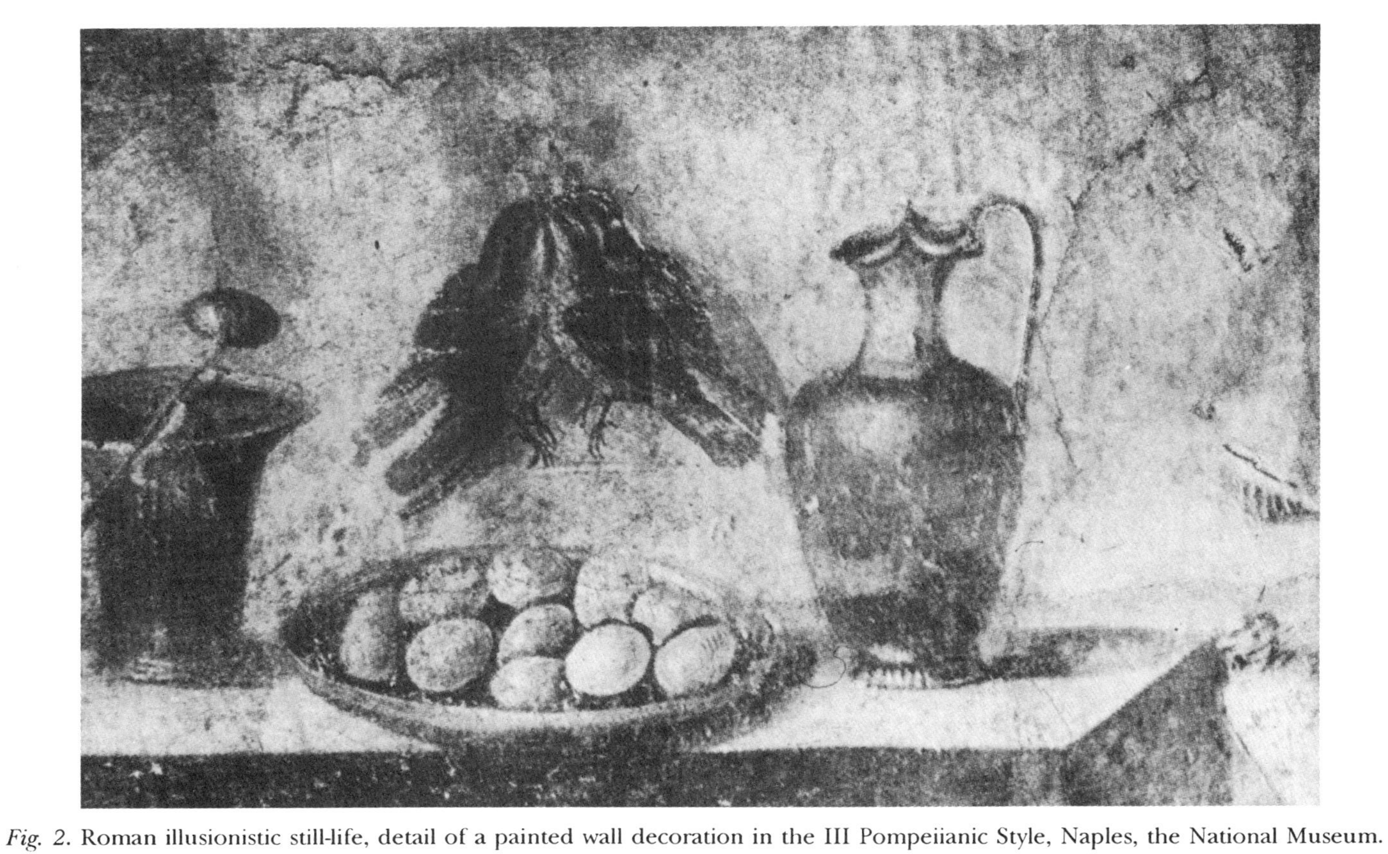

Fig. 2. Roman illusionistic still-life, detail of a painted wall decoration in the III Pompeiianic Style, Naples, the National Museum.

Fig. 3. Jan van Eyck, *The Virgin Mary Reading*, detail from the inner upper wing of the polyptic, signed by him in 1432, Gent, Cathedral of Saint Baafs.

Fig. 4. Massacio *The Tribute Money*, scene from the fresco decoration of the Brancacci Chapel from about 1425 in the Carmine church in Florence.

Les traductions françaises du Mantouan

CHARLES BÉNÉ

Avant d'évoquer les traductions françaises du Mantouan, il paraît bon de dire un mot du succès extraordinaire d'un poète aujourd'hui singulièrement méconnu.

Né à Mantoue en 1447, Battista Spagnuoli, dit Le Mantouan (pour souligner le fait qu'il était de la même patrie que Virgile), composa sa première oeuvre, les huit premières églogues de l'*Adolescentia*, pendant ses études à Padoue, poèmes qu'il publiera beaucoup plus tard, en 1498, corrigés et complétés, après son entrée au Carmel. C'est la lecture des oeuvres de Paulin de Nole qui le conduit à composer les trois livres de la *Parthenica Mariana*, véritable "Mariade," qui devaient paraître en 1481. Son intense activité littéraire ne l'empêcha pas d'être élu vicaire général du Carmel de Mantoue, puis, en 1513, prieur général de son Ordre.[1]

Son oeuvre littéraire eut un succès considérable. Marquons seulement l'hommage qu'Erasme lui a rendu, pendant toute sa carrière d'écrivain, tant dans sa Correspondance que dans ses publications.[2]

Nous n'insisterons pas sur le succès de cette oeuvre qui a connu une rapide diffusion dans toute l'Europe humaniste: éditions, éditions commentées se multiplient en Italie, aux Pays-Bas, en Pologne, en France; et qui suscitent des imitations chez plus d'un poète.[3]

---

[1] Cf. V. Zabughin, "*Un beato poeta: il Mantovano*," *Arcadia* 1 (1917): 61–90; *Poeti latini del Quattrocento* (Milano-Napoli: Ricciardi), 886–88.

[2] L'admiration d'Erasme pour le Mantouan, inspirée sans doute par C. Gérard à Deventer (Allen, t. 1, lettre 49), se maintiendra pendant toute sa carrière (cf. Allen, t. 5, lettre 1479 [1524] et même dans le *Ciceronianus* [1528]).

[3] Les oeuvres du Mantouan, après une première diffusion en Italie, trouvèrent aux Pays-Bas (Deventer) une nouvelle expansion, avant de se répandre en France. Cf. E. Coccia, *Le edizioni delle opere del Mantovano* (Roma, 1960).

Parmi les traductions françaises qui ont comme souligné ce succès, nous nous limiterons à trois d'entre elles: la *Parthenica Mariana*, traduite en 1523; les deux traductions de *l'Adolescentia*, celle de 1531 et celle de 1558. Mais si ces traductions portent témoignage de la permanence du succès du Mantouan pendant le 16e Siècle, elles portent aussi la marque de leur époque, et appartiennent, en fait, à deux générations très différentes. Car si deux d'entre elles, celle de la *Mariana* de 1523 et celle des *Eglogues* de 1530, offrent un texte complet, la deuxième traduction des *Eglogues* de 1558 porte profondément la marque des troubles qui commencent à marquer la France de Charles IX. Ainsi, dans ces traductions, c'est l'histoire religieuse et politique qui transparaît.

De l'oeuvre latine abondante du Mantouan, et malgré le succès extraordinaire que remportait l'*Adolescentia*, c'est la *Parthenica Mariana*, ou poème en l'honneur de la Vierge Marie, qui bénéficia de la première traduction française.[4]

Les trois livres de cette "Mariade" sont traduits en vers décasyllabiques, tout à fait dans la tradition de l'épopée médiévale. Editée en caractères gothiques à Lyon, en 1523, par Nourry, et traduite par Jean de Mortières, elle se présente comme une authentique oeuvre d'art, tout à l'honneur de l'imprimerie lyonnaise.

La traduction proprement dite, qui occupe la partie médiane de chaque page, est flanquée, à gauche, du texte latin de l'original, ce qui permet au lecteur érudit de se reporter, et de goûter, la poésie du Mantouan; et à droite de notes explicatives et bibliques. Ajoutons aux qualités de cette présentation du texte toute la richesse de l'illustration: si ces bois gravés, par leur facture, rappellent les illustrations de Josse Bade ou de Sébastien Brant, leur beauté tient aussi à l'inspiration évangélique des scènes représentées.

§ § §

C'est un chapelain bourguignon, Jean de Mortières, de Châlons-sur-Saône, qui a composé cette traduction, et il la dédie à une princesse qui nous est connue: Marguerite de France, duchesse d'Alençon et de Berry, dédicace qui ne surprenda personne quand on sait le rôle qu'elle a tenu tant sur le plan littéraire que spirituel.

La *Parthenice Mariana* se divise en trois livres d'une vingtaine de po-

---

[4] Un très bel exemplaire de cette traduction de J. de Mortières (Nourry, 1522) se trouve à la Bibliothèque Municipale de Lyon (cote 317054).

èmes chacun, et nous conduit de la prière d'Anne, la mère de Marie, pour que Dieu lui donne une descendance, au triomphe de Marie, après son Assomption. Si l'auteur suit l'essentiel de la tradition du Nouveau Testament, bien des chapitres sont de pure création poétique, telle la méditation de Marie, encore enfant, sur l'éminente dignité de celle qui sera choisie pour être la mère de Jésus.

La traduction de Jean de Mortières, qu'il est facile d'apprécier grâce au texte latin donné en marge, suit fidèlement l'original et ne s'en écarte guère, si l'on tient compte des contraintes inévitables de la versification. A plus d'une reprise, cette fidélité va jusqu'au scrupule quand il s'agit de rendre le mouvement du texte;[5] mais cette fidélité montre ses faiblesses lorsque le traducteur francise les mots latins. Souvent, heureusement, le mot francisé est éclairé grâce au procédé de la réduplication. Ainsi, au latin "magnifice mea mens extollit regem" devient: "mon sens, mon âme *extolle et magnifie* le roi du Ciel." Mais lorsque cette réduplication manque, on peut se trouver devant un texte bien rocailleux.[6] Heureusement, la réduplication est souvent mise au service de la vigueur ou de la tendresse. Au latin "Tunc anus laetata aduentu *carae* puellae," correspond cette traduction:

> Lors joyeuse, cette dame ancienne,
> Pour la veue de la cousine sienne,
> La pucelle *tant chère et tant aimée.*[7]

On notera aussi que si le traducteur reste souvent fidèle au vocabulaire, parfois de résonnance antique, du poète italien, il lui arrive de préférer, à juste titre, une couleur plus biblique. Ainsi, au début du chant de Marie, où le Mantouan avait écrit:

> Magnifice regem mea mens extollit Olympi.

Ce "roi de l'Olympe" deviendra, sous la plume du traducteur:

> Mon sens, mon âme extolle et magnifie
> Le roi du Ciel.[8]

Ainsi, les libertés du traducteur, légitimées par la transposition en vers,

---

[5] Cf. fol. 48r: Au latin: Vt ... Tunc ... Tu ne ... O ... O ... répondent: Après donc ... Lors ... Ne es-tu ... O ... O....

[6] "Extolle et magnifie" (fol. 50v). Mais on lit (fol. 48r): "le doulx spiramine"; "commis vitupères"; etc.

[7] Fol. 48r.

[8] Fol. 50v; mais Gabriel (42v) descend de "l'Olympe éternel"!

n'ont donc rien de chevilles paresseuses. Très souvent, le poète use de cette liberté pour introduire plus de chaleur, plus de force au texte original. Tendresse, par exemple, dans cette rencontre des deux futures mères; force par contre, dans cette transposition des versets du Magnificat:

> Et saturant des pauvres la famine,
> A délaissé en vain et en ruyne
> Ceux qui quièrent et colligent grand erre
> Les richesses et trésors de la Terre.[9]

On peut aimer ou ne pas aimer, et l'usage des mots francisés est certainement une faiblesse: mais la beauté de la présentation, comme la richesse des bois gravés, méritent considération, et montrent en tout cas le prestige du Mantouan en France en cette première moitié du 16e Siècle.

§ § §

Cette traduction devait être suivie, quelques années plus tard, d'une traduction française de l'oeuvre la plus célèbre du Mantouan, l'*Adolescentia.* On peut, pour cette traduction réalisée par Michel d'Amboise et éditée à Paris en 1531, parler mieux encore d'oeuvre d'art.[10]

Comme nous l'avons noté, ce sont les *Eglogues* ou *Adolescentia* qui seules connurent deux traductions françaises. Traductions très dissemblables, car si la première, celle de Michel d'Amboise, reproduit le texte complet des *Eglogues,* la seconde, réalisée en 1558 par Laurent de la Gravière, ne proposait que cinq églogues, et dans un contexte politique et religieux totalement différent.

Cette oeuvre d'adolescence, composée par Le Mantouan alors qu'il était étudiant à Padoue, ne comportait d'abord que huit églogues, d'inspiration virgilienne, consacrées à la vie amoureuse des rustiques. Elle portait même, d'après la découverte récente d'un savant américain, le titre de *Suburbanus.* Elle ne sera publiée que trente ans plus tard, en 1498, corrigée et complétée, par leur auteur, rentré au Carmel, de nouvelles églogues d'inspiration religieuse.[11]

---

[9] Cf. fol. 50v.

[10] Michel d'Amboise, *Les Bucoliques de Frère Bapt. le Mantouan* (Paris: Denys Janot, 1531) in 4° (BN, Rés.myc699).

[11] C'est à la Bodléienne que Lee Piepho a découvert une copie du *Suburbanus.* Découverte présentée au 7e Congrès Int. des Etudes Néo-Latines, Toronto (1988).

On ne saurait trop insister sur le succès immédiat qu'a connu l'*Adolescentia*. Les éditions se sont multipliées en Italie d'abord, et presque immédiatement dans les pays d'Europe, Deventer et Paris devenant des centres importants d'édition. Mais on l'accompagne aussi de commentaires, pour en faire un livre scolaire; et le succès est comme souligné par les traductions anglaises, allemandes, néerlandaises et françaises, tout au long du siècle.[12]

On comprend que ce poète, vénéré à l'égal de Virgile, ait exercé une influence profonde, tant sur la poésie bucolique, comme l'a montré Alice Hulubei, que sur la poésie proprement dite de l'amour, et même d'un Ronsard, comme nous avons tenté de le montrer au cours d'un récent congrès.[13]

§ § §

Les deux traductions françaises, avons-nous noté, sont aussi dissemblables que possible.

La plus ancienne, celle de Michel d'Amboise, appartient à la génération de la *Parthenice Mariana*. Comme la traduction de Jean de Mortières, elle est imprimée en caractères gothiques, avec en marge le texte latin du Mantouan, et illustrée de nombreux bois gravés. Le vers adopté est aussi le même: c'est le traditionnel décasyllabe. Mais là s'arrêtent les points de comparaison. Car, ni dans le contenu des Dédicaces, ni dans la conduite de la traduction, on ne retrouve l'esprit ou la fidélité de Jean de Mortières.

Les dédicaces qui ouvrent l'ouvrage, l'une à Mgr. de Créquy, l'autre au Seigneur de la Marche, montrent, par leur caractère ampoulé, le courtisan qu'était Michel d'Amboise.[14] La traduction proprement dite répond bien à la conception que l'on en avait au 16e Siècle. Si bien des passages sont traduits avec une certaine fidélité, la liberté du traducteur s'affirme, tant dans les suppressions que dans les additions très importantes qu'il fait subir au texte. Mais son souci de l'adapter à son propre génie, et au public français, en fait une oeuvre originale qui mérite mieux que le jugement sévère d'Alice Hulubei.[15]

C'est sans doute pour atténuer la rusticité des personnages, plus que par pudeur, qu'il supprime les deux vers "Dum vado ad ventrem ...

---

[12] Cf. A Coccia, op. cit. Des enquêtes sont en cours sur l'utilisation des oeuvres du Mantouan comme livres d'études (Pologne, Hongrie, Yougoslavie du Nord).

[13] Cf. A Hulubei, *L'églogue en France au 16e Siècle* (Paris: Droz, 1938); Charles Béné, "Le rayonnement du Mantouan en France au 16e Siècle," Congrès de Turin, 1987.

[14] Le Seigneur de la Marche est comparé successivement à Pompée, Alexandre, Cicéron, Virgile, Aristote ... et j'en passe!

[15] Cf. A Hulubei, op. cit., p. 85.

laxandum"; ou qu'il dit, de la jeune paysanne

> De ceintures d'argent éstoit serrée
> Pour le sien cors plus menu faire et rendre.

S'agit-il vraiment d'une paysanne, nus-pieds, entrain de glaner?[16]

A. Hulubei a bien montré aussi cette transposition qui substitue aux trois vers consacrés à Rome, 86 vers pour présenter Paris, ses monuments, et ses différentes professions. Mais pourquoi s'en tenir à cette critique négative? La satire a la vigueur de Rabelais et annonce Molière lorsqu'elle s'en prend, par exemple, aux gens de justice.[17] Il faudrait marquer aussi combien le poète s'enflamme pour peindre la première nuit des deux amants. A la sobriété discrète du Mantouan:

> Nox exspectata duobus venit . . .

Michel d'Amboise, emporté par son inspiration, évoque cette nuit d'amour:

> La nuit survint, tant désirée des deux:
> Entre mes bras, je me voyais tenant
> Mon coeur, ma joie, mon plaisir, mon soulas;
> De la baiser ne pouvais être las. . . .[18]

On pourrait multiplier les citations: on verrait que lorsqu'il suit le texte, il l'interprète, mettant par exemple l'accent sur l'allure séduisante de la jeune fille, mais négligeant de longs passages: visiblement, certains détails de la vie paysanne ne l'intéressent guère.

On ne saurait donc s'en tenir au jugement d'A. Hulubei: si bien des églogues du poète de Mantoue méritaient déjà les éloges qu'on lui a décernés, la première adaptation française, qui est en fait une oeuvre originale, par sa richesse, par la vigueur de la satire, par la violence de la passion exprimée, est, elle aussi un chef d'oeuvre, rehaussé encore par la qualité de sa présentation et de ses bois gravés.

§ § §

---

[16] Cf. *Eglogue* 4: 87; *Eglogue* 1: 65.

[17] Cf. *Eglogue* 5, pp. 111–113.

> (On voit) Des chicagneurs lettrez jusques aux dens,
> Qui mangent l'homme et dehors et dedans;
> Des sergenteaulx a verge et a cheval,
> Qui mangeroyent la teste a Parceval;
> Ung tas de rustres, un grand tas de satrapes. . . .

[18] Cf. *Eglogue* 1, pp. 156–57.

La deuxième traduction française de l'*Adolescentia*, réalisée près de trente ans plus tard, semble avoir échappé aux critiques. Elle montre à l'évidence la permanence du prestige du Mantouan au 16e Siècle, mais par ses profondes différences avec la première, elle marque surtout combien les temps avaient changé.[19]

Car, et il s'agit là d'une différence de taille, sur les dix églogues que comportait le modèle, cinq seulement sont traduites, et l'auteur s'en explique dans la Préface.

Ainsi, il a éliminé la 5e églogue, qui avait pour sujet "Les grands et les poètes." Et le poète nous dit, tout de go, qu'il l'avait traduite "me semblant à la vérité entre toutes la plus sententieuse." Mais c'est par crainte d'être malmené, ou châtié, qu'il a détruit son travail, "en sacrifice au Dieu Vulcain." Faut-il rappeler que ce genre de violences se pratiquait encore au 17e Siècle?

C'est pour des raisons religieuses, par contre, qu'il a renoncé à traduire les églogues 7, 8, 9, et 10. Il est vrai que si les deux premières, la 7e et la 8e, ont un caractère surtout descriptif (la 7e "sur la conversion des jeunes gens, et sa propre conversion," la 8e "Sur la religion des paysans"), les deux dernières étaient plus polémiques: la 9e critiquait vigoureusement les moeurs de la Curie, et la 10e abordait le problème délicat des Carmes "observants" et "non observants." Aussi précise-t-il, "pour le regard des autres, je n'y ai encore rien voulu, ni osé atteindre, à cause de la matière qu'elles contiennent, importante de tant, qu'elle doit être épluchée d'autre esprit que le mien." Faut-il noter que la controverse religieuse devient de plus en plus violente en 1558, et que cette prudence n'a pas de quoi étonner?

Cette Préface contient enfin une excuse aux dames qui montre bien les scrupules du traducteur. La 4e églogue avait pour titre "De natura mulierum," et le Mantouan développait à plaisir les arguments d'un antiféminisme particulièrement violent. Nos traducteurs ne sont pas en reste. Déjà Michel d'Amboise avait fait passer la même violence dans sa traduction de 1531. Laurent de la Gravière, quant à lui, connaît des scrupules qu'ont semblé parfaitement ignorer ses prédécesseurs. Il s'excuse auprès des dames, prétendant "qu'il a été contraint de faire ce que pour rien au monde il n'eût voulu entreprendre," car il veut "la conservation de l'honneur des dames," alors que le poète "tâche à découvrir leur malignité." Aussi craint-il que "pour s'être mêlé à la transcrire," elles lui fassent "d'exérables imprécations," et lui portent le "maltalent que l'auteur

[19] Laurent de la Gravière: *Les Eglogues de Fr. Baptiste Le Mantouan* (Lyon: Temporal, 1558) 8°.

mériterait." Et il les supplie de "ne le bannir de leurs bonnes grâces, lui qui n'a servi que de truchement."[20]

La lecture de ces cinq églogues montre la distance qui sépare cette traduction de celle de Michel d'Amboise. Sans, doute, une allure beaucoup plus "moderne": on a utilisé les caractères romains, et supprimé le texte latin et les commentaires marginaux; dans les noms propres aussi: Galla, gardé tel quel chez Michel d'Amboise, devient Catin sous la plume de La Gravière.[21]

Mais c'est d'abord par sa fidélité que cette nouvelle traduction s'affirme: plus de ces additions, de ces suppressions au gré du traducteur; c'est bien le poète italien que La Gravière a voulu rendre, et il l'a souvent fait avec bonheur.

Car cette fidélité ne l'empêche pas de tirer heureusement parti des libertés que donne la versification. Et il met cette liberté à profit pour garder, et même animer le mouvement du texte latin; la complicité des amants est mise en valeur; la présentation de la jeune fille trouve sous sa plume plus de séduction; la peinture du printemps est toute colorée et vivante; et les démarches qui précèdent le mariage sont vibrantes de naturel.

Ainsi, où le poète latin évoquait, à propos de la beauté de la jeune fille, celle de Diane Trivie, le traducteur propose:

> Quand je venais à comtempler sa face,
> Ses jeunes ans, son maintien, sa grâce,
> Je la jugeais plus belle et mieux parée
> Que ne fut onc Diane ou Cythérée.[22]

Il faudrait évoquer ce qu'il y a de vivacité, mais aussi de vérité, dans les rendez-vous furtifs des deux amants. Au latin: "O quotiens ... ibam ... sola tamen deerat mihi virgo" deviendra:

> O quantes fois, j'ai laissé à ma herse
> Mes boeufs liés, courant à la traverse
> En sa maison, quand seule l'y pensais ...
> Mais cependant je n'étais indigent
> Que de jouir de son corps bel et gent.[23]

---

[20] Cf. L. de la Gravière, op. cit., pp. 1–16.

[21] De même *Egl.* 1, Tonius devient Thibaut le Cornemuseux.

[22] le modèle proposait: Dicebam Triuiae formam nihil esse Dianae (1.47).

[23] O quotiens, misso cum bobus aratro,
Vt vacuis aliquando esset sola aedibus, ibam!

Laurent de la Gravière plaît, et l'on n'en finirait pas d'évoquer ses réussites, où le charme, la vigueur, l'émotion saisissent le lecteur.

Et si l'on a pu apprécier la création de Michel d'Amboise, la traduction de La Gravière vaut par sa précision, sa vigueur, son émotion. Cette traduction, réduite aux églogues champêtres et amoureuses, mérite d'être tirée de l'oubli. Et l'on se prend à regretter cette satire des grands, que le poète a dû sacrifier au Dieu Vulcain: perte très grave, sans doute, mais aussi, il faut le dire, signe des temps, où la peur règne dans le royaume.

Si les traductions du Mantouan parues en France témoignent de la permanence de son influence au 16e Siècle, elles offrent aussi des documents sur l'histoire littéraire, politique et religieuse du 16e Siècle. Mais elles sont plus que de simples documents: ici la beauté des bois gravés; ailleurs, la richesse de la création; ailleurs encore, la richesse et la sensibilité dans la traduction; le souci de l'adapter à un nouveau public: par bien des aspects, elles peuvent encore séduire aujourd'hui, et méritent, à ce titre, d'être tirées de l'oubli.

Université Stendhal de Grenoble

Omnia causabar: stiuam, dentale iugumque,
. . . sola tamen deerat mihi virgo (*Eglogue* 1.139–42).

John Barclay's Euphormio: Zur Rezeption eines neulateinischen Bestsellers in Frankreich

GÜNTER BERGER

Der satirische Roman des in Frankreich aufgewachsenen Autors schottischer Herkunft erregt schon mit der Publikation des ersten Teils (London, 1603, wahrscheinlicher Paris, 1605) europaweit großes Aufsehen,[1] das sich mit der Publikation des zweiten Teils (Paris, 1607) und dem Einschreiten der Zensur auf Intervention des päpstlichen Nuntius[2] eher noch vergrößert: Naturgemäß läßt sich die Verbreitung des Werkes durch Zensurmaßnahmen nicht stoppen, die nur bewirken, daß die nächsten 5 Editionen in den Jahren 1609–1616 ohne Angaben von Ort und Drucker erscheinen. Von 1619 an scheinen die Drucker keine Repressalien mehr zu befürchten, denn von diesem Zeitpunkt an weisen alle Editionen vollständige Angaben auf. Auch die Nachfrage steigert sich in ganz Europa weiter: Den 9 Ausgaben von Teil I und II von 1603 bzw. 1605–1616 stehen 11 aus den Jahren 1619 bis 1629 in Leiden (3), Amsterdam (2), Frankfurt (2), Trier, Straßburg, Rouen und London gegenüber.

In den 30er Jahren läßt der Erfolg mit 3 Ausgaben stark nach, der

---

[1] Die Auflagenübersicht nach David A. Fleming in seiner Edition John Barclay: *Euphormionis Lusinini Satyricon. [Euphormio's Satyricon] 1605–1607.* Translated from the Latin with introduction and notes by D. A. F., S. M., (Nieuwkoop, 1973), S. 355–57, im folgenden zitiert als *Euphormio.*

[2] Dazu übereinstimmend Pierre de L'Estoile, *Mémoires-Journaux*, edd. G. Brunet et alii, 12 Bde, (Paris, 1982) (Nachdr. d. Ausg. Paris 1875–1899), Bd IX, S.46 und Gillot in einem Brief an Scaliger vom 31.1.1608, vgl. Albert Collignon: *Notes sur L'Euphormion de Jean Barclay*, in: Annales de l'Est, 15, 1901, 32, A.1. Zur Indizierung vgl. *Index liborum prohibitorum et expurgandorum novissimus* (Madrid: D. Diaz, 1667), S. 698 f.

Abschwung setzt sich in den folgenden Jahrzehnten stetig fort, bis es im 18. Jahrhundert nur noch zu ganz vereinzelten Editionsversuchen kommt. Erstaunlicherweise spielt Frankreich bei dieser Editionstätigkeit, nachdem sie von dort ihren Ausgang genommen hatte, praktisch keine Rolle mehr, während auf der anderen Seite sowohl die Nachahmungen wie die Übersetzungen des *Euphormio* sich auf Frankreich konzentrieren. Zu den Texten, die sich in die Tradition des Werkes schon von ihrem Titel her einschreiben, zählen:

Isaac Casaubonus: *Misoponeri Satyricon* (1617)
Julien Colardeau: *Larvina Satyricon* (1619)
Claude-Barthélemy Morisot: *Alitophilis veritatis lacrymae, sive Euphormionis Lusinini Continuatio* (1614)
François Guyet: *Gaeomemphionis Cantaliensis Satyricon* (1628)

Während ansonsten nur eine ältere holländische (1683) und deutsche (1754) Übersetzung des *Euphormio* vorliegen, rivalisiert Sébastien Naus *L'oeil clairvoyant d'Euphormion dans les actions des hommes* (1626) mit den *Satyres d'Euphormion de Lusine* des Jean Tournet (1625), bricht aber nach dem 1. Teil ab, wahrscheinlich weil Nau im zeitlichen Wettlauf mit seinem Konkurrenten ins Hintertreffen geraten war. 1640 versucht Jean Bérault mit seiner *Satyre d'Euphormion* die älteren Übersetzungen aus dem Felde zu schlagen, indem er der seinen einen Schlüssel beigibt.[3]

All diese Versuche, den satirischen Roman einem gebildeten, des Lateinischen aber nicht ausreichend kundigen Publikum nahezubringen, scheitern. Einzig der Übersetzung Naus ist eine weitere (undatierte) Ausgabe bei T. Quinet vergönnt. Erst Drouet de Maupertuy gelingt seinen *Avantures d'Euphormion* (1711) ein relativer Erfolg, der sich in 3 weiteren Drucken aus den Jahren 1712–1733 manifestiert.[4] Während die beiden

[3] Das *Advertissement* macht zusätzlich auf die sprachliche Modernisierung und—wie schon der Titel—auf die Verständnishilfen in den beigefügten *Observations* aufmerksam.

[4] Ich zitiere die Übersetzungen nach folgenden Exemplaren: (Jean Tournet) *Les Satyres d'Euphormion de Lusine. Contenans la censure des actions de la plus grande partie des hommes en diverses charges & vacations.* Composées en langue latine par Jean Barclay. Et mises en françois par J.T.P.A.E.P. (Paris: Jean Petit-Pas, 1625) (Wien, Nationalbibiothek, B.E.8.R.28); *L'Oeil clairvoyant d'Euphormion dans les actions des hommes. Et de son règne parmy les plus grands et signalés de la cour. Satire de nostre temps.* Composé en latin par Jean Barclay et mis en nostre langage par M. Nau advocat en Parlement (Paris: Anthoine Estoct, 1625) (Wolfenbüttel, HAB, 51.18.Eth.); (Jean Bérault) *La Satyre d'Euphormion.* Composée par Jean Barclay mise nouvellement en François. Avec les Observations qui expliquent toutes les difficultés contenues en la première et seconde partie, Paris (Jean Guignard) 1640 (Paris, Arsenal 8° BL 17184); (Drouet de Mauper-

frühen Versionen, vor allem diejenige des Sébastien Nau, den enthüllenden ("L'Oeil clairvoyant"), aktuellen ("Satire de nostre temps") und strafenden ("censure") Charakter des Werkes, die Zielscheiben seiner Attacken ("les plus grands et signalés de la Cour" bzw. "la plus grandes partie des hommes en diverses charges et vacations") benennen, schweigt sich Bérault darüber aus und reiht Drouet seine Übersetzung mit der Bezeichnung "avantures" in einen anderen Gattungskontext ein, innerhalb dessen "satyrique"—der Untertitel lautet "histoire satyrique"—beinahe zum bloßen Akzidens wird. Auch das *Avertissement* unterstreicht den innovation Charakter seiner Version ("un Ouvrage presque tout neuf") hinsichtlich Stoff, Stil, Moral, Wahrscheinlichkeit und Schicklichkeit. Daß die zur Gattung des *Euphormio* gehörende Mischung von Prosa und Vers dem Gattungswechsel bei Drouet zum Opfer fällt, braucht kaum noch betont zu werden. Auf der anderen Seite verdankt sich der relative Erfolg dieser Version wohl gerade ihrer entschiedenen Distanznahme gegenüber dem Original.

Wie unterscheiden sich die Übersetzungen nun vom Original und voneinander? Welche Gründe und Intentionen lassen sich für einige der Abweichungen nennen?

Es fällt zunächst ins Auge, daß einzig der Version Béraults ein Schlüssel beigegeben ist, obwohl allen Übersetzern mit der Straßburger Ausgabe von 1623 ein Schlüssel zugänglich war;[5] Nau begründet seinen Verzicht damit, daß er keine "médisance" beabsichtige,[6] und begnügt sich mit ganz sparsamen, sehr allgemein gehaltenen Hinweisen, um den Leser den Rest selbst herausfinden zu lassen.[7] Tournet weist auf die Unzuverlässigkeit des kursierenden Schlüssels hin[8] und macht im übrigen deutlich, daß er nicht bereit sei, sein Wissen um die verschlüsselten Personen der Zeitgeschichte dem *profanum vulgus* nichteingeweihter Leser preiszugeben, während die historisch Gebildeten ("ceux qui sçavent le monde") des Schlüssels nicht bedürften.[9] Ausschlaggebend für diesen Verzicht könnte die Furcht vor Zensurmaßnahmen angesichts

tuy) *Les Avantures d'Euphormion, histoire satyrique*, 3 Bde, Anvers (Chez les héritiers de Plantin) 1711 (Paris, Arsenal, 8° BL 17185$^{1-3}$).

[5] Den auch die Edition Leiden 1623 enthält.

[6] *Au Lecteur*, nicht pag.

[7] Vgl. die Argumente zu Kap. II 1 –*Euphormio*, Kap. 18 und II 8 –*Euphormio*, Kap. 22/23.

[8] *Au Lecteur* zur Übersetzung der *Apologia* Barclays, S. 3f.

[9] *Epistre au* (sc. *du*) *traducteur*, nicht pag.

der besonders angespannten Lage nach der Verhaftung Théophile de Viaus sein.

Dies trifft freilich fast ein Jahrhundert später für Drouet nicht mehr zu, der jeden Entschlüsselungsversuch von vornherein mit dem Hinweis auf das Fehlen eines vom Verfasse autorisierten Schlüssels ablehnt.[10] Zu dieser Zeit ist jedoch die Form des Schlüsselromans längst obsolet, *satire personnelle* längst aus dem Bereich des literarisch Zulässigen verbannt. Andererseits geht Drouet an einem einzigen Punkt über seine Vorgänger und sogar Barclay hinaus: Er verschärft die Hofkritik[11] und walzt sie breit aus, indem er insbesondere die *grands* als Inkarnation aller Laster, Schwächen und "ridicules" darstellt.[12] Dagegen halten sich Tournet, Nau und Bérault an die Vorlage, die sich lediglich über ihren Standesdünkel, ihre belanglosen Konversationen, ausgeprägte Jagdleidenschaft, Topoi der Adelskritik also, mokierte.

Besonders der Zugriff des Hochadels auf hohe Kirchenämter erscheint Drouet ein Mißstand, den er unnachsichtig anprangert. An dieser Stelle tritt ganz deutlich der religiöse Eiferer Drouet de Maupertuy hervor, der sich 20 Jahre zuvor aus dem weltlichen Leben ins Kloster zurückgezogen hatte. Da er seine Version im Ausland anonym publizieren ließ, ging er mit seiner harschen, eifernden Kritik am Hochadel auch kein großes Risiko ein.[13]

Demgegenüber fällt mit der Kritik an kirchlichen Institutionen, insbesondere an den Jesuiten eine Hauptzielscheibe Barclayscher Satire bei Drouet begreiflicherweise völlig unter den Tisch. Um das Werk dieser kritischen Dimension zu entkleiden, fällt der gesamte zweite Teil dem Rotstift zum Opfer, und der "Übersetzer" läßt den Roman in autobiographischer Prägung mit der Abkehr des Protagonisten vom weltlichen Leben und seiner Aufnahme ins Kloster enden, wo er glücklich und zufrieden lebt,

> jusqu'à ce que le grand Thautates (sic) vienne rompre mes liens, & que mon ame en liberté, prenne son vol vers le Ciel, & s'aille heureusement perdre dans le sein de la Divinité.[14]

Mit diesem letzten Satz endet diese Version definitiv als Erbauungsroman,

---

[10] *Avertissement*, nicht pag.

[11] *Euphormio*, S. 20 - Drouet, Bd. I, S. 115-117.

[12] *Euphormio*, S.40/42 - Drouet, Bd. II, S.8-41.

[13] Das *Journal de Trévoux* zitiert übrigens in seiner Rezension der Edition Amsterdam (F. L'Honoré) 1733 vom Jan. 1734 auf S. 227-31 einen Ausschnitt aus genau dieser Passage.

[14] Vgl. Drouet, Bd. III S. 308.

nachdem ihr Verfasser schon zuvor den Textsinn immer dann nicht bloß verfälscht, sondern geradezu ins Gegenteil verkehrt hatte, wenn Barclay seinem Zorn auf die Jesuiten freien Lauf ließ.[15]

Diese Passagen bieten auch zwei der älteren Übersetzer Probleme, die auf ganz unterschiedliche Weise gelöst werden: Nau tendiert dazu, die gesamte ideologische Sprengkraft des Textes in einer treuen Übersetzung zu erhalten, verzichtet allerdings in den—im übrigen außergewöhnlich kurzen Argumenten—zu den Kapiteln des ersten Teils, die sich kritisch mit den Jesuiten auseinandersetzen,[16] auf eine Lehre, die sich in den übrigen Argumenten jeweils den Inhaltsangaben anschließt. Dagegen neigt Bérault im Zeichen erstarkter absolutistischer Macht dazu, den von Barclay als übermächtig beschriebenen Einfluß der Jesuiten selbst auf Herrscher zu negieren,[17] andererseits aber, jeden noch so leisen Versuch einer Einflußnahme, und gründe er sich nur auf die Neugier, hinter das Geheimnis herrscherlicher Kabinettstüren zu dringen, als unzulässig zu brandmarken.[18] Insgesamt versucht Bérault, der harschen Jesuitenkritik Barclays die Spitze zu nehmen, wenn er etwa in Euphormios Philippika gegen die Jesuiten als Verderber der Jugend den Vergleich "ut infernae artis mystae" ebenso wegläßt,[19] wie er an einer anderen Stelle ihre Anbiederungsversuche beim Protagonisten nicht mit der Giftmetaphorik des Originals charakterisieren mag. [20] Dasselbe gilt für Barclays scharfe Angriffe auf das Papsttum, die in der deutlichen Anspielung auf eine mögliche Beteiligung des Papstes an einem Attentat auf Fra Paolo Sarpi im Oktober 1607 gipfeln. Selbstverständlich meidet Jean Bérault diese Anspielung tunlichst, nachdem sie den wachen Augen der Zensur nich entgangen war.[21]

Wir wollen im folgenden nun der Frage nachgehen, auf welche Weise

---

[15] Vgl. z.B. *Euphormio*, S. 54—Drouet, Bd. II S. 95 f.; *Euphormio*, S. 72—Drouet, Bd. II S. 152.

[16] *Euphormio*, S. 52/54 und S. 72.

[17] *Euphormio*, S. 52/54—Bérault, S. 79 f.

[18] *Euphormio*, S. 184—Bérault, S. 290. Diese Passage wurde übrigens schon von der Zensur inkriminiert. In ähnlicher Weise fällt die explizite Erwähnung des Papstes, vgl. *Euphormio*, S. 268—Bérault, S. 422 unter den Tisch.

[19] *Euphormio*, S. 296.

[20] *Euphormio*, S. 306—Bérault, S. 488. Auch diese Stelle wurde Index, S. 699 gebrandmarkt.

[21] *Euphormio*, S. 318—Bérault, S. 510 und *Index*, S. 699. Einzig Tournet bietet durchgängig eine treue Übersetzung auch kritischer und von der Inquisition inkriminierter Passagen—wohl im Vertrauen auf den Schutz der Verschlüsselung, wie *ex negativo* der einzige Fall von Selbstzensur in seiner Version zeigt: Er verzichtet auf die Verse *Euphormio*, S. 204, in denen unverhüllt vom Papst und von Calvin die Rede ist.

ein Text wie der *Euphormio* von seinen Adressaten gelesen wurde, müssen aber sogleich einschränken, daß es sich lediglich um Elemente einer Rezeptionsgeschichte handelt. Zunächst einige Daten zum quantitativen Umfang der Rezeption: Das Werk ist in 80 von 105 Katalogen französischer Privatbibliotheken vorhanden, deren Besitzer etwa zwischen 1650 und 1750 gestorben sind. Dieser Anteil von 76% kann erst dann in siener außergewöhnlichen Höhe eingeschätzt werden, wenn man ihn mit anderen erfolgreichen Romanen der Epoche vergleicht, etwa Sorels *Francion*, der es zwischen 1623 und 1700 auf 35 Auflagen bringt, aber nur einen Anteil von 12% in diesen Bibliotheken erreicht. Diese Bibliotheksbesitzer sind häufig *curieux*, bzw. *amateurs*, wie man sie im 17. Jahrhundert nannte, die in bibliophilem Sammeliefer sich meist mit einer Ausgabe des *Euphormio* nicht begnügen, sondern ihn gleich mehrfach besitzen. Ihrer Gelehrsamkeit entsprechend geben sie dem lateinischen Original den Vorzug: In 63 Bibliotheken fand sich zumindest eine lateinische Ausgabe, 10 Bibliotheksbesitzer lasen den *Euphormio* in einer französischen Version und 7 konnten in ihrem Bücherkabinett zwischen Original und Übersetzung wählen. In Katalogen mit feiner bibliothekssystematischer Differenzierung, die wir seit Anfang des 18. Jahrhunderts zunehmend häufiger beobachten können, wird Barclays Werk meist unter der Rubrik "Satyrae, Criminationes, Apologiae" geführt und steht dort gewöhnlich Seite an Seite mit Petron, Rabelais und *Argenis*, zu denen sich zuweilen noch Apuleius und Erasmus' *Moriae Encomium*, seltener neulateinische Romane in der Traditionslinie des *Euphormio* wie das *Misoponeri Satyricon* des Casaubonus oder Morisots *Alitophilis veritatis lacrymae* gesellen. Damit wird deutlich, selbst wenn diese Klassifizierung eher auf die Systematik von Buchhändlern als auf die individuelle Katalogisierung des jeweiligen Besitzers zurückgeht, daß der *Euphormio* einer Tradition zugerechnet wird, die in Petron ihr Modell findet, an die im 16. Jahrhundert Erasmus und Rabelais anknüpfen und die mit John Barclay ihren Gattungserneuerer findet. In welcher Weise, aus welchem Bedürfnis heraus diese oft der *robe* entstammenden Gelehrten *curieux* unseren Roman lasen, läßt sich freilich nur ganz grob rekonstruieren. Vielleicht setzen sie auch in dieser Hinsicht eine Tradition fort, die sie ganz allgemein in ihrem Habitus hochhalten, ich meine die der humanistisch orientierten *curieux* um 1600, wie sie Pierre de L'Estoile verkörpert, dessen spezifischer Rezeption wir uns nun zuwenden wollen.

Pierre de L'Estoile (1546–1611)[22] stammt aus einer traditionsreichen

[22] Die biographischen Daten nach *Mémoires-Journaux*, Bd. I, S. XXVII–XL und M.

Familie der Parlamentsrobe, die enge Beziehungen zu den Spitzen der Pariser *robe*, den Séguier, Molé, de Thou unterhält. Obwohl weder selbst Gelehrter noch Literat zählt er dank seiner weitgespannten Interessen Casaubonus, Peiresc und die Brüder Dupuy zu seinen Freunden, hat aber darüberhinaus auch Kontakte u.a. zu einem Gelehrten wie J.-J. Scaliger. L'Estoile bewegt sich damit in einem Kreis von hochgebildeten, die humanistische Tradition fortsetzenden *robins*, die, beileibe keine Stubengelehrten, sondern äußerst wache Intellektuelle, von den Erfahrungen der Religionskriege tief geprägt, den "Renouveau catholique" nach dem Tridentinum mit äußerstem Argwohn betrachten und aus ihrer jesuitenfeindlichen Haltung keinen Hehl machen. So verwundert es nicht, daß diese Kreise um die Mitte der 1. Dekade des 17. Jhs. die Fortschritte der ultramontanen Reaktion mit großer Besorgnis registrieren. Um dieselbe Zeit wird L'Estoiles Tagebuch zur literarischen Chronik, in der John Barclays *Euphormio* ungewöhnlich breiter Raum gewidmet ist.

Zunächst aber bereitet es L'Estoile größte Schwierigkeiten, überhaupt an das Werk heranzukommen angesichts der auf Intervention des päpstlichen Nuntius durchgeführten Beschlagnahmeaktion.[23] So erhält er dank Pierre Dupuy im Februar 1608 für wenige Tage Einsicht in dessen Exemplar des 2. Teils, die er zu kurzen Exzerpten und zum Kopieren des beigegebenen Schlüssels nutzt.[24] Erst im August des folgenden Jahres leiht ihm sein Freund Christophe Justel[25] sein Exemplar des 2. Teils des schwer auffindbaren Buches aus, so daß er endlich die Muße zu intensiver Auseinandersetzung mit dem *Euphormio* findet.[26]

Soweit die äußeren Daten. Gehen wir nun zur spezifischen Lektüre L'Estoiles über! Die Gattungs–und Traditionszuordnung des Textes fällt ihm nicht schwer: Mit seinem "satyrique escrit"[27] und "Livret facétieux et utile"[28] knüpft Barclay nicht allein stilistisch an Petron an,[29] sondern ist überhaupt "tout Pétronique."[30] Die Mischung von Vers und Prosa,

---

Chopard: *En marge de la grande érudition, un amateur éclairé, Pierre de L'Estoile*, in: *Histoire et littérature. Les écrivains et la politique* (Paris, 1977), 205–35.

[23] Wie er im Februar 1608 notiert, vgl. *Mémoires-Journaux*, Bd. IX, S.46.

[24] Ebd., Bd. IX, S. 46-49.

[25] 1580–1649. Der protestantische Gelehrte und Historiker, Intendant des Duc de Bouillon organisiert den Aufbau der Universität von Sedan.

[26] *Mémoires-Journaux*, Bd. IX, S. 323 f und S. 348–83.

[27] Ebd., Bd. IX, S. 46.

[28] Ebd., Bd. IX, S. 383.

[29] Ebd.

[30] Ebd., Bd. IX, S. 324.

typisches Kennzeichen der menippeischen Satire, in deren Reihe sich das Werk einschreibt, wird ihm ebensowenig zum Problem: Beim Exzerpieren notiert er Prosa–wie Verspartien und spart auch gegenüber den letzteren nicht mit Lob.[31] Ganz selbstverständlich gilt ihm der *Euphormio* als Schlüsselroman und der Besitz des Schlüssels als unabdingbar für das Verständnis des Textes[32] wie für den Lektürenutzen.[33] Konsequenterweise also kopiert er den Schlüssel zuallererst und ordnet einigen der entschlüsselten Figuren, insbesondere der des Papstes, kurze Exzerpte zu. Offensichtlich bereitet dem gelehrten Leser die Enträtselung verschlüsselter Anspielung auch höchstes Lesevergnügen,[34] dient ihm das Verschlüsselungsverfahren mithin zugleich als Quelle von Nutzen und Freude. Damit liegt der *curieux* auch hier ganz auf der Linie gattungsadäquater Rezeption, wurde doch auch Petrons *Satyricon* als verschlüsselte Satire auf Nero und seinen Hof im 17. Jahrhundert gelesen.[35]

Im Besitz des Schlüssels exzerpiert L'Estoile ausgiebig Passagen aus den Ratschlägen des Kardinals Du Perron (bzw. wahrscheinlicher des Bischofs Cospéan) an den Protagonisten[36] und seiner flammenden Rede über die Mißstände innerhalb der kirchlichen Hierarchie.[37] Auch dem vergeblichen Versuch Euphormios, sich in wohlgesetzten Worten dem allmächtigen Sully als Musensohn zu empfehlen, widmet er breiten Raum.[38] Überhaupt scheinen in gut humanistischer Manier unserem Tagebuchschreiber Reden ganz besonders am Herzen zu liegen, notiert er doch u.a. noch die "harangue ... fort plaisante" eines Puritaners[39] und als Gengenstück zum schon erwähnten "grave discours"[40] Cospéans "un autre folastre de la femme d'Anemon."[41] In ähnlicher Weise spitzt er den schon bei Barclay vorhandenen Kontrast zwischen der Schilderung der Aufführung einer Tragödie über die kriegerischen Auseinandersetzungen

---

[31] Ebd.

[32] Ebd., Bd. IX, S. 46.

[33] Ebd., Bd. IX, S. 324.

[34] Ebd., Bd. IX, S. 348.

[35] Vgl. G. Berger: *Galanterie und Hofsatire: Petron und seine Übersetzer im Ancien Régime*, in: Komparatistische Hefte 4, 1981, S. 19-31, hier S. 21. Trotz gegenteiliger Beteuerungen der Autoren gelten auch die *histoires comiques* des 17. Jhs. bei ihren zeitgenössischen Rezipienten teils als Schlüsselromane, vgl. G. B.: *Der komisch-satirische Roman und seine Leser* (Heidelberg, 1984), S. 230–33.

[36] *Mémoires-Jounaux*, Bd. IX, S. 357f. –*Euphormio*, S. 234–36.

[37] *Mémoires-Journaux*, Bd. IX, S. 364–67 –*Euphormio*, S. 264–68.

[38] *Mémoires-Journaux*, Bd. IX, S. 361–64 –*Euphormio*, S. 248–56.

[39] *Mémoires-Journaux*, Bd. IX, S. 380–82 –*Euphormio*, S. 340–44.

[40] *Mémoires-Journaux*, Bd. IX, S. 360.

[41] Ebd. –*Euphormio*, S. 270.

in den Niederlanden[42] und der sich unmittelbar anschließenden Bettszene zwischen Euphormio und Anemons Frau[43] auch begrifflich zu, wenn er die entsprechenden Exzerpte in seinem Tagebuch mit folgender Überleitung verbindet:

> Ceste guerre d'Estat finie, nostre Aucteur passe à la description d'une autre, plus douce et aisée à composer, qu'il avoit avec la femme d'Anémon.[44]

Beide, Autor und Leser zollen damit ihrer humanistischen Bildung Tribut und huldigen dem Prinzip der *varietas* als einem besonderen Kennzeichen der *satura*.

Den satirischen Ausfällen Barclays gegen die katholische Kirche im allgemeinen und die Jesuiten im besonderen, Hauptzielscheibe seiner Kritik im 2. Teil des Werkes, steht L'Estoile anscheinend wohlwollend gegenüber, wenn er ihnen auch wenig Platz zugesteht, zitiert er doch die besonders kritische Spitze gegen den Papst als Anstifter eines Attentats auf Fra Paolo Sarpi.[45] Diese Angriffe auf die kirchliche Hierarchie hatte L'Estoile schon bei seiner ersten Lektüre vom Februar 1608 amüsiert registriert.[46] Freilich beläßt es der Memorialist nicht beim genießerisch-beifälligen Lesen, sondern wendet seine Lektüre durchaus instrumental an, wenn er etwa den *Euphormio* als Autorität gegen Bellarminos seiner Ansicht nach absurde und häretische Vorstellung zitiert, wonach der Papst

> non solum ut Pontificem errare non posse, sed etiam ut particularem personam, haereticum esse non posse, falsum alquid contra fidem pertinaciter credendo.[47]

Dagegen argumentiert er mit Barclays Darstellung einer erst historisch gewachsenen Autorität des Papstes.[48] Auch hierbei bleibt L'Estoile nicht wie ein Stubengelehrter stehen, sondern wendet diese historische Erkenntnis sogleich auf die Gegenwart an, wo er die päpstliche Macht vor allem von den Jesuiten propagiert und gestärkt sieht. Mit den Jesuiten landet er

---

[42] *Mémoires-Journaux*, Bd. IX, S. 368–73 –*Euphormio*, S. 274–84.

[43] *Mémoires-Journaux*, Bd. IX, S. 373 f. –*Euphormio*, S. 286.

[44] *Mémoires-Journaux*, Bd. IX, S. 373.

[45] *Mémoires-Journaux*, Bd. IX, S. 375 –*Euphormio*, S. 318.

[46] *Mémoires-Journaux*, Bd. IX, S. 46.

[47] *Mémoires-Journaux*, Bd. IX, S. 327 f.

[48] Vgl. *Euphormio*, S. 202: "paulatim assuetarum gentium animi hos antistites deorum paulo infra Numina adoraverunt, & omnia eos posse, in religionis parte fuit." Auch dieser Satz befindet sich im übrigen innerhalb eines längeren indizierten Abschnittes, vgl. *Index*, S. 699.

gleichsam beim nächsten Stichwort, und zwar ihrem bedrohlichen Einfluß auf die ihnen anvertraute Jugend, der sie es gar erlaubten, gekrönte Häupter zur Zielscheibe von "subtilibus iocis" zu machen.[49]

Der Transfer von Lektüre auf Lebenspraxis scheint für L'Estoile ein völlig normaler Vorgang zu sein: Als er etwa von der Amtsenthebung eines *financiers* erfährt, hat er dafür sogleich eine Sentenz aus dem wenige Tage zuvor ausgeliehenen *Euphormio* parat:

> Quicquid, mortales peccamus, aptissimas poenas Dii inveniunt, nec ingeniosiores sumus ad scelera, quam illi ad vindictam.[50]

In Form von Sentenzen sedimentierte Erkenntnisse beweisen derart ihre Allgemeingültigkeit in ihrer Aktualisierungsmöglichkeit im Alltagsleben. Und gerade Sentenzen gelten in der Poetik als wirksame Instrumente auf dem Wege zum Hauptzweck literarischer Produktion, der Förderung moralischen Nutzens.[51]

Die Funktion des Exzerpierens erschöpft sich damit für L'Estoile keineswegs im Notieren ästhetischer Genüsse, sondern zielt durchaus auf Gebrauch und Verwertung im Sinne einer Einordung und Bewertung lebensweltlicher Phänomene.

Für einen Leser wie unseren *curieux* um 1600 ist die Funktionsdifferenzierung funktionaler und theoretischer Texte wie die strikte Trennung von Literatur und Leben noch jenseits aller Vorstellung, gehören Literatur und Leben im Gegenteil aufs engste zusammen. Der Prozeß der Auflösung dieses unmittelbaren Zusammenhanges setzt bei den literarisch gebildeten Eliten Frankreichs erst mit der Herausbildung der *doctrine classique* etwa 20 Jahre nach dem Tode Pierre de L'Estoiles ein.

Bayreuth

---

[49] *Mémoires-Journaux*, Bd. IX, S. 328 –*Euphormio*, S. 268.

[50] *Mémoires-Journaux*, Bd. IX, S. 326 –*Euphormio*, S. 198.

[51] So sieht das auch Drouet, vgl. das unpag. *Avertissement.* Auf dem moralischen Nutzen unmittelbar lebenspraktisch anwendbarer Sentenzen insistiert z.B. auch Martin Crusius in seiner Epitome der *Aithiopika*; vgl. dazu G. Berger: "Rhetorik und Leserlenkung in der Aithiopika–Epitome des Martin Crusius," in *Acta Conventus Neo-Latini Guelpherbytani. Proceedings of the Sixth International Congress of Neo-Latin Studies.* Wolfenbüttel 12 August to 16 August 1985, ed. Stella P. Revard, Fidel Rädle, Mario A. Di Cesare (Binghamton, NY, 1988), 481–90.

Thomas Vincent's Paria

STEVEN BERKOWITZ

Paria is a long and complicated comedy. On 3 March 1628, a time of crisis in England and a time when he should have been doing more important things, Charles I visited Trinity College, Cambridge, and sat through the play—from 11 to 5 o'clock.[1] According to the epilogue, *Paria* had been severely cut for this royal performance.

Paria's plot will sound typical: Lidonia, a noble widow of Ancona, had twin sons, Archaicus and Fulgentius. The infant Fulgentius was stolen away on the day of his father's funeral. He grew up under the care of kind Laberio, a celibate merchant of Milan. Meanwhile, Archaicus came under the tutelage of the pedant Master Nicolaus and was taken to Padua for study. There he met Astraea and Flavia, daughters of the gracious old merchant Tiberius. Both loved him, while he loved the elder, Astraea. After wounding one of Flavia's local suitors in self-defense, Archaicus fled home to Ancona, promising to return within three months. This period having elapsed, the two sisters separately and secretly traveled to Ancona

[1] This date makes John Milton's attendance at least as likely as that he "hissed" *Fraus Honesta* or *Albumazar*. See David Masson, *The Life of John Milton*, 7 vols. (rev. ed. 1881; reprint, New York: Peter Smith, 1946), 1:221–25. See also Merritt Hughes' note on the *Apology for Smectymnus* in his *John Milton Complete Poems and Major Prose* (New York: Odyssey Press, 1957), 692. On the author, performance, and texts of *Paria*, see G. E. Bentley, *The Jacobean and Caroline Stage*, 7 vols. (Oxford: Clarendon Press, 1956), 4:854; 5:1232–33. See also the introduction to my facsimile edition forthcoming in *Renaissance Latin Drama in England: Second Series, Plays Associated with Cambridge University* edited by Marvin Spevack and James Binns (Hildesheim: Olms Verlag). Line references to *Paria* are to this facsimile. Quotations from Shakespeare are from the Riverside edition, G. Blakemore Evans textual editor (Boston: Houghton Mifflin, 1974). I am grateful to the National Science Council (R. O. C.) and to the SVD Section of Fu Jen University for funding my research on Renaissance Latin drama.

in order to be reunited with their lover. As the play opens, Lidonia is lamenting what she considers her son's recent unfilial and debauched behavior. Nicolaus realizes that Archaicus is suffering from love melancholy but dares not tell his mistress.

Phrygio, servant to Archaicus, tells his master that the two sisters are in Ancona. Archaicus tries to avoid Flavia, while seeking Astraea, who of course encounters his twin Fulgentius—now a young merchant called Fulvius, who has come to Ancona to collect substantial debts. Both Fulgentius and Astraea are confused and angered by their meeting. Flavia and Fulvius independently take up lodging in Babila's inn, where the braggart soldier Petruccius approaches all visitors for free meals. Petruccius fancies that he will win the hand of wealthy Lidonia. When Lesbia, the courtesan, asks Babila to arrange an evening assignation with the Captain, Babila and the courtesan's servant boy Brilla take this as the opportunity for the elaborate subplot, which involves Nicolaus, Petruccius, and Eleazer, a Jewish garment dealer, switching costumes.

Tiberius then arrives with his dim-witted servant Asellio to search for his daughters. Asellio is also searching for his cloak, lost or stolen as he left the ship. Much more confusion and near tragedy develop when Astraea in despair attempts to stab Fulvius who, despite his growing love for Flavia, thinks the sisters must be prostitutes playing a trick on him. Spurned by Fulvius, Flavia falls deathly love-sick. Archaicus then feigns madness to win back Astraea's pity and love.

The identities of Fulvius and Archaicus become clear when all the players come together at the inn. Astraea and Flavia are reconciled with their father, and Flavia agrees to accept Fulvius. Marriages ensue—not only do the two sets of young lovers wed, but also Lidonia and Tiberius effect a sober union. Moreover, Nicolaus announces that he has successfully wooed Lesbia. Finally, it is discovered that it was Eleazer who stole the infant Fulvius. For punishment he is forced to choose between being hanged or eating pork.

Vincent based *Paria* closely on Eusebio Luchetti's prose comedy *Le Due Sorelle Rivali* (Venice, 1609). Nevertheless, *Paria* represents a thoroughgoing rethinking of Luchetti's action, and the most memorable features of the characters of each play are frequently lacking in their counterparts. For example, there are few hints of Brilla's wit, Tiberius's magnanimity, or Nicolaus's pedantic charm in Luchetti's Brilla, Prasildo, and Nicocrosmo. The marriage of Vincent's "worn-out sparrow," Lesbia (*Exoleta Passercula* [Q12v]) to Nicolaus is new in *Paria* and caps the pedant's much expanded role, perhaps elaborated especially for the play's collegiate audience.

The general indebtedness of *Le Due Sorelle Rivali* to Plautus's *Menaechmi* is obvious. It appears, besides, from echoes not in Luchetti that Vincent went directly to the Roman comedy. For example, Lidonia's proverbial expression that water is not more similar to water than are the twins—"Aqua aquae non est similior, quam hic est alteri" (4496)—echoes the *Menaechmi*: "neque aqua aquae ... usquam similius, / quam hic tui, tuque huius autem" (*Plautus*, ed. Paul Nixon, 5 vols. [London: Heinemann, 1917], 2:478, lines 1089–90).

Although the outline of the Italian comedy's plot and its character-types are transmitted in Vincent's adaptation, where *Paria* is fleshed out it becomes relentlessly Stuart English. Combining components of romance, satire, and farce into something like Jacobean city comedy, *Paria* is distinguished by the resolute, social integration of its characters: jealous and negligent young lovers whose Neoplatonic passions are finally gratified, a liberal old father, a soldierly parasite whose boast to have rid the seas of pirates for the benefit of merchants (a likely allusion to Charles's controversial naval policy) is not disputed (868–74), a wayward son who is not really prodigal, a witty and honest innkeeper's wife, an engagingly lustful pedant, his aging (and poor) courtesan bride, a clever servant and a stupid who both triumph, and even a whining widow whose remarriage confirms the union of a noble with a merchant family. In the resolution of this comedy—in the marriages of Lidonia, Tiberius, and their children—the King and his company were shown the convenience of liquid assets for the fulfillment of gentle love, and thus the resolution of class conflicts (4983–87). Indeed, the admirably competent, if hot-blooded, young man Fulvius represents in himself the successful merging of ancient aristocratic nature and generous commercial nurture (4528–32).

It is worth noting that while he introduces or emphasizes class distinctions between characters, in his accommodative comedy Vincent almost eliminates the vulgarly mercenary motives prevalent in Luchetti's play. In Vincent's Ancona there are, except for the Jew Eleazer, of course, no predatory cheats and, therefore, no gulls. Tiberius's daughters and Asellio's cloak, even the clown's ducat, are restored. The near tragic errors of the day—Fulvius's taking Flavia for a whore or Astraea's jealousy—arise from insufficient trust, as Nicolaus explains, from appearances rather than "causes" (214–15).

Despite Vincent's continuing the long tradition of borrowing from the Italian for Cambridge drama, he also seems to be drawing from English plays.[2] One might expect that in portraying a miserly Jew Vincent could

---

[2] One may find in several of Shakespeare's works precedents for Vincent's

not evade the influence of *The Merchant of Venice*. And we find details not in *Paria*'s Italian source which may derive from Shakespeare's play: the association of Eleazer with the legal system and its abuses (1748–59, 2274–80, 2915), his ironic mention of the "dura lex" (5130) to which he is finally subject, pork as a Jewish abomination (5119), the window scene with Fulvius and Flavia (3213), Eleazer's meticulous locking of his house (2991), and Astraea's inscribed ring as a love token (1332). The innkeeper Jodocus's sarcastic remark to Tiberius that perhaps Fulvius and Flavia slipped out of the inn with her treasure chest to buy a long-tailed monkey in India (2200–3) recalls Jessica's night flight with Lorenzo and a casket of her father's jewels, as well as her trading Leah's ring for a monkey (*Merchant of Venice* 3.1: 118–23).

For *Paria*'s vivid portrayal of Eleazer, there is in Luchetti's Jew Sciamoel only the barest precedent. In the Italian comedy there is no connection between Sciamoel and the theft of the infant Fulvio, and after the closing of the subplot he does not reappear.

All in all, granting his comparative pettiness, Vincent's perfidious Jew revives the villainous energy of Shakespeare's Shylock and Marlowe's ever-popular Barabas. In act 5 scene 6, Vincent abandons both his source and the requirements of his plot to elucidate the difference between Christian and Jewish business ethics. Threatened with torture when his evasions are exhausted, Eleazer finally confesses. His defense is an indictment of his race:

ELEAZER: I did what your law forbids but our laws freely permit. Nothing is forbidden to us as long as we are dealing with you. Theft

---

reworking of a tale of mistaken identities, true and false transformations, and lovers separated by the consequences of street violence: *Romeo and Juliet* and *The Taming of the Shrew* quickly come to mind, but, in addition, one finds isolated echoes of tavern-scenes in *I Henry IV* and striking parallels between Tiberius and Brabantio, Desdemona's deceived father in *Othello*. The marked difference between the two *senes* Tiberius and Prasildo, centering on Tiberius's abused generosity, suggests that certain details in *Paria* not found in Luchetti may well be from *Othello*:

(1) *Othello*. Her father lov'd me, oft invited me,
(1.3.128); cf. *Paria* 325–29.

(2) *Brabantio*. For your sake (jewel)
I am glad at soul I have no other child,
For thy escape would teach me tyranny,
To hang clogs on 'em;
(1.3.195–98); cf. *Paria* 4269–80.

(3) *Iago*. Awake! what ho, Brabantio! thieves, thieves, thieves!
(1.1.79); cf. *Paria* 3095.

is not theft, if anyone steals anything from a gentile.
TIBERIUS: A pious opinion indeed!
ELEAZER: Hence it is that many of our people get rich so suddenly. For us profit arises in two thousand ways: by law, by injury, by theft, fraud, deceit, perjury, everywhere. But for you who live by justice and goodness there is only one way of acquiring goods.
TIBERIUS: Now he is speaking the truth. Wickedness is profitable, while poverty companions probity. Rarely does a good man get rich.
ELEAZER: And so having from boyhood embraced my father's customs, I engaged in all kinds of acts and, as opportunity allowed, I exercised each one. This trade of a peddler concealed all my other dealings. My grandfather and my father bequeathed me two very rich farms, usury and kidnapping. I tilled them with all eagerness and industry. If any other little profit offered itself, I scraped it together along the way.
TIBERIUS: How good for the state that there are so many farmers of this sort!
ELEAZER: At games, market places, triumphal processions, I was there in the crowd hovering like a kite looking for prey. If any good-looking boy wandered unattended, I lured him with caresses and sweets and took him home quickly. Soon I would carry him abroad and sell him for a lot of money. This was my treasury, this unimpeded road, if I had not now been caught, was leading me to wealth.
(4786–4823)

In 1628, then, when England had no Jews, Vincent's Eleazer is an imaginative reassemblage of familiar stage and folk elements. Yet these characteristics anticipate the alarm expressed by British merchants when in the 1650s Cromwell proposed readmitting Jews to England.

§ § §

Although there are few phrases which uniquely link *Paria* and *The Comedy of Errors*, the influence of this early comedy of Shakespeare is, as one might expect, pervasive. Vincent, like Shakespeare, moves his comedy from Plautine or Italian slapstick to resonant questions of identity uncomfortably near tragic. All Vincent's young lovers—and, indeed, their parents—suffer, but Fulvius, perhaps at once the most capable and the most innocent, wins our sympathy when immediately after repudiating his unrecognized mother, he prays for the wisdom of Oedipus to unravel the enigma in which he is emotionally and intellectually ensnared:

> Would that some Oedipus might with his cleverness cross my path now. Here I understand nothing of all the things that people say to me. I have gained a mother and a girlfriend, but have lost myself. I am someone, I do not know who, called Archaicus; I left Milan a Fulvius. (1952–59)

Shakespeare's Antipholus of Syracuse "to find a mother and a brother" loses himself in Ephesus (*The Comedy of Errors* 1.2.39–40), while, as we have just seen, Fulvius bewildered in Ancona laments: "I have gained a mother and a girlfriend, but have lost myself" ("Matrem atque amicam lucrifeci, atque meipsum perdidi" [1956–57]; cf. *The Comedy of Errors* 3.2.73–74 and *Paria* 3720, 4514). Moreover, Antipholus of Syracuse wonders that he is greeted by all, "[a]s if I were their well-acquainted friend, / And every one doth call me by my name" (*The Comedy of Errors* 4.3.2–3), while Fulvius is also mystified that he is saluted as a friend. But all call him by the wrong name: "nemo erat / Quin familiarem se ingereret, & falso nomine salutaret memoriter" (4353–56). There is poignancy, moreover, in Fulvius's not knowing that his name is in truth neither Archaicus nor Fulvius but Fulgentius. By contrast, Luchetti's Fulvio has always known that Virginio was his original name (H5v).

One final notice: whether Latin plays will ever make it into the Renaissance dramatic canon, *Paria* can participate in the radical revisioning of the Renaissance called new historicism.[3] The comedy subverts through contradiction the dominant ideology which promises the royal audience a successful resolution of social tension. For example, although he is, as Archaicus points out, a rich merchant, Tiberius holds the traditional idea that wealth is achieved by rapacious immorality. Thus he constitutes no threat to the legitimacy of the gentry. Eleazer's punishment—an invitation to dine on pork—is also a form of conversion, and so includes the exotic neighbor who, undiscovered, has been pursuing his vicious, but not undemanding, business for at least twenty years, without it seems achieving quick and easy wealth. Women as daughters are treated as inconvenient and potentially embarrassing property; but as a matron, as a proudly

[3] Compare treatment of *The Merchant of Venice,* which offers to the cultural materialist what Walter Cohen calls "an embarrassment of socio-economic riches" ("*The Merchant of Venice* and the Possibilities of Historical Criticism," *English Literary History* 49 [1982]: 765–89). More recently, Thomas Moisan has interrogated the reconciliations and mediations of the play in his " 'Which is the merchant here? and which the Jew': subversion and recuperation in *The Merchant of Venice,*" in *Shakespeare Reproduced: The Text in History and Ideology,* ed. Jean E. Howard and Marion F. O'Connor (New York: Methuen, 1987), 188–206.

fertile mother of twin sons, as she herself says, Lidonia is a figure of social substance. Yet the audience's estimation of the authenticity of her inherited position–which is the sole basis of her identity–is compromised by her long-winded pride, which in the Italian source is parodied by the innkeeper's ludicrous boast about his own Sienese origins. Finally, while the traditional disparagement of appearance in favor of inner reality is expressed overtly in *Paria*, it is clear that had Fulvius not looked like Archaicus, Flavia would never have fallen in love with him, nor, one imagines, would he with her had she not accidentally satisfied both his sexual fantasies and fears. That this love which represents the interaction of appearance and reality is celebrated merely points out one more disquieting contradiction which the comedy cannot resolve except by conventional closure. These contradictions are symptomatic, of course, of the political conflict which Charles's own paternalistic rhetoric also could not contain when two weeks later, 17 March, he addressed the newly elected members of his third Parliament as misbehaving children.

Fu Jen University, Taipei

Creating Humanist Myths: Two Poems by Ulrich von Hutten

ECKHARD BERNSTEIN

In his article "A New Look at the Reuchlin Affair,"[1] James H. Overfield has challenged the traditional view that the Reuchlin affair represented "a conflict between humanism and scholasticism in which the status, or even survival, of the two intellectual traditions was at stake" (p.171). He argued instead that "humanist support for Reuchlin was less universal than most writers have assumed" (p.171), blaming Ulrich von Hutten, and primarily him, for presenting "the Reuchlin affair as a climactic showdown between humanism and scholasticism." "Unfortunately," he concludes, "his interpretation has been the one which most historians have chosen to accept" (p.207). Although Overfield's evidence for the lack of universal support on the whole is convincing, his remarks on Hutten are disappointingly brief and need elaboration.

If Overfield is correct, how was Hutten able to shape the perceptions of the historians to such a remarkable extent? In order to create the image of the implacable enmity between scholastics and humanists Hutten was faced with two tasks: first, he had to paint his opponents, the adherents of scholasticism, in the blackest colors possible, establishing a valid "Feindbild." Secondly, however, he had to convince his audience, and perhaps himself, that there existed indeed a humanist movement and that it was a strong and unified one. He attacked the first task with all the wit, zeal and passion of which he was capable in a number of works, including his lengthy poem *Triumphus Reuchlini*, the *Epistolae obscurorum virorum*, a great number of personal letters and the introduction to his *Nemo*, and Over-

---

[1] *Studies in Medieval and Renaissance History* 8 (1971): 167–207.

field briefly, but for his purposes sufficiently, sketches these works and thus provides some documentation. But how was Hutten able to solve the second task, to demonstrate the existence of a unified humanist movement? It is with this aspect, one that Overfield ignores, Hutten's attempts to develop a particular humanist group consciousness, that this paper is concerned. In other words, I intend to take up the argument where Overfield left off. Two unlikely sources, namely two lengthy poems by Ulrich von Hutten can offer, I hope, some answers to this question. Since Hutten's efforts at fashioning a particular humanist group identity precede the Reuchlin affair, I have chosen one earlier work and one that was written in the midst of the Reuchlin controversy.

The first poem is the last elegy of Hutten's *Querelarum libri duo in Lossios* of 1510, the second the so-called "Carmen rithmicale" from the second part of the satirical *Epistolae obscurorum virorum* of 1517. Both describe fictitious journeys through Germany, both contain extensive catalogues of German humanists, and both were written in the decade between 1510 and 1520. In each case I will first briefly describe the poem itself and the context in which it was written and then discuss its contribution to answering our question.

The *Querelarum libri duo in Lossios*[2] are a collection of twenty poems totaling 1662 lines in which Ulrich von Hutten describes the ill-treatment he received from his former landlords in Greifswald, Wedeg and Henning Lötz. In the fall of 1509 Hutten had come as a student to this city following some unknown adventure on the Baltic sea. After initially being welcomed by the two Lötzes, father and son, and well-to-do citizens of Greifswald, Hutten, after a quarrel, decided to leave and try his humanist luck somewhere else. In the middle of the winter, on a bitter cold day in December with the rivers frozen, the young student set out on his journey. On his way, however, he was assaulted by servants of the Lötzes who robbed him of all belongings, including a small bundle of poems, and threatened to kill him.[3] Naked, shaken by fever, and with open wounds Hutten arrived in Rostock, where new friends from the university offered him food, shelter, and money.

This, briefly, is the incident that prompted Hutten to write the twenty

---

[2] *Ulrichi Hutteni, equitis Germani, opera quae reperiri potuerunt omnia*, ed. Eduard Böcking, 5 vols. Suppl. 2 vols. (Leipzig: Teubner, 1859–61; reprint 1963). Quoted as Böcking, followed by volume, page, and line. The *Querelae* are in Böcking 3:19–33.

[3] The most detailed description of that incident is in Elegy 2 of the second book, "Facinus Lossii," Böcking 3:23–25.

poems of the *Querelae* in which he not only describes with great rhetorical vehemence and obsessive repetition the alleged injuries he had suffered, but also tries to enlist the help and win the understanding of a variety of friends, acquaintances and benefactors, ranging from Duke Boguslav of Pomerania and his uncle Ludwig von Hutten to friends like Crotus Rubeanus and Eobanus Hessus and many others. The tenth elegy of the second book, called "Ad poetas Germanos,"[4] describes a fictitious journey his muse undertakes through Germany with the following mandate: "Sed pete Germanos ex ordine quemque poetas,/Patria vel quos hoc nomine terra colit" (line 9 f.). What follows is a detailed itinerary combined with a catalogue of fifty *poetae*, the name, of course, given to those men we now call humanists (i.e., men who were specifically occupied with literary matters).

Hutten's muse starts her journey in Rostock and then proceeds via Danzig to Frankfurt an der Oder. Silesia and Bohemia are the next stations in this literary pilgrimage. From Wittenberg, the following destination, the muse is instructed to hurry to Leipzig, Magdeburg, Erfurt, and nearby Gotha. After briefly visiting Würzburg the muse comes to Franconia, Hutten's native region, and the ancient city of Fulda. From there she repairs first to Westphalia and then to Cologne. After travelling up the Rhine with visits to Koblenz, Mainz, Speyer and Straßburg the muse ends her journey in Tübingen.

Since in each of these cities, one or several poets are visited, we have in effect a catalogue of German literary men at that time. Among them are such well-known names as Georg Spalatin, Rhagius Aesticampianus, Crotus Rubeanus, Eobanus Hessus, Mutianus Rufus, Johannes Trithemius, Hermann von dem Busche, Jakob Wimpfeling, Heinrich Bebel, and Johannes Reuchlin. In addition we find a great many men who have made it to this honors list only on the strength of their friendship with Hutten.[5]

The poem, however, is not merely a catalogue but a collection of thumbnail sketches of these *literati*. Taking advantage of Latin's penchant

---

[4] Böcking 3:64–81.

[5] There are, of course, some prominent names missing on that list. That Erasmus of Rotterdam, Conrad Celtis, Philipp Melanchthon, and Hermann von Neuenaar are not mentioned is understandable. Erasmus was living in England at that time, Celtis had died two years before, and Neuenaar and Melanchthon were too young. More surprising is the absence of the Viennese humanists Joachim Vadianus and Johannes Cuspinianus, as well as the absence of Conrad Peutinger from Augsburg and Willibald Pirckheimer from Nuremberg, Ulrich Zasius from Freiburg, and Beatus Rhenanus from Schlettstadt. There are explanations at least for Vadian, Peutinger and Zasius. All three had not published anything of note at this particular time and Beatus' *Life of Gailer von Kayersberg* appeared only in 1510.

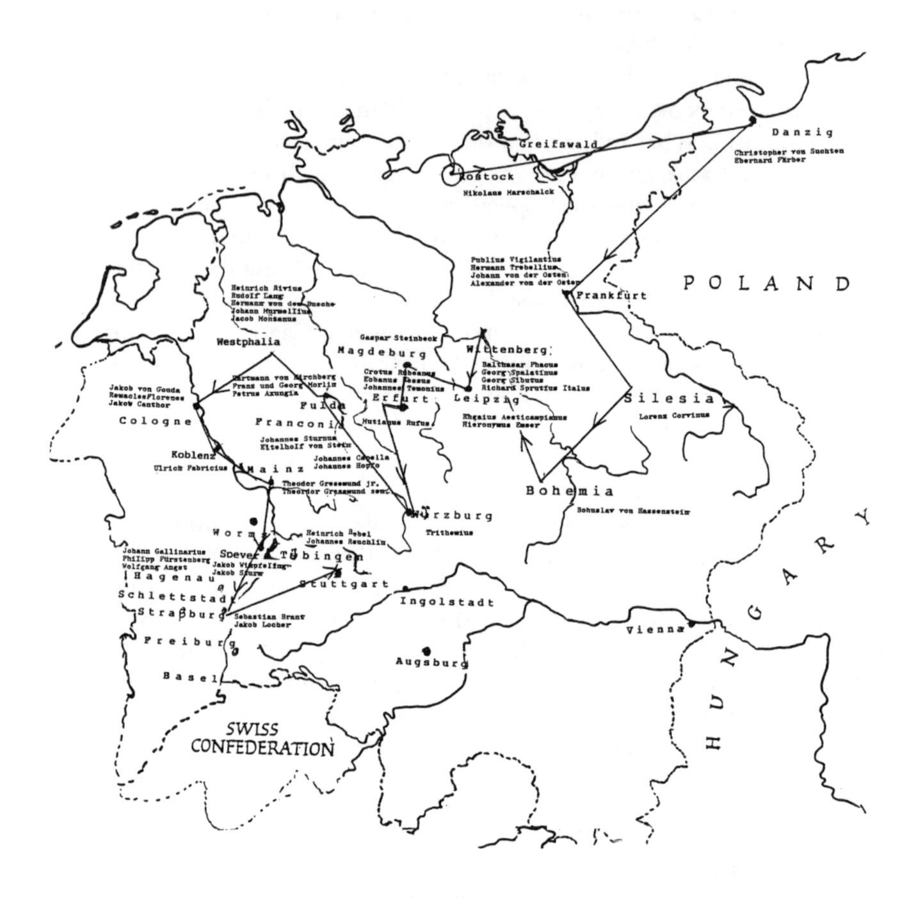

Fig. 1. Hutten's fictitious journey in the poem "Ad Poetas Germanos" from his *Querelae in Lossios* of 1510

for succinctness, Hutten in many of these sketches masterfully captures with a few strokes the very essence of a writer. A few examples must suffice. How better can one describe the fiercely independent spirit of Mutianus Rufus than with the phrase "Ipse sui totus" (line 91)? How skillfully does Hutten characterize the specific brand of humanism of the Dominican Jakob von Gouda when he says: " ... Qui miscet sacris Musica sacra suis" (line 182)? And is there a more concise way to encapsulate the essence of Jakob Wimpfeling's pious moralism and his dedication to the youth than with the phrase: "Non nisi quod sacrum est, studio complexe frequenti,/Qui quidquid scribas, utilitate scatet: /Multa, Jacobe, tibi debet Germana iuventus" (line 209 ff.)? And finally, with what an economy of words does Hutten synthesize the historic achievements of Johannes Reuchlin, who was also the first German to write a humanist comedy: "Dum triplice sacros explicat ore libros,/Inter Germanos ad comica scripta poetas/Primum ausus vetitas explicuisse manus" (line 232 ff.)?

We would, however, misunderstand the poem "Ad poetas Germanos" as well as the whole cycle of the *Querelae*, were we to interpret it merely as a colorful album of snapshots of the literary scene at the beginning of the sixteenth century. Renaissance poetics was a poetics of rhetoric, and rhetoric is the art of persuasion. A poem, like any other literary artifact, had the function of persuading the reader, to spur him on to action or change his mind. What was the object of Hutten's poem? Was it an attempt to enlist the aid of the German poets, who would rise in a show of solidarity for their beleaguered fellow humanist? Hutten seems to suggest this much when he says "Quod fecit nobis, faceret quoque Lossius illis" (line 237). But if the poem was a call to arms, a mobilization of all humanist forces, isn't there a grotesque discrepancy between the triviality of the incident and its literary treatment? And why should Germany's humanists come to the aid of this twenty-two year old student whose literary credentials at this point were very modest indeed. Most critics, even those favorably disposed to Hutten, therefore either criticize him for blowing up this incident out of all proportions or dismiss its treatment as a folly of youth. Hajo Holborn, for instance, argues that "this affair scarcely speaks well for Hutten ... he makes out of this episode a momentous question involving humanism as a whole and deserving wide publicity," adding that "Hutten's activist nature reveals itself unworthy of the occasion."[6]

The judgment is harsh and fails to take into account the biographical-

[6] Hajo Holborn, *Ulrich von Hutten and the German Reformation* (New York: Harper Row Publishers, 1966), 37 f.

psychological context and therefore also fails to appreciate the contribution Hutten made to the creation of a humanist group-identity. The significance of the *Querelae*, and especially that of the poem "Ad poetas Germanos," with its prominent position at the end, becomes clear only fully when we briefly recall Hutten's biography.[7] In 1499 his parents had sent the eleven year old boy to the cathedral school of the famous abbey in Fulda to prepare him for a career in the higher ecclesiastical hierarchy, a career which was open only to members of the nobility. Against the will of his parents, however, and to their great disappointment, the young Hutten left the school in 1505 or possibly earlier.[8] Instead of settling down to a comfortable life as a churchman, he began the restless life as a student, wandering in the next few years from university to university. By the time Hutten arrived in Rostock in 1510 and wrote *Querelae*, he had studied in Cologne, Erfurt, Frankfurt an der Oder, Leipzig and Greifswald. It was during that time that he became more and more attracted to that intellectual and literary movement which we now call humanism. He had begun writing Latin poetry, had followed his humanist teachers and had made many contacts with those who shared his interest in and fascination for the *studia humanitatis*. In applying himself so enthusiastically to these studies he had, however, not only crossed the plans of his ambitious father but had also broken with the traditions of the knights who in general did not belong to the humanist-intellectual elite of Germany.[9]

Seen from this perspective, Hutten's *Querelae*, and especially the last poem, begin to make much more sense. Having de facto rejected the traditions of the knightly class, Hutten sought a new identity in the "res publica litteraria" of the humanists. Up to this point, however, Hutten had published only five minor poems totaling a modest 164 lines.[10] With the writing of the *Querelae*, a substantial work by its very length and quality, Hutten hoped to provide the "entry ticket" to the humanist circle. If then the *Querelae* as a whole were meant as a journeyman's piece to gain entry into the humanist guild, the poem "Ad poetas Germanos" more specifically was meant to demonstrate not only the impressive number of the

---

[7] Cf. Eckhard Bernstein, *Ulrich von Hutten* (Reinbek bei Hamburg: Rowohlt, 1988).

[8] Cf. Heinrich Grimm, *Ulrich von Hutten: Wille und Schicksal* (Göttingen: Musterschmidt, 1971), 33 f.

[9] Men like Eitelwolf von Stein and Hermann von Neuenaar were the exceptions rather than the rule.

[10] They are: *In Eobanum Hessum Elegia*, *Laus Marchiae*, *De virtute elegiaca exhortatio*, *Ad lectorem Epigramma*, and *Elegia ad Trebelium*. Cf. Josef Benzing, *Ulrich von Hutten und seine Drucker* (Wiesbaden: Otto Harrassowitz: 1956), 1.

German humanists, but also their considerable achievements. At a time when humanists at most German universities were tolerated as mere outsiders, Hutten with this veritable "Who's Who" of German humanism in 1510 tried to persuade others, and perhaps himself, what a powerful and respectable group the humanists in reality were.

But were the humanists really such a cohesive group as Hutten wants his readers to believe? To be sure, there were numerous friendships between individual humanists. It is also true that Conrad Celtis, with considerable organizational talent, had founded so-called literary "sodalitates." But with his death in 1508 these had withered away, and they had been limited to southern Germany anyhow, with some branches in Bohemia and Hungary. The fact is that by 1510 the German humanists were quite a disparate group, even if we only look at Hutten's list. The reasons for that were as varied as the humanists themselves. There were generational differences: on the one hand there were the older humanists in their fifties and sixties (Wimpfeling was 60, Reuchlin 56, and Brant 52), on the other hand the younger humanist in their twenties (Richard Crocus was 21, Wolfgang Angst 25, and Hutten himself 22 years old). There were also considerable ideological differences: while Jakob von Gouda, for instance, was a pious churchman, Mutianus Rufus favored a paganistic Neoplatonism. There were sociological differences: Eitelwolf von Stein, Hutten and Hermann von dem Busche came from aristocratic families, while Crotus Rubeanus and Eobanus Hessus were the sons of peasants. Some humanists, finally, indulged in humanistic studies only in their leisure time as a "hobby," others pursued them with the intensity of a full-time vocation. To say that this heterogeneous company constituted a unified front was highly questionable. But this is of course precisely what Hutten was saying. What he had created with this catalogue was not an actual description, but a fiction, a myth—the myth of the strength, unity, and cohesiveness of the German humanist movement.

It would be tempting to stylize the conflict Hutten thematized in the *Querelae* as one between humanism and scholasticism. There is, however, no textual basis for such an attempt. To be sure, on the one hand there is Hutten and the allegedly combined forces of the German humanists. But who is on the other? Hennig Lötz – an insignificant law professor in a provincial German university town? Hutten's description of him as a mean, sadistic and vindictive old lecher is viciously one-sided. That Lötz is also an enemy of the muses does not make him a representative of scholasticism. In other words, at this point the humanism-scholasticism conflict does not interest Ulrich von Hutten. The notion of the strength of humanism precedes the Reuchlin affair and sprang, at this time, from

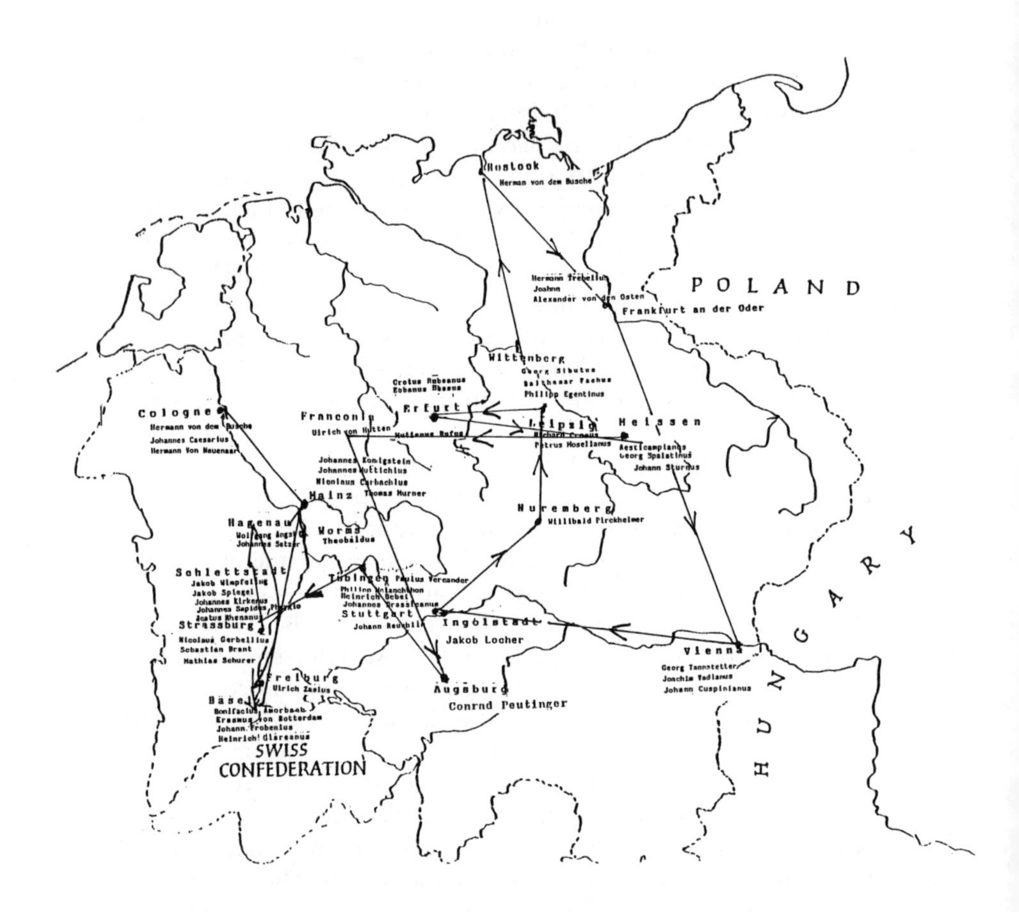

Fig. 2. Magister Schlauraff's fictitious journey in the *Epostolae obscurorum virorum* (II,9) of 1516

psychological motives as a means of possibly exorcising the inner conflicts within his own identity.

Six years later the literary and intellectual landscape of Germany had changed dramatically. The tensions between humanism and scholasticism had broken out, coming to a head in the so-called Reuchlin affair, that bitter controversy between the Cologne Dominicans and Johann Pfefferkorn on one side and the eminent scholar Johannes Reuchlin and a large segment of the German humanists on the other. Ulrich von Hutten first became an attentive spectator and later one of the most active participants in that acrimonious debate, shaping the perceptions of his contemporaries about this conflict more than any other humanist.

The literary fruit of the Reuchlin affair were the *Epistolae obscurorum virorum*, a fictitious correspondence presumably written by monks, scholastics and theologians but actually composed by Crotus Rubeanus and Ulrich von Hutten who wrote the majority of the letters of Part II, including the letter which contains the poem, the satirical "Carmen rithmicale" we are dealing with in this paper.[11]

The fiction of the letter is that a certain Philipp Schlauraff is sent by the Cologne theologians on a public relations tour to various humanist centers in Germany in order to enlist the help of scholars against the hated Reuchlinists. Schlauraff chooses to describe his experiences in a lengthy poem (185 lines), which, with its intentionally awkward meter (it approximates the leonine hexameter), naive mixture of Latin and German and barbarous Latin, is the very opposite of Hutten's elegant idiom modelled on the classical Roman poets.[12]

Schlauraff's fictitious journey starts in Wittenberg, goes via Rostock and

[11] Cf. Aloys Bömer, *Epistolae obscurorum virorum* (Heidelberg: Weissbach, 1924) and Walther Brecht, *Die Verfasser der Epistolae obscurorum virorum* (Straßburg, 1904). In addition to the standard arguments advanced by Brecht and Bömer, there are two more reasons suggesting why Hutten was the author of this particular letter. First we have the testimony of Johannes Cochlaeus, who on 9 September 1516 wrote to Willibald Pirckheimer: "I am sending you the *Marcus* of Hutten who dined with us tonight and read to us some new letters amid great laughter. By means of those letters one wandered through almost all Germany. He also mentioned you (in this letter) because you had written against usury which our master (Johannes Eck is meant) discussed in a disputation in Bologna. Hutten, however, denies that he is the author" (Böcking 1:126). The fact that Hutten denied having authored the letters was an understandable precaution at a time when the letters were about to be banned because of the anticlerical tone. The most convincing argument, however, for Hutten's authorship are the remarkable affinities and similarities in structure and "cast" between the two poems.

[12] Quoted after Böcking's edition, 6:198–203.

Greifswald to Frankfurt an der Oder. From there he turns to Vienna, Ingolstadt, Nuremberg, Leipzig, and Erfurt. Meissen, Franconia, Augsburg, and Tübingen are the next stages. Schlauraff then travels to Straßburg, Schlettstadt, Hagenau, Freiburg, Basel, and Worms. Via Mainz he returns home to Cologne. Compared with the trip from the *Querelae*, the itinerary in this case includes Vienna and the important imperial cities of Augsburg and Nuremberg as well as Ingolstadt. In southwest Germany Basel, Schlettstadt, and Hagenau are added.

Wherever this "cursor in theologia," as Schlauraff is called, turns, he is met with a hostile reception by the humanists. He is insulted, mocked, ridiculed, publicly embarrassed, and threatened. In Leipzig, for instance, Petrus Mosellanus urges his students to hang him, in Erfurt Eobanus Hessus threatens to knock his teeth out, and in Franconia Hutten himself vows to beat him with a stick, should he decide to stay. In addition to the threats Schlauraff also suffers physical injury. Spurred on by their teachers, Spalatin and Aesticampianus, students beat him up and pull him by his hair. As if this were not enough, the unlucky cursor is slapped in the face by Johannes Sturnus (line 80) and thrown down the stairs by Storchius (line 119). Even otherwise mild-mannered humanists like Beatus Rhenanus and Wolfgang Angst are caught up in their anger: Rhenanus hits the unfortunate Schlauraff over the head, while Wolfgang Angst pokes him with a stick in the eyes, and Johannes Setzer, the printer from Hagenau uses the fruit of his professional labors, a thick folio, to hit the fearless Anti-Reuchlinist so strongly in the side that he loses his wind (line 122). In Worms the physician Theobaldus temporarily forgets the oath of Hippocrates and instead of healing Schlauraff hits him hard on the head, a blow that results in a bump the size of a cheese.[13] Thoroughly intimidated Schlauraff retreats to Mainz only to be hit over the head once again, this time with a stool, by Huttichius, one of the members of the notorious "Kronengesellschaft," that circle of humanist friends who regularly met in the inn called "Zur Krone." Johann Königstein pushes him down the stairs, and Thomas Murner, whom he meets strolling along the Main, is only restrained by his professorial dignity from throwing Schlauraff into the cool waters of the river. Exhausted by so much verbal and physical abuse, Schlauraff returns to Cologne where he finds a congenial company of theologians.[14]

[13] "et statim unus Caseus/Stetit mihi in capite" (line 155).

[14] Although no less than eighteen humanists are the same in the two poems, (They are: Georg Sibutus, Balthasar Fach, Hermann von dem Busche, Hermann Trebelius, Jakob Locher, Eobanus Hessus, Crotus Rubeanus, Mutianus Rufus, Johann and

Whereas the tenth elegy of the second book of the *Querelae* offers sparkling gems of deft characterization, Schlauraff's "Carmen rithmicale" lacks such mini-portraits. This lack is quite understandable from the fiction of the poem, which like all the letters of the EOV is intended to demonstrate through self-revelation the ignorance, complacency, and narrow-mindedness of the scholastics. A precise knowledge of the individual achievements of the humanists would understandably have undermined this principle. For that reason Pirckheimer is referred to as a "quidam Pirckheymer" (line 40), the famous Freiburg jurist Ulrich Zasius as "unus vetulus qui vocatur Zasius" (line 135), and Erasmus a certain man "qui Erasmus dictur" (line 143). If details are mentioned, they are irrelevant gossip: of Georg Sibutus we learn that he "habet antiquam vetulam, que vendit bonam Cerevisiam" (line 8), and the only observation worthy of comment about Jakob Wimpfeling is that he wears "unum pellicium quod est bene impinguatum" (line 112). Schlauraff himself has only contempt for these "heretics," as he calls the humanists, while he himself is deeply steeped in the traditions of the Church and the ossified practices of the late medieval university.

Initially the controversy between the Cologne Dominicans and Reuchlin might have been, as has been suggested by Overfield,[15] a quarrel about the use of Jewish books. By 1514, however, it had developed into a *cause célèbre*, a showdown between humanism and scholasticism. Responsible for that change was above all Hutten, who had finally found an enemy worthy of his pen. Whereas in the *Querelae* the enemy had been a relatively unknown law professor, Henning Lötz, the opponent now was quite impressive: the university establishment, 200 years of outdated traditions of a rigid and arid philosophy and a monolithic church with the powerful instruments of intimidation and suppression. For Hutten, at least, the battle lines were clearly drawn: on the one hand were the progressive humanists, on the other the backward-looking theologians and scholastics.

Alexander von der Osten, Rhagius Aesticampianus, Johannes Sturnus, Johannes Reuchlin, Heinrich Bebel, Jakob Wimpfeling, Wolfgang Angst, Sebastian Brant, and Georg Spalatin), there are a number of interesting additions: new are the well known Viennese Humanists, Joachim Vadianus and Johann Cuspinian, as well as the Nuremberger Willibald Pirckheimer, the Englishman Richard Crocus, the Augsburg Humanist Conrad Peutinger, and the philological "wunderkind" from Tübingen, Philipp Melanchthon. New is also Erasmus of Rotterdam, who since his triumphal tour up the Rhine in 1514 had been regarded as a German Humanist, as well as Thomas Murner who had endeared himself to the Humanists because of his own quarrels with the Dominicans. New finally are two Cologne Humanists, Johann Caesarius and Hermann von Neuenaar.

[15] Overfield, 190.

But did this image correspond to reality? Were the humanists indeed such a powerful block, as Hutten suggests here, and as most critics believe they were at that time? They were not and Overfield has convincingly demonstrated this in his study. It is true that the support for Reuchlin was widespread but it was not by any means unanimous. Prominent humanists such as Jakob Wimpfeling, Sebastian Brant, Ulrich Zasius, Johannes Aesticampianus, and Jakob Locher never wrote a single line on behalf of the embattled scholar.[16] Others, like Mutianus, had their strong reservations, and Erasmus, as always, hedged and kept his options open.[17] In other words, the notion of a monolithic fraternity of humanists all rushing to support Reuchlin is, if not a fiction, at least a questionable claim. Just as a military leader tends to exaggerate the size of his troops to intimidate the enemy, so Hutten magnifies the size and unity of the humanist forces. That he presents the humanists, whose intellectual leadership was based on the power of the *word* and not physical superiority, as such a physically abusive group, must be ascribed to his heritage as a knight.[18] Again Hutten was essentially creating a myth of the power, influence and strength of a movement that really did not exist.

It would be foolish to deny the tensions that existed between humanism and scholasticism on the eve of the Reformation. What this paper wanted to suggest, however, was that the notion of a unified and cohesive humanist movement seems to have been, to a large extent the creation of the humanists themselves and that Ulrich von Hutten played a very important role in that mythmaking. Because the humanists, compared to their counterparts, were so articulate and ostensibly modern, historians have tended to accept their statements at face value, even when these were cast in the satirical mode, as in the case of the *Epistolae obscurorum virorum*. None of the charm, wit and sublime irony of this satire would be lost, however, if we start viewing it as what it was meant to be: a not too subtle piece of propaganda with its own myths about opponents and adherents of the humanist movement.

Holy Cross College. Worcester, MA

---

[16] Overfield, 192.

[17] Overfield, 195.

[18] As we know from his biography, he himself was not averse to occasionally resorting to violence: in Viterbo, for instance, he had stabbed one Frenchman in a quarrel.

Engelbert Kaempfer and the Myth of the Whirlpools of the Caspian Sea

ROBERT W. CARRUBBA

Seventeenth-century thinkers, scientists and travelers were puzzled by the Caspian Sea, the largest inland body of water in the world. Covering 143,630 square miles, the Caspian Sea extends 750 miles at its longest, averages between from 100 to 130 miles in width, and reaches its greatest depth at 3,264 feet. Among the almost countless number of streams and rivers which empty into the Caspian Sea are included the Volga, the largest of European rivers, the Ural, the Terek, and the Kura. The question, then, which confounded speculators was: How does the vast amount of water which accumulates in the Caspian Sea emerge from it without inundating the adjacent lands?

Perhaps the most ingenious answer is found in Athanasius Kircher's *Mundus Subterraneus*.[1] Kircher believed that the Caspian Sea was connected by underground channels to the Black Sea and to the Persian Gulf. When the water level in the Caspian Sea reached a height greater than that of the other two bodies, the Caspian's water would flow down and out at points marked by whirlpools whose existence travelers had reported. This explanation presented in the accompanying illustration by Kircher appeared to make good sense since the landlocked Caspian Sea has no outlets on the earth's surface. In support of this theory, the French missionary, Father Avril, had argued that leaves of a plant grown on the

---

[1] The celebrated scholar and mathematician Athanasius Kircher (1602–80), *Mundus Subterraneus* (Amsterdam, 1664), chapter 13, 85–89.

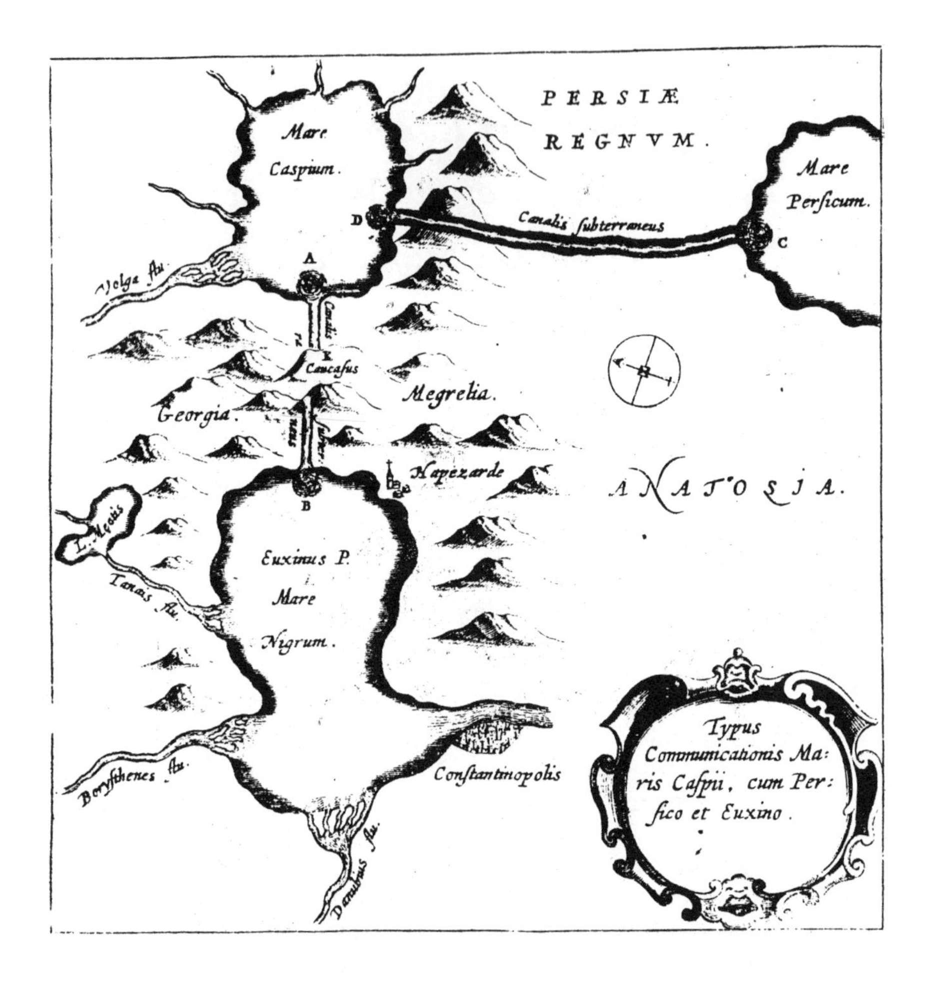

Fig. 1. Illustration from Athanasius Kircher's *Mundus Subterraneus*, p. 86, showing the supposed whirlpools (A,B,C,D) which mark the subterranean channels connecting the Caspian Sea with the Black Sea and the Persian Gulf.

shores on the Caspian were carried through an underground channel and could be observed floating on the surface of the Persian Gulf. Father Avril reasons:

> But I have two Conjectures which make me believe, that it rather discharges it self into the Persian Gulph, how far remote soever it may seem to be, then into any other Sea.
>
> The first is, because that in the Gulph of the Persian Sea, to the South, over against the Province of Kilan, there are two dangerous Whirlypools, or deep Abysses, which the Persian vessels that set Sail from that Coast, endeavour to avoid as much as they can. And the noise of the Water, which throws it self into that Gulph with a surprizing Rapidness, may be heard in calm Weather, so far off, that it is enough to terrify all those who are ignorant of the real Cause. The second Conjecture, which to me seems to be of more force then the former is grounded upon every years experience, by which they who inhabit all along the Persian Gulph, observe a vast quantity of Willow-leaves at the end of every Autumn. Now in regard this sort of Tree is altogether unknown in the Southern Part of Persia, which borders upon that Sea; and for that, quite the contrary, the Northern part which is bounded by the Sea of Kilan, has all the Sea-coasts of it shaded with those Trees; we may assure our selves with probability enough, that these Leaves are not carry'd from one end of the Empire to the other, but only by the Water that rowles 'em along through the Caverns of the Earth.[2]

Such was the prevailing solution, apparently supported by eyewitness testimony, during the latter part of the seventeenth century. But in the year 1683 the Swedish Embassy from Charles XI to the Shah of Persia left Stockholm and traveled through Russia on its way to Isfahan. Among those members of the delegation empowered to conduct trade negotiations was its secretary, Engelbert Kaempfer, the German scholar and scientist. Kaempfer was just beginning what would prove to be a most extraordinary journey of scholarship and science lasting a decade and including Russia, Persia, India, the East Indies, Siam, and Japan.[3] Dr.

---

[2] Reverend Philippe Avril, a Jesuit missionary, attempted to reach China. He left Europe in 1685, but was detained by the governor of Astrachan and forced to return to France. See *Voyages en divers Etats d'Europe et d'Asie* (Paris, 1692). The above English translation is taken from: *Travels into divers Parts of Europe and Asia, Undertaken by the French King's Order to discover a new Way by Land into China* . . . (London, 1693), 79–80.

[3] See: Karl Meier-Lemgo, *Die Reisetagebücher Engelbert Kaempfers* (Wiesbaden, 1968);

Engelbert Kaempfer was among the most learned scholars of his era and he surely was the most widely traveled. Upon leaving Moscow, the embassy traveled overland to Astrachan on the Caspian Sea where it boarded ship on an ill-starred voyage to Nisabad in Persia. Storm-tossed for twelve days, Kaempfer and his colleagues finally reached land on 22 November 1683. Kaempfer made diligent inquiries of the sailors and inhabitants of the region of the Caspian. Not a single person had ever seen any whirlpool. Clearly, the famous whirlpools of the Caspian Sea did not in fact exist. Nor did the supposed underground channels.

Based on eyewitness investigation, Kaempfer, in the *Amoenitatum Exoticarum* debunked the mythical whirlpools of the Caspian Sea.[4] But the nagging question of how the huge volume of water which empties into the Caspian Sea does in fact flow out still remained to be confronted. Before addressing alternative solutions, Kaempfer had to dispose of the apparent evidence presented by Father Avril. Relying on his own firsthand experience, Kaempfer disproved Father Avril's contention that leaves from the Salvia,[5] a plant supposedly found only on the shores of the Caspian Sea, can also be found floating during the autumn months on the waters of the Persian Gulf. Kaempfer spent two years on the Persian Gulf during which he had studied Persian history and customs, and investigated, among other things, Persian mummy, the torpedo fish of the Persian Gulf, and the harvesting of asafetida.[6] He took the opportunity to examine the vegetation around the Persian Gulf with regard to Father Avril's claim. Kaempfer concluded that Salvia leaves are not found floating in the waters and that one of two possible errors had occurred: either (a) Father Avril's informant had confused the Latin word Alga,[7] which is found on the shores of the Persian Gulf, with the Latin word Salvia; or (b) Father Avril had mistaken the leaves of Horau fruit mixed with Alga for the leaves of the Salvia Major which are

---

Engelbert Kaempfer, *Amoenitatum exoticarum politico-physico-medicarum fasciculi V, quibus continentur variae relationes, observationes & descriptiones rerum Persicarum & Ulterioris Asiae* (Lemgo, 1712); Engelbert Kaempfer, *The History of Japan*, trans. J. G. Scheuchzer, 2 vols. (London, 1727); John Z. Bowers and Robert W. Carrubba, "The Doctoral Thesis of Engelbert Kaempfer on Tropical Diseases, Oriental Medicine, and Exotic Natural Phenomena," *Journal of the History of Medicine and Allied Sciences* 25 (1970): 270–310.

[4] *Amoenitatum Exoticarum*, 253–58.

[5] Salvia: a large genus, of the family Labiatae, which grows in temperate and warmer climates. The name Salvia comes from the Latin *salvo* and suggests the reputed healing qualities of sage, Salvia officinalis.

[6] After voyaging from Russia and over the Caspian Sea, Kaempfer remained in Persia from 22 November 1683 to 30 June 1688, when he sailed for India.

[7] Alga: seaweed.

somewhat similar in shape and size. Kaempfer then appends a botanical description of the Horau or Amygdalus marina to clarify the issue.

Once the whirlpools of the Caspian Sea had been disproved, Kaempfer posited several solutions to the question of the outflow of water from the lake. The first theory, which Kaempfer found in ancient authors, proposes that all of the waters of the world are connected with one another and form a continuum through subterranean passages. Thus, the waters of the oceans, lakes, springs, and rivers form a circulatory system and respond to the pressures of the earth and the atmosphere. Kaempfer's theory is clearly articulated in Pliny.

> . . . the intention of the Artificer of nature must have been to unite earth and water in a mutual embrace, earth opening her bosom and water penetrating her entire frame by means of a network of veins radiating within and without, above and below, the water bursting out even at the tops of mountain ridges, to which it is driven and squeezed out by the weight of the earth, and spurts out like a jet of water from a pipe, and is so far from being in danger of falling down that it leaps upward to all the loftiest elevations. This theory shows clearly why the seas do not increase in bulk with the daily accession of so many rivers. The consequence is that the earth at every point of its globe is encircled and engirdled by sea flowing round it, and this does not need theoretical investigation, but has already been ascertained by experience.[8]

Pliny's explanation, which regards the human being as the microcosm and the natural world as the macrocosm, and which is based on the analogy of the circulation of the blood through the veins and arteries of the human body, prevailed through the Middle Ages, and persisted into the Renaissance and the seventeenth century. While Kaempfer is prepared to accept this theory as possible, he recognizes that the reader and others may not wish to. Kaempfer, of course, could not have known that the Caspian Sea is ninety-two feet below sea level.

The second solution offered by Kaempfer admits of three options: that the Caspian Sea returns its waters exactly as the oceans do by either: (a) the "quasi-mechanical" force of the fluctuations of the Caspian which drives its waters upwards through openings in the adjacent lands; or (b) by exhalation when the water is condensed through "magnetic mud" into little fountains; or (c) by exhalation when the water is condensed by the coldness of the air into rain. Kaempfer does not provide sufficient detail

---

[8] Pliny, *Natural History* 2.66.166.

for us to feel entirely comfortable that we understand the meaning of Option a. It appears that just as the ocean by mechanical motion of its waves and water level forces water up through openings in the adjacent lands, so the Caspian operates a smaller and independent system in the land area surrounding it. Option b is based on the observations of Becher that fountains or streams of water emerge from underground when condensed by a special type of mud. Becher reached his conclusion after studying conditions at Mount Saint Michel.[9] Option c, like Option a, has its roots in classical antiquity, not, however, in Pliny, but in Aristotle. The ocean, Aristotle contended, disposes of the vast quantities of water which flow into it by the process of evaporation. Instead of flooding the shores with excess water, the ocean disposes of an amount of liquid approximately equal to the inflow when the water evaporates, travels upward and then, because of the coldness of the air, condenses into rain and is once again deposited upon the earth and ocean. While the correspondence of intake and loss need not be exact in the period of a year, eventually, Aristotle observes, a balance is achieved. In Aristotle's words:

> The fresh and sweet water, then, as we said, is all drawn up because it is light, while the salt water because it is heavy remains....[10]

Kaempfer applies the Aristotelian theory to the Caspian Sea–the solution which modern science has confirmed as correct.

We must, however, caution that Kaempfer, while he ends his speculations with the correct solution, was by no means certain of its rightness. A practicing Christian and a minister's son, Kaempfer quotes Ecclesiastes (Chap. 1):

> All the rivers enter into the sea, and the sea does not overflow; to the place from whence the rivers come, they return so that they may flow again.

But exactly how this occurs, Kaempfer concludes, "the most wise King of mortals did not explain."[11]

---

[9] Johann Joachim Becher (1635–1682), German chemist, physician and adventurer, *Physica Subterranea* (Frankfort, 1669), 78–89. Given to ambitious schemes, Becher proposed a Rhine-Danube canal, the transmutation of sand into gold, and the establishment of colonies in South America.

[10] Aristotle, *Meteorologica* 2.2.355b.

[11] Kaempfer had more than the single verse seven in mind, for chapter one of Ecclesiastes, which focuses on the vanity of all temporal things, continues in verse eight: *All things are hard: man cannot explain them by word. The eye is not filled with seeing, neither is the ear filled with hearing.* Such a sentiment nicely captures the uncertainty with which the discussion of the whirlpools ends.

Appendix

Since Kaempfer's Latin text has not been translated into any language, I have provided an English version of his report on the whirlpools of the Caspian Sea and his description of the Amygdalus marina (*Amoenitatum Exoticarum*, pp. 253–58).

The Absence of Whirlpools in the Caspian Sea

The inland lake of Asia, which the Romans call the Caspian, the Russians term Galenskoi More (Hyrcanian Sea), the Persians name Derja Kulsum, and the Turks label Bohaar Korsurm (the closed sea), has wonderfully exercised the minds of philosophers, with no harm to those who are baffled. The issue in question is: that a basin enclosed on all sides accepts the force of rivers of near and distant origin without first overflowing, then crossing its shores and flooding the adjacent lands with a constant deluge. Athanasius Kircher, that Pliny of our era, has addressed the solution to this problem with a great effort. By an ingenious conjecture he energetically cuts through the earth and conducts water from the depths of the Caspian Sea on one side into the Black Sea and on the other side into the Persian Gulf. In this process, he relies on the condition of the aforementioned bodies of water and certain phenomena therein which that very learned gentleman, out of trust, believed that an untruthful reporter had in fact observed. He excited the puzzled minds of scholars so that they thought that they had escaped the impervious labyrinth of nature by grasping these whirlpools, so consonant with reason, so wonderful to the ordinary person and so precious to the mystics of nature, as if they were grasping the thread of Ariadne. And behold: all the travelers, who crossed this sea, henceforth freely confirm the presence of whirlpools which they have not seen, and in concert they do not hesitate to insert them on the hydrographic charts. To be sure, because they have been unduly persuaded of the existence of whirlpools, these writers escape the blame for sloth and negligence, and ever strive to please their readers with accounts of wonderful things.

I assert that these eddying whirlpools, visible indeed, and appearing on the surface of the sea, are pure figments (but on this side of the contempt of writers). As witnesses I have the Tartarean, Russian and Persian inhabitants around the Caspian Sea who have sworn by God and all things holy that they have not observed whirlpools. As witnesses I have the sailors and their seafaring comrades who have from childhood traveled on their ships the length and width of this sea and have discovered nothing unusual in it except the sharp rocks which are deadly to voyagers in the area of Hyrcania. And finally, we ourselves, the members of the Swedish Embassy to the Shah of Persia, come forward as witnesses who, having been tossed on this basin by changing winds for twelve days without sails and oars, discovered no whirlpools and, after skillful interrogation, discovered not one eyewitness among the neighboring peoples. Therefore, are all the many writers who report about them lying? They certainly are! In this region of the world, some men have a certain reserve and desire to please with the result that they always answer yes to questions; still other men have a certain peevishness so that, when annoyed with unclear speakers, they extricate themselves the more easily by affirming, when questioned, that which they do not understand or do not know. Consequently, with the same trust and ease with which travelers receive instructions from the local camel riders, barbarians and ignorant people, they again credulously expound to their readers the notions they have accepted.

Among the most recent assertors of whirlpools, the Reverend Father Avril, a Frenchman, deserves to be mentioned. In book two of his *Voyages* written in French, as he attempts to demonstrate the effluvium of the Caspian into the Persian Gulf, he posits two whirlpools around the Hyrcanian shore which absorb the sea with a dreadful tumult and crash but which he himself did not see. In an effort to bolster his contention, he says that leaves of the Salvia, which grow nowhere else but on the shores of the Caspian Sea, float during autumn in the Persian Gulf after they have been snatched up by the aforementioned whirlpools and carried through a subterranean channel. A specious argument! I did indeed perspire for two years on the shores of the Persian Gulf while sedulously examining its entire history, to the extent of my ability. But I would be lying if I said that I have ever seen a Salvia leaf among the vegetation which happens to float in or is tossed up by the waters, or is drawn out in the nets of the fishermen. The gulf nourishes Alga not Salvia and during the summer deposits an abundance of it on the shore. Perhaps the reverend father's informant, whose Latin was shaky and who was misled by the similar sound, substituted Salvia for Alga. Or perhaps the reverend father erred in taking the leaves of the Horau fruit, mixed with Alga, for the leaves of the Salvia Major whose shape and size they resemble, but whose wrinkles and other qualities, however, are different. This plant (which I will describe below) grows luxuriantly in the manner and size of Salix in depressed parts of islands and on the uliginous shore. At certain hours of the day it is constantly shaken by the incoming tide of the sea. The leaves, which are bent downward, and often the stems themselves are snatched up by the outgoing tide and frequently float in the sea. It is indeed unlikely that Salvia grows on the Caspian shores which on all sides are sandy and wild. I have heard no reports nor have I ever seen any plants while traveling through that region. I have encountered a certain species of it on a few and more fertile plains adjacent to the Volga, but some hundreds of leagues from the Caspian. Any removal of the leaves from there will prove useless, for in the vast stretch of river, sea and subterranean passage they will be battered by the water, will decompose and settle to the bottom. I add that if the Caspian Sea emptied itself by these whirlpools, of necessity the huge swirls of water both gliding out from the Caspian and belching forth in the Persian Gulf would reveal themselves with a prodigious tumult. Neither I, while sailing on the Caspian, nor others, as far as I have learned by inquiry, have ever seen any.

Where then, you will ask, does the horrendous mass of water which flows in remain if it is not absorbed by the aforementioned whirlpools? The Volga or the Rha river alone, which unburdens itself with eighty mouths, replenishes its waters over the course of five hundred and more miles from the west and the first territories of Russia. Between the metropolises of Shemakha in Shirvan and Rasht in Hyrcania, a distance of nearly sixty miles, I counted more than fifty swollen and rapid rivers, omitting the streams, flowing into the Caspian. The most famous among these, the Kura, after which Cyrus is named, equals our Elbe in size and exceeds it in velocity, in as much as it ultimately absorbs the Aras which draws the waters of almost all Armenia. What of the huge Ural river from the north beyond the sources of the Ob, the Syr Darya from Turkestan and deserts of Eastern Tartaria, the Oxus from India near the Himalaya Mountains, the begettor of the Ganges—all of which rivers deposit springs, rains, and melted snows into this guardian of the water of Asia? Perhaps we will not stray from the truth, if with the most ancient authors, we attribute to our sea a union with the ocean, or to put the matter more clearly, if we assert that through a subterranean abyss the Caspian comes together and forms a continuum with the ocean. Indeed, just as the ocean in many locations (as has been explored by taking soundings) extends downward to an immense depth, so it is likely that the same ocean also enters caves and openings running horizontally and obliquely. These connect both with certain inland lakes, those to be sure whose waters, increased by a perennial influx, imperceptibly recede, and with certain extraordinary pools and springs whose liquids are said to resemble the tides of the ocean by increasing and decreasing. Philosophers will never explain such phenomena short of this hypothesis of continuity. If so, we are no longer astonished that even if the Caspian Sea experienced a tenfold increase in water it would not swell up, since the lower mass immediately yields to the other flowing in, and from the common pressure of the air, encircling the globe of the earth, the same height is always maintained, which corresponds to the ocean and the common sphere of all the land. You will object: the lake will already have become sweet, if for as much sweet water it receives on the surface, it discharges an equal quantity of salt water from the bottom into the ocean. I reply that the same thing must be said to happen if the water flows out tumultuously through whirlpools. In truth, there is no difficulty in either case, if the salt streams flowing in and the roots of salt-laden mountains, which the waters perennially wash, restore the loss. If indeed you will deny this, I have no objection. In that case, we will again have a closed sea, no less so without a connection with the ocean than without whirlpools through which the sea may flow out; the latter of which we were obliged to demonstrate. Meanwhile, lest our lake be overwhelmed by so many waters, we will counter this flood with the dictum from chapter one of Ecclesiastes. Speaking of the ocean, it says: *All the rivers enter into the sea, and the sea does not overflow; to the place from whence the rivers come, they return so that they may flow again.* And in the case of the Caspian we will offer this judgement: that it returns its own waters to the adjacent lands in the same manner in which the ocean itself does, which, by Hercules, is burdened with the rivers of all the rest of the globe. But how does it return them? By what impetus are they driven? Or by a quasi-mechanical force of the fluctuating ocean, are the fluids of its water driven upwards through the openings of the earth, as if through siphons? Or by exhalation alone, whether condensed through magnetic mud, which the distinguished Becher observed, into little fountains, or condensed through the coldness of the air into rain? The most wise King of mortals did not explain this mystery of nature to us; nor will I, as a reporter, hazard an explanation based on dubious calculations and conjectures. Rather I turn to the second item, that is, the bitterness, which I will address, now that the whirlpools have been refuted. But first I will give the promised description of the plant.

Horau, or Marine Amygdalus, of the Persian Gulf

The Amygdalus marina is found in sandy locations subject to periodic flooding by the Sea. It sends its ramose and ligneous roots deep in order to escape injury from the waters by whose brine it is invigorated. It consists of a few trunks, of a thickness of one and one half spans, twisted, and protected with a testaceous coagulum. The uneven and fragile branches produce furcula which are leafy, two cubits and opposite at long intervals. It is covered with a bark that is hard, ash-colored, and somewhat wooly in furcula. The wood is hard and solid, catches fire with difficulty but retains it stubbornly; as it burns, however, the wood does not dissolve into coals but into ashes. The plant bears single leaves alternately opposite, attached with thick leafstalks weakening into yellow, flat, oblong, ending in a blunt tip, rigid, pinguid, fragile, with an unbroken circumference, an inner surface which is green and shiny, an outer surface that is incanous and slightly pubescent, with a salty taste, which may result from the sap or from the salty surface which the sea had so often flooded. It puts forth rather sparse flowers on the outermost extremities of the furcula. The flowers are pale yellow, imperfect for the most part, divided into four (sometimes five) labella which expand and bend backwards within the orb of a pea, are carnous and shapeless. The flowers have a very short style within and four pointed stamens. The amygdaline fruit follows the flower. The fruit has a grass-green pericarp, which through ripening is somewhat tough, and a stone inside that adheres firmly. Its kernel is divided into two parts and is insipid. Amygdalus marina has economic uses: as firewood, of course, and foliage to feed camels. For this reason, boats, launched with the outgoing tide, go forth in the cool of the night to thickets (with which the island of Kismis abounds) and with the incoming tide they return laden with cut stems. These they gather in bundles and offer for sale on the shore. I have found the same tree, in sufficient abundance, on the marshy shore of India under the Malayan name of Saga.

University of North Carolina at Charlotte

The Renaissance Commentators on Statius

PAUL M. CLOGAN

Publius Papinius Statius, the Neapolitan poet of the Silver Classical Latin literature, was one of the more popular and widely copied classical authors during the Middle Ages and Renaissance. The *Thebaid*, his major epic on the ancient legends of the house of Oedipus and of the Seven Against Thebes, was frequently copied, commented on and preserved in more than 112 manuscripts.[1] The *Achilleid*, his minor epic which was to relate the entire life of the hero of the Trojan War, was also frequently copied, annotated and preserved in some ninety-five manuscripts.[2] The *Silvae* was virtually unknown in the Middle Ages until Poggio discovered the famous lost *codex unicus* in 1416 or 1417. The majority of the manuscripts of the *Thebaid* and *Achilleid* contain glosses and frequently copious notes and often lengthy commentaries. There are at least nine full-length Latin commentaries on Statius: three written during the Middle Ages and six during the Renaissance. The commentary of Lactantius Placidus on the *Thebaid* was widely known in the Middle Ages and especially during the early Italian Renaissance as seen in the considerable number of fifteenth-century Italian manuscripts and incunabula.[3] Al-

---

[1] Concerning the manuscripts and textual history of the *Thebaid*, see *Achilleis et Thebais*, ed. P. Kohlmann (Leipzig: 1884), vii–xviii; *Thebais et Achilleis*, ed., H. W. Garrod (Oxford: 1906), v–xi; and D. E. Hill, ed., *P. Papini Stati Thebaidos Libri XII* (Leiden: Brill, 1983); Paul M. Clogan, "Medieval Glossed Manuscripts of the Thebaid," in *Manuscripta* 11 (1967): 102–112; and "Chaucer and the *Thebaid* Scholia," in *Studies in Philology* 61 (1964): 601–3.

[2] Regarding the manuscripts of the *Achilleid*, see Paul M. Clogan, ed., *The Medieval Achilleid of Statius: Edited with Introduction, Variant Readings, and Glosses* (Leiden: E. J. Brill, 1968), 11–17; and Paul M. Clogan, "A Preliminary List of Manuscripts of Statius' Achilleid," in *Manuscripta* 8 (1964): 175–78.

[3] See *Lactantii Placidi qui dictur commentarios in Statii Thebaida et commentariorum in*

though little is known about the medieval commentators, there is considerable information about the Renaissance commentators. This essay, part of the larger project of *Catalogus Translationum et Commentariorum,* will focus on the major Renaissance commentators including Domitius Calderinus, Franciscus Maturantius, Joannes Britannicus, and Joannes Bernartius with an eye to the development of the interpretation.

Domitius Calderinus was born at Torri del Benaco about January-March 1446 and he died at Rome January-May 1478.[4] He was educated at Verona and studied at Venice under Benedetto Brugnoli di Legnano and possibly taught there. About 1467 he went to Rome and became *secretarius familiaris et commensalis perpetuus* of Cardinal Bessarion, and as a result he associated with members of the "academia Bessarionea." Around

---

Achilleida, ed. R. Jahnke (Leipzig, 1898); see also Paul van de Woestijne, who would date Lactantius Placidus as a late fourth-century commentator who wrote in the period between Donatus and Servius, in *Les Scolies à la Thebaïde de Stace: Remarques et suggestions,* in *L'Antiquité Classique,* N. S. 19 (1950): 149-63. On the manuscripts of Lactantius Placidus, see Robert D. Sweeney, *Prolegomena to an Edition of the Scholia to Statius* (Leiden: Brill, 1969).

[4] S. Maffei, *Verona illustrata,* (Verona, 1731) 2: 220-33; Phillippus Bonamicus, *De claris pontificiarum epistolarum scriptoribus* (Rome, 1753), 203-5; G. Tiraboschi, *Storia della letteratura italiana* (Modena, 1776) 6.2: 346-48; G. B. Giuliari, *Della letteratura veronese al cadere del secolo XV e delle sue opere a stampa* (Bologna, 1876), *passim*; F. Gabotto-A. Badini Confalonieri, *Vita di Giorgio Merula* (Alessandria, 1894), 88-106; G. Levi, *Cenni intorno alla vita e agli scritti di Domizio Calderini* (Padua, 1900); A. Della Torre, *Storia dell'Accademia platonica di Firenze* (Florence, 1902), 9, 14 f., 819; R. Sabbadini, *Le scoperte dei codici latini e greci ne' secc. XIV e XV,* (Florence, 1905) 1: 125-6, 154, 167, 179-80; R. Malaboti, D. C. *Contributo alla storia dell' Umanesimo* (Milan, 1919); G. Mercati, *Per la cronologia della vita e degli scritti di Niccolo Perotti* (Rome, 1925), 69, 78, 82, 93 ff., 104; S. Timpanaro, "Atlas cum campare gibbo," in *Rinascimento* 2 (1951): 314-18; G. B. Picotti, *Ricerche umanistiche* (Florence, 1955), 19, 21, 64, 174; *Mostra del Poliziano nella Biblioteca Medicea Laurenziana* ... (cat.), a cura di A. Perosa (Florence, 1955), 14-15, 17, 31 ff., 63-64, 113; D. Maffei, *Alessandro D'Alessandro giureconsulto umanista (1461-1523)* (Milan, 1956), 41 ff., 95; G. Brugnoli, "La 'Praefatio in Suetonium' del Poliziano," in *Giorn. ital. de filol.* 10 (1957); 211-20; R. Weiss, "In memorian Domitii Calderini," in *Italia medioevale e umanistica* 3 (1960): 309-12; C. Dionisotti, "Umanisti dimenticati?" ibid. 4 (1961): 292-93, 295-96; I. Maier, *Les manuscrits d'Ange Politien* (Geneva, 1965), 63, 194, 214, 281, 292-93, 431; Id., *Ange Politien. La formation d'un poète humaniste (1469-1480)* (Geneva, 1966), 121 ff., 135, 422, 430; V. Rossi, *Il Quattrocento* (Milan, 1964), 308-9, 365; F. -R. Hausmann, *Giovanni Antonio Campano (1429-1477)* (Freiburg i. Br., 1968), 45, 141, 160, 173, 182, 189-90, 193-94, 204, 426 ff., 434-35, 439, 489; J.Dunston, "Studies in Domizio Calderini," in *Italia medioevale e umanistica* 11 (1968): 71-150; C. Dionisotti, C., *Poliziano e altri, ibid.* 151-85; *Enc. Ital. 8,* 384; P. O. Kristeller, *Iter Italicum, I-II, ad Indices.*

this time he assumed the Latin name Domitius in accordance with the practice of friends and students of Pomponio Leto. He was appointed professor of rhetoric at Rome by Paul II in 1470, and he continued in that office under Sixtus IV, who made him apostolic secretary in 1471. In 1472 he traveled with Bessarion to France, and in 1473 he traveled to Florence to work in the Bibliotheca Medicea where he met the young Poliziano, Bartolomeo Fonzio, and Marsilio Ficino. In 1476 he traveled to Avignon in the company of Cardinal Giuliano della Revere.

Calderinus was an irascible controversialist during his career, and his opponents included Niccolo Perotti on Martial and Angelo Cneo Sabino and Perotti on Juvenal. Shortly before Calderinus died G. Merula published an attack on the commentary on Martial, which was answered by Cornelio Vitelli. After he died, Poliziano severely attacked his scholarship and veracity.

His commentary on the *Silvae* was printed in Rome by Arnoldus Pannartz on 1 August 1475 and was reprinted at least ten times between 1475 and 1671. In addition to his commentary on the *Silvae,* Calderinus wrote commentaries on Cicero's letters to Atticus, Juvenal, Martial, Ovid's *Ibis, Metamorphoses* and *Sappho,* some passages of Propertius, Suetonius, and some of Virgil's minor poems; and he is said to have written commentaries on Catullus, Persius, and Silius. He died before finishing a Latin translation of Pausanias. In 1483, 1490, 1494, and 1498 editions of his commentary on the *Silvae* are very interesting from a humanistic point of view because they also contain the commentaries of Maturantius on the *Achilleid* and Lactantius Placidus on the *Thebaid.*

Franciscus Maturantius was born at Perugia in 1443 and studied at Vicenza, where he was a pupil of Ognibene da Lonigo.[5] Later he traveled for two years in Greece, especially Rhodes, studying Greek and collecting Greek manuscripts. In 1475 he was appointed secretary to Niccolo Perotti, governor of Perugia, and tutor to his nephews. He held office under Lorenzo Zane, governor of Perugia in 1483, and he was elected professor of eloquence at Perugia in 1486 and succeeded Ognibene da Lonigo at Vicenza in 1492. After a year of studying philosophy in Venice, Maturantius declined professorships at Rome, Venice, Udine, and Cesena and finally returned to teaching at Perugia in 1498. During the latter part of his life he was appointed to various chancellorships and ambassadorships.

---

[5] See G. Zappacosta, *F. Maturanzio, unmanista perugino* (Bergamo, 1970), G. Zappacosta, " 'De Sillabis' opusculum saec. XV ineditum," in *Latinitas* 18 (1970): 225–41; G. Zappacosta, "Amor Fugitivus," in *Latinitas* 19 (1971): 64–80; G. Tournoy, "Laurentius Abstemius," in *Bulletin de l'Institut historique belge à Rome,* 42 (1972): 189–210.

When he died in 1518, Christophorous Saxus, his former pupil, succeeded him as professor of eloquence at Perugia. Maturantius' commentary on the *Achilleid* was first printed in Venice in 1483 by Octavianus Scotus, the famous edition which also contains the commentaries of Lactantius Placidus on the *Thebaid* and Domitius Calderinus on the *Silvae.* From 1490 to 1508 Maturantius' commentary on the *Achilleid* was reprinted at least ten times. In addition to his explication of the *Achilleid,* he wrote commentaries on Cicero's *De Officiis, Philippics* and *Quaestiones Tusculanae,* and on *Rhetorica ad Herennium*; a life of the jurisconsult Pier-Filippo della Corgna; an *Opusculum de componendis versibus hexametro et pentametro*; and a chronicle of Perugia from 1492 to 1503. His letters are preserved in the Vatican Archives (MSS. 5358 and 5890) and the library of Perugia.

Joannes Britannicus was born at Palazzuolo and was a member of the same family as the printers Jacopo and Angiolo Britannico.[6] There is not very much information regarding his early education and career. He studied at Padua from 1470 to 1471 and taught Latin at Brescia for many years. By a decree confirmed on 31 March 1519, Joannes Britannicus and his descendants were given the right to hold office in Brescia. He published his commentary on the *Achilleid* in 1485 at Brescia where it was printed by Jacobus Britannicus. It was reprinted at Paris in 1618 by Tho. Blaise and at Leiden in 1671 by Hackius. Besides his commentary on the *Achilleid* and notes on the *Silvae,* Britannicus wrote commentaries on Horace, Juvenal, Ovid's *Metamorphoses,* and Persius, and edited Lucan, Pliny, Sallust, and Terence.

Joannes Bernartius was the last of the Neo-Latin commentators on Statius.[7] He was born at Mechlin (Mechelen) in 1568 and took the degree

---

[6] A. M. Querini, *Specimen variae literaturae quae in urbe Brixia . . . florebat* (Brixiae, 1739) vols. 1 and 2 *passim* (for Giovanni); 2: 334–36 (for Gregorio and Benedetto); G. M. Mazzuchelli, *Gli Scrittori d'Italia,* 2.4 (Brescia, 1763), 2106–10; V. Peroni, *Biblioteca bresciana* 1 (Brescia, n.d.): 196–202; L. Lechi, *Della tipografia bresciana nel secolo decimoquinto* (Brescia, 1854), *passim,* especially 93–94; F. Odorici, *Storie bresciane* (Brescia, 1860), 158–60; D. Fava, "G. B. e le sue Regulae grammaticales," in *Studi e ricerche nella storia della stampa del Quattrocento* (Milan, 1942), 131–43; G. Lanfranchi, *Breve storia di Palazzolo sull'Oglio. Note storiche di Palazzolesi illustri* (Bergamo, 1959), 180–84; V. Cremona, "L'umanesimo bresciano," in *Storia di Brescia* 2 (Brescia, 1963): 552–6; F. Chiappa, "Un'ipotesi circa l'identificazione del primitivo cognome dei 'Britannici' di Palazzolo," in *Mem. ill. di Palazzolo sull'Oglio* 3 (1969): 4–12; *Indice generale degli Incunabuli delle Bibliteche d'Italia,* 1: 278–80; *Gesamtkatalog der Wiegendrucke,* 5: 548–55.

[7] See E. Coemans, "Bernaerts J." in *Biographie Nationale de Belgique* vol. 2, col. 273–4; *Justi Lipsi Epistolarum Selectarum ad Belgas* (*Opera omnia* [Wesel, 1675], 2:729–

of licentiate in both Laws at Louvain, where he served as treasurer and dean of Bachelors. Because he was related to Justus Lipsius, Bernartius was called the latter's *enfant gâté*. Later in his career, he returned to Mechlin as counsel to the *Grand-Conseil*, and he died on 16 December 1601. He wrote commentaries on all three of Statius's works and a separate set of notes on the *Silvae*. The dedication of his commentaries on the *Achilleid*, *Thebaid*, and notes on the *Silvae* bears the date of 1 October 1593, and the edition was first printed in 1595 at Antwerp by Plantin-Moretus and was reprinted at least five times from 1595 to 1618. Bernartius' full-length commentary on the *Silvae* was first published in 1599 at Antwerp by Plantin-Moretus, again in 1618 at Paris by Tho. Blaise, and in 1671 at Leiden by Hackius. In addition to his commentaries on Statius, Bernartius wrote orations and occasional verse, a biography of Mary Queen of Scots, a treatise *De utilitate legendae Historiae*, a *De Lirani oppidi ab Hollandis occupati, per Mechlinianos & Antuerpianos admirabili liberatione, Commentariolus*, and a commentary on Boethius.

I edit here the text of the dedication, note to the reader, introduction, and beginning and end of Bernartius' commentary on the *Thebaid* from the 1607 edition.

Dedic. (1607 ed.): Reverendiss. et Ampliss. Domino Laevino Torrentio, Antverpiae Episcopo ... [*Inc.*] Non diu quaerenda aut reddenda mihi causa, Antistes amplissime, cur Statium Papinium, laboribus meis qua meliorem qua illustriorem redditum, lucem voluerim adspicere in nomine tuo.... perge amare Bernartium, qui nunc & aeternum erit vsu manucupioque tuus. Vale. Louanii Calend. Octob. M. D. XCIII.

Ad Lectorem: [*Inc.*] P. Statium Papinium volenter accipe mi Lector, vtilem (Deus bone!) magnumque Poetam.... neglectus hactenus nostris Aristarchis iacuit. no*n* Scholiis, non Notis, adeo. non Commentario illustratus. miror, imo indignor.... Hic trames quem calcaui, fulcru*m* quo superaui cliuos, libri veteres, quos studiose conquisitos varios cura ipse vidi. duos signate vere veteres. Elegantissimi Lipsii vnus erat, qui admirabile dictu quas notas sinceri codicis saepe pretulerit. alter, in Louaniensi hoc Athenaeo Buslidiani Collegii Trilinguis, optimae itidem notae. Laudo etiam interdu*m* codices duos vetustissimos bibliothecae S. Laurentii Leodie*n*sis: & vnum nihilo deteriorem, optimi Belgarum Caroli Langii. sed, vt vnicuique suum tribuam, eiusdem Langii industria. is enim tres illos codices, studiose composuerat, & suapte manu variantem lectione*m*

1064; and Issac Uri, *Francois Guyet* (Paris, 1886), 128–29, 234–44.

adnotarat libro, quem communicauit mihi Antuerpiensium Antistes, clarissimus Torrentius. sicubi discreparent, in Scholiis signate expressi. ad marginem libri, initiali littera, discriminaui. excusos quinque composui, apud Ald*um* duos anno MD.II, MD.XIX. alios Parisiis, Lugduni, Basilaeae. accessit his editio Veneta vetus, anni MCCCC.XC.... Denique adolescentiae nostrae memor haud graue sit vti Lesbia norma, & vt illa flectitur ad structuram, sic iudicium tuum accommoda huic tyroni.... finio, & te saluere iubeo quisquis es Lector.

Introd. inc.: Bellorum omnium quae inter Graecos priscis te*m*poribus fuere, si Troianu*m* excipias, celeberrimum semper habitum Thebanum illud, inter Oedipi filios, mirabili nescio magis, an miserabili exitu gestum. ante Christi naturale*m* annis circiter MCC.XXXVI.... / ... *Des.*: tantum moneo, a Diodoro Sophoclem, Euripidem, Lisimachum Alexandrinum, Senecam Iuniorem, nobilem etiam illum auctorem Thebaidos, scriptorum denique omne vulgus stare. plane vt ex formula Senatoria, *haec pars adhuc maior esse videatur,* praesertim accedente non Pedario Senatore, sed Consulari Papinio nostro quem iam aggredior. tu mihi dux vere Deus & manum hanc mentemque dirige.

Comm. inc.: Decertata odiis] decertate, pro *valde & pertinaciter certare.* sunt his igitur *alterna regna decertata odiis profanis,* pro quibus acriter & ad extremum certatum est, odiis externis & non fraternis, ... / ... *Des.*: XII. 798 *tot busta simul*) Pausanias in praeclara illa sua Graeciae descriptione, antiquae carae*que* eruditionis thesauros aperiens, multa ad Papinij nostri illustratione*m*, vti aduertere beneuole lector potuisti, contulit.... Haec ille. Plutarchus etiam Theseo, adiutorem Adrasto fuisse Theseum ad recuperanda illorum corpora, qui sub Cadmea ceciderant, refert, no*n* quod fuderit Thebanos, sed datis acceptisque hinc inde induciis.

According to Bernartius, Statius has lain hitherto neglected by the Aristarchuses (*Aristarchis*), for he knows of no scholia, notes, nor even a commentary on him. He is surprised and even angry at this neglect and in his note to the reader describes his own labors:

> This is the path which I have trod, this the staff by which I mounted the slopes–various ancient manuscripts which I have eagerly tracked down and carefully perused myself, two of them exceptionally old. One belonged to the most elegant Lipsius; frequently it exhibited some notable marks of a good codex; the other, in this Louvanian Athenaeum of the Trilingual Buslidian College, was likewise of the best quality. I sometimes mention two very ancient codices from the library of St. Laurence at Liège, and one which is by no means

> inferior belonging to that excellent Belgian scholar Charles Lang, but, to give each his due, [it owes its importance to the] industry of the same Lang. For he had carefully collated the three manuscripts and noted the variant readings on the manuscript which the bishop of Antwerp lent me, the famous Torrentius. I have carefully indicated in my notes where they differed and have differentiated them in the margin of my book with an initial. I have collated five printed texts, two from the Aldine press of the year 1502 and 1519, the others from Paris, Lyons, and Basel. There is also the old Venetian edition of the year 1490. . . . Finally please be good enough to think of my youth and to use the Lesbian rule[8] and as it bends to fit the structure, so fit your judgment to this tyro. . . . I conclude and I greet you, reader, whoever you are.

The work of these four Renaissance commentators manifests a new interest in and study of Statius during the period. Calderinus's commentary on the *Silvae*, which was virtually unknown during the Middle Ages, is the first extant commentary on that work. New interest in the *Achilleid*, Statius' minor epic, is seen in the three commentaries of Maturantius, Britannicus, and Bernartius. The story of the education and early life of Achilles was of particular interest in the humanists' view of education. Preserved in some ninety-five manuscripts, the *Achilleid* circulated as one of the six, and later eight, Latin texts in the popular schoolbook known today as the *Liber Catonianus*. For the first time editions of commentaries by different authors on all three of Statius's works begin to appear as well as editions of commentaries by a single author on three of Statius's work. Yet the present study is preliminary and incomplete. Information regarding the manuscript collections and early printed editions in Hungary, Czechoslovakia, Eastern Europe, and Russia has not been easy to obtain. Further research in the major libraries in these countries is necessary to complete this study for the *Catalogus Translationum et Commentariorum*.

University of North Texas. Denton, Texas

[8] On the "Lesbian rule" see Erasmus, *Adagia* I v 93 = LB II 217c, who cites Aristotle's *Nic. Eth.* 5.14 (=1137b 29–32) for the information that Lesbians used a leaden rule which changed shape to fit the shape of the stone. So Bernatius hopes that the reader will be similarly accommodating in his judgment of the work. I am indeed indebted to Professor Alexander Dalzell of Trinity College in the University of Toronto for this reference and explanation and for his careful editing of this article and also to my colleague Professor Anthony Damico of the University of North Texas for his help with the obscure Latin.

Aspects de l'exégèse de Charles de Bovelles

MARIE-MADELEINE DE LA GARANDERIE

Assurément Charles de Bovelles n'est pas à proprement parler un exégète. Ce mathématicien, ce métaphysicien ne s'est adonné à l'exégèse que de manière très ponctuelle: deux brefs commentaires du Nouveau Testament.[1] Mais le choix des textes est significatif. Choix de ce qui, dans l'Ecriture sainte, peut être dit—autant que de telles appréciations soient licites—le plus sacré. D'abord le prologue de l'Evangile de Jean, dont les premiers versets condensent les mystères de la trinité divine et de l'incarnation de la parole créatrice.[2] Tout l'essentiel, le "primordial" du christianisme est là, comme semble bien le suggérer, au titre même de l'ouvrage (*Commentarius in primordiale evangelium diui Ioannis*), l'emploi du mot, rare, *primordiale,* au lieu du terme courant: *primordium* (prologue).[3]

Quant au second texte, c'est l'Oraison dominicale, le "Notre Père" bien connu, mais qui, replacé dans son contexte évangélique (*Luc,* 9; *Matthieu,* 6),[4] n'est rien moins que la prière enseignée par le Christ lui-même.

---

[1] A quoi il convient d'ajouter les commentaires des psaumes 116 et 147 que l'on trouve dans un recueil publié à Lyon, chez Gryphe, en 1531.

[2] Ces mêmes versets qu'Erasme—dans sa Paraphrase (1523)—renoncera à paraphraser: "humanis rationibus de rebus divinis vestigare, periculosae cujusdam atque impiae audaciae est...." Notons que Bovelles (dans sa lettre–préface à l'évêque de Noyon Charles de Genlis, au fol. 3v) se plaît à souligner le caractère sacré du texte par une sorte de mise en scène: il imagine les apôtres réunis en prière dans le cénacle, tandis que Jean, sous l'inspiration de l'Esprit, jette sur le papier ces mots "In principio erat verbum." Nouvelle Pentecôte en quelque sorte....

[3] Hypothèse déjà avancée par J-C. Margolin voir (*infra* note 7).

[4] Comme Bovelles prend grand soin de le faire, insistant sur les prescriptions de l'Evangile de Matthieu (la prière sans ostentation, dans le secret).

Tandis que le prologue johannique est une révélation sur Dieu—plus précisément sur la relation du Fils au Père, et en quelque façon sur la vie intérieure de Dieu—l'Oraison dominicale définit la relation de l'homme à Dieu telle que le Fils de Dieu lui-même l'établit. Si donc le projet exégétique de Bovelles est de peu d'étendue, il est en revanche singulièrement ambitieux.

Il s'agit de deux ouvrages assez courts: 33 folios pour le commentaire du prologue de Saint Jean, 24 pour le Pater. Tous deux ont été écrits chez l'évêque d'Amiens François de Hallewin. Leurs dates s'entrecroisent en quelque sorte: l'étude du prologue, achevée le 23 juin 1511, sort des presses de Josse Bade le 3 décembre.[5] Le commentaire de l'Oraison dominicale, achevé le 7 juillet de le même année, est mis en vente par Jean Petit[6] dès le 8 octobre. Soit que ce dernier travail ait été rédigé en deux semaines après le premier, soit qu'ils aient été écrits concurremment, leur parenté est évidente. Mon propos sera non seulement de les présenter, mais de les éclairer par le rapprochement. Toutefois le commentaire du prologue de Saint Jean a déjà été l'objet d'une présentation très documentée par J-C. Margolin, et j'en ai à mon tour proposé une analyse à Genève en 1986.[7] C'est donc sur le deuxième texte que je me propose d'attirer plus longuement l'attention.

En 1511 Charles de Bovelles a environ trente deux ans. Après une suite de voyages (Suisse, Allemagne, Pays-Bas, Espagne, Italie), il vient de se retirer en Picardie. Il a déjà derrière lui presque toute son oeuvre philosophique et mathématique: ce qu'a matérialisé tout récemment, le 31 janvier 1511,[8] la réunion en un seul volume, chez H. Estienne, de six ouvrages philosophiques dont la composition s'échelonne depuis 1501—le *Liber de*

---

[5] Le commentaire du prologue de Jean y est suivi d'une *Vie de Raymond Lulle*, et Lulle est invoqué à deux reprises (fol. 3v et 6v) dans le commentaire lui-même. Sur l'influence de Lulle, qui dut s'excercer sur Bovelles par le truchement de Lefèvre d'Etaples (éditeur de quatre traités du Majorquais en 1499), mais que le voyage de Bovelles en Espagne, en 1505, avait certainement ravivée, voir M. Bataillon, *Erasme et l'Espagne* (Paris: Droz, 1937), 58; A. Llinarès, "Le lullisme de Lefèvre d'Etaples et de ses amis humanistes," in *L'humanisme français au début de la Renaissance* (Paris: Vrin, 1973), 127-36; P. Sharratt, "Le *De immortalitate* de Bovelles, manifeste et testament," in *Charles de Bovelles en son cinquième centenaire* (Paris: Tredaniel, 1982), 129-41.

[6] Jean Petit, avec le matériel typographique d'André Bocard.

[7] J-C. Margolin, "Bovelles et son commentaire du prologue johannique," in *L'exégèse au XVIème siècle* (Genève: Droz, 1978), 229-55; M-M. de La Garanderie, résumé de communication paru dans le bulletin de l'Institut d'Hre de la Réformation de l'Univ. de Genève (1985-1987), 15.

[8] Le recueil porte, à la fin, la date du 31 janvier 1510, soit 1511 nouveau style.

intellectu, le *Liber de sensu*, le *Liber de nihilo*, l'*Ars oppositorum*, le *Liber de generatione*, le *Liber de sapiente*—de cinq traités de mathématiques et de plusieurs lettres philosophiques. Les deux commentaires qui nous occupent ici ont donc été écrits dans l'élan et le sillage de ces oeuvres majeures. Ils en sont incontestablement tributaires.

L'étrangeté de ces travaux exégétiques frappe immédiatement le lecteur. Le moins étonnant des deux est le commentaire du prologue johannique. On est cependant surpris dès l'abord par le découpage du texte: non point en quatorze propositions, selon l'usage, mais en trente segments. Ce n'est manifestement pas l'analyse textuelle qui impose une telle fragmentation, mais la valeur symbolique du chiffre 30—qu'il s'agisse de l'âge du Christ, ou de la multiplication du 10 (chiffre de l'homme) et du 3 (signe de la trinité divine), ou peut-être de l'un et de l'autre. Première marque, en tous cas, de l'appropriation du texte par son commentateur. Aucune trace de la tradition patristique, aucune allusion aux controverses multiples dont s'est peu à peu, de ce texte difficile, dégagée l'interprétation orthodoxe. Bovelles, si j'ose dire, opère seul. Il se réfère éventuellement au reste de son oeuvre (ainsi—au fol. 9v—à son *De intellectu*). S'il se réfère évidemment à l'Ecriture sainte, et c'est bien le moins, il semble inclure dans l'Ecriture même l'oeuvre du pseudo-Denys. Le prétendu "converti de Saint Paul" a pour lui même autorité que Saint Paul, et offre à la pensée bovilienne ses résonances néo-platoniciennes et son architecture verticale. Les livres *Des noms divins*, *De la hiérarchie céleste*, et *De la hiérarchie ecclésiastique* sont très largement exploités.[9] Le nom du "divus Dionysius" est signalé onze fois en manchettes dans les marges du commentaire au prologue de Saint Jean.[10] Dans le commentaire de l'Oraison dominicale la présence dionysienne est plus obsédante encore, puisque le titre de l'ouvrage: *Dominica oratio tertrinis ecclesiasticae hierarchiae ordinibus particulatim attributa, et facili explanata commentatione* n'annonce pas seulement une explication doctrinale du texte, mais aussi, et d'abord, son intégration dans le "système dionysien." C'est donc à travers le prisme du pseudo-Denys que Bovelles lit l'Ecriture sainte. Dans ces conditions comment son exégèse va-t-elle procéder?

§ § §

L'exigence élémentaire de l'exégèse est la soumission au texte saint.

---

[9] *Des noms divins* (propositions 7, 15); *Hier. céleste* et *Hier. eccl.* (pr. 12).

[10] On trouve aussi, pr. 20, fol. 21 "sacer Dionysius."

Certes, chez Bovelles cette soumission est apparente; car le texte est suivi linéairement, segment après segment; les rapports de sens sont signalés, la structure d'ensemble appréciée (et nous verrons même que cette attention à la structure textuelle est caractéristique de la démarche de notre auteur). Le commentaire, toutefois, n'est pas philologique selon le mode des humanistes, Il n'est pas non plus, ou n'est que fort rarement, une pieuse paraphrase. C'est un commentaire rigoureusement didactique, qui, pour mieux persuader, a recours au procédé du dialogue fictif; "tu diras peut-être que ...," "persuade-toi bien que ...," "et voilà résolue la difficulté ...," etc. On trouve en marge fréquemment des mots comme *objectio, percunctatio, interrogatio, dubietas, instantia*; à quoi répondent *responsio, solutio, illatio....* Ce procédé didactique ne me paraît pas ici relever, purement et comme mécaniquement, de la scolastique. Il traduit plutôt l'exaltation et la tension d'un discours qui, dans sa rigueur et dans sa sécheresse mêmes (rigueur de la pensée abstraite, rigueur de la mathématique, passion de la logique) reste guidé par un désir ardent d'affirmer et de convaincre.

Pour persuader, Bovelles met en oeuvre tout l'appareil logique qui fait fonctionner tous ses livres. Il use évidemment des schémas binaires courants: comparaison, opposition, distinction. Ainsi distingue-t-il, à propos du début du prologue de Saint Jean, le *principium* de la durée et le *principium* de la substance, ou encore Dieu dans son unité (*sub conjunctione*) et dans la différence des trois personnes divines (*sub discretione*). Mais il privilégie les schémas ternaires. Tout, en effet, dans l'univers "va par trois," comme non seulement on le lit, mais on le voit figuré, par un tableau de 42 lignes, au *Livre du sage* (p. 136–37), et comme on le lit encore dans le commentaire du prologue johannique (fol. 9). Le 3, nombre de Dieu, éclate et reluit dans toute la création. La *triade* postule l'unité dans la diversité. Ainsi des trois facultés de l'âme, *intellectus, memoria, voluntas*; des trois parts du monde, *sol, luna, terra*; des trois moments de la connaissance, *conceptus, vox, scriptura*; des trois éléments du syllogisme, *major, minor, illatio*, etc. Transposées analogiquement de leur domaine propre à la théologie, selon l'opération que Bovelles désigne sous le nom d'*assurrectio* (transposition vers le haut),[11] ces triades permettent d'appréhender non seulement tout l'univers, mais le mystère de Dieu. Chacune d'elles toutefois enclôt un système de rapports qui lui est propre et qui ne saurait être adéquat à l'inaccessible réalité divine, laquelle

[11] Transposition vers le haut. Ev. de St Jean, pr. 3 à 6 (fols. 6 à 10). Voir J-C. Margolin, art. cité, 250.

reste impénétrable comme le proclame l'admirable conclusion du *De nihilo*.[12] Chaque triade fonctionne donc à la fois positivement et négative-ment, positivement par sa fécondité propre, négativement par l'évidence de son imperfection. Le meilleur éclairage du commentaire au prologue johannique est sans doute à chercher aux chapitres 23 à 30 du *De sapiente*: "toute connaissance est en quelque façon trinité," "l'homme est le miroir de l'univers," "seuls les chrétiens peuvent se glorifier légitimement de connaître la divine et sainte Trinité," "signes sensibles permettant de connaître la très haute Trinité divine." Il apparaît donc que, si la Trinité n'avait été révélée en l'Evangile et définie par les conciles, on la trouverait en quelque sorte comme à la fine pointe de la philosophie de Charles de Bovelles.

Une telle aventure intellectuelle n'est pas sans péril. Plus soucieux d'harmoniser et d'adapter que de déchiffrer, Bovelles inverse la relation exégétique. Ce qui "fait sens" pour lui, ce n'est pas le texte nu, c'est l'harmonie du texte avec sa propre vision du monde, laquelle trouve en Denys, le faux aréopagite, un miroir d'élection. Or cette vision s'ajuste souvent avec peine au credo de Nicée. Françoise Joukovsky a bien montré[13] quelles distorsions le néo-platonisme et notamment le plotinisme imposent à la pensée de Bovelles, concernant en particulier l'égalité des personnes divines, la place du péché, celle de la grâce.[14] Le christianisme de Bovelles gomme le pathétique de la chute et de la rédemption. En raison même de sa nature unitrine, Dieu se devait de créer le monde; en raison de sa nature unitrine il devait s'incarner. "*Opportuit igitur....*"

L'espace nous manque pour traiter des autres thémes qui mériteraient de retenir notre attention: thème de la lumière, thème de la femme (pourquoi le Christ s'est-il fait homme et non femme?), thème de l'aveuglement des Juifs, etc. Retenons seulement que le texte nous est donné à lire à travers la double grille de déchiffrement que sont—pour ne pas parler des relais

---

[12] "magis divinae illam eminentissimam substantiam honoramus atque reveremur sacris negationibus et privationibus, illam incognitam, ignotam et inscrutabilem esse attestantes, predicantes, efferentes."

[13] "Thèmes plotiniens dans le *De sapiente* de Ch. de Bovelles," in *Bibl. d'Hum. et Ren.* 43 (1981): 141–53; et *Le regard intérieur* (Paris: Nizet, 1982). Voir aussi P. Quillet "L'ontologie scalaire de Ch. de Bovelles," in *Ch. de B. en son cinquième centenaire* (Paris: Tredaniel), 171–79.

[14] Le commentaire du mot "grâce," à la pr. 30 ("Plenum gratiae et veritatis") est particulièrement étrange, le mot *gratia* désignant non plus le don gratuit de Dieu, mais la reconnaissnace que l'homme doit à Dieu, (comme dans l'expression courante "action de grâces"). Le découpage arificiel du texte explique sans doute ce genre d'aberration.

constitués par le Cusain, par Raymond Lulle, par Ficin, et bien entendu par Lefèvre d'Etaples–le corpus dionysien et le corpus bovillien lui-même.

§ § §

L'infléchissement est encore plus sensible dans le second ouvrage, le commentaire du *Notre Père*. L'auteur, là encore, s'approprie le texte, qu'il divise en neuf propositions–et non en sept demandes selon l'usage–dans le but de l'adapter (*aptabimus* ..., *accommodare studuimus* ...) aux neuf ordres, groupés eux-mêmes trois par trois (*tertrina*), de la hiérarchie ecclésiastique; ces ordres à leur tour correspondant (en vérité plus rigoureusement chez Bovelles que chez Denys lui-même[15]) aux neuf ordres de la hiérarchie céleste (Séraphins, Chérubins, Trônes, Dominations, Vertus, Puissances, Principautés, Archanges, Anges). De plus, le texte de l'Evangile s'efface en quelque sorte devant la classification dionysiennne, comme en témoigne la disposition des titres: les versets du *Pater* sont imprimés en seconde position, tandis que se détache–en première ligne et en milieu de ligne–le nom de la catégorie à laquelle chaque proposition, *particulatim*, est censée correspondre. Bovelles nous invite ainsi à descendre, à la suite de Denys, les divers degrés de la hiérarchie, depuis le plus sacré, celui des *pontifices*. Viennent ensuite les simples prêtres (*sacerdotes*), puis les ordres mineurs: *diaconi*, *subdiaconi*, *ministri*. Après eux les *monachi* (les moines non-prêtres). Puis la masse des laïques, la *plebs sancta*. Enfin deux catégories provisoirement exclues de ce peuple saint, les *energumini*, c'est-à-dire des baptisés, des initiés (pour parler comme Bovelles), qui ont succombé aux tentations, et sont comme en attente du pardon, des pénitents en somme;[16] puis les *catechumini*, qui sont, eux, en attente de l'initiation. Un tableau de correspondance (fig. 1) précède le commentaire et s'étale sur une double page–tandis que l'on trouve à la fin de l'ouvrage, symétriquement, le tableau de correspondance entre hiérarchie ecclésiastique (c'est-à-dire hiérarchie humaine, l'Eglise embrassant, en théorie, l'humanité entière), et hiérarchie céleste (fig. 2). Cet encadrement du commentaire signale et illustre bien l'étrange dessein de notre auteur.

---

[15] *Oeuvres complètes du pseudo-Denis*, trad. M. de Gandillac (Paris: Aubier, 1943), 311–12.

[16] Il ne s'agit évidemment pas d' "énergumènes," ni non plus de "possédés du démon," comme le propose, en se référant à Cassien, C. Demaizière dans la préface à son édition de *La différence des langues vulgaires*.... (Amiens, 1972), 34.

Pontifices

1 Pater noſter qui es ī celis.

Sacerdotes

2 Sanctificetur nomē tuum.

Diaconi

3 Adueniat regnum tuum.

Subdiaconi

4 Fiat voluntas tua ſicut in celo et in terra.

Miniſtri

5 Panem noſtrum quotidianum da nobis hodie.

Monachi

6 Et dimitte nobis debita noſtra.

Plebs ſancta

7 Sicut et nos dimittimus debitoribus noſtris

Energumini

8 Et ne nos inducas in tentationem

Cathecumini

9 Sed libera nos a malo

Omnes ſimul eccleſiaſtici gradus

10 Amen

Fig. 1.

Deus

Angelica hierarchia laudãs deũ

Angelica		Ecclesiastica
Seraphin	1	Pontifices
Cherubin	2	Sacerdotes
Throni	3	Diaconi
Dnationes	4	Subiaconi
Virtutes	5	Miniſtri
Poteſtates	6	Monachi
Prĩcipatus	7	Plebs ſãcta
Archageli	8	Energũini
Angeli	9	Cathecumĩ

Eccleſiaſtica hierarchia orãs deũ

¶ Hexaſtichon exhortatorium ad lectorem.

Mente deum nitida/ docet hic orare libellus:
Oret ſectator qui cupit eſſe dei.
Si penetrat breuis (vt dicunt) oratio celos:
Nil opus eſt vocum plurima congeries.
Non labiis igitur/preſſo ſed corde tonantem:
Nec longa ſtudeas conciliare prece.

FINIS.

Fig. 2.

De cet étrange dessein Bovelles s'acquitte d'une manière assez déconcertante. Ainsi les deux premières rubriques, celles des *pontifices* et des *sacerdotes* (*Pater noster qui es in coelis / Sanctificetur nomen tuum*) se perdent dans des questions purement formelles: distinction, dans la prière, de la substance et de l'accident, de la qualité et de la quantité, distinction (figure en losange à l'appui) de la prière directe et de la prière indirecte (ou *obliqua*) par laquelle se trouve justifiée, à propos d'un texte qui pourtant n'en a que faire, la médiation de la Vierge et des saints ... Et rien n'est dit sur les pontifes ni sur les prêtres, ni sur l'attribution de leurs noms aux deux premiers segments du texte. Le projet ne prend forme qu'à la troisième rubrique, celle des diacres (*Adveniat regnum tuum*). Là Bovelles semble s'arrêter pour admirer la composition harmonieuse du texte qu'il commente, sa *concinnitas*. Revenant alors en arrière, il justifie l'attribution des deux premières propositions aux deux premiers ordres. La première proposition—dit-il en substance—était la plus proche du divin et se situait en quelque sorte dans l'absolu, elle était *absolutissima*, se bornant à nommer Dieu sans rien lui attribuer ni lui rien demander; tandis que la seconde ne lui demandait que la louange de son nom. A quoi correspondaient les pontifes qui, les yeux levés au ciel, contemplent en silence[17] la divinité; puis les prêtres qui le louent en leurs saints cantiques. Après quoi l'on descend vers des propositions plus particulières, et des demandes concernant l'homme, les unes positives (comme la pain quotidien), les dernières négatives (la tentation, le mal à éviter). Ces dernières demandes étant, comme il convient (*decenter*) attribuées aux ordres inférieurs encore prisonniers du péché, *energumini, catechumini*.

A l'exception d'une belle méditation—dans la première rubrique—sur la bonté de Dieu qui veut être appelé Père, le commentaire de Bovelles, occupé trop évidemment par le jeu des "correspondances," n'est pas une prière.[18] C'est en revanche un commentaire doctrinal, mené certes avec un parti pris de brièveté (comme le proclame à maintes reprises la préface), mais avec le souci de traiter clairement tous les problèmes. Ainsi:

—Pourquoi demander à Dieu ce que de toutes façons il peut, et va, nous donner—ou (ce qui revient au même) pourquoi prier?

---

[17] Divinité qui elle-même habite dans le silence, comme l'exprime ce très beau passage de la rubrique *Diaconi*: "Nempe et Deus ipse in summo dicitur habitare silentio, in quo penitus omnis vox obmutescit, et a quo statim ubi digredimur, mox orationis vocisque (deum ipsum mire extollentis) multiplicitas oboritur."

[18] Cependant le sizain au lecteur, qui—à la suite de la table de correspondance entre les hiérarchies de la terre et du ciel—clôt l'ouvrage, insiste sur cet aspect (cf. fig. 2).

–Quel sens donner aux mots "pain quotidien?"
–Qu'est-ce que le péché? Quelles en sont les (trois) différentes formes, les (trois) différentes cibles, les (trois) différentes formes de réparation?
–Seul un être libre peut pécher. Qu'en est-il alors des anges, et, *a contrario*, des démons?
–Nous sommes tous sujets à tentation, et les démons sont bien réels, comme le prouve–unique anecdote du livre–l'histoire de ce cardinal en voyage, venu camper de nuit dans les ruines d'un temple païen, et qui a des visions effrayantes, entend les cris des démons, et finalement dissipe leur troupe par le pouvoir de sa parole; histoire rapportée d'après les *Dialogi de miraculis* de Cesaire de Heisterbach.[19]

Sans pouvoir entrer dans le détail des interprétations de Bovelles, je me bornerai à noter qu'elles sont toutes étrangères aux tendances de la Réforme, accordant notamment grande importance aux saints, et à la notion de mérite. On pourra aussi remarquer que la disjonction des propositions 6 et 7 (*dimitte nobis debita nostra / Sicut et nos demittimus debitoribus nostris*) enlève au mot *sicut* sa force, et gomme totalement la prescription du pardon des offenses. Mais ces question appartiennent à la catéchèse et ne sont pas ici mon propos. Au reste il me semble que l'intérêt de notre texte est ailleurs. Par delà un catholicisme bien traditionnel, par delà des modes d'argumentation qui sentent bien souvent l'école, Bovelles ne laisse pas de nous étonner. Dans le commentaire du Pater, mieux encore que dans le commentaire du prologue de Saint Jean, il découvre, il concentre en quelque sorte, et reflète une harmonie.

§ § §

Ce besoin, commun à tous les néo-platonismes, d'enserrer l'univers, matériel et spirituel, dans un réseau d'analogies, n'est-ce pas une sorte d'exorcisme? Exorcisme de nos angoisses: tout en ordre, chaque chose en son lieu.... Chez un mathématicien comme Bovelles, quelle sécurité pour l'esprit que de penser le monde soumis précisément aux lois de l'esprit, et répondant au *quod erat demonstrandum* qui achève les belles démonstrations! Traiter le prologue de Saint Jean non comme une "ouverture,"–ce qu'il est en fait–mais comme un tout, un *primordiale*; le découper en

[19] Cette oeuvre, pleine d'anecdotes et de "visions," du cistercien allemand (c. 1180–c. 1240) avait été imprimée à Cologne en 1475, puis en 1481.

trente segments, c'était déjà une façon de sculpter en quelque sorte un objet sacré et hautement symbolique. Plus encore, faire cadrer (fût-ce au prix de curieuses torsions) la prière du Christ avec la hiérarchie des hommes en l'Eglise, et indirectement avec la hiérarchie céleste, quelle symphonie!

Mais ce n'est pas tout. Au cours de son entreprise, dans son effort pour ajuster tant bien que mal le texte du *Pater* à l'architecture dionysienne, Bovelles expérimente la structure même du *Pater*; il en découvre l'axe (la proposition 4), et la division ternaire: 4 / 1 / 4. Il s'avise qu'un membre de phrase—"sur la terre comme au ciel"—pourrait constituer une sorte de pièce mobile qui, au prix de quelques variantes,[20] pourrait s'associer, en refrain, à chacune des propositions, comme pour former le poème de la terre accordée avec le ciel. Ainsi recompose-t-il le texte à la lumière de la loi interne qu'il croit y avoir découvert et dont il s'émerveille. Il le lit comme une oeuvre d'art, il en façonne à son tour une oeuvre d'art nouvelle. . . .

A cet égard l'AMEN final nous offre certainement le plus bel exemple. Là Bovelles paraît si fortement saisi par son entreprise même que les différents ordres de la hiérarchie ecclésiastique ne sont plus de simples catégories abstraites, de purs repères. On perçoit, à travers des variantes du vocabulaire, qu'ils ont pris une existence concrète. On passe en effet d'expressions comme "j'attribue," "j'opère le rapprochement," "j'institue la correspondance," à des termes comme "*ils* prient," "*ils* demandent." L'adaptation du texte à la hiérarchie n'est donc plus une simple *opération*, au sens mathématique du mot. Elle est théâtrale et musicale. Les personnages entrent en scène, ils ont pris voix, et chacun à son tour entonne sa partie. Puis, tous ensemble, *cuncti unica et concordi voce*, ils chantent l'Amen, la dixième proposition du *Pater*. C'est le *finale* de la prière qui monte de toute la terre (bien et dûment hiérarchisée) vers le ciel où les choeurs des anges lui font écho.

§ § §

Ainsi ces sortes d'exercices de théologie appliquée, quelque peu ingrats et étranges à première vue, laissent voir leur véritable fonction. Tout en paraissant suivre avec scrupule ses textes-supports, Bovelles en fait les

---

[20] Il faut beaucoup de subtilité en effet pour adapter la formule aux dernières demandes du Pater, puisque les habitants de ciel (anges et élus) n'ont ni offenses à se faire pardonner ni tentations à éviter.

annexe; il les transforme, il en fait des objets mesurés à son mode, témoins—avec la caution de Denys—de la cohérence universelle, et si bien ajustés au système bovillien qu'ils semblent tout à la fois en découler et l'étayer.

Université de Nantes, France

Latin Interpretations of Ptolemy's Geographia

O. A. W. DILKE

Over a thousand years after Ptolemy's death, the Greek scholar Maximus Planudes, at the monastery of Chora, Constantinople, embarked on a search for manuscripts of Ptolemy's *Manual of Geography*.[1] At that time Ptolemy was chiefly known as an astronomer, and some of his astronomical, mathematical and optical writings had been translated into Latin. But Planudes knew that Greeks, Romans and Arabs had used the *Geography*, and that it had been accompanied by maps. We know, though he may not have known, that in the tenth century the Arab historian Al-Mas'udi had found coloured maps in a Ptolemy manuscript.[2]

Planudes' search was only partly rewarded: in 1295 he found a text of it, but no maps. However, his manuscript indicated that the text should have been accompanied by twenty-six maps, and gave Ptolemy's suggestions for constructing rectangular regional ones according to proportions, applicable to each region, of longitude and latitude. Planudes therefore had new maps made; whether they were wholly reconstructed from Ptolemaic co-ordinates or were also dependent on maps is disputed.[3] A number of copies of the Greek text were made, most with twenty-six or twenty-seven maps,[4] but some (known as Recension B) with sixty-four to

---

[1] J. B. Harley and D. Woodward, ed., *The History of Cartography* i (Chicago, 1987), i.268; O. A. W. Dilke, *Greek and Roman Maps* (London, 1985), 157–60.

[2] M. Destombes, ed., *Mappemondes A.D. 1200–1500* (Amsterdam, 1964), 18; Masudi, *Le livre des prairies d'or* (Paris, 1962), i.76–77. According to him 4350 cities appeared on the map.

[3] A. Diller, "The Oldest Manuscripts of Ptolemaic Maps," *Transactions of the American Philological Association* 71 (1940), 62–67.

[4] J. Fischer, ed., *Claudii Ptolemaei Geographiae Codex Urbinas Graecus 82*, 2 vols. in 4 (Leiden and Leipzig, 1932), Tomus Prodromus I.219–89, 515–23, 551–54, and for the Latin maps of Recension A, *ibid.* 290–415.

sixty-six, and some with none.

Nevertheless, it is unlikely that the Western world would have been captivated by Ptolemy's *Geography* if this had not been translated into Latin. With some exceptions, the worlds of Greek and Latin scholarship were unduly separate. Not for over 100 years did Florentine scholarship set about remedying this. In 1395 Manuel Chrysoloras, sent as envoy from Constantinople to Venice, contacted classicists in Italy, and returned with the Tuscan scholar Jacopo d'Angelo da Scarperia (Iacobus Angelus). From 1397 to 1399 Chrysoloras, encouraged by the statesman and scholar Coluccio Salutati,[5] was teaching Greek in Florence; and although he had himself intended to translate the *Geography* into Latin, he handed over this task to Angelus. But in 1401 the latter became secretary to the Papal Curia, so that there was a delay in translating. The translation was completed in 1406, with dedication to Pope Gregory XII.

In his preface[6] Angelus contrasts the topographical precision of Ptolemy with the vague descriptions of such other ancient writers as Pliny the Elder. *Illi enim licet habitabilem universi orbis situm descripserint, non tamen ex eorum praeceptis plane captari potest qua arte totius orbis pictura formari valeat, ut proportio cuiusque partis ad totum universale servetur.* In other words, if we read, for example, Pliny, *Natural History III–VI*, we shall have no idea whether, say, India is bigger or smaller than Spain.

Angelus could in fact have made an exception to this lack of defined latitudes and longitudes in ancient writers. Ptolemy's predecessor Marinus of Tyre, whose work survives only in the former's extracts,[7] had perhaps a generation before him listed latitudes and longitudes, but unmethodically, sometimes recording latitude only, sometimes longitude only. The lack of precision by predecessors was undoubtedly a point for Angelus to stress, in contrast to the scientific approach, based on the astronomical background of the only extant writer to give latitude and longitude co-ordinates everywhere. The approach aimed at revolutionising world and regional cartography. Eighty-five years before Angelus' translation, the Venetian Marin Sanudo the Elder,[8] who presented his plea for a new

---

[5] L. D. Reynolds and N. G. Wilson, *Scribes and Scholars* (Oxford, 2nd ed., 1974), 119.

[6] To be found in numerous Latin manuscripts of the *Geography*; first printed at Vicenza, 1475.

[7] *Geog.* i.6.1 ff.

[8] O. A. W. Dilke and Margaret S. Dilke, "Famous Mapmakers: Marin Sanudo—Was he a great cartographer?," *The Map Collector* 39 (1987), 29–32; id., "Mapping a Crusade: Propaganda and War in 14th-century Palestine," *History Today* 39 (1989), 31–5.

crusade to the Pope at Avignon, had in some measure heralded a revival. In his *Liber secretorum fidelium crucis* (1321),[9] he had not only employed Pietro Vesconte of Genoa to map the Mediterranean, but had himself completely remodelled the map of the Holy Land, adding reference grid squares whose numbers appear also in his text. Nevertheless, such a grid was suitable only for a restricted area, and a return had to be made to co-ordinates for the cartography of the known world.

Angelus' other point is a much more doubtful one. He explains that Manuel Chrysoloras had used the Latin title *Geographia* for Ptolemy's title *Geographike Hyphegesis*, which may be rendered "Manual of Geography." Angelus, however, preferred *Cosmographia*, and felt that his master would have changed to that. *Cosmos enim graece mundus latine, qui terram caelumque ipsum, quod per totum hoc opus tamquam rei fundamentum adducitur, plane significat.* This is quite the wrong approach. Ptolemy did not call his work *Geographia*, as Angelus implies, but by the Greek phrase above, of which a possible Latin translation could have been *Geographiae introductio*, since the word *chartographia* was not yet in use.[10] Secondly, although the work is by an astronomer and uses astronomical data, it is not about the universe, so that, as later editors saw, *cosmographia* is a misnomer.

As to Angelus' translation of Ptolemy's text, on the one hand it represents no mean achievement, since no previous Latin translation of it and no annotation were available, and Ptolemy's Greek is by no means easy. On the other hand, after this translation had several times been revised, mathematicians were more than ever complaining that Angelus did not know mathematics well enough. As an example, he simply transliterated Ptolemy's word 'Επιτέταρτοζ meaning 5/4 as *epitetarti*. This unfamiliar word, referring in the context to the ratio of latitude to longitude at Rhodes, was badly corrupted in Renaissance editions, even the *editio princeps* (Vicenza, 1475) having *epitertati* (*sic*). It led to the 1932 translator, E. L. Stevenson,[11] mistaking the form Epitecartus, which he found, as if it were a geographer's name. A later Renaissance edition had *sesquiquarti*, which may have been more intelligible.

We may also think of Angelus' failure to comment on what has been called Ptolemy's major cartographic inaccuracy. Instead of accepting Eratosthenes' revised estimate of 252,000 stades for the circumference of

---

[9] Reprinted from J. Bongars, *Gesta Dei per Francos* II (Hanover, 1611), with introduction by J. Prawer (Toronto University Press, 1972).

[10] The Greek Χαρτογρᾶφος means "writing (adj.) on paper."

[11] *The Geography of Claudius Ptolemy* (New York, 1932).

the world, which whatever the length of his stade was reasonable enough, Ptolemy accepted Posidonius' revised estimate of 180,000 stades. As a result, among other defects, his equivalent for the length of the Mediterranean in degrees of longitude, always difficult to calculate in antiquity, was quite excessive.[12]

Angelus' translation was completed two generations before the *editio princeps* mentioned above, forerunner of so many Latin editions, which outnumber Greek editions by 15 to 1. This and its immediate successors[13] adopted Angelus' misleading title *Cosmographia*, his preface (often with a dedication as well) and his translation, the last two with little or no revision. But any reader of Latin will gather an increasing mass of information from the prefaces. Thus the Bologna editor of 1477[14] was proud of having the first printed maps made from copper plates, which could be either exactly repeated or modified, and so reach a wide public. We learn from his preface that Conrad Sweynheym, the German printer working in Italy, instructed certain *mathematici* between 1474 and 1477, when he died, in the art of producing copper plates. Unfortunately their printing of Roman numerals let them down, so that instead of M.CCCC.LXXVII (1477) they left out two letters, XV, and gave a totally wrong date for the edition, as if it had come out in 1462.

The largest number of early editions was published in Rome. The first Rome edition (1478)[15] has a preface by Arnold Buckinck, which starts from Hipparchus' celestial co-ordinates of heavenly bodies, based on a geocentric universe, and says *vir sagacis ingenii Ptolemaeus* did the same for the earth. However, so that arts as well as science may be represented and really good Latinity be incorporated, he has drawn on the services of the scholar Domitius Calderinus of Verona, so that the ears of his revered patron may not be offended by the ignorance of the scribes. Ptolemy's *floruit* is given too late a period, and in general Renaissance editors are hazy about his life.

The year 1482 was notable for two very different publications of Ptolemy's *Geography*. Of these, Berlinghieri's Florence edition does not particularly concern this conference, since it was in Italian *terza rima*. But

---

[12] Harley and Woodward, ed. (*op. cit.*, n. 1), i.168–70.

[13] Not, however, the Rome edition of 1478, which Tony Campbell, *The Earliest Printed Maps* (London, 1987), 132, includes.

[14] Facsimile edition, with preface by R. A. Skelton: *Theatrum Orbis Terrarum*, ser.1.i (Amsterdam, 1963).

[15] Facsimile edition, with preface by R. A. Skelton: *Theatrum Orbis Terrarum*, ser.2.vi (Amsterdam, 1966).

apart from this we should note that it was not intended as a translation but as a very free paraphrase. Perhaps Italian was regarded as largely the language of the arts, while Latin was also that of sciences. But in addition the mapmakers were wondering how much world cartography could or should, after over 1300 years, be updated. Clearly Berlinghieri could incorporate by this method a more current world map. His own was evidently recognised as such by the anonymous compiler of the Wilczek-Brown codex of Ptolemy maps, now at the John Carter Brown Library, Providence, R.I.[16] In that codex, instead of a manuscript world map to go with the manuscript regional maps, we find Berlinghieri's printed world map of 1482.

The other edition of the same year is that of Ulm,[17] with preface by Donis (=Donnus) Nicolaus Germanus dedicating the work to Pope Paul II. The first theme of his preface is his newly invented trapezoidal projection. Critics, he says, will undoubtedly accuse him of either clumsiness or rashness. *Nam plane nos aut ignorasse quid egerimus aut temere ausos esse tantum opus contaminare affirmabunt.* But was not Homer, the father of poetry, edited by Pisistratus, and Lucretius' *divinum opus* by Cicero? Readers, he adds, who have some inkling of geometry or cosmography will applaud, since Ptolemy himself gave two [actually three][18] different projections for a world map. One may comment that these trapezoidal frames were also applied by Donnus Nicolaus to regional maps, for which Ptolemy, as a simplification, proposed rectangular frames.

The other innovation of the Ulm edition was the inclusion of new maps, *tabulae novae* or *modernae*. Two famous regions, Spain and Italy, the editor points out, are in his time much better known topographically than they were in antiquity. Therefore in addition to the Ptolemaic maps in these areas, it seemed only right to incorporate new maps with the latest available information for comparison. There were also, he pointed out,

---

[16] L. Bagrow, "The Wilczek-Brown Codex," *Imago Mundi* 12 (1955), 171–74; O. A. W. Dilke and Margaret S. Dilke, "The Wilczek-Brown Codex of Ptolemy Maps," *Imago Mundi* 40 (1988), 119–24.

[17] Facsimile edition, with preface by R. A. Skelton: *Theatrum Orbis Terrarum*, ser.1.ii (Amsterdam, 1963). The original dedication (1466), as preserved in Codex Estensis latinus 463, was to Duke Borso d'Este; Pope Paul II died in 1471. The Ulm edition is derived not from this manuscript but from that at Schloss Wolfegg: see Fischer (*op. cit.*, n. 4), 344–47, 356. Among corruptions in its preface is *deuicisse* (col.2, line 28) for *deviasse*.

[18] The third projection, which occurs in Book VII of the *Geography*, is discussed by O. Neugebauer, "Ptolemy's *Geography*, Book VII, Chapters 6 and 7," *Isis* 50 (1959), 22–29.

regions remoter from the Mediterranean such as Scandinavia, where Ptolemy's knowledge had been very rudimentary. The one oddity which Donnus Nicolaus does not mention is the inclusion of a map of Palestine based closely on that of Marin Sanudo already mentioned. This map, wrongly ascribed by many modern scholars to Pietro Vesconte, was considered, despite being over 150 years old, as the most instructive and scientific available. Moreover such as map of biblical and crusader Palestine was needed to supplement Ptolemy.[19]

After Columbus' voyage of discovery, these *tabulae modernae* were gradually increased to include America. The Pesaro world map of ca. 1505[20] includes the words *mundus novus* on South America, but a more specific name was needed. The collaboration of Ringmann and Waldeseemüller at St. Dié in Alsace resulted in a proposal that the name America, derived from Amerigo Vespucci, should be adopted for the new continent.[21] This is discussed as a possibility in the *Cosmographiae introductio* of 1507, which was clearly a joint publication by them.

A curious and somewhat illogical edition of the *Geographia* was that published at Venice in 1511 by Bernardus Sylvanus of Eboli.[22] His idea was not to supplement Ptolemaic maps with contemporary ones, but actually to change the figures of latitude and longitude east of the Canaries in Ptolemy's text. The reader is first alerted to this in some elegant iambic trimeters by Ioannes Aurelius Augurellus (Giovanni Augurelli), beginning:

> Si forte primo dentur ingressu tibi,
> Hic, lector, obviam ulla, quae statim nova
> Inusitataque videantur, vel situ
> Priore mota vel figura et ordine
> Mutata vel dempta numeris et addita,
> . . . ne tu, quaeso, diligentiam
> Auctoris aspernare; namque operam is dedit. . . .

---

[19] For early maps of the Holy Land see K.Nebenzahl, *Maps of the Bible Lands* (London, 1986).

[20] Margaret S. Dilke and A. Brancati, "The New World in the Pesaro Map," *Imago Mundi* 31 (1979), 78–83.

[21] Ptolemy, *Geographia*, Strassburg 1513, facsimile edition with preface by R. A. Skelton: *Theatrum Orbis Terrarum*, ser.2.iv (Amsterdam, 1966), VII ff.; H. Jantz, "The New World in the Treasures of an Old European Library," in G. A. Kaldewey, ed., *The American Wolfenbutteliana* (New York, [1988]), 22–39, esp. 25–26.

[22] Facsimile edition, with preface by R. A. Skelton: *Theatrum Orbis Terrarum*, ser.5.i (Amsterdam, 1969).

For his preface Sylvanus prefers Latin prose, which may be translated: "I think I can envisage most readers frowning with amazement on seeing the maps drawn by me so different from those of my predecessors." On detail, he mentions north Britain as badly distorted by Ptolemy; and when we look at his co-ordinates and map, we find that N.E. Scotland goes no further than 16½° E. of the Canaries, while the Cantium (Kent) promontory reaches 17½° E. Probably the best solution would have been to leave Ptolemy's co-ordinates in the forms given in good manuscript tradition, but to add new ones by their side.

Evidently by this time it was felt not only at Venice but also at Nuremberg that after over 100 years it was high time Angelus' translation was revised. Both the 1514 and the 1525 Nuremberg editions complain of it, Pirckheymer (also called Bürckhaimer) in the latter claiming that Angelus was so poor at mathematics that often he did not even understand what he himself had written. On the other hand he claims that Werner, the 1514 editor, sometimes had hallucinations about the Greek. Pirckheymer's own translation seems to have relied on Regiomontanus for any mathematical points. In order to correct one such, an appendix by Regiomontanus was incorporated in the 1525 edition, giving notes on the penultimate chapter of Book VII. One may see the first changes in the opening words (*Geog.* i.1): (a) Angelus: *Cosmographia designatrix imitatio est totius cogniti orbis cum his quae fere universaliter sibi iunguntur.* The copy of the Vicenza *editio princeps* at the John Carter Brown Library has, in addition to other changes in i.1, *designatrix* crossed out and *designationis* inserted in ink after *est.* (b) Strassburg 1513 edition: *Geographia mutatio est per designationem totius cogniti orbis cum his quae fere universaliter sibi iunguntur.* (c) Nuremberg 1514 edition: *Geographia imitatio est picturae depraehensae terrae partis totius cum his quae tamquam ad totum ipsi coniuncta sunt.* (d) Pirckheymer, Strassburg, 1525: *Geographia imitatio est picturae totius partis terrae cognitae cum iis, quae sibi quasi universaliter sunt annexa.* Of these, (b) seems the best, except that *mutatio* is inferior for the Greek *mimesis* and may be a misreading of the handwriting.

Even Mercator, who can be said to have heralded modern scientific cartography, was among those who produced a Latin edition of Ptolemy's *Geography.*[23] Elegiac verses, addressed to him by Michaël ab Isselt Amerfortius, imagine God admiring Archimedes' astronomical sphere and wondering what He would have thought of Ptolemy's work.

Finally, two examples of the help that can be given by Latinists to study

---

[23] Cologne, 1578, maps only; 1584, maps and Pirckheymer's text.

of the cartographic texts of the Renaissance. In 1987, at the Paris International Congress of the History of Cartography, Donald L. McGuirk presented a paper on a Latin palimpsest caused by re-use of a metal plate on the Ruysch Ptolemy. One passage, as reconstructed by him read VBI SVT EXTREMICAE DIES MUDI. This must be incorrect, as there is no word *extremicae*, and should read *ubi sunt extremi cardines mundi.* A later sentence appeared as DICVTVR IRBORET DE EVROPA ET AROPHEI IN ASIA. These words appear to be translated by him as "disembarked from Europe and sailed into Asia." In fact, IRBORET should be IP(ER)BOREI, with contraction of *per*, i.e., *Hyperborei.* As to AROPHEI, it should be ARŌPHEI, i.e., *Aronphei,* described as an *insula deserta* of the Arctic in the 1508 Rome edition of Ptolemy.

The other is an introductory sentence in an edition of Pomponius Mela (Venice, 1482).[24] It reads: *Novellae etati ad geographiae vmiculatos calles huma | no viro necessarios flores aspirāti votū bn̄merēti ponit.* The explorer and map historian A. E. Nordenskiöld wrongly thought that the dedication, *votum benemerenti ponitur,* was to the man of humanity, *humano viro,* and a modern scholar makes no better sense. Certainly the Latin word order is as tortuous as what are called "the worm-like paths of cartography" *(geographiae vermiculatos calles).* But the dedication is to the first phrase, *novellae aetati,* i.e., to the Renaissance. So we may render: "Dedicated, as is justly deserved, to the Renaissance, which breathes into (*aspiranti*) the man of culture the flowers needed for the tortuous worm-tracks of mapwork." Such a sentiment epitomises the balance between the arts and science which that age sought to achieve.

---

[24] *Cosmographia geographia,* published by Erhard Ratdolt (Venice, 1482); *Cosmographia Pomponii* (Salamanca, 1498); Campbell (*op. cit.,* n. 13), 118–19, with translation by Dr. Lotte Hellinga. The world map is very Ptolemaic.

Signification Historique et Valeur Littéraire du De Unitate *de Reginald Pole*

NÖELLE-MARIE EGRETIER

Reginald Pole, l'auteur du *De Unitate*, est l'un des plus illustres représentants de l'Angleterre des Tudor en pleine transformation. Cousin de Henri VIII, un double lien l'apparentait au trône, dans ses veines coulait le sang des York et celui des Lancastre. Né en 1500, it était fils de Margaret Pole, Comtesse de Salisbury et nièce du roi Edouard IV; son père, Richard Pole, mourut alors qu'il était encore en bas âge. Reginald devint alors le protégé du roi qui finança généreusement ses études tant en Angleterre qu'en Italie. Henri VIII avait, sans aucun doute, quelque grand projet pour le jeune Pole aussi n'épargna-t-il rien pour assurer sa formation de grand seigneur. A l'époque, partisans et adversaires du divorce royal alimentent toute une littérature polémique en Angleterre. Lorsque le roi enjoint à Pole de se prononcer par écrit sur la question de sa "grande affaire," la réponse de Pole prend les dimensions d'un volume respectable désigné depuis sous le titre de *Pro Ecclesiasticae Unitatis Defensione* ou en abrégé *De Unitate*. Cet ouvrage de circonstance, motivé par un conflit entre le pouvoir spirituel et le pouvoir temporel, est à la fois affirmation d'une philosophie et d'une théologie. Il se divise en quatre grandes parties où l'auteur étudie principalement les questions de la suprématie royale et de la suprématie pontificale. Ce traité occupe une place importante dans l'histoire des sciences politiques en tant que tentative pour définir les conditions de l'état démocratique. On peut dire que, par bien des côtés, c'est l'oeuvre d'un humaniste érasmien qui a parfaitement intégré la philosophie nouvelle aux rigueurs de la scolastique.

Il y a dans le *De Unitate* une double intention: d'abord répondre aux questions du roi et lui montrer ses égarements, mais aussi, stigmatiser les novateurs en philosophie politique, les nouveaux mentors d'une société inquiète à la recherche de nouveaux fondements. Le traité s'inscrit dans l'effort que font les penseurs du siècle, théologiens et humanistes, pour définir un point de doctrine essentiel à l'intelligence et au fonctionnement de la société traditionnelle après les problèmes soulevés par la réforme allemande. Pole saisit le problème dans toute sa dimension historique, dans toute sa signification philosophique et théologique, dans toute sa résonance spirituelle. Comme tous les traités philosophiques et théologiques de l'époque, les deux premiers livres sont marqués au coin de la dialectique cicéronienne.

Dans le troisième livre, Pole délaisse l'exposé de philosophie politique ou de théologie destiné à étayer sa défense et il passe à l'accusation; ce sont des faits probants et parfois humiliants qu'il rappelle au roi tout au long de 33 feuillets. Il retrace les divers épisodes de l'histoire personnelle de Henri VIII jusqu'à sa rupture avec l'Eglise romaine. Le ton est tour à tour ému et violent; Pole retrouve l'accent des *Verrines* et des *Philippiques* pour dénoncer les excès de conduite du souverain, mais c'est aussi dans ce troisième Livre que l'inspiration biblique est la plus forte. Pole est le prophète, celui que Dieu a préservé du massacre pour être la voix qui crie dans le désert. Le changement de ton est total, aux lourdeurs et aux hésitations du début succèdent une clarté de vision, une vigueur dans l'expression à la fois très dure et très profonde bien caractéristique de style prophétique. La crise de conscience de Pole est poussée à son paroxysme par un double contexte: le meurte de John Fisher et celui de Thomas More d'une part, l'imminence du schisme d'autre part. Sa rigueur prophétique découle également d'une double certitude: l'unicité du chef de l'Eglise et l'impiété du roi. Après un long réquisitoire qui se déroule tout au long de ce troisième Livre, le quatrième est une exhortation pathétique à la pénitence. Ces pages, écrites avant le Concile de Trente, sont particulièrement révélatrices de la position philosophique et théologique de Pole. Il tente là, d'établir un équilibre entre la foi et la raison sans trop en préciser les modalités. On sait quelle réception fut réservée à cette courageuse admonition: son opposition à la politique anglaise entraîna la destruction de sa famille: son oncle, ses frères, son jeune neveu furent envoyés à la Tour. Lord Montague, son frère aîné, puis sa propre mère, la vénérable Comtesse de Salisbury, furent décapités.

Le *De Unitate*, malgré ses imperfections, demeure un grand ouvrage dont la valeur historique et théologique est incontestable. Que faut-il en penser du point de vue littéraire? Rappelons qu'il s'agit d'une lettre destinée au roi seul. Si le style en est lourd et diffus c'est que Pole s'attache plus au fond qu'à la forme. Le *De Unitate* ne représente pas exactement ce que Pole humaniste aurait pu produire sur le plan littéraire s'il avait eu pour seul souci d'écrire un ouvrage classique. L'ensemble, cependant, supporte la comparaison avec les oeuvres des meilleurs humanistes de la Renaissance. Pole écrit à une époque où confluent deux courants de culture: celui des lettres classiques et celui de la littérature chrétienne. Lorsqu'il rédige son ouvrage, il est certain qu'il s'efforce d'opérer en lui une synthèse de ces deux courants. Aussi, pour pouvoir porter un jugement sur cette oeuvre, il convient de la replacer dans le contexte littéraire du XVIème siècle. A cette époque, la majeure partie des oeuvres philosophiques et politiques sont rédigées dans un latin qui tend à s'affirmer avec un caractère propre. Le latin des humanistes, d'un normativisme rigoureux, se veut opposé au latin médiéval mais n'en procède pas moins d'une tradition séculaire ininterrompue. Latin artificiel, ordonné selon des règles strictes, c'est la langue d'une littérature savante et celle aussi des relations internationales. L'idéal cicéronien nourrit en partie l'inspiration des humanistes de la Renaissance. Cicéron est le maître à penser et à écrire. Pole, à la suite de Bembo, fut entraîné dans le cercle des cicéroniens de Padoue. S'il se tint à l'écart des excès auxquels se livrèrent bon nombre de ses amis vénitiens, il fut néanmoins influencé par l'esprit du groupe. Les pages du *De Unitate* témoignent de cette fidélité à Cicéron, fidélité qui est autant dans la syntaxe de la phrase que dans le vocabulaire employé. Pole cite nommément Cicéron à l'appui de sa thèse sur le pouvoir royal. Il développe son argumentation en longues périodes solidement articulées dont l'équilibre même traduit la rigueur de la pensée. Imitation de Cicéron certes, le latin de Pole demeure néanmoins un latin artificiel écrit par un Anglais. On y retrouve çà et là certaines formes héritées de la scolastique, de là son intérêt. Témoin d'un moment donné, il l'est également d'un pays donné: par une saveur bien anglaise, avec ses répétitions, ses pointes d'humour, ses nuances subtiles, autant d'éléments propres au génie d'une race et qui perdent de leur sel ou de leur poésie en passant par d'autres formes linguistiques. Les répétitions d'une même phrase ou simplement de quelques mots scandent le texte et sont destinées, semble-t-il, à opérer un double effet: imposer une idée et susciter un tourment secret. La même phrase revient plusieurs fois dans les trois premiers livres: "[ostendimus regem] nec lege, nec more, nec exemplo majorem, nec ultra denique vel naturali, vel e sacris scripturis ratione caput se Angliae ecclesiae constituere potuisse."

Pole aime l'apostrophe, il en use volontiers pour traduire son mépris ou sa douleur, son ironie ou sa colère: "O impostorem, o verum ambitiosum, superbum, arrogantem" (fol. 32–33); "Interfecistis, interfecistis, hominem omnium Anglorum optimum" (fol. 95). Au milieu des considérations les plus sérieuses, Pole demeure anglais par le tour humoristique de sa phrase. Il rit doucement des scrupules du roi! "quasi lex prohiberet eam retinere, cum annos totos viginti illam habueris sine ullo legis metu? Si lex te movit, cur tam sero movit? An tibi illius non veniebat in mentem? Ita credo, in viginti annorum spatio temporis satis non fuit ad cogitandum de lege" (fol. 76)? Pourrait-on mettre en doute la vertu d'Anne Boleyn ("concubina enim tua fieri pudica mulier nolebat, uxor volebat") (fol. 76)?

Nous retrouvons encore çà et là, dans la prose de Pole, des jeux de mots qui présentent certaines analogies avec les calembours de la comédie shakespearienne. Comme Thomas More, il aime les jeux de mots par homonymie occasionnelle, il joue, par exemple, sur le nom de son antagoniste Sampson: "O Goliad, Goliad, nec enim jam te Samsonem apellabo, in quo nullum Sampsonis signum, praeter nomen possum agnoscere" (fol. 11).

Le latin de Pole est encore caractérisé par ce procédé stylistique particuièrement cher aux Anglais: l'allitération. Le serpent siffle le conseil maléfique au premier père de notre race: "dolo tamen et callida interpretatione serpentis elusum est, qui cum flagraret hominis odio, studium simulans, se illi consiliarium obtulerat" (fol. 103). La lumière allumée par le Christ en nos intelligences éclipse toute autre source lumineuse: "Quod enim ex ratione lumen habemus, tale est, quale animantibus lumen lunae, quale etiam excluso et solis et lunae lumine lucernae lumen.... Quid ergo hic Princeps? malignam ne lunae, vel etiam lucernae lucem praeferes lumini solis" (fol. 125)?

Il faut se limiter, mais on voit combien le latin de Reginald Pole, malgré tout ce qu'il doit aux Cicéroniens padouans, trahit l'origine ethnique de l'auteur. Cependant son souci de pureté classique ne va pas jusqu'à éliminer tous les termes de la scolastique. On peut relever dans le texte des mots qui n'appartiennent pas au latin classique et d'autres qui ont subi une évolution sémantique au cours des âges, les emprunts au latin médiéval anglais n'y sont pas négligeables. L'auteur fait appel à tout un registre de termes religieux et politiques: *schismaticus, monasterium, Pontifex Romanus*, etc. ... ne proviennent naturellement ni de Plaute ni de Cicéron.

Pole avait fait à Padoue de solides études juridiques. Padoue était avec Bologne l'un des centres les plus réputés pour l'enseignement du droit avec Alciat et Zasius à une époque où se codifièrent de nombreuses lois et prescriptions. Dès lors, on comprend pourquoi dans le *De Unitate* l'emprunt le plus considérable au latin médiéval relève du vocabulaire juridico-politique. Des mots comme *legalia, dispensatio, prerogativa, recordari* ne sont attestés dans les écrits latins qu'à partir du 12ème siècle. De tels exemples pourraient être multipliés.

Le latin de Pole est donc un latin éclectique comme celui d'Erasme, ce qui peut sembler barbarie, ou du moins décadence, n'est très souvent que le raffinement subtil d'un art maître de ses procédés.

Le *De Unitate* est un ouvrage de la Renaissance à un autre titre: cicéronien par le style général, il est érasmien par les genres adoptés. Le commentaire du texte sacré que Pole utilise pour étayer son argumentation a été remis en honneur par Erasme. Il utilise d'ailleurs l'Ancien Testament dans la version des Septante, et les Pères qu'il cite sont ceux auxquels les humanistes se réfèrent et qu'ils commentent: Jean Chrysostome, Cyprien, Hilaire, Augustin et Jérôme. C'est la même théologie centrée sur le Christ des Evangiles. Fidèle à la méthode des Alexandrins, Pole recourt volontiers à l'allégorie pour expliquer l'enseignement biblique. Erasme avait remis en honneur *l'exemplum* hérité des écrivains classiques et des Pères, Pole y a recours dans le *De Unitate*. Il voit en Sampson un nouveau Cacus qui détourne de l'Eglise les brebis du Christ. Il exploite le mythe du Cerbère à trois têtes pour figurer l'inhumanité du roi. C'est pourtant l'histoire contemporaine qui lui fournit son exemplum le plus long: la vie et le meurtre de Thomas More et de John Fisher lui servent à concrétiser et à illustrer de manière saisissante les vérités dont il veut imposer l'évidence. Mais à l'exception de ces deux figures contemporaines, l'oeuvre de Pole est dominée par la Bible plus encore que par l'histoire et les poètes grecs ou contemporains.

Bref, si Reginald Pole s'est conformé aux canons de l'esthétique classique, son style est en premier lieu, d'inspiration biblique, un style caractérisé par l'abondance des images, leur vigueur et leur caractère fonctionnel. Il est, sous ce rapport, disciple de Saint Augustin: images en partie empruntées à l'Ancien Testament (parabole de la vigne, combat entre David et Goliath, la lèpre d'Osias. . . .) mais nous retrouvons aussi dans ces pages, les métaphores pauliniennes du Corps Mystique et de l'édifice. Son esprit, nourri de la parole inspirée, a communiqué à sa prose quelque chose de la poésie et aussi de la véhémence du texte sacré. Si Pole, en effet, écrit une prose théologique sobre et parfois terne, nous en avons déjà relevé le ton prophétique et le lyrisme. Pole, pour dénoncer le roi, se met en position de prophète et son style est marqué par la violence qui a présidé à son élaboration. Cette violence d'expression qui inquiète ses amis et indigne ses adversaires découle de la conviction profonde d'une mission personnelle à accomplir. Les outrances de langage étaient habituelles au XVIème siècle dans les écrits de caractère tant soit peu polémique. Là encore, le *De Unitate* apparaît bien comme un ouvrage de la Renaissance, il en trahit les grandeurs et aussi les faiblesses.

Université du Maine, France

Hercules in bivio und andere Scheidewege: Die Geschichte einer Idee bei Petrarca

K. A. E. ENENKEL

In einem der großen Prosatraktate Francesco Petrarcas, in *De vita solitaria*, begegnen wir nach einer tausenjährigen Abwesenheit plötzlich wieder einer literarischen Rezeption des Mythos vom Herkules am Scheidewege.[1] Dieser auffallende Sachverhalt, auf den Mommsen in einer Arbeit aus dem Jahre 1953 hingewiesen hat,[2] bedarf einer ideengeschichtlichen Klärung. Ich meine, daß die Argumente, mit deren Hilfe Mommsen das Erscheinen des Mythos interpretierte, grundsätzlich verfehlt sind und daß die Hintergründe des Neuauftretens dieses Mythos aufs neue geklärt werden müssen. In diesem Zusammenhang wird es notwendig sein die Verwendung zweier anderer Scheidewegkonzepte bei Petrarca in die Untersuchung miteinzubeziehen. Dies sind die Aufgaben des vorliegenden Referates.

Wovon handelt nun der Mythos von Herkules am Scheidewege und was ist seine Bedeutung? Der Inhalt der Geschichte, die von Xenophon und Cicero überliefert wurde,[3] ist, daß sich Herkules am Ende seines Knabenalters bzw. am Beginn seines Mannesalters an einen abgelegenen Ort zurückgezogen habe um tief über sein zukünftiges Leben nachzudenken; da wären ihm zwei Frauengestalten erschienen: Die Tugend (*Virtus*) und

---

[1] Text in Francesco Petrarca, *Prose*. a cura di G. Martellotti, P. G. Ricci, E. Carrara, E. Bianchi (Milano-Napoli 1955), S. 332.

[2] "Petrarch and the story of the choice of Hercules," in: *Journal of the Warburg and Courtauld Institutes* 16 (1953), S. 178–192, hier zitiert nach der neueren Ausgabe in: Th. Mommsen, *Medieval and Renaissance Studies* (New York 1959), S. 175–196.

[3] Xen., *Mem. Socr.* 2, 1, 21–34; Cic., *De off.* 1, 32, 118.

die Lust (*Voluptas*). Sie hätten ihm ihre Vorzüge angepriesen und ihn vor die Wahl gestellt; nach einigem Zögern hätte sich Herkules für die Tugend entschieden, wie es sich im übrigen für einen wahren Helden geziemt.

Es handelt sich hier nicht um einen alten Mythos religiöser Prägung, sondern um eine relativ junge Erfindung des Sophisten Prodikos von Keos, der mit der Erzählung eine bestimmte moralisch-pägaogische Botschaft vermitteln wollte. Prodikos stellte mit dem Mythos ein *exemplum* für eine vorbildliche Entwicklung des menschlichen Lebens auf; in dieser Hinsicht unterteilt er es in zwei Abschnitte, wobei dem Trennungspunkt, dem sog. "Scheideweg," besondere Bedeutung zukommt: An diesem Punkt muß eine Wahl getroffen werden, die für das gesamte weitere Leben des Menschen entscheidenden Charakter besitzt. Prodikos setzte dafür auch einen bestimmten Zeitpunkt als den richtigen fest: das Ende der Pubertät bzw. den Anfang des Erwachsenenstadiums.[4]

Bevor ich auf die petrarkische Verwendung des Herkulesmythos eingehe, ist es notwendig zwei andere Konzepte, die ähnliche Inhalte aufweisen, in die Betrachtung miteinzubeziehen: Die sog. *littera Pythagorica* und die christliche Zweiwegelehre. Im Hinblick auf eine möglichst genaue Interpretation empfielt es sich diese beiden Wegkonzepte zunächst analytisch zu behandeln. Das pythagoräische Y bezieht sich (s.die Gabelung des Buchstabens) auf eine Lebensentscheidung. Sie findet am Anfang des Erwachsenenalters statt.[5] Dabei schlägt der Mensch entweder den Pfad der Tugend (den rechten Zweig des Y) oder des Lasters (den linken

---

[4] In den Darstellungen des Herkulesmythos findet sich stets eine nähere Andeutung des Lebensalters, welches Herkules damals gehabt haben soll, s. Xen., *Mem. Socr.* 2, 1, 21: *Heeraklea, epei ek paidoon eis heben hoormato*. . . . ; Cic., *De off.* I, 32, 118: Herculem . . . , *cum primum pubesceret*. . . . ; Basilius Magnus, *De legendis gentilium libris*, PG 31, 573 A: *veooi onti tooi Heeraklei*; Petrarca, *De vita solitaria I*, 4, S. 332): *ineunte etate* und *Quod initio pubertatis fecisse Herculem*. . . . ; Salutati, *De laboribus Herculis*, ed. B. L. Ullman, Zürich, 1951, zitiert III, 7, 1 die Altersangabe aus Cic., loc. cit.; Obwohl die Terminologie zur Andeutung der Lebensalter Schwierigkeiten mit sich bringt (s.hierzu z.B. M.Dove, *The Perfect Age of Man's Life* [Cambridge U.P. 1986], S. 10–19 mit relevanter Lit. S. 15, Anm. 24); hinzuzufügen E. Eyben, *De jonge Romein* (Brussel 1977), hoofdstk.1: De afbakening van de jeugdperiode, S. 5–41), läßt sich hier m.E. mit ziemlicher Deutlichkeit feststellen, welches Alter gemeint ist: Der Lebensabschnitt, der unmittelbar auf das Knabenalter folgt, abwechselnd mit den Termen *adolescentia*, *iuventus*, oder *pubertas* angedeutet wird, und mit ca.15 Jahren beginnt.

[5] Servius, In *Aen.* VI 136 (ed. Thilo und Hagen): . . . *bivium autem Y litterae a iuventute incipere*. . . ; Lactantius, *Div. Inst.* 6, 3, 6 CSEL 19, 486: *cum primae adulescentiae limen adtigerit* und Isidorus, *Etym.* 1, 3, 7: *Bivium autem . . . ab adolescentia incipit.*

Zweig des Y) ein.[6] Ob Pythagoras wirklich der Erfinder dieses Konzepts war, läß sich nicht mit Sicherheit feststellen;[7] fest steht m.E. nur, daß es in der römischen Kaiserzeit, in der zweiten Hälfte des 1.Jh.n.Chr., allgemeine Bekanntheit genoß und dem Pythagoras zugeschrieben wurde.[8] Der Aussagebereich der *littera Pythagorica* ist dem der Herkuleserzählung sehr ähnlich: In beiden Fällen handelt es sich um eine Lebensentscheidung am Anfang des Erwachsenenalters. Das ist der Grund, warum die beiden Konzepte in der späteren Renaissance, vor allem in der emblematischen Literatur, des öfteren miteinander verbunden oder kontaminiert wurden.[9]

Das Symbol des pythagoräischen Y erfreute sich nun im gesamten Mittelalter einer großen Beliebtheit. Es eignete sich auch sehr gut für eine christliche Interpretation; die Wegzweige von *virtus* und *vitium* konnten als Wege der christlichen Tugend bzw. der (christlichen) Sünde aufgefaßt werden; die Wegziele wurden vom Irdischen ins Transzendente gesetzt: Der Weg der Tugend führte dann zum ewigen Leben (*ad beatam vitam*), der Weg der Sünde zum ewigen Verderben (*ad labem interitumque*). Dies zeigt z.B. die Interpretation des Bischofs Isidor von Sevilla in seinen *Etymologiae* I 3, 7. Zudem ermöglichte das Symbol eine neue, dem mittelalterlichen Denken willkommene Interpretation: Als christliche Tugend par exellence galt stets mehr die vollständige Widmung des menschlichen Lebens an Gott, d.h. das Einschlagen des Lebensweges der *vita contemplativa*. So konnte die Wegwahl zwischen *virtus* und *vitium* von der Wahl zwischen *vita contemplativa* und *vita activa* ersetzt werden. Der Eintritt in einen Orden wurde dann als Einschlagen des rechten Pfades des Y gedeutet.[10]

Die christliche Interpretation der *littera Pythagorica* wurde durch das Vorhandensein einer christlichen Zweiwegelehre im Neuen Testament

---

[6] s. die genaue Beschreibung bei Servius, In *Aen.* VI 136.

[7] Brinkmann und de Ruyt nehman an, daß es erst von alexandriner Neupythagoräern dem Pythagoras zugeschrieben worden sei; s. A. Brinkmann, Ein Denkmal des Neupythagoräismus, in: *Rheinisches Museum für Philologie* 66 (1911): S. 618; F. de Ruyt, *L'idee du 'bivium' et le symbole pythagoricien de la lettre Y*, in *Revue Belge de Philologie et d'Histoire* 10 (1931): S. 137–44; zustimmend W. Harms, *Homo viator in bivio*, München 1970, S. 43.

[8] Dies müssen wir aus der Persius-Stelle Sat. III 55 schliessen. Die *littera* fügt sich gut in das antike Denken, das die Jugend als Krisenperiode betrachtete, s. Eyben, op. cit., S. 66–110.

[9] s. Harms, op. cit. passim.

[10] Salimbene, *Cronica*, M(onumenta) G(ermaniae) H(istorica) 32, S. 38: Ego frater Salimbene, qui, quando perveni ad bivium Pythagorice littere, id est finitis tribus lustris . . . ordinem fratrum minorum intravi.

erleichtert; es handelt sich hier um die Matthäuse-Stelle 7, 13–14. Das enge Tor und der schmale Weg versinnbildlichen hier die Annahme eines Christus geweihten Lebens, das weite Tor und der breite Weg die aufs Weltliche ausgerichtete Lebenswahl der Vielen; die Wegziele sind wie in der christlichen Interpretation der *littera Pythagorica* transzendent, der schmale Weg führt zum ewigen Leben (*ad vitam*), der breite zu ewigem Verderben (*ad perditionem*). Die christliche Zweiwegelehre impliziert einen eigenständigen Beschluß des Menschen: Der Mensch selbst muß sich dazu durchringen, den schmalen Weg zu wählen. Wie die Herkuleserzählung und die *littera Pythagorica* nimmt sie auf das gesamte folgende Leben Bezug, hat also definitiven Charakter. Einen wichtigen Unterschied stellt aber die Tatsache dar, daß diese Entscheidung unabhängig vom Lebensalter stattfinden kann und also auch noch dem gealterten Menschen eine sittlich-religiöse Umkehr ermöglicht. Wie die *littera* wurde sie im Mittelalter mit dem Eintritt in einen Klosterorden in Zusammenhang gebracht, stellte dann also die Wahl für Christus im engeren Sinne, die Wahl für die *vita contemplativa*, dar.

Die frequente Darstellung der Herkuleserzählung in der bildenden Kunst der Renaissance hat Panofsky zur Abfassung seines inspirierenden Buches "Herkules am Scheidewege und andere antike Bildstoffe in der neuren Kunst" veranlaßt.[11] Hier konstatiert er das vollständige Fehlen einer Abbildung des "Herkules am Scheidewege" im Mittelalter. Im Bezug auf die Literatur des Mittelalters muß, soweit ich sehe, mutatis mutandis dieselbe Feststellung getroffen werden. Panofsky erklärte diesen auffallenden Sachverhalt–ausgehend von der bildenden Kunst, aber mit weitreichenderen Folgen–vor allem mit Hilfe von zwei Argumenten;[12] 1. Die Herkuleserzählung wäre für das mittelalterliche Denken ungeeignet gewesen, weil darin von der *Virtus* die Rede sei. Für das Mittelalter, das nur einzelne *virtutes* gekannt habe, sei der Gesamtbegriff *virtus* unannehmbar gewesen. 2. Die Herkuleserzählung wäre für das mittelalterliche Denken unbrauchbar gewesen, weil sich der mittelalterliche Mensch nicht als "wählendes Subjekt," sondern als "umkämpftes Objekt" gefühlt habe. Mommsen hat in seiner Arbeit über den Mythos bei Petrarca die Argumente Panofskys en bloc übernommen und noch ein weiteres hinzugefügt: Eine Geschichte mit Herkules wäre grundsätzlich zu heidnisch gewesen um eine christliche Verwendung zuzulassen.[13]

---

[11] in: *Studien der Bibliothek Warburg* 18 (1930).

[12] Panofsky, op. cit. S. 153–56.

[13] Mommsen, op. cit. passim; die übernahmen von Panofsky S. 177–78.

Ich meine, daß sich diese Erklärungen bei einer diachronen ideengeschichtlichen Betrachtungsweise als prinzipiell unrichtig herausstellen. Die funamentalste Abweisung des Mythos für das mittelalterliche Denken beinhaltet das Argument Mommsens. Dieses verstößt gänzlich gegen die neueren Erkenntnisse der Mythenforschung. Bereits seit den Arbeiten von Von Bezold und vor allem von Seznec ist deutlich geworden, daß die antike Mythologie im Mittelalter keineswegs untergeht, sondern daß der Euhemerismus und besonders die allegorische Mytheninterpretation reiche Möglichkeiten für ein Fortleben bieten.[14] Das gilt auch für Herkules, der im Mittelalter ein weitläufiges Nachleben als christlicher Tugendheld hatte.[15] Als konkretes Beispiel möchte ich hier Albricus, einen Mythographen des 12. Jh., anführen, der Herkules, als Personifikation der christlichen *virtus* interpretierte.[16] Daß eben auch die Erzählung von Herkules am Scheidewege in christlichem Kontext funktionieren konnte, ziegt ihre übernahme bei Basilius dem Grossen, in dem verbreiteten Werk *De legendis gentilium libris* (PG 31, 573 A–C).

Nun zu den Argumenten Panofskys: zu 1. Es ist, meine ich, eine verfehlte Ansicht, daß das Mittelalter die *virtus* im Singular und im nicht näher spezifizierten Sinn nicht gekannt habe. Ich habe an die These Panofskys, bevor ich Gegenbeispiele hatte, nicht geglaubt, weil *virtus* einen polyinterpretablen Begriff darstellt, der also auch in einem christlichen Kontext ein reiches Interpretationspotential bieten würde. Es ist in diesem Rahmen unmöglich, das Thema erschöpfend zu behandeln; ich muß mich hier auf einige Gegenbeispiele beschränken: In einem Gedicht des 11. Jh., das eben das Thema der *littera Pythagorica* behandelt, finden wir folgende Verse: *pueritia/que non facile noscitur,/ utrum vitiis/ an virtuti animum/ subicere velit.*[17] Es ist hier sogar auffallend, daß (die nicht näher definierte) *virtus* in der Einzahl auftritt, während die Sünden/ Laster im Plural stehen. Schon oben genannt wurde der Unstand, daß Albricus Herkules als die Personifikation der *virtus* interpretierte; man sehe auch die Besprechungen der *virtus* in der Summa Theologica des Thomas von Aquino.

[14] F. Von Bezold, *Das Fortleben der antiken Götter im mittelalterlichen Humanismus*, Neudruck der Ausgabe 1922 (Aalen 1962); J. Seznec, *La survivance des dieux antiques*, in: *Studies of the Warburg Institute* 11 (1940), neur in engl.ü.: *The Survival of the Pagan Gods. The Mythological Tradition and its Place in Renaissance Humanism and Art* (Princeton 1972/2).

[15] M. Simon, *Hercule et le christianisme* (Paris 1955).

[16] = *Mythographus* III 13, 2: *a gloriosa virtute, id est ab Hercule, superatur Anteus (=libido).*

[17] s. K. Strecker, ed., *Die Cambridger Lieder* (Berlin 1955), Nr. 12.

Für die bildende Kunst läßt sich die These Panofskys augenfällig falsifizieren: In einer um 1156 entstandenen Miniatur zur Clavis Physicae des Honorius von Autun finden wir eine Frauengestalt mit Schleier abgebildet, die die überschrift trägt: "*VIRTUS*."[18] zu 2.Dieses Argument Panofskys betrifft die Essenz der mittelalterlichen Verwendung der Wahlmythen. Wenn Panofsky recht hätte, daß der mittelalterliche Mensch sich nicht als "wählendes Subjekt," sondern als "umkämpftes Objekt" gefühlt habe, dann wäre die richtige Schlußfolgerung, daß das Mittelalter grundsätzlich kein Bedürfnis an Lebenswahlmythen gehabt hätte; war dem aber so?–Die große Beliebtheit der christlichen Zweiwegelehre, der *littera Pythagorica*, und noch eines dritten Wahlmythos, des Parismythos, im Mittelalter, zeigen an, daß die Theorie Panofskys nicht stimmen kann. Heuristisch muß man hier auch die Haltung mittelalterlicher Autoren zur philosophischen Frage des *liberum arbitrium* berücksichtigen; dabei geht hervor, daß mittelalterliche Autoren nich einfach eine negative Haltung eingenommen und die Renaissance en bloc für den freien Willen plädiert hätte:–es gibt es kaum eine Schrift zu diesem Problem, die so optimistisch ist wie der einflußreiche Traktat *De gratia et libero arbitrio* des Bernard von Clairvaux aus der 1.Hälfte des 12.Jh.

Ich glaube deshalb nicht, daß die Erklärungen Panofskys und Mommsens stichhaltig sind. Ich meine, daß es ein anderer Umstand war, der eine stärkere Rezeption der Herkuleserzählung verhindert hat und der zugleich anderen Konzepten den Vorzug gab; dieser Umstand liegt in einer Änderung des moralphilosophischen Denkens: Im Unterschied zur Antike finden wir im gessamten Mittelalter einen starken Primat der *vita contemplativa* über die *vita activa*. Diese Vorliebe affiziert die Symbole der Wegwahl: D.h., ein Wegwahlsymbol, das im Mittelalter Erfolg haben will, muß einen potentiellen Eingang für die *vita contemplativa* besitzen. Herkules war aber immer mit der aktiven Tugend identifiziert worden; der Herkulesmythos war deshalb ungeeignet, eine Lebenswahl für die *vita contemplativa* zu verkörpern. Demgegenüber konnte sowohl der rechte Zweig der *littera Pythagorica* als auch der schmale Weg der christlichen zwei-Wege-Lehre unschwer mit einer Wahl für die *vita contemplativa* identifiziert werden. Diese Konzepte erhielten deshalb den Vorzug. Darüberhinaus gab es sogar noch einen konkurrierenden Mythos, der ebenfalls einen Wegeingang zur *vita contemplativa* besaß und deshalb besser in das mittelalterliche Denken paßte: den Parismythos. Dieser

[18] Paris, Bib. Nat. M. S. Lat. 6734; Abbildung in G. Pochat, *Geschichte der Ästhetik und Kunsttheorie* (Köln 1986), S. 155.

Mythos bietet die Wahlmöglichkeit zwischen der *vita activa* (Iuno), der *vita contemplativa* (Minerva) und der *vita voluptaria* (Venus).[19] Der Parismythos erfreute sich dementsprechend im Mittelalter einer weiten Verbreitung. Ich glaube also, daß es die Vorliebe für die *vita contemplativa* und das gleichzeitige Vorhandensein von brauchbaren konkurrierenden Symbolen war, welche das Mittelalter von einer aktiven Rezeption des Herkulesmythos abgehalten haben. Gegen diesen Hintergrund müssen wir Petrarcas Verwendung der Wahlkonzepte betrachten.

Im Unterschied zu der vorhergehenden Periode des Mittelalters hat Petrarca nun den Herkules-Mythos zweimal aktiv rezipiert, beide Male in *De vita solitaria* (I 4, S. 332 und II 13, S. 550). Beleuchten wir die näheren Umstände: Seine Quelle war hierbei Ciceros *De officiis*. Es ist interessant Petrarcas und Ciceros Behandlung einer komparatistischen Betrachtung zu unterwerfen. Cicero konnte die ursprünglich optimistische Tendenz der Erzählung bei Prodikos/Xenophon nicht mehr ohneweiteres teilen: Er meint zwar auch, daß das Jugendalter eine Scheidewegsituation impliziere und läßt den auf Nachdenken (*deliberatio*) basierten freien Entschluß als ethisches Postulat bestehen (§ 117: *debemus . . . constituendum est*); jedoch ist er der Meinung, daß die meisten diesem Anspruch nicht genügen könnten. Im Normalfall schlage man denselben Lebensweg ein wie seine Eltern oder ahme die Masse nach. Trotz dem Zweifel an der Gültigkeit des Postulats für die Mehrzahl der Menschen läßt er beträchtliche Ausnahmen zu, worunter er sich zweifellos selbst zählte: Diese Individuen vermögen aus eigener Kraft den richtigen Weg einzuschlagen: *Non nulli tamen . . . sine parentium disciplina rectam vitae secuti sunt viam* (§ 118).

Im Vergleich dazu ist Petrarcas Behandlung des Herkulesmythos in *De vita solitaria* I, S. 332 viel pessimistischer; dies fällt schon auf grammatischer Ebene auf: Der Gandanke wird in der Form eines Irrealis präsentiert (*esset-obstaret-cogitaret-diverteret*). Petrarca schließt also die Möglichkeit einer richtigen Wegwahl aufgrund eigener, freier Willensentscheidung für sich und seine Zeitgenossen klar und deutlich aus (*id non facimus*). Wenn jemand ausnahmsweise den richtigen Weg eingeschlagen hat, dann war dies nich sein Verdienst, sondern kam zur Gänze von aussen, aufgrund göttlicher Eingebung, zustande. Cicero definierte die Wegewahl noch als Willensentscheidung (*a nostra voluntate proficiscitur* § 115), bei Petrarca ist dies nicht mehr der Fall. Damit korrespondiert Petrarcas meist überaus pessimistiche Haltung zur Frage des freien Willens; sie läßt sich vor allem in seinen theologischen Äusserungen erkennen, worin er stets zuungun-

---

[19] s. z. B. Albricus = Mythographus III 11, 22–23.

sten der eigenen Leistung des Menschen die *gratia* und die *misericordia* Gottes betont. Manchmal hat es hier sogar den Anschein, als ob sich Petrarca in Richtung der *sola-gratia*-Lehre Luthers bewegte.

Zwei Faktoren bestimmen m.E. Petrarcas pessimistische Haltung im Bezug auf die Wegwahl: Auf der einen Seite seine allgemein negative Einschätzung des Jahrunderts, in dem er lebte, auf der anderen die Art und Weise, wie er seine persönliche Entwicklung beurteilte. In Petrarcas Denken finden wir einen ausgesprochenen Zeitpessimismus: Sein Jahrhundert betrachtet er als das schlechteste aller bisher dagewesenen. Petrarca glaubt nicht an die sittliche Kraft seiner Zeitgenossen. Zu allen anderen übeln schreibt er ihnen einen geradezu krankhafte Trieb zur Nachahmung zu (*Vit. Sol.* I, S. 386–90), der eigenständiges Denken bzw. einen selbstständigen Beschluß vonvorheherein unmöglich mache; die Zeitgenossen sind für ihn Blinde, die von Blinden geführt werden und deshalb in den Abgrund stürzen müssen (*Vit. Sol.* I, S. 394). Es ist interessant, daß wir ein ganz ähnliches Bild in der Behandlung der Wegwahl in *De vita solitaria* wiederfinden: *per tenebras alienis vestigiis insistentes sepe periculosas et inexplicabiles ingredimur vias* (*Vit. Sol.* I, S. 332).

Der zweite Faktor lag in Petrarcas Beurteilung seiner persönlichen entwicklung. Diese Betrachtungsweise ist besonders fruchtbar, weil sich Petrarca ausführlich mit seiner eigenen Persönlichkeit auseinandergesetzt hat und wir zahlreiche Äusserungen hierzu besitzen. Zwar ist die Chronologie seiner Entwicklung umstritten,[20] jedoch nicht, daß er eine solche durchgemacht hat. Wie u.a. aus seiner Autobiographie in Briefform, der *Epystola posteritati* hervorgeht, war er nicht der Ansicht, daß er in seiner Jugend die richtige Entscheidung getroffen habe. Er spricht Täuschung, Irrtum und *vanitas*.[21] Ab 1336/7 geriet er in einige aufeinanderfolgende moralische Krisen, die sich in den 40er Jahren fortsetzten und in deren Folge er sich um eine persönliche Bekehrung bemühte. Das autobiographische Werk *De secreto conflictu curarum mearum*, die *Psalmi penitentiales* und einige Briefe sind die literarischen Zeugen dieser Bemühungen. In den 40er Jahren, in denen auch die Stelle in *De vita solitaria* geschrieben worden war, fühlte sich Petrarca bereits als alter Mann, der dem Tod nahe ist, und verglich sich mit einem herumirrender Reisenden, dem der Einbruch der Nacht droht; man sehe z.B. seine flehentliche Bitte an Gott

[20] s.hierzu zuletzt H. Baron, *Petrarch's Secretum, Its Making and its Meaning* (Cambridge Mass. 1985) mit der relevanten Literatur.

[21] Posteritati, ed. Fracassetti, S. 1: *Adolescentia me fefellit ... senecta autem correxit* und S. 5: *pueritiam sub parentibus, ac deinde sub vanitatibus meis adolescentiam totam eqi....*

aus dem Jahre 1348 in den *Psalmi Penitentiales*: "Führe mich vor Sonnenuntergang zurück auf deine Wege, denn es wird schon Abend...."[22] Danach richtet sich die moralische Forderung der Wegwahl in *De vita solitaria*; es genüge, wenigstens im Alter seinen Irrtum zu erkennen und zum rechten Weg zurückzufinden: *idcirco, quam sibi personam vel natura vel fortuna vel error aliquis imposuit, si iuvenis non potuit, quisque secum senex cogitet et (quod errans viator solet) ante vesperam quantumlicet saluti sue consulat* (*Vit. Sol.* I, S. 332).

Den besten Aufschluß darüber, wie Petrarca sein Verhalten am *bivium* beurteilte, vermittelt eine Stelle aus dem *Secretum*, die merkwürdigerweise im Zusammenhang der petrarkischen Verwendung des pythagoräischen Y noch nicht genannt wurde.[23] Im dritten Buch versucht dort Petrarcas literarischer Beichtvater, der Hl.Augustinus, zum Ausgangspunkt des spirituellen Notstandes sienes Schützlings Franciscus vorzudringen; er fordert diesen deshalb auf den gesamten Lebenslauf zu überdenken; Franciscus findet nun den Ausgangspunkt des übels interessanterweise eben am *bivium* des pythagoräischen Y: AUG.: *Quid reperis iqitur?* FRA.: *Litere velut pithagoree, quam audivi et legi, non inanem esse doctrinam. Cum enim recto tramite ascendens ad bivium pervenissem modestus et sobrius et dextram iuberer arripere, ad levam–incautus dicam an contumax–deflexi.... Ex tunc autem obliquo sordidoque calle distractus et sepe retro lacrimans conversus dextrum iter tenere non potui ... tunc, profecto tunc, fuerat illa morum meorum facta confusio.* Diese Äusserungen Petrarcas stimmen mit den in der *Epystola posteritati* getroffenen überein: Er ist der Ansicht, daß seine Knabenzeit sittlich einwandfrei gewesen sei und daß er erst am *bivium* den falschen, den linken, Pfad eingeschlagen habe; interessant ist auch, daß er in der Secretum-Stelle sein falsches Verhalten am *bivium* mit der Begegnung mit einer Dame identifiziert. Es handelt sich um die uns wohlbekannte Laura. Natürlich wäre allzu einfach, wenn eine Frau für die sittliche Fehlentscheidung verantwortlich gemacht werden sollte; aber für Petrarca war Laura-Laurea mehr als bloß ein Mädchen: sie war für ihn das Symbol für bestimmte Bestrebungen innerhalb seiner Persönlichkeit, das Streben nach Sinnendingen und das Streben nach irdischem Ruhm mittels seiner Poesie. Diese Bestrebungen konnten nun sehr wohl für das sittliche Fehlen verantwortlich gemacht werden.

---

[22] Ps.Pen.3, ed. H. Cochin, Paris 1929: *Reduc me in vias tuas ante solis occasum, advesperascit enim et nox est amica predonibus. Coqe ire, si vocare parum est, denique ut libet, modo ne peream.*

[23] *Prose*, S. 130–32.

Petrarca war also der Ansicht, daß er an der Wegwahl versagt habe, und bemühte sich deshalb um eine Spätbekehrung. Die Spätbekehrung war sicherlich im 14.Jh. ein weit verbreitetes religiöses Phänomen. Eine interessante–humanistiche–Parallele sehe ich in Coluccio Salutati, der nach Meinung seines rezenten Biographen Ronald Witt im Jahre 1381/2, also mit 50 Jahren, eine moralisch-religiöse Krise durchlebte.[24] Nun hat Salutati danach in seinem Werk *De laboribus Herculis* ebenfalls den Mythos vom Herkules am Scheidewege behandelt: Es ist, meine ich, kein Zufall, daß Salutati dabei offene Kritik an den Autoren des Mythos, Prodikos und Xenophon, übt und die Richtigkeit des Postulates bezweifelt.[25]

Betrachten wir die Frequenz der drei Scheideweg-Konzepte im Werk Petrarcas, so fällt auf, daß die christliche Zweiwegelehre am häufigsten vorkommt, daß die *littera* einige Instanzen aufweist,[26] und daß letztlich die Herkules-Erzählung nur zweimal aufscheint. Diese Beobachtung stimmt mit Petrarcas Beurteilung seiner persönlichen Lage überein. Für ihn, der eine Spätbekehrung erstrebte, besaß die christliche Zweiwegelehre die größte Anziehungskraft. Das heißt aber nicht, daß Petrarca die anderen Wegwahlkonzepte, die *littera* und die Herkuleserzählung kritisierte oder verurteilte. Das geht z.B. deutlich aus der Verwendung der *littera* im *Secretum* hervor: *Litere velut pithagoree . . . non inanem esse doctrinam* (S. 130). Es ist nicht richtig, aus der schwächeren Frequenz mit Mommsen schelchtweg auf eine "apparent reserve" Petrarcas gegenüber dem Konzept zu schliessen;[27] so läßt sich z.B. in der Wiedergabe des Mythos im *De vit. sol.* II 13, S. 550 keine Kritik, sondern nur ein lobender Tenor feststellen. Petrarca hat nicht wie Salutati den Mythos als ethisches Postulat kritisiert. Für ihn blieb die jugendliche Entscheidung am Scheideweg ein sittliches Ideal, auch wenn er selbst es, als sittlich Schwacher, nicht erfüllen konnte.

Ich habe oben die These aufgestellt, daß das Mittelalter den Herkulesmythos nicht verwenden konnte, weil er keinen Eingang für die *vita*

---

[24] R. G. Witt, *Hercules at the Crossroads. The Life, Works, and Thought of Coluccio Salutati* (Duke U.P. 1983), S. 205–7. Ich schliesse mich der Meinung derer an, die den Inhalt von De seculo et religione nicht als Ausfluß leerer Rhetorik betrachten.

[25] ed. B. L. Ullman, Zürich 1951, III 7, 1–4, vol. I, S. 181–83; Kritik S. 182, § 2.

[26] z.B. *Ep. metr.* 3, 32, ed. D. Rossetti 1831; *Fam.*, ed. V. Rossi, 3, 12, 5; 7, 17; 12, 3, 5–11 und *Secr.* III, *Prose*, S. 130–32.

[27] op. cit., S. 192; es ist ebenfalls unrichtig, Petrarcas weniger frequente Rezeption des Mythos mit Mommsen (loc.cit.) damit zu begründen, daß sich Petrarca davon bewußt gesesen wäre, daß die Geschichte eigentlich zu heidnisch wäre. Auch für Petrarca konnte Herkules ohneweiteres eine Rolle in christlichem Kontext spielen s.z.B. *De vit. sol.* I, S. 322, bei der Besprechung der Seelsorge.

contemplativa besaß. Wie war nun Petrarcas Haltung zu diesem Problem? In vielen seiner Schriften hat Petrarca seiner persönlichen Vorliebe für die *vita contemplativa* Ausdruck gegeben, am ausführlichsten in *De vita solitaria.* Warum konnte er aber dennoch und gerade in *De vita solitaria* den Herkulesmythos verwenden? Der Grund ist darin zu suchen, daß Petrarca in *De vita solitaria* nicht mehr den absoluten und theoretischen Primat der *vita contemplativa* vertritt; für ihn sind beide Lebensformen prizipiell gleichwertig. An einigen Stellen scheint er sogar der *vita activa* die Palme zu geben, wenn er verspricht, daß er, würde er dazu im Stande sein, das aktive Leben ergreifen und Anderen helfen würde.[28] In diesem Sinne konnte Petrarca auch den Herkulesmythos verwenden: Die Wahl des Herkules, der aktiven Tugend, bedeutete keinen moralisch weniger wertvollen Standpunkt mehr. Wenn Petrarca in *De vita solitaria* die *vita contemplativa* verteidigt, betont er stets, daß es sich um eine persönliche Vorliebe handle, und daß eine andere Charakterstruktur gegebenfalls eine andere Lebenswahl nahelege; eine solche differenzierte und bescheidene Haltung wirkt sympathisch. Sie hat der *otium-negotium*-Diskussion neue Dimensionen eröffnet, indem sie sie offener gestaltete und das Element des Persönlichen hinzufügte. In ihr können wir Petrarcas Beitrag zum *vita activa:vita contemplativa*-Problem erblicken.

Rijksuniversiteit Leiden

[28] z.B. *Vit. Sol.* I, S. 322 und S. 328: *Optarem, fateor, talis esse, qui possem prodesse quam plurimis . . . profecto, quisquis in tuto est . . . peccat in legem nature, nisi quibus potest laborantibus opem fert.*

French Latin: Literary Hybridizing in the Renaissance

ROBERT J. FINK

The purpose of this paper is, first, to draw attention to an obscure Latin monograph published anonymously and dated Lyon, 1555; second, after briefly describing the text, to identify its genre as a hybrid form and; third, to suggest to you that looking closely at such texts can help to explain one of the apparent contradictions of the French Renaissance: that humanists using classical genres and following the classical rules and practice of composition in purest Ciceronian Latin actually contributed to the liberation of their own vernacular writing and eventually of French literature in general from the constraints of traditional normative rhetoric.

The text, then, entitled *Ad principes christianos cohortatio pacificatoria,*[1] was the work of Jacques Peletier du Mans who by this time was a highly reputed author of translations, poetry and treatises on a variety of subjects. In 1558, three years after the appearance of the original Latin title, Parisian publisher André Wechel brought out a French version whose text, apart from a few excerpts discovered in Lacroix du Maine and DuVerdier's *Bibliothèque françoyse,*[2] has never been found. There is no reason to doubt that the French version was by Peletier's own hand.

---

[1] Anonymous (Jacques Peletier du Mans), *Ad principes christianos cohortatio pacificatoria* (Lyon: Jean de Tournes, 1555).

[2] Antoine du Verdier, *Bibliothèque françoise*, ed. Rigoley de Juvigny (Paris: Saillant and Nyon, 1772–73), 1:561–63.

Antoine du Verdier, *Bibliothèque françoise*, ed. Rigoley de Juvigny (Paris: Saillant and Nyon, 1772–73), 2:115–17.

The *Cohortatio* is an elaborate, twenty-seven page discourse in the form of an oration in which the first person speaker appeals directly to Emperor Charles V and French King Henri II to make peace. The orator speaks to Charles and Henri in turn, urging each to make peace with arguments that are not just abstractions but are appropriate to their personalities and political positions and ambitions. He refers, for instance, to their relative ages, their personal histories and military careers and to the actual military situation. Each argument, and they go on for twenty-seven pages, is tailored to suit the circumstance of one or the other ruler and, in the apparent conviction that the author is speaking for Jesus Christ himself, is put with great forcefulness and authority. He tells Charles for instance that he is too old to keep up this war and Henri that he will only bankrupt his country and lose the personal glory he already has as well as his soul. The old notion of a single European Holy Empire politically united under one head has long since given way to the new nationalism and the leaders had better come to terms with reality and learn to live in peace. Since neither is strong enough to annihilate the other, peace is the only possible alternative to their impossible dream of domination. It is also the perfect opportunity for each to satisfy his own personal aspirations: Charles can retire covered with glory and Henri can be secure in his rôle as national hero. They can both take comfort in the knowledge that Europe will remain united in its common Christian faith of which they themselves are the exemplars. Meanwhile they can conduct themselves as true–and equal–rulers by providing their subjects with what they need most: protection of their religion, which is being attacked from within, and justice for all. This is God's will for them both and it is God, not they, who is master of destiny. Above all, they should look to their future–eternal beatitude and glory for posterity.

This, then, is a simulated deliberative oration with all requisite parts very clearly distinguishable: the *exordium* with its *captatio benevolentiae* and effected modesty; the *narratio* and *confirmatio* setting out the facts and proofs with accompanying objections and refutations, a model epideictic digression and the brief but sufficient *conclusio*. The writing betrays a genuine feeling for Ciceronian stylistic practice and it has all the amplitude, rhythms, and richness of diction that the master could have hoped to pass on. In other words, its rhetorical credentials are impeccable.

Of course, rhetoric had in one way or another determined almost all forms and modes of public communication in Europe since ancient times. Various schools of thought on the subject alternatively stressed the character and qualities of speaker, speech or audience, producing theories about the ideal man, the orator, about the ideally ordered, expressed and delivered discourse and about the open-minded but perspicuous audience prepared to be convinced, persuaded or moved. Being a simulation, the *Cohortatio* has incorporated all three: *Ethos, Logos,* and *Pathos* into the text, which raised a question as to its genre. Rhetorical production had been continuously subjected to classification so as to isolate, compare and judge particular rhetorical events or instances. Thus the various genres within the main classes of discourse, verse, prose and drama were universally recognized and this facilitated both meta-textual discourse or treatises and renewed creativity, one of whose manifestations was what I would like to call grafting.

In verse, for example, various types of persuasive speeches were grafted onto the stock of epic poems (Homer); in prose, historical discourse was enriched by the splicing in of real or imagined debates (Thucydides, Herodotus). Grafting, however, was not limited to changing genres part way along a narrative line: in tragedy, conflict among characters was developed and resolved by passing it through a situational form proper to a court of law and so subject to the rules of judicial rhetoric; dialectical argumentation was frequently arranged in accordance with theatrical rather than strictly logical modes, taking the form of dialogue. Since the lyric love poem had entirely internalized participants in its discourse, that is both poet and beloved, there was no external speaker or narrator to be interrupted but as with tragedy, situations resembling those of any of the oratorical genres were regularly exploited. The same may be said of philosophical or political odes and epigrams in which speaker and audience, *Ethos* and *Pathos* were wholly fictionalized and incorporated into the text. In every case, however, the original genre received the foreign graftings without changing or appearing to change its identity.

The genre of the Renaissance text at hand, *Cohortatio pacificatoria*, is apparently that of a prose oration, upon which has been grafted elements belonging to other, more literary, genres such as the dialogue and the lyrical or philosophical poem with their fictionalized characters whose individual temperaments colour the arguments and influence the reader's intellectual and emotional reception of them. In this case, the reader may substitute himself for the orator, the *Ethos*, as he reads, that is to say, as he mouths the words, assuming the forceful, sincere, intelligent, persuasive personality of the first-person speaker as well as his arguments. He does not at this level position himself with Charles and Henri, who are given no lines, who are silent receptors of the reader's harangue, but he talks to them–persuasively. Another foreign element, proper to tragedy rather than to oratory, is apparent in this text: the confrontation of protagonists in an imagined situation: two powerful monarchs are, in the mind's eye of the reader seated before an authoritative orator listening to the voice of reason. Should the reader resist the urge to play the part of orator, he may read this work as a spectator watches a drama and react to the interplay of the characters. On yet another level, considering the final cause of the oration's function: to convince the reader of the necessity for peace and persuade him to engage in the lofty pursuits for which peace is a condition, the latter may well filter out the theatrics of the literary instance and focus his attention on the argument. He is thus, like Charles and Henri, receptor of the speech's message as long as he is moved by the arguments, and is most likely to be this kind of *Pathos* on second or third reading.

It is evident that manipulation of the oration of such a radical kind does indeed deprive the text of its generic identity. No longer recognizable as the text of an oratorical instance, it has become, thanks to printing and publication, that of a literary instance which the reader may experience in a variety of ways as he pleases. The product of this combining of generic elements can no longer be distinguished as one genre onto which parts of another will have been grafted, but a genre unto itself, a true hybrid, the product of a creative act.

And so, the *Cohortatio*, by demonstrating that pure Ciceronian classicism can be creative, constitutes an incentive to contemporary humanist writers to imitate the ancients, but with at least this kind of freedom and originality. However, creativity has its price and, consciously or not, the creation of a new genre not traceable to classical antecedents *ipso facto* called into question the validity of rhetorical norms in its case. Peletier, of course, adhered to those norms with the utmost rigour, but was it necessary? Future writers, following his example would be free to develop the genre for like purposes of social commentary by elaborating on one or another of its parts: characterization, situation, personal relationships or modes of expression.

But let us not slip into the trap of hagiography here: hybridizing is not the exclusive invention or domain of Jacques Peletier du Mans. There were after all Utopias and Praises of Folly, religious polemics and various other examples which readily come to mind. In the main, the thrust of Renaissance writing was not after all retrogressive but innovative as the subsequent evolution of vernacular literature proves. Freedom from normative rhetoric would inevitably follow from this and other kinds of neoclassicizing activities: the art of free composition in poetry, of free narrative in the novel and, much later, in cinema.

I should like to point out in passing that this phenomenon of hybridizing also effectively contributed to the rejoining of the classical and classicizing current of French literature and that of the Middle Ages whose genres had other sources of inspiration, those of ancient celtic and germanic mythology, and other norms of invention, disposition and delivery.

Cohortatio either advocated or illustrated the use of the vernacular. Here was a text which, with its contemporary subject matter and protagonists, almost begged to be expressed in French. Since it was an original work in a modern genre, its author's choice of language was strictly his own, unfettered by any obligation of respect or justice to imitate his elders. The same would be true of any future writers working in this genre. Yet Peletier composed and published it in Latin and as a matter of fact it stood up as a piece of excellent classical Latin writing. But why did he do it if it wasn't necessary and if he was so interested in the vernacular? As if to stay such a question, Peletier produced his own French version which he had published in 1558 (unfortunately lost except for those few excerpts quoted by Lacroix du Maine and DeVerdier). Whatever his motives for favouring the Latin, the *Cohortatio* was, at least, now reaching two reading publics and could convince and persuade both purists and those who either couldn't read Latin or who approved the use of French for weighty subjects.

A reading of that part of the French text which is extant and which includes at least one fairly extensive passage, shows it to be quite as vigorous, varied in tone and effective as the Latin. Let me quote a short passage, to illustrate how lively it can be. Peletier is evoking a conversation between Pyrrhus and his counsellor Cinéas about the merits of pursuing his wars in Italy:

> C'est à vous ausquels touche ce que le prudent Cynéas répliqua à Pyrrhe, Roi des Epyrotes, autant véritablement que familièrement. Pyrrhe (dit-il) quand tu auras surmonté les Romains, subjugué toute l'Italie, gagné la Sicile, & puis la Lybie, occupé le Royaume Macédoine, & toute la Grèce, que ferons-nous plus? Voilà une belle demande, dit le Roi: nous vivrons lors en repos, nous deviserons joyeusement & privement les uns avec les autres. Et donc, dit Cynéas, pourquoi ne jouissons-nous dès maintenant de ce repos & de ces devis, quand nous avons le moyen, plutôt que chercher ce que nous avons comptant, aux dépens du sang de tant de gens, par tant de dangers de nos vies, & par l'événement incertain de nos affaires? Cet homme de singulier esprit & jugement, amena le Roi à ce point, qu'il lui fit confesser, que tranquilité parmi les choses de ce monde, est celle qui plus se doit desirer; & par même moyen, il tira cela de lui, que tous les apprêts de guerre qu'il faisoit, ne s'adressoient ailleurs qu'au fait de la paix.[3]

---

[3] Verdier, 1:562–63.

Judging from the texts available, the two versions of this work are equally successful. Once the possibilities of this new genre are exploited, however, by treating other contemporary subjects, by further fictionalizing and developing the characters of speaker and audience, their situations and their relationships, French will be inevitably more attractive as time passes. A humanist author like Peletier, because he understood the underlying values of Roman rhetoric, was able through a piece like the *Cohortatio* to free his work of rhetoric's superficial restraints as well as slavish attachment to its language and with it to help nudge the national literature into an era of unparalleled creative production.

Acadia University, Nova Scotia

Historiography and Humanism in Early Sixteenth-century Scandinavia

KARSTEN FRIIS-JENSEN

At the beginning of the sixteenth century many states of northern Europe saw it as a necessity to produce a history of their own country in polished Latin, intended first of all for a public abroad. Italian humanist historiography of the fifteenth century set the standard, on several levels. The strong chauvinism of Italian humanists, claiming Italy to be the true and only heir to the classical tradition and thus to civilization in general, was in itself a challenge. The primary aim for the new writers of patriotic history was to show that their country also represented old and important cultural traditions, if possible with links to the classical world. The Italian insistence on a polished classicizing Latin as the only acceptable medium for such historical works was met with more wholehearted approval, in principle at least.

The French humanist Robert Gaguin published a history of France in Latin in 1495. An Italian humanist, Paulo Emilio, was commissioned by the French king to write a more official work. The first part of his history of France was printed in 1517 by a man who will be mentioned several times in this paper, the Parisian printer and humanist Jodocus Badius Ascensius. Emilio's work was clearly a stylistic improvement compared with Gaguin's. In England another Italian, Polydore Vergil, wrote the official work of history, published in 1534. In Germany, native humanists were at work. The circle around Emperor Maximilian concentrated mainly on the history of the Holy Roman empire, and of that part of Germany which had been Roman, whereas northern Germany found its historiographer in the Hamburg diplomat Albert Krantz.[1] Scandinavian humanists

[1] A short survey of early sixteenth-century historiography is found in Denys Hay,

also worked on national history, but visible results were late in appearing. The first humanist work of history by a Scandinavian was Johannes Magnus's history of the Swedish kings, printed in 1554. Paradoxically, Magnus's very ambitious Swedish history was to all intents and purposes an answer to the publication in 1514 of a more than three-hundred-year-old medieval chronicle, Saxo Grammaticus's history of Denmark. I shall now try to give an idea of Saxo's role in the early Danish and Swedish humanist movements.[2]

First a few facts about Saxo's work.[3] Saxo wrote the history of the Danes and their kings in sixteen books from the eponymous King Dan, some twenty generations before Christ, and down to his own time, ending with events that took place in 1185. The first nine books of the work are dominated by what we would call legendary material, but sources begin to flow more abundantly in the Christian period, comprising the last seven books from the tenth century onwards. Saxo does not connect the Danes with any of the mediterranean peoples, neither Greeks, Trojans, nor Old Testament tribes. To Saxo the Danes are apparently autochthonous. Apart from mentioning the birth of Christ, Saxo lacks explicit references to the categories of universal history. Saxo's history of Denmark is thus a secular, patriotic work of history. Saxo writes a highly polished and elegant Latin. His classical model is not Cicero, but rather Silver Age writers such as Curtius Rufus and Valerius Maximus. Moreover, the first part of the work is embellished with poems in many classical quantitative metres. Saxo's metrical technique is highly developed, and in the poems his models for language and subject matter are the Roman poets of the Golden Age, particularly Vergil and Horace.[4]

Annalists and Historians. Western Historiography from the Eighth to the Eighteenth Centuries (London: Methuen, 1977), chap. 6.

[2] In Karsten Friis-Jensen, "Humanism and Politics: The Paris Edition of Saxo Grammaticus's Gesta Danorum 1514," *Analecta Romana Instituti Danici* 17–18 (1988–89): 149–62, I have discussed the ideological background to the *editio princeps* of Saxo in more detail, whereas Johannes Magnus's history of the Swedish kings was not commented upon.

[3] Latest edition *Saxonis Gesta Danorum* eds. J. Olrik, H. Ræder and F. Blatt, 2 vols. (Copenhagen: Levin and Munksgaard, 1931–57), English translations and commentaries *Saxo Grammaticus: The History of the Danes. Books I–IX* trans. Peter Fisher, comment. Hilda E. Davidson, 2 vols. (Cambridge: Brewer, 1979–80), *Saxo Grammaticus: Danorum Regum Heroumque Historia. Books X–XVI* trans. and comment. Eric Christiansen, 3 vols. (Oxford: BAR, 1980–81), latest monograph in English Karsten Friis-Jensen, *Saxo Grammaticus as Latin Poet: Studies in the Verse Passages of the Gesta Danorum*. Analecta Romana Instituti Danici. Supplementa, vol. 14 (Rome: Bretschneider, 1987).

[4] See Friis-Jensen, op. cit., (n. 3) passim.

Saxo's history of Denmark is an unusual achievement, also when seen in its proper context, the so-called "Renaissance of the Twelfth Century." In fact it must have been altogether too difficult for many readers of the later Middle Ages. In the fourteenth and fifteenth centuries there are only few traces of the original version. On the other hand, an epitome written in current medieval Latin, and omitting the difficult verse passages, soon gained popularity.[5]

Prior to the printing of Saxo, in the late fifteenth century, there are clear signs of an awakening interest in the original version. A grammatical handbook, printed in Copenhagen in 1493, includes a section on versification with the express purpose of enabling the student to read the poems of Boethius (in the *Consolation of Philosophy*), Saxo Grammaticus, and other poets.[6]

A few years later, the Hamburg humanist and diplomat Albert Krantz began to write his history of the Scandinavian kingdoms, a part of a larger historiographical project, namely to write the history of that part of Germania which lay outside the Roman empire.[7] Krantz is therefore not a writer of national, patriotic history in the same sense as the French and English historiographers already mentioned. Owing to Germany's particular status as a federation of territorial states, German patriotic feelings had some difficulties in finding a specific focus. Krantz's allegiances lay primarily with the Hanseatic League, and his North-Germanic territory comprised Saxony, the Baltic Slavs, and Scandinavia.

Krantz had access to a manuscript of Saxo, and used him extensively. Although he discarded what he found untrustworthy, still, many legends and the whole implicit chronological construction remained. Saxo's early history was simply too useful for Krantz's project to be rejected. Krantz also acknowledged his debt to Saxo several times, most detailed at the end of the Norwegian part: "It has pleased me to copy this passage word for word from our Saxo and insert it here, in order to introduce from time to time the very voice of the author whom I have followed in these Antiquities. In this way posterity can observe the care which men of Danish descent already at that time bestowed on writing. Such considerable

---

[5] The so-called *Compendium Saxonis*, ed. in *Scriptores Minores Historiae Danicae Medii Aevi*, ed. M. Cl. Gertz, 2 vols. (Copenhagen: Gad, 1918–22), 1:195–470.

[6] See *Tre latinske Grammatikker*, eds. Erik Dal and Jan Pinborg (Copenhagen: Munksgaard, 1979) 176 and 245 f.

[7] See Manfred Grobecker, *Studien zur Geschichtsschreibung des Albert Krantz* (Diss. Hamburg, 1964), with further references.

literary ability did not seem to agree with either that age or that region, since then and there—in the most distant part of the barbarian world, as the Italians say, and at a time when the knowledge of illustrious literature seemed to be long since neglected even in Italy, that mother of fine arts—the Dane Saxo nevertheless wrote a work which I regard with admiration. And if I could not decide the matter openly by palpable evidence, I would not be convinced that something like that could be learned at that time and in those regions."[8]

Krantz combined his praise of Saxo's style with a dig at the Italian humanists. He obviously resented their calling all non-Italians barbarians, and took pleasure in pointing out that Saxo's fine Latin style was highly unusual among his contemporaries, also according to Italian standard.

Although Krantz finished his history of the Scandinavian kingdoms in 1504, the work remained unpublished for almost half a century. But Krantz's activities as a diplomat in the service of the Hanseatic League brought him in frequent contact with representatives of the Danish government. His admiration for Saxo's work may therefore have contributed to the decision to print Saxo.

The *editio princeps* of Saxo was published in 1514 by the Parisian printer Jodocus Badius Ascensius, in collaboration with the Danish humanist Christiern Pedersen.[9] In this case Christiern Pedersen seems to have acted as the agent of the Danish government, the young King Christian II and his aristocratic councellors. The Paris edition is accompanied by three introductory letters which are our main source for the understanding of the events that led to the publication of the book: one from the king's chancellor to the editor Christiern Pedersen, the other two addressed to the chancellor by the editor and the printer.

Saxo's literary qualities are praised more than once in these letters. The learned printer Badius apparently considers Saxo's merits the result of a

---

[8] Albert Krantz, *Chronica Regnorum Aquilonarium* (Strasbourg: Ioannes Scottus, 1546), p. 744: "Haec ad uerbum libuit ex Saxone nostro transferre et inserere, ut per interualla autoris, quem in his Antiquitatibus secuti sumus, uocem intermisceamus, ut uideant posteri, quae cura scribendi fuerit iam tum ea tempestate Danici generis hominibus. Non uidebatur tanta literarum instructio neque seculo congruere neque regioni, quando in ultima (ut uocant Itali) barbarie illis temporibus, quando illustrium literarum memoria uidebatur etiam in Italia (bonarum artium matre) iamdudum intermissa, Saxo tamen Danus in patria sua tum ea scripsit, quae admiramur. Et nisi manifestis attestationibus rem in propatulo in eis regionibus tale aliquid compertum iri."

[9] Cp. Philippe Renouard, *Bibliographie des impressions et des oeuvres de Josse Badius Ascensius, imprimeur et humaniste, 1462–1535*, 3 vols. (Paris: Paul and Guillemin, 1908), 3:249 ff.

good French education. In this he may be right, although it has never been possible to prove definitely that Saxo studied in France. We know, on the other hand, that Saxo's editor, Christiern Pedersen, had been educated at Paris, as Badius likewise points out. Christiern Pedersen's studies in France and his collaboration with the printer Badius in several editorial projects of national interest for Denmark may in fact have been of decisive importance for the breakthrough of the Danish humanist movement.

The founding of the University of Copenhagen in 1479 was without doubt a positive development, and some of the first professors seem to have been of a humanist orientation.[10] Many students still went on to universities abroad, for instance Greifswald, Rostock, Cologne, and Louvain. But prior to Christiern Pedersen's Paris printings, very few texts have been retained that actually show traces of humanist influence. The humanist circle in Paris, of which Badius was an important member, clearly influenced Christiern Pedersen, and the edition of Saxo is the main monument to his activities. His antiquarian interest, his according to contemporary standards sound scholarship,[11] the whole context in which the introductory letters place the edition, all herald a new spirit. The edition was, to quote Badius, "an omen of a better and more learned century in Denmark" (non sine melioris doctiorisque in Dania saeculi praesagio).

Badius also stresses the political relevance of Saxo's patriotic work by drawing parallels between Saxo's two patrons King Valdemar and Archbishop Absalon, and Christiern Pedersen's patrons King Christian and his chancellor. By calling King Christian a descendant of King Valdemar, Badius underlines his legitimate right to the Danish throne. Saxo's own strong emphasis on the dynastic history of the medieval Danish kings thus becomes a foil to the present ruler.

The political situation in Scandinavia at the time was precarious. The personal union between the three Nordic kingdoms under the house of Oldenburg had to be renewed when Christian II succeeded his father in 1513. He was crowned without difficulties in Denmark and Norway, but Sweden resisted successfully for several years. An advantageous marriage consolidated Christian's position. The bride was a Habsburg princess, the future Emperor Charles's sister Elisabeth. The publication of Saxo may even have been connected with this marriage.

---

[10] See e.g., Jan Pinborg, op. cit., pp. 244 ff.

[11] Cp. Erik Petersen, "Humanism and the Medieval Past: Christiernus Petri as a Humanist Scholar," in *Acta Conventus Neo-Latini Bononiensis,* ed. R. J. Schoeck, Medieval & Renaissance Texts & Studies, vol. 37 (Binghamton, NY, 1985), 172–76.

Some months after the edition had been printed, carrying an idealized portrait of Christian II on the title page, Elisabeth was married to Christian by proxy in Brussels. Next summer a Danish delegation brought the queen home. At the departure from the Netherlands the Danish orator gave an eloquent Latin speech, whose text is known. And to my surprise, I discovered that he had woven a long quotation from one of Saxo's poems into his oration. When eulogizing King Christian, he uses a flattering characterization in Saxo of one of the earliest heroic kings. Again, Christian is being linked with the ancient kings of Denmark, although without help the allusion to Saxo must have been impossible to catch for the foreign audience.[12]

In any case, Saxo's history of Denmark won rapid circulation, and was reprinted twice during the sixteenth century. Erasmus of Rotterdam's famous words of praise in the dialogue *Ciceronianus* from 1528 are a clear indication of the qualities humanists found in Saxo. The hypercritical Ciceronian of the dialogue says of Saxo: "I like his lively and ingenious spirit, his way of speaking that is never drab or sleepy, and also his wonderful abundance of words, his many proverbs and his admirable variation in rhetorical figures; I like all of this and cannot marvel enough at the way in which a Dane at this point in time could acquire such mastery of speech; but there is hardly a trace of Cicero to be found in him."[13]

Erasmus is only concerned about Latin style in this work, so that we cannot expect him to discuss historical method. But in Latin patriotic historiography the humanists showed a similar preoccupation with style, to the neglect of method.[14] Even Saxo's more dubious legends did not necessarily give offence, and the speeches in his work, inspired as they were by classical historiography, were fully in consonance with the humanists' own efforts.

For Danish history writers the publication of Saxo proved to be of the greatest importance.[15] His authority remained undisputed for a long

[12] See Karsten Friis-Jensen, op. cit., (n. 2) pp. 150 ff.

[13] *Erasmus von Rotterdam: Ciceronianus & Adagia selecta*, ed. Theresia Payr. Ausgewählte Schriften, vol. 7 (Darmstadt: Wissenschaftliche Buchgesellschaft, 1972), 272: "Probo uiuidum et ardens ingenium, orationem nusquam remissam aut dormitantem, tum miram uerborum copiam, sententias crebras et figurarum admirabilem uarietatem, ut satis admirari non queam, unde illa aetate homini Dano tanta uis eloquendi suppetierit; sed uix ulla in illo Ciceronis lineamenta reperias."

[14] Polydore Vergil is probably the best historian, according to modern critical standards, among those mentioned.

[15] Sixteenth- and seventeenth-century Danish historiography has been admirably

time, and their task in a way consisted in either writing a continuation to him, or translating him into Danish. Despite many attempts in the course of the sixteenth century, a complete official history of Denmark in elegant Latin did not see the light until more than one hundred years after the publication of Saxo, and moreover written by historiographers called in from the Netherlands. The upheavals of the Reformation explain the lack of results in the early part of the period, but the demand to emulate Saxo's greatness may also have acted as a psychological stumbling block.

In the meantime, the Danish government in the 1540s supported the printing of Albert Krantz's almost half a century old history of the Scandinavian kingdoms, both in the original Latin and in a German translation. No less than Philip Melanchthon seems to have acted as a go-between in the affair.[16] Krantz was one of Saxo's ardent admirers, as we have seen, and in general Denmark was most fully and most positively treated among the three kingdoms. That should be enough to explain the official Danish interest in Krantz.

In 1523, Sweden liberated herself finally from the Scandinavian union. The resulting rivalry between Denmark and Sweden in fact inspired the most extraordinary work among those written by Saxo's followers. That was Johannes Magnus's *History of the Kings of the Swedes and the Goths*, finished about 1540, and published posthumously in Rome in 1554.[17]

Johannes Magnus went in exile in 1526 as the last catholic archbishop of Sweden. The coolness between him and the new regime in Sweden grew steadily. Nevertheless Johannes Magnus remained an ardent Swedish patriot all his life, and in the long years of exile he collected material for a patriotic history of Sweden. A fundamental part of his patriotism was a burning hatred for everything Danish. As a writer of Swedish history he had to take issue with Saxo and Saxo's picture of Sweden as a barbarian country which for long periods was nothing more than a Danish vassal state. Moreover, he simply must outdo Saxo's imposing series of about one hundred Danish kings.

Johannes Magnus solved the problem by taking up the medieval identi-

---

surveyed by Ellen Jørgensen, *Historieforskning og Historieskrivning i Danmark indtil Aar 1800* (Copenhagen: Hagerup, 1931).

[16] See Ellen Jørgensen, op. cit., pp. 85 and 221.

[17] *Historia Ioannis Magni . . . De omnibus Gothorum Sveonumque regibus . . . opera Olai Magni Gothi fratris . . . in lucem edita* (Rome: I. M. de Viottis, 1554). A recent monograph on the Magnus brothers gives an excellent picture of their intellectual background: Kurt Johannesson, *Gotisk renässans. Johannes och Olaus Magnus som politiker och historiker* (Stockholm: Almqvist and Wiksell, 1983).

fication of the Goths of the Great Migration with the Swedish tribe of the same name. He diligently explored the various classical and early medieval sources concerning the migrations of the Goths and their kingdoms in Europe and Africa. In a bold combination of this material with biblical genealogy and some of Saxo's most shadowy figures he created a series of 143 Swedish kings, from Noah's grandson Magog to his own contemporary Gustavus Vasa.

We do not know when Johannes Magnus began to read Saxo. But another of his sources was Albert Krantz, who often mentions Saxo, as we saw. In 1525, Johannes Magnus came across a manuscript of Krantz's *History of the Nordic Kingdoms* in Lübeck, and he at once had a copy made of the part dealing with Sweden.[18] If not before, he now realized how important it was to emulate Saxo.

Saxo was vital for Johannes Magnus as a historical source, but the form of Saxo's work also influenced him. He may have contemplated writing parts of his history as a mixture of prose and verse, like Saxo did in his first eight books. A verse monologue, in sapphic stanzas, is put into the mouth of one of the early kings.[19] The sapphic stanza is one of Saxo's favourite metres, and Saxo's poems are likewise only used for dialogue. But the sapphic poem remained the only verse in Johannes Magnus: it was probably too time-consuming to write just as good classicizing poetry as Saxo had done, even for a well-educated sixteenth-century humanist.

The speeches in Johannes Magnus are not written to emulate Saxo alone, because they belong to the genre as such. In one speech, however, Saxo plays a very important role, and this speech is moreover almost the climax of the whole work.[20] It is ascribed to one of the leading Swedish patriots of the early sixteenth century, Hemming Gadh, but modern historians have been able to prove that it is entirely a fabrication on the part of Johannes Magnus himself.[21] The speech is an eloquent diatribe against the Danes and their machinations, and almost all illustrations of its thesis are taken from Saxo.

Johannes Magnus quotes Saxo for saying about himself and his Danes:

---

[18] As we know from a note in the MS; see P. Wieselgren, "Rörande en handskrift af Alberti Kranzii . . . Regnorum Aquilonarium . . . Chronica," *DelaGardiska Archivet* 2 (1832): 152–53, and cp. Kurt Johannesson, op. cit., p. 40.

[19] This feature was also mentioned by Ellen Jørgensen, op. cit., p. 87.

[20] Johannes Magnus, op. cit., pp. 753–76.

[21] An extensive literature on this speech exists; the most important contribution is perhaps Egil Petersen, "Hemming Gadhs Tale mod de Danske," *(Dansk) Historisk Tidsskrift* VI:4 (1893): 464–73.

"we do not count lying and deceit as despicable faults" (de se et suis Danis ait: Nos mentiri et fallere inter uitia sordesque non ducimus).[22] This unfortunate phrase runs as a red thread through the whole speech, applied to all Danes of all times. Moreover, the speaker makes his own frame of reference quite explicit: at the end of the long speech he compares his task to that of Cicero, speaking against Verres, Catiline, and Anthony.[23] Johannes Magnus also cannot resist the temptation to allude to the famous beginning of Cicero's first speech against Catiline. Hemming Gadh says somewhere: "My aim is, finally to stop the Danes abusing our patience" (me ... moliri ... quod Dani ... tandem desinant nostra patientia ... abuti).[24] Saxo is here in very good humanist company.

As we have seen, soon after the appearance of the *editio princeps* Saxo won a status almost comparable to a classical writer. His stylistic qualities combined with his glowing patriotism made him an unexpected trump card for Denmark when the other rivalling states of Europe had to engage humanists to produce patriotic history.

University of Copenhagen

[22] Johannes Magnus, op. cit., p. 754. In fact Saxo makes a distinction between his own time and the heroic old days: he writes, à propos an isolated dubious character (a Swede) in Book IV (4, 10, 1 p. 102, 13 Olrik/Ræder): "Crediderim nostri temporis mores huius uiri auspiciis inchoatos, qui mentiri ac fallere inter uitia sordesque non ducimus."

[23] Johannes Magnus, op. cit., p. 776: "Nec me quisquam quasi nimis prolixa oratione utentem increpet: sed ad memoriam reuocet Romanum Ciceronem, qui multo extensioribus actionibus in unum Verrem, atque alterum Catilinam usus fuisse probatur, totque Philippicas in solum M. Antonium exaggerat. Ego autem cum innumerabilibus Verribus, et Catilinis, Antoniisque adeo ingens bellum assumpsi, ut" eqs.

[24] Ibid., p. 771, cp. Cic. Catil. 1, 1 "Quo usque tandem abutere, Catilina, patientia nostra?"

Fanciful Journeys in Vives' Early Writings

E.V. GEORGE

Among Juan Luis Vives' experiments in various literary forms prior to 1522, there is a striking series of three instances of a narrative type which I shall call the fanciful journey, defining it as a visit to a place inaccessible to Vives the traveler on the literal geographical map of his world and in his own era. The works in question are the *Genethliacon Iesu Christi* (from the "Kalends of January," probably no later than January, 1519, our style); the *Aedes Legum* (April, 1519); and the *Somnium* composed as a satirical preface to the 1520 *Somnium et Vigilia in Somnium Scipionis* (March, 1520).[1] The following survey of selected aspects of these journeys is offered as possible evidence of stylistic development on Vives' part.

We start with a look at how Vives visualizes the entrance into the worlds of the three journeys. First, the *Genethliacon Iesu Christi,* in which Vives travels across the Mediterranean from Valencia to Palestine, arriving

---

[1] See the discussion of the dates of pieces in the *Opuscula Varia* by Constant Matheeussen in *J. L. Vives: Early Writings*, ed. C. Matheeussen, C. Fantazzi, and E. George (Leiden: E. J. Brill, 1987), xv–xx. The *Genethliacon* was presented to Jean Briard of Ath on the "Kalends of January," further unspecified. As Briard died on 8 January 1520, and the *Genethliacon* dedication makes no mention of his death, this date is "an all but certain *terminus ante quem*" for the actual publication of the *Opuscula varia* volume (Matheeussen, p. xix). For the "Kalends" to have been as late as January 1520 itself (in our dating style) would also be highly unlikely. Matheeussen (op. cit., p. xviii.) accepts April 1519 as a highly probable date for the *Aedes*. The *Somnium* preceding the *Dream of Scipio* commentary appeared in March 1520. See P. S. Allen, ed., *Opus Epistolarum Des. Erasmi Roterodami*, vol. 4 (Oxford: Oxford Univ. Press, 1922), ep. 1106, line 103 and note. It was augmented and revised in 1521 (Basel, Froben). A fourth work dedicated 1 April 1519, the *Anima senis*, resembles in some ways the three considered here but does not involve a journey.

at the moment of the birth of Christ, encountering the holy family along with the shepherds, and engaging in a dialogue with the Virgin Mary. The adventure begins as follows:

> Quum e plaga mediterranei maris ad nostram Valentiam spectante, quae paullo ad orientem inclinatior e conspectu Libyae, fretum ad occidentem relinquit Herculeum, munita nave solvissemus ora, perpetuo cursu Baleares, Sardiniam, Siciliam praetervecti, Asiaticam Cretam adnavigavimus ... et nos ad maris litus iter agentes, Canopum profectos ... postero die gens colona multiiugis vehiculis in Palaestinam adduxit.
> Derelictus ego, a sociis variis negotiis complicatis, serena nocte, eo coelo ... intentius perscrutabar.... (p.3)[2]

The voyage itself is sketched briefly, and may be taken as little more than a hurried excuse to mention the Cretan and Egyptian landfalls, chosen because the former is the home of the impious cradle of Jupiter, the latter of the degraded rituals and worship of Serapis and other Nilotic deities, symbols antithetical to the incarnation of the true God which is about to occur. The narrator's companions are mentioned only cursorily; there is no interest in providing a believable sequence of events leading up to the trip, or in telling how it was that the traveler was free to make it, or what enabled him to move through time as well as space.

We turn now to the opening of the *Aedes Legum*, in which Vives comes to the temple of Law, where he engages an ancient gatekeeper in conversation on the need for renewal of legal study:

> Cum in humanam societatem venissem a deo nostro imperatore (sumus etenim homines hominum causa creati "neque nobis nati solis", ut aiebat Plato), pedetentim in locum munitissimum pariter et amoenissimum quendam me contuli, quo nihil in terris affirmabant illi principi deo gratius atque iucundius. civitatem eam appellabant, ubi concilia coetusque hominum iure sociati, ubi iustitia et pax, ubi humanitas, fides, hospitalitas et aliae quae in hominibus hominum causa sunt virtutes. in medio quodam eiusce civitatis loco natura vallatissimo atque saeptissimo, unde tutari civitas facile poterat, arx quaedam.... (*Aedes* 1, ed. Matheeussen)[3]

---

[2] Citations of the *Genethliacon Iesu Christi* are from *Ioannis Ludovici Vivis Opera Omnia*, ed. Gregorius Majansius, (Valencia: Montfort, 1788), 7:3–18.

[3] Citations of the *Aedes legum* are from *Ioannis Lodovici Vivis Valentini Praefatio in Leges Ciceronis et Aedes Legum*, ed. Constant Matheeussen (Leipzig: Teubner, 1984).

This time the venue is allegorical, rather than a single literal spot on the earth. Again *cum* precedes a pluperfect subjunctive and an active verb involving Vives as a subject. Matheeussen plausibly takes the opening as an echo of the first words of Scipio Aemilianus' narrative in the *Dream of Scipio* ("Cum in Africam venissem M'. Manilio consuli . . . tribunus ut scitis militum, nihil mihi fuit potius," etc.). The association applies to the first words of the *Genethliacon* as well, but in the *Aedes* the connection is confirmed by other allusions, notably the echo of the Scipionic remark about political activity winning divine favor.[4] Thus the connection of the *Aedes* with a kindred philosophical work at once provides signposts by which the reader may judge what the drift of the encounter will be.

But there are artistic problems. What does Vives mean when he says he "came into human society from God" his commander? Is this intended to refer to his own birth? That is what the allusion to the *Dream of Scipio* implies.[5] But this implication is either nonsense or humor; it is hard to tell what we are supposed to envision. Another possible interpretation is that *since* he was created by God, he came to the *locum munitissimum*, et cetera. Here, we are to assume that the thoughtful philosopher of politics knew where he was going, and indeed *me contuli* sounds like an action performed by deliberate choice. But the nature of his ensuing questions to the old guardian of the House of Laws presents the picture of a visitor to an unknown place. In short, we see here by contrast to the *Genethliacon* an immediate effort to make the context and the theme more specific by philosophical allusions, but once again with confusion in portrayal.

Finally, the *Somnium* accompanying the Commentary on the *Dream of Scipio*, a nocturnal excursion to the realm of the god Sleep, where various events occur more or less directly connected with Vives' hopes for educational reform, involving an otherworldly "senate meeting" which sanctions humanist renewal of education and a final interview with Cicero, who provides suitable data for the Spaniard's projected commentary. This narrative opens as follows:

> Hesterna nocte, studiosi iuvenes, cum de enarrando vobis Scipionis somnium cogitarem, Somnus me suam in aedem repente induxit

---

Translations are my own.

[4] See the following note.

[5] "Nihil est . . . illi principi deo, qui omnem mundum regit, quod quidem in terris fiat acceptius quam consilia coetusque hominum iure sociati, quae civitates appellantur. Harum rectores et conservatores hinc profecti huc revertuntur" (Cicero, *Somnium Scipionis* 3.5).

> ipsumque somniantem ostendit Scipionem, ex quo me iussit percontari totius illius lucubrati et vigilati somnii enarrationem. Operae pretium fuerit singula a capite ipso cognoscere et describere vobis templum illius dei, cui vos tam crebro tam libenter sacrificatis, ne ignoretis eum locum in quem piis animis operaturi sacris saepe convenitis. (*Somn.* 1)[6]

The *cum* precedes an imperfect subjunctive this time, and the main verb describes not further action by the narrator but an initiative by the god Sleep during a specific appropriate moment in the course of Vives' own activity. The audience, namely the Louvain students to whom Vives is preparing to lecture, is sharply defined and specific. The writer wastes no time in turning the topic, sleep and dreams, into a gentle reproach directed at the lazy habits of his youthful hearers. Sleep's realm is vividly detailed, using Ovid's *Metamorphoses* Book 11 as a springboard. Among the three introductions we are studying it is here that Vives presents himself, his listener, and the events in the clearest focus with the least doubt about exactly what is going on.

Another facet of the fanciful journeys that shows maturation of style is the way in which the author includes himself as a character in the experience. In all three pieces, Vives is in some way the inquisitive learner. In the *Genethliacon*, Vives seeks out opportunities to elevate the Virgin's wisdom and learning by contrast with his own secular stupidity and the worthlessness of his secular erudition. His idea is to present, much as he does in ordinary life for Briard or others, a little product of his scholarship as a gift:

> . . . ad blandam benignamque Matrem conversus, "quam tibi, dulcis et sacra Virgo, placeret," inquam, "si ex astris quid sit tuo isti Filio fati eventurum praenuntiarem?" Illa vero me tam delirantem limis nonnihil intuita (qui Virginis mos semper fuit) in viam reducere brevi ac facili compendio volens, "et qua," inquit, "hunc putas natum coniunctione? quibus signis?" Tum ego: "Dicam equidem, tametsi varietas visa est in coelis. . . ." (p. 5)

Vives launches into an astrological analysis of the position of the planets and the signs of the zodiac, concluding:

> . . . non desunt qui Martem esse asserant in mortis contubernio: idcirco hoc momenti natum, crucis candidatum praefantur.

[6] Citations of the *Somnium* are from Juan Luis Vives, *Somnium et Vigilia in Somnium Scipionis*, ed. and trans. Edward George, (Greenwood, SC: Attic Press, 1989).

> Tum illa ingenio mitissimo puella: "Et quam," inquit, "toto (ut dicitur) erras coelo! An tu solus ignoras huius esse utramque genesim inenarrabilem, ineffabilem?" (p. 6)

And beginning with the angel Gabriel's words, Mary embarks on a scripturally based explication of her divine son's future. Coming to a portrayal of the Father, the Son and the Paraclete as three suns which have converged into one, she challenges him: "tu nunc his signorum ortibus et obitibus, his vagantium fixorumque siderum coniunctionibus variisque aspectibus, quis erit puer hic, si vales, coniicito" (9–10). Vives demurs:

> Quamvis mihi, o sacratissima Virgo, hominem ingenio monstrares celerrimo et perspicacissimo, etsi nonnihil sane divinam hausisset sapientiam, eum ego haudquaquam puto vel mediocri modo enarrare posse quantus infantulus iste tuus futurus sit; tantum abest, ut ego, vir nihili, neque litteras doctus (ut aiebant) neque natare, ea ipsa contingere ac penetrare satis tuto mysteria queam. (p. 10)

Obviously, Vives' offering has been a hopeless waste of time. He listens quietly as Mary occupies four pages with further remarks on Jesus' impact on human history. She charges him (p. 14) to act as "gentili populo salutiger," and to carry news of this wonderful birth. When Vives tries to evade any such responsibility, Mary replies with a classic humanistic litany of erudition: why should gentiles find Jesus' resurrection unbelievable, since they accept the resurrection of Arcas the son of Callisto, the beneficiaries of Aesculapius, Er of Pamphylia, and others? She is as conversant with secular learning as with sacred. Having neutralized the value of Vives' astronomical lore, she now preempts his territory in yet another respect. Vives' uselessness is confirmed.

On his excursion to the *Aedes Legum*, Vives meets a cantankerous doorkeeper at the entrance to the edifice, and politely inquires, "Parens optime, quis hic habet?" The man replies: "Filie, si aves, audibis. Nam ex nostris mihi videris congerronibus nosque amare." Vives is gratified: "Quae tua est humanitas! Congerro vero tuusne sum, parum scio; gerro certe, et magnus quidem, sum." Vives aims first of all to be agreeable: the impression he makes will be chosen to suit his need to get along with his interlocutor so as to find out as much as he can.

The old gatekeeper laments the burial of true legal knowledge under the obscuring avalanche of comments by Accorso, Bardo, and others, and longs for a renewal of legal studies by cultivators of ancient wisdom such as Vives:

> Vtinam a tehe tisque aliis similibus sociennis, qui veteres ollas et veras sophias calendari et exterebrare commalaxatis, prosferarem uti

> huc innuberetis et aedituaremini; neque tudicularet prognariter impancrare has allodapas et atroces copias fastidilitas....
>
> If only I were to get my wish from you and your colleagues like you who strive to study (?) and investigate the ancient and true wisdom, that you would enter here and protect this dwelling, and bravely withstand the alien and savage bounties (? of commentaries)!
>
> (*Aed.* 10)

Complimented though he is, Vives is left in the dark by the gatekeeper's archaic language: "Hui, tum inquam, Quid iste mihi sermonis tam diu a me auscultatus loquitur?" (*Aed.* 11). He is not Evander or an Aborigine, protests the humanist. The caretaker is disappointed, for, as he says, "nullus perscrutari domum hanc legum rite possit, qui plene veram tersamque Latinitatem et antiquariam hanc modice saltem non imbiberit" (*Aed.* 11). But later, when Vives asks whether he will be granted entrance to the most sacred and mysterious recesses of the edifice of Laws, the old man responds: "Quid prohibet? Tu certe quam illiterati illi multo rectius, verius, clarius" (*Aed.* 14). The point in the larger context is that Vives as a philosopher is qualified to pursue expertise in law, and better qualified than *bêtes-noires* such as Accorso, Bardo and others.

In the flow of the excursion, however, Vives, while admitting to limitations, establishes himself as an authority entitled to speak in this ambience on a footing of respectability, as when he reassures an inquirer that there are signs of hope on earth; people of learning are resorting once again to the wise ancients (*Aed.* 20). Still, he wears his status diffidently in artistic terms:

> ... quam multa ... tecum disserere vellem, ... nisi vererer ne ego, qui e foribus solum (ut vides) leges salutavi, alieno decore conspicuus exsistam ac
>
> "ne, si forte suas repetitum venerit olim
> grex avium plumas, moveat cornicula risum,
> furtivis nudata coloribus."
>
> (*Aed.* 21)

He is not hindered, however, from providing the doorkeeper with a brief disquisition on the Aristotelian notion of *epieikeia*. This is unusual; the traveler in adventures such as these ordinarily does not go anywhere to teach others, but to learn. Here Vives feels at the same time inferior to and a peer of his interlocutor. There is inconsistency in his self-portrayal. Perhaps it comes from an attempt to refine the simple pattern of inferiority he established in the presence of the Virgin in the *Genethliacon*. He is aiming at a more subtle and complex depiction of himself, but merely produces sentiments that do not mesh with each other.

Inspection of the *Somnium* discloses that Vives alludes to himself without the self-uncertainty of the *Aedes*. He is quite nearly a nonentity until well into the visit, when Insomnium, the being who fabricates realistic dreams, recognizes him:

> Insomnium ... cum attentius perspexisset, agnovit congerronem. "Papae! Tu es Vives," inquit, "cui ego saepe soleo persuadere eum modo cum Cicerone modo cum Quintiliano ... versari et suavissime disputari?" "Ipsissimus," inquam.... (*Somn.* 46)

Implicitly Vives, precisely because his soul is so susceptible to the utter enchantment of the early greats, is a dupe. Paradoxically, his gullibility is directly proportional to his legitimate and worthy dedication to the classics. Self-deprecation and astuteness now go hand-in-hand.

Similarly, upon recognizing Cicero, Vives cleverly cozens him into a useful conversation by pretending to be a partisan of Pompey's party. Here is a level of sophistication unobserved in the *Genethliacon* or the *Aedes*: the visitor adopts a pose in order to collect the information he came to get. Cicero, flattered, gladly agrees to put himself at the humanist teacher's disposal. The relationships portrayed surpass considerably the scenes in the *Genethliacon* and the *Aedes* for subtlety; Vives accepts his low-profile position, equanimously absorbs aspersions on his capabilities, and finally coaxes what he wants out of the great orator. Vives has arrived at a level of coherence in a convincing narrative previously unexhibited in this "fanciful journey" series, and at a remarkably sophisticated use of the device of self-deprecation.

Finally, the *Genethliacon*, like the *Aedes* and the *Somnium*, is connected with a scholarly treatise. For in December of either 1517 or 1518, Vives dedicated to Serafin de Centelles, Count of Oliva, a work titled *De tempore quo, id est de pace, in qua natus est Christus* (Vives, *Opera Omnia*, ed. Majansius, vol. 7:20–32). It is taken up mostly with a recitation of events in Palestine and the rest of the Roman world leading up to the birth of Christ, with a focus on the wars of that period and their sweeping termination with Augustus' third closure of the gates of the temple of Janus, the age-old symbol of peace in the Roman world. A brief conclusion to the *De tempore* alludes to prophecies of peace to come with the Messiah. The general point is that secular history, with peace following long savage conflict, confirms the prophecies. It is time for a census in the wake of the gate-closing; Joseph and Mary are off to Bethlehem.

In the dedicatory epistle to the *Genethliacon* we find a phrase echoing the title of the historical work just described ("Christi Iesu fecimus γενεθλιακόν, eo dumtaxat tempore, quo et ipse natus est, et alii rerum humanarum passim fata praenuntiant"). But there is a noteworthy variation from the use of the Janus-reference in the *De tempore*, where the information had confirmed the connection between sacred and secular history. The *Genethliacon*, rather, asserts emphatically that it is sacred not secular history which is in control, and that the peace signified by the temple closing is temporary at best. Mary says:

> Quid quaeso sibi vult Iani Quirini, seu potius Monstri cuiusdam, tertium ab Octavio clausa nostris diebus porta, velut non mox saevissima bella Romanis secutura sint? Hinc, hinc pax orietur ex humili lutea casula, non vasto marmore, auro, ac gemmis refulgenti Romano capitolio .... (*Geneth.* p. 10)

A true symbol becomes a secular deception. Vives contravenes the relationship between sacred and secular history he had posited in the *De tempore*, even though we have seen one hint that he might have had his mind on the one piece while composing the other. The assumption, then, that the *Genethliacon* is no later than New Year's 1519 again gives us a picture of progression in literary competence from the *Genethliacon* to the *Aedes* and the *Somnium*: this time, from looser to more systematic incorporation of literary inventiveness with scholarly analysis.

The above remarks suggest, I hope, that a clearer picture of Vives' literary and personal development can indeed be hoped for by expanding the method applied here to his other early writings. Further, there is some pertinence to chronological questions. A hypothesis of stylistic development proceeding from the *Genethliacon* to the *Aedes* to the *Somnium*, if sound, corroborates Matheeussen's implicit argument that New Year's day 1520 is an improbably late date for the *Genethliacon* (see note 1 above). In addition, the similarity of topic but the clash in some details of treatment between the *De tempore* and the *Genethliacon* raises questions about how much time lapsed between the two compositions. Noreña assumes they both refer to the same Christmas season.[7] If they do, Vives will have put the symbol of the temple of Janus to radically different uses in two pieces composed simultaneously or nearly so. This may have happened: but the detail urges us to leave room for the alternative mentioned by Matheeussen, that the "December 1518" date for the *De tempore* may also refer to

[7] Carlos Noreña, *Juan Luis Vives* (trans. Antonio Pintor-Ramos, Madrid: Ediciones Paulinas, 1978), 84.

the last week of December 1517 (our style) as well as to 1–24 December 1518.

Texas Tech University

The Reconstruction of a Genre: Carolus Sigonius and the Theorization of Renaissance Dialogue

DONALD GILMAN

In his *Discorso dell'arte del dialogo* (1586), Torquato Tasso defines the dialogue simply and succinctly as the imitation of discussion.[1] A type of discussion is, of course, argumentation, and the dialectical dialogue, which is one form of this literary kind, becomes accordingly an imitation of disputation. Dialogue, then, is not a treatise postulating and elaborating one single statement. Rather, the presentation of varying opinions requires the use of interlocutors who reveal individual characteristics, attitudes, and personalities. Combining the roles of poet and logician, the writer of dialogue reproduces in prose the traits and thoughts of fictitious personages and, at the same time, records the subtle and sophisticated forms of their reasoning. For Tasso, the dialectical dialogue includes the topics, but transcends the generic limits, of philosophy. It is, in short, an artistic representation of argumentation which is a mimesis, or imaginative imitation, of man's search for truth.

Tasso's theorization of dialogue was not totally original. In fact, his *Discorso* can be described, in many ways, as a vernacular summary of a Latin treatise, *De dialogo liber* (Venice, 1561), by his teacher at Padua, Carolus Sigonius (ca. 1524–1584).[2] As professor of Greek at Venice

---

[1] Torquato Tasso, *Discorso dell'arte del dialogo* in *Tasso's Dialogues*, ed. and trans. Carnes Lord and Dain A. Trafton (Berkeley, Los Angeles, and London: University of California Press, 1982), 16–41, especially, 18–23.

[2] Carlo Sigonio, *De dialogo liber*, ed. Johannes Jessenius (Leipzig: Henry Osthausus,

(1552–1560) and, later, as professor of rhetoric at Padua (1560–1584), he defended the revival of classical Latin; commented on selected works of Aristotle, including the *Rhetoric*; and edited fragments of Cicero's lost writings (*De consolatione*, 1583). His interests also extended to history. Working diligently in archives and libraries, and taking advantage of archaeological findings, he published his *Fasti consulares* (1550), which chronicles the history of Rome, and his *De regno Italiae* (1580), which traces the development of the Italian kingdom from the invasion of the Lombards in 568 to the end of the thirteenth century. The quantity and significance of his historical writings have shifted attention away from his contributions in philology and literary criticism, in general, and from his definition of dialogue, in particular.

Sigonius's eighteenth- and nineteenth-century biographers, L. A. Muratori (1732–37), J. B. Krebs (1840) and G. Franciosi (1872) allude to his treatise on the dialogue,[3] and scholars, such as Moustapha Bénouis and C. J. R. Armstrong, have noted the significance of this work.[4] Only Bernard Weinberg and, more recently, K. J. Wilson have examined some of the principal points of Sigonius's theory.[5] However, in the preface to Sigonius's *De dialogo* published in Leipzig in 1596, the editor Johannes Jessenius reminds us of the importance of this treatise.[6] According to

---

1596). All page references correspond to this edition. A more modern edition is provided in *Opera omnia*, ed. P. Argelati, 6 vols. (Milan: Palatinus, 1732–37), 6:431–88. For a summary of his life and humanist contributions, see entries in the *Bibliographie universelle* and the *Encyclopaedia Britannica*, and J. E. Sandys, *A History of Classical Scholarship*, 3 vols. (Cambridge: Cambridge University Press, 1908–21), 3:143–45.

[3] L. A. Muratori provides a biography and account of the writings of Sigonius in *Opera omnia*, op. cit., as well as J. P. Krebs, *Carl Sigonius* (Frankfurt-a.M.: H. L. Brönner, 1840), and G. Franciosi, "Della vita e delle opere di Carlo Sigonio," *Scritti varii* (Florence: Le Monnier, 1878).

[4] Moustapha Kemal Bénouis, *Le dialogue philosophique dans la littérature française du seizième siècle* (The Hague and Paris: Mouton, 1976); and C. J. R. Armstrong, "The Dialectical Road to Truth: The Dialogue," in *French Renaissance Studies 1540–70: Humanism and the Encyclopedia*, ed. Peter Sharratt (Edinburgh: Edinburgh University Press, 1976), 37–38.

[5] Bernard Weinberg, *A History of Literary Criticism in the Italian Renaissance*, 2 vols. (Chicago: University of Chicago Press, 1961) 1:455–57, 482–85; K. J. Wilson, *Incomplete Fictions: The Formation of English Renaissance Dialogue* (Washington D. C.: The Catholic University of America Press, 1985), 11–14, 18, 29–33, 57.

[6] The characteristics of ancient dialogue that Sigonius describes have been examined in more recent studies: e.g., Rudolf Hirzel, *Der Dialog*, 2 vols. (1895; reprint, Hildesheim: G. Olms, 1963); and Michel Ruch, *Le préambule dans les oeuvres philosophiques de Cicéron: essai sur la genèse et l'art du dialogue* (Paris and Strasbourg: Les Belles Lettres, 1978). Eva Kushner, "The Dialogue of the French Renaissance: Work

Jessenius, Greek and Roman practitioners of the genre, Plato, Xenophon, and Cicero, established the form. In spite of the suitability and adaptation of this literary kind to the didactic purposes of analyzing and synthesizing ideas, Sigonius was the first to present the precepts of this genre. By collecting and studying the scattered observations of Plutarch, Athenaeus, Ammonius, and perhaps most significantly, Diogenes Laertius, Sigonius attempts to reconstruct the ancient theory of dialogue. His recovery of this doctrine, though, must not be viewed as a compilation of isolated statements. Rather, in drawing forth ancient rules, he situates this genre within a sixteenth-century critical context that enables him to describe dialogue as a poetic expression of dialectical discourse.

I. Imitation: Dialogue as Poetry

According to Sigonius, dialogue integrates the arts of poetry, rhetoric, and dialectics. Like poetry, it is an imitation of human actions; like oratory, it employs prose rather than verse. By borrowing the definition of dialogue proposed by Diogenes Laertius in his *Life of Plato* (3.48), Sigonius sees the substance of the genre as disputation. This division into the *verba* of poetic and oratorical forms and into the *res* of dialectics clearly adumbrates Tasso's later definition of dialogue as an "imitazione di ragionamento."[7] But the thoughts enunciated by the respective interlocutors direct attention to the portrayal of character. Argumentation, then, cannot be separated from the representation of personages. And if dialogue is the imitation of human actions that, in turn, reflect the reasonings of fictional interlocutors, Sigonius recognizes a need to defend the genre as a poetic form.

The delineation of characters with varying thoughts and attitudes requires an openness of form that goes beyond technical treatise or demonstrative discourse. For Sigonius, dialogue is not the elaboration of a truth that can be quantified and logically verified. On the other hand, it is not simply the representation of an exchange of words. The articulation of ideas becomes, in this literary kind, the actions of man; for, through a series of questions and answers and of statements and retorts, adversaries

---

of Art or Instrument of Inquiry?" *Zagadnienia Rodzajów Literackich* 20 (1977): 23–35, and John McClelland, "Dialogue et rhétorique à la Renaissance," *Le Dialogue*, ed. Pierre R. Léon and Paul Perron (Ottawa: Didier, 1985), 157–64, study sixteenth-century interpretations of ancient concepts of dialogue.

[7] Tasso, op. cit., 20.

placed in an imaginary setting submit to a conflict that enables them to elicit the probable from the possible and to attain a resolution instructive to the reader. In placing dialogue in a *via media* between the thematics of expository prose and the techniques of direct discourse, Sigonius views dialogue as a hybrid form. Like Aristotle who classifies the mimes of Sophron and Xenarchus and Socratic conversations as a nameless art which is conveyed by words alone (*Poetics* 1447b), Sigonius recognizes the qualities that distinguish dialogue from established poetic forms. But the character portrayal implicit in the definition of dialogue requires Sigonius to rework Aristotle's thoughts. Sigonius, though, does not depart entirely from Aristotelian thought; for, in justifying dialogue as a poetic form, he follows Aristotle's methodology of examining literary kinds through their use of things, means, and manners:

> Res, quas poetae imitando simularent, aut graviorum, aut leviorum hominum, aut qui his interiecti essent, actiones esse invenit; instrumenta, quae ad imitandum afferrent, orationem esse, concentum, et rhythmum; modus ineundae imitationis, cum iidem aut perpetua uterentur narratione, aut quasi agentes inducerent, aut utrumque. (p.30)

The repetition of the word *imitatio* reflects the centrality of mimesis in Sigonius's theory of dialogue. For Sigonius, the imitation of the "actions of men" consists in the copying of words that convey a "serious or light character or a mixture of the two." Plato's three modes of imitation are useful to his theorization: "(1) pure narrative, in which the poet speaks in his own person without imitation, as in the dithyramb; (2) narrative by means of imitation, in which the poet speaks in the person of his characters, as in comedy and tragedy; and (3) mixed narrative, in which the poet speaks now in his own person and now by means of imitation."[8] Obviously, the second and third sorts of discourses conform to Sigonius's conception of the imitation of human actions in dialogic form, and thereby enable him to define dialogue as a genus of poetry.

By defining the speech of men as the object of representation, Sigonius offers guidelines by which the reader-critic may classify a poetic work. History, or the chronicling of events in narrative, would not meet his

[8] Richard McKeon, "Literary Criticism and the Concept of Imitation in Antiquity," in *Critics and Criticism, Ancient and Modern*, ed. R. S. Crane (Chicago: University of Chicago Press, 1952), 151; quoted by K. J. Wilson, *Incomplete Fictions*, op. cit., 7. The classification of these modes of discourse is based upon Plato, *Republic* 392d–394c.

criterion of imitation of the actions of men, and is therefore distinguished from dialogue. Further, the physics of Empedocles and the verses of Lucretius reproduce a picture. But in copying the nature of things, they imitate an object, and their theory of mimesis does not satisfy the requirements of a faithful rendering of the actions of man. Rather, he perceives, through the image, the manners and distinguishing features of the represented person: "ex ea mores, at [ac] perturbationem animi perspicere videaris" (p. 5). The selection of the object of imitation is therefore neither random nor accidental. Instead, both the poet and orator who engage in the creative process direct their attention to the object to be reproduced by words. By identifying with the source, they attain a similitude of speech and embellish it with dignity of words, elegance of style, and copiousness of rhetorical figures. In empathyzing with the origin of speech, the poet or orator captures idiosyncrasies that individualize character. This finding and subsequent copying of distinguishing characteristics disclose the essential and reflect a verbal re-creation of the perceived person.

Dialogue is, according to Sigonius, a form of poetic imitation. Mimesis, he contends, originates with the copying of words. Through use of Plato's description of discourse, and through application of Aristotle's method of classifying genres, Sigonius demonstrates that the selection and expression of speech distinguish poetic genres from expository writings. Philosophical topics inform the subject matter of dialogue. The recording of human speech, though, reflects the actions of man, and thereby differentiates dialogue from the matter-of-fact form of demonstrative discourse. The categorization of dialogue as a genus of poetry satisfies definition but raises questions of form. Sigonius turns attention to the means whereby writers convert abstract precept into concrete techniques that elucidate the actions (or speech) of men.

II. Characterization: Dialogue and the Resources of Rhetoric

The rhetorical precepts of verisimilitude and decorum serve as principles in elucidating the actions (or thoughts) of men. Although dialogue is a poetic form, the adversarial roles of the interlocutors suggest a conflict of ideas that results in instruction. Ultimately, the validity of thought depends upon the logic of exposition and the knowledge of topic; and Sigonius later describes the place of dialectics in the didactic purpose. But the acquisition of knowledge implies a predisposition to accept the concepts being proposed and explained. Like the orator, then, the writer of dialogue must draw upon rhetorical techniques of persuasion. Thus, the dialogist confronts the contradiction between the reality of ideas that is the substance of debate and the illusion of expression that characterizes personage and setting. In attempting to bridge this irreconcilability, Sigonius acknowledges the importance of verisimilitude and decorum as the means to create a semblance of truth that, in turn, enhances credibility.[9]

As we recall, the writer of dialogue employs prose rather than verse. The use of prose links dialogue with oratory; and it also reflects the customary speech of men, thereby confirming the application of verisimilitude to the writing of this genre. In presenting arguments that lead to probable conclusions, the dialogist recognizes the need to create a semblance of truth that induces belief. The framework of imaginative scenes and scripts impedes credibility, but the techniques associated with verisimilitude enable the writer to fabricate a framework compatible with reality: "hoc autem poeticum eius est potestatis, atque naturae, ut cum adest, efficiat, ne res, ut est ficta, sic videatur" (p. 58). The precept of verisimilitude is associated with the notion of decorum, or appropriateness of character portrayal. Like Cicero, in his *Orator* (21.71), Sigonius sees the importance of drawing upon the thoughts, speech, and mannerisms suitable to the respective interlocutor.

Sigonius relates Cicero's principles of propriety to the writing of dialogue. For Cicero, the rhetor keeps in mind thought and language appropriate to the speaker and credible to the audience.[10] The "thought" to which Cicero refers becomes for Sigonius action and temperament. By identifying thought with action, Sigonius reinforces the mimetic nature of dialogue and, at the same time, describes his ideas of character portrayal. His emphasis on the deeds and nature of character recalls Aristotle's words on appropriateness in his *Rhetoric* (3.7), which calls for the use of style corresponding to the emotion and character of its subject. If man acts according to his situation, then the language of anger must be used to express outrage, and words of disgust suitably convey impiety or

---

[9] For an examination of the concept and uses of decorum theorized by sixteenth-century critics, see especially Vernon Hall, *Renaissance Literary Criticism: A Study of Its Social Content* (New York: Columbia University Press, 1945); Weinberg, op. cit.; and Baxter Hathaway, *The Age of Criticism: The Late Renaissance in Italy* (Ithaca: Cornell University Press, 1962), 115, 131–35, 152, 233.

[10] "Est autem quid deceat oratori videndum non in sententiis solum sed etiam in verbis" (*Orator* 21.71).

foulness. Characters, moreover, should conform to actual personages; and, by drawing on the thought and temperaments of real individuals, the writer incorporates individual characteristics into an illusion of truth. Plato, he continues, violates this precept; for, as we learn from Athenaeus, the elder Parmenides is far removed in age from the younger Socrates. Cicero, on the other hand, selects Cato who, renowned for his oratorical skills, expresses the subtlety of arguments as if he were alive and present. Characters must assume the roles of confirming, teaching, refuting, and listening, and thereby represent a particular stance. But Sigonius stresses that the writer's use of language goes beyond speech. The setting must also complement the fictitious illusion. October 16th, for example, establishes a specific time for Cicero's depiction of debate in his *Tusculan Disputations*. And if discussion touches upon literature or philosophy, an estate or rustic surroundings away from the distractions of work contribute to an expression of the verisimilar.

III. Substance: Dialogue and Dialectics

Sigonius designates dialectical discourse as the subject matter of dialogue. Accordingly, the structure of dialogue is bipartite: (1) a prologue serves as an introduction; (2) the debate, like the narrative of a poem, contains the substance of the work that examines the veracity of a thesis. The initial statement defined in the prologue begins an orderly progression that leads to a reasonable conclusion of the disputation. Sigonius, though, continues to emphasize the importance of rhetorical tropes and techniques. In the prologue, the reader must be informed of the proposition to be discussed; but, like the orator attempting to capture the listener's attention, the dialogist softens the intellectual with the mundane. In Cicero's *De divinatione*, for example, an interlocutor asks a question in a restrained way, whereas the history of rhetoric recounted in the *Brutus* begins indirectly through a discussion of an unpaid literary debt. In each case, however, the initial statement is expressed and elaborated through the employment of *sententiae* and a description of customs.

The reference to the depiction of everyday happenings recalls the remarks on decorum and verisimilitude. But Sigonius relates the word *sententia* to Aristotle's use of the term *dianoia*, which affords an opportunity to interrelate rhetorical and dialectical aspects of the dialogue. Like Aristotle who sees rhetoric as the counterpart of dialectics (*Rhetoric* 1.1), Sigonius insists on the role of argumentation as the substance of a poetic genre that includes the resources of the orator. In criticizing previous arts of rhetoric that appeal primarily to emotions, Aristotle argues for argumentative modes which result in the affirmation or refutation of thought or in the demonstration of universal ideas. Syllogism and enthymeme are the means to confirm a thought, and they become for Sigonius tools of the dialogist. The three types of arguments defined by Aristotle represent, according to Sigonius, the modes of exposition that the writer of dialogue is to employ. But the dialogist must adhere to the principles of decorum, and the interlocutors propose arguments appropriate to their respective professions. Philosophers, he notes, profess scientific knowledge based upon demonstration, and dialecticians deal with generally accepted opinions. Whereas philosophers treat of self-contained, eternal truths, dialecticians examine probable premisses which, as starting points, result in an understanding of principle or a definition of elements. Sophists participate in contentious arguments, seeking victory on premisses that appear generally accepted but, in reality, are misleading.

Theoretically, all three sorts of disputants may express their arguments in dialogic form. Earlier, Sigonius accepted Laertius's definition of dialogue as a "discourse consisting of questions and answers on some philosophical or political subject" (*Life of Plato* 3.48). In shaping subject matter to a suitable structure, Laertius defines two sorts of dialogues: *expositio*, or instructive discourse; *inquisitio*, or dialectical discussion. Similarly, Sigonius appropriates the subject matter of dialogue to instruction or examination, and its structure must therefore conform to these purposes. But Aristotle, in his *Sophistical Refutations* (165 a38–b11), designates four sorts of discourse used in dialogue: didactic, dialectic, examination-arguments, and contentious arguments. Thus, Sigonius must accommodate Aristotle's analyses of argumentation to Laertius's thoughts on dialogic structure. According to Sigonius, sophistical or contentious arguments are inappropriate to the genre; and he compresses the other modes of argumentation to Laertius's *expositio* (instructive demonstration) and *inquisitio* (dialectic discussion and examination-arguments).

Expositio, as Sigonius terms the demonstrative dialogue, is adapted to the purpose of instruction. After the postulation of the topic, the interlocutors examine the existence, nature, causes, and consequences of the subject under discussion. A thesis, or principle, emerges from the initial proposition; and, as debate ensues, interlocutors express opinions. At the end of the discussion, though, the varying thoughts return to the initial principle, thereby instructing the reader or listener in the ramifications of the subject which has been demonstrated through analysis and synthesis. Sigonius does not limit demonstrative debate to particular topics; and, like Laertius, he views such thematically diverse dialogues as Plato's *Timaeus*,

Phaedrus, and *Laws* as representative of instructive argument.

Whereas *expositio* represents a means to exhort or advise through use of discussion, *inquisitio* reflects a use of the Socratic method which leads to match-winning or truth-hunting. Sigonius defines two sorts of dialogue that belong to this later classification: (1) *obstetricus*, or the *maieutic*, or art-of-the-midwife, dialogue; (2) *tentativus*, or *peirastic*, debates that Aristotle had termed as examination-arguments. In describing the *maieutic*, or midwife sort, Sigonius relies upon Plato's definition of the Socratic method in *Theaetetus* (150b–151a). Similar to the midwife sterile in body, Socrates is lacking in wisdom and, through a series of questions, draws forth knowledge. Unlike the interlocutor in the *expositio*, Socrates does not propose any statement. Rather, through the use of inquiry, he enables his respondents to advance from ignorance and misconceptions to a discovery of "many fair things" within themselves. Thus, Socrates does not instruct; and, by employing a negative approach that drives the respondent to self-contradiction or to a concession of ignorance, he enables the interlocutor to recognize his confused conception and ignorant thoughts. Sigonius provides two reasons for Socrates's use of *maieutic* approach: refutation of sophistic learning; training of minds in a method resulting in valid opinions. The use of elenchus compels the respondent to deny a position and, for Plato, represents a method that trains minds in the art of argumentation. Sigonius, though, sees a greater application of this approach, for such inquiry, he notes, restores an understanding of knowledge.

Although Sigonius views the *tentativus*, or examination-argument, as a form of inquiry, this sort of dialogue also shares characteristics of *expositio*. In describing this type of discourse, Sigonius relies upon a speech by Hippias in Plato's *Protagoras* (337e–338a). A discussion of topics that may lead to wisdom requires seriousness of purpose and dignity of speech. Socrates, Hippias says, should not confine his words to extreme brevity, and Protagoras should avoid excessive eloquence. Hippias does not prescribe the techniques of such a middle course. But Sigonius continues to see the value of numerous sharp questions which, characteristic of *maieutic* debate, serve as an effective instrument in combating sophistry. The *maieutic* method, though, could also be employed in contentious or sophistical contests. In countering such misapplication, Sigonius emphasizes the didactic purpose of dialogue; and he contends that, through the inclusion of demonstrative discourse characteristic of *expositio*, the practitioner of examination-arguments assists the reader in his search for truth.

Form accompanies substance. With Sigonius's stress upon the poetic and rhetorical characteristics of dialogue, his comments on the style of dialogue reinforce the artistic aspects of the genre. Dialogues consist of two possible patterns. In open style that records an interchange between teacher and student, the student, or *discipulus*, asks a question to which the teacher or *magister*, responds fully and accurately. Examples of this sort include Plato's *Laws* and Cicero's *Brutus*. Demonstrative argument can be adapted to this structure; and, although the presentation of ideas often takes precedence over characterization, the use of collateral circumstances, similarities, oppositions, and contradictions enable the writer to fulfill the expectations of decorum and verisimilitude. Unlike the openness of the *magister-discipulus* form, the closed style emphasizes disputation and a concision of diction that may seem to obscure the truth sought by the interlocutors. Both forms, though, have defects. Dialogue is not a treatise; and, if a writer indulges in long explanations on mathematics, he must add touches of brilliance through a description of characters and customs. And if dialogue intends to refine intellectual insights, argumentation must be dulled through techniques of pleasantness as prescribed by Hermogenes. Comedy results from ridiculous and amorous characters, and tragedy depicts the fall of admirable personages. Analogously, dialogue describes a harmony of contentions that results in keener souls.

IV. Conclusion

Like all Renaissance genres, dialogue eludes precise and rigid definition. But as we have seen, Sigonius offers a description based upon an analysis of ancient comments and a reading of classical models. In theory, any definition implies exclusionism; but, in practice, especially with dialogue, description requires inclusionism. Sigonius was certainly aware of the numerous arts of disputation that sixteenth-century humanists had inherited from their medieval forebears. Rudolph Agricola, in his *De inventione dialectica* (1534), associates dialectics with dialogue; Johannes Sturm, in his *Partitionum dialecticarum libri* (1539), devotes one of four books of this dialectical treatise to dialogue; and Melanchthon, in his *De elementis rhetoricis* (1542), views Cicero's art of disputation as a use of dialectics embellished by the techniques of rhetoric.[11] By 1550, then, dialogue could be viewed as a mixture of forms. If we may use Zeno's metaphor, it combines aspects both of the "literature of the fist," or the philosophical argument, and of the "literature of the palm," or rhetorical composition.[12] In assimilating Aristotle's forms of reasoning with the precepts of

[11] Armstrong, op. cit., 37–40.

[12] W. S. Howell, *Logic and Rhetoric in England, 1500–1700* (Princeton: Princeton

decorum, Sigonius integrates the methods of argumentation with the stylistic techniques of rhetoric. But dialogue was also a poetic form; and, although the dialogist does not center attention on narrative, his use of mimesis, or imaginative imitation of the words of man, qualifies him nevertheless to assume the place of poet. As Jessenius notes (A2r°–v°), Sigonius was the first to formulate a definition of dialogue which permitted the refinements and expansions by Speroni and Tasso.[13] In spite of these later revisions, Sigonius establishes the expectation of a genre which humanists could shape to the contours of themes and thoughts. The dialogue, then, was no longer solely characterized by the cut-and-thrust of dialectical discourse used in the learning of scholastic philosophy or in the training of disputation. As we have seen, Sigonius unites, and even expands the limits of, the literatures of fist and palm, and thereby theorizes a more inclusive genre reflecting the argumentation of philosopher and the artistry of poet and orator.[14]

Ball State University, Indiana

Univ. Press, 1956), 14–15, studies the Renaissance reception of this metaphor which, formulated by Zeno of Citium, was interpreted by Cicero (*Orator* 32.113 and *De Finibus* 2.6.17), Quintilian (*Institutio oratoria* 2.20.7), and Sextus Empiricus (*Adversus Mathematicos* 2.7).

[13] Sperone Speroni, in his *Apologia dei dialogi*, defended his use of dialogue before the Inquisitors in Rome, subsequently published in his *Opere*, 5 vols. (Venice: Domenico Occhi, 1740), 1:266–452.

[14] Jon R. Snyder, *Writing the Scene of Speaking: Theories of Dialogue in the Late Italian Renaissance* (Stanford: Stanford University Press, 1989), chap. 2, has recently commented on Sigonius's theory of dialogue. Since his study appeared after the preparation of my work, I could not unfortunately take his views into account. However, as he describes Sigonius's adaptation of ancient precepts to an individual, innovative concept of dialogue, my analysis of Sigonius's investigation into, and reconstruction of, an ancient theory of the genre complements Snyder's approach.

Scaliger, Vinet, and the Text of Ausonius

ROGER GREEN

The *editio princeps* of Ausonius, who was a popular poet in the Renaissance, appeared in 1472, and the following fifty years saw his corpus gradually augmented, interpreted, and made available to a wide readership. The next fifty years, broadly speaking, belong in particular to textual critics.[1] This paper will investigate an episode of Ausonian scholarship in the sixteenth century which has become highly controversial in the twentieth.

A year or so before 1558 Stephanus Charpinus (Étienne Charpin) discovered near Lyons the manuscript now at Leyden as *Voss. Lat.* F 111. (Or rather rediscovered, since it was known to Sannazaro early in the sixteenth century, but all he did was transcribe a very small part of it, and very few were aware of even that much[2]). In 1558 Charpinus published a new edition of Ausonius at Lyons which incorporated this new material and in which he said, quite correctly, that he had greatly added to the text of Ausonius. The new material naturally attracted many other scholars, including Willem Canter, Pierre Pithou, Theodore Poelmann and Adrianus Turnebus, and in particular the subjects of this paper, Élie Vinet, who had already produced an edition of Ausonius in 1551, and Joseph Scaliger, who when the discovery had been made was still in his teens.

Both Vinet and Scaliger are rightly regarded by modern editors as major contributors to the text of Ausonius: between them they provide

---

[1] See my earlier paper, "Ausonius in the Renaissance," in *Acta Conventus Neo-Latini Sanctandreani*, ed. I. D. McFarlane. Medieval & Renaissance Texts & Studies, vol. 38 (Binghamton, NY, 1986), 579–86.

[2] See now C. Vecce, *Iacopo Sannazaro in Francia* (Padua: Editore Antenore, 1988), 70-83.

some 300 useful emendations. In about forty-five cases the attribution of emendations to one or the other has proved controversial. Editors by and large give Scaliger the credit for these, but Vinet was vigorously championed by the French scholar Henri de la Ville de Mirmont,[3] who is followed at a cautious distance by Anthony Grafton in his recent biography of Scaliger.[4] More about de la Ville de Mirmont (henceforth "Mirmont") in a moment, but first let me present a few facts about the case. Scaliger worked on the text of Ausonius during the summer of 1573; he published his *Ausonianae Lectiones* in 1574 and a text in 1575. Both were printed at Lyons by Antoine Greyff.[5] Vinet began his second edition in about 1562, and sent it to Greyff at the latter's request in 1567 or 1568. It was never printed there, but appeared at Bordeaux, coming from the new press of Simon Millanges first in a very small edition in 1575 and then together with a large commentary in 1580.[6] Scaliger was thus the first into print: his *Ausonianae Lectiones* preceded Vinet's text by about a year, and his text, which did not in fact incorporate all his emendations, preceded it by a month or so. So it seems that editors are right to attach Scaliger's name to the disputed emendations, unless there is good evidence that Vinet made them first. Mirmont thought there *was* good evidence, so I now turn back to him.

The fact that such a valuable manuscript of Ausonius should have ended up at Leyden seemed strange and rather irksome to French scholars of the late nineteenth century. One of them, Reinhold Dezeimeris, hoped to get it back, but was unsuccessful.[7] As a *pis aller* a facsimile of it was produced under the direction of Mirmont. Not content with that, Mirmont added an introductory volume and two volumes of detailed commentary in which he assembled all the emendations known to him of the text of the manuscript. His second aim, as a bitter preface makes clear, was to rescue Vinet from the dishonour placed on him by Scaliger

---

[3] H. de la Ville de Mirmont, *Le Manuscrit de l'Ile Barbe* (Bordeaux and Paris, 1917), 1:165–200.

[4] A. Grafton, *Joseph Scaliger: A Study in the History of Classical Scholarship*, vol. 1: *Textual Criticism and Exegesis* (Oxford: Clarendon Press, 1983), 129.

[5] See L. Desgraves, "Ausone Humaniste Aquitain," *Revue Francaise d'Histoire du Livre* 46 (1985), 199 f.

[6] Desgraves, 199 f. and 202–4.

[7] R. Dezeimeris, *Actes de l'Académie nationale des Sciences, Belles-Lettres et Arts de Bordeaux* 41 (1879), 317–26; subsequently published elsewhere (see Mirmont, Pref. VII).

and by recent editors.[8] In the introduction he gives a short biography of Vinet and an account of his relations with Scaliger, using uncompromising language in which everything is very much black and white. Vinet is the modest hero inspired by the pious quatrain on Phoebus-born Ausonius placed on the Collège de Guyenne in 1543[9] but subsequently distracted by all sorts of other matters; Scaliger on the other hand is a vain, dogmatic, and mendacious tyrant. According to Mirmont the young Scaliger misappropriated the results of Vinet's work and passed some things off as his own, and later, after Vinet's death in 1587, further turned the knife by accusing Vinet of plagiarism.[10]

Before we descend further into melodrama, let us consider the available evidence. This consists of the emendations themselves, which I will consider shortly, and the prefaces, which I will deal with first. Several letters in fact passed between the two men, but only one remains, the one dated 29 August 1573; this was printed as a preface to Scaliger's *Ausonianae Lectiones*.[11] Vinet's view of these matters is given in the preface to his commentary of 1580.[12] Vinet says that his work progressed in the following way. After seeing the edition of 1558 he expressed his views with due politeness to its careless editor, Charpinus. It was several years later (probably 1564) when he first saw the manuscript, which Cujas, who owned it, had lent to Turnebus. Vinet made various emendations to the text and sent his version to Greyff at Lyons at the printer's request. (The date of this can be deduced as either 1567 or 1568, probably the former.) Nothing happened, at least in Lyons. Sometime after that (the date is not known) some emendations made by Vinet were revealed to Scaliger by one Jacobus Salomo, and at least one of them was warmly praised by Scaliger. In 1572 Vinet wrote to Scaliger, who was now in the vicinity of Lyons, to ask him to give Greyff a prod and try to speed things up; he wrote two letters in fact, and received two replies. Scaliger gave his help, but actually did more than he had promised, producing the edition and commentary already mentioned. Vinet withdrew his text and had it printed by Millanges at Bordeaux as quickly as a severe shortage of paper allowed.

---

[8] Mirmont, Pref. XI.

[9] Mirmont, 1:8.

[10] Mirmont, 1:198.

[11] pp. 3–6. Also in L. Desgraves, *Elie Vinet, Humaniste de Bordeaux 1509–1587*, Travaux d'Humanisme et Renaissance 156 (Geneva: Droz, 1977), 136–37.

[12] Fol. aa 2–3.

Nowhere in all this narrative does Vinet complain about Scaliger or anyone else. The only place where one might detect recrimination is in the statement "but Scaliger thought he should do more than he promised." He even speaks of Scaliger's *benevolentia*; he calls Salomo, the intermediary, *benevolus et doctus*, and does not as one might expect curse or even censure the printer for procrastination. It might even seem as if Vinet did not greatly object to the delay; he was always a man with, so to speak, a very long fuse. Conceivably the printer was holding out for a commentary to accompany the text; if so, he was not the first of Vinet's printers to be disappointed in him.

Now for Scaliger's letter. What does the suspect have to say for himself? He gives an account of his dealings with Greyff, which (in modern jargon) were reactive rather than proactive. He states that he put the works of Ausonius in a new order: this is quite correct. He says that he noted changes that others had made to the text in the previous fifty years, and identified the authors of these changes: this is partly true, but it must be said that acknowledging predecessors was never Scaliger's strongest suit. Scaliger writes in a flamboyant style, whereas Vinet's was sober; but the only place where one is tempted to suspect his sincerity is where Scaliger says that if *he* were to attempt a commentary he would only be gleaning where Vinet had harvested. Finally Scaliger launches into an interesting though irrelevant defence of Ausonius, Bordeaux, and the Collège de Guyenne against the cultural snobbery of Paris and the Gallic nobility.

To Mirmont all this is a smoke screen. He denounces Scaliger as "ce grand travailleur vaniteux et plat, impudent et hypocrite."[13] Grafton does not go over the top, but speaks of Scaliger's "considerable effrontery" in dedicating it to Vinet.[14] However strongly we may feel that Scaliger had in some way stolen a march on Vinet, it is important to keep things in proportion. Scaliger's work contained about 250 emendations, of which not more than fifty can have been taken from Vinet. At the same time it would be wrong to suggest that Vinet was an indifferent scholar. He too made many useful emendations, some better than Scaliger's. But one cannot deny Scaliger's greater fecundity, as Mirmont does, or the generally higher quality of his emendations, as Mirmont might have done if he had been able to recognize it.

We must now turn to the readings themselves. In writing my own text and commentary on Ausonius I naturally noted all emendations worthy of

[13] Mirmont, 1:175.

[14] Grafton, 129.

consideration, and came up with these forty-five of disputed origin. Since Vinet and Scaliger were working on an almost virgin text, it is only to be expected that some of the manuscript's errors would receive their obvious resolutions from both critics. Many of the emendations they share are trivial, the sort of thing that any competent Latinist could provide immediately: about a third fall into this category. About half of the emendations fall into a further category of "easy," the sort of thing that a competent Latinist could provide fairly quickly. It is of course sometimes easy to spot a mistake but much harder to see a satisfactory correction; and it is also easy, with hindsight, to underestimate the difficulty of spotting an error, except where a violation of metre is concerned. But if anything I have been conservative in my assessment of these emendations.

That leaves half a dozen emendations common to both scholars. They are: *Protrept.* 51 *ecquando* for various readings of VPHZ; *Par.* 4:25 *flesti* for *fletu* (V); *Par.* 13:8 *sauciis* for *sociis* (V); *Prof.* 21:27 *deceret* for *doceret* (V); *Ecl.* 13:3 *dicat alta* for *dicata* (V); *Mos.* 438 *Vivisca* for *vivifica* of all manuscripts. These are not in any way exceptional, though in some cases it must be said that additional corruption complicates the matter. They are good but not brilliant. The best of them is *Vivisca* in *Mos.* 438. The word *vivifica* makes a sort of sense—early scholars accepted and attempted to explain things much worse—and is grammatically and metrically acceptable. But the word *Vivisca*, which is certainly right, is commended on literary, palaeographical and topographical grounds. Not many of us, I suppose, carry in our heads the knowledge that Bordeaux was the capital of the Bituriges Vivisci; but Scaliger and Vinet were not only local men, they were also keen antiquarians, and so either of them might have divined this correction. We happen to know in this one case (from Vinet, not Scaliger) that Vinet thought of it first, but if we did not, then we might fairly conclude that both men had arrived at it independently.

The purpose of this brief analysis has not been to evaluate the work of Scaliger and Vinet on the text but to try to facilitate the attribution of the disputed emendations. I cannot say that there are any of such brilliance that they compel the conclusion that they could not have been made independently. It would be quite easy to believe that most of them did occur independently to both scholars. And it does not seem possible to assert that some of them bear the characteristic imprint of one or the other—as one might venture in the case of certain other scholars, such as Heinsius, the third great benefactor of the text of Ausonius.

The problem remains therefore, and a solution must be given on the basis of the circumstantial evidence. It seems very likely that Scaliger saw some or perhaps all of Vinet's emendations and then used them more or less consciously in his own edition; it may well have been the sight of Vinet's text that spurred him to turn his attention to Ausonius. To believe the reverse of this, that Vinet took them from Scaliger, would be very difficult. The problem would be not that Vinet always acknowledges his sources, as frequently declared by Mirmont; there is no clear evidence to the contrary, but his claim can only be checked in about three cases. It would be that it is virtually incredible that the much slower Vinet should have suddenly galvanised himself into action or thrown aside his distractions, and taken over what Scaliger had just published. And why restrict himself to such a small proportion?

If nothing else, I hope that my analysis has shown that the whole affair is in fact a storm in a teacup. I do not mean that the matter of principle thought to be involved is a trivial one: the misappropriation of another scholar's work is rightly regarded as a serious matter. I mean that the emendations concerned were not such as to be worth fighting over. It is clear that Mirmont greatly exaggerated the situation, influenced no doubt by the stressful times in which he lived. So did a recent reviewer of Grafton who, though underestimating the amount of common material, wrongly described Grafton's charge against Scaliger as one of "conscious theft."[15] The episode that we have just examined is a classic case of much heat and no light. If modern scholars had looked at the problem with the same dispassionate consideration that Scaliger and Vinet seem to have used, this unnecessary controversy might never have arisen.

St. Andrews

[15] H. D. Jocelyn, in *Liverpool Classical Monthly*, vol. 9, no. 4 (April 1984), 129–30.

Allegory, Rhetoric and Spirituality: Erasmus's Early Psalm Commentaries[1]

M. J. HEATH

Erasmus never found the time to write a complete commentary on the book of Psalms.[2] It is not clear from his writings on the first four psalms what form it would have taken, but they do tell us something about the method of exegesis he might have chosen.

Of course, he knew all about the traditional theory of the "four senses of scripture," the literal, allegorical, moral, and anagogic,[3] to which he alludes in the commentary on Psalm 2: "In many psalms the theme is twofold: the historical, which underlies it like the foundations of a building, and the allegorical or anagogical which, beneath the cloak of historical events, conceals, or rather reveals, the gospel story, or instruction in true piety, or an image of eternal bliss." He illustrates this scheme with a conventional exposition of the story of David and Goliath [201D–F]. However, he was often rude about the traditional theory, which he associated with the despised schoolmen and found too constricting.[4] In his

---

[1] Numerical references in the text [in square brackets] are to vol. 5 of the Le Clerc edition of Erasmus, *Opera omnia* (Leiden, 1703–6 [LB]); the translations of this material are my own.

[2] It crossed his mind more than once to do so: see the end of Psalm 2 (LB 5 213C) and the dedicatory epistles to Psalms 3 and 4 (Epp 1427 and 1535).

[3] On the tradition, see H. de Lubac, *Exégèse médiévale: les quatre sens de l'Ecriture* (Paris, 1959–64) and, for a slightly different account from mine of Erasmus's adaptation of it, G. Chantraine, "Erasme, lecteur des psaumes," *Colloquia Erasmiana Turoniensia* (Paris, 1972), 2:691–712.

[4] See for example passages in the *Moria*, in *The Collected Works of Erasmus* (Toron-

exposition of the First Psalm [182E] he complains about certain theologians "with unwashed hands and feet" who, when they get their dirty hands on holy scripture, will always force it, however reluctant and unwilling it may be, into the prescribed mould. Erasmus's own flexible twofold division, into literal and concealed meaning, removes the obligation to find all four senses in any given passage.

Of these two, Erasmus usually has little time for the literal or historical sense; he reminds us of Paul's dictum about the "letter which kills" [2 Cor. 3:6. cf. 220D] and dismisses the "contentious and unprofitable speculations" [243D] of the rabbis, who all disagree with one another about the historical details:

> I do not disapprove entirely of looking at what the Hebrew commentators have to say, especially the older ones, but I do not think that they have very much to offer, seeing that their commentaries are pretty much stuffed with vapourings and old wives' tales–not to mention their desire to discredit *our* interpretations, and their hatred of Christ. [202C]

So Erasmus concentrates on the concealed meaning. In the *De copia,* he identified no less than five loose categories which reflect but do not coincide with the traditional scheme of exegesis:

> Whenever we are endeavouring to turn men towards piety or away from wickedness, we shall find very useful anecdotes drawn from the Old or the New Testament. The hidden meaning of these can be variously handled; it can be explained in terms of human life, or of the body of the Church joined and connected to Christ the head, or of the fellowship of heaven, or of those early days when the faith was newborn, or of our own times. [CWE 24, 635]

Or–almost anything! In fact, Erasmus usually has little to say on the most abstract of these categories, the anagogic or eschatological: on Psalms 1 and 2, for example, he says no more than a few words on their possible application to the Day of Judgment [196C–D and 225E]. He expounds the First Psalm "Blessed the man" / *Beatus vir* "above all according to the tropological sense," he says;[5] this preoccupation with ethics reflects the period in which the exposition was written, as it often echoes the long adages published in the same year, 1515, and above all the *Institutio*

---

to, 1969–[CWE]), 27:134 and the *Ecclesiastes* in LB 5 1035A.

[5] "Iuxta tropologiam potissimum"; this is part of the subtitle in the early editions.

principis christiani. The final passage underlines Erasmus's relative unconcern here with the allegorical or religious lesson:

> If we wish to be called blessed [like the man in the psalm] let us ensure that it is not only in our prayers and devotions, but also in our lives and deeds, that we reflect the only source of bliss, Jesus Christ. [198B]

On the other hand, the commentary on the Second Psalm, "Why did the nations rage?"/ *Quare fremuerunt gentes* appeared seven years later, in the midst of doctrinal controversies, and is thus dominated by the religious lesson: Erasmus's analysis of what is obviously a prophecy concerning the Messiah proves (in exhaustive detail) that the psalm foretells the whole story of the redemption of mankind; it revolves around the characteristic Erasmian antithesis between the folly of the Cross and the wisdom of the world. The brief paraphrase on the Third Psalm (1524) embodies a new point of view, as Erasmus himself adopts the persona of the psalmist and addresses the Lord directly; he makes a parallel exegesis by applying the story of Absalom's revolt to the persecution both of Christ and of modern Christians. This is clearly an example of one of the modes of exegesis proposed in *De copia*, dealing with "the body of the Church joined and connected to Christ the head." Finally, the *concio* on the Fourth Psalm (1525), the longest of these pieces, also contains a dual exegesis: first the psalmist's words are attributed to Christ on the cross, though in this case Erasmus emphasizes less the folly of the cross than its redemptive and consolatory functions, and Christ's promises are applied to the church in general; secondly Erasmus descends to the individual plane and addresses a homily (*concio*) to his contemporaries:

> Therefore I would request that those of you who have nodded off should rouse yourselves, and those who are still awake should pay even closer attention. [361 B]

Interestingly, this sermon is the least eloquent, the most terse in style, of all these commentaries, almost as if Erasmus were repenting of his earlier verbosity and constraining his rhetoric to make his style "more conducive," as he put it, "to that reform of morality which is my principal aim."[6]

It is obvious from this brief summary of the commentaries that Erasmus treated each psalm somewhat differently, adopting the style and level of

---

[6] This quotation is from the exposition of the first psalm (LB 5 174B); in the final section on Psalm 4, Erasmus is apparently returning to this initial purpose.

exegesis which the material, and his own current preoccupations, seemed to warrant. But what literary criteria did he use to arrive at a general estimate of the psalmist's meaning? Erasmus seems to have regarded oratory as more useful, indeed more salutary, than dialectic in the exposition of theology,[7] and in the commentary on the First Psalm he discusses the preacher's choice of language, which should aim to produce a lasting impression on the audience, even at the expense of precision: "some words are more impressive than others, some more meaningful, some more impassioned, some more pleasant; very important to the preacher is a knowledge of the rhetorical figures"[190D].[8] The vital thing is to avoid the brain-numbing dullness of the Scotists.

In fact Erasmus the satirist and dialogist is well attuned to the dramatic style of the Psalms and takes delight in analysing their rhetorical twists and turns. He identifies antithesis as the basic figure in the Psalms, in which admonition to the wicked alternates with consolation to the faithful, but he also comments on the psalmist's exploitation of such figures as periphrasis, anaphora, synecdoche, hypallage, and metonymy.[9] Above all, Erasmus the literary critic appreciates the metaphorical qualities of the Psalms, and defends stoutly what some commentators had seen as a frivolous and unbecoming usage. He is well aware, for example, that the divine nature is changeless and unmoving, but accepts that the frequent attribution of human characteristics to God in the psalms was a means of increasing understanding: God's wrath and laughter in the Second Psalm, for example, convey most vividly the effect on us of his vengeance, and his capacity for irony, for instance in frustrating the Jews' elaborate plots against Christ [212E, 216E–F and cf. 256F]. At one point he criticises St. Hilary, who objected austerely to metaphorical utterances about Christ, such as the First Psalm's description of him as a tree [173D–F and cf. 185A]; Erasmus's pedagogy had always stressed the usefulness of vivid and lifelike imagery. In expounding the typology of the Psalms, Erasmus also exploits the fact that the range of Hebrew metaphor is very limited, mostly to

---

7 See Marjorie O'Rourke Boyle, *Erasmus on Language and Method in Theology* (Toronto, 1977), 55 and 63 ff.; this subject was discussed at the Toronto congress in the seminar on Erasmus and literary criticism (papers by Erika Rummel, Laurel Carrington, and Robert D. Sider) and in the paper by Dominic Baker-Smith.

8 At this point Erasmus quotes an ornate example taken from a hymn by Notker Balbulus: see *Notkeri poetae liber ymnorum*, ed. W. von den Steinen (Berne and Munich, 1960), 78; I am grateful to Clarence Miller for identifying its source.

9 See LB 5 194 and 205C for general comments on the rhetorical structure and, for individual figures, 184C, 191B, 199D, 204E, 216E, 265F and 268A.

natural phenomena, and thus it is not difficult to find resonances and reverberations throughout holy writ: in this case, the tree in Psalm 1 reminds him of so many others, from the tree in Eden to the tree by the waters in the Apocalypse; most importantly for Erasmus's Christology, the list includes the vine and its branches, and the cross [185A–F]. Christ's own unpretentious use of metaphor does nothing to impair Erasmus's case [cf. 183E]. His own commentaries are often inspired by the Psalms' welcome directness and vividness of style; as well as adding metaphors of his own, for example on the arboreal theme [196C], he includes passages of well-paced dialogue or invective [e.g., 197A and 205E] and compelling visual images, such as that of the prophet in his watch-tower halfway between heaven and earth [261B].

One oddity about Erasmus's literary appreciation of the Psalms is of course his ignorance of Hebrew. To fill the gap he turned to Jerome and, interestingly, to Nicolas of Lyra,[10] for information on the most obscure and controversial readings, but his concern for effect rather than accuracy, shocking to many contemporary theologians, led him to conclude that the Greek and Latin versions provided all the inspiration necessary to the commentator [e.g., 193D]. Discussing the meaning of the word *bar* in Syriac and Hebrew, he makes a less than respectful pun about not "cudgelling our brains with the complexities of these *barbaric* languages" [230D] and later skips merrily away from a Hebrew conundrum with the remark that "no language is more confusing nor more open to misinterpretation and disagreement" [267D]. Modern Hebrew scholars have demonstrated the coherence of the psalms as songs of praise or prophecy in the Jewish tradition, but Erasmus had to gloss over apparent logical lapses:

> It is not essential that every part of a prophecy should fit perfectly into either an historical or an allegorical reading, because often certain elements are included to ensure chronological coherence whilst others, which are out of place in the historical context, compel us to have recourse to allegory. [213D]

Erasmus's cavalier approach to the texts is nowhere clearer than in his comments on a particularly knotty verse of Psalm 4 [v. 2] where the Hebrew, Greek and Latin versions all seem to suggest something different:

---

[10] See LB 5 200E, where Erasmus chides the 14th-century Franciscan for disrespect towards Jerome, but also 202B, an unacknowledged borrowing from Nicolas's *Postilla super psalterium*.

> The large number of different readings here should not surprise anyone. There can be no doubt that what the psalmist wrote, at the behest of the holy spirit, was simple and unambiguous; but God allowed these differences, the work of copyists and translators, to appear in the holy books, so that these extra difficulties would rouse us from our torpor. [274D]

Thus even in this technical linguistic sphere, the main value of the psalms lies in their capacity to inspire; the supreme example is St. Augustine, whose fumbling exposition of Psalm 4, as a novice, may have been utterly wrong, but led him on to greater things [286F].

Although Erasmus the poet, dramatist, and philologist is kept fully occupied by the Psalms, it is striking how Erasmus the classical scholar is almost redundant: his very first comment on Psalm 1 reminds us that we are not dealing with the hymns of Orpheus or Homer [171A], and later he says: "I think it more fitting to expound holy writ in terms of holy writ" [283C], at a point where the "good things" in Psalm 4:6 ["Who will show us these good things?"] would normally lead to a discussion of Aristotle's categories of good things. Only on Psalm 1, written during his "ethical" period, does Erasmus draw on pagan philosophers (but in vaguer terms than in the *Institutio*, for example) and even in this first commentary he repeats his strictures on Aristotle as a theologian [183C], partly as a rebuke to the schoolmen, but especially as a mark of respect for the truest source of wisdom, scripture. As for the other commentaries: there are three classical allusions on Psalm 2,[11] none at all on Psalm 3 and, in a surprisingly anti-syncretic passage on Psalm 4, the most he will grudgingly allow is that "perhaps a few pagan philosophers did conceive some vague notion of God's nature" [246B]; he goes on to rebuke apparently pious pagan poets for not believing what they wrote [249E]. Even when embellishing his style, as always, with his own adages, he is careful here to label them "profane" or "Greek" proverbs, to distinguish them, no doubt, from the biblical books of Proverbs or Wisdom. Thus, although Erasmus did not hesitate to apply to these sacred texts the classical critical principles embodied in *De copia*, in expounding their meaning he found little use for Ancient philosophy or literature.

Neither did he enlist the help of the Jewish commentators, as I mentioned earlier. In fact, a deep vein of contempt for the Jews runs through

[11] All syncretic allusions: to the *Iliad* (213D), to the fable of King Log (220B) and to the myth of Phæton (228F).

these works, accompanied by some uncharitable gloating over their downfall [e.g., 216B–C and 248–49]. The Jews had not welcomed the Messiah precisely because they had interpreted these psalms and other prophecy too literally; the violence of Erasmus's invective against the Hebrew traitors (with their pagan fellow-conspirators) may be explained by his conviction that the truth had lain within their grasp but, in their impiety, they had failed to embrace it; in their blindness, they had failed to see it. It is also likely, though, that Erasmus's scorn here for Judaism and Pharisaism embodies a veiled attack on the Christian formalism which so disgusted him: in these works it is only rarely [e.g., 290D–E]–and cautiously–that he alludes directly to such controversial doctrinal questions. There is no place here for contemporary satire: even an apparently slighting reference to the death of Leo X–"his destination is uncertain" [230F]–can be given a pious gloss: Erasmus will not arrogate to himself God's prerogative of judgment.[12]

The positive function of these commentaries is thus to expound the *philosophia Christi*. If Erasmus exhorts us to approach the portals of these psalms with due awe and reverence [e.g., 171–72], it is especially because each in its different way is a prophecy of Christ, as the Fathers agree. That is why they were of special interest to Erasmus among Old Testament texts, since he viewed Christ as the true centre of all exegesis:[13] "this level of meaning is almost inexhaustible in the Psalms" [232A]. According to Erasmus, Psalm 1 teaches that the remedy against temptation is to meditate upon and imitate Christ, Psalm 2 describes the folly and passion of Christ, Psalm 3 holds him up as the exemplar of perseverance, and Psalm 4 foretells his words upon the cross. Erasmus's desire to be consistent and comprehensive can lead to just the sort of logic-chopping which he despised in his medieval predecessors (though his cause is doubtless better): he admits, for example, that the verse [Ps 2:9] "You shall rule them with an iron rod; you shall break them like a pot of clay" hardly sits comfortably with the mildness and clemency of Christ; he is therefore grateful for Hilary's helpful suggestion that a rod is only a sceptre, an emblem of authority, like the praetor's rod in ancient Rome (in a tight spot, he will accept classical assistance), and that iron is used as a symbol of durability rather than of harshness; he adds from his own stock the

[12] Cf. Ep. 1342, where Erasmus makes this very point, and Ep. 1248, a eulogy of Leo. Erasmus's principal concern is to illustrate the ephemerality of earthly life.

[13] See Boyle (n. 7 above) 88–93; also 70 and 106 on approaching the scriptures with reverence.

notion that the "pot of clay" is one that has not yet been fired in the oven, that the clay is still damp, and that there is thus a chance of rescuing the material, to be reshaped by the heavenly potter [225D–227D]. Erasmus justifies such subtlety on the grounds that his aim is to edify humanity:

> Salvation is not imperilled by a slight departure from the original sense of the scripture, so long as the new reading conforms to piety and truth; even if our interpretation does not entirely fit into its original context, our labours will have been more or less worthwhile if our reading contributes to moral improvement, and fits in with other scriptural texts. [274D]

The exposition of Psalm 1 was Erasmus's first published work of scriptural exegesis, and these four commentaries may be seen in part as an extension of his contemporary work on the New Testament, since what he seeks in them is Old Testament ratification and clarification of the promises in which the Evangelical is to trust. Divinely inspired, the psalms are almost like an extension to the New Testament:

> Despite its extreme brevity, this [first] psalm deals with vital universal themes ... Although it is short, this one psalm [the fourth] would enable us to win salvation, if we understood what we read, and put that understanding into practice. [174B, 291D]

It was still possible in 1525—but only just—to propose "slight departures from the original sense," but it is noticeable that Erasmus's later commentaries on the Psalms were mostly contributions to Reformation controversy, especially the *De puritate, De bello Turcico* and *De Ecclesiae concordia.* But in the first four, at least, Erasmus was inspired by the divine rhetoric of the Holy Spirit to summon *all* Christians to abandon their worldliness and embrace Christ.

King's College London

*Erasmus's Suspicions of Aleander as the Instigator of Alberto Pio**

CHRIS L. HEESAKKERS

It is a well-known fact that Erasmus was easily inclined to consider his writing opponents to be mainly the mouthpieces of numerous anonymous adversaries. The insinuation that an author writes "impulsu," or "instinctu alieno," occurs frequently, not only in the correspondence, but also in the apologetical writings. This holds good for early opponents still fairly politely faced like Dorp, and Lefèvre d'Etaples as well as for deeply despised enemies such as Lee and Stunica.[1] It holds particularly for an adversary such as the Italian nobleman Alberto Pio, Prince of Carpi, the author of the most voluminous attack on Erasmus's oeuvre, covering in twenty-four books the whole field of Christian dogmatical and moral doctrine. It was evident in Erasmus's eyes, that Pio, not a theologian but a destitute landlord and a diplomat by profession, was incapable of composing a wide-ranging work like that. Pio, who as a former legate of the French king spent the last years of his life in Paris, would, according to Erasmus, not have found the time to go through the large corpus of his works and would also have lacked the necessary theological equipment for it. It was his opinion that Pio must have employed the aid of a horde of

---

* For the abbreviated titles of Erasmus's works used in this paper, see the *Opera omnia Desiderii Erasmi Roterodami. Instructions for Editors*, North-Holland, 1986, pp. 42–44 and p. 47.

[1] For this topic, cf. H. J. de Jonge's note to *Apolog. resp. Iac. Lop. Stun.*, *ASD* IX.2. p. 63, ll. 39–40; for Dorp, cf. also Ep. 337, ll. 23–25; and for Lefèvre d'Etaples, cf. *Apolog. ad Fabr. Stap.*, *LB* IX,17C. See also Epp. 998, 1.47 (Latomus) and 1384, 1.67 (Hutten).

monks and theologians, willing to scrutinize severely every line written by their most hated antagonist.[2]

Apart from these anonymous assistants, however, Erasmus assumed one particular and all but nameless instigator to be behind the work of the Italian Sunday theologian. He had connected the name of this presumed instigator with that of Pio from the very beginning, in 1525, of the long lasting polemics. In a later period he even remembered that already in 1520, five years before the polemics started, he had been informed of the hostile activities of an imperial legate, a "Caesaris Orator," in Rome. He only then realized that this legate was no other than the Prince of Carpi, whose later activities were evidently inspired by the very same informer of that time.[3] This informer had been the controversial messenger of the papal bull against Luther at the Diet of Worms, the "diplomatophorus," as Erasmus ironically used to call him in this connection, Jerome Aleander.[4]

Even before the name of Pio occurs in Erasmus's correspondence, his trouble-making conversation in Rome was connected by Erasmus with Aleander. Allen quite naturally identifies the anonymous Italian critic who, in a letter in August 1524, is said to have publicly proclaimed all over Rome that he by far preferred the scholarship of Aleander to that of Erasmus, even in the field of theology,[5] as the Prince of Carpi. In reaction to these rumours, Erasmus decided to approach Aleander directly in writing, to assure him that, far from being jealous, he could only feel honoured to be compared with such a great scholar as his addressee.[6] Even if irony is not lacking in this letter, nevertheless Erasmus seems to a certain extent to be sincere, since a few days before he had written in the same vein to an impartial countryman.[7]

In the next year, 1525, Erasmus appears to know about the identity of

---

[2] In his *Apolog. adv. rhaps. Alb. Pii*, Erasmus repeatedly calls them "variae operae"; other designations are amanuensis, artifex, collector, congestor, delator, famuli, famulitium, pharmacologus, rhapsodus, schediastes, sycophanta, and indefinite indications such as quisquis, monachus aut theologus quispiam, etc.

[3] *Resp. ad ep. Alb. Pii*, *LB* IX, 1099C–D.

[4] As an indication for Aleander the term is found in *Resp. ad ep. Alb. Pii*, *LB* IX, 1105D, 1118B (both in Greek form), 1119B; *Apolog. adv. rhaps. Alb. Pii*, *LB* IX, 1125F; Epp. 2443, 1.319 (Greek); 2565, 1.14.

[5] Cf. Ep. 1479, ll. 130–39.

[6] Cf. Ep. 1482, ll. 56–59.

[7] Cf. Ep. 1479, ll. 131–34.

his Roman critic, now referred to as Pius ille Carpensis.[8] After he had been assured of the amiable personality of this new opponent by one of his Italian correspondents, Celio Calcagnini,[9] he addressed Pio directly and asked for an explanation of his hostile feelings and statements or otherwise a disclaimer to the rumours.[10] Apparently he already took it for granted that Pio was incited by someone else,[11] but it is not clear if he then already presumed Aleander to be the instigator in question. An argument against this supposition would be that Erasmus in a contemporary letter made clear that he still obviously valued his long-standing but precarious friendship with the Italian scholar who had developed into an influential diplomat and prelate.[12] His following letter referring to Pio, however, coupled Pio and Aleander without any reservations as being the leaders of the anti-Erasmian pagan band in Rome: "Romae paganum illud sodalitium iam pridem fremit in me, ducibus, vt ferunt, Aleandro et Alberto quondam Principe Carpensi."[13]

These suspicions of a close collaboration between the two Italians were further strengthened by the fact that Pio's answer to Erasmus's first letter mentioned above arrived in Basel more or less simultaneously with an anonymous pamphlet, entitled *Racha*, the authorship of which Erasmus immediately ascribed to Aleander.[14] He obviously felt so absolutely sure of his ground that he openly denounced Aleander as the author of the *Racha* in a letter to Pope Clement, complaining about "the two booklets, one sent to me by Alberto, Prince of Carpi, and another that circulated in your Holiness's household, without author's name, but for evident stylistic reasons betraying the Bishop of Brindisi, Jerome Aleander, as the author."[15] From now onwards, Erasmus considered the two works, the anonymous *Racha* with its presumed author Aleander, and Pio's *Epistola*

[8] Cf. Ep. 1576, ll. 38–41.

[9] Cf. Ep. 1587, ll. 233–34: "Eo Principe nihil humanius, nihil modestius agnoui."

[10] Ep. 1634, dated 10 October 1525.

[11] Ep. 1634, ll. 4–5, five years later almost repeated verbatim in a letter to Alciati, Ep. 2329, 1.94.

[12] Cf. Ep. 1621, ll. 9–11.

[13] Ep. 1719, ll. 34–36.

[14] Cf. Ep. 1744, ll. 130–34.

[15] Cf. Ep. 1987, ll. 5–8. For Erasmus this identification of the author is an evident fact; cf. such statements as in Epp. 2077, ll. 49–50; 2443, 1.290. In a similar way in 1532 Erasmus was to undauntedly attribute Scaliger's *Oratio*, Paris 1531 (Ep. 2564, 2 n.), to Aleander for reasons of "stilus" and "phrasis"; cf. Epp. 2575, 1. 6; 2581, ll. 1–13; 2613, ll. 43–44.

paraenetica answering Erasmus's letter, as the wings of a diptych depicting him as the cause of all the troubles in the German church. In his letters to others, time and again Alberto Pio and Jerome Aleander appear as twins of one and the same anti-Erasmian breeding.[16]

Erasmus's first letter to Pio in Rome, dated 10 October 1525, was the overture of the long lasting polemics with the Italian prince. Pio spent several months on an answering letter, dated Rome 15 May 1526, many times as long as the one he had received from Erasmus. When Pio had this letter printed four years later, in Paris in 1529, the scene was moved from the Italian to the French capital and the controversy became fully public. Continued until 1532, it would number five more documents of increasing size and grimness.[17] Although Aleander was not mentioned by name in Erasmus's contributions to the controversy, he haunts the background throughout the polemics. In his *Responsio* to Pio's printed letter, Erasmus informed his addressee that in 1520 he had already heard about the hostility of a Roman "Caesaris orator" whom he now understood to be Pio. His informant for this had been the former Papal legate at Worms, that is Aleander, "your most devoted complice," "alter tibi iuratissimus sodalis." Later on in the work Aleander was pointed to as "ille διπλωματοφοροσ, magna pars animae tuae et, vt ego sentio, magna

[16] Cf. Epp. 2029, ll. 50–51; 2042, ll. 16–17; 2077, ll. 51–52; 2371, 1.37; 2375, ll. 79–80; 2565, ll. 18–19. Even in a seemingly neutral context such as the *Ciceronianus*, *ASD* I, 2, pp. 669–70, their names are joined. Cf. also *Apolog. adv. rhaps. Alb. Pii, LB* IX, 1118B: "magna pars animae tuae."

[17] The polemics number six documents: A) 10 Oct. 1525: Erasmus's letter to Pio, Ep. 1634; B) 15 May 1526: Pio's answering letter, reworked and printed in Paris, 7 Jan. 1529, as: *Alberti Pii Carporum comitis illustrissimi ad Erasmi Roterodami expostulationem responsio accurata et paraenetica. Martini Lutheri et asseclarum eius haeresim vesanam magnis argumentis et iustis rationibus confutans*; C) 13 Feb. 1529: Erasmus's *Resp. ad ep. Alb. Pii*, answering doc. B; D) 16 April 1530: Pio's answer to doc. C, 9 March 1531, in Paris published as *Alberti Pii Carporum Comitis illustrissimi et viri longe doctissimi, praeter praefationem et operis conclusionem, tres et viginti libri in locos lucubrationum variarum D. Erasmi Roterodami, quos censet ab eo recognoscendos et retractandos*. The work is preceded by a re-edition of the documents A, B, and C; E) 1531: Erasmus's *Apolog. adv. rhaps. Alb. Pii*, answering doc. D; F) 1532: *In Elenchum Albertii Pij breuissima scholia per eundem Erasmum Roterodamum*, added to Erasmus's *Dilut. Iodocus Clicthov.* (Basel, 1532). There were two more sequels to the controversy: *Antapologia pro Alberto Pio comite Carpensi in Erasmum Roterodamum*, by Sepulveda, Rome 1532, and the unpublished *Examen vanitatis duodecim articulorum Martini ad veritatis disciplinae christianae censuram sub incude rev. patris domini Ambrosii Flandini*, for which cf. S. Seidel Menchi, "La discussione su Erasmo nell' Italia del rinascimento," in *Società, Politica e Cultura a Carpi ai tempi di Alberto III Pio, Atti del Convegno internazionale (Carpi, 19–21 Maggio 1978)* (Padova, 1981), pp. 291–382.

pars huius calamitatis," "that messenger of papal bulls, great part of your soul, and in my view, actor of great parts in these catastrophic events."[18]

The Diplomatophorus returns, again without further indication, in Erasmus's Apology against Pio's last and posthumously edited work, the exceptionally voluminous "Of Alberto Pio the most illustrious and by far the most learned Count of Carpi, Twenty-three Books, not counted the preface and the epilogue, against the places in the various works of Erasmus that should in his opinion be revised and withdrawn."[19] In Erasmus's Apology, however, we encounter another, rather malicious hint as to Pio's presumed accomplices that can only be understood as pointing to, amongst others, Aleander: "I easily accept that Pio in Rome wrote against me on the instigation of some others, whose identity does not escape me; one is a Jewish man, people I never could well get along with."[20]

The insinuation that Aleander was Jewish by descent, seems to occur for the first time in 1520 in the *Acta Academiae Louaniensis contra Lutherum*. This pamphlet was anonymously published at Cologne in view of the coming Diet of Worms, probably during the days both Erasmus and Aleander were in Cologne, Oct./Nov. 1520. Although the *Acta* later were included in the collected works of Luther, its authorship has to be ascribed to Erasmus.[21] The introductory letter to the *Acta* gives a very unsympathetic portrait of Aleander as being of Jewish descent, ironically adding that he possibly was not even baptised and, to judge from his behaviour, certainly did not believe in resurrection.[22] The *Acta* itself names Aleander as belonging to the same brood as Judas Iscarioth, willing to betray the cause of the Gospel, even for three instead of thirty drachmes.[23] That Erasmus was the first to call Aleander a Jew, seems to be confirmed by Hutten's charge in his *Expostulatio* against Erasmus and by Aleander's complaint, as reported by Erasmus in his *Spongia*, his refutation of Hutten's charge.[24]

---

[18] See above, n. 3, and *Apolog. adv. rhaps. Alb. Pii, LB* IX, 1118B.

[19] For the Latin title, see above n. 17, doc. D. For diplomatophorus, cf. above n. 4.

[20] *Apolog. adv. rhaps. Alb. Pii, LB* IX, 1124B.

[21] See *Erasmi Opuscula. A Supplement to the Opera Omnia*, edited with introductions and Notes by W. K. Ferguson (The Hague, 1933), p. 312.

[22] Cf. *Erasmi Opuscula* (above n. 21), pp. 316–17, ll. 6–11.

[23] Cf. *Erasmi Opuscula* (above n. 21), p. 324, ll. 72–73.

[24] Cf. *Spongia, ASD* IX, 1, p. 150, ll. 716–717; Ep. 1166, ll. 84–85; cf. also *Coll., ASD* I, 3, p. 680, ll. 148–49. Other references in *Erasmi Opuscula* (above n. 21), pp. 316–17; J. Paquier, *Jérôme Aléandre de sa naissance à la fin de son séjour à Brindes (1480–1529)* (Paris, 1900), pp. 10, 14, 173, 186, 201, 218, 242, 260.

What was Erasmus's image of Aleander at the beginning of the polemics with Pio in 1525? At the time Erasmus first heard about Pio's hostile activities, he had already had a somewhat ambivalent and precarious kind of relationship with Aleander throughout almost two decades. Their acquaintance dated from their concurrent stay of about six months in 1508 at Aldus's printing house in Venice, where they had shared not only house and board, but also their room and even their bed.[25] Erasmus was impressed and fascinated by Aleander's scholarship and his knowledge of the three theological languages. He assisted at Aleander's lectures on Plutarch's *Moralia*.[26] An intimate friendship between the two of them developed.[27] Like the other members of the Aldine Neoacademia,[28] Aleander helped Erasmus to enlarge his collection of Proverbs by providing him with Greek manuscripts.[29] When Aleander contemplated leaving Venice for a career in France, Erasmus strengthened his resolve against all other advice and willingly provided him with a letter of recommendation.[30] Aleander started a correspondence with Erasmus who was still in Italy, which because of the lack of encouraging response, never took off.[31] About four years later, when Aleander, living in Orléans, was informed that Erasmus was in Paris and had written a letter to a friend in Orléans, he felt disappointed not to have been written to by Erasmus, but he nevertheless immediately travelled to Paris to see his former roommate. Unfortunately Erasmus had already left the city.[32] We know of these events thanks to Aleander's first extant letter to Erasmus, in which the author proves himself fairly content with the development of his career. No answer from Erasmus, who may have scented some conceit in the other's letter, has come down to us.

Again four years later, in 1516, Erasmus was invited to come to Liège,

---

[25] Cf. Epp. 2443, ll. 285–86; 2644, ll. 12–14; Allen I, p. 55, ll. 98–101. Cf. also Aleander's statement in Th. Brieger, *Aleander und Luther 1521. Die vervollständigten Aleander-despeschen nebst Untersuchungen über den Wormser Reichstag, 1. Abteilung*, Gotha 1884, p. 52, ll. 7–8.

[26] Cf. Brieger, *o.c.* (above n. 25), p. 52, ll. 8–10.

[27] Cf. Epp. 1195, l. 50; 1219, ll. 16–17; *Adag.*, *LB* II, 419C; *Spongia*, *ASD* IX, 1, p. 149, ll. 687–88.

[28] Cf. Allen's Introduction to Ep. 256.

[29] Cf. Erasmus's letter to Botzheim, Allen I, p. 35, ll. 11 sqq.; *Adag.* 1001, *LB* II, 405D.

[30] Cf. Epp. 256, ll. 88–90; 1195, l. 51; 2443, ll. 287–88.

[31] Cf. Ep. 256, ll. 6–8.

[32] Cf. Ep. 256, ll. 13–22.

to enjoy the city in the company of many friends. One of them, to quote the letter of invitation, would be the Liegian prince-bishop, Erard de la Marck's then chancellor, Jerome Aleander.[33] For unknown reasons the meeting did not take place, and again four years went by. Years, as we know, full of overpowering events, which radically changed the political, social, and particularly the ecclesiastical situation in the German Roman Empire. In this new situation, the two scholars were finally, after twelve years, to meet again. Aleander came to the Netherlands to win over the newly chosen emperor for the promulgation of the Pope's bull *Exsurge* against Luther. He must soon have noticed the traces of strong Lutheran tendencies among the people of the southern Netherlands. During this period he presently became aware of Erasmus's difficulties with the Louvain theologians in their crusade against Lutheranism. To most members of the Faculty of Theology, Erasmus was as bad as, or even worse than Luther. Aleander, on his arrival in the Netherlands, was certainly disposed to view Erasmus from the same point of view, as appears from his concern with the famous letter Erasmus had written to Luther one year before.[34] Against the author's will, this letter had been printed and soon a copy of it had arrived in Rome. Aleander had revealed his worry about Erasmus's kindness to Luther in a message to his former Liegian patron, Erard de la Marck.[35] From then onwards, distrust would predominate in Erasmus's view of the personality and the activities of Aleander.

Aleander, on his side, was filled with suspicions about Erasmus's part in the Lutheran question, and these suspicions soon became convictions. One of his extensive reports to his superior, Cardinal Giulio dei Medici, the future Pope Clement, leaves no doubt about that. It seems almost naive that Aleander, according to this report, still expected Erasmus to pay him a friend's visit during his stay in Antwerp or Louvain, where he was to organize his first anti-Lutheran book burning.[36] In some lines earlier in the report, Erasmus is depicted as the "fomes malorum," the kindling-wood of all the fires of dissent in Flanders and the Rhine region.[37]

[33] Cf. Ep. 381, ll. 8–11.

[34] Ep. 980.

[35] Cf. Allen's Introd. to Ep. 1038; Epp. 1482, ll. 6–8; 1496, ll. 21–23.

[36] Cf. Brieger, *o.c.* (above n. 25), p. 52, ll. 11–13. Erasmus on his side believed that it was Aleander who avoided a meeting; cf. *Spongia, ASD* IX, 1, p. 150, ll. 696–97; *Responsio ad ep. Alb. Pii, LB* IX, 1104C-D; Ep. 1482, 1.

[37] Cf. Brieger, *o.c.* (above n. 25), p. 52, ll. 2–4.

Aleander shows himself easily disposed to believe the statements being made that Erasmus suspected the Bull against Luther to be a forgery.[38] Within a few weeks they both arrived in Cologne, where Erasmus, according to Aleander, paid nightly visits to the Electors in order to corrupt them.[39] Nevertheless, on the initiative of Erasmus, a meeting was arranged. Erasmus refused an invitation to have dinner with Aleander, probably for fear of being poisoned,[40] but the conversation was an unexpected success. Common memories revived and the reciprocal charges of slanderous talk, though not completely groundless, were soon swept away in waves of laughter. They separated, to quote Erasmus's version, "with a kiss, the symbol of old friendship."[41]

Erasmus's report of the meeting, given in his *Spongia*, seems to be sincere. Aleander, however, frankly confirmed that he, for the sake of the Faith and of his mission, dexterously hid his real opinion as to the part Erasmus was playing in the Lutheran tragedy.[42]

After Aleander had left for Worms new rumours about his malicious plans against Erasmus soon surfaced, but once again the air was cleared by means of letters.[43] This time too there is reason to quesion Aleander's sincerity since his contemporary report from Worms blamed Erasmus alone for the progress of Lutheranism in Holland.[44] Later in 1521 the two had a serious but satisfactory talk of five hours in Brussels where Aleander accused Erasmus of giving rise to the rumour of his being born a Jew.[45] Relations obviously became friendly again. In Louvain, where Aleander was ready to show his disapproval of Stunica's attack on Eras-

---

[38] Cf. Brieger, *o.c.* (above n. 25), p. 52, ll. 13–14; p. 271, ll. 5–6.

[39] Cf. Brieger, *o.c.* (above n. 25),p. 52, ll. 20–21. Aleander probably has Erasmus's brief encounter on 5 November 1520, with the Elector Frederic of Saxony in mind, for which cf. *Spongia, ASD* IX, 1, p. 182, ll. 422–24. According to Erasmus's later statement, Frederic was the only prince he had met with in Cologne; cf. Ep. 1512, l. 19.

[40] Cf. *Spongia, ASD* IX, 1, p. 150, ll. 703–705, to combine with Ep. 1188, ll. 33–37.

[41] Cf. *Spongia, ASD* IX, p. 150, ll. 706–7; ll. 709–10; Brieger, *o.c.*, (above n. 25), p. 53, ll. 14–15.

[42] Cf. Brieger, *o.c.* (above n. 25), p 53, ll. 2–4, and also p. 271, ll. 12–14.

[43] Cf. *Spongia, ASD* IX, 1, pp. 150, ll. 710–14.

[44] Cf. Brieger, *o.c.* (above n. 25), p. 81, ll. 14–15. Aleander suspected Erasmus to be the author of several Lutheran publications, among which even Luther's *Babylonian Captivity*; cf. Ep. 1218, ll. 13–16: "ex his mihi tribuit Captiuitatem Babylonicam." Cf. Paquier, *o.c.* (above n. 24), p. 229.

[45] Cf. *Spongia, ASD* IX, 1, p. 150, ll. 715–17. Cf. Paquier, *o.c.* (above n. 24), p. 280.

mus[46] and to forbid anti-Erasmian sermons,[47] the two found themselves coincidentally lodging in the same inn,[48] and brought their Venetian past to life in night-time scholarly conversations.[49]

I cannot escape the impression that Erasmus for a time had sincerely hoped for full restoration of his former friendship with the Roman prelate. Several statements in his letters show his readiness to believe Aleander misled by the mendacious machinations of his Netherlandish enemies[50] who only wanted to alienate them from each other, as they both finally had understood.[51] On a hint of Vives, Erasmus inserted an honourable mention of Aleander in his next edition of the Annotations on the New Testament.[52]

Aleander on his side was certainly less sincere. Simultaneously with their stay in Louvain, where he had sworn to surpass everybody else in friendly feelings towards Erasmus, he assured his Roman patron, as he had done before, that he on every occasion had dissimulated his real opinions about the Dutchman "for the sake of the Church of God and his Vicar."[53]

Soon after Aleander had left the Low Countries to accompany the newly chosen Pope Adrian from Spain to Rome, Erasmus was to discover his double-facedness[54] and now definitely lost all confidence in him. He considered the man who now held sway in Rome able to dissimulate under any circumstance whatsoever.[55] Although Erasmus kept up the semblance of friendly relationship with Aleander for a long time,[56] he had become quite willing to interpret every sign of hostility coming from Rome as a symptom of Aleander's secret activities. Thus he has his label ready for the newly started campaign of the Roman nobleman soon to be revealed as the Prince of Carpi, whom he, moreover, might have remem-

---

[46] Cf. Epp. 1235, ll. 33–34; 1236, ll. 57–58.

[47] Cf. Epp. 1342, ll. 133–47; 1581, ll. 377–85; 1582, ll. 42–43.

[48] Cf. Epp. 1233, ll. 171–75; 1244, ll. 1–4.

[49] Cf. Ep. 1342, ll. 105–10.

[50] Cf. Epp. 1218, ll. 12–13; 1219, ll. 15–17; 1268, ll. 63–65; 1605, ll. 7–9.

[51] Cf. Ep. 1236, l. 16: "sed sero sensimus vtrique."

[52] Cf. Ep. 1256, ll. 67–69, and Allen, ad loc.

[53] Cf. Ep. 1268, ll. 65–67, and on the other side Brieger, *o.c.* (above n. 25), p. 271, ll. 12–14.

[54] Cf. Epp. 1553, l. 50; 1605, ll. 8–9.

[55] Cf. Epp. 1437, ll. 112–13; 1549, ll. 10–11, and the ironical understatement, 2029, l. 49: "homo . . . non superstitiose verax."

[56] Cf. Epp. 1605, l. 7: "Aleandrum tum amo, tum suspicio"; 1621, l. 9 (above n. 12).

bered as the former patron of Aldus[57] and the Roman acquaintance of the Liegian bishop Erard de la Marck who had welcomed Aleander in Rome after his return from Liege in 1516.[58] And, as we have seen, Erasmus saw one more proof of his convictions in the circulation of the pamphlet *Racha*, which he considered to be Aleander's personal, direct contribution to the campaign. He maintained his opinion unchanged throughout the controversy with Pio, even when the latter showed no signs of recognition at Erasmus's allusion to Aleander with the indication "diplomatophorus," as mentioned above.

It has already been said that right from the beginning Erasmus connected Pio's activities with the person of Aleander. In Pio's last work, the *Twenty-three Books*, Erasmus assumed not only Aleander's instigation, but also his direct assistance in collecting the blameworthy texts: "Ni me fallit animi coniectura, Aleander huic et addit animum et loca suppeditat."[59] According to a letter to Pirckheimer, it was said that Aleander, now living in Venice, precisely for this reason subjected all the works of Erasmus to a close investigation.[60]

Now the question is whether Erasmus's suspicions as to the close collaboration between Pio and Aleander and particularly as to the latter's share in the *Twenty-three Books* were right. Here, a quiet and late, but confident and plain negation from Aleander stands against Erasmus's repeated and resentful assertion. Aleander's negation sounds rather sincere and I think that he this time merits our credit. It is connected with the negation of the authorship of a recently published *Oratio*, a reaction to Erasmus's *Ciceronianus*. In a letter, now lost, Erasmus accused Aleander of hiding behind the author's name, Julius Caesar Scaliger.[61]

On 1 April 1532 Aleander sent Erasmus his answer in two letters.[62] The first opens with Pio's name: "Alberto Pio I have met no more than three or four times in the past decade and your cause was not the subject of our talks. As far as I know, I did not write him for seven years and I certainly have not seen him the past five years." Aleander goes on to

---

[57] In his *Epistola paraenetica* (above n. 17, doc. B) Pio pointed to the possibility that he might have met with Erasmus at Aldus's in Venice in 1508.

[58] Cf. Paquier, *o.c.* (above n. 24), p. 117.

[59] Ep. 2329, ll. 105–6.

[60] Cf. Epp. 2371, ll. 34–36; 2466, ll. 98–99.

[61] Cf. Ep. 2644, l. 9.

[62] Epp. 2638 and 2639.

assure Erasmus that Pio's first sign of life after the Sacco di Roma had reached him was the posthumously published final attack in *Twenty-three Books* on Erasmus. Only thanks to the insertion of the preceding documents of the controversy in Pio's last work did he now know about the polemics. Then Aleander immediately goes on to deny the authorship of Scaliger's *Oratio*. To prove his sincerity,[63] he informs Erasmus that he, Erasmus, owed his cherished, eight-year old letter from Pope Adrian to his, Aleander's, pen.

It is a proven fact that Aleander is right in the last two cases, that is, Scaliger's *Oratio* and Pope Adrian's *Breve*. This makes it wise to start with the assumption that he also was sincere in his first assertion, the denial of having had any part in Pio's *Twenty-three Books*. And there are some indications which support this assumption. After the arrival of Erasmus's letter, on 28 January 1532, Aleander, once again pontifical legate on his way to the German Diet of Regensburg, wrote from Cologne to Giovan Battista Sanga about the alleged authorship of Scaliger's *Oratio*. In it he ironically observed how productive an author he must be and how much leisure he must have, to be able to compose books for others, such as the Prince of Carpi, and whoever the other, called Scaliger, may be.[64] Actually, there was no reason for Aleander to deny to Sanga, a possible contribution to Pio's work which enjoyed approval among the Italian churchmen. I may add that, twelve years before, Erasmus had rebuked with a similar argumentation Aleander's assumption of his being the author of numerous Lutheran pamphlets at the Diet of Worms.[65]

A second indication of Aleander's sincerity is found in the report of the meeting Erasmus's correspondent Jacob Spiegel had with him in Speyer. Here too, Aleander casually and unemotionally blamed the spokesman who had erroneously convinced Erasmus of his part in Pio's work. Spiegel, at least, obviously found no reason to distrust the statement.[66]

Finally, I must remind you that Erasmus's suspicions were partly occasioned by the simultaneous arrival in Basel of Pio's *Epistola paraenetica*

---

[63] Ep. 2638, l. 33. For Adrian's *Breve* and Aleander's share in it, cf. Ep. 1324 and Allen's Introduction.

[64] Cf. H. Laemmer, *Monumenta Vaticana historiam ecclesiasticam saeculi XVI illustrantia* (Freiburg i.Br., 1861), p. 99.

[65] Cf. Ep. 1218, 1.17: "O me fecundum, qui tot libellis scribendis sufficiam."

[66] Cf. Ep. 2572, ll. 7–16. It is not clear whether the crushing statement, "Fuit Carpensis irrequieto animo, ingenio vafro et perfido," renders the purport of Spiegel's conversation with Aleander, or merely Spiegel's own opinion.

and the anonymous *Racha* ascribed to Aleander. Recently, however, it has been argued on good grounds that the *Racha* was not written by Aleander but by the Augustinian Cardinal Giles of Viterbo.[67] This implies that Erasmus was wrong in one of his basic assumptions concerning Aleander's relationship with Pio.

All these considerations point to the conclusion that Erasmus probably was wrong throughout in his suspicions concerning the part Aleander played in Pio's attack. The Aleander of 1530 was less powerful and less omnipresent than he had grown to be in Erasmus's mind. And although he considered the recent condemnation of Erasmus by the Faculty of Theology in Paris the prelude of a deserved general ecclesiastical condemnation, he probably was not eagerly looking forward to this condemnation, nor did he want personally to promote it.[68] His last letter to Erasmus, written at Regensburg on 4 July 1532, was kind and placative, and patiently prayed him to renounce his earlier insinuations. He offered Erasmus a reconciliation or rather, in his own eyes, a continuation of their friendship and for the future he promised letters of a more pleasant persuasion.[69]

Apparently Aleander did not succeed in convincing Erasmus of his honest and friendly feelings. The latter continued to consider him the guiding spirit behind almost every new attack on his work, be it from the Parisian Theologians[70] or from Ciceronians such as Scaliger, and, as late as 1535, Pietro Cursio[71] or Etienne Dolet.[72]

The corollary to Aleander's being a less hostile and less involved adversary is that Pio was a more independent and theologically a more competent and more dangerous opponent than Erasmus had imagined.

---

[67] See E. Massa, "Intorno ad Erasmo: Una polemica che si credeva perduta," in: Charles Henderson, Jr. (ed.), *Classical, Mediaeval and Renaissance Studies in honor of B. L. Ullman.* (Rome, 1964), pp. 435–54.

[68] Cf. Laemmer, *o.c.* (above n. 64), p. 94. Aleander suggests, that he had tried to prevent this development by asking Erasmus eleven years before, that is, in about 1521, "che'l mutasse alcune cose nelli soi scritti et alcune altre mitigasse" (ibid.).

[69] Cf. Ep. 2679, ll. 42–49, and ll. 66–67.

[70] Cf. Ep. 2565, ll. 3–7. Erasmus's assumption that Aleander had passed through Paris on his way to Regensburg was erroneous, cf. Allen, ad loc. On another occasion, he at least added a reserving "vt suspicor," to his assumption, cf. 2587, ll. 9–11. Aleander himself justifiably denied the Parisian visit in the last letter mentioned, cf. Ep. 2679, ll. 22–29.

[71] Cf. Ep. 3032, ll. 358–59, and Allen, ad loc. Cf. also Ep. 3052, ll. 29–30.

[72] Cf. Ep. 3052, ll. 26–27.

The history of the reception of Erasmus's work in Italy in the sixteenth century, as revealed in the studies of Silvana Seidel Menchi, furnishes clear proof of how skillfully Pio had put his finger on the sore points in it, at least from the counterreformatory point of view.[73]

University of Amsterdam

---

[73] Cf. S. Seidel Menchi, "Alcuni atteggiamenti della cultura italiana di fronte a Erasmo (1520–1536)," in *Eresia e Riforma nell'Italia del Cinquecento. Miscellanea I.* (Florence, 1974), pp. 71–133; the same, *o.c.* (above n. 17); the same, *Erasmo in Italia 1520–1580* (Torino, 1987). —For corrections to the English I am greatly indebted to Mrs. Jane Zaat-Jones.

Ehrenfried Walther Graf von Tschirnhaus (1651–1700) als neulateinischer Schriftsteller

JOHANNES IRMSCHER

Ehrenfried Walther Graf von Tschirnhaus, geboren am 10. April 1651 auf seinem Familiengut Kieslingswalde bei Görlitz, gestorben am 11. Oktober 1708 in Dresden, wirkte, Theorie und Praxis miteinander verbindend, als Philosoph, Pädagoge, Mathematiker, Physiker, Chemiker, Politiker, Wissenschaftsorganisator und nicht zuletzt als Erfinder und Techniker.[1] Er gehört der Generation von Gottfried Wilhelm Leibniz (1646–1716) zu und ist wie dieser als Universalgelehrter von einer heute schon kaum mehr faßbaren Weite und in ideologiegeschichtlicher Hinsicht als Frühaufklärer zu kennzeichnen. In allen solchen Beziehungen ist Tschirnhaus in letzter Zeit Gegenstand wissenschaftlicher Aufmerksamkeit gewesen, und das besonders auch in der Deutschen Demokratischen Republik, wo namenlich Eduard Winter der Forschung wesentliche Impulse vermittelte.[2] Dagegen ist der Neolatinistik Tschirnhaus vorerst ferngeblieben,[3] so daß es vielleicht nicht unbegründet ist, sein Leben und Oeuvre und vor allem auch seine lateinische Diktion hier und heute vorzustellen.

Der Sproß einer alten Adelsfamilie erhielt seinen ersten Unterricht gemeinsam mit seinen beiden Brüdern im Elternhaus durch den Magister

---

[1] Siegfried Wollgast, *Ehrenfried Walther von Tschirnhaus und die deutsche Frühaufklärung* (Berlin 1988), 54.

[2] Eduard Winter, *Der Freund B. Spinozas E. W. v. Tschirnhaus* (Berlin 1977), 16.

[3] Bei Jozef Ijsewijn, *Companion to Neo-Latin Studies* (Amsterdam 1977), z.B. bleibt er unerwähnt.

Nathanael Heer, dem die Brüder nach Lauban folgten, als dieser als Prediger dorthin berufen wurde;[4] Lauban gehörte damals zu dem Sechsstädtebund der Oberlausitz. Es darf angenommen werden, daß Heers Unterricht die Fundamente auch für den aktiven Gebrauch der lateinischen Sprache legte, war doch das Lateinische bis ins 18. Jahrhundert hinein in der theologischen Fachliteratur weithin in Gebrauch.[5] Jedenfalls ermöglichte es diese Vorbereitung, daß Tschirnhaus fünfzehnjährig in die Prima des Görlitzer Gymnasiums eintreten konnte; gewiß kennzeichnete seine wenigen Gymnasialjahre ein stupendes Selbststudium auf dem Gebiete der Mathematik und der Naturwissenschaften,[6] aber dahinter stand ja der gymnasiale Lehrplan, in dem der Lateinunterricht mit Einschluß des Lateinschreibens und Lateinsprechens einen weiten Raum einnahm. 1668 bezog Tschirnhaus die Universität Leiden, damals eine hervorragende Pflegstätte der Mathematik[7] im Sinne des René Descartes, der nicht nur durch die deduktive Methode für Philosophie und Wissenschaft eine neue Orientierung gab, sondern zugleich zu jenen französischen Autoren gehörte, die sich ihrer Muttersprache und des Lateinischen mit gleicher Meisterschaft bedienten.[8] Die Medizin wußte Tschirnhaus in sein Studium einzubeziehen, das er durch anderthalbjährigen Offiziersdienst unterbrach, als 1672 Truppen Ludwigs XIV. in den Niederlanden einfielen. Auf einen kurzen Zwischenaufenthalt in der Oberlausitzer Heimat folgte eine bis 1679 sich ausdehnende Kavalierstour, die nach Holland, England, Frankreich, Italien und Sizilien, ja bis nach Malta führte.[9] Sie brachte den angehenden Gelehrten in vielfältige Kontakte zu Koryphäen der Mathematik, Naturwissenschaft und Technologie, darunter auch Leibniz. Seit 1682 verehelicht, lebte Tschirnhaus fortan auf seinem Gute Kieslingswalde, ehrenvolle auswärtige Angebote ausschlagend, seinen umfassenden Studien. Wir können hier auf diese sowie ihre praktischen Ergebnisse ebensowenig eingehen wie auf die nicht immer leichten persönlichen Geschicke Tschirn-

---

[4] O. Liebmann in: *Allgemeine deutsche Biographie*, 38 (Leipzig 1894), 722 ff. (Liebmann verzeichnet auch das ältere biographische Schrifttum.)

[5] Trillitzsch bei Johannes Irmscher, *Lexikon der Antike*, 9. Auf. (Leipzig 1987), 399.

[6] Zu dieser Lektüre gehörten laut Liebmann a.a.O. 722 die zwei Folianten der "Encyclopaedia septem tomis distincta" (Herborn 1629) des reformierten Polyhistors Johann Heinrich Alstedt sowie die gleichfalls lateinisch abgefaßten Schriften des jesuitischen Polyhistors Athanasius Kircher.

[7] Rudolph Zaunick bei Ehrenfried Walther von Tschirnhaus, *Medicina mentis*, deutsch von Johannes Haußleiter (Leipzig 1963), 6.

[8] Ijsewijn a.a.O. 89.

[9] Zaunick a.a.O. 7 Fig. 1.

haus,' sondern beschränken uns auf sein lateinischsprachiges Oeuvre.

1686 erschien in Amsterdam ohne Verfassernamen die "Medicina corporis seu Cogitationes admodum probabiles de conservanda sanitate," 1687 am gleichen Orte die "Medicina mentis sive Tentamen genuinae Logicae in qua disseritur de Methodo detegendi incognitas veritates."[10] Die vorangestellte Dedicatio an König Ludwig XIV. von Frankreich ist mit den Initialen E. W. de T. gezeichnet, der vollständige Name des Autors wird in der holländischsprachigen Kopie des Druckprivilegs genannt, die ihrerseits noch vor der Dedicatio zu lesen ist. Beide Tschirnhaus-Texte waren zusammen gebunden; das gedruckte Deckblatt nennt den gemeinsamen Titel "Medicina mentis et corporis." Eine Editio nova, auctior et correctior mit wesentlich erweiterter Praefatio amici autoris ad lectorem (welche darum auch ausdrücklich auf demTitelblatt erwähnt wurde) kam in Leipzig 1695 heraus; sie wurde 1733 nach Tschirnhaus' Tode ebenfalls in Leipzig wiederholt, und zwar mit voller Verfasserangabe auf dem Titelblatt.[11] Bereits 1687 hatte Ameldonck Block eine holländische Übertragung beider Schriften vorgelegt. Er muß also Einblick in die entstehende lateinische Ausgabe erhalten haben.[12] Ein solches Verfahren, neben der lateinischen Ausgabe gleichzeitig eine solche in der Nationalsprache–des Autors oder des Verlegers–vorzulegen, war im. 16./17. Jahrhundert weitverbreitet. Eine von Tschirnhaus selbst bearbeitete deutsche Ausgabe der "Medicina corporis" brachte es auf drei Auflagen: 1688, 1705 und 1708.[13]

Es ist darauf hingewiesen worden, daß Tschirnhaus, da er das Lateinische literarisch-stilistisch nicht vollkommen beherrschte,[14] sich der Mithilfe seines Studienfreundes Pieter van Gent bediente. Eine solche literarische Zusammenarbeit ist weder heute noch war sie früher etwas Ungewöhnliches. Sie stellt weder die lateinischen Sprachkenntnisse von Tschirnhaus[15] in Frage noch seine Qualität als neulateinischer Schriftsteller; denn die Nichterwähnung des Mitarbeiters im Titel der Ausgabe

---

[10] Die Ausführungen von Johannes Heinz Horn bei Rugard Otto Gropp, *Festschrift Ernst Bloch zum 70. Geburtstag* (Berlin 1955), 125 f. zur Titelgestaltung sind zu korrigieren.

[11] Zaunick a.a.O. Tafel IX.

[12] J. Haußleiter bei E. Winter, *E. W. von Tschirnhaus und die Frühaufklärung in Mittel- und Osteuropa* (Berlin 1960), 133.

[13] Haußleiter, *Tschirnhaus* a.a.O. 306 f.

[14] Zaunick a.a.O. 13.

[15] Tschirnhaus hat gelegentlich sogar lateinisch korrespondiert; Belege gibt Curt Reinhardt in: Programm Fürsten- und Landesschule St. Afra in Meißen 1903, 18 f.

zeigt ja eindeutig, daß er die Verantwortung für deren innere und äußere Gestalt auf sich nahm. Überdies hatte er schon vor der "Medicina mentis" 1682 und 1683 in den "Acta eruditorum," die im Jahre vorher der Leipziger Professor Otto Mencke als erste wissenschaftliche Zeitschrift in Deutschland ins Leben gerufen hatte,[16] fünf mathematische Abhandlungen zur gleichen Thematik, nämlich "Inventa nova exhibita Parisiis Societati Regiae Scientiarum,"[17] "Nova methodus tangentes curvarum expedite determinandi"[18] "Nova methodus determinandi maxima et minima,"[19] und "Methodus auferendi omnes terminos intermedios ex data aequatione" ("Methode, von einer gegebenen Gleichung alle Zwischenglieder zu beseitigen"),[20] "Methodus datae figurae rectis lineis et curva geometrica terminatae aut quadraturam aut impossibilitatem eiusdem quadraturae determinandi,"[21] zum Druck gebracht. Die Abhandlungen fanden den Widerspruch der Mathematiker,[22] gegen ihre Sprachform hatte der Professor der Eloquenz Mencken offenbar jedoch nichts einzuwenden gehabt.[23] Möglicherweise und völlig legitim hat sich auch hier Tschirnhaus kundiger Hilfe bedient. Was übrigens Pieter van Gent anlangt, so war der Leidener Studienfreund von Tschirnhaus, dessen Geburts- und Todesjahr nicht mehr zu ermitteln sind, ausgebildeter Arzt, der jedoch von dieser Ausbildung augenscheinlich nicht allzuviel Gebrauch machte, sondern sich mit wissenschaftlichen Aufträgen, die ihm zum Teil Tschirnhaus besorgte, und Stundengeben mehr schlecht als recht durchs Leben schlug.[24] Man wird daher füglich fragen müssen, ob das Latein des Helfers wirklich so viel besser war als das des Meisters.

Das früheste der Tschirnhausschen Bücher, die "Medicina corporis" von 1686, ist von dem Autor in der zweiten Auflage unverändert gelassen worden und hat dank der deutschsprachigen Ausgaben wohl das weiteste

---

[16] Kirchner bei Karl Löffler und Joachim Kirchner, *Lexikon des gesamten Buchwesens*, 1 (Leipzig 1935), 16 f.

[17] D. T. (so die Sigle des Autors = De Tschirnhaus), *Acta eruditorum*, Jg. 1682, 364 f.

[18] D. T., *Acta eruditorum*, Jg. 1682, 391 ff.

[19] D. T., *Acta eruditorum*, Jg. 1683, 122 ff.

[20] D. T., *Acta eruditorum*, Jg. 1683, 204 ff.

[21] D. T., *Acta eruditorum*, Jg. 1683, 433 ff.

[22] Herbert Oettel bei Haußleiter, *Tschirnhaus* a.a.O. 28.

[23] Dieser gab im Gegenteil auch in späteren Jahren Tschirnhaus in den Acta eruditorum Raum (vgl. die bibliographischen Angaben bei Alfred Kunze, *Neues Lausitzisches Magazin* 43, 1866: 34 ff. und 37 f.).

[24] Haußleiter, *Tschirnhaus* a.a.O. 399; E. Winter, *E. W. von Tschirnhaus und die Frühaufklärung in Mittel- und Osteuropa* (Berlin 1960), 6 f.

Publikum erreicht; es umfaßt in der Amsterdamer Erstausgabe 59 Seiten. Vorangestellt ist die Vorbemerkung eines vermeintlichen Freundes des Autors, da dieser selbst zur Abfassung einer Präfation nicht bereit gewesen sei; zugleich sucht der Freund scheinbar berechtigte Zweifel zu vertreiben, ob der Autor der "Medicina corporis" der gleiche sei wie der Verfasser der "Medicina mentis," die ja erst im folgenden Jahr herauskam! Das Werk selbst gibt in barocker Umständlichkeit eine Anleitung zur Lebenskunst, zur Erhaltung der Gesundheit. Zu diesem Zwecke werden zwölf Regeln aufgestellt, auf die jeweils eine Probatio folgt. Allenthalben mahnt der Verfasser zur Mäßigung und einer naturgemäßen Lebensweise. Tschirnhaus kennt hier keine Autoritäten, sondern stützt sich auf die Experientia[25]–auf die eigene wie auf die anderer, so wenn er die Beschreibung eines Heilverfahrens im "Journal des Savants" von 1680 aufgreift.[26] Im Zeichen der Experientia wird–als einziger Autor mit Namen–der Venezianer Lodovico Cornaro genannt,[27] der nach den Ausschweifungen der Jugend durch Enthaltsamkeit ein Alter von fast hundert Jahren erreichte, worüber er in seinen "Discorsi della vita sobria" (1558) berichtete.[28] Indem Tschirnhaus eine wichtige Denkkategorie seiner Epoche, die Experientia, zur Maxime einer gesunden Lebensführung machte, bereitete er moderne medizinische Denkweisen vor; seine Schrift sollte unter solchen Aspekten untersucht und gewürdigt werden.

Ein Jahr nach der "Medicina corporis" erschien die "Mediana mentis," Tschirnhaus' Hauptwerk, 224 Seiten in der Erstausgabe, von der sich die Editio nova von 1695 durch Korrekturen und Erweiterungen nicht unwesentlich unterscheidet. Der Gedanke, daß der Mensch, aus Animus und Corpus bestehend, für beide der angemessenen Medicina bedürfe, wurde bereits von Cicero im Anfang des dritten Buches der "Tusculanae disputationes" ausführlich erörtert und im Anschluß an griechische Vorbilder[29] die Philosophie als Animi medicina bezeichnet.[30] Daß Tschirnhaus seinen Titel bewußt an Cicero anlehnte, ist nicht zu beweisen, hat aber viel Wahrscheinlichkeit für sich. Der Untertitel formulierte eindeutig sein philosophisches Anliegen: "Tentamen genuinae Logicae, in qua disseritur

[25] *Medicina corporis* (Amsterdam 1686), 12.

[26] *Medicina mentis* a.a.O. 46.

[27] *Medicina mentis* a.a.O. 2.

[28] *Der Große Brockhaus*, 4 (Leipzig 1929), 231.

[29] Aufgeführt von Reinhold Klotz, *Cicero's philosophische Schriften*, 2 (Leipzig 1841), 329 Anm. 14.

[30] Tusc. disp. 3,3,6 (M. Tullius Cicero, *Tusculanae disputationes*, recogn. M. Pohlenz [Leipzig 1918], 319).

de Methodo detegendi incognitas veritates"–"Versuch einer echten Logik, wobei über die Methode gehandelt wird, unbekannte Wahrheiten aufzudecken." Die Dedikation an den Sonnenkönig Ludwig XIV. hält sich im Stile solcher Widmungen in jener Epoche mit der Besonderheit, daß sie herausheben konnte, daß der Autor auf Veranlassung Ludwigs Mitglied der Pariser Akademie geworden war–freilich ohne die Jahrespension,[31] deren er für seine Forschungen dringend bedurft hätte. In der Ausgabe von 1687 folgt darauf wie in der "Medicina corporis" der Brief eines Amicus autoris ad lectorem von ähnlichem Inhalt, welcher in der Ausgabe von 1695 durch eine ausführliche Praefatio autoris ad lectorem ersetzt wurde. Sie beginnt mit einem Lobpreis der Allmacht Gottes (was man denen ins Stammbuch schreiben sollte, die Tschirnhaus für den Atheismus in Anspruch nehmen zu müssen glauben[32]), nennt im Gegensatz zu der "Medicina mentis" Autoritäten–Descartes,[33] Arnauld,[34] Malebranche,[35] Mariotte,[36]–begründet die Zusammengehörigkeit von Medicina mentis und Medicina corporis und beschreibt das Ziel des Autors, nicht die gesamte Philosophie, sondern allein die Prima philosophia zu erfassen, worunter er nicht unnütz spekulierende Metaphysik, sondern eine Nutzen bringende Logik verstanden wissen will; Ratio und Experientia, so lesen wir weiter, sind dabei für ihn leitende Prinzipien. Das Vorwort beizugeben aber schien ihm erforderlich, weil die Erstausgabe gelegentlich Mißverständnisse hervorgerufen hatte. Der Stil der Präfation ist sicher von barocker Umständlichkeit, ihr Latein jedoch im ganzen verständlich.

Kommt man nun freilich zum Texte selbst, so wird deutlich, daß dessen Inhalt weit weniger auf Logik im gebräuchlichen Wortsinne als vielmehr auf Metaphysik tendiert, auf Metaphysik als aristotelische Prima philosophia, das heißt Lehre vom Sein als solchem und ihren Prinzipien.[37] Zur Erleichterung des Benutzers hat Tschirnhaus seine Ausführungen in drei Teile mit entsprechenden Überschriften gegliedert und überdies Randnotizen beigefügt, welche es ermöglichen, Inhaltsübersicht und Gedankengang zu rekonstruieren.[38] Aber gerade eine solche Rekonstruktion ver-

---

[31] Winter, *E. W. Tschirnhaus* a.a.O. 13 ff.

[32] In diese Richtung zielt z.B. Horn a.a.O. 128 und 134.

[33] 1596–1650.

[34] 1612–1694; vgl. Friedrich Ueberweg, *Grundriß der Geschichte der Philosophie der Neuzeit*, 10. Aufl. von Max Heinze (Berlin 1907), 104.

[35] 1638–1715; Ueberweg a.a.O. 109 ff.

[36] 1620–1684; Haußleiter, *Tschirnhaus* a.a.O. 402.

[37] Jürß bei Irmscher a.a.O. 372.

[38] So geschehen durch Haußleiter, *Tschirnhaus* a.a.O. 31 ff.

deutlicht die Unzulänglichkeiten des Opus, die offenbar dem Verfasser selbst bewußt waren und von den Kritikern vollends herausgekehrt wurden.[39] Daß das Lateinische zum Idiom nicht nur der Philosophie, sondern auch der Mathematik und der physikalischen Theorie geworden war, ist nicht Tschirnhaus' Verdienst; er steht vielmehr in einer literarischen Tradition, deren sprachliche Mittel er indes nicht voll beherrschte—trotz der Unterstützung durch seinen Helfer van Gent und trotz der stets gesuchten Beratung durch kundige Freunde. Es ist gewiß nicht zufällig, daß Tschirnhaus seine "Medicina corporis" späterhin auf deutsch bearbeitete und seine "Gründliche Anleitung zu nützlichen Wissenschaften" von vornherein auf deutsch herausbrachte.[40]

Trotz aller solcher Einschränkungen gehört Ehrenfried Walther Graf von Tschirnhaus in der Kreis der neulateinischen Schriftsteller, bedürfen die sprachlichen Traditionslinien, in denen er stand und die sprachlichen Wirkungen, die er übte, durchaus noch der Erhellung—beispielsweise machte der Buchtitel "Medicina mentis" Schule.[41] Auf seine philosophischen Positionen (Einwirkung des Spinozismus),[42] auf seine wissenschaftstheoretischen Auffassungen (Bedeutung des Experiments) und seine technologischen Ergebnisse (Neuerungen bei der Glasherstellung, Verbesserung des Brennspiegels, Entwicklung von Porzellan) kann hier nur hingewiesen werden, dagegen sind die neolateinischen Desiderate aufs neue nachdrücklich herauszuheben: Thesaurierung des Wortschatzes, semasiologischen Untersuchungen, Erfassung von Syntax und Stil für die Generalia der Epoche und die Specialia des einzelnen Autors.

Akademie der Wissenschaft, Berlin

[39] Winter, *E. W. von Tschirnhaus* a.a.O. 26 f.

[40] Die Belege bei Haußleiter, *Tschirnhaus* a.a.O. 306 ff.

[41] Belege bei Haußleiter, *Tschirnhaus* a.a.O. 48 Anm. 6.

[42] Über Spinozistisches Gedankengut in *De medicina mentis* vgl. u.a. H. J. De Vleeschauwer, *Tijdschrift voor philosophie* 4 (1942), 352 f.

An Eighteenth-Century Refutation of Epicurean Physics: The Anti-Lucretius *of Melchior De Polignac (1747)*

HOWARD JONES

The re-establishment of classical atomism belongs in the seventeenth century. In 1692 the classical scholar Bentley could refer to it as complete: "The mechanical or corpuscular philosophy, though peradventure the oldest as well as the best in the world, had lain buried for many ages in oblivion and contempt, till it was happily restored and cultivated anew by some excellent wits of our own age."[1] He goes on to refer specifically to the work of Robert Boyle and the Fellows of the Royal Society; and indeed, as the ballad that heralded the formation of the Society proclaims:

> The new Collegiates doe assure us
> Aristotle's an Asse to Epicurus.[2]

Yet the experimental work of Boyle, which more than any other single factor finally secured the acceptance of atomism in England, was but the closing of a long debate to which the following had contributed in varying degrees: in England, the group of experimenters who gathered around their patron Henry Percy, the "Wizard" Earl of Northumberland, around the beginning of the seventeenth century, a circle which included the

---

[1] Richard Bentley, *Eight Boyle Lectures: Sermon IV, Works*, ed. Alexander Dyce (London, 1838; reprint, Hildesheim, 1971), 3:74.

[2] From "The Ballad of Gresham College," ed. Dorothy Stimpson, *Isis* 18 (1932): 103–17.

mathematicians Thomas Hariot, Walter Warner, and Nicholas Hill, the author of the first, if confused, account of classical atomism in English, the *Philosophia Epicurea, Democritiana, Theophrastica* of 1601; the "Newcastle circle," a small group of English emigrés under the patronage of William Cavendish in Paris during the 1640s, numbering among them William Petty, Kenelm Digby, and Lady Margaret Cavendish; Dr. Walter Charleton, scholar of Oxford and physician to Charles I, whose solid reputation as a High Churchman gave acceptance to his *Physiologia Epicuro-Gassendo-Charletoniana* of 1654, a translation and adaptation of the atomistic writings of Pierre Gassendi; the French scientist Gassendi himself, whose grand synthesis of Epicurean philosophy in the *Animadversiones in Decimum Librum Diogenis Laertii* (1649) and the *Syntagma Philosophicum* (1658) established atomism as a serious rival to Cartesianism; in Italy, Sebastion Basso, Claude Berigard, and Jean Chrysostome Magnen; and in Germany, Daniel Sennert and Joachim Junge.

It is in the nature of a debate, of course, that there be at least two sides, and it is certainly the case that the promoters of atomism had not gone unchallenged—by supporters of the Aristotelian concept of substantial forms, by university men who saw in the 'new science' and its adoption by the majority of members of the newly formed Royal Society a challenge to their authority, and by staunch churchmen who feared for the integrity of established religion. Melchior de Polignac was last in a line. A devout member of the Catholic church he was convinced that the classical atomism resurrected by its modern defenders was inseparable from its Epicurean parent and synonymous with the rejection of a deity, the denial of the immortality of the soul, and the glorification of sensuality as the end of living. If its defeat required a refutation of the new physics, he was prepared to accept the challenge.

Polignac was born of distinguished ancestry at Puy-en-Velay in southern France in 1661, and after an education at the Jesuit College of Clermont and the Sorbonne he became a cleric at the court of Louis XIV, and began a long career as a dignitary of the Church and diplomat in the service of France. From 1693–97 he served the court as Ambassador to Poland, and in 1716 was appointed Auditeur de Rote at Rome. He represented France at the Congress of Gertruydenberg in 1710 and at the Council of Utrecht in 1713. In the same year he was appointed Master of Music at the Chapel Royal and made Baron of Versailles and Cardinal of the Church. Following a temporary exile at his abbey at Bonport he spent the years 1724–32 as Minister de la Paupite in Rome where he assisted at the election of three popes. Well connected at the French court he numbered Mme. Pompadour, Voltaire, and Fontenelle among his close friends. As a collector he owned a vast library, as well as a fine display of ancient statues and monuments (many taken from the Villa of Marius which he uncovered at Frascati); his art collection contained works by Titian, Van Dyck, Raphael, Leonardo da Vinci, and Michaelangelo. He was respected in the world of letters, succeeding Bossuet to the French Academy and holding honorary membership in both the Academie Royale des Inscriptions et Belles Lettres and the Academie Royale des Sciences.[3]

The inspiration for his anti-Epicurean poem came as a result of a conversation he held with Pierre Bayle on his return from Poland in 1697. To each of Polignac's observations on the subject of religion Bayle replied with a quotation from Lucretius; and the popularity of the Latin poet during the period is attested by the fact that, while between 1580 and 1650 there had appeared only two editions of the *De Rerum Natura*, between 1650 and 1708 there appeared six new editions and two translations in France alone.[4] If Lucretius could thus furnish weapons for the sceptics, then he must be disarmed. The task was to occupy Polignac for the rest of his life, and the result was the *Anti-Lucretius sive de Deo et Natura*, nine books of Latin hexameters totalling more than 12,000 lines. Polignac did not himself see the poem published; at his death in 1741 the manuscripts were taken in hand by his friends the Abbé de Rothelin and the Abbé Cerati, rector of the University of Pisa, and finally put through the press by Le Beau, Professor of Eloquence at the University of Paris, who composed the Preface for the first edition of 1747.[5] But the poem had long circulated in manuscript and was much in vogue in the salons and at the Court (portions were translated for Louis XIV by the Duke of Bourgogne); during its composition Polignac received encouragement and advice from such people as Malebranche and Boileau, and the poem was

[3] For a fuller account of Polignac see the following: C. H. Foucher, *Histoire du Cardinal de Polignac* (Paris, 1780); A. Jacotin, *Preuves de la Maison de Polignac* 5 vols. (Paris, 1898–1905); P. Paul, *Le Cardinal de Polignac* (Paris, 1922); Hedwidge de Polignac, *Les Polignac* (Paris, 1960); A. Counson, "Lucrèce en France: L'Anti-Lucrèce," *Musée Belge* 6 (1902), 403–22; C. A. Fusil, *L'Anti-Lucrèce du Cardinal de Polignac* (Paris, 1918), chap. 1; E. J. Ament, "The Anti-Lucretius of Cardinal Polignac," *TAPA* 101 (1970): 29 ff.

[4] For details see Cosmo A. Gordon, *A Bibliography of Lucretius* (London, 1962), 30.

[5] For the various editions of the *Anti-Lucretius* see Gordon, op. cit., 297–300. All references in the present paper are to my own copy of the edition of 1748 printed in Amsterdam by M. M. Rey; it contains the full title, *Anti-Lucretius sive de Deo et Natura*, the dedication to Pope Benedict XIV by Abbé de Rothelin, the original preface by Le Beau, and a tribute to the author written in Latin elegiacs by Ger. Nicolaus Heerkins of Groningen.

early held in esteem by Voltaire, though he was later to call it a "poème sans poésie, et philosophie sans raison."[6]

Polignac's treatment of the fundamental principles of Epicureanism and Lucretius's exposition of them is comprehensive. The first book of the poem is a vehement attack upon Epicurean ethics and the concept of pleasure (*voluptas*) as the *summum bonun*; to Polignac, unconvinced by attempts to restore Epicureanism to an original purity, it is nothing but a selfish and corrupting devotion to lust. In the second and third books Polignac attacks the two pillars of Epicurean physics, void and atoms. Book 4 is devoted to a criticism of atomic motion and in particular the Epicurean notion of a *clinamen* or swerve of atoms designed to account both for creation and for freedom of will. Book 5 is a reply to the third book of the *De Rerum Natura* in which Lucretius argues for the mortality of the soul. The sixth book is an engaging digression in which Polignac enters the ongoing debate concerning the nature of animal soul, inclining to the Cartesian view of the animal as an automaton. The seventh book treats the question of the generation and reproduction of animals and Polignac uses the genetic theories of Swammerdam against Epicurean and Aristotelian explanations. The eighth and last complete book of the poem offers an impressive survey of the astronomical advances of the age, in which Polignac defends the Copernican system and heaps praise upon Galileo, Tycho Brahe, Huygens, and above all Kepler.

A full assessment of Polignac's critique of the essentials of Epicurean physics would require an examination of all of books 2–4 of the poem. However, at the risk of doing some disservice to the author, but in the interest of economy, we may get the measure of Polignac's approach from an examination of his treatment of atoms in book 3.

Book 3 opens with a brief summary of the principal features of the Epicurean concept of atoms: they are the smallest units of matter, eternal, independent and indivisible; they are infinite in number because the existence of an infinite void demands it: if the number of atoms within an infinite void were finite, then the creation of compound bodies through a protracted process of fortuitous atomic combinations could never have taken place, nor could created things avoid destruction.[7] Further, the atoms are

---

[6] Voltaire, *Oeuvres*, ed. Beuchot (Paris, 1834–40), 12:325; 61:201.

[7] See *De Rerum Natura* 1.1008–51 (cf. Epicurus, *Ep. ad Hdt.* 42), where Lucretius makes the following points not summarised by Polignac: (a) that because of the ceaseless motion of the atoms those at the outer edge of the world are ejected into the surrounding cosmos, and unless there is a constant supply of new atoms entering from the outside, the world will gradually be diminished (1029–41), and (b) that these new

endowed with free movement in the void, since this too is necessary for creation. Polignac will attack each of these points in turn; the system, he assures Quintus, is so much stage-scenery; looked at from the rear stalls it gives the appearance of truth; once back-stage the illusion is destroyed; the trappings and machinery are laid bare, and the whole is seen for what it is:

> Nil praeter telasque leves leviterque perunctas
> Cernis, et avulso ruit omnis machina clavo (103–4).

A. Limitations of atoms in power and number.

1. *111–181*—The atom does not exist *per se*:

(a) Nothing can be said to exist independently unless it is unlimited in every way; but the atom, far from being completely unlimited, lacks some of the powers which even dependent creatures possess, e.g., mind; therefore, the atom does not exist in its own right.

(b) The existence of the atom is not *necessary*: the loss of a single atom does not affect the security of the world as a whole; it can be replaced by void; but if a single atom is dispensable, why not two or four or all atoms? Once you admit an immense void, there is no need for atoms; matter becomes a stranger to the world. Why then is it to be considered infinite and independent?

2. *182–284*—The atoms are not infinite in number:

(a) The Epicureans posit an infinite void which is larger than the whole mass of atoms; the number of atoms is thereby limited and cannot also be infinite.

(b) Since there are not enough atoms to fill the void, there is room for matter to be increased; but if it can be increased it must *now* be limited. Moreover, if matter can be increased, it can also be decreased; but whatever can be increased or decreased by parts being added or taken away cannot be called infinite.

(c) Each atom is itself finite and no total of finite units can make an infinite; it will either be possible to add one further unit to the total or

---

atoms, as they rush at the outer rim, serve to prevent the disintegration of the world by their blows; but an infinite supply of them is needed if the succession of blows is to be maintained (1042–51). For analysis of the entire section see C. Bailey, *Titi Lucreti Cari: De Rerum Natura*, 3 vols. (Oxford, 1947), 2:772–77. We may note that the infinity of atoms is rejected by Gassendi (*Animadversiones in Decimum Librum Diogenis Laertii*, 127).

it will not be possible; in either case a limit is established.

3. *285–483*—There is not an infinite number of atoms of each shape:[8]

(a) Take the number of cubed atoms; they do not fill all space at one time, otherwise there would be no room for atoms of other shapes; therefore, if no one type of atom can fill all of space, no one type is infinite in number. Further, since it is agreed that the number of shapes is limited and has been shown that the number of atoms of each shape is also limited, the total number of atoms must be finite (285–331).

(b) If there were an infinite number of atoms of every shape this would mean that there would be an infinite number of examples of every species of thing; this is not so; therefore, the number of atoms of each shape is limited.

Lucretius is mistaken, then, in claiming an infinite number of atoms and infinite number of atoms of every shape. The incalculable range of combinations among just a limited number of atoms of a fixed number of shapes is sufficient to account for the variety of forms in the natural world. One need look only at the game of chess to appreciate what a multitude of variations can be achieved with but a few pieces.

B. The atoms are not indivisible

1. *523–76*: If the atoms are to have shape—and this is necessary if they are to combine to form compound bodies—then they must have parts. If they have parts, they are divisible. Moreover, even if you deny the atoms shape, they will still have parts; as units of matter they have extension, and everything that has extension is infinitely divisible. Polignac expectedly strikes at the heart of the question, finding it impossible to conceive of extended matter which is not infinitely

---

[8] Lucretius's main argument for an infinite number of atoms of each shape is given in book 2, 522–68; it is a position which he is more or less forced to adopt, since he has already argued that the total number of atoms is infinite (1, 1008–51), while the number of atomic shapes is limited (2, 478–521). Polignac agrees with Lucretius that the number of atomic shapes is limited; on the other hand he criticises him for viewing this as simply a part of the nature of things evidenced by the limit to the appearance of new forms, referring it rather to the purposeful operation of Mind. The other Lucretian argument against an infinite number of atomic shapes—that because the shape of the atom is determined by the arrangement of the *minimae partes* which compose it, too great a variety of atomic shapes would entail the possibility of an atom large enough to see (2, 478–99)—is completely ignored by Polignac.

divisible. It is a simple statement of the Cartesian position rather than an argument.[9] What is surprising, however, is that Polignac does not direct his attention at all to the question of *minimae partes,* a concept adopted by the atomists in a deliberate attempt to resolve this very difficulty; a concept which Lucretius himself took great pains to explain and which Gassendi also adopted.[10]

2. *577–677*: The principle of infinite division is capable of being proven by examples both perceptible and geometrical. Among the former Polignac points to the extremely diffusible nature of hammered bronze, smoke, dye, and sulphur. Chief among the geometrical illustrations is the case of concentric circles, where the innermost circle can be divided into as many parts as the outermost.

3. *702–43*: Polignac refutes Lucretius' argument (1. 615–27) that infinite division would mean the equality of the smallest and the largest objects by arguing that while two bodies may be infinitely divisible, it is a case of division not into equal but into decreasing parts, and so the sum of the parts will not be the same. He then offers an ingenious application of Lucretius' mistaken belief in the equality of infinities to the Epicurean doctrine of an infinite number of atoms of each shape: if infinities are equal, then, according to the atomists, there will be as many atoms of one shape as there are of all shapes; also, the total number of atoms of one shape will have to include the total number of atoms of all shapes.

4. *744–802*: A treatment of the Epicurean argument that what exists must be simple; therefore, there must exist bodies that are indivisible; indeed, if there were no such bodies there would be no beginnings of matter; for just as the beginning of number is "one," so the beginning of a compound body is "one," and bodies are made up of several "ones."

Polignac replies by agreeing that whatever exists is "one"; but what is meant by "one" here is not the same as when we say that something is "one" because it lacks parts; in this latter sense only God and the human mind are "one" and incapable of division; matter can no more be "one" than Mind can be divided; only that which does not have extension can be

---

[9] Cf. Descartes, *Principia Philosophiae*, part 2, Princ. xx.

[10] Gassendi, *Syntagma Philosophicum*, Opera 1, 267.

"one." As to the comparison with number, it is true that any number is made up of "ones"; yet an uneven number can be divided mentally into two equal parts; and in the physical world a line of matter made up of points unequal in number can be divided actually into two equal parts; thus "one" is divisible and the units of matter are sectile.

The basis, then, of Polignac's arguments against limited division is a dogmatic assertion of the Cartesian position that whatever has extension is divisible into parts; and despite his attempt to provide perceptible and mathematical illustrations it is clearly a position which he feels is in no real need of argumentation. As a presentation of the Cartesian view it is adequate enough; as a criticism of the Epicurean position it is less satisfactory. It is true that those of Lucretius' arguments which depend upon the independent existence of void and matter have in a sense been met by Polignac's earlier denial of void; but there are others to which Polignac pays no attention. He does not discuss, for example, the Epicurean argument from the immutability of species; nor does he examine the view that limited division is necessary for the re-creation of species within a fixed space of time; and, as we have remarked, the concept of *minimae partes* is completely ignored.

C. The atoms are not eternal

1. *873–918*: Since atoms are divisible into parts and both atoms and their parts have shape, there must exist spaces between the parts which make the atoms dissoluble. Moreover, even if it were the case that the parts were joined in such a way that there were no spaces in between, it would be necessary to attribute this to the skill of a designer. In either case, then, the atom is not eternal.

2. *938–1014*: Since the atoms and their parts have shapes which are appropriate for the creation of gross bodies, we must assume that these shapes were the gift of a designer.

The atoms, then, are not independent, uncreated, and indestructible units motivated by chance; if they exist at all, it is as the creations of a prior and superior Being who fashioned matter with deliberate design and who maintains a continuing control over his creation. Thus, in the final sections of book 3 the reader is reminded that despite Polignac's genuine interest in the technical aspects of science and philosophy his motivation is fundamentally a religious one. Early in book 2 he had warned Quintus what was at stake in the argument:

If what Epicurus says is true, you need not cringe with terror at the

> Thunderer; but if it false, then you must believe in God and fear him (163–64)

and this third book closes with a panegyric of the Divine as fulfilling all the requirements of a Supreme Being.

In book 3 Polignac has taken his reader over difficult terrain. The physical details of Epicurean atomism do not offer the poet promising material; but Polignac has been uncompromising in his treatment, and like Lucretius himself has succeeded in presenting these details in verse which is not only technically exact but also at times flowing and even picturesque. Yet one cannot miss remarking that in much of his argumentation Polignac is attacking positions which no longer boasted defenders; the seventeenth century had produced an atomism which was in many important details no longer the atomism of Epicurus and his classical followers; Gassendi had insisted, for example, that the atoms are not eternal but the creations of God, and it was this purified atomism that Charleton, Boyle, and Newton had espoused in England. Nor can it be claimed that the ultimate objects of Polignac's attack—the *libertins* and the *philosophes*—relied upon classical atomism as a defence for their moral beliefs; Polignac has confused with Epicureanism a contemporary movement in the direction of sensualism which has little to do with the classical philosophy.

It has been remarked by more than one Lucretian scholar that while superstition and uncertainty may have played a disturbing role in the lives of Epicurus's contemporaries, Lucretius's own age found no difficulty in outwardly observing the formal demands of religion while attaching little importance to their substance; that Lucretius, in his polemic against "religio," was doing little more than flailing at shadows. If there is truth in this, then it is a strange irony that almost two thousand years later Lucretius's bitterest foe should be found doing much the same as Lucretius himself. I would like to be able to claim that this assessment of the *Anti-Lucretius* is original. However, one of Polignac's earliest readers came to a similar conclusion—Voltaire, who remarked of the poem: "c'est employer de l'artillerie pour détruire une chaumière."

McMaster University, Hamilton, Ontario

The Prologues of Comoedia sacra *and Their Classical Models*

EMILY KEARNS

Among the writers of Latin biblical and sacred comedy of the 1530s onwards, there are few who feel reluctance to express the aims and intentions of their works. Dedicatory letter, accompanying poem, or, within the play itself, prologue or epilogue: in any or all of these areas of the play's printed text the author may choose to expound his purpose. Such passages naturally have a special importance for all those interested in the theoretical background of this type of classicising writing; but there are distinctions to be made between these various parts of the text. I have chosen to centre this short study on the prologue not only because of the importance of the themes which most prologues treat, but also because of the prologue's relationship with Plautine and particularly Terentian exemplars—adaptation of classical models being itself a matter of central theoretical concern—and because of its curious position as *both* part of the performance *and* part of the prefatory material.

In Roman comedy the prologue is spoken directly to the audience, often out of character, and forms no part of the action. The scholar Donatus, whose work on comedy was a familiar text by the late fifteenth century, makes the prologue one of the four essential parts of a comedy, and distinguishes by their subject-matter four different kinds. We might prefer a simpler distinction. Whereas typically Plautus uses the prologue to set the scene and explain the background to the plot, Terence's manner is quite different: in all six plays he uses the device to defend his compositions against the attacks of hostile critics, and hence if only implicitly to put forward something of his own literary theory. This was to be the formative model for *comoedia sacra*. That might seem unsurprising, granted that, in the post-classical world, it was of course Terence who was both more highly esteemed and more read, were it not that earlier imitators of Terence had evidently not found much to interest them in prologues of either type. Hroswitha, for example, who consciously presents her work as a kind of more improving version of Terence, writes no counterpart to the Terentian prologue. Her public statement of her aims is contained in a preface to each play; within the play itself, as it might be performed, the author remains invisible. Prologues of a sort start to appear, usually in addition to the prefatory letter of the printed text, in the comedies of the late fifteenth century, such as Jacob Wimpfeling's *Stylpho* (1480), where the prose drama is introduced by a short prologue in elaborate, periodic prose, quite unlike anything in the Roman dramatists. The appearance of prologues in such pieces seems largely motivated by a desire to conform with the text-books and to a lesser extent with the models, rather than by any internal need. Although these plays were performed as well as read, the published version probably reached a larger audience, and it was natural that the author's main statement of his aims should still appear in the letter prefacing the play's printed edition.

It is only with Reuchlin's two short comedies, *Henno* (= *Scaenica progymnasmata*, 1490) and *Sergius* (c 1504) that anything like the ancient prologue starts to emerge. The two verse prologues, short as the plays themselves are short, include in each case a plea for attention, an outline of the plot, and a comment on the author's achievement in the play, thus corresponding to Donatus' "mixed" type of prologue. Reuchlin himself apparently wrote no dedicatory letter for the publication of his plays, concentrating on the play as performance. The prologues themselves state no more about his aims than the classically-derived but not comic conceit that he wishes to bring Greek and Roman pastimes to Germany.[1]

True *comoedia sacra* begins with Gnapheus' *Acolastus* of 1529,[2] which

---

[1] *Scenica progymnasmata* (=*Henno*), *prologue*:

> optans poeta placere paucis versibus
> sat esse adeptum gloriae arbitratus est
> si autore se Germaniae schola luserit
> Graecanicis et Romuleis lusibus.

Compare the figure in Hor. *Carm.* 3.30.13–14, Virg. *Geo.* 2.176, and many other places in classical Latin poetry.

[2] This honour is often accorded to Macropedius' *Asotus*, which although published in 1537 is stated by its author to have been written some thirty years previously. This would have been a remarkable anticipation of what is essentially a new genre, and while Macropedius may very well have composed a prodigal-son drama at that date, I find it hard to believe that the revision undergone for the printed edition was not in effect a re-writing.

shows a different pattern, suggestive of a status somewhere between the play conceived primarily as literary artefact and the play primarily as performance. The text opens with the traditional letter of dedication, addressed both to the dedicatee (explicitly) and (clearly also) to the reader: it deals with the general issue of a modern writing Terentian comedy, with his choice of subject-matter, and with various more technical aspects of his adaptation of the genre. Here the writer is Gulielmus Gnapheus, addressing his friend Ioannes Sartorius and beyond him the literary public; in the prologue, which follows in the text after the *dramatis personae*, the author again embarks on introduction and *captatio*, but now he has become 'the dramatist,' addressing not a reading public but an audience, through the medium of one of his characters on stage. The speech is more purely Terentian in subject-matter than are Reuchlin's prologues; it alludes to the paraphernalia of a real theatre–*in apparatu scenico tituli*–and affects to detect in one of the audience embarrassment at the description of his literary misdemeanours. Yet the appearance is, at least in part, illusory. This prologue is not the transcription of a performance, but is conceived primarily as a written text designed to evoke the idea of performance. While Reuchlin wrote his plays for performance and afterwards did not (apparently) even supervise their publication himself, in his preface Gnapheus writes more tentatively: "Quod si iuuet comoediam hanc public spectandam exhibere...." If we can take this at face value, no production had taken place at the time of publication, but the play, although originating as a written, literary text, had been composed with at least half an eye to performance; publication may in fact have been a direct herald to production. *Acolastus*, then, is as it were suspended between the play as production and the play as a printed book, but the latter seems to be uppermost in Gnapheus' mind.

The emphasis seems to have been otherwise with the plays of this genre which followed, for stimulating which the success of *Acolastus* was largely responsible. Though Gnapheus was a schoolmaster, he writes first and foremost for the republic of letters; his successors, themselves too mostly schoolmasters, were clearly not averse to the praises of the literary world, but on the whole seem to have thought first of reading and especially producing the plays as a suitable occupation for their classes. In a note *ad lectorem* prefaced to *Hecastus*, Macropedius apologises for the large number of parts in the play, a device necessary, he says, to give a role to a greater number of boys. The shape of the play when published is dictated by the circumstances of performance.[3]

[3] The text of Crocus' *Joseph* includes the date and names of the original boy actors,

We should bear this difference in mind when we contrast Gnapheus' use of the prologue with the practices of his successors. A good deal of Gnapheus' motives for the particular form of the prologue to *Acolastus* will have been the desire to make his play as Terentian as possible. He tackles the more technical literary points in his preface and postpones the Christian moral and explanation to the interestingly un-Terentian feature of the epilogue or *peroratio*.[4] In the prologue he deals almost entirely with possible attacks on his *noua impudentia* in challenging comparison with Roman comedy, and launches a counter-attack on those content with bad productions (or possibly bad imitations) of Plautus and Terence. This is very much in the spirit of Terence's prologues: the only real difference, and it is an important one, is that while Terence defends himself against (presumably) real past attacks from one rival poet in particular, Gnapheus, since this is his first play, can only imagine and anticipate hostile reactions to this drama.[5] Without any external need he evokes an atmosphere of controversy and presents himself as the bold spirit who dares to follow the ancients (though at the same time modestly acknowledging their superiority), and who is unjustly attacked by an inferior crowd of calumniators—whose attacks, however, only serve to highlight his own genius. Gnapheus thus conforms to the preferred persona of countless fifteenth- and early sixteenth-century Latin writers, setting himself in a self-styled 'progressive' milieu.[6]

---

so that here publication seems to be secondary to performance and forms a record of it; but the inclusion of this list is also a bow to the play as text, in that it provides a neat modern version of the didascalia or record of performance transmitted in the manuscripts of many classical plays. Not only by the mere act of publication does the play become text; the author himself may deliberately exploit the ambiguity between oral and written. On this topic in general, see also Jean Lebeau, *Salvator Mundi: L"exemple" de Joseph dans le théâtre allemand au XVIe siècle* (Nieuwkoop, 1977) 109–14.

[4] Epilogues are the norm in *comoedia sacra*, and presumably derive largely from vernacular models; the only classical exemplars are from tragedy. The vernacular connexion is demonstrated by their appearance in both the German and the Latin plays of Sixt Birck, while Macropedius introduces the further popular feature of the Fool into several of his epilogues. Evidently, having decided on a hyper-Terentian prologue, Gnapheus was forced to use an epilogue in order to point the moral. This is not so inappropriate; the fact that the play *has* a clear message is, after all, the least Terentian thing about it.

[5] A later comic prologue, that of Macropedius' *Bassarus* (1540), can use the Terentian device in its exact form, referring to criticism of the previous year's play.

[6] Possibly Gnapheus even wished to distract attention from a more real controversy, hinted at in lines 5–6 of the prologue: "verum enimuero hic nouis/de dogmatis ne μῦ quidem." Such Lutheran content as the play does possess is discreetly handled.

When actually performed,[7] the use of a Terentian, rather than the Plautine, scene-setting type of prologue goes further: it carries apologetic (literary, and potentially theological) from the written text into the live performance, and brings theoretical concerns in front of the audience. But in the prologues of the immediate successors to *Acolastus*, the strictly controversial tone typical of Terence (corresponding to Donatus' *relativus* type) is less prominent. There is also a change in subject-matter with a switch towards the moral and religious. This second change is not too surprising. Where writers wish to claim a moral or religious purpose for their play, it becomes natural to make that claim at the play's first appearance, which regularly after Gnapheus is the first performance. The audience is alerted to the play's orientation, and the statement forms a nice variation on the *captatio* traditional in the comic prologue: "Listen, you will be instructed. . . ." Although this pattern is not found universally, it is very common and forms the basic message of the prologues of such works such as Zovitius' *Ruth* (1534), Crocus' *Joseph* (1535) and Papeus' *Samarites* (1537). Such prologues sometimes also contain a few brief points on literary matters. That of Macropedius' *Asotus* actually deals with these points in some detail in an "address to the learned," but more normally the detailed defence of the poet's use of metre, observance of or failure to observe the unities, and similar points, will be placed in the prefatory letter, so excluded from the actual performance. The moral point must be got over immediately; metrical niceties could await publication. The preface itself, however, also frequently contains more religious-moral material, giving a lengthier and more heavily documented treatment of the appropriateness and usefulness of the comedy, or of comedy or even classical learning in general.[8] More often than not there are areas of overlap between preface and prologue, while the prologue is made to treat matters of far greater complexity than the Terentian model ever approached.

Perhaps the most striking example of what by Roman standards would be a heavily over-loaded prologue occurs in the *Anabion* or Lazarus play of Iohannes Sapidus, written in 1539.[9] Here there is a return to the Terentian *relativus* type of prologue, in the form of a long and detailed

[7] It is of course theoretically possible that the printed text could have been substantially revised before publication, but there is no evidence for radical changes.

[8] The extreme example is the preface to Crocus' *Joseph*, which in effect forms a separate essay on the desirability of the study of selected classical texts.

[9] Outside strictly *sacred* comedy, we might compare the prologue of *Bassarus* (1540).

defence of his own comedy and of *comoedia sacra* in general against possible lines of attack. But the length (nearly 200 lines) and the number of topics touched on give a completely un-Terentian effect. Like Gnapheus, Sapidus postpones an explicit Christian reading of the play until the epilogue; in the prologue, he invokes a whole set of acerbic critics, each blaming some aspect of his work (either making some purely "literary" point or more radically questioning the whole basis of *comoedia sacra*), and some reflecting objections made to the genre in actuality. Here we see another reason for the popularity of the specifically Terentian form of the prologue: it was the perfect classical vehicle for engaging in controversy on the very lively issue of the relation of classical forms to modern, especially Christian, needs. But Sapidus does not abandon the role of direct instructor; in giving detailed answers to each group of hypothetical critics, he goes very much further than Terence in establishing by contrast with his enemies a positive canon of what is desirable. There is no question of leaving the audience to enjoy the play simply as story-telling while the readers of the printed version may contemplate its moral aims: the aim of this theatre is to instruct, and the prologue is there to ensure that the audience is properly prepared for instruction.

Plautus and Terence, of course, show few signs of concern about such high moral aims. But the consensus of ancient literary *theory* is another matter; by the Roman period most types of narrative literature were commonly held to provide useful models of virtues to be imitated and vices to be avoided. Donatus applies this dictum specifically to comedy (5.1) and the idea, just hinted at in Gnapheus,[10] is made much more emphatic in a great many prologues in *comoedia sacra*.[11] Observing the blameless behavior of a Ruth, a Joseph or a Solomon will inspire both audience and young performers and make them better people, while Zovitius also claims (though in preface, not prologue) that contemplating the villains of the piece will deter them from evil living. It might almost be said that Donatus' view can be applied more easily to *comoedia sacra*, which usually has a clear distinction between good and bad characters, than to

---

[10] "ii [i.e., the *boni*] numquam vitio vortent sui/quod senserint studio fieri. . . ." (*Acolastus*, prologue lines 51–52.)

[11] A simple example is *Asotus*, prologue lines 69–71:

> paucis vos monendos censui
> quos absque fructu huic parabolae neutiquam
> dabitis operam, nec poenitebit ocii.

Plautus and Terence, where many characters show a more realistic mix of virtues and vices. From a post-classical, Christian perspective, certainly, the moral utility of ancient comedy, with its conspicuous indulgence towards young men's love affairs, might seem questionable. It was in this regard that Hroswitha claimed superiority for her plays over those of Terence, and some Renaissance authors use the prologue to do the same: Zovitius, for instance, marshalling all possible arguments claims that Ruth is a more useful character than the heroines of Plautus and Terence, because she is more virtuous. Sixt Birck goes further, and in a witty prologue of the controversial type uses the criterion of moral excellence to show that his play *Susanna* is more useful not only than ancient comedy but also than its recent predecessors in the genre.

In this area, then, although employing a topos foreign to the classical prologue, typically the author is using the prologue to advertise conformity with well-established classical values. If he claims to surpass classical models, that too is an ancient commonplace. A second criterion of excellence with sometimes appears in the prologue has a much more oblique relation to classical precepts and models. Donatus quotes Cicero for the opinion that comedy is "imitatio vitae, speculum consuetudinis, imago veritatis."[12] This was a favourite passage among our authors, and will very likely have been the starting-point for the claim in some prologues that the play offers not only usefulness but truth.[13] For Cicero, presumably, "truth" meant something like "realism," things as they generally are; but in a Christian context it has quite other associations, and in this area authors move by and large from being self-consciously "classical" to being equally self-consciously "Christian." At its simplest level, the stories of Susanna and Joseph may be perceived as true, in comparison with the parallel classical story of Hippolytus, because being related in scripture they are historical events–and thus, to become less simple, God's creation, not man's.[14] When, as frequently, it is a parable which is dramatised, this

[12] Donatus, *De comoedia* 5.3 (Cicero fr 10 Grilli).

[13] The clearest example is the prologue to *Joseph*, lines 6–9:

> apporto namque non Plauti aut Terenti
> quas esse fictas nostis omnes fabulas,
> vanas, prophanas, ludicras ac lubricas:
> verum veram sacramque porto et seriam....

[14] Thus Crocus contrasts the *fabulae* of Plautus and Terence with the *historia* of Joseph (*Joseph*, prologue lines 15–20: note the reference to Donatus' quotation from Cicero in the phrase *vitae speculum*, and the conclusive summing-up *ne quid maius*

point might seem more difficult to apply, but this does not prevent Macropedius from relating his prodigal-son story *Asotus* to truth. It is after all a story of divine origin, another form of God's creation, and truth is ultimately identical with Christ himself:

> sed auribus spectantium probam indimus
> e veritatis ore lapsam fabulam.
> quid fabulam? non fabulam, sed mysticam
> e fonte puritatis haustam parabolam. . . .
>
> (*Asotus*, prologue, lines 6–8)

"True" then means something more than "historically accurate"; rather it covers the whole of the fourfold interpretation of scripture, embracing the various allegorical senses as well as the literal one, and historical truth is seen as the guarantee for a greater spiritual truth. The dramatised form of such a "true" story then will equally be true on several levels.

Ciceronian truth has now been metamorphosed in something quite different, so that for those who emphasize its importance, like Crocus and Macropedius, it is able (in contrast with the criterion of usefulness) to form a clear disjunction from classical models and an indisputable claim to superiority. But it is clear none the less that the two criteria of Truth and Usefulness were not felt to be in conflict. Truth after all is bound to be useful, particularly if one concentrates on its allegorical applications, and where it is used as a commendation it tends to be mentioned in close connexion with moral utility. Yet for the historian looking back on these texts there is something almost emblematic about the confrontation of the two ideas. In stressing Usefulness, authors are extending a classical commonplace, with reference to morality alone; in stressing Truth, they have totally transformed Cicero's dictum by introducing Christian revelation. When describing their aims, no less than when working out the details of their treatment, authors are caught between two value-systems imposing often separate demands. In this light the critics who appear in Sapidus' prologue can be seen as the externalised form of internal pressure on the dramatist; some people, he says, don't approve of using poetry—that is, classical forms—to treat Christian themes, while others find sacred subjects tedious. Can the apparently exclusive systems, each with its own ideals, be reconciled? The whole endeavour of writing sacred comedy presupposes

---

dicam, sed verius.) James A. Parente, Jr. (*Religious drama and the humanist tradition* [Leiden 1987] 43–44) compares Holonius, *Lambertias* A iii^{v}–iv, but also points out (p. 29) that such a distinction was not universal.

that they can, even if to us the results may seem uneven. What is clear is the importance of this problem of relating classical and contemporary, highlighted in the prologue's ambiguous form and contrasting claims.

St. Hilda's College, Oxford

De Regni Poloniae cum regnis vicinis praesertimque Germanico rationibus mutuis ab Ioanne Zamoscio in oratione a. 1573 Lutetiae Parisiorum typis excusa adumbratis

ANDRZEJ KEMPFI

Es war sicherlich angebracht in der treuen Freundschaft mit den Tschechen auch Kraft der geheiligten Staatsverträge auszuharren, man hat auf die Gemeinschaft der Herkunft und der Sprache, auf das Andenken an die Gründer einerseits des polnischen, andererseits des tschechischen Staates, die Gebrüder Lech un Tschech, Rücksicht nehmen sollen. Und was ist über die Unger zu sagen? Sie haben immer treu in Freund und Leid hinter uns gestanden, wir haben ihnen ebenfalls als der ungarische Staat schwere Stunden durchmachte Hilfe geleistet, wir für sie, sie für uns pflegten auf die Feinden unter Einsatz des Lebens zu stürzen; überhaupt hatten beide Völker solche Liebe füreinander, dass, auch wenn die Herrscher es wollten, Ungar gegen Polen und Polen gegen Ungar gleichsam Kraft eines stillschweigenden Abkommens nie bereit gewesen sind mit bewaffneter Hand gegeneinander aufzutreten.... Abstand werde ich nehmen von der uralten Vertrautheit Polens und Litauens mit Schweden zu reden sowie über die jüngste Verschwägerung des schwedischen Königs mit dem unseren.... Sonst was die Deutschen anbelangt, wir haben zwar Krieg um den Besitz Preussens mit den Teutonischen Rittern geführt und mit dem Kaiser Heinrich V haben wir uns auf den Feldern um Breslau herumgeschlagen. Doch diese Kriege sind in keiner Weise aus irgendeinem angeborenen Unwillen der beiden Völker enstanden. Sie wurden auch nicht förmlich von der Seite des Kaisertums angesagt, sondern sind auf die private Veranlassung im Zusamenhange mit den privaten Streitigkeiten zustandegekommen. Im übrigen haben wir mit den Deutschen in einer wahren und dauernden Freundschaft gelebt."

Dem obigen aus dem Lateinischen ins Deutsche übersetzten Zitat erlauben wir uns eine nicht geringe historische Bedeutung beizumessen. Es handelt sich um einen für die westeuropäische Öffentlichkeit bestimmten, doch von einem Polen geschriebenen und im Jahre 1573 in Paris gedruckten Text. Wie ersichlich besteht das Thema der Ausfürung in der Eröterung der Beziehungen der Polen zu ihren Nachbarvölkern: Tschechen, Ungarn, Schweden, Deutschen. Gerade die Aussage, die das polnisch-deutsche Verhältnis betrifft, erweist sich als ganz besonders interessant, sie widerspricht ja der Annahme, dass die gesamte Vergangenheit der polnisch-deutschen Beziehungen in ständigen Kämpfen bestanden hätte, einer Annahme, die noch heute hier und da zu hören ist. Es lohnt sich diese Aussage auch im lateinischen Original hier zu zitieren: "Bellum nobis fuit pro Prussia cum Marianis militibus, cum Henrico quoque quinto imperatore Vratislaviensibus in campis dimicavimis. Verum haec bella nec ab insito gentium a natura dissidio, quod nullum est, profecta nec publico Germaniae imperii decreto suscepta, sed privatis consiliis privatas ob controversias concitata fuerunt. Caeteroqui nobis vera et perpetua cum Germanis amicitia mansit."

Der Gedanke über das Fehlen von Abneigung zwischen den Polen und den Deutschen wird in der Passage fortgesetzt und der Autor schreibt wie folgt: "Wozu sollte ich hier noch die heiligen Bündnisse, die die deutsche Kaiser mit uns geschlossen und öfters erneuert haben erwähnen? Wozu sollte hier die Rede sein von dem von Dienstbereitschaft gekennzeichneten Abkommen mit den ehrwürdigen deutschen Geschlechtern von Oesterreich, Bayern, Brandenburg, Stettin, Mecklenburg? Was nutzt es die Verwandschaft unserer Könige mit den Herrscherhäusern von Osterreich, Bayern, Sachsen, Brandenburg, Hessen und Stettin aufzuzählen? Was nutzt es die mit den Herrscherfamilien von Brandenburg und Stettin ausgetauschten Gefälligkeiten anzuführen?"

Die Aussagekraft der Passage, die das Verhältniss der Polen zu ihren Nachbarvölker und darunter den Deutschen darlegt, ist um so grösser als deren Verfasser ein hervorragender und zugleich literarisch begabter Staatsmann gewesen ist. Sie ist entnommen der Rede deren Originaltitel wie folgt lautet: *Ioannis Sarii Zamoscii Belzensis et Zamechensis praefecti ac in Galliam legati oratio qua Henricum Valesium regem renuntiat. Lutetiae Parisiorum: ex officina F. Morelli typographi regii a. 1573.* Diese Pariser Rede von Ioannes Zamoyski ist als ein beachtenswertes Stück der lateinischen

Beredsamkeit in der europäischen respublica litteraria des XVI Jahrhunderte zu bezeichnen. Der im Erscheinungsjahr der Rede am Beginn einer grossen politischen Laufbahn sich befindende Zamoyski war Mitglied der Botschaft die im Jahre 1573 aus Krakau nach Paris entsandt worden ist und dem französischen Prinzen Henri Valois die vom polnischen Reichstag durchgefuhrte Wahl seiner Person zum Thron Polens angekündigt hat.

Die Rede ist durch Festlichkeit und ausdrücklichen Nationalstolz gekennzeichnet. In der Eigenschaft eines Tribuns des polnischen Adels und eines Verehrers der alten Respublica Romana, apotheosiert Zamoyski die adelige Freiheit sie als Grundlage der Staatspolitik behandelnd. Gleichzeitig versäumt er nicht die Richtlienien des polnischen Raison d'etat darzulegen sowohl bezüglich der Gewährleistung der Rechte der polnischen Andersgläubigen, wie auch der auswürtigen Politik. Die finale an den neugewählten König gerichtete Apostrophe des personifizierten Vaterlandes tritt den Lesern mit den Elementen eines wirklich rührenden Lyrismus entgegen.

Dass nach einer Veröffentlichung in der Pariser Muretus Typographie Zamoyskis Rede auf dem französischen Boden Leser gefunden hatte, bezeugt uns eine—ebenfalls Henri Valois gewidmete—Beschreibung Polens aus der Feder des Humanisten Louis Le Roy [lateinische Namensform Regius], eine Beschreibung der nicht vergönnt wurde gedruckt zu werden und die zwischen den Manuscripten der Pariser Biblioteque Nationale erhalten ist. Ahnlich wie Zamoyski hat Regius nicht versäumt mit einer Charakteristik der Nachbarlander Polens hervorzutreten und wie dies der mit Reguis sich befassende Herr Kollege Jerzy Starnawski festgestellt hat—verraten seine Ausführungen mit jenen von Zamoyski deutliche Verwandschaft. Mit Zamoyskis Pariser Rede erweist sich Regius so vertraut, dass er sie im Jahre 1574 selbst ins Franzosiche übersetzt. Sonst sind aus dem Anlass der Besteigung des polnischen Throns von Henri Valois mehrere Descriptiones Poloniae in der europaischen respublica litteraria erschienen mit Ioannes Krasinskis "Polonia ad serenissimum et potentitissimum utriusque Poloniae regem Henricum Primum Valesium" (Bononiae 1574) an der Spitze.

Wenn man die Literatur nachschlägt die dem Grosskanzler und Kronfeldherrn von Polen Ioannes Zamoyski gilt, fällt sofort auf, dass vielfach von ihm als einem ausgesprochen Feind Habsburgs und somit dem Anschein nach der Deutschen im allgemeinen die Rede ist. Nun dass er wirklich ein entschiedener Habsburggegner war, darüber besteht kein Zweifel; wir wissen das er sich nach dem Tod von Stephan Bathory tatkräftig dem Einzug in das Land des im Grundsatz schon zum König von

Polen gewählten Habsburgischen Erzherzog Maximilian widersetzt hat, Maximilians Heer im Jahre 1588 auf dem Schlachtfeld bei Byczyna in Oberschlesien aufs Haupt geschlagen und ihn selbst–was zu einer Sensation in ganz Europa geworden ist–zwanzig Monate lang auf der Burg in seinem Landsgut Krasnystaw nicht weit von der von ihm im Jahre 1580 nach italienischen Mustern aufgebauten Stadt Zamość in Ostpolen gefangen gehalten hat. "Habsburg–heisst es in einer die Elektion des Königs betreffenden Rede Zamoyskis–ist der Feind Polens. . . . Die Polen sollten daher wachsam sein dass sie nicht dem Machtstreben dieses Hauses zum Opfer fielen, nicht demnächst den Status einer Provinz einnähmen [im lateinischen Original: colonia quasi aut provincia Germanica], denn dann werde der Name Polens im deutschen aufgehen und ein deutscher König auf dem polnischen Thron alle Ruhmestaten polnischer Virtus sich allein zugute schreiben."

Doch was auch immer sich sagen liesse über die entschlossene antihabsburgische Orientation Zamoyskis, sie sollte keineswegs identifiziert werden mit der Deutschfeidlichkeit im allgemeinen. Ein Beleg des grundsätzlichen Fehlens einer solchen prinzipiellen Deutschfeindlichkeit in Zamoyskis Gesinnung tritt uns entgegen eben in der diesbezüglichen Enuntiation seiner Pariser Rede. Dazukommt dass dies deutlich bekräftigt wird von den regen Zamoyskis Beziehungen mit den in Deutschland tätigen Humanisten, vor allem mit Iohann Caselius in der braunschweiger Helmstedt in Niedersachsen. Die Interessierten verweisen wir auf die im Jahre 1929 in Zamość erschienene Untersuchung Stanisław Kots "Helmstedt i Zamość."

Als eine Sache von grossen Belang die wir der Aufmerksamkeit empfehlen ist ebenfalls die Feststellung bezüglich der Beurteilung der Kriege Polens mit dem Teutonischen Ritterorden zu bezeichnen. Dies gilt um so mehr als fast die ganze Geschichte Polens vom dreizehnten bis zu Anfang des sechszehnten Jahrhunderts unter dem Zeichen der Auseinandersetzung mit diesem Orden steht und bis heute jedes polnische Kind von dem über die als "latrones cruce signati" bezeichneten Deutschen Ritter in der Schlacht bei Grunwald am 15 Juli 1410 davongetragen Sieg bescheid weiss [deutscherseits spricht man von der Niederlage bei Tannenberg]. Ja, Polen haben gegen diesen Orden nicht lediglich mit den Waffen sondern auch mit dem Wort auf den Konzilen gekämpft–ich habe im Sinn Paweł Włodkowic Auftreten auf dem Konzil zu Basel und seine Polemik gegen die von dem Deutschen Orden verfochtene damals These dass den heidnischen Völkern kein Recht auf Souverenität zustehe. Doch wie dies aus der Passage ersichtlich ist, Zamoyskis Autorität steht dafür dass dies nicht bedeutet dass diese Kriege aus irgendeiner angeborenen Feindschaft der beiden Völker füreinander zustangekommen seien und in der Konsequenz nicht als eine Erscheinung des vermutlichen ewigen Ringens zwischen dem Polentum und dem Deutschtum zu betrachten sind.

Die Bewältigung dieser noch heute hie und da Anhänger findenden Hypothese über das vermutliche ewige Ringen beider Völker wurde ab 1972 zum Ausgangspunkt der Eröterungen der gemischten polnisch-deutschen Kommission gemacht, welche mit der Aufgabe beauftragt worden ist die Richtlinien für die Darstelung der Geschichte der polnisch-deutschen Beziehungen in den Schulbüchern beider Länder herauszuarbeiten. Ich habe hier im Sinn die gelehrte Kommission die nach der Unterzeichnung am 7 Dezember 1970 des Staatsvertrages zwischen der Volksrepublik Polen und der Bundesrepublik Deutschland und der darauffolgenden Besserung der gegenseitigen Kontakte bei dem Braunschweiger Georg Eckerts Institut für internationale Schulbuchforschung errichtet worden ist und die inzwischen entgegen pessimistischen Prognosen sichtbare Fortschritte gemacht hat.

Es sei noch hinzugefügt dass die wie gesagt ein beachtenswertes Stück der lateinischen Beredsamkeit in der europäischen respublica litteraria des XVI Jahrhunderts darstellende Pariser Rede Zamoyski keineswegs als einziges Dokument des persönlichen literarischen Engagements des grossen polnischen Staatsmanns zu betrachten ist. Ioannes Zamoyski hat sich schriftstellerisch betätigt schon zur Zeit seiner Studien an der Universität zu Padwa indem er ein nachher in Venedig im Jahre 1563 (zweite Ausgabe Strasburg 1608) herausgegebenes wertvolles altertumswissenschaftliches Werk *De Senatu Romano libri duo* geschrieben hat. Und die Höhen des kunstvollen Rede zu der er sich im reifen Alter emporgehoben hat beurteilen sie selbst, liebe Leser, aus folgender Stelle der Proklamation zur Eröffnung der Akademie in Zamość im Jahre 1594, einer Stelle in welcher—nicht ohne Anspielung auf den sowohl die Tapferkeit wie auch den Ziegenbock, den Zamoyski im Wappen trug, bezeichenden Namen Booz—zwei Akademien, die alte in Krakau und neue in Zamość, mit den Säulenhallen Booz und Iachin (siehe das altestamentliche Buch der Königen) des Salomontempels verglichen werden:

> Tu—Academia mea Zamoscensis—velis Patriae meae charissimae Booz esse. Accitus enim a Salomone Hiram de Tyro, in porticu Templi Hierosolymitani duas ex aere fusas columnas statuit, quarum dextram Iachin, sinistram Booz appellavit: uniuscuiusque autem columnae capitello, opus in modum lilii [aiente textu Biblico] praefixit. Ecclesiae et Regni Poloniae dextra: Iachin, id est firmitas, Alma Academia Cracoviensis est.... Sinistra eiusdem columna Booz, in fortitudine, aut in hirco, tu sis velim Academia mea Zamoscensis. Te

et illam contra virtute munitus quis assurgat? Quis utriusque decora convellere audeat? super utriusque capita purpurei ab Oriente et Occidente spargentur flores, manibus dabuntur lilia plenis; quia ab utriusque laureae dabuntur, virtutis et eruditionis tesserae immortales. Amplificate utraeque bonum Patriae! bonos ei viros cives bone suppeditate! Sit vobiscum beata, sit florens, sit florens, sit incolumis.

Stimmt es nicht dass di Pracht der Rhetorik deren Probe wir gerade demonstriert haben nicht nur beachtenswert is sondern auch den bestern Mustern der neulateinischen Beredsamkeit sicherlich nicht nachsteht?

Warsaw

Ioan. Sarij Zamoſcij, Belſenſis, & Zamechē-ſis Præfecti, ac in Galliā Legati, Oratio:

QVA HENRIC. VALESIVM
Regem renunciat.

LVTETIÆ PARISIORVM.
Ex Officina Federici Morelli Typographi Regij.
M. D. LXXIII.
CVM PRIVILEGIO REGIS.

Fig. 1. Titelblatt der Pariser Zamoyskis Rede

Cultura e linguaggio figurativo nei codici miniati benedettini della Biblioteca Nazionale Centrale di Firenze

GIOVANNA LAZZI

Sempre conservativa, legata alle tradizioni e al culto, la cultura monastica più difficilmente e lentamente assorbe conquiste e innovazioni. Dotata di un preciso orientamento, in obbedienza alla "regola," la biblioteca benedettina segue delle direttrici ben precise,[1] che si esprimono nella oculata scelta dei testi sia agiografico-teologici che classici, diventando così lo specchio e de l'esegesi e dello stratificarsi delle sollecitazioni culturali più moderne sul primitivo nucleo costitutivo. Il patrimonio librario dei conventi, pervenuto alle raccolte pubbliche a seguito delle successive ondate delle soppression, ad esclusione della parte, invero abbastanza consistente, rimasta in possesso dei monaci, é stato spartito, limitatamente all'area fiorentina, tra la Biblioteca Laurenziana (soprattutto gli splendidi libri di coro), l'Archivio di Stato (le filze e i registri dei documenti) e la Biblioteca Nazionale Centrale (il nucleo fondamentale della biblioteca).[2]

Il codice miniato assume, in questo ambito, un ruolo particolare proprio per la sua qualità—si fanno decorare solitamente i manoscritti più significativi—indicando precise scelte e categorie d'importanza o testuale

---

[1] M. Elena Magheri Cataluccio—A. Ugo Fossa, *Biblioteca e cultura a Camaldoli* (Roma: ed. Anselmiana,1979).

[2] Sulle soppressioni conventuali a Firenze cfr. Osanna Fantozzi Micali-Piero Roselli, *Le soppressioni dei Conventi a Firenze. Riuso e trasformazioni dal sec.XVIII in poi* (Firenze: L. E. F., 1980), e Domenico Fava, *La Biblioteca Nazionale Centrale di Firenze e le sue insigni raccolte* (Milano: Hoepli, 1939), 50-52, 79-80, 142-43.

o di gusto. E se il linguaggio figurativo si pone stilisticamente al passo con i tempi, il contenuto iconografico consente una più approfondita esplorazione rivelando l'assorbimento di idee e teorie diversificate.

A prescindere dai libri di coro, in cui la decorazione si impone per motivi didascalico-celebrativo-cultuale, la scelta dei volumi da decorare si indirizza nei secoli XI–XIII principalmente verso testi esegetico-agiografici e giuridici: l'immancabile *Decretum Gratiani* (ad esempio Conv. Soppr. A.1.402; Conv. Soppr. A.2.376) o quello di Burcardo (Conv. Soppr. F.4.255), Vite dei Santi (ad esempio Conv. Soppr. A.1.1213), tra cui il noto Passionario II.I.412, i Commenti alle Epistole di S. Paolo (Conv. Soppr. C.6.1903) o ai Salmi (Conv. Soppr. B.6.1901; Conv. Soppr. G.1.715 contedinte il commento ai Salmine di Pietro Lombardo, Conv. Soppr. D.7.822 con il Commento di Origene *In Canticum Canticorum*).[3] Il formulario decorativo si adegua in casi particolari a stilemi ben codificati, come nel *Decretum Gratiani*,[4] rappresentato, tra gli altri, dal Conv. Soppr. A.2.376, raffinato esemplare di stile tardo geometrico toscano che già si protende al secolo XIII,[5] dove la figura del Cristo benedicente e soprattutto il "presbiter infirmus" che orna il testo della causa XVII, non si distaccano da un "corpus" illustrativo entrato ormai a far parte di una tradizione. In manoscritti di questo genere il legame tra testo e decorazione é assai chiaro; altrove, soprattutto nel caso di codici aniconici, l'illustrazione può apparire crittografica e, apparentemente, solo esornante. Eppure talvolta basta un'iniziale a fare da spia e a tracciare la strada per un'interpretazione. La "Virgo casta et desponsata," ad esempio, che illustra il passo corrispettivo del *Pantheron* (Conv. Soppr. E.4.841, c.49r),[6] localizzabile alla metà circa del XII secolo, induce ad analizzare l'intero apparato miniato del codice, sostanzialmente omogeneo, che si avvale unicamente di elementi zoofitomorfi, la cui funzione allegorico-simbolica sarà rintracciabile solo con un minuzioso esame comparativo e testo-immagine. Basti, come esempio, la protome semimostruosa di c.72v, circondata di foglie variegate di verde e rosso, una delle quali fuoriuscendo dalla bocca ne costituisce la lingua, significativamente posta nell'iniziale all'incipit del paragrafo *de invasoribus ecclesiasticarum rerum*

---

[3] Per una breve scheda descrittiva e attributiva di questi codici cfr. *Codici miniati benedettini* (Firenze: Biblioteca Nazionale, 1982).

[4] Sui problemi concernenti l'illustrazione del *Decretum Gratiani* e il relativo corpus di immagini cfr. Anthony Melnikas, *The Corpus of the miniatures in the manuscripts of Decretum Gratiani* (Roma: Studia Gratiana, 16–18, 1975).

[5] *Codici Miniati*... (1982), cit. 24–25, scheda di Adriana Di Domenico (da ora AD).

[6] Ibid., 22–23, scheda A.D.

predonibus ac furibus, in una chiara allusione a forze diaboliche e malefiche, pertinente al testo.

Più tardi, procedendo nel XIV e soprattutto nel XV secolo, i libri miniati si fanno particolarmente vari, quanto al contenuto testuale, testimoniando l'ampliarsi e lo sfaccettarsi della cultura, anche monastica. Il cospicuo fondo dei Conventi Soppressi della Biblioteca Nazionale Centrale di Firenze, fornisce, pertanto, abbondante materiale per una indagine in questo senso, pur se necessariamente con il limitativo valore della campionatura.

Il linguaggio figurativo, adeguandosi alle esigenze illustrative del testo, nella scelta del repertorio iconografico segue l'evolversi della produzione libraria, articolandosi, tuttavia, con connotazioni precise all'interno delle diverse congregazioni conventuali. Al di là di certi interessanti personalismi—come le iniziali fitomorfe che illustrano i codici di Don Simone monaco "reclusus" nell'Eremo di Camaldoli, come si firma di nei suoi libri,[7] e che probabilmente si diletta di minio dipingendo palmette di tipo bolognese all'incipit delle opere, o gli ingenui disegni di un altro eremita Camaldolese, quel Girolamo da Praga, che nel 1425 illustra il suo *Liber diversorum*[8] di deliziose vignette che tradiscono, nel loro linguaggio delicato e quasi naif, l'opera di un dilettante, talvolta nostalgico della terra d'origine, come mostra la raffigurazione dell'*Ecce Homo* (c.73v) carica di patos—l'illustrazione libraria monastica si pone al passo con i tempi.

Inizialmente Camaldoli chiede codici a Bologna, prima del formarsi della scuola miniatoria aretina, e ad altre zone della Toscana e in particolare si rivolge a Lucca, fervido centro culturale, per i manoscritti musicali; Vallombrosa gravita prevalentemente su Firenze, successivamente S. Maria degli Angeli, ove si realizzerà il connubio fra umanesimo e vita monastica,[9] organizza il suo "scriptorium"creando un personalissimo stile, quasi un marchio di fabbrica.[10] Grandi artisti—Don Simone, Lorenzo Monaco, Silvestro dei Gherarducci[11]—si impegnano a far "rider le carte" dei suoi

---

[7] La sottoscrizione compare nel manoscritto segnato Conv. Soppr. A.4.254, c.Iv "Iste liber est Heremi Camaldulensis quem scripsit Dominus Symon in eodem Heremo reclusus"; cf. *Codici miniati* . . . (1982), 32, scheda di Giovanna Lazzi (da ora G.L.).

[8] Conv. Soppr. G.3.1130; cf. *Codici miniati* . . . (1982), 34, scheda AD e M. Elena Magheri Cataluccio—A. Ugo Fossa, *Biblioteca e Cultura* . . . . (1979), 448.

[9] M. Elena Magheri Cataluccio—A. Ugo Fossa, *Biblioteca e Cultura* . . . . (1979), 102.

[10] Per una nota sui manoscritti di S. Maria degli Angeli cf. Serenella Baldelli Cherubini, "I manoscritti della Biblioteca Fiorentina di S. Maria degli Angeli attraverso i suoi inventari" *La Bibliofilia*, 74 (1974), 9-47.

[11] *Codici liturgici miniati dei Benedettini in Toscana* (Firenze: Centro d'Incontro della

splendidi Corali, ma anche nei codici più usuali la "Scuola degli Angeli" esplica il suo inconfondibile linguaggio. I colori sordi e violenti dei codici trecenteschi si ammorbidiscono, già all'inizio del '400, sotto un'ondata di luce, che li rende brillanti e smaltati: verdi, arancio, azzurri lumeggiati di giallo o di biacca esaltano le composizioni fitomorfe che giocano sul tema della foglia d'acanto, della palmetta, del fiore con inesauribile fantasia, in una serie di composizioni infinita. Tuttavia una rigorosa euritmia, una razionalissima partizione dello spazio, e all'interno dell'iniziale e bilanciata nel fregio, una simmetria esasperata fanno muovere il pennello del monaco che crea pagine splendide per il cromatismo esaltato dal brillar dell'oro, ma non dimentica le finalità del libro. Esemplare, proprio nella sua aniconicità, nonostante le barbare mutilazioni di cui é stato fatto oggetto, il *Breviario* Conv. Soppr. G.1.808, datato 1413,[12] ove la decorazione fitomorfa impiantata sull'iterazione del motivo della spirale e della croce, é di evidente simbologia cristiana.

Ma se nelle iniziali decorate il significato simbolico appare sottilmente allusivo e non sempre é in nostro possesso una sicura chiave di lettura, più scoperto e chiaro sembra, invece, il senso di certe immagini figurate. Il volto corrucciato di Frate Martino, il venerato autore delle Costituzioni dell'Ordine, (Conv. Soppr. C.8.380),[13] memore dell'Orcagna e parente dei profeti dei Corali Laurenziani,[14] sembra mitigato dalla struttura delle pieghe del saio, che si corripondono ad una ad una in gotiche cadenze e dalla pannosità serica della stoffa, di un bianco abbagliante di luce. Il tratto somatico fortemente caratterizzante esalta l'individualità del personaggio che presenta il suo libro come un monito e un invito. Nel linguaggio figurativo conventuale il libro non si identifica ancora con l'uomo, come nel dotto raffigurato nelle iniziali dei codici umanistici, ove il volume tenuto nelle mani dall'autore rappresenta il frutto del suo essere, la "dignitas hominis," "faber fortunae suae." Nel linguaggio monastico il libro assume un significato sacrale. E' il testo dell'ordine che Martino

---

Certosa di Firenze, 1982), introd. di Maria Grazia Ciardi Dupré Dal Poggetto, cf. anche la relativa bibliografia; Mirella Levi D'Ancona, "La Miniatura fiorentina tra Gotico e Rinascimento" in *La Miniatura Italiana tra Gotico e Rinascimento.* Atti del II Convegno di Storia della Miniatura Italiana vol. 1 (Firenze: Olschki, 1985), 451-64.

[12] *Codici miniati* . . . (1982), 37, scheda G.L.

[13] L'immagine di Frate Martino segue un'iconografia codificata; cf. Giovanni Benedetto Mittarelli-Anselmo Costadoni, *Annales Camaldulenses ordinis Sancti Benedicti*, (1755-73), t. V, 12-13.

[14] Anna Maria Ciaranfi, "Lorenzo Monaco miniatore" *L'Arte*, 35 (1932): I, 285-317, 379-99.

presenta, quello a cui il monaco deve uniformarsi per il suo "itinerarium" verso Dio. Nelle biblioteche dei conventi il libro era oggetto di culto e testimonianza della tradizione, sovente ornato, anche nel suo aspetto esteriore, di belle legature, talvolta venerato tra le reliquie.

Nei codici più tardi, quando intervengono sul manoscritto i pennelli dei maestri più noti,—il Torelli, Gherardo e Monte, Francesco d'Antonio ecc.—una maggiore uniformità stilistica pervade la produzione miniatoria e soltanto l'abito monastico distingue Ricciardo da S. Vittore o S. Antonino da Leonardo Bruni o dal Bracciolini. La figura di S. Antonino, ad esempio, si pone a mezzo busto nell'iniziale del ms. A.4.2555 vol.2,[15] ancora di profilo, secondo gli stilemi del più antiquato ritratto umanistico di ispirazione medaglistica, con un libro chiuso tra le mani, che regge e mostra quasi in atto di offerta, un ricco piviale broccato d'oro sulla tonacella bianca, la mitria vescovile sulla testa. Il volto, dal bulbo oculare pronunciato, le rughe sulla fronte, il naso appuntito, il colorito marmoreo si accomuna ai molti manoscritti coevi dal Torelli a Ricciardo. Come per il dotto umanista, pochi sono i tratti connotanti in ritratti dalla tipologia sempre più stereotipa:[16] non il libro, comune al laico come al monaco, ma, caso mai, l'abito e gli attributi del ruolo: la mitria del vescovo, il lucco del funzionario della Repubblica, il saio del monaco.

Tuttavia il senso dell' Umanesimo non sta soltanto nella caratterizzazione dell'individuo, nell'esaltazione del dotto, nella valorizzazione della natura. Una rinnovata umanità pervade anche la scena religiosa: ecco in un Offiziolo (Conv. Soppr. G.1.804),[17] la madre di Dio, giovane, bionda, vestita secondo la foggia di moda, scherzare affettuosamente con il suo bambino, che, avvolto nel bozzolo delle fasce bianche e rosse, reclina dolcemente la testa verso la sua spalla. Tutto attesta la quotidianità di un atto calato in un tempo reale e non sublimato nell'astratto metafisico dell'eternità atemporale a cui il retaggio bizantino aveva abituato. L'Umanesimo riporta anche la scena religiosa nelle coordinate spaziotemporali del presente ove agisce l'individuo-persona. Così le Visitazioni e le Nascite

---

[15] *Codici miniati* . . . (1982), 56, scheda G.L.

[16] Sul ritratto dell'umanista nel codice miniato quattrocentesco cf. ad esempio la breve nota di André Chastel, *Arte e Umanesimo a Firenze* (Torino: Einaudi, 1964) 30–31; Anna Rosa Garzelli, *Miniatura fiorentina del Rinascimento 1440–1525. Un primo censimento* (Firenze: Giunta Regionale Toscana, La Nuova Italia, 1985), 191; Giovanna Lazzi, *Per un itinerario iconografico nei codici miniati di Leonardo Bruni presenti nelle Biblioteche fiorentine* in "Leonardo Bruni cancelliere della Repubblica." Atti del Convegno, in corso di pubblicazione.

[17] *Codici miniati* . . . (1982), 35, scheda G.L.

sacre diventano scene reali, anzi mondane, dove le donne sfoggiano le cotte di broccato, dove il letto si addobba dei lini più pregiati. Anche l'oro del campo delle lettere, lungi dall'evocare il fondo astratto delle pale due-trecentesche, il bagliore metafisico delle icone, crea con i suoi sbattimenti di luce un contrasto luministico cromatico ancora evocativo della divinità, ma di stampo neoplatonico.

Inseribile e comprensibile in questo ambito culturale ma certamente rivestita di connotazioni particolari appare la presenza a S. Maria degli Angeli del codice oggi Conv. Soppr. A.6.1147. I bellissimi disegni, che rappresentano le costellazioni extrazodiacali secondo la tradizione di Igino,[18] tracciati con eleganza e sicurezza di tratto da mano fiorentina all'interno del quarto decennio del '400, testimoniano il rinnovato interesse e la rivalutazione dell'astrologia, i suoi collegamenti esoterico-religiosi, la considerazione del mondo naturale che l'uomo studia e di cui conosce i segreti. Se solitamente le figure delle costellazioni si pongono a corredo didascalico illustrativo di un testo, in questo caso formano esse stesse il corpus del codice e le note che le accompagnano, di mano posteriore, altro non sono che un mero apparato esplicativo, come in un libro modello, forse un prontuario illustrativo concepito per esser trasferito sulla volta di S. Maria degli Angeli, in analogia con il consimile "cielo" della Sacrestia Vecchia di S. Lorenzo.[19] Considerando che il Brunelleschi nel 1434 poneva mano al Coro degli Angeli—la famosa Rotonda—e che il manoscritto é stato messo in relazione con un codice viennese datato 1435,[20] l'ipotesi si presenta assai allettante e non priva di fondamento.[21] Il manoscritto dovette comunque, costituire un vero modello iconografico, almeno per il Convento, se, oltre un secolo più tardi, veniva copiato per illustrare la "Istituzione compendiaria della Cosmografia" di Filippo Fantoni (Conv. Soppr. A.9.482).[22]

Il "timbro" della nuova cultura si riconosce in modo eclatante nei

---

[18] *Codici miniati . . .* (1982), 38, scheda G.L.; *Firenze e la Toscana dei Medici nell'Europa del '500: Astrologia, Magia, Alchimia,* (Firenze: Ed. Medicee, 1980), 358.

[19] Alessandro Parronchi, *Il cielo notturno della Sacrestia Vecchia di S. Lorenzo* (Firenze: Biblioteca Medicea Laurenziana, 1979), 7.

[20] Patrick McGurk, *Catalogue of Astrological and Mythological illuminated Manuscripts of the Latin Middle Ages. IV Astrological Manuscripts in Italian Libraries (other than Rome),* vol. 33 (London: The Warburg Institute, 1966); Fritz Saxl, *Verzeichnis Astrologischer und Mythologischer Illustrierter Handschriften des Lateinischen Mittelalters.* vol. 2. Die Handschriften der National-Bibliothek in Wien (Heidelberg: Carl Winter Universitätsbuchhandlung, 1927), 150–55, tavv. IX–X.

[21] Alessandro Parronchi, "Astrologia e Arte nel '400" in *Ghiberti e la sua arte nel '3–'400* (Firenze: ed. Città di vita, 1979), 87–92.

[22] *Codici miniati . . .* (1982), 39; scheda G.L.

fiorentinissimi codici a "bianchi girari," vera cifra decorativa che contrassegnano manoscritti umanistici anche quanto al contenuto, probabile frutto delle ben organizzate botteghe laiche che fiorivano in città e a cui anche i conventi non disdegnavano di rivolgersi.

Particolarmente significativa a S. Maria degli Angeli, pur se in un codice modesto decorato dai consueti racemi a risparmio, la presenza della traduzione ficiniana del Pimander[23] (Conv. Soppr. C.3.742), testimone dell'interesse per le dottrine ermetiche ove "pia philosophia" e "prisca teologia" si trovano unite e in accordo in una concatenazione ininterrotta, nel desiderio di mediare la filosofia orientale e la rivelazione cristiana. La presenza di questi e altri testi, adorni dei tipici tralci bianchi, quali la traduzione bruniana delle Vite di Plutarco (Conv. Soppr. B.3.874) o il *De Temporibus* di Matteo Palmieri (Conv. Soppr. A.2.2638), riflesso di una cultura assai sfaccettata e in fermento, trova giustificazioni precise in ambito fiorentino. L'Umanesimo del Traversari, il Convento di S. Maria degli Angeli, il clima politico e sociale della città, non potevano lasciar immune il pur conservativo ambiente conventuale. Significative penetrazioni si affiancano ai testi agiografici, alle Summae, al sapere enciclopedico, per aprire altre vie, per coinvolgere anche il monaco in un cammino più personale. Così il linguaggio figurativo assume nuove pregnanze, nuovi stilemi iconografici, un rinnovato interesse per il mondo e la natura. Codici stranieri affluiscono—e già nel passato—con l'apporto di esperienze espressive diversificate. Sono francesi, franco-fiamminghi, fino a quel particolarissimo manoscritto di Badia (Conv. Soppr. A.4.2554)[24] il cui "portoghesismo" non può che evocare la figura dell'Abate Gomezio.[25]

L'omogeneo nucleo benedettino della Biblioteca Nazionale di Firenze, dunque, se non può vantare gli splendidi cicli corali della Laurenziana, è

---

[23] Sull'importanza della traduzione ficiniana del Pimander cf. tra l'altro Eugenio Garin, "Magia e astrologia nel Rinascimento" in *Medioevo e Rinascimento* (Bari: Laterza, 1951), 150–69, in part 156–57; sulla fortuna del Pimander Paul Oskar Kristeller, "Marsilio Ficino e Lodovico Lazzarelli. Contributo alla diffusione delle idee ermetiche nel Rinascimento" in Annali della R. Scuola Normale Superiore di Pisa, Lettere, Storia e Filosofia, 16 (1938), 237–62; Paul Oskar Kristeller, *Supplementum Ficinianum* (Firenze: Olschki, 1937), 26; Paul Oskar Kristeller, *The Philosophy of Marsilio Ficino* (New York: Columbia University Press, 1943).

[24] *Codici miniati* ... (1982), 51, scheda di Alessandro Guidotti, che mi ha gentilmente comunicato di essere intento ad uno studio speciale sui problemi iconografici concernenti questo codice.

[25] Rudolph Blum, *La Biblioteca della Badia fiorentina e i codici di Antonio Corbinelli*, (Città del Vaticano: Biblioteca Apostolica Vaticana, 1951) 14 segg.; il governo dell'Abate Gomezio si svolse negli anni 1419–39.

comunque in grado di testimoniare, proprio in virtù dell'alta percentuale numerica e dell'eterogeneità del materiale librario, le persistenze e le variazioni iconografiche nel linguaggio figurativo dell'illustrazione dei codici in rapporto alla cultura del momento che condiziona la scelta dei testi e delle immagini.

Biblioteca Nazionale di Firenze, Italy

Zur Problematik von "vita activa" und "vita contemplativa" in den Disputationes Camaldulenses *von Cristoforo Landino*

MANFRED LENTZEN

Die Frage nach der besten Lebensform ("vita activa" oder "vita contemplativa") ist seit alters her immer wieder neu gestellt, reflektiert und diskutiert worden, wobei jeweils anderslautende Antworten gegeben worden sind. Es gab Epochen, in denen mystische und monastische Vorstellungen das der Kontemplation hingegebene Leben favorisierten und solche, in denen der politische und soziale Druck zum aktiven Engagement im Staat aufrief bzw. zwang, und schließlich auch solche, in denen für eine harmonische Verbindung beider Lebensweisen (was schon Platon vorgeschwebt hatte) geworben wurde. Die Diskussion über "vita activa" und "vita comtemplativa" bzw. Praxis und Theorie, um aristotelische Begriffe zu verwenden, spiegelt somit das Verhältnis von Individuum und Gesellschaft, das den jeweiligen historischen und politischen Gegebenheiten entsprechend stets anders aussehen muße. Was Italien betrifft, so zieht z.B. Petrarca das "otium" und die "vita solitaria" der "vita occupata" vor. Seinen Argumenten schließen sich die Anhänger der "devotio moderna" an. Gegen Ende des 14. und am Anfang des 15. Jahrhunderts wird im Rahmen des Florentiner Bürgerhumanismus eine aktive Teilnahme an der Verwaltung des Staats gefordert. Die existenzbedrohenden Kriege zwischen Mailand und Florenz, zwischen imperialer Machtgier und republikanischem Freiheitskonzept verlangen das politische Engagement des in den "studia humanitatis" geschulten "civis Florentinus." Salutati, Bruni, Palmieri u.a. propagieren den Vorrang der "vita activa" und hoffen, auf diese Weise den bedrohten Staat vor der Tyrannei zu retten. In der zweiten Hälfte des 15. Jahrhunderts ändert sich die Situation mit der Gründung der Platonischen Akademie in Florenz, deren erste Sitzungen gegen 1462 in der Villa von Careggi noch zu Lebzeiten Cosimo de' Medicis stattgefunden haben. Die Akademie wird unter Leitung Ficinos zum Hort der platonisch-neuplatonischen Spekulation und wendet sich weitgehend von der Teilnahme am öffentlichen Leben ab.[1] Einer der wichtigsten Vertreter der Florentiner Accademia Platonica ist Cristoforo Landino, der gegen 1472 seine berühmten *Disputationes Camaldulenses* verfaßt, deren erstes Buch ganz dem Problemkreis "vita activa"—"vita contemplativa" gewidmet ist.[2]

Landino läßt in diesem ersten Buch der Camaldolensischen Gespräche, das, wie die übrigen drei Bücher auch, als Dialog strukturiert ist, als Hauptgesprächspartner Leon Battista Alberti und Lorenzo de' Medici auftreten. Alberti hält zwei große Reden, Lorenzo eine. Die drei Teile des Dialogs, der in das Jahr 1468 gelegt wird, ließen sich in ihrer Gesamtheit als These, Antithese und Synthese fassen. Dabei spiegeln die vorgetragenen Auffassungen einerseits sowohl die politische wie auch die intellektuelle Situation der Zeit wider, andererseits entwerfen sie ein Konzept, nach dem der jeweilige Herrscher (in diesem Falle Lorenzo) den Staat sinnvoll und zum Wohle und Nutzen aller zu lenken in der Lage wäre. Schauen wir uns die drei Reden des ersten Buchs der *Disputationes Camaldulenses* näher an! Die erste Oratio ist ein Plädoyer für den Vorrang der "vita contemplativa" aus dem Mund Leon Battista Albertis. Der Argumentation liegt im wesentlichen die Begriffswelt der platonisch-neuplatonischen Philosophie, so wie sie im Rahmen der Accademia Platonica diskutiert wurde, zugrunde. Landino shceint es darauf anzukommen, durch Alberti wichtige Aspekte der philosophischen Spekulation des Kreises um Ficino vortragen zu wollen. Die Beweisführung zugungsten der "vita contemplati-

[1] Zum Komplex "vita activa"—"vita contemplativa" vgl. bes. den von Brian Vickers herausgegebenen Band: *Arbeit, Muße, Meditation; Betrachtungen zur "vita activa" und "vita contemplativa"* (Zürich, 1985). Ferner Fritz Schalk, "Il tema della "vita activa" e della "vita contemplativa" nell'Umanesimo italiano," in: E. Castelli (Hrsg.), *Umanesimo e scienza politica* (Milano 1951), 559–66; ders., "Aspetti della "vita contemplativa" nel Rinascimento italiano," in: R. R. Bolgar (Hrsg.), *Classical Influences on European Culture, A. D. 500–1500* (Cambridge, 1971), 225–38; K. A. E. Enenkel, "Der andere Petrarca: Francesco Petrarcas "De vita solitaria" und die "devotio moderna," *Quaerendo*, 17, 2 (1987), 137–47.

[2] Ausggabe der *Disputationes Camaldulenses* von Peter Lohe (Firenze 1980). Die im Text angegebenen Seitenzahlen beziehen sich auf diese Ausgabe.

va" geht davon aus, daß die Seele das eigentliche Prinzip des menschlichen Lebens ist (vitae principium, 13). Das Wesen des Menschen besteht im Denken mit Hilfe des Intellekts (mens). Dabei wird eingeräumt, daß der Intellekt den Menschen befähigt, sowohl in der richtigen Weise sich zu betätigen wie auch die Wahrheit zu erforschen (in agendo ac speculando, 14). Diese doppelte Funktion der "mens" kann einmal durch die Auffassung antiker Autoritäten gestützt werden und zum anderen durch die Figurenpaare Rachel-Lea bzw. Maria-Martha aus dem Alten und Neuen Testament. Wichtig aber für die weitere Argumentation ist die Aufstiegskonzeption der Seele (ascensus), wodurch die "actio" des Menschen zu einer sekundären Lebensform wird. Die Erforschung der Wahrheit (investigatio veri) erfolgt in mehreren Stufen bis hin zur Anschauung der himmlischen Wesenheit Gottes (ad ipsius usque dei incorpoream divinamque essentiam intuendam, 16). Die Etappen des Aufstiegs werden durch "ratio," "intellectus" und "intelligentia" markiert (16): der Verstand (ratio) ermöglicht es, die wahre Natur der Körper zu erfassen (corporum natura); mit der Vernunft (intellectus) gelingt es der Seele (animus noster), die zwar unkörperlichen, aber doch geschaffenen Geister zu erfassen (incorporeos quidem, sed tamen creatos spiritus), und mit der "intelligentia" schließlich vermag sie das, was ungeschaffen ist (id, quod increatum est), zu schauen. Die "ratio" ist also so etwas wie das diskursive Erkenntnisvermögen des Menschen, "intellectus" und "intelligentia" hingegen beinhalten sein übersinnliches Erkenntnisvermögen. Über diese drei Stufen schwingt sich die Seele, gleichsam mit den beiden Flügeln "iustitia" und "religio," zur Erkenntnis Gottes und damit zum "summum bonum" empor und gelangt in den Genuß von Nektar und Ambrosia. Dem ascensus-Konzept ratio-intellectus-intelligentia wird an die Seite gestellt der Aufstieg von den moralischen (virtutes morales) zu den spekulativen Tugenden (virtutes intellectuales; virtutes quae a mente sunt, 17), wobei die letzteren sich gliedern in "intelligentia," "scientia" und "sapientia."[3] Mit der "Intelligenz" erfassen wir die Prinzipien der Dinge (principia rerum), mit der "Wis enschaft" die aus den Prinzipien sich ergebenden Wirkungen und Folgerungen (progressus effectusque a principiis manantes) und mit der "Weisheit" schließlich beides zusammen (sapientia untrunque percipit, 17).

---

[3] Schon im 3. Buch des Dialogs *De anima* (ca. 1471) findet sich eine ausführliche Erörterung der moralischen und intellektuellen Tugenden. Vgl. Manfred Lentzen, *Studien zur Dante-Exegese Cristoforo Landinos, mit einem Anhang bisher unveröffentlichter Briefe und Reden* (Köln Wein 1971), 77 ff., bes. 85 ff.

Landino hat in die erste Rede Albertis zwei Exkurse eingebaut, die letztlich nichts anderes zum Ziel haben, als die Aufstiegskonzeption des Florentiner Neuplatonismus auch noch aus anderen Perspektiven zu beleuchten. Es handelt sich einmal um die Frage, ob die Erforschung der Wahrheit eine Angelegenheit des Intellekts (mens) oder des Willens (voluntas) sei. Alberti favorisiert die Position des Vorrangs der "voluntas," da der Wille die Triebfeder ist, die den Menschen zur Erkenntnis des Wahren antreibt[4], und zwar in einer fünffachen Stufenfolge: cogitatio, meditatio, contemplatio, admiratio, und speculatio (19 ff.). Das Denken (cogitatio) sammelt die Einzeltatsachen und scheidet das Falsche aus; die "Meditation" ist eine Art geistiger Übung und schreitet bereits über die auf die Erforschung der Wahrheit sich beziehenden Prinzipien hinaus; die "Kontemplation" wird als ein scharfes und sicheres Hinsehen der Seele gefaßt, das der Erkenntnis des Wahren dient; die "Bewunderung" drückt den Zustand der Betroffenheit aus (stupor dicitur, 21), der bei einer unser Fassungsvermögen überschreitenden Wahrnehmung eintritt; die "speculatio" schließlich versetzt den Menschen in die Lage, in den durch bestimmte Ursachen hervorgerufenen Wirkungen gleichsam Abbilder der Wahrheit (veritatis simulacra quaedam, 21) zu sehen. In der "Spekulation" wird somit die höchste Stufe der Erkenntnis erreicht. Der zweite Exkurs ist den Bewegungen (motus) der Seele gewidmet (auf der Basis der Theorien von Dionysius Areopagita). Drei Arten von "motus" werden unterschieden, die geradlinige (rectus), spiralförmige (obliquus) und kreisförmige (orbicularis) Bewegung (21 ff.). Der Mensch bewegt sich zunächst geraldlinig, wenn er seinen Weg von der Sinneswahrnehmung zur übersinnlichen Erkenntnis antritt; wird er von einem göttlichen Lichtstrahl erfaßt (lumen divinum), so bewegt er sich in spiralförmiger Weise. Das Schauen der Wahrheit in einem Zustand der "inmobilitas" erreicht er indes erst durch den "motus orbicularis," durch den er den Engeln gleich wird.

Nach einer kurzen Charakterisierung der "vita activa," die an den Prinzipien der Eloquenz, der Frömmigkeit und vor allem an den moralischen Tugenden (iustitia, fortitudo, temperantia, prudentia) orientiert sein müsse, zieht Alberti sein Resümee: Da der Mensch sich durch seinen

---

[4] Alberti unterscheidet die Perspektive des *Ziels* der Betrachtung und die des *Strebens* nach Warheit; im ersten Fall hat der "intellectus" den Vorrang, im zweiten die "voluntas." Am Rande sei erwähnt, daß im zweiten Buch der *Disputationes Camaldulenses* (über das "summum bonum") Ficino den Primat des Intellekts vertritt; vgl. M. Lentzen, op. cit., 111 ff.

Intellekt (mens) auszeichnet, dessen Ziel die "cognitio" ist, ist die spekulative Lebensform der tätigen eindeutig vorzuziehen (25). Wenn Landino durch den Mund Albertis für die "vita contemplativa" Partei ergreift, so tut er das–wie seine Argumentation gezeigt hat–mit dem Ziel, die platonisch-neuplatonische Aufstiegskonzeption zu propagieren; die erste Rede Albertis spiegelt somit das Denken der Platonischen Akademie in Florenz.

Die zweite Oratio wird von Lorenzo de'Medici gehalten (26 ff.). Als Reaktion auf Alberti tritt er für den Primat der "vita activa" ein; er argumentiert als Politiker und Staatsmann, dem es auf die Erhaltung und auch den Machtzuwachs des Gemeinwesens ankommt. Das politisch Machbare und Notwendige verliert er in seinen Überlegungen nicht aus dem Auge. Die Gesichtspunkte, die ihn für das tätige Leben plädieren lassen, sind im wesentlichen folgende: Zunächst wird der Mensch als eine Einheit aus Seele und Körper (animus–corpus) gesehen. Die Erhaltung und Vervollkommnung beider Bestandteile würden am besten durch die "vita activa" gewährleistet, die sich auf die moralischen Tugenden (virtutes de vita et moribus; virtutes morales) stütze. Verbürge die "actio" die Entfaltung sowohl des Körpers wie auch der Seele, so die "veri investigatio" (26) lediglich die des Intellekts (mens). Ein zweiter Beweisgrund ist die Tatsache, daß der Mensch von Natur aus für die Gemeinschaft geschaffen ist und somit seine Aufgabe darin besteht, eine "civitas" zu bilden. Derjenige, der dem "otium" frönt, entzieht sich seiner von Gott vorgesehenen Bestimmung. Auch der "sapiens" habe die Pflicht, sein Wissen für den Staat nutzbar zu machen, damit auf diese Weise Schaden von der Gemeinschaft abgewendet werden kann. Lorenzo führt zur Stützung seiner These Beispiele an, u. a. Phidias, Numa Pompilius und auch den Apostel Paulus, dessen Werk ohne die von ihm betriebene "actio" unvorstellbar wäre. Weiterhin wei es eine allgemein akzeptierte Auffassung (consensus omnium nationum, 34), daß der "negotiosus" stets dem "otiosus" vorzuziehen sei. Als letztes Argument wird auf Gottes Gebot, den Nächsten zu lieben wie sich selbst verwiesen; da dem Menschen aber am nächsten der Staat stehe, müsse man ihm primär dienen.

Eine Stelle in Lorenzos Rede ist von besonderem Interesse, die nämlich, in der er sein Bild einer idealen Stadt entwirft (28 ff.). Ein "sapientissimus vir" steht am Stadttor und prüft die Einlaß Begehrenden, ob sie durch Klugheit (prudentia) oder Kunstfertigkeit (artificium) dem Gemeinwesen dienen können. Alle, die eintreten wollen, werden aufgenommen; als aber dann der Philosoph (sapiens otiosus oscitansque, 29) erscheint, stellt sich die Frage, welchen Platz man ihm zuweisen soll. Durch zwei Gleichnisse, das vom Schiff und das vom menschlichen Organismus, wird die Nutzzlosigkeit des der bloßen Spekulation und Kontemplation sich hingebenden Menschen dokumentiert, Auf dem Schiff wäre der Philosoph, der weder Steuermann noch Ruderer sein will, nichts als überflüssiger Ballast, und wenn im Organismus, in dem jedes Glied, jedes Organ seine Obliegenheiten zu erfüllen habe, auch nur ein Teil ausfralle oder mitzuarbeiten sich sträube, dann sei die Funktionsunfähigkeit vorprogrammiert (30 f.). Lorenzo trägt also rein politisch-pragmatische Gesichtspunkte vor, die gleichsam einen reibungslosen und störungsfreien Geschäftsablauf garantieren.

Albertis zweite Rede (als Antwort auf den Medici-Herrscher) stellt eine Art Synthese dar und ist als ein Lebensentwurf anzusehen, den Landino als Modell sowohl für den Herrscher wie für den sich den "studia humanitatis" hingebenden Intellektuellen bzw. Humanisten gewertet wissen will (36 ff.). Alberti bleibt dabei, daß der Mensch nichts Vornehmeres habe als den Intellekt (mens), dessen Ziel die "investigatio veri" sei. Wenn Maria, gemäß der Bibel, die "optima pars" gewählt habe, so würde dadurch die Rolle Marthas nicht abqualifiziert, wenn sie auch nicht denselben Stellenwert besitze. Wenn die "speculatio" die *beste* Lebensform sei, so sei die "actio" immerhin noch gut. Alberti akzeptiert, daß der Mensch ein Einheit aus "mens" und "corpus" darstellt, für ihn hat aber die Tugend ihren Ursprung in der "bis cognoscendi" (41); mithin können die "actiones," die an die "virtutes morales" oder civiles gekoppelt sind, ohne die "mentis investigatio" nicht durchgeführt und vollendet werden. Dies zeige sich auch schon daran, daß Martha von Maria Hilfe erbittet (und nicht umgekehrt). Das tätige Leben kann also ohne eine vorausgehende Erforschung der Wahrheit nichts ausrichten. Damit wird die "vita activa" in der Weise an die "vita contemplativa" geknüpft, daß die praktische Tätigkeit ohne Erkenntnis des "verum" erfolglos ist. Mit einer dem Mathematiker und Physiker Paolo Toscanelli in den Mund gelegten Verteidigung des zurückgezogenen, den Wissenschaften gewidmeten Lebens kann Alberti die enge Verflechtung von "actio" und "speculatio" dokumentieren (38 ff.). Für Toscanelli ist nur der in der Lage, das Gemeinwesen zu leiten, der im Besitz der Wahrheit ist. Die Wahrheit wiederum ist die Bedingung der Tugend, diese ihrerseits garantiert die "concordia civium." Wie Lorenzo in seiner Rede das Bild einer idealen Stadt entwirft, so auch Alberti. Sein Ideal sieht indes etwas anders aus (44 f.): bei ihm erhält der Philosoph die beste und vornehmste Wohnung, und er lebt auf öffentliche Kosten. Er wird in allen wichtigen Angelegenheiten um Rat gefragt, und die Lenkung des Staats richtet sich nach seinen Erkenntnissen. Was den Schiffsvergleich angeht, so ist der Philosoph keineswegs überflüssiger Ballast, vielmehr wird die Route eingeschlagen, die nach seinem Wissen die beste ist. Hinsichtlich des menschlichen Organismus verweist Alberti auf die herausgehobene Funktion des Verstandes (mens), der die Sinne (sensus) berät. In einem zusammenfassenden Rückblick wird das Ideal in einer Verbindung beider Lebensformen gesehen: so wie Maria und Martha als Schwestern miteinander verbunden und beide Gott wohlgefällig sind (47). Damit knüpft Alberti wieder an die platonische These an, daß der Philosoph, der sich der theoretischen Kontemplation hingibt, immer wieder in die politische Gemeinschaft zurückkehren muß, um das Leben der Mitbüurger zu teilen und die Polis teilhaben zu lassen an der Erkenntnis der Wahrheit.[5]

Albertis Konzept muß, wie schon angedeutet wurde, als eine Art Modell gewertet werden. Die zweite Rede des "uomo universale" verfolgt mit Sicherheit auch pädagogische Absichten, und zwar in zweifacher Hinsicht. Zum einen soll Lorenzo daran erinnert werden, daß die Lenkung und Verwaltung des Gemeinwesens stets vom Prinzip der Wahrheit, die letztlich die Voraussetzung von Gerechtigkeit und Freiheit ist, bestimmt sein muß. Bloße Machtausübung allein garantiert noch nicht das Wohl aller Bürger—sofern ihr nicht die "investigatio veri" zugrunde liegt.[6] Zum anderen wird den Humanisten in Umkreis der Platonischen Akademie klargemacht, daß sie über die theoretische Reflexion und Spekulation nicht ihre Pflichten gegenüber der Gesellschaft vernachlässigen bzw. vergessen dürfen und sich nicht in einer ausschließlich für die Kontemplation geschaffenen Akademie ins Abseits drängen lassen sollen—ein Ziel, das Lorenzo sicherlich im Auge hatte, um politische freie Hand zu haben. Das erste Buch der *Disputationes Camaldulenses* ist somit von einer eminent realitätsbezogenen Bedeutung, so daß der—im wesentlichen von marxistischer Seite vorgetragenen—Auffassung, daß sich in Landinos Dialog "nirgends auch nur der Anflug eines Verweises auf konkrete sozial-politische Probleme des realen Staates Florenz" fände und der Autor "völlig im Bereich der ethischen Theorie und der philosophischen Spekulation" verharre,[7] in keiner Weise zugestimmt werden kann. Überdies stimmt die Position, die der Alberti des Dialogs einnimmt, im großen und ganzen mit der des historischen Alberti überein: derjenige von "Della famiglia" tritt

---

[5] Vgl. hierzu Gerhard Huber, "*Bios theoretikos* und *bios praktikos* bei Aristoteles und Platon," in: Brian Vickers, op. cit., 21–33.

[6] Bezüglich der pädagogischen Wirkung auf Lorenzo vgl. auch M. Lentzen, "Le lodi di Firenze di Cristoforo Landino. L'esaltazione del primato politico, culturale e linguistico della città sull'Arno nel Quattrocento," *Romanische Forschungen*, 97 (1985), 36–46.

[7] Vgl. Heinz Entner, "Der Beitrag der Humanisten," in: Robert Weimann (Hrsg.), *Realismus in der Renaissance. Aneignung der Welt in der erzählenden Prosa* (Berlin-Weimar 1977), 246–96, bes. 274–76.

für ein ausgewogenes Gleichgewicht zwischen "vita activa" und "vita contemplativa" ein, in seinen übrigen Schriften neigt er jedoch mehr dem "otium cum litteris" zu, um in seinem letzten Werk, *De iciarchia*, der "vita contemplativa"–wie in der ersten Rede in Landinos Dialog–den Vorzug zu geben.[8]

Die Konzeption, die Landino in Albertis zweiter Rede propagiert, ist im wesentlichen auch die, die die Deutung der ersten Hälfte der *Aeneis* (in den Büchern III und IV der *Disputationes Camaldulenses*) wie auch die der *Divina Commedia* (1481) bestimmt. Der Held des vergilischen Epos hat sowohl an der "vita activa" (Karthago) wie an der "vita contemplativa" (Latium) teil, wobei die Irrfahrten als ein allmählicher Aufstieg zur Anschauung Gottes interpretiert werden. In der *Divina Commedia* ist u. a. Matelda die Gestalt, die in sich sowohl die "virtutes morales" wie die "virtutes intellectuales" vereinigt und demnach die harmonische Verbindung der beiden menschlichen Lebesformen symbolisiert.[9]

Vergleicht man die Auffassungen Albertis in Landinos Dialog mit den Entwürfen, die gegen Ende des 14. und zu Beginn des 15. Jahrhunderts vorgelegt wurden, so fällt auf, daß z. B. Salutati ein auf den ersten Blick ähnliches Konzept verficht. "Vita activa" und "vita contemplativa" sind für ihn verschiedene Formen intellektueller Aktivität; der Mann der "actio" kontempliert, der der "contemplatio" handelt. Aber aufgrund der politischen Situation von Florenz–hierauf wurde bereits ganz zu Beginn hingewiesen–favorisiert Salutati die tätige Lebensweise, die für ihn gleichsam die beste Form der Kontemplation ist. Als Exemplum eines derartigen Lebensentwurfs erscheint ihm Christus.[10] Was Salutati von Landino unterscheidet, ist das Fehlen der platonisch-neuplatonischen Konzeption des Aufstiegs der Seele.

Auch Lorenzo Valla setzt sich für eine Verbindung beider Lebensformen ein, wenn er vom "negotiosum otium" spricht. Er verwirft sowohl die "tranquillitas" des stoischen Weisen die platonische Trennung von Körper und Seele, die die Grundlage des Konzepts der "contemplatio rerum divinarum" ist. Seine Vorstellungen sind diesseits gerichtet, und

---

[8] Vgl. August Buck, "Matteo Palmieri als Repräsentant des Florentiner Bürgerhumanismus," in ders., *Die humanistische Tradition in der Romania* (Bad Homburg-Berlin-Zürich 1968), 253–70, bes. 268 f.

[9] Vgl. M. Lentzen, *Studien zur Dante-Exegese Cristoforo Landinos*, 94–110.

[10] Zu Salutati vgl. Victoria Kahn, "Coluccio Salutati on the Active and Contemplative Lives," in: Brian Vickers, op. cit., 153–79; und Paul Oskar Kristeller, "The Active and the Contemplative Life in Renaissance Humanism," ebenfalls in: Brian Vickers, 133–52.

seine egalitaristische Idee der Errettung aller Menschen hat mit Landino nichts gemein.[11] Der Verfasser der *Disputationes Camaldulenses* liefert also in der langen Diskussion über die beste Lebensform einen originellen Beitrag, der nur vor dem Hintergrund der philosophischen Spekulation im Rahmen der Platonischen Akademie von Florenz verständlich wird.

Universität Münster

Die Aufstiegsschemata in Albertis 1. Rede
(Disputationes Camaldulenses, *Buch I)*

1. *Die Stufen der "investigatio veri"*
   ratio
   intellectus
   intelligentia

2. *Die Tugenden*
   virtutes morales (oder: virtutes civiles; virtutes de vita et moribus)
   virtutes intellectuales (oder: virtutes quae a mente sunt)
      intelligentia
      scientia
      sapientia

3. *Die "voluntas" treibt zur Erkenntnis des Wahren an über die Stufen:*
   cogitato
   meditatio
   contemplatio
   admiratio
   speculatio

4. *Die "motus" der Seele*
   motus rectus
   motus obliquus
   motus orbicularis

[11] Zu Valla vgl. Letizia A. Panizza, "Active and Contemplative in Lorenzo Valla: The Fusion of Opposites," in: Brian Vickers, 181–223.

Une étoffe bigarée....
Dolet critique du style érasmien

KENNETH LLOYD-JONES

Notre but ici est de souligner l'importance d'un aspect jusqu'ici peu étudié de la pensée rhétorique d'Etienne Dolet: la démonstration matérielle de sa critique du style érasmien, formulée au cours de la polémique qu'il mène contre Erasme au sujet du cicéronianisme.

En 1528, au moment où Erasme publiait son *Ciceronianus*,[1] texte où il déployait toute sa verve satirique pour condamner tant les excès stylistiques que les tendances paganisantes de ceux qui pratiquaient une imitation excessive de Cicéron, Dolet étudiait à l'Université de Padoue.[2] Puisque'il avait comme maître le célèbre latiniste Simon de Villeneuve (Villanovanus), professeur formé par celui en qui tous reconnaissaient le plus grand des cicéroniens, le défunt Christophe de Longueil (Longolius), on conçoit sans difficulté l'effet sur le jeune Dolet de ce brillant texte polémique. Quoique sa riposte à l'attaque d'Erasme, le *De Imitatione Ciceroniana* (connu aussi sous le nom de l'*Erasmianus*),[3] n'ait pu être

---

[1] *Dialogus, cui titulus Ciceronianus, sive De optimo genere dicendi* (Bâle: Froben, 1528); texte et traduction italienne, éd. A. Gambaro (Brescia: La Scuola Editrice, 1965); traduction anglaise de B. I. Knott in *Collected Works of Erasmus* 28 (*Literary and Educational Writings*, éd. A. H. T. Levi), (Toronto: Univ. of Toronto Press, 1986).

[2] Pour tout détail biographique, le texte de référence continue à être R. C. Christie, *Etienne Dolet: The Martyr of the Renaissance*, éd. rév. (Londres: Macmillan, 1899); voir aussi C. Longeon, "Etienne Dolet: Années d'enfance et de jeunesse," *Réforme et Humanisme* (Montpellier: Univ. de Montpellier, 1977), 37-61, ainsi que sa *Bibliographie des Oeuvres d'Etienne Dolet, écrivain, éditeur et imprimeur* (Genève: Droz, 1980).

[3] *Dialogus, De Imitatione Ciceroniana, adversus Desiderium Erasmum Roterodamum, pro Christophoro Longolio* (Lyon: Gryphe, 1535): éd. E. V. Telle, *L'Erasmianus sive Ciceronia*

publiée que sept ans plus tard, lorsque Dolet s'était établi chez les imprimeurs humanistes à Lyon, il y a tout lieu de croire que Dolet se mit à la composition de celle-ci dès qu'il eut pris connaissance du texte d'Erasme, vraisemblablement l'année même de sa parution.[4]

E. V. Telle a déjà étudié de façon magistrale les positions stylistiques et intellectuelles adoptées par Dolet au cours de son *De Imitatione Ciceroniana*.[5] Il nous semble, cependant, que quoique ce texte représente la réponse définitive de Dolet, elle se situe sur un plan essentiellement idéologique et théorique. Nous aimerions donc insister ici sur l'importance d'un texte jusqu'à récemment plus ou moins ignoré par la critique, mais qui constitue un effort de démontrer sur le plan pratique, devant le grand public, la supériorité de l'imitation cicéronienne—les *Orationes Duae in Tholosam*.[6] La réussite de ce texte devait révéler de façon matérielle l'insuffisance de l'humanisme érasmien en face des problèmes qui menaçaient la "république des lettres" dans la France des années 30, en prônant l'imitation, tant stylistique que conceptuelle, de Cicéron et de son idée de la fonction sociale de l'éloquence et de l'orateur.[7] L'échec de ces grandioses ambitions, en revanche, marqua à jamais la vie et l'oeuvre de Dolet, et le mit sur le chemin qui le mena au bûcher de la Place Maubert en 1546.

Les *Orationes* trouvent leur origine dans le fait que Dolet, étudiant de droit à l'Université de Toulouse en 1533, est élu orateur de la "nation française," c'est-à-dire, de l'association des étudiants de France (ceux qui viennent du nord de la Loire). Le 9 octobre, il prononce un discours en latin où il proteste les efforts du Sénat pour supprimer les diverses associations nationales, dont les rivalités mènent souvent à des bagarres dans les rues, parfois avec des conséquences mortelles. Puisqu'une grande partie de sa défense de la nation française consiste à condamner les

nus d'Etienne Dolet (Genève: Droz, 1974).

[4] Voir K. Lloyd-Jones, "Dolet et la rhétorique: les *Orationes in Tholosam*," *Etienne Dolet (1509–1546), Cahiers V. L. Saulnier* 3 (Paris: Univ. de Paris-Sorbonne, 1986), 79–92, ainsi que notre "Renaissance Rhetoric: Dolet's *Orationes in Tholosam* (1533–1534)," *Neo-Latin Bulletin* 4-2 (1988): 14–18.

[5] Telle, *Erasmianus*, 9–95 et passim.

[6] *Orationes Duae in Tholosam. Eiusdem Epistolarum libri II. Eiusdem Carminum libri II. Ad eundem Epistolarum amicorum liber* (Lyon: Gryphe, 1534). Avec M. van der Poel, nous espérons publier bientôt une édition des *Orationes* avec traduction française et commentaire.

[7] Pour une plus ample discussion de ces aspects des *Orationes*, voir K. Lloyd-Jones, "From Sewers to Triumphal Arches: Dolet's Ideal of Civic Oratory," à paraître dans *The Renaissance, Papers from the 1987 CEMERS Conference*, Medieval & Renaissance Texts & Studies (Binghamton, NY).

autorités locales et à attaquer les Gascons de Toulouse, un orateur pour la nation d' Aquitaine, Pierre Pinache, prend la parole quelques semaines plus tard, en accusant Dolet d'avoir débité des propos séditieux; Dolet lui répond aussitôt, dans un discours où il cherche à couvrir de mépris son malheureux adversaire. Ainsi que nous l'avons démontré ailleurs,[8] les deux discours de Dolet (du moins sous leur forme imprimée) suivent avec une fidélité absolue les principes de l'éloquence classique énoncés dans les manuels comme la *Rhetorica ad Herennium*, ou le *De Inventione* de Cicéron. Le premier discours, du genre délibératif, cherchant à convaincre le public de tout ce qu'il y a d'ignoble dans le comportement des autorités toulousaines, et le second, du genre démonstratif, cherchant à démontrer le mérite de l'orateur et à couvrir d'opprobre le nom de son adversaire, suivent les divisions classiques depuis l'*exordium* jusqu'à la *conclusio*, et contiennent de nombreux exemples des figures agréées; les échos de Cicéron s'y trouvent en abondance—tournures idiomatiques, imprécations typiques, clausules et ainsi de suite—et les trois styles (*oratio gravis, oratio media,* et *oratio tenuis*) sont soigneusement alternés afin que la variété et le ton des discours soient adaptés à la question et au moment, selon les critères rhétoriques du *decus*. Il n'est guère surprenant que Pinache, croyant sans doute lui porter un coup mortel, taxe Dolet de n'être autre chose qu'un "religiosus Ciceronis imitator"[9]—expression calculée, avec justesse, afin d'endommager gravement la réputation de Dolet dans le bastion d'orthodoxie qu'est Toulouse.

Il est donc d'autant plus remarquable que, au lieu de chercher à minimiser la portée des propos de son adversaire, Dolet n'hésite pas à affirmer la satisfaction qu'il éprouve à se faire traiter de la sorte: c'est que, en répondant à Pinache, Dolet va pouvoir attaquer Erasme, et l'accusation d'être "un fervent imitateur de Cicéron" lui fournira l'occasion de dresser une de ses critiques les plus précises des idées rhétoriques de l'humaniste hollandais.

"Par le dieu immortel," s'écrie Dolet, "que pourrait-il y avoir de plus splendide pour moi, de plus beau, de plus salutaire" que d'être appelé un fervent imitateur de Cicéron? Et c'est toute la notion de l'imitation envisagée par Erasme qui est alors mise en cause:

> Quid me per deum immortalem lautius? quid pulchrius? quid denique beatius?... Quod si per omnia scriptorum genera inconsulte

[8] Voir Lloyd-Jones, "Dolet et la rhétorique...," passim.

[9] C'est Dolet même qui rapporte l'expression de Pinache (*Oratio* II:35), ainsi que presque tout ce que nous savons du discours de l'orateur aquitain.

nostri temporis oratorum exemplo vagarer, nec aliquem unum mihi imitandum proponerem, aut si tuo Batavique rhetoris iudicio inexhaustam Ciceronis copiam atque ubertatem, ita tenuem contractamque arbitrarer, ut latine loqui cupienti non omnia abunda suppeditare posse diffiderem, risu me iure proscinderes, ab iis non dissimilem, qui eo orationis genere utuntur, quae ex verborum undique accersitorum corrogatorumque congerie, et immenso historiarum, exemplorum, adagionumque cumulo, velut cento undequaque consutus, constet: quaeque nullam neque elegantiam, neque venustatem, neque gravitatem prae se ferat, formamque inconditam habeat, et minime aequabilem: sicque verbis distenta sit et exuberans, rerum pondere inanis (*Oratio* II:35–36).

Abscence de critère de sélection chez celui qui cherche un modèle, refus de reconnaître la supériorité du latin "classique," manque de principe organisateur chez celui qui cherche à pratiquer l'éloquence—il n'y a guère de pointe dans cette tirade qui ne vise pas un aspect spécifique de l'idée de l'imitation, de la pensée sur la création originale et de la notion de l'*auctoritas* telles qu'Erasme les développe dans le *Ciceronianus*. Il semble assez clair que Dolet, dans cet extrait, pense à un passage comme le suivant, où Erasme/Buléphore précise le genre d'imitation qu'il favorise:[10]

Amplector imitationem, sed quae adiuvet naturam, non violet; quae corrigat illius dotes, non obruat; probo imitationem, sed ad exemplum ingenio tuo congruens, aut certe non repugnans, ne videare cum gigantibus θεομαχεῖν. Rursus imitationem probo non uni addictam praescripto, a cuius lineis non ausit discedere, sed ex omnibus autoribus, aut certe praestantissimis, quod in quoque praecellit maxime tuoque congruit ingenio decerpentem ... ut qui legit non agnoscat emblema Ciceroni detractum, sed foetum a tuo natum cerebro, quemadmodum Palladem aiunt a cerebro Iovis, vivam parentis imaginem referentem, nec oratio tua cento quispiam videatur aut opus mosaicum, sed spirans imago tui pectoris, aut amnis a fonte cordis tui promanans.

Dans une semblable perspective, afin de flétrir non seulement le caractère de Pinache mais aussi son incompétence rhétorique, Dolet emprunte à Cicéron son portrait d'un Marc Antoine débauché et dégoûtant:

Illa sic obscoene et turpiter facta, obscoeni turpisque hominis furorem

---

[10] Erasme, *Ciceronianus* (éd. Gambaro): lignes 4206–24.

> non extinxere, concionem non ullo rhetoricae ornatu expolitam, sed tam multis compotationibus nocturnis elucubratam, quam crapulam, et stomachi cerebrique cruditatem exhalantem, in me foede evomuit, eademque nos se contaminaturum dissipat (*Oratio* II:67).

Pinache, tout comme Marc Antoine, est souvent critiqué pour la piètre qualité de son latin et de son éloquence,[11] mais c'est bien sûr toute la latinité d'Erasme qui est mise en cause ici. Il ne s'agit pas alors d'une invective conventionnelle destinée à jeter du blâme sur l'adversaire lors d'une joute oratoire: un tel passage, en condamnant l'incapacité de l'orateur à digérer et à faire siennes ses sources, représente une de ses critiques les plus vives de la notion de l'éloquence chez Erasme.

Là où l'idéal érasmien est ancré dans l'authenticité du *moi*, l'idéal de Dolet vient moins du coeur que de l'esprit, et se nourrit de tout ce qui nous distingue de la bête—notre *virtus*, notre *humanitas*, l'adresse, la culture, la technique, la discipline. Idéal austère peut-être, difficile sans doute, mais qui rend honneur à nos efforts pour nous améliorer, et qui a du moins le mérite d'être réalisable dans ce monde, à la différence de la transcendance érasmienne. Lorsque Dolet fera dire à son héros Villeneuve, au cours de l'*Erasmianus*, que ce que nous écrivons à la suite de l'effort intellectuel est plus riche et plus significatif que ce qui relève de la simple conversation,

> Pleniora sunt & uberiora quae chartis reponimus, quam quae inter nos confabulamur: stilum cogitatio alit & auget, formaturque meditatione oratio, & ad habitum venustiorem adolescit (*Erasmianus*: 94),

c'est toute une esthétique de l'éloquence qui s'engage, et il est évident que la spontanéité et le "naturel" érasmiens n'ont rien à y contribuer.

La théorie de l'imitation qui se dégage des *Orationes* est profondément ancrée dans la capacité de l'écrivain à reconnaître les mérites linguistiques et stylistiques de son modèle; tout y est question de goût, de ce qui est *decus*:

> Nec tamen in ea sum sententia, ut nullum praeter Ciceronem nobis legendum est. Placet quisquis pure, emendate, probateque, non inquinate, aut abiecte loquitur, nec novum loquendi genus, aut immodicum obscuritatis studium, barbarieive sordes: nec humilem frigidamve scriptionem, aut proverbialem nescio quam orationis

[11] Cf. les *Philippicae* II:63, V:20 et passim: pour la *latinitas* de Pinache et de Marc Antoine, cf. *Oratio* II:25, et *Phil.* XIII:43.

> farraginem, linguae Latinae splendori & sublimitati anteponit (*Oratio* II:36).

L'on pourra objecter avec justesse que tout cela n'est pas trop loin de certains aspects de la pensée d'Erasme sur la même question: J. Chomarat a déjà fait valoir le fait que la théorie de l'imitation chez Erasme[12]

> suppose un jugement porté sur le modèle: il faut reconnaître ses qualités et ses défauts, son fort et son faible, ce qui implique déjà quelque connaissance des règles de l'art.... Imiter c'est choisir.

Mais aucune langue ne se distingue de sa fonction expressive. Absorber Cicéron, c'est faire siens une langue et un langage qui expriment des positions et des perspectives nettes, qu'on le veuille ou non. C'est là évidemment la base même de l'opposition d'Erasme au cicéronianisme, et sur ce point précis l'on n'aurait sans doute pas tort de se demander si Dolet épouse une position tellement différente de celle d'Erasme. L'importance des notions de la discrimination, de la digestion et de l'absorption des sources est explicitement reconnue au cours de l'*Erasmianus*:

> Ciceroniani nomen ei tribuam, qui Ciceronem diligenter legerit, qui Ciceronem intus & incute noverit, qui Ciceronem una lectione (ut tuus Erasmus librorum helluo) non vorarit aut absorbserit: sed sensim delibarit, degustarit, regustarit, exhauserit, beneque concoxerit (*Erasmianus*: 63).

L'on pourrait poser la question de la manière suivante: malgré des ressemblances indéniables entre certaines de leurs positions, est-ce que le désaccord qui les sépare reflète des différences stylistiques, ou plutôt conceptuelles? Mais ce serait là ne pas tenir compte du fait que la rhétorique même n'autorise pas une distinction aussi artificielle. La différence entre les procédés stylistiques de Dolet et d'Erasme entraîne une différence majeure entre leurs intentions rhétoriques.

Ainsi que nous l'avons déjà proposé, les *Orationes* préparent la voie à l'*Erasmianus*: tandis qu'il n'y a aucune incompatibilité de pensée entre les deux textes, il est pourtant évident que certaines différences existent entre les *Orationes* et l'*Erasmianus*, grâce en partie aux différences de format et d'intention. Tel serait le cas, par exemple, pour l'argument développé par Dolet/Villeneuve lorsque le narrateur déclare qu'il n'y a aucun lien

---

[12] J. Chomarat, *Grammaire et Rhétorique chez Erasme* (Paris: Les Belles Lettres, 1981), 823–24.

nécessaire entre le caractère moral de l'orateur et la valeur morale des idées qu'il avance:

> nec mihi placet ficta illa oratoris diffinitio, ut vir bonus sit, praescribens. Non fides eloquentem, non mores facundum, non vitae integritas, disertum quenquam aut doctum efficit. Tribuit eloquentiae facultatem & disciplinarum peritiam, tum ingenii felicitas, tum immensus labor, atque vehemens exercitatio (*Erasmianus*: 107 et suiv.).

J. Chomarat, évoquant ce qu'il appelle "le rejet par Dolet de la définition antique, cicéronienne pourtant, de l'orateur comme *vir bonus dicendi peritus*," parle de ce passage capital dans les termes suivants:[13]

> pour communiquer sa conviction, il faut que [l'orateur] en ait une; selon Dolet ce n'est pas nécessaire, il est possible de feindre; une canaille est quelquefois grand orateur; mais cet amoralisme est moins dicté par le cynisme ou le machiavélisme que par l'esthétisme. Un discours est beau indépendamment des circonstances où il est né, de sa réussite ou de son échec immédiat, de la sincérité et de la moralité de son auteur.

Selon les arguments d'Erasme, en revanche, ce serait précisément dans la sincérité, dans l'authenticité du *moi* de l'auteur que le texte trouverait toute sa valeur et son éloquence, lorsque celles-ci sont consacrées au service de questions moralement défensibles.

Nous croyons avoir montré, pourtant, en ce qui concerne les *Orationes* du moins, qu'il serait excessif de parler d'un "rejet" de la conception cicéronienne de l'orateur.[14] Quoi qu'il en dise dans l'*Erasmianus*, il faut croire que si Dolet insiste tant sur sa propre honnêteté, sa propre innocence et sa propre *virtus* au cours des *Orationes*, ce n'est pas entièrement dans un effort de se soustraire à l'attention des autorités. Il s'agit aussi de trouver le moyen de rassurer ceux à qui il consacre son éloquence–ses amis, sa confrérie, sa patrie, sa *societas*; il faut leur affirmer qu'il mérite leur confiance, qu'il est en effet "vir bonus peritus dicendi," et digne, par conséquent, de parler pour la "res publica." L'argument qu'il développe dans l'*Erasmianus* est le fruit incontesté de l'esthétisme, et le jugement qu'en fait C. Longeon nous semble tout à fait juste:[15]

---

[13] J. Chomarat, "Dolet et Erasme" (in *Cahiers V. L. Saulnier* 3: voir note 4): 24.

[14] Voir Lloyd-Jones, "From Sewers to Triumphal Arches. . . ," passim.

[15] C. Longeon, "Cohérences d'Etienne Dolet," *Acta Conventus Neo-Latini Sanctandreani*, éd. I. D. McFarlane, Medieval & Renaissance Texts & Studies, vol. 38 (Bing-

Il plaide ainsi pour un orateur qui soit un authentique professionnel, défini par sa compétence dans l'art de persuader et non pas par des certitudes morales.

Le champ de références de l'*Erasmianus*, du moins du passage dont il s'agit ici, n'est pourtant pas celui des *Orationes*; dans le dialogue contre Erasme, Dolet propose une défense vigoureuse de l'autonomie *littéraire* de l'orateur, tandis que les *Orationes* insistent plutôt sur la valeur civique de sa tâche. La remarque de M. Fumaroli s'applique de façon fort juste ici:[16]

> C'est un acte de courage, et même de témérité, qui fait de Cicéron et de l'imitation cicéronienne les garants d'un art littéraire profane [. . .] qui refuse de céder au "soupçon" moral et religieux. Dolet revendique contre Erasme une véritable séparation de la Religion et de l'art littéraire.

La *praxis* des *Orationes*, même si elle ne contredit pas l'argument "esthétique" de l'*Erasmianus*, nous révèle que la position de Dolet est plus nuancée dans les discours. La consécration de nos talents au bien-être de la république est en soi un acte d'engagement moral, et seul celui qui est irréprochable a le droit de parler pour la patrie. Que personne n'aspire à gagner la confiance de ses compatriotes à moins de posséder "la renommée la plus éminente et l'érudition la plus exceptionnelle" (ad quos nisi & nomine amplissimo, & eruditione eximia liceat prorsus adspirare nemini [*Oratio* I:19])—et tout Cicéron est là pour nous rappeler que la gloire n'est réservée qu'aux bons, que l'érudition ne vaut rien si elle ne mène pas à la sagesse.

Lorsque Dolet, dans les *Orationes*, condamne Erasme pour ses attaques contre le cicéronianisme, il s'y prend entièrement par le biais des différences entre leurs conceptions stylistiques—mais ces différences, placées dans le contexte de la pratique rhétorique, entraînent des perspectives conceptuelles incompatibles. Dolet dresse systématiquement une caricature du style érasmien qui fait ressortir à quel point ce style constitue une trahison à toutes les valeurs que Dolet identifie avec la rhétorique—valeurs qui relèvent de la plus haute idée de la fonction de l'éloquence. Erasme, à la différence de l'orateur cicéronien, refuse de prendre un modèle particulier pour guider son style, préférant choisir à sa discrétion parmi

---

hamton, NY, 1986), 366. Cf. aussi Telle, *Erasmianus*, 354.

[16] M. Fumaroli, *L'Age de l'éloquence: Rhétorique et "res literaria" de la Renaissance au seuil de l'époque classique* (Genève: Droz, 1980), 111.

tous les écrivains dont il dispose. La théorie de l'imitation chez Dolet suppose elle aussi la formation nécessaire pour savoir choisir un (mais un seul) modèle en connaissance de cause. Il y a cependant, pour Dolet, une sorte de vantardise, d'arrogance intellectuelle, chez un Erasme qui, devant tous les maîtres de l'Antiquité, n'arrive pas à en choisir un seul qui trouve grâce à ses yeux.

Voilà pourquoi les écrits d'Erasme ne seraient qu'un amas de mots tirés d'un peu partout, un immense monceau d'histoires, "une pièce d'étoffe bigarrée cousue de morceaux venus de n'importe où." Il y a absence totale d'art et d'adresse, de forme et de structure; ses écrits sont gonflés de la suffisance de leur auteur qui, du fait qu'il ne s'engage jamais, s'exprime toujours "circumspecte cauteque" (*Oratio* II:60), ainsi que l'*Erasmianus* ne cessera de le rappeler. L'éloquence qui défendra les valeurs de la République, de cette nouvelle République des Lettres dont la citoyenneté est ouverte à tous à l'époque où Gargantua informe son fils que "la lumière et dignité a esté [...] rendue ès lettres,"[17] doit être rigoureuse et universellement appréciable. Pour se libérer de l'"infélicité et calamitez des Gothz," pour "yssir de ceste tranquillité et repos d'estude, et apprendre la chevalerie et les armes pour défendre [la] maison et [les] amys secourir en tous leurs affaires contre les assaulx des malfaisans," il faudra une autre voix que celle d'Erasme.

Trinity College, Hartford, CT

[17] Rabelais, *Pantagruel*, chap. 8.

The Beginnings of Catullan Neo-Latin Poetry

WALTHER LUDWIG

The starting point for my research on Catullus in the Renaissance was an observation which is probably familiar to all of you. There is a characteristic Catullan style. It uses Catullan metres, especially the typical hendecasyllabic, the favorite Catullan vocabulary, Catullan word forms, modes of expressions, topics and themes. These elements remind the reader immediately of Catullus, may he be mentioned as a model or not. Poems of such kind were written for many occasions, on various subjects in Italy and other countries in the centuries of the Renaissance. Pontano, Janus Secundus, Lotichius, and others may come to your mind. But we do not know how and when this Neo-Catullan poetry began, how it developed, how wide spread it was and how it influenced the vernacular literatures. There are a few more or less detailed studies on some specific aspects like the Catullan poetry in France or in England or the general relationship of Catullus and Pontano, but on the whole the questions which I just raised remain unanswered in modern research literature. This is even the case in regard to the beginnings of Neo-Latin poetry in Catullan style. The relevant literature tells you that it began in the Italian Quattrocento and usually some poets are mentioned who are said to have imitated Catullus, but they are listed without any order and differentiation and without any attempt to determine the origin of this poetical style more closely. In most cases poets like Poliziano, Pontano, Marullo, Beccadelli, Navagero, and Flaminio appear in the random lists of such imitators, sometimes Lovato and Mussato are included, and the term 'imitator' is often used so broadly and vaguely that it comprises anything from the use of a Catullan word to the variation of a Catullan poem, from the development of certain stylistic features to the choice of certain topics. The most recent work which dealt with the influence of Catullus neglected Neo-Latin poetry totally. John Ferguson wrote in the chapter 'Influence' of his survey on Catullus, published in 1988, "much work needs to be done on the influence of Catullus on the early Renaissance in Italy and France," but did not mention Neo-Latin poetry at all among the fields on which Catullus had an impact. Such restraint is not justified even in view of the scant literature on the subject. It can only be explained by the unfortunately still existing blindness of some classicists in front of the phenomenon of Neo-Latin. All this caused me to ask: how was Catullus received after his rediscovery? Where and when did the composing of poems in Catullan style originate? What were the motifs? What was considered to be Catullan and what was reproduced? What was the purpose of these poems? And finally: Which impact did these poems have on the later Catullan poetry of the Renaissance?

The still existing controversy, whether the Catullus manuscript which is the source of our tradition was brought from France to Verona around 1300 or if this manuscript always lay in Verona and was rediscovered around that time, is not immediately relevant to our problems. It may only be stated that there is no evidence that Lovato knew Catullus around 1265, as some scholars believed, following an article of Guido Billanovich in 1958. He thought that the word connections *acrior ignis* and *imbre madet*, which occur in a poetical letter of Lovato from 1268, are proof that Lovato had read Catullus by that time. As I demonstrated in an article in the Rheinisches Museum of 1986, these word connections do not go back to Catullus, but to Seneca and Statius. But did Lovato and/or Mussato imitate Catullus at a later time? The problem here is first, whether certain words and word connections, which in identical or similar forms appear in texts of these early humanists and in Catullus, but also in other ancient authors, do come from Catullus or not. In each case a close comparison of the different contexts is necessary. Sometimes we will only be able to decide such questions with higher or lesser degrees of probability. But in whichever way such parallels are evaluated, the use of some single Catullan words or word connections in the hexameters and distichs of Lovato and Mussato can never be interpreted as an attempt to compose poems in Catullan style. It would always be only the use of ancient word material which they took from Catullus as well as from other ancient authors. Augusto Sainati wrote in 1972 that Mussato imitated the passer poem of Catullus "in una svelta poesiola." But in that epigram Mussato only says that he does not write poems like Virgil's first Eclogue or like Catullus's *passer*-poem, and the phrasing of this statement is not even specifically Catullan. I recommend to use the term *imitation* more restrictively. Otherwise we have to call almost any relationship of a later text to an earlier one an imitation and have to find new terms for those phenomena which more properly are designated with this term.

It is then further necessary to see how far the text of Catullus was known in the fourteenth century and how it was received. For this purpose I checked the manuscript tradition and all the instances where Catullus is mentioned or quoted in texts of that century. The result was the observation that the text of Catullus was distributed very slowly and that a very small number of humanists in northern and middle Italy came to know it. They studied this text and quoted sometimes passages from it for moralistic, antiquarian, philological or, in case of c. 16 with its distinction between the *vita* and the verses of a poet, for learned poetic reasons. The various metres were observed and defined, some *ioci* appreciated. Petrarch once used the term *nugae* as a formula of modesty for his own writings. But nobody in the whole century tried to write poems in Catullan style. Catullus was one of the rediscovered ancient authors and as such important, but he was not among the most favorite authors of anybody; he stood, so to speak, in the second row. His rediscovery had not yet lead to his renaissance.

In the first half of the fifteenth century, his text was considerably wider distributed. The first warnings against reading Catullus in school appear. In this time Latin poetry in Catullan style began. In modern literature Antonio Beccadelli, called Panormita (1394–1471), is often named as a prominent imitator of Catullus. I checked his poem collection *Hermaphroditus* from 1425 and the letters of humanists related to it and found that Panormita did not yet imitate the style of Catullus, but that he was most important in preparing the way for the Catullus-imitations of Pontano. Panormita mentions Catullus at the head of a list of ancient authors who, as he says, all wrote poems full of *lascivia*, and he defends his own obscene elegiacs with the Catullan distinction of the *castus et pius poeta* and the *versus molliculi et parum pudici*. Catullus and other ancient poets protect and legitimize his audaciously obscene and sexually oriented poetry. But if you check these poems, only very few borrowings from Catullus are to be found. They restrict themselves on the use of the verbs *pedicare* and *irrumare*, on some obscene motives from c. 97 and on the tag of the thousand kisses. Panormita never tried to imitate the Catullan style or the typical hendecasyllabics. Martial and the *Carmina Priapea* were his more prominent models, but he pointed to Catullus as a patron of frivolous poetry.

Before Pontano could follow this hint, Cristoforo Landino (1424–1504) came to Catullus by another way in Florence. He wrote a poem collection titled *Xandra* in 1443/4. It contains mainly elegies, but also two hendecasyllabic poems and three Sapphic odes. On the whole a cycle of love poems, it is primarily oriented on Propertius. But Landino mentions also

Catullus among his favorite authors, and in order to show himself in the role of a pathetic and unhappy lover, he also uses thoughts and expressions from Catullus's c. 8 and 87. He reproduces in his hendecasyllabics specifically Catullan words and stylistic features like the diminutives and the polysyllables. In a Sapphic ode he incorporates structural elements from c. 11. These are, according to my knowledge, the earliest attempts to use the thoughtline of specific Catullan poems and to imitate the Catullan style. But the instances are rather rare and not very prominent, and Landino did not continue this use of Catullus in his later poems. These are reasons why he probably did not have much influence on the later development of the Catullan style in Neo-Latin poetry. In addition, his poems were not printed before the eighteenth century.

The successful foundation and propagation of the Catullan style in Neo-Latin poetry is to be ascribed to Pontano (1429–1503). We may observe three different phases in this process. He had come to Naples in 1448, where he found Panormita, who became his close friend. Stimulated by the *Hermaphroditus*, Pontano wrote in 1449 a poem collection titled *Pruritus sive de Lascivia*, the second version of which he dedicated to Tito (Vespasiano) Strozzi at Ferrara in 1451. The problem with this collection is that neither of its two versions is completely transmitted. But we have various manuscripts which contain parts of that collection. By comparison of the order of the poems in the different manuscripts and by an analysis of their content, I have been able to reconstruct the *Pruritus*-collection, at least to a certain degree. It contained poems which opened and closed the book, and at least seven erotic, partially very obscene poems, three poems addressed to friends and one invective on a bad contemporary poet. Ten poems are in Catullan hendecasyllabics, one is a Sapphic ode; glyconics, distichs, and hexameters occur. The metres and themes indicate that poetry in Catullan style was intended. The title *Pruritus* and the first poem declare as a function of the *novus libellus* to make the reader prurient. Catullus and Martial occasionally said their *versus molles et iocosi* should provoke a *prurire* on the side of the reader. Pontano surprises the reader with exposing this aim right at the beginning. His collection stands in the tradition of the *Hermaphroditus*. The *Carmina Priapea* provided some ideas and expressions in both cases. But in the *Pruritus*, there is also a conscious imitation of Catullus. If you analyse its hendecasyllabics, you find that Pontano observed the stylistic peculiarities of Catullus closely and reproduced them in concentrated form. This concerns the take-over of typically Catullan words and expressions as words of value and vituperation, deminutives, polysyllables, generalizing pronouns, comparatives and comparisons, particles, intensifications, repetitions, and reversals. Then, there are several poems which are modelled as variations to specific Catullan poems (*Am.* 1.5, for instance, in which the author plans to give his *nivea columba* to his *puella*, is a variation of the *passer*-poems; sexual connotations in the invisaged activities of the *columba* clearly indicate that Pontano wanted his poem to be allegorically understood and that he, therefore, interpreted the *passer*-poem itself in a similar way, as, later on, Poliziano). Finally, Pontano followed Catullus in his general themes, the erotic pleasures with *puellae*, the witty conversation with *amici* and the rude invectives against enemies, and gave the whole a light and gay, joking and pleasurable, exclusive and sometimes rough and very obscene tone.

A second phase of Pontano's Catullus-imitation is shown by his *Liber Parthenopaeus*, which he dedicated to his friend Lorenzo Bonincontri in Naples in 1457. This book comprises the first twenty-eight poems of his printed *Liber Amorum I*. Pontano placed in this book four poems from the *Pruritus*, but only those which do not contain elements of crude obscenity and invective. Again he assembled a variety of metres in this book; eight poems are in hendecasyllabics. The poems are mostly erotic in content. Motives of the Roman elegists occur. But above all, Pontano wanted to be measured on Catullus. He wanted his verses to be *molles, lepidi, leves, iocosi*. He states in the closing poem (*Am.* 1.28) that he tried to follow the *nequitiae*, the *procacitas* and the *elegantia* of Catullus and claims that poems of this sort were not heard in the last thousand years. He emulated also the Catullan poems of Landino; apparently he intended to come closer to the frank style of Catullus. An analysis of the metres, the themes, the stylistic features and the content of the poems shows that he tried to imitate Catullus on all these levels. The difference in the *Pruritus* is to be seen first in the quantity of these imitations, second in the avoidance of crude obscenities. But he loved erotic representations. The general atmosphere of the book is cheerful and optimistic. He may show himself in the role of a frustrated *exclusus amator*, or an unhappy love may provoke the idea of death. But, in the same poems or in the next ones, such emotions are replaced by hopes for more pleasurable events—a reconciliation may occur or the lover consoles himself with an other *puella*, who compensates his loss to his full satisfaction. There is never a desperation without recovery, never the pathetic love for the one and only beloved. It seems Pontano thought that he followed Catullus also in this emotional condition.

These Catullan poems of Pontano gave impulses to other humanists to try the Catullan style too. The strongly increased distribution of the text of Catullus and the recognized principle of the imitation of the ancients could independently lead to imitations of Catullus. But Michele Marullo

(1453–1500), the most important imitator of Catullus in the fifteenth century next to Pontano, is known to have been a younger friend of Pontano at Naples. Not later than 1489, when he came to Florence, he must also have known Landino's poems. He published at Rome in 1489 two and at Florence 1497 two further *Libri epigrammaton*, which again show various metres, hendecasyllabics included. Some poems show the typical stylistic elements of Catullus. Marullo also took specific Catullan poems as models, some not yet used by Pontano. But, contrary to Pontano, Catullus is not the declared and not the most prominent poetical model, and love is only one of several themes. Above all, there is a decisive difference between the love poems of Marullo and Pontano: Marullo praises the beauty of Neaera, assures her of his unchangeable love, complains about her refusals, confesses his torments and accuses *Amor* of cruelty, but he never describes the happy pleasures of love, not even in his desires. Only once he uses the Catullan term *basiationes*–but he presses his hundred kisses on a picture of his beloved. In Pontano's *Liber Parthenopaeus* kisses were a dominant motive, and he showed his readers the love play up to and after the climax. Marullo is very conscious of this contrast to Pontano. He explains and defends his position in a poem to an unknown *Quintilianus*–there are reasons to suppose that this is a pseudonym for his poetry teacher *Iovianus Pontanus*. *Quintilianus* had censured Marullo's liber as *nimium castus ... nimiumque pudicus*, but approved of his *ingenium*. According to the often quoted c. 16 of Catullus, he apparently even wanted from a *poeta castus et pius* the writing of *versus molliculi et parum pudici*. Marullo, on the contrary, was in favour of *carmina casta*: they please Apollo and the Muses and as, he says, *vetat ingenuus verba inhonesta pudor*. The reference to Catullus does not bring him to compose obscene poems: *Tu licet Marsumque feras doctumque Catullum/et quoscumque alios Martia Roma legit/ non tamen efficies, ut Phrynae scribere malim ... / Sit procul a nobis obscoena licentia scripti: / ludimus innocuae carmina mentis opus*. And in accordance with his own poetical practice, he lists the permitted themes of love poetry: *Sit satis auratos crines laudare Neaerae, / sit satis in duram multa queri dominam / et facere iratum saevo convincia Amori, / ... caetera Thespiadum prohibet chorus*. The imitation of Catullus in the sense of Pontano was not permissible. Landino probably approved. The Carmelite Baptista Mantuanus condemned at the same time in an elegy *Contra poetas impudice loquentes* any erotic poetry: in his view *casta carmina* were exclusively destined *ad sanctos usus*. The distinction between the poet's life and poems was wrong.

It is remarkable that, just at the end of the eighties of the fifteenth century, Pontano returned to his Catullan poetry: between 1489 and 1501, he composed two books entitled *Hendecasyllabi*, the first poem books of modern times devoted exclusively to this metre, as well as the largest collection of such poems: altogether seventy poems with more than 1800 verses. One should take into consideration that Pontano wrote these poems when Marullo had announced his opposing poetic view and when Mantuanus had raised his principal objections from a Christian position. Pontano did not care. He chose a title *sola metri lege*, which Pliny the Younger had used before him, and recommended his two books in the opening poems to the inspiration of the Catullan Muse. The poems, dedicated to his friend Marino Tomicelli, deal with the pleasurable life at the spa of Baiae near Naples, where the most charming *puellae* and his best *amici* meet. Some poems are modelled on specific Catullan ones, but this occurs not as often comparatively as in his earlier Catullan collections. The general Catullan style of Pontano, in which certain Catullan peculiarities occur more often than in Catullus, is brought to a mastership of its own. The tone is playful and joking, the atmosphere serene, cheerful, and full of laughter. At the same time, Pontano shrinks from no taboo in his erotic representations, although he avoids specifically obscene words. This inclusion of sexual actions is not only strictly against the moralistic poetical code of Marullo, it surpasses even Catullus by far. But Pontano always connects Catullan motives with such representations. This seems to show that Pontano even here wants to be seen as following Catullus or at least as being on a way opened by Catullus. The dominant term of the *Hendecasyllabi sive Baiarum libri II* is *voluptas*. He used it at various prominent places in the collection and *Voluptas* appears personified in the last poem as the last word, where he wishes his future readers: *Sic vobis in amore nil amarum, / nil insit nisi dulce, sic amando / et noctes pariter diesque agatis, / assistat lateri et comes Voluptas*. The term *voluptas* was, of course, known to Pontano and his contemporaries as the leading Epicurean term. In Lorenzo Valla's dialogue *De vera voluptate* (1433/49) the poet Maffeo Vegio had defended the Epicurean position. To defend the *voluptas* of Epicurus as the highest aim, was, in the fifteenth century only possible under the protection of *poetica licentia*. The poetical example of Catullus and his differentiation between the *castus et pius poeta* and his *versus molliculi et parum pudici* made possible and legitimized for Pontano a poetry of Epicureanism, which he kept apart from his Christian beliefs. Thus, Catullus had a role in the complex process in which certain humanists separated themselves more or less from the precepts and/or doctrines of Christianity.

In this way, the basic lines of origin and early development of the new Catullan poetry may be drawn. Other humanists, less prominent as Catullan poets, could be mentioned. At the beginning of the sixteenth century Pontano and Marullo are regarded to be the best Latin poets of modern times, regardless of the fact that Erasmus accused them of paganism. It is not yet investigated which impact they had on the development of Catullan poetry in the sixteenth century, in which it spread on the transalpine nations. We do not yet see the full extent of this Neo-Catullan poetry. But some observations allow the supposition that Catullan poets of the sixteenth century were not alone in studying Catullus for this purpose, but were also influenced by their Catullan predecessors in the fifteenth century, especially by Pontano. In this way, Pontano's view and use of Catullus guided humanists far into the seventeenth century in what they saw in Catullus and how they tried to imitate his poetry.[1]

Universität Hamburg

---

[1] This paper is the condensed version of a forthcoming considerably larger article on the same topic, titled "Catullus renatus–Anfänge und frühe Entwicklung des catullischen Stils in der neulateinischen Dichtung." [Meanwhile it appeared in: W. Ludwig, *Litterae Neolatinae*, Munich 1989, p. 162 ff.]

Sur les traces de Louis Aleaume, Seigneur de Verneuil, poète neo-latin

JEAN-CLAUDE MARGOLIN

Verneuil-sur-Seine, petite ville du département des Yvelines, toute proche de Conflans-Ste-Honorine, était, au début du XVIe siècle, la résidence d'un seigneur français, Etienne Aleaume.[1] Il avait acquis en 1517 le fief de Verneuil et de Vernouillet. Nous avons des renseignements sur sa famille, son épouse, ses enfants, et aussi sur sa piété et son sens du beau, grâce à un magnifique livre d'Heures qui lui a appartenu[2] et qui contient, outre quelques miniatures particulièrement "parlantes," des

---

[1] Le nom d'ALEAUME (ou ALLEAUME, voire ALEAULME) figure dans plusieurs Biographies (comme le *Dictionnaire de la Biographie française*) et Dictionnaires des Blasons ou Armoriaux (comme ceux de Rietstap ou de d'Hozier). Mais les noms d'Etienne et de son fils Louis y figurent rarement, et plusieurs confusions sont à craindre dans les rapports généalogiques à établir. La branche qui nous intéresse est originaire de l'Orléanais. Tout au début de sa notice consacrée à Louis Aleaume, son ami Scévole de Sainte-Marthe précise, dans les *Eloges des hommes illustres qui depuis un siècle ont fleuri en France dans la profession des lettres* (trad. fr. de G. Colletet des *Gallorum illustrium . . .*, Paris, 1644), que son père (donc Etienne) était un "homme riche et de noble race, Seigneur de Verneuil, petite ville qui n'est éloignée de Paris que d'une journée. . . ." Voir la notice très brève du *DBF* sur *Louis* Aleaume. Je tiens à remercier Soeur Marie-Claire Tihon, qui m'a aiguillé sur la piste de Louis Aleaume et de ses parents, grâce à un article intitulé "Un poète de la Renaissance, Seigneur de Verneuil, Louis Aleaume," et publié dans le n° 4 de la brochure *Notre-Dame de Verneuil*, 16–19.

[2] Il l'a fait orner selon ses désirs. La magnifique reliure est selon toute vraisemblance d'origine: reliure à compartiments d'un goût exquis en maroquin noir, incrusté de pièces de maroquin grenat et de filets d'or, figures géométriques et entrelacs; tranches dorées. Ouvrage détenu par la Bibliothèque de l'Arsenal, n° 1175 (328 A. T. L.).

renseignements manuscrits (souvent peu lisibles) à la fin du livre, sur les derniers feuillets qui étaient restés blancs. Ce Livre d'Heures, qui mériterait à lui seul toute une monographie, a été sommairement décrit dans un article actuellement sous presse.[3] Nous retiendrons seulement des indications fournies par ce manuscrit de 135 feuillets, la devise franco-latine des armes de la famille: IBI REQVIES / NON CY MAIS LA,[4] expression de la piété chrétienne, en attente du repos éternel, ainsi que quelques précisions chiffrées: c'est ainsi que, contrairement à la notice du *Bulletin de la Société archéologique de l'Orléanais*[5] consacrée au fils aîné d'Etienne Aleaume et de Jeanne Tenon, ce Louis auquel nous nous intéressons, le futur poète néo-latin, n'est pas né à Verneuil en 1520, comme ses frères et sa soeur, mais à Paris, le 9 mai 1524.

Nous savons qu'il fit d'excellentes études humanistes à Paris dans le second quart du siècle, tout en ignorant quels furent le ou les collèges fréquentés, ou les maîtres de son adolescence. Il devint par la suite avocat–il sera cité avec éloge par Antoine Loisel dans son *Dialogue des avocats du Parlement de Paris*–et accomplira une brillante carrière juridique et administrative à Orléans, d'où sa présence, dans toutes les monographies de l'Orléanais,[6] parmi les "hommes illustres." En 1569, il est pourvu de l'office de lieutenant général au baillage et siège présidial d'Orléans, le siège étant devenu vacant par suite de la révocation de Jean Hue, réformé déclaré. Au cours de sa carrière, il prendra une part active à la réforme de la Coutume d'Orléans, en 1583. Pendant les guerres civiles, il s'efforcera de tempérer les violences, impuissant toutefois à empêcher les massacres, comme celui des protestants à Orléans. Il conservera sa fonction jusqu'à sa mort, en 1593. Il eut droit à des funérailles solennelles, dont maints détails sont rapportés par un article de la *Revue Orléanaise* de 1847 d'après des documents d'archives.[7]

Il était lié avec tous les savants, lettrés et poètes de son temps, en particulier l'Orléanais Germain Audebert,[8] qui a célébré en vers latins

---

[3] A paraître dans la *Bibliothèque d'Humanisme et Renaissance*, t.51 (ou 52).

[4] Voir entre autres, Laurence Urdang et Ceila Dame Robbins Editors, *Mottoes* ("A complete list of more than 9000 mottoes from around the World and throughout History") (Detroit, 1987), 625–26 (34 "mottoes" relevant de la catégorie thématique REST, ou REPOS). Voir n° 12 ("Mon repos au ciel"), n° 7 ("In caelo quies"), etc.

[5] Tome 18, n° 212 (1917), 356–59.

[6] Entre autres, *Les hommes illustres de l'Orléanais* (Orléans, 1852), t.1, 11.

[7] Voir aussi *Recherches historiques de la ville d'Orléans*, par D. Lottin père (Orléans, 1837), t. 2, 110.

[8] Sur Germain Audebert, voir, outre l'art. de la *Biographie universelle*, t. 2, 399–400,

Venise, Rome et Naples, et son fils Nicolas,[9] Scevole de Sainte-Marthe (qui lui consacre une notice de deux pages dans sa galerie des hommes illustres de son temps),[10] Jean II Brinon[11] (dont il épousa la cousine, Marguerite Brulart), et, par l'intermédiaire de celui-ci, tous les poètes de la Pléïade que Brinon recevait magnifiquement en son château de Médan, Ronsard tout le premier, ainsi que Jean Dorat, leur commun maître. Nul doute qu'au contact de ces poètes, Louis Aleaume ait pris le goût de la versification latine (on ne lui connaît pas de poèmes en français). Ses dédicaces à de hauts personnages du royaume ou à d'autres, qu'il a contribués lui-même à sortir de l'anonymat, montrent assez l'étendue, et parfois l'intimité de ses relations.

Sa modestie ne lui permit pas de publier ses poèmes latins de son vivant. C'est à son fils Gilles que nous devons de connaître ces *Poematia*, puisqu'il prit sur lui, non sans scrupule de conscience (comme nous le devinions d'après sa préface) de les publier en 1595. Il devait lui-même mourir en 1597.

Il s'agit d'une plaquette, fort rare (elle ne dut pas être tirée à un très grand nombre d'exemplaires, et beaucoup ont disparu depuis cette date), publiée sans date, sans lieu d'impression et sans nom d'éditeur. On peut lire sur la page de titre (l'exemplaire que nous avons utilisé est celui de la Bibliothèque nationale, cote *Ye 8003*):

LVD. ALEALMI / PRAESID. PROV. / AVREL. / V.C. / POEMATIA

c'est-à-dire: *Ludovici Alealmi Praesidialis provincialis aurelianensis viri clarissimi poematia.*

Le second exemplaire disponible de la Bibliothèque nationale (*Rés. p Ye. 1020*) ne présente aucune différence par rapport au précédent (une note au crayon, au verso de la page de titre, renvoie à l'article de Basseville, du *Bulletin de la Société archéologique de l'Orléanais*).

Signalons encore que les poèmes de Louis Aleaume ont été reproduits, avec quelques variantes ou additions, et un ordre légèrement différent, au

---

et celui de la *Nouvelle Biogr. génér.*, t. 3–4, col. 599, l'article de Jacques Boussard, "L'Université d'Orléans et l'humanisme au début du XVIe siècle," *Humanisme et Renaissance* 5 (1938): 209 sqq.

[9] Voir P. de Nolhac, "Nicolas Audebert, archéologue orléanais," *Revue archéologique* 2 (1887): 315–24.

[10] Voir n. 1. Dans la traduction de Colletet, 454–55.

[11] Que Ronsard appelait "l'Orphée du jour d'huy." Voir P. de Nolhac, *Ronsard et l'Humanisme* (Paris: Champion, 1921), *passim.*

tome Ier du recueil de *Deliciae poetarum Gallorum*,[12] qui date de 1609 et où ils occupent les pages 1–53, en tête du volume. D'autre part, plusieurs de ses poèmes se trouvent dans le recueil des poésies de Germain Audebert, le "Virgile orléanais," édition de Hanovre, 1603.[13] En revanche, il y a tout lieu de penser que la mention qui figure dans le catalogue de la Bibliothèque Beauharnaise, imprimé à Orléans en 1683 (chez Jean Boyer) est inexacte. On lit en effet, page 10: *Lud. Alealmi proeludia, Duaci, 1555 in–8*, mais, par ailleurs, aucun ouvrage imprimé à Douai au XVIe siècle ne porte ce titre.

§ § §

La rareté de ce petit volume est-elle une raison suffisante pour sortir de l'ombre le personnage qui en fut l'auteur, dans les loisirs que lui laissaient les devoirs de sa charge? Apparemment non. Mais, comme nous le verrons par une rapide analyse de son contenu, ces poèmes, tout conventionnels qu'ils soient par leur forme et (souvent) par les thèmes qui y sont traités, ont un intérêt biographique et historique certain: non seulement ils fournissent des éléments relatifs à leur auteur, comme c'est le cas pour la plupart des poètes néo-latins du XVIe siècle, mais surtout des renseignements sur ses amis, ses relations, ses "réseaux" socio-professionnels, les alliances familiales qu'il a contractées, ainsi que sur des événements qui ont marqué l'époque ou remué l'opinion publique, comme la fameuse comète de 1577, qui suscita toute une littérature,[14] ou encore le duel de Jarnac. Le très long poème qui ouvre le recueil, et qui porte le titre paradoxal d'*Obscura claritas*, est tout à fait dans l'esprit de la poésie baroque de l'époque (dernier tiers du siècle), comme son objet, puisqu'il s'agit d'une énigme, que près de 600 vers donneront à déchiffrer (si l'on y parvient!). On notera une élégie consacrée à la reine Catherine de Médicis, et plusieurs "tombeaux," fidèles à la tradition, ceux de son ami, le célèbre Christophe de Thou, de Noël Brulart, son beau-père, de Jean Brinon, mort prématurément à l'âge de trente-six ans à peine, des compliments aux Audebert, père et fils, sur leurs accomplissements poétiques, etc. Il ne dédaigne pas l'humour ou les "jocoseria" de la tradition humaniste, comme on le voit dans son poème héroï-comique sur un buveur

---

[12] Francfort, J. Rosa, 3 vol. in-16.

[13] *Venetiae, Roma, Parthenope, Postrema Editio ab auctore ante obitum recognita* (Hanoviae, 1603).

[14] Voir le livre de Clarisse Doris Hellman, cité plus loin.

d'eau (que ce breuvage fit mourir) et un buveur de vin (auquel le jus de la treille assura le salut), renouvelant à sa manière le vieux débat médiéval sur l'eau et le vin.

La métrique qu'il utilise le plus couramment est l'hexamètre dactylique ou le distique élégiaque, mais il n'est pas moins habile au maniement d'autres mètres utilisés par les classiques.

§ § §

Dans l'adresse de son fils,[15] Gilles Aleaume, à ses amis ("Aeg. Aleaulme Lud. s. Amicis S."), le nouveau président et le lieutenant général (il avait succédé dans cette charge à son père) rappelle que ces poèmes ont été le fruit des loisirs et des distractions de son père, mais que ce dernier ne songeait pas à les présenter au public. Il a hésité longtemps avant de se décider à le faire, mais son amour filial l'a emporté même si ces poèmes concernent essentiellement un cercle d'intimes..." "Hanc igitur, sylvam dedico lubens vobis, Amici...." Et il demande l'indulgence de son père: "At vos mihi, Manes, este boni: si quid pecco, iste quidem et pietatis vis est." Il commettrait en effet une plus grande impiété en laissant à jamais disparaître ces vers.

La plaquette de 1595 comporte 40 fols. (sign. A–E7, et chiffr. 1–39) plus un fol. blanc. C'est un petit in-8° à caractères italiques. Nous examinerons ces 26 poèmes d'après ce texte, la comparaison avec le recueil de Gruterus de 1609 n'offrant pas d'intérêt suffisant (sans compter la mauvaise impression du recueil des *Delitiae,* qui en rend la lecture difficile). D'après le *Bulletin du Bibliophile* de Techener, année 1896, page 407, des vers d'Alleaume, célébrant la mémoire de Laure d'Avignon (sans doute les mêmes que ceux de la pièce n° 17 des *Poematia*) seraient inclus dans l'ouvrage de G. Baussonnet intitulé *Paraphrases* en l'honneur de la Sacrée Vierge Marie, publié à Reims en 1611 (Constant), mais nous n'avons pas pu le vérifier par nous-même. Signalons enfin, en l'honneur de Gilles, le fils dévoué, que l'on trouve une pièce de lui en tête d'un volume de vers intitulé Tumulus Michoelis Violaei et imprimé à Orléans, chez Fabien Hotot, en 1692.

§ § §

On examinera d'abord, et avec plus de détails, le long poème liminaire, qui représente à lui seul à peu près le tiers de l'ensemble des *Poematia*

---

[15] C'est le seul que signalent ses biographies.

(fols. 1–12 v), 582 vers. Fidèle à la tradition ludique et poétique des énigmes versifiées, mode humaniste puisée chez les Grecs (Simonide, Archiloque, Bion, et surtout Symphosius) et chez les Latins (Aulu-Gelle, et surtout Ausone), Aleaume se souvient peut-être de modèles plus récents de logographes, comme ceux du Flamand Alexandre Sylvain,[16] de l'Allemand Lorichius,[17] de l'Italien Giraldi,[18] ceux de Charles de Bovelles[19] ou de Scaliger.[20] Toujours est-il que, par vagues successives de vers clairs et obscurs, où l'on croit saisir l'objet occulté par la reconnaissance de quelques-unes de ses caractéristiques, pour être un peu plus loin balloté dans l'incertitude par des vers qui annulent l'hypothèse précédente, le lecteur patient, bon latiniste et amateur de ces jeux, finira (on doit l'espérer!) par trouver la solution en regroupant tous les fragments de ce "puzzle" verbal. On se contentera ici d'évoquer, à différents "moments" de l'énigme, quelques vers, en rappelant que l'objet à deviner s'exprime à la première personne (c'est aussi une convention) vantant ses qualités et ses bienfaits:

Le voici se comparant à des défenses d'éléphant ("tornatos Indo de dente cylindros") ou à des fûts de colonne ("caesas referunt Pario de monte columnas"), insistant un peu plus loin sur son brillant ou sa luminosité ("Absque ulla candens macula"), pouvant être brisé, mais jamais recourbé ("frangi interdum patiens, nescia flecti"). Les adjectifs employés au féminin nous feront désigner l'objet par "elle," même s'il proclame (à la fin) son caractère asexué ("nec foeminea nec mas"), son absence de langue ("illinguis") et pourtant son bavardage (582 vers!) digne du sexe féminin ("Foeminei vitio generis, me garrula prodo"). A la différence des humains, il (ou elle) vit et meurt alternativement, revit, meurt à nouveau "Castoris instar." Même mort (ou morte), il (ou elle) conserve, par sa chaleur, "vestigia vitae." Cette particularité de renais-

---

[16] Voir l'étude de Henri Helbig sur l'auteur et ses oeuvres, précédant une publication de ses oeuvres choisies (avec une notice de G. Colletet), (Paris: Liège, F. Renard; Brockhaus: A. Claudin et Leipzig, 1861).

[17] Voir l'art. de l'*Allgemeine deutsche Biographie* (= ADB), s.n. Voir son *Aenigmatum libri tres* (Francfort: C. Egenolf, 1545).

[18] Voir l'*Interpretatio symbolorum Pythagorae* de Lilio Gregorio Giraldi, (Bâle, 1551).

[19] Dispersés dans son oeuvre, notamment ses *Proverbes*, et dans le Ms. 1134 de la Bibliothèque de la Sorbonne.

[20] Voir la section de ses *Poemata* intitulée *Aenigmata* (éd. de 1574, 546–81), et une autre intitulée *Logogriphi* (614–33). Voir à ce sujet P. Laurens, "Les Lacs, l'Escale: les *Logogryphes* de J. C. Scaliger," in *Acta Scaligeriana* (Agen: Société Académique, 1986), 221–33.

sances et de morts continuelles revient à plus d'une reprise: mais l'individu en question demeure "exanguis," "enervis" et "exos" (sans os). Il (ou elle) se consume en un jour ("absolvor eodem / quo fieri sum coepta die"). Nous arrêterons ici ces quelques "flashes" sur ce mystérieux objet, qui se révèle être—du moins le pensons-nous—une chandelle ou un cierge (mais le mot *candela* n'est, bien entendu, jamais exprimé). Le choix de cet objet n'a rien d'original: les faiseurs d'énigmes le connaissent bien, on le trouvera encore au XVIIe siècle dans les *Enigmes* de l'abbé Cotin,[21] l'emblématique s'en est emparée assez tôt, on la voit parfois associée au soleil, dénonçant la vanité ou la sottise de vouloir éclairer un espace que le soleil illumine; l'art et la littérature baroques utiliseront fréquemment cet accessoire.

Nous laisserons les poèmes dans lesquels Aleaume rend à ses amis Audebert l'hommage de son amitié admirative, rappelant seulement que dans son poème n° 4 sur la *Venise*[22] de Germain Audebert, il développe, pour venir en aide à son ami auquel ses concitoyens d'Orléans reprochaient de les abandonner pour l'Italie et d'honorer une cité étrangère au lieu de chanter la gloire de sa ville natale, cette idée qu'Orléans doit être plus fière d'avoir enfanté Audebert que Venise d'avoir été célébrée par ses vers.

Le poème *Soteria* (22r–25v) a pour principal intérêt de nous faire connaître que l'auteur a dû être gravement malade, car, après avoir rendu hommage aux médecins qui l'ont soigné, il rend surtout des actions de grâces au Christ, son véritable sauveur. Ici encore, même si le poème nous intéresse d'un point de vue biographique, nous avons affaire à un *topos* des plus classiques: Erasme lui-même n'y a pas échappé.[23]

Nous nous arrêterons davantage sur le petit poème de 18 vers (9 distiques) consacré à la Comète de l'année 1577, non pas qu'il soit remarquable ni par l'inspiration ni par la forme, tout à fait classique, mais parce qu'il est un témoignage, parmi des dizaines d'autres—de prédicateurs, de poètes, mais surtout d'astronomes et d'astrologues de toute l'Europe—que suscita l'apparition d'une comète en novembre 1577, qui fut aperçue dans les régions les plus éloignées les unes des autres, et qui succédait, comme signe céleste ou "prodige," à l'apparition de l'"étoile nouvelle"[24] de

---

[21] *Enigmes et descriptions énigmatiques* (édit. orig. 1638).

[22] Venetiae. . . , (Venise: Alde, 1583).

[23] Par exemple, dans son poème votif à la gloire de sainte Geneviève, sa protectrice qu'il associe au Christ, dans le recouvrement de sa santé (in C. Reedijk, *The Poems of Desiderius Erasmus* [Leyde: Brill, 1956], n° 131, 350 sqq.).

[24] Voir l'article de Jean Céard, "Postel et l' "étoile nouvelle" de 1572," dans *Guillaume Postel 1581–1981* (Paris: Editions de la Mesnie, 1985), 349–58.

1572. L'histoire de l'apparition de la comète de 1577 est bien connue, dans son retentissement intellectuel et du point de vue de l'histoire des idées et des mentalités grâce à l'étude extrêmement fouillée de Clarisse Doris Hellman, *The Comet of 1577. Its place in the History of Astronomy*,[25] qui date de 1944. L'auteur recense, dans un long Appendice, 111 brochures ou traités différents relatifs à cette comète: certains noms d'auteurs sont très peu connus, mais nous y rencontrons aussi ceux de David Chytraeus, luthérien militant, d'Otho Brunfels, de Nicolas Bezelius, médecin et chirurgien flamand, de Jacob Heerbrand de Tübingen, d'Antoine Crespin, du Norvégien Jans Nielsen, de l'Italien Hannibal Raimondo, de Junctinus ou Giuntini, un autre Italien, de Blaise de Vigenère, de l'Anglais Thomas Twyne, des deux savants dont la réputation avait dépassé les frontières de leur pays, Cornelis Gemma, le fils de Gemma le Frison, et surtout de Tycho Brahé. Louis Aleaume, qu'il est bien pardonnable à l'auteur de ce volume de ne pas avoir connu, et dont le modeste poème ne peut guère rivaliser avec le *De illustri stella caudata*[26] de Brahé ou le *De cometo sidere quod hoc mense Novembri Anno 1577 videmus* ...[27] de Chytraeus. Notre poète ignorait d'ailleurs vraisemblablement la plupart des traités, brochures ou feuilles volantes qui se multiplièrent avec une rapidité remarquable, et le plus souvent sans concertation de la part de leurs auteurs; mais le seul fait que ce phénomène céleste, chargé de toutes les valeurs et de toutes les intentions qu'on lui associait alors, ait été, soit directement observé, soit simplement imaginé par Aleaume, mérite notre attention.

Triste quod attonitis sydus se miscuit astris
  Et caelum longa terruit omne coma,
Quo terrore latens vix nostras Phoebus ad oras
  Obliquum hiberno mittit ab axe diem.
Persephone radios evitatura minaces,
  Ultro ad raptorem fugit anhela suum,
Caetera continuis lacrymarunt sydera nimbis,
  Nec bene discussa nunc quoque nube micant....

On retrouve dans ces vers et dans ceux qui suivent le stock habituel d'images empruntées à la mythologie courante, et le caractère traditionnel-

[25] Hellman, (New York: Columbia University Press), 1944.

[26] *De illustri stella caudata ab elapso fere triente Novembris Anni 1577, usque in finem Ianuarii sequentis conspecta* ... (Uraniburgi, 1588); (Hellman, 337).

[27] Rostoch, 1577 (Hellman, 346).

lement funeste ou lugubre de la comète, phénomène insolite, y est souligné:

Funeste étoile que celle qui s'est mêlée aux astres épouvantés,
Et la longue chevelure qui remplit tout le ciel de terreur;
Terrorisé, Phébus se cache, et c'est avec peine que, vers nos rivages,
Il envoie de son axe hivernal un jour oblique.
Perséphone, pour éviter les rayons menaçants,
De son plein gré, s'enfuit à perdre haleine auprès de son ravisseur.
Les autres astres ont versé des larmes sous d'incessants
nuages de pluie,
Et, la nuée maintenant dissipée, ils ne scintillent pas encore!

Les dix distiques qui relatent un événement d'un tout autre genre et qui dut faire suffisamment de bruit à l'époque pour qu'il soit passé en proverbe (30v–31r) évoquent le duel (*monomachia*) qui opposa *Iarnacus* (Jarnac, c'est-à-dire Guy Chabot comte de Jarnac) à *Castaneus* (c'est-à-dire La Châtaigneraie) et qui eut lieu le 10 juillet 1547 sur le plateau de Saint-Germain en présence du roi Henri II et de la cour.[28] On sait qu'à la suite d'intrigues "au sommet" politico-sentimentales, La Châtaigneraie, bretteur renommé, et dont François de Guise fut le parrain, devait rencontrer le comte de Jarnac pour lequel Diane de Poitiers nourrissait une haine durable. Chacun comptait sur la victoire de La Châtaigneraie quand Jarnac, d'un revers d'épée, lui coupa les jarrets (*poplitibus*); vainqueur, il n'acheva pas son adversaire, devenu dès lors inoffensif. C'est le fameux "coup de Jarnac" sans rapport, sinon de toponymie, avec la célèbre bataille de Jarnac, où les catholiques, commandés par le comte d'Anjou (futur Henri III) écrasèrent les protestants commandés par le prince de Condé qui y fut tué (12 mars 1569). Voici les premiers vers de cette "chronique de la Cour," dont il est difficile de dire si Aleaume l'a composée au moment où s'était produit l'événement (il aurait alors 23 ans) ou plus ou moins de temps après:

De Iarnaci et Castanei monomachia

Ut movere pares contraria cominus arma

---

[28] Sur La Châtaigneraie et le duel en question, voir la notice de la *Biogr. Univ.* (t. 8, p. 18–19) et les *Mémoires* de Vieilleville (ou de Vincent Carloix, son secrétaire), publiés par le P. Griffet en 1757 (Paris: H.L. Guérin et L.F. Delatour). De la Châtaigneraie, François Ier disait:
Châtaigneraie, Vieilleville et Bourdillon
Sont les trois hardis compagnons.
Quant à Gui Chabot de Jarnac, il était le beau-frère de la duchesse d'Etampes, partageant avec La Châtaigneraie, la faveur de Henri II.

Acer Iarnacus, Castaneusque ferox.
Quo non par hominum concurrere fortius unquam,
Nobilis Elei vidit arena Iovis.
Mars stetit attonitus, dubius quem vincere mallet,
Vincere sic pariter dignus uterque fuit.

Il est difficile de passer sous silence le court poème (5 distiques élégiaques, 31v–32r) adressé à la reine Catherine de Médicis elle-même[29] ("D. Catherinae Medicaeae"), vraisemblablement pour célébrer le mariage qu'elle contracta avec le dauphin Henri en 1533, mariage arrangé par François Ier et sa diplomatie en direction de l'Italie. Ainsi est célébrée l'arrivée en France de cette "fleur florentine" de l'illustre famille des Médicis, nièce du pape Clément VII.[30] Vers qui ne sont ni meilleurs ni pires que les innombrables poèmes encomiastiques, célébrant un personnage, une victoire, une ville. On peut supposer que le poème est contemporain de l'événement (car le contraire serait peu vraisemblable), qu'il s'agit donc des vers de la jeunesse de Louis Aleaume.

Miserat hunc nobis florem Etruria, florem
Translatum ex hortis, gens Medicaea, tuis,
Quem secum ambrosios late dispergere odores
Gaudebant junctis lilia nostra comis.
Nec mala tempestas aut his aut obfuit illi,
Dum florere simul fata Deusque dabant.
Sed simul ac superis ille est subductus ab oris,
Latior ut campis floreat Elysiis,
Lilia et ipsa suo penitus defecta vigore,
Pronum inclinarunt mox ruitura caput.

L'Etrurie nous avait envoyé cette fleur,
Fleur que tu avais transplantée, race des Médicis, de tes propres jardins
Et nos lys, confondant leur chevelure avec la sienne,
Se réjouissaient de ce qu'elle exhalât au loin,
Mêlée à leur parfum, sa senteur [d'ambroisie].

On aura remarqué évidemment le jeu de mots hautement significatif et emblématique sur "lilia nostra"—c'est-à-dire les fleurs de lys de la monarchie française, des lys blancs—et la "fleur d'Etrurie," incarnation de

[29] Voir J. H. Mariéjon, *Catherine de Médicis,* (Paris : Tallandier, 1979), chaps. 1 et 2.
[30] Julien de Médicis.

Florence "la fleurie," dont le blason, comme on sait, est le lys rouge. Ce bouquet bien odorant des lys blancs et rouges qui symbolise l'union de la couronne française avec l'Etat florentin, le plus puissant alors de l'Italie, n'aurait pas été dédaigné, malgré son peu d'invention, des poètes humanistes ou même des maniéristes. L'ensemble du poème joue d'ailleurs sur la famille du mot *flos*: *floreat, florere, florem*.

Nous négligerons le "tombeau" de Jean Brinon,[31] personnage trop connu et ami intime de Louis Aleaume (32v–33r), jetterons un regard sur les 35 vers consacrés à la mémoire de Noël Brulart,[32] procurateur du Roi, qui fait naturellement partie de ces "hommes illustres" de l'Orléanais: ces poèmes évoquent, sans originalité, avec les images et le ton qui conviennent en pareille circonstance, les "vertus" personnelles et civiques des personnages. Du Président Christophe de Thou,[33] illustre magistrat de la non moins illustre famille de Thou, nous n'évoquerons le "tombeau" de Louis Aleaume (33v–36r) qu'en raison des liens profonds qui unissaient les deux hommes, de la date tardive du poème qui devait précéder de peu celle de son auteur (mort en 1593) et surtout de l'"aura" qui entoura les derniers moments de ce grand personnage, qui fit preuve d'une admirable "constance" à l'instant suprême, digne émule de Socrate—un Socrate chrétien—et des plus célèbres stoïciens.

Dans un style très différent—ce sera notre dernier échantillon—il faud-

[31] *Jani Brinonis* ... ("Insigne rerum si lubet mortalium...."), pièce n° 21.

[32] *Natalis Brulartii Procuratoris Regii*... pièce n° 20. Sur ce personnage, voir le *Dictionnaire de Biographie française* (n° 11 des Brulart). Procureur général depuis le 29 mai 1540, il mourut le 23 septembre 1557, dans une crise de folie (selon les *Mémoires* de Henri de Condé). Il a laissé plusieurs ouvrages et mémoires politico-juridiques et politico-religieux (sur l'Eglise gallicane).

[33] CL.V. CHRISTOPH, THVANI CELII, EQVITIS, Supr. apud Gall. Cur. Praesid. primarii memoriae sacrum.... Il serait intéressant de comparer ce long poème, en tenant compte des "choses vues" (ou rapportées) et des lieux communs qui abondent en pareille matière, avec le témoignage de Guillaume du Vair qui, dans son traité *De la Constance et consolation ès calamitez publiques*, où il développe le thème, redevenu à la mode, de la *consolation* (comme celles de Sénèque, voire celles de Cardan), consacre un passage à Christophe de Thou (au livre 3) qui nous fait évoquer inmanquablement les pages célèbres du Phédon, où Socrate, qui attend une mort imminente, disserte avec ses disciples sur l'immortalité de l'âme: "Ce bon seigneur ... le premier de nostre senat en France, levant la teste de dessus le chevet et s'appuyant sur le coude" se plaint, pour commencer, que beaucoup n'aient plus confiance en la vie future: "Helas, nous en reculons le plus loing que nous pouvons la pensée, et qui pis est, beaucoup la décroyent du tout.... Ils font ce qu'ils peuvent pour faire mourir leur âme avec leur corps et vont emprunter des raisons chez les philosophes anciens pour combattre et renverser l'unique but, le seul loyer et la dernière fin de la Philosophie."

rait évoquer la pièce 24, où l'on retrouve l'humour et le goût des jeux de mots chers aux "jocoseria" humanistes,[34] hérités des anciens: il s'agit de deux personnages, l'un nommé Blanc (*Canus*) et surnommé *Linus* ou *Linos* (c'est-à-dire "toile de lin," ou "vêtement de lin"), qui, ayant bu de l'eau, contrairement à ses habitudes ("insolentissimus") étant en proie à la fièvre, en était mort; l'autre, un certain Janus Jametius (Jean Jamet?), vieillard sobre (*abstemius senex*), qui souffrait d'une hernie (*hernia laborans*) et que le vin guérit de sa maladie (*vini auxilio a morbo sit liberatus*).[35] Ces vers, que la place nous manque de citer ici, n'auraient, certes, pas suffi à valoir à notre poète le titre de Virgile de Verneuil-sur-Seine!

§ § §

En présentant ces quelques échantillons des *Poematia* de Louis Aleaume, je n'ai pas voulu crier au chef-d'oeuvre inconnu, loin de là. Je ne pense même pas qu'une édition critique, avec analyse attentive de la métrique, des tournures, du vocabulaire de ces poèmes, s'impose pour le développement de nos études. Aleaume a bien assimilé la culture humaniste de sa jeunesse, qu'il a pu avoir plusieurs occasions de développer, sinon dans sa vie professionnelle, du moins dans les rencontres fréquentes chez ses amis lettrés, notamment chez Jean Brinon, qui tenait table ouverte dans son château de Médan, et où se réunissaient les meilleurs esprits du temps, dont Pierre de Ronsard et d'autres représentants de la Pleïade. Le principal intérêt de ces vers, ici comme chez des dizaines, voire des centaines de poètes néo-latins du XVIe siècle[36]—ceux que Lucien Febvre qualifiait irrévérencieusement d'"Apollons de collège"[37]—c'est, comme nous l'avons dit, d'éclairer quelques aspects de la vie sociale et des goûts

---

[34] Voir notre article, "Le paradoxe, pierre de touche des 'jocoseria' humanistes," dans *Le paradoxe au temps de la Renaissance* (Paris: Touzot, 1982), 59–80.

[35] Cf. d'Erasme l' "Epitaphe pour un bouffon pris de vin" (Epitaphium scurrulae temulenti), visant dans ses vers héroï-comiques le Portugais Hermicus, qu'il avait rencontré à Rome, et dont il parle encore sur le même sujet (son goût immodéré du vin) dans un adage (n° 3702) justement intitulé "Vinaria angina," où le personnage, obèse et malade, est présenté au moment où il se fait apporter du vin de Corse vieux de quatre ans, terminant sa vie. Aleaume connaissait-il ce poème? A-t-il voulu en prendre le contrepied, en montrant que l'on peut mourir du fait de l'eau, et revivre du fait du vin? Il est difficile de le savoir, et la question elle-même offre un intérêt très relatif!

[36] Qu'il s'agisse de Visagier, de Dolet, de Boyssoné, d'Arlier, etc.

[37] Dans le chapitre "Les bons camarades" de *Le problème de l'incroyance au XVIe siècle* (Paris: Albin Michel, 1942 et 1968), 32.

intellectuels de l'auteur, de recueillir des témoignages sur les événements politiques, militaires, voire scientifiques ou socio-culturels du temps. Il semble à peu près certain que Louis Aleaume, dont les fonctions officielles devaient être assez absorbantes, a composé ses poèmes (rien ne nous permet d'affirmer qu'il n'en ait pas composé d'autres) comme un "peintre du dimanche" se met à son chevalet. Aux historiens de chercher à identifier un certain nombre de personnages qui apparaissent dans les poèmes d'Aleaume, comme ce médecin Massac[38] ou ce Dessaeus,[39] tombé sur le champ de bataille de Térouane.

C'est encore au Livre d'Heures manuscrit de son père, Etienne Aleaume, premier Seigneur de Verneuil, que les *Poematia* nous renverront avec un plus grand profit intellectuel (sans compter la joie des yeux), car ce document nous plonge immédiatement dans la vie profonde et quotidienne d'un gentilhomme pieux du temps de François Ier, et nous y saisissons, beaucoup mieux que dans des vers "à la mode," mais assez artificiels, un caractère d'authenticité.

Université de Tours

[38] Pièce n° 8: "*Ad Raimundum Massacum medicum et poetam*" (27r°–v°).
[39] Pièce n° 18: "*Dessaei Teroane occisi*" (31v°).

Johannes Murmellius' Scoparius *(1517–18): Another German Defense of Humanistic Study*

JAMES V. MEHL

During the 1975 Tours Colloque, Joël Lefebvre identified Strasbourg, Cologne, and Vienna as "centres de gravité" in the development of German humanism.[1] His argument was based on the appearance of a number of defenses of poetry by German humanists, published in those cities between about 1460 and 1520. That series of defenses, according to Lefebvre, culminated in 1518 with the publication of works by several leading humanists: Hermann von dem Busche's *Vallum humanitatis*, Johannes Murmellius' *Scoparius*, and Joachim Vadianus' *De poetica et carminis ratione*. Vadianus' *De poetica* has already been treated by Peter Schäffer.[2] During the last congress of this association, I attempted to interpret Busche's *Vallum humanitatis*.[3] I should now like to turn my attention to Murmellius' *Scoparius*.

Prior to the brief analysis of the *Scoparius* by Lefebvre,[4] only short accounts of Murmellius' last major work could be found in the older Murmellius biography of Reichling and in the biographical articles by

---

[1] Joël Lefebvre, "Le poète, la poésie et la poétique: Eléments pour une définition et pour une datation de l'humanisme allemand," in *L'Humanisme allemand (1480–1540): XVIIIe Colloque international de Tours*, ed. Joël Lefebvre and Jean-Claude Margolin (München: Fink; Paris: Vrin, 1979), 285–301, here 285.

[2] Peter Schäffer, ed., trans. and comm., *Joachim Vadianus: De poetica et carminis ratione*, 3 vols. (München: Fink, 1973–77), esp. vol. 3.

[3] James V. Mehl, "Hermann von dem Busche's *Vallum humanitatis* (1518): A German Defense of the Renaissance *studia humanitatis*," *Renaissance Quarterly*, 42 (1989): 480–506.

[4] Lefebvre, 287–88.

Bömer and Nauwelaerts.[5] However, none of these treatments has added appreciably to the useful commentaries in Bömer's critical edition of the *Scoparius*, published at the end of the last century as part of Murmellius' complete works.[6] My purpose here is to summarize and to interpret Murmellius' arguments in the *Scoparius*, as another German defense of humanistic study. I shall also place its publication within a biographical context. Unfortunately, limitations of time and space do not allow extensive comparison of arguments in the Murmellius text with other Northern and Italian defenses of poetry. Furthermore, a comparison of textual differences in the 1517 Deventer and the 1518 Cologne editions, and how those emendations may be explained by events of the Reuchlin affair, will have to be explored in another paper.

Along with Alexander Hegius and Rudolf von Langen, Murmellius ranks as one of the most famous "schoolteacher humanists" of the Lower Rhineland and Westphalia during the late fifteenth and early sixteenth centuries. Born in 1480 in Roermond (a fact memorialized often in his signature–Johannes Murmellius Ruremundensis), he attended the famous Latin School of Hegius in Deventer. In 1496 Murmellius continued his studies at the University of Cologne, where he received his undergraduate and two graduate degrees.[7] Through the patronage of Langen, he was appointed assistant rector at the cathedral school in Münster. It was in that Westphalian town that Murmellius pursued his early career as a teacher, headmaster, proponent of educational reform, and prolific author. Nauwelaerts, who has compiled the most current bibliography of his writings, lists forty-nine publications down to 1517, many of which were reprinted.[8] They include original works of poetry, editions of the pagan and Christian classics, and practical textbooks to encourage the reform of Latin grammar and rhetoric, intended for both teachers and students. Murmellius' *Pappa puerorum*, by far the most popular of his handbooks, was reprinted thirty-one times and used in every part of Europe.[9] Following a dispute with the headmaster of the cathedral school,

[5] Dietrich Reichling, *Johannes Murmellius: Sein Leben und seine Werke* (1880; reprint ed., Nieuwkoop: De Graaf, 1963), 107–15; Aloys Bömer, "Johannes Murmellius," *Westfälische Lebensbilder* (Münster: Aschendorff, 1930–), 2:396–410; M. A. Nauwelaerts, "Joannes Murmellius Roermond 1480-Deventer 1517," in *Historische Opstellen over Roermond en Omgenving* (Roermond: n.p., 1951), 201–34.

[6] Aloys Bömer, ed., *Ausgewählte Werke des Münsterischen Humanisten Johannes Murmellius*, 5 vols. (Münster: Regensberg, 1892–95), vol. 5.

[7] Nauwelaerts, 202–3.

[8] Ibid., 228–33.

[9] Ibid., 220–21; Reichling, *Johannes Murmellius*, 150–51; Bömer, "Johannes Murmel-

Timann Kemner, Murmellius by 1509 had become rector of St. Ludger's School in Münster, where he introduced the study of Greek.[10] In 1512 Langen persuaded him to return as co-rector of the cathedral school, where he continued the efforts of Johannes Caesarius in Greek instruction. But within a year Murmellius accepted appointment as rector of the Latin school in Alkmaar. During the summer of 1517 that unfortunate city was sacked by troops involved in the Gelderland wars, forcing Murmellius, his wife, and young son to flee to Zwolle. Again, a dispute with the headmaster there, Gerhard Listrius, prompted him to take a position in Deventer. After only about a month in Deventer, Murmellius died unexpectedly (October 2, 1517) at the age of thirty-seven.[11] There were widespread rumors at the time that Murmellius had been given poisoned wine by Listrius, prompted by the controversy in Zwolle, but the more likely cause of death was an attack of pneumonia or the plague.[12] It was during these last years of personal difficulty and tragedy that Murmellius was preparing his *Scoparius* for the press.

The *Scoparius* was not only Murmellius' last major work, but represented the culmination of his efforts as a humanist reformer. Nauwelaerts has described it as "zijn humanistische geloofsbelijdenis," his humanistic creed.[13] Murmellius' prefatory letters to two former colleagues at Zwolle, Hermann Stüve and Alexander von Meppen, indicate that the manuscript was already in preparation in that city and that it was carried along on the hasty trip to Alkmaar.[14] Reichling suggests that the first edition was printed during the months of August or September by the Deventer printer Albert Paffraet, since Murmellius had only just arrived in the city at that point.[15] But internal evidence from the document itself shows that the collection of literary selections had been long in preparation. The selections, many of which have been carefully traced and documented in

lius," 2:403–6.

[10] C. G. van Leijenhorst and Ilse Guenther, "Johannes Murmellius," in *Contemporaries of Erasmus*, ed. Peter G. Bietenholz, 3 vols. (Toronto: University of Toronto Press, 1985–87), 2:470–71.

[11] Bömer, "Johannes Murmellius," 2:398–401.

[12] Nauwelaerts, p. 216; Leijenhorst and Guenther, 2:471; M. E. Kronenberg, "Heeft Listrius schuld aan de dood van Murmellius?" *Bijdragen voor vaderlandsche Geschiedenis en Oudheidkunde* 9 (1930): 177–203.

[13] Nauwelaerts, 222.

[14] Ibid.; Reichling, *Johannes Murmellius*, 106–8.

[15] Reichling, *Johannes Murmellius*, 108; see also ibid., 164, for the bibliographical listing of these early editions.

the critical apparatus of Bömer, range from unpublished letters to a great variety of printed works of ancient, patristic, and Renaissance authors, including Italian, French, and German humanists. Murmellius had obviously been collecting and sifting his sources for some years.

The title of the collection was deliberately fashioned: *Scoparius ... in barbariei propugnatores et osores humanitatis ex diversis illustrium virorum scriptis ad iuvanda politioris literaturae studia comparatus*; that is, "The broom against the defenders of barbarism and enemies of humanism, composed from the different writings of famous men, for the purpose of assisting the study of literature."[16] The *Scoparius* was to be a useful tool or instrument, a "broom" to sweep away the dirt and cobwebs of the scholastic way of thinking that had so obscured the purity and cleanliness of the schoolhouse. To insure that this intention was clear, Murmellius had printed on the title page several lines from Plautus' *Stichus*: "Everything must be tidied up. Bring some brooms here, and a long pole, too, so that I could throw out the spiders' work entirely, condemn their weaving, and discard all of their webs."[17] In the context of the Plautus play, these lines were spoken by Pinacium, a servant ordering a house-cleaning in preparation for the return of Epignomus. The point of the analogy is evident: just as a thorough cleansing of the house was needed for the happy return of Epignomus and his exotic treasures from the East, so too is a thorough sweeping of the schoolhouse required for the proper return of the gems of ancient wisdom to be found in the study of literature.

This humanistic intention is further established by a quotation taken from the ancient philosopher Heraclitus, which Murmellius related in his prefatory letter to his friends Stüve and Meppen.[18] The line is based on Heraclitus Fragment 74: "Here, too, are gods."[19] Murmellius had read the passage in Aristotle: "There is a story which tells how some visitors once wished to meet Heraclitus, and when they entered and saw him in the kitchen, warming himself at the stove, they hesitated; but Heraclitus said, 'Come in; don't be afraid; there are gods even here'."[20] Just as

[16] As it appears on the title page of the 2nd ed. (Coloniae: Quentell, 1518). I have used the copy in the British Library: 8463.de.7.

[17] Plautus, *Stichus*, Loeb Classical Library Plautus 5 (Cambridge, Mass.: Harvard Univ. Press, 1968), 42–43.

[18] In Bömer, ed., *Ausgewählte Werke*, 5:3.

[19] As cited in Philip Wheelwright, ed. and trans., *The Presocratics* (New York: Odyssey Press, 1966), 75.

[20] Aristotle, *Parts of Animals*, Loeb Classical Library Aristotle 12 (London: Heine-

Aristotle had used the story as a way to encourage his readers to continue their investigation of his biological work, so too was Murmellius prompting his former colleagues (and the reader) to consider carefully his own study of the *humaniora*.

Murmellius sustained his analogy of the *scoparius*, the broom, in the very organization and format of his text. As the broom is a binding together of individual pieces of reed, he brought together some 131 different selections, or chapters, in his collection. The pieces vary widely in their subject, authorship, purpose, and length. Again, limits of time preclude a more detailed summary of the contents of each selection; in any case, Bömer has already provided such a summary.[21] Rather I would like to refine certain groupings of the selections, already suggested in part by Bömer, as a means of clarifying Murmellius' argument in the *Scoparius*. In a sense, the *Scoparius* was a *fasciculus*, a collection of "bundles" of documents bound together and then interwoven to form a useful tool, a broom, to promote humanistic reform of education.

These "bundles," or groupings, are only suggested by Murmellius in periodic headings and brief commentaries in the *Scoparius*. My efforts here to identify and to interpret those themes should likewise be viewed as suggestive. Each of the six groups or categories that I have listed below is characterized by a specific criticism or attack against certain "defenders of barbarism and enemies of humanism," referred to in the book's title. At the same time, Murmellius usually included selections and references for correction or reform of those abuses.

Group I: Against Alexander de Villa Dei and the glossators of his medieval grammar (Nos. 1–31 in the Bömer ed.).

Group II: Against scholastic theologians, to be corrected by cultivating a biblical humanism (Nos. 32–50).

Group III: Against jurists and those grammarians that support them, to be corrected by reading purified pagan and Christian classics, along with appropriate humanist commentaries (Nos. 51–62).

Group IV: Against those who misuse and corrupt Latin and Greek grammar (Nos. 63–84).

Group V: Against sophists and dialecticians (Nos. 85–122).

Group VI: Against unlearned clerics, to be corrected by a return to the humanistic study of language and literature (Nos. 123–131).

mann, 1968), 101.

[21] Bömer, ed., *Ausgewählte Werke*, 5:v–xxiii.

These themes are intertwined and supported by each other. Murmellius reinforces his textual unity in a concrete way by taking different selections from a single source and placing them, as appropriate, through the entire work.

In keeping with his earlier interests as a humanist teacher and author, Murmellius directed his main attack against those who continued to treat Latin and Greek as medieval languages, that is, as scholastic corruptions of the original classical languages. Instruction in late medieval Latin was based largely on the *Doctrinale*, which had been written in 1199 by the French grammarian Alexander de Villa Dei.[22] That popular Latin textbook had undergone numerous revisions, including attempts to make it compatible with the new humanistic way of learning.[23] Alexander had used rhymed verses as a pedagogical method for students to remember Latin vocabulary and grammatical rules. From the humanist perspective, that approach not only trivialized linguistic study, but contributed to a corruption of the Latin language itself.

In his critique of Alexander, Murmellius cited several of his own works, including the *Pappa puerorum*, where he relied on the dialogue form as a linguistic basis for learning Latin (19–25).[24] His supporters in the attack included a number of important fifteenth-century Italian educators and grammarians: Sulpicius Verulanus (1), Aldus Manutius (2), Antonius Illuminatus (4), Mapheus Vegius (12–14), and Paolo Vergerio (18). From the North he referred to Rudolph Agricola (26) and Jacob Wimpfeling's *Isidoneus Germanicus* (3). As a corrective to Alexander, Murmellius quoted from the first pages of Erasmus' *De ratione studii* (28), where it is recommended that students should learn Greek before taking up Latin grammar.

Murmellius' charge against the scholastic theologians was oblique rather than direct. Nowhere did he mention those theologians, especially the

---

[22] Dietrich Reichling, ed., *Das Doctrinale des Alexander de Villa-Dei: Kritisch-exegetische Ausgabe*, Monumenta Germaniae Paedagogica, vol. 12 (Berlin: Hofmann, 1893). For additional references on the *Doctrinale*, see Erich Meuthen, "Die 'Epistolae obscurorum virorum'," in *Ecclesia Militans: Studien zur Konzilien- und Reformationsgeschichte*, ed. Walter Brandmüller, Herbert Immenkötter, and Erwin Iserloh, 2 vols. (Paderborn: Schöningh, 1988), 2:53–80, here 56.

[23] Terence Heath, "Logical Grammar, Grammatical Logic, and Humanism in Three German Universities," *Studies in the Renaissance* 18 (1971): 9–64; Wolfgang Maaz "Zur Rezeption des Alexander von Villa Dei im 15. Jahrhundert," *Mittellateinisches Jahrbuch* 16 (1981): 276–81.

[24] In order to facilitate the documentation here, as well as in the following references to the *Scoparius*, the appropriate numerical citations of selections in the Bömer edition will be indicated in parentheses.

Cologne Dominicans, who had recently opposed Reuchlin and placed restrictions on the teaching of humanistic subjects. Instead, Murmellius advocated the study of the so-called wisdom books of the Old Testament—Psalms, Proverbs, Ecclesiasticus—together with the gospels, as the best way for students to learn "doctrina" (32). Those Old Testament books contained religious truth expressed as "divine poetry." He quoted from the Church fathers Eusebius (37) and Jerome (33–36, 43–45), the latter claiming that the writings of Pindar, Alcaeus, and Sappho were nearly equal to the metered wisdom contained in the Hebrew scriptures (44). Among the moderns, Murmellius referred to Erasmus' *Paraclesis* (42), Baptista Mantuanus' *Apologeticon* (47–48), and especially Giovani Pico della Mirandola's biblical commentaries (39–41, 49–50). In these ways, Murmellius was recommending a kind of biblical humanism to replace the scholastic approach to theological study.

He next extended his argument to include the jurists, focusing on the canon lawyers and the grammarians who supported them, who had been so responsible for corrupting Latin usage. As an illustration of the change, Murmellius included a passage from Angelo Poliziano, where it is pointed out that grammarians are no longer called "grammatici," but "grammatistae," and the educated men of letters no longer "litterati," but rather "litteratores" (52). A major cause of such corruptions of the language, according to Murmellius, was the continuing widespread use of faulty Latin grammar textbooks. He even provided a list of the worst offenders: "Isidorus, auctor alioqui pius et non omnino contemnendus, Papias, Eberardus, Hugutio, *Catholicon*, Mammaetractus, Aimo, *Breviloquus*, *Gemma gemmarum*, *Vocabularius rerum*, Joannes Garlandinus, Nicolaus Lyranus, Accursius, *Aurea legenda*, *Glossulae decretorum*, *Glossa notabilis* et id genus reliqua" (54). Bömer has provided a precise identification of these "unlearned expositors of words."[25] Several of these medieval grammarians are also decried in Valla's *Elegantiae* and Mantuanus' *Apologeticon* (55–56).

As a corrective to those medieval grammarians, whose glosses had obscured the true meaning of the classical languages, Murmellius himself contributed two chapters filled with useful references for the reader. In one he recommended the best dictionaries, lexicons, and other works dealing with questions of philology, to be consulted when reading classical texts (57). Besides such older, but still helpful, works as Varro, Festus Pompeius, Aulus Gellius, Macrobius, and Priscian, Murmellius approved the most current works of scholarship by Renaissance humanists, includ-

---

[25] Bömer, ed., *Ausgewählte Werke* 5:xv.

ing, among others, Lorenzo Valla, Niccolò Perotti, Ermolao Barbaro, Guillaume Budé, and Erasmus. A number of Greek lexicons are likewise suggested, including specialized dictionaries for the Attic dialect. In another chapter–the longest and probably the most important in the *Scoparius*–Murmellius recommended the best humanistic commentaries written for sacred and especially profane literary works (62). This checklist has also been summarized by Reichling and discussed by Nauwelaerts.[26] In addition to the numerous learned commentaries on the familiar Greek and Latin classics, Murmellius suggested that his own comments be consulted for Boethius' *De philosophiae consolatione*. He even noted several recent commentaries for the modern authors Petrarch, Sabellico, Poliziano, Mantuanus, Giovanni Pico, and Lefévre d'Etaples.

In the remaining selections, Murmellius basically returned to his theme of grammatical abuse. He cited examples of corrupt grammar, and their correction, in Vergil (63), Cicero (72), and several other classical authors, as well as particular Latin phrases: "en umquam" (65), "insubidus" (68), "popa" (71), and "labarum" (73). Again, it was an arrogance bred of "Aristotelian instruction" (i.e., scholasticism) that had caused the enemies of the *studia humanitatis* to write and speak such debased language (66). He agreed with Raphael Regius (75), as well as Budé (76, 78), Francesco Filelfo (79), and Georgius Valla (80–82), that unlearned "grammatici," "leguei," and "philosophastri" were the major culprits. But chief among the offenders were the lawyers of his own time, who had substituted a "Gothica lingua" for the eloquent style of the ancient jurists (77). This had resulted in a "barbarian" vocabulary, whereby lawyers now say "guerra" for "bello," "causus legis" for "specie," "vasallus" for "cliente," and so on (84). He pointed out that such legal practices had been denounced and satirized by several humanists, including More in his *Utopia* and Erasmus in *The Praise of Folly* (83).[27]

Murmellius next directed his ridicule towards the kinfolk of ignorant lawyers, the sophists and dialecticians. Aristotle himself is cited as a major authority against the sophists (86). Besides a quotation from Ecclesiasticus, Murmellius drew upon passages from the early Christian fathers, where the false wisdom of sophists and logicians is denounced: in Seneca,

---

[26] Reichling, *Johannes Murmellius*, 112–13; Nauwelaerts, 223–24.

[27] These brief references concerning lawyers may be found in the *Utopia*, ed. Edward Surtz, S. J. (New Haven and London: Yale Univ. Press, 1964), 114–15, and in *The Praise of Folly*, ed. Clarence H. Miller (New Haven and London: Yale Univ. Press, 1979), 85.

Prudentius, Jerome's commentaries, and Augustine's *De doctrina christiana* (98–105). As a means of confirming those ancient and patristic authors, Murmellius again relied on Italian and Northern humanists, especially Giovanni Pico (90, 91, 117, 121), Agricola (93-96, 120), Reuchlin (107, 111–12), and Erasmus (108–10, 113–16).

Murmellius turned against the unlearned clergy ("indoctos sacerdotulos") for his final criticism in the *Scoparius*. No doubt he had in mind the same group of foolish priests, monks, and would-be teachers that was satirized by the authors of the *Epistolae obscurorum virorum*. Again, the proof of their ignorance was their incorrect and barbarous use of grammar (126). There is a selection from Filippo Beroaldo, warning that ministers of the Church who speak in solecisms and barbarisms can only but confuse the meaning of the holy Word (127). The corrective, Murmellius suggests, is stated in the very canonical decrees of the Church. He listed a number of statements by early fathers and popes who promoted a learned clergy (128). For instance, in addition to the prophets and evangelists, Jerome approved the reading of Vergil and Terence. Murmellius also affirmed Augustine, who suggests that the correct study of language is prerequisite for a spiritual life (129). In a final poem and salutation Murmellius argued that only through a more cultivated study of literature will Christian students learn the correct approach to true theology ("veram theologiam") and to living a virtuous life (131).

In his orientation and arguments, then, Murmellius followed a long tradition of Italian and German humanist defenses of poetry.[28] In keeping with his earlier activities as a reform-minded teacher, headmaster, and author, he collected a variety of ancient, patristic, and Renaissance sources that supported his views on the need for basic educational changes. Towards the end of his brief, but productive, career, Murmellius fashioned selections from those sources, often tying them together with commentaries of his own, to form a rather tightly woven argument. He intended this instrument or tool to be used as a *scoparius*, a broom to sweep away the filth and cobwebs that had so obscured the cleanliness of the schoolhouse, just as the servant in Plautus' *Stichus* had pushed a broom to cleanse his master's house. The six thematic arguments of the *Scoparius*, like so many

[28] For the Italian defenses, see especially Concetta Carestia Greenfield, *Humanist and Scholastic Poetics, 1250–1500* (London and Toronto: Associated University Presses, 1981). For the German defenses, see the studies cited by Schäffer and Mehl, as well as the discussion in James H. Overfield, *Humanism and Scholasticism in Late Medieval Germany* (Princeton: Princeton Univ. Press, 1984).

sections of a broom, were loosely grouped and interwoven. Murmellius attacked Alexander and his glossators because instruction based on their faulty grammar had led to serious corruptions and misunderstandings of language and texts among other grammarians, dialecticians, jurists, theologians, and clergymen. As a means of overcoming the problems implicit in scholastic education, the "schoolteacher humanist" recommended his own primer, the *Pappa*, along with many approved humanist editions, commentaries, dictionaries, and other learning aids. For only by reading corrected texts of the Greek and Latin classics and the Bible, along with approved commentaries, Murmellius contended, could the Christian student achieve proper expression in language and the wisdom to lead a virtuous and spiritual life.

Compared with other German defenses of the period, the *Scoparius* was less original, more crude, and rather labored in its argument.[29] These characteristics may be explained, in part, by its apparently hasty compilation and publication during the tragic final months of Murmellius' life. In 1509 Ortwin Gratius, as a young humanist professor, had struggled to adapt his arguments supporting humanistic study into the scholastic forms of a quodlibetical disputation at the University of Cologne.[30] In 1518 Busche, still fighting the battle for Reuchlin's cause, constructed his *Vallum*, or strong fortress, in defense of the *studia humanitatis*. In the same year, Vadianus composed his *De poetica*, a polished treatise advocating the study of poetry and other humanistic subjects. Murmellius' *Scoparius* is significant precisely because it reflects the more practical, down to earth, interests and intentions of one of Germany's leading humanist teachers on the eve of the Reformation.

Missouri Western State College

---

[29] Lefebvre, 287–88.

[30] James V. Mehl, "Ortwin Gratius' Orationes Quodlibeticae: Humanist Apology in Scholastic Form," *The Journal of Medieval and Renaissance Studies* 11 (1981): 57–69.

The Liturgical Context of Erasmus's Hymns

CLARENCE H. MILLER

Sometimes we tend to forget that Erasmus was a priest and an Augustinian canon regular in good standing throughout his life.[1] Though he never functioned as a pastor or held ecclesiastical office, he certainly would have said mass regularly and read the divine office daily. Hence the missal and the breviary[2] would have been quite as well known to him (though perhaps less consciously) as his favorite classical authors. Erasmus's liturgy is understandably not as familiar to his modern students. Hence the Toronto editors of one of his letters[3] misidentified a quotation from a sequence for the Transfiguration. And when the modern editor of Erasmus's poems[4] pointed out in Erasmus's hymn to St. Michael "a rather striking parallel" with a sequence attributed to Alcuin, we will find the

---

[1] In *The Spirituality of Erasmus of Rotterdam,* Biblioteca Humanistica & Reformatorica, vol. 40 (Nieuwkoop: De Graaf, 1987), Richard L. DeMolen has recently reminded us of Erasmus's religious and sacerdotal commitment.

[2] To say *the* missal and *the* breviary is misleading, since neither was standardized until the Council of Trent and there was a bewildering variety of both in Erasmus's time, especially of the breviary. I have had to be content with the Windesheim breviary, which may or may not have been used at Steyn while Erasmus was there; the edition I have consulted was also adapted for Cambrai, where Erasmus lived from 1492 to 1495: *Breuiarium consuetudinem ad Canonicorum regularium instituti diui patris Augustini episcopi. congregationis Windesimensis . . . In quo . . . addita quaedam sunt. quae etiam alijs extra diocesim Traiectensem degentibus. & precipue Cameracensi conuenire possint* (Antwerp: for Henricus Eckertanus de Homberch, 24 September 1519), microfilm of the copy in the British Library, cited as *Windesheim-Cambrai Breviary.* I have also consulted the missals and other breviaries from the continent and England which are available in modern editions.

[3] As I have pointed out in *Renaissance Quarterly* 31 (1978): 60.

[4] Cornelis Reedijk, *The Poems of Desiderius Erasmus* (Leiden: E. J. Brill, 1956), 230, note on lines 30–36.

similarity less remarkable if we realize that Alcuin and Erasmus are not versifying the same passage in Revelations 8:3–4 but are adapting the liturgical version of that passage in the versicles, antiphons, and responses for matins on Michael's feastday,[5] in the Mass for Michael's feastday,[6] and in the mass of the angels[7]—a passage which was also incorporated in medieval hymns.[8]

I wish to consider four of Erasmus's poems (and four of his best, I might add) which have a direct relation to a liturgical setting.[9] His hymns to St. Gregory and St. Ann,[10] written about 1489 while he was still at the Steyn monastery dedicated to St. Gregory, are modelled on the hymns of the breviary and are suitable for the divine office, though we do not know if they were ever so used. His suite of four angel hymns (to Michael, Gabriel, Raphael, and all the angels),[11] which were probably written between 1489 and 1491,[12] were composed, as Erasmus himself report-

---

[5] *Windesheim-Cambrai Breviary*, pars aestivalis, fols. 119–119v (sigs. v3–v3v). See also *The Hereford Breviary, Edited from the Rouen Edition of 1505*, ed. Walter H. Frere and Langton E. G. Brown, 3 vols., Henry Bradshaw Society nos. 26, 40, and 46 (London: Harrison and Sons, 1904–1915), 2:339–42.

[6] *Missale Romanum Mediolani, 1474,* [and] *A Collation with other Editions Printed before 1570,* ed. Robert Lippe, 2 vols., Henry Bradshaw Society nos. 17 and 33 (London: Harrison and Sons, 1899–1907), 2:275.

[7] *The Sarum Missal,* ed. J. Wickham Legg (Oxford: Clarendon Press, 1916), 329, 459.

[8] *Analecta hymnica medii aevi*, eds. Clemens Blume and Guido M. Dreves, 55 vols. in 27 (Leipzig: O. R. Reisland, 1886–1922), 10: no. 266; 37: no. 231. A similar passage was in the ordinary of the mass (*Missale Romanum,* 1:200).

[9] His paean to Mary and his poems on the earthquake and eclipse at the Crucifixion, on the harrowing of hell, and on the shed where Christ was born (Reedijk, nos. 19–21, 33) are not closely related to the liturgy, either in length, sources, or character. His hymn to St. Geneviève (Reedijk, no. 131), which I have discussed in "Erasmus's Poem to St. Genevieve: Text, Translation, and Commentary," *Miscellanea Moreana: Essays for Germain Marc'hadour*, Moreana 100, Volume XXVI, eds. Clare M. Murphy, Henri Gibaud, and Mario A. Di Cesare, 481–515, is a votive poem, with no direct relation to the liturgy.

[10] Reedijk, nos. 17 and 22. According to evidence presented by Harry Vredeveld, the hymn to St. Ann might well have been written about 1498–99. I refer to the accessible edition of Dr. Reedijk, though I have had the benefit of the new Latin text and commentary which Harry Vredeveld is preparing for the Toronto *Collected Works of Erasmus.* For the Lorettan sequence I also rely on the edition of Léon Halkin in *Opera omnia Desiderii Erasmi Roterodami*, V-1 (Amsterdam and Oxford: North Holland Publishing Co., 1977), 87–109, taking into account the corrections made by Prof. Josef IJsewijn in *Humanistica Lovaniensia* 31 (1982):217.

[11] Reedijk, nos. 34–37.

[12] According to the evidence presented by Harry Vredeveld.

ed,[13] at the urging of a great man who presided over a church dedicated to St. Michael.[14] They were probably intended to be put up near images of the angels in the church, as the wording of the last poem suggests;[15] but, though Erasmus tempered his style so as to bring them closer to prose, the great man rejected them because he found them to be so poetic as to seem like Greek.[16] The presence of these poems near images of the angels at mass on angelic feastdays is suggested by a reference to the incense of High Mass.[17] Finally, in 1523 Erasmus wrote and published separately his mass for the Virgin of Loreto, including a poetic introit and sequence. It had been written at the request of Thiébaut Biétry, parish priest at Porrentruy, and was indulgenced by the archbishop of Besançon for use within his diocese so that it became an actual part of the liturgy.

If we compare these poems with their medieval sources and analogues, we see Erasmus is more selective in the episodes he includes than some of his medieval predecessors. He ignores the legend of St. Ann as the mother of all three New Testament Marys[18] and focuses on the vivid episode of the high priest's rejection of Ann and Joachim from the temple and the appearance of the angel to them. Omitting all but one of the many miracles attributed to Gregory in *Legenda Aurea*[19] and some medieval hymns,[20] he recounts only how a column of light revealed Gregory when he had fled to the woods to avoid becoming pope; his humility made him suitable for the highest office. After a brief mention of Gabriel's appearances to Daniel and Zachary, Erasmus limits himself to the annunciation, omitting many other messages sometimes included in medieval hymns, such as informing Joseph that Mary was not adulterous, telling the shepherds of Christ's birth, warning Joseph to flee into Egypt and the magi not

---

[13] *Opus epistolarum Des. Erasmi Roterodami*, ed. Percy S. Allen et al., 12 vols. (Oxford: Clarendon Press, 1906–1958), *1*: Ep. *I*, p. 3, line 30–p. 4, line 2.

[14] Erasmus's phrasing suggests that it was the lay patron rather than the pastor.

[15] Reedijk, no. 37, lines 65–68.

[16] A more practical objection, perhaps, is their length.

[17] Reedijk, no. 37, lines 65–66.

[18] Franz J. Mone, *Lateinische hymnen des Mittelalters*, 3 vols. (Freiburg: Herder, 1853–1855), *2*: no. 782. *Analecta hymnica* 9: no. 131; 10: no. 168; 33: no. 38; 34: no. 197; 42: nos. 165–66; 44: nos. 37–40; 52: no. 107; 55: nos. 61 and 65. The story also appears in the fourth and fifth lessons for matins of Ann's feastday in *Windeshein-Cambrai Breviary*, pars aestivalis, fol. 96 (sig. q4).

[19] *Legenda aurea Jacobi a Voragine*, ed. Theodor Graesse, 3rd ed. (Breslau: Wilhelm Koebner, 1890), 188–202.

[20] See Mone, 2: nos. 957 and 962. *Analecta hymnica,* 10: no. 249; 19: no. 250; 22: no. 195; 29: nos. 201 and 284; 33: no. 102; 48: no. 41.

to return to Herod, consoling Christ in Gethsemani, comforting Mary after Christ's death, and telling the women that Christ had risen from the tomb.[21] Here the omissions are clearly deliberate, since Erasmus opens the section on the annunciation with the question: "Cuncta quid frustra sequimur canendo?" ("Why should we vainly try to sing all your deeds?").[22] Finally, the Lorettan sequence (which has, as far as I know, no precedents in its subject matter) makes no mention whatever of the legend which gave the shrine its fame: the angelic transportation of the *santa casa* of Mary and Joseph from Nazareth to Italy. Instead Erasmus limits himself to the symbolic associations of the laurel which gave the shrine its name.[23]

Erasmus is equally fastidious in the varying style of these four hymns. As we would expect, he eschews the accentual, rhyming patterns of most medieval hymns. The hymn to St. Gregory is written in third-asclepiadean strophes, rare during the later Middle Ages until they were revived by the humanists in the fifteenth century. The hymn to Gregory is brief, plain, dignified, instructive, entirely suited for actual use as a matins hymn. The angel poems, written in sapphic strophes, are longer and loftier, with some epic touches and some high coloring, for, as Erasmus says in the introduction to the suite, it is fitting that the fiery ranks be celebrated in words of fire.[24] And the angel poems lack the contorted classicism of such a poem as the poetic dialogue between Erasmus and his friend Cornelis Gerard.[25]

The hymn to St. Ann is written in quatrains of quantitative iambic dimeters, pretty clearly in imitation of the last great classical hymnist, Prudentius, whose poems Erasmus admired; he even wrote a commentary on two of them for More's daughter Margaret Roper.[26] In his title Eras-

---

[21] *Analecta hymnica*, 16: no. 141; 19: no. 142; 23: no. 177; 34: no. 192; 44: no. 135.

[22] Reedijk, no. 35, line 17.

[23] We should not make too much of Erasmus's critical intentions in this omission, since the story, given currency by a phamphlet of Mantuan and not fully discredited until this century, was still recent and recognized as only a pious legend when Erasmus wrote. Bulls issued by Julius II and Leo X recommended pilgrimage to the shrine but refrained from endorsing the story on which it is based. The first published attempt to give the pious legend a spurious historical basis did not occur until 1531, eight years after Erasmus wrote his liturgy. See Henri Leclercq, "Lorette" in *Dictionnaire d'archéologie chrétienne et de liturgie*, ed. Fernand Cabrol et al., 15 vols. (Paris: Letousey et Ané, 1907–1953), 9: 2473–2511.

[24] Reedijk, no. 34, lines 15–16.

[25] Reedijk, no. 14.

[26] Erasmus, *Opera omnia*, ed. Jean LeClerc, 10 vols. (Leiden: Pieter van der Aa, 1703–1706), 5: 1337–58.

mus called it a "rhythmus," which meant "verse" or "poem" but also had overtones of the accentual, rhymed poems of the later Middle Ages. Though Erasmus's verse is quantitative, the accents do frequently coincide with the long syllables of the iambs, as they often do in Prudentius. But unlike Prudentius Erasmus also has more than a hint of rhyme or at least half rhyme.[27] He also favors vivid and dramatic narrative over the denser theological texture of Prudentius, which he understood full well, as his commentaries on Prudentius show. The implied doxology in the two concluding lines of the hymn to St. Ann is even more subtle than in the explicit strophe at the end of the hymn to St. Gregory, where the persons of the trinity are invoked. "Indivisa quibus Numinis unitas / Est sub nomine triplici" ("who are united indivisibly in their divinity under the diversity of a triple name").[28] "Triplici nomine," which refers to the three different names, is singular and echoes "numinis," their single godhead. At the end of the hymn to Ann we are told that if Ann asks help for us from Mary, and Mary asks it from her son, he will not refuse her, "Neque filio negat pater, / Amans et ipse filium" ("nor will the father refuse his son, for he, too, loves his son").[29] The suggestion of the Holy Spirit, the love between the father and the son, completes the Trinitarian theme in an appropriate familial context.

But Erasmus's most daring and original experimentation with liturgical hymnology is to be found in his Lorettan sequence. To see how this is so, it is necessary to sketch briefly how the sequence evolved from its origin in the ninth century until the time of Erasmus.[30] In its earliest form the text of sequences typically consisted of a series of prose couplets of unequal length, with a single line at the beginning and at the end. Both lines in each couplet had an equal number of syllables so that both could be sung to the same melody. The form emerged when words were provided for long melodies that had been added to the last syllable of the alleluia after the gradual of the mass. As perfected by Notker of St. Gall in the late ninth century, the lines of the couplets, though they had no rhyme or metrical feet, did frequently match each other in accentual patterns and

[27] Reedijk, no. 22: lines 1, 3; 5, 7; 9, 10; 26, 28, 29; 49, 50; 53, 55; 69, 70; 74, 75; 88, 90.

[28] Reedijk, no. 17, lines 31–32.

[29] Reedijk, no. 22, lines 94–95. I have corrected "filum" to "filium."

[30] I am relying mainly on Willi Apel, *Gregorian Chant* (Bloomington, Indiana: Indiana University Press, 1958), 442–64. The textual and musical details are often complicated and disputed, but the main outlines of what was available to Erasmus are clear enough.

corresponding word-lengths, partly so as to provide a good fit for the same melodic line. During the next three centuries assonance and rhyme began to be added to the ends of the couplets until Adam of St. Victor, at the end of the twelfth century, established a new pattern: pairs of rhyming, accentually metrical strophes, which may be illustrated by the opening pair of strophes from St. Thomas Aquinas's sequence for the feast of Corpus Christi:

Lauda Sion salvatorem
lauda ducem et pastorem
in hymnis et canticis.
Quantum potes tantum aude,
quia maior omni laude:
nec laudare sufficis.[31]

In this form, often with a triplet instead of a couplet in each strophe, literally thousands of sequences were written in the next three centuries. Often they were composed to fit a popular sequence melody.

Erasmus's scattered remarks about the sequences of his time[32] show that he considered many of them trivial, inept, and unworthy of use in divine worship because they introduced too much unlearned and legendary material and because they were so long that they displaced or deemphasized more important parts of the mass. His strictures were apparently not unjustified, since the Council of Trent swept away all the sequences except four: *Victimae paschali* (Easter), *Veni sancte spiritus* (Pentecost), *Lauda Sion salvatorem* (Corpus Christi), and *Dies irae, dies illa* (Mass for the Dead). And anyone who has spent some hours reading the volumes devoted to sequences in *Analecta hymnica* can testify that many of them seem tinklingly monotonous and trivial.

Hence we are not surprised that Erasmus's own sequence is relatively short (thirty lines) and that he avoided the late-medieval rhyming pattern by returning to the original scheme established by Notker. In fact, we know from the testimony of Heinrich Glarean, a musician friend of Erasmus, that he especially admired two of Notker's sequences.[33] Like

---

[31] *Missale Romanum*, 1:256.

[32] His pronouncements are conveniently gathered and translated by Clement A. Miller, "Erasmus on Music," in *The Musical Quarterly* 52 (1966): 335–38.

[33] Heinrich Glarean, *Dodechachordon*, translated, transcribed, and annotated by Clement A. Miller, American Institute of Musicology, Musicological Studies and Documents No. 6 (n.p., 1965), 158, 170.

Notker he frequently matches word-lengths in corresponding positions in each line of a couplet.[34]

But Erasmus's innovations are even more remarkable than his return to the antique form of the sequence. Not content with Notker's prose patterning of accents, he wrote each couplet in a different quantitative meter—a dazzling display of metrical virtuosity.[35] This variety enabled him to vary the length of the couplets, as Notker had done, but it also meant that the rhythms of the music, which Erasmus would have wished to follow the long and short syllables of the verse,[36] would not be monotonously limited by the verse.[37]

At the same time, Erasmus also seems to be including indirectly a dominant feature of late-medieval hymns and sequences, their accentual meter; for here, more than in early hymnists like Prudentius or Erasmus himself in his hymn to St. Ann, the word accents tend to coincide with the quantitatively long syllables.[38] He also incorporates a structural principle never found (so far as I can tell) in the Notkerian sequence but very common in late medieval hymns and sequences: the sense, syntax, and parallelism show that he has combined pairs of couplets to form seven quatrains (the last of which is extended by a two-line coda). Each quatrain except the second consists of a long couplet followed by a shorter one, just as late-medieval sequences (and classical strophes too) tend to consist of three long lines followed by a shorter one. Moreover, the quatrains are arranged

---

[34] See the capitalized words in the appended text of the poem. The texts of Notker have been edited, with commentary and analysis, by Wolfram von den Steinen in vol. 2 (Editionsband) of *Notker der Dichter und seine geistige Welt*, 2 vols. (Bern: A. Franke, 1948).

[35] The scansion is given and the meters are identified in the appended text of the poem. They were first noted by Prof. Josef IJsewijn in a review of Professor Halkin's edition of the liturgy (*Humanistica Lovaniensia* 31 (1982): 217). I had the pleasure of noticing them independently and should point out that the thirteenth couplet is in greater asclepiadeans, not elegiambics; also it seems to me that the verse of the last couplet should be called anapestic dimeter, not dactylic tetrameter, since dactylic verse would not allow the anapestic substitution in the first foot, but this verse is so odd that it is hard to know what to call it.

[36] See *Opera omnia*, ed. LeClerc, 9:943C–E. Glarean made the length of the notes correspond to the length of the syllables in his setting of the first eight lines of Reedijk, no. 85 (*Dodecachordon*, pp. 220–21).

[37] Erasmus's sequence does not fit any of the popular melodies to which sequences were written; at least I could not find one that it fits. But perhaps this is not surprising, since the quantitative meter would make it very difficult to match the line lengths and the total number of syllables required by an existing melody.

[38] See the underlined syllables in the appended copy of the poem.

to form three sections commonly found in hymns and sequences: the first three quatrains invoke the earthly choir and join to it the angels, virgins, martyrs, and saints in heaven; the next three praise Mary by means of analogies with stars, flowers, and trees, especially (of course) the laurel; the last extended quatrain asks Mary for help. Each of the three sections begins with an especially long couplet and ends with an especially short one.

Surely Erasmus's sequence is an amazing synthesis of techniques drawn from classicism, humanism, and the Middle Ages, early and late.

I hope that examining these four hymns in their liturgical context has suggested how selective they are in content and how skillful and varied they are in technique.

Erasmus's Lorettan Sequence

1. a. SUME NABLUM, sume citharam, virginum decens chorus

   b. VIRGO MATER est canenda, virginali carmine, (16/15)

   Trochaic tetrameter catalectic

2. a. Vocemque referent accinentes ANGELI.

   b. Nam virgines amant et ipsi VIRGINES. (13/12)

   Iambic trimeter

3. a. IUNGET CARMINA LAUREATA TURMA,

   b. VITAE PRODIGA, SANGUINISQUE QUONDAM. (11)

   Phalaecean hendecasyllables

4. a. MARTYR carnificem VINCIT ET edomat,

   b. CARNEM virgo: decet LAURUS ET hunc et hanc. (12)

   Lesser asclepiadean

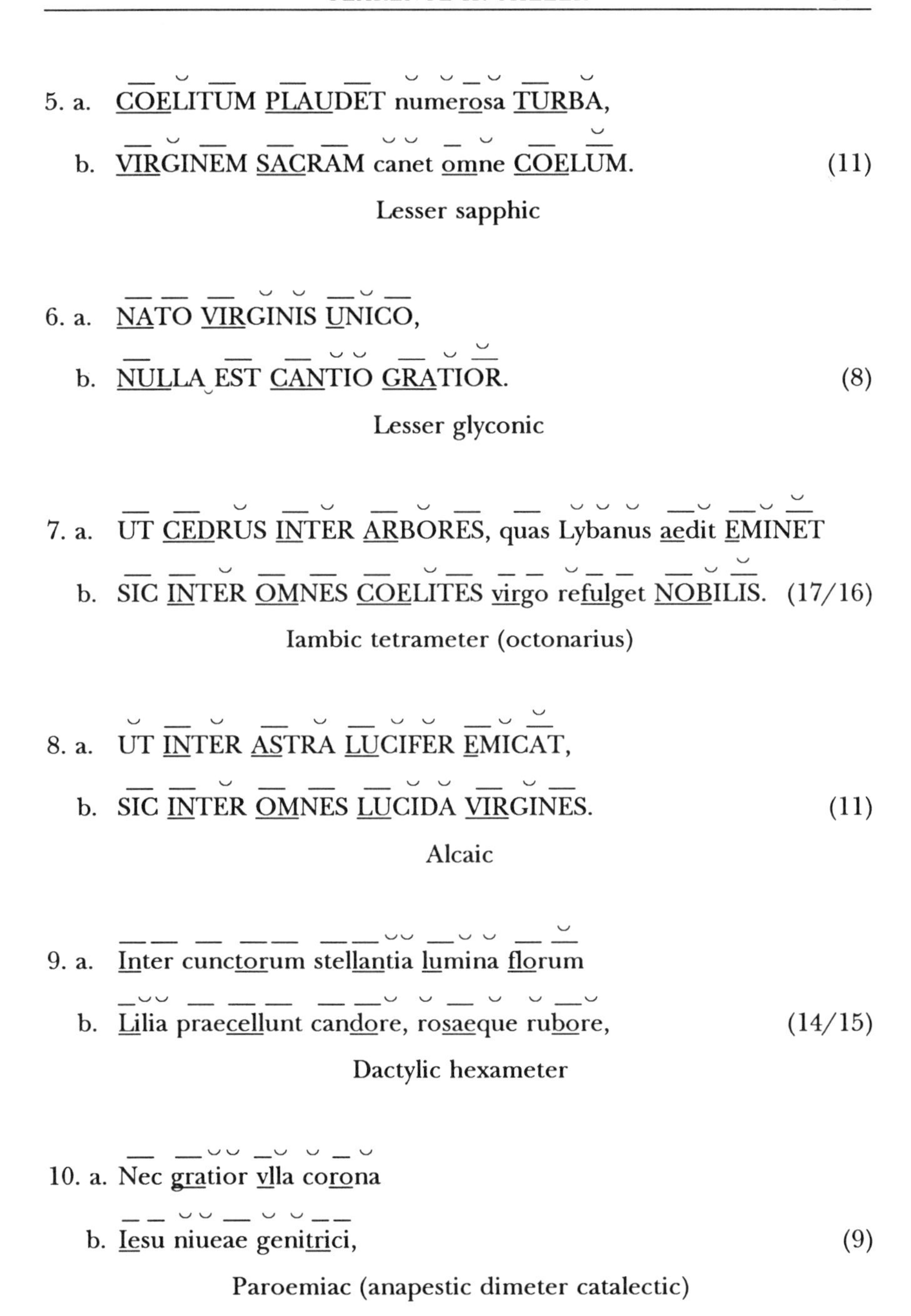

5. a. COELITUM PLAUDET numerosa TURBA,
b. VIRGINEM SACRAM canet omne COELUM. (11)

Lesser sapphic

6. a. NATO VIRGINIS UNICO,
b. NULLA EST CANTIO GRATIOR. (8)

Lesser glyconic

7. a. UT CEDRUS INTER ARBORES, quas Lybanus aedit EMINET
b. SIC INTER OMNES COELITES virgo refulget NOBILIS. (17/16)

Iambic tetrameter (octonarius)

8. a. UT INTER ASTRA LUCIFER EMICAT,
b. SIC INTER OMNES LUCIDA VIRGINES. (11)

Alcaic

9. a. Inter cunctorum stellantia lumina florum
b. Lilia praecellunt candore, rosaeque rubore, (14/15)

Dactylic hexameter

10. a. Nec gratior vlla corona
b. Iesu niueae genitrici, (9)

Paroemiac (anapestic dimeter catalectic)

11. a. Inter odoriferas non GRATIOR ARBOR ULLA LAURO,

b. Pacifera est, dirimens fera PRAELIA, FULMEN ARCET ARDENS, (17/18)

Greater archilochian

12. a. BACCAS HABET SALUBRES,

b. IUGI NITET VIRORE. (7)

Iambic dimeter catalectic

13. a. Esto virgo FAVENS, QUI MODULIS te celebrant piis,

b. Iram auerte DEI, NE FERIAT fulmine noxios. (16)

Greater asclepiadean

14. a. LAURUS esto, gaudeasque

b. USQUE Lauretana dici, (8)

Trochaic dimeter

15. a. Licet in VASTI FINIBUS ORBIS,

b. Plurima PASSIM FUMIGET ARA. (10)

Anapestic dimeter

St. Louis University

Anna Maria van Schurman's Appeal for the Education of Women

LEO MILLER

Two thousand years ago, in the days when the Emperor Nero was presiding in supreme lordship over the vices of imperial Rome, an obscure lecturer of the Stoic persuasion, Gaius Musonius Rufus by name, was teaching the extraordinary doctrine that daughters should be given the same schooling as sons, and that women would be rightfully admitted to academies of philosophy.[1]

Two thousand years later Musonius is all but forgotten, and in vast areas of our globe the principles he taught still do not begin to be considered.

So the story of Anna Maria van Schurman, who made some of the same proposals 350 years ago, is both extraordinary and typical. She was born into the Dutch Renaissance in 1607 when girls were typically taught at home to cook, to sew, and to recite the catechism. Born into a cultured home, Anna was given lessons in French and taught to play musical instruments. But it was her brothers, one two years older and one four years older than she, who were regularly tutored at home by their father, in Latin grammar, to prepare them for higher schooling. One day, when Anna was about eleven, papa noticed that whenever his sons stumbled in their paradigms, little Anna prompted them with the correct answers. Formal schools of advanced studies for girls were then non-existent, but from then on she was given encouragement and the opportunity to study with private tutors.[2] With an inborn genius for languages she not only

---

[1] The writings of Musonius, Greek text with English translation, are printed in Cora E. Lutz, *Musonius Rufus, The Roman Socrates,* Yale Classical Studies, vol. 10, (New Haven: Yale Univ. Press, 1947), 3–147.

[2] See her personal memoirs in A. M. á Schurman, *EUKLERIA, seu Melioris Partis*

mastered Latin, but went on to acquire the tongues for Scripture studies, Greek and Hebrew, Syriac, and Chaldee. To gain access to the texts of the Coptic church, she compiled a grammar of Ethiopic.

Talented she was in many ways. She engraved pictorial designs by diamond on glass, and worked in tapestry: some of her creations are museum treasures to this day. Her portrait drawings and her etchings brought her into the company of the professional artists, Meerevelt, Lievens, and the Honthorsts.[3] She soon became widely known for learned discourses on philosophical questions in letters she exchanged in Latin and Greek with Dutch savants, with sympathetic correspondents in England, with the French polymaths Salmasius, Mersenne, Gassendi, and Descartes.

In the Netherlands she became a national celebrity. Latin verses were composed to sing her praises, composed by Jacob Cats, Daniel Heinsius, Constantine Huygens, Caspar Barlaeus, and many others. In turn she won recognition for her own Latin poems returning the compliment to these men and other versifiers.[4]

When the burghers of her city, prospering in the third generation of Dutch independence, launched a new university at Utrecht in 1636, the incoming rector Gisbert Voetius turned to Anna Maria van Schurman to contribute the customary Latin ode required for the inaugural ceremonies. She composed the kind of ode that was wanted, replete with the sentiments and allusions appropriate to such an occasion, framing beginning and end with the traditional emblems of Utrecht, opening with the

---

Electio. Tractatus Vitæ ejus Delineationem exhibens. Altonæ ad Albim, Ex Officina Cornelii van der Meulen, 1673.

[3] Exhibits in Rijksmuseum, Amsterdam (Rijksprentenkabinett and other departments; in Fries Museum, Leeuwarden; and in Museum 't Coopmanshûs, Franeker. Th. Mercuur, *Anna Maria van Schurmann 1607–1678,* issued 1978 by Rijksuniversiteit Utrecht, to accompany exhibition at its Universiteitsmuseum.

[4] Much of her correspondence is printed in her *Opuscula* and the Beverovicius publications, described below; likewise her verses, and verses to her. Some letters survive at the museums above and the British Library, Harleian MS. 6824. Verses from her and to her are found in many publications: Constantine Huygens, *Momenta Desultoria, Poematum Libri XIV,* The Hague, 1655, and his *Korenbloemen,* The Hague, 1667, passim; *Alexandri Mori Poemata*, Paris, 1669, 123; Antonius Vivianus in the 1644 Beverovicius *Epistolocæ Quæstiones*; and others. Contemporary letter writers often report or ask news of her: Gui Patin. Epistola LXX, *Clarorum Virorum Epistolæ ex Musæo Johannis Brant*, Amsterdam, 1702; Samuel Bochartus, *Geographis Sacra*, Leyden, 1692, 6; Nicholas Heinsius, in P. Burmann, *Sylloges Epistolarum a Viris Illustribus Scriptarum,* Leyden, 1727, III, 601–2; Antonius Clementius, *Claudii Salmasii Epistolarum Liber Primus*, Leyden, 1656, viii, etc.; and many others.

stern realities of lowland floods, passing to the significance of the new academy for seafaring Netherlanders cruising to far-off transoceanic shores. Then abruptly in the middle there comes a two line interruption, a digression, a painful parenthetical aside and a private sigh:

> At quae (forte rogas) agitant tua pectora curæ?
> [But, perhaps you ask, what grief aches there in your breast?]
> Non hæc Virgineis pervia Sacra choris.
> [No girls will gather in these hallowed halls.][5]

So much she allowed herself, and then she returned to the accepted theme in hand.

In the Netherlands, the classic land of controversy between predestinarian Calvinists and free-will Arminians, during that decade a practical issue was agitated among theologians and physicians: *De Termino Vitæ*, on the bounds of human life: was the life span of each person predetermined by divine providence, not to be tampered with by mortals and their means, or was it in some measure indeterminate, so that physicians might properly intervene to prolong an invalid's life? About 1632 Jan van Beverwyck (Latin, Beverovicius), professor of medicine and burgomaster of Dordrecht, initiated a wide epistolary discussion of these issues, and presently he collected and published the responses he had received. This led to a series of successively larger collections, printed 1634, 1636, 1639, and 1651, with many contributors, including Hugo Grotius, Simon Episcopius, Gerard Vossius, and Gabriel Naudé. Most striking, in the 1639 printing, the response by Anna Maria van Schurman received special notice on the initial title page and her essay was accorded special placement in a *pars tertia* with its own additional title page: a segregation that seems to have been intended as an honor.[6] (It should be noticed that a much longer

---

[5] *Inclytæ & Antiquæ Urbi Trajectinæ Nova Academia Nuperrime Donatæ Gratulatur*, in *Opuscula*, 1652, pages 300–2. Translation mine, L. M.

[6] All of these have very long titles. The 1639 text will suffice here. Appended to the 1636 edition, it reads *Joh. Beverovicii Epistolica Quæstio, De Vitæ Termino, Fatali an Mobili? Cum doctorum Responsis. Pars Tertia et Ultima, nunc primum edita. Seorsim Accedit Nobilissimæ & Doctissimæ Virginis Annæ Mariæ a Schurman de eodem argumento Epistola* (etc.), Lugdunum Batavorum, Ex Officina Ioannis Maire. The Latin 1639 edition was reprinted in 1651. It had been turned into Dutch, again featuring Anna Maria van Schurmann, in *Pael-Steen van den Tyt Onses Levens*, Dordrecht, 1639. Other exchanges between Beverovicius and Anna Maria van Schurmann are printed in a different work, *Epistolicæ Quæstiones cum Doctorum Responsis*, etc., Roterodami, Sumptibus Arnoldi Leers, 1644 and his *DD. Virorum Epistolas et Responsa*, etc., Roterodami, excudebat Rudolphus a Nuyssel, 1665.

treatise *De Termino Vitæ* by Menasseh Ben Israel was published that same year in response to Beverwyck but it was printed entirely separately. While some of the sources in Anna's and in Menassah's analyses overlap, there is no sign of any cross consultation between them, although there is indication elsewhere that they were at some time acquainted.)[7]

The necessity of schooling for women was then uppermost in her mind. As early as 1632 she mentioned in a letter to Andreas Rivetus, the Leiden theologian, that she was drafting something on that issue in French. About 1638 she had recast her arguments into a Latin dissertation and she sent it to Rivetus. An exchange of letters followed, which apparently was not entirely private. In his letter of 18 March 1638 Rivetus summed up the smug dogmas of the divinity school: *Multum vales ad persuadendum, sed hic tamen frustra es*, "you are powerful in persuasion, but you are nonetheless wrong, your efforts are in vain." God, he told her plainly, (God, whose will was clearly known to Andreas Rivetus) has destined men and women in different directions. Surely she must remember how Odysseus demonstrated that fact when he exposed Achilles who was trying to hide among the maidens. Since women are not suited for political power or responsibility in the church, why should they seek to study for those roles. The Apostle Paul bade women not to teach or hold authority over men, but to abide in silence. True, he would grant her that women should not be condemned to the colander and the spindle alone, but, said he, the proper scope of women's education had been set forth a century before by Ludovicus Vives, *De Institutione Fœminæ Christianæ*. (Vives had written, for Henry VIII's first wife Catherine, directions on how to fit demoiselles to become wives of courtiers, mothers of their children, and retired widows in due course). The war-winning roles of Deborah and Jael in the Hebrew Scriptures were rare exceptions, he went on, and see how Joan of Arc came to a bad end, even her admirers questioning her maidenly virtue (*Rivetus was French by nationality*). He adduces the *practical problems*: it is simply improper to mix boys and girls in a coeducational setting, and it is just impossible to find a corps of erudite to staff a women's college, so better women should read what they need in their home-learned vernacular, in humility and in modesty.

Faced by such obduracy, Anna Maria van Schurman restrained her feelings as best she could. In her letters she rebutted Rivetus's gross fallacies and gross unfairness with eloquence and with reason, but tactical-

[7] Menasseh Ben Isreal, *De Termino Vitæ Libri Tres*, etc., Amstelodami, Typis et Sumptibus Authoris, An. 1639.

ly she drew back from the advanced positions taken by contemporary women whose writings she admired: Lucretia Marinella of Venice, who had written *La Nobiltà e l'Excellenza delle Donne con diffetti e mancamenti di gli huomini*, and her friend by correspondence Marie de Jars de Gournay, who in France had written *De l'Egalité des Hommes et des Femmes*. She first published her tract in 1641, *Dissertatio de Ingenii Muliebris ad Doctrinam & Meliores Literas Aptitudine*, moderating her tone and her content to meet Rivetus's objections, which she knew others would argue against her, and she included her exchanges with Rivetus in the same volume, issue by Elzevir of Leiden.

She set it up in the format of a university disputation of that age, as an exercise in logic, defining subject and predicate, major premise and minor, fourteen arguments in favor, followed by refutation of five objections. She poses a *Problema Practicum: Num Foeminæ Christianæ Convenit Studium Literarum*, which may be properly interpreted as "Is advanced education consistent with the role of women as conceived by the Church in the Netherlands."

In the *study of letters* Anna Maria van Schurman includes "all disciplines": languages, history, grammar, logic, rhetoric, physics and metaphysics, mathematics, music and poetry, Hebrew and Greek for the Scriptures. Pathetically, she makes many concessions: not all women are equally capable, not all women are equally free from burdensome family responsibilities, or able to draw on adequate family resources. If only women will at least be admitted to the world of culture, she will not insist on training women in the arts of forensic jurisprudence, or in military strategy, nor seek to have them prepared for preaching in the temple, arguing in court, lecturing in the university and politics in general.

Her arguments follow the a priori patterns of the university logicians: women have the potential, women desire learning, women need more solid activity, learning makes for love of God and greatness of soul, learning teaches reverence and arms against seductive heresies, ignorance is simply not fitting for women. In the same format she rebuts objections: women's intellect is too feeble (she cites mediocrities among male graduates), women's mind does not incline to study, facilities are lacking, higher learning is not suited to women's "vocation." Each objection is answered in terms of formal logic, major and minor premise in turn, the way degree candidates used to argue in those days. And still realistically confronting the conditions of her time, she pleads: if the universities will not open their doors, at least parents should take responsibility and provide private tutors at home. So she rests her case, having meanwhile cited in support texts from Aristotle and Plato and Nazianzenus and the Christian Scriptures in their original Greek, from Livy and Pliny and Erasmus among others in Latin, a demonstration which is a powerful and eloquent lesson in itself.

How much positive effect her writing had is hard to say. It was translated in 1646 into French by Guillaume Colletet, *Question célèbre, s'il est nécessaire ou non que les filles soient sçavantes*; into English in 1659, *The Learned Maid, or Whether a Maid May be a Scholar*; and it is echoed by her British counterpart and correspondent Bathsua Pell Makin in her *An Essay to Revive the Ancient Education of Gentlewomen* (1673). In the Netherlands it was reprinted three times in the collection of her writings, 1648, 1650, and 1652, in a volume of *Opuscula*, which was issued not by herself but at the insistence of her scholarly (male) devotees, initially the Leiden theologian Frederic Spanheim.[8]

The story of Anna Maria Schurman turns into very different channels in later years. She was never married: whether she did not see herself yielding to the usual round of wifely domestic duties, even when she was sought in marriage by men of high repute in poetry and in public life, whether there was a peculiar influence from the father, or pressure of family responsibilities. It seems that the particular influence of her religious environment, which reacted negatively to her most ardent ambitions, acted as a discouragement to productivity in their avenues, while at the same time it disabled her from responding to other liberating influences. Descartes in particular wrote with regret in a letter to Mersenne in effect that the baneful influence of Voetius was a barrier to any efforts to open new vistas to her.[9] So, to the amazement and unhappiness of her earlier admirers, of whose adulation she seems to have grown weary, in middle age she turned to a charismatic radical preacher Jean de la Badie, and

---

[8] These publications were (including correspondence with Rivet and others): *Nobiliss, Virginis Annæ Mariæ à Schurmann Dissertatio, De Ingenii Muliebris ad Doctrinam, & Meliores Litteras Aptitudine. Accedunt Quædam Epistolæ Ejusdem Argumenti.* Lugdunum Batavorum, ex Officina Elzeviriana, 1641. *Nobiliss. Virginis Annæ Mariæ à Schurmann Opuscula Hebræa, Græca, Latina, Gallica, Prosaica & Metrica.* Lugdunum Batavorum, ex Officina Elzevirorum, 1648.
—Editio Secunda, Auctior et Emendatior, Lugdunum Batavorum, ex Officina Elzevirorum, 1650
—Editio Tertia, Auctior & Emendatior, Trajecti ad Rhenum, ex Officina Johannis à Waesberge, 1652.

[9] Descartes to Mersenne, in *Renati Descartes. Epistolæ. Amstdodami. Ex Typographia Blaviana, 1682,* Pars II, Epistola xlv, page 185: "Voetius iste generosæ puellæ de Schuermanna indolem etiam corrupit; cum enim antea ingenium haberet ad Poësin, picturam, cæterasque disciplinas elegantes præstantissimum, ille jam abhinc quinque aut sex annis illam ita possidet, ut tota sit nunc in Theologiæ controversis quod quidem ingeniosos omnes ab ejus consortio demum arcuit."

joined with him to be equal co-leader of a small Quaker-like sect in a community of devout pietists forced to move from place to place seeking refuge from persecution by their self-styled Christian neighbors.[10]

La Badie had begun as a Jesuit in France, broke from them, and was accepted by Huguenot congregations, but he continued to evolve his religious ideas into a more radical Christianity of the inner light. Exactly when their association began to develop is unclear. La Badie came to Geneva in 1659, when he was beginning to have difficulties in keeping, or obtaining, a regular church appointment because of his novel preachments. It was in Geneva that Anna Maria's brother was first attracted to La Badie, but the date is not precisely recorded. It was also in 1659 that the poet John Milton, who was himself a thoroughly unorthodox radical in religious doctrine, tried to arrange for La Badie to come to London and take over the French church there, whose pastor Jean D'Espagne had just died. Milton's letter, 21 April 1659, says that he extended the invitation on the recommendation of (his colleague in the Interregnum administration) John Dury, who was widely known in the Netherlands and Switzerland as the advocate of Protestant church unity.[11] Milton's letter does not mention that John Dury's wife was the former Dorothy Moore, who had been a close friend of Anna Maria van Schurman in the 1640s; they wrote to each other in Hebrew, and Dorothy Dury also composed a (then unpublished) proposal for women's education in England.

La Badie did not go to London, but after a while developed his own congregation of loyal followers which moved back and forth between the Germanies and the Dutch provinces. In La Badie's personality and in the tenets which he preached Anna Maria van Schurman found an appeal which drew her totally away from her former pursuits. She quickly became his recognized full equal sharer in the leadership of his community. Perhaps among the so-called orthodox there were those who whispered,

---

[10] On her turn to LaBadie, see letter of J. Græevius to N. Heinsius, 13 April 1670, in P. Burmann, *Sylloges*, IV, 88; Caspar Burmann, *Traiectum Eruditum . . . Vitas, Fata et Scripta Exhibens*, (Utrecht, 1738), 348–55; Andreas Wickelius, Petrus Lindgren and Hans Pet. Schoenbeck, *Dissertatio Historica de Vita et Meritis Annæ Mariæ Schurmanniæ*, Lundae, Litteris Berlingianis, 1796, very valuable for many seventeenth-century citations. La Badie was much discussed in late seventeenth-century discourses on heretical thought, and is amply treated in many scholarly reference works.

[11] John Milton, *Epistolarum Familiarium Liber Unus . . .* Londini, Impensis Brabazon Aylmeri, 1674, 60–62. His nephew Edward Phillips, under "The Modern Poetesses," in the 1675 *Theatrum Poetarum*, 254, included "Anna Maria Schurman, an Hollandish Lady, of the most celebrated Fame of any of her Sex that I have heard of in Europe at this day. . . ."

or snickered, about relationships which might be something or other more than ideological; but however we today may assess their doctrinal vagaries or their communal mode of living, least of all may we pass any judgment on suffering souls if in their mature sixties they might have found a fulfillment which had escaped them in earlier years.

When La Badie died in 1674, Anna Maria van Schurman carried on his work. Among other visitors, William Penn, the great Quaker leader, came to talk with her and observe her community. La Badie had published a great deal, and she continued: she prepared a hymnal, *Heylige Gesangen*, with a supplement *Bedenckingen over de Toekomste van Christi Koninckrijk* ("Considerations on the Coming of the Kingdom of Christ");[12] and above all she wrote a full length spiritual autobiography and apologia for their creed, *Eukleria seu Melioris Partis Electio*, composed in elegant Latin, so that it would be read by the learned scholars and theologians from whom she had broken off all connection, but who still remembered her very well.[13]

Our Neo-Latin Congress meets this year in Canada, in the city of William Lyon McKenzie, who in a real sense is the great-grandfather of this document which I hold in my hand, the Canadian Constitution Act of 1982, La Loi Constitutionelle de 1982. In it we may read Article 15 guaranteeing equal benefit of the law to all without any discrimination based on sex, and another Article 28 guaranteeing all its rights and freedoms equally to male and female. Wherever we have achieved such progress, we may congratulate ourselves for our good fortune, and as Neo-Latinists we can remind the world to pay tribute and render honor to the memory of Anna Maria van Schurman among the many whose struggles made possible our freedoms, our equality.

New York City

---

[12] *Heylige Gesangen, uyt het Frans vertaelt*, Amsterdam, by Jacob van de Velde, 1683.

[13] Besides recent Dutch publications in the Netherlands, notice should be taken of: Una Birch (Pope-Hennessy), *Anna van Schurman, Artist. Scholar, Saint*, London, 1909; Joyce L. Irwin, "Anna Maria van Schurman: The Star of Utrecht," in J. R. Brink, *Female Scholars ... Before 1800*, Montreal, 1980; and Cornelia N. Moore's paper on *Eukleria* at the 1988 Modern Language Association convention.

Quaenam apud Thomam Campanellam in Theologicis *ad Plautum ad Terentium et ad Vergilium redeant*

ANGELA MINICUCCI

In amplissimo opere illo de *Theologia*, quod anno 1613° inchoatum Thomas Campanella anno 1624° perfecit, sescenties Augustinum Calaber philosophus revocat saepiusque Ambrosium Hieronymum Tertullianum Lactantium. Innumeros praeterea alios scriptores memoria repetit et Latinos et Graecos cuiusque aetatis, et gentiles et christianos, et vetustiores et recentiores. Cum praelongum sit omnia de omnibus Latinis scriptoribus recensere a Thoma in *Theologicis* memoratis, ea tantum attingam quae ad Plautum, ad Terentium et ad Vergilium attinent ne fusior fiat dissertatio haec.

Theologica quae scripsit Thomam Campanellam exornare iuvit atque interdum corroborare quodam modo et confirmare sententiis plurimorum scriptorum Latinorum. Saepius enim auctorum nomina multa invenias qui plus minus ea attigerunt vel Thomae attigisse videntur quae ipse perpendit atque considerat.

Quod tam multos scriptores eorumque sententias continuata et nominum et rerum serie una simulque saepius protulit saepius mirata sum dubitanter. Fuerit vir ille omni doctrinarum copia imbutus ornatusque vigueritque praeter ceteros mira ac fere incredibili memoriae vi tamen plures saepius esse rata sum scriptores eorumque locos quam ut Thomas uno eodemque tempore animo complecti valeret cursim raptimque. Quae vero res mentis facultatem atque, ut ita dicam, memoriae terminos mihi visa est excedere atque exsuperare. (Ut inter omnes constat, litterarum testimonia suo de more, prout res quaeque postulabat, e singulari ac permagno illo omnium rerum thesauro plerumque hausit ac deprompsit in sua ipsius memoria abdito). Quae quidem volutanti mihi verisimile visum est Graecorum et Latinorum nomina eorumque sententias in paginas a Thoma exaratas quandoque perfluxisse ex operibus aliorum scriptorum recentiorum, quae ei in manibus fuere. Itaque hoc mihi visum est pervestigandum nonne eadem vel similia a Latinis scriptoribus derivata invenirem et apud Thomam et apud alios scriptores Thomae notos. A Caesaris Baronii *Annalibus Ecclesiasticis* initium duxi. Res bene processit: *Annales* enim pervolvens ex eis vidi in *Theologica* Calabri philosophi multa migrasse ex operibus deprompta non modo veterum scriptorum christianorum sed etiam superiorum scriptorum et Latinorum et Graecorum: cuiusmodi inventa aliquot infra proponere operae pretium mihi esse videtur.

§ § §

Plauti et Terentii fabularum locos haud multos in *Theologicis* invenias. Qui quidem loci mihi considerandi videntur una cum locis utriusque poetae a Thoma in operibus de arte poetica revocatis necnon cum sententiis viri illius doctissimi et de Plauto et de Terentio. Quae omnia una considerans vidi mihique aperui Campanellam multa hausisse et e Ioannis Boccaccii *Genealogia deorum gentilium* et e Caesaris Baronii *Annalibus Ecclesiasticis*: quod ad Plautum et ad Terentium attinet, una cum *Annalibus Genealogia* quoque in numero habenda est fontium quos Calaber ille praesto habuit adhibuitque.

Opus illud de arte poetica a Thoma anno 1596° Romae in coenobio S. Sabinae dicato Italice conscriptum legenti patet adulescentem illum singularem in ipso flore aetatis (XVIII enim annos natus erat) Plauti et Terentii comoedias quodam modo novisse earumque studiose perlegisse aut nonnullas aut certe partes aliquot. Quo in opere poetam laudavit utrumque qui liberae rei publicae temporibus vera populum fabulis suis scaenicis edocuisset res pertractans ad hominum vitam attinentes. Thomae enim sententia optimi cuiusque poetae est cives vera, bona et utilia docere eosque carminibus adiuvare. Ei vero persuasum usque fuit "poema," ut ait, ad bona suadenda "instrumentum" esse omnium optimum, immo vero "magicum." Comoedias plurimi fecit quae cum speculum essent hominum vitae cunctae tum instrumentum omnium aptissimum ad mores corrigendos. Eius enim sententia virtutes et vitia, quibus hominum omnium vita referta scatet, comici poetae depingentes et proponentes ridendo castigant mores et ad recte vivendum cives invitant atque impellunt quodam modo.[1]

---

[1] Tommaso Campanella, "Poetica" in *Tutte le opere di Tommaso Campanella*, a cura

Si quis ea legit quae de comoedia et anno 1596° et anno 1612°[2] disseruit eius vestigans naturam notasque peculiares atque ea aperiens quae essent a poeta assequenda, ei manifestum erit sibi eum ante oculos posuisse intentoque animo perpendisse fabulas a Plauto et a Terentio compactas quasi exempla omnibus numeris perfecta atque absoluta, quae comoediarum scriptores imitarentur fere omnia.[3] Mea quidem sententia Plauti et Terentii comoedias partim Thomas legit ipse partim oblique novit per alios scriptores. Laudes quas Plauto et Terentio tribuit cum laudibus a Ioanne Boccaccio tributis ita congruunt atque concinunt ut adfirmare non dubitem eas a Certaldensis *Genealogia* in opus perfluxisse de arte poetica a Calabro scriptore Italice exaratum.[4]

Adulescens enim ille doctissimus Plautum et Terentium passim nominatim revocat. *Captivorum* mentionem facit propter res novas atque inopinatas a Plauto mirum in modum inventas atque contextas. Terentii *Andriam* et *Eunuchum Hecyrae* anteposuit ob praecepta de moribus plura et crebriora. *Andriam* eum iuvit in epitomen cogere. Verba Parmenonis haec memoriter ex *Eunucho* revocat: "fraudes bellum pax rursus" (cf. vv. 59–61).[5]

In *Poeticorum* libro anno 1612° Neapoli in taeterrimis vinculis exarato de comoedia fuse agens Terentium se ipsum defendentem memorat saepiusque ad Plautum redit. Comoedias optimas eas esse contendens in quibus exemplum fortunae insit cum exemplo virtutis et amoris coniunctum *Captivos* profert. Quam fabulam pulcherrimam habitam exponit breviatam.

E plautinis salibus unum tantum revocat lepide, ut ait, dictum. Illudendi enim causa Plautum dixisse affirmat "proh, fundum" cum vellet "profundum" dicere. Qua in re erravit ille quidem. In versu enim *Captivorum* 182°:

---

di L. Firpo. Scritti letterari (Milano: A. Mondadori editore, 1954), 336, 408–13, 412; (volumen hoc infra litteris memorabitur *SL*); "Poeticorum liber unus" in *SL*, 906–12, 934, 1034, 1152–62 etc.

[2] Anno 1612° Th. Campanella *Poeticorum* librum memoratum conscripsit.

[3] Comoedia una a Sfortia Oddi conscripta plautinis omnibus ei videtur anteponenda eo quod auctor e proposito homines voluit monere praeceptisque imbuere de recta vivendi ratione ita ut ad bonam frugem adducerentur et quasi cogerentur: cf. Tommaso Campanella, "Poetica" in *SL*, 413.

[4] Giovanni Boccaccio, *Genealogie deorum gentilium libri*, a cura di V. Romano, 2 voll. (Bari: G. Laterza e Figli, 1951), 2:707. Boccaccii *Genealogiam* Th. Campanella perbene novit hausitque ex ea multa de arte poetica: cf. Angela Minicucci, "I libri XIV e XV della *Genealogia deorum gentilium* e gli scritti di poetica di T. Campanella" in *Boccaccio in Europe*, ed. G. Tournoy. Proceedings of the Boccaccio Conference, Louvain 1975 (Leuven: Univ. Press, 1977).

[5] Tommaso Campanella, "Poctica" in *SL*, 409–11.

profundum vendis tu quidem, haud fundum, mihi

legendum est "profundum" neque "proh, fundum." Thomae praesto editio fuisse videtur mendose "proh, fundum" exhibens. Quam editionem nondum potui invenire.

Captivos, *Andriam* et *Eunuchum* melius quam ceteras utriusque poetae fabulas Campanella novisse videtur. In *Menaechmis* et in *Captivis* deos inductos laudat. *Amphitryonem* improbat propter Iovem et Mercurium "prave," ut ait, "operantes." *Poenuli* locum de Punico mercatore Punice loquente (cf. vv. 930–49) semel atque iterum in posteriore *Poetica* revocatum Thomas oblique per Hieronymum novit, ut ipse ait.[6]

Quem locum in libro quoque *Theologicorum* XVIII memoria repetivit.[7] In libro *Theologicorum* X *Aulularia*e mentionem facit avarorum sollicitudines curasque a poeta in scaenam eleganter allatas esse affirmans.[8]

Quid sit indulgentia exquirenti Thomae illud Terentii occurrit "nimis mihi indulgeo" e thesauro memoriae haustum. Quae verba poeta Phaedriam adulescentem in *Eunucho* (cf. v. 222) dicentem facit, haec Thomas per errorem Menedemo tribuit, viro illi aetate provecto qui–ut scriptum legimus in fabula cui index *Heautontimorumenos* (cf. vv. 96–150)–ad peccatum in filium luendum operibus nimii laboris se frangere voluit.

Quanti facienda sit verecundia docens Thomas Campanella testimonia haec affert, alterum ex *Adelphis* deprromptum: "erubuit: salva res est" (cf. v. 643), alterum e Ciceronis epistula XXII libri *Familiarium IX*: "amo verecundiam ... Atqui hoc Platoni placuit."[9] Quo loco Zenoni a Cicerone revocato Platonem supposuit eo fortasse quod paulo ante Platonis sententiam protulerat de verecundia legum et virtutum custode. Praeterea apud Ciceronem in eadem epistula mentio inest Platonis verecundiae.[10] Ex *Adelphis* locum quoque hunc exscripsit posuitque perperam in primo versu "malum" cum recte legendum esset "malo":

---

[6] Tommaso Campanella, "Poeticorum liber unus" in *SL*, 1158, 1160, 1214, 1036, 1060–62, (cf. "Poeticam" quoque Italice conscriptam: 347 et 412), 1064, 1196. Aloisii Firpo sententia (cf. *SL*: 1427 n. 11) Campanella ad Hieronymi rediisse videtur "Epistulam" 53:276 (cf. *PL* XXII col. 545).

[7] Tommaso Campanella, *Cristologia*: Theologicorum liber XVIII a cura di R. Amerio, 2 voll. (Roma: Centro internazionale di Studi Umanistici, 1958), 2:130.

[8] Tommaso Campanella, *Delle virtù e dei vizi in particolare*: Theologicorum liber X a cura di R. Amerio (Roma: Centro internazionale di Studi Umanistici, 1976), 72.

[9] Tommaso Campanella, *I Sacri Segni*: Theologicorum liber XXIV a cura di R. Amerio, 6 voll. (Roma: Centro internazionale di Studi Umanistici, 1966–69), De Sacramentis 5, 1:116.

[10] Tommaso Campanella, ibid., De Sacramentis 4, 1:16; Terentii *Adelphorum* v. 643; Ciceronis *Ad Fam*. 9:22, 1 et 5.

malum coactus qui suum officium facit,
dum id rescitum iri credit, tantisper cavet;
si sperat fore clam, rursus ad ingenium redit
(cf. vv. 69–71).

Haud per errorem Thomam puto scripsisse "malum": casum enim ablativum in accusativum consulto mutans, mea quidem sententia, clariorem fieri ratus est loci significationem, cum "malum cavet" valeret "cavet ne male faciat, ne peccet."[11] "Ieiunium" affirmans "ad luxuriam domandam . . . laudabiliter in omni lege commendatum" illud Terentii profert: "sine Cerere et Libero friget Venus" (cf. *Eun.* 732).[12]

Ex *Annalibus* Caesaris illius Baronii quasi e fonte uberrimo plurima hausit Thomas Campanella. Ut exemplum unum proferam, in libro *de vita Christi* II de sole obscurato et de tenebris longe lateque obortis simul ac Iesus in crucem sublatus est sententias invenias et Origenis et Phlegontis, scriptoris illius Hadriani liberti, et Eusebii et Tertulliani et S.Luciani et Dionysii Areopagitae: quas sententias omnes paucis immutatis e I *Annalium* volumine Campanella exscripsit neque Baronium memoravit. Item hoc contendens quattuor minimeque tribus clavis Iesum cruci esse affixum (". . . vix enim invenies clavum," ait, "qui 2 pedes simul cum ligno transfigere valeat") plautinae *Mostellariae* locum quendam revocat in *Annalibus* inventum Baronium haud memorans.

Antequam Thomas Campanella *Theologica* sua scripsit iamdiu in quaestione fuit numerus clavorum quibus Redemptor cruci est suffixus. Baronius Gregorii Turonensis sententiam revocans de quattuor minimeque tribus clavis adhibitis Romanorum morem corpora in crucem agendi quodam modo illustrat vel potius illustrare conatur testimonio hoc nisus e *Mostellaria* (cf. vv. 359–60) deprompto:

Ego dabo ei talentum, primus qui in crucem excucurrerit;
sed ea lege, ut offigantur bis pedes, bis bracchia.

Quo e loco Baronii sententia efficitur Christi pedes singillatim esse transfixos. Qua quidem in re Baronius haud recte Plauti versus illos est interpretatus, qui de pedibus et de brachiis sunt "bis" i.e. semel atque iterum vel dupliciter perforandis: cui poenae novi generis irrogandae geminatus clavorum numerus fuit adhibendus ita ut brachia binis offigerentur clavis et pedes aut duobus clavis una simulque impositi et coniuncti

[11] Tommaso Campanella, ibid., 128.

[12] Tommaso Campanella, *Delle virtù e dei vizi in particolare* cit., 84. Cf. Cic. *de n.d.* 2:23, 60: "Fruges Cererem appellamus, vinum autem Liberum, ex quo illud Terentii: Sine Cerere et Libero friget Venus."

aut binis disiuncti. Itaque *Mostellariae* loco aut sex aut octo clavi minimeque quattuor manifesto significantur. Baronium secutus Thomas quoque Campanella plautinum locum illum revocat quo sententiam suam confirmet de quattuor clavis adhibitis. At Baronium secutus Thomas quoque a vero deerravit neque vim intellexit plautini loci.

De vino myrrhato dicens quod Christo datum est bibendum paulo ante quam cruci est suffixus testimonia nonnulla de vino id genus profert a Plinio a Martiale a Paulo iurisperito tradita. Quae testimonia apud Baronium inventa in suam rem convertit, Baronii nullam faciens mentionem. Hac in re *Persae* versus 87–88 neglexit a Plinio revocatos vina odoribus condita attingente: quem Plinii locum apud Baronium exscriptum invenit una cum testimoniis reliquis de myrrhino.[13]

§ § §

Vir quidam doctissimus de studiis ad Campanellam attinentibus optime meritus mihi dixit olim Thomam Vergilii opera parum leviterque novisse: pluries enim eum eclogae III Sibyllae vaticinia de puero illo singulari tribuisse quae in IV ecloga inessent. Quae audiens stupore perculsa sum haud mediocri: verisimile enim mihi minime videbatur virum illum omni doctrinarum ac litterarum copia imbutum eumque poetam egregium parum leviterque Vergilium novisse. Quid verum esset statui tum exquirere. Campanellae operibus et Italicis et Latinis diligenter pervestigatis hoc vidi mihique fuit compertum perspectumque Thomam Vergilii opera perbene novisse eumque adamasse non modo propter singularem illam poeticam facultatem qua praestitit, non modo propter animi naturam atque habitum misericordiam et humanitatem usque redolentis sed etiam propter sententiarum amplitudinem et gravitatem ad res quoque et philosophicas et theologicas attinentium. Sescenties apud Thomam in omnibus operibus Vergiliana invenias. Erravit ille quidem semel atque iterum falso tribuens III versus aliquot eclogae IV. Erravit praeterea Damonem pro Daphnide memorans; erravit in IV eclogam transferens versum hunc *Pharmaceutriae*: "carmina vel coelo possunt deducere lunam" (cf. *Ecl.* 8.69).[14] At errata huiusmodi non sunt plurimi facienda. Qui memoriae

[13] Tommaso Campanella, *Vita Christi*: Theologicorum liber XXI a cura di R. Amerio, 2 voll. (Roma: Centro internazionale di Studi Umanistici, 1962–63), 2:8–10; 1:116–20; *Annales ecclesiastici auctore Caesare Baronio*... 38 voll. (Lucae: typis L. Venturini, MDCCXXXVIII–MDCCLIX), 1:153, 152, 147. Cf. Plin. *N.H.* 14:13, 89; 15:92.

[14] Tommaso Campanella, *Articuli prophetales* a cura di G. Ernst (Firenze: La Nuova

vi viguit singulari poetarum versus suo de more memoriter proferre solitus est: qua in re memoriae lapsu erravit interdum. At haec hactenus. Quod ad Vergilium apud Thomam attinet alia sunt maioris momenti.

Ea considerans e pythagorico et e platonico fonte hausta Vergilium poetam esse platonicum Campanella affirmare non dubitavit. In *Theologicis* crebra est poetae mentio. Cum eo quasi cum theologo Thomam iuvit interdum de rebus theologicis disputare. Quae nunc propere cursimque attigi ante alibi pertractavi plurima recensens quae apud Calabrum philosophum ad Vergilium redeunt de rebus potissimum theologicis.[15] Quae ante scripsi minime iterans perpauca tantum adiungam atque adnectam. Campanellae penitus persuasum fuit omnia in rerum natura sensu quodam esse praedita. In libro *Theologicorum* XIV corvos ait peculiari sensu monitos "pluvias praevidere" et alcyones tranquillitatem maris, Vergilii recordatus qui corvos induxit e pastu agmine magno decedentes pluvia impendente et alcyones imbribus desinentibus pennas in litore pandentes (cf. *Georg.* 1.381–82, 398–99). In libro IV corvorum pluvias praesentientium mentionem iam fecerat Vergilium non memorans. Alibi quoque in *Theologicis* Mantuanus adest non memoratus. De re obscura ac perdifficili disserens "hoc opus," ait, "hic labor" illud Vergilii (cf. *Aen.* 6.129) proferens proverbii instar vulgatum.[16]

Vergiliana fere innumera in *Theologicis* passim invenias. Sticheomantiam attingens Alexandrum Severum inducit *Aeneida* evolventem quicquid fortuito occurrat lecturum atque oculos in versu defigentem: "tu regere imperio populos, Romane, memento" (cf. *Aen.* 6.851): quibus verbis summam Augusti dignitatem praenuntiatam esse percontanti. De "prophetia," ut ait, daemoniaca et de angelica agens Vergilium Thomas

---

Italia, 1977), 82, 114, 87–88; "Poetica" in *SL*, 415; *Magia e grazia*: Theologicorum liber XIV a cura di R. Amerio (Roma: Centro internazionale di Studi Umanistici, 1957), 216.

[15] Tommaso Campanella, *La filosofia che i sensi ci additano = Philosophia sensibus demonstrata*, trans. Luigi De Franco (Napoli: Libreria Scientifica Editrice, 1974), 175, 809 (*Philosophia* ... Italice reddita mihi una praesto fuit); Angela Minicucci, "Virgilio nell'opera di Tommaso Campanella" in *Atti* del Convegno virgiliano di Brindisi nel bimillenario della morte. Brindisi 15–18 ottobre 1981 (Perugia: Istituto di filologia latina dell'Università, 1983); "De Vergilio apud Thomam Campanellam" in *Atti* del Convegno nazionale di studio su Virgilio. Torino 1–2 maggio 1982 (Torino: CELID Editrice, 1984).

[16] Tommaso Campanella, *Magia e grazia* cit., 80; *De homine*: Theologicorum liber IV a cura di R. Amerio, 2 voll. (Roma: Centro internazionale di Studi Umanistici, 1961), 82; *Dio e la predestinazione*: Theologicorum liber I a cura di R. Amerio, 2 voll. (Firenze: A. Vallecchi editore, 1949, 1951), 2:76.

affirmat "propriissime" Sibyllam descripsisse vaticinantem "subeunte diabolo ... cum corporis commotione, distorsione oris et inconditis actibus." Ulixis socios in lupos et in alias bestias mutatos Vergilium ait revocasse (cf. *Ecl.* 8.70; *Aen.* 7.15–20). Salmonea inducit faces incensas iacientem Iovis fulmina simulantem (cf. *Aen.* 6.585–91) adnectitque "non imitabile fulmen ... nos imitamur bombardis."[17]

Quid plura? Tanta admiratione tantaque reverentia Vergilium Calaber philosophus est prosecutus ut eius sententias nonnullas de re theologica una cum sententiis similibus ac congruentibus Ieremiae et Isaiae et David et Salomonis et Lactantii et Ambrosii et Augustini et Ioachimi de Flora et Iustini et Thomae Aquinatis proferre non dubitaverit, ut ante scripsi ostendique.[18]

Alia quaedam perpauca e *Theologicis* deprompta nunc mihi addere liceat. Una cum Dante semel atque iterum Thomas memorat Vergilium. De malis artibus dicens vocabulum "doli" eadem significatione adhibitum affirmat et in *Aeneide* et in psalmo quodam (cf. *Aen.* 2.34; *Ps.* 104, 25). Quae sit otii natura indagans ad Vergilium ita redit: "... ociosus est ... etiam qui multa operatur, sed quae non sunt debita et utilia relictis debitis utilibusque. Sic vocatur Aeneas otiosus apud Virgilium dum moenia Chartaginis et non Romae curat" (cf. *Aen.* 4.271: "... aut qua spe Libycis teris otia terris"? Adiectivum "otiosus" numquam invenitur apud Vergilium). Et apud Vergilium quandoque et in Sacris Litteris verbum "faciendi" idem valere ratus est ac "sacrificare." Veteres considerans philosophos qui contenderunt "... indesinenter nasci et mori mundos...; ... interire et renasci ex ruinis intereuntium mundorum ... mundos" sententias una proponit et *Ecclesiastae* (cf. I:9: "nihil sub sole novum") et Vergilii (cf. *Ecl.* 4.36: "atque iterum ad Troiam magnus mittetur Achilles"). A David "prophetice intuente ut praesentia quae erant futura" ad Vergi-

---

[17] Tommaso Campanella, *Magia e grazia* cit., 90, 98, 222; *De remediis malorum*: Theologicorum liber XVII a cura di R. Amerio (Roma: Centro internazionale di Studi Umanistici, 1975), 178.

[18] Thomae Campanellae Stylensis ord. Praed. *Universalis philosophiae seu Metaphysicarum rerum iuxta propria dogmata partes tres, libri 18* (Parisiis, MDCXXXVIII; rursus edidit A. Firpo, Torino: Bottega d'Erasmo, 1961), 3, 14:143; 15:170; 17:237; 18:250; *Articuli prophetales* cit., 87–88; *La prima e la seconda resurrezione*: Theologicorum libri XXVII et XXVIII a cura di R. Amerio (Roma: Centro internazionale di Studi Umanistici, 1955), 27:36, 68, 70; 28:182; *Origine temporale di Cristo*: Theologicorum liber XIX a cura di R.Amerio (Roma: Centro internazionale di Studi Umanistici, 1972), 102, 128; *Metaphysicarum rerum* ... cit., 3, 16:200–201; *Magia e grazia* cit., 98; *Escatologia*: Theologicorum libri XXIX et XXX a cura di R. Amerio, 2 voll. (Roma: Centro internazionale di Studi Umanistici, 1969), 1:46 etc.

lium facile sermonem transfert qui eadem de Sibylla testatus sit. Item de hominum condicione, si quando omnes omni culpa vacui ad integritatem et innocentiam redibunt, testimonia affert una et Isaiae (cf. 9:8: "... neque nocebunt serpentes ... sed delectabitur infans....") et Vergilii (cf. *Ecl.* 4.24: "occidet et serpens ...").[19]

Plurimi igitur, ut manifestum est, Vergilium Campanella fecit qui multa protulisset notis insignita et gravitatis et veritatis. Qua de re pluries eum iuvit una cum Sacrarum Scripturarum locis locos proferre Vergilii cum sacris scriptoribus re concinentes.

Opus Fundatum Latinitas in urbe Vaticana

[19] Tommaso Campanella, ibid., 52, 132; *Delle virtù e dei vizi in particolare* cit., 44, 110; *I Sacri Segni* cit., De Sacramentis 3, 2:100; *Escatologia* cit., 1:218–20; *De remediis malorum* cit., 252; *Cosmologia*: Theologicorum liber III a cura di R. Amerio (Roma: Centro internazionale di Studi Umanistici, 1964), 184.

Printed Commonplace Books in the Renaissance

ANN MOSS

The existence of commonplace books in the Renaissance is common knowledge. Access to the world of neo-Latin culture, that is to say to the world of the educated élite in Early Modern Europe and its dependencies, was gained through humanist education, and one of the most characteristic features of humanist pedagogy was the commonplace book every student reader of Greek and Latin literature was earnestly advised to keep. The Lutheran schoolmaster David Chytraeus in his *De Ratione discendi* of 1564 summarises almost a century of almost identical observations on the subject:

> So that the more lustrous passages in the designated authors and ornaments of discourse such as notable aphorisms, examples, similitudes, words, phrases and figures may be the more easily imprinted on the memory and available and ready for use as occasion requires, it is extremely useful for students to have a book of commonplaces arranged in a definite order, that is to say, in headings under which they may transcribe everything worthy of recall out of what they hear or read in their texts, apportioning their excerpted material to the separate sections of their notebooks. In this way students will construct an index to the major texts and a store-house from which to draw an abundant array of excellent subject matter, aphorisms, similitudes, exemplary narrations, etc., whenever they are required to speak or write on any matter. (Fol C 3 v°)[1]

---

[1] I have deliberately chosen Chytraeus as a typical, not an original promoter of the commonplace book. The advice on commonplace books given by more eminent humanists, Vives, Erasmus, Melanchthon, Agricola, had already been collected since the early 1530s in a volume *De Ratione studii*, reprinted several times in the middle years of the century.

Such a prescription goes to the core of humanist teaching and focusses our attention on distinctive features of the literary culture that teaching produced. Chytraeus presupposes a canon of approved writers privileged for entry into the commonplace book. Whatever the ostensible subject of these writers, Chytraeus proposes a paradigmatic approach to them, which essentially identifies their productions as rhetoric. This approach involves the break-down of any given passage into its constituent places, or topics; the recognition of particular figures of thought or speech; the juxtaposition, under appropriate headings in the note-book, of the treatment of analogous themes and the use of parallel modes of expression by various writers; and ultimately, but as an integral part of the process of reception, the genesis of verbal composition which is basically a reproduction or an assembly or a variation of antecedent texts. Prescriptions for commonplace books correlate exactly with contemporary literary commentaries, where suitable passages for extrapolation are signalled by asterisks or quotation marks, and marginal notes suggest the heads under which they might be placed. Books in every scholastic discipline are indexed by topics, or "digested into commonplaces," as the publicity jargon of the day expresses it. The role of memory in reading and of imitation in writing, and of intertextuality in both, is reinforced by the commonplace book. Yet, despite its centrality to the humanist enterprise, there has as yet been no overall history of the Renaissance commonplace book, much less any attempt to provide a descriptive bibliography even of printed examples (which were far outnumbered at the time by manuscript note-books for private use). It is not my intention here to embark on such a history, but merely to indicate how interesting that history might be, by briefly glancing at a very few of the earliest of these books and by suggesting the sort of questions they raise.[2]

[2] One of the main problems to be faced in any such history is the extremely confused terminology of "places" in Renaissance dialectic and rhetoric. The present paper deliberately side-steps the issue, but it is confronted in the two most valiant attempts so far to survey the field of commonplace books: M. J. Lechner, *Renaissance Concepts of the Commonplaces* (New York, 1962, Westport, 1974); E. Mertner, "Topos und Commonplace" in *Toposforschung. Eine Dokumentation*, ed. P. Jehn (Frankfurt, 1972), 20–68. These studies are full of insights, but partial in historical coverage. For further information, but again limited in scope, see: P. Porteau, *Montaigne et la vie pédagogique de son temps* (Geneva, 1935); B. L. Ullman, "Joseph Lang and his anthologies" in *Middle Ages, Reformation, Volkskunde. Festschrift for John G. Kunstmann* (Chapel Hill, 1959), 186–200; A. Buck, *Die humanistische Tradition in der Romania* (Bad Homburg, 1968), 133–50; W. J. Ong, *Rhetoric, Romance, and Technology* (Ithaca, New York, 1971); B. Beugnot, "Florilèges et *Polyantheae*. Diffusion et statut du lieu commun à

In the beginning of humanist education, or very near it, was the school of Guarino of Verona (1370–1460), at which "the practice of making extracts . . . and of collecting parallel passages from different authors" was well-established.[3] But this was not the beginning of commonplace books. Despite its crucial role in the recovery of classical culture, the origins of the Renaissance commonplace book lie neither in humanist schools nor in antiquity itself. The pattern was set in the Middle Ages, not by odd random sequences of extracts, but by thoroughly systematic methods of information retrieval developed from the thirteenth century onwards for the benefit of preachers. These were in effect commonplace books. They extrapolated from a canon of authors, the excerpts were entered under heads inevitably chosen to suit the moral and doctrinal preoccupations of sermon-writers, and they were usually meticulously cross-referenced. The purpose was rhetorical: to supply material for persuasive discourse and to authenticate it by reference to authoritative texts. A history of the humanist commonplace book needs to look at the organisation of these preaching manuals, and, more particularly, at those which were printed, and, by implication, sold and used at the end of the fifteenth century and at their subsequent publishing history. At the very moment that Northern humanism was taking off, printed medieval commonplace books display the wide range of investigative and exegetical techniques to which the commonplace-book formula had already been adapted.

The simplest form of the preaching commonplace book is exemplified by the *Manipulus florum* of Thomas of Ireland, written in 1306 (first printed at Piacenza, 1483). The preface to the early printed editions stresses the virtues of orderly classification, and the work is a retrieval system for finding apposite quotations from the Fathers and the Doctors of the Church, and from Cicero, Seneca, Valerius Maximus and Aulus Gellius on an extensive list of moral and doctrinal topics arranged in strict alphabetical sequence. No rhetorical or interpretative strategies are indicated. The work survived as a useful reference tool, printed and plundered throughout the sixteenth, seventeenth and even eighteenth centuries, by Catholics and Protestants alike.[4] Compiled slightly later, and

l'époque classique," in *Le lieu commun*, ed. R. Melançon, *Etudes françaises*, 13 (1977): 119–41; A. Compagnon, *La Seconde main, ou le travail de la citation* (Paris, 1979).

[3] Battista Guarino, *De ordine docendi et studendi* (1459), quoted in W. H. Woodward, *Vittorino da Feltre and other humanist educators* (New York, 1963), 173.

[4] For an exhaustive analysis and history of this work, see R. H. Rouse and M. A. Rouse, *Preachers, Florilegia and Sermons: Studies in the "Manipulus florum" of Thomas of Ireland* (Toronto, 1979).

destined to a much shorter printed career, was the *Lumen animae* (Augsburg, 1477). Its third part is an alphabetical commonplace book of topics suitable for sermons, in the manner of the *Manipulus florum* (and indeed largely derived from it), but the first and longest part is an encyclopedia in which a diversity of natural phenomena are described and moralised in great detail. The commonplace-book formula for building up matter cumulatively and selectively from a proliferation of disparate texts here functions as a complement or an adjunct to a very different process, whereby discourse is generated through interpretation, that is, by translation from one code of meaning to another.[5] Our next example, the *Summa predicantium* of John of Bromyard, who died in 1352, was printed at Nuremberg in 1484. Bromyard integrates the commonplace-book formula much more fully into yet another way of unfolding concepts in words. The *Summa* is an extremely well indexed, workable retrieval system, arranged alphabetically by topics which are further subdivided by divisions and distinctions to produce the branch-patterns characteristic of the development of a medieval sermon. Quotations, mainly Biblical, but also examples derived from ancient sources, are drawn in to illustrate and confirm each proposition. In this case the commonplace book organises not only extrapolated quotations, but a strategy for deploying them by distinctions, producing ramifications which are radically different from the linear composition favoured by humanist dialecticians. And yet, Bromyard is reprinted later in the neo-Latin period.

Not all printed commonplace books available around 1500 were reference tools for professional religious, though these tend to be the most systematically organised. There was also a less strong secular tradition of which the most notable medieval survival was probably the early fourteenth-century *Compendium moralium notabilium* of Hieremias of Montagnone, of which there is a single printed edition in 1505. Montagnone's aim was to produce a digest of moral wisdom, with extracts from a very comprehensive array of Christian and pagan authors, from Plato down to Montagnone's own time. The way the headings, or *tituli*, are arranged distinguishes this primarily secular work from its clerical counterparts with their easily searched alphabetical order. Montagnone proposes a topography of moral science, beginning with religion and the good, and then dividing all possible aspects of the active life under titles which are subdivisions of the four cardinal virtues. Despite the alphabetical index append-

[5] See M.A. Rouse and R. H. Rouse, "The texts called *Lumen animae*," *Archivum fratrum praedicatorum*, 41 (1971): 5–113.

ed, this is a display rather than an information retrieval system. The texts are very diverse, include many extracts from poets, and within each subsection are ordered with a philologian's scruple for chronological priorities, so that the reader may see who borrowed what from whom. Yet, even though Montagnone devotes several columns to rhetoric and poetic (under the general head of *eloquentia*), the quotations chosen are descriptive and prescriptive rather than exemplificatory.

The isolated printing of the medieval Montagnone contrasts sharply with the activity round another publication which has much of the commonplace book, the *Margarita poetica* of Albrecht von Eyb (1420–1475) with its fifteen, often revised and amplified versions between 1472 and 1503. Here we have moved into quite another universe of discourse, in which the production of texts is to be stimulated by copious verbal variation. The purpose of the finding mechanism explained in the preface and worked by an alphabetical list of commonplace-book headings is all about finding words, rather than matter, "words which can make the letters we write richer and more elegant in language, especially when we have seen our way to appropriating to our own kind of letter-writing, by a process of imitation, the passages from the poets here set out in order" (1472 edition, fol. cxxix). For most of the time Eyb deals specifically with written rather than with spoken language. The book is loosely related to contemporary letter-writing manuals, but derives its values from the practice and, to some extent, the particular text books in use in fifteenth-century Italian schools, and transmits to Northern Europe the humanistic rhetoric of stylistic elegance based on the imitation and quotation of model authors, which Eyb had learnt during his years in Italy. The most interesting feature of the work is how he adapts the commonplace-book method to new preoccupations and old habits, assembling his prose and verse extracts according to author rather than topic (though they are indexed according to topic), choosing a preponderance of "good" classical authors, but interspersing them with some Biblical quotations of the proverbial sort, with some recent humanistic writers, but also with some more at home in the company of the elementary *octo auctores morales* of the traditional medieval curriculum. Those eight authors were in fact largely assemblies of commonplaces in the more banal sense, juxtaposed aphorisms or similes frozen into unalterable versified sequences and so disfigured as to be incapable of recalling any original text to which they might once have belonged. How to open up the curriculum to the almost infinitely extendable, adaptable, manoeuvrable, but barely disciplined material stored in Eyb's commonplace book was a question which vexed many a Northern humanist, and lies at the origin of, for example, Josse

Bade's careful commentary on his headed extracts called *Silvae morales* (Lyons, 1492) and of Jacob Wimpfeling's *Adolescentia* (Strasburg, 1500), a commonplace book hedged round with salutary injunctions. What really stabilised the rhetorical commonplace book and enabled a methodical exploitation of its resources was neither exegesis nor moral caution so much as the dialectical process of verbal composition promoted first by Rudolphus Agricola (1443–1485).[6] At the same time as the hey-day of the *Margarita poetica*, Agricola's place-logic came to provide the skeletal framework of any connected passage of writing, to be fleshed out and ornamented from the stored riches of the commonplace book. It is on the assumption of a firm dialectical substructure underpinning new compositions built up by commonplaces that major influences like Erasmus and Melanchthon and a host of other humanists provide the headings, the layout, the extrapolated quotations, synonyms, aphorisms, adages, similitudes, apophthegms, examples and epithets for hundreds of different commonplace books, which, with their more fastidious choice of source-material and with a purer Latinity, soon made the *Margarita poetica* redundant.

Even this small example of printed commonplace books compiled before 1503 shows I hope, how nicely they exemplify, and, to some extent, create the range of thought-patterns and the different matrices of style and language available at the dawn of Northern humanism. It is not possible here to attempt further analyses of later commonplace books, but it is possible to give a sense of just a few of the issues they raise about neo-Latin culture and its influence.

We return first to the subject of literary imitation. For humanist teachers and their pupils, the analysis of pre-existing texts led as a matter of course to the generation of new ones. Humanist commonplace books make the assumption that the reader is a potential writer and propose themselves as mediators between the old texts they harvest and the new texts they hold in germ. The headings under which excerpts are classed (and which tend to become standardised as commonplace books coalesce during the course of the Renaissance) are overwhelmingly moral (and not at all dissimilar to the headings in the preaching reference books). They are partly imposed by editors seeking to underscore the moral content of their largely pagan material; are partly a by-product of the assumption that

[6] See especially Agricola's letter *De Formando studio*, dated 1484, published in conjunction with other advice on compiling commonplace books in the manual *De Ratione studii* from the 1530s on.

literature is epideictic rhetoric, whose purpose is to praise or blame; and partly a reflection of the thought-patterns actually discoverable in ancient literature and consciously adopted. But the effect of thinking about texts in terms of such headings is a uniform belief that there is a universe of ideas proper to literature, to which all writing can and should refer and to which Latin and Greek writing in particular has given privileged and paradigmatic expression. Yet, at the same time as the subjects of literature seem invariable, the production of language is seen as variety itself, with open-ended lists of juxtaposed quotations stimulating the pursuit of abundance, versatility and inventiveness. Variation on a theme or commonplace is the hallmark of Renaissance poetry, and so is the manipulation of allusions to ancient texts, juxtaposed with each other or with the new text to produce new meanings. The pleasures of Renaissance poetry are as often as not the pleasures of intertextuality and recognition, which poets learnt to give us by absorbing and reproducing the contents of the commonplace books that they and their original readers had in common.

The connection between commonplace books and literary imitation has at least two major corollaries, both of which bring us to the heart of the humanist enterprise. One is the creation of a literature which is a code of references and allusions understood only by an educated élite. The other is that the commonplace-formula for writing raises in acute form the question of the role of the new writer, the unique individual who wanders like Seneca's honey-producing bee through anthologies culled from ancient masters.[7] When the commonplace-book mentality is adopted by vernacular writers, the question is further complicated by the problematic relationship of ancient languages and ancient models to modern languages and forms. Pierre de Ronsard saw the commonplace book as a prototype for a solution to the dilemma, enabling him to "run through his books, collecting, sorting, selecting all the finest materials to paint a picture in a hundred colours, of which he alone is master."[8] It is precisely the arrangement of intertextual references which enables him to dominate them and to speak with his own individual voice. Michel de Montaigne, as ever, is more complex, but his *Essais* are a continuous dialogue between French

---

[7] Seneca's image (*Epistulae morales*, 84) finds a place in most prefaces to commonplace books, though editors may choose to emphasise different features in it. For a splendid analysis of Renaissance literary imitation starting from this crucial metaphor, see G. W. Pigman, "Versions of imitation in the Renaissance," *Renaissance Quarterly*, 33 (1980): 1–32.

[8] *Hylas*, lines 417–26, in Pierre de Ronsard, *Oeuvres complètes*, ed. P. Laumonier, 20 vols (Paris, 1914–1975), 15:252.

and Latin, himself and his quotations. Most of his Latin quotations are additions to the major revision and amplification of the *Essais* published in 1588, and he called them "emblems," a semi-technical term used for amplification by additional quoted excerpts as from a commonplace book. Montaigne finds himself by assaying himself against commonplaces, and finds his true reader, his critical reader, in him who can recognize both commonplaces and private places in the *Essais*.[9] There is also a much more general sense in which the commonplace book may be said to have invented the critical reader. It was by bringing together analogous excerpts from different poets under common heads that J. C. Scaliger, in the book called *Criticus* of his *Poetice* (Lyons, 1561), provided the apparatus for his detailed critical comparisons, in which we recognise the principles of what we call literary criticism.

If the influence of commonplace books in their role as vehicles of the humanist revolution in literature was considerable, their influence on religious thinking was no less so. We have noted the survival from the Middle Ages of commonplace books for preachers, but it was only after they had been reformed that they became a dominant mode of theological exposition. A method of indexing Sacred Scripture according to commonplaces is clearly set out by Erasmus in his *Ratio* of 1518, with a cross-reference to the chapter "ratio colligendi exempla" in his *De Copia* which makes it obvious that the method for making a commonplace book there described in the context of secular studies differs in no way from the one he now prescribes for religious purposes.[10] Here too it will be a tool for analysing texts, furnish the memory, and supply ready material for exposition and disputation. Even more crucially, it will isolate and juxtapose difficult passages, and so enable the illumination of Scriptural text by Scriptural text, which for Erasmus was the true exegetical method. Theological commonplaces in the sense of axiomatic truths of the faith had had a place, but a relatively minor one, in medieval systematics. What happens in the first half of the sixteenth century seems to be that philological Humanists like Erasmus substitute their favourite method of analysis (by commonplaces) for the *quaestiones* and *distinctiones* they reject, and in so

---

[9] See, for example, the opening paragraphs of *Essais*, I xxvi and II x. For a beautifully judged assessment of the role of commonplaces in the *Essais*, see F. Goyet, "A propos de ces 'pastissages de lieux communs': le rôle des notes de lecture dans la genèse des *Essais*," *Bulletin de la Société des Amis de Montaigne* (July–December, 1986), 11–26.

[10] *Ratio seu methodus compendio perveniendi ad veram theologiam* in *Opera*, ed. J. Clericus (Leyden, 1703–1706), V, col. 130.

doing reinforce the centrality of the text, the Word, and also place it well within the competence of the educated layman. All this coincides with (and probably to some extent assists), the drift of the Reformation. The most famous of all *Loci communes* were the work of a humanist theologian, Philip Melanchthon, who from 1521 established the method of drawing up heads, or articles of religion, derived from and supported by quotations from the Scriptures, as the new dogmatics of the new religion: "for the doctrine of the Church is not derived from demonstrations, but from sayings."[11] It also became the ground on which the debate with the Catholics was conducted, thereby engendering commonplace books with a Catholic bias aimed at supplying weapons for controversy, as well as provision for sermons now based on and amplified by the places of rhetorical invention learnt in the humanist schoolroom.[12]

In his advice for making commonplace books for secular studies, *De Locis communibus ratio* (1531), Melanchthon contended that the places, or heads, into which the book was to be divided were far from arbitrary or conventional.[13] They were "the forms or rules of all things, drawn from deep-seated patterns in nature." This conviction enabled him to transfer the commonplace-book formula without difficulty to dogmatics, but raises wide issues with which any history of the commonplace book will have to grapple. Was its effect to inhibit new thought, because it implied that every new text, every new discovery had to find a place in the corpus of received wisdom, which was itself the Book of Nature? Is the prestige of commonplace books and their lengthy survival in the education system to be explained by the fact that they contained the consensus, even connived with the *doxae* of the dominant political and social power-structure? To begin to answer these questions one would have to examine not only the titles of places and the range of quotations transcribed, but also the order

---

[11] From Melanchthon's preface to the 1543 edition of the *Loci communes*, in *Opera*, ed. C. G. Bretschneider and H. E. Bindseil (Brunswick, 1834–1860), XXI, col. 604. For an account of Melanchthon's *Loci communes* which pays some attention to the commonplace context, see Q. Breen, "The terms *loci communes* and *loci* in Melanchthon," *Church History*, 16 (1947): 197–209; also P. Joachimsen, "*Loci communes*: eine Untersuchung zur Geistesgeschichte des Humanismus und der Reformation," *Luther-Jahrbuch* (Berlin, 1926), 27–97; K. Kolb, "Teaching the text: the commonplace method in sixteenth-century Biblical commentary," *Bibliothèque d'Humanisme et Renaissance*, 49 (1987): 571–85.

[12] A typical example is the *Sylva locorum communium* of Luis of Granada (1504–1588), which was first published in 1582, to be used in conjunction with his *Rhetorica ecclesiastica sive de ratione concionandi*.

[13] *Opera*, ed. cit., XX, col. 698.

in which the places were arranged, sometimes following alphabetical convention, but sometimes complex patterns of subordinates and contraries, which reveal deep-seated notions of how things connect and which things are mutually opposed. Yet it is of the nature of the commonplace book that the quotations it gathers tend to pull away from the norms to which they are attached. The very function of the places as ever-expanding receptacles of multiple quotations is to add, not foreclose, to produce linguistic variations more admired for their inventiveness than for their referentiality, perhaps to invite self-contradiction and the scepticism that may go with it. By the end of the sixteenth century commonplace books could go to extremes. At one end there was the carefully supervised and censored selection operated in Jesuit schools; at the other, collections of political aphorisms from very diverse sources proposed in a positivist spirit as issues of contemporary debate.[14] Like Montaigne (and both were learned humanists, both actively involved in political life), Francis Bacon had a very ambivalent attitude to the commonplace book, but he too recognised its potential for discovery:

> Aphorisms, since they lay before us only certain portions and, as it were, bits and pieces of knowledge, invite others to add and contribute something in their turn.[15]

University of Durham

[14] Most notably the *Politica* of Justus Lipsius (Leyden, 1589). For an overview of political compilations, see S. Anglo, "Aphorismes politiques: évolution d'une fragmentation systématisée," in *L'Automne de la Renaissance 1580–1630*, ed. J. Lafond and A. Stegmann (Paris, 1981), 271–79.

[15] Francis Bacon, *Works*, ed. J. Spedding, R. L. Ellis and D. D. Heath, 14 vols (London, 1857–1874), 1:665–66.

Zu den 'Amores' (1542) des Simon Lemnius

LOTHAR MUNDT

Man kann Lemnio den Ruhm eines geschickten Poetens nicht absprechen. Nur sind diese Elegien etwas zu frey geschrieben."[1] So urteilte Johann Christian Götze 1743 im ersten Band seiner 'Merckwürdigkeiten der Königlichen Bibliothek zu Dreßden' über die fast genau 200 Jahre früher (1542) gedruckten 'Amores' des Simon Lemnius.

Nicht ganz 200 Jahre später (im 1929 erschienenen zweiten Band seiner 'Geschichte der neulateinischen Literatur Deutschlands') schrieb Georg Ellinger in ähnlicher Tendenz, den milden Vorbehalt Götzes aber mit der moralisierenden Prüderie des 19. Jahrhunderts übersteigernd:

> Die Tatsache, daß jede Idealisierung des Sinnengenusses fehlt, und daß man es nur mit den Ausbrüchen der rohen Begierde und den Vorstellungen einer verdorbenen Phantasie zu tun hat, schädigt den Gesamteindruck und beeinträchtigt unwillkürlich auch die Vorzüge. Trotzdem lassen diese sich nicht verkennen.[2]

Diese Urteile über die 'Amores' des Lemnius, denen sich manche ähnlich akzentuierte beifügen ließen, sind sicher nicht unbeeinflußt von der Kenntnis jener Affäre, die den Namen des Autors dem Gedächtnis der Nachwelt zwar dauerhaft einprägte, deren Nachwirkungen aber eine sachbezogene Würdigung seines literarischen Schaffens lange Zeit verhindert haben: ich meine seinen bekannten Streit mit Luther in den

---

[1] Johann Christian Götze, *Merckwürdigkeiten der Königlichen Bibliothek zu Dreßden*, Bd. 1. (Dresden, 1743), S. 286.

[2] Georg Ellinger, *Geschichte der neulateinischen Literatur Deutschlands im 16. Jahrhundert*, Bd. 2. (Berlin, 1929), S. 98.

Jahren 1538/39, der mit der Veröffentlichung einer Luther mißliebigen Sammlung von Epigrammen an der Universität Wittenberg begonnen hatte und mit dem nach der Flucht des Lemnius aus Wittenberg erschienenen dramatischen Pamphlet 'Monachopornomachia' beendet wurde.[3]

Kurz nach der Herausgabe dieses Werkes war Lemnius in seine Heimat Graubünden zurückgekehrt und hatte in der Stadt Chur eine Anstellung als Lehrer an dem dort gerade gegründeten Gymnasium erhalten. Nachdem er dieses Amt aus nicht völlig zu klärenden Gründen[4] nach ca. drei Jahren wieder verloren und die Stadt Chur verlassen hatte, veröffentlichte er im Jahre 1542 die Elegiensammlung 'Amorum libri IIII.' Von dem Werk, das ohne Angabe eines Druckortes erschien, sind heute nur noch drei Exemplare nachweisbar (in Chur, Zürich und Dresden).[5] Eine von mir veranstaltete Neuedition mit deutscher Übersetzung ist 1988 als Band 2 der Reihe 'Bibliotheca Neolatina' (Verlag Peter Lang, Bern, Frankfurt a.M., New York) erschienen.[6]

Die vier Bücher umfassen 12 Texte in elegischem Versmaß, deren Umfänge zwischen 74 and 440 Versen schwanken. Hinzu kommen zwei kurze Einleitungsgedichte, ebenfalls in elegischen Distichen, überschrieben 'Ad lectorem' und 'Cupido,' letzteres zum Teil eine Variation des ersten Distichons von Buch I der 'Ars amatoria' des Ovid. Ein kompositorisches Prinzip, das etwa dem der 'Amores' des Celtis vergleichbar wäre, ist nicht zu erkennen; die Texte sind locker aneinandergefügt. Dem Titel des Buches werden eigentlich nur die Elegien der Bücher I-III und die 4. Elegie von Buch IV, insgesamt acht Texte, gerecht. Die restlichen vier, die im Unterschied zu den anderen Elegien historischen Persönlichkeiten gewidmet sind, behandeln andere Themen, sind aber, mit einer Ausnahme (IV,5), durch Einbettung in bestimmte Rahmenhandlungen mit dem Hauptthema verbunden.

Die eigentlichen Liebeselegien enthalten Schilderungen von glücklichen und (in der Mehrzahl) unglücklichen erotischen Beziehungen zu verschie-

---

[3] Diese Affäre ist dargestellt und dokumentiert in: Lothar Mundt, *Lemnius und Luther. Studien und Texte zur Entstehung und Nachwirkung ihres Konflikts (1538/39)*. 2 Bde. (Bern, Frankfurt a. M., New York 1983); (= Europäische Hochschulschriften 1,612; auch in: Arbeiten zur Mittleren Deutschen Literatur und Sprache 14).

[4] Dazu: Lothar Mundt, Von Wittenberg nach Chur. Zu Leben und Werk des Simon Lemnius in den Jahren ab 1539. In: *Daphnis* 17 (1988), S. 163-222, hier: S. 176 ff.

[5] Chur, Kantonsbibliothek Graubünden (Bb 33); Zürich, Zentralbibliothek (St 435_3); Dresden, Sächs. Landesbibliothek (8° Lit. Lat. rec. A. 1042).

[6] Simon Lemnius, *Amorum libri IV. Liebeselegien in vier Büchern. Nach dem einzigen Druck von 1542 hrsg. u. übers. von Lothar Mundt*. Bern, Frankfurt a.M., New York 1988 (= Bibliotheca Neolatina 2). Alle im folgenden angeführten Stellenangaben beziehen sich auf diese Edition.

denen Mädchen. Fünf davon haben die Form von Briefen, die an diese Mädchen gerichtet sind.

Ich möchte auf den Inhalt eines der heiteren Texte näher eingehen, da sein Aufbau, sein Figuren- und Motivarsenal typisch sind für die von Lemnius angewandten Gestaltungsprinzipien. Die Elegie—es handelt sich um den Schlußtext von Buch I—setzt ein mit der anmutigen Schilderung eines Frühsommerabends in einem Landstädtchen. Beim Spaziergang durch die Gassen begegnet der Dichter den Göttern Apoll und Merkur, die ihn fragen, ob er für die Nacht schon ein Mädchen habe, und ihm eines empfehlen, das sich in der Nähe aufhält. Es handle sich um die Tochter des Bacchus und einer von diesem vergewaltigten Dryade. Der Dichter geht nun ohne weiteres auf Leukis—so heißt das Mädchen—zu und nimmt sie mit sich nach Hause. Als die beiden gerade bei raetischem Wein sitzen und die ersten Küsse getauscht haben, erscheint eine Gruppe von Satyrn vor der Haustür, um Leukis zu rauben. Der Dichter kann die Satyrn durch gutes Zureden besänftigen, und diese ziehen unverrichteterdinge wieder ab. Die beiden Liebenden steigen nun in ein höhergelegenes Gemach des Hauses, das vier Fenster—in jeder Himmelsrichtung eines—besitzt. Nachdem sich der Dichter an den Schönheiten des nun nackt vor ihm stehenden Mädchens erfreut hat, beginnt das Liebesspiel, dessen Schilderung von einer nach den Begriffen der Zeit geradezu heidnischen Unbefangenheit—ohne dabei eigentlich lasziv[7] zu sein—gekennzeichnet ist. Als der Morgen heranbricht, sehen Aurora und Phoebus die beiden auf ihrem Lager, und beide Götter denken gerührt an eigene Liebesfreuden.

Genau den gleichen Aufbau hat die folgende Elegie, mit der Buch II eingeleitet wird. Die Rolle des Kupplers spielen hier allerdings nicht Apoll und Merkur, sondern Venus, die dem Dichter in einer schönen Gartenlandschaft begegnet und ihn in einer langen, mit vielen Beispielen aus der antiken Mythologie gespickten Rede dazu ermahnt, seine Jugend zum Lieben zu benutzen, da das Greisenalter zur Liebe kaum noch geeignet sei. Der Dichter solle gleich in die Stadt gehen; dort werde ihm auf dem Markt eine 'nigra puella' in den Weg laufen. So geschieht es auch. Der Dichter spricht das Mädchen unter Berufung auf Venus an und lädt sie in sein Haus, dessen anmutige Lage er ihr ausführlich schildert. Nach der Liebesnacht, die sie dort erwarte, werde sie ein bedeutendes Geschenk

[7] So die gängigen Urteile. Vgl. Peter Wiesmann, Simon Lemnius. In: *Bedeutende Bündner aus fünf Jahrhunderten. Festgabe der Graubündner Kantonalbank zum Anlaß des 100. Jahrestages ihrer Gründung*, Bd. 1. Chur 1970, S. 120; Franz Wachinger, Lemnius und Melanchthon. In: *Archiv f. Reformationsgeschichte* 77(1986), S. 143.

erhalten. Das Mädchen willigt sogleich ein. Vor der Haustür wartet auf sie ein schwarm 'Freier' ('proci'), die dem Dichter– ebenso wie die Satyrn in der Elegie I,3–sein Mädchen streitig machen wollen. Diese werden aber ebenso ausmanövriert, und alles weitere läuft dann entsprechend ab–nur daß die noch verbleibenden Abschnitte der 'quinque lineae amoris'[8] (visus, allocutio, tactus, osculum, coitus)–insbesondere der letzte–noch breiter und noch konkreter ausgemalt werden.

Es ist kein Zufall, daß die beiden Texte mit Schilderungen lieblicher Landschaftsszenerien einsetzen: in *allen* Elegien, die von erfüllter Liebe oder der Erinnerung daran handeln, fehlen nie Hinweise auf die Anmut der umgebenden Landschaft oder die Pracht und Fülle der Vegetation. Die Funktion des locus amoenus ist hier im wesentlichen die gleiche, wie sie Klaus Garber für die antike Bukolik konstatiert hat:[9] Steigerung des Liebesgenusses durch das Erleben der Schönheit der umgebenden Natur, Verführungs–und Lockmittel für den Mann und Ausdruck der Vitalität, der lebenspendenden Kraft des Eros.

Die Elegien traurigen Inhalts–sie sind, wie bemerkt, in der Mehrzahl–enthalten heftige Klagen über die Abwesenheit und grausame Härte der Geliebten und ebenso heftige Selbstvorwürfe des Dichters über sein eigenes Fehlverhalten, das zur Trennung geführt hat. Bei den Fehlern, die der Verfasser sich selbst zum Vorwurf macht, handelt es sich um unbegründete Eifersucht, zu große Schüchternheit und Mangel an liebenswürdiger Zuwendung zur Geliebten. Liebeskrank, mit vernachlässigtem Äußeren irrt er, von allen Freunden und Bekannten grausam verlacht und gemieden, in der Stadt und im Hause umher und vergrößert noch sein Leiden, indem er sich alle früher genossenen Schäferstündchen lebhaft vor Augen führt.

In einer dieser von Liebesklagen erfüllten Elegien (I, 1) erscheint dem Dichter Apoll in Begleitung der neun Musen und macht ihm Vorwürfe, daß er sich immer wieder in nutzlose Liebeshändel stürze. Die Schädlichkeit und die Gefahren der Liebe werden an zahlreichen Beispielen (u. a. Phyllis, Hippolytus, Narcissus, Myrrha) aufgezeigt. Lemnius solle sich wieder mehr um Minerva und die Musen kümmern, dann könne ihm die Liebe nichts mehr anhaben.

Spielt die Frau in den heiteren Elegien die Rolle einer allen Wünschen

---

[8] Vgl. Heinz Schlaffer, *Musa iocosa. Gattungspoetik und Gattungsgeschichte der erotischen Dichtung in Deutschland.* (Stuttgart 1971); (= Germanist. Abhandlungen 37), S. 77.

[9] Klaus Garber, *Der locus amoenus und der locus terribilis. Bild und Funktion der Natur in der deutschen Schäfer- und Landlebendichtung des 17. Jahrhunderts* (Köln, Wien 1974); (= Literatur und Leben 16), S. 181.

des Mannes gefügigen Partnerin, so in den traurigen die Rolle einer sich nach anfänglicher Hingabe grausam verweigernden beleidigten Schönen. Im Mittelpunkt aber steht immer der Mann: sei es als Liebe Genießender und Liebesgenuß Spendender oder als an der Liebe Leidender.

Mit einer Ausnahme (I,1) haben alle diese traurigen Elegien die Form von Briefen, bei denen, wie nicht anders zu erwarten, Ovids 'Heroides' als Vorbild gedient hatten. Besonders ausgiebig wurde Ovids 15. Heroide, der Brief Sapphos an Phaon, ausgewertet. Lemnius' Elegie III,2 (Ad Illyrida) ist in den zentralen Passagen eine Adaptation dieser Vorlage— bis hin zur leicht variierenden Übernahme einzelner Verse, Versteile oder Versgruppen. Ein großer Teil der Änderungen war natürlich wegen des Wechsels der Geschlechterrollen nötig, denn alle Klagen Sapphos macht sich der Dichter selbst zu eigen, während die Rolle Phaons auf ein Mädchen übertragen ist. Eine dieser variierenden Übernahmen ist besonders deshalb interessant, weil sie bisher— seit der grundlegenden Lemnius-Biographie von Paul Merker—als autobiographische Selbstcharakteristik gewertet wurde.[10] Es handelt sich um die Stelle, in der Sappho beklagt, daß ihr Leben schon immer unter einem Unstern gestanden habe, und, um dies zu belegen, auf Ereignisse in ihrer Kindheit hinweist (v. 59 ff.). Mit sechs Jahren habe sie ihre Eltern verloren. Ihr Bruder habe sich in eine Hure verliebt und sich dadurch Schande und finanzielle Einbußen zugezogen. Beides wiederholt Lemnius fast wörtlich (v. 207 ff.) und läßt nur anstelle eines Bruders eine *Schwester* sich durch eine Mesalliance ins Unglück stürzen. Ob hier wirklich eine Parallelität der Biographie der Ovidschen Sappho mit der des Lemnius gegeben war oder ob der Autor sich hier nur selbst in eine literarische Rolle hineinstilisiert hat, wird für immer ungeklärt bleiben müssen. Das Beispiel lehrt aber, wie vorsichtig man bei der biographischen Ausdeutung neulateinischer Dichtung verfahren muß. Warum Lemnius sich gerade den Sappho-Brief als Vorlage gewählt hat, ist unter dem eben angedeuteten Aspekt leicht verständlich: zum einen war dies naheliegend, da es sich bei Sappho gewissermaßen um eine Kollegin im Dienste der Musen handelte, deren Existenz zudem geschichtlich verbürgt war,[11] zum anderen lag in der Anverwandlung an

[10] Paul Merker, *Simon Lemnius. Ein Humanistenleben.* (Straßburg 1908) (= Quellen u. Forschungen zur Sprach- u. Culturgeschichte d. german. Völker 104), S. 5.

[11] Hierin unterscheidet sich die Epistula Sapphus von den anderen Epistulae Heroidum Ovids, deren Verfasserinnen und Verfasser ausnahmslos Gestalten des Mythos sind. Auch überlieferungsgeschichtlich hat der Sappho-Brief eine Sonderstellung; er wurde erst ca. 1420 wiederentdeckt, nachdem er über 1000 Jahre verschollen war. In neuerer Zeit war seine Echtheit umstritten. Hierzu: Heinrich Dörrie, *P. Ovidius Naso. Der Brief der Sappho an Phaon* (München 1975); (= Zetemata 58); ders.,

die Rolle, die Ovid der berühmtesten Dichterin des Altertums zugewiesen hatte, die Möglichkeit, den eigenen Ruhm bzw. den Anspruch darauf zu unterstreichen.

Die Elegien des vierten Buches sind, ausgenommen die Heroide 'Ad Marullam' (IV, 4), wie schon erwähnt, nicht eigentlich erotischen Inhalts. Sie sind sämtlich Persönlichkeiten aus Graubünden gewidmet, an deren Wohlwollen dem Dichter gelegen sein mußte und denen er offenbar beweisen wollte, daß er auch über ernstere Themen zu schreiben imstande und willens war. Die Elegie IV, 1 ist eine Huldigung an den Freund Wolfgang Salet, einen sehr wohlhabenden Bürger der Stadt Chur. Eine Verbindung zum Hauptthema des Werkes wird durch die Einleitung geschaffen, in der der Dichter sich selbst als Gefolgsmann in Triumphzug der Venus darstellt (in Anlehnung an Ovid, *Amores* 1,2).

Text IV, 2 ist Jakob Travers, dem Hofmeister des Bischofs von Chur, gewidmet; eigentlicher Adressat ist aber, wie aus dem Text hervorgeht, dessen Vater Johannes Travers (1483–1563), damals der ein flußreichste Bündner Staatsmann, selbst humanistisch geprägter Schriftsteller, der in den Jahren nach der Rückkehr des Lemnius aus Deutschland wiederholt helfend und fördernd in sein Leben eingegriffen hat. Der Brief an Johannes Travers wurde von einem früheren Lemnius-Forscher (Gerhart Sieveking) nicht ganz zu Unrecht, aber doch wohl etwas zu emphatisch als "Beichte" des reuig aus Deutschland heimkehrenden Dichters an seinen großen Landsmann bezeichnet.[12] Lemnius bedauert in diesem Brief, daß er mit seinen Jugenddichtungen zu sehr im Banne des 'Trankes der Kirke' gestanden habe, den ihm mißgünstige Landsleute in seiner Jugend zu trinken gegeben hätten, um sein Talent zu ruinieren. Der Bann sei jetzt aber gebrochen, und er, Lemnius, wolle sich nun ernsten vaterländischen Themen zuwenden. Er plane, eine zweite Ilias zu schreiben, in der die militärischen Leistungen seiner Landsleute in dem für die Schweizer siegreichen Krieg von 1499 gegen Kaiser Maximilian I. und den Schwäbischen Bund, ein Denkmal zu setzen. Dieses Versprechen machte der Dichter dann einige Jahre später wahr mit der Abfassung des Epos 'De bello Raetico (Raeteis).' Der Ernst dieser 'Beichte' wird allerdings sehr durch den Ausgang der Rahmenhandlung relativiert, mit der der Autor den Brief an Travers in die erotische Hauptthematik seines Werkes

---

Der heroische Brief. Bestandsaufnahme, Geschichte, Kritik einer humanistisch-barocken Literaturgattung (Berlin 1968), S. 76, Anm. 13; S. 80 f.

[12] Gerhart Sieveking, "Die Beichte des Simon Lemnius an Gian Travers," In: *Rätia* 6(1944), S. 179–90.

eingefügt hat. Diese Rahmenhandlung beginnt damit, daß dem Dichter, als er an dem lauschigen Ufer eines Flüßchens eingeschlafen ist, im Traum Venus und Apoll erscheinen. Venus fordert ihn auf, nur die Liebe zu besingen, Apoll dagegen ermahnt ihn, von derlei Tändelkram abzulassen. Als der Dichter aufgewacht ist, entschließt er sich, Apoll zu gehorchen, und schreibt den schon charakterisierten Brief an Travers. Als dieser Brief aber beendet gewesen sei, da sei, so heißt es, Cupido durch die Luft herbeigeflogen und habe das liebeleere Herz des Dichters mit seinem Pfeil durchbohrt, so daß es nun wieder vollkommen von der Liebe beherrscht werde.

Sehr ähnlich ist die Einrahmung der folgenden, dem französischen Gesandten in Graubünden, Jean de Castion, gewidmeten Elegie, mit dem Lemnius diesem seinem Mäzen anscheinend mit seiner Vertrautheit mit dem Geschichtswerk des Livius imponieren wollte. Venus, die mit ihrem Gefolge am akidalischen Quell fröhliche Tänze aufführt, bekommt Besuch von ihrem Sohn Cupido, der sie bittet, ihn nicht in die Alpentäler Graubündens, zu dem bekannten gelehrten Dichter, zu schicken und diesem etwas Ruhe zu gönnen, damit er sich stärker den Musen widmen könne. Daraufhin erscheint die Muse Erato dem Dichter, überreicht ihm eine venezianische Ausgabe des Livius und empfiehlt ihm, diese zu lesen, um damit die Glut der Venus zum Erlöschen zu bringen. Der Dichter schildert nun, was er einen Monat lang im Livius gelesen hat, und dies ist eigentlich der wesentliche Inhalt der Elegie. Inzwischen aber ist Venus mit Sohn und Gefolge vom akidalischen Quell aufgebrochen und im Triumph in die raetischen Alpen gezogen (die Schilderung des Trimphzugs auch hier nach Ovid, Amores 1,2). Nun kennt Cupido keine Gnade mehr und verschießt seine Pfeile ebenso auf den Dichter wie auf die jungen Männer und Mädchen Raetiens. So findet natürlich das Livius-Studium ein Ende, und der Dichter gibt sich weder ganz der erotischen Lyrik hin.

Auf die letzte, dem Reformator des Engadin, Philipp Gallicius, gewidmete Elegie des Bandes (IV, 5), die inhaltlich, bis auf bestimmte Motive im Einleitungsteil, gänzlich aus dem Rahmen fällt, kann ich hier nicht näher eingehen, da zu ihrem Verständnis eine eingehende Schilderung der biographischen Zusammenhänge zur Zeit der Entstehung des Werkes nötig wäre.[13]

Was das Werk des Lemnius für uns besonders interessant macht, sind zweifellos die unerhört offenen und direkten sexuellen Schilderungen,[14] für die es weder in der römischen Liebesdichtung[15] noch, soweit wir

---

[13] S. o., Anm.4.

[14] Vor allem: *Amores* I, 3, 83-124; II, 1, 127-82; 2, 29-102.

[15] Zwar begegnet man auf Schritt und Tritt dem Einfluß Ovids (der mehrfach

wissen, in der neulateinischen Literatur der Zeit eine Parallele gibt, abgesehen von einem anderen Werk des Lemnius selbst, nämlich der 'Monachopornomachia', wo aber sexuelles Geschehen ganz anders, unter entgegengesetztem Blickwinkel, dargestellt wird, und zwar im Grunde als etwas, was die menschliche Persönlichkeit herabwürdigt und bei seiner ungeschminkten Offenlegung gegenüber der Mitwelt nur moralisch kompromittierend oder lächerlich wirken kann. Hat also Lemnius in der 'Monachopornomachia' bewußt Auffassungen seines Zeitalters, die er selbst anscheinend nicht mehr teilte, aufgegriffen und zu polemischen Zwecken gegen seine Feinde gewendet, so setzt er sich in den 'Amores,' wo dieser polemische Zweck entfiel, mit größter Selbstverständlichkeit darüber hinweg und preist hier nun Sexualität vorbehaltlos als positive menschliche Kraft. Auffallend und auch bezeichnend für die Veränderung der Perspektive ist der—bei aller Offenheit in der Sache—sehr sparsame und abgemessene Gebrauch obszönen Vokabulars in den 'Amores' im Vergleich zu seiner forcierten Verwendung in der 'Monachopornomachia.'[16]

Auch in den erotischen Dichtungen des Johannes Secundus sucht man Textpassagen, die den sexuellen Schilderungen in den 'Amores' vergleichbar wären, vergeblich. Allenfalls Nr. XIV der drei Jahre vor Lemnius' Werk (1539) erstmals im Druck erschienenen 'Basia' wäre hier zu nennen.[17] Ellinger verwies auf Einflüsse aus Italien und Frankreich, mit denen natürlich aufgrund der geographischen Lage Graubündens auf jeden Fall zu rechnen ist, und zwar auf Titus Vespasianus Strozza und den französierten Italiener Publius Faustus Andrelinus.[18] Konkrete Textbeispiele, anhand derer sich etwa eine Abhängigkeit des Lemnius von diesen Vorgängern nachweisen oder zumindest als wahrscheinlich annehmen ließe, führte Ellinger jedoch nicht an.[19]

---

verwendete Topos der männlichen Potenzprotzerei z. B.—*Amores* I, 2, 121–22.167; 3,119–24; II, 1, 157-58.161–63. 167–68.179–80; 2, 95–96; IV, 5, 53–56—in Anlehnung an Ovid, *Amores* III, 7, 23–27), aber die Ausmalung erotischer Szenen in der Unverblümtheit, wie wir sie bei Lemnius finden, war für Ovid natürlich undenkbar. Selbst die Priapea, die dem Autor sicher bekannt waren (vgl. *Amores* I, 2, 166 u. II, 1, 152 mit Priap. VI, 6) können als Stoffquelle ausscheiden.

[16] S. dazu Mundt, *Lemnius u. Luther*, Bd. 1, S. 145 ff.

[17] Ioannes Nicolai Secundus, *Basia. Mit einer Auswahl aus den Vorbildern und Nachahmern* hrsg. von Georg Ellinger (Berlin 1899); (= Latein. Litteraturdenkmäler d. 15. u. 16. Jahrhunderts 14), S. 11 f.

[18] Ellinger, *Geschichte*, Bd. 2, S. 98. In einer früheren Arbeit nannte Ellinger auch den Franzosen Johannes Vultejus. (Georg Ellinger, Simon Lemnius als Lyriker. In: *Festgabe Friedrich von Bezold dargebracht zum 70. Geburtstag von seinen Schülern, Kollegen und Freunden* [Bonn, Leipzig, 1921], S. 226).

[19] Der Verweis auf des Andrelinus titelgleichen Elegienzyklus 'Amorum libri

Eine Sexualauffassung, die in ihrer Freizügigkeit der des Lemnius nahekommt, findet man durchaus bei Giovanni Pontano (1426–1503): etwa in den Zyklen 'Parthonopeus sive Amores' oder 'Eridanus';[20] ein Abhängigkeitsverhältnis des Lemnius gegenüber Pontano ist aber nicht erkennbar. Zu nennen wäre in diesem Zusammenhang auch die erotisch-*satirische* Literatur der frühen italienischen Neulateiner, etwa der frivole 'Hermaphroditus' des Antonio Beccadelli, genannt Panormita (1394–1471) oder die 'Facetiae' von dessen Freund Poggio Bracciolini (1380–1459). Diese Literatur unterliegt aber ganz anderen gattungsmäßigen Gesetzen und Traditionen und muß daher hier außer Betracht bleiben.[21]

---

quattuor' (auch bekannt unter dem Titel 'Livia'; entstanden ca. 1485–95), der sich in Ellingers Aufsatz von 1921 findet, wurde in dem 1929 erschienenen 2. Band seiner 'Geschichte der neulateinischen Literatur Deutschlands' getilgt. Die Formulierungen wurden abgeschwächt. Hieß es 1921 noch: "... mit ... Andrelinus hat Lemnius nicht bloß den ... Titel seiner Gedichtsammlung gemein, sondern er steht auch unter seinem Einflusse." (S. 226), so schrieb Ellinger 1929 vorsichtiger: "... auch der Einfluß des ... Andrelinus läßt sich nicht verkennen." (S. 98). Dies mag jedoch eher für gewisse sprachliche Eigenheiten oder für die Verwendung von Bildern und Motiven gelten als für konkrete Inhalte. Zu letzteren vgl. die Angaben in Bd. 1 (1929) von Ellingers Werk (S. 125 ff.). Bei meiner eigenen Lektüre der Elegien des Andrelinus in der Ausgabe Venedig 1501 (Exemplar der Landesbibliothek Detmold) fand ich kaum Parallelen, die so augenfällig wären, daß man berechtigt wäre, von einer mutmaßlichen Abhängigkeit des Lemnius von Andrelinus zu sprechen.

[20] Joannes Jovianus Pontanus, *Carmina. Ecloghe. Elegie. Liriche.* A cura di Johannes Oeschger (Bari 1948); (= Scrittori d'Italia 198), S. 63–121; 379–444. Vgl. im 'Parthonopeus' die Texte 'Ad vicinos' (S. 96 f.) und 'De improbitate puellae meae' (S. 98), im 'Eridanus' die mit 'Ad Stellam' überschriebenen Gedichte IX und XVII in Buch I (S. 389 f., 395 ff.).

[21] Um sich den Unterschied deutlich zu machen, vergleiche man z. B. den Ovid (Her. 15, 23–24) imitierenden Lobpreis der Geliebten bei Lemnius, *Amores* III, 2, 67–70 und IV, 4, 31–34 mit Beccadellis auf ebendieselben Ovid-Verse zurückgehender 'Laus Aldae' (Hermaphroditus II, 3):

Si tibi sint pharetrae atque arcus, eris, Alda, Diana;
Si tibi sit manibus fax, eris, Alda, Venus.
Sume lyram et plectrum, fies quasi verus Apollo;
Si tibi sit cornu et thyrsus, Iacchus eris.
Si desint haec, et mea sit tibi mentula cunno,
Pulcrior, Alda, deis atque deabus eris.

Führtest du Köcher und Bogen, so wärest du Artemis, Alda;
Nähmst du die Fackel zur Hand, wär'st Aphrodite du ganz;
Trügest du Lyra und Plectrum, du wärest mir Phöbus Apollo;
Hättest du Trinkhorn und Stab, wär'st du Dionysos selbst.
Wenn dir dies alles auch fehlt, wenn nur meinen Schwanz du im Schlitz hast,
Schöner scheinst, Alda, du mir dann als der ganze Olymp.

Interessanter noch als die Suche nach möglichen Vorbildern ist die Frage nach den möglichen Verbindungslinien der bei Lemnius zum Ausdruck kommenden souveränen Sexualauffassung zur Liebespraxis und-ideologie der Gesellschaft seiner Zeit, für die Liebe und Sexualität bekanntlich nur im Rahmen der Ehe und zum Zweck der Fortpflanzungeinen legitimen Platz hatten. Mag es auch unwahrscheinlich sein, daß der Autor in jedem Fall konkretes eigenes Erleben geschildert hat, wie er es in dem Einleitungsgedicht 'Ad lectorem' behauptet (Si quid erit forsan, de me tu scripta putabis. / Ista Venus nostra est, iste Cupido meus!), so muß man doch zumindest voraussetzen, daß er dergleichen für denkbar oder auch wünschbar gehalten hat, d. h. daß die realen Verhältnisse solche Gedanken in irgendeiner Weise gefördert und begünstigt haben müssen. Hieran schließt sich die weitere Frage nach einer denkbaren Funktion neulateinischer Literatur, soweit sie nicht eindeutig christlich geprägt war; etwa so: ob vielleicht diese Literatur aufgrund des Freiraums, die ihr die tradierte Autorität der lateinischen Sprache verschaffte, in der Lage war, eine oppositionelle oder kompensatorische Funktion gegenüber einer ganz anderen sozialen Wirklichkeit und ihren Moralkategorien einzunehmen, und zwar ohne daß die Autoren, die diese Literatur hervorbrachten, sich dieser Funktion bewußt gewesen sein müssen. Eine Beantwortung dieser Frage ist in Anbetracht unserer geringen Kenntnis der neulateinischen Literatur und des Mangels an Quellendokumentationen und Untersuchungen zum Selbstverständnis neulateinischer Dichter natürlich noch nicht möglich.

Freie Universität Berlin

Text und Übersetzung zit. nach: *Antonii Panormitanae Hermaphroditus*. Lateinisch nach der Ausgabe von C. Fr. Forberg (Coburg 1824), nebst einer deutschen metrischen Übersetzung der Apophoreta von C. Fr. Forberg. Besorgt u. hrsg. von Fr. Wolff-Untereichen. Mit einem sexualwissenschaftlichen Kommentar von Dr. Alfred Kind (Leipzig, 1908; repr., Hanau, 1986), S. 70 f. (Der 'Hermaphroditus' war vor seinem ersten Erscheinen im Druck [Paris, 1791] nur in Abschriften verbreitet.) Auch in den zahlreichen Textauszügen, die Eduard Fuchs im Ergänzungsband zu Band 1 seiner 'Sittengeschichte' (Illustrierte Sittengeschichte vom Mittelalter bis zur Gegenwart. Renaissance. Ergänzungsband. Privatdruck. München o. J.) mitteilt, wird man kaum etwas finden, was den 'Amores' an die Seite gestellt werden könnte.

Partes orationis et partes pingendi: Rhétorique antique et peinture au XVIIe siècle dans le De pictura veterum *de Franciscus Junius*

COLETTE NATIVEL

"Ces fameux anciens qui portèrent la peinture au plus haut point de sa perfection et la rendirent admirable observaient exactement dans leurs ouvrages cinq parties qui sont proprement ses principes fondamentaux parce que sans eux, elle n'est qu'un art chimérique et une simple barbouillerie de couleurs. Mais avant que d'en donner l'instruction, je veux référer l'honneur de cette recherche à Franciscus Junius, hollandais, qui depuis vingt et cinq ans a mis en lumière un beau traité de la Peinture des anciens."[1]

C'est cette présentation élogieuse du *De pictura ueterum* qui introduit l'*Idée de la perfection de la peinture*. Fréart de Chambray y reprend point par point la division qui nous occupe et traduit ainsi l'argument du livre 3 où Junius l'expose:[2] "Les anciens observaient exactement dans leurs tableaux cinq parties: l'invention ou l'histoire, la proportion ou la symétrie, la couleur, laquelle comprend la juste dispensation des lumières et des ombres, les mouvements où sont exprimées les actions et les passions et enfin, la collocation ou position régulière des figures en tout l'ouvrage."[3]

Junius n'a pas trouvé cette division dans les rares ouvrages traitant de

---

[1] Roland Fréart de Chambray, *Idée de la perfection de la peinture démontrée par les principes de l'art* (Au Mans, 1662), 9. Franciscus Junius, *De pictura ueterum libri tres* (Amsterdam, 1637); nous renvoyons à la 2° éd. latine (Rotterdam, 1694).

[2] *Idée*, p. 9; *de pict.* 3, *argumentum*.

[3] Fréart omet que Junius y ajoute la recherche de la grâce.

peinture qui nous restent des anciens: il s'est appuyé sur les *partes orationis* de la rhétorique antique: *inuentio, dispositio, elocutio, memoria, actio*. Dans le *De pictura*, le même nom désigne les deux premières. La proportion et la couleur sont l' *elocutio* du tableau: Cicéron déjà parlait de *uarietas colorum* et de *color orationis* à propos des figures de pensée et de mots.[4] Le mouvement, enfin, correspond à l'action. Seule donc manque la mémoire: Junius en a déjà longuement souligné le rôle dans la formation du peintre et rappelait, dans le livre 1, la fonction mnémonique des tableaux peints.[5] Le dessin qui n'apparaît pas ici n'est pas oublié: il est étudié avec la *symmetria*.

Junius adapte sans mal à cette partition picturale les exigences auxquelles Cicéron soumettait l'orateur idéal. Un beau tableau visera au même triple but qu'un beau discours: "sicut optimi oratores ac poetae, ita pictores quoque et docent et delectant et permouent." On reconnaît les *officia dicendi* fixés dans le *De optimo genere dicendi* dont Junius poursuit la citation.[6] Leur rappel clôt une série de conseils qui, inspirés de Quintilien et destinés à étayer la démarche critique de l'amateur, nous serviront de fil conducteur.

"D'abord, il faudra peser ce qu'enseigne la disposition bien adaptée d'une invention dépourvue de stupidité et de quelles forces elle inspire et emplit nos esprits."[7] Sans cesse, Junius souligne la fonction didactique de l'art: "Une peinture doit viser non seulement au plaisir, mais encore à l'utile"; "des tableaux riches en matière insinuent dans nos esprits une leçon de morale ou d'histoire."[8] L'invention et la disposition rempliront cet office. Comme en rhétorique, l'invention est le fruit d'une solide culture générale. Junius lui consacre le développement le plus long de son analyse.

Cette insistance sur la partie la plus intellectuelle de la création picturale situe le *De pictura* dans la tradition des grands traités d'art humanistes. La peinture n'est plus une vile activité manuelle, elle procède avant tout de l'esprit. Le peintre savant (*doctus pictor*) est formé comme l'était l'orateur cicéronien. C'est à ce modèle, complété par celui de Quintilien,

---

[4] *Orat.* 65; *de orat.* 3.199.

[5] *De pict.* 1.4.V et 1.2, *passim*.

[6] *De pict.* 3.7.2; *opt. gen.* 3.

[7] *De pict.* 3.7.2: "Ac primo quidem trutinanda est apta non stultae inuentionis dispositio, quid doceat et quibus mentes nostras uiribus inspiret atque impleat." *Cf.* Quint., *inst.* 2.5.8.

[8] *De pict.* 3.1.12; 3.5.7: "argumentosae tabulae . . . historicum aliquem aut moralem sensum animis nostris insinuent."

que Junius se réfère pour définir le vaste programme pédagogique tracé au livre 2 et sur lequel il revient ici.[9] "Eruditis hominibus nunquam deesse potest argumentum":[10] un seul problème doit s'offrir au peintre, le choix de sa matière. Adaptée à son sujet et à ses forces, elle sera aussi "surabondante, débordante, plus déployée qu'il ne faut."[11] Ce choix de l'abondance, de la grandeur, de la nouveauté, de l'originalité était celui de Cicéron qui faisait dire à Antoine dans le *De Oratore*: "Sumendae res erunt aut magnitudine praestabiles aut nouitate primae aut genere ipso singulares."[12] Outre sa culture, l'artiste partagera les deux vertus majeures de l'orateur, *sapientia* et *prudentia*. "Car la peinture n'est pas autre chose que l'expression parfaite d'une certaine sagesse (*sapientiae*) qu'on tire de l'ensemble des bons arts,"[13] écrit Junius en s'inspirant d'une définition cicéronienne de l'éloquence. Cette sagesse permet au peintre de concevoir cette idée de la Beauté vers laquelle tend son oeuvre. Quant à la *prudentia*, la sagesse pratique, il devra l'exercer, nous le verrons, à toutes les étapes de sa création.

L'invention brillera de quatre qualités: *ueritas, occasio, aequitas, magnificentia*—toutes empruntées à la rhétorique. Junius, avec Lucien, lie la vérité à l'utile: "Utile enim ex sola ueritate colligitur."[14] De plus, la peinture est *imitatio ueritatis*: par deux fois, Junius cite le précepte classicisant de Vitruve: "Pictura sit imago eius quod est seu potest esse."[15] Et il rappelle la critique horatienne d'une licence excessive en peinture et en poésie.[16] Il retrouve chez Cicéron ce souci de vérité et utilise l'analyse du *Brutus*[17] sur les évolutions parallèles de l'éloquence et de la sculpture dans le sens d'un plus fidèle rendu de la vérité. Sa quête prime même celle de la beauté: on peindra la sueur et la poussière qui maculent la robe du cheval.[18]

---

[9] *cf.* mon art.: "La rhétorique au service de l'art: éducation oratoire et éducation de l'artiste selon Franciscus Junius," *XVIIe Siècle* 157 (Oct.-Déc. 1987); 385–94.

[10] *De pict.* 3.1, sommaire du §.1.

[11] *De pict.* 3.1.3; *cf.* Quint. *inst.* 2.4.7.

[12] *De or.* 2.347: "Il faut choisir une matière remarquable par sa grandeur ou originale par sa nouveauté ou unique en son genre."

[13] *De pict.* 3.1, sommaire du §7: "Quum pictura nihil aliud sit quam perfectio quaedam sapientiae ex omni bonarum artium orbe mutuatae."

[14] Luc. *h. conscr.* 9; *de pict.* 3.1.12 (Trad. de Junius): je ne cite le texte grec que s'il contient un concept délicat.

[15] Vit. 7.5.1; *de pict.* 3.1.12 et 1.3.12.

[16] *De pict.* 1.3.12; Hor. *ars* 1 *sqq.*

[17] *Brut.* 70–71; *de pict.* 1.3.1.

[18] *De pict.* 3.1.12; *cf.* Philstr. *Im.* 15.2 (332k).

La convenance (*occasio*, καιρός qui consiste dans le respect des circonstances et l'adaptation au sujet des éléments de l' *inuentio* manifeste la *prudentia* du peintre. Quintilien et au-delà Cicéron sont encore les sources essentielles: le sacrifice d'Iphigénie où Timanthe avait peint le visage d'Agamemnon voilé de peur d'en mal exprimer l'inexprimable douleur, cité en exemple dans l' *Institution oratoire*, suscitait déjà l'admiration de l'Arpinate.[19]

Le peintre respectera aussi les bienséances: c'est ainsi que Junius entend les termes *aequitas* et δικαιοσύη puisqu'il précise qu'un tableau ne doit pas représenter de scènes lascives ou trop violentes. Ce souci moral adapté aux exigences du XVIIe siècle contribue à donner cette noble image de l'artiste, *uir doctus*, mais aussi *uir bonus peritus pingendi.*[20] Comme l'éloquence, l'art a une fin morale.

L'ultime qualité de l'invention est la grandeur ou le sublime. Junius emploie comme synonymes les termes *granditas, magnificentia*, μεγαλοπρέπεια, σεμνότης et ὕψος. La grandeur donne à la peinture son poids, son autorité si on évite les écueils de l'enflure. Son étude se fonde sur Cicéron, Quintilien et le pseudo-Longin. Avec celui-ci, il considère qu'elle est innée, mais admet qu'on peut la cultiver par la fréquentation des meilleurs modèles.[21] Comme Cicéron, il en trouve le principe dans l'élévation de l'âme. Il cite l'*Orator*: "Omnia profecto qui se a caelestibus rebus referet ad humanas excelsius magnificentiusque et dicet et sentiet."[22]

On voit donc aisément l'importance qu'il accorde à la matière: la disposition (*collocatio siue oeconomica totius operis dispositio*) mettra en valeur ses éléments tout en respectant son abondance. Elle aussi joindra l'utile à l'agréable. Junius rappelle ces mots de Xénophon: "Rien n'est plus utile ou beau aux yeux des hommes que l'ordre."[23] Mais surtout, ayant cité la page célèbre du *De Oratore* où Cicéron méditait sur le bel et nécessaire ordre du monde,[24] il relève une nouvelle analogie entre un tableau et un

---

[19] *De pict.* 3.1.13; Quint. *inst.* 2.13.13; Cic. *or.* 70–74. Junius n'utilise pas le terme cicéronien attendu, *decorum*.

[20] L'idée est développée en 2.8–11.

[21] *De pict.* 1.1.15–19. Le *De pict.* est un des premiers traités qui se fonde sur une lecture du ps. Longin.

[22] *Or.* 119: "Vraiment, il dira et sentira tout avec plus d'élévation et de grandeur, celui qui, se fondant sur les choses célestes, les rapportera aux choses humaines"; *de pict.* 1.1.18.

[23] Xen. *Oec.* 8.3: "Nihil est tam utile aut tam pulchrum hominibus quam ordo"; *de pict.* 3.5.2.

[24] *De or.* 178–80; *de pict.* 3.5.2.

discours: leurs diverses parties doivent s'enchaîner de la même facon, car un tableau, discours muet (*mutum alloquium*), se lit comme un texte. Junius, comparant peinture et poésie, mentionnait au livre 1, la formule de l'*Enéide–perlegere oculis*–appliquée à un tableau.[25] Il l'utilise ici pour souligner que celui-ci doit présenter l'action dans son développement, avec logique et sans heurts. Il s'attache surtout à la peinture d'histoire qui met en perspective différents épisodes en respectant leur chronologie sans toutefois obéir aux lois de l'histoire écrite. En effet, elle peut exercer un choix des éléments en fonction de son propre sujet et représenter sur une même toile des événements éloignés dans le temps. Sans cesse Junius, on le voit ici encore, dégage la spécificité de la peinture par rapport aux autres genres, même si, et cela est habituel en son siècle, il s'appuie sur eux pour la définir.

La disposition contribue enfin à la clarté de l'oeuvre–*euidentia*, notion qui sera approfondie plus loin.

Un tableau doit encore nous charmer. Le dessin et la couleur rempliront cet office. Junius poursuit ainsi ses conseils à l'amateur: "Il faudra ensuite examiner combien les pigments des couleurs mis en valeur par les lois d'une exacte proportion nous charment et de quels agréments ils flattent nos sens."[26]

La contemplation de l'oeuvre s' accompagne de plaisir esthétique: certes Junius revient souvent, nous le disions, sur sa valeur éthique, mais il n'est pas insensible à sa beauté plastique. Dans les chapitres sur la proportion et la couleur, il donne deux définitions cicéroniennes de la *pulchritudo*. L'une provient du *De officiis*: "Pulchritudo corporis apta compositione membrorum mouet oculos et delectat hoc ipso quod inter se omnes partes cum quodam lepore consentiunt."[27] L'autre, plus complète–elle introduit la couleur–est extraite des *Tusculanes*: "Corporis est quaedam apta figura membrorum cum coloris quadam suauitate eaque dicitur pulchritudo."[28] Ces formules suscitent plusieurs remarques.

---

[25] *De pict.* 1.4.II et 3.5.6; Vir. *Aen.* 6.34.

[26] *De pict.* 3.7.2: "Inspicienda deinde colorum pigmenta iustae proportionis legibus commendata quantum oblectent et qua iucunditate sensus nostros permulceant." *Cf.* Quint. *inst.* 2.5.8.

[27] Cic. *off.* 1.98: "La beauté d'un corps attire le regard à cause de la disposition appropriée de ses membres et plaît pour cette raison précise que toutes ses parties s'accordent entre elles avec une certaine grâce"; *de pict.* 3.2.1.

[28] Cic. *Tusc.* 4.31: "Pour un corps, il existe une certaine configuration appropriée des membres, liée à une certaine douceur du coloris: c'est cela qu'on appelle beauté"; *de pict.* 3.3.11.

D'abord nous y retrouvons une notion déjà mentionnée tant elle est fondamentale dans la pensée antique dont Junius se fait le moderne porte-parole, celle d' *aptum*. La beauté repose sur la convenance, la justesse, "l'adaptation des parties au tout et des parties entre elles."[29] La recherche de cette harmonie, Junius l'écrit après saint Augustin et Plutarque, fait de la peinture une soeur de la musique.[30]

La beauté ensuite a quelque chose d'indéfinissable, "certaine douceur du coloris," "certain agrément" qui la font échapper aux lois d'un art trop strict. Junius ne donne pas de règles précises pour l'emploi des couleurs, pas plus qu'il n'étudie en mathématicien les proportions. Il laisse au domaine de la *prudentia* de l'artiste cette part de flou, "ce je ne sais quoi de plus"[31] qui n'est pas autre chose que la grâce. Enfin, et Junius se fonde encore sur le *De officiis*, la beauté est inséparable de la santé qu'elle soit la virile *dignitas* ou la *uenustas* féminine.[32]

A l'étude de la couleur est associé un long développement sur l'*ornatus* issu pour l'essentiel de l' *Institution oratoire*. Tout en soulignant avec Philostrate l'importance de l'ornement, "puisque les arts eux-mêmes ont été inventés pour l'ornement," il en énumère avec Quintilien les qualités: *uirilis, fortis, sanctus*,[33] il sera adapté à son sujet (*accommodatus*).[34] Cicéron refusait la recherche gratuite de la *concinnitas* et, avant lui, les stoïciens pour qui la beauté de la forme ne devait pas l'emporter sur le fond. C'est le sens de cette maxime de Sénèque: "Non faciunt meliorem equum aurei freni."[35]

Dans ces conditions, le plaisir esthétique naît d'une sorte de sentiment instinctif du beau, d'un goût de l'harmonie inné et que, Cicéron l'avait montré, seul l'homme ressent:[36] à plusieurs reprises, Junius cite les formules de cet auteur—*tacitus sensus, naturalis sensus*.[37] Ainsi s'explique que doctes et ignorants goûtent également ce plaisir, même si ceux-ci n'en savent expliquer la raison. Ce goût se manifeste d'abord par une attirance

---

[29] Stob. *Ecl. eth.* 5; *de pict.* 3.2.1.

[30] Aug. *lib. arb.* 2.16.41.; Plut. *M.* 45C; *de pict.* 3.2.2.

[31] Mart. 6.61 (Izaac ed., Paris, 1965); *de pict.* 3.6.1.

[32] Cic. *off.* 130; *de pict.* 3.2.4.

[33] Philstr. *u.Ap.* 7.6: "In ornatum enim intenta est omnis ars, quandoquidem et ipsae artes ad ornatum sunt adinuentae." Quint. *inst.* 8.3.6:"viril, vigoureux et pur"; *de pict.* 3.3.11.

[34] Quint. *inst.* 11.1.7; *de pict.* 3.3.12.

[35] Sen. *epist.* 41.6: "Un mors doré n'améliore pas un cheval"; *de pict.* 3.3.13.

[36] Cic. *off.* 14; *de pict.* 3.2.1.

[37] *De pict.* 3.7.9, n. a; Cic. *de or.* 3.151 et *or.* 203.

du regard: la première définition de la beauté que nous citions comprenait l'expression *mouere oculos*. La couleur surtout, selon Sénèque, "ravit le regard" et Junius ajoute avec Plutarque qu'elle touche plus les spectateurs que les traits nus.[38] Elle est plus efficace parce qu'elle donne davantage l'illusion de la vie.

Mais, peu à peu nous abordons le dernier point tant est ténue la frontière qui le sépare du plaisir. *Mouere oculos*, certes, mais plus encore que les yeux, ce sont les âmes qui doivent être émues. *Imitatio ueritatis*, art d'illusion, la peinture est aussi art d'émotion.

L'ultime devoir de l'orateur—*mouere*—était dévolu à l'*actio*, véritable éloquence du corps destinée à traduire les mouvements de l'âme. Les conseils de Junius à l'amateur s'achèvent ainsi: "Il faudra enfin considérer comment les très puissants sentiments de l'action et de la passion jouent un rôle dominant, font irruption dans nos coeurs et rendent nos âmes semblables à ce que nous contemplons."[39] Ce passage, toujours inspiré de Quintilien, décrit bien la mission essentielle de l'*actio*: elle doit transporter le spectateur, lui faire éprouver les mêmes passions que celles qu'il voit peintes au point que son âme en soit altérée. Cette aptitude d'une oeuvre à entraîner la foule était pour Cicéron le critère de sa réussite. Junius transpose à l'art ce fameux passage du *Brutus*: "Toi, artiste, que demandes tu de plus? La foule éprouve du plaisir à regarder, se laisse mener par ta peinture, se réjouit, souffre, rit, admire et, la peinture lui inspirant toute sorte de sentiments, elle est induite à la pitié ou à la haine."[40]

Junius plaide donc pour une rhétorique de l'effet: une peinture doit avant tout émouvoir et le critique se garder d'un jugement trop vétilleux sur ses autres aspects.[41] Dès le livre 1, comparant poésie et peinture, il affirmait la supériorité de celle-ci, "plus apte à exciter les mouvements de l'âme et plus appropriée à la facon de sentir de la foule que l'éloquence même."[42] Plus loin, il citait Quintilien: "Une peinture, oeuvre silencieuse

[38] Sen. *dial.* 4.2.1: "Maxime oculos rapit color"; *de pict.* 3.3.11. Plut. *M.* 16B: "In picturis color magis mouet lineatura"; *de pict.* 3.3.12.

[39] *De pict.* 3,7,2: "Considerandi denique sunt potentissimi actionis et passionis affectus, quemadmodum dominentur atque in pectora irrumpant animosque nostros similes iis quae spectamus efficiant."

[40] Cic. *Brut.* 183-89; *de pict.* 1.5.4: "Tu, Artifex, quid quaeris amplius? Delectatur spectans multitudo, ducitur pictura, gaudet, dolet, ridet, miratur et pictura quosuis affectus inspirante ad misericordiam et odium inducitur."

[41] *De pict.* 3.7.2.

[42] *De pict.* 1.4.IV: "Pictura utpote aptior ad ciendos animorum motus atque ad

et d'un aspect toujours identique, pénètre si profondément notre plus intime sensibilité qu'elle semble parfois vaincre la puissance même de l'éloquence."[43] Il en voulait pour preuve que jadis plaideurs et naufragés exhibaient pour apitoyer l'assistance des tablettes où étaient figurés leurs malheurs. Il en trouvait l'explication chez Horace: la vue, plus fidèle que l'ouïe, restitue mieux ce qu'on lui confie.[44]

Mais c'est surtout par la notion d'ἐνάργεια et l'analyse qu'en développent le pseudo-Longin et Quintilien qu'il justifie cette psychagogie de la peinture. L'ἐνάργεια est, selon Quintilien, une qualité du récit qui ne semble pas tant dire une chose que la montrer si bien que "les mouvements de l'âme suivent tout comme si nous participions à l'action."[45] Junius, s'il prend à son compte cette définition, aborde ce concept un peu différemment.

D'abord, il ne suit pas la distinction établie au livre 8 de l'*Institution oratoire* entre une ἐνάργεια qui serait plutôt la clarté de l'exposition—*perspicuitas*—et une ἐνάργεια qui, elle, appartient à l'*ornatum*, que certains appellent hypotypose, Quintilien *euidentia* et grâce à laquelle les choses "semblent sous nos yeux."[46] Pour Junius, *euidentia* désigne la clarté de la disposition aussi bien que l'évidence du récit: il traduit indifféremment les mots grecs σαφήνεια et ἐνάργεια par *perspicuitas* ou *euidentia*. D'où son étude tant à propos de la disposition au chapitre 5 du livre 3, que de l'action qui donne à la représentation toute sa vivacité, au chapitre 4 du même livre.

D'autre part, Junius combine les textes du pseudo-Longin et de Quintilien pour énoncer une théorie originale de la création picturale. Au chapitre 4 du livre 1, réfléchissant sur ses rapports avec la poésie, il adapte à la peinture une distinction du pseudo-Longin entre l'imagination poétique et l'imagination oratoire. L'une vise à l'étonnement—ἔκπληξις—(*admiratio uel consternatus attonitae admirationis*, l'autre—l'imagination oratoire, pour le rhéteur, picturale, pour lui—à l'évidence. L'ἐνάργεια est donc étroitement liée à une certaine qualité de l'imagination (φαντασία) qu'il

sensum uulgi ipsa eloquentia accommodatior."

[43] Quint. *inst.* 11.3.67: "Pictura tacens opus et habitus semper eiusdem, sic in intimos affectus penetrat ut ipsam uim dicendi nonnunquam superare uideatur"; *de pict.* 1.4.IV.

[44] Hor. *ars* 180–83.

[45] Quint. *inst.* 6.2.32: "quae non tam dicere uidetur quam ostendere et affectus non aliter quam si rebus ipsis intersimus sequentur."

[46] Quint. *inst.* 8.3.62: "Magna uirtus res de quibus loquimur clare atque ut cerni uideantur enuntiare."

précise. Il continue son parallèle en citant plus amplement le traité *Du sublime* toujours modifié en fonction de la peinture: "Les inventions des poètes contiennent des éléments trop fabuleux et dépassent toute mesure et probabilité. Au contraire on trouve toujours d'une facon éminente une possibilité de mise en oeuvre et une vérité profonde dans l'imagination du peintre."[47]

Ce qui donc distingue peinture et poésie, c'est que celle-ci s'égare hors du vrai et, par sa liberté d'invention, tend surtout au plaisir, tandis que celle-là, comme le discours, tire son efficacité de sa clarté et de sa vérité. Ayant ainsi conçu en imagination ce qu'il va représenter, le peintre, totalement pénétré de sa vision et des passions qu'il veut exprimer, est seul capable de le rendre avec force sur sa toile. *Si uis me flere*. . . .[48]

Cette conception souligne vivement l'importance de l'image mentale: Junius y revient au sujet de l'action, démarquant Quintilien à qui il emprunte cette définition des φαντασίαι: "Ce que les Grecs appellent φαντασίαι nous pouvons le nommer *uisiones*. C'est par leur intermédiaire que l'âme se représente les images des choses absentes de telle sorte que nous croyons les voir de nos yeux et les avoir présentes devant nous. Qui les concevra bien sera tout puissant sur les mouvements de l'âme."[49]

Avant d'être matérialisé par des traits et des couleurs ou des mots, un tableau est donc une image dans l'âme du créateur. Une fois peint, il suscite dans l'âme des spectateurs les mêmes sentiments qu'éprouvait le peintre en le concevant. Junius énumère des exemples tirés des deux Philostrate et de Pline l'Ancien pour illustrer concrètement ce qu'il entend par ἐνάργεια, mais on le comprendra aussi en lisant le tableau du sac d'une ville qu'il brosse au chapitre 5 du livre 1. Tout n'y est qu'étude de mouvements, d'expressions; chaque élément, trouvé chez les historiens anciens et Quintilien, est choisi pour sa vérité et son efficacité.[50]

Cette étude appelle plusieurs conclusions. C'est d'abord le constat de la haute conception que Junius se fait de la peinture: comme la grande

---

[47] Longin, *sub.* 15.8: Οὐ μὴν ἀλλὰ τὰ μὲν παρὰ τοῖς ποιηταῖς μυθικωτέραν ἔχει τὴν ὑπερέκπτωσιν καὶ πάντη τὸ πιστὸν ὑπεραίρουσαν τῆς δὲ ἑητορικῆς φαντασίας κάλλιστον ἀεὶ τὸ ἔμπρακτον καὶ ἐνάληθες; *de pict.* 3.3.4.

[48] Hor. *ars* 101; *de pict.* 3.4.4.

[49] Quint. *inst.* 6.2.29: "Quas φαντασιας Graeci uocant nos sane uisiones appellemus, per quas imagines rerum absentium ita repraesentantur animo ut eas cernere oculis ac praesentes habere uideamur. Has quisquis bene conceperit, is erit in affectibus potentissimus"; *de pict.* 3.4.4.

[50] *cf.* mon art.: "Le *De pictura* de Franciscus Junius (livre 1): une compilation," *XVIIe Siècle* 150 (Janv.-Mars 1986): 331-38.

éloquence cicéronienne, elle doit répondre aux exigences de l'esprit, du sens esthétique et des passions.[51] On se demandera aussi si Junius, oubliant sa spécificité, n'opère pas une *reductio picturae ad rhetoricam*. Je ne le crois pas, car si la qualité qu'il cherche dans la peinture est l'éloquence, il exige aussi de l'éloquence le pittoresque. Sa réflexion sur l' ἐνάργεια et plus profondément sur l'imagination donne à son analyse toute sa richesse et lui permet de dépasser le mécanique parallèle qu'était devenue l'étude des rapports entre peinture et rhétorique.

Le jugement de Fréart qui nous a servi d'introduction ne me semble donc pas exagéré. Si Junius n'est pas l'initiateur de cette division de l'art, répétée, avec quelques variantes, d'Alberti à Zuccaro, c'est lui qui l'a développée, lui a donné la caution de la pensée antique et en a fait l'instrument sur lequel s'appuiera la critique classique.

Nice, France

---

[51] *Cf.* Alain Michel, *Rhétorique et philosophie chez Cicéron*, (Paris: PUF, 1960), 153–57.

Grotius's Fame as a Poet

HENK NELLEN AND EDWIN RABBIE

The type of poetry which is commonly referred to as "occasional poetry" was, and is perhaps still even now, considered to be inferior. For many years the appreciation of Pindar's poems, for instance, was determined by the prejudice that owing to its occasional nature his poetry did not by any means measure up to the "truly" immortal works of Greek literature such as those of Homer and the tragic poets. If this view were justified, this would be the end of our lecture: for we would not dare to demand the attention of this eminent audience, not even for as little as twenty minutes, for a poet whose works largely belong to that very category of occasional poetry.

In our days Grotius enjoys little fame as a poet; outside the limited circles of specialists his present renown is exclusively based on his works on international law. But in his own times and certainly up to 1800 this was completely different, as appears from a large number of sources. During his own life collections of the poems he wrote as a young man were published both in Holland and abroad, and his most famous poems appear in Dutch and foreign anthologies until the beginning of the nineteenth century. As late as 1867 the influential German classicist Lucian Müller expresses his final judgment of Grotius's significance as a Neo-Latin poet as follows: "I do not hesitate to declare him to be the most noteworthy of all Latin poets of this country [viz. Holland]"[1]–a staggering statement, considering that Müller apparently regarded generally recognised celebrities such as Janus Secundus and Daniel Heinsius as inferior to Grotius.

Grotius wrote the bulk of his Neo-Latin poetry as a young man.[2] From

---

[1] L. Müller, *Hugo Grotius als Latijnsch dichter beschouwd* (Haarlem, 1867), p. 78.

[2] For numerical data see A. Eyffinger, *Inventory of the Poetry of Hugo Grotius* (Assen

1591, when he was eight years old, onwards he produced a large number of Latin verses, which–apart from his very first experiments–display an astounding technical and poetical skill. This period ended in 1608, when he embarked on a political career and devoted his attention to other matters: the exercise of his duties and his gradual involvement in religious-political controversies put an end to what he later called the "lusus" of his youth.

Grotius's youthful poems, which we know rather comprehensively from a collection edited by his brother Willem in 1617,[3] may perhaps not all be among his most outstanding poetic products, but do deserve many positive epithets: entertaining, at times amusing, ingenious, modern, virtuosic, moving in the epicedia, exuberant in the epithalamia, biting in the mockery of the epigrams, panegyric in the laudatory poems. A living document, the collection–more so than any other source–allows us a private view of the grandeur as well as the *petite histoire* of the coteries of Leyden and The Hague at the beginning of the seventeenth century. We may be grateful to Willem de Groot for going through with the publication of the collection in spite of his brother's hesitations.

Some of the poems in the collection may rightly be considered part of the most beautiful Neo-Latin poetry known to us. Macaulay once said that there were three poems of Catullus which he was unable to read without being moved to tears;[4] if we may extend the list by adding one of Grotius's, it would be the poem on the portrait of Joseph Scaliger.[5] It is one of the seven poems which Grotius wrote on the occasion of his death and is entitled "In imaginem Scaligeri paulo ante mortem expressam." Departing from the emotions brought about in him by a portrait of Scaliger which had been painted shortly before his death, Grotius successfully conjures up a suggestive image of the loss he has suffered. Using this technique he creates a strong pathetic effect which time and again deeply moves the reader; "divinum epigramma," posterity called it.[6] It is the

---

1982), pp. 236–37 and passim.

[3] *Hugonis Grotij Poemata, Collecta & magnam partem nunc primùm edita à fratre Gvilielmo Grotio*, Ludun. Batav. Apud. Andr. Clouquium. Anno 1617 [henceforth: *PC*]; see J. ter Meulen-P.J.J. Diermanse, *Bibliographie des écrits imprimés de Hugo Grotius* (La Haye, 1950) [henceforth: *BG*], no. 1.

[4] G. O. Trevelyan, *The life and letters of Lord Macaulay* (London etc., 1908), chap. 14, p. 665. The poems were Catullus 8, 38, and 76.

[5] *PC* no. 152 p. 360.

[6] On the back of the portrait in question, which is in the Senate Chamber of Leyden University, is glued a note written by G. van Papenbroeck, in which he renders

"abnormal" character of the poem on the mortally ill but mentally unaffected Scaliger which elevates it above the great mass of funeral odes on famous and less famous persons produced in those days by poets and poetasters.

Another example of Grotius's originality in presentation is the poem on the death of his younger brother Frans.[7] From the original manuscript[8] it is clear that the poem was not written until after his death; yet, the reader gets an unmistakable impression that the poet composed it while sitting at his dying brother's bedside. He prays to God that the seriously ill man may be invigorated by sleep, and although he pretends to realise that recovery is no longer possible, he continues to hope until the very end. The effect of the poem is not unlike that of tragic irony: from the title the reader knows already that Frans has died of his illness, whereas this is not mentioned in the poem itself.

We would now like to take a closer look at two of Grotius's poems, one of his last youthful works and one dating from the period of his exile. We have chosen these two poems because our sources allow us to demonstrate how they were received and what their effect was. Thus we may gain some insight into the extent of Grotius's fame as a poet.

The first poem was written by Grotius in 1609 on the occasion of the death of the Leyden professor of theology Jacobus Arminius. When a professor at Leyden University died, it was customary for one of the deceased's colleagues to deliver a funeral oration after the burial. This oration was then published, thus enhancing the fame of the deceased, but, of course, also adding to the renown of the speaker himself. Such publications usually included a number of epicedia composed by colleagues, friends and students.

Arminius died at the relatively early age of 49, after a professorship of six years which had been full of conflicts and which had thus put a severe strain on his health. Even before being appointed, this moderate theologian had been sharply criticised for lack of orthodoxy, and his professorship was marked by a series of conflicts with his strictly Calvinistic *collega proximus* Franciscus Gomarus, who waged a holy war against his moderate

---

the text of the poem preceded by the qualification cited above; cf. *Icones Leidenses, de portretverzameling van de Rijksuniversiteit te Leiden* (Leiden, 1973), no. 31.

[7] *PC* no. 52 pp. 259–66.

[8] Leyden University Library ms. Pap. 10, fo. 18r–v. The title of the poem in this manuscript, which was not added afterwards, is: "Anapaesti in morbum fratris Francisci Grotii, ex quo obiit," as in the published version.

views. Arminius was continually accused of heresy, and, though by nature averse to conflict, had no intention of renouncing his opinions; an escalation was inevitable. When he died on 19 October 1609, numerous co-religionists were prepared to continue to refine and spread his doctrine and a serious religious conflict developed in Holland.

In such circumstances, it was impossible to write a funeral ode on Arminius without taking sides, at least if one did not want to resort to meaningless generalities. It is doubtful whether Grotius immediately realised this, for he went to great lengths to try to persuade his friend Daniel Heinsius to contribute a poem, even though he knew that Heinsius did not approve of Arminius's theological views.[9] Apparently, Grotius himself did not feel at all hindered by the circumstances: he composed four poems, three epigrams and a long σκάζων of 84 lines, in which he expressed his admiration for Arminius.[10]

In this last poem Arminius is portrayed as a man who, while searching for the truth, realised the limitations of human knowledge and thus recognised the appropriateness of modesty and tolerance. In order to illustrate this characteristic of Arminius, the poet uses the opposition between heavenly bliss and terrestrial misery. Whereas in their search for the truth the living continued to wander around helplessly in the dark, the dead, among whom now also Arminius, were granted true knowledge. A most traditional subject matter, of course, but rendered especially effective by Grotius's master-hand: it brings to light the senselessness of the theological disputes which had made Arminius's life so difficult. The poet then goes on to argue that the truth was not furthered but only hindered by such theological quibbling, his aversion to which he expresses quite openly. The confusion of tongues resulting from the petty discussions benefits only the enemies of Christendom. Those who think that they have a monopoly on the truth and try to force their views on others are off the right track and only bring misery to the church, as is now clear for all to see. Rather than wanting to have the last word on salvation and damnation, the true believer ought to stay well clear of such quarrelling, study the Scriptures and defend the truth, even though it might sometimes be wiser to preserve the peace by remaining silent:

---

[9] P. C. Molhuysen [a.o.], *Briefwisseling van Hugo Grotius* [Rijks Geschiedkundige Publicatiën] [henceforth: *BW*] ('s-Gravenhage, 1928–), I, 176 d.d. 21-10-1609.

[10] The poems were published in *Petri Bertii Oratio in obitum ... Iacobi Arminii ...* (Lugduni Batavorum, 1609), pp. 46–48 (= *BG* no. 268). The *PC* contains only the σκάζων (no. 75, pp. 304–7).

> Damnatus aliis ipse neminem damnat,
> modestiaeque limitem premens donat
> nunc verba vero, nunc silentium paci.

Grotius points out that Arminius propagated and tried to follow these rules until the very end of his life, and then concludes the poem with a number of verses which could be interpreted as a direct attack on Gomarus: he presents Arminius as praying in heaven that the theologians may strive for unity rather than bragging about their own personal discoveries:

> Det [sc. Deus] non loquentes sua reperta doctores;
> det consonantes semper omnium linguas
> aut corda saltem, praepotente vi flammae
> caliginosas litium fuget sordes,
> ut spiret unum tota civitas Christi
> vitamque terris approbet, fidem caelo.

This poem was placed after the text of the funeral oration, which was delivered on 22 October 1609 by Petrus Bertius, a co-religionist of Arminius, and which was published in that same year.[11] In the heated atmosphere of those days such an unequivocal declaration of support could not remain without repercussions. Immediately Bertius clashed with the implacable Gomarus and was forced to defend Arminius's reputation in a lengthy and sharp exchange of polemics. For Grotius, too, the publication caused trouble: owing to either ill will or negligence on the part of Bertius or his assistants, Grotius's poem was published with a number of printing errors. Most of these turned out to be harmless, but one passage of the σκάζων now suggested that Arminius alone (*solus*) had felt love for the kingdom of heaven, whereas the poet had meant to say that Arminius had been full of love (*totus*) for it.[12]

When Gomarus saw the poem, he had to admit that it was moderate in message and beautiful in style, but—not surprisingly—was annoyed by the passage mentioned above, as it seemed to shed a dubious light on his role

[11] See note 9 above.

[12] Molhuysen, *BW* I, p. XIX, assumes ill will on Bertius's part, although there is no clear evidence for this. The *editio princeps* edited by Bertius contains a number of other deviations from the text which had been authorised and was later published by Grotius. It cannot, therefore, be ruled out that Bertius was speaking the truth when he reduced the entire business to an annoying misunderstanding (*BW* I, 179 d.d. 21-12-1609): either the differences were due to negligence on the part of the copyist who had transcribed Grotius's autograph for the printer or they were simply the result of printing errors.

in the dispute with Arminius. Gomarus was afraid that an outsider like Grotius would be taken at his word, whereas he himself would automatically be portrayed as partial and, therefore, untrustworthy. Through a mutual acquaintance Gomarus communicated his annoyance to Grotius,[13] who then had a corrected version of the epicedium published, in the introduction to which Bertius's behaviour was criticised.[14] Moreover, he did his best to apologise to the offended theologian. In a letter to Gomarus[15] he argued that he had by no means intended to insult him. He had only wanted to praise Arminius's talent, eloquence and peacefulness. As for the dispute between the two scholars, Grotius said that he did not quite understand the details, but that he was merely concerned with the unity of the church, which had to be preserved in spite of any difference of opinion.[16]

In this letter, the twenty-six-year-old Grotius displays such self-confidence that it must have seemed outright arrogance to the strict Gomarus; its tone is similar to that of the poem, which must have been difficult to swallow for a man such as Gomarus, even without the printing error, whether intentional or otherwise.

It may be concluded that the nature of Grotius's poem is that of a manifesto: here, for the first time, he expresses his favourite view on the unity of the church, an ideal which would continue to inspire him all his life. As such, this occasional poem goes beyond its immediate "occasion" and its perfunctory character. The commotion which it brought about shows that Grotius's popularity and influence as a poet were such that someone who was directly involved, like Gomarus, felt obliged to respond. Coincidentally, as a result of the matter of Bertius and the printing error, it became clear that poems such as that discussed here were addressed to the forum of public opinion, and that Grotius's voice did in fact count. In this way, an occasional poem can practically function as a political or religious manifesto.

Our second example, a poem dating from a much later period, from 1636, is similar to the Arminius-poem in that it contains a statement of principles, as a result of which it rises above its formal status of occasional

---

[13] See *BW* I, 180 d.d. 21-12-1609 from J. Rutgersius.

[14] See *BW* I, p. 156 n. 4.

[15] *BW* I, 181 d.d. [24-12-1609].

[16] "Caeterum, quae Arminio tecum ac cum bonis multis disconvenere, ea nec satis scio nec si sciam temere me interponam. Habet ista res suos iudices ... Dolent mihi haec dissidia. Sed numquam diu fuit ecclesia sine illis, numquam erit. Restat ut feramus alter alterum...."

poem. In this case, too, it is clear that as a poet Grotius was read by and sollicited reactions from a wide audience. This was, of course, furthered by his fame, which ensured that all his statements in this field were considered important and worthy of attention.

In the Sala Regia of the Vatican there is a large fresco by Giuseppe Porta "Il Salviati" dating from 1563. It shows us how in 1177 Frederic Barbarossa had submitted to Pope Alexander III after his defeat in the struggle for hegemony in Northern Italy.[17] In an inscription under the fresco the contribution of Venice, an ally of the Pope, to the victory was described rather more elaborately than truthfully.[18] In 1632 Pope Urbanus VIII had the inscription painted out, following recent historical insights. The introduction, three years later, of a new inscription, in which the role of Venice was not mentioned at all,[19] resulted in a diplomatic conflict, which ran so high that the Venetians even considered expulsion of the papal nuncio.

In February of 1636 Grotius heard of this. He became highly interested and mentioned the matter in several letters. In a letter to his brother Willem[20] he even incorporated a poem which showed his strongly antipapal views. This is in accordance with other statements made by Grotius in his correspondence during this period, to the effect that the Pope had far too much influence on French society and politics.[21] Thus he is led to express in his poem an opinion which is in conflict with the true events regarding the disputed inscription: Grotius unquestioningly assumes that the Venetian, anti-papal version of the incident was the right one.

The qualities of this poem are less conspicuous than those of the

---

[17] Illustration in A. Venturi, *Storia dell'arte italiana* IX-7 (Milano 1934), p. 423; see also W.R. Rearick, *Maestri veneti del cinquecento* [= Biblioteca di disegni, 6] (Firenze, 1980), pp. 22-23.

[18] The inscription ran as follows: "Alexander Papa tertius Frederici Imperatoris iram et impetum fugiens abdidit se Venetiis, et a Senatu perhonorifice susceptum Othone imperatoris filio navali proelio a Venetis victo captoque Fredericus pace facta supplex adorat, fidem et obedientiam pollicitus. Ita Pontifici sua dignitas Venetae reipublicae beneficio restaurata est." (text after L. von Pastor, *Geschichte der Päpste seit dem Ausgang des Mittelalters* XIII-2 [Freiburg i.B., 1929], p. 718 n. 2; with slight differences Grotius, *BW* VI, no. 2465, p. 509 [to Willem de Groot, d.d. 7-2-1636]).

[19] The new inscription ran as follows: "Fridericus primus Imperator Alexandrum tertium Pontificem, quem diu insectatus fuerat, post constitutas cum eo pacis condiciones et damnatum schisma Venetiis supplex veneratur" (text after Pastor op. cit. p. 718 n. 4; identical text Grotius loc. cit.).

[20] *BW* VI, 2465 d.d. 7-2-1636.

[21] Cf. *BW* VII, 2536; 2893; VIII, 2957; 3043; 3088.

epicedium on Arminius discussed above; this is clearly a competently but rapidly composed product, which deserves attention for its message rather than for its poetical beauty. The addressee is Frederic Barbarossa, the famous emperor: his enemies, Venice and Rome, who had defeated him in coalition, are now in conflict with one another over him. The Pope refused to attribute his victory to the Venetians, and the latter now regret the services they have rendered him in the past; they fear that they might well suffer the same fate as Barbarossa. Grotius concludes the ten-line poem with a taunting remark concerning the secular power of religious leaders:

> Nolite in fastum titulo pietatis abuti:
> esse iubet regum libera colla Deus.

According to Grotius, the Pope used piety as a disguise for abuse of power, but God wishes the necks of kings to be free—a nice allusion to the representation on the fresco, which, as Grotius apparently assumed, depicted Pope Alexander with his foot on the neck of Frederic Barbarossa.

The poem is significant not only because of its anti-papal message, but also because, as in the case of the first example, it evoked considerable response, which can even now be analysed. Another recipient of the poem, besides Willem de Groot, was the Parisian scholar Jacques Dupuy, who sent it on to Nicolas Fabry de Peiresc. The latter, a famous humanist and an important link in the contacts among scholars in this period, confirmed on 24 March 1636 the receipt of "les vers de Mr. Grottius sur l'inscription contentieuse"; he greatly admired them, and found them to be completely in accordance with a talent such as Grotius's.[22] In Holland, too, the poem circulated: Grotius gave it to the English ambassador to Paris, who passed it on to his Dutch colleague, who felt that the verses were important enough to be sent to Holland. There they finally reached André Rivet, the court minister, who was later to become Grotius's most fervent antagonist in theological matters. Rivet even made a French translation, in order that Stadholder Frederik Hendrik could also read the poem. Thus, "everyone who was anyone" in Holland got to see it, and Willem de Groot wrote to his brother that it met with general acclaim.[23]

---

[22] *Lettres de Peiresc aux frères Dupuy*, ed. Ph. Tamizey de Larroque, 3 vols. [Collection de documents inédits sur l'histoire de France, deuxième série] (Paris, 1892), 3, p. 461.

[23] *BW* VII, nos. 2503, 2505, 2544 d.d. 10-3-1636, 10-3-1636, 9-4-1636 from Willem de Groot, from Nicolaas van Reigersbergh and to Willem de Groot, respectively.

The poem on Barbarossa is then not mentioned in Grotius's correspondence until three years later, in November 1639, Willem de Groot asks his brother whether he wants it to be included in a new edition of his poetry (a project which was never realised). Willem himself is uncertain about this, because he expected this poem not to be well received in Rome.[24] Grotius agreed with his brother, and did not wish the poem to be published in print, since it would be incompatible with his ideal of the unification of the churches, which he was propagating more and more openly, eventually even without reservation in large numbers of publications and pamphlets.[25]

Reconsidering, finally, the reactions to the two "occasional poems" discussed above, it may be concluded that both were influential and effective beyond their immediate scope. As we stated already, Grotius's personal position and reputation played a considerable role: like, for instance, Daniel Heinsius and Claudius Salmasius, he was regarded as one of the "aces" of the scholarly world of his time, and any written statement by his hand was, therefore, automatically treated as important. Yet, time and again we see that Grotius's poems, however insignificant the occasions for which they were written may have been, constitute an important testimony and at any rate provide us with instructive information about the poet himself. Moreover, even in the tiniest epigram, in the shortest treatise the highly personal tone of the author may be perceived; a case in point of the saying "le style est l'homme même."

Grotius's own statements about his poems, unfortunately handed down to us only sporadically, show that he did not view his poetry as essentially different from his other writings: he considered the poem on Arminius, for instance, to be a declaration on a par with his theological treatises concerning the desirability of unity within the church. He regarded it as a manifesto, and occasionally quoted from it.[26] Also his opponents were of the opinion that his poetry constituted an essential part of his oeuvre. Thus, in 1643[27] André Rivet reproached him for having changed his

---

[24] *BW* X, no. 4386 d.d. 14-11-1639: "Poemata tua dum perlego et hoc rogandum duxi, an [epigramma quod] de victoria Barbarossae ... scripsisti non aliquam tibi invidiam [sit creaturum] ... Romae apud pontificem."

[25] *BW* X, no. 4405, d.d. 26-11-1639 to Willem de Groot: "Sententiam tuam de omittenda ... historia Barbarossae et causas quas adfers, probo."

[26] *Verhooren en andere bescheiden betreffende het rechtsgeding van Hugo de Groot*, ed. R. Fruin [= Werken uitgegeven door het Historisch Genootschap gevestigd te Utrecht, N.R. 14] (Utrecht, 1871), pp. 3-4; *BW* V, 2055.

[27] Andreas Rivetus, *Apologeticus pro suo de verae et sincerae pacis ecclesiae proposito contra Hugonis Grotii votum* ... (Lugd. Batavor., 1643), pp. 288-91.

attitude towards Theodorus Beza; in an epicedium dating from 1606,[28] thirty-seven years earlier, Grotius had literally praised him to the skies, but later Beza's intransigent Calvinism had induced him to form a much more negative judgment.

Thus, Grotius's poetry, especially during his youth, constitutes a complement to his other writings which is indispensable for a proper understanding of the author, his life, his connections and his intellectual development. But, unfortunately, this importance goes hand in hand with the inaccessibility of Grotius's poetry for the modern reader. The often convoluted Latin, in the tradition of the Silver Epic, the impenetrable mythological apparatus, the frequent allusions to *loci* in classical Latin poetry, the importance of the historical details of the situation in which the poem has been written, all these obstacles which the modern reader encounters on the road to a proper understanding of this great poet necessitate a modern edition of Grotius's poetry with an elaborate commentary. As stated above, such editions further the understanding of Grotius's life and works. But above all we believe that his poetry itself, owing to its intrinsic qualities, amply justifies such an undertaking.

Grotius Institute,
Royal Netherlands Academy of Arts and Sciences,
The Hague

[28] *PC* no. 70 pp. 295–98.

Indis Americanis quae cum veteribus Helvetiis intercedere necessitudo sit visa Sepulvedae Bartholomaei Casai adversario novi orbis ad antiquum referendi specimen

KARL AUGUST NEUHAUSEN

I

Quoniam triennio ante, auditrices auditoresque maxime honorabiles, cum Guelpherbyti supremus Societatis Internationalis Studiis Neo-Latinis Provehendis congressus agebatur, solus equidem orationem Latino habui sermone conscriptam,[1] eo dignius est commemoratione, quod hoc in conventu primo extra Europae fines et in Americae quidem universitate studiorum tam praeclara agendo is quoque collega, qui me prior verba fecit, Latinam linguam tamquam totius orbis Neo-Latini patrium sermonem ausus est usurpare.[2] Atque cum eundem ita nunc excipiam, ut de similibus disseram rebus, facilior redditus est aditus ad quaestionem mihi deinceps tractandam. Verum quia dolendum est alterum collegam, ne primus hic prodiret orator,[3] impeditum esse, claudo agmen non trilogiae cuiusdam, ut erat promissum, sed bipertitae tantum sessionis ad primordia pertinentis historiae Americanae Latinarum litterarum monumentis mandatae.

---

[1] *Acta Conventus Neo-Latini Guelpherbytani*, pp. 117–26. Lepido fiebat errore, ut quasi humanistis ascribendus omnium etiam aequalium solus in voluminis illius indice (p. 691) collocarer.

[2] Haec est oratio infra pp. 811–22 typis mandata.

[3] Heinz Hofmann de iis praecipue libris, qui 'Columbeis' inscribuntur, Anglice dicturum se pollicitus non potuit huc convenire.

Americam igitur novum orbem, quo nihil umquam accepimus esse maius inventum, quinque saeculis ante a Christophoro illo Columbo detectam quadriennio post totum fere per orbem terrarum sollemniter celebratum iri et aliis ubique hoc iam tempore est curae pronuntiare et hac in sede perquam accommodata admonuit collega ante me modo locutus, cum dilucide enarraret atque expediret varia carmina epica, quae singula eiusdem illius Columbi nomen insigne vel fronte prae se ferunt. Considerantibus autem nobis memoriaque repetentibus, quando cur quomodo novus ipse mundus antiqui hominibus orbis mediique aevi prorsus ignotus ab Hispanis Anglis aliisque Europam tum incolentibus in universum sive repertus sive expugnatus sit et subactus, hoc potissimum esse statuendum videtur illa documenta, quibus Americae origines inde ab eo anno, quo Columbus huc appulit, descriptae sunt atque explicatae, multo maiorem certe partem, quam vulgo creditur, Latinis utique exarata litteris esse tradita posteris.[4]

Atque huius quidem rei gravissimae testimonia vel maxime egregia bini continent catalogi, qui vix aptius inscribi potuerunt (si Latine licet vertere) quam: "Novus orbis in Europae vetere quadam bibliotheca obvius" et "Latina America in Saxonia Inferiore conspicua"; exhibuit enim alterum librum laudatum duodecim,[5] alterum tribus abhinc annis[6] admodum nobilis ipsa Bibliotheca Augusta, ubi novissima tum Neo-Latina habebantur triennalia. Iam vero, siquidem permulti praeterea variique interim commentarii eandem illam rem concernentes publici sunt facti iuris, exempli gratia aliquot opera recentiora sub uno velut aspectu collocata unicuique vestrum praebui prompta ita quidem, ut confiderem, si qua praetermisisse visus essem, quibus aliquantum tribui oporteret momenti, eadem sua quemque sponte mecum esse communicaturum.

Sed quamquam haud ignoro Bibliothecaeque etiam illius Augustae scrinia perscrutatus ipse habeo plane cognitum innumerabiles investigandos exstare Latinos quosdam fontes, qui quidem ad explorandas res pristinis Novi Orbis temporibus gestas plurimum valeant, sed qui cum adhuc abditi lateant e tenebris in lucem quam primum sint protrahendi, hodie tamen equidem alia progrediendum via censeo. Nam veritus, ne

[4] Infinita enim silva quaedam ac materies Latinae patebit et prosae orationis et poesis ad res omni in America gestas spectantis, si quis perlustraverit ea, quae in appendice proposui.

[5] Catalogus hic *Die Neue Welt in den Schätzen einer alten europäischen Bibliothek* inscriptus veniit Guelpherbyti anno 1976°.

[6] Hic cuius est titulus *Lateinamerika in Niedersachsen von Kolumbus zu Bolívar* catalogus foras est datus Guelpherbyti anno 1985°.

parum recte perspiceretur, quid sibi vellent ea, quae iam edita essent ac propagata, in medio malui ponere non tam, quae neglecta iacerent aut oblivione obruta, quam quae in illarum rerum peritissimae cuiusque personae manibus versari viderentur. Itaque eam retractandam constitui sumere commentationem intra quadriennium solito longius latiusque diffusam, cuius maiore exprimitur inscriptione, quatenus ad Indos Americanos attineat humanismus, minore autem indicantur Hispanorum in novi quibusdam orbis partibus conquisitiones Latinis illustratae litteris.[7] Textus enim huius commentationis appendice comprehensi tantum existimabantur valere, ut superiore anno iterum imprimendi curarentur eo fasciculo, qui seorsum emissus inscribitur "Mundus Novus" ideoque, ut addita confirmatur subscriptione, pertinet ad expugnatam Americam Latinis litteris memoriae proditam.[8]

II

Principem vero locum et in hoc libello et in illa commentatione optimo iure obtinent Bartholomaeus Casaus et Ioannes Genesius Sepulveda ambo ex eadem orti Hispaniae regione aequales, qui scriptores Latini saeculo decimo sexto excellentes praeter ceteros tum Christianos Indorum Americanorum existimatores floruerunt.[9] Atqui eidem, quamvis uterque esset non modo Catholicae Romanorum addictus Ecclesiae sacerdos, verum etiam theologus eminens idemque humanista litteris antiquis ita imbutus ut qui maxime, mirum quantum inter se dissentiebant. Alter enim, quia persuasum ei erat Indos Americae indigenas advenis Europaeis suo ipsorum orbe terrarum potitis neutiquam inferiores sed moribus ingeniisque omnino pares vel potius iisdem aliquatenus etiam praestare, defendendae eius gentis universae tuendaeque patrocinium tot decennia tanto studio suscipere perseveravit, ut quemadmodum humanistarum Petrarca sic ipse Indorum pater illorum appellaretur; alter autem, quando-

---

[7] E. Schäfer: "Die Indianer und der Humanismus–Die spanische Conquista in lateinischer Literatur" (1984) (v. infra p. 557).

[8] J. Klowski: *Mundus Novus–Lateinische Texte zur Eroberung Amerikas* (1987).

[9] Non igitur est casu factum, ut auctores hi duo deinceps in eo quoque volumine, quod *Humanismus und Neue Welt* inscriptum nuperrime edidit W. Reinhard, et singuli quidem dilucide doctissimeque tractarentur. Ea enim, quae de Sepulveda (*ib.* pp. 143–66) disseruit H. Pietschmann ("Aristotelischer Humanismus und Inhumanität? Sepúlveda und die amerikanischen Ureinwohner"), excipit illa commentatio, quam B. Rech inscripsit "Bartolomé de las Casas und die Antike" (*ib.* pp. 167–97).

quidem sibi persuaserat eisdem illis novi qui dicitur orbis veteribus incolis dominos extrinsecus advectos indole opibus potentia adeo superiores esse, ut his illi cuncti cedere deberent, nihil antiquius habuit quam ut evinceret aequum esse ab Hispanis imprimis Indos Americae primicolas tamquam natura humiles feros vitiisque contaminatos nulla interposita dubitatione subigi, quo facilius perdomiti aut sua sponte aut–si aliter nequiret perpetrari–per vim ad Christianam religionem converterentur.

Quod quidem quibus subductis rationibus atque calculis Sepulveda acerrimus usque Casai pertinacissimusque adversarius probari voluerit, cum ex aliis tum ex hac arbitror colligi posse sententia, quam scriptam legimus in illius Apologia pro eo libro, quem de iustis belli causis confecit:[10]

> Cum igitur duae viae sunt, quibus ad barbarorum conversionem procedi posse videatur, altera per monitionem solum doctrinamque et praedicationem difficilis, longa et multis periculis impedita, altera per subiectionem barbarorum facilis, brevis et cum multis barbarorum commoditatibus expedita: utra progrediendum sit, non est prudentis hominis dubitare.

Huius autem periodi editores a me laudati[11] nihil ad eandem explanandam putaverunt opus esse nisi septenas notiones in vernaculum transferri sermonem.[12] Vereor tamen, ut effugere quempiam possit, cuius ad exemplar Sepulveda hoc loco legentium animos intenderit advertere nomine scilicet celeberrimi scriptoris naviter omisso. Etenim Caesar primo in libro commentariorum de bello Gallico, postquam de Helvetiorum belli initiis coepit referre, illorum relictis finibus suis in Romanam provinciam invasurorum causas condicionesque hisce verbis describit:[13]

> Erant omnino itinera duo, quibus itineribus domo exire possent: unum per Sequanos, angustum et difficile, inter montem Iuram et flumen Rhodanum, vix qua singuli carri ducerentur, mons autem altissimus impendebat, ut facile perpauci prohibere possent; alterum

---

[10] Eandem exhibeo sententiam, quam primus protulit Schäfer (v. n. 7, p. 86) quamque idem una cum altero collega curavit iterum imprimendam (v. n. 8, p. 15).

[11] Ad plura Sepulvedae scripta Latina mox edenda cf. ea, quae Pietschmann (v. n. 9) indicavit.

[12] Schäfer et Klowski (v. n. 8, p. 15). Triennio ante Schäfer (v. n. 7, p. 86) non plus quam duo vocabula Germanice tantum verterat.

[13] *Bell. Gall.* 1.6.1–2 ed. W. Hering (Lipsiae, 1987) 3.

per provinciam nostram, multo facilius atque expeditius, propterea quod inter fines Helvetiorum et Allobrogum, qui nuper pacati erant, Rhodanus fluit isque nonnullis locis vado transitur.

Id igitur tralaticium quoddam duplicis itineris specimen ne Herculei quidem illius bivii imagine notissima minus idoneum, quod suis quisque finibus eligat adaptandum, quomodo Sepulveda imitatus ad suum ipsius usum converterit, enodare atque interpretari nostra nunc interest plurimi.

III

Ac primum quidem, etiamsi quis Sepulvedae sententiam a me prolatam leviter strictimque attigerit, facile animadvertet illum eandem fere, qua Caesar usus erat, adhibuisse componendi structuram. Namque Caesar incipit ita, ut certiores nos faciat fuisse duo tum itinera, quibus Helvetii Celtarum gens ex agris suis exire atque in Romanorum fines proficisci possent; Sepulveda exorditur argumentari, cum asserit duas esse vias, quibus primicolas Americae barbaros ad Catholicam fidem appareat posse converti. Unde manifestum est vel theologum hunc vel philosophum ab illo gestarum rerum scriptore eo dumtaxat differre, quod et pro praeterito substituit praesentis formam *sunt* et vice *itineris*, quod quidem nomen apud Caesarem angustius valeat, *viae* vocem idcirco fungentem inducit, quod haec latissime patet eademque ei vis ac *rationis* notioni ita subiecta est, ut verborum iunctura, quae est *via ac ratione procedere*, in locutionem abierit admodum tritam.

Perspicuum porro est Sepulvedam Caesaris illud exemplum quam diligentissime secutum affirmare duas vias inter se maxime contrarias distinguendas esse: alteram nempe difficilem longam impeditam, alteram facilem brevem expeditamque. Quam autem arte Sepulveda presserit Caesaris vestigia, vel ex eo perspici potest, quod verborum etiam seriem, quam ab illo mutuatus est, omnino conservatam retinuit; nam *altera per monitionem solum doctrinamque et praedicationem* necnon *altera per subiectionem barbarorum*, quae sententiae membra apud Sepulvedam hoc ordine coagmentata deinceps occurrunt, respondere Caesarianis illis vocum iuncturis, quae sunt *unum per Sequanos* et *alterum per provinciam nostram*, in aperto est. Accedit, ut adiectivis iis praecipue verbis, quibus duplex illud tamque diversum sive itinerum sive viarum declaratur genus, Sepulveda Caesaris exemplo nixus arguatur ambitum circumscripsisse verborum; perinde enim atque ille utitur cum vulgaribus adiectivis, qualia sunt verba *difficilis* ac *facilis*, tum rariore *expeditus*.

Cetera autem elementa e Caesaris illa sententia deprompta compluribus Sepulveda causis adductus alia alio commutavit modo. Rhetorica enim instructus arte quia varietate quadam vocum animos didicerat delectari, duo illa Helvetiorum itinera, quibus bina Caesar attribuerat adiectiva verba, partim invertendo partim quaedam addendo ita auxit atque amplificavit, ut duas suas vias trinis afficeret adiectivis eiusdemve generis ornamentis. Id itaque effecit Sepulveda, ut Helvetiorum illud *iter angustum et difficile* exaggeratum transformaretur in *viam difficilem longam multisque periculis impeditam*, alterum autem iter a Caesare perhibitum *multo facilius atque expeditius* fieret via *facilis brevis et cum multis barbarorum commoditatibus expedita*. Reliqua rursus, quae a Caesare illic relata cernebat, cum ad ea, quae sibimet ipsi demonstranda proposuerat, omnino non quadrare viderentur, praetereundo removit et sustulit.

Quibus initis rationibus Sepulveda, quamvis tot tantaque eius sententiae membra cum Caesariana periodo congruant, eadem tamen ad id, quod ipse suis verbis exprimere atque effingere studebat, tam apte convenienterque accommodavit, ut et propriae scriptoris eius virtutes eluceant nec parum liqueat, quam severum ille se quamque superbum Indorum Americanorum praebuerit iudicem. Quid enim cunctis his de hominibus Sepulveda senserit iudicandum, vel inde cognosci potest, quod tribus omnibus locis, ubi illorum mentionem facit, nomen eorum proprium evitandum ratus nullum nisi 'barbarorum' nomen ipsum, quod ne Caesar quidem saepius aequo adhibuerat, ut Helevtios Germanos ceterasque nationes Romanorum cultus atque humanitatis expertes nuncuparet, idem in peiorem partem accipiendum Sepulveda ut alibi fere sic intra unius quoque sententiae nobis examinandae spatium tam exiguum ter Indis Americanis tamquam deterioribus turpitudinis instar inussit notae. Quae cum ita sint, in proclivi est intellectu, quantopere suam de barbaris Americanis opinionem Sepulveda pro recta veraque habendam lecturis inculcare temptaverit.

Enimvero, simulac quaesivit denique, utrum illa difficili via progrediendum esset an multo faciliore, ipse confestim negat prudentis cuiusquam esse dubitare, utram interrogatus sit praelaturus. Consimiliter igitur atque Aristoteles, cui summo quidem auctori qualis intercederet necessitudo cum Indis Americanis patefecit originum 'orbis novi' eruendarum Nestor ille Americanus,[14] Sepulveda antiquis eiusdem novae quae vocatur telluris incolis communia quaedam esse contendit cum comparandis veteribus

---

[14] Scilicet Lewis Hanke in eo libro, qui inscribitur *Aristotle and the American Indians: A Study in Race Prejudice in the Modern World* (Londinii, 1959).

Helvetiis. Quemadmodum enim olim illi Gallorum Celtarumve primi Caesari tum subigendi, priusquam pacati Romanorum in imperium redigerentur, expeditius iter difficiliori duxerunt anteponendum, ut eo celerius commodiusque in provinciam quandam Romanorum pervenirent, sic Sepulveda comprobare conatur certo esse certius primicolas Americae ipsos quoque barbaros, quo facilius converti possent, non per difficilem longamque illam viam eo perducendos esse sed 'per subiectionem' alteram viam multo expeditiorem eo videlicet consilio, ut idem in Hispanorum imprimis dicionem potestatemque redacti sub eorum dominationem subiungerentur. Hactenus ergo Indos Americanos Europaeis quibusdam hominibus vincendos cum Helvetiis Caesaris hostibus[15] conferri posse Sepulvedae placuit.

IV

At vero Bartholomaeus Casaus ut alias sic hac quoque de re decernenda longe secus est censendus fuisse iudicaturus. Sepulveda enim, si recordari libet, haudquaquam ait nullius Christiani, immo *prudentis* non esse hominis dubitare, utra sit via procedendum. Quocirca prudentem illum quidem, sed omnia vel ad sua tantum vel rei publicae commoda referentem subiciendi per vim viam a Sepulveda commendatam altera pluris aestimare non cunctari concedamus profecto necesse est. Casaus autem, quippe qui vir vere Christianus aliis magis quam sibi consulere soleret, si Caesaris illud de duobus Helvetiorum itineribus dictum similitudinis cuiusdam deducendae causa arcessivisset, dubium non est, quin contra ac Sepulveda conclusurus fuerit ea ipsa, quam ille quasi nimis difficilem repudiavit, progrediendum esse via; numquam enim destitit idem eximius suorum patronus Indorum monere non suae salutis eos causa 'per subiectionem'—id quod Sepulveda ita poposcit, ut eam nimirum rem, quae ipsi arrisit, acu tangeret—, sed—quas Sepulveda res singulas adversarii sententiam adumbrans non minus circumscripte amplexus est—'per monitionem solum doctrinamque et praedicationem' debere converti. Aeque consentaneum est coniectare eundem perpetuo illorum amore commotum recusaturum fuisse, ne confiteretur eos 'cum multis' ipsorum 'commoditatibus', ut asseveravit Sepulveda, aut iam subactos esse aut umquam subici posse.

---

[15] Nova nuper hanc ad rem saepenumero tractatam contulit Franz Fischer: "Caesar und die Helvetier: Neue Überlegungen zu einem alten Thema," *Bonner Jahrbücher* 185 (1985): 1–26.

Immo veri simillimum est Casaum iratum ita Sepulvedae contradicturum fuisse, ut quodcumque illius subiectionis genus indigenis Americae et commonefaceret semper damno detrimentoque fuisse et praedicaret numquam emolumento fore aut fructui.[16]

Nec vero nostrum nunc est omnem hanc tam gravem de Indis Americanis iuste tractandis controversiam inter Sepulvedam et Casaum summae auctoritatis humanistas exortam eandemque adhuc nondum diremptam disceptare. Sufficit enim allato eo testimonio, quo quidem haud scio an nullum exstet aptius ad universam illam quaestionem discutiendam documentum quoddam Latinum, primum exposuisse, quatenus Sepulveda et suam ipsius et Casai gravissimi adversarii de primicolis Americae sententiam ad duorum itinerum veteribus Helvetiis oblatorum exemplar referendam descripsisset, deinde eandem hanc normam totamque rem, de qua Sepulveda et Casaus disputaverunt, Carneadeo more in utramque partem disseri posse. Quae quidem satis evidenter ostendisse me spero.

Appendix

Librorum atque commentationum et ad detectam expugnatamque Americam et ad omnem Novi Orbis historiam Latinis litteris mandatam pertinentium conspectus

Fundamenta harum quoque rerum investigandarum iecit J. Ijsewijn praeclaro illo libro (pp. 191–200), qui *Companion to Neo-Latin Studies* inscriptus anno 1977° prodiit primus universas Neo-Latinas quae vocantur litteras complexus.

Novissima quaeque continet id "Instrumentum Bibliographicum Neo-Latinum," quod idem ille editor in singulis *Humanisticorum Lovaniensium* voluminibus quotannis imprimendum curat copiosissimum.

A. Recentiora opera inde a duodecim annis edita

1. *Die Neue Welt in den Schätzen einer alten europäischen Bibliothek* (= Ausstellungskataloge der Herzog August Bibliothek, Nr. 17), (Guelpherbyti, 1976).

---

[16] Huius quoque disputationis causas dilucide expedivit idem ille Lewis Hanke et recentiore quidem eo libro, quem inscripsit *All mankind is one–A study of the disputation between Bartolomé de Las Casas Ginès de Sepúlveda in 1550 on the intellectual and religious capacity of the American Indians* (Illinois, 1974).

2. Quinn, David B. (Ed.), *New American World–A Documentary History of North America to 1612*, Vol. 1-5 (Londinii, 1979).

3. Kohl, Karl-Heinz (Ed.); *Mythen der Neuen Welt–Zur Entdeckungsgeschichte der Neuen Welt* (= Ausstellungskatalog im Auftrag der Berliner Festspiele) (Berolini, 1982).

4. Meyn, M. et alii (Edd.), *Die großen Entdeckungen* (= *Dokumente der europäischen Expansion*, Vol. 2) (Monaci, 1984).

5. Schäfer, Eckard, "Die Indianer und der Humanismus—Die spanische Conquista in lateinischer Literatur," *Der altsprachliche Unterricht* 27 (1984), fasc. 6 (= Neulateinische Literatur im Lateinunterricht), pp. 49–70 et 82–91.

6. Piper, Wulf (Ed.), *Lateinamerika in Niedersachsen von Kolumbus zu Bolívar* (= Ausstellungskataloge der Herzog August Bibliothek, Nr. 48) (Guelpherbyti, 1985).

7. *Gold und Macht: Spanien in der neuen Welt, Eine Ausstellung anläßlich des 500. Jahrestages der Entdeckung Amerikas* (Viennae, 1986).

8. Reinhard, Wolfgang (Ed.), *Humanismus und Neue Welt* (= Mitteilung XV der Kommission für Humanismusforschung), Acta humaniora 1987. Continet id volumen et alia et:
(a) Pietschmann, Horst, "Aristotelischer Humanismus und Inhumanität? Sépulveda und die amerikanischen Ureinwohner," pp. 143–166;
(b) Rech, Bruno, "Bartolomé de Las Casas und die Antike," pp. 167-197.

9. Klowski, Joachim (Ed.), "Utopia—Mundus Novus," *Der altsprachliche Unterricht* 30 (1987), fasc. 2.

10. Klowski, Joachim et Eckard Schäfer (Edd.), *Mundus Novus: Lateinische Texte zur Eroberung Amerikas* (Stutgardiae, 1987).

11. Knefelkamp, Ulrich et Hans-Joachim König (Edd.), *Die Neuen Welten in alten Büchern: Entdeckung und Eroberung in frühen deutschen Schrift–und Bildzeugnissen* (= Ausstellung in der Staatsbibliothek Bamberg) (Bambergae, 1988).

12. Hofmann, Heinz, "La scoperta del nuovo mondo nella poesia latina: i 'Columbeidos libri priores duo' di Giulio Cesare Stella," *Columbeis*, Vol. 3 (1988): 71–94.

B. Opera usque ad annum Columbi totiusque Novi Orbis ab eodem detecti memoriae dedicandum copiosissima editum iri promissa

1. Meyer Reinhold, J. Rufus Fears, Wolfgang Haase (Edd.), *The Classical Tradition of the Americas*, Voll. 1–5; cf. *Wolfenbütteler Renaissance Mitteilungen*, 12 (1988): 99.

2. Cetera publici facienda iuris continet fasciculus novissimus hic: Briesemeister, Dietrich et Raabe, Paul (Edd.), *Mundus Novus: Lateinamerika und Deutschland* (Programm: Neue Welt–Alte Welt. 500 Jahre Begegnung mit Amerika 1492–1992), N. 1 (1989).

The Dedicatory Letter as a Genre: The Prefaces of Guarino Veronese's Translations of Plutarch

MARIANNE PADE

The humanists' prefaces have been studied for various reasons: recently they have been seen predominantly as sources for literary history and for the sociology of humanist literature, that is especially the relationship between humanists and their patrons. A stylistic analysis of Quattrocento prefaces to translations from the Greek, undertaken some years ago by Lucia Gualdo Rosa,[1] has demonstrated their close stylistic similarity to Latin prose prefaces of late Antiquity,[2] a similarity which was enhanced by the analogous circumstances under which these prefaces were composed: the society of the late empire, as well as that of the Italian city states, favoured *clientela* relations; and many literary works of late Antiquity were compilations and imitations which, like translations, would not call for *inventio*. Dedicatory letters are furthermore a very conventional kind of writing, and their form, once established, would not often be subject to change.

Contrary to what might be expected, the preface is only incidentally a

---

[1] Lucia Gualdo Rosa, "Le lettere di dedica delle traduzioni dal greco nel '400. Appunti per un'analisi stilistica," *Vichiana* n.s. 2 (1973), fascicolo I–II, 68–85. Another attempt at a comprehensive analysis is in Karl Schottenloher, *Die Widmungsrede im Buch des 16. Jahrhunderts*. Reformationsgeschichtliche Studien und Texte 76–77 (Münster: Aschendorff, 1953).

[2] Tore Janson, *Latin Prose Prefaces. Studies in Literary Conventions*. Acta Universitatis Stockholmiensis. Studia Latina Stockholmiensia XIII (Stockholm: Almqvist & Wiksell, 1964).

comment on the work it accompanies, and so it has little in common for instance with the *accessus*. What matters seems to be the relationship between the writer and his dedicatee. The traditional *loci* include an ecomium of the dedicatee; praise of the work which has been translated, compiled or imitated both for its inherent value and for its special significance to the recipient; and profuse protestations of the translator's or compilator's humble status in comparison either with the exalted dedicatee or with the author in question. Important is also the effort to connect one's work to the classical *auctores* by quotations and allusions of various kinds. The work is usually said to have been undertaken at the explicit request of the dedicatee, who in return is asked to scrutinize it and judge its quality, but the exact relationship of the translator/compilator and the person to whom the book is dedicated is seldom apparent.

Guarino's Translations of Plutarch's Vitae

Guarino Veronese (1374–1460)[3] made numerous translations from the Greek, many of which were later sent to friends or patrons. If we may judge from quotations in his letters and from the number of translations, his favorite Greek author was Plutarch, and of his *oeuvre* Guarino cared especially for the *Lives*,[4] a predilection shared by many at the time. With emphasis on the Plutarchean translations, Guarino's prefaces will be the subject of this paper.[5] By analyzing his letters of dedication I shall try to demonstrate how the established pattern would change according to the purpose of the gift, and as Guarino's own position in society changed.

---

[3] For the life of Guarino, cf. Remigio Sabbadini, *Vita di Guarino Veronese*. Giornale Ligustico 18 (Genova: Sordo-Muti, 1891), and his *La Scuola e gli Studi di Guarino Guarini Veronese* (Catania: Fr. Galati, 1896). An earlier treatment is in Carlo de'Rosmini, *Vita e disciplina di Guarino Veronese e de' suoi discepoli*, 4 vols. (Brescia: N. Bettoni, 1805–1806).

[4] For Guarino's work on Plutarch, cf. Sabbadini, *La scuola e gli studi*, 130–136.

[5] The prefaces to Guarino's translations are printed in *Epistolario di Guarino Veronese*, a c. di Remigio Sabbadini, 3 vols. Miscellanea di Storia Veneta, ser. 3, No. 8, 11 e 14, (Venezia: 1915–1919). I have edited the preface to the *Alexander and Caesar* in "Guarino, his princely patron, and Plutarch's *Alexandri ac Caesaris*: an ineditum in *Archivio di S. Pietro H 31*," *Analecta Romana Instituti Danici* XVII–XVIII (1988–1989), 135–49. In the following I shall refer to the prefaces edited by Sabbadini only by the numbers they have in the *Epistolario*. They are: *Flaminius*, no. 6; *Dion*, no. 21; *Themistocles*, no. 66; *Philopoemen*, no. 377; *Phocion*, no. 651; *Pelopidas and Marcellus*, no. 706; and *Lysander and Sulla*, no. 667.

More often than not a translation would be dedicated to somebody. In the Renaissance, Plutarch's *Lives of Famous Greeks and Romans* were considered a wonderful collection of "mirrors for princes," and they were incessantly sent with dedications to secular and ecclesiastical magnates. Guarino apart, only a few dedicated their Latin *Lives* to other humanists: Leonardo Bruni sent Latin *Vitae* to Coluccio Salutati and Antonio Loschi; Francesco Barbaro dedicated the *Aristides and Cato* to his brother Zaccharias; and Antonio Beccaria sent the pair *Alcibiades and Coriolanus* to the physician Matteolo Perugini. A few *Lives* have no dedications: most of these were made by Iacopo Angeli da Scarperia, Leonardo Bruni and Guarino, and they were completed in the first quarter of the fifteenth century.[6]

Guarino translated thirteen different *Lives* and some *Comparationes*. He made several revisions of his own translations, usually, it seems, when he had found a worthy dedicatee. The first was the *Life of Alexander* which Guarino undertook while studying with Manuel Chrysoloras in Constantinople from 1403 to 1408, but he probably made a revision of it in 1412 when it was published together with the *Caesar*. During the years Guarino taught in Florence (1411 to 1414), he further completed three Roman *Lives* of famous republican heroes: the *Flaminius*, *Marcellus*, and *Coriolanus*. The next five years of his life Guarino spent teaching Greek and Latin in Venice, and there he translated six Greek *Lives*: the *Dion*, *Pelopidas*, *Themistocles*, *Phocion*, *Eumenes*, and *Philopoemen*. Finally, he presented Leonello d'Este with the pair *Lysander and Sulla* on the occasion of his wedding in 1435.

Of these translations, only the *Coriolanus* and *Eumenes* lack dedications. It seems, however, that only half of them were undertaken with one particular dedicatee in mind; the rest were published with dedications several years after they were completed, although this is not always clear from the accompanying letters. Undoubtedly many of them were originally made for teaching purposes, and so they would be literal versions with no pretensions to stylistic elegance. They would serve as a help to Guarino's students to read the Greek original. Such a version would have to be revised before it was published. When the dedication was thus written years after the translation, it will not necessarily reflect interest which Guarino originally had in the Greek text.

---

[6] Vito R. Giustiniani, "Sulle traduzioni latine delle Vite di Plutarco nel Quattrocento," *Rinascimento* 1, 2. ser. (1961), 3–62.

Guarino's Dedicatory Letters

A. Structure

Guarino hardly ever dedicated his Latin *Lives* to anybody he did not know fairly well. One exception to this seems to be the *Alexander and Caesar*, which were probably presented to a North Italian prince around 1412.[7] The rest were dedicated to influential people in the cities where he lived, to other humanists, close friends and pupils. In a number of instances several of these functions were united in the same person. In his prefaces one finds all the traditional *loci*, but in varying order and not always with the same emphasis. Their use seems to be determined by Guarino's relationship to the dedicatee and by the occasion of the dedication rather than by the nature of the work in question. The style of the dedications changes over the years; in the early ones there is usually a very factual description of why the translation was undertaken, while later on Guarino would begin the letter with a small moral or philosophic essay which would lead elegantly to the actual dedication. In his first prefaces Guarino would write about matters pertaining to method of translation, but this theme afterwards disappears entirely. In later years he omits to ask the recipient to be the judge of the translation, which surely reflects the growing esteem in which Guarino was held. Only once, in his very first translation, the *Ad Demonicum* of Pseudo-Isocrates, does he explicitly say that the work was undertaken at the request of the dedicatee, Floro Valier.[8]

In the early years, Guarino adheres closely to the traditional formal structure, and his prefaces are with few exceptions built up in a uniform manner. In 1411 he sent the *Life of Flaminius* to the Florentine noble Roberto de'Rossi. Guarino's choice of text is extremely important, but this cannot be seen from the preface. Flaminius was the great Roman philhellene, and Rossi would have been flattered by the association, since he had been one of the early admirers of Manuel Chrysoloras and instrumental in inviting him to Florence. In the preface Guarino first tells why he translated the life. Unexpectedly he had had some time free, and there was no better way to use it than to undertake a translation. The result would please others and the work itself was a healthy intellectual exercise. Guarino sent the translation to Rossi because he was well educated in both Greek and Latin.[9] Then follows a eulogy of Rossi's achievements as

[7] See my *Guarino, his princely patron.*

[8] No. 2: " 'Habes quod tota mente petisti' [*Aen*, 4.100] Flore Valeri. Id enim crebra a me violentia precatus extorsisti. . . ."

[9] No. 6: "Nuper Roberte suavissime, cum ex labore in otium vel invitus incidissem,

a translator of Aristotle's *Analytica Posteriora*, where his version is said to compare favorably with the medieval one. Guarino asks Rossi to act as a judge of his own translation, but he expresses this with some irony: he uses a very elaborate image about his own inferiority as a translator compared to Rossi, describing himself as Thersites, the ugliest man in the army of Agamemnon, who could expect no praise from Ulysses/Rossi.[10] Guarino's humility in this passage forms a contrast to his tone at the end of the letter, where he claims to be the intellectual relative of Rossi through their common parent, Manuel Chrysoloras.[11]

Rossi was the social superior of Guarino, and he belonged to the inner circle of Florentine humanists, whom Guarino would somehow have to please while teaching in that city. What is explicitly stressed in the letter is not Rossi's social rank, but his Greek learning, where Guarino could claim to be his equal, though he professes the opposite. The purpose of the letter, and of the Latin *Flaminius*, was to better Guarino's position among the intellectuals of Florence; though he did not think himself inferior in learning, he could not entirely overlook differences in social standing.

Eventually Guarino, not content with the milieu in Florence, sent the *Alexander and Caesar* with a solemn dedication to a person of very high rank. This was sometime before 1414, probably around 1412. The dedicatee is explicitly said to have offered Guarino patronage,[12] and Guarino was presumably applying for a position at court—which as far as we know he did not get. The formal structure is almost exactly as in the previous letter, but Guarino elaborates two points far more than he did then. One is the effect of the dedication: "Their own merits as well as their author will secure these two great men, Alexander and Caesar, a great reputation in posterity, but it would add infinitely to their esteem," Guarino says to his addressee, "if they were dedicated to your name, just as people came from afar to visit the celebrated statue in Olympia, not only because it was

---

cuius rationem in presentia tibi reddere institui, exercendi simul ingenioli ac memoriae causa T. Q. Flaminii vitam ex Plutarcho latine convertere aggressus sum."

[10] No. 6: "tu mihi iudex censorque sis vehementer exopto . . . ," and "nec enim eo temeritatis et ignorantiae adductus sum ut ullam Thersiti formae ac decoris laudem ab Ulixe tribui potuisse putem, cum Homerus 'illo deformiorem neminem Troiam petisse' cecinerit."

[11] "Accedit inter nos necessitudo quaedam atque propinquitas ex . . . Chrysolora. . . . Ille communis utrique parens dulcissimusque praeceptor arctissimo [*codd.*; *Sabbadini* artissimo] nos ita quodam cognationis genere conciliavit, sicuti quos uno procreatos genitore eademque ortos familia cernimus."

[12] ". . . que coram te patrocinium michi. . . ."

sculpted by Phidias, but because it was dedicated to Jove." The second point is the description of the differences in their social standing, the thought of which almost made Guarino desist from his plan: as happened to Aeneas, when he met first Creusa, his dead wife, and later Polydorus, the son of Priam, Guarino became "chilled to the marrow, he could feel the hair / on his head rise, the voice clot in his throat."[13]

Whereas the quite early prefaces are all very traditional, the later often differ from them in tone and structure. Guarino may use the established scheme jokingly; so, for instance in the dedication of the *Philopoemen* to his friend, the lawyer Mazo de'Mazi, where he makes the hero implore him to be translated as he missed his friend Flaminius, the Latin half of the pair.[14] The preface to the *Nicocles* of Isocrates; this he translated for Leonello d'Este in 1433, is an example of the way Guarino departs from the traditional structure. The greater part of the letter is an essay on the nature of man and the obligations of kings, which leads to the future responsibilities of Leonello and the speech of Isocrates, where he can find valuable advice. Other prefaces, as for instance the dedication to Nicholas V of the *Strabo*,[15] are built up in a similar manner. However, in the preface of *Nicocles*, Guarino abandons the solemn tone at the end, showing his much more informal relations with Leonello. Having said that Leonello would need a Nestor to counsel him, he then makes Leonello interrupt him with the ironic comment: "So you think you will serve as a Nestor," to which he answers, "No, of course not."[16]

B. Themes

Another important aspect is how this traditional form was employed by the author, and what relational structures existed between author, dedicatee and text.

A central notion in similar writings is that of *humanitas*, and this word has a special function in Guarino's prefaces: it is the *humanitas* of Roberto

---

[13] *Aen.* 2, 774 and 3, 48, translated by Robert Fitzgerald, King Penguin, Harmondsworth 1985.

[14] No. 377: "Is [*Philopoemen*] meam tacitus implorare fidem visus est, ut cum superiori tempore T. Flaminium aequalem suum et honoris aemulum latinum fecissem, et socium distraxissem, solum ac destitutum se nequaquam esse paterer. Audivi hominem et orantem exorare sivi."

[15] No. 889.

[16] No. 675: ". . . ut Agamemnoni Nestorem, sic et tibi fidelem ac prudentissimum consiliarium addidero. . . . 'An te ipsum Nestorem vel sentis vel appellas?' inquies. Minime medius fidius. . . ."

de'Rossi which will make him consent to be the judge of Guarino's work,[17] and when Guarino dared to send the *Alexander and Caesar* to a prospective patron, it was again because of the *humanitas* of the recipient.[18] In the first case the word is connected with *mansuetudo*, in the second with *comitas*. In a solemn passage where Guarino praises Leonello's virtues, he calls him *humanissime princeps*, referring amongst other things to Leonello's *mansuetudo, clementia* and similar virtues.[19] Elsewhere too, Guarino invokes Leonello's *humanitas*.[20] Here and in Guarino's other writings, it seems that *humanitas* is a virtue which belongs to patrons or persons of high social rank, presumably (one might venture to guess) because it was more important to invoke this virtue with people in power. In Guarino's description of Leonello, it appears that one way to achieve *humanitas, mansuetudo*, and *clementia* is through the imitation of great men, in other words, the reading of history. Here we find the connection between learning and human qualities which is so important in Coluccio Salutati's definition of *humanitas*.[21]

If the differences in social standing were great enough, then *humanitas* was important as a mediator between Guarino and the dedicatee. Their relationship may also be described in terms of *munificentia* and *gratia*: Francesco Barbaro had presented Guarino with a Greek manuscript of Plutarch, and as a token of his *gratia*, Guarino sent to Barbaro the *Dion*, although it was not an adequate return for the gift;[22] and when citizenship had been granted to Guarino in Ferrara, the dedication to Leonello

---

[17] No. 6: "Quod quidem ad onus amice et benivole suscipiendum tua te, scio, persuadebit humanitas et mansuetudo, . . ."

[18] "Quocirca inceptum pene omiseram, nisi humanitas et diuina ferme comitas tua occurrisset. . . ."

[19] No. 667, the preface to the *Lysander and Sulla*: "Nec vero te perturbet, humanissime princeps, quod . . . aliqua facinora crudelitatis offendes, potissimum cum te . . . ad mansuetudinem placabilitatemque animare coner et incendere, ad quam cum tuopte ingenio tum studiis et magnorum hominum imitatione et exemplo pronus duceris et quae tanti in principe et in eo qui excelso maiestatis gradu pollet momenti est, ut quisquis clementia, ut tu, insignitus sit, . . ."

[20] No. 706, the preface to the *Pelopidas et Marcellus*: ". . . , si modo tuam humanitatem exoravero. . . ."

[21] See Eckhard Kessler, *Das Problem des frühen Humanismus: seine philosophische Bedeutung bei Coluccio Salutati*. Humanistische Bibliothek. Abhandlungen und Texte. Reihe I: Abhandlungen Bd. 1 (München: Fink, 1968).

[22] No. 21, the preface to the *Dion*: "Qua quidem in re cum pro mea parvitate ingens magnificum ac principale munus intueor, . . . nam ut verae officium liberalitatis absolveres, in eum tuum collocare beneficium maluisti, unde parem tibi referri posse gratiam ne minima quidem tibi spes esset, . . ."

of the *Pelopidas and Marcellus* was again a poor token of his gratitude.[23] The *gratia-munificentia* relation coexists with other types of relations: elsewhere Guarino uses emotional terms like *caritas, amor* and *benevolentia* about his relationship to both Barbaro and Leonello, and the feelings are seemingly reciprocal.

On the level of contents, it also seems to have been important to establish links between the text and its recipient. Guarino often praises the erudition and prudence of his dedicatees. Erudition was not a purpose in itself, though one sometimes has that impression. It was rather the means to obtain prudence and experience, qualities which were essential for anyone engaging in public affairs,[24] and it furthered human qualities like leniency and clemency. Also Plutarch is erudite, very much so, and Guarino several times emphasizes the *prudentia* of Plutarch's heroes, thereby establishing the connection with the dedicatees by means of analogy. The wise, old statesman, general and admiral, Carlo Zeno, is presented with his Athenian counterpart, Themistocles, the *prudentia* of the one mirroring that of the other;[25] and when Barbaro began his term as *podestà* in Vincenza, he could take advice from Phocion, who was known as a prudent counsellor both in war and peace.[26]

Only once do we have a formal exposition of the utility of history, and this is in the preface to the *Pelopidas and Marcellus*; elsewhere the translations, the study of literature and the whole complex of *studia humanitatis* are described in words that recall Cicero's praises of the effect of rhetoric. Guarino often hopes that his translation will please people, using the word

---

[23] No. 706: "Cogitanti mihi, Leonelle princeps, et priora illa et recentiora haec tuae in me magnificentiae merita, quibus ut quasi tuae caritatis et benivolentiae cumulum adiungeres . . . , est enim grave, homini verecundo praesertim, gratiam referre non posse, . . ."

[24] No. 706, the preface to the *Pelopidas and Marcellus*: "Praeterea qui privati sunt vel ipsa antiquitatis peritia, quae non parva prudentiae pars est, ad magistratus et imperia digniores evandunt."

[25] No. 66: "In hoc ipsum vitae genus [*i.e., a scholar's life*] te pro summa prudentia tua non sine probabili causa venisse certo scio, cum post illustrissimas res tuas terra marique gestas, quibus et pacis et belli magister optimus evaseras, . . ." about Carlo Zeno, and "In ea vero lectitanda mirifice te oblectaturum esse confido, cum aliis de causis tum quia summae prudentiae virum, maximae auctoritatis civem, eximiae integritatis praetorem, incredibilis prudentiae consiliarium, rei denique militaris instructissimum imperatorem aspicies,"about Themistocles.

[26] No. 651: "Tibi itaque Phocionem adduco, fidelem profecto et sapientem pacis atque belli consiliarium, in quibus quidem artibus adeo, uti nosti, mirifice excelluit, ut nescias fortissimine ducis et strenui militis an prudentissimi senatoris et boni oratoris laudem magis illi tribuas."

delectare, which is also used of *studia humanitatis*. In the preface to the *Themistocles*, where he writes about the *studia humanitatis* in general and specifically about the study of history, he says the mind should enjoy the reading of literature, that such studies are a pleasure, and as an example he mentions Alexander and Caesar who were so attracted by the sweet pleasure of reading that they used literature as a remedy against excessive sorrow or lust.[27] He quotes Chrysoloras, who had said that the reader should be allured by the enjoyability of the subject material.[28] The words used are *iocunditas, amoenitas, voluptas, allicere*, and they occur repeatedly when Guarino writes about literature. This quality of literature is closely connected to diction and style, as is evident from the letter to Roberto de'Rossi. His merits as a translator are that Aristotle, who before was coarse and ungraceful in Latin, now appeared in a sweet, ornate and elegant style.[29]

The humanists usually stressed that the historical writers furnished their readers with examples to follow or examples to avoid, but although Guarino no doubt agreed with that, he rarely states the point explicitly. One passage where he does so is in the preface to the *Lysander and Sulla*. Here Sulla is presented as a rare specimen of cruelty; in translating his *Vita*, Guarino is imitating the ancient Spartans, who induced young boys to sobriety by showing them the hideous sight of a drunken slave.[30] One suspects that these rather harsh words are part of the ideological war waged between the adherents of monarchical and republican government in these years. Caesar, the great monarchical symbol, had been assailed by the writers of republican Florence. In return Guarino, educator of the prince

[27] No. 66: "Quod cum plurimorum tum vero Macedoniae regis Alexandri et Augusti Caesaris eruditissimorum hominum testimonio probari licet, quos tanta lectionis amoenitate allectos fuisse constat, ut omnem et voluptatis et molestiae magnitudinem quottidiana illius admixtione condirent lenirentque."

[28] No. 66: "..., quae [*i.e., the events of the life of Themistocles*], ut a summo vero gravissimoque philosopho Manuele Chrysolora praeceptore meo accepi, non sine quadam animi delectatione lectorem alliciunt tenent afficiunt."

[29] No. 6: "is [*Aristoteles*] enim antea sentus incultus horrens per Latinorum gymnasia versabatur, ut qui propriis exutus indumentis nullo dictionis lepore aut amoenitate lectorem alliceret; nunc autem tua cultus eloquentia, tuis florens ornamentis, tua gratissimus suavitate visetur legetur amabitur."

[30] No. 667: "Verum enimvero crudeles ac probos illorum mores perinde ac speculum idcirco tibi propono, ut bona cum inspectes, ad ea te conformes, vitia vero fugias et abomineris; fit enim ut in alienis personis turpitudinem acriore censura notemus et execremur. Quamobrem Spartanos cum servum in conviviis ebrium deprehenderent, eum accitis filiis demonstrare solitos accepimus, ut ebrietatis ineptias deformitatem spurcitiasque subtilius in mancipiis intuentes abhorrerent."

Leonello, presented Sulla in a way which would certainly enrage any Florentine patriot who hailed him as the republican founder of their city.

There is one last point I wish to discuss here, and that is the role of Manuel Chrysoloras in Guarino's prefaces. More often than with anyone else, Guarino attributes to him virtues like *munificentia* and *liberalitas*, which are princely virtues *par excellence*: to have brought back Greek literature to the Latins is to bring light where it was dark, to awake to new life the ancient splendors of Roman culture, and to enrich the whole of Italy; in short, it is an act of munificence which equals the *beneficia* of any *signore*, and Chrysoloras, accordingly, deserved great gratitude.[31] Guarino, in a way, continued the work of his teacher, and his lavish praises of Chrysoloras, though undoubtedly heartfelt, were meant also to reflect credit on his own work, making his *gratia*, the translations, markedly more significant.

Aarhus

[31] Cf. No. 6: "..., ex cuius [*Chrysolorae*] opera et liberalitate manavit quicquid graecarum hisce temporibus litterarum nostrates hausere"; the preface to the *Alexander and Caesar*: "qui profugas dudum ex Latio litteras grecas ex innata liberalitate reducens ad nostrates id in primis meditatus est, ut greca latinis imperciens tam precioso patrimonio et immortali beneficio uniuersam ditaret Italiam. 0 singularem munificencie claritatem, ..."; No. 667: "Quocirca ingentes utrique Chrysolorae grates habendae sunt laudesque cantandae, quorum beneficio...."

The Latin Correspondence of Jean de Pins Ms. 215 of the Municipal Library of Nîmes

JAN N. PENDERGRASS

In his *Panegyric of Saint Louis*, held at the University of Poitiers around 1509, and published in 1510,[1] Christopher Longolius makes a passionate appeal to the nationalist sentiment of his compatriots, and to the intellectual community as a whole, in an effort to ennoble the French nation both intellectually and morally, rendering its achievements equal, if not superior to those of the Italian peninsula. It is a period of awakening national pride, if not chauvinist rapture. After having extolled the illustrious accomplishments of his Gallic forefathers, disdainfully passing over what he considered to be times of barbarian decay, Longolius then goes on to enumerate the major humanist representatives of the new school of learning in late fifteenth- and early sixteenth-century France and in other regions outside of Italy. Among those cited, one finds names such as Guillaume Du Bellay, Germain de Brie, Guillaume Budé, Claude de Seyssel, Badius, Gaguin, Erasmus, Lefèvre d'Étaples, Clichtove, Bovelles, Symphorien Champier. Also cited among these founding champions of the early sixteenth-century French humanist movement is Jean de Pins, who, as Longolius maintains, is to be considered a skillful narrator.[2] In 1510, Jean de Pins was but at the beginning of a long career, and yet he had already acquired a privileged and lasting place in the famed "sodalitas" of new learning.

---

[1] *Christophori Longuolii Parisiensis oratio de laudibus divi Ludovici*, Paris, H. Estienne, 1510. On the date his speech was given, and for a resumé of its contents, see Th. Simar, *Christophe de Longueil, humaniste (1488–1522)*, Louvain, 1911 (Recueil de Travaux de l'Université de Louvain, fasc. 31), 14 ff.

[2] "narrabit . . . Pinus scite" (*Oratio*, f. Cii v). The entire passage is cited by Simar, *op. cit.*, 22–26.

Jean de Pins' initial renown (founded essentially on two minor publications he had made during his early years of study in Italy[3]) was soon to be surpassed, however, as he went on to become one of the most respected statesmen and clergy members of his time. He was an influential senator in two French Parliaments (Toulouse[4] and Milan), French ambassador to Venice (1516–1520) and to Rome (1520–1522), before his election as bishop of Rieux (1523), where he played an important rôle in ecclesiastical, political and cultural affairs until his death in 1537. Two useful biographies have been written about him. One, by Léonard Charron, appeared in 1748.[5] It is admittedly encomiastic in nature and contains general biographical information followed by an important selection of his political correspondence in French. Another genealogically oriented study by Gentil Cormary was published in 1933,[6] correcting some of the minor errors of his predecessor. Yet it is interesting to note that neither of these authors had ever been able to consult an important manuscript collection of Jean de Pins' Latin correspondence. They admit having learned of its existence, but were, despite their laudable efforts, unable to discover its location.[7] Beyond what could be learned through independent sources, such as dedications of scholarly works, the published correspondence of other humanists, de Pins' own scholarly publications or archival documents, they knew but little of his early years of formation (notably about his studies in Italy), and less still of the humanist circles that had formed around him, or to which he had adhered. His relations with Erasmus of

---

[3] Besides contributions to an edition of Codrus Urceus' *Orationes* (Bologna, 1502), de Pins published two other works during his years of study in Italy: a *Philippi Beroaldi Bononiensis vita* (Bologna, per Benedictum Hectoreum, 1505), containing a prefatory epistle addressed to Étienne Poncher, bishop of Paris, and a *Divae Catharinae Senensis vita*, published together with a reprint of *Vita Philippi Beroaldi* (Bologna, 1505), dedicated to Louis d'Amboise, bishop of Albi. Subsequent publications are his *Divi Rochi Narbonnensis vita* (Venice, 1516); an *Allobrogicae narrationis liber* (Venice, 1516), addressed to Guillaume and Antoine Du Prat, sons of chancellor Antoine Du Prat; and a now rare posthumous edition of his *De vita aulica*, Toulouse: ex typographia Iacobi Columbei [1540] (cf. Bibliotheca Bibliographica Aureliana, vol. 58, Baden-Baden, 1975, p. 77).

[4] See notice in Fleury Vindry, *Les Parlementaires français au XVIe siècle*, vol. 2, fasc. 2 (Paris, 1912), 186–87.

[5] L. Charron, *Mémoires pour servir à l'éloge historique de Jean de Pins, évêque de Rieux, célèbre par ses ambassades, avec un recueil de plusieurs de ses lettres au roi François I, à Madame Louise de Savoye, mère de sa Majesté, Régente du Royaume, et aux principaux ministres d'État* (Avignon: chez Charrier, 1748).

[6] Gentil Cormary, *Jean de Pins, évêque de Rieux (1470–1537)*, Albi-Castres, 1933.

[7] Charron, *op. cit.*, VIII–IX, 88–89, 98–99; Cormary, *op. cit.*, 121–22.

Rotterdam, with François Rabelais and Christopher Longolius have since been studied in some depth; yet little has been said of his numerous other connections with prominent educators, statesmen, clergymen or military leaders versed in the urbanities of humanist learning. A modern critical edition of de Pins' personal correspondence would therefore represent a significant contribution to the study of the early years of humanism in Southern France. New information concerning known public figures would come to light; more obscure individuals would be called to the attention of specialists and provide new avenues for research.

Yet the question remains as to where this mysterious collection of letters now is. Germain de La Faille, a seventeenth-century historian of Toulouse, is said to have possessed it at one time.[8] The last person known to have consulted it was the highly industrious literary historian of Nîmes, Francis Graverol. In March of 1691, he had obtained permission from the owners of the manuscript to transcribe a rather large portion of the letters. That is the last time any qualified mention has been made of the original, which seems to have disappeared towards the end of the seventeenth century.

Due to the unfortunate loss of the original, the Graverol manuscript, now preserved in the Municipal Library of Nîmes (Ms. 215), has become all the more important, as it is the only remaining collection of de Pins' Latin correspondence known to exist. The Graverol transcription, had it come to his attention, would certainly have provided valuable insight to L. Thuasne, who has linked our author to Rabelais and Erasmus.[9] The correspondence has only come into use since its initial discovery by John L. Gerig, who in turn passed his knowledge on to Preserved Smith[10] and P. S. Allen.[11] Subsequent studies by count Jean de Pins,[12] a descendant of

[8] Marquis de Pins (along with several other contemporaries) writes: "La Faille, en son traité des Nobles de Toulouse, dit avoir ce recueil en main." BM Nîmes, Ms. 215.

[9] Louis Thuasne, "Rabelaesiana: Lettre de Rabelais à Erasme," in *Revue des Bibliothèques* 15 (1905), 203–8.

[10] See Preserved Smith, *Erasmus, a Study of His Life, Ideals and Places in History*, (New York: Harper & Bros., 1923), 447.

[11] See *Opus epistolarum Des. Erasmi Roterodami*, ed. P. S. Allen and H. W. Garrod, (Oxford, 1906–1958), vol. 3, 510–11 n. 36. M. Dégert, however, speaks in some detail on the contents of the Graverol Cartulary several years earlier in a *mémoire* published in the *Bulletin de la Société Archéologique du Midi de la France*, nouv. série no. 37 (1907), 81–95.

[12] Jean de Pins, "Autour des guerres d'Italie," in *Revue d'Histoire Diplomatique*, 61 (1947): 215–46 and 62 (1948): 88–113; and "Jean de Pins et Longueil," in *Bibliothèque d'Humanisme et Renaissance* 12 (1950): 183–89. See also contributions by chanoine Jean

our humanist, have also contributed much to the study at hand. However, no in-depth study of the surviving collection has ever been conducted, no list of de Pins' literary correspondents has been presented.

It is not surprising that the Graverol manuscript has long gone unnoticed. The General Catalogue of the Municipal Library of Nîmes mentions only our author's name, the date Graverol had completed his transcription (4° Id. Mart. 1691) and the dimensions of the volume. No mention appears of the dates or the persons to whom the letters were sent.[13] It is for this reason, most probably, that the collection has gone unnoticed in the latest volume of Kristeller's *Iter Italicum*,[14] a painstaking survey of humanist manuscripts in and outside of Italy. As we await the final transcription and edition of the Graverol codex, it seems appropriate that researchers be reminded of the existence of this Latin correspondence, and more important, that they gain a more detailed knowledge of its contents.

Although Graverol's copy is an incomplete transcription of the original manuscript, he was nonetheless a meticulous scholar. In miscellaneous notes at the end of his transcription, Graverol provides a brief description of the original collection which is now missing. As he states there, the original collection had belonged to the inheritors of a certain Bernard Medon, identified as a former councillor of the seneschal of Toulouse. It had contained 118 letters of Jean de Pins' correspondence, of which Graverol claims to have copied only the first 53 in their entirety.[15] This statement is reinforced in a separate marginal note at the end of lettre no. 53, where he writes: *J'ay fini la 53e lettre* (I have finished the 53rd let-

---

Contrasty, "Jean de Pins, évêque de Rieux (1522–1537)," in *Revue Historique de Toulouse* 23, no. 73, (1936): 137–47, and by the same author, *Histoire de la cité de Rieux-Volvestre et de ses évêques*, (Toulouse, 1936).

[13] *Catalogue général des manuscrits des bibliothèques publiques des départements*, vol. 8 (ancienne série: Toulouse-Nîmes), (Paris, Imprimerie Nationale, 1885), 634: "Ms. 215: Recueil no. 25, venant de Graverol—Copies de bulles ... Discours de Sadolet ... Lettres écrites et reçues par Jean *Pinus* (de Pins).... Papier; hauteur 280 millimètres. Le manuscrit est d'une seule main, daté à la fin ainsi que suit: *Ex bibliotheca Francisci Graverol Nemausensis, 4° idus martii 1691*."

[14] P. O. Kristeller, *Iter Italicum, accedunt alia itinera*. A finding list of uncatalogued or incompletely catalogued humanist manuscripts of the Renaissance, vol. 3 (London–Leiden, 1983).

[15] "Jay copié ce dessus d'un manuscrit appartenant aux héritiers de Monsieur Bernard Medon, vivant conseiller au senechal de Toulouse, lequel manuscrit contient en long 118 lettres de Pinus, desquelles je n'en ay extrait que 53 entières" (Ms. 215 fol. 170r). On B. Medon, see *Biographie toulousaine*, vol. 2, (Paris, 1823), 42.

ter).[16] He then continues his transcription of letters, with numerous abridgements, over some 15 pages, arriving at a total of 69 letters attributed to Jean de Pins. In reality, only 68 of those letters can be attributed to our humanist, as one of them (no. 17) was written by a brother—probably Jean de Montbrun—and then forwarded to senator Jean Séguier of Toulouse, as evidence that he and his family were diligently protecting their friend's property from the ravages of unruly mercenary troups. Yet contrary to what we might be led to believe through Graverol's previous statement and his marginal note at the end of letter no. 53, several of the remaining 16 letters are not necessarily abridged. Letter no. 60, addressed to pope Clement VII,[17] does not appear to have been truncated, probably because it was sufficiently interesting, or sufficiently brief, that Graverol was willing to copy it from beginning to end. Four other letters show no sign of abridgement: no. 61, an undated letter to Erasmus, no. 62 addressed to Pierre Gylli, prior of Durenque, no. 64 to the highly respected first president of the Parliament of Toulouse, Jacques Minut, and no. 68 to the Supreme Pontiff Adrian VI.[18] It therefore appears that the first section of the manuscript contains, in fact, not 53 complete letters, but 58. Clearly eleven of the first 69 letters were abridged by Graverol.[19] We can assume that he had grown tired of this tedious labor, or else had simply lacked the time necessary for completing his work with all due attention.

If we take a closer look at one formal aspect of these letters, it becomes clear that Jean de Pins is at least in one sense a true Ciceronian: chronological considerations are of little importance in the collection. A great majority of the 69 letters or extracts of letters copied by Graverol are incompletely dated, or contain no date at all. Forty-five are without any

---

[16] *Ibid.*, fol. 164r (p. 47 of the Pinus collection).

[17] Although the name of this pope is not indicated in the address, and no date appears in the letter, comte J. de Pins has tentatively placed this papal missive in 1525, during the papacy of Clement VII. See *Revue d'Histoire Diplomatique* 62 (1948): 111–13. The bishop of Rieux is considered to have contributed to the ratification of the Truce of Toledo, of August 11, 1525.

[18] Although undated, this letter "Ad Pontificem Maximum" contains what may be interpreted as references to de Pins' future legation to the Conference of Verona (winter of 1519–1520). We can therefore ascribe it to the months preceding November 1519, during the papacy of Adrian VII.

[19] Those letters are nos. 54, 55, 56, 57, 58, 59, 63, 65, 66, 67, 69. At the end of no. 63, Graverol notes a very brief excerpt from yet another letter not contained in the manuscript: ". . .huic cruentae et sanguinariae belluae, sub cuius impotenti dominatu et imperio vivimus. . . ." The transcriber does not mention the name of the addressee or the date this brief excerpt was written.

indication as to the date or geographical origin, thirteen do not indicate the year, only eleven furnish both place and date. This unfortunate circumstance will undoubtedly make the chronological classification of the letters a somewhat difficult task, but not impossible. References to known historical events or to public figures will in many cases permit letters to be dated with relative precision.

The earliest dated letter (no. 3) was written from Vienne in Southern France on August 18, 1509. As the author confesses, he is troubled that an unnamed friend has experienced difficulties with a brother, and urges him to make peace. The remaining ten dated letters originate all from Toulouse, and range from Sept. 1, 1512 to January 29, 1515. Many of the undated letters appear to have been written approximately during the same period. Others, however, must be placed during his years as an ambassador under Francis I (1516–1522) or shortly thereafter as bishop of Rieux (1523 or later). Most of his correspondence from the later years of his existence in Rieux and Toulouse, if we can assume that it was contained in the original manuscript, is unfortunately missing in the copy Graverol had made. Only a few of the letters can be situated, on grounds of internal evidence, in the early 1530's. Such letters are nos. 61, 62 and 65 addressed to Erasmus and to Pierre Gylli, where it is a question of loaning out a Greek manuscript copy of Josephus' *Jewish History* belonging to de Pins' personal library. The same is true of letter no. 64, where de Pins intercedes in favor of young Étienne Dolet, who had been imprisonned for violence and "contempt of senate" in 1534. According to our bishop's *plaidoyer*, Dolet is a young man of excellent and rare qualities, who excels not in one, but in various poetic meters—elegiac, lyric, iambic and hendecasyllabic, attaining in each the perfection of Ovid, Tibullus and Horace. He further notes that what had begun as mere literary competition between Dolet and a fellow student of Aquitaine, had later degenerated into armed conflict, but argues that in the end no harm had been done.[20] In a period of history where student violence often led to capital

[20] Quodque magis mihi mirum videri solet, sic carmine excellit, ut nihil supra desideres, idque etiam vario metrorum genere, quod solet esse difficilius. Nam si elegiacum tentet, Ovidium aut Tibullum putes; si lyricum, iambicum aut hendecasyllabum scribat, Horatium tibi plane effingi censeas... Coeperant nuper inter hunc et Pinmachum quendam Aquitanum contentiones quaedam litterariae intercedere, quibus ego primum gaudere coeperam, quod ita utriusque et ali ingenium et augeri facundiam putabam, idque iam olim clarissimos viros etiam in senatu exercuisse cognoveram, Ciceronem et Crispum Sallustium, Messalam et Polleonem Asinium, et paulo supra nostram aetatem Vallam et Poggium, Gazam et Trapezuntium, Galeotum

punishment, Dolet was indeed fortunate to have found in Jean de Pins such an eloquent patron. Through the bishop's influence and the good will of first president Jacques Minut, to whom the letter is addressed, Dolet spent only a brief time in the prisons of Toulouse.

The affairs of Church and State intermingle as freely in Jean de Pins' correspondence as they do in his "curriculum vitae." There are a good number of letters addressed to ecclesiastical dignitaries such as the bishops of Grasse and of Toulon, Denis Briçonnet (no. 26) and Agostino Grimaldi (nos. 1, 12), to the bishops of Paris (no. 42,) and Angoulême (no. 49), to the two popes already mentioned, Adrian VI and Clement VII, or to the often neglected Barthélemy de Castellane (nos. 4, 7, 8, 28, 35, 37, 63), whose name appears regularly in the epistolary collections of Erasmus, Jacopo Sadoleto, Alciato, Bembo..., and in the Provençal humanist circle of Denys Faucher, Jean Visagier and Antoine Arlier.[21] Other letters are addressed to Jean de Pins' professional colleagues and friends at the Parliament of Toulouse, to senators Jean de Langeac (nos. 18, 20, 36), Étienne Sacaley (no. 6), Jean Séguier (nos. 13, 14, 15, 16) and first president Pierre de Saint-André (no. 32), whose son reaps lavish praise as a budding poet. In his letter to Saint-André, Jean de Pins depicts a typical scene at the palace chapel, where he was one day seated next to his senatorial colleague Jean Séguier. As the devotional service was progressing, Séguier suddenly leans over to his friend, whispering humorously into his ear:

> I have something, he says, that you will desire above all else, yet for which you will find it necessary to sacrifice your entire wealth should you wish to purchase it.

De Pins responds in a similar vein:

> I shall even take out a loan and pay interest if my wealth will not suffice, provided that this mysterious treasure of yours is truly worth that much to me. However, in order to avoid your tormenting me

---

et Merulam, quorum ingenii monumenta etiam ad posteros maximum fructum attulerunt, atque ididem [*sic*] ego de his futurum speraveram. Verum, ut video, longe in contrarium vertit. Nam illi et iuvenes adhuc et pravis factiosisque partium studiis incensi facile a litteris ad arma prosilierunt, sed in quibus nihil adhuc (ut audio) detrimenti acceptum est... (fols. 166v–167r, p. 52–53). This "Pinmachus quidam" is obviously the same individual as described by R. C. Christie (*Étienne Dolet, a Martyr of the Renaissance*, ed. [1899], 101) as the Gascon Pierre Pinache. Cf. the slightly different version of this same letter in Dolet's *Orationes*, pp. 149–51.

[21] On Barthélemy de Castellane's relations to Arlier and his circle of Provençal humanists, see the notice in *Correspondance d'Antoine Arlier*, Ep. 48 n.1 and *passim*.

> any longer with such annoying delay, I shall let you be sole judge of both that very costly merchandise of yours and my price for it.

At that point, Séguier, smiling radiantly, pulls forth an eloquent threnody, written by the first president's son, Martin de Saint-André, on the deceased Anne of Brittany.[22] The remainder of de Pins' letter is spent in exaltation of the author's dubious merits. Apparently, the senators of Toulouse, despite their tremendous workload, could always find occasions for discussing literary novelties and for entertaining dialogue, albeit, at times, to the detriment of their spiritual enlightenment.

Still other letters are sent to representatives of the Parliament of Paris, to first president Antoine Du Prat (no. 9), who later becomes chancellor of France and promptly receives a congratulatory epistle from de Pins (no. 59), or to the Parisian senators and court magistrates, Gilles Anthonis (nos. 23, 27, 34), Francis Disque (no. 31) and Francis Deloynes (no. 53). Letter no. 23 to Gilles Anthonis is particularly interesting, as it conveys precious biographical information on de Pins' early years as a student in Italy. From the letter, it is clear that the author had not contacted his friend for quite some time, and that he deems it necessary to recount what had become of himself over the years. His *récit* begins around 1500, an extremely difficult period, as our humanist states, infested with wars and brigandage. Anthonis had just left for Paris, de Pins for Italy:

> Shortly after you had gone to Paris [he writes]..., I left for Italy. There, I spent several days in Venice, hearing lectures by Marco–Antonio Sabellico, and then in Padua, where I heard Giovanni Calfurnio, both celebrated for their knowledge of Greek and Latin. Forced to leave because of troubled times and the threat of a Venetian war..., I went to Ferrara in order to hear the lectures of Battista Guarini, son of the great [Guarino] Guarini, and did that

---

[22] Assederat hodie mihi vicinus in sacello palatii, dum res divina peragitur, Seguerius noster senator, egregius homo—ut nosti—tui tuorumque omnium amantissimus. Is, ut saepe solet, facete nobis in aurem insusurrans: "Habeo," inquit, "quod summopere cupias, sed in quo tuum omne tibi patrimonium profundi oporteat, si comparare velis." Ad quem ego: "Versuram etiam faciam et aliunde faenerabor, si non id tibi satis videatur, et dummodo tuum istud quicquid est tanti etiam apud nos aestimetur. Verum ne nos diutius tam molesta cunctatione distorqueas, et tuae huius carissimae mercis et mei quoque pretii, ut libet, te unum solum arbitrum facimus." Tum ille subridens protulit e sinu funebres elegos, quos de divae Annae reginae obitu ut immaturo sic omnium quoque qui saeculo nostro unquam auditi sunt maestissimo et accerbissimo dominus filius tuus dominus Martinus Carcassonensis episcopus edidit (Ep. 32 fol. 155r, p. 29). Anne of Brittany died January 9, 1514.

> assiduously for as long as I had the freedom to do so. Shortly thereafter, however, when civil strife and domestic sedition had begun to trouble the public peace, I was called away to Bologna by a letter from my younger brother Antoine de Pins, who despite his youth was in the service of M. d'Aubigny, commander of the Neapolitan army. Upon my arrival in Bologna, learning of Filippo Beroaldi's growing fame, captivated by the man's amiable character and moved by his incredibly vast science, I abandoned my plans of returning to Padua (for tensions between France and Venice had by then calmed, and peaceful conditions appeared to prevail). And so it is that I remained with him [Beroaldi], frequenting his school assiduously for two years. For the remaining five years (which is approximately how long I stayed there), I returned to those previous studies I had once so propitiously begun here in your presence ...[23]

The letter ends with the author's repeated apology for having neglected to write for such a long time.

Looking elswhere, we can see that de Pins also maintains steady relations with the humanist circles of Albi, centered around bishop Louis d'Amboise, and of Rodez, under the patronage of Georges d'Armagnac. Letters of mutual estime are exchanged with Germain de Brie (nos. 44, 45, 52), whose poetry delights the refined palate of our humanist, and with Jacques Robertet (nos. 19, 21), who must patiently endure chiding praise of his jealously concealed talents. Pierre Gylli (no. 62), to whom de Pins had opened his library,[24] is asked to relinquish the Greek manu-

---

[23] Paulo post enim quam tu hinc Parisios abiisti..., in Italiam me contuli, ibique primum Venetiis plusculos dies Marcum Antonium Sabellicum, deinde Patavii Calphurnium Brixiensem, viros tum Graecis cum Latinis litteris clarissimos, audivi, pulsusque inde temporum iniuria et iam instantis Veneti belli metu..., Ferrariam petii, ut ibi Baptistam Garinum magni Garini filium audirem, quod quidem feci diligenter quamdiu id mihi per otium licuit. Paulo mox vero inde quoque, ubi iam civili bello et seditione domestica publicum otium turbari coeperat, Bononiam sum litteris evocatus ab Antonio Pino fratre minore natu, qui tum admodum iuvenis Aubinio duce Neapolitanam militiam sequebatur. Quo simulac appuli, audita Philippi Beroaldi Bononiensis fama, quae tum passim et fere ubique gentium miro successu vulgari coeperat, captusque amoenissimo hominis ingenio et incredibili fere omnium rerum eruditione ductus mutavi repente consilium, quod iam mecum de repetendo Patavio ceperam; nam et illic quoque rebus inter Gallos Venetosque compositis quieta omnia ac tranquilla futura videbantur. Mansi itaque apud illum et in eius schola frequens biennio. Quinquennium reliquum (tot enim fere annos Bononiae egimus) ad pristina studia me retuli, quibus hic te praesente nescio quam bonis avibus initiari coeperam (Ep. 23: fol. 151r, p. 21).

[24] Besides having obtained a copy of Josephus' *Jewish History* from de Pins'

script copy of Josephus he had borrowed, so that it can be forwarded to Erasmus. With Alain de Varènes (no. 33), our humanist is willing to exchange books. The list goes on with a number of other interesting "personae" of early sixteenth-century France, ambassadors such as Giovanni Giacobono (no. 69), financial administrators such as Jean Grolier (no. 54), jurisconsultants,[25] educators,[26] theologians[27] and their likes.

This first section covers 54 pages in Graverol's manuscript, and is followed by a collection of twelve more letters, mostly excerpts, written to Jean de Pins by humanist friends. All but two of the letters are dated, and those dates range from 1518 to 1535. Of the two undated letters, one is a congratulatory epistle from Agostino Grimaldi (no. II.11) and must have been composed shortly after de Pins' nomination as ambassador to Rome in 1520. The second, from Celio Calcagnini (no. II.10), can be dated perhaps in the latter part of 1519 (or early 1520), as it contains allusions to the French ambassador's official request of repatriation, some time prior to his delegation to Rome. Calcagnini councils his friend to persevere in his rôle as a diplomatic emissary, not to return home so quickly:

> First of all [advises Calcagnini], so that you do not fruitlessly consider returning home, remember that you must assume first one, then another mission, of which the first will be extremely brief and hardly disagreeable, yet the second of which will be quite long and exceedingly difficult, imposing burdens on you and great dangers..., yet in the end I trust you will return home safe and sound, and not without greatly increasing your personal wealth, for through the favor of a benevolent patron, you will surely attain pontifical rank, spending your old days in blissful leisure.[28]

collection, Gylli had also borrowed, in 1532, a Greek manuscript copy of Saint Theodoretus, on which he based his translation and commentary of *Divi Theodoreti episcopi Cyrenensis explanationes in duodecim prophetas* (Lyon, 1533).

[25] For example, letter no. 46, to Jean de Montaigne, professor of law; no. 38 to Claude de Seyssel (Ysselius).

[26] Cf. letter to Jean Le Maure (no. 67).

[27] Letter no. 47 to Guillaume Castel, of Tours; no. 24 to John Major.

[28] Primo ne quid frustra de reditu in patriam cogites, scito unam atque alteram tibi in Italia legationem obeundam esse, ac priorem quidem illam perbrevem neque multum molestam, alteram verum et longam satis et apprime difficilem, et in qua labores et ingentia pericula tibi subeunda erunt..., sed tandem domum salvus sospesque redibis nec sine magno rei tuae familiaris compendio, nam viri cuiusdam optimatis praesidio, favore ac benevolentia pontificalem dignitatem assequeris, in qua tu posthac foelici otio consenesces (Ms. 215: fol. 169 v, p. 58). According to the Venetian ambassador in Paris, de Pins had officially requested his replacement as early

A further excerpt of the same letter informs us that de Pins had once been, in Paris, a student of Girolamo Balbi, with whom Calcagnini had become acquainted during his recent sojourn in Hungary.[29] We can therefore assume that our humanist had studied under Balbi, in or shortly prior to 1493, at approximately the same time he had introduced himself to the Parisian humanist Robert Gaguin.[30] There are further letters or excerpts from Girolamo Fondulo (nos. II.1, II.2), Erasmus (nos. II.3, II.4, II.5, II.6, II.12), Germain de Brie (no. II.4), cardinal Lorenzo Pucci (no. II.7), archbishop Federico Fregoso (no. II.8) and Agostino Giustiniani (no. II.9), bishop of Nebbio and famed professor of Hebrew sojourning in Paris from 1517 to 1522.[31]

These final letters are then followed by Graverol's remarks, as has been stated, and a list of "incipits" from various speeches, official translations and miscellaneous writings that Graverol had not found the leisure to transcribe from the original Codex. The final piece of the collection is a seventeeth-century letter from Marquis de Pins to the Grand Vicar of Pamiers, listing what little knowledge he had been able to accumulate concerning his illustrious ancestor. He, too, indicates knowledge of the original manuscript, yet does not appear to have been able to locate it.[32]

University of Georgia

---

as April 15, 1517 (cf. *Revue d'Histoire Diplomatique* 61, p. 245). His request is later mentioned in a letter to chancellor Antoine Du Prat (no. 59) dated from Venice, March 13 (probably 1519). Cf. Marino Sanuto, *I diarii*, edd. N. Barozzi *et al.* (Venice, 1879–1903), xxvii, col. 629, 630.

[29] tum verum ob praeclaram hominis illius memoriam, qui ut te discipulum olim dum in Gallia Parisiis ageret, sic me posthac in Pannonia aequalem et amicum praecipuum habet (Marginal note, Ms. 215: fol. 169v). Calcagnini had accompanied Ippolito d'Este to Hungary in 1517, remaining there probably until late 1518.

[30] Cf. L. Thuasne, *Gaguini epistole,* (Paris, 1903), vol. 3, p. 374, n.1.

[31] On Giustiniani's stay in Paris, see Abel Lefranc, *Histoire du Collège de France,* (Paris, 1893), 45 ff. and L. Delaruelle, "Le Séjour d'Augustin Giustiniani à Paris (1518–1522)," *Revue du Seizième Siècle* 12 (1925): 322–37.

[32] A portion of this letter has been paraphrased in the preface to Charron's work, *op. cit.*, pp. viii–ix.

Humanist Poetry and Its Classical Models: A Collection from the Court of Emperor Maximilian I

JOHANN RAMMINGER

The *Complurium eruditorum uatum carmina ad magnificum uirum D. Blasium Hoelcelium sacri Caesaris Maximiliani consiliarium Moecenatem eorum precipuum* (hereafter CBH) were edited in late summer or early fall of the year 1518 in Augsburg during the Imperial Diet by Petrus Bonomus, then Bishop of Trieste, formerly secretary of the emperor.[1] Our anthology comprises letters and poems by politicians and intellectuals connected with the court of Maximilian I; besides Bonomus and Hölzel they include, e.g., Sbruglio, Muzio, Peutinger, Celtis, Stabius, Bartholini and Cuspinian. The earliest of the pieces go back to the 1490s, the latest were composed for the publication.[2] Most of the contributors are the

---

[1] I used the copy in the Bayerische Staatsbibliothek, Munich. For the bibliographical data see Stephan Füssel, *Riccardus Bartholinus Perusinus: Humanistische Panegyrik am Hofe Kaiser Maximilians I.*, Saecula Spiritalia, 16 (Baden-Baden, 1987), 229.

[2] Composed for the edition were, e.g., Sbrulius' poem *Ad lectorem* (a1^v), the prose letters of Bonomus to Hölzel (a2^r), Peutinger to Bonomus (a2^r), and Ricius *ad lectorem* (a3^r), Mucius' *carmen Isagogicon* (a4^r–a4^v) and Spiegel's poem in praise of the book (i1^v–i2^r). For the others there is little evidence. Bonomus's remarks in the introductory letter suggest that the original collection was quite old, but had been augmented by him with some pieces of later dates; this is borne out by the evidence of the poems themselves. One poem mentions the death of Frederick III (in 1493, the poem by M. Transsilvanus, c3^v–d1^r). In 1518, Celtis had been dead for ten years, Bebel died in the spring or summer of 1518 (see Wilfried Barner *et al.*, eds., Introduction to: *Heinrich Bebel, Comoedia de optimo studio iuvenum; Über die beste Art des Studiums für junge Leute* [Stuttgart, 1982], p. 168 and n. 176). If the end of Bartholini's ode *Sed mecum . . . fran-*

ones we usually find involved in the literary projects of the Imperial court.[3] No fewer than eight of the twenty-one contributors had by the time of the publication been crowned poet laureate by Maximilian.[4]

At first glance there seems to be little which distinguishes our collection from countless similar products of the early sixteenth century. Extravagant praise, formulated in the most commonplace phrases, can be found over and over again in the poetry of that age, and hardly any of the poems published is outstanding as a poetical achievement. The CBH represent the average quality of this type of poetical production at Maximilian's court. Nevertheless our collection occupies a special place in the history of German humanist literature. As it was printed only a few months before Maximilian's death, it represents a last synthesis of the literary aspirations of the Imperial court, especially since Luther's theses had been published the year before and soon were to change the German political and literary scene entirely.

---

cicus || *Vates plectra feret* (b2^{v}, vv. 42 f.) alludes to Celtis (see n. 26 below), it, too, would predate Celtis' death in 1508 and presumably belong to the years 1504–1506, when Bartolini was in Germany (for biographical details see Füssel, pp. 36–37). Gadius' marriage poem (e1^{r}–e3^{r}) may be dated to 1511, Celtis' *Carnorum pręses quod factus ... es* (d4^{r}–d4^{v}) and other poems can be referred to the time of Hölzel's appointment in Carinthia. Further poems dated by Jan-Dirk Müller, *Gedechtnus: Literatur und Hofgesellschaft um Maximilian I,* Forschungen zur Geschichte der älteren deutschen Literatur, 2 (München, 1982) 261, 303 n. 67, and 373 n. 47.

[3] We catch a glimpse of their daily life in a letter by I. Spiegel to Erasmus of 31 Aug. 1518, written in Augsburg (Allen, no. 863), in which he writes about an oration delivered by Erasmus Vitellius at the diet on Aug. 22: *Aderant enim viri non pauci, tum exquisite docti tum in iudicando naris emunctissime, Antistes Tergestinus* [=Bonomus], *Peutingerus, Huttenus, Bartholinus, Spalatinus, et Stabius ille in nullo doctrine genere non versatus* ... An earlier production similar to ours, but on a smaller scale, had been the *Episodia sodalitatis Danubianae ad Conradum Celten, dum a Norico gymnasio ad Viennam Pannoniae concesserat,* 18 short poems printed in Vienna around 1497; among the contibutors we find Cuspinianus, Stabius, Ulsenius, and the *duo Bonomi.* The poems are published in Kurt Adel, ed., *Conradi Celtis quae Vindobonae prelo subicienda curavit opuscula* (Leipzig, 1966), 6–11.

[4] Celtis (1487), Cuspinianus (1493), Bebel (1501), Stabius (1502/3 by Celtis), Sibutus (1505), Sbrulius (1513), Ursinus (1517), Bartholini (1517). A lacuna may be the absence of another poet laureate: Vadian (crowned in 1514). On May 1st, he was still in Vienna, in Sept. 1518 he had been in St. Gallen for some time (cf. his dedicatory letter to Konrad Grebel: Conradin Bonorand and Heinz Haffter, eds., *Die Dedikationsepisteln von und an Vadian,* Vadian-Studien, Untersuchungen und Texte. Herausgegeben vom Historischen Verein des Kantons St. Gallen, 11 [St. Gallen, 1983], p. 131 no. 30; Bernhard Milt, *Vadian als Arzt,* Vadian-Studien, 6 [St. Gallen, 1959], 42). The most probable reason for his absence is that he simply was not acquainted very well with Hölzel (cf. Conradin Bonorand, *Vadians Weg vom Humanismus zur Reformation und seine Vorträge über die Apostelgeschichte 1523,* Vadian-Studien, 7 [St. Gallen, 1962], 56.

The purpose of the publication is discussed in the introductory pieces. The poems will secure *immortalitas* for the patron and his generous deeds. They show Hölzel's *precipuam, et prope diuinam ... modestiam, probitatem, eruditionem, prudentiam, summamque benignitatem* (Ricius, a3r). They praise him as being a famous poet and are by famous poets themselves (Sbrulius, a1v, vv. 1–2). They will be frequently read by Hölzel's friends (*sub doctorum uirorum oculos crebro reuocanda, et mihi et cęteris amicis, futura communia*, Peutinger, a2v), reminding them of the love they felt for their patron (the poems are *amoris gratissima pignora*, Peutinger, a2v).

We lack several facts which would be important for an evaluation of Hölzel's position in respect to our collection. E. g., who organized the publication? Was it Bonomus? Or Hölzel? Was the latter involved in the publication in any way? Why had Bonomus this sudden urge to collect poems about Hölzel which had been neglected for years? Some of the poems which had been sent to Hölzel singly must have been known to him previously.[5] Had he collected any or all of them already?[6]

That our collection should be addressed to an Imperial counsellor, is

---

[5] In the Augsburg municipal library there is a single printed sheet with some epigrams by Celtis. The poet seems to have sent it to literary acquaintances; the preserved copy has a handwritten dedication: *Domino Blasio Patrono et Pręfecto r̄ario nostro semper memorando Conradus Celtis at amicis om̄ibus nostris Aulicis mittit.* We may imagine a similar use for some of our poems (cf. Ulsenius, f 3r: *Vlsenius pridem medicus nunc carmina mittit*; Gadius, f 1r: *A me missa brevis tibi venit Epistola*). The Celtis print has been published by Dieter Wuttke, "Eine unbekannter Einblattdruck mit Celtis-Epigrammen zu Ehren der Schultzheiligen von Österreich," *Arcadia* 3 (1968):195–200.

[6] In his letter to Hölzel Bonomus remarks: *Collectos igitur in unum corpus quosdam nostros illius temporis lusus / et quę deinde ab amicis de te scripta comparare potuimus* (a2r). That might suggest that the CBH are a more or less fortuitous collection of every poem the editor could lay his hands on. This, however, is not so. Some of the contributions were sollicited for the CBH (see n. 2 above). Furthermore, our collection is only a selection from a larger pool of poems to and about Hölzel, some of which were surely known to Bonomus. Of the two poems by Bonomus himself in the oldest part of the cod. Oenipont. 664 only one found its way into the CBH: the first part of the exchange between Bonomus and Hölzel about a girl friend of the latter (c1r, see n. 35 below; the ms. has been edited in part by Antonius Zingerle, *De carminibus latinis saeculi XV. et XVI. ineditis,* Beiträge zur Geschichte der Philologie, I. Theil [Innsbruck, 1880]). The version of this poem we find in the ms. (fol. 126v: Zingerle, no. 52) is obviously older. A second poem, pleading Hölzel's intervention with the emperor on Bonomus' behalf for a grant of money (fol. 135v), was omitted in the CBH (this poem was overlooked by Zingerle in his discussion of the contents of the ms.: p. XXXIII). More poems dedicated to Hölzel are found in the second part of the same ms. (see Zingerle, pp. XXXIV f.). Another poem is mentioned by Johanna Felmayer, "Blasius Hölzl: Eine markante Persönlichkeit am Hofe Kaiser Maximilians," *Tiroler Heimatblätter,* 37 (1962), 93–104, esp. p. 103 n. 1. See also n. 5 above.

not unusual.[7] Some of the poems simply praise Hölzel in general, but most of them are more specific. Their unifying theme is the hommage to Blasius Hölzel announced in the title: Hölzel is the *maecenas praecipuus* of the poets paying their tribute to him in this volume. This expression refers to a specific rôle: that of a sponsor of literature. The poems make it clear that the "Maecenas" theme is not a thoughtless application of a topos common in the laudatory poetry of the period; it would have been possible to praise a friend amply without it.[8] Rather, the term is used to specify his position in respect to the contributors to our volume.

The rôle of a "Maecenas" is defined in a contemporary document, Ulrich von Hutten's famous letter to Willibald Pirckheimer (written at the same Augsburg diet in 1518),[9] with the following words:

> quibus [principibus] nos magnis passim nominibus applaudimus, Maecenates nonnumquam vel Augustos etiam vocantes, non quod ullae hoc aliquando illorum virtutes mereantur . . . , verum spe quadam ad pristinae bonitatis emulationem excitandi. . . . aliquos iam enim coegimus pudore sui benefacere nobis.

Our poems have been discussed in relation to this text with good reason.[10] Hölzel's munificence towards the poets could not have been

---

[7] Karl Schottenloher, *Die Widmungsvorrede im Buch des 16. Jahrhunderts,* Reformationsgeschichtliche Studien und Texte, 76/77 (Münster, 1953), 187–88.

[8] As appears, for example, from the posthumous edition of poems for the court musician Paul Hofhaimer (there, Cardinal Lang is the *maecenas*): *Harmoniae poeticae Pauli Hofheimeri, uiri equestri dignitate insigni* (sic), *ac musici excellentis, quales sub ipsam mortem cecinit, qualesque ante hac nunquam uisae, tum uocibus humanis, tum etiam instrumentis accomodatissimae. Quibus praefixus est libellus plenus doctissimorum uirorum de eodum d. Paulo testimoniis. Vna cum selectis ad hanc rem locis e poetis accommodatioribus, seorsim tum decantandis, tum praelegendis* (Norimbergae apud Iohan. Petreium. Anno M. D. XXXIX). This collection is discussed in my article "Die Biographie Hofhaimers im Spiegel der Widmungsgedichte seiner Odensammlung von 1539 (RISM 1539–26)," paper presented at the symposium "Paul Hofhaimer—Zentren seines Lebens," 23–25 Jan., 1987, Radstadt, Austria; forthcoming in *Hofhaymeriana. Acts of the Symposium,* and in my forthcoming edition of the *Harmoniae poeticae.*

[9] Eduard Böcking, ed., *Vlrichi Hutteni equitis opera quae reperiri potuerunt omnia. Ulrichs von Hutten Schriften,* I (Leipzig, 1859), 200.

[10] Jan-Dirk Müller, "Deutsch-lateinische Panegyrik am Kaiserhof und die Entstehung eines neuen höfischen Publikums in Deutschland," in *Europäische Hofkultur im 16. und 17.Jahrhundert: Vorträge und Referate gehalten anläßlich des Kongresses des Wolfenbütteler Arbeitskreises für Renaissanceforschung und des Internationalen Arbeitskreises für Barockliteratur in der Herzog August Bibliothek Wolfenbüttel vom 4. bis 8. September 1979,* ed. August Buck, Georg Kauffmann, Blake Lee Spahr, Conrad Wiedemann, II. Wolfenbütteler Arbeiten zur Barockforschung, 9 (Hamburg, 1981), 133.

praised so highly if it had not been real to some extent. Some poems contain appeals to him for money, pieces of land, and other gifts.[11] One refers to an occasion when Hölzel entertained his "protégés" (if that is what they were) in Linz.[12] The poems frequently contain applications to be received into the group of Hölzel's *amici*.[13] Despite their topical character even these may in some cases have had a factual background, perhaps in connection with the Augsburg *sodalitas litteraria*, of which Hölzel was a member.[14] The poems define the relationship between Hölzel and his poets quite clearly: he gives presents or provides help in practical difficulties. In consequence the poets acclaim him in their works, recompensing him with fame and immortality as a result.[15]

There are considerations which raise some doubts about the picture painted by our poems. Even if most of the contributors were dependent in some way on court patronage, was Hölzel an adequate protector? He had made an impressive career in the Imperial financial administration.[16] But, as we see from the poems, there was one fundamental limitation to his munificence: in most cases he could not satisfy appeals on his own, but only on behalf of the emperor. The poets did not belong to his circle, but

---

[11] M. Transsilvanus: *equum et nummos* (g1^v), Celtis: *Si centum numeres mihi ducatos,* | | *Quos Cęsar mihi largiter dicauit* (c3^r, vv. 11–12), Bonomus: *Rex mihi iampridem Pucini tradere turrim* | | *Pollicitus / moneas is tibi saepe iubet* (b3^v), Gadius: *Aurea nam mihi das fulgentia serta smaragdo:* | | *Et sponsalitium munus habere iubes* (f1^r). Another example is provided by Celtis: *Non sat erat / tunicam te tribuisse mihi.* | | ... | | *Mox scythicas pelles et mollia vellera madros* | | *Donas* (e3^v).

[12] Celtis: *conuiuales epulas et pocula lęta* (c2^r, v. 5).

[13] This reception into the circle of Hölzel's 'friends' is the theme of a curious poem by Pinicianus, which purports to describe an edifice Hölzel is having built for himself (d2^v–d3^r); it is constructed of different kinds of wood (the German for wood is "Holz", a pun on "Hölzel") and is more precious than Solomon's temple or Fugger's house, *nam uariis surgit uatibus ista suis* ("because it consists of so many different poets"). But in the end Hölzel notices the absence of a particular tree, the pine (i.e., Pinicianus), which he immediately takes care to have added to the structure; *sic est cygneis. additus anser aquis* ("so the goose was added to the waters of the swans").

[14] Cf. Hermann Wiesflecker, *Kaiser Maximilian I: Das Reich, Österreich und Europa an der Wende zur Neuzeit*, III (München, 1977), 29. Heinrich Lutz, "Die Sodalitäten im oberdeutschen Humanismus des späten 15. und frühen 16. Jahrhunderts," in *Humanismus im Bildungswesen des 15. und 16. Jahrhunderts*, ed. Wolfgang Reinhard, Mitteilung der Kommission für Humanismusforschung, 12 (Weinheim, 1984), 25–60.

[15] Cf. Hieronymous Emser: *Post ego / quum dabitur coelum uidisse serenum.* | | *Te graviore canam carmine* (f4^r, vv. 39–40). A poem by Stabius ends with the following appeal: *Sis Stabio auxilio, ... quem pressat egestas* | | *Et uersu te ad sydera tollet* (e3^v, vv. 11–12).

[16] A short account of his life is given by Wiesflecker (see n. 14) V (1986), 261–65.

to the emperor's or other courts, as Stabius phrased it: *Qui mihi fautor pius et patronus: | | Caesaris qui conciliat fauorem* (dl^v, vv. 33–34).

We may pursue this line of thought a little further. The editor Bonomus himself had a social position at court which was clearly equal, if not superior to Hölzel's. He was even sent for when Maximilian was dying. Although he composed poetry, this was only a minor leisure occupation for him. He was not a professional man of letters like, e.g., Bebel or Celtis. He would not even have been interested in benefitting as a poet from Hölzel's patronage. As the introduction gives us to understand, he undertook the edition as an act of friendship for the sake of their old *contubernium*, when they had both been *amanuenses* at court (a2^r). In their friendship poetry was hardly more than a secondary issue.

Hutten's reference to the famous patrons of antiquity recommended a norm for the behaviour of a patron. But the ancient model had another, equally important function. It served as a literary standard for poetical descriptions of cases of patronage. As such it determined the literary profile of Hölzel's sponsorship to a large extent.

The term "maecenas" refers to the most prominent literary patron in antiquity,[17] who gave his name to this type of sponsor: C. Cilnius Maecenas, the patron of Horace, Vergil and other poets of Rome's Golden Age.[18] Our poems frequently invoke him and other sponsors known from classical literature. Individual poet-patron relationships varied as widely in antiquity as in the Renaissance, but the essential points of ancient literary patronage can be briefly outlined as follows.[19] The basic framework for personal services and obligations was the concept of

[17] In speaking of "patronage in antiquity" I refer to a span of time beginning with Catullus (i.e., the middle of the first century B.C.), and ending with Martial and Juvenal in the middle of the second century A.D. Earlier cases of literary patronage are not sufficiently well documented to influence the picture Renaissance poets had of ancient patronage. Later poetry remained without importance in that respect because of the changes Roman literary production underwent; also the Renaissance held it in low esteem (e.g., Joachim Vadianus, *De poetica et carminis ratione*, ed. Peter Schäffer, I [München, 1973], 50–51. The *De poetica* was first published in 1518).

[18] The way Horace presents his relationship to Maecenas in his poems reflects the development of the relationship itself. See Eckard Lefèvre, "Horaz und Maecenas," in ANRW, 31, 3 (Berlin / New York, 1981), 1987–2029; Gordon Williams, *Tradition and Originality in Roman Poetry* (Oxford, 1968), 44–51.

[19] My account is based on Peter White, "*Amicitia* and the profession of poetry in early imperial Rome," *JRS* 68 (1978), 74–92; Ludwig Friedländer, *Darstellungen aus der Sittengeschichte Roms in der Zeit von August bis zum Ausgang der Antonine*, I, 9th ed. (Leipzig, 1919), 224–32.

amicitia. The term can denote any kind of friendly relationship. *Amicitia* was not necessarily a relationship on equal terms. The "minor friends" (the *amicorum numerus* of Horace, sat. 1, 6, 62) which concern us here were expected to fulfill numerous duties for their sponsor.[20] They were in a way attached to the house of their *dominus*; in some cases they lived there. They were expected to turn up at the *salutatio* in the morning, accompany their "friend" to the forum, to court, even on trips; they might be back at night to collect their *sportula* and could expect an invitation to dinner (even if they were served food of lower quality!). At various occasions they received gifts, which might take the form of a piece of land, a house, or money to meet the requirements of the equestrian census (and to allow them to live off its interest). A poet in the house of a rich 'friend' was not treated any differently from any other *familiaris.* He was expected to produce verses for domestic occasions, sometimes even to extemporize. In his turn the poet could expect a well-to-do *amicus* to sponsor his recitations and generally to further his recognition as a poet. The patron's favourable judgment was vital for the circulation of a book. The main recompense a poet could offer was the promise of eternal fame through his praise. But that was not always taken too seriously by the *dominus,* if we believe the cool assessment of Martial's poetry by Pliny the Younger: "they [Martial's poems] are not likely to last, but he wrote them as if they were" (epist. 3, 21).

The vocabulary the Romans used to describe this sponsorship was curiously imprecise. The word 'client' was obviously felt to be too blunt; understated terms like *amicus* and *amicitia, sodalis, contubernium, familiaris* were preferred;[21] *colere* was the term for the behaviour of the "lesser" friend, *fovere* and *favere* denoted the attitude of the *potior.* The term *patronus* was not applied to this kind of relationship in antiquity.

The classical model is obviously the one we find applied in our poems. If we compare Renaissance patronage to its ancient counterpart, we can see some analogies. Sometimes there might be a morning reception to attend, poets might still be attached to the entourage of a nobleman; they would no longer receive money in order to fulfill the requirements of the equestrian census, but perhaps be provided with a position at a court or a living from a piece of land.

The literary application of the classical model to Renaissance conditions, however, posed several problems. In employing the Roman vocabu-

---

[20] Hor. sat. 2, 6, 42–46.

[21] O. Hey, *TLL,* I, 1907, 77–1908, 1, s.v. *amicus.*

lary the Renaissance poet had to be careful to avoid any disrespect; most of the ancient terms would not have sounded appropriate if applied to a Renaissance prince.[22] Notably the term *amicus* could no longer refer to a dependent position, but solely to that of a peer; terms like *contubernium* and *familiaris* or *sodalis* would have suggested an undue cameraderie. For example, Bartholini could not have described his position at the Salzburg court as a *contubernium* with the Archbishop; significantly enough Bonomus used the term to describe the time when he and Hölzel had been together in Innsbruck, holding similar, inferior court appointments at the beginning of their careers.

Hölzel's situation was hardly analogous to that of his ancient namesake. Both men were politically active, but while Maecenas had an independent social status, Hölzel's depended entirely on his career as a "civil servant." While Maecenas had a vast private fortune at his disposal, Hölzel was a man of mediocre means and could merely administer the funds of the emperor. While Maecenas could compete with the Emperor Augustus as a protector of the arts, Hölzel played an intermediate and secondary part in the network of court patronage of his day. We may conclude that as a sponsor of poets Hölzel was and could only be inadequate, compared not only to the archetype, the *priscus Maecenas* (Ulsenius, f 3^r), but also to the other sponsors at court. This must have been clearly evident to his contemporaries, for whom patronage was a vital issue.

On the other hand, the relative weakness of Hölzel's social position made him especially suited to be styled as "Maecenas." I will give two examples from our collection. The first one is a poem by Heinrich Bebel, in which he applies to be received amongst Hölzel's "friends" (d3^r–d3^v). He begins by praising Hölzel for prudently favouring the poets and gaining immortality, like Maecenas and Messalla. Lately, however, he has been slack in granting favours. Nevertheless he wants a poem, but *Frustra: sum mutus / conticuitque lyra* (v. 10). The poet proceeds to give the reason for his reticence: *non est qui floci pendat homerum:* | | *Croesus habet laudes: carmina nulla iuuant* (vv. 13–14). With all his fame, a poet has to go hungry: *Carmina sola famem / famam licet addere, praestant* (v. 17). Only if the poet were received *dulces ... inter amicos* (v. 19) would he be willing to praise Hölzel in return.

[22] For the problems of the status of the court poets see Uwe-K. Ketelsen, "Literarische Zentren—Sprachgesellschaften," in *Deutsche Literatur; Eine Sozialgeschichte,* III: *Zwischen Gegenreformation und Frühaufklärung: Späthumanismus, Barock,* ed. Harald Steinhagen (Reinbek bei Hamburg, 1985), 117–37, esp. 129–30.

If this poem had been intended as an appeal for patronage, it would have been formulated in a remarkably ineffective way. If anything, it would have the opposite effect. To insult the prospective patron, who here basically is charged with avarice, would hardly have been an auspicious beginning for a poet-patron relationship. Neither a Renaissance nor an ancient sponsor would have cared to receive such an impertinent poem.

But its humorous tone and circular logic prevent us from taking it literally. The poem fulfills the patron's wish while pretending to deny it.[23] The witty presentation of a hungry poet's thoughts on his art is much more important than its apparent purpose. The poem presupposes the *amicitia* it seems to apply for; but this "friendship" is not the dependent status in the house of a nobleman, but a closer aquaintance on an equal footing. The poem cannot be understood as an appeal for help. Hölzel's Maecenas is no more real than Bebel's hunger or denial of a poem. Obviously Bebel expects not only the average reader, but also Hölzel to be amused by his "jeux d'esprit." We are meant to regard it as a (rather successful) employment of classical topoi (e.g., a phrase lifted from Horace, a wordplay from Cicero),[24] with which the poet pays his friend a subtle compliment by giving him a central position in the poem and thus acknowledging his literary interests.

My second example is Bartholini's ode *Qui primus ratibus proscidit aequora,* one of the more sophisticated contributions to the collection (b1^v–b2^v).[25] In a grand adaption of the introductory poem to the first book of Horace's odes he presents himself applying for the patronage of Hölzel. Bartholini defines his goal as a poet by contrasting his profession with three others. He starts with the most different from his own: the merchant sailing perilous seas in his quest for riches (vv. 1–9). The second is the soldier, risking his life like the merchant, but with a different aim: to earn eternal fame through his deeds (vv. 10–15). Similarly lead by the desire for public recognition, are the participants in athletic and literary contests, and the court poets praising noblemen (vv. 16–25). Bartholini's own life is far removed from these. *His* companion has been Calliope, the muse of epic poetry, who despises the rewards of lyrics and avoids the masses (vv. 26–32). The poet will be content to gain the recognition of his

---

[23] A ploy used several times in our collection (e.g., n. 35 below).

[24] For example, the *fames–fama* wordplay already occurs in Cic. Att. 1, 16, 5. The poem may have been inspired by Theocritus, 16 (I would like to thank Minna Skafte Jensen for the reference).

[25] I am enlarging an interpretation by Füssel, 236–43.

patron. He will then praise his sponsor, and furthermore be joined by another poet (i.e., Celtis, vv. 33–44).[26]

Bartholini's ode is quite Horatian in contents and style. Meter, structure and verbal analogies ensure that the reader will recognize the connection. Horace had found his theme and arrangement in Greek poetry. We might assume that in reusing Horace Bartholini only followed the latter's example. But Horace had thoroughly romanized the Greek model; the poem reflected his own experience and aspirations.[27] If we understand Bartholini's poem as a description of his literary ideals like Horace's, Bartholini's transfer does not seem entirely successful. Such modernization as he attempted, still reflects more of the Roman than of his contemporary world.[28] Without knowledge of the Horatian model Bartholini's poem could not be understood. E.g., Horace's ode referred to the Olympic and Isthmian games. This was not merely an allusion to earlier themes of Greek poetry. Winning these games could still be considered a major achievement in an athlete's or poet's career in Horace's times. When Bartholini's ode mentioned these same games, the reference had an entirely different function. There were no more Isthmian games to be won. The Horatian formula had become a symbol for the cheaper fame accorded by "the masses," which the reader could not understand if he were not familiar with Horace's ode.

While Horace claims his rank as *vates lyricus* on the strength of the subsequent poems, Bartholini proceeded differently: the one poem both formulated the poet's aspirations and was proof of his mastery in what the Renaissance considered the highest standard of lyrical poetry.[29] The speaker of Bartholini's ode is confident of the superior qualities of the poem; the appeal for recognition which had been vital for Horace is now an empty formula. The appreciation and distribution of Bartholini's poetry does not depend on Hölzel's judgement any more than on any other reader's. The privileged position the patron still enjoys in the poem is not a reflection of his actual importance, but the result of the process of imitation.

---

[26] Füssel, 243.

[27] Hans Peter Syndikus, *Die Lyrik des Horaz*, I (Darmstadt, 1972), p. 24 n. 9 and p. 25 n. 11; R. G. M. Nisbet and Margaret Hubbard, *A Commentary on Horace: Odes book 1* (Oxford, 1970), p. 5 ad 1.

[28] E.g., the insertion of the *portus Iccius* seems to echo Caesar, Gall. 1, 1, 2.

[29] Eckart Schäfer, *Deutscher Horaz. Conrad Celtis, Georg Fabricius, Paul Melissus, Jacob Balde: Die Nachwirkung des Horaz in der neulateinischen Dichtung Deutschlands* (Wiesbaden, 1976), 1–38 passim.

The poet's "declaration of independence" from the patron's judgement changed the very nature of the relationship between them. The poet was no longer dependent on the patron, while the latter's fame rested entirely on the poetry of the sponsored poets, or so the Renaissance poets assure us, claiming the precedent of antiquity. Without Horace and Vergil Maecenas would be forgotten, without Tibullus Messalla, etc.[30] This concept had already been formulated by Petrarch in the famous speech at his coronation on the Capitol in Rome in 1381.[31] It is expressed in a catalogue of patrons of antiquity given by Gadius:

> Vtque tui similes narrem, quis nomina Galli
> Sciret: Vergilio ni celebrata forent.[32]
> Quis moecenatem: nisi doctus horatius illum
> Cantasset: uarium musa maronis amat.
> Parthenius / priscusque uigent per carmina Marci.[33]
> Et messala tuis culte tibulle modis.
> Statius hos: illos commendat carmine Naso
> Viuit et ingeniis quisquis in orbe fauet.
>
> (d2^r, vv. 17–24)

Here the patron has become a requisite in the process of imitation, he is a means to define the poet and his product. In comparing him to Maecenas, the poets compared themselves to Horace, Vergil etc. The comparison indicated their own poetical models. The patron was an essential part of the classical literary pattern; the individual selected for that rôle was virtually immaterial for the execution of the design.

This accounts for the presence of numerous earlier appeals for help in our collection, for which there would otherwise be little reason. Their original purpose was outdated by the time of publication. As a patron Hölzel would have felt flattered by the public display of his generosity only if these requests had actually been granted. But if we take some expostula-

---

[30] Cf. Ursinus: *Quum Moecenatem dederint te numina nobis:* | | *Ni dederint / fuerint inuida, Vergilium* (b1^v). Similarly, Horace had already claimed the precedent of Homer's epics (carm. 4, 9, 25–8).

[31] See Carlo Godi, "La 'Collatio laureationis' del Petrarca," *Italia medioevale e umanistica,* 13 (1970), 1–27, esp. 22 (par. 9, 13–16).

[32] The famous *laudes Galli* in Vergil's 10th eclogue.

[33] The patrons of Martial: Ti. Claudius Parthenius (see Martial 4, 45, 2. 4, 78, 8. 5, 6, 2 etc.) and Terentius Priscus (to whom Martial dedicated the 12th book of his epigrams).

tions with Hölzel literally, a number of them had been unsuccessful.[34] Therefore they contributed little to the glory of Hölzel as "Maecenas."

What they did show, however, was Hölzel as one of the "literati" at court engaged in an urbane discourse with each other.[35] The underlying concept is that of a "civitas doctorum," an (albeit invisible) community of intellectuals, which, although geographically dispersed, would unite from time to time in common enterprise. This idea underlies many collections of prose and poetry of that time.[36] The poems praise Hölzel by suggesting that he belongs to that community of intellectuals and shares their ideals, but not exclusively. The same fame is secured by the other contributors still living.[37]

Our considerations do not preclude real sponsorship on Hölzel's part. At a Renaissance court entirely fictive praise of this kind would have been impossible. But reality played a subordinate rôle in the design of our poems. The formative factor was the ancient poetry considered authoritative. The classical prototype was remodelled in several respects to suit the modern circumstances. The result was a synthetic pattern of literary relations between the "literati" on the one side and Hölzel on the other. This pattern had a double layer of significance. The equation: Horace to Maecenas equals modern author to Hölzel suggests that Hölzel would have been incited by these poetic appeals to imitate his ancient counterpart's munificence. We have seen traces of the fact that the parties concerned were well aware that neither of them was (or expected the other to be) a second Maecenas or Horace. The poems represent a type of civilized literary intercourse, in which the participants assumed rôles adapted from Roman literature. These "impersonations" did not need to

---

[34] Cf. Celtis d3ᵛ and f3ᵛ, Transilvanus f2ᵛ.

[35] Hölzel himself is introduced as a poet in an exchange of poems between him and Bonomus about a girlfriend of his (c1ʳ–c1ᵛ). Bonomus, asked to praise Hölzel's *puella* in a poem, charges his friend for concealing her and assumes that she is actually not respectable at all. Unless Hölzel produces her, he is not going to make a poem about her: *Non uisam laudare nequit mea musa* (here again the promise—or in this case denial—of a poem is in fact the poem itself). Hölzel's reply speaks about her beauty and ends saying that, *Sit tamen illa licet scortum,* she hides this fact so well that she should be praised for that. Further references to Hölzel's literary efforts are Sbrulius: *Concinit clarum liber hic poetam* (a1ᵛ, v. 1); Gadius: *A me missa breuis tibi uenit Epistola, reddis* | | *Litterulas / reddis carmina carminibus* (f1ʳ, vv. 3–4). This is quite congruent with the ancient model, since Maecenas was also a poet (and a bad one at that).

[36] E.g., Reuchlin's *Epistulae clarorum uirorum* or Hofheimer's collection (see n. 8).

[37] "Die Auszeichnungswirkung der Wiedmungsvorrede hob den Dichter ... zu gesteigerter Wertschätzung in der Gesellschaft" (Schottenloher, 195).

(and could not) match the real persons precisely. The recreation of an aspect of ancient Roman culture considered exemplary in Renaissance thought was, however, successful enough to serve its main purpose: the claim to status in the literary community at Maximilian's court and the expression of the literary ideals shared by them.[38]

Thesaurus linguae Latinae, Munich

[38] Müller, "Deutsch-lateinische Panegyrik," 133–40.

Cowley's Anacreontiques
and the Translation of the Greek Anacreontea

STELLA P. REVARD

In 1656 Abraham Cowley published among his *Miscellanies* eleven paraphrastic translations into English from the Greek anacreontea, the collection of 61 hemiambic lyrics that the Renaissance thought the genuine work of the sixth-century BC Teian poet, Anacreon. These eleven imitations are not only esteemed by many critics as the most finished of Cowley's work, "his happiest vein," but also conspicuously the best among the English translations of the anacreontea. Some critics even go so far as to suggest that they surpass the Greek originals in their sprightliness.[1]

Cowley's *Anacreontiques* come at a pivotal time in the history of vernacular translation, just at the moment when the anacreontea were attaining their peak of popularity. Within a ten-year span Thomas Stanley, Robert Herrick, and Cowley himself published their versions. Although this popularity did not fade until the nineteenth century—both Byron and Thomas Moore translated Anacreon—the seventeenth-century translators and particularly Cowley stand out as the most accomplished. In order to understand Cowley's success at this medium, we must look back to the beginning of interest in the anacreontea, when humanist poets, such as Thomas More and Joannes Secundus, were just turning out the first translations in Latin.

The anacreontea were not freely available poets until 1554, when Henri Estienne published 55 of the 61 poems with his own Latin translation,

---

[1] For critical appraisals see Michael Baumann, *Die Anakreonteen in englishen Übersetzungen* (Heidelberg, 1974), 73–79; A. H. Bullen, "Preface," *Anacreon*, trans. Thomas Stanley (London: A. H. Bullen, 1906), xii–xiii; Michael Hilton, *The Anacreontea in England to 1683* (D Phil Thesis, Wolfson College, Oxford, 1980), 93–100.

following the Greek text of a manuscript lent him by John Clement, a protégé of Thomas More. Estienne made the manuscript available to his circle of friends, and Ronsard published the first of his French imitations shortly before the appearance of Estienne's edition. Some few of the anacreontea had been known independently before the publication of the first edition, for they are quoted by Latin authors–Aulus Gellius, for example–and included among the epigrams of the Greek Anthology, a printed edition of which, in Planudes' version, had been current since 1494.[2] Hence, some poets of the early sixteenth century–More, Alciati, Secundus, Macrin, among them–had already turned out Latin epigrams based on them. After the publication of Estienne's edition, many more appear, both in Latin and in the vernaculars. Estienne includes Helye André's Latin translation of the anacreontea. together with his own translation, in his second printed edition in 1556. Remy Belleau publishes a French translation of the anacreontea in 1556, following Estienne's first edition. Eilhard Lubin produces a third Latin translation in 1597, printing versions of the anacreontea that are more literal than either Estienne's or André's. The first full English translation of the sequence comes in 1651. Availing himself of Estienne's edition and earlier Latin, French, and English versions of the anacreontea, Thomas Stanley produces an English sequence which, although it may not actually inspire Cowley's *Anacreontiques*, certainly must affect Cowley when he comes to arrange and publish his own versions in 1656. Both Latin and vernacular translations continue throughout the seventeenth century. William King reprints a number of Cowley's anacreontiques in *Songs and Ayres* (1668), together with versions by other poets. Still more Latin translations of the sequence appear, with William Baxter in 1691 and Joshua Barnes publishing separate editions.[3]

Cowley translates only a fifth of the anacreontea that were available to him, and in ordering those poems he translates he does not follow the sequence either of Greek or Latin or vernacular editions. Translators of the anacreontea commonly follow the order of Estienne's edition, which deviates significantly from the order of the manuscript. (Modern editors more or less restore the manuscript order.)[4] Yet certainly Cowley is affected by his predecessors both in choosing the poems he translates and

---

[2] Baumann, 13–15; Bullen, xv–xviii.

[3] Baumann, 14–15.

[4] Modern editions of the anacreontea include Theodor Bergk, *Poetae Lyrici Graeci*, Vol. III (Leipzig, 1843, 1853, 1866, 1878, 1914); J. M. Edmonds, *Greek Elegy and Iambus, with Anacreontea* (London: William Heinemann, 1931).

in arranging them in a readable sequence. With only two exceptions, he includes all of the most popular anacreontea. Only the Cupid poems—"The Beggar Cupid" and "Cupid and the Bee"—are excluded, remarkable exclusions, however, since the Cupid poems had won the hearts of French and English translators alike, with versions by Ronsard, Spenser, Watson, Lodge, and Herrick, as well as many others.[5] Cowley's *Anacreontiques*, however, have little to do with playful amorousness, so he banishes the little winged god, though he does not banish love as a subject. Apart from retaining Estienne's no. 1 as his first poem and Estienne's no. 2 as his third, Cowley completely reshuffles the order of poems. From Estienne's edition, he adopts the practice of giving titles to the anacreontea, a practice followed also by later translators; he retains, however, few of Estienne's actual titles, either selecting his own or perhaps following Stanley's choices. (See table no. 1) His choice of titles reflects, I think, close use of Estienne's edition and his notes and knowledge of Stanley's recent translation.

Both Estienne and Stanley assert an influence on the choice and by implication the title of Cowley's no. 1. Estienne had argued that this lyric, θέλω λέγειν 'Ατρείδας, ought to be first in the sequence because, like the introductory poems of Ovid's *Amores*, it announces the subject of the sequence as love. Estienne, and following him Stanley, point out the close resemblance between Ovid's opening line, "Quum Thebae, cum Troia foret, cum Caesaris acta, / Ingenium movit sola Corinna" (Where Thebes, Troy, or the deeds of Caesar might have been, Corinna only moves my wit) and the opening declaration of the poem that they place first, "I would sing of Atreides; I would sing of Cadmus; but my lyre will only speak of love." Similarly, this anacreontic's farewell to heroes and heroic themes and Ovid's "Heroum clara valete / Nomina" are parallel.[6] Estienne's and Stanley's discussion of the affinities of classical amatory elegy and the Greek anacreontea persuade Cowley to adopt this anacreontic as his introductory poem and to entitle it not "To the Lyre," but "Love," using it as the apology for his collection. Indeed, Cowley doubles the use of the word *love* in the opening anacreontic; in the original Greek it appears three times, in Cowley's rendering six.

Cowley's careful choice of words in translating the anacreontea persuades me that he knew and used not just Estienne's and Stanley's editions

---

[5] See Hilton for a discussion of the Cupid poems in their various versions.

[6] Henri Estienne, "Observationes in Anacreontis carmina," in *Anacreontis et Aliorum Lyricorum aliquot poetarum Odae* (Paris, 1556), 71; Thomas Stanley, "Excitations upon Anacreon," in *Poems* (London, 1651), 81–82.

of the anacreontea, but the translations of other poets. Cowley is clearly aware that the word φρόνημα in the anacreontic, "Beauty," is problematical. Estienne renders it as "prudentia," but André and Stanley prefer to translate it as "courage" (Stanley, p. 83). An earlier English translator, A. W., in *A Poetical Rhapsody* (1602–21) had selected the word *wisdom*, and this is what Cowley selects, doubling it with *wit*, to suggest both arms and amor.[7]

> Wisdom to Man she did afford
> Wisdom for Shield, and Wit for Sword.[8]

Similarly, in his second anacreontic, "Drinking," Cowley, like translators before him, is unhappy with the adjective *black* (μέλαινα), traditional though it may be in Homer and Sappho as an epithet for earth. Only Lubin retains it, both Estienne and André substituting the Latin *fecunda* or *ferax* (fertile or fruitful) and Stanley concurring with the English *fruitful*. But Cowley, no slavish translator, is interested neither in the liberal or the gloss but in sharpening the wit of the poem. Hence, he reaches back to a word that George Buchanan had used in his Latin translation, *sicca* (thirsty), which Cowley with paraphrastic freedom renders: "The thirsty *Earth* soaks up the *Rain*, / And drinks and gaps for drink again" (1–2).[9]

In the anacreontic "Gold" Cowley is attentive both to word choice and to the translators' notes as he reshapes the theme of the original. The Greek poem is a lament on the difficulty of love, make more difficult by a lack of money (silver in the original). Translators, following Estienne, substitute the Latin *aurum* or gold for silver. Stanley, however, goes on to say that the real subject of the poem is female avariciousness, citing in his notes the complaints by Propertius, Theocritus, and Lucan on women who weigh their lovers' purses before giving their favors (p. 109). Estienne's original title for this poem is "To Love"; Stanley retitles it "Gold" and Cowley apparently follows him. He also appears to be following Stanley in interpolating a curse on the woman, as well as the man, "who this traffick first began" (10). As the word *love* dominates the first anacreontic, the four-letter world *gold* takes over from the four-letter *love*: "*Gold* alone does passion move, / *Gold Monopolizes* love" (7–8). *Gold* appears as the first word in seven lines of the poem. In the final line Cowley turns the lament

[7] A. W. in *A Poetical Rhapsody* 1602–1621, ed. Hyder Edward Rollins (Cambridge, MA: Harvard Univ. Press, 1931).

[8] Quotations from Cowley follow the text of the *Anacreontiques* in the 1656 edition of the *Miscellanies*.

[9] See George Buchanan, *Poemata* (Basileae, 1564).

of the Greek upside-down by commenting, tongue-in-cheek, "*Gold*, alas, does *Love* beget."

Cowley's "The Grasshopper," his paraphrase of the "Tettix" or Cicada poem of the Greek profits even more from the notes and translations of his predecessors. First of all, he follows the example of the English poets Lovelace and Stanley and turns the southern singer, the cicada, into an English grasshopper. The lore of the happy grasshopper is rich in Greek literature. Cowley would have known some of the sources Stanley cites, notably the passage from Philostratus' "Life of Apollonius Tyanaeus" (lib. 7, cap. 5), where Demetrius praises the happiness of the grasshoppers singing in the summer heat (107). He also might have known the passage from *The Shield of Heracles* (393–401), where its all day singing is described or the number of epigrams from the *Greek Anthology* (A.P. VII, 195, 196, 198–201; Planudes IIIa 21, 5) where its special blessedness is praised. Cowley's 34-line paraphrase is almost twice as long as the Greek original. Cowley elaborates on the basic elements of the Greek lyric and includes allusions to the larger tradition. The Greek merely says that the *tettix* is drunk on a little dew; Cowley elaborates that it is "Fed with nourishment divine" (3), alluding to the tradition that as a favorite of the gods, the cicada or grasshopper was miraculously sustained by dew alone. Estienne and André use the Latin word *felix* (happy) for the cicada, and Cowley, picking it up, repeats the word throughout his paraphrase, making happiness the *leit motif* of his poem: "Happy *Insect*, what can bee / In happiness compar'ed to Thee?" (1–2). For the Greek poet the *tettix* is wise, noble, song-loving, and unperturbed, hence almost like to the gods. The translators temper this view. For Estienne, the cicaca has no experience of evil and suffering; for Belleau, it is free from affection or passion. The Neapolitan neo-Latin poet Angerianus and the French Ronsard contrast the singer's state with their own as excluded lovers. Angerianus complains that the cicada sings happily under the soft leaves, while he sighs before the closed doors of his mistress. Ronsard, transforming the cicada into a gentle loving lark, says that she tells her love to the winds and need not fear the disdain of a proud lover.[10] For Cowley, however, the wisdom of the grasshopper lies in its use of pleasure for its own sake, a pleasure hardly attainable on earth by human beings: "*Voluptuous*, and *Wise* with all, / Epicurean Animal!" (32–33).

[10] See Hieronymus Angerianus, in *Carmina Iluustrium Poetarum Italorum* (Florence, 1719), 1:274–75; Pierre de Ronsard, *Les Odes*, ed. Charles Guerin (Paris, 1952), IV, xxii. Ronsard's adaptations of Estienne's numbers 11, 19, 15 should also be compared with Cowley's.

Cowley's "The Epicure" takes even more liberties with the text. That we should find so free a treatment of this anacreontic is not surprising, however, in that it is one of the most imitated of the series, having been available to Latin and vernacular poets alike in its version in the *Greek Anthology* (A.P. xi, 147). Both Thomas More and Joannes Secundus translate it more or less literally, with Secundus, however, adding here and there a flourish to the text.[11] Where More states directly, "Aurum non ego persequor," (Gold I do not pursue), Secundus makes a triple denial, "Non me argentum, non gemma, nec aurum / Detentat," (Neither silver, nor gems, nor gold tempt me). While More attempts to render the short, end-stopped anacreontic line, Secundus turns the hemiambics into elegiac couplets, smoothing out the short phrases into longer more melodic ones: "Cura est vnguento fluat vt mihi barba fragranti, / Cura vt odoriferis cingam mea tempora sertis." Further, Secundus inserts a line at this point before returning to the literal text, commenting on the pervasiveness of care at this time of life: "Curae sunt dubiae tantum presentia vitae / Tempora."

Yet these liberties are few in comparison with those that other translators take. Salmon Macrin freely substitutes Midas for Gyges as an example of a wealthy tyrant; Ronsard and later Baïf do the same in their versions of this anacreontic, substituting, however, the great Turk or the Tartar. Further, when Macrin arrives at the sections of the lyric where pleasure is summoned, he is not content merely to perfume his beard or crown his head with roses. Beckoning young girls to his side, he exhorts:

> Sat mihi Iuventae tempora floridae
> Inter decoras ducere virgines
> Ventura securo quid orbi
> Afferat hora boni malive ...[12]

> Let it be enough for me to spend my time
> Of flowering youth among lovely virgins,
> Secure, whatever the hour of the world
> May bring either of good or ill;

Like Macrin, Baïf in his French version extends both the renunciation of empire and the invitation to pleasure. Once crowned with flowers, he welcomes his loved one into his embrace:

---

[11] Thomas More, *Epigrammata* (Basil, 1563), 205–6; Ioannes Secundus in *Poetae Elegantissimi Opera* (Paris, 1561), 91v–92r.

[12] Salmonius Macrinus, *Carminum Libri Quatuor* (Paris, 1530), 4:63v–64r.

Me couronner la teste,
De chapeaux que m'a preste
La delicate main
D'une de que soudain
Bras & mains il retienne
Luy disant. Toute mienne,
Ma mignarde, mon coeur
Qui fais tante rigueur
Ma barbotante bouche
Lèvres sur lèvres bouche.[13]

Probably it is this same lyric that the English poet Robert Herrick is imitating in his "A Lyrick to Mirth." Eliminating the dismissal of wealth and summoning love and wine, he begins with the last element of the Greek original, the determination to enjoy life while time permits.

While the milder Fates consent,
Let's enjoy our merryment:
Drink, and dance, and pipe, and play;
Kisse our *Dollies* night and day:
Crown'd with clusters of the Vine;
Let us sit, and quaffe our wine;
Call on *Bacchus*; chaunt his praise;
Shake the *Thyrse*, and bite the *Bayes*:
Rouze *Anacreon* from the dead;
And return him drunk to bed:[14]

For Cowley also the call to pleasure becomes the dominant motif of the anacreontic. He transposes the opening line of the Greek to line 6 and reduces the dismissal of riches to a single sentence: "we contemn / *Gyge's* wealthy *Diadem*" (5–6). Joining the command to bind the temples with roses from line 8 of the original with he call for wine found in no. 6 or no. 21 of Estienne's sequence (poems Cowley does not directly translate), Cowley begins:

Fill the *Bowl* with rosie Wine,
Around our temples *Roses* twine,

[13] Jean Antoine de Baïf, *Les Ieux de Ian Antoine de Baïf* (Paris, 1572), 32r–33r.

[14] Robert Herrick, *Poetical Works of Robert Herrick*, ed. L. C. Martin (Oxford: Clarendon Press, 1956), 39.

And let us chearfully awhile,
Like the *Wine* and *Roses* smile. (1–4)

But it is not just translators and editors who influence Cowley's *Anacreontiques*. A number of the anacreontea had been turned in the sixteenth century into epigrams, which in turn had been attached to the illustrations of the Renaissance emblem books and so had entered the emblem tradition. Two of these, the first by Sambucus, the second by Alciati, may have influenced Cowley's renderings of "Beauty" and "The Swallow." When an anacreontic becomes an epigram, its point is often sharpened in order to illustrate the moral maxim of the emblem it illustrates. Both Sambucus and Alciati shorten the anacreontic they imitate and make it deliver a swift epigrammatical thrust. In the emblem, "Pulchritudo vincit" (Beauty conquers), Sambucus pictures a woman in the foreground supported by a Cupid; in the background the diverse animals–horse, lion, hare, fish, bird–whom nature has supplied with defenses appear. Sambucus closely follows the Greek anacreontic in the first six lines; in the final six he diverges; omitting any reference of nature's gift of wisdom to man, he proceeds immediately to woman:

Concessit at loco horum
Formam, placere possit.
Qua, vincere & seueros
Ignes, acuta tela
Tantum potest venustas.[15]

So [Nature] conceded to them [Women]
Beauty in its place, by which
It is possible both to please
And to conquer raging fire and sharp weapons,
Such great power had Beauty.

The shift in emphasis is small, but telling. The epigram makes the generalization that the anacreontic only implies–that beauty has the power both to please and to conquer. The epigrammatist even manages to make (*venustas*) the final word in his poem.

Cowley in "Beauty" follows the epigrammatical tradition and reworks the nine lines of his anacreontic to express a generalizing moral and to extend that moral to a witty observation not in the original Greek. First of all, Cowley makes Beauty both arms *and* armor:

[15] Ioannes Sambucus, *Emblemata* (Antwerp: Platin, 1564), 144.

Beauty is both; for with the *Faire*
What *Arms*, what *Armour* can compare? (13–14)

Having made beauty both an offensive and a defensive force, Cowley goes on to allude to a story outside the confines of his original anacreontic. It is the paradoxical tale of Beauty's queen, Venus, who best puts on arms, not when she dresses in Mars' armor, but when she undresses. Several well-known epigrams from the Greek Anthology tell the story from different vantage points, and neo-Latin and vernacular poets in turn produce imitations of the Greek epigrams. The first of these, attributed to Leonidas of Alexandria (*Appendix Planudea*, IV. xvi. 171), directly questions Venus on putting on Mars' armor. Cowley's friend, the poet Richard Crashaw, renders it in this way:

What? *Mars* his sword? faire *Cytherea* say,
Why art thou arm'd so desperately to day?
Mars thou has beaten naked, and ô then
What need'st thou put on armes against poore men?[16]

The second, a Latin epigram attributed to Ausonius (lxiii [xlii]), records Pallas' quip on seeing Venus armed: "Why bear arms, since you conquer naked?" Both Ludovico Ariosto and Antonio Minturno wrote imitations in Latin, and Crashaw has an English version.[17] Cowley is certainly aware

[16] Richard Crashaw, *The Poems, English, Latin, and Greek, of Richard Crashaw*, 2nd ed., ed. L. C. Martin (Oxford: Clarendon Press, 1957), 161.

[17] See Ludovicus Areostus, *Carmina* (with Pigna and Calcagnini) (Venice, 1554). In the epigram, Pallas, on seeing Venus in armor, says:

Nil opus est ferro, ferri cum nuda potentem
Exueris spolijs omnibus ipsa Deum. (p. 296)

Also see "De Venere Armata" in Antonio Sebestiano Minturno, *Epigrammata, et Elegiae* (Venice, 1564).

Armatum Venerem aspiceret cum caesia Pallas,
Vis Cypri indicium sic subeamus? ait.
Quae tenerum ridens, clypeos attollere contra,
Audes: si vici nuda, quid arma ferens? (p. 3)

Crashaw's version of the same epigram runs thus:

Pallas saw *Venus* arm'd, and streight she cry'd,
Come if thou dar'st, thus, thus let us be try'd,
Why foole! saies *Venus*, thus provok'st thou mee,
That being nak't, thou know'st could conquer thee?
(p. 161)

of this epigrammatical tradition, though how many of the originals or imitations he knew we cannot be sure. The final lines of his anacreontic, "Beauty," apply Pallas' famous quip on Venus to women in general and add a coda to the original Greek anacreontic.

> Who can, alas, their strength express,
> Arm'd, when they themselves undress,
> *Cap a pe* with *Nakedness*? (22–23)

In a different way the emblem tradition exerts its influence on "The Swallow." Alciati in his emblem book has reduced the ten-line anacreontic on the swallow (Estienne's no. 12) to two elegiac couplets; he has made the swallow herself a figure illustrating *Garrulitas* (Talkativeness).

> Quid matutinos Progne mihi garrula somnos
> Rumpis & obstrepero Daulias ore canis?
> Dignus Epops Tereus, qui maluit ense putare,
> Quam linguam immodicam stirpitus eruere.[18]

> Why, noisy Procne, do you shatter my morning sleep
> And sing your Daulian songs with a clamoring mouth?
> The Hoopoe Tereus was justified when he settled matters with his sword,
> And tore out at the root your unrestrained tongue.

Alciati has made the swallow of the anacreontic into an allegorical figure with an uncontrolled mouth; she is Noisiness herself. He replicates the *garrulitas* of his title by repeating the adjective *garrula* and garnishing it with the phrases *ore obstrepero* and *linguam immodicam*. The barbarity of the original story of Tereus and Procne is forgotten with Alciati's exasperated outcry that Tereus' action was only a desperate man's final defense against an uncontrollably talkative woman. Cowley might well have known Alciati's popular emblem. His own swallow is very like the emblematic figure of *Garrulitas*:

> Foolish *Prater*, what do'st thou
> So early at my window do
> With they tuneless *Serenade*? (1–3)

He too submerges the barbarity of Tereus with an easy quip: "There his

---

For other versions of this epigram, see James Hutton, *The Greek Anthology in Italy* (Ithaca, 1935); *The Greek Anthology in France* (Ithaca, 1946).

[18] Andreas Alciatus, *Omnia Emblemata* (Antwerp, 1573), 207.

Knife had done but well" (6). There, however, the resemblance between Alciati's emblem and Cowley's emblematical swallow ends.

Cowley's swallow is an equivocal figure. She is both the foolish talker of the emblem tradition and the bird which, having wintered in the south, brings back the spring. Cowley has combined in his anacreontic the two swallow poems of the anacreontea—Estienne's no. 12 and no. 33. In the first the swallow's early morning singing drives away the dream of the beloved; in the second the swallow is asked why she builds her nest in the spring and deserts it to fly south in the fall, while Love is forever building and unbuilding his nest in the lover's heart. Cowley has retained only the essential elements from both poems; he banishes all reference to love. He has used the poem, moreover, as the final anacreontic in his collection. He doubles at the end "The Grasshopper," the king over all, whose happy song brings joy and hope for retirement and rest, with "The Swallow," the harbinger of farewell, whose foolish prating drives away his dream, a dream not identified with the beloved, but with some unequalled joy, now never to be attained. This bitter-sweet song is a curious conclusion to a sequence that begins with a trio of lyrics celebrating the cavalier pleasures—Love, Beauty, and Drinking, and whose dominant figure is the old ever-green epicure Anacreon, tallying up his loves and enjoying in the shade of the myrtle tree the days of wine and rose. The anacreontea, however, had often been both in England and France the kind of verse that belonged to the courtly poet and that celebrated the courtly way of life. Secundus, Ronsard, Baïf on the continent and Sidney, Spenser, Jonson, Herrick, Lovelace, Stanley, and Cowley himself in England had pleaded the case of king and court. The last flowering of the anacreontea came in England just at the time of the English Civil War, when the celebration of love, wine, and merriment was at best nostalgic. Cowley, a royalist supporter, had spent much of the 1640s in exile; on his return to England in the 1650s he might well have felt that the Puritan, like the foolish prating swallow, had interrupted his royalist dream. Such a mood might well explain the melancholy close to his jovial collection.

Although Cowley did not publish his anacreontics until 1656, many may have been written earlier. His interest in the Greek anacreontea went back to his university days; adaptations of two anacreontea appear as songs in *Love's Riddle* (London, 1638), a pastoral drama written when he was a student. The anacreontics that he published in 1656 are mature pieces, carefully chosen, polished, and arranged in a well-ordered sequence. Cowley is one of the few poets who produced a collection of anacreontea that is neither a full sequence nor a mere random sampling. His collection demonstrates, moreover, that he was a master not only of the Greek tradition of anacreontea and epigram, but also of the rich legacy of Latin and vernacular translation of these poems that had begun over 150 years before.

Southern Illinois University

Figure 1

Cowley	Stephanus (Estienne)	Stanley	Edmonds
I. Love	1. εις λυραν (To the Lyre)	1. The Lute	23. Of his Lyre: that it would only play of Love
II. Drinking	19. εις το δειν πινειν (On the Necessity of Drinking)	19. (Untitled)	21. To his Comrades, to justify himself in Drinking
III. Beauty	2. εις γυναι κας (To Women)	2. Beauty	24. The Power of Beauty
IV. The Duel	14. εις ερωτα (To Love)	14. The Combat	13. A Fight with Cupid
V. Age	11. εις εαυτον (To Himself)	11. The old Lover	7. Age can still Play
VI. The Account	32. εις τους εαυ το ερωτας (To his own Loves)	32. The Accompt	14. A Catalogue of Loves
VII. Gold	46. εις ερωτα (To Love)	46. Gold	29. Another by the same, on a dart
VIII. The Epicure	15. εις εαυτον (To Himself)	15. (Untitled)	8. Wine Better than Love
IX. Another	4. εις εαυτον (To Himself)	4. (Untitled)	32. Another Love Poem by the Same
X. The Grasshopper	43. εις τεττινα (To the Cicada)	43. The Grasshopper	34. Another, a little poem to the cricket
XI. The Swallow	12. εις χελιδονα	12. The Swallow	10. To the Swallow, not to disturb his Love-Dreams
	33. εις χελιδονα (To the Swallow)	33. The Swallow	
		25. The Nest of Love	

Le lettere familiari di Leonardo Bruni: Alcuni esempi della loro diffusione in Italia nel primo '400

LUCIA GUALDO ROSA

Quando, alcuni anni fa, decisi, insieme con Paolo Viti e con l'aiuto di alcuni amici, di intraprendere il censimento descrittivo dei codici contenenti lettere familiari di Leonardo Bruni, sapevo bene di accingermi ad un'impresa difficile e poco ragionevole. Ancora oggi mi capita non di rado di ripetere a me stessa, con Agostino Sottili: "Ho i miei dubbi che una tale decisione sia stata la migliore, e per tutta una serie di motivi."[1]

Al normale scoraggiamento che minaccia chiunque intraprende una ricerca di troppo lungo respiro, si accompagna l'inquietante impressione di camminare sulle orme del fantasma, non certo benevolo, di Ludwig Bertalot. Si sa, infatti, che il Bertalot, dopo aver dedicato tutta la sua vita di studioso alla ricerca codicologica, fu incaricato nel 1935 dall'Istituto Storico Italiano per il Medio Evo di realizzare l'edizione critica dell'epistolario del nostro umanista. Di tale impegno, portato avanti fino alla morte (1960), non restano che degli appunti, in parte scritti a margine di una copia assai mal ridotta dell'edizione del Mehus, in parte ordinatamente raccolti in un grosso quaderno nero. Questo materiale, toccato in eredità all'Istituto per il Medio Evo, è stato la "causa causans" di questo censimento.[2]

---

* Quaesto articolo sarà pubblicato, in edizione un po' ampliata, nel volume miscellaneo *Per un censimento dei codici dell'epistolario di Leonardo Bruni*, in corso di stampa, a cura di L. Gualdo Rosa e di P. Viti, nella collana "Nuovi studi storici," dell'Istituto Storico Italiano per il Medio Evo in Roma.

[1] Sottili, "I codici del Petrarca nella Germania Occidentale," *Italia medioevale e umanistica* 10 (1967): 420.

[2] Sulla vicenda Bertalot, rinvio alla prefazione che Raffaello Morghen preparò per

Tuttavia, se nei momenti peggiori temo che sul nostro lavoro si riverberi l'ombra infausta di quel lontano fallimento, nei momenti migliori, che sono per fortuna i piú frequenti, sento di essermi messa nella via regia percorsa dall'umanesimo italiano alla conquista dell'Europa e che la diffusione capillare delle lettere del Bruni, prima in Italia e poi nel resto del mondo, merita di essere seguita con la stessa attenzione con cui da anni si va studiando la fortuna delle opere del Petrarca.

Del resto, se dell'utilità scientifica di un censimento di questo genere non si può oggi seriamente dubitare, dal punto di vista della cooperazione internazionale, indispensabile per lo studio dell'umanesimo, è già un risultato assai confortevole che intorno al nostro progetto si sia raccolta un'équipe di studiosi italiani e stranieri di tanto prestigio.[3] Grazie al comune amore per il Bruni, è nata o si è approfondita tra noi un'amicizia di tipo veramente umanistico, cementata da una ricca e divertente corrispondenza, scritta in italiano, in inglese, in spagnolo; e chissà che nei secoli futuri a qualcuno non venga in mente di raccogliere e pubblicare questo nostro epistolario, fiorito ai margini di un epistolario piú illustre.

Per ora vorrei soffermarmi su quelle che ritengo siano le piú antiche testimonianze della diffusione delle lettere bruniane su territorio italiano; una diffusione che immediatamente si configurò come contributo al rinnovamento in senso umanistico dello stile epistolare.

Di fatto le prime lettere del Bruni le troviamo inserite nella piú antica raccolta di modelli epistolari composti da un maestro del nuovo ciceronianismo, Gasparino Barzizza. Una di queste lettere, indirizzata a Ognibene Scola, in molti di questi codici è addirittura attribuita a Gasparino. Si tratta della lettera "Solent qui errati ..." (II 17 dell'ed. Luiso, X 4 dell'ed. Mehus), datata 28 novembre 1407. Piú che per il contenuto, la lettera si distinque per l'eleganza dello stile; il contenuto è riassunto infatti abbastanza efficacemente in tre manoscritti—evidentemente imparentati tra loro—dove, prima della lettera, di legge: "Leonardus Aretinus fatetur se erravisse non scribendo amico."[4]

---

il volume di F. P. Luiso, *Studi su l'epistolario di Leonardo Bruni*, a cura di L. Gualdo Rosa, Studi storici, 122-24 (Roma 1980), VI-VII.

[3] Per i criteri con cui è stato impostato il censimento e per i nomi dei collaboratori, rinvio a L. Gualdo Rosa -P. Viti, *Epistolario di Leonardo Bruni. Censimento dei Codici* (Firenze 1987); l'opuscolo fu pubblicato a cura della Banca Commerciale Italiana, in occasione del seminario del 30 ottobre 1987. Ai nomi dei collaboratori indicati allora, possiamo oggi aggiungere quello di Claudio Griggio, che, già benemerito degli studi bruniani, ha accettato di descrivere per noi i codici delle biblioteche di Padova e di Venezia e quello di Marianna Pade che ci ha fornito un'accurata descrizione dei due codici della biblioteca reale di København.

[4] Bruxelles, Bibliothèque Royale, MS. II 1443, ff. 184v-185 (cfr. P. O. Kristeller,

Il tema, in sè topico e banale, è trattato dal Bruni con una certa originalità e non poca ironia; tuttavia lo stesso Bruni non la ritenne degna di essere inserita nell'edizione ufficiale dell'epistolario, da lui preparata all'inizio del 1440.[5] Infatti, come scrive Guarino in una lettera che fu usata come prefazione dell'edizione dell'epistolario bruniano apparsa a Lovanio intorno al 1485, il Bruni, imitando in ciò il Cicerone delle lettere ad Attico, aveva accolto, nella sua edizione definitiva, solo quelle lettere che avessero un certo significato per la storia politica, religiosa o culturale di cui l'autore era stato un protagonista.[6]

E tuttavia, proprio per la tipicità del suo argomento, la lettera piacque moltissimo, tanto che si conserva, a quel che mi risulta finora, in ben 51 manoscritti. Tra questi meritano di essere segnalati cinque codici, in cui la troviamo–insieme alla prima lettera del libro IX–in appendice all'edizione dell'epistolario in otto libri;[7] e sei manoscritti in cui è inserita, con altre

---

Iter Italicum, III. *Alia itinera*, I; *Australia to Germany* [London-Leiden 1983], 122b-123a; descritto da Dirk Sacré per il nostro censimento col n° 5); London, British Library, Cotton Tiberius B VI, ff. 181v-182 (cfr. Th. Smith, *Catalogus librorum manuscriptorum bibliothecae Cottonianae* [London 1696], repr. C. G. Tittle [Cambridge 1984], 23-24; Kristeller, *Iter*, IV, *Alia itinera, II; Great Britain to Spain* [London-Leiden 1989] 135b; nel nostro censimento, a cura di Martin C. Davies, n.° 8); London, British Library, Harley 2268, f. 69 (è il modello da cui deriva il codice precedente; cfr. R. Nares e altri, *The Harleian manuscripts in the British Museum*, II [London 1808], 633-35; Kristeller, *Iter*, IV, 154b–158a, censimento di M. Davies, n° 9). In realtà, mentre nei due codici inglesi si legge il regesto cosí come l'ho dato nel testo, il codice di Bruxelles lo dà in una forma un po'piú ampia: "Leonardi Aretini epistola, in qua fatetur se errasse non rescribendo amico suo."

[5] La data dell' "edizione" dell'epistolario curata direttamente dal Bruni e limitata ai primi otto libri, si deduce proprio dalla lettera di presentazione di Guarino da Verona di cui mi occupo alla nota seguente. La lettera di Guarino, indirizzata al discepolo Prosdocimo de' Prosdocimi per esortarlo allo studio e all'imitazione dell'epistolario bruniano, è datata XI Kalendas Maii (21 aprile) 1440.

[6] Cfr. Guarino da Verona, *Epistolario*, ed. R. Sabbadini, II (Venezia 1915), n° 762, 395-96: "ut nulla in re antiquitati cederet, non communia in epistolis scripsit, sed sui temporis historiam de Romana curia et scismate deque fluctuantis naviculae tempestate atque aliis plerisque rebus dignissimis ... texere videtur." Per l'incunabolo di Lovanio, edito da Rudolf Loeffs intorno al 1487 (GW 5608; BMC IX, 161; Hain *1564) e contenente l'epistolario in nove libri, cfr. F.-R. Hausmann, recensione agli *Studi* del Luiso, *Mittellateinisches Jahrbuch* 17 (1982): 314-15.

[7] Si tratta dei seguenti manoscritti: Bern, Burgerbibliothek, MS. 221, f. 87 (cfr. H. Hagen, *Catalogus codicum Bernensium. Bibliotheca Bongarsiana* (Bern 1874), 273; nel censimento dei codici svizzeri curato da me, n° 8); Biblioteca Apostolica Vaticana, MS. Chigi lat. HV 164, f. 21v (cfr. Kristeller, *Iter*, II, [London-Leiden 1967], p. 474b); Hamburg-Altona, Christianaeum, MS. R aa 4/6.2 (Cfr. Kristeller, *Iter*, III, p. 448a; censimento curato da Ursula Jaitner, n° 17); Paris, Bibliothèque Nationale, MS. 8575 (Dupuy 923/Regius 5388), f. 201v (cfr. *Catalogus bibliothecae regiae*, IV, Parisiis H44 p. 472b; censimento dei codici francesi, curato da me, n° 11); Wolfenbüttel, Herzog-

cinque lettere bruniane e diverse lettere di Cicerone, in quella "Subtilis et brevis epistolandi ars," composta, intorno al 1475, dall'umanista tedesco Martinus Prenninger (o Brenninger).[8]

Ma i codici piú antichi e piú interessanti sono quelli in cui la lettera, generalmente attribuita al Barzizza, è inserita in una delle piú antiche collezione delle lettere di Gasparino, resa famosa dagli studi del Bertalot, del Sabbadini e, piú di recente, di Daniela Mazzuconi:[9] con lievi oscillazioni, questa raccolta, di origine padovana, è attribuita al secondo decennio del '400.

In tre di questi codici—il Vaticano latino 5126, l'Ambrosiano H 49 inf. e il MS. 303 della Biblioteca Capitolare di Verona—la lettera allo Scola è seguita anche dalla trascrizione dell'indirizzo: "A tergo. Prestantissime

---

August-Bibliothek, MS. 9.1.Aug.4° (folio 73), f. 175 (cfr. O. V. Heinemann, *Die Hss. der Herzoglichen Bibliotheken Wolfenbüttel*, 2. Abteilung. *Die Augusteischen Handschriften*, IV [Wolfenbüttel 1900], 142–43; Censimento di U. Jaitner, n° 19). Alla fine del nostro censimento, i manoscritti di questo tipo risulteranno sicuramente piú numerosi.

[8] I codici che contengono l' "ars epistolandi" del Prenninger sono i seguenti: Erlangen, Universitätsbibliothek, MS. 639 (olim 762), datato 1475, ff. 99–113 (cfr. H. Fischer, *Die Lateinischen Papierhandschriften der Universitätsbibliothek Erlangen* [Erlangen 1936], 360–65; n° 3 del censimento di F. R. Hausmann); München, Bayerische Staatsbibliothek, clm 14644, dat. 1485, ff. 1–25 (cfr. E. Eutner, *Frühhumanismus und Schultradition in Leben und Werk des Wanderpoet Samuel Karoch von Lichtenberg*... [Berlin 1968], 152; n° 23 del censimento di F. R. Hausmann); München, ibidem, clm 18801, ff. 111–37 (cfr. *Catalogus Codicum Latinorum Bibliothecae Regiae Monacensis*, II, 3 [IV, 3], [Monachii 1878], 211; n° 25 del censimento de Hausmann); Paris, Bibliothèque Nationale, MS. 11347, datato 1483, ff. 131–56 (Kristeller, *Iter*, III, 249 ab; n° 16 del mio censimento dei codici francesi); Seitenstetten, Stiftsbibliothek, MS. 178, ff. 7–27 (cfr. Kristeller, Iter, III, p. 516a; n° 8 del censimento di Paolo Viti dei codici austriaci); Wien, Nationalbibliothek, MS. 3123, ff. 2–17 (cfr. *Tabula codicum manuscriptorum ... in Bibl. Pal. Vindobonensi asservatorum*, II [Vindobonae 1868], 206–8; n° 14 del censimento di P. Viti).

Per Martinus Prenninger, detto Uranius, cfr. L. Bertalot, *Humanistische Vorlesungsankundingen in Deutschland im 15. Jahrhundert*, in Id. *Studien zum italienischen und deutschen Humanismus*, hrsgg. von P. O. Kristeller, I (Roma 1975), 245–46; e W. Zeller, *Der Jurist und Humanist Martin Prenninger* (Tübingen 1973), 17, 85–91, 172. Le lettere del Bruni comprese nell'antologia del Prenninger sono le seguenti: ep. IV 2(2) al Niccoli (*Cum Johanne qui aliquot* ...); ep. V 3(6) al Filelfo (*In bonam queso partem* ...); ep. I 4 (2) a Coluccio (*Scripsi antea tibi* ...); ep. II 17 (X 4) a Ognibene Scola (*Solent qui errati* ...); ep. VI 2 (2) a Niccolò Albergati (*Ego vero gratias habeo* ...); ep. VII 15(8) a Giacomo Foscari (*Reddite mihi*).

[9] Cfr. L. Bertalot, *Die älteste Briefsammlung des Gasparinus Barzizza*, in Id. *Studien*, II, 35–37; R. Sabbadini, "Dalle nuove lettere di Gasparino Barzizza," *Rendiconti del R. Instituto Lombardo di Scienze e Lettere* 62 (1929): 883–86; D. Mazzuconi, "Per una sistemazione dell'epistolario di Gasparino Barzizza," *Italia medioevale e umanistica*, 20 (1977): 183–88.

prudentie et [eloquentie] viro, domino Omnebono de la Scola, fratri optimo et suavissimo."[10] In questa antica collezione di lettere del Barzizza, troviamo inoltre assai spesso due lettere del Barzizza attribuite al Bruni e indirizzate a Lorenzo Bonzi,[11] e un'altra lettera del Bruni, riconosciuta come sua, e ben piú importante del biglietto di scuse inviato ad Ognibene. Si tratta della lettera che comincia: "Etsi sciam quae tu nuper...," inviata dal Bruni a Coluccio Salutati e da lui inserita nell'epistolario ufficiale (I, 6, ed. Mehus, I, 3. ed. Luiso). In questa lettera il Bruni ringrazia Coluccio per averlo raccomandato ad Innocenzo VII,[12] racconta dell'ottima accoglienza che quella commendatizia cosí autorevole ed affettuosa ha avuto in curia; ma al tempo stesso critica acerbamente il suo rivale, Iacopo d'Angelo da Scarperia, e non risparmia nemmeno il Salutati, sia per aver scritto una lettera di incoraggiamento all'odiato Iacopo, sia per errori imperdonabili nello stile epistolare. Come per molte lettere umanistiche, anche di questa importante ed antica lettera del Bruni esistono due redazioni: una, riveduta e corretta per essere inserita nell'epistolario ad edificazione dei posteri, l'altra, tramandata dai corrispondenti, in redazione piú ampia e non purgata dalle critiche al suo maestro.[13] Nella collezione di lettere del Barzizza, formatasi come abbiamo detto nel secondo decennio del '400, si trova ovviamente la redazione piú ampia; tra i codici che contengono questa collezione, l'unico a darci l'indirizzo (almeno a quanto ho potuto per ora verificare), è il Vat. lat. 5126, dove si legge: "A tergo. Litteratissimo nostre etatis viro, Colucio Salutato canzellario Florentinorum, patri

---

[10] Per il Vat. lat. 5126, f. 105 r/v, cfr. Kristeller, *Iter*, II, 369b-70a; per l'Ambrosiano lat. H 49 inf., cfr. Kristeller, *Iter*, I (London-Leiden 1963), 325a; (vedi inoltre Laurentii Valle *Epistole*, edd. O. Besomi-M. Regoliosi (Padova 1984), 46-47; e C. Griggio, *L'epistolario di Francesco Barbaro. Tradizione manoscritta e a stampa*, in cor so di stampa, Ma3, p. 201); per il codice di Verona, Bibl. Capitolare 303, ff. 73v-74v, cfr. Kristeller, *Iter*, II, 299a.

[11] Si tratta della lettera che comincia con *Pollicitus eram* ... (n° 185 del censimento della Mazzuconi) e di quella che comincia con *Lepide tetigisti* ... (n° 109 dello stesso censimento). Le due lettere, come rileva la stessa Mazzuconi, sono attribuite al Bruni in numerosi manoscritti. Nel Vat. lat. 5126 (ff. 105v-107v) si leggono immediatamente dopo la lettera ad Ognibene Scola, che manca di ogni attribuzione; sicché l'*inscriptio* che le precede—*Leonardus Aretinus*—potrebbe essere stata, nell'archetipo, la naturale conclusione dell'indirizzo che chiude la lettera precedente.

[12] La lettera di Coluccio ad Innocenzo VII (cfr. Coluccio Salutati, *Epistolario*, a cura de F. Novati, IV, 1 [Roma 1905], 105-9), fu inserita dal Bruni al terzo posto del I libro dell'epistolario da lui "pubblicato" nel 1440; si trova pertanto in tutti i manoscritti che conservano l'edizione d'autore.

[13] Per le parti escluse dall'edizione definitiva e per altre notizie, cfr. Luiso, *Studi*, 7-8.

optimo."[14] Il codice Vaticano, inoltre, è anche l'unico di questi codici a darci la data ("Victurbii, kalendis decembris"), che era sfuggita al Luiso ed era quindi finora ignota. Tuttavia, sia la data che l'indirizzo si trovano, non si sa attraverso quali passaggi, anche in due codici assai meno autorevoli, il 5350 e il 14134 della Bayerische Staatsbibliothek di München, descritti da Frank-Rutger Hausmann.[15] In questi due manoscritti, databili alla metà del '400 e di provenienza tedesca, la lettera del Bruni a Coluccio è inserita in una collezione di lettere di Poggio Bracciolini, alcune delle quali indirizzate allo stesso Bruni.

Se la presenza della data e dell'indirizzo ci induce ad accostare tra loro tre manoscritti distanti come contenuto e come origine, molto piú profondi sono i legami che legano il codice della Capitolare di Verona ad altri due codici che contengono la collezione delle lettere del Barzizza: il MS. 132 b 4° di Hamburg—descritto da Ursula Jaitner[16]—e il Canonicianus misc. 125 della Biblioteca Bolleiana di Oxford, descritto da Martin Davies.[17] In entrambi, oltre alle ovvie affinità di contenuto, troviamo infatti un comune errore nell'*explicit* ("incudi *redeas*" per in "incudi *reddas*"); per il codice di Hamburg c'è inoltre l'identità di alcune *inscriptiones*, che dimostra inequivocabilmente un rapporto diretto o una comune derivazione.[18]

---

[14] Cfr. Vat. lat. 5126, f. 110. La lettera, preceduta dall'*inscriptio* "Leonardi Arretini ad Petrum Ystrum," si legge ai ff. 108v–110. Anche questa *inscriptio* evidentemente errata, deve essere stata in origine la sottoscrizione della lettera precedente, che in questo manoscritto, evidentemente tra i piú vicini all'archetipo, è la lettera di dedica dei *Dialogi ad Petrum Histrum*. L'errore passò poi in altri codici, dove questa dedicatoria o è assente, o non è vicina alla nostra lettera. (Cfr. ad esempio i codici citati qui alla nota 18.)

[15] München, Bayerische Staatsbibliothek, clm 5350, ff. 104v–105 (cfr. A. Sottili, "I codici del Petrarca nella Germania Occidentale," IV, n° 120, *Italia medioevale e umanistica* 13 [1970] 351); München, ibidem, clm 14134, f. 175 r/v (cfr. Sottili, *Codici*, n° 140, 412); la presenza dell'indirizzo e della data nel secondo manoscritto non è segnalata dal Sottili, ma dallo Hausmann che descrive i due codici nel suo censimento bruniano (n° 17 e n° 22).

[16] Hamburg, Staats-und-Universitätsbibliothek, MS. Phil. 132 v 4°, ff. 55v–56v (cfr. Kristeller, *Iter*, III, pp. 562b–63a; n° 16 del censimento di Ursula Jaitner). Il codice, datato 18 novembre 1443, contiene anche, ai ff. 51v–52, la lettera *Solent qui errati* ... attribuita al Barzizza e, ai ff. 92–94v, l'ep. II 18 (*Fides sacerdos* ...) edita solo dal Luiso. Vi si leggono inoltre, attribuite al Bruni, le due lettere al Bonzi, citate qui alla nota 11.

[17] Oxford, Bodleian Library, Canonicianus Misc. 125, f. 41 r/v (cfr. H. O. Coxe, *Catalogi Codicum Manuscriptorum Bibliothecae Bodleianae pars III, Codices Graecos et Latinos Canonicianos complectens* [Oxonii 1854], 597–603; n° 26 del censimento bruniano del Davies). Il Canonicianus, assai vicino per contenuto sia al codice de Amburgo che a quello di Verona, contiene anch'esso l'ep. II 17 (X 4) *Solent qui errati*, e la II 18 (*Fides sacerdos* ...).

[18] Cosí al f. 51v del codice di Amburgo—come al f. 73v del MS di Verona—prima

Piccole scoperte, dunque: una data, finora sconosciuta, la presenza di un indirizzo o di errori comuni che collega tra loro codici apparentemente lontani ecc.

Qualcosa di piú consistente ci offrono invece altri manoscritti, dove le lettere del Bruni, sempre adoperate come modelli retorici, si trovano inserite in mezzo ad altri modelli, lettere di Cicerone, o lettere fittizie di stile ciceroniano. Si tratta di una nuova redazione della lettera inviata dal Bruni, nell'estate del 1421, all'amico Bartolomeo d'Arezzo, e pubblicata per la prima volta negli *Studi* del Luiso, come ventitreesima del IV libro.[19] La versione della lettera pubblicata dal Luiso ci dà il nome del destinatario e ci fornisce tutti gli elementi concreti indispensabili per capirne il contenuto. Bartolomeo d'Arezzo si era raccomandato al suo illustre concittadino, Leonardo Bruni, per ottenere una cattedra all'università di Firenze[20] e avrebbe dovuto succedere ad un certo Simone, anch'egli di Arezzo, che era malato e sembrava doversi ritirare dall'insegnamento. Leonardo risponde che, avendo parlato con un suo autorevole amico, Matteo Castellani, ne ha avuto risposta nettamente negativa. Egli suggerisce tuttavia al suo corrispondente di venire personalmente a Firenze, per seguire da vicino il suo affare. La nuova redazione della lettera, da me trovata prima in due importanti codici della Biblioteca Nazionale di Napoli,[21] e poi, a ondate successive, in altri sette manoscritti,[22] elimina ogni riferimento personale; resta solo, in alcuni

---

dell'ep. II 17 (X 4) *Solent qui errati*, si legge: "Idem Gasparinus Pergamensis ad quendam amicum suum"; al f. 55v del MS di Amburgo—e al f. 78 di quello di Verona—prima dell'ep. I 6(3) a Coluccio (*Etsi sciam* . . .), si legge: "Leonardi Aretini ad Petrum Histrum"; al f. 92 del codice di Amburgo, come al f. 90v del MS di Verona—si legge: "Leonardi Aretini elegans oratio feliciter incipit," come comune "inscriptio" dell'*Oratorio in funere Othonis* (inc.: *Plenam lacrimarum atque meroris* . . .) ecc. Per l'*inscriptio* dell'ep. I 6(3) vedi comunque qui, nota 14.

[19] Cfr. Luiso, *Studi*, pp. 98, 167–68 (ep. X 10).

[20] Non molto possiamo aggiungere a quanto il Luiso dice a commento di questa lettera, traendolo da *Statuti dell'Università e studio Fiorentino dell'anno MCCCLXXXVII, seguiti da un'appendice di documenti dal MCCCXX al MCCCCLXX*, ed. A. Gherardi (Firenze 1881), 187, 198, 201–2, 389. La voce *Castellani Matteo*, curata da C. Galvani per il *Dizionario biografico degli Italiani* vol. XXI, (Roma 1978), 630–32 non dice infatti niente sul ruolo svolto dal Castellani nel governo dell'università.

[21] Napoli, Biblioteca Nazionale, MS. XIII G 33, f. 115v (132v) (cfr. Kristeller, *Iter*, I, p. 432b; ma assai piú dettagliata la descrizione dello stesso autore in Id., "Un'ars dictaminis di Giovanni del Virgilio," *Italia medioevale e umanistica* 4 [1961]: 191–92); e Napoli, B. N., MS. V F 19, f. 107 r/v (cfr. Kristeller, *Iter*, I, p. 414b; e L. Valle *Epistole*, p. 55). I due codici presentano in pratica lo stesso testo ma da piú indizi sembra che il MS. V F 19 derivi dal precedente.

[22] Bologna, Biblioteca Universitaria 2720, f. 182 r/v (cfr. L. Frati, "Indice dei

esemplari, il nome Bartolomeo dell'*inscriptio* e poi quello che evidentemente interessava di piú al raccoglitore delle lettere bruniane, e cioè un modello di risposta apparentemente sollecita, ma in sostanza negativa, ad una richiesta di raccomandazione. Il confronto tra i due testi, che pubblico in appendice, renderà evidente la differenza.

Interessante è anche la notevole diffusione di questa edizione rifatta, diffusione che fa nascere il sospetto che questo rifacimento, indubbiamente elegante, possa risalire addirittura allo stesso Bruni.

La lettera effettivamente spedita, che il Luiso dichiarava di aver trovato in due manoscritti, si trova in realtà, insieme con la richiesta di Bartolomeo d'Arezzo, nel solo codice 349 della biblioteca Classense di Ravenna.[23] L'altro codice segnalato dal Luiso, il Laurenziano 90 sup. 65, contiene infatti la redazione ridotta; anzi, insieme con i due napoletani, ci

---

codici latini conservati nella R. Biblioteca Universitaria de Bologna," *Studi Italiani di filologia classica* 17 [1909]: 95–97 e Griggio, *L'epistolario*, Bn U 3, p . 83); Firenze, Bibl. Medicea Laurenziana, MS. 90 sup. 65f, 83v (82v) (cfr. A. M. Bandini, *Catalogus codicum Latinorum* . . . , III [Florentiae 1776], coll . 645–54); Roma, Bibl. Casanatense, MS. 294 (D V 13) , f. 13 (cfr. M. Ceresi, *Catalogo dei manoscritti della Casanatense* [Roma 1952], 105–11); Biblioteca Apostolica Vaticana, Reg. lat. 1832, ff. 86–87 (cfr. Kristeller, *Iter*, II, 410b; É. Pellegrin e altri, *Les manuscrits des classiques latins de la Bibliothèque Vaticane*, II, 1, [*Fonds Patetta, et Fonds de la Reine*] [Paris 1978], 440–43); ibidem, MS. Reg. lat. 1834, ff. 106v–107 (cfr. Kristeller, *Iter*, II, 315 ab); ibidem, Urb. lat. 886, f. 88 (cfr. C. Stornaiolo, *Codices Urbinates Latini*, II [Romae 1912], 619); ibidem, Vat. lat. 2951, f. 87 (cfr. Kristeller, *Iter*, II, p. 410b). Di questi nove manoscritti, sei sono degli zibaldoni da classificare in modo piú o meno netto come "scolastici," in quanto destinati allo studio o all'insegnamento della nuova retorica umanistica; tre (il Casanatense e i due Reginensi), pur conservando un testo piuttosto scadente, contengono collezioni piustosto cospicue di lettere bruniane, raccolte anche per il loro interesse contenutistico (cfr. L. Bertalot, *Forschungen über Leonardo Bruni Aretino*, ora in Id. *Studien*, II, 409, nota 1).

[23] Cfr. Ravenna, Biblioteca comunale e Classense, MS. 349, f. 105 r/v (lettera di Bartolomeo a Bruni) e f. 106, lettera del Bruni a Bartolomeo (cfr. S. Bernicoli, in G. Mazzatinti, *Inventari delle biblioteche d'Italia*, IV [Forlí 1894], 219–22). Poiché a tutt'oggi questo è l'unico manoscritto che ci conserva la lettera effettivamente spedita, non credo si debba apportarvi alcuna correzione. E non solo nell'ortografia, che uniformo alla lezione del codice (è noto che il Luiso preferiva invece normalizzarla secondo l'ortografia classica), ma nemmeno nella data, che il Luiso nel testo latino lascia cosí come la dà il Ravennate (17 giugno); ma poi nel regesto e in nota dice di preferire la data del 10 agosto che si legge nel Laurenziano (e in tutti gli altri manoscritti che hanno la redazione rielaborata). Tutte la argomentazioni del Luiso, fondate su un'eccessiva coerenza logica, non valgono contro la tradizione manoscritta. Una giornata afosa può benissimo essersi avuta anche in giugno; cosí come è possibile che il Bruni si rivolgesse a Matteo Castellani, personaggio comunque assai autorevole, anche se dal febbraio 1420 al luglio 1421 lasciò temporaneamente l'ufficio di riformatore dello Studio, perché impegnato in altri incarichi (cfr. *Statuti*, 198).

conserva il testo nettamente piú antico e piú autorevole.[24] Ché anzi il codice Napoletano XIII G 33 e il Laurenziano conservano la lettera del Bruni in una collezione di lettere—di Cicerone, di umanisti, o pseudo-lettere di tipo ciceroniano—precedute da un volgarizzamento. L'identità di molti di questi testi e dei relativi volgarizzamenti, mostra che i due codici, o almeno le due sezioni che contengono la lettera bruniana, derivano da un archetipo comune.[25] Abbiamo in questi due codici un esempio non troppo comune di didattica attiva dello stile epistolare; oltre a far imitare e tradurre le lettere piú caratteristiche di Cicerone, e dei piú autorevoli maestri dello stile ciceroniano, i maestri adattavano ai loro scopi le lettere degli umanisti o ne costruivano altre fittizie, mettendo insieme frasi particolarmente eleganti degli autori piú apprezzati. Nel codice di Napoli, in cui tutti i testi latini sono accompagnati da glosse marginali di tipo retorico, la lettera del Bruni ha subito un'ulteriore trasformazione, che il codice conserva in volgare e in latine: ai nomi moderni si sono sostituiti

---

[24] Non è facile stabilire uno stemma per la trasmissione di un testo scolastico, certo non lineare. L'autorità dei due codici napoletani e del fiorentino è comunque dimostrata dal fatto che essi conservano insieme lezioni nettamente preferibili come *Unis* (lin. 2), *primo* (lin. 3), *possit* (lin. 9) e *feras* (lin. 10), ma anche una lezione non buona, come *quod* (lin. 4). Particolarmente importante e caratterizzante la lezione *Unis*, che è una vera e propria citazione di Cicerone *Fam.* II 7, 3., 3 e XIII 24, 3, 2. Tanto è vero che nella lettera fittizia che si legge solo in N' (cfr. qui alla nota 26), rimane la formula "Quoniam unis tuis disertissimis litteris." E' ovvio che nella realtà le lettere spedite da Bartolomeo d'Arezzo dovevano essere due, tanto che il Bruni si vede costretto a rispondere proprio dall'insistenza dell'amico: ma la realtà non interessa i maestri di retorica.

[25] Ai ff. 81–83v (82v) del Laurenziano si leggono le stesse lettere con gli stessi identici volgarizzamenti, che sono nel Napoletano XIII G 33, ff. 104v–15v. Vi si legge del Bruni, oltre alla redazione minore della lettera a Bartolomeo, senza volgarizzamento, anche una importante lettera al Niccoli, l'ep. IV 21 (*Audivi ex familiaribus* . . .) preceduta dal volgarizzamento (*Ho inteso da nostri amici che heri te partisti melanchonuso* . . .). In entrambi i codici si trovano inoltre le stesse lettere umanistiche con volgarizzamento (come le definisce il Kristeller), che hanno tutta l'aria di composizioni scolas tiche. Ne diamo qui gli *incipit* latini con le rispettive collocazioni: *Esti verecundia impediar*. . . :
F, ff. 66 r/v e N', f. 109v–10; *Officium in me tuum*. . . : F, ff. 66v–67 e N', f. 110 r/v; *Cum non sim nescius*. . . : F, f. 67 r/v e N', f. 111; *Intellexi quam maximas*. . . : F, ff. 67v–68 e N', f. 111v; *Vellem libenter te*. . . ; F, f. 68 e N', f. 111v–12; *Negotium M.Bruti*. . . : F; f. 69 e N', f. 112 r/v; *Quam sit (Quantum esset) morosus M.Antonius*. . . : F, f. 69v e N', f. 112: *Quod mihi M.Antonium hominem*. . . : F, ff. 69v–70, e N', ff. 113v–114: *Marco Bruto uno omnium*. . . : F, f. 70v e N', f. 114v;
Quoniam mihi persuadebam. . . : F, f. 71 (70) e N' f. 116.
Tutti questi testi, con i respettivi volgarizzamenti, meriterebbero uno studio approfondito, che ci aiutasse tra l'altro a capire da quale scuola derivano le due importanti raccolte.

nomi di ambiente ciceroniano (Marco Antonio e Clodio). Ne risulta una curiousa composizione che merita di essera letta.[26]

Assistiamo comunque in questo caso (ma in un certo senso anche per la lettera ad Ognibene Scola) ad un tipico esempio di quel processo di astrazione retorica, al quale i nostri umanisti sottomettevano la loro corrispondenza privata, sia quando la volevano rendere pubblica, inserendola in un epistolario, sia quando se ne volevano servire (o autorizzavano altri a servirsene) come strumento didattico e come modello di stile. Essi tendevano—secondo la brillante definizione di Giorgio Pasquali—a trasferire la loro lettera dal regno del contingente a quello dell'eterno.[27] La lettera a Bartolomeo, dopo essere stata purificata da tutte le banalità del quotidiano, raggiunse finalmente il livello piú alto dell'astrazione, quando fu eliminata dall'edizione definitiva dell'epistolario.

Università della Tuscia (Viterbo)

[26] Cfr. Nap. XIII G 33, f. 115v: Per che se conteneva in una ornatissima tua lettera che devessemo levare ogne speranza de quello perteneva al facto dellu officio de Marco Antonio mio fratello, per quisto breve tempo non troppo accuratamente vi respondo: che serria ben facto che vui fossevo ad veder vestre cose. Ad cio che non intervenga ad vui quello e intervenuto ad me; che, portando bon novella ad Clodio nostro vicino, me dixe era impacciato in nella raccolta del grano; per che niuno in quella faccenda lu porria passare de consiglio o de prudentia.

Quoniam unis tuis disertissimis litteris legebatur nobis esse spem omnem deponendam de eo quod ad negocium magistratus M. Antonii fratris mei attinet (*d.m.*: Attinet. Spectat), hoc brevissimo tempore non nimis accurate respondeo. Optimum esset te tuis rebus adesse, ne tibi accidat quod mihi; qui, cum ad Clodium vicinum nostrum bonos nuntios afferrem (*d.m.*: afferre, portare), respondet in messe se esse continuum. Nemo enim in ea re consilio aut prudentia sibi preesse posset. Vale.

[27] Cfr. G. Pasquali, *Storia della tradizione e critica del testo* (Firenze, 1952^{2}), 457.

Appendice

SIGLE DEI CODICI:

B=BOLOGNA, BIBL. UNIVERSITARIA, MS. 2720, F. 182 R/V;
C=ROMA, BIBL. CASANATENSE, MS. 294 (D V 13), F. 12;
F=FIRENZE, BIBL. LAURENZIANA, MS. 90 SUP. 65, F. 83 R/V (82 R/V);
N'=NAPOLI, BIBL. NAZIONALE, MS. XIII G 33, F. 115V (130V);
N''=NAPOLI, BIBL. NAZIONALE, MS. V F 19, F. 107 R/V;
R'=BIBL. APOSTOLICA VATICANA, MS. REG. LAT. 1832, F. 85;
R''=BIBL. APOSTOLICA VATICANA, MS. REG. LAT. 1834, FF. 106V-107;
U=BIBL. APOSTOLICA VATICANA, MS. URB. LAT. 886, F. 88;
V=BIBL. APOSTOLICA VATICANA, MS. VAT. LAT. 2851, F. 87.

1. Leonardus ... suo *om.* N''; dulcissimo *om.* F; dulcissimo suo *om.* N'; Leonardus Ar. B. suo p.s.m. B; Leon. s.d. Beno suo R'. 2. Binis litteris tuis CR''V; Binis R'U; In his B; litteris disertissimis F; cogor *om.* F; in *post* hoc *add.* BCR'R''V. 3. extuans CFN'N''R'R''UV; primo FN'N''; quoad V; negocium magistratus B. 4. quod FN'N''; tua *omm.* CF; cupidus B; attinet *om.* V; seponenda V. 5. Arecto B; retro R'; ut *post* veniunt *add.* R''V; afferunt bonos nuntios F. 6. advertat CFU. 7. rebus tuis BCFU. 8. iura meliora CUV; ipse *post* tu *add.* F; neque *pro* aut C; tibi *omm.* R''V. 9. prodesse B; prodesse alibi preesse R'; posset BCR'R. 10. feres B CR'R''U V. 11. tibi *om.* F, *post* minus *add.* CR'R''V; rescribam BR'R''U; scrivam F; Ex... sextiles *om.* V; idibus F; nonas *pro* ydus B; sextilis U.

Unis tuis disertissimis litteris cogor hoc brevissimo tempore sudans atque estuans respondere. Et primum, quod ad magistratus negocium—quem tu, pro omni tua dignitate cupiebas—attinet, omnis spes deponenda est. De amicissimo tuo, qui Aretio veniunt, bonos nuntios afferunt; quod utinam sequatur. Sin secus—quod avertat Iupiter—optimum esset te tuis rebus adesse. Nemo enim meliora iura habet quam tu habeas, neque consilio aut prudentia tibi preesse possit. Vale. Et siquid inpresentiarum tardius respondi, equo animo feras. Sum enim in re continuus; que res facit ut minus tibi accurate respondeam. Ex Florentia, IIII ydus Sextiles.

Redazione autentica della lettera (ed. Luiso, ep. IV 23): dal MS. di Ravenna, Biblioteca Comunale e Classense, 349, f. 107.

Leonardus Aretinus salutem dicit Bartholommeo suo.

Binis litteris tuis cogor, in hoc brevissimo tempore, sudans et estuans respondere. Primum, ad negotium Studii quod attinet, deponenda est omnis spes. In quo illud fuit potissimum, quod, animadversa re, non nimium propagavimus intentionem nostram. Nam dominus Matteus Castellanus–in quo spes erat maxima–aperte respondit vanum fore laborem, quantumcunque conaremur. Quo responso, destiti. De domino Symone, qui veniunt Aretio bonam spem afferunt salutis: que utinam sequatur. Sin vero succumbet–quod avertat Iuppiter–optimum esset te presentem rebus tuis providere. Nam iura nemo meliora habet quam tu habes. Sed contentio erit cum illius propinquis qui benefitiis inhyant. Quare, nisi quid impediat, venias suadeo. Presentia quidem tua et consilio et opere proficiet. Vale. Florentie, die XVII Iunii. Ego sum in re continuus; que res facit ut minus frequenter rescribam.

La Culture du style *dans les* Epistolae *de J.-L. Guez de Balzac*

PHILIPPE-JOSEPH SALAZAR

Le *Ioannis Ludovici Epistolarum Liber Vnus* parut en 1637, dans le *Recueil de Nouvelles Lettres de Monsieur de Balzac.*[1] Durant cette année climatérique pour les Belles Lettres françaises, qui virent la parution en français du *Discours de la Méthode* et l'apparition sur scène du *Cid*, ce recueil d'épîtres latines serait ainsi un rappel à l'ordre ou l'adieu du créateur de la prose d'art française à la néo-latinité humaniste. Œuvre charnière peut-être que ces *Epistolae*, correspondance avec le passé, sorte d'entretien final avec les sources de l'imitation classique. Pour reprendre une expression de Giorgio Manganelli, dans sa confection d' "héroïdes," "e poetarum fabulis"—pour parler comme l'Erasme du *De conscribendis*—,[2] qu'échangent Hamlet et la Princesse de Clèves, Balzac offre à son public mi-mondain mi-humaniste un dialogue qui, par delà et à travers la variété de ses correspondants, s'entretient avec des "dèi ulteriori," la lettre néo-latine, ses sources d'invention, ses modèles d'élocution, ses "offices."

Jean Jehasse et Bernard Yon ont récemment réédité ces lettres dans leur version de 1637; ils y lisent la naissance du mythe du Romain. J'y distinguerais, pour ma part, dans une optique néo-latine, un effort presque mélancolique accompli par Balzac pour recueillir, *ad posteros*, sa parole latine et léguer, dans la gloire grandissante du vernaculaire, une "pra-

---

[1] J.-L. Guez de Balzac, *Livre unique d'épîtres latines*, éd. J. Jehasse et B. Yon (Saint-Etienne: Presses de l'Université de Saint-Etienne, 1982). Voir B. Beugnot, *Guez de Balzac, bibliographie générale, supplément I* (Montréal: Presses de l'Université de Montréal, 1969) et *Supplement II* (Saint-Etienne: Presses de l'Université de Saint-Etienne, 1979) pour la bibliographie de Balzac.

[2] Voir J. Chomarat, *Grammaire et Rhétorique chez Erasme* (Paris: Belles-Lettres, 1981).

tique" vigoureuse de l'art d'écrire une lettre. Ici nulle polyanthée, nulle sylve, nul palais des lettres, mais, en mineure, seize épîtres d'un art de la mémoire de la lettre néo-latine telle que pratiquée par l'*unico eloquente.*

Seize lettres en effet où, sous l'apparence d'un classement "rythmique," peut-être même hâtif, se dissimule une véritable volonté de disposition, un geste magistral d'esthète littéraire. Un regard attentif porté à la *dispositio* des lettres révèle en effet que ce recueil brosse un tableau presque ironique dans sa perfection d'une *varietas* des sujets et des récipiendaires dans l'*unitas* du projet. De fait, réagençant la chronologie selon la règle de l'art, Balzac lègue au "pays latin" une leçon de composition: les quatre épîtres au Cardinal de Richelieu ouvrent le recueil, datées de 1630, 1633, 1634 et 1636, deux lettres du 1er janvier encadrant en chiasme les deux épîtres centrales; puis, deux séries analogues de lettres mènent par deux fois le lecteur de 1632 à 1637 (lettres V à IX et X à XIV), dans un bel effet de symétrie; enfin les *epistolae* XV et XVI, datant l'une de 1631 et l'autre de 1637, redoublent et synthétisent les deux termes chronologiques de la correspondance vécue. En faisant légèrement violence aux mots, il semblerait que les *Lettres latines* empruntent, *cum grano salis*, la division rhétorique d'un discours: l'exorde des épîtres à Richelieu, le développement des deux groupes de cinq lettres, la péroraison des deux missives finales.

Toutefois cette disposition d'ensemble n'apparaît pas à la lecture suivie. Elle se dissimule sous un apparent négligé, une fois passée l'ouverture sur le mode encomiastique, peut-être réminiscente de toute "rhétorique au Prince," où le lecteur ne saurait pénétrer dans le texte qu'une fois l'hommage rendu au lecteur archétypal, princier, premier dont l'autorité rejaillit sur l'oevre. De surcroît, comme à la tutelle prestigieuse mais hasardeuse du Prince répond la constante et vigilante protection des vrais amis, les amertumes que celle-là engendre trouvent dans la douceur de celle-ci leur équilibre. Les lettres initiales et finales forment ainsi un tout. De fait, à bien examiner les deux séries de lettres qui forment le corps du recueil, il serait possible de saisir leur ingénieux art de la diversion et la variété des lieux de l'invention tel un jeu d'anamorphoses: les lettres V et X se font écho l'une à l'autre sur le lieu de la Folie littéraire, les lettres VI et XI développent le *topos* du Prince parfait, les épîtres VII et XII tentent un essai d'histoire littéraire, les épîtres VIII et XIII s'unissent dans une méditation sur la vérité de l'éloquence, les *epistolae* IX et XIV, dans une brillante discussion de Descartes et Corneille, de Machiavel et de Térence ressaisissent la question de l'imitation et du génie. Terme à terme et face à face les lettres, en une disposition copieuse, font dialoguer des sujets par dessus les correspondants, dans une sorte d'univers rhétorique clos sur lui-même. L'épistolier y joue d'un art de l'allusion et de l'imprévu sous lequel se dissimule l' harmonie des thèmes. En cela il tend un miroir aux jeux de la Fortune, un fil qui court à travers le recueil, dont les brutalités inattendues ne sont que l'apparence d'un destin peut-être déjà joué.

Il nous faut donc revenir, pas à pas, sur cette leçon de composition que Balzac donne dans son *Liber Vnus* et sur la teneur de cet ouvrage réellement unique. De toute évidence, le repli sur le style moyen français et l'intimité dont a parlé B. Beugnot est ici en voie de réalisation: l'*ingenium* de l'épistolier tire profit de l'intimité créée par l'usage du latin, intimité de langue, intimité de culture, langue d'initiés. Il confie donc à cet *aptum* du texte et des lecteurs les délices et les peines d'une intimité: "teque habeam ferè unum, in quo conquesciam, & in cuius sinu omnes curas ac dolores deponam meos," écrit-il à Chapelain. A tous égards cette correspondance est "curatius scripta," pour citer Pline le Jeune, le modèle peut-être le plus prégnant des *Epistolae*.[3]

Les correspondants de chair et de voix auxquels, selon la formule de Démétrius, l'épistolier offre "un tableau de son âme," se voient réordonnés les uns par rapport aux autres, dans l'ordre "curatius" d'une oeuvre close sur elle-même.[4] Plus que jamais le rapport entre la vive voix du français, déployée sous les aspects protéiformes des *Entretiens* de 1657, et la voix intelligible du latin se dévoile dans ces lettres latines, telle une opposition entre le ciel des Idées et le désordre du monde sensible.[5] Traversant la biographie de Balzac, les *Epistolae* seraient comme l'héritage de sept ans de prose néo-latine, avant les sept ans de silence menant aux *Oeuvres diverses* de 1644.

Une analyse des quatre épîtres liminaires révèle bien vite que Balzac y compose, dans la demie fiction d'une correspondance suivie avec le Cardinal, une gamme d'arguments et de traits qui impriment au recueil entier son mouvement: éloge du Cardinal dont dépend la paix civile, la floraison des arts et la direction du vrai goût littéraire, une définition des conditions politiques et culturelles propres à une entière rénovation de la société française. Or, sous ce programme sans grande originalité, coule la véritable source des épîtres: Balzac y lance le thème de l'*otium* et du

[3] B. Beugnot, "Style ou styles épistolaires," *Revue d'Histoire Littéraire de la France* LXXVIII (6) (novembre–décembre 1978).

[4] Voir F. Gamberini, *Stylistic Theory and Practice in the Younger Pliny*, Altertumswissenschaftliche Texte Nund Studien, XI (Hildesheim-Zürich-New York: Olms-Weidemann, 1983).

[5] J.-L. Guez de Balzac, *Les Entretiens*, 2 vols., éd. B. Beugnot (Paris: Didier, 1973).

negotium, cet *otium* auquel il se condamne et ce *negotium* auquel il aurait aimé prendre part. Cette confluence des courants de la vie privée et de la conduite des affaires mène ainsi Balzac à la rencontre de Richelieu: face à l'homme privé, dont l'absence loin de Paris est un prodige de publicité, se trouve l'homme public dont la présence envahit tout y compris la retraite du premier, témoin incessant et vigilant de la réconciliation de Balzac avec les lettres: "carissimam mihi imaginem ... cujus quotidiano conspectu animus aeger ... recreatus."[6] Or, ce dialogue de l'oisiveté et du négoce, ce jeu de retraite et d'évocation, dont le canon me semble être, outre Pline,[7] l'Ovide des *Tristes*, se soutient d'une opposition entre un style de vie qualifié de "solutius viuendi genus" et de "pudor quidam subrusticus," consacré à "studentem parandae bonae menti," et les dangers inhérents aux "aulicis artibus."[8] Le style de vie de la Cour, son "cultus" tout en extériorité, s'éloigne par deux fois de cette pudeur humaine, éminemment intériorisée, prônée par Balzac: ce sont ces "paroles dorées" à l'Italienne, ce sont tous les périls de tous les bavardages.[9] Or Balzac tente une analyse de l'art de la louange, dont l'excès est l'un de ces dangers, dans la lettre II qui, reprise à mon sens du discours de Laelius dans le *De Amicitia*, trace un trait d'union entre la culture aulique et la culture, disons, amicale.[10] Si l'art épistolaire est un ressaisissement de l'amitié vive dans l'absence de la lettre elle doit, tout comme la vraie louange, se passer des fictions flatteuses. En d'autres termes l'échange épistolaire doit servir de modèle à toute relation transparente, urbaine, humaine. Ceci explique donc pourquoi ces quatre lettres au Cardinal, du point de vue tant de l'invention que de la composition de recueil, trouvent leur écho dans les deux lettres finales. Un paradoxe donne à ces épîtres leur énergie: la *réelle urbanitas* habite l'*urbs* toute intellectuelle de la correspondance littéraire et non la Ville de pierres et de pouvoir, cette "politiorem Lutetiam." La rusticité et l'urbanité peuvent se fondre l'une en l'autre.[11]

Les épîtres XV et XVI, adressées à Silhon et Chapelain, sont quant à

---

[6] Ep. II, p. 63.

[7] Pliny, *Letters*, éd. W. M. L. Hutchinson, 2 vols., Loeb Classical Library (Londres: Heinemann, 1953), VII, 9.

[8] Ep. III, p. 66.

[9] Voir M. Fumaroli, *L'Age de l'Eloquence* (Genève: Droz, 1980), p. 691 et suivantes.

[10] Cicéron, *L'Amitié*, éd. L. Laurand (Paris: Belles-Lettres, 1961), p. 51.

[11] Ep. XIV, p. 121.

elles un miracle d'équilibre, et ce, à plusieurs égards: la figure du Cardinal, cette "carissimam mihi imaginem" s'est dédoublée, telle une Idée platonicienne, dans ses deux amis qui sont, en même temps, deux exemples de bons courtisans; de surcroît c'est bien par une apologie de l'amitié que ces lettres ferment le recueil: l'amitié vraie est un hâvre contre la maladie et les ennemis, images de la Fortune, et Balzac d'évoquer le cercle complet de leurs amis: Colletet, Cospéan, Ogier, Gomberville, Lhuillier, Laelius évoquant le cercle de Scipion l'Africain. Il trace autour du vrai style le cercle magique de l'amitié. Ici l'urbanité et l'humanité règnent. Bref, dans la traversée de la chronologie parallèle des quatre premières épîtres et des deux lettres de conclusion, Balzac établit un jeu presque plotinien d'où émane la vraie parole, transparente et latine, hors de l'"inani verborum strepitu," ces paroles françaises sans cesse au bord des lèvres de la barbarie.

Au coeur du recueil les dix épîtres centrales reprennent, développent et amplifient les lignes de force ainsi tendues. La lecture de ces lettres s'agence donc aussi bien selon la chronologie, mime appauvri d'une correspondance qui placerait le lecteur anonyme dans la situation des récipiendaires, que selon une architecture d'échos et de renvois, fiction de profondeur et ouverture de perspectives qui nourrissent la lecture d'une simulation de vivacité. Au demeurant la différence toute contemporaine entre une lecture savante et une lecture innocente n'a ici aucune prise: le plaisir, le *pathos* et l'instruction vont l'amble dans cet art néo-latin. C'est en ce sens que, comme on l'a noté dans la récente édition des *Epistolae*, le recueil présente une manière de *theatrum mundi* mais non pas tant du *negotium* que de l'art épistolaire et de ses "offices."

Relevons-en donc les lieux.

Le premier lieu sur lequel Balzac arrête sa plume surgit dans la lettre V: un mot l'emblématise, "insanitas." Balzac vilipende les folies qui pervertissent le goût et corrompent les lettres et produisent un style qui ne s'adresse plus aux héritiers de l'humanisme mais à des sauvages, un style "Ætiopibus." La folie littéraire agitent ces auteurs qui "librosque quotidie euomant insipientiae suae testes." Au "rendu" littéraire réplique une innutrition qui se nourrit à l'"innoxia vita" menée par Balzac. Dans la lettre X, double de la Ve, Balzac oppose en effet les poisons semés par les mauvais auteurs à l'innocence de ses écrits. C'est alors qu'à cette autre innocence, la congénialité de la lecture amicale, qui encourage les vertus et guérit les vices, Balzac affronte l'audace adultère de certains critiques: "Ea est . . . adulterae, vt sic dicam, manus audacia" et qu'il confronte la fausse renommée des querelles à la vraie gloire d'être bien lu et bien compris.[12] Quel est ce lecteur idéal, qui peut remédier à l'"insanitas" du monde littéraire? Dans la lettre V, Richelieu, "optimum omnis doctrinae & elegantiae disceptatorum," dans la lettre X, Voiture, "vir optime & dicendi peritissime." Si d'une lettre à l'autre et d'une folie à l'autre, Balzac a changé de registre, c'est que le fil qui relie les deux lettres se noue pas tant sur la question de l'auteur du jugement–Richelieu ou Voiture–que sur les moyens littéraires de répliquer aux jugements faux: là, il interdit à Priésac de le venger par un libelle, trop proche de la satire, genre lui-même soupçonné de folie puisque, "non ingeniosam," elle peut "altius vulgi animum penetrare"; ici, il envisage de répondre "civiliter." De l'un à l'autre un choix littéraire s'est accompli: le libelle n'eût fait que nourrir l'"obscenitas" du "champ littéraire," la réponse lui conserve partie de sa "dignitas."

Aprés avoir ainsi décrit le désordre qui règne dans les relations littéraires et comment il affecte la restauration d'un "cultus" selon ses voeux, Balzac entretient son correspondant de Gustave de Suède. La turbulence littéraire et le chaos politique forment doublet. Prince parfait, soldat lettré, le roi protestant–revers du roi catholique Louis XIII dont *Le Prince* avait frappé l'avers de la même médaille–incarne en effet une sorte d'atticisme politique dans un univers de passions hamletiennes, la raison et la mesure dans l'"inclementia" et l'"asperitas" nordiques, bref l'idéal d'urbanité au sein de la Barbarie: "Spartanum vel Atheniensem diceres matre peregre profectâ in Barbariâ." Gustave de Suède est l'objet d'un traitement sur le mode de l'éthopée et de la prosopographie. Cette lettre illustre à la perfection le style du *laus hominum* tel que pratiqué par Pline le Jeune.[13] De fait, la série d'expressions employées par Balzac "plurima humanitate temperatus ... mira in ore dignitas ... firmissima proceri corporis compages" pourraient être appliquées au style-même de Balzac. Cette apologie figurale sert de définition à la beauté du langage littéraire: le panégyrique du Roi mort est une apologie du beau style balzacien. On peut d'ailleurs se demander si, dans cet éloge d'un prince parfait malgré son "apostasie," Balzac ne glisse par la figure de l'Empereur Julien, modèle de culture en dépit de son reniement religieux, dont lui, Balzac, eût voulu être, dans un théâtre des lettres, le Libanios. Quoi qu'il en soit de cette incertitude allusive, c'est bien le thème du Prince que reprend la lettre XI au sujet de l'ouvrage du même nom: le choix de Gustave et de Louis XIII répond à un désir de vérité, de vraisemblance, de mesure–

[12] Ep. X, p. 95.
[13] Ep. VI, p. 77. Sur Pline voir Gamberini, p. 286.

d'humanité. Balzac oppose ses portraits au fard, au faux et à la fiction des louanges auliques, qui postulent un Prince idéal au lieu d'essayer de discerner dans le Prince de chair et d' esprit l'unité harmonieuse et sublimée de la variété humaine. Cette essence allusive de la vertu royale trouve ainsi son écho dans l'humanité du bon style littéraire.

Les lettres VII et XII, que nous apparions de nouveau, continuent, à leur façon, cette méditation sur la beauté des mots et la vérité des choses. Il faut toutefois bien voir que l'apologie de Saint-Cyran, à la dialectique "recta sinceraque," entretenue par une nature secrète et solitaire, fait contre-poids au développement sur le poétique, objet de la lettre XII. La toile de fond commune à ces deux épîtres, c'est cette "sophistica lues" dont l'infection affecte autant les "lettres sacrées" que les belles lettres. Malgré l'écart qui tient à distance la prose sacrée de la prose d'art, Balzac ne parle que d'une seule et même chose: la vérité des mots appliqués aux choses, qu'elle concerne l'exégèse, pédagogie de l'âme, ou les belles lettres, pédagogie de l'esprit et du coeur. L'intelligence d'un style dépend essentiellement, avance Balzac au cours de sa poétique comparée de Ronsard et de Malherbe, d'un principe de constance. Il reproche en effet à Ronsard d'osciller entre l'Antiquité et son siècle, jouant d'un style "(cultus) . . . inter nostram ac priorem aetatem medius." Au contraire l'art malherbien se nourrit des qualités d'être "constans," "perspicax" et "castigatus," ce qui empêche cette hésitation entre deux styles, acte d'autant plus héroïque à accomplir qu'un tel mouvement de pendule existe dans les habitudes de lecture du public: on lit encore sous Louis XIII ces "Bardos . . . & Gallicos Faunos, & insanos vates," tout autant que "fuit . . . Ennianus Populus saeculo Virgiliano."[14] Cette "superstition" de la vétusté est insupportable, elle suscite la préciosité de l'archaïsme, double artistique de la sophistique sacrée. De même cette indécision ne saurait brouiller la prose et la poésie, "alterum genus ne incurrat in alterum." En d'autres termes la vérité véhiculée par un style de discours est tributaire d'un certain *decorum*.

Les lettres VIII et XIII, qui ont en commun d'être adressées à deux hommes d'Eglise, amplifient ce traitement de la culture littéraire. Balzac y saisit l'occasion de soulever la question de la dualité du style au regard du "docere." Il envisage la mission pédagogique du bon style de deux

[14] Ep. XII, p. 105. La question d'une poésie "bardique" se trouve ici formulée très exactement: il faudrait suivre la trame de cette réflexion sur la poésie vaticinante jusqu'à sa pleine formulation au XVIIIe siècle, dans ses rapports à la transformation du concept de sublime.

façons, dans son rapport à la philosophie et à l'histoire. Se demandant comment il est possible de dénaturer un texte artistique, "torquens innocentissima verba, minimas etiam syllabas excutere ad vivum," afin de le faire coïncider avec un discours philosophique, Balzac est conduit à distinguer le philosophe de l'écrivain au nom de l'"usus communis" et de la "loquendi consuetudo."[15] L'"oratoria libertas" s'arrêterait devant le savant "ratio intelligendi disserendique." Cet acte de contrition et de soumission serait la défaite de la prose—et Balzac dans un poème de Noël, où il franchit la barrière du "genus," brosse un tableau de son abandon de la pourpre littéraire—si Balzac ne se retirait dans la prose elle-même et ne réclamait pour le *cultus* épistolaire un droit à exprimer une part de la vérité des choses. Cette revendication de liberté est analogue à celle de Descartes qui divorce, au même moment, le discours philosophique du discours apologétique, dans l'alliance de la biographie et de la réflexion métaphysique.[16] Telle est, par corollaire, la relation qui unit le discours historique à l'Histoire. Selon Balzac le débat autour de Plutarque s'articule aux deux éléments suivants: son style composite peut-il enseigner la vérité des faits, l'enseignement historique doit-il se couler dans un langage "aequabile et temperatum" pour relever véritablement du *docere*? Comment définir le rapport de l'*ingenium* de l'écrivain à la transparence des mots et des choses?

Tel est le sujet des lettres jumelles IX et XIV. Balzac se fait le témoin et le critique, dans l'épître IX, de deux exemples d'ingéniosité assez cruels puisqu'il choisit la publication de deux oeuvres aussitôt ressenties comme magistrales dans le monde des lettres françaises, *Le Discours de la méthode* et *Le Cid*, pour reprocher à son correspondant, Charles de Berville, de "frustrer" ses amis de son "profuturum saeculis opus." Amicale raillerie mise à part, Balzac soulève à propos de Descartes et de Corneille la question le plus épineuse de l'*ingenium* littéraire, comment lire une oeuvre de génie?[17] Le style cartésien pêche par excès, par ampleur, par dilatation. Balzac conseille de "(coercere) stilum." Ce qui compte c'est le poids des mots. Expression difficile à saisir sauf si on la compare à la critique de Corneille: Balzac hésite à y définir le style dramatique de celui-ci de

[15] Ep. VIII, p. 85.

[16] Ph. J. Salazar, "Balzac lecteur de Pline le Jeune: la fiction du *Prince*," *XVIIe Siècle* 168 (3): 292-302.

[17] M. Fumaroli, "Genèse de l'épistolographie classique," *Revue d'Histoire Littéraire de la France* LXXVIII (6) (novembre-décembre 1978): 886-905.

"grande" ou d'"immodicum," d'"alium" ou d'"enorme."[18] Soit, la difficulté que l'on éprouve à juger un style génial provient non pas du plaisir indéniable qu'il procure au lecteur, mais d'une indécision sur la nature de ce plaisir. A deux reprises Balzac se demande s'il ne s'est pas laissé tromper par "l'imposture de la récitation" ou la fidélité de sa mémoire.[19] Bref le poids d'un style génial, en prose ou en vers, irrite l'"aptum" nécessaire à une bonne intelligence du lecteur et de l'auteur. Le sublime, car c'est de cela qu'il s'agit ici, change de nature s'il se transporte du domaine latin au domaine français. Le sublime d'un Ogier, "ingenium igneum, & concitatissimae sublimitatis,"[20] diffère de celui d'un Descartes ou d'un Corneille: Balzac entrevoit combien "l'effort héroïque" pour s'écarter de la norme s'incarnera avec plus d'aisance dans le vernaculaire que "son assomption communément acceptée," pour citer Marc Fumaroli, et combien le consensus espéré sur "le langage des honnestes gens," sur la simplicité et le naturel du style littéraire français portera toujours en lui l'embryon d'une esthétique sinon trouble du moins inquiétante.[21] Lorsque Balzac insiste sur l'art de Térence, sur cette rivière qui "fluat leniter & pure, nihil secum turbidum, neque alienum deferens," et qu'il vante les qualités humaines de la comédie latine et ses "voluptés innocentes," il brosse l' éloge d'un art fidèle à la vraie nature humaine–dans l'*Eunuque*, pièce "divine," choisie expressément par Balzac, Gnathon emblématise au contraire toutes les sophistiques–;[22] mais il y met en quelque sorte les auteurs français en garde contre ce "coeco impetu"qui risque, privé de la "possession des Muses," d' entraîner les lettres modernes vers l'intempérance et le désordre.

University of Cape Town

[18] Ep. IX, p. 90 et 92.

[19] Ep. XIV, p. 115: Balzac n'incrimine pas sa mémoire à proprement parler mais demande le secours de la mémoire de Thoreau de Saint-Chartres–ce qui revient au même.

[20] Ep. XV, p. 124.

[21] M. Fumaroli, "Rhétorique d'école et rhétorique adulte," *Revue d'Histoire Littéraire de la France* LXXXVI (1) (janvier 1986): 33–51.

[22] Cette méditation sur Gnathon vient du *De Amicitia* où Cicéron analyse l'amitié, la flatterie et critique, en sourdine, la philosophie cynique. Il faudrait reprendre, dans les *Epistolae* ce fil de la "caninam facundiam" (Ep. V, p. 71) dans son double rapport à l'encomium et au stoïcisme.

Bartholomaeus Coloniensis: Two Fables

PIETER SCHOONBEEG

Contrary to any suggestion its geography might make, the northern and eastern parts of what is now the Netherlands were the first to be touched by Italian humanism. In the proud and prosperous cities of the Hanseatic League around the middle of the fifteenth century, an awareness of intellectual and cultural studies grew that was already rapidly reaching its zenith in Italy. The first enthusiasm for these new *studia humanitatis* was centered in the Cistercian monastery of Aduard just to the northwest of the city of Groningen; hence the term *Adwert Academy*. Its "members" were teachers and clerics and they had a tremendous influence on future generations. Bartholomaeus Coloniensis was a product of this intellectual atmosphere.[1] He was highly thought of by his contemporaries. In his twenty-third letter Erasmus remarks: "Pretaerea Bartholomaeum Coloniensem a literatorum numero secludendum censuerim minime."[2]

Born in about 1460, probably in Cologne, Bartholomaeus was educated at Alexander Hegius's school in Deventer, where he stayed on as a teacher after his studies. From Deventer he moved to Zwolle where, still teaching, he remained until 1506. That same year he succeeded Johannes Grovius as rector of St. Mauritius's school at Münster. In 1511 he moved to Alkmaar to replace Bastius as rector of the Latin School. One of his colleagues here was Alardus of Amsterdam who later was to edit Agricola's works. In 1513 he returned to Deventer, and three years later he died at Minden.

---

[1] See for the following C. G. van Leijenhorst in *Contemporaries of Erasmus. A Biographical Register of the Renaissance and Reformation*, eds. P. G. Bietenholz and Th. B. Deutscher (Toronto, 1987), vol. 3, s.v. Zehender.

[2] Desiderius Erasmus, *Opus Epistularum*, eds. P. S. Allen, H. M. Allen, and H. W. Garrod (Oxford, 1906–1958), I, ep. 23.

His extant works are: In prose an *Epistula mythologica* (Deventer: J. de Breda 1489/90) which was called by a German editor of the last century "eine Humoreske aus der Zeit des deutschen Frühhumanismus."[3] In 1500 he published a book entitled *Canones cum declarationibus eorundem in tabulas computi ecclesiastici* (Zwolle: P. Os), which in later editions appeared with an additional *Libellus de magnitudine terrae, lunae et solis*, and in 1515 appeared a *Tractatus de diversis rebus ponderabilibus* (Deventer: T. de Borne). There is also a *Libellus isagogicus seu introductorius in primum, secundum et tertium tractatus Petri Hispani* and a "Letter to Pancratius."[4]

His poetical work consists of a collection of various poems that is called *Silva Carminum* (Deventer: J. de Breda, 1491), an eclogue (or, as the manuscript calls it, *egloga bucolici carminis*)[5] and a *Libellus elegiacus de septenis doloribus Mariae*, published in the year 1514 (Deventer: J. de Breda). Three other poems have come down to us that are connected with his Alkmaar years: one of them is entitled *De miraculoso sanguine civitatis Alcmariensis carmen heroicum*, celebrating a Holy Blood-miracle that took place in Alkmaar in 1429 and was commemorated annually.[6] The second poem, *Carmen de Sancto Matthia*, is written in elegiac distichs and addressed to the tutelary saint of Alkmaar's principal church. The last poem, in acslepiadei minores, is in praise of St. Lawrence, patron of the city.[7] Bartholomaeus also wrote several commendatory poems for other books.

The two fables that are my particular object in this paper can be found at the end of the *Silva Carminum*. They are both written in elegiac distichs; the first consists of seventy, the second of 144 lines.

The fable-literature of classical antiquity was, for its Greek part, written in prose (Aesopus) and choliambs (Babrius); in Latin, Phaedrus, using Aesopus as his main source, wrote iambic senarii and Avianus, drawing principally on Babrius, used the elegiac distich. Its contents are tersely phrased

---

[3] D. Reichling, *Epistola Mythologica*. Humoreske aus der Zeit des deutschen Frühhumanismus (Berlin, 1897).

[4] P. O. Kristeller, *Iter Italicum* (London-Leiden, 1983), III, 156[a] (Czechoslovakia, KYNZVART, Zámecká Knihovna, 20 K 23) and 611[a] (Michelstadt FRG, Evangelische Kirchenbibliothek C 376).

[5] Kristeller, ibid., 121[b] (Brussels, Bibliothèque Royale Albert Ier, 20589).

[6] E. H. Rijkenberg, "De geschiedenis en de reliquie van het mirakel van het H. Bloed te Alkmaar," *Bijdragen voor de Geschiedenis van het Bisdom Haarlem* 21 (1896), 377–97.

[7] Dr. W. Lampen O.F.M., "Twee gedichten van Bartholomaeus van Keulen op Alkmarr's patroonheiligen," *Haarlemsche Bijdragen, Bouwstoffen voor de Geschiedenis van het Bisdom Haarlem* 52 (1935), 112–27.

scenes, mostly from animal life, with a moralizing application, story and application usually not running to more than ten or twenty lines.

The fables of the Aesopus-Phaedrus tradition were known to the Middle Ages from the so-called Romulus-collection, a prose version dating, according to some, from late antiquity, according to others, from somewhere between the tenth and twelfth centuries.[8] They were also known through the distichs of the Anonymus Neveleti, identified later with Gualterus Anglicus, from the twelfth century. In 1465 Perotti gave an epitome of the Phaedrus-fables and thirty others, these last known as the *Appendix Perottina.*

The great number of extant manuscripts shows that the spread of Avianus's fables must have been enormous in the Middle Ages. Owing to their simple metre and their rather tame spirit in comparison to Phaedrus's fables, they were used as schooltexts from a very early date on. Their influence on mediaeval fables written in hexameters of elegiac distichs was great.

Further development of the fable in the Middle Ages brings into existence, on the one hand, the animal epic, like the *Roman de Renart* and the *Ysengrimus,* which criticises contemporary society and contains strong elements of allegory and parable. On the other hand, the traditional fable lives on and is used in sermons, where it becomes, in accordance with the system of biblical exegesis developed by Origenes, a *signum* or *significatio* that can be interpreted in many kinds of ways, *mystice, spiritualiter* etc.

Between 1476 and 1480, so more than ten years before Bartholomaeus Coloniensis's fables appeared in print, Heinrich Steinhöwel published his fable-collection.[9] It contained a biography of Aesopus by Planudes, the Latin prose-text of the Romulus-collection with a German translation, the Latin distichs of the Anonymus Neveleti and some prose-fables by Petrus Alphonsi and Poggio. Another famous collection of fables, that of Martinus Dorpius, a Louvain professor of Divinity, appeared about thirty years later.[10] In between Bartholomaeus published his two fables.

---

[8] For this and the following see A. Tietze in *Lexikon des Mittelalters*, eds. L. Lutz, J. M. McLellan (Munich and Zurich, 1977), vierter Band, erste Lieferung, s.v. Fabel, -dichtung; *Pauly's Real-Encyclopädie der classischen Altertumswissenschaft*, ed. G. Wissowa (Stuttgart, 1896), zweiter Band, s.v. Avianus; *Pauly's Real-Encyclopädie der classischen Altertumswissenschaft*, eds. G. Wissowa, W. Kroll (Stuttgart: 1938), 38ster Halbband, s.v. Phaedrus. The fables can be found in L. Hervieux, *Les fabulistes latins depuis le siècle d'Auguste jusqu'à la fin du Moyen-Age*, 5 vols., (1893–1899); repr. Hildesheim and New York: Georg Olms, 1970).

[9] Ulm, s.a. (c. 1476–1480).

[10] *Aesopus Dorpii* (Antwerp, 1524).

Not counting their length, these fables seem, at first, to be what their title pronounces them to be: scenes from animal life with a moralizing application. Taken together, their common ancestry is obvious: Phaedrus's *Fabula de corvo et vulpe* in Avianus's metre, after various mediaeval and Renaissance versions chiefly known to us from La Fontaine's *Le corbeau et le renard*. There are, however, striking differences. To begin with, the first fable is entitled *Fabula de gallo et vulpe in qua latenter deridetur inanis gloria cuiusdam poetae*. A bird, by the not only groundless, but in this case hilariously exaggerated flattery of a fox, is coaxed into doing something that will prove highly deleterious to itself. Although the story is broadly the same as Phaedrus's and its successors, the changed title connected with this story has no parallel in the vast corpus of post-classical fable-literature. There is, incidentally, in the Romulus-collection a *Fabula de gallo et vulpe*, but its story and its ending are completely different.[11] But there is more. The main object of the fox in the orthodox version of the fable is a piece of cheese in unlawful possession of the raven. The fox tries to get hold of it by flattering the bird into singing and thus opening its beak. Bartholomaeus's variation on Phaedrus's theme, however, introduces a fox that, not satisfied with so small a reward, aims at making a meal of the bird itself, in the end successfully.

The second fable seems at first to be traditional in its title and in the moral precept the title contains: *Fabula de corvo et vulpe in qua latenter praemonemur ne fidem adhibeamus adulatorum blanditiis*. But again all similarity to its classical and mediaeval predecessors ceases here. Within the space of the first ten lines it becomes evident that the fox has malicious intentions on the life of the raven. Simulating a grave illness, it tries to convince the bird that it is the only one that can cure him, simply by embracing and kissing him, a piece of advice that he was given, so he says, by the priestess of the oracle at Delphi. The raven immediately spots the pitfall and, indignant for being considered stupid enough to succumb to the flatteries of the fox, compares these to seemingly harmless animals that have an unexpected but effective weapon like scorpions and bees. The fox, not to be outbidden, replies at length with a long catalogue of similar animals, assuring the raven that it is unjust and groundless to

[11] This is the fable on which Chaucer's *The Nun's Priest's Tale* is based. There is, however, some resemblance to a fable in the *Directorium humanae vitae* of Johannes de Capua (see Hervieux, ibid., V, 201) and to one in the *Speculum sapientiae* of (ps.-) Cyrillus. See J. G. Th. Grässe, *Die beiden ältesten lateinischen Fabelbücher des Mittelalters* (Hildesheim, 1965), 51–52.

compare him to those animals. This only makes the bird angrier. It curses the fox by wishing it several unpleasant fates and then, contrary to the traditions of the genre, it rises uninjured and majestically into the air or, as Bartholomaeus puts it in epic phraseology, "geminisque alis sese auras sustulit in liquidas," leaving behind a disappointed fox and a probably dumbfounded reading-public.

Consideration of these fables as simply two pieces of fifteenth century Neo-Latin gives the following impression. Reading the fables is great fun. The Latin is lucid, instantly intelligible and, if not always up to rigidly classical standards, amusing by its unusual, variegated and at times extravagant modes of expression. Bartholomaeus is fond of variation: for example, he uses five different paraphrases to denote an oak, he has some six words to describe the agreeeable sound of musical instruments or voices, and several words for the cither and the flute. He loves long, composite words (e.g., *dulcifluus, dulcisonus, glandifer, multiforus, anguicomus, semicaper*, and the like), among them some that do not occur in classical Latin and cannot be found in Du Cange's dictionary. The metre is, broadly spoken, faultless; the structure of the distichs as to the distribution of dactyls and spondees over the lines, is comparable to the practice of the classical elegiac poets. In matters of caesura and dihaeresis there is nothing exceptional in these poems, but they do show a high rate of elision.

Two problems can be discussed with regard to the first fable. First, although the public was highly conversant with fable-literature either through the use the schools made of Latin–and even sometimes of Greek fables or through the translations and versions in the vernacular that had already been in existence for some time–Bartholomaeus evidently had a motive for presenting the contents of a very well-known fable in a new form, which bears the name of another equally well-known fable. The second problem arises from the fact that the word *fabula* or its Greek counterpart had, amongst others, the meaning I already indicated but never served the purpose of teaching *one* person a moral lesson or of ridiculing *one* person, as is here apparent from the title and the *epimythium*.

As to the first question: The change of the title appropriate to the contents (i.e., the change from *De corvo et vulpe* to *De gallo et vulpe*) may have been caused by the end that is envisaged in the title, the "latens derisio cuiusdam poetae." The contemporary in-crowd may have seen the link between the *gallus* and the name, nationality or unusual sexual appetite (cf. appendix 1, 42 sqq.) of the intended poet. Regarding the problem that the word *fabula* is here not used in its accepted sense, the solution may be that this poem, though superficially a fable, should be considered as just another one of Bartholomaeus's satirical poems.

The second fable bears the title *De corvo et vulpe,* accompanied by its traditional moral "ne fidem adhibeamus adulatorum blanditiis." The poet, however, takes even fewer pains to conform to his model: the customary piece of cheese is no more mentioned than in the first fable and the raven is not even flattered on account of its good voice. On the contrary, the poet speaks of "garrula murmura" (line 6) and makes the fox speak directly to the raven of "clamosas voces" (line 13) and "nimia garrulitate" (line 14), of "obtundere" (line 15) and "vocibus horrendis" (line 16). Then, after a verbal contest that brings to mind a coloratura-opera in which two singers try to outdo each other by the briliance and virtuosity of their arias, the fable reaches the stupendous conclusion already mentioned: the raven, traditionally the victim of its own vanity and the flatteries of the fox, does not comply with the request of the fox and so evades a certain death. This ending, alien to the *Fabula de corvo et vulpe,* has a parallel: oddly enough, this parallel is the fable in the Romulus-collection, entitled *De gallo et vulpe.*

Apart from these obvious differences in content between Bartholomaeus's fables and the conventional representatives of the genre, there is another disparity that at first is even more striking. Compared to "normal" fables, these two are very long; and, what is more, their inordinate length is filled by a completely different vocabulary and phraseology. The conventional classical fable is tersely and sometimes rather boringly worded. This obtains even more for its post-classical successors. In Bartholomaeus's fables, however, there is never a dull moment. Within the scope of this paper these poems cannot be discussed in detail, but a few passages can be shortly described.

In the first fable, the opening speech of the fox (lines 5–12) consists of eight verses full of poetical commonplaces; however, looking back on it after having read the whole of the two fables, it is comparatively modest. But the cock immediately almost buries it under seventeen lines of mythological erudition: there is the story of the dying swan, of Phaethon who fell into the river Po when trying to drive the chariot of the Sun; there are Orpheus, the monster Argos guarding Io, the Sirens, Arion and his dolphin, and finally "nigra Persephone" and the Phlegeton.

Another example can be found from line eighty onwards in the second fable. In the preceding lines the fox has explained the situation: he is ill and to embrace the raven will cure him. For this the fox has promised the raven immortal fame. The raven's answer (lines 80–89) is negative: he compares the flattering words of the fox to innocent-looking animals like scorpions and bees, with their hidden sting, and to the melodious but fatal sound of the fowler's flute. The fox, pretending to be indignant, answers this implicit accusation with a long list of more or less dangerous animals with whom there is no cause to compare him. He mentions (lines 91–110) the basilisk, the ox, the snake, the scorpion, the horse, the bear, the wild boar, the porcupine, and the lion. Besides, the fox adds, I cannot bite because a coughing-fit robbed me of my teeth long ago.

Of these bombastic enumerations from various fields of learning, there are more in these fables, but these catalogues of *Priamel*-like forms do not belong to the fable-genre. The same obtains for the epic words and phrases and the almost baroque modes of expression in which these poems abound.

What people in the second half of the fifteenth century considered to be a fable can be gathered from the already mentioned collection of Heinrich Steinhöwel: short stories in prose or poetry, mostly about animals, with an attached moral. That people still thought so about thirty years later is shown by the enormous popularity of the fable-collection of Martinus Dorpius: here are contemporary versions of old fables, but also new fables by men like Poliziano. But the overall impression is still the same. The fables of Bartholomaeus Coloniensis do not fit in at all, and they cannot be seriously considered fables: their length, their exorbitant vocabulary and the evidently intentional clash between title, contents and tradition preclude this. It seems likely that these poems should be regarded as an elaborate and amusing parody of the fable as a genre.

Groningen State University, the Netherlands

Appendix I

[From *Bartholomaei Coloniensis Silva carminum. In qua primo philosophia miris laudibus super aurum argentumque et lapides preciosos extollitur. Deinde Secta diogenis cynici cum quibusdam epigrammatibus ponitur. Ceterum. Zoilus detractor omnium doctorum virorum acerrime reprehenditur. Postremo ponuntur due fabelle in quarum altera latenter deridetur inanis gloria cuiusdam poete et in altera latenter premonemur ne adulatorum blandiciis fidem adhibeamus*, ed. Jacobus de Breda, Deventer, 1491.]

b iij r. sqq.: Fabula de gallo et vulpe in qua latenter deridetur inanis gloria cuiusdam poetae.

Arbore de querna uoces iactauit inanes
  Gallus et horrendos edidit ore sonos.
Hunc ubi glandifera comprendit in ilice uulpes,

Risit et in gallum subdola uerba dedit:
"Galle, decus uolucrum, nostram nunc accipe mentem
Auribus arrectis uerbaque nostra bibe:
Ecce per umbrosas siluas, per inhospita tesqua,
Per ualles imas, per iuga celsa rui.
Et uolucrum citharas et dulcia acanthidos ora
Lusciniaeque chelyn saepius aure bibi, 10
Sed tibi dulcisonae uolucres, me iudice, cedunt,
Vt cedit querrulae rauca cicuta lyrae."
Talia ubi dixit, cristatus rettulit ales:
"O uulpes, merito carmina magnificas,
Quom cantu exsupero moribundi gutter oloris
Qui Phaetontei stagna colit fluuii,
Et mihi multiforae buxi modulamina cedunt
Quae Phryx tibicen pollice et ore mouet.
Bistonii uatis plectrum, quod leniit Orcum
Anguicomasque deas, ora mea exsuperant. 20
Fistula quae somnos Argeis suasit ocellis,
Non poterit modulis aequiualere meis.
Quae proram aeratam scopulis Acheloia proles
Cantando impinit, me resonante tacet.
Et lyra quae tumido delphina sub aequore fouit,
Cedere carminibus cogitur illa meis.
Vox mea semicaprum Pana et Dryadas Satyrosque
Capripedes mulcet carmine dulcifluo.
Aurea plectra gero quis subterranea regna
Nigrae Persephones et Phlegetonta adeo." 30
Huic dixit uulpes: "O formosissme galle,
Quis dedit hanc citharam qua Phlegetonta petis?"
Dixit. Gallus ait: "Muscosa biuerticis antra
Parnasi rupemque Aoniam incolui
Atque ego Pegaseis sitibunda labella sub undis
Prolui et arenti fauce fluenta bibi.
Cuius odoratos hederae cinxere capillos,
Calliopea mihi haec aurea plectra dedit
Proque hederis iussit serratam surgere cristam
Ex capite, ut uates doctus in orbe uocer." 40
Dixit. Tum gallo uulpes caudata loquuta est:
"Ecce ego Calliopes te reor esse procum
Succensumque eius tenero te suspicor igne et
Illaqueatum eius mollibus illecebris.

Quom uetitos thalamos, ueluti petulans Epicurus,
Appetis, uxorum copia grata tibi est."
Hunc ubi servmonem finiuit callida uulpes
Et finem uerbis blandisonis posuit,
"Sim licet in Venerem foedo procliuior hirco
Et boue lasciuo spurcior," ales ait, 50
"Haud tamen Aonides coitu tentabo petulco
Nec nitidas Musas lubrico amore sequar.
Quis nisi spurcus amor de turre Pyrenea trusit,
Thespiadum amplexus furtaque dum petiit?"
Haec ubi gallus ait, uulpecula poplite flexo
Procubuit supplex talia uerba mouens:
"Galle, poeta sacer, quernis elabere ramis
Glandiferasque trabes desere et ima pete
Et caput excultum cristis frontemque uerendam
Appone, ut supplex osculer ora tua, 60
Ora quibus cedunt Thracis resonantia uatis
Plectra et Phoebeiae carmina amoena lyrae."
Haec ubi bestia ait, gallus nodosa reliquit
Robora gramineique ima soli petiit
Sinciput exermumque armato dentibus ori
Fraudosae uulpis praebuit intrepidus.
Mox caput oblatum morsu lacerauit acerbo
Carniuorax uulpes alitis exta uorans.
Galle, poeta sacer, quid inanis gloria prodest
Quae tibi non uitam contulit, immo necem?

Notes to Appendix I

3. *Eupolem.* 2.399; 6. Verg. *Aen.* 1.152, ibid. 2. 303, Claudian. 1.210; 7. Hor. *Ep.* 1.14.19; 16. *Sil.* 7. 149, ibid. 17. 496; *Poet. min.* (Baehrens) 4.153. 8; 17. Ov. *M.* 12. 158, cf. Sen. *Ag.* 358; 18. Catull. 63. 22;19. Sil. 11. 473; 20. Drac. Romul. 10. 439; 23. Verg. *Aen.* 10. 223, Stat. *Theb.* 5. 335, *Poet. min.* 4. 153. 1; 24. cf. Sil. 12. 187; 28. Ven. Fort. *carm.* 8. 19. 2; 33. cf. Sil. 15. 775, Stat. *Theb.* 1. 628, Sid. *carm.* 22. 233; 45. cf. Verf. *Aen.* 6. 623; 47. Prud. *Ditt.* 71; 55. Stat. *Theb.* 6. 590; 61. cf. Ov. *M.* 11.2; 62. Ov. *Ep.* 15(16). 182.

Appendix IIo

Fabula de coruo et uulpe in qua latenter pramonemur ne fidem adhibeamus adulatorum blanditiis.

In patulae fagi ramis Phoebeia uolucris
  Ariddulas uoces gutture fudit ouans.
Forsan flabra Noti aut pluuiam nubesue crepantes
  Fulmine terrifico uaticinata fuit.
Callida humi strata uulpes fertur sub eisdem
  Ramis, quae accepit garrula murmura auis,
Haec animo uoluit qua fraude aut arte uolucrem
  Illaqueet, tandem repperit illa uiam.
Nam se aegram finixit gemitumque et flebile murmur
  Edidit, hac coruum fallere fraude studens. 10
Hinc caput erexit tremulisque ululatibus ora
  Soluit et illacrimans haec, nisi fallor, ait:
"Inclute corue, precor, clamosas supprime uoces,
  Me miseram nimia garrulitate premis.
Desine, corue, precor, moribundam obtundere uulpem
  Vocibus horrendis, desine, corue, precor.
Fronde sub hac diros ego humi proiecta dolores
  Perdius et pernox languida sustinui.
Stamina quae neuit Lachesis, disrumpere tentat
  Atropos et mortem iam properare iubet." 20
Haec ubi ait uulpes, obmutuit et caput atrae
  Illisit terrae, se exanimem simulans.
"Quid fles? Quid quereris? Lacrimis quid rumpis obortis
  Lumina? Dic uulpes," decolor ales ait,
"Estne fames uel dira lues aut quispiam acerbus
  Morbus qui exagitat te? Mihi fare, rogo."
"O corue, esurie si me marcescere credis,
  Falleris augurio," subdola bestia ait,
"Contestor superos quod me igne geluque uicissim
Febris anhela coquit nocte dieque furens. 30
Dum uigor omnis abit, dum languentes calor artus
  Deserit et frigus membra tremore quatit,
Me puto Hyperboreae stellis glacialibus Vrsae
  Suppositam semper quo fera saeuit hiems,
Aut gelidis niuibus quas nubifer Apenninus
  Seruat, cuius apex sidera clara tenet.

Dum uero frigtus tremebundos deserit artus
   Et mea membra calor torquet ut ante gelu,
Vsque adeo exuror truculentis febribus, ut me
   Expositam Libycis aestibus esse rear. 40
Aut Aetnae iniectam, flammas quae pumice mixtas
   Candida siderei torquet ad astra poli.
Hanc pestem herbarum succis herbaque uirenti
   Pellere tentaui: Profuit herba nihil.
Saepe deos precibus pulsaui, ut morbida membra
   Curarent: Fusae nil ualuere preces.
Hinc tripodas Phoebi, quis Dephica terra superbit,
   Ilicet accessi, ut nimina consulerem.
Mox ubi fatidicum numen Phoebeia sacerdos
   Pectore suscepit, talia uerba dedit: 50
'Falleris, ah demens, si morbum pellere tentas
   Viribus herbarum multipliciue prece.
Morbus quo afficeris fatali elapsus ab astro
   Dicitur: hinc herbis pellier ille nequit.
Hippolytum Elysiis quamquam reuocauit ab aruis
   Herba, tamen pestem hanc pellere nulla potest.
Si uero, o uulpes, aegros curarier artus
   Opts, consilium sume salubre meum.
Pennigerae turbae decus est Phoebeius ales
   Et gratus Stygiis caelixolisque deis. 60
Hunc ubi frondosae prospexeris arbore fagi,
   Procumbas et opem sollicites precibus.
Ille feram pestem stomacho liquidisque medullis
   Pellet, grata genis fixerit oscla tuis.'
Hinc, pie corue, precor: fer opem, miserere misellae
   Vulpis et apta genis oscula fige meis,
Vt morbum expellas qui frigore et igne uicissim
   Languidolos artus nocte dieque premit.
Quod nequit herba uirens, quod non ualet herbidus humor
   Efficere, hoc osclo, corue, potes facili. 70
Quas ego fundo preces si librae lancibus aequis
   pensas, his cernes iustius esse nihil.
Pestibus euulsis si aegros curaueris artus,
   Laudibus immensis te super astra feram,
Sed si restiteris precibus, quod abominor, istis,
   Dic, pie, dic, corue, ad cuius opem fugiam?"

Hisce quidem uerbis sermonem belua clausit
Et finem imposuit blanisonis precibus.
Haud mora nocticolor coruus prorupit in hasce
Voces: "Blanditiis non ego credo tuis: 80
Faucibus est blandus sed cauda saeuus adunca
Scorpius, hamus inest melliferisque apibus.
Aequoreis scopulis impacta est concaua puppis
Dulcia Sirenum carmina quae petiit.
Fistula dulcisona est miserum qua callidus auceps
Alituum uulgus pellicit in laqueos.
Qui blandam uulpem caecarum retia fraudum
Texere subdubitat, mente carere puto hunc."
Hos ubi sermones accepit subdola uulpes,
Ingemuit querulosque edidit ore sonos. 90
"Me miseram insimulas fraudum et me texere rete
Fraudis ais, quamquam mens mea fraude caret.
Di mihi sint testes quod mens mea nescia fraudum est,
Occultant nullum quod mea uerba dolum.
Quod fugis inbellem uulpem, fortissime corue,
(Venia sit dicto) est dedecus atquepudor.
Haud ego letiferos gesto, ut basiliscus, ocellos.
Non, ut bos toruus, cornua adunca gero.
Non uirus gesto sub lingua, ut squameus anguis,
Nec mortem cauda, ut scorpius, incutio. 100
Calcibus haud ferio, ut sonipes, nec ego unguibus uncis
Bestiolas nemoris uenor, ut ursa ferox.
Non, ut aper, saetis nec, ut hystrix, squaleo spinis,
Nec gesto fauces, ut leo, carniuoras.
Escas, quas mihi fors dederat, gingiua ego inermi
Contriui, nam dens nullus in ore fuit.
Denticulos, quibus omniparens natura beauit
me, tussis iamdudum expulit ore meo.
Quid metuis? Quid, corue, fugis languentem et inermem
Vulpem quae texit retia nulla doli?" 110
Hinc uulpes uerbis finem imposuit labiisque
Occlusis tacuit, murmura quaeque premens.
Tunc Phoebi uolucris furiali concita bile
Effudit tales ore tonante sonos:
"Esto quod exermes, fallax uulpecula, fauces
Gestes, sit quoque dens nullus in ore tuo,
Non tamen est tutum fraudosae lambere faucem

Vulpis quae uiuas saepe uorauit aues.
Te simulasti aegram et commenta es febris anhelae
Pestem, ut me rabidis dentibus obtereres. 120
Sed frustra annosum tentasti fallere coruum
Quem caecae fraudis retia nulla latent.
Di tibi dent inpem uitam, quod non uerita es me
Tentare alloquiis blanditiisque tuis.
Hi tibi sint hostes qui duram fertilis agri
Terram proscindunt uomere adunco aratri.
Hi tibi sint hostes qui pascunt bucera opacis
Armenta in siuis rureue gramineo.
Hi tibi sint hostes qui lanigerium pecus alto
Monte aut ualle ima pascere saepe solent. 130
Cuius aues dudum rapuisti rustica anus te
Percutiat baculo te excerebretque colo.
Te catuli oppugnent, te dentata ora Molossi
Insani expugnent, te ora canina necent."
Sermonem his uerbis coruus clausit geminisque
Alis sese auras sustulit in liquidas.
Hinc fallax uulpes detectis fraudibus eius
Siluarum solitas maesta adiit latebras.
Dulces blanditias sapiens, ut toxica melle
Oblita, deuitat blandiloquosque fugit. 140
Auribus oppletis cera uersutus Vlysses
Sirenum molles praeteriit modulos,
Veliuolas naues fundo ne impingeret imo
Aut saltem aequoreis laederet in scopulis.

Notes to Appendix II

1. Verg. *Ecl.* 1. 1, Stat. *Silv.* 2. 4. 17; 3. Claudian. 26. 205; 9. Stat. *Theb.* 8. 619; 11. Verg. *Aen.* 7. 395, cf. Ov. *M.* 7. 190/1; 13. Cypr. Demetr. 1, Aug. *invang. Ioh.* 6. 2; 18. Gell. 2. 1. 2; 23. Verg. *Aen.* 4. 30, cf. Ov. *M.* 2. 656; 24. Val. Fl. 5. 340; 28. cf. Ov. *Ep.* 16. 234; 30. cf. Ov. Pont. 1. 10. 5; 33. Stat. *Theb.* 1. 693; 35. Ov. *M.* 2. 226; 36. cf. Ov. F. 1. 308; 40. cf. Claudian. 8.27; 42. Sen. *Phaedr.* 663; 45. Aldh. Virg.

31, Beda Cuthb. 4,2 c. 578 B; 47. Ov. *Ars* 3. 789; 49. Plin. *Ep.* 8. 8. 5; 59. Ov. *M.* 2. 544; 62. Ov. *M.* 9. 683; 74. *Anth. Lat.* 1. 2 630. 9; 81/2. cf. Ov. *M.* 15. 371; 82. Ov. *M.* 15. 383; 85. Ov. *M.* 11. 73, Paul. Nol. *carm.* 1. 2; 87. cf. Sil. 4. 580; 105. Iuv. 10. 200; 127. Ov. *M.* 6. 395; 129. Ov. *F.* 1.384, ibid. 2.681, ibid. 4.715, Mart. 9. 71. 1/2, Lucr. 5. 866; 133. Sol. 2. 45; Ov. *M.* 1.475

La Danse macabre, *the English Dance of Death, and William Drury's* Mors Comoedia

HUBERTUS SCHULTE HERBRÜGGEN

I La danse macabre

The medieval Dance of Death[1] depicts an allegorical processional dance of representatives of all human estates, from pope and emperor down to beggar and baby, being lead to the grave by an emaciated or skeletoned figure of Death. It found expression in late Medieval churchyard murals, often accompanied by didactic verses with a *memento mori* moral. Such monuments were and many still are known all over Europe, from Portugal to the Eastern Baltic, and from Scandinavia to Italy and the Balkans, as the existence of corresponding technical terms in the various languages indicate: e.g., English *dance of death*, German *totentanz*, Danish *dødedans*, Dutch *dodendans*, French *danse macabre*, Spanish *danza de la muerte*. The origin of the allegory seems to be shared between France and Germany.

---

[1] On the subject see Francis Douce, *The English Dance of Death* (London, 1833); Thomas T. Wildridge, *The Dance of Death in Painting and in Print* (London, 1887); Aldred Scott Warthin, *The Physician of the Dance of Death* (New York, 1931); Henri Stegemeier, *The Dance of Death in Folksong. With an Introduction of the History of the Dance of Death* (New York, 1939); J. M. Clark, *The Dance of Death in the Middle Ages and in the Renaissance* (Glasglow, 1950); T. S. R. Boase, *Death in the Middle Ages* (London, 1972); Leonard Kurtz, *The Dance of Death and the Macabre Spirit in English Literature* (1934; repr. Genève, 1975); Erwin Koller, *Totentanz. Versuch einer Textembeschreibung* (Innsbrucker Beiträge zur Kulturwissenschaft, Germanistische Reihe, 10), (Innsbruck, 1980).

French monumental representations of the *danse macabre* are widespread and well researched, La Chaise-Dieu, Auvergne (c. 1400), SS Innocents in Paris (c. 1425) and Kenmaria in Brittany (c. 1440) being perhaps those known best.[2]

When, during the Middle Ages, thinking was focussed on the life to come and when, furthermore, Death's ubiquity was brought home to everyone by endless waves of the plague that swept Europe, it was little wonder that the subject of death's triumphant dance, starting as mere illuminations without accompanying texts, found its way into the decorative margins of manuscript *books of hours* for private devotion.

German Blockbooks[3] took up the subject and added a text, closely followed by the new art of printing. Guyot Marchant saw a market for it when he first published *La danse macabre* in Paris in 1485, followed, before 1500, by fourteen other editions.[4] Accompanied by the French verses from the cemetery of SS Innocents, the book was enlarged both in text and in pictures almost from edition to edition. Apart from a Latin version of 1490,[5] there seem to be no early German,[6] English or other vernacular editions of Marchant's *Danse* among the incunabula,[7] but the subject of the *danse macabre* was passed on in *Le Kalendrier des bergiers*, the *Shepheard's Calendar*, the *Schäfer-Kalender*.[8]

---

[2] Cp. Jean-Georges Kastner, *Les Danses des morts* (Paris, 1852); E.-H. Langlois, *Essai historique, philosophique et pittoresque sur les danses des morts*, 3 vols. (Rouen, 1851).

[3] Xylographic books: Heidelberg, c. 1465; Munich, c. 1480.

[4] *Gesamtkatalog der Wiegendrucke*, VII (Leipzig, 1938), 7943–57. Cited as *GW* with number.

[5] *(C)Horea ab eximio Macabro versibus alemanicis edita . . .*, (Paris: Guy Marchant for Geoffroi de Marney, 1490); *GW* 7957.

[6] *Der Doten danz mit figuren* (Heidelberg: Heinrich Knoblochzer, c. 1488), fol., though, seems to rely on some of Marchant's woodcuts and verses.

[7] Pollard & Redgrave, *A Short-Title Catalogue of Books Printed in England . . . 1475–1640*, 2d ed., vol. 2 (London, 1976), 22407–22423.

[8] As recent studies have shown, a considerable part of the literary and illustrative material of the *Danse* found its way into another best-selling book of Marchant's, *Le Kalendrier des bergiers*, first published in 1491 and from there, after the turn of the century, by way of a "British" (Duff) and English translations into England. Cp. by the present author, "Der Schäfer-Kalender: Zur unbeachteten Rolle des *Kalendrier des bergiers* als Übermittler des *Danse macabre* in die englische Literatur," *Feschrift Otto Schäfer zum 75. Geburtstag am 29. Juni 1987*, ed. Manfred von Arnim (Stuttgart, 1987), 237–88.

II The Dance of Death in England[9]

The earliest known pictorial representation in England seems to have been the "The Dance of Paul's," murals painted c. 1426–1430 on the walls of the cemetery of old St. Paul's, which were destroyed in 1549.[10] Another early example of c. 1465 is the sculptural Dance of Death in the chapel of the Earl of Rosslyn at Roslin near Edinburgh.[11] Dance of death wall paintings in the Guild Chapel at Stratford-upon-Avon,[12] partly destroyed early in the nineteenth century, must have been known to young Shakespeare and may have prompted his well-known lines in *Measure for Measure* (III, i, 11f).[13]

When John Lydgate, Benedictine of Bury St. Edmond's, visited Paris in 1426, he made a verse translation of the "Danse macabre" poem at St Innocents. His verses were soon circulated in manuscripts.[14] At the cost of Jenkyn Carpenter they were made to accompany the painted "Dance of Paul's" in the cloysters of that cathedral. Sir Thomas More refers to them in his *Four Last Things*.[15]

How Death seizes everyone in the midst of life, is the subject of *Everyman/Elckerlijk*.[16] The origins of that late medieval morality play seem to be shared between England and the Netherlands. In Hugo von Hofmannsthal's modern German version it continues to attract an annual audience of many thousands at the Salzburg Festivals.[17]

---

[9] The subject of the English Dance of Death was first treated by Francis Douce; modern studies include Leonard Kurtz and J. M. Clark: cf. n. 1.

[10] John Stow, *A Survey of London*, ed. C. L. Kingsford (Oxford, 1908; repr. 1971), I, 109, 327 f.

[11] Cp. the present writer's "Der Totentanz von Rosslyn (Schottland): Ein Beitrag zu einem neuen Forschungsvorhaben," *Jahrbuch der Universität Düsseldorf 1981–83* (Düsseldorf, 1986), 165–75.

[12] Clifford Davidson, *The Guild Chapel Wall Paintings at Stratford-upon-Avon* (New York, 1987).

[13] ". . . thou art Death's fool; / For him thou labour'st by the flight to shun / And yet run'st toward him still."

[14] Ed. Florence Warren and Beatrice White, E.E.T.S., 181 (London, 1931).

[15] *The vvorkes . . . in the Englysh tonge* (London, 1557), 77 (= sig. e_7).

[16] *Den spyeghel der salicheyt van elckerlyc Hoe dat elckerlyc mensche wert ghedaecht gode rekeninghe te doen* (The mirror of everyman's salvation . . . .), a Flemish morality by Petrus Dorlandus van Diest, was printed at Delft by Snellaert c. 1495, at Antwerp by Govaert Bac in 1501 and by Willem Vorsterman 1525. For English editions cf. *STC*^{2}, 10604–10606.5.

[17] Cp. *Jedermann in Europa: Vom Mittelalter bis zur Gegenwart*, exhibition catalogue of the Max Reinhardt- Forschungs- und Gedenkstätte, ed. by Edda Fuhrich-Leisler,

The Dance of Death found its way also into the printing press in England. It seems appropriate, that Lydgate, again, leads the way. As far as is known, his verses were first printed in part in an English book of hours printed in Paris for the English market by Jean Bignon for Richard Fakes in 1521.[18] The earliest extant publication of his full text appeared in the appendix to Richard Tottel's edition of Lydgate's *Fall of Princes*, London, 1554.[19]

A metrical Dance of Death in poignant dimeters, in which Death alone speaks, dramatizes a series of woodcut male and female figures of estate being seized by death, ornamenting the borders in the so-called "Queen Elizabeth's Prayer Book" (1569).[20] It shows the continuance of our late medieval subject even across the radical religious changes of the reformation and under the very eyes of a calvinistically educated Supreme Head of the Church of England.

The vital force of the subject is demonstrated by a number of surviving broadsides or single sheet prints, distributed in the late sixteenth and early seventeenth century. They turned the traditional ecclesiastical serenity of the homiletic dialogue between Death and its victims into popular street songs or ballads sometimes embracing satire.[21] From hence it will be but a step to the Dance of Death caricatures of the eighteenth and nineteenth centuries.

In one word: the Dance of Death was alive and popular in England beyond the reformation and well into the seventeenth century. It is precisely at this stage in the history of the Dance of Death that Drury's Latin school drama comes into play.

Gisela Prossnitz, and Fritz Fuhrich (Salzburg, Schloss Arenberg, 1978).

[18] Cp. the present writer's "Ein frühes liturgisches Beispiel für den englischen Totentanz: *Hore beate marie virginis ad vsum Sarum* Paris, (1521?)," *Festschrift Dieter Wuttke* (München, 1989) (in press).

[19] *STC*², 3177.

[20] Cp. the present writer's "Ein anglikanischer Beitrag zur Geschichte des englischen Totentanzes: John Day's *Christian Prayers and Meditations*," in *Motive und Themen in der englischsprachigen Literatur als Indikatoren literaturgeschichtlicher Prozesse: Festschrift zum 65. Geburtstag von Theodor Wolpers*, ed. H.-J. Müllenbrock und A. Klein (Tübingen, 1990) 73–93.

[21] Cf. Douce, 76; Kurtz, 142 f.; Warren, 100 f.

III William Drury's Mors Comoeda, 1620

The Author

William Drury (Latinized Gulielmus Druraeus) alias Bedford (b. 1584)[22] was the third son of William Drury, D.C.L. (1527–1579), of Brett Hall, Tendrig, Essex, master of the Prerogative Court of Canterbury. Baptized on 11 Oct. 1584, he was five when his father died.[23] In 1605 he was sent to Omers (being contemporary there with Thomas V More, S.J. (1586–1623, the martyr's great-grandson). In 1610 he was ordained priest and sent to England two years later. As a seminary priest, he suffered imprisonment in the gatehouse, awaiting banishment. He was released through the good services of the Spanish ambassador in London, Didacus Sarmiento d'Acuna, Count Gondomar. Being a gentleman of singular ability, he was appointed on 8 Oct. 1618 by Matthew Kellison, President of the English College at Douay, to teach music, poetry and rhetoric there and to serve as confessor. At Douay, two of his tragi-comedies (*Aluredus* and *Reparatus, sive Depositum*) were acted, besides his Latin farce, *Mors*. He dedicated his plays to his patron, Count Gondomar.

On 2 August 1621 he returned to England with Francis Green, *ut in vinea Anglicana laborent*,[24] and was several times imprisoned. The date of his death seems not known.

The English College, Douay

After the accession of Elizabeth I (1558) and her Protestant settlement, many Catholics fled to the Continent. In order to provide university education for the younger generation, William (later Cardinal) Allen founded in 1568 the English College at Douay, a town with a young university of five faculties in which the English influence was strong already. Its first chancellor, Dr Richard Smith, was former fellow of Merton and Regius professor of divinity. The attraction of the College was

---

[22] Recent biographical studies have provided a fair number of fresh dates: Godfrey Anstruther O.P., *The Seminary Priests*, vol. II, Early Stuart 1603–1659 (Great Wakering, 1975, 87–89).

[23] The *Inquisitio Post Mortem* mentions Dryry (Drury) House in Dryry Lane, London, which lends its name to London's Theatreland.

[24] *The Douay College Diaries*, Third, Fourth and Fifth, 1598–1654, ed. Edwin H. Burton and Thomas Williams, vol. I (Catholic Record Society, 10) (London, 1911), 186.

due to its being both safe in the Spanish Catholic Netherlands and conveniently close to the Channel coast. Allen's foundation, the first in Northern Europe after the Tridentine Council, was intended and proved successful as a *seminarium*, a "seed-bed," for English priests. Douay also became the most important publishing centre for those books of piety and religious controversy which were proscribed in England, and it was at Douay that the Catholic English version of the Old Testament was printed in two volumes between 1609 and 1611. Having about some 80 students per year reading the humanities, the English College nourished most of the future English bishops, many famous writers,[25] and some outstanding Catholic laymen.[26] In fact, the preservation of the Catholic faith in England was largely due to Douay College.

Mors Comoedia

Drury's comedy *Mors* was apparently written in 1618. *The Douay Diaries* give an account of the first performances on January 8 and 11, 1619:

> 1619 Januarius Die 8◦ Comoediam[27] a Domino Gulielmo Druraeo compositam scolares privatim in refectorio egerunt, quae spectatoribus adeo placuit, ut fama ejusdem per civitatem ab iisdem disseminata aliqui iique ex precipuis Magistratus, nomine aliorum per alios ad Reverendum Dominum Presidem[28] supplicarunt, ut iterum curaret exhiberi. Quorum votis annuit Reverendus Dominus Praeses; unde 11° huius mensis scolares nostri eandem publice etiam sub dio (quia loci prioris angustia omnium votis minime satisfecisset) maiori cum alacritate ac applausu exhibuerunt; unde unus magistratuum qui praesens aderat aliquot vini totas nomine aliorum actoribus ipsis est elargitus.[29]

A manuscript of *Mors* seems not extant. It was printed thrice, first in 1620,[30] with Latin *encomia* by George Leyburne, Thomas Blackloe,

---

[25] Among them Harding, Stapleton, Sanders, Reynolds and Campion.

[26] (Charles Dodd), *The History of the English College at Douay* ... (London, 1713). Convenient summaries, quoting sources, by Bernard Ward in *The Catholic Encyclopedia*, vol. V (London, 1913), 138–41, and T. H. Clancy in *The New Catholic Encyclopedia*, vol. IV (New York etc., 1967), 1020.

[27] The name of the comedy is not mentioned here; since two of Drury's three plays are tragi-comedies, the entry may well refer to *Mors Comoedia*. I gratefully acknowledge Professor James A. Parente's advice.

[28] Dr. Matthew Kellison, the fourth president.

[29] *Douay Diaries* (cf. note 24), 148.

[30] In: *Aluredus, sive Alfredus*, Douay: Joannes Bogardus, 1620. (Copies: British

Thomas Metcalf, and Robert Blundeston, all students of the college at that time. It was reprinted twice in Drury's *Dramatica Poemata.*[31]

Mors is a comedy. According to Aristotelian theory,[32] comedy deals in an amusing way with common, everyday characters (not heroes) in ordinary situations (unlike those in tragedies), and according to Donatus[33] it contained various dispositions of town-people being shown what is useful in life and what has to be avoided. In the Middle Ages a comedy was seen as a poem with a bad start and a happy ending, in the Renaissance as serving a corrective and educational purpose and as giving pleasure and entertainment at the same time. Drury's *Mors Comoedia* partakes of all such notions.

It belongs to a genre of plays called school (or university) drama, because they were written by scholars, performed by schoolboys or students, acted before a school or college audience and, last but not least, many of them were written in Latin, the *lingua franca* throughout the Western academic world. By the time of Drury, the genre had established a tradition of its own, particularly in England, where performances of Roman comedies (Terence and Plautus) were very popular. It could also look back to early vernacular examples in England such as *Ralph Roister Doister* (1553), a knockabout comedy following Roman models in unities, plot and motivation or to *Gammer Gurton's Needle*, played at Christ's College, Cambridge.

If, generally, the university drama pursued didactic purposes (fluency in Latin, use of rhetoric, humaneness), the continental reformers, at the instance of Luther and Melanchthon, placed such plays at the service of religious controversy. The Jesuits soon followed suit. Their school drama sought to inculcate moral virtues and to deter from vices which, in the age of counter-reformation, included Lutheran heresy (in *Mors*, Act III, vi, Luther and the Devil are synonyms). By 1586, the Jesuit *Ratio atque Institutio Studiorum* provided for the performance of Latin (later also vernacular) tragedies and comedies, to be acted annually in all their schools. As time went on, the plays became more and more ambitious,

---

Library: 840.a.4.; G.17412).

[31] At Douay: Petrus Bogardus, 1628 (no. 2), 89–144. (Copies: British Library: 238.1.28 (in an old vellum binding with the gilt stamp of George III (1740–1800). Oxford, Bodleian Library: 8° Z. 211.Jur.; Douce DD.64) and at Antwerp: Petrus II Bellerus, 1641 (no. 2), 93–156, "editio ultima et recognita," 1641 (Copy: British Library: 11712.1.10.; G.17414).

[32] *Poetics*, cap. III.

[33] *In P. Terenti Afri. Comoedias, Examinata. Interpretatio.*

spectacular and sumptuous so that their performances attracted, as did Drury's *Mors*, also the general public of the town.

The plot may be summarized as "Death duped."[34] A rich old miser (Chrysocancrio) has a son (Scombrio), eager to remove his father. He thus sends his servant (Crancus) to find Death, and engages him to kill the old man. He even gives himself into his hands under certain conditions. The Devil, who joins them, promises him his father's riches, if he is willing to be his after death. Scombrio agrees on sly conditions.

When, after a while, the old man seems to have disappeared, both Death and Devil demand their dues, truly *media in vita*, as their victim is still alive. They only now detect their having been duped by his and his servant's slyness. Before the judge they both lose their case. Whereas Chrysocancrio promises to lead a better life, Death and the Devil depart duped.

Drury's characters stem from different provenances. The Italian *commedia del arte* supplies a number of stock types: Pantaloon as the simple, rich and aged father (Chrysocancrio), the role of Harlequin is doubled here as two smart and witty servants (Crancus, Grinco), there is also Scaramuch, the braggard captain (Frangicostonides), the *dottore* (here just mentioned). Other characters are taken from the medieval morality play, e.g., personified figures of Death and "a devil." Death, the title hero, plays an acting (though minor) part. Along with his counterpart "a devil," he appears in the stereotype role of the looser and both remain in the end as cheated cheaters. Another medieval figure is a witch (Grampogna), the only female in the play. She, too, plays a harmless role, as it were taken rather from a puppet show, and nothing like a satanic temptress.

Most characters remain quite flat and lack both depth and profile. Just as the devil has none of the metaphysical qualities of the fiendish adversary or *diabolos*, the miser, too, embodies only "the type" and lacks any profound wickedness of his classical (in Herodot or Ovid), his biblical (as Samuel's sons or Jehoiakim), his medieval (as Everyman) or Renaissance counterparts (in Poggio or Macropedius).

---

[34] Prof. Clarence H. Miller points out similarities in Ben Jonson's *The divell is an asse* (first published in the second volume of Jonson's *Works* [London, 1631] (*STC*[2] 14753.5).

IV Summary

Like any drama, Drury's *Mors* may be viewed from different formal and material angles. If led by Drury's title, we view it, as it were, from the point of death and his major manifestations in medieval and Renaissance art and literature, the medieval allegory of the "Dance of Death" must needs come into view. Within its history Drury's *Mors* appears precisely at the moment when the medieval notion of a grim and greedy Death, who seizes popes, emperors and all other estates alike, and who snatches his victims *media in vita,* is no longer prevalent. Partly through the Protestant reformation (which, for its sphere, did away with popes) and partly through the rise of the national state (which did away with emperors) that traditional notion gave way. From the traditional serenity of church art depicted on the walls of the choir or the cloister and from the high ranks of poetry and the morality play, it had "sunk" (apparently between 1568 and 1680) to unassuming broadsides, peddled in the market square for the entertainment of the masses (with the next step even further down to the world of caricature lying only just behind the corner).

If, on the other hand, one takes the title in all its seriousness, it suggests a striking contrast by juxtaposing fearful Death with playful comedy. It thus puts death into its metaphysical relativity: if men's destiny is eternal life, then indeed, physical death is but transitory, is but a *porta vitae,* and Christian belief triumphs in the resurrecting victory of Easter Sunday over the gloom of Good Friday. Even in a counter reformation school drama of somewhat modest literary qualities.

Düsseldorf

The Seventeenth-Century Taxonomy of Arts and Sciences in G. J. Vossius's De artium et scientiarum natura *and John Milton's "Curriculum" in* Of Education

PAUL R. SELLIN

Although the Yale commentary on John Milton's *Of Education* might seem definitive regarding the "curriculum" of studies that he envisions,[1] a number of problems touching the rationale underlying Milton's epistolary essay and the broader significance of his educational program still ask resolution. They are too complex to treat fully in the space available here. However, if we compare the scheme of studies that Milton proposes in *Of Education* with the Hellenistic taxonomy of the arts and sciences set forth by the Dutch polymath Gerardus Joannes Vossius (1577–1649) in his *De artium et scientiarum natura,* some provocative features of Reformed thinking about education and intellectual activity in the seventeenth century emerge, I think, with unusual clarity.[2] As rector

[1] Ernest Sirluck, "Introduction," chap. 4, and Donald C. Dorian, edition of and commentary on *Of Education, Complete Prose Works of John Milton,* D. M. Wolfe, gen. ed. vol. 2: 1643–48 (New Haven: Yale Univ. Press, 1959), 184–216 and 357–415, resp. (hereafter cited as *PW*). But cf. L. B. Langston, "Milton, J. A. Comenius, and Hermetic Natural Philosophy," *Dissertation Abstracts International,* 5 (April, 1978): 6144A. I am indebted to Professors J. W. Binns and Philip Rollison for their suggestions.

[2] *Gerardi Joannis Vossii De artium et scientiarun natura ac constitutione libri quinque*

of the Latin school at Leiden (which bloomed during his fifteen years at the helm), as regent of the States' Theological College at the University of Leiden, where his liberal Remonstrant sympathies made him so suspect to ultra-orthodox Calvinists after 1619 that he left the *Statencollege* for a professorship *ordinarius* at the university proper, and as the founding rector and professor of the *Illuster Gymnasium* (the first institution of higher learning at Amsterdam established in 1632), Vossius was not only an encyclopedic professional classicist famous the world over for his learning, but a liberal Reformed theologian, honored in England by co-religionist Puritans and Prelates alike.[3] More important for our purposes here, he was also a practical educator, renowned for handbooks on, among other things, the very rhetoric that Milton's own tutors at Cambridge saw fit to use.[4] This is *not* to claim that Vossius's book is Milton's direct source, however. Whereas Milton's pamphlet was first published in 1644 (*PW*, 557), during the first phase of the Puritan revolution, *De artium et scientiarum natura* was posthumous, not seeing light until 1650. Inasmuch as our perception of the subjects and arts we intend to inculcate have a way of determining the character of educational programs we embrace, the branches of learning informing a given curriculum are essential to understanding the rationale behind it.[5] Hence, even though *Of Education* slight-

---

antehac diversis titulis editi, separately paginated in *Gerardi Joan. Vossii Operum tomus tertius Philologicus* (Amsterdam: Ex typographia P. & J. Blaeu, 1696), pp. i–xviii, 1–279 and Index, in *Gerardi Joan. Vossii Opera in sex tomos divisa. Quorum series post praefationem exhibetur*, 6 vols. (Amsterdam: Ex typographia P. & J. Blaeu, 1695–1701), vol. 3 (hereafter cited as *A & S*).

[3] See C. S. M. Rademaker, *Gerardus Joannes Vossius (1577–1649)* (Zwolle: Tjeenk Willink, 1967).

[4] Harris Francis Fletcher, *The Intellectual Development of John Milton*, 2 vols. (Urbana: Univ. of Illinois Press, 1956, 1961), 2:214, 217–18, 256–58, 261, 323, 621, 644, 664.

[5] Cf. Bernard Weinberg regarding cinquecento classifications of poetics, *A History of Literary Criticism in the Italian Renaissance*, 2 vols. (Chicago: The Univ. of Chicago Press, 1961), 1:1–2. For additional background, see Richard McKeon, "Rhetoric in the Middle Ages" and "Poetry and Philosophy in the Twelfth Century: The Renaissance of Rhetoric" in *Critics and Criticism Ancient and Modern*, ed. R. S. Crane (Chicago: Univ. of Chicago Press, 1952), 260–96, 297–318, and "The Organization of Sciences and the Relations of Cultures in the Twelfth and Thirteenth Centuries" in *The Cultural Context of Medieval Learning*, eds. J. E. Murdoch and E. D. Sylla, Boston Studies in the Philosophy of Science, vol. 26 (Dordrecht and Boston: D. Reidel Publishing Company, 1975), 151–84; Paul O. Kristeller, "The Modern System of the Arts," chapter 9 in *Renaissance Thought II: Humanism and the Arts*, Harper Torchbooks (New York, Evanston, and London: Harper and Row, 1965), 174–89; and among the various essays in *Arts libéraux et philosophie au moyen âge*, Actes du Quatrième Congrès International de Philosophie Médiévale, 27 August–September 1967 (Montreal/Paris: Institut

ly antedates Vossius's treatise, the seventeenth-century hierarchy of arts and sciences that the Dutch scholar recorded is nonetheless useful in arriving at some of the key thought behind the kinds and order of studies that turn up in Milton.

Let us begin by consulting the digest of Vossius's "Distribution of the Arts and Sciences" that is appended to this essay.[6] The first point to note is an essential, if obvious difference between Milton and Vossius. That is, the moment one glances at Vossius's scheme, it becomes immediately apparent why Milton's "curriculum" fails initial expectations of twentieth-century readers looking for an orderly sequence of educational "units."[7] *Of Education* does *not* take student experience as its organizing principle, presents no simple linear progression from the lowest level of study up a single ladder to the highest in unbroken sequence. On the contrary, if viewed from a student's perspective, it seems to suffer from an odd incoherence that we rather too quickly ascribe to haste or informal, perhaps overly compact epistolary style. That is, Milton's outline of subjects proceeds unevenly, incorporating seeming redundancies and repetitions, as if within such a short and self-consciously condensed essay it were possible for him to suffer uncharacteristic lapses in attention, at times forgetful of what he says about grammar even from one sentence to the next, acting unsure of when a language like Italian should be taken up, or neglecting to present information on a matter like versification at the proper time and then having to double back to insert it later (e.g., *PW*, 382–83, 369, 404). But if we read Milton's program in light of the distribution adopted in Vossius's treatise, it soon becomes apparent that the "curriculum" in *Of Education* consists of at least three separate strands, all proceeding parallel to each other up through a taxonomy that, despite Milton's occasional concessions to exigencies of practical pedagogy, looks nevertheless very much like Vossius's five-fold system. It is the assumed

---

d'Études Médiévales/Librairie Philosophique J. Vrin, 1969), especially those by Henri I. Marrou, James A. Weisheipl, John E. Murdoch, Jean-Charles Falardeau, and Louis-M. Regis, *passim.*

[6] This schematization of Vossius's treatise has been reproduced with the kind permission of the William Andrews Clark Memorial Library from P. R. Sellin, "The Last of the Renaissance Monsters: The *Poetical Institutions* of Gerardus Joannis Vossius and Some Observations on English Criticism," in *Anglo-Dutch Cross Currents in the Seventeenth and Eighteenth Centuries,* ed. A. Lossky (Los Angeles: William Andrews Clark Memorial Library, 1976), Appendix, 38–39.

[7] Robert H. Sundell, "Of Education," *A Milton Encyclopedia,* gen. ed. W. B. Hunter, 8 vols. (Lewisburg: Bucknell Univ. Press, 1978–80), 6:17; cf. *PW,* 195, n. 58.

taxonomy, not the sequence of studies, that provides the essential organization underlying *Of Education*.

The first of Milton's strands or tracks is the Latin one, of course, since Latin is fundamental to everything in both systems. With respect to this strand, let us note a second important difference between the Dutch scholar and his younger contemporary. That is, Vossius's first, or lowest level, the "vulgar" arts, which occurs at the bottom of our diagram, does not appear in Milton's scheme for Latin at all. In Vossius's system, the various levels of the arts are directly associated with social strata (*A & S*, I.i.1), and the same assumptions that Vossius adopted regarding liberal studies and social class patently underlie *Of Education* too. Inasmuch as Milton aims at a "compleate and generous"—that is, a "noble"—education, his program is for a governing elite, not the gross, unfranchised "vulgar" (*PW*, 377–78; cf. *A & S*, I.i.1). Obviously, mechanic skills proper to mere crafts- or bourgeois tradesmen are not relevant to the much more crucial task of fitting the sons of Puritan gentlemen supporting the revolution to perform "justly, skilfully, and magnanimously all the offices both private and publike of peace and war" (*PW*, 378–79). Hence, *Of Education* skips over this rung of the ladder entirely.

The arts on the second level of Vossius's scheme, the "popular" arts, are another matter, however. They are all arts common to nobility and patricians as well as plebians, for they are basic to any future acquisition of philosophical learning and exercise of political power (*A & S*, I.i.1). As one can see on the appended diagram, they consist of such elementary matters as basic literacy (reading and writing), painting/drawing (or drafting?), learning to sing from notation, and physical training in martial arts (*A & S*, I.ii.1–v. 59). As everyone familiar with *Of Education* will surely agree, the first concerns in Milton's view of studies are exactly of this kind. Students must begin, he tells us, with the "chief and necessary rules of some good [Latin] Grammar," and since the "speech" of his students is also at the same time "to be fashioned to a distinct and cleer pronunciation," his line of thought proceeds exactly parallel to Vossius's in this respect (*PW*, 382–83). Note too that, although "boxing" is not precisely identical with the fencing and "wrestling" that Milton prescribes elsewhere in his pamphlet (*PW*, 403), an underlying concern with the development of physical skills useful in war is common to both systems (*PW*, 381, 407–11).

When Milton turns to the next step in his scheme, he in effect enters the third level in Vossius's hierarchy, just as one might expect. That is, the Latin strand embraced in *Of Education* now enters the world of "encyclopedic" or "polymathic" studies. Essentially this phase consists of traditional "liberal" arts, conceived not as ends in themselves but as no more than a set of preparatory studies necessary to uphold the "splendid estate of the nobility," as Vossius puts it (*A & S,* I.i.1)–in other words, much the same elite as Milton envisions in *Of Education.* Although Milton's phrase, "Next to make [the youngsters] expert in the usefullest points of grammar" may at first seem redundant in light of his previous remarks about the "necessary rules" of grammar and pronunciation (*PW,* 382–83), his procedure here in fact runs exactly parallel to Vossius's own return to grammar (*A & S,* II, i.1–iii.12), a reiteration that becomes necessary if the program is to enable students to turn from the *Artes Populares* to *Philologia* and enter into studies preparatory for the "liberal" arts proper. Inasmuch as *Of Education* later reveals that "the prosody of a verse" also belonged among the "rudiments" of grammar (*PW,* 403–4), it seems likely that, like Vossius (*A & S,* II.ix.1–8), Milton thinks of grammar on this level as encompassing Latin versification, not just vocabulary, forms, and syntax. I daresay that students would also be likely to encounter the tropes and schemes of rhetoric under the same rubric, much as they are subsumed under the more general heading of "philology" in Vossius (*A & S,* II.iv.1–2; viii.1–9). As for Milton's seeking to buttress these tasks with "some easie and delightfull" book of Education "withall to season them and win them early to the love of vertue and true labour" (*PW,* 383–84), what is this but taking Vossius's word *philologia* quite in its literal sense? In any event, it comes as no surprise after consulting Vossius that Milton should thereupon proceed directly to the "rules of Arithmetick" and "soon after the elements of Geometry" (*PW,* 386). This is exactly what we find in the Dutch Neo-Latin scheme too (*A & S,* III.i.1–xiv.7), and it is perhaps worth observing that with respect to mathematics, Milton does not appear to be so original as some commentators insist (*PW,* 386–87, n. 82). Milton's next step does depart sharply from Vossius, however. That is, he completely passes logic by (cf. *A & S,* IV.i.1)–evidently a bugbear so truly detested that he deliberately discards it–and proceeds instead to "easie grounds of Religion and the story of Scripture" (*PW,* 387). Hereby, of course, he begins to lay the groundwork for later study on Vossius's fifth level; namely, theology or *doctrina inspirata/revelata,* as sons of the Reformed church like Vossius and Milton would indeed tend to term it (*A & S,* V.xxiii).

The last step in the Latin curriculum is designed to give students their first sample of level four, the level Vossius calls true "philosophy" (*A & S,* V.i.1), the final end at which the entire course of preparatory studies has been aimed. This is exactly what happens in Milton's Latin strand too. However, in Milton this phase consists of no more than an initiation into the "Authors of *Agriculture*," the study of whom he wants to coordinate with either geography or a "compendious method of naturall Philosophy" (*PW*, 387–90), presumably but an introductory Latin survey of the studies on this level still to come, since the original, primary texts themselves would in fact have been couched in Greek, not Latin.

For without Greek, so Milton's thinking seems to run, it is impossible to read such "philosophy." Greek, not Latin or the vernacular, is the language of true "science." Accordingly, the Hellenic strand must intrude into his scheme at this point, and so students will have to return to the level of Vossius's *artes populares* and begin anew with acquisition of basic language skills, this time in the Greek on which access to the world of natural and ethical philosophy is going to depend (*PW*, 390; cf. *A & S*, V.iii.1–19). Thereafter Milton recommends hastening "after the same manner" through the Greek curriculum indispensable to picking up "encycliopaideic" subjects such as the principles of arithmetic, geometry, and geography that want of Greek evidently precluded from the Latin track earlier (*PW*, 391; cf. *A & S*, III.i.1). As Milton's Greek program makes especially clear, the true objective in *Of Education* is not *Encycliopaideia*, as is sometimes suggested, but "philosophy" proper. That is, if the end of "learning" is to "repair the ruins of our first parents" and arrive "cleerly to the knowledge of God and things invisible" by the "orderly conning over" of "the visible and inferior creature" (*PW*, 366–69), then *Polymathia* can be no more than a stepping stone to greater and nobler learning (cf. *A & S*, V.i). In light of *De artium et scientiarum natura*, it also seems apparent that in this stage of Greek studies, philosophy to Milton really means what Vossius terms "operative" *sapientia* as opposed to *speculativa*—that is, "applied science" rather than "theoretical" (*A & S*, V.v.1; vi.1). Indeed, Milton's emphasis in *Of Education* falls explicitly on things "usefull to be known," the "solid things" in the "convaying" instrument "language" (*PW*, 369). Hence, the subjects to which he now turns all seek a "reall tincture of natural knowledge" (*PW*, 394): viz., fortification, architecture, "Enginry," navigation, the "History of Meteors," mineralogy, "plants and living creatures as farre as Anatomy," medicine—all complete with laboratory and field work, and fortified with readings in the versified scientific treatises inherited from classical antiquity, ranging from the Orphic Hymns and Hesiod to Lucretius and the rural Virgil (*PW*, 391–96).

Finally, Milton's third and last strand emerges. As one can see in my diagram of Vossius's scheme of the arts and sciences, "philosophy" divides into two branches, Natural Philosophy and Ethical Philosophy. Of these two, *Physike* is lesser and therefore anterior to *Ethike* (*A & S*, V.iv.1–9).

Indeed, if emphasis is to be upon applied science, then right use, as even we moderns are finally coming to realize—witness contemporary strife over nuclear policy and the technology of weapons systems—is of the essence. Almost as if in direct imitation of Vossius, Milton now turns to the crowning study of *prudentia* (or *philosophia activa*), starting with ethics, the "knowledge of vertue and the hatred of vice," as he puts it (*A & S*, V.iv.2; xviii.1–2; *PW*, 396–97). Naturally, any such study of "personall duty" inevitably depends upon the "morall works" of antiquity, primarily Hellenic, tempered with the "determinat sentence" of the Psalms and Proverbs of the Old Testament, and the Gospels and "Apostolic scriptures," preserved of course in the Koine of the New.

Then at last, and only then, comes the grand immersion in politics proper. The first branch of this "science" is "Economics" (Vossius's "Domestic politics"—we might say "Estate Management"), a study to be reinforced, logically enough, by exposure to dramatic literature that treats of "household matters": ancient comedy and tragedy in Greek and Latin (*PW*, 397–98; *A & S*, V.xix.7–11). It is also a subject important enough to warrant sending students back once again to Vossius's lower levels, this time in order quickly to acquire Italian, for Italian is, after all, the language of the main Renaissance culture that has "been most industrious after" such domestic "wisdom" (*PW*, 369).

"The next remove," as Milton puts it, is clearly equivalent to what Vossius terms "civil" politics (*A & S*, V.xix.7). For the English poet, this branch encompasses knowledge, not only of the "beginning, end, and reasons of politicall societies" but the grounds of law and "legall justice," beginning with Judaic law and extending through Greek and Roman to "the Saxon and common laws of England, and the Statutes." However, since these are matters of but "humane" and therefore limited "prudence"—the very term, we should note, that Vossius uses to denote this branch of philosophy—they must be supplemented with "highest matters"; namely, theology and church history (Vossius's fifth level), the need for firsthand perusal of which presumably necessitates Milton's recommending still another return to grammar and the lower arts, on this occasion in order to gain skills in Semitic tongues of the Bible sufficient to the purpose (*PW*, 398–400; *A & S*, V.ii.1–4; xxii.1).

Many take note of Milton's postponing the study of eloquence until the final stage of his "curriculum," but in light of Vossius, this is not so very remarkable. In commencing this branch of study with an emphasis on reading histories, heroic poems, and Greek tragedies of "regal argument" plus "all the famous political orations" (*PW*, 216), Milton does not exactly allow literature and creative writing to crown the study of "liberal" arts, as people sometimes like to suggest.[8] In Vossius as well as Milton, *eloquentia* constitutes a body of arts that, despite their importance, nonetheless remains subservient to the more architectonic "sciences" of politics and ethics (*A & S*, V.xx.5–6). That is, the final stage in human, or "earthly," learning consists of cultivating those "organic arts" that "our noble and gentle youth" should know and learn to use skilfully, not as goods in and of themselves, but in order to rule well. They are, first, a "graceful and ornate Rhetorick," fit to appear in "Parliament or counsell" as well as in the "pulpit," an art which is to unfold from the "well-coucht heads and Topics" of logic, the *application* of which has been deferred until now. And second, a "sublime," not common, art of poetry, to be devoted to "Religious, . . . glorious and magnificent use . . . both in divine and humane things" (*PW*, 405–6). From such remarks it seems to me patently evident that when Milton speaks of "Poetry" as a "science" "subsequent, or indeed rather precedent" to rhetoric, he is saying something rather more simple and hoary than profound or innovative. The study of rhetoric and *poesis* is indeed subsequent to politics and ethics, but the former arts are in no sense "precedent" to either of the latter. As in Vossius, both poetry and rhetoric are, to quote the very Aristotelian expression Milton himself uses, but "organic" instrumentalities ancillary to the further–i.e., higher and more architectonic–ends of "politicall societies." In giving poetry "precedence" over rhetoric, Milton is only saying that although poetry may be the last of the "philosophical" disciplines to be studied, its potential for effecting right ethical and political ends exceeds even that of forum, council, and pulpit if used properly. From this perspective, poetry is no more "precedent" to *Ethike* than criticism to *poesis* (*A & S*, V.xxi.1–8). Professor Rajan's influential essay to the contrary, politics, not poetry nor poetic inspiration, remains the queen of "humane" learning in *Of Education*.[9] Of the art of criticism that Vossius places "subsequent" to both poetry and rhetoric (*A & S*, V.xxi.1–8; cf. *PW*, 216)–i.e., documents assessing (like Dryden's *Essay on Dramatic Poesie* or Pope's *Essay on Criticism*) whether literature serves its proper ends with respect to society–Milton says nothing specific, interestingly enough, but his opinion of modern poetasters probably gives some idea of how he envisions such an art (*PW*, 405, n. 185).

Some quick conclusions are now perhaps in order. First, comparing

[8] Cf. Sundell, 18.

[9] B. Rajan, " 'Simple, Sensuous and Passionate'," *RES* 21 (1945): 293–94; cf. 296–97, 300–301.

Milton with Vossius indicates that *Of Education* is much less original than appears if studied only in light of purely English settings of the 1640s.[10] However, the proper context for trying to view Milton's educational program is not that of broader humanist thought generally, as many assert,[11] but specifically that of the late cinquecento, in which the tendency to link poetics with the moral sciences becomes marked.[12] Secondly, this is evidently an orientation that Milton shares with thoroughly Reformed Neo-Latin thought obtaining in influential intellectual circles on the continent rather than with "Puritan" viewpoints predominating in Britain at the start of the revolution. Thirdly, both Vossius and Milton seem to reflect an important shift away from the outmoded trivium and quadrivium, certainly as Milton saw them. To speak, as does the commentary to the Yale *Complete Prose Works* of "the trivium," as standing "at the beginning and end of Milton's whole program" (*PW*, 194–95) distorts the picture.[13] While the statement is not very helpful because it literally holds true for almost any educational scheme, whether ancient or modern, this formulation makes the English poet seem far more old-fashioned than I think he really is. Quite unlike John Donne, who lamented all the "cohaerence" lost half a generation before, Milton does not flinch before the "Baconian"[14]—should we not rather read "Hellenist" here?—challenge of the "new" science to old learning. As Professor Dibon has indicated,[15] there was a revolution in Protestant university education on the continent at the end of the sixteenth century. Vossius but codifies this change, in my opinion, and Milton embraces it with gusto. Moreover, the English revolutionary's preference throughout is always for "operative" sciences, never "speculative" ones, like metaphysics, that great stumbling block for even the most enlightened of Reformed universities. Unlike Vossius, who at least acknowledges existence of the field (*A & S*, III.ii.7; V.iv.7–12), Milton ignores metaphysics completely, and this fact (not to speak of his dislike

---

[10] Cf. Michael Lieb, " 'The Sinews of Ulysses': Exercise and Education in Milton," *JGE* 36 (1985): 245–56.

[11] E. g., Marjorie H. Nicolson, *John Milton: A Reader's Guide to His Poetry* (New York: Farrar, Straus and Giroux, 1971), 121.

[12] Weinberg, 1:1–2, 16–31, 36–37.

[13] Cf. William Melczer, "Looking Back without Anger: Milton's *Of Education*," *Milton and the Middle Ages*, ed. J. Mulryan (Lewisburg: Bucknell Univ. Press, 1982), 93–100.

[14] Cf. Nicolson, 121.

[15] Paul Dibon, *La Philosophie néerlandaise au siècle d'or* (Paris/Amsterdam *et al.*: Elsevier, 1954), 1:1–126, 220–59.

of and suspicious caution vis-a-vis the sister study of logic) reflects at the very least a marked antipathy towards the theoretical and abstract as opposed to the practical or "prudential." Furthermore, as the emphasis upon "philosophy" natural and ethical suggests, Milton is one with the likes of Vossius in drawing upon the world of professional classics, particularly the Hellenic, for his inspiration. Anything but enamoured, evidently, of cramped pietism that too often informed the mainstream of revolutionary Puritanism seeking to alter religion, state, and schooling in England when he composed *Of Education*, he preferred the magnanimous values of an Athenian *politeia* as not the early but the later sixteenth and the early seventeenth century conceived it, an ideal city state ruled by enlightened patricians serving the common good. Would it be too much to suggest that with Vossius, Milton shares a Reformed vision of not so much a "liberal" as a "philosophical" education? One conceived on the continent in the tradition not of Zwingli or the Comenians indeed, as some thought in pre-Yale days (cf. *PW,* 184–86), but of Beza and anti-Ramist programs[16] espoused by Reformed institutions of higher learning above all in the Dutch republic, then still a loose union of sovereign provinces largely run, appropriately enough, by more or less "Aristocratic" city oligarchies? As for critical theory, lastly, it seems quite clear, as I have argued elsewhere,[17] that Vossius regarded poetry and poetics as an instrumental "science," as ancillary to ethics and politics as preaching and political oratory. Despite Milton's seeming modernity to many, the argument in *Of Education* makes no attempt to nudge poetry into the category of—to use Aristotelian terminology—a "productive," or as we might say, a "fine" art. In 1644, at least, Milton publicly claims to think of poetry not as art for the sake of art, or art for the sake of form, or art for the sake of the artist, but art for the sake of society and betterment of human existence.

University of California, Los Angeles

---

[16] Juergen Moltmann, "Zur Bedeutung des Petrus Ramus fuer Philosophie und Theologie im Calvinismus," *Zeitschrift fuer Kirchengeschichte* 68 (1952): 295–318.

[17] Sellin, 14–15.

APPENDIX

Distribution of the Arts and Sciences According to *Gerardi Joannis Vossii, De artium et scientiarum natura* (1650)

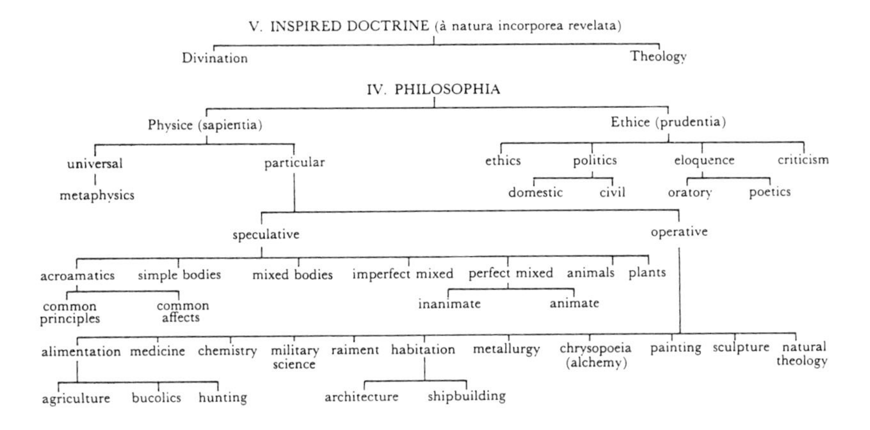

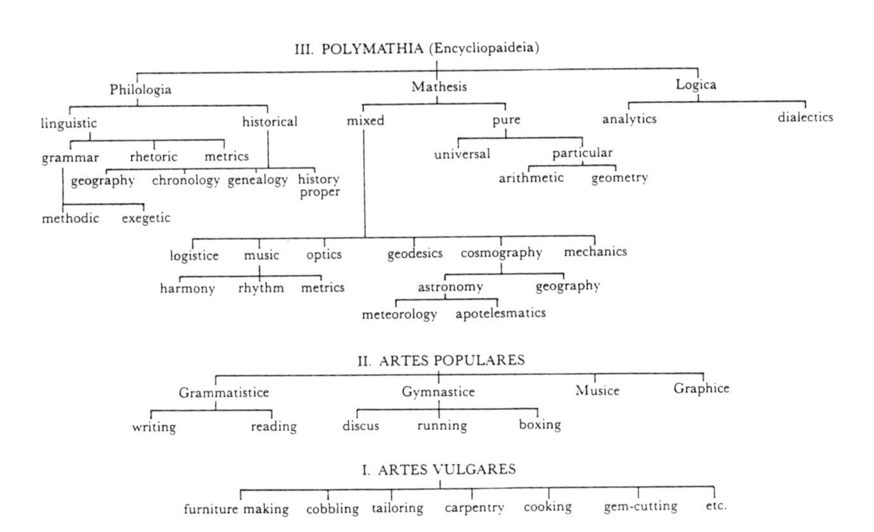

Marc-Antoine Muret: The Teaching of Literature and the Humanistic Tradition

PETER SHARRATT

In any discussion about the teaching of literature in the Renaissance Marc-Antoine Muret (1526–1585) is worth considering because he spent his whole life in colleges and universities in France and Italy (teaching Greek and Latin as well as law and philosophy), lectured and wrote about the theory of education, and was at the same time a scholar and editor of some standing, a sensitive critic and a practising playwright, poet and orator.[1]

After dissatisfying studies in the traditional mould of arts-course scholasticism and law he came to a humanist classical awakening through the study of Alciati and Budé: "Visus mihi sum de caelo decidisse, aut in alium quendam orbem delatus esse" he declares jubilantly in a text which anticipates Ramus's and Descartes's accounts of their intellectual conversions.[2] He first taught in various French provincial colleges (Auch, Ville-

---

[1] There is no recent general work on Muret. Charles Dejob's study, however, remains useful, *Marc-Antoine Muret. Un professeur français en Italie dans la seconde moitié du XVIe siècle* (Paris, 1881; repr., Geneva: Slatkine, 1970). This should be supplemented by Pierre de Nolhac, *Ronsard et l'humanisme*, (Paris: Champion, 1921), and various studies on particular points, and a recent work, *Commentaires au Premier Livre des "Amours" de Ronsard*, eds. Jacques Chomarat, Marie-Madeleine Fragonard and Gisèle Mathieu-Castellani (Geneva: Droz, 1985).

[2] Cf. *De toto studiorum suorum cursu, deque Eloquentia ac caeteris disciplinis cum Jurisprudentia conjungendis. Oratio XV. Habita Romae Anno M.D. LXVIII*, 142. All my

neuve d'Agen, and Bordeaux where Montaigne was among his pupils) before moving to Paris. He next went into more or less voluntary exile in Italy after being accused of homosexual practices and there spent the second half of his life, working in Venice, Padua and Rome where he was ordained priest in 1576. The main thrust of his teaching was literary, though this must be understood broadly since he insisted on alternating rhetorical texts with philosophical ones, and his teaching of law was a lengthy interlude before a final phase of teaching history and ethics in tandem.

At the time Muret wrote there was much confusion about the meaning and scope of the term "literae humaniores" and related expressions: they were sometimes understood more or less synonymously with "bonae artes" or "artes liberales," that is with Greek and Latin literature, including all that was written on any of the liberal arts. But the notion of the seven liberal arts was a theoretical one and the list had been modified and enlarged over many centuries, until it embraced not only subjects like poetry and history, but also law, medicine and theology; and the encyclopedia of the arts was seen as equivalent to philosophy according to the all-embracing Ciceronian definition, and ultimately literature, the liberal arts, the study of humanities, and culture became indistinguishable. The confusion arises because the terms were not always used synonymously, for example, when attempts were made to distinguish literature from either philosophy or history, or when teachers of one discipline resented teachers of other subjects intruding in their domains. In the case of Muret, the matter is further complicated by his strong belief in the cross-fertilization of disciplines, and by his desire to define afresh the role of the teacher of literature who will no longer be the old "grammaticus" teaching little boys, but someone who will initiate maturer students into the study of a new independent discipline. Muret owed much both to the experience of the para-university Collège Royal, and to the stimulating humanist atmosphere of the Paris colleges in which Dorat, Turnèbe, Buchanan, Lambin, and Ramus were revolutionizing the teaching of literature, and to the literary milieux of Ronsard and his Pléiade of poets.[3]

---

references are to Muret, *Orationes, Epistolae, et Poemata*, ed. Jacobus Thomasius (Leipzig: Johannes Grossius, 1690).

[3] On the scope of the liberal arts see Jean-Claude Margolin's edition of Erasmus's *Declamatio de pueris statim ac liberaliter instituendis* (Geneva: Droz, 1966), 85, 389; and Marie-Madeleine de la Garanderie, *Christianisme et Lettres profanes (1515–35)* (Lille: Université de Lille III; Paris: Champion, 1976), 162–68, 171 (on Guillaume Budé). It is worth looking at Estienne's *Dictionarium latino-gallicum* (Paris: Robert Estienne,

In his early years in Venice Muret published three inaugural speeches usually referred to together as *De studiis literarum*, but bearing individual titles: *De laudibus literarum* (1554), *De utilitate ac praestantia literarum humaniorum adversus quosdam earum vituperatores* (1555), and *De philosophiae et eloquentiae conjunctione* (1557). The first of these is a public display to the Senators of Venice of his capabilities, in order to obtain a chair of literature, and stresses the value to the state of learning, and more precisely of "literarum disciplina," both to preserve the state and increase its prosperity; the aim of government is "felicitas publica" which depends on the happiness of the individual, and therefore on his virtue which in turn depends on literature or learning. No state can flourish properly without "literarum cultura." Muret is not saying that it is impossible for the unlettered to be useful citizens but that all civic leaders must have a literary formation if they are to be ready for their duties in peace-time and in war. It will be noted that the liberal arts are praised not for their inherent merit but for their usefulness. Lambin too believed strongly in the usefulness of literary studies to the state and his own penchant was towards moral and political exhortation. Yet Muret is also concerned with the effect that learning ("discendi cupiditas") has on the individual, as the example of Archimedes, Chrysippus and Solon shows, as well as with the pleasure which literature provides. The subject was delicate since literature was often attacked because of its immorality and its futility, either on the moral and psychological grounds of Plato's *Republic*, or on the religious grounds of the Christian rejection of "voluptas," from St. Basil through Vives to T. S. Eliot and beyond. Like many of his contemporaries Muret speaks pejoratively of literature as the seductive song of the sirens and as the fruit of the lotus. Pierre Galland, for example, in a reply to Ramus's work on university reform (1551) was worried that the new vogue for literature would lure students away from pure philosophy, Turnèbe attacks imaginative writing explicitly, and, for both, the poet is meretricious and a corrupter of youth. Lambin, too, points to the dangers of rhetoric and of poetic fable.[4] Muret, however, distinguishes two kinds of pleasure:

1538) for a translation or definition of some of the relevant terms: *Literae*. Les sciences, et estudes contenues par lettres et liures. *Literatura*. Escripture, ou le scauoir des sciences qu'on a. *Humanitas*. (i) Le debuoir qu'ung homme doit à l'autre. C'est aussi l'esguillon que nature a mis en nous d'aimer et secourir l'ung l'autre. (ii) *Humanitas etiam pro eruditione*, Enseignement et institution des sciences liberales. Humanitatis studia, artes ipsae liberales dicuntur.

[4] Cf. Jean Jehasse, *La Renaissance de la critique. L'Essor de l'Humanisme érudit de 1560 à 1614* (St.-Etienne: Publications de l'Université de St.-Etienne, 1976), and the

letters, he says "titillatione quadam honestissimae voluptatis alliciunt" and this leads to moral improvement, preserving the reader from unacceptable pleasure, and he adds, "Nimirum ut major lux minorem, ita minoris voluptatis sensum perceptio majoris extinguit" (16). Yet he has admitted that literature is pleasurable, and that sensibility matters.

The second speech develops the relationship between imaginative literature and moral teaching, and states the intellectual value of literary training, for understanding the philosophical content of poetic fables: "sub eis, velut involucris, atque integumentis, omnis doctrina elegans, omnis ingenuo homine digna cognitio, omnis denique sapientia continetur" (26). The teacher must be eloquent, because of the persuasive power of literature in the controlling of emotions, and because he prepares young men who will guide the people; he must also aim at encyclopedic learning. Arts like physics, medicine, and civil law are self-contained, literature alone embraces everything: "Nos uni sumus, quibus omnis illa liberalium artium varietas non pertractanda quidem, ac pernoscenda penitus, sed degustanda tamen, et delibanda necessario est" (28). As he tells us himself, he put his own legal training to good use when he taught the *Verrine Orations*, and will draw on his knowledge of philosophy when he comments on the *De Finibus*. "Quid astrorum ratio? Quid terrarum situs?" he concludes, and asks, "Nisi qui haec utraque utcunque teneat, satisne se quisquam idoneum poetarum interpretem profiteri potest?" (29). Once more it is clear that he is trying to establish a new status for men of his profession.[5]

The third speech, on the joining of philosophy and eloquence, works out in some detail this other Renaissance commonplace, which sums up the Renaissance ideal of education, that sound learning and good powers of communication together form the true humanist. Once more Muret is attempting to define the role of the teacher of literature. His colleagues restrict themselves to explaining speeches and poems, to the neglect of

---

various prefaces and dedications of Lambin to which he refers; cf. also my articles "Peter Ramus and the reform of the university: the divorce of philosophy and eloquence?" in *French Renaissance Studies. Humanism and the Encyclopedia (1540–1570)*, ed. Peter Sharratt (Edinburgh: Edinburgh Univ. Press, 1976), and "The rôle of the writer and the uses of literature. Critical theory in the prefaces to the editions of the classics in sixteenth-century France" in *Acta Conventus Neo-latini Turonensis* (Paris: Vrin, 1980), 1249–56. Bacon, it may be noted, in the preface to the Great Instauration, observes that knowledge should not be sought for pleasure of the mind, nor for lesser selfish reasons, but for "the benefit and use of life."

[5] Erasmus, too, insists that the teacher of literature must aim at omniscience, cf. *De ratione studii ac legendi interpretandique auctores* in *Collected Works of Erasmus*, ed. Brian McGregor, vol. 24 (Toronto: Toronto Univ. Press, 1978), 672–75.

philosophical and historical works, whereas he wants to embrace the whole literary output of antiquity, "ut sciamus, quid homines sapientissimi de humanis animis senserint" (31–32). His adversaries want to confine each teacher to his own discipline, "clamantque regendos esse professionum fines, suisque quamque limitibus ac terminis coercendam" (33). But philosophy without eloquence is arid, barbaric and sordid, and eloquence without philosophy is vain and empty. "Oratio" and "ratio," "copia rerum" and "copia verborum" should be inseparable. Here philosophy is assimilated to literature: "A philosophis omnis doctrina liberalis, a philosophis omnis historia, a philosophis omnis artium varietas sumi potest" (36). Philosophy like literature is necessary to the rulers of the state, to lawyers and administrators and all who use eloquence, and the role of the teacher (whether of literature or philosophy, or both together), is therefore paramount.[6]

There is one important later speech on the purpose of literature to which I shall return, but wish first to say something of Muret's life-long interest in theology and moral and political philosophy since this illuminates the highly moral view he had of literature. In *De dignitate ac praestantia studii Theologici* (Paris, 1552) he treats theology as the most important of the liberal arts, Homer's golden chain, or Jacob's ladder, linking the divine and the human; it is the fire which Christ, the true Prometheus, brought down from heaven. Three speeches delivered in Rome underline his moral outlook: *De Moralis philosophiae laudibus* (1563), in which he says that the teaching of political philosophy is particularly appropriate in Rome, the source of empire, law and religion, *De Moralis philosophiae necessitate* (1564) where he says that it brings freedom, repose and public and private "salus," and *De sui cognitione, deque omnibus humani animi facultatibus* (1565). His views on the practical working out of ethical principles may be seen in his *De justitiae laudibus* (1565) and his account of teaching them in *De toto studiorum suorum cursu, deque Eloquentia ac caeteris disciplinis cum Jurisprudentia conjungendis* (1567). He takes up the subject in various other speeches and commentaries on Plato and Aristotle.[7]

---

[6] There is a vast bibliography on this subject. Recent accounts closely related to the present topic will be found in: Nelly Bruyère-Robinet, *Méthode et Dialectique dans l'oeuvre de La Ramée* (Paris: Vrin, 1984); Kees Meerhoff, *Rhétorique et Poétique au XVIe siècle en France. Du Bellay, Ramus et les autres* (Leiden: Brill, 1986); James J. Murphy and Carole Newlands, *Arguments in Rhetoric against Quintilian.* Translation and text of Peter Ramus's *Rhetoricae Distinctiones in Quintilianum* (Illinois: Northern Illinois University Press, 1986); and Anthony Grafton and Lisa Jardine, *From Humanism to the Humanities. Education and the Liberal Arts in Fifteenth- and Sixteenth-Century Europe* (London: Duckworth, 1987).

[7] These speeches appeared under different titles in their separate original editions,

To return to the teaching of literature: the speech *De utilitate, jucunditate ac praestantia literarum* (1573), which extends literature to include "earum artium quae in litteris continentur," deals with the professional or occupational purpose of studying literature. He sets before his wealthy young pupils four kinds of people: the idle, pleasure-seeking rich, poor boys who have to follow a trade, soldiers, and scholars of literature. He contrasts literature with other arts: although agriculture and commerce are vital to the state, the cultivation of the spirit is nobler than that of the soil, small trade is sordid and great is perilous and based solely on gain; painting and sculpture are not sordid, and provide "honesta voluptas," preserve the memory of famous men and invite us to imitate them, but it is only through literature that we know of the ancient artists, who can represent only the body, and of their works which can be seen only in one place and are ephemeral. Literature reproduces thoughts, behavior, actions and is eternal. Military glory depends on literary records. Muret next develops, rather reluctantly, the argument that literature can be financially rewarding, as it was, or could have been, for Thales, Gorgias, Isocrates, Seneca. The ending of the speech is more idealistic: "Literae inditos nobis a natura honestatis igniculos excitant; luxuriantes quasique fruticantes cupiditates stringunt ac coercent, easque rationis finibus regunt" (208). Unlike Montaigne, he thought the path to learning and virtue was not easily accessible.

So far we have looked at Muret's theory of the teaching of literature and this may be checked against his learned editions, such as those of Catullus, Tibullus and Propertius, or of Cicero, and may also be compared with his commentaries, including his personal and urbane *Variae lectiones*. From all of these there emerges a highly refined view of imaginative writing and especially of poetry, which is a divinely inspired, prophetic force, producing in the poet "mirificum quoddam ingenii acumen," and not reducible to art. Poetry works on our emotions by imitation—"Omnis autem imitatio videri vult id quod non est: itaque quodam genere mendacium est" (330)—proceeding by "veritatis similitudinem." The poet must be learned, teach the reader or hearer to speak well and invite him to virtue. It is this elevated (and new) ideal which the teacher of literature must aspire to.[8]

It is also possible to compare Muret's general statement of his views with the detailed plan of study he drew up, *De via ac ratione tradendarum*

---

but are easily findable in the collected works.

[8] Cf. *Cum explanaturus esset Aeneida Virgilii. Oratio habita Romae III.Non.Novemb. M.D.LXXIX.*

disciplinarum: his chosen pupil is "honesto loco natus, modicis opibus instructus, ea corporis firmitate, ut studiorum laborem perferre possit, ingenio neque agresti, et hispido, nec molli et effoeminato, sed eleganti, et ad honestatem propenso praeditus"(397) which does, it must be said, make his task rather easier.

The basis of his scheme is the study of Latin and Greek literature, (taken together, and not consecutively as Vives and some others wanted) "instrumentum ... ad parandam doctrinae copiam." At the age of five or six ("Sextum aetatis ingressus annum") the boy will learn the two alphabets, "per ludum iocumque," "non metu, ac verberibus, sed praemiolis" which recalls other Renaissance educationalists from Erasmus to Montaigne, so that he can read the two languages easily and quickly enough. In his seventh year he will learn the first principles of both grammars, declensions and conjugations, in his eighth "incipiat jam aliquid audire, aliquid legere, idque ejusmodi, ut et ad formandos mores non nihil conferat, et voluptatem potius adferat, quam magnam ullam animi contentionem requirat," by means of Aesop's fables, Phocylides' *Carmina* in Greek and Gabriel Faerno's fables in Latin. For the next two years he will study Xenophon's *De institutione Cyri* in the morning and Caesar's *Commentaries* in the afternoon, in his eleventh year the comedies of Terence, Plautus, Aristophanes (in expurgated versions); the twelfth and thirteenth years will be devoted to Theocritus, Moschus, Bion's *Idylls*, together with Virgil's *Bucolics*, Hesiod with the *Georgics*, and both books of Homer with the *Aeneid*, not all in class, however, since the aim for the pupil is "ut sine cortice ... nare possit." The master must see that he speaks every day and writes at least every other day. At the onset of puberty he will engage in "progymnasmata, id est, praeludia quasi quaedam, et praecursiones ad eloquentiam" especially from Theon the Sophist. Muret laments the loss of this old-fashioned eloquence in favor of modern pantomimic gesticulation and verbiage. All this is followed by a frighteningly impressive list of authors to be studied by this comparative method, including historical works and therefore geographical works which in turn call for works on mathematics. At full puberty, around the age of eighteen, he will turn to analytics and dialectic, "non ex barbarorum lacunis, sed ex Aristotele ipso, et Graecis Aristotelis interpretibus." After this exhaustive preparation (he admits it is an ideal from which you should take what you can), the young man will be ready for a life of literary leisure and will never lack spiritual nourishment, or for studies in medicine, law or theology.

As well as providing this detailed, if somewhat utopian scheme of education, Muret also spoke of his general views on teaching-method. In his *De doctoris officio deque modo Jurisprudentiam docendi* (1569) he declares "curandum esse ei, primum ut vera doceat; tum ut propria ejus artis, in qua versatur, aut certe cum eo quod agitur conjuncta et cohaerentia" (150). He must teach clearly, methodically and in appropriate language. The legal writers of forty years previously, for example, were often misinformed about antiquity, had a spirit of contradiction, filled their books with extraneous matter from grammar and logic, lacked structure and logical organization and wrote in bad Latin. Legal writing needs a clear, unornamented everyday style.

The problem of what is relevant to any art was a very real one, as the writings of Ramus and the controversies surrounding them make clear. Muret does not enter into these controversies but he touches very closely on the subject when he discusses the classical commonplace about the perfect orator. In his preface to the second Catilinarian oration of Cicero, he attacks the classical idea that the orator should have an encyclopedic knowledge: "nam cum ita late patere oratoris officium tradidissent, ut ex omni artium numero nullam relinquerent, qua non instructum esse eum atque ornatum oportere dicerent, neque praeclarum illud nomen eloquentis cuiquam tribuendum putarent, nisi qui idem et grammaticus esset, et dialecticus, et earum rerum quae in naturae obscuritate positae sunt, intelligens, et gubernandae reip. et gerendi belli peritus: eundemque esse uellent et musicum, et geometren, et arithmeticum, et astrologum, et medicum, et architectum: nulla ut res esset coelo, terra, mari, de qua non ille copiosissime disputare, atque ornatissime posset" (600–601). You might as well insist that he be a good cook or a good cobbler because he happens to mention food or shoes. "De iustis, iniustis, utilibus, inutilibus, honestis, turpibus, dicere oratoris officium est: non de quadratis, et circulis, de conis, et pyramidibus disputare" (602). The error is due to the Stoic conception of the wise man and to Vitruvius's idea of the architect.

It seems to me that there is an unresolved contradiction here in Muret's thought since, as we have seen he did think that the teacher of literature should strive for encyclopedic knowledge, and for him, as for many of his contemporaries, the teacher is an orator, and indeed a prime example of the eloquent philosopher. Perhaps it is just that like Vives, Ramus, Sanctius and others he believed that these other arts were in no sense part of rhetoric and not strictly part of the role of the orator, and was alarmed at the way some writers had extended Cicero's and Quintilian's ideas.[9]

---

[9] As Robert Bolgar says in *The Classical Heritage and its Beneficiaries* (Cambridge: Cambridge Univ. Press, 1954), 346, "The whole of Humanism in its manifold variations was to some extent implicit in Quintilian's conception of the perfect orator. The *Institutio oratoria* had described a discipline whose aim was to produce virtuous men

Muret was born eleven years after Peter Ramus but the two overlapped in Paris for only about three years. Ramus lacked Muret's literary sensibility, but he did use literature to illustrate his philosophical and scientific texts and his theory of "analysis" and "genesis" constitutes an original approach to literary criticism and to creative writing. His educational theory "Quod sit unica doctrinae instituendae methodus," with his account of the method of nature and the method of prudence, stresses that the arts should be kept separate in theory but not in practice. Like Muret, too, he was concerned with the end product of education "in forum, in senatum, in concionem populi, in omnem hominum conventum."[10]

A recent account of the question of the perfect orator and its place in the humanist ideal of education is to be found in Grafton and Jardine *From Humanism to the Humanities. Education and the Liberal Arts in Fifteenth- and Sixteenth-Century Europe* (1987). The authors argue that "utility" is of first importance for Ramus, as is the social position his pupil will play in society, and that this institutional reform, which made his doctrine acceptable to the business world, was one of the causes of opposition to him. There is, of course, room for discussion about the importance of moral training in Ramus, and indeed about the relation between moral and civic responsibility, yet there is much truth in the idea that Ramus "explicitly (though not necessarily deliberately) achieved the final *secularization* of humanistic teaching—the transition from 'humanism' to 'the humanities.' " Muret, in spite of his insistence on the usefulness of a liberal education, still hankered after the old ideal that the purpose of teaching literature was intellectual and moral. Towards the end of his life, however, he became increasingly aware that the ideal did not work in practice, that the teaching of literature was in a state of crisis, not to say decadence and disintegration. Jean Jehasse has argued that this decadence (from the mid-1570s) corresponds to the explosion (*éclatement*) of the old encyclopedia to include new arts and especially new sciences, as well as to the rise of literary criticism, accompanied by various factors of social and political unrest. Muret nowhere makes clear that he was aware of any of this, but

skilled in all branches of knowledge and capable of presenting their ideas in brilliantly persuasive words." Other writers have pointed to the close link between oratory and teaching, rhetoric and pedagogy, e.g., W. H. Woodward, *Studies in Education during the Age of the Renaissance* (Cambridge, 1906); Carlos G. Noreña, *Vives* (The Hague: Nijhoff, 1970).

[10] *Pro philosophica Parisiensis Academiae disciplina oratio* (Paris: David, 1551), 50. Reference should be made to the studies mentioned in n. 6, and to my article "Recent Work on Peter Ramus (1970–86)," *Rhetorica* 5 (Winter 1987): 7–58.

it does help to explain his uneasiness and his disillusionment.[11]

§ § §

Today, as so often before, there is a new crisis in the humanities in education which centers on the relation between liberal and professional education and their place in different social, political and economic structures, especially with reference to scientific, technological and commercial studies. It has been argued recently by Peter Scott *The Crisis of the University* (1984) that "no single discipline today can aspire to be a sufficient framework in which the most important ideas that arise from human experience can be incorporated, an overarching context for intellectual life."[12] It is true that the old humanist encyclopedic ideal developed into the study of the humanities, as Grafton and Jardine have shown, and that this in turn gave way, with some overlapping, to a study of philosophy, then history, then English literature, then social studies, and that there is now something of a gap.[13] It is time, I believe, for teachers of literature to return to a broad concept of their discipline, going beyond the still prevailing nineteenth-century view of good quality imaginative literature in the three traditional genres, and embracing all writing (even if imaginative writing remains at the center)–historical, philosophical, political and social. All this is the domain of the teacher of literature. Moreover, it is time to return to the old idea of the *artes sermocinales* which cover all discourse, whether written or oral (and, we might add, transmitted by whatever means). There is also a need to link eloquence (expression and communication) with philosophy; this will be achieved in two ways, firstly by considering criticism, with F. R. Leavis, as "a constructive or creative process,"[14] and insisting on literary creation not just in early schooldays, but also in the university, and secondly by extending the definition of literature to include all learning, encouraging cross-fertilization, and reviving the ideal of the encyclopedia. All of this constitutes a new notion of the role of the teacher of literature. (There is, of course, much debate about what "teaching literature" means: some, like L. C. Knights, take it for granted that the term has a meaning which everyone is aware of; Northrop Frye, and Jean Ricardou, on the other hand, have shown that you cannot teach literature as you can physics, mathematics or drawing,

---

[11] Jehasse, op. cit., 11, 103.

[12] Peter Scott, *The Crisis of the University* (London: Croom Helm, 1984), 271.

[13] Ibid. 31.

[14] F. R. Leavis, *Education and the University* (London: Chatto and Windus, 1943 [1961]), 70.

but only the criticism of literature, a discourse about literature.[15] Yet most would agree that it is possible to acquire a "competence in literature" (F. R. Leavis) or "literary competence" (Jonathan Culler), which does not seem far from the Ciceronian "literarum scientia" to which Muret and his contemporaries aspired.[16] There is broad agreement today that the study of literature develops "intelligence and sensibility,"[17] which echoes the traditional view of "animi cultura" and is very close to what Muret says, and these concepts have been minutely analyzed and refined by many educationalists in the last fifty years. There is perhaps less agreement about the ethical value of the teaching of literature, yet all commentators list the personal values which a study of literature can help to develop, and all stress the value to the state of the formation of mature, responsible, tolerant citizens with a common culture, though some point to the dangers inherent in this.[18]

Although teachers still consider the study of literature to be largely non-vocational (liberal as opposed to servile, gainful mechanical arts or sciences), many emphasize the practical uses to which it may be put, and all, I imagine, believe that is useful in some way or other.

My contention is that a study of Muret's views of teaching literature may help us to return to a broader, less specialized definition of the subject, to reassert its place in the university curriculum, redefine its relation to other subjects, and convince the skeptical of its necessity for the well-being of our society.

University of Edinburgh, Scotland

---

[15] L. C. Knights, "Literature and the Teaching of Literature," in W. Roy Niblett, *The Sciences, the Humanities and the Technological Threat* (London: Univ. of London Press, 1975), 134; Northrop Frye, *Anatomy of Criticism* (Princeton: Princeton Univ. Press, 1957), 11; Jean Ricardou in Michel Mansuy, ed., *L'Enseignement de la littérature. Crise et perspectives* (Paris: Nathan, 1977), 19.

[16] Leavis, op. cit., 88; Jonathan Culler, "Structuralism and Literature" in *Contemporary Approaches to English Literature*, ed. Hilda Schiff (London and New York: Heinemann Educational, 1977), 64; Cicero, *Brutus* 47, 153.

[17] Leavis, op. cit., 7.

[18] This is not the place to give a bibliography of the whole subject; my own principal debts are to works by Karl Jaspers, F. R. Leavis, Raymond Williams, and several contributors to the volume edited by W. Roy Niblett (see n. 14), especially David Edge, "On the Purity of Science," 42–63, and Max Black, "Some Tasks for the Humanities," 79–89.

Civil Society and State, Law and Rights: Some Latin Terms and Their Translation in the Natural Jurisprudence Tradition

M. J. SILVERTHORNE

In the course of translating from Latin into English some writings of the natural law school of the seventeenth century, I have had some difficulty in choosing appropriate translations for several key-words in the area of political and legal philosophy. The most perplexing have been *civitas* and *jus* and to a lesser extent *imperium* and *summum imperium*. Others that have given some difficulty include *respublica, status,* and *regimen*; *potestas, potentia,* and *vires*; *civis* and *subditus*; *societas* and *socialitas*; *pactum* and *contractus*. The translator faces, of course, the usual difficulties of translation, that the semantic range of any one of these words does not correspond exactly with the semantic range of any one English word, and this is compounded by the fluidity in the usage of the Latin words. But the greatest risk of misunderstanding, and of misleading the reader who relies on the translation, arises from the fact that the various uses of the Latin words carry a large element of what one might call ideological connotation. I intend to illustrate the various uses of the Latin words by showing how variously certain key words were understood. My evidence consists partly of lexical remarks in the authors themselves, partly of their usage and partly of the variety of equivalents found by contemporary translators.[1]

[1] Seventeenth-century Latin political vocabulary does not seem to have received much attention, and the work that has been done is not easily available. In particular, there is as yet no dictionary or word list, and one appreciates the value of the Society's recent decision to begin working towards a dictionary.

The texts in question are Thomas Hobbes, *De Cive* (1642),[2] Samuel Pufendorf, *De Officio Hominis et Civis* (1673),[3] and an extensive and influential commentary on the latter by Gershom Carmichael, regent and professor of moral philosophy at Glasgow University, which was published in 1724.[4]

Pufendorf and Carmichael are consciously writing in a particular tradition of natural law which they regarded as having been created in reaction against scholastic natural law doctrine by Hugo Grotius. Carmichael announces this intellectual debt in the preface to his commentary. "This [moral] science had been most highly esteemed by the wisest of the ancients who devoted themselves to its study with great care. It then lay buried under debris together with almost all the other noble arts until a little after the beginning of the last century when it was restored to more than its pristine splendour ... by the incomparable Hugo Grotius in his outstanding work *On the Laws of War and Peace*. And from that time the most erudite and celebrated scholars in Europe, as if aroused by the sound of a trumpet, have vied with one another in the study of this noblest and most useful branch of learning."[5] This school goes by the name of the "natural jurisprudence" tradition.[6]

Despite Carmichael's emphasis upon Grotius's originality, Grotius was clearly indebted (though the extent and nature of the debt is a matter of controversy) to previous writers on natural law and particularly to Vasquez, Suarez, and other Catholic theologians, chiefly in Spain, who in the

---

[2] An English translation of *De Cive* appeared in 1651 under the title *Philosophical Rudiments Concerning Government and Society*. Richard Tuck in his review of Howard Warrender's edition of *De Cive* in *Political Studies* 33 (1985), 308–15 has given reasons for thinking that most of this translation is not by Hobbes himself, as had always been assumed.

[3] My translation is due to appear in an edition of this work by Professor J. H. Tully, McGill University, to be published by Cambridge University Press.

[4] S. von Pufendorfii, *De Officio Hominis et Civis juxta Legem Naturalem Libri Duo, Supplementis et Observationibus in Academicae Juventutis usum auxit et illustravit Gerschomus Carmichael* (Edinburgh, 1724). Professor J. W. Moore of Concordia University and I plan to publish selections from Carmichael and other commentators in the near future.

[5] Carmichael, op. cit., "Lectori benevolo," vi.

[6] An account of the identity of this tradition may be found in Jean Barbeyrac, "An Historical and Critical Account of the Science of Morality, and the Progress it has made in the World from the earliest Times down to the Publication of this Work" in S. Pufendorf, *Of the Law of Nature and Nations*, trans. B. Kennett (London, 1729), section xxix–xxxi ("Grotius therefore ought to be regarded as the first who broke the ice ..."); following Pufendorf's own view of the matter as expressed in his Preface.

sixteenth century revived, amplified and revised the natural law teaching of St. Thomas Aquinas.[7]

Hobbes clearly stands somewhat apart from this tradition, but his treatise *De Cive* takes up many of the topics and something of the general plan of treatises in the tradition, and clearly has a complex relationship of influence and opposition to it. Pufendorf's *De Officio Hominis et Civis* published thirty years after *De Cive* is an attempt to come to terms with Hobbes by a student of Grotius,[8] and it is clear that in writing several passages in *De Officio*, Pufendorf had the very text of *De Cive* before him, since there are verbal echoes and close parallels in sequence and structure of thought.[9]

Pufendorf's *De Officio* (1673), together with the large work *De Jure Naturae et Gentium* (1672) of which it is a compendium designed for students, had a large success in its time, going through several editions, attracting ever-increasing layers of commentary and being translated into all the major European languages.[10] John Locke included both works in a short list of books on ethics and political though which he recommended in 1703 as suitable for the education of a gentleman.[11] The second of his two *Treatises*, though differing profoundly on such questions as the justification of property and the right of resistance, still follows the form of Pufendorf's work and discusses many of the same questions. Both of Pufendorf's books were edited and translated into French by Jean Barbeyrac. *De Jure Naturae et Gentium* appeared at Amsterdam in 1706 as *Du droit de la nature et des gens* and *De Officio* as *Les devoirs de l'homme et du citoyen* in 1707. The former was translated into English complete with Barbeyrac's notes by Basil Kennett in 1729. Through Barbeyrac in particular Pufendorf became very well-known in the first half of the eighteenth century. Among those who studied Barbeyrac's Pufendorf are Montesquieu, Edward Gibbon, and Jean-Jacques Rousseau, and in various editions and commentaries Pufendorf's works were widely used as textbooks in European universities until the middle of the century.

The normal language of this long, capacious and diverse tradition of

---

[7] E.g., J. St. Leger, *The "etiamsi daremus" of Hugo Grotius: a Study in the Origins of International Law* (Rome, 1962).

[8] Cf. R. Tuck, *Natural Rights Theories: their origin and development* (Cambridge, 1979), 156–58.

[9] See below 7.

[10] S. Othmer, *Berlin und die Verbreitung des Naturrechts in Europa* (Berlin, 1970).

[11] From Maurice Cranston, *John Locke, a biography* (London, 1957), 244.

natural law was Latin. In its development all writers share some similar vocabulary and yet use it in diverse fashion. There are on the one hand a number of key words typical of the tradition, among which are those mentioned earlier in the paper—*civitas, imperium, jus* and *lex, pactum,* and *contractus,* etc. On the other hand, given the diversity of religious and political positions argued within this tradition, it was natural that these key words should be used in a variety of senses; and these are seen with particular clarity in contemporary translations. I turn first to the uses and translations of *civitas*.

Civitas and civilis societas

Civitas is the word normally used in the Latin works of Grotius, Hobbes, Pufendorf and his commentators for an independent political entity.[12] The twentieth-century translator's first inclination is to translate *civitas* normally as "state." The difficulty with this is that seventeenth century translations into English do not use the word "state" in this sense of independent political entity. The translation of *De Cive,* published in 1652, uses "civil society" very frequently. A well-known translation of *De Officio Hominis et Civis* by Andrew Tooke which achieved a fourth edition in 1716 uses "civil society" (e.g., 2.8.11) and "community" and even "society" indifferently as in 2.5 *passim*. In the chapters of the *Second Treatise* where he is dealing with topics which in Latin natural law treatises have titles which include the word "civitas," John Locke has "Of political, or civil society" (c. 7) "Of the beginning of political societies" (c. 8) "Of the end of political society and government" (c. 9).

Thus to translate "civitas" we have seventeenth century authority for "civil society," "political society," "commonwealth" and "community." What we do not have authority for is "state."

By far the most common translation of *civitas* in English was "civil society."[13] But "civil society" is not of course a direct translation of

---

[12] Locke, too, explicitly recognizes *civitas* in this sense at *Second Treatise of Government,* chap. 10, para. 13, where he speaks of "any Independent Community which the Latines signified by the word *Civitas*" and argues himself for the translation 'commonwealth.' That translation requires further explanation, as does Hobbes, *Leviathan,* Introduction p. 5 "For by Art is created that great LEVIATHAN called a COMMON-WEALTH or STATE (in Latine CIVITAS) which is but an Artificiall Man." Suarez by contrast normally uses *respublica,* e.g., *De Legibus ac Deo Legislatore* 1.2.1.

[13] Cf. R. Derathé, *Jean-Jacques Rousseau et la science politique de son temps* (Paris, 1970), 382.

civitas; it is rather the translation, or almost transliteration, of *civilis societas*. This, I think, gives a clue to the origin and ideological significance of taking "civil society" as a translation of *civitas*. The tradition of treating *civilis societas* as a synonym of *civitas* gained currency, according to James Schmidt,[14] because both were chosen by Leonardo Bruni to translate a famous phrase from the first paragraph of the first book of Aristotle's *Politics*. There Aristotle, distinguishing the three different types of "community," "association" or "society" κοινωνία, says that "the sovereign and inclusive community is ἡ καλουμένη πόλις καὶ ἡ κοινωνία ἡ πολότική. Bruni translated this phrase *civitas appellatur et civilis societas*, finding it a suitable rendering in the linguistic and historical context of his day because he had a "sense that Florence was the *polis* reborn."[15] The consequence is that the phrase *civilis societas*, from Bruni's choice of it in connection with Aristotle's *polis* in a Florentine humanist translation, carries an inevitable connotation of the classical city, with suggestions of republicanism, constitutionalism and aristocratic participation in government.

There is nothing inevitable, there is in fact something paradoxical in treating *civitas* and *civilis societas* as equivalent. The phrase itself *civilis societas* is sufficiently flexible. *Civilis* had the authority of Cicero as a translation of πολιτικός but both words have a wide range of meanings, from "civic" or "civil" to "political" and to the more specific sense of "related to the *polis*."[16] And *societas* has its own variety of meanings. Like κοινωνία, it is of course a legal word meaning "partnership" or perhaps "association," but classical usage also included "society." Thus when *civilis societas* was translated "civil society," several choices had already been made to cut out areas of the possible semantic ranges of *civilis* and *societas* which might not be acceptable. Moreover, when seventeenth century writers chose "civil society" as a translation of *civitas* (rather than of *civilis societas*), they were making a very definite commitment, in choosing to equate a word which essentially means an independent community (*civitas*) with a phrase (*civilis societas*) which inevitably

[14] James Schmidt, "A raven with a halo: the translation of Aristotle's *Politics*," in *History of Political Thought* 7 (1986), 295 ff. and 299 n. 14.

[15] Schmidt op. cit., 314. For the linguistic context see Nicolai Rubinstein, "The history of the word *politicus* in early-modern Europe" in A. Pagden, ed., *The Languages of Political Theory in Early Modern Europe* (Cambridge 1987) 41 ff., especially 45–49.

[16] Cicero proposes *civilis* as a translation of πολιτικός at *de Finibus* 4.5 to serve as the name of the fourth division of philosophy which the Academics and Peripatetics add to the Stoics' threefold division into logic, physics and ethics.

carried overtones of a particular kind of government whose model was the classical city. If then a twentieth century translator chooses to render *civitas* as "civil society," he should be aware that he is implicitly locating his author in a certain political tradition.

None of this is relevant, however, to the translation of Pufendorf. Born near Leipzig in 1631, he spent his life at the courts of German princes and at the royal court of Sweden. To render *civitas* in Pufendorf's *De Officio*, published at Lund in 1673, I have thought it appropriate to use the word "state." It was first noticed in 1677 that the German word *Staat* was being employed in the sense of Italian *stato*, French *estat* and Dutch *staat* and that the word had a connection with absolutism; the word *Staatsmann* as *homme d'état* is also first noticed at this time.[17] Pufendorf's political doctrine is clearly in support of absolutism; and in one of his latest writings, *De habitu Christianae religionis* (Brême 1687), he does in fact consistently employ the word *status* for "state," as if he had seen the difficulty of using the tainted *civitas* (which he had used throughout *De Officio*) and had gone back to the Latin root of *estat* and *stato* to express his meaning.[18] When, finally, Barbeyrac translated *De Officio* into French, which unlike English, by this date (1707) had long had *état* in common usage, he included it among his options for translation of *civitas*, along with *société civile* and *corps politique*.

One may illustrate the tensions set up by the different traditions by comparing a variety of translations of a crucial passage. At. 2.6.6 a *civitas* (as a *potestas . . . quae omnibus sit metuenda*) is said to come into being only when men have united their wills and strengths by conferring them upon one man or assembly of men. *Ubi autem et voluntatum et virium unio facta fuerit, tunc demum multitudo hominum in validissimum corpus, civitatem nimirum, animatur.* Tooke translates "And when there is a union made of their wills and forces, then this multitude of men may be said to be animated and incorporated into a firm and lasting society" (293). Tooke here gives "society" (not even "civil society") for *civitas*. Barbeyrac, by

[17] *Trübners Deutsches Wörterbuch*, ed. A. Gotze (Berlin, 1935–1947) vol. 6, 509 s.v. "Staat" and "Staatsmann." Cf. also K. H. F. Dyson, *The State Tradition in Western Europe* (Oxford, 1980) 27, "its political use during the seventeenth century developed under French and Dutch influence." Pufendorf rarely uses *societas civilis* and then always in a sense having to do with society rather than with state.

[18] E.g., paragraph thirty-two: Circa primam statuum sive civitatum originem constat, homines, animadversis vitae segregis incommodis atque periculis, quaerendae securitatis causa inter se convenisse super sua in unam societatem conjunctione. Quoted at Derathé, op. cit. 380.

contrast, chooses *état*; *Du moment que cette union de volontés et de forces est ainsi faite, elle produit le corps politique, que l'on appelle un Etat, et qui est le plus puissante de toutes les sociétés.*[19]

Finally, Kennett translates the equivalent passage in *De Jure Nature et Gentium*: "When this union of wills and of forces is once complete, thence at last ariseth what we call a Commonwealth, or civil state, the strongest of all moral persons, or societies."[20] One notes that Kennett hedges, using "Commonwealth, or civil state" but following it up with "society." In other passages Kennett varies between "commonwealth" (e.g., 7.1.1), "civil society" (7.1 title), "civil state" (7.2 title) and "community" (7.1.4).

The problem for the translator of *civitas*, then, in a seventeenth century text is to know to what tradition his author belongs and to choose his translation of this keyword accordingly. It makes all the difference whether he chooses "state" or "civil society."

imperium and summum imperium

The translations offered for *imperium* and related phrases seem to follow the same ideological lines as those for *civitas*. One may give a few examples, though I have no space to work this out here. *Imperium* itself usually comes out as "government" or "power," though the second section of Hobbes's *De Cive* has "Dominion" as its title, where one might have expected "government," in contrast to the use of "Liberty" as the title of the first part.

Summum imperium is particularly interesting. Hobbes uses "sovereign power" freely along with "sovereign" in *Leviathan*; however, the translator of *De Cive* in dealing with *summam potestatem, sive summum imperium sive dominium* in 5.11 gives "supreme power, or chiefe command, or dominion." John Locke, however, in places where *summum imperium* would occur in Latin, chooses "supreme power" and simply does not use "sovereign." Presumably this is a reflection of his opposition to absolutism and divine right.[21] Tooke in his translation of Pufendorf's *De Officio Hominis et Civis* gives the title of 2.7 *De Partibus Summi Imperii* as "Of the several parts of Government." At 2.8.1 he translates *summum imperium* as "supreme power," and in general avoids "sovereign"; for instance, chapter 11 *De*

---

[19] *Les Devoirs de l'homme*, edition of 1820 Paris, 280. Cf. Derathé 381.

[20] *Of the law of Nature and Nations* trans. Basil Kennett, (London, 1729).

[21] Cf. Derathé, op. cit., 383–84; J. Franklin, *John Locke and the Theory of Sovereignty* (Cambridge, 1978).

Officio Summorum Imperantium, which seems to call out for "sovereigns," is translated "The duty of supreme governors" (which, I believe, is not contemporary idiom in any school of thought). Barbeyrac, by contrast, in dealing with the same chapters, has for the title of 2.7 "Des parties de la souveraineté en général"; at 2.8.1 he uses "la souveraineté"; and for the title of 2.11 he has "Des devoirs du souverain."

Once again, then, in a crucial area of terminology the twentieth century translator is left to make the choice of how he will present his author. For Pufendorf "sovereign" seems to be appropriate for much the same reasons as "state" is appropriate for *civitas*, because it seems to fit his absolutism, his employment of *civis* and *subditus* as synonyms[22] and because the English thinker closest to him, Hobbes, used "sovereign."

jus and lex

A comparison of the treatment of *jus* and *lex* by Hobbes and Pufendorf shows how little an author's own definition of a word may correspond to general usage. In a well-known passage of *Leviathan* (1.14) Hobbes says: "Though they that speak of this subject use to confound *jus* and *lex*, *right* and *law*, yet they ought to be distinguished; because RIGHT consisteth in liberty to do, or to forbear: whereas LAW determineth, and bindeth to one of them: so that law, and right, differ as much as obligation and liberty: which in one and the same matter are inconsistent." Comparison with Pufendorf and others shows this to be very much a "persuasive" definition.

The distinction between *jus* as "right" (in a subjective sense) and *lex* as "law" does not figure prominently in classical usage. Though *jus* does sometimes mean subjective "right" usually with reference to a legal right, it more often means objective right or "law."[23] Indeed it is commonly argued that the concept of subjective right which Hobbes wishes to signify by *jus* did not exist in the classical world but developed during the later Middle Ages.[24]

---

[22] The description of the general duties of the good citizen at *De Officio* 2.18.3–4 makes clear why there is no distinction between a citizen and a subject.

[23] In the sense of "law" (e.g., Var. *L.* 5.165) *jus institutum a Pompilio . . . ut (porta) sit aperta*; with a wider interchangeability of *jus* and *lex* Cic. *Har.* 32 *si minus civili jure perscriptum est, lege tamen naturae, communi jure gentium sanctum est.*

[24] M. Villey, "Droit subjectif (la genèse du droit subjectif chez Guillaume d'Occam)" in *Seize essais de philosophie du droit* (Paris, 1969), 140 ff.; R. Tuck, op. cit., chap. 1 "The first rights theory."

Can we then take Hobbes's distinction between *jus* and *lex* as standard for the seventeenth century? Alas, no. Suarez and Grotius had both given much more complex and thorough analyses of the meanings of *lex* and *jus* and of their relations. *Jus* as subjective right is only one of the three categories of meaning assigned to *jus*, and both authors acknowledge it as perfectly proper to use *jus* in one of its senses as synonymous with *lex*.[25] We cannot even apply Hobbes's distinction consistently to a writer so close to Hobbes as Pufendorf. It is indeed true that on many occasions in Pufendorf *jus* is best rendered as "right" (in a subjective sense) and *lex* as "law," for example, the *lex naturae* is often distinguished as the "law of nature" from *jura naturalia* ("natural rights"). But in two fundamental passages which I wish to discuss, *jus* is used almost synonymously with *lex*.

At *De Officio* 1.2.2 Pufendorf gives a formal definition of *lex*. Here of all places one would expect him to make a sharp distinction from *jus* if he is going to make such a distinction. But he does not. The exposition is as follows: *Norma illa vocatur Lex, quae est decretum, quo superior sibi subjectum obligat, ut ad istius praescriptum actiones suas componat.* But what is *obligatio*? Pufendorf continues by asking, and answers: *Vulgo ... obligatio dicitur vinculum juris, quo necessitate adstringimur alicujus rei praestandae.* It is impossible to get a subjective sense out of *juris* in *vinculum juris*, since Pufendorf paraphrases *vinculum juris* as *quasi fraenum aliquod nostrae libertati*.[26] *Jus* here then is "right" in the objective sense; like *lex* it has the effect not of expressing our liberty (as in Hobbes's subjective definition) but of restraining it.

The second fundamental passage in which *jus* occurs in an objective sense is *De Officio* 1.3.7–8. Pufendorf is explaining the "fundamental law of nature" (*fundamentalem legem naturalem*). It is "that every man should so far as he can promote and preserve sociality (*socialitas*)." Consequently, Pufendorf continues, "since he who wills the end wills also the means to that end," *omnia quae ad istam socialitatem necessario et in universum faciunt, jure naturali praecepta.* Clearly here the actions which make for sociality are enjoined by *jus naturale*, and *jus* is being used in an objective sense of "right" which is equivalent to "law." Tooke saw this and translated *jure naturali praecepta* as "are commanded by the natural law" and Barbeyrac has "*prescrit par le droit naturel.*" It is not then a question of a liberty, in Hobbes's terminology, but of an "obligation."

---

[25] F. Suarez op.cit., 1.2.1–8; H. Grotius, *De Jure Belli ac Pacis* 1.1.3–9.

[26] Tooke translates *vinculum juris* as "a moral Bond" and the following phrase as "a kind of a Moral Bridle [is] put upon our Liberty."

It is particularly striking that Pufendorf is willing to use *jus* as "law" in this passage since a comparison of his text with the equivalent passage in Hobbes's *De Cive* shows that he is directly replying to Hobbes, asserting the duty of sociality as the foundation of duties against Hobbes's view of the right of self-preservation. Pufendorf, as we have seen, speaks of sociality as the *fundamentalem legem naturalem* and of its derivatives as *jure naturali praecepta*. Hobbes had spoken of self-preservation as the *Iuris naturalis fundamentum primum*, and had immediately explained that he was taking *jus* in a subjective sense; *Neque enim Iuris nomine aliud significatur, quam libertas quam quisque habet facultatibus naturalibus secundum rectam rationen utendi. Itaque Juris naturalis fundamentum primum est, ut quisque vitam et membra sua quantum potest tueatur.* And Hobbes had continued as Pufendorf continues (but in the language of rights rather than of duties), that since the right to the means follows the right to an end, everyone has the right (*jus*) to use and to do whatever may be for his self-preservation.

Thus Hobbes's "persuasive" definition of *jus* and *lex* does not square with the usage of his period and is explicitly repudiated by Pufendorf.

Further studies along these lines might throw light not only upon the Latin usage but upon contemporary uses of the vernacular equivalents. Such studies of an author's vocabulary are a valuable clue to the tradition of thought or even to the ideology within which he is working. In the case of seventeenth-century Latin political works analysis of contemporary translations seems particularly valuable.

McGill University

Texts Discussed:

Thomas Hobbes, *De Cive*, 1642. An English translation, long attributed to Hobbes, probably wrongly, appeared in 1651. References are to: Thomas Hobbes, *De Cive, the Latin Version*, ed. Howard Warrender (Oxford, 1983); Thomas Hobbes, *De Cive, the English Version*, ed. Howard Warrender (Oxford, 1983).

S. Pufendorf, *De Iure Naturae et Gentium* (Lund, 1672).

——, *Les droits de nature et des gens*, edited and translated by Jean Barbeyrac (Amsterdam, 1700), itself translated into English by Basil Kennett in 1729.

——, *De Officio Hominis et Civis juxta Legem Naturalem* (Lund, 1673).

——, *The Whole Duty of Man According to the Law of Nature*, translated by S. Tooke, 4th ed. (London, 1704).

——, *Les Devoirs de l'homme et du citoyen*, translated and annotated by Jean Barbeyrac (Amsterdam, 1707).

Martial in the Renaissance: Three "Lost" Commentaries Found

JOYCE MONROE SIMMONS

Some works are lost inadvertently when they are destroyed or accidentally hidden. Others are condemned to obscurity through neglect as critical tastes change. Such was the fate of three early seventeenth-century commentaries on the epigrams of Martial. They had been neglected since the late nineteenth century and have been ignored by all subsequent commentators on Martial despite the recent resurgence of interest in him. They are valuable for their help in assessing what Renaissance humanists thought about Martial and the genre epigram. This brief description of the commentaries and their authors will serve to suggest their value to students of the Renaissance.

The story of Martial in the Renaissance begins in antiquity. From the first century A.D. we can trace an unbroken line of critical attention and imitation, a line culminating in the editions and commentaries of the Renaissance, the last great age of the epigram. Juvenal and Pliny the Younger were influenced by him. Later, the works of the Church Fathers display knowledge of Martial.[1] At the end of the fourth century Ausonius, professor of rhetoric and poet, chose Martial as a model for imitation. In seventh-century Spain, Martial appears in the *Etymologiae* of Isidore of Seville.[2] During the Carolingian revival, while Martial was not so popular

---

[1] J. Wight Duff, *A Literary History of Rome in the Silver Age*, ed. A. M. Duff, 3rd ed. (London: Benn, 1964), 420–21; Harald Hagendahl, *Latin Fathers and the Classics: A Study of the Apologists, Jerome and Other Christian Writers*, Studia Graeca et Latina Gothoburgensia (Göteborg, 1958), 183, 258, 284.

[2] Anthony A. Giulian, *Martial and the Epigram in Spain in the Sixteenth and Seventeenth Centuries*, Univ. of Pennsylvania Publication of the Series in Romantic Languages, no. 22 (Philadelphia: Univ. of Pennsylvania Press, 1930), 11.

as Vergil, Horace, or Terence, we find the epigrams included in a catalogue of books in the library of Charlemagne in about 790.[3] Two great encyclopedias of the Middle Ages, the *Policraticus* of John of Salisbury and the *Speculum Quadruplex* of Vincent of Beauvais, cite Martial as well. As the early humanists' interest in style and eloquence escalated into an attempt to reconstruct and relive every aspect of ancient life, long before the first printed edition of the epigrams, Martial received attention from Italian humanists Lovato Lovati (1241–1309), Geremia da Montagnone (1255–1321), and Boccaccio.[4]

The printed editions of the fifteenth and sixteenth centuries continue the tradition of serious critical attention to Martial in their methodical, systematic way. The earliest printed edition of the epigrams appeared in Rome in about 1470. Between that year and 1670 at least 145 separate editions were brought out with ever-increasing items in the critical apparatus.[5] The 1470 edition of Martial featured the text alone, but a 1471 edition provided by way of introduction Pliny's epistle to Cornelius Priscus on the occasion of Martial's death (book 3.21).[6] The epistle subsequently became standard for many editions through the Renaissance. It was again included in Georgius Merula's (c. 1424–94) 1472 edition, along with Merula's defense of his work. In 1474 Domitius Calderino issued a commentary with the text, a summary of his lectures given at Rome. At the end of the work Calderino included a defense of his work, too, evidence of a controversy involving him, Merula, and Niccolo Perotti (1430–80), whose *Cornucopia* (1489) on the *Liber Spectaculorum* and book 1 occupies one thousand folio pages. It was Calderino's edition, however, with Pliny's

---

[3] L. D. Reynolds and N. G. Wilson, *Scribes and Scholars: A Guide to the Transmission of Greek and Latin Literature* (Oxford Univ. Press, 1968), 82–86.

[4] Ibid., 102–10; and Frank-Rutger Hausmann, *Martialis, Marcus Valerius*, in *Catalogus Translationum et Commentariorum: Medieval and Renaissance Latin Translations and Commentaries*, ed. F. Edward Cranz and Paul Oskar Kristeller (Washington, D.C.: Catholic Univ. Press, 1980–), 4:251–52.

[5] The best accounts of the early printed editions may be found in Hausmann, above, and in the introductions to the editions of Martial by Ludwig Friedlaender, *M. Valerii Martialis epigrammaton libri*, 2 vols. (Leipzig: Hirzel, 1886), and, before him, F. G. Schneidewin, *M. Val. Martialis epigrammaton libri* (Leipzig: Teubner, 1881).

[6] Material concerning the Renaissance editions of Martial was compiled from the descriptions listed in the *National Union Catalog: Pre-1956 Imprints* (London: Mansell, 1968–); the *British Museum General Catalogue of Printed Books: Photolithographic Edition to 1955* (London, 1965); and the *Catalogue général des livres imprimés de la Bibliothèque Nationale* (Paris: Imp. nationale, 1924–).

epistle, his own biographical sketch of Martial, and his defense that became the reigning commentary until 1500.

Beginning in 1491 and onward the commentaries of Calderino and Merula are frequently bound together in various editions. In 1514 an alphabetical index of places and figures in Martial appears; a 1515 edition adds an explanation of words in Martial borrowed from the Greek. In 1518 Pietro Crinito's life of Martial begins to be included. A 1522 Leyden edition contained most of the material named thus far and also resurrected some annotations on Martial by Angelo Politian (1454–95) and others.

In 1535 the first expurgated edition of Martial appeared, the work of Franciscus Sylvius (Jacques du Bois) (1478–1555), and such chastened texts came forth regularly from this point onward. The 1579 edition of Hadrian Junius added two indexes, "Annotations and Corrections," and "Names of Those Who Wrote on Martial." One final sixteenth-century edition that deserves notice is the 116-page commentary on the *Liber Spectaculorum* by Theodore Marcilio (Musambertius) (1584). In 1601 another edition appeared, this time bound with an assortment of the by-now obligatory apparatus items and also the 255-page *Animadversiones* on Martial by Desiderius Heraldus (1600), a commentary on books 1–12. The Heraldus is subsequently cited as authoritative while the Marcilio more often only to be condemned. Scholars at the turn of the seventeenth century, then, had at their disposal a considerable corpus of scholarship which was as important as textual advances and which reflected the growing field of the study of antiquity and the scholars' tendency to carry old material along with the new.

Though Schneidewin's and Friedlaender's surveys of seventeenth-century editions leap from the Gruter (1602) to the Scriverius (1619), actually, the early part of the seventeenth century marks a high point of interest in Martial, with at least twenty-six separate editions between 1600 and 1620, and a total of at least 61 editions between 1600 and 1670. Included among these are commentaries which address themselves to interpretation, the "*poetae mens*," rather than to emendation. Three in particular stand out in this respect. First is the *Hypomnemata* or notes on the *Liber Spectaculorum* and first four books of the epigrams by Lorenzo Ramirez de Prado. It appeared only once in Paris, 1607.[7] Next is the "gelded" edition with full commentary by the seemingly indefatigable

[7] Lorenzo Ramirez de Prado, *Hypomnemata ad librum Spectaculorum et quator primos epigrammaton M. Valerii Martialis collecta ex schedis succisivis Domini Laurentii Ramirez de Prado* (Paris, 1607).

Jesuit Matthias Rader which he put through three editions from 1601 to 1628. These remained popular, being reprinted as late as 1784. I quote from the 1000-page third edition of 1627.[8] Finally there is the three-volume 1619 edition of Peter Scriverius with its composite commentary.[9]

Friedlaender praised the text of Scriverius but took no notice of the rich prefatory material and commentary.[10] Further, the Ramirez and Rader have been lost to classicists since Friedlaender dismissed them as "out-of-date" ("*veraltet*")[11]–out-of-date, I believe, for their image of Martial as a *doctus poeta*, one who had achieved perfection in art through diligent study of the best models; out-of-date for asserting the connection between poetry and learning that is implicit in their readings; out-of-date at a time when a preference for originality denied imitation as a creative endeavor, mistook it instead for copying, and in the process divorced succeeding scholarly generations from the tradition in whose preservation these humanists saw the beginning and end of their work.

Lorenzo Ramirez de Prado (1583–1658) was born into a noble Spanish family. There has been some controversy over the authorship of the *Hypomnemata*, which has also at times been attributed to Baltasar de Cespedes, the famed grammarian and the young Ramirez's professor at the University of Salamanca.[12] Both the circumstances of the work's publication and its brash criticisms of Joseph Scaliger, Justus Lipsius, and Janus Gruter placed Ramirez in numerous hot controversies with many, including ultimately the Spanish authorities. His later public life was devoted to law, politics, and diplomacy, including appointment in 1626 to the Office of the Inquisition. The catalogue of his personal library shows Ramirez to have been a man equally devoted in private to letters, and one who maintained a life-long interest in Martial. He owned virtually every important Martial commentary, including the 1619 Scriverius and the 1627 Rader.[13]

---

[8] Matthaeus Rader, *Matthaei Raderi de Societate Jesu ad M. Valerii Martialis epigrammaton libros omnes, plenis commentariis novo studio confectis explicatos, emendatos, illustratos, rerumque et verborum, lemmatum item, et communium locorum variis et copiosis Indicibus auctos, curae tertiae, plurimis locis meliores* (Mainz, 1627).

[9] Petrus Scriverius, *M. V. Martialis nova editio: ex museo P. Scriverii*, 3 vols. (Leyden, 1619).

[10] Friedlaender, note 5 above, 1:121.

[11] Ibid., 1:125.

[12] Hausmann, note 4 above, 290–92.

[13] Joaquin de Entrambasaguas, *La Biblioteca de Ramirez de Prado* (Madrid: Imprenta Soler, 1943), vii–xxxx.

The *Hypomnemata* is a delight to read for its vigorous style and individual response to the epigrams. Ramirez's uncovering of intricate combinations of figures and ornaments in his rhetorical analysis bears witness to the technical skill of Martial. As one of the few to grapple with the very real issue of obscenity in the epigrams, a topic at last receiving attention today, Ramirez offers readings of a number of these difficult poems.[14] At one point he digresses to defend himself: "I love this poet for many reasons, but above all because he is the most assiduous master of refinement (*urbanitatis*). I hate the supercilious who think him obscene. May I perish if anything obscene offends in him. For he writes everything to one end: that he may with a laugh and mocking gesture (*subsannatione*) deter us from vices and coarseness of manners."[15] In these respects Ramirez's commentary serves Martial well.

In contrast to Ramirez, Matthias Rader, of course, purged all of the obscene epigrams from his edition. This German Jesuit, born in 1561, is often better remembered today as the object of two vicious attacks by John Donne, first in an epigram and then in an anti-Jesuit tract, *Ignatius his Conclave* (1611).[16] The Jesuits were not the first to purge Martial, but Donne viewed such tampering with texts as a Jesuit effort to manipulate learning. Rader's commentary belies such charges and reveals a man of vast erudition and little rancor toward other scholars. Of the three commentaries it is the most learned and the longest, treating all fifteen books of epigrams.

Rader discloses his threefold plan for the commentary in the preface: to reach the mind of the poet ("*poetae mentem*"), that is, his innermost thoughts; to illustrate them with parallel passages ("*geminis dictis*") from various others; and to fortify his readings with other evidence.[17] He has annotated Martial, he states, as Servius and Donatus had for Vergil, as Acron and Porphyrion had for Horace, and the anonymous commentator for Juvenal. With the subject of his commentary as no less serious or

---

[14] See, for example, Ramirez, 166, for a reading of Martial 2.28. For a more recent treatment of obscenity in the epigrams, see J. P. Sullivan, "Synchronic and Diachronic Aspects of Some Related Poems of Martial," in *Contemporary Literary Hermeneutics and Interpretation of Classical Texts*, ed. Stephanus Kresic (Ottawa: Ottawa Univ. Press, 1981), 215–25.

[15] Ramirez, 53.

[16] See John Donne, *The Satires, Epigrams, and Verse Letters*, ed. W. Milgate (Oxford: Clarendon Press, 1967), 54; and *The Complete Poetry and Selected Prose of John Donne*, ed. Charles M. Coffin (New York: Random House, 1952), 544.

[17] Rader, note 8 above, Preface.

complex than those of the others, he characterizes Martial as especially learned ("*doctus*"), and more riddling ("*aenigmatodes*") and obscure ("*tenebricosus*") than others. Clearly, he says, such a poet was in need of greater illumination ("*maiore face*"). And this Rader provides.

While only a small part of the Scriverius commentary is devoted to the *poetae mens*, the work is valuable for its personal glimpse of a circle of seventeenth-century Martial scholars. Peter Scriverius (1576–1660) was an independent scholar living in Leyden. His edition, some 950 pages long, is in three volumes, the first containing interesting prefatory material and the much-praised text of the poems. The second, *Animadversiones in Martialem*, contains notes to the text, mostly emendations, by Scriverius, begun in 1604 and completed for the 1619 publication date. In these pages he makes frequent attacks on Ramirez.[18] Elsewhere he laments the loss of that first generation of Leyden scholars—Lipsius, who died in 1606, Joseph Scaliger, in 1609, and Casaubon, in 1614—and expresses the hope that the Jesuit Andreas Schottus and Janus Gruter will take their place.[19]

The third volume contains 280 pages of additional notes and emendations excerpted from the works of eight famous Renaissance scholars, some from earlier times but others friends and contemporaries of Scriverius who each append a personal letter with their contribution, bringing this circle of scholars again to life as they recover and refine the text of Martial. There are letters from Justus Lipsius, Pontanus, Janus Gruter, and Janus Rutgers. In his letter to Scriverius, Scaliger urges restraint on the part of Scriverius in the counter-attack on Ramirez, advice which apparently went unheeded.[20] The final three excerpts, from fifteenth- and sixteenth-century Martial scholars, were selected by Scriverius himself: the notes of Jean Brodeau (1519–1563), published for the first time therein; twenty-five pages of notes from Hadrian Turnebus; and selections from the *Miscellanea* of Politian.

Among the edition's dedicatory poems are two to Scriverius by Hugo Grotius, also from Leyden, and another, an epigram of entreaty to Martial as "*vatum optime*," "*culte*," and "*pater*" of jests and wit, by Johan Pannonius, the fifteenth-century Hungarian poet attached to the household of Guarino.[21] Another epigram, by Gerardus Vossius, describes a Martial wasting away with wounds and sores until he is saved by the work of three

[18] Scriverius, note 9 above, 2:77, 84, 113.

[19] Ibid., 2:49.

[20] Ibid., 3:167.

[21] Ibid., 1:13, lines 1–4.

Dutchmen–Junius, Gruter, and Scriverius.[22]

Taken collectively, the commentaries, in addition to shedding light on particular epigrams, establish a fuller image of the Renaissance Martial, one that is at odds with the popular Renaissance image of him merely as a witty satirist that we find in vernacular imitations of the day. In contrast, we see here a poet recognized to be in the mainstream of the traditional imitative process. The commentators are far-reaching in recording *gemina dicta*, covering not only similarities of expression but metaphors and places. They draw from Catullus and mostly the Augustan poets, but also mention, among others, both Greek and Latin Anthologies, the *Disticha Catonis*, the fables of Publilius Syrus, the *Priapea*, and Renaissance writers as well.

Among prose writers the favorites are from the Silver Age. A noticeable characteristic of the commentaries is their persistence in aligning, in over 200 places, the style and substance of Martial with the works of Seneca, an association that has largely been lost today. New readings of particular lines and whole epigrams emerge when bathed in the light of Stoic philosophy and Senecan style.

The rhetorical analysis of the epigrams observed in the commentaries further serves to support certain conclusions about the epigram genre itself in the Renaissance and to dispel popular misconceptions about the form in the Renaissance.In a theory derived from Lessing's 1771 essay, the epigram is commonly thought of today as a short, witty, often satirical poem consisting of two parts: the anticipation (*Erwartung*) and conclusion (*Aufschluss*). As a theory it has persisted as a basis for discussion even though it was long ago found inapplicable to either the *Greek Anthology* or Martial, and more closely defines epigram in the restricted sense of its modern use. The commentaries show no awareness of a bi-partite structure of anticipation and conclusion. Instead the commentators often analyze the epigrams' arguments as comparisons, either *a maiore, a minore, ab aequali,* or *a contrario*. As a simple example, Rader describes the epigram on the arena of Domitian (Mart. 5.65) as a *comparatio a minore* to the feats of Hercules.[23] These commentaries contain considerable evidence to support the idea that, at least for Renaissance readers, the basis of epigram, like the basis of wit, lies rather in comparison itself.[24]

---

[22] Ibid., 3:2.

[23] Rader, note 8 above, 411–12.

[24] Further support for this idea may be found in J. C. Scaliger's discussion of epigram in his *Poetice* (1561), book 3, cap. 126, 170.

In place of a bi-partite structure the commentators appear to perceive the distich as the structural "unit" of epigram, not surprisingly, since the distich is often the metrical unit as well. Each distich has its rhetorical strategy, figures and wit. Longer epigrams are shown to exploit the distich structure to allow for movement in diverse directions, for the commentators recognize "wit" and "point" throughout the epigram, not just at its conclusion. As such, the epigram's form is its function. Here the meaning of Mario Praz's suggestion that the Renaissance epigram was the "poetical counterpart of the false perspective," or *trompe l'oeil*, becomes clear.[25] Readers of epigrams enjoy having their worlds turned upside down, their normal perspective manipulated, with, say, the feats of Hercules appearing small compared to an emperor's arena, or with a seemingly tragic event being made to seem felicitous, or even a long tragic poem being made to seem trivial compared to the art of a mere epigram.

The epigrams of Martial have a special value to those who can see, as Renaissance readers did, the beauty of things "writ small." Appreciation of the form captures the paradoxical nature of the genre itself: trifling yet belabored, small yet of great value, constrained yet extravagant, like a gem. These three commentaries of the early seventeenth century can contribute to the critical interpretation of Martial in the Renaissance, and as such can be of use to future commentators of Martial and students of the Renaissance.

Tallahassee, Florida

---

[25] Mario Praz, *Mnemosyne: The Parallel Between Literature and the Visual Arts* (Princeton: Princeton Univ. Press, 1974), 126.

The Herculean Lover in the Emblems of Cranach and Vaenius

PEGGY MUÑOZ SIMONDS

The emblem book was a major Neo-Latin literary genre during the sixteenth and seventeenth centuries in Europe. Such books, which were also translated into or originally composed in the vernacular, basically consisted of a collection of verse epigrams. Each epigram was accompanied by either a motto or a short topical statement, and most were illustrated—at first by crude woodcuts but later by more sophisticated engravings. The literary purpose of this tripartite genre appears to have been the writing of endless (and often quite subtle) variations on those traditional themes or *topoi* which seemed appropriate to the poet for commentary on personal or national problems and events.

But all Renaissance emblems did not follow the usual tripartite form of motto, picture, and verse; indeed some were called "blind emblems" because they had no pictures, while others—such as certain oil paintings incorporating a verse into the picture—did not include a motto, nor did they appear in a book. Still other emblematic paintings included a motto but not a verse. To further complicate matters, Renaissance decorators often reproduced only the pictures from popular emblem books on ceilings, tapestry borders, and embroidered fabrics, assuming that the viewer would already know the motto and its verse, which he usually did. In any case, emblems, whether written in Latin or in a vulgar tongue, became an established genre among educated people soon after the publication in 1531 of the first *Emblemata* by Andrea Alciati in Augsburg.

The purpose of this paper is to explore the changing relationship between Hercules and Amor within this widespread emblem tradition. I shall discuss not only three printed emblems by Otto van Veen (1556–1629) but also two unusual and interesting painted emblems by the

German artist Lukas Cranach the Elder (1472–1553). We know that Cranach and his son produced for wealthy buyers a number of such painted emblems, which were usually on the subjects of "Hercules and Omphale" or "Venus consoling Cupid who has been stung by bees." Each of these oil paintings contains either a Latin epigram, which comments on the visual scene, or simply a motto to indicate the topos, while the picture itself makes the artist's commentary clear in visual terms.[1] I shall demonstrate here a philosophical shift in the attitude of emblematists in northern Europe toward the theme of the Herculean lover between the mid-sixteenth century when Cranach was at work in Saxony and the early seventeenth century when Otto van Veen, or Vaenius, published his trilingual *Emblemes of Love* in Antwerp.[2]

Appearing in 1608, the English edition of this beautifully illustrated book contains verses also in Latin and Italian. Another edition of the same year offers the same poems in Latin, Dutch, and French versions. The English translator of the *Amorum Emblemata* is believed to have been Richard Verstegan, an Englishman of Dutch descent.[3] Primarily an artist, Vaenius himself was a student of the painter Federigo Zuccari for seven years in Rome, and he later became Rubens' master in the Netherlands between the years 1596 and 1600. According to Mario Praz, "Vaenius's Cupids" were certainly inspired by those of Raphael's "Logge" seen during his student years in Rome.[4] Moreover, like the sonneteers of the period, Vaenius as a humanist took a Neoplatonic view of the figure of Cupid or Amor, who then became for him an entirely appropriate companion for virtuous Hercules. But, as we shall see, the most intriguing aspect of van Veen's *Emblemes of Love* is the way in which the Netherlandish artist conflates various Herculean topoi to arrive at a very different version of the Herculean lover from that of Cranach and other earlier emblematists.

Hercules is, of course, best known in Western art and literature for his heroic virtue rather than for his exploits as a lover (fig. 1). Indeed a favorite Renaissance topos concerns the hero's decision to turn resolutely

---

[1] For an overview of Cranach's works see E. Ruhmer, *Cranach,* trans. Joan Spencer (London: Phaidon Press Ltd., 1963).

[2] *Amorvm Emblemata* or *Emblemes of Love* (Antwerp, 1608). The engravings were done by Cornelius Bol from original drawings by Vaenius. Further references to this work will be indicated in my text.

[3] See Hester M. Black, "The Stirling Maxwell Collection of Emblem Books in Glasgow University Library," *The Bibliotheck* 8 (1977): 160.

[4] *Studies in Seventeenth Century Imagery,* 2 vols. (London: The Warburg Institute, 1939), 1:99.

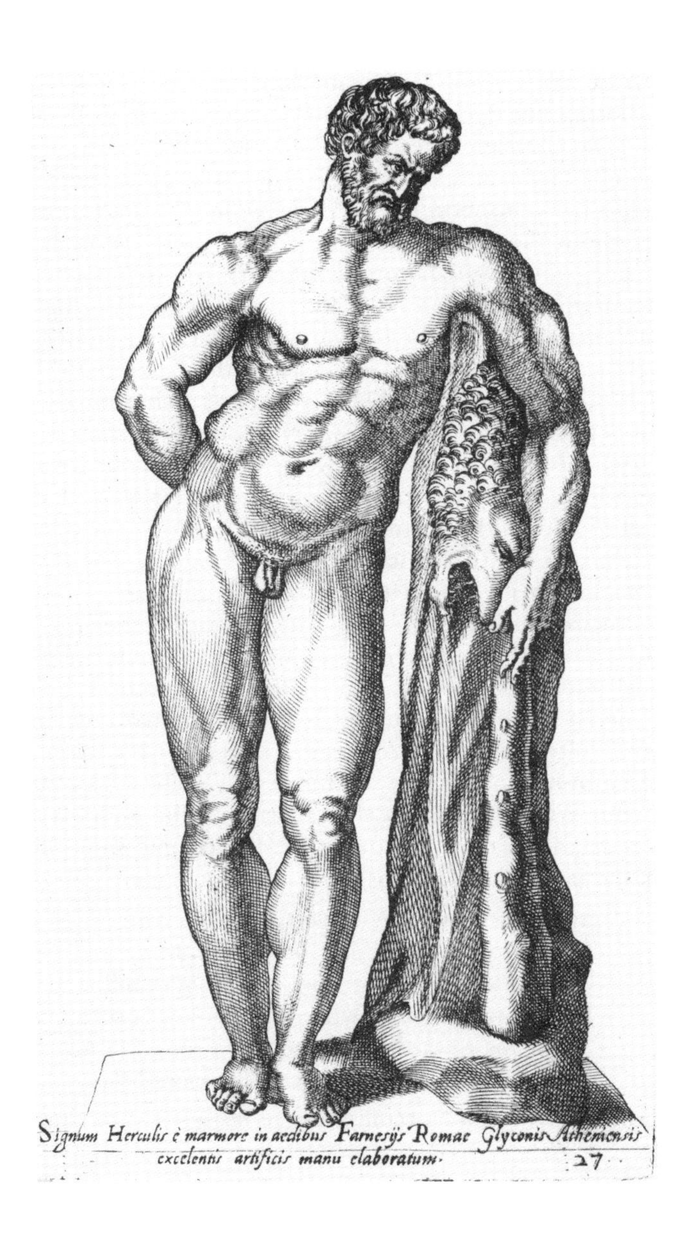

Signum Herculis è marmore in aedibus Farnesijs Romae Glyconis Atheniensis
excelentis artificis manu elaboratum.
27

Fig. 1. An engraving of the Farnese Hercules from Giovanni Battista de' Cavalieri, *Antiquarum Statuarum Urbis Romae* (Rome, 1585). Reproduced with permission from the Folger Shakespeare Library (NB 1380 C2 1585 Cage).

away from the pleasures of love and sexual dalliance in order to climb the rocky path of virtue toward ultimate fame, and emblems and paintings commemorating this decision are usually entitled "Hercules at the Crossroads" or "The Choice of Hercules."[5] The moral fable of the young hero approached by Virtue and Vice was first told by a sophist named Prodicus. Later related by Xenophon in his *Memorabilia* (2.1:21–34), it was widely used throughout the Hellenistic period as an *exemplum* by fathers determined to keep their sons heroically at work on their studies and away from the softening temptations of local courtesans.[6] During the Renaissance, emblematists found the topos useful for the very same reason.

A typical visual example of "Hercules at the Crossroads" (fig. 2) was painted by Lukas Cranach the Elder as part of a charming series on the life and labors of Hercules, a series which is now on display at the Herzog Anton Ulrich-Museum in Braunschweig, West Germany. Turning away from naked Vice, or sensual pleasure, a seated Hercules reaches out for the hand of Virtue. In this painting we find a motto or *inscriptio* above the visual scene rather than an explanatory verse epigram. The motto informs us that, "Sollicitant iuvenem virtus ac blanda voluptas" (Both virtue and alluring pleasure move youth), suggesting the difficulties for Hercules of the decision. Cranach's commentary on this statement is the picture itself, which clearly indicates Hercules making the correct moral choice between heroic virtue and alluring sensuality. In 1586, a similar emblem appeared in Geffrey Whitney's English emblem collection *A Choice of Emblemes* under the Latin motto "Bivium virtutis et vitii" (The crossroads of virtue and vice). But Whitney's *pictura* shows virtue as the goddess Athena and vice as Venus with Cupid to emphasize the cosmic importance of the choice. In the last verse Hercules proclaims,

> But heare, I yeelde oh vertue to thie will,
> And vowe my selfe, all labour to indure,
> For to ascende the steepe, and craggie hill,
> The toppe whereof, whoe so attaines, is sure
> For his rewarde, to haue a crowne of fame.
> Thus HERCVLES, obey'd this sacred dame.[7]

Not surprisingly, when Hercules does at last give in to Cupid's arrow,

---

[5] For a full discussion of the topos, see Erwin Panofsky, *Hercules am Scheidewege* (Leipzig, 1930).

[6] See Xenophon, *Memorabilia*, trans. E. C. Marchant, Loeb Classical Library (London: William Heinemann, 1923), 95–103.

[7] Whitney, *A Choice of Emblemes* (Leyden: Christopher Plantin, 1586), 40.

Fig. 2. "Hercules at the Crossroads" by Lukas Cranach the Elder, Nr. 712. Reproduced with permission from the Herzog Anton Ulrich-Museum, Braunschweig, West Germany.

Fig. 3. "Hercules and Omphales" by Lukas Cranach the Elder, Nr. 25.
Reproduced with permission from the Herzog Anton Ulrich-Museum, Braunschweig, West Germany.

he becomes an object of satiric mockery in literature and art. Deriving from Ovid's *Heroides* IX, this topos is called "Hercules and Omphale."[8] It concerns the period when the hero was sold as a slave for three years to the queen of Lydia as punishment for killing his friend Iphitus during a spell of madness. Since Omphale found the muscular Hercules to her liking, she invited him to become her lover and soon enslaved him emotionally as well as physically. But the ancients believed that passionate love—perhaps suitable for women—actually effeminizes a man. Because this negative attitude toward passion appealed to moralizing Christian humanist scholars and to the emblematists among them, the affair between Hercules and Omphale became an obvious opportunity for satire on the foolishness of military men in love. Enslaved by his passion for the Lydian queen, the hero must now amuse her by dressing in female clothing and by learning the art of spinning, instead of practicing his usual warlike activities. She, in turn, often wears his lion skin and brandishes his club in painted renditions of the scene.[9]

Lukas Cranach's 1537 painting of the topos (fig. 3) includes both a Latin moral verse and a description of a bearded but effeminized Hercules in Omphale's court. Both verse and picture are designed to provoke laughter at the hero so degraded by love. As Sir Philip Sidney explains in his *Defense of Poesie,* "So in Hercules, painted with his great beard, and furious countenaunce, in a womans attyre, spinning, at Omphales commaundement: for the representing of so straunge a power in Love, procures delight, and the scornefulnesse of the action, stirreth laughter."[10] Cranach's satiric epigram reads as follows:

> HERCULEIS manibus dant Lydae pensa puellae
> Imperium dominae fert deus ille suae.
> Sic capit ingentis animos damnosa voluptas
> Fortiaque enervat pectora mollis amor.
>
> The Lydian girls give tasks to the hands of Hercules;
> He submits to the rule of his mistresses.

---

[8] Ovid, *Heroides and Amores,* 2nd ed., trans. and rev. by G. P. Gould, Loeb Classical Library (Cambridge, MA: Harvard Univ. Press, 1977), 113–17.

[9] William Shakespeare makes the same point about the relationship of the passionate lovers in *Antony and Cleopatra* when Cleopatra exults: "Ere the ninth hour, I drunk him to his bed;/ Then put my tires and mantles on him, whilst/ I wore his sword Phillippan" (II.v.21–23).

[10] Quoted in G. Karl Galinsky, *The Heracles Theme* (Totowa, NJ: Rowman and Littlefield, 1972), 210.

Thus ruinous sensuality enslaves the will of the great one,
And passion weakens the strong heart by its effeminacy.[11]

This painted emblem clearly warns through ridicule against the dangers for males of sexual passion. The distaff held by Hercules is the traditional symbol of the female sex and has been substituted in this painting for the hero's usual phallic club. The bearded hero's dress, obviously inappropriate for a military hero, is that of a Renaissance lady.

In apparent contrast to these orthodox views of a piously loveless or a foolishly lovelorn Hercules, we find three later emblems by the artist Otto van Veen in his 1608 *Emblemes of Love,* a work very much influenced by Renaissance Platonism. The three emblems which concern us here present the Herculean lover as a positive image rather than as an object of satire. For example, on pages 32 and 33, Vaenius offers an emblem under the astonishing motto "Virtutis Radix Amor" or "Love is the Cause of Virtue." Without love, he seems to suggest, the military man cannot achieve virtue at all. In his illustration, Vaenius depicts a thoroughly heroic Hercules wearing his lion's skin and leaning on his club after killing the hydra (fig. 4). However, we also note a rather pained look on his face. Although the defeated hydra lies vanquished between the hero's feet, Amor—on the left side of the picture—is apparently the true victor over the hydra since he shot an arrow into Hercules' breast before the hero tackled the monster. Cupid conquers the conqueror, who then gains sufficient strength from love's arrow to subdue the monster with his club alone and without even cauterizing the hydra's multiple heads in accordance with details of the original myth. But, needless to say, Vaenius is not really suggesting here that sensual love causes virtue but rather that passionate spiritual or Platonic love inspires the hero with sufficient strength to overcome his enemies.

The emblematist cites as the sources of his emblem both Plato and Cicero, neither of whom would ever have argued on the side of sensuality. Vaenius paraphrases Plato in the following Latin sentence: "Anima immersa corpori, Amoris expergiscitur stimulis: & hinc primi ad honesta impetus capiuntur" (Immersed in the body, the soul arouses itself by the stings of Love; and from this the first beginnings of the virtues are taken). According to Cicero, in another Latin paraphrase by Vaenius, "Sine studio & ardore quodam Amoris in vita nihil quidquam sit egregium" (Without a certain zeal and passion of love, nothing whatever would be admirable). This statement derives from a speech of Crassus in *De Oratore*

[11] Translated by Roger T. Simonds.

Fig. 4. "Virtutis Radix Amor" from Otto van Veen, *Amorvm Emblemata or Emblemes of Love* (Antwerp, 1608), p. 33. Reproduced with permission from the Folger Shakespeare Library (STC 24627a.5 copy 1).

Fig. 5. Anteros chastizing Eros from Otto van Veen, *Amorvm Emblemata* (Antwerp, 1608), p. 69. With permission from the Folger Shakespeare Library (STC 24627a.5 copy 1).

(I.xxiv.134–XXX).[12] The English verse by Verstegan, which also accompanies the emblem, explains that,

> Moste great and woorthie deeds had neuer bin atchyved,
> If in respect of loue they had not bin begunne,
> Loues victorie hath made more victories bee wonne,
> From loue-bred virtue then thus were they first deryued.

It would seem, therefore, that Vaenius's love god is not wanton Eros at all but Plato's second love called Anteros, or the spiritual love of the cardinal virtues: Justice, Fortitude, Temperance, and Wisdom.

In fact, Anteros, the mythical younger brother of Eros, is depicted elsewhere (fig. 5) in *Emblemes of Love* in the act of chastizing Eros for his sensual excesses (pp. 68–69).[13] This second love god is therefore a fit companion for virtuous Hercules and vice versa. Because Anteros inspires mankind to true love, which includes acts of charity and martyrdom, he also teaches the Herculean lover that love is as heroic a venture for mankind as is military heroism on the battlefield. Although Alciati first introduced the opposing figures of Eros and Anteros into emblem literature in 1531, the mythographer Vincenzo Cartari finally tells the full story of their competition in the 1556 edition of his *Le imagini de i dei de gli antichi* and in the later illustrated edition of 1571.[14] Cartari also associates Hercules with Anteros in an interesting context. He describes a Roman statue of Amor standing between the figures of Mercury and Hercules; this juxtaposition means, he says, that Love is both reasonable and virtuous.[15] Like most humanist painters, Vaenius undoubtedly knew Cartari's book, which influenced his view of Hercules and Amor.

Vaenius next provides an emblem of Hercules in full battle array. The hero is shown holding Amor firmly by the hand while leading him up the steep and narrow path to fame (fig. 6). Hercules looks down at Cupid in a kindly and paternal fashion, while the little love god gazes up at his guide with an attitude of worshipful admiration (pp. 53–54). Here the topos of the "Choice of Hercules" has been cleverly conflated by Vaenius

---

[12] See Cicero, *De Oratore*, Vol. I, trans E. W. Sutton, Loeb Classical Library (London: William Heinemann, 1947), 95.

[13] Praz points out (op. cit, 99) that the topos of "Cupid Crucified" was introduced by Ausonius, who was inspired by a wall-painting of Zoilus. See Vol. I, Book VIII, of Ausonius, trans. H. G. E. White, Loeb Classical Library (London: William Heinemann, 1919), 207–15.

[14] See *Le imagini de i dei de gli antichi* (Venice: Vincentio Valgrisi, 1571), 500–501.

[15] Ibid., 501–2.

with the topos known to art historians as the "Education of Cupid," a thematic reference to the revival and love of classical learning. However, in most cases, Cupid's teacher is Hermes, or Mercury, rather than Hercules, a demi-god known more for his muscles than for his brains. In Vaenius's emblem, the motto is "Virtute Dvce" ("Virtue the guyd of loue") which is borrowed from Cicero's letter to the young Plancus in *Letters to his Friends*. Here Cicero tells the young man that, "Omnia summa consecutus es virtute duce, comite fortuna" or "You have gained all the

Fig. 6. "Virtute Dvce" from Otto van Veen, Amorvm Emblemata (Antwerp, 1608), p. 53. With permission from the Folger Shakespeare Library (STC 24627a.5 copy 1).

highest distinctions–virtue your guide, fortune your comrade."[16] Vaenius's Latin verse reads as follows:

> Herculis insignis virtus dux praesit Amori;
> Hunc ne praecipitem deuius error agat;
> Vtque sui capiat felicia praemia voti.
> Laus est, cum virtus dux in Amore praeit.

According to the English translation,

> Hercules leadeth loue and loue thereby doth gayn,
> Great courage to performe what-so loues dutie byndes,
> For loue by virtues led no difficulties fyndes,
> To vndergo for loue attempts of anie paynes.

This conflation of two motifs by Vaenius is an effective way of presenting the reader with the other half of the Virgilian proposition that "Love conquers all," which we saw dramatized in the previous emblem arguing that "Love is the Cause of Virtue." Now Love, himself, must choose, as had the young Hercules, between sensual pleasure and spiritual enlightenment, but he needs help. Once instructed by heroic virtue, Cupid then moves resolutely upward on the Platonic ladder of love, represented here by the mountain path, instead of downward to a degrading animal passion. Vaenius surely intends us to recognize at this point the mutuality of the relationship between Hercules and Love. Without passion, Virtue can accomplish very little. On the other hand, without virtuous guidance, Love can mistake his goals and/or lack the determination to achieve them. Rather than making the conventional claim that Hercules is effeminized by his contact with Love, Vaenius suggests more wisely that Love gains masculine courage and purpose from his association with virtuous Hercules.

The third Hercules-Eros emblem by Vaenius asserts that "Amor Addocet Artes" or that "Love is the Schoolmaster of artes" (pp. 82–83). To illustrate this motto, Vaenius depicts an interior scene within which the roles of teacher and pupil are reversed (fig. 7). Now it is Love who, while singing a spinning song from a music book, instructs Hercules in the art of transforming natural fibers into the thread from which the fabric of civilization is woven. A subdued Hercules sits on a stool and clenches his distaff tightly between his massive knees. His fingers hold the thread most

---

[16] See Cicero, *Letters to His Friends*, trans. W. Glynn Williams, Loeb Classical Library (London: William Heinemann, 1928), 2:10.3.2.

delicately, while his spindle seems to pierce the handle of his club, which has been abandoned on the floor. Although Hercules is clearly uncomfortable during this lesson from Love, he is not effeminized by it since he is shown draped in his usual lion skin rather than attired in female clothing. The aggressive passion of the Herculean lover is directed here into an artistic form by Love and restrained from excess by a proper musical measure in the song of Cupid.

The Latin epigram apparently inspired by Ovid tells us that,

> Ingeniosus Amor varias nos edocet artes;
> Rebus nosque habiles omnibus ille facit.
> Illius inuento concordant carmina neruis:
> Molliaque Alcides pensa trahebat herae.

> Cupid doth teach by note the louer well to sing,
> As sometyme Hercules he learned for to spinne,
> All artes almoste that bee did first from loue beginne,
> loue makes the louer apt to euerie kynd of thing.

Fig. 7. "Amor Addocet Artes" from Otto van Veen, *Amorvm Emblemata* (Antwerp, 1608), p. 83. With permission from the Folger Shakespeare Library (STC 24627a.5 copy 1).

Yet art is, after all, the transformation of rough nature into a civilized form of expression which provides both instruction and pleasure for humanity.

Vaenius's amusing emblem on the submission of Hercules to Love's instruction in the arts echoes the earlier topos of "Hercules and Omphale" since the hero is pictured with a distaff. However, I believe that this emblem is even more concerned with another popular topos of the Renaissance, namely that of "Pleasure Reconciled with Virtue," which derives in turn from the original "Choice of Hercules."[17] The mature Hercules finally recognizes (in Vaenius's version of the topos) that, although Vice must be eschewed by the hero, Virtue and Pleasure should not be always separated. As Mercury tells Hercules in Ben Jonson's masque of 1618, "Pleasure Reconciled to Virtue,"[18]

> The time's arrived that Atlas told thee of: how
> By unaltered law, and working of the stars,
> There should be a cessation of all jars
> 'Twixt Virtue and her noted opposite
> Pleasure (ll.180–84)

Only through art and skill, however, can these opposites be joined in harmony: "For what is noble should be sweet, / But not dissolved in wantonness" (ll. 299–300). Indeed, G. Karl Galinsky tells us that in Jonson's masque, "Virtue and Pleasure cease to exist as ethical polarities but are elegantly transformed into two different ways of life, the life of pleasure merely enhancing what virtue has to offer."[19] Vaenius attempts a similar harmonizing of nobility and sweetness in his emblem through the conflation of "Hercules and Omphale" with the theme of "Pleasure Reconciled with Virtue." Love and Hercules are now happily united through the arts as an emblem of perfect concord.

Bethesda, MD

---

[17] For an extended discussion of "Virtue Reconciled with Pleasure," see Edgar Wind, *Pagan Mysteries in the Renaissance*, rev. and enlarged ed. (New York: W. W. Norton & Co., 1968), 81–96.

[18] See Ben Jonson, "Pleasure Reconciled to Virtue" in *Inigo Jones: The Theatre of the Stuart Court*, 2 vols., eds. Stephen Orgel and Roy Strong (Berkeley and Los Angeles: Univ. of California Press, 1973), 1:277–88. Line numbers will be indicated in my text.

[19] Galinsky, 213.

Grotius and Legal Tradition: A Study in Ambivalence

ROGER T. SIMONDS

In Hugo Grotius's famous work on international law, *De iure belli ac pacis* (1625), there is a curious ambivalence toward the European legal tradition. It is clear that what Grotius does is rooted in that tradition, but he seems to go out of his way to obscure or minimize his relationship to it. A study of his treatment of the theory of legal interpretation brings out this ambivalence, as I shall argue.

Grotius's reputation as a founding father of modern legal and political thought rests on two pillars: his advocacy of a "natural law" theory of jurisprudence, and his development of the theory of international law. His position is said to be modern in the sense that it seems for the first time to divorce legal and political theory from theology and from traditional European concepts of imperial sovereignty.

In the field of international law, Grotius is famous for having advanced the principle of freedom of the seas, the doctrine of the just war, and the theory that treaties between sovereign nations constitute a valid body of law independently of any international political power. This theory is connected with the natural law doctrine in the sense that the notion of legal validity as applied to agreements between sovereign powers implies that there are legal principles independent of the positive laws of those powers themselves.

The concept of natural law is of course very ancient and is a commonplace among the classical philosophers, poets, rhetoricians, and jurists. What was new in Grotius, it is said, was the idea that certain principles of natural law are valid independently of the divine will itself. This is the famous "impious hypothesis" in the Prolegomena (section 11) to Grotius's work: "What we have been saying (about the natural law) would have a degree of validity even if we should concede that which cannot be conceded without the utmost wickedness, that there is no God, or that the affairs of men are of no concern to him."[1]

Certainly Grotius is no atheist, and his background and sympathies are Protestant. Yet his emphasis on the independence of natural law seems to align him more with the intellectualist than with the voluntarist side of theological controversy. The intellectualists held that God wills the good because it is good; the voluntarists held that what is good is good because God wills it.[2] Such an abstract dispute over the relations between intellect and will in God might seem to have no practical import. Yet on the one view it will be possible to construct a theory of ethics and jurisprudence without recourse to theology; on the other view it will not. At the same time, it is clear that Grotius does not want to abandon voluntarism altogether. In the next section (12) of the Prolegomena he states that there is "another source of law besides the source in nature, that is, the free will of God, to which beyond all cavil our reason tells us we must render obedience."

This intellectualism represents an apparent shift in Grotius's point of view from his earlier unpublished work, *De iure praedae* (On the Law of Prize and Booty) of 1604, a manuscript discovered only in 1864. In that work he seems to take a simple voluntaristic position, equating the natural law with the divine will.

Closer inspection, however, shows that his early work is more consistent with his later work than it appears to be at first sight. Already in 1604 we see him formulating and struggling with the problem which was to be the focus of his *magnum opus* in 1625. That is, he has already seen that his ideas about international relations require him to develop some sort of natural law theory, and he has decided that he will have to develop it without depending on legal, philosophical or theological tradition in any essential way.

In this early work Grotius shows that he was well aware of the intellectualist/voluntarist debate, which he locates in the classics, although he must have known that it was raging among the theologians of his own time; and he thinks he has the solution. He writes:

---

[1] Hugo Grotius, *De jure belli ac pacis libri tres*, vol. 2: *The Translation*, by Francis W. Kelsey (Oxford University Press, 1925), 13. Further references to this work are given in the text. For general discussion of the importance of Grotius in the "natural law" tradition, see A. P. d'Entrèves, *Natural Law* (London: Hutchinson & Co., 1951), 50–54.

[2] See M. B. Crowe, "The 'Impious Hypothesis': A Paradox in Hugo Grotius?" in *Tijdschrift voor Filosofie*, 38, nn. 3–4: 379–410.

> Ausonius has declared that, 'Law is the unerring mind of God'. This was the sentiment that inspired Orpheus—and after him, all the old poets—to say that Themis and Dike [Right and Justice] were the judicial assessors of Jove; whence Anarchus has correctly inferred ... that a given thing is just because God wills it, rather than that God wills the thing because it is just. According to the somewhat more subtle contention of Plutarch, however, the goddesses Right and Justice are not so much the assessors of Jove, as Jove himself is Right and Justice, and the most ancient and perfect of all laws. It is the latter view that Chrysippus also adopts when he asserts that Jove is the name given to 'that force inherent in the constant and eternal law, which guides our lives, so to speak, and instructs us in our duties.'[3]

The implication is that God's will and God's intellect are really one and the same, a suggestion which anticipates the philosophy of Spinoza. Thus the apparent voluntarism in Grotius's earlier work is only a *façon de parler*; he believes he has transcended the distinction. The later work, in contrast, retains the intellectualism/voluntarism distinction but solves the problem by affirming both sides of the question. That is, as we have noted, he now recognizes two independent sources of law, apart from human positive laws and conventions: nature herself and the will of God.

The introductory chapter of the early work makes his project quite clear. Quoting Dio, Cicero, Sophocles, and Lactantius in support of the proposition that international disputes must be resolved by appeal to customary, unwritten, natural and heavenly laws, he continues:

> If those persons [who base their judgment on written laws] do not read the works of the authors above cited, they ought at least to pay heed to the words of their own Baldus, who has wisely ruled that in any controversy arising between claimants of sovereign power the sole judge is natural reason, the arbiter of good and evil. Other quite learned authorities uphold this same doctrine. Nor does it differ greatly from the popular maxim that he who seeks for a statutory law where natural reason suffices, is lacking in intelligence. Therefore, it is from some source other than the Corpus of Roman laws that one must seek to derive that pre-eminent science which is embodied, according to Cicero, in the treaties, pacts, and agree-

---

[3] *De iure praedae commentarius*, vol. 1: *A translation of the Original Manuscript of 1604* by Gwladys L. Williams, with the collaboration of Walter H. Zeydel (Oxford Univ. Press, 1950), 8. Further references to this work are given in the text.

> ments of peoples, kings, and foreign tribes, or—to put it briefly—in every law of war and peace. (6)

Then follows a short paragraph in which Grotius suggests that an appeal to Holy Writ would be the ideal solution, except that by and large Holy Writ gives only historical accounts, in which ordinarily the wrong course of action is described, or it gives the Hebrew law rather than the divine law.

> The true way, then, has been prepared for us by those jurists of antiquity whose names we revere, and who repeatedly refer the art of civil government back to the very fount of nature. This is the course indicated also in the works of Cicero. For he declares that the science of law must be derived, not from the Praetor's edict..., nor yet from the Twelve Tables..., but from the inmost heart of philosophy.... Nevertheless, it will be of no slight value as a confirmation of our belief, if the conviction already formed by us on the basis of natural reason is sanctioned by divine authority, or if we find that this same conviction was approved in earlier times by men of wisdom and by nations of the highest repute. (7)

Who are "those jurists of antiquity whose names we revere"? Grotius does not name them, but in a marginal note he simply mentions certain titles in Justinian's Digest.

Now he spells out the method to be followed: first, laying down certain general rules and laws, "presenting them as preliminary assumptions which need to be recalled rather than learned for the first time, with the purpose of laying a foundation upon which our other conclusions may safely rest" (ibid.).

In the sequel, Grotius devotes a chapter to spelling out nine "rules" and thirteen "laws," from which supposedly the solutions of actual controversies in international law could be deduced. These rules and laws, however, are extremely general. Among them one finds, inter alia, that "what God has shown to be His Will, that is law"; that "what the common consent of mankind has shown to be the will of all, that is law"; that it is permissible to defend one's own life, to acquire for oneself "those things which are useful for life," that no one may inflict injury or seize possession of what is possessed by another, that evil deeds must be corrected and good deeds recompensed.[4] But how can we bridge the gap between

[4] See appendix A, 369–70, where all of the "rules" and "laws" discussed in chapter 2 are conveniently presented.

these general propositions and concrete cases? What principles are available to guide us in taking such a leap?

It seems that Grotius in 1604, a mere twenty-one years old, had not yet discovered the importance of this question. Or perhaps he was not certain how to deal with it. Clearly, if he were serious in pursuit of what he calls the pre-eminent science embodied in international treaties, pacts and agreements, he would have to deal sooner or later with the problem of interpreting these agreements.

In the *De iure belli ac pacis* Grotius does present a chapter on this topic, not near the beginning, where one might expect to find it, but as the sixteenth chapter of the second book. The basic ideas in it can be described quite simply.

There are thirty-two numbered sections in the chapter, which is organized into five main topics as follows: (1) the presumption in favor of the ordinary or natural senses of words; (2) what to do in the event of ambiguity or apparent contradiction; (3) the effects of the difference between favorable and odious agreements; (4) extensive and restrictive interpretation based on intent; (5) presumption in favor of the promisor in an obscure agreement. The ideas presented are for the most part thoroughly traditional and familiar to anyone well versed in Western jurisprudence, although they are sometimes dressed in unfamiliar language.

At the outset, he argues (quoting Cicero) that in promises what you meant, not what you said, is binding. "But because internal acts are not of themselves perceivable, and some degree of certainty must be established, . . . natural reason itself demands that the one to whom the promise has been made should have the right to compel the promisor to do what the correct interpretation suggests. . . . The measure of the correct interpretation is the inference of intent from the most probable indications. These indications are of two kinds, words and implications . . ."(409).

He then lays down the rule that "if other implications are lacking, words are to be understood in their ordinary sense" (ibid.), that is, natural or current usage. But he gives no reason for this rule, other than to quote a line from Horace's *Art of Poetry*, and in fact it goes potentially counter to what he had stated first about promisors being bound by thoughts rather than by words. It is a somewhat weaker form of the Roman-law principle, that the words in a legal instrument are to be understood in their proper and common senses (*communis usus loquendi*) unless it is manifest that the maker had other senses in mind.[5] Grotius does give an amusing illustra-

[5] In Justinian's *Digest* (D 32,1,69,pr) we have the maxim: *Non aliter a significatione*

tion from Polybius, who says that the Locrians "took oath that they would keep [an] agreement as long as they should stand on that ground and should bear heads on their shoulders; then they threw away the earth which they had placed in their shoes, and the heads of garlic which they had laid on their shoulders, as if in that manner they could free themselves from the ... obligation" (410).

Ambiguity and apparent contradiction, he tells us (in his second topic), call for conjectures as to the true meaning. If there is a real contradiction, then a later agreement between the parties prevails over an earlier agreement. The presumption is that ordinarily contradictions are apparent only, so that one should favor an interpretation which reconciles the different parts with one another (411). These ideas, again, are thoroughly traditional,[6] but Grotius gives no citations. He does go on to explain the basis of conjectures as to meaning: they depend, he says, on the subject-matter, or on the effect, or on the connection. By "subject-matter" he seems to mean the special circumstances of an agreement. For instance, "in a division one-half of the ships ought to be understood of whole ships, and not as one-half of each ship cut in two, as the Romans maintained in taking advantage of Antiochus" (412). By "the effect" he means the result of interpreting an instrument in a particular way. If this result is "contrary to reason" then some other interpretation must be found. By "the connection" he means the context of a word in a particular instrument or the context of an instrument in others by the same maker.

Passing on to his third main topic, Grotius divides promises into four types, that is, favorable, odious, mixed, and median. This division, according to his marginal note, is from Alciati (413). It is in effect a special case of the general classical distinction between more beneficial and less beneficial statutes or instruments, a beneficial instrument being one which confers greater rights or privileges than the common law already allows.[7]

---

verborum recedi oportet, quam cum manifestum est aliud sensisse testatorem. Although this rule is stated with respect to wills, the glossators and commentators extended it, with ample justification, to cover all sorts of legal instruments. That the *significatio* of words "should be understood not according to individual opinions but according to common use" is affirmed by Celsus in another text (D 33,10,7).

[6] See for example D 1,4,4, to the effect that later imperial enactments are "worth more" than earlier ones. Also D 1,3,24 ("It is uncivil to adjudicate by or respond to some particular part of a law without taking the whole of it into account") and various texts (e.g., D 22,1,4; 28,7,12; 50,1,1) where the principle is applied that no provision in an instrument should be interpreted as superfluous or redundant if some other sound interpretation is available.

[7] This understanding of "beneficial" was apparently first formulated by Accursius (gloss on D 1,3,25) by inference from various classical texts.

As expected, Grotius tells us that "in agreements that are not odious the words should be taken with their full meaning according to current usage; and, if there are several meanings, that which is broadest should be chosen, just as the masculine gender is taken for the common gender, and an indefinite expression for a universal" (414).

Grotius's fourth topic is what he calls "interpretation from conjectures outside of the meaning of the words in which the promise is contained" (421). By "outside the meaning" he means beyond the range of ordinary and proper signification. This kind of interpretation consists in broadening or narrowing the sense of a term if the result otherwise would be unjust, unlawful or demonstrably contrary to the maker's intent.

Among other examples of broad or extensive interpretation, Grotius gives what he takes to be a stock illustration, the condition in a will that an expected posthumous child has died. Suppose that in fact no posthumous child is born; then the condition is understood by extension to cover that situation, since it is presumed that the maker wanted to provide for the non-existence of a child, not merely for the death of an existing child. Grotius adds the comment, "It is, in fact, possible to find this very example in the writings not only of the jurists but also of Cicero and Valerius Maximus" (422), as if to suggest that its appearance in the latter two authors somehow gives it greater value. As an example of narrow or restrictive interpretation, Grotius says that "a person who has promised to return a sword which he received in trust will not return it to a madman, lest he bring danger either to himself or to other innocent persons" (425). He cites Quintilian for this example, which is at least as old as Plato's *Republic* (331C).

At the end of this part of his chapter, Grotius adds the following statement, in which he mentions Roman law for the first and last time in the body of the text. "I shall not ... admit the rule, which has been adopted by some writers [meaning Alciati in particular], that the contracts of kings and peoples ought to be interpreted according to Roman law as far as possible, unless it is apparent that among certain peoples the body of civil law has been received as the law of nations in respect to the matters which concern the law of nations. Such a presumption ought not rashly to be admitted" (429).

Finally, in the very last section of the chapter, we find what I have called the fifth main topic, the presumption in favor of the promisor in an obscure agreement. Whether more weight should be given to the words of one who offers or of the one who accepts a condition, Grotius tells us, is a point which interests Plutarch in his Symposiacs. The one who accepts or promises ought to be favored, he argues, because the mere offer of a condition creates no obligation unless it is accepted. This reasoning is not very persuasive. But there is in Roman law the same general principle (D 2,14,39), the reason for it being that the maker of an obscure agreement could have made it clear by a more careful choice of words, so that the risk of misunderstanding falls on him.

I have referred to some of Grotius's notes mentioning sources. Legal literature is famous for mentioning sources, but usually they are professional ones, that is, texts in the corpus of civil law, canon law, glossators, or commentators. It is striking that in this one chapter there are no fewer than 150 citations, supplied by Grotius himself either in marginalia or in footnotes; of these only fifty-two refer to professional legal literature, and only twelve mention specific civil or canon law texts.[8] In some places he quotes or paraphrases these texts without mentioning their origin.[9]

In the methodological statement which I quoted from Grotius's earlier work he takes the view that the only criterion available for settling international disputes is natural reason, and that therefore the appeal to Roman law is not appropriate. And I have noted his rejection of Roman law at the end of the later work. But he asserts that the method of drawing legal wisdom from the fount of nature, from the heart of philosophy, is recommended by "those jurists of antiquity whose names we revere," and according to his own note these are none other than the jurists whose works are represented in Justinian's *Digest.* He thus finds authority within the legal tradition itself for the idea that he should form his own opinions independently of the legal tradition. There is some truth in this idea, certainly, if one believes that the heart of philosophy is also the heart of jurisprudence. What is odd about Grotius is that after having announced that he was going to recreate jurisprudence on the basis of natural reason he only reiterates in a rather sketchy way the main outlines of a doctrine which was well developed and exhaustively discussed by jurists and commentators centuries before. And it is not clear that he has discovered any new or more persuasive reasons for adhering to the principles laid down.

---

[8] Apart from the professional literature (*Corpus iuris civilis, Corpus iuris canonici,* glossators and commentators), Grotius cites Aristotle, Cicero, Isocrates, Livy, Horace, Polybius, Thucydides, Polyaenus, Augustine, Servius, Tertullian, Frontinus, Plutarch, Valerius Maximus, Homer, Procopius, Justin, Demosthenes, Diodorus Siculus, Appian, Dionysus of Halicarnassus, Ammianus, Menander Protector, Lucan, Quintilian, Seneca, Pliny the Elder, Tacitus, Philo, Isaeus, Gellius, Donatus, and Ovid.

[9] As an example, the sentence "For as in all things the absence of a single one of the causes is sufficient to prevent the result, and all causes need to concur that the effect may be produced . . ." (421) contains a paraphrase of a well known maxim by Paul (D 50,1,1): *Regula est, quae rem quae est breviter enarret . . . et, ut ait Sabinus, quasi causae coniectio est, quae simul cum in aliquo vitiata est, perdit officium suum.*

Grotius himself, I am convinced, being extraordinarily well versed in the classics and fully trained as a lawyer, must have been aware that in reconstructing the theory of legal interpretation he was plundering the past rather than improving on it. But if his aim was to provide a theoretical basis for international relations, free from the traditional imperialisms which were in contention with the new idea of national sovereignty, he had to provide something which looked new even if it was not really new. He was trying to reach a general international audience, not a special professional one. If his argument was challenging and intriguing but not obviously sound, that fact may have contributed to his success. All participants in the modern debate over political theory have found support in his work and have found something to criticize. Hence, if his ambivalent attitude toward the legal tradition was a fault, it was perhaps a fortunate fault. He brought old ideas in jurisprudence, clothed in non-technical language, to the attention of the general reader; and by choosing his illustrative examples from the remote past, he managed to avoid taking sides in the political and religious controversies of his own time. Thus his voice seemed to be the voice of pure natural reason, but the message it conveyed was an ancient and traditional one.

The American University

Danish Neo-Latin Epic as Anti-Swedish Propaganda

KAREN SKOVGAARD-PETERSEN

In the sixteenth and seventeenth centuries a number of Latin historical epic poems were written in Denmark, dealing with the history of Denmark. Some of these are annalistic in nature, i.e., they recount the history of Denmark over a longer period of time. They are normally dedicated to the reigning Danish king, and can be characterized as versified, panegyrical, national history. Others are, like classical epic poems, centered around a single conflict. In this paper I shall deal with three such "classical" epics.

The three poems are united by their common theme, namely a Danish-Swedish war. During this period Denmark and Sweden were constantly competing with each other, often with open warfare as the result. This tense situation was expressed in a great number of polemic literary works in both countries. The goal was to denigrate each other, not least in the eyes of outsiders. Historical writing in Latin was a useful tool in this literary battle, and historical epic also served the cause of national propaganda.[1] These three epic poems are very much engaged in polemics against Sweden. In the following I shall provide examples illustrating the way in which authors utilize classical epic models in order to accomplish their own polemic ends.

The largest of these epics is *Margaretica* (10 books, 6666 lines) from 1573, written by Erasmus Laetus (1526–1582), who was by far the most prolific Danish Neo-Latin poet. At this point in time the so-called Nordic

---

[1] This article only deals with Danish poems. A survey of Swedish anti-Danish poems in the 1550s and 1560s is found in: Kurt Johannesson, "Retorik och Propaganda vid det äldre Vasahovet," in *Lychnos* 1969–70. Stockholm, 1971.

Seven Years War between Denmark and Sweden had just ended, more or less indecisively. *Margaretica* deals with a great Danish victory over Sweden some 200 years earlier, in 1389, but the poem nevertheless contains a large number of allusions to the recent Seven Years War—which therefore, indirectly, is made to look like a great Danish victory.

It is not just any previous Danish victory over Sweden Laetus has chosen as his subject matter. The poem deals with the victory of the ruling Danish Queen Margaret over the Swedish King Albrecht (Laetus has appropriately dedicated the poem to a contemporary ruling queen, Elizabeth of England). This victory paved the way for the so-called Union of Kalmar between Denmark and Sweden which lasted until 1523, under the rule of Danish kings. Once the union was dissolved, the Swedish kings were at pains to distance themselves from this previous dependence; so when Laetus chose precisely this battle as the subject of his epic, it was clearly intended as a provocation.

In one of the central scenes Queen Margaret lies awake at night in fear of the numerous threats of war which had been given by the Swedish king. The scene has models in the *Aeneid* where Aeneas often lies awake with the gnawing uncertainty as to where he is going to lead the Trojans. Like Aeneas, Margaret receives the answer in a dream. This answer, given by her deceased husband, is a description of the glorious Danish kings who are to reign over the Union of Kalmar—that is if she now responds to the challenges of the Swedish king by going to war. This prophecy is modelled upon Anchises' foretelling to Aeneas of the future greatness of Rome in the sixth book of the *Aeneid*. Thereby the union between Denmark and Sweden is made to form a counterpart to Rome in the prophecy of Anchises, a suggestion that must have been highly provocative to Swedes at the time.

Virgil's *Aeneid* is in fact the most important literary model for *Margaretica*. Among other things, Laetus has borrowed a number of features from the description of the Trojan war, in the second book of the *Aeneid*, for his portrayal of the battle itself—Sweden of course playing the part of the defeated Troy.

In addition, the figure of Queen Margaret has much in common with Aeneas, but unlike Aeneas she shows practically no signs of human weakness. She is a perfect monarch, while her opponent, the Swedish King Albrecht, is a tyrant pure and simple.

Albrecht's intention with the war is to conquer the Scanian provinces (today the southernmost area of Sweden which was part of Denmark until 1658). With this Laetus is clearly alluding to the Swedish king during the recent Seven Years War, Erik 14, who had declared, correspondingly, that his highest goal was to make the Scanian provinces Swedish. However,

Erik 14 did not achieve his goal, and thus Laetus can use this in his polemics as an example of Albrecht's—and indirectly of Erik's—ridiculously exaggerated ambitions.

When Laetus published *Margaretica*, in 1573, Denmark was still the leading country of the North. Eighty-five years later, in 1658, the balance of power between the two countries was completely reversed. In the course of the Thirty Years War, Sweden had become one of the leading European powers, and had now conquered the Scanian provinces along with a number of other areas from Denmark. The Swedish king Charles 10 Gustav even planned to bring the whole of Denmark under his rule. At a certain point he actually controlled most of the country, but the Danish capital Copenhagen was still left to conquer. Consequently, he surrounded the city in the autumn of 1658.

Even this rather unflattering situation could become glorious in Danish anti-Swedish epics. The Swedish siege of Copenhagen is the subject of no fewer than two Latin epics, owing to the fact that the Swedish king was not successful in his attempt to take Copenhagen, and Denmark thus remained independent.

One of these poems, *Amagria vindicata* (1 book, 926 lines), is written by the Danish philologist and scientist Ole Borch (1626–1690).[2] It deals with a single encounter, in which the Danes overcame the Swedes on the island of Amager a little outside Copenhagen. The poem is almost solely concerned with the Swedish King Charles who has surprisingly many traits in common with his Swedish predecessor Albrecht in Laetus' *Margaretica*. Just as Laetus' Albrecht is convinced that he will conquer the provinces of Scania, Charles considers it a small matter to conquer the whole of Denmark. Both kings are advised against these presumptuous projects; and both entirely ignore the warnings. They do not become aware of their unjust greed until they have suffered well-deserved defeat.

One morning Charles tells his men that he has had a dream the night before, in which one of his great predecessors on the Swedish throne Gustav Adolf (who died in the Thirty Years War) appeared before him (*Amag.* 167–70):

> Adfuit & toto Gustavus luridus ore
> Hei mihi! quam pallens? quam loti sanguine vultus?
> Exhaustaeque genae, capitisque orbata capillis
> Area, & a Lycio praecordia fossa tumultu?

---

[2] The *Amagria vindicata* was probably written shortly after 1660, but it was not published until 1693 (see the Bibliography).

Here Borch quotes Aeneas' description of Hector, who appeared to Aeneas in a dream, shortly before the fall of Troy (*Aen.* II.270–79):

> in somnis, ecce, ante oculos maestissimus Hector . . .
> raptatus bigis ut quondam, aterque cruento
> puluere perque pedes traiectus lora tumentis.
> ei mihi, qualis erat . . .
> squalentem barbam et concretos sanguine crinis
> uulneraque illa gerens, quae circum plurima muros
> accepit patrios.

In the same way as Aeneas is surprised at Hector's miserable appearance, Charles is surprised at the sight of the badly injured Gustav. Both figures appear in a wounded state as they looked at the moment of death.[3] And just like Aeneas, Charles only partially comprehends the fact that it is a bad omen when this formerly great hero and fellow countryman suddenly appears in such a pitiful state. Charles simply declares that only women and children are scared by that kind of dream (*Amag.* 171–73):

> Talibus at trepident puerilia pectora visis,
> Effoetaeque nurus: non vana insomnia Regem
> Terruerint. . . .

He does admit, however, that he was shaken by a strange chill (*Amag.* 181): Sed mihi nescio quid frigusculi in ossa penetrat—a phrase that recalls Aeneas' account from the ominous beaches he arrives at right after his flight from Troy (*Aen.* III.29–30): mihi frigidus horror/membra quatit gelidusque coit formidine sanguis. But even this sign of warning is dismissed by the Swedish king. He proclaims confidently that the Danes shall be conquered in any event (*Amag.* 182): Quidquid id est, Dano delebitur omne cruore—echoing Laocoons foreboding pronunciation regarding the Trojan horse (*Aen.* II.49): quidquid id est, timeo Danaos et dona ferentis. Thus, in Charles' speech, we find a number of allusions to the vague premonitions of imminent danger among the Trojans, before the fall of Troy and during the flight from the city. With this, the defeat of the Swedes is alluded to, in this poem as in Laetus' *Margaretica*, by means of the fall of Troy in the *Aeneid*.

It is no coincidence that Charles is the same type of tyrant as Albrecht. Borch has clearly copied his own Swedish scoundrel from Laetus' Al-

---

[3] Borch's words *Lycio tumultu* are almost certainly a reference to the battle of Lützen in 1632 where Gustav Adolf died.

brecht. Indeed, in Borch's poem Albrecht is the great and awful example of a Swedish king who suffers well-deserved defeat at the hands of Denmark. In his dream, Charles is warned, not only by the appearance of Gustav Adolf, but also by the Swedish saint, the holy Birgitta, who lived in the fourteenth century and was a contemporary of Albrecht. She addresses him thus (*Amag.* 157): semialberte ... nimium fremis—Albertus being the Latin form of Albrecht. This is likely to be an allusion to Laetus' *Margaretica*, where Albrecht's *fremitus*, his blustering behaviour, is a continuous theme. The first words of *Margaretica* actually are: Alberti Sueonum fremitus ... canimus, and the last: Alberti fremitus fatali in sede quieuit. In Borch's poem Charles is a new Albrecht, that is, yet another boastful Swedish king who finally suffers a crushing and deserved defeat to Denmark.

Margaret's dream in Laetus' poem and Charles' dream in Borch's poem function in much the same way. In both poems the dream is an attempt to persuade the principal character with the help of historical examples of Swedish crimes and defeats. Margaret is encouraged in her dream to take up the fight against the Swedes, as her deceased husband not only describes to her the future Union of Kalmar, but also reminds her of earlier Swedish crimes which must now be punished. Charles is warned, in his dream, against the war with Denmark: First, saint Birgitta tells him about his coming defeat and death (in 1660), then he sees a former enemy, the duke of Kurland,[4] call forth the punishment of the gods upon him, and finally the ominous figure of Gustav appears. Unlike Margaret, Charles does not obey the divine advice given in the dream, and continues the war with Denmark in spite of the warning.

For the reader,however, these dreams also point beyond the plot itself. The battle is placed in a greater historical perspective: In both dreams the battle is portrayed as a consequence of Sweden's previous crimes, and in turn, a number of later Swedish defeats are presented as consequences of precisely this battle. It is one of the characteristic features of classical historical epics that the subject is placed in a historical perspective through various forms of prophecies and accounts of previous history—thus appearing as an event of particular significance in the history of the nation. Laetus and Borch have borrowed this feature in their dream scenes, and given it a polemical turn by limiting their account to a series of historical Swedish crimes and defeats and Danish triumphs.

Another traditional epic characteristic that lends the subject of the

---

[4] The Swedish troops had in 1658 captured Mitau, the capital residence of duke Jacob of Kurland, and taken him prisoner.

poem particular weight and significance is the interest of the gods in the action. This feature is utilized to the fullest in the second epic on the siege of Copenhagen in 1658, the *Hafnia Liberata* (1 book, 1351 lines) of Henrik Harder (1642–1683), who later became better known as a writer of epigrams.[5] Here, the plot begins with the fury Megaera who is aggravated at the prevailing peace in the North—a lot of wonderful wars are going on in the rest of Europe, but in the North peace seems to have come to stay. She seeks out her sister in the underworld and encourages her to help stir up a war in the North again. They agree that it would be best to ally with the Swedes, since the Danes cannot be convinced to use delusion and cunning, so they proceed to the Swedish court and have their snakes poison the hearts of the king and his men. The Swedes are thus joined with the evil of the furies, and the entire subject of the poem, the siege of Copenhagen, is then presented as a battle between Good and Evil.

Harder has taken this introduction from Claudian's poem *In Rufinum* (from around 400 a.d.). Here the fury Allecto is correspondingly irritated by the peace that exists in the world under Emperor Theodosius. She, too, becomes allied with her friends in the underworld, where Megaera, also here one of the leading furies, suggests the young Rufinus as a means to disturb the peace, and then Rufinus is presented as the quintessence of everything evil. With this Harder suggests a parallel between Rufinus and Charles, both of whom are tools of the furies in their attempts to bring about unrest.

Of course the design of the furies is in vain. Claudian's Stilicho and Harder's Danish king are both able to conquer the enemy with whom the furies have confronted them. They fight with the gods on their side. In Harder's poem God is offended by the Swedish violation of peace, and once he has decided to save the besieged city, the Swedish defeat is only a matter of time.

All these poems are unmistakably on the side of the Danes in the conflict. A correspondingly propagandistic message is found in Claudian, who continuously tried to promote the policy of Honorius and his general Stilicho in his poems. As far as I can see, however, only Harder has made use of Claudian, in describing the Danish-Swedish war as a struggle between the powers of good and evil. But the distinctions between good and bad are very clear-cut in all the poems. None of them make the Swedish king into a tragic hero who is able to arouse the sympathy of the

[5] Like Borch's *Amagria vindicata* Harder's *Hafnia Liberata* was not published until 1693 (see the bibliography), but probably written in the early 1660s.

reader (as for instance Turnus in the *Aeneid*). Throughout, the central and unmisunderstandable message is that Sweden deserved to lose and Denmark to win.

To sum up: I have tried to point out how classsical historical epic is transformed into national polemics. In the poems of Laetus and Borch, the divine messages in the dreams are modelled upon central prophecies in the *Aeneid*. Thereby the subject of the poem is placed in a wider perspective of national history; but this perspective is, in these two poems, simply an enumeration of Swedish shortcomings and Danish successes. Similarly, in Harder's poem, another epic device, the involvement of supernatural powers, contributes towards associating the opponent parts, Danes and Swedes, with Good and Evil, respectively. Finally Harder's use of Claudian is perhaps worth noticing. In Claudian's straightforward propagandistic poetry, court poets of later ages must have found a more readily adaptible model than in the subtle narrative of Virgil's *Aeneid*.

University of Copenhagen

Bibliography

Borch, Ole. "Amagria vindicata." In *Deliciae Poetarum Danorum*, edited by F. Rostgaard. Copenhagen, 1693.

Henrik Harder. "Hafnia Liberata." In *Deliciae Poetarum Danorum*, edited by F. Rostgaard. Copenhagen, 1693.

Kurt Johannesson. "Retorik och Propaganda vid det äldre Vasahovet." In *Lychnos* 1969–70. Stockholm, 1971.

Laetus, Erasmus. *Margaretica*. Frankfurt am Main, 1573.

Latin Epigrams on Etienne Dolet

MALCOLM C. SMITH

French Neo-Latin poets exchanged epigrams in the 1530s (and later) on any and every pretext.[1] It is not surprising, therefore, that many epigrams are dedicated to Dolet, or have him as their subject. But the epigrams on Dolet are of particular interest. For one thing, they seem to be exceptionally numerous: I have discovered well over twenty people who wrote Latin epigrams on Dolet, and a total of about one hundred poems.[2] Many of them give insight into the particularly complex and intriguing personality of Dolet. Many have historical interest, for Dolet is impor-

---

[1] As Lucien Febvre showed in his admirable portrait of this scholarly milieu in *Le problème de l'incroyance au seizième siècle, La religion de Rabelais* ("L'évolution de l'humanité"), éd. revue, Paris, 1962, I, i, 18–104.

[2] The genre of the epigram is not rigidly defined. J. C. Scaliger, in the section of his *Poetices libri septem* dealing with the epigram ([Lyon,] 1561, B.L. 833 1.24, 169–71), notes that epigrams are of varied lengths, and adds: "Recipit autem omne genus Poeseωs, διαλογικον, sive δραματικον, et διηγηματικον, et μικτον. Epigrammatum autem genera tot sunt, quot rerum. Tot versuum generibus explicantur, quot sunt versuum genera. Tot versibus verborumque generibus, speciebus, formis, figuris, modis componuntur, quot sunt in quocunque linguæ, nationis, populi, gentis ambitu genera, species, formæ, figuræ, modi verborum" (170). Guillaume Colletet, in his *Traitté de l'épigramme et traitté du sonnet*, defines the epigram as "Tout Poëme succinct, qui désigne et qui marque naïfvement, ou une personne, ou une action, ou une parole notable; ou qui infere agreablement une chose surprenante de quelque proposition advancée, soit extraordinaire, ou commune," and adds that "la jurisdiction de l'Epigramme s'estend sur toutes les matieres, et sur toutes les choses morales, naturelles, feintes, et imaginaires" (ed. P. A. Jannini, Genève, 1965, 31). Colletet's treatise is an excellent introduction to the genre, especially in the scholarly edition by Jannini. I have accepted as an epigram any poem which its author described as such, or which is succinct, witty and pointed in the conclusion, especially if it offers a verdict upon a person. I have included one poem (that by Beza on Dolet's death) which the author classifies in a different genre.

tant for the history of scholarship and printing, as well as for his eventful life (which included five spells in prison, mostly on religious charges) and momentous death (he was executed in 1546, supposedly for denying the immortality of the soul).[3] Often, these epigrams say as much about the people who wrote them as they do about Dolet. This is to the best of my knowledge the first attempt to list them, and I hope in due course to publish them.[4] Since the poems are by definition short, it seems sufficient to give the author's name in references: the sources are cited in an appendix.

Dolet was distinctive (and hence an appropriate subject for epigrams) in three ways. Firstly for his scholarship and prowess as a writer. Many of the epigrams on Dolet deal with this. For some commentators, his *Fata Francisci regis* qualified him as the new Virgil and his *De Imitatione Ciceroniana* as the new Cicero. For Godefroy Béringier, Dolet is the equal of both Cicero and Virgil.[5] Guillaume Durand declares that his Latin poetry is the equal of that of the ancient Greeks and Romans. Nicholas Bourbon,

---

[3] Dolet was imprisoned (a) in Toulouse, in March 1534, on a charge of exciting a riot and contempt for the *Parlement*; (b) after the murder of the painter Henri Guillot (or Guillaume), known as Compaing, 31 December 1536; (c) in July or August 1542, on suspicion of heresy, probably at the instigation of printers at Lyons; (d) on 6 January 1544, after two packets of heretical books addressed to Dolet had been seized on entry into Paris, and an order for his arrest sent to Lyons (he escaped two days later to Piedmont); and (e) after publishing his *Second Enfer* with his translations of *Axiochus* and *Hipparchus*. See R. C. Christie, *Etienne Dolet, the martyr of the Renaissance, a biography*, London, 1880, respectively 131; 296–313; 401–3, where the charges are related (he was released in October 1543); 425; 431–61. He was arrested for the last time either at Lyons or at Troyes by 7 September 1544, condemned principally for his translation of a passage of the *Axiochus* which taken in isolation denies the immortality of the soul, and condemned to death on 2 August 1546. Nor were these his only unfriendly encounters with authority: see Christie, 154–55 (his retreat from Toulouse to avoid a second arrest there), 157–58 (his banishment from Toulouse) and 385 (trouble over *Cato Christianus* and epigrams).

[4] Michael Maittaire compiled a collection of biographical statements on Dolet, including some epigrams, in his *Annales typographici*, 5t., Hagæ Comitum, 1715 (B.L. 823 h), III, i, 9–113, which I have drawn on. Another very useful source is Claude Longeon's *Bibliographie des œuvres d'Etienne Dolet*, Genève, 1980.

[5] On Dolet as a latter-day Virgil and Cicero, see the flattering comment of Béringier in the epigram cited above, and the sardonic remark of Scaliger in his *Poetices libri septem*, cited by Maittaire (III, i, 16): "[...] suo arbitratu Vergilianas gemmas suæ inserit pici, ut videri velit sua. Ignavus loquutulejus, qui ex tessellis Ciceronis febriculosas quasdam conferruminavit (ut ipse vocat) orationes; ut docti iudicant, latrationes: putavit tantum licere sibi in divinis operibus Virgilianis." On echoes of Virgil in Dolet, see V. J. Worth, "Etienne Dolet: from a neo-Latin epic poem to a chronicle in French prose," in I. D. McFarlane, ed., *Acta Conventus Neo-Latini Sanctandreani* (Binghamton, 1986), 423–29.

commenting on Dolet's oratory, applies to it successively the terms *flumina, lumina, fulmina* and *numina*. Aneau commented that Francis I would be an Augustus to Dolet and Dolet a Virgil to Francis. Several, including Bourbon, Macrin and (curiously) the illustrious Catholic scholar and controversialist Gentian Hervet (whose epigrams glowingly praise Thomas More and John Fisher as well as Dolet) gratify his insatiable thirst for eternal renown. But not all the epigrams on Dolet as a scholar and author are eulogious. George Buchanan tartly comments that it is small wonder that Dolet's poems lack meaning, as their author lacks a mind; and, in another epigram, that Dolet (as no-one can deny) offers splendid words, but that that is all he offers. Several mock Dolet's supposed claim to be Cicero incarnate: Ducher claimed that he had the soul not of Cicero but of Villanovanus, whose Ciceronian scholarship he had stolen (*De Cloaco et Duro*). Gouvea noted that Cicero's soul had lost its power when spread through Dolet's colossal body. And some (Ducher, Gouvea, Scaliger) criticize his versification.[6]

Dolet was egregious secondly for his personality. To put it mildly, several contemporaries found him difficult to get along with—and the epigram is an ideal medium for those with scores to settle. Thus, epigrammatists focused on his ingratitude, his unsociability, his austerity, his treachery, his conceit.[7] From the outset of his career as orator and writer he manifested a tendency to antagonize authority, and this immediately worried even his friends, many of whom, as we shall see, later distanced themselves from Dolet by writing hostile epigrams. And Dolet, who had no mean opinion of himself, had a propensity to belittle others—notably Erasmus, whose friends (Ducher, Binet ...) retaliated in epigrams directed at Dolet.

The third interesting thing about Dolet is his views on religion, which are presented—perhaps caricatured—by epigrammatists. In order to understand what preoccupied them, it is necessary to examine briefly Dolet's religious views. He cavalierly dismissed dogmatic theology, and

---

[6] Dolet was sensitive to this criticism and replied to it in a prefatory letter in his *Carminum libri quatuor*, 1538.

[7] Even those modern scholars who feel drawn to Dolet have noted these negative aspects. See notably the studies by Claude Longeon: "Cohérences d'Etienne Dolet," in I. D. McFarlane, ed., *Acta Conventus Neo-latini Sanctandreani* (Binghamton, 1986), 363–69; and the introductions to his editions of Dolet's *Le Second Enfer* (Genève, 1978) (11) and *Correspondance* (Genève, 1982) (7) and to his *Bibliographie d'Etienne Dolet* (Genève, 1980) (xx–xxii, xxiv). Among the characteristics which Longeon notes are his instability, irascibility, conceit, intransigence, self-justification, naivety, vindictiveness, suspiciousness and recklessness. On his love of fame, see especially F. Joukovsky, *La gloire dans la poésie Française et latine du XVIe siècle* (Genève, 1969), 191–92.

notably that of Erasmus.[8] He did not profess atheism in any extant document,[9] but we have reliable witnesses to his utterance of such views orally. One is Joannes Angelus Odonus, who visited Dolet in Lyons when Dolet was working at Sebastian Gryphius's printing house: Odonus declared, in a letter to Gilbertus Cognatus dated October 29, 1535, that the University or *Parlement* of Paris might be preparing to have him executed for his atheism—which was public knowledge, for Dolet's own words declared him to be an "impious fellow, without God, without faith, without religion." Dolet, he wrote, perceptively and prophetically, is "For the sake of a slight breath of applause, [...] rushing to certain destruction both of body and soul."[10] Another commentator on Dolet's religious views is Bonaventure Des Périers who worked with Dolet from the summer of 1535 until May 1536 correcting the first volume of Dolet's massive *Commentarii Linguæ Latinæ* [11] and who, in his *Cymbalum mundi* of 1537, implicitly accuses

---

[8] Dolet felt particular scorn for theologians: his *De imitatione Ciceroniana* of 1535 rails against "the insolence, the intolerable conceit and the lunacy not just of Erasmus but of the whole sect of Lutherans." Ranking Erasmus among the Lutherans was a solecism, and an intentionally offensive one, insinuating that Erasmus's refutations were counterproductive—and that dogmatic theologians are all indistinguishable, and all equally noxious. Religion, Dolet urges, "consists entirely in an inner stirring of the soul, in religious awe, in reverence—and is not brought about by words: if you debate about it, or write freely and verbosely about it, then reverence will wither, religious awe will gradually be removed, belief in God will be destroyed and religion will decline into mere commonplace and be dissipated." The *De imitatione Ciceroniana*, though ostensibly philological, is a work of theology, or anti-theology—and highly readable. See the edition by E. V. Telle: *L'Erasmianus sive Ciceronianus d'Etienne Dolet (1535)* (Genève, 1974), especially p. 34–37 of the facsimile, where the passages I have translated here are found. Dolet's cavalier dismissal of Erasmus amounts, needless to say, to caricature: Erasmus, too, saw the need for silence in the face of the divine (see J. C. Margolin, "Erasme et le silence," *Mélanges Saulnier* (Genève, 1984), 163–78). Dolet's abrasive attack on theology recalls another adversary of Erasmus, the renegade Carthusian Otto Brunfels, the founder of modern Nicodemism: the links between the two are explored in my forthcoming study of contemporary views on Dolet.

[9] Scholars have frequently pointed this out, from Maittaire onwards: "At invisum 'αθεον nomen, quod Doleto inurit Scaliger, illi convenire nondum mihi fuit satis compertum. Quantum ex aliquibus eiusdem operibus conjicio, non tantum Deum esse aperte professus est, sed a religione Christiana minime alienum et generalioribus ejusdem dogmatibus imbutum esse se indicavit" (III, i, 17; cf. 101 and notes there). But it is meaningless to say that there is no atheism in Dolet's writing. To consign such thought to print was to write one's own death sentence.

[10] See Christie, *op. cit.*, 216–20. Odonus's attack may have been known to Dolet: see Dolet's *Correspondance*, ed. Longeon, 1982, 62 and n. 4. On Odonus's visit to Dolet, see Longeon, *Bibliographie*, xxv–xxviii.

[11] See Longeon, *Bibliographie*, xxvi and notes 42 and 43 there; see also E. Droz,

Dolet of militant atheism.[12] By 1538, denunciations of Dolet's atheism come thick and fast—and from former friends.[13]

This is the background to epigrams on Dolet published by his close friend and fellow-epigrammatist Joannes Vulteius. Vulteius published some thirty epigrams in praise of Dolet in 1536 and 1537. In 1538, in poems clearly alluding to Dolet though not by name, he accuses him of being a covert atheist—and says he took singularly little trouble to conceal his views.[14] Vulteius's *In quendam irreligiosum Luciani sectatorem* fits absolutely the portrait given in the *Cymbalum mundi*. Nor was Vulteius the only epigrammatist to castigate Dolet for atheist views. The reason why Vulteius and others publicly distanced themselves was that Dolet's reputation made him a dangerous man to know. Friendship with radical thinkers aroused suspicion: at least one humanist was questioned by the Inquisition for his friendship with Dolet.[15] Dolet was an especially dangerous friend for those who had themselves come under suspicion for their religion, as many of Dolet's friends had.

Was Dolet really an atheist? Might one argue that his "real" position is better represented by his work in publishing edifying biblical books? Witnesses like Odonus, Des Périers and Vulteius, who all knew Dolet, leave little or no room for such speculation. Their presentation of Dolet

---

"Pierre de Vingle, l'imprimeur de Farel," in G. Berthoud *et al.*, *Aspects de la propagande religieuse* (Genève, 1957), 74.

[12] I accept the traditional attribution of the *Cymbalum mundi* to Des Périers: see L. Sozzi, *Les contes de Bonaventure Des Périers*, Torino, 1965, 36. It is in my view inconceivable that during the many months that Des Périers and Dolet worked together, and in Lyons in the 1530s, they failed to discuss religion; I propose to examine Des Péziers's attack on Dolet's atheism elsewhere.

[13] Clément Marot is one, assuming his epigram *Contre l'inique*, written around 1538, is, as has been supposed, directed at Dolet—cf. Chassaigne, *op, cit.*, 195–97. But Lionello Sozzi surmised that the epigram was directed at Des Périers—see "Marot, Dolet, Des Périers e l'epigramma *Contre l'inique*," *Studi francesi*, V, 1961, 83–88. A mysterious attack on Dolet by Jean Binet may refer to his atheism: see J. Dupèbe, "Un poète néo-latin: Jean Binet de Beauvais," *Mélanges V. L. Saulnier* (Genève, 1984), 613–28, 625 n. 82.

[14] That the enemy denounced by Vulteius is Dolet has been argued before, notably by Lucien Febvre in *Le Problème de l'incroyance au seizième siècle, la religion de Rabelais* (Paris, 1942), 48–60. My reading of the *Cymbalum mundi* strongly corroborates this interpretation. Dolet's religion (or lack of it) was attracting increasingly frequent comment.

[15] Diogo de Teive's friendship with Dolet was held against him at his trial by the Inquisition in Portugal: see R. Trinquet, *La Jeunesse de Montaigne*, Paris, 1972, 500 n. 99.

is borne out by Cardinal Philibert Babou de La Bourdaisière, who apparently also knew Dolet: "[...] Dolet un des premiers, [...] commençant par assez legeres opinions et de peu d'importance, tomba en peu de temps es plus execrables blasphemes que j'ouys jamais."[16] Dolet had a public and cosmetic position represented by his pious publications and by his (nebulous) declarations of belief, and a semi-public and real position which was atheism. Having been guided to this conclusion by people who can be trusted, one can say that it is borne out by contemporary polemicists (from both sides of the religious divide) whose testimony one is more inclined to treat with caution.[17]

Dolet's obsession for self-justification and fame led him to a mistake which was to prove fatal: instead of playing down the allegations of atheism, he denied them–thus keeping alive the question, "Is Dolet an atheist?" In a dedicatory letter to Jacopo Sadoleto in his *Cato Christianus* of 1538, he drew attention to the fact that his enemies alleged he was an atheist but claimed that the *Cato Christianus* would itself dispel that charge. Guillaume Durand, in an involuntarily revealing epigram published in this work, urged Dolet's detractors to stop describing him as "void of religion" and to conclude from his book that he is a "learned teacher of religion." These claims availed nothing: the book was condemned.[18] Dolet added a further profession of faith in his *Genethliacum* of 1539 and, in a tract against Floridus Sabinus published in 1540, refuted the allegation (which Sabinus had made the year before) that he had denied the immortality of the soul.[19] However, the manner of Dolet's protests of orthodoxy remains truculent. And their content remains nebulous. The same contempt for dogmatic theology which made the *De Imitatione Ciceroniana* such an electrifying document pervades or underlies his subsequent statements on religion. None of these statements silenced his foes: Sabinus attacked him for irrelig-

---

[16] Cited from Michel de Castelnau's *Mémoires*, 1660, I, 355–56 by Maittaire, III, i, 111, note.

[17] Calvin declared, in his *Traitté des scandales*: "Chacun sçait qu'Agrippa, Villeneuve, Dolet, et leurs semblables ont tousjours orgueilleusement contemné l'Evangile: en la fin, ils sont tombez en telle rage, que non seulement ilz ont desgorgé leurs blasphemes execrables contre Jesus Christ et sa doctrine, mais ils ont estimé, quant à leurs ames, qu'ils ne differoient en rien des chiens et des pourceaux" (ed. O. Fatio, Genève, 1984, 136–38). Cf. the verdict of Proteolus [Gabriel Du Préau?] cited by Maittaire, III, i, 106, note (m), from Bayle, *Dict.*, II, 1012.

[18] See C. Longeon, *Documents d'archives sur Etienne Dolet* (Saint-Etienne, 1977), 27.

[19] See Christie, *op. cit.*, 336–38 and 273–75.

ion again in 1541.[20] Dolet's uncompromising attitude towards powerful foes remained with him until the end—and doubtless hastened the end: shortly before his death he published a virulent denunciation of the Inquisitor Matthieu Orry.[21]

That Dolet's erstwhile friends had reason to distance themselves was soon to become graphically apparent.... And his death, like his life, inspired epigrammatists, some writing long after his death. One epigram is friendly to Dolet: Théodore de Bèze, in his *Poemata* of 1548, has a picture of the Muses dampening with their tears the flames which are consuming Dolet—until Jupiter instructs them to stop delaying his entry into heaven (the poem was not reprinted in later editions).[22] But most are hostile. Jean Binet noted that Dolet, who had written of the destiny of Francis I, has not foretold his own, and ought rather to have followed Christ than adopted atheism and the fate that went with it. Andreas Frusius commented gruesomely that Dolet's desire to shine brightly had been met in the manner of his death and, in another epigram, that Dolet used to rejoice in his belief that the soul is mortal but now grieves at the fact that it is not. Estienne Pasquier commented that the flames had failed to purify Dolet and that he had sullied the flames; Jacques Servert, author of a work titled *L'Anti-martyrologe* published in Lyons in 1622, attributed to Dolet an epigram at the moment of his execution: "Dolet is not grieving (*Non dolet ipse Dolet*), but the pious crowd is"—and attributed to a bystander the cruel rejoinder, "The pious crowd is not grieving, but *dolet ipse Dolet*."

A good epigram moves swiftly and inevitably towards a conclusion which is startling but which on reflection seems inevitable. Dolet's life—brief, unpredictable, striking, memorable—has the qualities of the epigram. And it resembles the epigram most intimately and poignantly in that the most disconcerting, moving and memorable point comes at the end: the epigram, wrote Guillaume Colletet, must have a "conclusion artificieuse, surprenante, et dont la pointe vive et aiguë soit capable d'émouvoir et d'enlever l'esprit du Lecteur."[23] And just as the good

[20] See Christie, *op. cit.*, 275–76.

[21] Dolet described Orry in the following terms: "soy disant Inquisiteur de la foy (je ne sçay si plus tost se debvroit appeller inquietateur d'ycelle [...] je n'en cogneus jamais ung plus ignorant, ung plus maling et plus appetant la mort et destruction d'ung Chrestien" (Dolet, *Préfaces françaises*, ed. C. Longeon, Genève, 1979, 169.

[22] On this, and other epigrams by Bèze which I have recently proved have Dolet as their (unnamed) subject, see my "Théodore de Bèze and Philaenus, *Bibliothèque d'Humanisme et Renaissance*," LII, 1990, 345–353.

[23] Colletet, *op. cit.*, 83.

epigram carries throughout the seeds of its own ineluctable conclusion, the life of Dolet prepares the end: the rootless youth, the precarious livelihood, the defiance of the system, the disparagement of privileged but untalented colleagues, the unbridled love of intellectual freedom in a society which limited its exercise, the idealism which ultimately would not bow to expediency–these characteristics stirred friend and foe into action and, ultimately, into action which cost Dolet his life. His life and his death were an epigram: doubtless subconsciously, his contemporaries discerned just how apposite the epigram is as a vehicle for their verdicts upon him.

Royal Holloway and Bedford New College
(University of London)

Bibliography

Barthélemy Aneau, in Dolet's *Francisci Valesii Gallorum regis Fata*, Lugduni, apud Doletum, 1539, B.L. G9713 (3), 78.

Godefroy Béringier, in Dolet's *Carminum libri quatuor*, Lugduni, 1538, B.L. G9713 (1), Z2vo.

Théodore de Bèze, *Poemata*, 1548, B.L. 11403 aaa 35, 51.

Jean Binet, B.Nat. ms. n.a. lat. 2070 (two poems; cf. *Mélanges sur la littérature de la Renaissance à la mémoire de V.-L. Saulnier*, Genève, 1984, 621, n. 52); manuscript verse in the B.Nat. copy of Dolet's *Francisci Valesii Fata* (see Christie, *op. cit.*, 466).

Nicolas Bourbon, Παιδαγωγειον, Lugduni, 1536, B.L. 11403 aaa 14, 26 (two poems), 33 and 45; also Dolet, *Carminum libri quatuor*, 1538, Zro (two poems).

Jean Boyssoné, Latin poems in defence of Dolet: see H. Jacoubet, *Les Poésies latines de Jehan de Boyssoné*, Toulouse, 1931.

George Buchanan, *Franciscanus et fratres* [s.l.], 1584, 160–61 and 166; and another poem cited by Christie, *op. cit.*, 478, n. 1.

Claude Cottereau, in Dolet's *Genethliacum Claudii Doleti*, Lugduni, apud Doletum, 1539, B.L. G9713 (2), C2ro (two poems).

Estienne Dolet, poem on his own impending execution: in Jacques Severt, *L'Anti-Martyrologe*, Lyon, 1622, cited by Christie, *op. cit.*, 458–59.

Gilbert Ducher, *Epigrammaton libri duo*, Lugduni, 1538, B.L. 11409 aa 23, 12, 38, 90, 96, 104, 104–5 and 105.

Guillaume Durand, in Dolet's *Cato Christianus*, Lugduni, apud Doletum, 1538, John Rylands Library, 3 d 1, 7; another epigram in Dolet's *Francisci Valesii Fata*, 78.

Andreas Frusius, *Epigrammata in haereticos*, Antuerpiæ, 1606, B.L. 11408 a 41 (two poems).

Joannes Gigas, four epigrams against Dolet in *Sylvarum liber*, Vitebergæ, 1540 according to Christie, *op. cit.*, 466.

Antonius Gouvea, *Epigrammata*, Lugduni, 1540, B.L. G17437 (2), 16; this and three others on Dolet in Leodegarius a Quercu, *Flores Epigrammatum ex optimis quibusque authoribus excerpti*, t.1, 1555, B.L. 11403 a 29, 313vo, 314vo, 315vo and 316vo; and another in Dos Reys, *Corpus illustrium Poetarum Lusitanorum*, Lisbonæ, 7v, 1745–48, VII, 454.

Janus Guttanus, in Dolet's *Genethliacum Claudii Doleti*, C2vo.

Gentian Hervet, *Epigrammata*, Lugduni, apud Doletum, 1541, B.L. 8411 aa 24, 72.

Jean Salmon Macrin, in Dolet's *Carminum libri quatuor*, Y4vo.

Estienne Pasquier, *Poemata*, 1585, B.L. 11408 aaa 58 (2), 5ro; and a poem from his *Tumuli* cited by F. Berriot, *Athéismes et athéistes*, Lille, 1976, 392.

François Rabelais, in Dolet's *Carminum libri quatuor*, 75–76.

Georgius Sabinus, in *Delitiæ poetarum Germanorum huius superiorisque ævi illustrium*, Pars V, collectore A.F.G.G. [Janus Gruterus], Francofurti, 1612, B.L. 238 i 21–22, 1138 (two poems).

Julius Caesar Scaliger, *Poemata omnia*, 1600, B.L. 1213 1 4, 182, 184 (three poems), 330, 377, 382, 401 and 588.

Maurice Scève, in Dolet's *Genethliacum Claudii Doleti*, C2vo.

Hubert Sussaneau, *Ludorum libri*, Parisiis, 1538, B.L. 1070 d 14, 16ro–vo, 16vo, 25vo–26ro, 27vo and 34ro–vo.

Pierre Tolet, in Dolet's *Genethliacum Claudii Doleti*, C4vo.

Simon Vallambertus, in Leodegarus a Quercu, *Flores*, 129vo.

Joannes Vulteius, *Epigrammatum libri duo*, Lugduni, 1536, B.L. 1213 k 5 (1), 8 (two poems), 11, 12 (two poems), 13, 16, 25, 26, 29, 48, 73–74, 100, 102, 106, 110, 134, 152, 158, 161, 173; further poems are found in the 1547 edition (B.L. 1213 f 1), 31, 190, 206, 220–22, 230, 230–33, 248–49, 250 (two poems) and 254; more poems in his *Hendecasyllaborum libri quatuor*, Parisiis, 1538, B.L. 11405 a 52, 9ro–10ro, 10ro, 10ro–11ro, 22ro–vo, 28ro (two poems), 30vo–32vo, 42ro–vo, 47vo–48ro, 71vo–72vo, 81vo, 84ro–vo, 92ro and 96vo (two poems).

Macarius Mutius's De Triumpho Christi: *Christian Epic Theory and Practice in the Late Quattrocento*

CARL P. E. SPRINGER

This paper examines a little work of the late quattrocento which deserves to be better known than it is, a biblical epyllion of 317 lines entitled *De triumpho Christi,* written (along with two prose prefaces) by an Italian knight from Camerino by the name of Macarius Mutius.

Unfortunately we know very little about Mutius himself except that he was an ambassador who was sent, among other places, to the court of Louis XII of France.[1] In the two prefaces to his poem, Mutius makes several references to his official duties as a *legatus* which have prevented him from writing as much as he would have liked. Eventually he solved the problem of lack of time by writing while travelling. He composed *De triumpho Christi* on horseback, while *en route* to Rimini. Despite his other duties, Mutius did manage to become an author of sorts. He was a correspondent of Politian[2] and a fairly prolific poet. Works of Mutius which survive or which he himself mentions in the prefaces to *De triumpho Christi* include one entitled *Dryas* (dedicated to Pope Julius II)[3], an encomium in

---

[1] Sent by (perhaps) Guidobaldo da Montefeltro c. 1500, according to Mario Cosenza, *Biographical and Bibliographical Dictionary of the Italian Humanists* (Boston, 1962), vol. 3, 2405–6.

[2] See Ida Maier, *Ange Politien: La formation d'un poète humaniste (1469–1480)* (Geneva, 1966), 429–32. For a letter to Uranius Advogarius preserved in Bologna at the Biblioteca Universitaria, see Paul Oskar Kristeller, *Iter Italicum* (Leiden, 1965), vol. 1, 26.

[3] A copy survives in Rome in the *Biblioteca Nazionale Centrale Vittorio Emanuele II,* according to Kristeller, *Iter Italicum*, vol. 2, 122.

praise of St. Sebastian, a *Parthenodia* in praise of the Virgin Mary, a short work on the crucifixion of Christ, and others.

The best known work of Macarius Mutius, however, is undoubtedly *De triumpho Christi*, printed in Venice in 1499.[4] It went through a number of editions and was especially popular in Germany in the sixteenth century. This paper briefly reviews the main arguments of *De triumpho Christi*'s two prefaces (described by Mario Di Cesare as "admirable")[5] and examines their application in the poem itself. I would suggest that in his theory and practice of Christian epic, Mutius points the way to the more ambitious and better known Neo-Latin biblical epics of the sixteenth century.

I

In the first preface Mutius attacks the content of pagan poetry. The poet could be a valued member of society, according to the knight from Camerino, if he wrote works (as he should) celebrating *mystica cerimoniarum sacra aut divinos hymnos aut heroum et fortium virorum gesta.*[6] Such poetry serves a useful instructive purpose. Unfortunately, most pagan poets chose unworthy topics. The eloquence of authors like Petronius, Apuleius, and Lucian was not applied *ad humanae vitae institutionem et politicae rei utilitatem.* Quite the contrary:

> Quos clarissima ingenia doctrinam singularem et scribendi elegantiam meretriciis amoribus et impurissimis scortorum lenociniis maculare et divinae poetices dignitatem, sanctitatem, et gloriam ad libidinem suam traducere ac turpiter foedare non puduit.

Even when the pagan poets wrote religious verse they still managed to be lewd and lascivious. They told stories of the father of gods and men

---

[4] A colophon in the first edition of *De triumpho Christi* informs the reader that it was printed in Venice, 29 March 1499 during the reign of Augustino Barbadico. The printers/publishers of *De triumpho Christi* are mentioned in the colophon. They are the presbyter Franciscus Lucensis, *cantor ecclesiae S. Marci* (See F. J. Norton, *Italian Printers* 1501–1520 [London, 1958], 134–35) and Antonius Francisci, *Venetus litterarum artifex* (see Mario Cosenza, *Biographical and Bibliographical Dictionary of the Italian Printers and of Foreign Printers in Italy* [Boston, 1968], 33).

[5] Mario Di Cesare, *Vida's Christiad and Vergilian Epic* (New York and London, 1964), 79.

[6] Here and elsewhere in the paper I use the text of the 1499 edition (with some minor alterations, mostly orthographic).

disguising himself as a "mooing bull" and swimming across the sea with a girl on his back. Small wonder that Zoilus castigated Homer and Plato was forced to ban him from his ideal city. Even allegory, the traditional way of finding some good in pagan poetry, does not meet the exacting standards set by our impatient poet / ambassador:

> Maneo tamen in sententia, quod tenuem frugem sparsam et magno et confuso acervo abstrusam ad iacturam potius quam ad lucrum accedere arbitror, si longae inquisitionis labor consideretur et temporis ratio, quae non parvi ducenda est, habeatur.

Despite the shortcomings of traditional pagan poetry, Macarius Mutius has discovered (to his dismay) that contemporary poets—all of them presumably Christian—are no more inclined than the ancient pagan writers to deal with lofty and divine subjects, even though they have the ability to do so:

> Ecce florent nostra tempestate ingenia. Vigent studia. Quotusquisque tamen est qui ad illustrandas sacras litteras stilum accommodet?

Certainly there is good precedent for biblical verse. The Bible itself is filled with poetry. Quoting Jerome, Mutius observes:

> Quid Psalterio canorius? Quod in morem nostri Flacci et Graeci Pindari, nunc iambo currit, nunc Alcaico personat, nunc Sapphico tumet, nunc semipede ingreditur.

The Book of Job, of course, as everyone in the Renaissance knew, was written in hexameters and pentameters. In addition, there were the examples of the great Christian poets of Late Antiquity who turned the Bible into verse: Juvencus, Sedulius, Arator, and Prudentius, names familiar to every fifteenth-and sixteenth-century schoolboy.[7]

Mutius tells his readers that he has determined to remedy the situation by writing a biblical poem himself. He is not a professional poet and in the best tradition of *captatio benevolentiae*, he begs the reader's forgiveness and indulgence. After all he is a very busy man, but he has done what he could (cf. Mark 14:8):

> Quid enim ab homine occupatissimo et qui studia litterarum iampridem posthabuerit, amplius expectant, qui omnia ad trutinam revocant? Dedi quod potui.

---

[7] For a discussion of the reception of the biblical epics of late antiquity in the Renaissance period, see Carl Springer, *The Gospel as Epic in Late Antiquity: The Paschale Carmen of Sedulius* (Leiden, 1988), 135 ff.

It occurred to Mutius while riding his horse to Rimini that in the life of Christ a poet could find a wealth of suitable subject material.[8] The idea of a poem which concentrated on Christ's descent into hell especially appealed to him: *tollebat animum ea cogitatio ac sublimem rapiebat et dulcedine quadam novitatis pertentabat.*

In the second preface Mutius abandons his polemic against pagan poetry and turns instead to defending biblical poetry against its detractors (*excipient haec quidam cum risu, certo scio, et contemnent*). One reason, writes Mutius, that contemporary poets give for not writing Christian poetry is a stylistic one. Christ is a name, they say, which is inimicable to the Muses (*a fonte sororum ut aiunt aversum existimant*). Mutius points out that there is nothing about the sound of the name of Christ itself which makes it unfit for verse. In fact, Virgil, Statius, and Silius Italicus all use the word *crista* (plume) in their poetry–and the word *crista* is very close to *Christus*.

A second objection to biblical poetry is that its themes are too lofty and exceed the power of the poet to describe (*quod poeticam facultatem excedere fortasse arbitrantur*). This is an objection which Mutius takes more seriously: *negare non ausim eam esse divinarum rerum vim atque dignitatem ut nullo stilo assequi possimus*. Nonetheless, Mutius continues, it should be observed that the pagan poets dealt with lofty and divine subjects such as the triune nature of divinity (the three deities, Neptune, Jove, and Pluto, who ruled the three distinctive realms of the universe are a sort of pagan trinity, according to Mutius). Even such a profound mystery as transubstantiation finds parallels in pagan poetry. Virgil writes of wine turning into "foul blood" (*fusaque in obscoenum se vertere vina cruorem*). Certainly Ovid's *Metamorphoses* contain miracles just as incredible as the transformation of bread and wine into the body and blood of Christ.

But even if the poet were to leave such divinely mysterious subjects alone, certainly the life of Christ on earth is not too lofty to consider in verse, especially those parts of his life in which he is clearly human. Christ's childhood, for instance, presents a wealth of appropriate material for the poet. And yet, complains Mutius, "our Muses despise" the subject (*pueritiam Christi musae nostrae despiciunt.*) They prefer to tell of Romulus's and Remus's upbringing or the stories of the youthful Achilles or Ascanius.

---

[8] For biblical texts treating of the descent into hell, see, among others, 1 Peter 3:19 and 4:6. The most extensive treatment in antiquity was the apocryphal Gospel of Nicodemus (see the useful discussion in C. Reedijk, *The Poems of Desiderius Erasmus* [Leiden, 1956], 189).

And, finally, what about the poetic possibilities of Christ's descent into hell? Homer, Virgil, and other pagan poets told of heroic journeys into the underworld. But what did their heroes accomplish in comparison with Christ? Orpheus did not succeed in rescuing Eurydice. Odysseus and Aeneas did nothing more except to chat with shadows. Hercules brought back Cerberus. But what benefit did that monster give to the world? By contrast, Christ redeemed mankind and rescued the souls of Old Testament heroes of faith like Adam, Abel, Job, David, and Moses. But, Mutius, concludes:

> Quid pergo molestus esse? Quid plura ingratis auribus ingero eorum qui sanam doctrinam non sustinent? Iam carmina ipsa testentur an possit Christus versibus celebrari. Vale.

II

It is interesting to see how Mutius's criticism of pagan poetry's content and his apology for the style of Christian poetry are translated into practice in the *De triumpho Christi* itself. First of all, and most noticeably, the author's strenuous objection to the content of pagan poetry seems to lead to an extremely restricted use of pagan mythological characters. Even though Mutius borrows heavily from Virgil's language, he refuses to give any significant dramatic role to the traditional characters of classical mythology. This is not to say that Mutius does not adopt some of the terminology of Virgil's underworld. Hell is Orcus or Tartarus; the Styx river and the Cocytus still flow through Mutius's underworld. He also employs the standard personifications of nature found in classical mythology: Mutius's Dawn is, as one would expect, married to Tithonus and the poet is not reluctant to refer to the sun as Titan.[9] But the pagan mythological figures are present in name only in this Christian epic, relegated for the great part to the realm of terminology.

This is clearly different from the practice of such nearly contemporary poets as Jacobus Bonus whose *Sub figura Herculis Christi praeludium* (1526) treats of hell as a "classical-Dantesque landscape inhabited by classical figures such as Pluto, Vulcan, Erebus, Medusa, Charon, Cerberus, Allecto,

[9] Barbara Lewalski, *Milton's Brief Epic: The Genre, Meaning, and Art of Paradise Regained* (Providence, 1966), 57, overstates the case when she declares that the poem "rejects all use of or allusion to pagan mythology."

Centaurs"[10] and other creatures, or Jacopo Sannazaro's (1456–1530) *De partu virginis* in which we find Jesus' feet being kissed by Neptune as he walks across the Sea of Galilee. Even the fairly conservative Mantuan (1447–1516) finds no incongruity in allowing Thetis, Ceres, and Aeolus to pay homage to the Virgin Mary in the first *Parthenice.*[11] The closest parallel to Mutius's practice in this regard is Marcus Hieronymus Vida (bishop of Alba from 1533–1566) who also uses only Christian supernatural agents in his *Christiad,* but at the same time retains the "classical atmosphere and furniture of Hell-Avernus."[12]

In the second place, as Mutius's extreme defensiveness on this score in the second preface would indicate, he is aware of the stylistic problems involved in transforming biblical narrative into hexameters. One major structural problem facing the biblical poet was how to tell a story (like the life of Christ) which is panoramic in scope while maintaining some kind of unity. Mutius solves the problem deftly. His poem achieves the same kind of annalistic effect which biblical poets as early as Juvencus (a contemporary of Constantine) had tried to achieve. Mutius compiles a long catalogue of Old Testament heroes and heroines, beginning with Adam and continuing all the way down to the innocents slain by the soldiers of Herod. His poem, short as it is, therefore, reaches back to the creation of man. It also extends forward to the last judgement. In the final lines of the poem, Mutius tells of Christ's ascension into heaven, accompanied by the souls of the Old Testament believers and prays that he too will find a place there on the last day.

Unlike such traditional biblical poets as Juvencus and Mantuan, however, Mutius does not begin his epyllion *ab ovo.* Instead he treats of a strictly limited subject, the events of one day, the day on which Christ descended into the underworld. The actual focus of this poem is restricted to the descent into hell. Old Testament characters are introduced only because these are the souls whom Christ has come to the underworld to rescue. This concern with observing the unities of time and place, of course, has more affinities with the classical aesthetic than with the biblical.[13] Again

---

[10] Lewalski, 57.

[11] Thomas Greene, *The Descent from Heaven: A Study in Epic Continuity* (New Haven and London, 1963), 167.

[12] Lewalski, 62–63.

[13] It is also worth noting, incidentally, that Mutius chooses to concentrate on a martial subject, a topic especially well suited for epic, according to Horace ("res gestae regumque ducumque et tristia bella"), thus avoiding a charge that was frequently made against other biblical poetry, namely, that its peaceful subject was not suited for the epic genre (cf. Lewalski, 72).

an obvious parallel to Mutius's practice is Vida's *Christiad* which manages to recount the entire life of Christ but whose dramatic setting is actually just a few days before Christ's death.[14]

It should be observed that there is much about the epic theory and practice of Macarius Mutius that is unoriginal. Christian poetry was not so completely nonexistent in the late fifteenth century as Mutius would have his readers believe. There were a number of Mutius's contemporaries who were writing biblical poetry in the period. Nor was the knight from Camerino the first poet to come up with the idea of writing about the harrowing of Hell in verse. Venantius Fortunatus, André de Coutances, and others had all tried their hand at versifying this particular subject.[15] We should also note that there is little in Mutius's two prefaces that is actually original with him. One suspects that he borrowed many of his conventional ideas and arguments from some convenient source such as the *Apologeticon* to Mantuan's first *Parthenice*.

On the other hand, we do know that Mutius's short epic was quite popular in the next century. A number of different editions of *De triumpho Christi* appeared between 1500 and 1567. As mentioned above, Mutius was especially popular in Germany. Editions of his poem were produced in Erfurt, Cologne, and Strasburg[16] and it is likely that his epic inspired a number of German poets (including Eobanus Hessus, Matthias Funk, and Johannes Spangenberg) to write on the same subject. It is also quite possible that Mutius's poem was the inspiration for Erasmus's epyllion written on the same subject.[17] As late as the eighteenth century, we find the youthful Goethe undertaking to write a poem on the same theme, with the title *Poetische Gedanken über die Höllenfahrt Jesu Christi* (1765).[18] In Italy, too, Mutius was popular and well respected throughout the sixteenth century. The *De triumpho Christi* was reissued a number of times in Venice

[14] Most of the events of Christ's life are represented as being told to Pilate by his father Joseph and his disciple John in the third and fourth books of the poem.

[15] For a brief survey of *De triumpho Christi*'s poetic predecessors, see Reedijk, 190.

[16] I have been able to locate the following editions: Venice (1501, 1532, and 1567), Strasburg (1509 and 1514), Deventer (c. 1512), Erfurt (c. 1515), and Cologne (1515 and 1550).

[17] In a paper presented to the Seventh International Congress of the International Association for Neo-Latin Studies, Harry Vredeveld argued persuasively that *De triumpho Christi* influenced Erasmus's *Carmen heroicum de solemnitate paschali atque de tryumphali Christi resurgentis pompa et descensu eius ad inferos* and that the latter work should be dated to 1499 rather than to c. 1489 (as it is by Reedijk, 189–90).

[18] See the comments of Georg Ellinger, *Geschichte der neulateinischen Literatur Deutschlands* (Berlin and Leipzig), vol. 1, 324.

and Mutius's work was reprinted in Antonio Possevino's (1593) *Tractatio de poësi*.[19]

Despite his influence in the sixteenth century, literary historians have not taken Mutius very seriously. Saintsbury observes that little will be found in *De triumpho Christi* "but rhetoric."[20] Georg Ellinger speaks of "the meager literary worth" of the poem. While it would be difficult to argue that this work is a literary masterpiece in any sense of the word—the modesty which Mutius expresses in the prefaces concerning his abilities as a poet and literary critic is well justified—Mutius's biblical epic may merit more than passing attention from the student interested in the evolution of the Neo-Latin biblical epic.

The two most striking features of the *De triumpho Christi* are Mutius's consistent refusal to use pagan mythological characters in dramatic roles and the strictly classical structure and unity of his poem. Mutius was not the first biblical poet to reject pagan mythological characters. The fourth-century Juvencus deserves that distinction. Nor was Mutius the first biblical poet to begin a poem *in medias res*. Poems like the fifteenth-century *Develis Perlament* or *Parlamentum of Feendis* and Jerome Valle's *Jhesuida* (1473) use sophisticated narrative devices like flashback or recitals, more commonly associated with Virgilian than biblical narratives. It is the *combination* of these two emphases, however, that marks Mutius's epic theory and practice as unusual. He rejects emphatically the dramatic role of all pagan supernatural beings and *at the same time* embraces classical notions of style and unity. It is this juxtaposition of elements in the *De triumpho Christi*, I would suggest, that helps to make "this little work" (to quote Mario Di Cesare) "in ways other than chronological, the final word in Quattrocento religious epic."[21]

Illinois State University, Normal

---

[19] See B. Weinburg, *A History of Literary Criticism in the Italian Renaissance* (Chicago, 1961), vol. 1, 337.

[20] G. Saintsbury, *A History of Criticism and Literary Taste in Europe* (New York, 1961), vol. 2, 326.

[21] Di Cesare, 79.

"Le Renvoi des Ambassadeurs Grecs" de Jan Kochanowski et "L'Histoire de la destruction de Troye la Grant" de Jacques Millet

JERZY STARNAWSKI

Le drame de Jan Kochanowski "Le Renvoi des Ambassadeurs Grecs" (1578) est traduit par Józef Brykczyński en français dans l'anthologie *Chefs-d'oeuvre du théâtre polonais* ... sous la direction d'Alphonse Denis.[1] Le traducteur a intitulé le drame de Kochanowski: "Congé des Ambassadeurs grecs." La traduction fut réimprimée à cause d'un anniversaire de Kochanowski en 1884 dans une revue française bien connue.[2] Au XXe siècle c'est une traduction d'André Mary (1931)[3] qui a remplacé la traduction de Brykczński. Toutes les deux sont en prose d'où l'oblitération des vers non rimés, ainsi que des stichomyties d'epeisodion 1^{r}. Dans cet article la traduction d'André Mary sera citée. Mais avant tout il faut citer l'introduction d'Alphonse Denis qui a précédé la traduction de Brykczyński. Denis était d'avis que l'action du drame de Kochanowski ne se déroule de façon peu développée mais en même temps il reconnait que la présentation des personnages est très exacte.

Le personnage de Cassandre inspire véritablement de l'intérêt; ses

---

[1] *Chefs-d'oeuvre du théâtre polonais. Félinsky, Wenzyk, Niemcowitz, Oginsky, Mowinsky, Kochanowski* (Paris, 1823), 523–50.

[2] *Revue des Chefs-d'oeuvre, anciens et modernes* 4.2 (1884): 372–90.

[3] Jean Kochanowski, *Choix de poèmes suivi du "Renvoi des Ambassadeurs Grecs."* Version francaise d'André Mary (Paris, 1931), "Le Renvoi des Ambassadeurs Grecs," 23–44.

paroles prophétiques peignent assez bien le trouble dont elle est agitée. On trouve dans la scène d'Antenor et de Paris une vivacité de dialoque à laquelle on est loin de s'attendre, et qui développe, d'une manière ferme et rapide, les caractères mis en opposition, en même temps qu'elle offre une exposition digne d'un ouvrage conduit d'une manière plus savante. On peut juger que l'esprit de l'auteur a, bonne heure, été nourri de la lecture des poètes grecs et latins.[4]

Les sources du drame de Kochanowski sont connues: ce sont les antiquités grecque et romaine. Mais le critique de l'an 1823 remarque aussi:

> Cependant je ne voudrais pas jurer que Kochanowski, qui passa quelques années en France avant de travailler pour le théâtre, n'ait eu connaissance d'un de nos plus anciens drames, "La destruction de Troye la Grant," translatée du latin en français, composée par le maître Mirtel, l'an 1540.[5]

Jacques Millet est l'auteur du drame "L'Istoire de la destruction de Troye la Grant" (1450) dédié à Charles VII. Ce drame fut réimprimé à Paris en 1450 et en 1498, à Lyon en 1500 et en 1544. Il était beaucoup lu à l'époque de la Renaissance mais est tombé dans oubli ensuite. Il est sujet de trois thèses de doctorat en Allemagne vers la fin du XIXe siècle. L'affinité entre les drames de Millet et de Kochanowski n'est pas proche. L'oeuvre de Millet est bien longue (2700 vers). Elle est divisée en quatre parties (quatre jours) selon l'usage des auteurs dramatiques à l'Ouest de l'Europe des XVe, XVIe et XVIIe siècles. Une analogie existe dans la présentation des personnages ainsi que de leur fonctions dans le déroulement du drame. Kochanowski a présenté Anthénor comme modèle d'un bon citoyen. Il l'a choisi parmi les héros de l'*Iliade*. Il est bien possible que Kochanowski qui a fait ses études à Padoue choisit Anthénor, fondateur légendaire de cette ville (une présomption de Tadeusz Ulewicz).[6] Mais il est aussi possible qu'il a subi l'influence de la tragédie française du XVe siècle.

Anthénor joue un rôle prépondérant dans le drame de Kochanowski et aussi dans le drame de Millet. Chez Kochanowski c'est lui, Anthénor, qui

---

[4] *Chefs-d'oeuvre du théâtre polonais* . . . , 523.

[5] Ibid.

[6] T. Ulewicz, L'introduction dans: J. Kochanowski; *Odprawa posłów greckich* (*Le Renvoi des Ambassadeurs Grecs*), 10ème édition (Wroclaw, 1962; 11ème éd. 1969; 12ème éd. 1974).

annonce le sujet de drame:

> C'en est fait. Ce que j'avais prévu est arrivé, et je l'ai annoncé depuis longtemps: les vaillants Grecs ne souffrent pas le tort et n'endurent pas l'outrage. Aujourd'hui leurs ambassadeurs sont à Troie: ils exigent qu'Hélène soit remise entre leurs mains, Hélène que naguère Alexandre, en hôte déloyal, ravit à son époux et emmena dans sa nef à travers les plaines salées. Rendons-la, nous maintiendrons la paix; mais que les envoyés reviennent, apportant notre refus, et nous saurons, le jour même, que les Grecs ont débarqué et engagent la bataille.

Chez Millet dès le commencement de la première journée où le roi l'a fait venir il est présenté comme un bon citoyen. Dans sa harangue au roi il assure qu'il va "pour vous servir loyalement en tous cas" avec son fils Polydame.

Quand le roi "souffre grand douleur," Anthénor adresse une longue harangue aux dieux en les implorant de surveiller le roi de près. C'est particulièrement Castor et Pollux qui doivent veiller sur Priam. Anthénor se rend compte du danger qui menace sa patrie et à chaque instant rénouvelle ce souvenir. Dans un long monologue il implore Apollon:

> Phoebus, qui gouverne la terre
> Par influences merveilleuses,
> Défend le roi Priam de guerre
> Et de toutes choses périlleuses.

Invité à s'avancer vers le roi il répond:

> Je suis tout près quand on voudra.

Au début de la deuxieme "journée" il tâche de déterminer le roi à bien préparer la défense. Pas seulement ses actes mais aussi les paroles de Huppon le caractérisent:

> Or est Anthénor très puissant
> Et en conseil fort profitable
> Et est aussi bien advenant
> En guerre, et très redoutable;
> Et à chacun fort dommageable:
> Où il soit—les mains des ennemis
> Pour cette cause raisonnable
> Il faut avoir en ce admis.

Le drame français du XVe siècle est un peu chaotique: l'action se déroule à Troyes, des Greces ainsi que des habitants de Troye dialoguent. L'auteur présente alors une rencontre d'Anthénor avec Agamemnon. Tous les deux sont adversaires bien préparés à la lutte. Après cette rencontre Anthénor décide de poursuivre le combat à outrance, et dit au roi: "Si je puis, j'aurai vengeance / D'Agamemnon, ou je mourrai."

Parys, nommé par Kochanowski Alexandre, est présenté par le dramaturge français comme personification de l'orgueil. Pendant la "journée" le prince royal dit avec fierté à son père, lui présentant le tragique conflit:

> Nous sommes assez grand' puissance
> Pour mettre en notre obéissance
> Tous les Grecs.

Hélène est comme dans l'oeuvre de Kochanowski peu réelle, indécise. Voilà le monologue d'Hélène chez Kochanowski:

> J'ai le pressentiment que cet infâme Alexandre ne jouira pas long temps de sa conquête. Les Grecs victorieux troubleront bientôt sa tranquilité. Comme un loup vorace qui a jeté le désarroi dans le troupeau, il a déguerpi au loin, tandis que les Grecs le pourchassent comme les bergers avec leurs chiens. Et il s'en faut de bien peu que le loup n'abandonne la brebis et ne s'enfuie éperdu dans les bois. Comment va se faire mon retour? Sans doute dans le fond d'un vaisseau, parmi les galères grecques, avec des chaînes au cou. De quel front saluerai-je mes frères chéris? Accablée de quelle honte, ô mon cher époux, je paraîtrai à tes yeux, et te rendrai compte de mon infortune! Oserai-je te regarder en face? Plût au ciel que tu n'eusses jamais vu Sparte, malheureux Priamide! Que pouvait-il me manquer? Issue de noble lignage, j'étais entrée dans la demeure d'un prince vertueux. Dieu m'avait donné la beauté, des enfants, et, par -dessus tout, une renommée sans tache. Tout cela, je l'ai perdu par la faute d'un homme félon. Mon pays est loin, je n'ai pas un ami, et mes enfants, j'ignore s'ils vivent. Je suis ici presque comme une esclave, couverte d'opprobre, en proie aux vilenies de chacun. Et ce que le sort me réserve encore, ô Dieux! vous le savez!

Chez Millet Hélène se déclare "votre prisonnière" (prisonnière des Troyens) qui doit "obéir de toute manière." Elle se désole d'être la cause de guerre. Elle aime les Troyens mais elle aime aussi les Grecs, étant Grecque de naissance. Au cours de la troisième "journée" Anthénor lui répète trois fois les paroles consolantes: "Dame ne soyez si troublée / Mais veuillez reprendre bon coeur. . . ."

Pendant la quatrième "journée" dans le drame de Millet Anthénor cause avec Ménélas (nouvelle preuve de confusion entre Troyens et

Grecs—Ménélas ne prend pas part à l'Ambassade comme chez Kochanowski) et lui dit qu'Hélène a peur donc pour cette raison elle n'est pas renvoyée. En présence du danger qui devient de plus en plus proche, Hélène serait peut-être prête à retourner. Le titre du drame de Millet est "La destruction de la Troie." La destruction n'est pas encore accomplie mais seulement proche. L'atmosphère devient de plus en plus tragique et cette progression du tragique représente peut-être la plus grande valeur artistique de la tragédie.

La prophétie de Cassandre est un autre trait caractéristique d'une grande maîtrise. Conformément à la coutume de tous les dramaturges d'imprégner leurs tragédies de rhétorique, le rôle du monologue prophétique est du premier ordre dans la tragédie de Kochanowski:

> Cruel Apollon, pourquoi me tourmentes-tu vainement? Tu m'as donné l'esprit de prophétie, mais tu ne m'as pas permis d'être en crédit auprès des hommes. Tous mes oracles s'envolent dans le vent, et l'on n'y prête pas plus attention qu'à des contes fabuleux et aux songes d'un malade. A quoi bon avoir enchaîné mon coeur et détruit ma mémoire? Pour qui parle-t-il, ce démon qui s'agite en ma poitrine et qui s'exprime par ma bouche? Mon être est dominé, torturé par un hôte importun: je me défends en vain, il me fait violence, je ne me possède plus, je ne suis plus à moi. Sais-je seulement où je suis? Je ne vois plus la lumière du jour, la nuit étend ses voiles devant mes yeux. Voici que nous avons deux soleils qui éclairent deux Ilions. Une biche s'avance sur la vaste mer: une biche malheureuse et de mauvais augure. Défendez les rivages, pasteurs, ne laissez pas cette hôtesse incommode toucher terre nulle part. Pays infortuné, bords maudits où cette biche mettra le pied, lugubre forêt où elle entrera, ou reposera son flanc au soyeux pelage! Le sang va ruisseler sur les traces de ses pas; elle apporte avec elle le mort, l'incendie et la dévastation. O ma belle patrie, ô murailles, ouvrage des Immortels, quel destin vous attend? Et toi, mon frère, vigilant gardien de la Cité, soutien de notre maison, tu seras traîné autour de nos remparts par les chevaux de Thessalie: et si ton malheureux père veut ensevelir ton corps glacé, il devra l'acheter aux brigands à prix d'or. Ame sublime, la patrie est morte avec toi; vous reposerez dans le même tombeau. Mais toi, féroce détrousseur de cadavres, tu tomberas bientôt à ton tour, percé par la flèche d'un valet . . . Maintenant l'arbre puissant gît à terre, mais du tronc s'élance un nouveau rejeton qui croît avec une rapidité soudaine . . . Quel est ce cheval étrangement grand qui demeure seul sur le champ de bataille? Ne le

> faites pas entrer à l'étable, je vous en supplie: ce cheval rue et mord; brûlez-le plutôt, si vous ne voulez être brûlés vous-mêmes. Gardes! Veillez, la nuit vient, la nuit profonde. Un grand feu va jaillir, tel que dans la ville on y verra comme en plein jour, mais quand le jour renaîtra, on ne verra plus rien. Alors, mon père, n'aie plus foi en tes dieux, ne tends plus tes mains suppliantes devant les autels consacrés: un lionceau cruel s'élance derrière toi, qui va te déchirer de ses griffes acérées et soûler de ton sang sa gorge avide. Tous tes fils seront tués, tes filles emmenées en servage, les autres immolés sur la tombe des morts. Et toi, ma mère, on te verra appeler tes enfants, non avec des pleurs, mais par de longs hurlements.

Dans la tragedie française Cassandre prophétise trois fois—chaque fois d'une autre façon—la ruine de Troie. La tension se renforce: la patrie va succomber, ses défenseurs seront tous morts, les Grecs seront maîtres de Troie. A un seul monologue lyrique de Kochanowski correspondent cinq monologues: la prophétie de la débâcle devient le motif dominant de la tragédie.

Entre l'oeuvre de Kochanowski et celle de Millet existe un intervalle de plus de cent ans. Pendant cet intervalle beaucoup de changements se sont produits mais pas dans tous les domaines. A côté d'autres coïncidences encore une mérite d'être mentionnée: les deux poètes étaient enclins à regarder le temps d'Homère par le prisme de l'époque où ils vivaient. Chez Kochanowski c'est la diète qui est l'organe du gouvernement de Troie et Agamemnon reçoit le titre d'un "hetman";[7] dans le drame français Priam donne à ses chevaliers le titre des "barons" et ceux-là lui parlent de magnifiques victoires que Troie avait remportées jadis et c'est au moment où la guerre devient un danger de plus en plus menaçant.

Pourtant la tragédie succincte et compacte de Kochanowski n'est pas sans analogie avec le long drame français. Le rôle d'Anthénor est l'analogie principale dans les deux drames. L'hypothèse de Denis mérite d'être mentionnée comme intéressante et non sans valeur. A l'époque où l'on n'a pas encore commencé à étudier "Le Renvoi des ambassadeurs grecs" avec des méthodes modernes, on a beaucoup cité l'hypothèse de Denis, mais seulement dans sa première partie concernant une caractéristique générale, sans prendre en considération la coïncidence avec Millet. Le fragment de sa critique fut répété par Charles Forster dans un essai de synthèse "De l'art dramatique en Pologne"[8] et par Wojciech Sowiński

[7] Dans la traduction d'André Mary, c'est Agamemnon qui commande l'armée?

[8] Dans: *La Pologne historique, littéraire, monumentale et illustrée*, direction de Léonard Chodźko. t.3 (Paris, 1839–42), 17–26.

dans un article "Coup d'oeil historique et littéraire sur l'art dramatique en Pologne."[9] A l'époque des études modernes consacrées à l'oeuvre de Kochanowski le premier traité concernant le drame de Kochanowski est complètement tombé dans l'oubli.

Université de Lodz

[9] Ibid., t.7 (Paris, 1846), 281–88.

*Erasmus and Aurelius and Their Lives of Jerome: A Study of Cooperation and Dependence**

KARIN TILMANS

In one of the first rooms of the Rijksmuseum in Amsterdam we find a small early-sixteenth-century painted panel titled: "Spes Nostra" (figure 1). The name of the painter is unknown, so he is referred to as the Master of the "Spes Nostra." The words "Spes Nostra" refer to the pregnant girl sitting in the background; they stem from the well-known medieval hymn "Salve Regina." In this song Maria is called mankind's hope, she is showing her child at the hour of death. But it is not so much Maria nor Elizabeth, seen touching her belly, that intrigues us most in this beautiful painting. As becomes obvious from other figures, the panel was ordered by the religious congregation with which the three main characters of this paper had a special relationship. The painting was apparently commissioned by the Dutch Congregation of Sion. This congregation consisted of a group of Dutch monasteries of Augustinian canons and brothers, with Saint Jerome as their patron. It was in this order that both Erasmus and Aurelius took vows before 1490. In the foreground we see the Church Fathers Jerome (left) and Augustine (right) and four impressive regular canons in white dress and with a black cope. This was the normal dress of Erasmus before 1513, when he decided to put aside his monk's habit. His friend, the poetry teacher Cornelius Aurelius, who was nine years older than he, went into the monastery after 1485 and did wear the Augustinian frock until his death in 1531.[1]

---

* This publication was made possible through financial support of the Netherlands Organization for Scientific Research (NWO).

[1] On this painting see: H. Schulte Nordholt, "Meester van Spes Nostra. Allegorie

For some reasons it is even tempting to see a portrait of Aurelius in one of these four regular canons. At the time the painting was commissioned, Aurelius was one of the outstanding members of the Congregation. Besides he was the biographer of the patron of the Congregation, S. Jerome, and in a way he deserved to be portrayed. Can it be Aurelius whom we see in the left foreground of this painting?

By introducing Aurelius and his life of Jerome I hope to show why this one of the four canons has my vote. The most important facts of Aurelius's life you can find in my thesis;[2] in this paper I concentrate on his *Vita gloriosi Jheronimi*, written between February 1508 and July 1516. This *Vita* has been preserved in a contemporary, early-sixteenth-century manuscript which is kept at the Athenaeum Library in the Dutch city of Deventer. Before we speak about the cultural and intellectual background of this *Vita* and its possible influence on the *Vita Hieronymi* of Erasmus, we should first have a closer look at the manuscript and its contents. The work is in a contemporary copy, apparently made for the library of the so-called Heer Florens house, where Aurelius had stayed in the fourteen-seventies while studying at the Lebuinus school in Deventer. The *Vita gloriosi Jheronimi* was copied by the same person who made a copy of his *Marias*, the famous imitation of the *Parthenice* of the Italian Christian poet Baptista Mantuanus or Spagnuoli. This work was sent by Aurelius to his Deventer friends before his journey to Paris in August 1497 and apparently he later did the same with his biography of Jerome. In both cases the brethren found the works interesting enough to copy them, or they ordered copies directly from the scriptorium of the Leiden monastery Lopsen, where Aurelius lived and worked at that time. In any case we know with certainty that the *Vita Jheronimi* is not an autograph, because we know the handwriting of Aurelius from examples in the Vulcanius collection presently at Leiden.[3]

---

op de vergankelijkheid," *Openbaar Kunstbezit* (1962), p. 35; *Geert Grote en de Moderne Devotie* (Utrecht, 1984), pp. 34–35; J. D. Bangs, *Cornelis Engebrechtsz's Leiden. Studies in cultural history (ca 1450–ca 1500)* (Assen, 1979), pp. 23–24 and p. 197.

[2] See my *Aurelius en de Divisiekroniek van 1517. Historigrafie en humanisme in Holland in de tijd van Erasmus*, Hollandse Studiën 21 (Hilversum, 1988).

[3] On the Vulcanius MSS, containing autographs of Aurelius see my thesis, p. 54, pp. 198–200. Aurelius kept his own copy of the *Vita Jheronimi* as appears from the legacy of his books to his friend Johannes Theodericus Harius in 1531: M. E. Kronenberg, "Werken van Cornelius Aurelius (Donkanus) in de bibliotheek van kanunnik Mr. Jan Dirksz. van der Haer (anno 1531)," *Het Boek* XXXVI (1963–1964), p. 76, nr 6. Most probably the copy was made in Deventer, and not in the scriptorium of Leiden, as appears from the marginal glosses.

The Deventer manuscript bears the title *Vita gloriosi Jheronimi doctoris ecclesiae eximii et zelatoris precipui* and consists of 123 folia, compared with the seventeen folia of the *Vita Hieronymi* of Erasmus; it is an extensive work. Let me summarize the content: first there is a prologue in three parts (figure 2). The first part is called "Prologus universalis," apparently intended for the general reader, in which Aurelius tries to explain the degree of eloquence and the command of rhetoric needed to do justice to the reputation and importance of the patriarch Jerome. The second part, which is called "Divisio prologi pro relligiosis [*sic*] in refectorio de ordine dicendorum," was intended to be read aloud for the special kind of public Aurelius apparently wanted to address with this work: his fellow regular canons and the friars of the Modern Devotion. This part of the prologue gives a general historical background of the life of Jerome and explains the composition of the biography. The third part, the so-called "prologus communis," treats his method of historiography and the sources he used for this biography, and mentions the places where he found them.[4]

The *Vita* itself is divided into four books: the first book describes Jerome's youth in Istria and his education. The second deals with his travels through Germany and the Middle East. In the third book we can read about the stay of Jerome as cardinal in Rome and here Aurelius gives special attention to the role of Jerome as spiritual adviser to a number of aristocratic Roman ladies. After 385 Jerome stayed in the Middle East, where he had founded a convent with two of these ladies in Bethlehem and where he could dedicate himself solely to literary studies. This last episode is the subject of the fourth and longest book.[5] Between the second and third books of the *Vita* we find a dedication-epigram of Aurelius in elegiac distiches (figure 3).[6] This *Epigram* is interesting for three essential points which I would like to underline: 1st, the printer's terminology used by Aurelius for this manuscript; 2nd, the emphasis of the author on the historical method; and 3rd, the origin and the sources of the *Vita*.

All these three points need some comment here, because they help to clarify the relation between this *Vita* and that of Erasmus. First the printer's terminology. Aurelius consistently called this work an "editio," of

---

[4] MS. Deventer SAB, I.32, f. 25–27 *prologus universalis*; f. 28–29 *prologus de ordine dicendorum*; f. 30 *prologus communis*.

[5] MS. Deventer SAB, I.32, f. 30–52: (*liber primus*); f. 52v–77r (*liber secundus*); f. 81–106 (*liber tertius*); f. 107–147 (*liber quartus*).

[6] MS. Deventer SAB, I.32, f. 77v-79r: *Epigramma Cornelii Aurelii super editione quattuor librorum in vitam gloriosi Hieronymi*. This same epigram we find in the autograph MS: MS. Leiden UB, Vulc. 66, f. 82.

which he states in the epigram that it appeared outside his own region. He does this not only in the poem dedicated to George van Scheveningen, rector of the Hieronymus convent of Delft, and to Gerard Bartoldszn. van Noortwijk, the sexton of the house. Also in 1524, in a letter to the famous Sacramentarian Cornelis Hoen, he refers to the last book of the *Vita Hieronymi* "a me edito."[7] As Rizzo showed in her book *Il lessico filologico degli umanisti* the Italian humanists of the quattrocento tried to prove that their manuscript works were of the same value and importance as the printed editions of their colleagues and that for this reason they applied terms like "editio" to a manuscript.[8] In the Dutch *respublica litteraria* at the time of Aurelius we find a similar attitude.

The stress of Aurelius on the *Vita Jheronimi* as an "editio" becomes even more significant when we consider the fact that there was some competition on his part to get his *Vita* published before that of Erasmus came out. On the first of July 1516 the greatest Aurelius-admirer ever to live, namely Alardus of Amsterdam, professor of theology at the Louvain university, wrote to Erasmus, who was perhaps already at Louvain: "Please do not fail to give as much work as you can to assist the efforts which your friend Cornelis has expended on Jerome."[9] These words are interesting because they suggest in the first place that Aurelius had already finished his *Vita Jheronimi* by July 1516, and in the second place that Erasmus knew about this work. To verify this last point we have to see whether there is possibly some textual relationship between the two *Vitae*.[10] For that I have chosen a few passages from both *Vitae* to compare.

First I will take a closer look at the passage which both authors devote to the *patria* of Jerome, the place where he was born and the question whether this was already at that time a part of Italy. Under the heading *nativitas* Erasmus gives a short exposition:

> Natus est igitur vir eximius Hieronymus,... in oppido Stridonis, quod iam tum a Gothis omnia populantibus eversum fuisse, testis est

---

[7] MS. Leiden UB, Vulc. 66, f. 1r: "Is enim vir nobilis, et comes in Hispania, operante Spiritu Sancto, ut in ultimo libro in *Vita Jheronimi* a me edito habetur expressius, odore librorum gloriosi Jheronimi allectus...," edited by C. Burman, *Hadrianus VI sive analecta historica de Hadriano sexto* (Utrecht, 1727), pp. 248.

[8] S. Rizzo, *Il lessico filologico degli umanisti* (Rome, 1973), p. 70.

[9] P. S. Allen, ed., *Opus epistolarum Des Erasmi Roterodami*, II (Oxford, 1910), pp. 271, letter 433, lines 35–36: "Non committas, oro, quin Cornelii tui labores in Hieronymum exantlatos quanta maximas possis, iuves industria."

[10] On the manuscript and the edition of Erasmus: *Erasmus von Rotterdam. Vorkämpfer für Frieden und Toleranz*, Katalog des Historischen Museums Basel (Basel, 1986), pp. 182–83.

> ipse in Catalogo Scriptorum Illustrium, olim Dalmatiae Pannoniaeque confinium. Id hodie nonnulli, quorum de numero Blondus est, idem esse volunt cum eo quod hac tempestate vulgus Sdrignam appellat, oppidulum in Histria, Italiae regione situm inter Petram pilosam, Portulam, et Primontem, ut horum temporum utamur vocabulis.[11]

By referring to Flavio Biondo and to the word "in volgare" for Stridon Erasmus showed that he was aware of the Quattrocento-discussion about the origin of the Italian *volgare* and the role of Latin or the "sermo litteratus" in the development of Italian. But at the same time he did not consider important the question whether Hieronymus could be called an Italian or not. For the Dutch historian Aurelius, on the other hand, the argument about the relation between the native language and the *patria* was far more important. For the description of the fatherland of Jerome, Istria, the peninsula in the North of the Adriatic, he used the works of Pliny the Elder and also of Biondo. Interesting are the observations Aurelius made about the problem of the vernacular languages. The language in Istria was apparently related to Italian; but it was not right, according to him, to call Jerome an Italian for that reason alone. He compared the situation with that in Holland. The Dutch vernacular was similar to that of its neighbours, especially the Frisians, the Utrechters, Flemings, Brabanders and so-called Maaslanders. But still the Dutch formed their own "nation" and were therefor entitled to their own *patria* and name:

> Ceterum quod Stridonem Jheronimiani ortus consciam in Pannoniae Dalmatiaeque confinio ipso etiam auctore Jheronimo positam legimus, re quoque nostra est nobisque non parum suffragatur. Siquidem qui Jheronimum Dalmatam non Italum dicunt, meminerint nos qui Hollandiam utique incolimus Phrisiis et Anthonianis, Belgis et Bathasiis confines quidem esse, minime tamen eisdem efferri nominibus aut earundem regionum quod proxime eas commoremur, nos continuo esse vernaculos ac gentiles.[12]

A theme which both *Vitae* have in common, and on which it is interest-

[11] MS. Basel UL, IX.56, f. 88. *D. Erasmus, Opuscula, a supplement to the Opera omnia*, ed. W. Ferguson, (The Hague, 1933), p. 139, lines 136–44. On the position of Flavio Biondo in the Volgare-discussion: M. Tavoni, *Latino, grammatica, volgare. Storia di una questione umanistica* (Padua, 1984), p. xi.

[12] MS. Deventer SAB, I.32, f. 32v. See also my thesis *Aurelius en de Divisienkroniek*, p. 38 for the discussion of this passage.

ing to compare the viewpoints of both authors, is the neglect of classical studies in former and even in their own times, and the enlightening example provided by the education and works of Jerome. The most important innovation which Jerome brought about, according to both authors, was the study of classical Latin, of Greek and of Hebrew and the use he made of this trilingual knowledge for his biblical studies. Erasmus praised Jerome's study of Hebrew in the following words:

> Proinde cum ipsa re compertum haberet, litteras arcanas nec intelligi posse nec tractari quemadmodum oportet, nisi cognitis his linguis quibus primum nobis proditae sunt, sermonis Hebraici difficultatem improbo studio pervicit, et barbarae peregrinaeque linguae non solum intelligentiam, sed et peculiarem sonum ac vernaculum stridorem est assecutus.[13]

Aurelius made a greater effort in his *Vita* to get the usefulness of the Greek accepted. On this last point there was as much difference of opinion, he argued, as in Jerome's day. He used his exposition on the importance of Greek to express his disapproval of the neglect of classical studies in his own environment:

> Nam si quis aut Latine pureque loqui nititur aut nostram [Vulgatam] cum Grecis codicibus longe discrepare affirmat, is continuo hiis nostris Atheniensibus et sciolis, vel (ut verius loquar) archadibus et barbaris barbarus quoque videbitur et insanus....[14]

In the praise of the Greek language which followed, Aurelius tried to create the impression that he knew at least the rudiments of this language. A very profound knowledge it was not, although he was the first Dutchman, even before Budé, to use a (wrong) Greek word for encyclopedia, namely [εν]κικλιπεδιαν.[15] As far as the classical meaning of the expression 'ενκικλιοσ παιδεια is concerned, it is illuminating to compare the education of Jerome in the liberal arts, described by both Erasmus and Aurelius. For Jerome's higher education, his father Eusebius sent the young son to Rome. His family and friends had great expectations for the talented young man, and besides, Rome furnished an excellent center of learning as Erasmus stated:

---

[13] *Erasmus, Opuscula*, p. 152, lines 527–32.

[14] MS. Deventer SAB, I.32, f. 44r. See my thesis, *Aurelius en de Divisiekroniek*, p. 39.

[15] MS. Leiden UB, Vulc. 66, f. 4r. See my thesis, *Aurelius en de Divisiekroniek*, p. 40 note 44.

> Quis non iam nunc in summam erectus spem, novum quiddam de hoc praesagiat puero? Primum reputans talem parentum animum, deinde felicissimam indolem, ingenium foecundum ac facile, pectus ardens et infatigabile. Praeterea Romam educatricem, id temporis, opinor, aliquanto quam nunc incorruptiorem.[16]

With "Victorinus rhetor et Donatus grammaticus" as teachers, Erasmus continues, Jerome took practice in the *bonae litterae*. After rhetoric, Erasmus gives the most attention to the formation of Jerome in philosophy:

> Sub huiusmodi praeceptoribus, iam adultior in bonis litteris, nullum doctrinae genus intactum reliquit. Porphyrii Eisagoogen, Aristotelicam, Platonicam, Stoicam, ac ceterorum omnium philosophiam attigit.[17]

In the citations of authors in the *Vita* there is a certain tendency toward and preference for Neoplatonic philosophers. As far as history is concerned, this discipline of the *studia humanitatis* is treated as subordinate to rhetoric, as appears from the following:

> In rhetorica tamen sese studiosius exercuit, degustatis omnibus, sed his praecipue quae propius ad eam conferant facultatem, historia, cosmographia, et antiquitatis notitia.[18]

The final goal of Jerome's education was, after all, a theological and Christian one, according to Erasmus: Jerome saw it rightly as a necessity for all Christians to be formed in classical literacy and eloquence, in order to improve in the end the literacy and eloquence of Christianity:

> ...quod intelligeret apud Latinos ad id usque temporis paene infantem esse theologiam, et ob hanc causam permultos a divinorum voluminum abhorrere lectione, sperans futurum ut plures sacris litteris delectarentur, si quis theologiae maiestatem dignitate sermonis aequasset; partim ut esset aliquando quod ethnicis obiici posset, Christianos ut infantes et elingues despicientibus.[19]

When we then turn to the chapters on the education of Jerome in the *Vita gloriosi Jheronimi* of Aurelius, we are struck by two points: first the far

---

[16] *Erasmus, Opuscula*, p. 141, lines 197–201.
[17] *Erasmus, Opuscula*, p. 143, lines 231–34.
[18] *Erasmus, Opuscula*, p. 143, lines 236–38.
[19] *Erasmus, Opuscula*, p. 143, lines 239–44.

more programmatic, clarifying presentation of the *studia humanitatis* as a practical educational course, Aurelius apparently was hoping to establish something which was novel for his Dutch readers; and secondly the immense importance Aurelius seemed to attach to education in history.

It was Jerome, Aurelius stated, who had given the proper example of how every regular cleric should be educated. Before he ventured into the field of biblical studies, Jerome practiced the different disciplines of the *studia humanitatis*. The fact that Aurelius dedicated a separate chapter to Jerome's historical training, whereas the other disciplines (grammar, rhetoric, poetics and philosophy) were dealt together in only one chapter, is typical of the historical preoccupation of the author.[20] In a letter of dedication to the *Compendium de origine et gestis Francorum* of the French historian Robert Gaguin, Aurelius had first given his theory on the criteria for impartial,true and eloquent historiography.[21] Now in the *Vita Jheronimi* Aurelius tried to convince his readers that knowledge of the pagan and Christian history was indispensable for every Christian and certainly for every cleric. In this general plea for the study of the past, Aurelius used the famous topoi, which he illustrated with citations from classic authors. The writing of history "quae veritatis magistra est, nuncius fidelis, testis verus, benignus interpres, perhenne monumentum et indubitata firmaque memoria..." was more important and precious than classical sculpture, the triumphal arches and the Egyptian pyramids. Alexander the Great had understood this: not from the beautiful building of Athens would posterity know his glorious deeds, but through the historiographers. And Jerome also understood, according to Aurelius:

> neque se unquam sine veterum historiis atque scriptis, retroactorum temporum et annorum supputationem posse luculenter comprehendere, neque plurima sibi pro divinarum rerum gestarum consequentia* quam maxime** necessaria nisi per consulum et regum annales atque successus facile perscrutari.[22]

Like Jerome, Aurelius continued, a Christian humanist studied the classics not only to learn to write correct Latin, but also—and this was no less

[20] MS. Deventer SAB, I.32, f. 39–41 (liber 1 caput 4 on *grammatica, poetica, retorica, philosophia*); f. 41–43 (liber 1 caput 5 on *historia*). The title of the history chapter is: "Quanta se diligentia Jheronimus ad legendas gentilium et christianorum historias post artes liberales contulerit et quantum exinde sibi et ecclesiae profecerit."

[21] See my thesis *Aurelius en de Divisienkroniek*, pp. 31–33.

[22] MS. Deventer SAB, I.32, f. 41v: * ms. *consequenda*; **: ms. *maxima*.

important–to learn to judge and convince, keeping in mind the words: "Omnia probate, quod bonum est tenete" (1 Thess. 5.21). An important complement to the historical erudition of Aurelius was the knowledge he had gained from the works of Cornelius Tacitus, his *Germania, Historiae* and *Annales*. In the list of historians which Jerome read and studied, we find this name first: "Jheronimum . . . legisse Cornelium Tacitum, Quintum Curtium, Sallustium, Titum Livium, Trogum, Justinum, Suetonium. . ."[23]

The reading of classical historiography could develop not only pragmatic historical insight, but also a better feeling for literary style. The style of the historian as well as that of the theologian should be 'nitidus et cultus'; on this point both authors fully agree. They both praise and recommend in their *Vitae* Cicero's style as the best, and they both devote their best efforts to recommend the Ciceronian ideal as legitimate for any Christian writer. Aurelius did try to prove the usefulness of Ciceronianism–and in this *Vita* he is concentrating especially on *De Oratore*–with some specific examples and more generally in the explanation of his own approach to this biography. Two passages might show this. By reading Cicero's passus on history in *De Oratore* (book II) in which Herodotus and Thucydides are mentioned, Jerome got the splendid idea to learn Greek, Aurelius argued. The words of Marcus Antonius in Cicero's *De oratore* II, 9, 36 were in fact the motto and leitmotiv for him when writing his own *Vita Jheronimi*:

> Nam ut Anthonius in secundo libro *De Oratore* testatur, qui laudare quempiam cupit, non solum intelliget exponenda sibiesse genus propinquos, opes, valitudinem, formam, vires, ingenium, ceterarumque rerum bona, quae sunt aut corporis aut extraneae. . .Verumeciam exponenda erunt in eo quem laudare cupimus quid sapienter et magnifice, quid liberaliter et pie, quid fortiter et grate, quid iuste et humaniter, quid denique cum aliqua virtute aut fecerit aut tulerit, aut eciam quid aliis ad profectum dignitatemque contulerit.[24]

The Ciceronianism which Erasmus defended with Jerome as his spokesman, is rather well known, especially through the work of Prof. Olin on Erasmus and Saint Jerome.[25] Fortunately, according to Erasmus, Jerome

---

[23] MS. Deventer SAB, I.32, f. 41v.

[24] MS. Deventer SAB, I.32, f. 87r.

[25] J. C. Olin, "Erasmus and Saint Jerome: the close bond and its significance," Seventh Annual Birthday Lecture, *Erasmus of Rotterdam Society. Yearbook Seven* (1987): 33–53; J. C. Olin, "Erasmus and Saint Jerome: An Appraisal of the Bond," *Proceedings of the Erasmusconference 10–12 November 1986 Rotterdam* (in press).

was not the last to defend Cicero and more than once Erasmus mentions in his *Vita Hieronymi* Italian and Dutch humanists who had understood the importance of the bond between Cicero and Jerome: Valla, Politiano, Barbaro, Pico and "noster Rodolphus Agricola."[26]

I come now to the conclusion of my paper on Erasmus, Aurelius and their lives of Jerome. It is obvious that the inspiration of Erasmus by Jerome and his works had already originated in the religious Dutch milieu to which both Aurelius and Erasmus belonged. It was not due to John Colet, whose lectures on Jerome Erasmus heard at Oxford in 1500, that he started to work on the study of scripture, the reform of theology and especially on Jerome.[27] It would not only be an overestimation of the influence of Colet on the development of Erasmus's theological scholarship, but also at the same time it is an underestimation of the role of his former friend and correspondent, Cornelis Gerard, better known as Aurelius. It was Aurelius who recommended to Erasmus in 1489 the letters of Jerome as the best example of classical rhetoric and Christian piety, before Erasmus answered arrogantly: "As for your inciting me to read through these letters, I am most grateful. But I have long ago read them. . . ."[28]

Whatever may be the truth of that contention, it has been convincingly proved that Aurelius had an important influence on the early religious poetry of Erasmus, and that he added a long citation from the mouth of Jerome to the *Apologia adversus barbaros* of Erasmus, written already before the letter mentioned earlier.[29] It was possibly under the influence of Aurelius that Erasmus turned to theology and especially to the study of Jerome, as has also been argued by Prof. IJsewijn.[30] For this we also find proof in the years 1497/1498 when both are staying in Paris. At that time Aurelius is studying manuscripts with works of Jerome in the library of the

---

[26] *Erasmus, Opuscula*, p. 185, lines 1385–88; see also p. 176, lines 1132–35.

[27] On this point I disagree with Olin in his paper for the Erasmus conference at Rotterdam: see note 25.

[28] Allen, *Opus epistolarum* I (Oxford, 1906), p. 103, lines 20–21: "Quod autem ad eas lectitandas me invitas, habeo gratissimum. Iam olim tamen eas non modo legi, . . ."

[29] See C. Reedijk, *The poems of Erasmus* (Leiden, 1956) pp. 47–54, 169–70.

[30] J. IJsewijn, "Erasmus ex poeta theologus, sive litterarum instauratarum apud Hollandos incunabulis," in *Scrinium Erasmianum* I (Leiden, 1969), pp. 375–89. See also my "Cornelius Aurelius (c. 1460–1531), praeceptor Erasmi?" in F. Akkerman and A. J. Vanderjagt, ed., *Rodolphus Agricola Phrisius 1444–1485*, Proceedings of the International Conference at the University of Groningen 28–30 Octobre 1985 (Leiden, 1988), pp. 200–210.

Celestini, and for that goal he received help from Jacques Lefèvre d'Étaples and Josse Clichtove. He is doing this research because he intended to write a biography of the patriarch. Erasmus must have known of his plans. Then after 1500 Erasmus starts his far more ambitious project of the *Opera omnia*-edition, whereas Aurelius did write his *Vita Hieronymi*. When he has finished, before July 1516, he looks for support from Erasmus to find an editor. This request is without success, not only because Erasmus intends to publish his own *Vita Hieronymi*, but also because they have different views of the most important aspects of Jerome's life: Aurelius admired Jerome the learned monk and stressed particularly his historical education, while Erasmus rather idealized Jerome the wandering scholar and philosopher. Nevertheless we can conclude that the bond Jerome-Erasmus was not unique, but rather exemplary for Northern Christian humanism. The life of Jerome had something recognizable for every humanist, inside or outside the monastery. Jerome too had met with opposition and he was one of the first Christians to recognize the importance of Cicero. Finally, his plea for the *studia humanitatis* inside the monastery was one which appealed immensely to Northern humanists. In this sense the bond Erasmus-Aurelius-Jerome becomes one of true identification and dependence.

University of Groningen

Fig. 1

Prologus auctoris in vitam gloriosi Jheronimi.
doctoris ecclesie eximii et zelatoris precipui

Cornelium Asinam romanorum consulem Kar-
thaginenses per legatum fictus officio servi-
tiorum suorum senatoresque adduxerat: in vincula
coniecerunt. Sed tandem fractis penorum animis et iam rebus
ad defectionem inclinantibus: duces petende pacis consilium
agitabant. Cum Amilcar princeps Affrice [illegible]
[illegible] ne se ad romanos negabat consules: ne eodem modo
sibi [illegible] quo ab ipsis Cornelio consuli in-
certas meminerat [illegible] Hannone certior: romane fidei
[illegible] estimator nichil tale timendum ratus [illegible]
merito sibi poterat evenire quod Cornelio accidisset: [illegible]
[illegible] ad romanorum colloquium [illegible] fiducia tende-
[illegible] et fidem quam constanti [illegible] non longe fe-
[illegible] apud illos rebus suis [illegible]. Huius itaque viri
ego [illegible] erectus fiducia spero me facile apud
omnes [illegible] perfecto eruditori [illegible]
[illegible] minime [illegible] nullum pro merito [illegible]
certe pro [illegible] studio veniam haud temere
[illegible]. Neque enim laudem michi [illegible] sic [illegible]
[illegible] ipse [illegible] scribendo, quam nec mereor: neque gra-
[illegible] ac ingenio impar [illegible] labor-

[illegible]

[illegible] ipse diffiteor. Ego equidem nullum prorsus in me
oratoris esse splendorem, nullamque vernantis eloquentie venustatem: que divinas [illegible] gloriosi Jheronimi laudes
vel minima ex parte posset attingere. Clarorum enim sunt omnia
in hoc clarissimo christiane fidei doctore omnipotentis opera:
que nulla mortalis ingenii possunt viribus [illegible] illustrari.
Sed quoniam opus hoc quod [illegible] ad alias [illegible]
illi [illegible] patres de sancto Jheronimo [illegible] oppidi
certe viri religione et vita [illegible] a me potissimum fieri
contenderent, et ego ut verum fatear, non tam caritative cor-
[illegible] imperio, quam eorum me [illegible] adiuvandum pro-
mo. [illegible] coactus [illegible]. Neque
enim eorum michi [illegible] preces neque [illegible]
[illegible] quos utique [illegible] esse. michi [illegible]
semper [illegible] qui et in divum sanctum Jheronimum [illegible]
devotissime [illegible]. ac de me plurimis ab annis optime
meriti. Postremo vel ea que [illegible] operis
causam michi fuisse ut [illegible] arbitror. Cupiens
enim omnibus [illegible] Jheronimianus et [illegible]
[illegible] qui [illegible] gestum [illegible]
et [illegible] Jheronimo [illegible] fide dignissimum [illegible]
[illegible] conabor. Dignum itaque [illegible] etsi nullo [illegible]
[illegible] tamen et benevolentia ad [illegible] de me [illegible]
[illegible] in [illegible] postulata ut de-
[illegible] illis: ita et [illegible] deo potuisse videri: si vel hoc

[illegible] quod in me est ingenii [illegible] in opere [illegible]
[illegible]. [illegible] enim [illegible] gloriosissime vir omnium [illegible]
[illegible] et [illegible] qui ad eruditionem [illegible] et [illegible]
ecclesie splendorem ac utilitatem omnes suos labores [illegible]
vigilias lucubrationesque ac ipsam denique vitam infatigabili
studio et [illegible] et [illegible]. Nonne iste est Jheronimus [illegible]
[illegible] sollicitudine et cura divina fides catholica per varios
[illegible] scrupulos varie fluctuantes, ad veritatis tramitem [illegible]
[illegible] unitatem reducta est. Nonne is [illegible] est Jheronimus
[illegible] incredibili diligentia et labore factum est ut sine [illegible]
in loco sine alibi [illegible] de altissima fide [illegible]
ac divinarum cognitione et recte [illegible] copiosissime
possimus disserere. Nonne hic denique Jheronimus est [illegible]
[illegible] doctrina teste Aurelio Augustino in [illegible]
[illegible] in latina lingua ecclesiastice [illegible]
[illegible] potuerit. Legi enim [illegible] sine ulla controversia
omnium confessione atque consensu, plane constat [illegible]
[illegible] Jheronimum ignoravit. Cum [illegible]
[illegible] fide [illegible] pontifices [illegible]
ut in [illegible] atque [illegible] suum [illegible] arbitrium
et quecumque ille [illegible] scripserat illa
[illegible] aut [illegible] aut [illegible]. Quid plura [illegible].
Cum Cornelios et [illegible] si Fabios et Marcellos si Scipiones
aliosque quamplures qui vel pro tuenda patria, vel pro augenda

Fig. 2

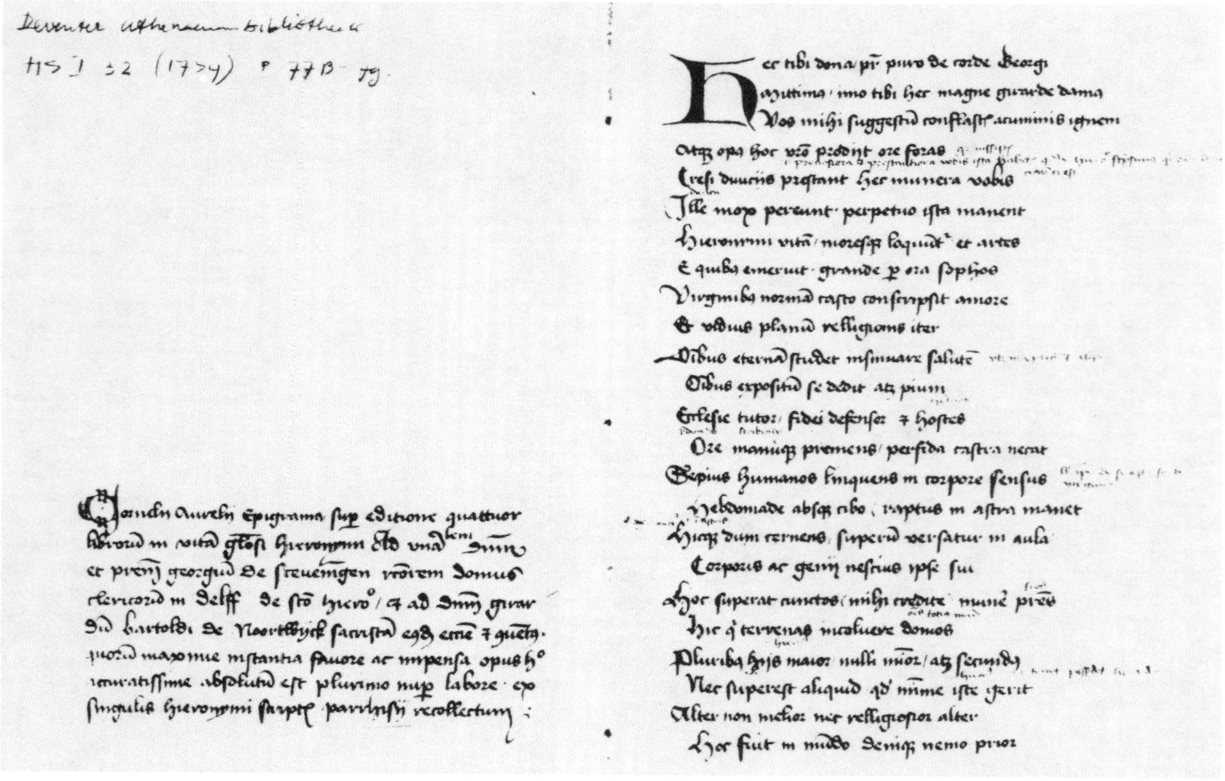

Cornelii Aurelii Epigrama sup[er] editione quattuor
librorum in vita[m] gl[ori]osi Hieronimi [illegible] una cum domino
et priori georgio de Streuengen rectorem domus
clericorum in Delff de s[an]c[t]o hiero[nimo] / et ad dominum [illegible]
[illegible] bartoldi de Noortwyck sacrista [illegible]
quorum maxime instantia favore ac impensa opus hoc
[illegible] absolutum est plurimo nup[er] labore ex
singulis hieronimi scriptis [illegible] recollectum :

Hec tibi dona pr[ior] puro de corde Georgi
[illegible] / imo tibi hec magne [illegible]
Nos mihi suggestio [illegible]
Atque opa hec [illegible] prodeunt ore foras
[illegible] durius prestant hec munera vobis
Ille mox pereunt perpetuo ista manent
Hieronimi vita[m] moresque loquuntur et artes
E quibus emeruit grande p[ro] ora [illegible]
Virginibus normam casto conscripsit amore
Et viduis planum religionis iter
Omnibus eternam studet insinuare salutem
Omnibus expositum se dedit atque pium
Ecclesie tutor fidei defensor et hostes
Ore manuque premens perfida castra necat
Sepius humanos linquens in corpore sensus
Hebdomade absque cibo raptus in astra manet
Hicque dum cernens superum versatur in aula
Corporis ac [illegible] nescius ipse sui
Hoc superat cunctos mihi credite nunc [illegible]
Hic qui terrenas incoluere domos
Pluribus hic maior nulli minor atque secundus
Nec superest aliquid quod nunc iste gerit
Alter non melior nec religiosior alter
Hoc fuit in mundo denique nemo prior

Fig. 3

Erasmus's Precationes

J. TRAPMAN

Prayers were an important matter to Erasmus.[1] This is demonstrated by the frequency with which he criticized or ridiculed their abuse: the mindless rattling off of all too often misunderstood Psalms, praying for things inconsistent with christian ethics, and invoking the help of some saint specialized in a particular illness.

Erasmus's criticism is comprehensible only if we assume that he was convinced of the value of sincere prayer. Although in the *Enchiridion* prayer and knowledge are called the weapons of the christian soldier,[2] the subject of prayer itself is barely touched upon, which led Alfons Auer to conclude that Erasmus was not that strongly committed to praying.[3] We should bear in mind, however, Erasmus's view that, first, neither of these weapons should ever be laid down; and, second, that knowledge (that is to say, knowledge of the Scriptures) teaches us *what* to pray and therefore is relevant, though indirectly, to prayer.[4] Moreover, prayer is, of course, not really susceptible to extensive examination, because it is largely performed privately, in "the inner chamber" to use the words of Matthew 6:6. That Erasmus accorded prayer a central role appears most clearly from his comments on the Sacrament of penance. Without rejecting this sacrament,

---

[1] The study of the *Precationes* (with the exception of the *Precatio Dominica*) has long been neglected. See, however, Lee Daniel Snyder, "Erasmus on Prayer. A Renaissance Reinterpretation," in *Renaissance and Reformation* 12 (1976) no. 1: pp. 21–27; L. -E. Halkin, "La piété d'Erasme," in *Revue d'Histoire Ecclésiastique* 79 (1984) no. 3–4, pp. 671–708, esp. 691–706.

[2] *Enchiridion*, Holborn, p. 29, line 16.

[3] A. Auer, *Die vollkommene Frömmigkeit des Christen nach dem Enchiridion* ... (Düsseldorf, 1954), p. 56.

[4] *Enchiridion*, Holborn, p. 28, line 28–p. 30, line 19.

Erasmus considers it possible, even preferable, to confess one's sins directly to God—that is to say, to obtain remission of sins through prayer.[5]

We have at our disposal an extensive treatise by Erasmus, the *Modus orandi Deum*,[6] that is devoted to prayer specifically, and his book of prayers, the *Precationes*, published in 1535. There are also numerous statements about prayers and praying scattered throughout his other writings as well as actual prayers incorporated in some of these writings.[7]

The *Modus orandi Deum* (published in 1524, revised and enlarged by almost one fifth in 1525) is Erasmus's manual for praying. He himself claimed that, in the *Modus*, he took a stance against Luther by defending the invocation of saints.[8] This is true, albeit that the *Modus* is mostly a defense of current practices that should be tolerated, unless they entail impiety or superstition. In this respect, Erasmus tends to be willing to interpret much "in a charitable manner." Of course Erasmus was aware that such a lenient interpretation would allow the borderline between "pietas" and "impietas" to fade, but it is only in his controversy with Alberto Pio that he actually put this into words.[9]

As the title indicates, the *Modus* primarily focuses on the prayer to God. Of the many bible texts that Erasmus cites and comments upon one receives particular emphasis: "Pray without ceasing" (in the Revised Standard version: "Pray constantly"), from 1 Thess. 5:17. How can this exhortation be brought into line with Christ's antipathy against prayers that consist in "vain repetitions" (Mt. 6:7) or as Erasmus liked to call this, using the Greek word, "battologia."[10] Time and again, he opposed "battologia" and very effectively, as, for example, in his *Annotationes*.[11] According to Erasmus, the words "Pray without ceasing" should not be taken literally, but as an indication of an inner attitude, a consistent orientation towards God, that does not necessarily have to be expressed in words. The

---

[5] *Exomologesis sive Modus confitendi*, LB V: col. 157B–E; cf. the colloquy "Pietas puerilis" in ASD I, 3: 178, lines 1728–34.

[6] ASD V, 3: 111–76.

[7] See e.g., *Querela pacis*, ASD IV, 2: p. 84, lines 541–50 (on the Pater noster); prayers in *Christiani matrimonii institutio*, LB V: col. 676DE, and in *De immensa Dei misericordia*, LB V: col. 557BC. For prayers incorporated in the *Colloquia*, see below.

[8] In a letter to John, cardinal of Lorraine, of 22 March 1525, Ep. 1559, lines 120–22.

[9] *Apologia adversus rhapsodias Alberti Pii* (1531), LB IX: col. 1164B: "Et periculum est ne istae commodae interpretationes inducant nobis pro religione superstitionem. . . ."

[10] *Modus orandi*, ASD V, 1: p. 138, line 578–p. 140, line 674.

[11] *Annot. in Mt.*, LB VI: col. 35E; see *De copia*, ASD I, 6: p. 55, n. to line 545.

enduring desire to live godly–that is what constant prayer means.[12] A prayer in the narrow sense, whether said aloud or not, must meet one condition: it should come straight from the heart and if it does, it is not bound to a particular place. The "colloquy with God"–one of Erasmus's definitions of praying[13]–can be conducted anywhere; any place can be turned into a shrine: bedroom, kitchen, workshop, ship, carriage, bath, even the "latrina." In essence, the heart is the temple of God.[14]

As I mentioned earlier, Erasmus condemns "battologia," by which he means meaningless repetitions. Prayers that arise from passionate emotions, however, can be full of repetitions, like the Psalms. These are, according to Erasmus, forms of "holy battologia."[15] Praying methods that are based on repetition, such as the Rosary and the Litanies, are not mentioned by Erasmus in this context. Such forms of praying he considered to be an aid for the weak at best, although he is sympathetic towards the Office of the Holy Cross,[16] doubtless because it was christocentric and short.

Viewed against this background, Erasmus's *Paean* to the Holy Virgin and his *Obsecratio*[17] seem rather incongruous. The *Paean* consists mostly of a list of Mary's traditional titles of honor: "the new Eve," "the tower of David," etc. and of less traditional (we would say "Ciceronian") titles, like "the true Diana."[18] The *Obsecratio* addresses Mary as the "Star of the Sea," the only hope of the mortals who drift about on the dangerous seas of life in the frail ship of their body.[19] Half of the *Obsecratio* is in the nature of a litany, invoking Mary in some 60 "obsecrationes," for instance: "by your conception, by your birth, by your childhood, your purity, humility," etc. And as in medieval prayerbooks, the stages of Christ's

---

[12] *Modus orandi*, ASD V, 1: p. 130, line 332; cf. p. 138, line 605.

[13] Op. cit.: p. 134, line 483: "Psalmorum liber quid aliud habet quam perpetuum cum Deo colloquium?"; cf. Ep. 2994, lines 12–13: "mitto Precationes aliquot, quibus iam nunc insuescas cum Deo colloqui. . . ."

[14] *Modus orandi*, ASD V, 1: p. 166, lines 585–86, and p. 173, lines 827–30.

[15] Op. cit.: p. 140, lines 679–80. Cf. *Enarratio in Ps. 33*, ASD V, 3: p. 120, line 953–p. 121, line 978, with reference to, *inter alia*, *Adag.* 149 ("Bis ac ter, quod pulchrum est"), LB II: col. 89E.

[16] *Modus orandi*, ASD V, 1: p. 172, lines 802–3.

[17] *Paean Virgini Matri dicendus*, LB V: col. 1227E–1234C; *Obsecratio ad Virginem Matrem Mariam in rebus adversis*, LB V: col. 1233E–1240A.

[18] "Tu vera illa Diana . . . ," "Tibi Lucinae nomen unice convenit. . . ," LB V: col. 1230A.

[19] LB V: col. 1233E–1236A; 1233E: "spes unica calamitatum nostrarum"; 1235F: "succurre, quaeso, mea servatrix, mea salus, meum unicum certissimumque perfugium. . . ."

passion are recounted in a very realistic manner describing, for example, the bitter tears, the wounds, and the "thousand streams of red blood flowing from all over the body."[20]

The two prayers to Mary just mentioned were written, together with a prayer to Jesus, some time before the year 1500. They are the earliest prayers of Erasmus we know of. On a number of occasions Erasmus informs us that he wrote these prayers at the request of Anna van Veere and in deference to the wishes of Jacob Batt. In a letter to the young Adolf van Veere that precedes the *Lucubratiunculae* he says he made the prayers to suit Adolf's tender age.[21] In a letter to John Colet of December 1504, Erasmus says that he wrote the *Enchiridion* (that made up part of the *Lucubratiunculae*) "to counteract the error of those who make religion in general consist in rituals. . . ." He creates the impression that the *Enchiridion* is the only part of the *Lucubratiunculae* that has his full support, saying: "as for all the rest, I wrote them almost against the grain, especially the *Paean* and the *Obsecratio*."[22] This explicit mention of the two prayers to Mary, by the way, was added only in 1521.[23] In 1523, in the famous letter to Botzheim containing the catalogue of his writings (complemented in 1524), Erasmus reiterates his reservations with regard to the prayers to Mary. The prayer to Jesus, on the other hand, he had written, he says, "magis ex animo meo," more from the heart.[24]

Obviously, then, the style of Erasmus's *Paean* and *Obsecratio* greatly differs from that of his other prayers. This is true of their contents as well. Erasmus never rejected the moderate worship of Mary,[25] but that is not what we find in these prayers. Not only is the Holy Virgin exuberantly praised here, she is also invoked as the "mater misericordiae," who can mitigate the wrath of her son, that severe judge.[26] Elsewhere, however, Erasmus teaches that sinners facing the severe justice of God or Christ must appeal to the mercy of the Father or the Son himself.[27]

---

[20] LB V: col. 1237E: "Per mille purpurei sanguinis rivulos toto corpore prosilientes."

[21] Ep. 93, lines 101–3.

[22] Ep. 181, lines 42–54; trans. in CWE 2: p. 87, lines 54–55; 60–61.

[23] Ep. 181, critical apparatus to lines 53–54.

[24] Allen, vol. 1: p. 20, lines 18–21.

[25] L. -E. Halkin, "La Mariologie d'Erasme," in *Archiv für Reformationsgeschichte* 68 (1977), 32–55.

[26] *Paean*, LB V: col. 1229BC and 1234A-C.

[27] Cf. *De praeparatione ad mortem*, ASD V, 1: p. 354, line 327–p. 355, line 362; p. 373, line 818–p. 374, line 846; p. 386, lines 139–71.

Let me return briefly to Erasmus's apology against Alberto Pio of 1531. In it, he denies showing Mary too little deference, referring to the *Paean* and *Obsecratio*, "that have been printed so many times." The latter is true: even in 1518, when the *Enchiridion* was published with a new preface addressed to Volz, the old material from the *Lucubratiunculae* was reprinted, although now it comes after the *Enchiridion*.

The discussion with Pio is interesting because, while Erasmus wishes to establish his orthodoxy, he also writes critically about the veneration of Mary. His reservations are so strong that in fact he is criticizing what he had said about Mary in the *Paean* and the *Obsecratio*, the two prayers he had adduced earlier in order to prove his orthodoxy! Thus he asserts that the "Star of the Sea" (Stella maris) is Christ, rather than Mary.[28] He also acknowledges that, in taking a sympathetic view of certain devotional practices (he does so regularly himself), one may simultaneously and inadvertently legimitize superstition.[29]

The two prayers to Mary are not reprinted in the volume that now requires our attention, the *Precationes aliquot novae* of 1535, dedicated to the 14-year-old David Paungartner, son of a prominent citizen of Augsburg.[30] To start with, its title: "some *new* prayers, to which are added new ones, through which the young may learn to speak with God ..." (*Precationes aliquot novae ac rursus novis adauctae, quibus adolescentes adsuescant cum Deo colloqui* ...). It would seem that this title was devised by the publisher to arouse the interest of the public. After all, considering the contents, one would sooner have expected the title to read "some prayers, to which are added new ones...." As it is, the volume pretends to be wholly "new."

In fact, the volume had for the most part been published before and only the first part was new. Besides prayers to the Father, the Son, the Holy Spirit, and Mary, it contains prayers for various occasions, such as illness, travel, holy communion, etc. A dedicatory letter, again to David Paungartner,[31] introduces the second part, the so-called *Eiaculationes*, short prayers composed mainly of texts from the Psalms. These are followed by a dozen equally short prayers from another source, to which I will return shortly. By now, we have arrived at page 75. The nearly one hundred pages that follow contain familiar material: (a) the prayer to Jesus

---

[28] Cf. also the prayer of the "navigaturus" in *Precationes*, LB V: col. 1204E.

[29] *Apologia adversus rhapsodias Alberti Pii*, LB IX: col. 1163E–1164D; cf. n. 9 above.

[30] Ep. 2994, Freiburg, 13 February 1535.

[31] Ep. 2995, probably same date.

that is one of Erasmus's earliest compositions (dating back to about 1500);[32] (b) the prayer "Pro pace ecclesiae," written in 1532, and also invoking Jesus[33] (this prayer is often confused with the previous one); and (c) the *Precatio Dominica*[34] of 1523, which Erasmus on occasion described as "a paraphrase of the Lord's Prayer."[35]

Thus, the *Precationes novae* of 1535 include prayers from the period between 1500 and 1535, the latter half of Erasmus's life. The readers have noticed that, whereas the early prayer to Jesus is included, the *Obsecratio* and the *Paean*, written shortly before, are not. The latter are the prayers to Mary, with whose texts, as we have seen, Erasmus soon became dissatisfied and that, certainly after 1519, he was not very happy about.

Moreover, Erasmus must have been well aware of the fact that the *Obsecratio* and the *Paean* would have been totally unacceptable to adherents of the Reformation; had he reprinted these texts, he would unnecessarily have estranged them from himself—which would not have been in agreement with his prayer "pro pace ecclesiae." Although in the *Modus orandi* he does defend the invocation of Mary and the saints, he does so in the moderate manner we have come to know so well from his other writings. However, Erasmus was always at pains to point out that praying to God and to Christ is to be preferred under all circumstances ("tutius"[36] etc.).

Taking a closer look at the *Precationes* with this background in mind, we find that the prayers to, successively, the Father, the Son, and the Holy Spirit, are followed by a prayer "ad virginem Matrem," whose first line is "Ave Maria." This prayer is striking in that it is not a prayer in the proper sense of the word. Nothing is asked of Mary, not even her intercession. In the editio princeps this is emphasized by the running titles: whereas those of the first prayers read "precatio ad patrem," "precatio ad filium," or "precatio ad spiritum sanctum," that of the prayer to Mary reads "*salutatio* ad virginem matrem."

I suppose that this book of *Precationes* was read by Protestants too, and it seems likely that it was compiled with an eye to this particular readership as well. In this connection it should be noted that the *Precationes* include prayers for the sick and dying, but not for the dead. Finally, I

[32] *Precatio ad Virginis filium Iesum*, LB V: col. 1210E–1216B.

[33] LB V: col. 1215E–1218D.

[34] LB V: col. 1217–1228C.

[35] Allen, vol. 1: p. 21, lines 16–17; cf. *Explanatio Symboli*, ASD V: p. 320, line 449.

[36] Cf. the prayer "Tempore pestilentiae" in *Precationes*, LB V: col. 1206B.

would like to note that the wording of the penitent's prayer and of the prayer to be said before holy communion is such that no adherent of the Reformation could have had any qualms about using them.

Erasmus composed the so-called *Eiaculationes* from bible texts, according to the method he had recommended in the *Modus orandi*.[37] The dedication (the second one) discusses only this type of short prayer:[38] prayers composed like a mosaic of bible texts and intended for use in all kinds of situations. There are twenty-two of these short prayers, some of them consisting only of a single line. These are followed by another thirteen short prayers and the early prayer to Jesus of about 1500.

This last prayer being twenty-five pages long, it obviously does not belong to the category of "eiaculationes." However, its typographical design may easily create the impression that it does belong there: the large capitals in which the title "Eiaculationes" is printed would seem to indicate that it is a heading to all of the following text. It is only when we get to the *Precatio Dominica*, that we encounter these large capitals again in the title. Traces of this typography are to be found also in the Clericus-edition and there too it creates the impression that the *Precatio ad Iesum* is to be counted among the "eiaculationes." However, the Maire-edition of 1641 did not make this mistake.

Do the thirteen prayers following the biblical prayers belong to the category of "eiaculationes" as well? In the dedication, only the biblical prayers are mentioned. We may assume, however, that this group of thirteen prayers is actually yet another set of "eiaculationes." The question to be asked here is: can these prayers be considered "precationes novae"?

In the Amsterdam-edition of the *Colloquia* (*ASD* I, 3), it is pointed out that of the prayers included in the *Colloquies* three short ones were to be printed in the *Precationes* of 1535.[39] One might think, then, that Erasmus had added the other ten prayers around 1535. But in this case, too, the running titles of the editio princeps again suggest otherwise. The biblical prayers have "Eiaculationes e scriptura sacra" as their running title,

---

[37] ASD V, 1: p. 161, line 405–p. 162, line 435.

[38] Ep. 2995, lines 3–5: "Eas appelavimus Eiaculationes, quod breves quidem sint, sed quoniam erumpunt ab ardenti mentis affectu, celerius penetrant in coelum." Cf. the colloquy "Epicureus," ASD I, 3: p. 733, lines 489–90: "Penetrat autem et brevis precatio coelum . . ." (for the medieval proverb "brevis oratio penetrat coelos" see *Proverbia sententiaeque Latinitatis Medii ac recentioris Aevi*, n.s., vol. 7, ed. P. G. Schmidt, [Göttingen, 1982], no. 35313).

[39] ASD I, 3: p. 173, n. to lines 1578–83; p. 198, n. to lines 2365–66; p. 214, n. to lines 2916–20.

whereas the next thirteen, the ones we are concerned with now, have "Precationes e scriptis Erasmi." So these must have been existing prayers and this information compels us to look further. As it turns out, we do not have to look very far: these prayers too are to be found in the *Colloquia* (except for one, which is taken from Erasmus's *Liturgia Virginis Lauretanae*[40]). The same is true of the two prayers whose source is given as "ex Chrysostomo"–no doubt they found their way into our volume through the *Colloquia*, that is to say through the "Convivium religiosum."

The colloquies that served as the source for these prayers are "Pietas puerilis" (five prayers),[41] "Convivium religiosum" (four prayers),[42] "Convivium profanum" (two prayers)[43] and "Apotheosis Capnionis" (one prayer).[44] The passages taken from the *Colloquia* are not all of them formal prayers; in some cases they had to be modified and transposed from the third person to the second person. In "Convivium religiosum," for example, the host, Eusebius, says at one point (I am quoting from Thompson's translation):

> "Now may Christ, who makes all men to rejoice, and without whom nothing is truly pleasing, deign to attend our feast and rejoice our hearts by his presence." Then Timotheus says: "I hope he will deign to do so. But since every place is filled, where will he sit?" Eusebius: "May he mingle with all our food and drink, so that everything taste of him, but most of all may he penetrate our hearts!"[45]

In the *Precationes*, Erasmus transformed this passage into a prayer by

---

[40] The prayer "Ad Evangelium de nuptiis in Cana" (LB V: col. 1209F); cf. *Liturgia Virginis Lauretanae*, ASD V, 1: p. 107, lines 364–67 (in the *Precationes* the words "eiusdem [sc. Mariae] suffragiis adiuti" are omitted!).

[41] No. 1 ("Mane a somno experrecti"), cf. ASD I, 3: p. 173, lines 1553–58; no. 2 ("Euntis ad ludum litterarium"), cf. p. 173, line 1577–p. 174, line 1583; no. 3 ("Quum recitantur haec ex Paulo, Expurgate vetus fermentum . . ."), cf. p. 176, lines 1679–83; no. 4 ("Quum legitur Evangelium de seminante"), cf. p. 176, lines 1684–86; no. 6 ("Accedentis ad sacram synaxim"), cf. p. 177, lines 1693–1700.

[42] No. 7 ("Ad Christum pro vera pietate"), cf. ASD I, 3: p. 234, lines 94–97; no. 10 ("Alia [sc. consecratio mensae]"), cf. p. 241, lines 307–9 and 311–12; no. 12 ("Alia ex Chrysostomo"), cf. p. 240, lines 291–94; no. 13 ("Alia ex Chrysostomo in Matthaeum"), cf. p. 261, lines 935–37.

[43] No. 9 ("Consecratio mensae"), cf. ASD I, 3: p. 198, lines 2365–66; no. 11 ("Gratiarum actio"), cf. p. 214, lines 2916–26.

[44] No. 8 ("Pro consensu dogmatum"), cf. ASD I, 3: p. 273, lines 208–15.

[45] ASD I, 3: p. 241, lines 307–9; trans. Craig R. Thompson, *The Colloquies of Erasmus* (Chicago and London, 1965), 56.

rewriting it in the second person and omitting Timotheus's interruption. The result is a prayer, where we find this rather unconventional line: "May you mingle with all our food and drink ..." etcetera.

Another example is the prayer for consensus on dogmatic issues ("pro consensu dogmatum") which Erasmus had so much at heart. This prayer refers to the "gift of tongues," which enabled the apostles to preach the Gospel to all, while the pseudo-apostles were building their "impious tower of Babel." The prayer "pro consensu dogmatum" begins as follows:

> O God, thou lover of mankind, who has deigned to confer the gift of tongues, by which thou didst once from heaven through thy Holy Spirit instruct the apostles for the preaching of the Gospel, grant that all men everywhere may preach in every tongue the glory of thy son Jesus, ...[46]

This prayer is taken from the end of the colloquy *Apotheosis Capnionis* (1522), where, however, the "gift of tongues" carries the more specifically humanistic tone of "knowledge of languages" rather than "ability to preach to all." For instead of the general words "who has deigned to confer" the colloquy in question reads: "who through thy chosen servant John Reuchlin has renewed to the world the gift of tongues."[47] This prayer must have appealed to many a christian humanist. For example, a copy of the original version (that is: including Reuchlin's name) was found among the papers of an erstwhile friend of Erasmus's Gerardus Geldenhouwer, papers that were published only in our century, under the title of *Collectanea*.[48]

The *Modus orandi* seems to suggest that prayers should preferably be addressed to the Father, in conformity with the Bible and the Liturgy.[49] We have seen, however, that Erasmus addressed his prayers not only to the Father, but also (a majority) to the Son. In this respect, Erasmus is in line with medieval devotional practice. This leads us to Erasmus's dying words, which I would like to discuss briefly.

We know that the tradition according to which Erasmus on his deathbed invoked Mary is not reliable. Its most important source, Amerbach,

---

[46] LB V: col. 1210B.

[47] ASD I, 3: p. 273, lines 208–11; trans. Thompson, op. cit.: p. 86.

[48] *Collectanea van Gerardus Geldenhauer Noviomagus*, ed. J. Prinsen (Amsterdam, 1901), 77; J. Lindeboom, *Het Bijbelsch Humanisme in Nederland* (Leiden, 1913), 183 (neither author has identified the source of this prayer).

[49] ASD V, 1: p. 144, line 829–p. 146, line 866.

has it that the dying Erasmus so concentrated himself on Christ, that only the sweet name of Jesus was on his lips. The classic account of Erasmus's last moments is that of Beatus Rhenanus and is included in the introduction to Erasmus's posthumously published edition of Origen (1536). Rhenanus tells us how Erasmus had placed all his trust in Christ and had died, repeating the words: "O Iesu misericordia" (O Jesus, have mercy), "Domine, libera me" (Lord, deliver me), "Domine, fac finem" (Lord, bring the end), and then, in Dutch, "lieve God," which Rhenanus translated as "chare Deus" (dear God).

Nicolaas van der Blom, in his article on Erasmus's last words, thoroughly analyzes all the information we have on this subject.[50] He convincingly argues that the Dutch words "lieve God" need not have been Erasmus's very last words. But this is not what concerns us here. It is the meaning of these two Dutch words that interests us. Nowhere in the Dutch religious language could Van der Blom trace the combination "lieve God," but he did find the combination "lieve Heere" (dear Lord). He believes that a contamination occurred in the tradition, although, in his opinion, the word "lieve" was indeed uttered by Erasmus.

In my view, it is very likely that Erasmus spoke the words as they have been handed down to us. The combination "lieve God" does occur in Dutch medieval prayers, for example in prayers where Jesus' suffering and wounds are meditated upon. These prayers invoke "the merciful God," "the blessed God," "the perfect God" or "the dear God," but in all cases this "God" is Christ, who in these and other prayers is also called Father, even "almighty Father."[51] Erasmus too, occasionally called Jesus "parens" or "conditor."[52] Would it be possible that Erasmus had learnt such prayers in his youth and that a familiar expression had come back to him when his end was near? Anyway, it is possible that in medieval Dutch the words "lieve God" (dear God) refer to Christ. If we accept this, then the accounts claiming that Erasmus invoked Christ only are true in an unexpected sense.

In *De praeparatione ad mortem*, Erasmus suggests what texts a dying person could use to express his faith: "Lord Jesus, receive my spirit" (Act.

---

[50] N. van der Blom, "Die letzten Worte des Erasmus," in *Basler Zeitschrift für Geschichte und Altertumskunde* 65 (1965) no. 2, 195–214, esp. 212–14.

[51] D. A. Stracke, "De originele tekst der XV Pater op het lijden des Heeren en diens latere lotgevallen," in *Ons Geestelijk Erf* 17, vol. I (1943), 71–140, esp. 85–96.

[52] *Precatio ad Virg. filium Iesum*, LB V: col. 1211CD; cf. *Precationes*, Ad filium, LB V: col. 1198C.

7:58) or "Into thine hand I commit my spirit" (Ps. 31:5).[53] The latter words were spoken by Jesus on the cross and naturally were addressed to the Father. But in the prayer "on the occasion of serious illness" included in the *Precationes*, the distinction between the Father and the Son has become blurred, as it is in many medieval prayers. Thus, in that prayer, the line "into thine hand I commit my spirit" is addressed not, as would be expected, to God the Father, but to Christ.[54]

Koninklijke Nederlandse Akademie van Wetenschappen

List of Abbreviations

LB = *Desiderii Erasmi Roterodami Opera omnia*, [ed. J. Clericus], 10 vols, Leiden, 1703–1706; reprint, Hildesheim, 1961–62.
ASD = *Opera omnia Desiderii Erasmi Roterodami*, Amsterdam etc., 1969–. In progress.
Allen = *Opus epistolarum Des. Erasmi Roterodami*, ed. P. S. Allen, H. M. Allen, and H. W. Garrod, 12 vols., Oxford, 1906–1958.
Ep. = Epistola in Allen, quoted by number and line.
CWE = *Collected Works of Erasmus*, Toronto, 1974–. In progress.
Holborn = *Desiderius Erasmus Roterodamus. Ausgewählte Werke*, ed. H. and A. Holborn, Munich, 1933; reprint, Munich, 1964.

[53] ASD V, 1: p. 390, lines 239–43.
[54] LB V: col. 1203D.

English, Scottish, and Irish History in Continental Jesuit Drama

FRIEDRICH-K. UNTERWEG

In the course of a good two hundred years between the beginnings of Jesuit drama and the dissolution of the order in 1773, the Jesuits adapted an enormous variety of subjects for performances on their college stages. When they realized that their plays were an excellent medium for their moral-didactical and religious-propagandist purposes, they made great efforts to reach as great an audience as possible, and thus kept enlarging their traditional canon of plays by adding new and attractive themes. The performances of their plays were often characterized by great magnificence and soon proved to be *the* cultural event of a town or city. Often the plays were attended by hundreds of visitors from the surrounding regions.

In view of the immense number of plays about very different subjects, it is quite difficult to obtain a general view of the subject-groups and to make reliable statements about the rank and popularity of certain subjects within the Jesuits' canon of dramatic works.

In her stimulating study *Geschichte, Politik und Gesellschaft im Drama des 17. Jahrhunderts*, Elida Maria Szarota has pointed out that in Jesuit plays—unlike humanist dramas—the importance of historical subjects gradually grew after the end of the sixteenth century.[1] In a later article she stressed the important rôle of Spanish and English history for Jesuit dramatists and discussed ten plays dealing with Henry II and his chancellor Thomas Becket, Henry VIII, and the martyrs John Fisher and Thomas More, Mary Stuart, Charles I, and Thomas Cromwell.[2]

---

[1] Bern and Munich 1976, 10.

[2] "Englische Geschichte auf den Jesuitenbühnen," in *From Wolfram and Petrarch to*

As an Anglicist, I wondered if any other subjects of English, Scottish, or Irish history had been treated by the Jesuits, wondered which subjects had been the most popular and for what reasons they might have been adapted for college performances.

The following paper is the result of an analysis of bibliographies, play-lists, and subject-catalogues of Jesuit-dramas, including the *index materiorum* of Elida Maria Szarota's monumental edition of *periochae*, in which two dozen plays dealing with British history are listed.[3] The paper is a preliminary survey of a field of research which has proved to be far greater and much more varied than I had expected after reading Szarota's article in honour of Leonard Forster.[4] This is, however, only one reason for the introductory character of the survey. The other reason is that some of the apparently extant *periochae* could not be found and therefore could not be analysed or compared with other texts on the same subject before I had to finish this paper.

As may be seen from the following chronological list of plays, more than a hundred and fifty plays dealing with English, Scottish, or Irish history were performed between 1594 and 1771 in about sixty different Continental Jesuit colleges. In view of the fact that particularly some minor play-lists of the non-German-speaking provinces require further verification, it is likely that the real number of plays is even higher. On the basis of my experience with my project *Thomas Morus Tragoedia*, about which I read a paper during the Wolfenbüttel Congress,[5] I would assume that in fact nearly two hundred Jesuit dramas dealt with English history in the broadest sense of the word. If this assumption proves to be correct, English, Irish, or Scottish history was dealt with at least once a year in some college.

Goethe and Grass. Studies in Honour of Leonard Forster. eds. D. H. Green, L. P. Johnson, and Dieter Wuttke (Baden-Baden, 1982), 489–500.

[3] *Das Jesuitendrama im deutschen Sprachgebiet. Eine Periochen-Edition*. Vol. 4, "Indices" bearbeitet von Peter Mortzfeld. (München 1986), 104–5.

[4] I am very much indebted to Dr. Hermann Wiegand, Mannheim, for informing me about Szarota's above-mentioned article which is 'hidden' in Forster's Festschrift.

[5] See *Acta of the Neo-Latin Congress at Wolfenbüttel, August 1985*. eds. Mario DiCesare and Fidel Rädle (New York 1988), 365–74.

Chronological List of Plays

1594	Ingolstadt	*Martyrium seu caedes innocentis Mariae Stuartae Scotorum Reginae.*	lost?
1605	Dillingen	*S. Edmundus.*	lost?
1607	Paderborn	*Prima S. Edmundi pueri innocentissima aetas.*	lost?
1612	Rome	*Thomas Morus, Tragoedia.*	Lat. MS, 46fols.
1614	Lucerne	*Sanctus Edmundus Cantuarensis Archiepiscopus Christi visione dignatus.*	lost?
1615	Augsburg	*Summarischer Inhalt Des Schawspiels von Ametano oder von einem unbußfertigen Engellaendischen Hauptmann welcher von wegen seiner Ritterlichen Thaten dem Koenig Cenredo sehr lieb gewesen von ihme offtermaln zur Beicht angemahnt aber dieselbig allzeit außgeschlagen and endtlich in der Verzweiflung gestorben.*	Ger. progr., 6pp.
1617	Ingolstadt	*Drama de S. Guthberto adolescente Anglo.*	lost?
1617	Olmütz	*Sanctus Eduardus Angliae Rex ab exilio in regnum revocatus.*	lost?
1619	Eichstätt	*Tragoedia de Milite Anglo nolente confiteri.*	lost?
1620	Krumau	*Sanctus Edmundus adolescens gloriosae virgini desponsatus.*	lost?
1620	Tournai	*La Mort de Thomas Morus.*	lost?
1621	Lucerne	*Summarischer Inhalt der Tragedi Von dem heiligen Oswaldo Khoenig in Engelland.*	Ger. progr., 8pp.
1622	Ingolstadt	*Tvndalvs redivivvs. Summarischer Inhalt der Action von Tundalo einem Irrlaendischen Kriegsmann welcher durch ein wunderbarliche vision oder Gesicht sein Gottloses Leben in einen Gottseligen Wandel verendert hat.*	Lat./Ger. progr., 8pp.

1622	Dillingen	*Synopsis Comicotragoediae De Gvilielmo Adolescente Hiberno Nobili.*	Lat. progr., 8pp.
1622	Roermond	*Tragoedia Thomas Morus.*	Lat. progr., 8pp.
1625	Courtrai	*Thomas Morus, Cancellier von Enghelant.*	Lat./Dut. progr., 8pp.
1625	Eichstätt	*Summarischer Inhalt der Tragoedi Vom Koenig Henrico Henrici II. Koenigs in Engellandt aeltesten Sohn.*	Ger. progr., 8pp.
1626	Constance	*S. Thomas Cantuariensis Archiepiscopus, & Martyr. Das ist: Tragoedien Von dem H. Thoma Ertz-Bischoffen vnnd Martyrer zu Candelberg in Engellandt.*	Lat./Ger. progr., 13pp.
1628	Schlettstadt	*Thomas Morus.*	lost?
1628	Lucerne	*Tria castitatis lilia, SS. Edmundus, Casimirus et Elzearus.*	lost?
1629	Burghausen	*Edmundus Das ist Spiegel der studierenden Jugent in einem Dramate vorgestellt.*	Ger. progr., 7pp.
1629	Freiburg/Br.	*Gutbertus adolescens drama.*	lost?
1631	Ingolstadt	*Thomas Morus, Das ist: Tragoedia von Thoma Moro des vor Gott und der Welt berühmten Engelländischen Reichs Cantzler Wellicher vor 96 Jahren von dem Gottlosen Wieterich Henrico, dem Engelländischen König, wegen Verfechtung wahren Glaubens vnd H. Römischen Stuelß Tyrannischer weiß hingerichtet worden.*	Ger. progr., 12pp.
1632	Krems	*Sanctus Edmundus Cantuariensis.*	lost?
1633	Lucerne	*Gutbertus adolescens.*	
1636	Cologne	*Sanctus Edmundus puer.*	Lat. MS
1641	Freiburg (Switzerl.)	*Sanctus Patricius.*	Ger./Fren. progr., 8pp.
1643	Landsberg	*S. Edmundi pueritia.*	lost?
1644	Innsbruck	*S. Edovardus Rex Angliae.*	Lat./Ger. progr., 8pp.
1645	s. l.	*Historia von einem armen Waißlein Victoria genannt, Auß den uhralten Irrländischen Chronicis gezogen.*	Ger. progr., 8pp.
1647	Bamberg	*Thomas Morus.*	lost?
1648	Munich	*Comoedia seu potius drama de caritate Sancti Gregorii Magni adversus juventutem Anglicanam.*	lost?
1650	St. Omer	*Morus sive Morum integritas suo sanguine pupurata.*	Lat. MS, 30pp.
1651	Krems	*Maria Stuarta Scotiae Regina Ab Anglica tyrannide capite truncata.*	lost?

1651	Dillingen	*Sanctus Edmundus.*	lost?
1652	Bamberg	*Winredus Anglus.*	lost?
1654	Aachen	*Carolus II. Scotiae rex, musico-drama.*	lost?
1654	Cologne	*Comoedia de admirabili Conto A S. Columba Scotiae Episcopo Pauperi dato.*	Lat. progr., 4pp.
1656	Cologne	*Eduinus Angliae Rex In regnum suum restitutus.*	Lat. progr., 4pp.
1656	Luxemburg	*Thomas Morus. Tragédie.*	French progr., 4pp.
1657	Ingolstadt	*Kenelmus puer Per dolum nutritij Et ambitionem Germanae sororis Innocue et crudeliter necatus. Erbärmlicher Mordt Kenelmi Eines Unschuldigen Knaben und Königs in Mercien, durch List seines Nöhr-Vaters durch anstifftung und Ehrgeitz seiner aignen Schwester vollbracht.*	Lat./Ger. progr., 8pp.
1659	Hall	*Maria Stuart.*	lost
1660	Cologne	*Superbia Correcta Seu Insolens Fastus Elati Regis Ludicro Schemate Ab Anglo Monitore Senio Castigatus.*	Lat. progr., 4pp.
1660	Cologne	*Ulfadus et Rufinus Duo Britanni fratres illustres regali purpura, sed fuso pro Christo sanguine longe illustriores.*	Lat. progr., 4pp.
1661	Feldkirch	*Kenelmus Merciorum Regis filius Per Sororis ambitionem et dolum Nutritij innocue trucidatus Erbärmlicher Mordt Kenelmi Eines Unschuldigen Knabens und rechtmässigen Erbens des Königreichs Mercien durch Ehrgeitz seiner Schwester unnd List seines Nöhr-Vaters angestifft und vollzogen.*	Lat./Ger. progr., 10pp.
1662	Düsseldorf	*Edvinus Rex Angliae. (Ethelfredi Protectoris sui ambitione profugus Genii Tutelaris ope, Regno et Ecclesiae Catholicae restitutus.)*	Lat./Ger. progr.?
1662	Constance	*Kenelmus per dolum nutritij et ambitionem germanae sororis innocue et crudeliter necatus. Erbärmlicher Mordt Kenelmi, Eines unschuldigen Knaben und König in Mercien durch Anstifftung und Ehrgeitz seiner einen Schwester vollbracht.*	Lat./Ger. progr., 7pp.
1664	Düsseldorf	*Humfredus dux exercitus Coenredi, Regis Angliae.*	Lat./Ger. progr.
1666	Constance	*Thomas Morus Supremus Angliae Cancellarius.*	Lat./Ger. progr., 8pp.
1666	Lucerne	*Thomas Morus Angliae Cancellarius Pro Authoritate, Immunitate, Veritate Apo-*	Lat./Ger. progr. 16pp.

		stolico-romanae sedis Passus Londini An. M. D. XXXV. VII. Julij ipso die Translationis S. Thomae Cantuar.	
1666	Steyr	*Thomas Morus.*	lost?
1668	Freiburg/Br.	*Edvinus Umbriae Rex.*	lost?
1669	Munich	*Agon Christianus Landulphi et Ruffini Angliae Principum. Landulph und Ruffin Fürsten und Martyrer in Engelland In einem Schawspil fürgestellt.*	Lat./Ger. progr., 8pp.
1669	Brigue	*Kenelmus puer, rex Merciae.*	lost?
1671	Burghausen	*Ulfadus Christianae Religionis Idea. Das ist: Ulfadus Ein dapfferer beständiger Verfechter deß Christlichen Glaubens*	Lat./Ger. progr., 8pp.
1671	Vienna	*Languetta Regina Scotia.*	Lat. MS 59pp.
1672	Ingolstadt	*Primitiae insulae Vectae Deo Duorum Principum Adolescentum Sanguine consecratae Die Erst-Zeitige Frücht Der Insel Wigcht Gott Auffgeopfferet, In dem Bluet zwayer Königlichen Printzen.*	Lat./Ger. progr., 8pp.
1673	Landsberg	*Thomas primus Angliae Cantuariae Archiepiscopus et Martyr. Thomas Grooss Cantzler in Engelland Ertzbischoff zu Cantelberg In einem Schaw-Spil vorgestellt.*	Lat./Ger. progr., 8pp.
1677	Innsbruck	*Georgius Clarentiae Comes perduellionis veris Optione mortis ab Eduardo Quarto Angliae Rege data mori In vino Cretico eligit.*	Lat. progr. (MS), 4pp.
1678	Ellwangen	*Orthodoxae Veritatis Prodigiosa vis in Hibernia ad Christum conversa per D. Patritium Britanniae Thaumaturgum. Wunderwürdige Krafft Catholischer Warheit in der zu Christo bekehrten Insel Irrland durch den Apostolischen H. Bishoff Patritium grossen Patronen in Hohenstatt.*	Lat./Ger. progr., 8pp.
1678	Munich	*Via mirabilis Divinae Providentiae Principem Hedvinum ad Terrenum et Caeleste Regnum evehentis. Wunderbarlicher Weeg Der Göttlichen Vorsichtigkeit, Durch welche Fürst Hedvinus so wol yu dem irrdischen als himmlischen Königreich erhöhet wird*	Lat./Ger. progr., 8pp.
1679	Eichstätt	*Certamen Gratiae et Naturae in Richardo Comoedia Gnaden und Naturkamff In Richardo Weilandt Königen in Engellandt Nachmahlen Eystättischen Schutz und Schirm Patronen.*	Lat./Ger. progr., 8pp.
1679	Freiburg (Switzerl.)	*Früchte Der Buss und Widerwärtigkeit einsmals beschauen In Richardo Roberti Königs in Schotland Sohn.*	Lat./Fren. progr., 8pp.

1679	Ingolstadt	*SSS. Archus, Hereneus et Quardanus Nobiles Angli ob Fidem Christianam Patria Exule. Glückseeliges Elend Der Dreyen Heyligen Archi, Herennei, und Quardani, Welche von des Catholischen Glaubens wegen Auss Engelland Vertriben Zu leichten.*	Lat. MS and Lat./Ger. progr., 8pp.
1680	Emmerich	*Thomas Morus.*	lost?
1682	Constance	*Alter Regius David peccans et poenitens. Dass ist Lasteren verlohrner, hernach aber von dem gnadenreichen Aug der Göttlichen Barmhertzigkeit wol Angesehner, und zur endlichen Buss bekehrter Jüngling.*	Lat./Ger. progr., 8pp.
1682	Munich	*Englischer Beystandt So Gott dem Menschen verschaffet zu Verwahrung der köstlichen Freyheit wider allen Anfall der fünff Sinnen und Arglist dess bösen Feinds in einem Schauspil Gesangweiss in Teutscher Sprach vorgestellet.*	Ger. progr., 8pp.
1683	Paderborn	*Infelix Ambitio Joannis Dudlaei, Ducis Northumbriae in tragoediam reducta.*	Lat./Ger. progr.?
1687	Ingolstadt	*Thomas Morus de vitae statu eligendo deliberans.*	Lat. progr., 4pp.
1687	Neuss	*Triplex victoria Ecclesiae militantis in Hungaria sub Imperatore Leopoldo I., in Gallia sub Ludowigo XIV, in Britannia sub Jacobo II.*	lost?
1688	Graz	*Thomas Morus Kanzler von England.*	lost?
1690	Vienna	*Mansuetudo principum Laureata Messe Diadematum Coronata in gloriosissimo Scotorum rege Kennetho.*	Lat. MS, 96pp.
1693	Luxemburg	*Thomas Morus, martyr.*	lost?
1694	Innsbruck	*In morte vita Sigberto et Pendae Regiis Vectae Anglicanae Insulae Principibus A Divina Providentia parata.*	Lat./Ger. progr., 8pp.
1696	Porrentruy	*Carolus Dises Namens der Erste König in Engelland Schot- und Irrland ein Trauerspihl von Cromwell gehalten.*	Ger./Fren. progr., 8pp.
1697	Lucerne	*Edvinus Allae, Regis Deirae Filius Tragico-Comoedia.*	Ger. progr., 8pp.
1698	Hildesheim	*S. Edmundus juventutis decus.*	lost?
1700	Ingolstadt	*Carolus I. Magnae Britanniae Rex Carolus der Erste Engel-, Schott- und Irrländischer König von den Seinigen hingerichtet.*	Lat./Ger. progr., 8pp.
1700	Eichstätt	*Angelica Custodia in Emmanuele Hyberniae Comite spectata. Englischer Schutz An Emmanuel Graffen auß Irrland erzeigt.*	Lat./Ger. progr. 8pp.

1700	Lucerne	[*Corona Gloriae mundi contemptu parta a S. Jodoco Anglicano principe.*]	lost?
1701	Ellwangen	*Carolus I. Magnae Britanniae Rex Tragoedia.*	Lat./Ger. progr., 8pp.
1701	Innsbruck	*Thomas Morus Ex Angliae Cancellario Regis Regum Purpuratus.*	Lat./Ger. progr., 8pp.
1702	Eichstätt	*Victrix Constantia in Thoma Moro Angliae Cancellario.*	Lat./Ger. progr., 8pp.
1702	Neuburg	*Maria Stuarta Scotiae Regina Tragoedia Königliche Unschuld Von Königlicher Falschheit Biss zu dem Schwerdt-Todt unterdruckt in Maria Stuarta in Schottland.*	Lat./Ger. progr., 11pp.
1702	Wiener Neustadt	*Thomas Morus Angliae cancellarius.*	lost?
1704	Constance	*Eduardus.*	lost?
1705	Eichstätt	*Eduardi Angliae Regis Sacrum Connubium Eduardi Königs in Engelland Heilige Ehe-Verbündnuss.*	Lat./Ger. progr., 8pp.
1706	Ellwangen	*Justitia in mercatore Anglo triumphans ostensa.*	lost?
1706	Klagenfurt	*Ludus Divinae Providentiae in Languila (= Languetta?) Redereti Scotorum regis conjuge.*	lost?
1709	Hildesheim	*Thomas Morus mori quam impias Henrici VIII. nuptias approbare praeoptans.*	lost?
1709	Eichstätt	*Maria Stuarta Scotiae Regina Tragoedia Königliche Unschuld Biss zu dem Schwerdt-Todt underdruckt Maria Stuarta Königin in Schottland.*	Lat./Ger. progr., 8pp.
1710	Mindelheim	[*Corona Gloriae Contemptu Parta A S. Jodoco Anglicano Principe Wechsel Der Irrdischen mit der Himmlischen Reichs-Cron Von dem heiligen Engelländischen Printzen Jodocus Verachter der Welt glücklich getroffen.*]	Lat./Ger. progr., 8pp.
1711	Baden	*Thomas Morus.*	lost?
1711	Ellwangen	*Liberalitas Regia Regno Donata. Das ist Elfredus Britanniae Rex Durch Almusen zu seinem Reich von Gott erhoben.*	Lat./Ger. progr., 6pp.
1712	Ellwangen	*Thomas Morus Angliae Cancellarius Purpuratus Verae Religionis Defensor.*	Lat./Ger. progr.
1713	Hall	*Thomas Morus Ein unbewegliche Tugend-Saul Und Heldenmüthiger Verfechter Der Wahren Kirchen in Engeland.*	Lat./Ger. progr., 8pp.
1714	Ingolstadt	*Joannes Baptista Fischerus Episcopus Rofensis Tragoedia I. B. Fischer Wegen Beschützung der Catholischen Wahrheit zum Todt verurtheilt.*	Lat./Ger. progr., 8pp.

Square brackets indicate subjects which the Jesuits mistook to be British history, but which, in fact, are non-British.

1716	Kaufbeuren	*Liberalitas Regia Regno Donata Oder das von Elfredo Durch Allmosen wider eroberte Engelländische Königreich.*	Ger. progr., 8pp.
1717	Mindelheim	*Fortitudo Christiana Paternae Impietatis Victrix in Landulpho et Ruffino regiis Angliae principibus.*	Lat./Ger. progr., 7pp.
1718	Heiligenstadt	*Thomas Morus.*	lost?
1718	Feldkirch	*Thomas Morus.*	lost?
1719	Eichstätt	*Richardus Ex Angliae Rege Peregrinus Unde Regia Eystadij Origo.*	Lat./Ger. progr., 8pp.
1720	Munich	*Henricus Henrici II. Angliae Regis Filius.*	Lat./Ger. progr., 8pp
1721	Burghausen	*Anglorum par nobile Fratrum Landulphus et Ruffinus Verus Fortitudinis Christianae Typus.*	Lat./Ger. progr., 8pp.
1721	Salzburg	*Thomas Morus, ein Opfer des katholischen Glaubens.*	Lat./Ger. progr., 8pp.
1722	Neuburg	*Conscientiae malae tor/-mentum In Odoardo ad Tumbam Pelagij converso.*	Lat. progr., 4pp.
1723	Munich	*Thomas Morus Gloriosus Victor et Victima Pro Sede Apostolica.*	Lat. MS and Lat./Ger. progr., 8pp.
1724	Freiburg/Br.	*Cromvellius Tragoedia. Das ist entsetzter Hochmuth.*	Lat./Ger. progr., 8pp.
1724	Ingolstadt	*Sanctus Thomas mundi et carnis Victor.*	Lat. progr., 4pp.
1725	Eichstätt	*In Funere Vita Seu Ulferus Rex Angliae ex filiorum funere renatus.*	Lat./Ger. progr., 8pp.
1725	Mannheim	*Thomas Morus Angliae Cancellarius.*	Lat. MS
1726	Augsburg	*Thomas Morus Tragoedia. Gut und Blut Vor die Warheit Ritterlich aufgesetzet Von einem Engelländischen Cantzler Thoma Moro.*	Lat./Ger. progr., 8pp.
1726	Brigue	*Carolus I. Magnae Britanniae Rex Tragoedia Das ist Untreuer Welt-Lohn in Carolo dem ersten Engel-, Schott- und Irrländischen König.*	Ger. progr., 8pp.
1726	Constance	*Joannes et Franciscus Dudley.*	Lat./Ger. progr., 8pp.
1727	Olmütz	*Heroica in adversis constantia Thomae Mori ...*	printed book
1728	Molsheim	*Thomas Morus.*	lost?
1730	Fulda	*Thomas Morus. Tragoedia.*	lost?
1731	Hildesheim	*Luctus Fortunae in familia Stuartica in duobus Carolis depressa et exaltata.*	lost?
1733	Ieperen	*Thomas Morus.*	lost?

1733	Neuss	*Carolus Stuartus per Cromwellum et Fairfaxium securi subjectus. Tragoedia.*	Ger. progr., 8pp.
1734	Landsberg	*Lambertus Simnellus Lixa Rex Comicus Angliae.*	Lat./Ger. progr., 8pp.
1735	Coblenze	*Coenredi Anglorum Regis Aula poenitentiae ab Humfred spretis Coenredi Regis et Drithelmi Redivivi infeliciter neglectae theatrum.*	Ger. progr., 8pp.
1735	Ingolstadt	*Hymenaeus Parthenius in morte S. Eduardi Regis Angliae Spectatus.*	Lat. progr., 4pp.
1736	Jülich	*Siegreicher Jugend- und Tugend-Kampff das ist Obsiegende Lieb- und Hertzens-Reinigkeit in Niceta einem englischen Jüngling.*	Ger. progr.?
1736	Coesfeld	*Thomas Morus.*	lost?
1736	Munich	*Annulus Sponsalitius a Divo Edmundo B. Virgini Mariae oblatus.*	Lat. progr., 4pp.
1737	Ingolstadt	*Fructus precum nocturnarum in Richardo.*	Lat. progr., 4pp.
1740	Ellwangen	*Sanctus Patritius.*	Lat. progr., 4pp.
1741	Brigue	*Thomas Morus Tragoedia Das ist Die bis in den Tod unüberwindliche Beständigkeit Einstens in Thoma Moro Engelländischen Ertzkantzler gesehen.*	French progr.?
1741	Coblenze	*Aula sancta seu Regia Scotiae domus cum rege patre et quina prole Edoardo, Elfrido, Carolo, Alexandro, Mechtildo totam se Deo in ereme consecrans.*	lost?
1741	Linz	*Thomae Mori constantia.*	lost?
1741	Sitten	*Marianische Hochzeit Vorgestellet in dem Todt des Heiligen Eduardi Königs auss Engelland.*	Ger. progr., 8pp.
1742	Burghausen	*Ormundus Tragoedia.*	Lat./Ger. progr., 8pp.
1743	Trèves	*S. Richardus Anglo-Saxonum in Britannia Rex cum utroque filio SS. Wunibaldo et Willibaldo, spreto regno Gloriosus Christi exul.*	Lat./Ger. progr., 6pp.
1744	Augsburg	*Sanctus Edmundus.*	Lat. progr., 4pp.
1746	Lucerne	*Thomas Morus Tragoedia Das ist Die bis in den Tod unüberwindliche Beständigkeit Thomae Morio Engelländischen Cantzlers.*	Lat./Ger. progr., 8pp.
1746	Munich	*S. Thomae Cantuariensis Pietas a Deipara ostento comprobata.*	Lat. progr., 4pp.
1747	Dunkerque	*Thomas Morus.*	lost?

1747	Jülich	*Pieta in motu immobilis sive Sanctus Edmundus Angliae Rex Bello obrutus exitiali dirissimisque motus tormentis in Romano-Catholica Fide et Justitia immotus.*	Lat./Ger. progr., 12pp.
1747	Klagenfurt	*Eduardus Angliae Rex insidiis Alfredi novercae peremptus.*	lost?
1749	Landshut	*Sanctus Patritius Drama.*	Lat. progr., 4pp.
1750	Sitten	*Thomas Morus Gross Cantzler von Engelland, In einem Trauerspill.*	Ger. progr., 8pp.
1751	Neuburg	*Constantia Coronata Tragoedia Edvins König in Northhumberland Standhaffte Begierd Des Heil. Tauffs Eine Urquelle Alles Zeitlich- und Geistlichen Glücks.*	Lat./Ger. progr., 8pp.
1752	Feldkirch	*Carolus I. Britanniae Rex. Tragoedia.*	lost?
1755	Solothurn	*Thomas Morus.*	lost?
1758	Ingolstadt	*Constantia Christiana Thomae Mori Das ist Christliche Standhaftigkeit Des Engleländischen Gross-Cantzlers Thomas Morus.*	Lat./Ger. progr., 8pp.
1758	Munstereifel	*Ulfadus et Ruffinus Martyres, A Parente Ulfero Occisi Tragoedia.*	Lat./Ger. progr., 8pp.
1760	Krems	*Wolpherus Merciorum Rex.*	lost?
1762	Feldkirch	*Coenredus Merciorum rex religiosus.*	lost?
1764	Constance	*Thomas Morus Kanzler in Engelland.*	Lat./Ger. progr., 8pp.
1764	Straubing	*Henricus Henrici Das ist Heinrich des zweyten Namens Prinz von Engeland.*	Lat./Ger. progr., 23pp.
1766	Eichstätt	*Sanctus Richardus Angliae Rex Exul Voluntarius.*	Lat./Ger. progr., 8pp.
1768	Landshut	*Sanctus Richardus Angliae Rex.*	lost?
1769	Innsbruck	*Euphemia Tochter Eduards III. Königs von England.*	lost?
1770	Jülich	*Carolus Primus Angliae, Scotiae et Hyberniae, inaudita judicii forma Cromwelli potissimum et Fairfaxii artibus ad universae Europae indignationem Constituta Capitis damnatus.*	Lat./Ger. progr., 8pp.
1771	Münstereifel	*Carl I. aus dem Stuartischen Hause, König in Engel-, Schott- und Irrland. Ein Trauerspiel.*	Ger. progr., 8pp.

About two thirds of the dramas listed seem to have been handed down to posterity. As is customary with Jesuit dramas, they have come down to us in the form of *periochae*—mostly bilingual programmes of four to sixteen pages with an *argumentum*, a summary of the scenes and a list of the actors—thus enabling the non-Latin speaking audience to follow the Latin performances of the plays.

Eight dramas about Thomas More, Saint Edmund, Queen Languetta, the Saints Archus, Herenus, and Quardanus or the Scottish King Kenneth, are extant in the form of Latin manuscripts.[6] As far as I know, all have remained unedited, although the editing of two More-dramas is now in progress.

My words "seem to have been handed down" refer to the fact that a considerable number of the plays in question could not be found despite the fact that we have clear evidence that a *periocha* was printed. Moreover, many of the shelf-marks Jean Marie Valentin lists in his bibliography are now obsolete and some of the archives he names do not have the *periochae* in question.[7] In view of this, I fear that at least ten percent of the listed *periochae* must be classified as "lost" because of damage during World War II, or other losses.

As far as the remaining third of the dramas is concerned, not more than the year and place of performance and the play's title—often in the short *Litterae Annuae*-version—could be discovered. As we have no evidence at all of the printing of a *periocha* or the existence of a manuscript, these plays have also been classified as "lost?" in my list.

By now the reader of the list must wonder if it really is a list of individual plays or merely a list of performances of a smaller group of original plays. The striking similarities of several titles, e.g., *Thomas Morus, Gross-Cantzler von England* (1750), and *Thomas Morus, Kanzler in Engelland* (1764), or *Carolus dises Namens der Erste Koenig in Engelland, Schott- und Irrland* (1696), and *Karl der erste aus dem Stuartischen Hause, Koenig in Engel-, Schott-, und Irrland* (1771), seem to indicate that not all of the items are independent or new treatments of a subject. Comparisons of *periochae* prove, however, that simple reperformances of plays from other colleges without any variations were an exception.[8] In addition, Szarota's edition

[6] Cf. 1612. Rome; 1636, Cologne; c. 1650, St. Omer; 1671, Vienna; 1679, Ingolstadt; 1690, Vienna; 1723, Munich and 1725, Mannheim.

[7] The librarians of the Ordensbibliothek Eichstätt and of the Provinzialbibliothek Amberg informed me, for example, that their shelf-marks had been changed years ago and in the Bibliothèque des Jésuites and the Paulinum Münster I could not find the periochae Valentin claims to be there.

[8] Here, I should like to express my gratitude to all the libraries that kindly

of *periochae* shows that different treatments of the same subject were common practice in the Jesuit order—the degree of individual characteristics of the dramas varying with the abilities of the *choragus* who prepared the subject for the performance and wrote the *periocha*.[9]

Leaving the previous considerations aside, the above chronology underlines the fact that the Jesuits considered English history particularly congenial to their purpose and, furthermore, that they dealt with far more subjects than Szarota's article seems to indicate.

The number and variety of the subjects they adapted for college-performances becomes even more evident if the chronological order of the list is replaced by a systematical one.

During a period of roughly one hundred and eighty years, more than fifty different subjects from English, Scottish, or Irish history were re-enacted on their stages.

Among the subjects presented are *Sanctus Edwardus Angliae Rex, The Tragedy of the English Soldier who did not want to confess,* the *Tragedy of the holy Oswald, King of England,* the *Action of Tundalo, an Irish soldier who abandoned his sinful life after a miraculous vision, Gutbertus adolescens drama, Sanctus Edmundus puer, Carolus Secundus, Scotia rex, Ulfadus and Ruffinus, two British brothers, noble through the royal purple, but far nobler after the shedding of their blood for Christ,* or *Sanctus Patritius*, to name but a few of those not included in Szarota's article.[10]

All in all, the Jesuits dealt with more than a thousand years of British history, presenting events of heathen England[11] in the same manner to their audience as incidents which had taken place less than half a century before, such as the life and death of Charles I, which in 1696 was presented on a Jesuit stage for the first time.[12]

---

provided microfilms or copies of numerous *periochae* and allowed me to use their archives, especially to the Provinzialbiblithek Amberg, the Ordensbibliothek Eichstätt, the Universitätsbibliothek and the Staatsbibliothek Munich, the Historisches Archiv der Stadt Köln, the Staats- und Stadtbibliothek Augsburg, and the Bibliothèque des Jésuites, Chantilly. Apart from this, I should like to thank Dr. H. Frings of the Beethoven Gymnasium, Bonn who allowed me to browse in 'his' collection of well-preserved *periochae*.

[9] Cf. Szarota, *Jesuitendramen. Eine Periochenedition*. Vol. 1, part 1, 1585–87, vol. 2, part 1, 2296–97 or vol. 3, part 2, 2237–43.

[10] English translations mine. For the full Latin or German titles see 1619, Eichstätt; 1621, Lucerne; 1622, Ingolstadt and 1660, Cologne.

[11] E.g., the life of Ulfadus in *Ulfadus Christianae Religionis Idea*. Burghausen 1671.

[12] Cf. 1696, Porrentruy. A German/French periocha is kept in the Staats- and Stadtbibliothek Augsburg.

The fact that most of the plays listed may without difficulty be linked with historical events or persons, should, however, not lead to the assumption that the plays accurately mirrored the historical facts as they are known to us. In many a commentary on a *periocha*, Szarota has pointed out that just the opposite is true, because the Jesuits mainly used sources written by members of their order from a Catholic point of view, which often provided a merely partial report of the events.[13] Moreover, one should not forget that their plays were primarily written to ensure the success of the Counter-Reformation, to lead apostates back to the Catholic faith and to reinforce the belief of their disconcerted contemporaries. Therefore, historical accuracy was of far less importance than the impact of their plays. Consequently, the Thomas More of their dramas, for example, is—unlike the historical figure—not a fearful man who retreats when the conflict with King Henry reaches its climax, but rather an eager martyr who—regardless of the danger to his own life and without taking his family into consideration—stands up for his convictions.[14]

Most of the characters in the plays are painted in black and white, as is often already indicated in the title of a drama: Henry VIII is presented as a "godless tyrant," Mary Stuart as "Royal Innocence" who is killed by Elizabeth or "Royal insidiousness" and Thomas More is characterized as a man of "invincible steadfastness." Cromwell (Oliver as well as Thomas, who is the hero of the play *Cromwellus Tragoedia* of the year 1724) is as mean a councillor as Mary's brother Murray, who in the end is responsible for her death. Their positive counterparts are Thomas Becket and John Fisher, who in vain try to fight against the intrigues of the corrupt courtiers or the power-hungry young nobles.

The typical stress on the second part of the maxim "delectare et movere" is also responsible for a number of fictitious and very emotional scenes in the plays under discussion. A young nobleman, for example, awaits his execution, but is taken out of prison on a cloud, after having fervently prayed to Saint Catherine.[15] The rude soldier Tundalus, who leads a most sinful life, is moved to begin a virtuous life after he has had a horrifying vision of hell.[16] Numerous other examples could be added, but are for brevity's sake not discussed here.

[13] Cf. Szarota, "Englische Geschichte," 494ff.

[14] See among others *Thomas Morus Tragoedia*, Munich 1723, II, 1 or *Thomas Morus*, Ingolstadt 1631, II, 2.

[15] Cf. *Comicotragoedia de Guilielmo* . . . , Dillingen 1622, IV, 3.

[16] Cf. *Tvundalus Redivivus*, Ingolstadt 1622, II, 2–7. See also Szarota's commentary in *Jesuitendramen. Eine Periochenedition*. Vol. 1, part 2, 1815ff.

For reasons which I will explain below, the Jesuits had a preference for English history. As may be seen from the following tables only thirteen subjects stemming from Scottish or Irish history were treated in twenty plays–Mary Stuart and Saint Patrick being the most popular figures in these groups.

Plays dealing with Scottish History

Maria Stuart (d. 1587), Queen of Scots (1542 - 1587)

1594	Ingolstadt	1651	Krems	1659	Hall
1702	Neuburg	1709	Eichstätt		

Other subjects

1654	Aachen	1654	Cologne	1671	Vienna
1679	Freiburg	1682	Constance	1690	Vienna
1706	Klagenfurt	1741	Coblenze		

Plays dealing with Irish History

Saint Patrick (373 - 463), bishop

1641	Freiburg (CH)	1678	Ellwangen	1740	Ellwangen
1749	Landshut				

Other subjects

1622	Ingolstadt	1622	Dillingen	1645	s.l.
1700	Eichstätt				

As for English history, the following tables are meant to give an idea as to which subjects were frequently dealt with and to show that the Jesuits' interest was mainly focused on historical events of periods after the Norman Conquest. According to these tables, the fate of the English Lord Chancellor and author of the famous *Utopia*, Sir Thomas More, was the most popular subject of the matter in hand. Certainly, the life of St. Edmund, the fate of Charles I, the conflict between Henry II and Thomas Becket or the life of Edward the Confessor, were also quite often presented on Jesuit stages, yet the number of More-dramas is even higher than the sum of the plays written about these four different subjects. The undisputed dominance of More-dramas is further enlarged by the fact that at least three other plays, *Roffensis, Tragoedia*, 1612, *Fisherus Episcopus Roffensis Tragoedia*, 1714, and *Cromwellus Tragoedia*, 1724, also dealt with the reign of King Henry VIII and his breach with Rome.

The reasons which made British history and especially the above mentioned subjects so popular among Jesuit authors may only be assumed, but not clearly proven. Szarota has suggested that the defeat of the Spanish Armada and England's subsequent rise to become a world-power directed the Jesuit's attention to remarkable events and figures in Eng-

Most popular English subjects on Jesuit stages

Sir Thomas More (1477/78 - 1535), lord chancellor of Henry VIII.

1612	Rome		1620	Tournai		1622	Roermond
1625	Courtrai		1628	Schlettstadt		1631	Ingolstadt
1647	Bamberg	c.	1650	St. Omer		1656	Luxemburg
1666	Konstanz		1666	Lucerne		1666	Steyr
1680	Emmerich		1687	Ingolstadt		1688	Graz
1693	Luxemburg		1701	Innsbruck		1702	Eichstätt
1702	Wiener Neustadt		1709	Hildesheim		1711	Baden
1712	Ellwangen		1713	Hall		1718	Heiligenstadt
1718	Feldkirch		1721	Salzburg		1723	Munich
1725	Mannheim		1726	Augsburg		1727	Olmütz
1728	Molsheim		1730	Fulda		1733	Ieperen
1736	Coesfeld		1741	Brigue		1741	Linz
1746	Lucerne		1747	Dunkerque		1750	Sitten
1755	Solothurn		1758	Ingolstadt		1764	Constance

Saint Edmund (1170? - 1240), Archbishop of Canterbury

1605	Dillingen	1607	Paderborn	1614	Lucerne
1620	Krumau	1628	Lucerne	1629	Burghausen
1632	Krems	1636	Cologne	1643	Landsberg
1651	Dillingen	1698	Hildesheim	1736	Munich
1744	Augsburg				

Charles I. (1600 - 1649), King of England (1625 - 1649)

1696	Porrentruy	1700	Ingolstadt	1701	Ellwangen
1726	Brigue	1731	Hildesheim	1733	Neuss
1752	Feldkirch	1770	Jülich	1771	Münstereifel

Henry II. (1113 - 1189), king of England (1154 - 1189), and
Saint Thomas Becket (1118? - 1170), Archbishop of Canterbury

1625	Eichstätt	1626	Constance	1673	Landsberg
1720	Munich	1724	Ingolstadt	1746	Munich
1764	Straubing				

Edward or Eadward, called The Confessor (d. 1066), King of the English

1617	Olmütz	1644	Innsbruck	?	1704	Constance
1705	Eichstätt	1735	Ingolstadt		1741	Sitten
1747	Klagenfurt					

Edwin or Eadwine (585? - 633), King of Northumbria

1656	Cologne	1662	Düsseldorf	1668	Freiburg/Br.
1697	Lucerne	1751	Neuburg		

A good thirty other subjects of English history were treated in about forty-five plays performed between 1615 and 1769.

land's history.[17] England had been christianized comparatively early but then, in the reign of King Henry VIII, it established the Church of England and rejected the pope as head of the Catholic church. There can be little doubt that the Jesuits carefully observed all developments in this lost province, as they, at least secretly, hoped to win it back for Roman Catholicism. Moreover, in times of religious struggles, the Jesuits searched for historical situations in which the conflict between spiritual and secular power had been fought out.[18] In addition, they tried to find historical characters whose fates could be used as examples in teaching pupils and their parents to find answers to their everyday problems. British history proved to be a rich source of material for their purposes: it provided negative or ideal heroes as well as conflicts between *sacerdotium* and *imperium* or the popular conversion-tales.

The above arguments may be considered a satisfactory explanation of the Jesuits' general interest in English, Irish, or Scottish history, but they are not a convincing reason for the extraordinary popularity of a small group of plays which stand in sharp contrast to the large number of subjects only dealt with occasionally.

Therefore, I should like to point out a few characteristics of the repeatedly staged plays and to illustrate why Thomas More played such an eminent rôle in Jesuit drama.

The dramas under discussion can be divided into two major groups. The plays on Saint Edmund, Edward the Confessor, and Saint Patrick clearly revolve around a positive hero. The rest deal with historical events that had aroused great interest on the continent. Moreover, due to the intrigues of a number of negative heroes, they share a conflict-structure which reaches its climax in the death of the protagonist, be it Thomas More, Mary Stuart, Charles I, or Thomas Becket.

The christianization of foreign countries and the involved risks had at all times been very popular with the Jesuits. No wonder they wrote plays about Saint Patrick, who, equipped with the ability to perform miracles, succeeded in converting the Irish at the beginning of the fifth century. There can be little doubt that this wonder-working, which reached its climax in his opening of the gate to hell, and which could be presented in a most horrifying way on the well-equipped stages, very much appealed to

[17] Szarota, "Englische Geschichte," 490.

[18] Szarota, *Jesuitendramen. Eine Periochenedition*, vol. 1, part 1, 46.

the audience. Apart from this, St. Patrick was an ideal hero for the students, as purity and devoutness had determined his whole life.[19]

This applies also to Saint Edmund, the Archbishop of Canterbury, who appears in at least thirteen plays and who was one of the most attractive medieval characters, not so much because of his political qualities as because of his personal qualities. With regard to the moral-didactic purposes of the Jesuits, he was an absolutely ideal subject. Even as a child, St. Edmund had been a model of self-discipline. His austerity towards himself was balanced by extreme tenderness towards others. He soon won fame as a public preacher of extraordinary eloquence and at the pope's bidding, he preached the crusade over a great part of England. In the light of such a biography, it is no surprise that Jesuit dramatists quite often presented St. Edmund as a model according to which their pupils could shape their own lives.[20]

Compared with St. Edmund, Edward the Confessor was a less popular character on the Jesuit stages. As I mentioned above, he is another positive hero, whose virtues are worthy of imitation. He protected orphans and widows, founded Westminster Abbey, was at peace with everybody and a welcome party in the drawing up of contracts. His generosity, justice, kindness and humility are stressed repeatedly. To my mind, Edward the Confessor was for the Jesuits a personification of their "idea boni principis", which is illustrated in a drama of the same title, staged in the college of Mindelheim in 1703.[21] Thus, plays about Edward were not only instructive for the students of a college, but they also served as a mirror of contemporary magistrates or princes.[22]

Contrary to Szarota's opinion, Charles I appeared more than once on a Jesuit stage. In addition to the only play she seems to know, I was able to find titles of another eight and *periochae* of another six dramas on the subject. Considering that Charles I died a non-Catholic, it is indeed surprising how often the subject has been treated. An explanation for its

---

[19] Cf. *Orthodoxae veritatis prodigiosa* . . . , Ellwangen, 1672 and Szarota, *Jesuitendramen. Eine Periochenedition.* Vol. 1, part 2, 1769–71.

[20] Unfortunately most of the St. Edmund plays are lost. The *periochae* of the plays Burghausen, 1629, and Augsburg, 1744, which are kept in the Staatsbibliothek Munich and the Stadtbibliothek Augsburg respectively, give, however, a good idea of the Jesuits' presentation of the subject.

[21] *Idea boni principis per varia Spectacula In Documentum, Solatium & Exemplum afflictae Germaniae proposita*, . . . The Lat./Ger. *periocha* is reprinted in Szarota's edition, vol. 3, part 2, 827–34.

[22] Cf. particularly *S. Edovardus Rex Angliae*, Innsbruck 1644, *passim*.

popularity is to be found in the partial portrait of the King's character and life. In the extant dramas, Charles is portrayed as a king who favoured Catholics, re-established Catholic rites and planned to reunite his kingdom with Rome.[23] He becomes, however, a victim of Oliver Cromwell's intrigues, the latter stirring up his English subjects against the King. Under Cromwell's leadership they decide to execute Charles in order to keep Catholicism out of England. This partial presentation of the historical event that shocked the world in 1649, allowed them to depict Charles as a martyr for the Catholic faith, although this word is not mentioned *expressis verbis*.

In contrast to him, Mary Stuart is, in fact, portrayed as a martyr for the Catholic Church in the two *periochae* extant. I am quite convinced that the Jesuits dealt with her fate mainly in order to illustrate the consequences of Henry VIII's breach with Rome, Elizabeth being his child by Anne Boleyn. On the other hand, the unusual fact that two heroines were the focus of attention on a Jesuit stage might have promoted the subject's popularity. Mary Stuart is depicted as completely innocent and as a victim of the intrigues of her half-brother James Murray, who hopes to become king after her death. Queen Elizabeth, however, fears that Mary could succeed to the throne and re-establish Catholicism in England. Her decision to have Mary executed is therefore a preventive measure she has to take for the good of her state.[24]

The characterization of Mary as a weak-minded sacrificial lamb is in clear contrast to Becket's committed stand in church matters. Fearless, he fights against the king's attempts to curtail the traditional privileges and rights of the Church. As Szarota has illustrated, the conflict between Henry II and Thomas Becket had in many respects been very attractive for Jesuit dramatists.[25] Firstly, it could be used to symbolize the conflict between the German princes and the emperor during the Thirty Years War. Secondly, the subject provided the opportunity to present an ideal prince of the church, who had dared to oppose the king's wishes. Thirdly, the subject also allowed the inclusion of the conflict between Henry II and his rebellious son, who had tried to seize his father's throne. As

[23] Cf. *Carolus, Dises Namens der Erste Koenig in Engelland/Schott= und Irland...*, Porrentruy 1696, "Inhalt" and III, 4 and *Carolus I. Magnae Britanniae Rex Tragoedia*, Ingolstadt 1700, *Argumentum*. See also Szarota, "Englische Geschichte," 494–95.

[24] Cf. ibid, 497–99 and *Maria Stuarta Scotiae Regina Tragoedia*, Neuburg 1702, *Argumentum*.

[25] Cf. *Jesuitendramen. Eine Periochenedition*, vol. 1, part 1, 45 ff. and "Englische Geschichte," 490–92.

father-and-son-conflicts played an important rôle in Jesuit education, the subject was particularly attractive. Yet, it never grew as popular as the conflict between Henry VIII and his chancellor Thomas More, who had refused to accept the king as the Supreme Head of the Church and who had been executed for that offence in 1535.

Thomas More's extraordinary popularity on the Jesuit-stage is based on various characteristics of the subject and his person. His conflict with the king had taken place 350 years after the struggle between Henry II and Becket, and thus was of greater topicality for the Jesuits. Moreover, Thomas More's fate was strongly influenced by a woman, namely Henry's second wife Anne Boleyn, who in Jesuit plays is portrayed as a sinful herodias, who led the king to repudiate his first wife and to renounce the true faith. Her deeds served as an awful example of the consequences of a "schaedliche Weiber-lieb," of harmful women's love, as the *choragus* of the Ingolstadt play put it.[26]

The main reasons for the subject's popularity are, however, substantiated in the person of Thomas More himself. Unlike the heroes of the dramas discussed above, he was neither a clergyman nor a sovereign, but a layman in a position of high rank. Surrounded by his wife and his children he led a devout life, completely in keeping with Jesuit ideals. He was renowned as a very capable statesman, an impartial judge, a wise councillor and, what is stressed by the Jesuits, an author of religious writings. No wonder they made him a hero of their plays, the more so as the audience seemed to have loved him more than other protagonists. I think they loved him for his encouraging example and for his steadfastness which even the sight of Fisher's bloody head could not shake.[27] To my mind, it was, in particular, the willingness of the layman Thomas More to die for his faith which deeply impressed the audience and made them weep when he laid his head onto the block![28]

Universität Düsseldorf

---

[26] Cf. *Constantia Christiana Thomas Mori...*, 1758, *Argumentum* and "Zweytes Singspiel." See also *Thomas Morus Tragoedia*, Lucerne 1746, *Argumentum* and *Thomas Mohrus*, Mannheim 1725, *passim*.

[27] Cf. Thomas Morus Tragoedia, Rome 1612, III, 8 or *Thomas Morus Supremus Angliae Cancellarius...*, Constance 1666, II, 7.

[28] An event which is described in the *Litterae Annuae* of the Collegium Ellwangen for the year 1712.

Observations on J. L. Vives's Theory of Deliberative Oratory in De consultatione *(1523)*

MARC VAN DER POEL

One of Vives's less well known rhetorical treatises is *De consultatione*, "On political deliberation" or "On deliberation." Vives wrote this short work during his stay at Oxford in 1523, at the request of Louis of Flanders, a nobleman, who was at that time the ambassador of Emperor Charles V at the English court.[1] This work has been somewhat neglected by modern scholars, overshadowed as it is by some of Vives's other rhetorical writings both in length and in number of editions. It has been criticized strongly by the Spanish scholar Bonilla y San Martín, who considers it a bad political treatise and who writes, among other things, that it lacks originality and that its method is confused and arbitrary.[2] Bonilla clearly misjudges Vives's work, which is a truly rhetorical treatise on deliberative oratory. The aim of this presentation is to analyze briefly some sections of this short essay, mainly in order to illustrate its rhetorical focus and thus contribute to evaluating it fairly.

After a short survey of the contents we will point out a few interesting adaptations made by Vives to classical deliberative oratory, especially his

---

[1] Oxford-London 1523; *Opera*, ed. G. Mayansius (Valencia, 1782; reprint, London: Gregg Press Ltd. 1964) 2:238–62. Spanish translation in *Obras completas*, trans. Lor. Riber (Madrid: M. Aguilar, 1948) 2:807–28.

[2] A. Bonilla y San Martín, *Luis Vives y la filosofía del Renacimiento* (Madrid: Imp. del Asilo de huérfanos del S. C. de Jesús, 1903), 402–4.

treatment of *inventio*. For although Vives draws heavily on ancient sources (especially Aristotle, Quintilian and Cicero, as Bonilla y San Martín already stated),[3] he by no means follows them slavishly, but seems to rearrange them and, in addition, give new meaning to certain concepts.

When one looks at the global arrangement of *De consultatione*, one notes that Vives treats in succession the *inventio, dispositio* and *elocutio* of the *genus deliberativum*, omitting *memoria* and *pronuntiatio*, the fourth and fifth tasks of the orator. More than four fifths of the work, which comprises twenty-five pages in Mayansius's edition, is concerned with the *inventio*. The structure of *De consultatione* comprises a section which Vives refers to as *materia* or *seminarium universae inventionis*, and a section which he labels *de exercenda facultate*.[4] The section on *materia* comprises first of all an extensive survey of the *loci argumentorum a persona* which are relevant to the *genus deliberativum*.[5] Secondly, Vives describes the subject matter of deliberative oratory and discusses the general rhetorical goals at which the deliberative orator must aim.[6] In the part called *de exercenda facultate* Vives discusses first of all the way in which to handle the raw material of *inventio*. After having developed this point, he justly remarks that he has in fact not only dealt with *inventio*, but also with *dispositio*.[7] Next, he briefly discusses the *partes orationis* and the *elocutio*.[8]

After this brief summary let us now look at two interesting points in which Vives is clearly adapting the ancient theory to his own standards and, more in general, to those of his time. The first aspect concerns Vives's views on the range of deliberative oratory and its character in general.

It is quite striking that when Vives discusses the *loci argumentorum* (or *consideranda*, as Vives says himself) at the beginning of the treatise, he

---

[3] One can mention at least three specific points of reference: Aristotle, *Rhet.* 1.4.1–2; Cicero, *Inv.* 2.52.157 ff. and Quintillian, *Inst.* 3.8. See notes 5, 6, and 24.

[4] The first section covers pp. 238–45, the second pp. 245–62.

[5] This part begins with a brief mentioning of all the important aspects which must be taken into consideration in the deliberative process: "Ante omnia considerandum qui sit cui consulimus, tum qui nos, deinde qui alii consultores, et quibus de rebus, quo loco, quo tempore, ac rerum statu; quae sic volo esse a me posita, ut non longis intervallis cogitanda sint, sed velut uno oculorum aspectu colligenda, conferendaque inter sese . . ." (ed., Mayansius, 238–39). Compare, e.g., Quint., *Inst.*, 3.8.15.

[6] The definition of the subject matter is apparently derived from Arist., *Rhet.* 1.4.1–2: "Deliberatio omnis ac electio de futuris est, non necessariis, neque impossibilibus, sitis in manu deliberantis, ut agere ea possit, et non agere . . ." (ed. Mayansius, 241).

[7] ". . . hactenus *de inventione*, sub qua nonnullis in locis *dispositionem* quoque sumus complexi . . ." (ed. Mayansius, 258).

[8] Ed. Mayansius, 258–60 (*partes orationis*), 261–62 (*elocutio*).

concentrates on the *loci a persona*:

> in deliberante, et nobis, et ceteris consultoribus, denique in unaquaque persona, haec considerari debent, quae ante ipsam, quae cum ipsa, quae post ipsam; ante ipsam sunt majores ejus, et veteres omnes, hinc patria, tum quidquid actum, vel dictum est, quod ad ipsum possit quoquo modo pertinere, aut ad rem de qua deliberatur, velut exempla ex historia, ex fabulis, oracula, praedictiones, apophthegmata, sententiae, dicta vulgaria, proverbia; cum ipsa, quae in animo, quae in corpore, quaeque extra.[9]

Vives proceeds to discuss these last three points in great detail.[10] An explanation for this focus on the *loci a persona* at the beginning of the treatise can possibly (and, one might add, at least partly) be found in the fact that according to Vives the range of deliberative oratory is much wider than it is described in ancient theory. In the classical sources, deliberative oratory is generally confined to political matters, that is, matters related to the polis.[11] Quintilian vaguely suggests that other than political matters can be subject for discussion in deliberative oratory.[12] Vives states bluntly: "De omnibus quaecunque sunt in nostra potestate consultamus, de operibus manuum, et actionibus animi."[13] He immediately adds that these subjects are treated after consideration of the ambition and ability to proceed to an action.[14] At this point, the three categories of credentials, that is, the physical and psychological constitution and the social status and material condition, all three mentioned at the beginning of the treatise, are relevant. Indeed, concerning ambition, the counsellor must evaluate the possible objective motives to aspire to a physical or mental action, as well as the possible affective, emotional elements influencing the ambition. Ambition is however limited by the ability to

---

[9] Ed. Mayansius, 239.

[10] Ed. Mayansius, 239–40. It is remarkable that Vives's discussion of the *loci a persona* seems more elaborate than one finds in the classical sources and that, as we will see, he concentrates in his discussion of the *res expetendae* on the category of *honestum* (ed. Mayansius, 242–43). Compare for instance Cicero's discussion of the *loci* in *De inventione*, in which more attention is paid to the *loci a re* than to the *loci a persona* (*Inv.* 1.24.34–25.36, *loci a persona*; 1.26.37–28.43, *loci a re*).

[11] See, e.g., Aristotle, *Rhet.*, 1.4.7.

[12] Quintilian, *Inst.*, 3.8.14–15.

[13] Ed. Mayansius, 242.

[14] ". . . tranctantur haec perpensa voluntate et facultate, nam qui et potest, et vult, faciet, utique non facturus si alterum desit . . ." (ed. Mayansius, 242).

proceed to an action. It is in this area that, as Vives explains, the physical condition and the character, and also the financial and social condition must be taken into account.[15]

A second factor explaining the focus on the *loci a persona* right at the beginning of the treatise becomes manifest in the section *de exercenda facultate*. In this section Vives, following basically the classical theory of ethos, states that the counsellor, in order to reach his goal of persuasion, must do all he can to ensure the impression that he is a friendly and a good and wise man.[16] Although Vives does not explicitly refer here to the credentials mentioned at the beginning of the treatise, his discussion of the subject makes clear that he is dealing exclusively with the *loci a persona*. For in the process of establishing his authority, it is very important that the counsellor knows which attitude to take towards his hearer, who can be his equal, but who can also be his superior or inferior. This last point seems to be a somewhat new aspect in deliberative oratory, at least, that is how Vives presents it to the reader. In the old days of free republics, he explains, it was allowed to attack any person who did not agree. Even then it was a rule that one should not speak evil of those who had a good reputation. This is true even more so for us Christians, he says, but he adds that the counsellor must also bear in mind that one must use a different tone towards equals—say, members of a City Council—than towards a superior—say, the emperor.[17] In short, we read, the sixteenth-century counsellor must always adapt his behavior to the standards of modesty and gravity.[18] It is obvious that the consideration of all the credentials, as mentioned at the beginning of the treatise, of the persons involved in the deliberative process is essential in doing so.

Let us now briefly take a look at a second area where Vives seems to modify ancient theory. We have seen that he defines the vast field of human activities (the *opera manuum* and the *actiones animi*) as the subject matter for deliberative oratory and that in each deliberative process,

---

[15] Ed. Mayansius, 242.

[16] "Duo sunt in consiliis potentissima ad persuadendum, opinio probitatis, et opinio prudentiae . . ." (ed. Mayansius, 245); "Ergo tota oratione danda opera est, ne quid dicas quod opinionem vel probitatis, vel amicitiae, vel prudentiae imminuat, augeat potius quantum licebit . . ." (ed. Mayansius, 247). Compare the general remarks on ethos in Aristotle, *Rhet.* 1.2.4; 1.8.6; 3.7.6–7, and the treatment of ethos in Quintilian, *Inst.* 6.2.13–19.

[17] Ed. Mayansius, 249.

[18] ". . . quum nihil magis deceat consulentes, quam modestia et gravitas" (ed. Mayansius, 249).

ambition (*voluntas*) and capability (*facultas*) must be taken into account. Vives measures the whole area of human actions on a moral scale defined by two opposites, good and bad. Ultimately, he says, every deliberation is concerned with just these two notions, for man's *voluntas* is by nature directed towards the good.[19] The emphasis on the natural morality of man, which is one of the premises of Vives's entire philosophical thought,[20] induces an adaptation of the classical analysis of the rhetorical goals to aim at (*res expetendae*) and thus also modifies Vives's general viewpoints on the *loci*. The ancients were not entirely consistent in their treatment of this subject. Aristotle equates the good with the useful and states that the useful is the main goal in deliberative oratory.[21] Cicero and Quintilian, both following the Stoic tradition, make a distinction between the honest and the useful and accept that either one of these can legitimately be a goal to strive for,[22] although they claim that of course the honest is the more important goal.[23] Vives focuses on the *bonum* and subdivides it, in Aristotelian fashion, into *bonum per se* or *honestum* and *bonum propter aliud* or *utile*. He critically discusses Cicero's analysis of these concepts in the second book of *De inventione*.[24] In the process of doing

[19] "... quoniam omnia ad voluntatem deliberantis referuntur, illud enim modo quaeritur, ut velit, aut nolit, voluntasque in bonum semper fertur, ... fit, ut omnis deliberatio sit de bono, et hinc de contrario hujus malo ..." (ed. Mayansius, 242).

[20] C. Noreña, *Juan Luis Vives* (The Hague: M. Nijhoff, 1970), 200ff. ("The Naturalistic Emphasis"). Also quite illustrative of Vives's claim that man's will is directed by nature towards the good is the introduction to book III of *De anima et vita*, dealing with the *affectiones*: "Condidit omnia Rex naturae, ut illis de suo impartiretur esse, quo essent, de sua vero beatitudine, ut bene essent ... ad quae sua assequenda et conservanda munia, attribuit facultates, ad esse quidem, pronitatem, ut se quicque ab injuria tueatur corrumpentis, quoad ejus possit efficere, ad bene autem esse, appetitum boni, aversionem a malo, ut in bonum feratur appetitus, a malo declinet et fugiat ..." (ed. Mayansius, 3:421).

[21] Arist., *Rhet.* 1.6.1.

[22] See Cicero, *Off.* 1.9–10 for the Stoic viewpoints. In *Inv.* 2.52.157–8 Cicero discerns three *genera rerum expetendarum*, the *honesta*, things to be sought for their own sake, such as *virtus*, *scientia* or *veritas*, the *utilia*, things to be aimed at for their practical use, such as *pecunia*, and things which are mixed, such as *amicitia* and *bona existimatio*, which are also termed *honesta*. Quintilian also accepts that either *honestum* or *utile* is a legitimate aim to strive for (*Inst.* 3.8.30). Compare also, e.g., Erasmus's discussion of this topic in *De conscribendis epistolis*; he distinguishes six groups of *loci*, *honestum, utile, tutum, iucundum, facile, necessarium* (ASD I, 2 (1971), ed. J.-Cl. Margolin, 366; *honestum* is discussed on pp. 366–69, *utile* on 369–70, *tutum, iucundum, facile* and *necessarium* are explained briefly on 399).

[23] Cic., *De orat.* 2.82.334; *Inv.* 2.57.173; Quint., *Inst.* 3.8.1.

[24] Ed. Mayansius, 243; Cic., *Inv.* 2.52.157–56.170.

so, Vives presents his own theory on the *bonum*, especially the *bonum per se*. First of all, Vives excludes, as already mentioned, the *utile* from the goals to aim at.[25] Secondly, Vives's definition of *honestum* is entirely different from Cicero's and illustrates his concern for Christian values. *Honestum* comprises first of all things connected with God, such as faith or knowledge and adoration of the Divine; moreover, it covers things connected with human beings, among which are mentioned first of all the social values expressed in the Gospel, such as love for one's neighbor, justice and beneficence. Finally, Vives allows room for the classical values, such as glory and power, but he qualifies their validity carefully.[26]

Thus it becomes clear that to Vives much, if not all, of the deliberative process is to be centered around Christian values. Interestingly, this focus also influences significantly Vives's precepts on the use of *exempla* and the handling of emotions, the *affectus*. As to the *exempla*, Vives simply stresses that they must come from primarily Christian sources.[27]

Quintilian speaks of the importance of arousing emotions, such as anger, fear, ambition, hatred and reconciliation, thus voicing a widely accepted view in ancient rhetorical theory.[28] Vives on his part says that emotions must not be aroused, for this would be contrary to the necessity of gravity and probity. This does not mean, however, that emotions should be absent from the deliberative speech—for then the discourse would

---

[25] "... et inter honestum quidem ac utile, si modo Christianos nos esse meminimus, nulla erit controversia: olim Romanus populus saepe numero in deliberationibus illud usurpabat, *Vincat utilitas* ... nos vero dicamus, *Honestas vincat*, seu potius, *vincat religio*" (ed. Mayansius, 251). Vives may have in mind Quint., *Inst.* 3.8.30, where an example is given from Roman history illustrating the prevalance of the *utile* over the *honestum*. Vives describes the category of the *utile* as follows: "illa ... praecipua, quae ad tuendam vitam sunt reperta, nec in praesens modo comparantur, sed in posterum quoque prosunt ... quae ad delicias, voluptatesque per omnes sensus, et quae animo sunt jucunda," and finally "speciosa et magnifica" (ed. Mayansius, 244).

[26] "In honesto potissima esse convenit quae ad Deum pertinent; hujus generis sunt pietas, ardor rerum supremarum, cognitio et adoratio illius omnipotentis naturae, quam cognitionem Dominus in Evangelio pronuntiat esse vitam aeternam ... secundum locum obtinent quae ad homines, ut caritas in illos, quod est Christi praeceptum, tum justitia, propulsatio injuriae, liberalitas, beneficentia ... post haec acumen ingenii, judicium, eruditio, dignitas, honor, laus, gloria, gratia, auctoritas, potentia, et per quam nonnulla ex his parantur generis claritudo; quae si ultro contigerint, et moderate utaris, in emolumentum aliorum, pulchrae res sunt, et magnificae ..." (ed. Mayansius, 243).

[27] Ed. Mayansius, 254. Vives also allows didactic fables, which figured among the standard *exempla* in ancient theory and practice.

[28] Quint., *Inst.*, 3.8.12.

cease to be rhetorical, but rather that the counsellor must try to balance emotions in order to secure moral standards.[29]

Although our discussion of *De consultatione* has been far too general to come to any definitive conclusions, it seems possible to sum up a few general points and formulate a few observations, which will perhaps stimulate further discussion and study of this work. First, *De consultatione* is not confusedly written and slavishly modelled after ancient sources, as has formerly been pointed out. It would seem appropriate to carry out a detailed comparison between Vives's work and that of other humanist theorists of deliberative oratory. Such an analysis would make it possible to determine to what extent, if at all, Vives is innovative in this field. Second, the need for high moral, more specifically Christian, standards is evident in every paragraph of the treatise. This need not be a surprise in a work written by Vives, and it is consistent with early sixteenth-century rhetorical theory in general. It seems more important to note that Vives extends the range of deliberative oratory from political matters to human deeds, both physical and mental, on the one hand, and that, on the other hand, in all sections of his theory, man, both as an individual and as a social being, is the touchstone by which all things are judged. One might say this particular interest for the human individual is not surprising in a writer like Vives. However, the definition of the range of deliberative oratory in terms of all human activities does seem unusual. One could

---

[29] "Affectus non sunt in hoc genere, ut in aliis nonnullis, concitandi et perturbandi, propterea quod alienum id videtur a gravitate et probitate, quae in consultationibus exigitur, vellicantur tamen nonnumquam, idque vel ex rebus ipsis per amplificationem, si ostendantur esse graviores, atrociores, majores, meliores, honorificentiores, utiliores, jucundiores, tutiores, quam primum intuenti videantur, praesertim accommodatis his ad aliquem affectum quo maxime teneatur, vel proximum ei, ut atrocitas atque indignitas iracundo proponatur, injuria vel contemptus superbo, alienum bonum invido, honor ambitioso, divitiae avaro, ambiguum dictum suspicaci, periculum meticuloso, labor segni" (ed. Mayansius, 254). Vives treats the *affectus* in considerable detail at 254–56. The fundamental importance of a proper handling of *affectus* is explained by Vives in *De ratione dicendi*, when he calls them the "facultas animi, qua de bono vel malo opinato movemur" (*De ratione dicendi* 2.14, ed. Mayansius, 2:164); compare the definition of *affectus* by Aristotle (*Rhet.* 2.1.8), whose treatment of the subject greatly influenced Vives, but whose definition lacks the moral quality inherent in Vives's definition. In the same chapter, Vives stresses that a careful balancing of emotions is necessary. To this end, it is important, among other things, to consider the psychological and material aspects of the persons involved (in other words, the credentials mentioned at the beginning of *De consultatione*). In the chapter on *decorum* (*De ratione dicendi* 2.16), he again stresses that the *affectus*, if handled improperly, are likely to harm the communicative process (ed. Mayansius, 192–93).

perhaps suggest and argue that through the broad definition of the field of deliberative oratory, Vives aims not only at the political counsellor in the strict sense, but at any educated member of Christian society who masters the principles of rhetoric. Thus, the vast range of *opera manuum* and *actiones animi*, defined as the subject of deliberative oratory, would comprise any topic an intellectual writer, any *orator* or *rhetor*, might choose to write upon, with the restriction that it be treated according to Vives's moral standards. If this makes sense, then *De consultatione* could perhaps be useful to help understand the nature and purpose of many sixteenth-century writings with a rhetorical structure written by authors who profess to write as a *rhetor* or *orator*. *De consultatione* should then not only be considered as a treatise on a specific kind of oratory with limited range, but also as a theoretical description of the function of rhetoric in the early sixteenth-century intellectual community.

Instituut Griekse en Latijnse Taal en Cultuur Nijmegen

Antiquitas Superata: In carminis epici Ubertini Carrarae (1642–1716), cuius index est Columbus, *librum sextum observationes selectae*

HERMANN WIEGAND

Multi fuere poetae et Itali et peregrini, qui carminibus heroicis res gestas Christophori illius Columbi celebrarent, quod Americae quam vocant inventor esset.[1] Inter quos extant et aliquot auctores Latini, quorum plerique vestigia Vergilii summi poetae subsecuti Columbum ut alterum Aenean ad sidera tollunt. Quamquam fortasse supervacaneum esse videtur eorum seriem reddere, tamen faciam, ut appareat, quatenus Carrarae carmen cum eorum carminibus cohaereat quidve novi ad historiam Columbi poeticam Latinam afferat. De Laurentio Gambara, qui, si partem libri tertii *Syphilidis* Fracastorii excipias,[2] primus hac via ac ratione usus est, post Genofevam Demerson[3] disserturus est Henricus Hofmann.

---

[1] De historia poetica Christophori Columbi disseruerunt i. a. viri docti Carlo Steiner, *Cristoforo Columbo nella poesia epica Italiana* (Voghera, 1891); Antonio Belloni, *Gli epigoni della Gerusalemme liberata. Con un' appendice bibliografica* (Padova, 1893); Marcos A. Moringo, *América en el teatro de Lope de Vega* (Buenos Aires, 1946); Ernst Wetzel, *Der Kolumbus-Stoff im deutschen Geistesleben* (Breslau 1935); confer etiam: E. Ceva Valle, "Columbo," in *Dizionario letterario delle opere e dei personaggi* (Milano, 1950), 1:306; Elisabeth Frenzel, "Kolumbus" in eiusdem *Stoffe der Weltliteratur* (Stuttgart, 1976), 416–21; "Columbo" in *Grande Dizionario Enciclopedico UTET* (Torino, 1967), 5:108; "Colombo" in *Enciclopedia Italiana* (1950), 10:811; G. Bianchi, *Cristoforo Colombo nella poesia italiana, Parte primera, Poesia epica* (Venezia, 1892) (quem librum non vidi). Cf. etiam "Colombo, Cristoforo" in *Dizionario biografico degli Italiani* (Roma, 1982), 27:168–200.

[2] Usus sum editione: *Girolamo Fracastoro, Lehrgedicht über die Syphilis*, ed. Georg Wöhrle (Bamberg, 1988; =Gratia 18), 3. v.102 sqq.

[3] Geneviève Demerson, "La tradition antique dans la première épopée co-

Reliquorum poetarum praestantiores ordine temporum breviter recensebo, sed ita, ut ea tantum in medium proferam, quae meae de Carrarae carmine commentatiunculae usui fore possint. Petrus Angelius Bargaeus libro sexto *Syriadis*, quam iure quodam appelles *Hierosolymam liberatam* Latine confectam,[4] vaticinium de "Ligurum decore"[5] inseruit, quo nomine poeta Christophorum tamquam alterum Godefredum terrae sanctae liberatorem ornat, ut Italiae gloriam novi orbis Christianitati addicti vindicet. Magis quam Bargaeus Vergilium imitatus est Julius Caesar Stella[6] carmine iuvenili *Columbeide*, quod primum publici iuris factum esse videtur Londini anno 1585.[7] Quo in carmine Stella nobilis Romanus Francisci Benci S. J. discipulus pro Iunone Vergiliana diabolum inimicum consilio Dei Christianorum inducit, qui mentem Ascanii cuiusdam ad tumultum contra Columbum faciendum concitat, ut ille cursum navium mutet retroque in patriam vertat. At is oratione Vergiliana Deum orat, ut se adiuvet, quia nec praedae nec imperii cupidine commotus novum orbem adire velit, sed ut omnes gentes Deum verum agnoscant et colant. Dei nuntius mentes nautarum in melius mutat, et Christophorus vel Ascanium persuadet iter reliquum conficere. Breviter Stella his verbis usus Spiritus Sancti mentionem facit:

> . . . Tibi quae corda abdita, sancte
> Spiritus, aethereos afflas qui sensibus ignes?. . .[8]

ut divinitus mutatas mentes indicet.

Proximus ordine Vincentius Placcius Hamburgensis admodum adulescens laudes Columbi carmine epico uberrime notis adornato praedicavit. Cuius *Atlantis retecta* ter edita[9] discrepat cum aliis poetis, qui de America inventa cecinerunt, cum Atlantidem, quam more Claudiani et saeculi sui ipsius persona ficta inducit querentem, quod nondum inventa

---

lombienne . . ." in *Colloque l' épopée gréco-latine et ses prolongements européens, Calliope 2.* ed. R. Chevalier, (Paris, 1982), 237–54.

[4] Cf. Petri Angeli Bargaei *Poemata omnia* . . . , (Romae: Ex typographia Francisci Zanetti, M.D.LXXXV), *Syriados libri sex priores*, 6.168–69.

[5] Eodem loco 168, V. 19.

[6] De quo se retulisse mihi scripsit Henricus Hofmann. Vide nunc: Heinz Hofmann, "La scoperta del nuovo mondo nella poesia latina: i *Columbeidos libri priores duo* di Giulio Cesare Stella," in: *Columbeis III* (Genova, 1988), 71–94.

[7] Iulii Caesaris Stellae Nob. Rom. *Columbeidos libri priores duo* (Lugduni, 1585).

[8] Eodem loco C 3^v, V. 18 sq.

[9] Prima: Hamburgi 1659; altera ibidem 1665; tertia eademque definitiva editio in: Vincentii Placcii *Carminum puerilium et iuvenilium libri IV* (Amstelodami: Apud Petrum Le Grand, M.DC.LXVIII), 1–82. Editionem cum versione Germanica praeparo.

sit, non more illo Platonis[10] civitatem legibus ac institutis satis ornatam fingit, sed rudem et omnis fere cultus egentem, quae mores Christianos ac religionem veram desideret. Placcius pro diabolo Stellae, cuius carmen ignorare videtur, Vetustatis personam fingit, quae quia retegi non vult sororem Discordiam instigat, ut Rodericum quendam nobilitate superbum ad coniurationem in Columbum humili loco natum virtuteque sui ipsius fretum ideoque despectum conflandam adducat. Hieronymum Benzonem secutus[11] memorat Columbum oratione nautis habita pollicitum esse se in patriam cum eis rediturum, nisi intra triduum terra iam diu expectata appareat.

Eiusdem Societatis Jesu ac Carrara sacerdos fuit Nicolaus Parthenius Giannettasius Neapolitanus, qui exeunte saeculo XVImo carmen didascalicum composuit, quo artem nauticam docuit.[12] In cuius carminis libro octavo dissimili modo ac plerique poetarum, quos iam memoravimus, Columbum describit: huius enim poetae eximii Columbus Uraniae nymphae ac Apollinis filius more summorum virorum Romanorum cupiditate dignitatis ac gloriae accensus ardet magnum illud opus detegendi orbis novi perficere. Mater a filio, quod se moretur, incusata Columbum magna nympharum caelestium comitante caterva ex insula quadam Fortunata in regiam caelestem ducit–imitatur Somnium illud Scipionis auctor–unde prospiciat et orbem veterem et novum, in quo insulam Haiti, quae acceptura sit naves eius. Sed antequam iter faciat, Oceanum, Doridem, Ammericen placandos esse. Haec omnia more poetarum veterum finguntur.

Priusquam ad poetam nostrum veniamus, necesse est mentionem faciam ultimi poetae Latini–quem quidem novi–qui carmen epicum Columbianum condidit, dico Aloisium Mickl, qui postea fuit abbas Hohenfurtensis Bohemus; is adulescens undeviginti annorum carmen, cui index *Plus ultra*, composuit (anno 1730), quo monstrat iure quodam divino Columbum illud "Non plus ultra," quo proverbio antiquitas vetuit naves ultra columnas Herculis provehi,[13] superavisse. Affirmare ausim carmen Carrarae Micklio notum fuisse. Editori eius sane exempla poeseos Columbianae prorsus ignota erant.[14] Non solum structura carminis Mick-

---

[10] Vide Platonis *Timaeum* 22a sqq. et eiusdem philosophi *Critiam*. Cf. et *Novam Atlantidem* Francisci Baconis.

[11] Usus sum Latina versione Urbani Calvetonis, *Novae novi orbis historiae, id est rerum ab Hispanis ... hactenus gestarum* ... (s. l.: Apud Eustathium Vignon, M.D. LXXXI), 27.

[12] Nicolai Parthenii Giannettasii ... *Piscatoria et Nautica* (Neapoli, 1686), 236–46.

[13] De hoc loco cf. librum Heydenreichii (A. 29), passim.

[14] *Plus ultra. Ein lateinisches Gedicht über die Entdeckung Amerikas durch Columbus verfasst von ... Joh. Christian Alois Mickl*, ed. Rudolf Schmidtmayer S. Ord. Cist. (Wien, 1902).

liani quadrat Carrarae carminis conformationi, sed etiam singula: Eodem nomine quo Carrara Mickl e.g., hostium Columbi ducem Androphagum nuncupat; canoae Caribum eodem fere modo describuntur a Micklio ac a Carrara; Superstitionem auctricem refert belli contra Columbum ineundi Mickl ut Carrara & etc.

Ne autem longius a proposito digrediar, iam necesse est convertamur ad *Columbum* Ubertini Carrarae. Carmen, cuius auctor sententia Hoeferi[15] renovator poeseos Latinae saeculo XVIIImo nominari potest, in lucem prodiit primum anno 1715 (Romae apud Rocchium Barnabo), iterum anno 1725, tertium autem anno 1730 Augustae Vindelicorum recusum est. De eo egerunt hoc saeculo Mario Segre geographus anno 1925,[16] cuius librum anno insequenti P. Petrus Tacchi Venturi S.J.[17] recensuit, et proximo abhinc anno (postquam iam annuntiavi hanc commentationem) Marius Martini Soranus[18] civis patriae poetae, qui adiecit commentationi suae textum (satis mendosum) libri primi cum versione Italica Gregorii Redi aequalis Carrarae, necnon carmina tria minora, quae una cum *Columbo* ea sunt poetae nostri, quae ad nos pervenerunt amissis aliis, in quibus et carmina vernacula lingua scripta fuerunt. Segre diligenter fontes et historicos et litterarios operis exquirit, exempla affert quaedam selectiora styli; monstrat Carraram consilio quidem operis Vergilium, coloribus autem maxime praeter Ovidium Lucanum et Statium secutum esse.[19] De vita Columbi agit, quomodo eam tractaverit Carrara, disputat de imagine, qua ille populos Americae repraesentaverit, quaerit, quid poeta de insulis Fortunatis, de Atlantide, de Ulixe prodiderit. Hunc enim indigenae libro sexto ad oram insulae appulisse perhibent eamque patrio nomine Ithacam appellasse; Columbus eam mutato nomine Hispaniolam nuncupavit. Huic commentationi autem vita Carrarae praemissa est, quam Venturi ex tabulario Societatis Jesu Romano correxit. Martini vitam auctoris denuo fusius exponit paraphrasique Italica summam totius operis retractat additis singulorum librorum argumentis ab ipso auctore conscriptis, quae ex unico manuscripto primus edit.

Rebus sic stantibus utile non putavi fore integrum opus denuo fusius

---

[15] Cf. *Nouvelle Biographie generale*, ed. Michaud, (repr. 1964), 8–9, 815 sq.

[16] Mario Segre, *Un poema Colombiano del Settecento, Il "Columbus" di Ubertino Carrara* (Roma: Instituto Cristoforo Colombo, 1925).

[17] P. Tacchi Venturi S. J., *Il "Columbus" dell' Arcade Eudosso Pauntino, Estratto da L' Arcadia anno 1926* (Roma, 1926).

[18] Mario Martini, *Ubertino Carrara, Un Arcade Umanista* ... (Sora: Centro di studi Sorani, 1987).

[19] Cf. Segre (A. 16), op. cit., 147 sqq.

tractare; itaque eam partem elegi explicandam, qua navigatio ab insula Magna Canaria ad Hispaniolam usque continetur, quae pars est media eademque summa operis. Ita procedam: Praemissa brevissima vita auctoris explicatoque argumento structuraque carminis locos quosdam libri sexti praestantiores examinare temptabo, ut ostendam, qua voluntate quoque consilio Carrara opus confecerit. Natus est igitur Ubertinus Carrara nobili genere Sorae, in civitate regni olim Neapolitani die 13mo mensis Martis anno 1642; Societatem Jesu ingressus est die 21mo mensis Aprilis anni 1662. Per viginti tres annos artem rhetoricam in praeclarissimo Societatis Jesu collegio Romano professus est. Socius Academiae Christinae Sueciae reginae iam ab anno 1679 factus sodalis Arcadiae quam dicunt Romanae creatus est anno 1694 sub nomine Eudoxi Pauntini. Carmen *Columbum* per quadraginta annos elaboravit, anno ante mortem in lucem edidit, obiit autem die sexto mensis Ianuarii 1716.[20]

Opus eius magnum duodecim libros continet, quorum sex priores iure dicas Odysseam alteram, posteriores autem Iliada, ita ut structura carminis Carraram Vergilii imitatorem esse ostendat. Primo libro exposito auctoris consilio—dicit se illum velle virum canere, qui novum orbem veteri adiecit —invocatis Musa fautoreque operis Benedicto Pamphilio Bibliothecae Vaticanae tum praeside Columbus naves Gadibus solvit. Discordia tamquam altera Iuno Vergiliana labaro crucis exterrita Proteum incitat, ut mare perturbet. Tempestate orta Aretia, quae Veneris Vergilii personam gerit, ad Summum Tonantem querelam defert et convocato concilio caelestium, quod fata ab inimica sua prohibeantur, conqueritur. Cui Deus respondet fata mutari non posse. Venturum esse diem, quo die Christophorus novum orbem retecturus sit Auriaque, regis Cubani filia sibi ob pietatem dilecta Americo illi Tusco nuptura nomine mutato America futura sit. Quam Auriam poeta et Laviniae et Camillae virginum Vergilianarum moribus praeditam fingit. His dictis placata Aretia Teneriffam se confert, ut omnia adventui Columbi praeparet, quem tempestas a sodalibus distraxit, quorum naves duce Vasco, quem Ilioneo Vergilii conferas oportet, ad Canariam insulam appulsae sunt. Teneriffae in porta Iani Aretia hunc versum invenit inscriptum: "Ianua pandetur nulli, quae ducit ad Indos," quem ita mutat: "India pandetur, patriam cui Ianua fecit;" ut alludat ad patriam Columbi Ianuam vel Genuam. Discordia indefessa Theromantidi sacerdoti imperat, ut sodales Columbi phantasmatibus Bacchicis in Canariae detineat—agnoscis imitationem Circae Homericae. Theromantis sodalibus more Ovidiano fabulam de Eutychies et Bacchi

---

[20] Eodem loco, 13 sqq.; Martini (A. 18), op. cit., 1 sqq.

sacris nuptiis narrat. Libro tertio Aretia Columbo vaticinatur futura in clipeo depicta, qui clipeus ad exemplum Vergiliani libri octavi procusus monstrat imperatores domus Austriacae orbi universo dominaturos. Sequenti libro Columbus tamquam alter Perseus aegide usus sodales fascinatione Theromantidis liberat, quae frustra inferos carmine arcessere conatur. Ut taedium itineris fallat, Columbus libro quinto de pugna navali apud Malacam Isabella regnante contra Mauros commissa narrat. Libro sexto torpor maris sociis navigationis causa est rebellandi contra Columbum auctore Alvaro quodam, qui praetorem navis interficere conatus tandem in mare proicitur. Sed Fernandus Christophori filius, cum parricidis obstiterit, in aquas praecipitatus mergitur mortuusque habetur. Spiritu Sancto adiuvante malacia tollitur. Atlantis illa sub mari visa index est terrae propinquae, quae statim apparet. Cuius incolae Berecynthiae matris statua, quam Ulixes attulerat, disrupta advenas ut deos colunt vetante id Columbo, qui eos verum Deum hoc effecisse docet. Libro septimo scaena mutatur. Cum tempestas Discordia instigante insulam Cubam devastaverit, oraculum imperat, ut Auria, regis Arviragi filia monstro immoletur. Hostia a Columbo ab Aretia praedocto servatur. Carrarae haec fingenti Ovidii fabula de Perseo et Andromeda exemplo fuit, quod virum doctum Martini fugit.[21] Liber octavus vice carminis didascalici est: Amicitia inter Arviragum et Columbum pacta advenae et indigenae sibi invicem divitias suas monstrant, in quibus animalia, fruges suaves, bombardas necnon alia nova inventa. Columbus futuras nuptias Auriae sive Americae cum Americo Tusco praedicit. His irata Superstitio vitia Europaea mundo novo immittit, ut litem inter Hispanos efficiat. Qua lite placata Duellum, Bellonae filius, Androphagum, regem Cannibalum Auriae procum, qui ut Mezentius Vergilii divos contemnit, adducit, ut aemulum suum Columbum cum sociis Cubanis perditum eat. Libro decimo fata Fernandi Columbi narrantur, qui more Dantis Aligherii vivus a Nerina nympha in conclave Aletiae sub mari situm ducitur, ubi multa de rerum natura docetur. Tandem emersus a Vasilinda, Androphagi sorore Iuthurnae personam gerente, invenitur, quae eum fratri commendat socium, quia necem patris ab Alvaro Hispanisque ulcisci velit. Bellum inter Cannibales, filios Noctis, et Cubanos, filios Solis, eorumque socios Hispanos summa vi apud Avanam, Cubae caput, geritur. Occisis multis pugnantibus, in quibus erant Vasilinda ac Androphagius, alter Turnus, Fernandus filius patrem Columbum, quem falso Alvarum esse putat, auctore Duello aggreditur. Cognita re inter se conciliantur, poetae Carrarae autem

[21] Martini, op. cit., 52.

inter Barbaros Indos lingua Latina loqui iam desueto Romam redire in animo est.

Argumento totius operis examinato diligentius inspiciamus locos quosdam selectos libri sexti, ut consilium auctoris in carmine pangendo eluceat. Eius libri initio simile a Vergilio sumptum, sed proprie mutatum ac amplificatum, invenitur: Auctor, ut monstret Columbo semper mundum novum in animo esse, eum cani Umbro comparat, qui sollerter ea quoque observat, quae non videat, et eum venatorem terrae appellat. Eo maxime a Vergilio differt Carrara, quod simili uno non contentus alia addit, quibus desiderium eius vehemens terrae novae videndae exprimat. Quippe inter alia aegroto similem Columbum repraesentat, qui febribus vexatus aquam haurire vult, quae nusquam est. Spem novi orbis potiundi navigatori sidera nova nondum visa addunt, quae novis hominibus lucere oportet. At socii spe deiecti inconstantia mentium contra ducem murmurant. Malacia, id est pigritia maris, statim exorta Alvarus quidam "indolis Afrae" homo arrepta occasione orationem habet, cuius argumentis percipias, qua mente ac voluntate Carrara *Columbum* perfecerit. Sunt ea:

> En quo verbosi Liguris vesania tandem
> Perduxit miseros: en quos invenimus Indos.
> Stamus ubi vivis vel respiramen ademptum;
> Scilicet hoc etiam restabat, ut improbus iste
> Praedo, domos postquam, dulces cum coniuge natos
> Abstulit, & terram, raperet post omnia Coelum,
> Quin ipsum mare quo vehimur: non cernitis? haesit
> Torpens unda, nec ire licet *vetitumque* redire.
> Ni fallor, locus hic *sacer* est, hominique *negatum*
> *Tangere*: summa Parens rerum, quo fessa diurnis
> Membra ministeriis tandem requiescere possent,
> Hac, procul ex hominum vulgo, regione remotâ
> Quaesivit somnos ac si pudor esset, alumnis
> Cerni posse suis, & non operosa videri.
> Illius arcanum quod vestigare cubile
> *Sacrilegis ausi remis*, has pendere *poenas*
> Cogimur: una tamen superest via, grande *piandi*
> *Delictum*, si causa mali *cadat hostia Ductor.* [22]

---

[22] Ubertinus Carrara, *Columbus Carmen Epicum* . . . , (Romae; Typis Rocchi Bernabò, MDCCXV) 6, p. 130, v. 159–76 (numeratio versuum mea est).

Eadem fere argumenta profert Fernandus, cum libro XIImo de patris conatu narrat.[23]

Iam relationes saeculi decimi sexti, quibus Carrara usus est, nautas contra ducem murmuravisse narravere. Fernandus Columbus in vita patris auctor est eos patrem in mare praecipitare voluisse.[24] Columbum cum eis pactum esse memorat, ut, nisi terra intra triduum appareret, vela mutare vellet. Quam rem et nonnulli poetae perhibent. Sed plerique alias afferunt causas, quibus moti nautae seditionem conflaverint: Apud Fernandum Columbum nautae ducem peregrinum sententiis doctissimorum omnium terrarum scriptorum repugnantem, oderunt, apud Benzonem nautae Columbo–id quod auctor Italus aegre fert–ut impostori Genuensi maledicunt.[25] Poetarum voces omnium afferre non possum. Ascanio illi apud Stellam auctorem diabolus mutata forma penuriam longa navigatione perferendam cassamque spem reditus perfidiamque Ligurum notam[26] proponit. Vincentii Placcii nautis nobilitas generis ipsorum causa est seditionis contra ignobilem navis praetorem excitandae,[27] Micklii viros tempestas maris Vergiliana metu implet maximo.[28]

Argumenta Alvari apud Carraram aliunde sumuntur, antiquitatem enim redolent. Mare hominibus vetitum esse ac sacrum plurimi poetae veteres persuasum habuerunt. Supersedeo locos singulos afferre. Titus Heydenreich in libro, cui titulus est "Lob und Tadel der Seefahrt"[29] (Laudes et Vituperationes Navigandi) omnes fere locos ad rem pertinentes auctorum veterum eorumque imitationes in litteris, quas Romanicas appellant, collegit.[30] Notissimus est locus ille Horatii in Propemptico Vergilio dicato:

Nequiquam deus abscidit
   prudens Oceano dissociabili
terras, si tamen impiae
   non tangenda rates transsiliunt vada.

---

[23] Op. cit., p. 260–61, v. 588–652.

[24] Cf. *Vita di Cristoforo Colombo, descritta da Fernando, suo figlio*, tradotta da Alfonso Ulloa, Nuov. ed. (Londra, 1867), 67.

[25] Cf. A. 11, op. cit., 26.

[26] Cf. A. 7, op. cit., B 3^r sq.

[27] Cf. A. 9, ed. definitiva, op. cit., 37 sq.

[28] Cf. A. 14, op. cit., 1, v. 446 sqq.

[29] Titus Heydenreich, *Lob und Tadel der Seefahrt, Das Nachleben eines antiken Themas in den romanischen Literaturen* (Heidelberg, 1970).

[30] Op. cit. (A. 29), 15–48. Non nominat Carraram.

audax omnia perpeti
gens humana ruit in vetitum nefas[31]

quem locum Carrara imitatus esse videtur. Ex carminibus Columbianis unius tantum loci reminiscor, cuius iam mentionem feci: in In Nauticis Giannettasii mater Urania Columbum adhortatur, ut antequam per mare naviget, Oceanum placet:

Ante sed Oceanus placandus, & humida Doris,
Nate, tibi, facilisque simul Dea divitis Orbis
Ammerice [. . .][32]

Frustra quaeres in libro doctissimo Heydenreichii locos, ubi de hominibus dis maris iratis immolandis agatur. Quod Columbum hostiam dis maris caedendam putat Alvarus Carrarae, pluribus e fontibus hausisse videtur poeta: Sinonem Vergilii, qui se ipsum hostiam nominat,[33] imitatus est—versu 106to libri sexti Carrarae nautae tumultuantes Columbum "Italum Sinonem" appellant—necnon eiusdem poetae Palinurum, qui tamquam hostia a dis poscitur.[34] Fatum instans Iphigeniae quoque poetam in animo habuisse credam.[35] Denique e diverso ab his fonte Carraram hausisse contendere ausim: Ionae dico prophetae sacrificium.[36] Dubium enim esse non puto, quin sacerdoti Carrarae sors illius prophetae ante oculos fuerit, cuius nomen Hebraeum "Iona" viri docti interpretantur "columbam."[37] Hanc sententiam eventus rei, quem Carrara quidem fingit, probare videtur: Alvarus primus coniuratorum praetoria rostra ascendere conatus ipse patitur, quod Columbo destinaverat.[38] Columbus autem, ut animos nautarum tranquillet seque ipsum confirmet, Spiritum Sanctum invocat, ut veniat seu forma linguae igneae seu specie columbae.[39] Consulto vates noster Spiritum Sanctum hic propio nomine appellavisse videtur mythologicam circumscriptionem Vergilianam evitans, qua libro

---

[31] Horatius, carmen 1.3.21 sqq.

[32] Cf. A. 12, op. cit., 245.

[33] Cf. Vergilii Aeneidem 2.154 sq.

[34] Op. cit., 5.835 sqq.

[35] Cf. e.g., Lucretium 1.82 sqq.

[36] Cf. Hans Schmidt, *Jona, Eine Untersuchung zur vergleichenden Religionsgeschichte* (Göttingen, 1907), 96 sqq.

[37] Cf. e.g., Hieronymum Lauretum, *Silva allegoriarum totius Sacrae Scripturae* (repr. München, 1971), 579: Ionas, id est columba.

[38] Carrara, op. cit. (A. 22), 6, 132, v. 230–44.

[39] Op. cit., 6, 134, v. 294 sqq.

primo usus erat, cum concilium deorum, cui Summus Tonans vaticinatur fata Columbi,[40] fingeret. Hoc loco poeta indicat antiquitatem, cuius personam Alvarus ille gerit, a Deo Christianorum navigationi Columbi propitio superari, ideoque eum Iovem Tonantem nuncupare nequit. Quare e Trinitate Divina hic Columbus Spiritum Sanctum oret, ut veniat, duae sunt causae: prima, quod pro tempestate Vergiliana[41] torporem maris inducit seditionis apertae causam, quem torporem qui tollat solus idoneus est flatus Spiritus Sancti; altera, quod similitudine nominis fretus non solum praenomen Christophori pro omine habuerit, sed etiam nomen gentile columbam Sancti Spiritus referens, cui quadrat quoque nomen "Ionae" vel Columbae prophetae.[42]

Quod hoc loco observavimus, antiquitatem superari a Christianismo, causa esse quoque videtur, cur Carrara ab reliquis poetis Columbianis quodam modo differat in describendis novi orbis incolis. Iam feminas Magnae Canariae Ovidium imitatus[43] libro secundo ornatu Bacchico vestiverat. In hoc sexto libro apparatus ille antiquus magis in aperto est: Adiuvante Spiritu Sancto, cuius flatus nautis pro prodigio est, iter pergentes sub mari sitas ruinas civitatis magnae vident, quam Ergastus quidam eos docet esse Atlantidem Platonicam civitatem olim et legibus et iustitia ornatissimam. Non casu hae ruinae speciem quandam ruinarum Romae prae se ferunt, illius dico Romae, quae ob superbiam moresque Christo repugnantes corruerit:

> Quaedam strata solo, quaedam inclinata iacebant
> Fragmina, spirabantque tamen vel naufraga fastum.
> Tale quid adveniens dominam novus accola Romam
> Aspicit in Caveâ, frendens ubi carcere coeco
> Tigris erat, patrii nemoris, rupisque relictae
> Saevior exilio: donec spectante Senatu
> Pascerent humano jejunia longa cruore,
> Et sua terribiles trepidarent gaudia Cives;
> At nunc mole ruinarum, & squallore verendo
> Obruitur decus antiquum, stat pensilis horror
> Semirutae majestatis, titubatque vetustas
> Casum ferre gravem: spectacula prisca requirens

[40] Op. cit., 1, 21–23, v. 379–469.
[41] Qua usus est libro primo, op. cit., 18 sq., v. 308 sqq.
[42] Cf. epistolam Columbi apud Heydenreichium, op. cit. (A. 29), 158.
[43] Cf. Carraram, op. cit., 1, 33–34, v. 122–78 et Ovidii Metam. 3. 511 sqq; 4. 1–32.

Hospes nulla videt, lacerum premit herba cadaver
Spectatorque sui est nunc funeris Amphitheatrum.[44]

Spectaculum illud non tam est, ut vult Martini, signum destructionis, mortis, fragilitatis,[45] quam signum interitus antiquitatis paganae.[46] Ergasto enim ruinae praesagiunt terram novam meliorem renascentem, quae profecto mox videtur. Incolae eius terrae—quae est insula Hispaniola—non sunt illi "nudi sine ponderibus, sine mensura, sine mortifera denique pecunia, aurea etate viventes sine legibus," quos describit Petrus Martyr de Angleria,[47] quem plurimi auctores secuti sunt, sed hos Carrarae poetae Indos Ulixes erroribus suis huc iactatus illos mores "delirantis Areopagi"[48] docuit deamque Berecynthiam colendam. Cuius simulacrum iam corruit tremore terrae, cum advenirent Hispani labarum crucis erigentes. Quo facto re vera evenire videtur, quod prodigium illud a Sancto Spiritu datum pronuntiaverat: Superari antiquitatem quamvis cultissimam a duce Christiano. Non diutius quaerendi sunt fontes huius partis operis Carrarae, quos Segre non invenit.[49] Ulixes ut Alvarus personam gerit antiquitatis paganae; cuius tumulus imaginibus magnarum ab Ulixe rerum gestarum ornatus significat vanitatem gloriae a summis viris antiquitatis petitae. Qua in re enarranda Carrara certe locum illum libri primi *Aeneidis* in animo habuit, ubi Aeneas nube tectus in templo Iunonis imagines belli Troiani contemplatur:

Artificumque manus inter se operumque laborem
Miratur, videt Iliacas ex ordine pugnas,
Bellaque iam fama totum volgata per orbem,
Atridas Priamumque et saevum ambobus Achillem.
Constitit et lacrimans: "Quis iam locus," inquit, "Achate,
Quae regio in terris nostri non plena laboris?
En, Priamus! Sunt hic etiam sua praemia laudi."[50]

---

[44] Cf. Carrara op. cit., 6, 137, v. 400–413.

[45] Martini, op. cit. (A. 18), 50.

[46] Carrara refert ad vituperationes Romae antiquae Christianas. Quibus opponit libro IIIio ecclesiam S. Petri Teneriffae aedificandam, op. cit., p. 61 sqq., v. 332 sqq.

[47] Cf. Petrus Martyr de Angleria, *Opera* . . . , repr. ed. intro. Dr. Erich Woldan (Graz, 1966), 46.

[48] Carrara, op. cit., 6, 146, v. 690.

[49] Cf. Segre (A. 16), op. cit., 124.

[50] Vergilius, Aeneis 1, 455 sqq.

Cui loco Vergiliano velim conferas contrarium *Columbi* Carrarae:

> Singula quae docti postquam monimenta laboris
> Vidit (scil. Columbus) & explicuit, nec non miseratus inanem
> Curam hominum de victuro post funera busto,
> Tanquam non etiam tumulos sua fata manerent....[51]

Spolia illa antiquitatis vati nostro instrumenta sunt ad veram gloriam ducis Christiani augendam: vincit enim antiquitatem cultam, non feram barbariem.

Quanti Carrara ipse materiam operis aestimaverit, testatur in libro quarto: Columbo socios quaerenti occurrit Poesis ipsa, quae enumerat exempla veterum poetarum, qui summos viros cecinerint: Homeri Iliadem, Thebaidem Statii, Pharsalia Lucani, Valerii Flacci Argonautica, Aeneidem Vergilii.[52] Quin Columbo inter hos summos viros antiquitatis primus dignitatis gradus debeatur, Carrara non dubitat; itaque vel Vergilius summus poeta vix sufficiat res gestas eius enarrare:

> Tu quoque, si prisco vixisses tempore, magnam
> Arboris in nostrae partem, Columbe, venires;
> Praelatumque duci Phrygio te clara Maronis
> Forsan in Heroem legisset Buccina, si non
> Actis pressa tuis timuisset fabula vinci.[53]

Carrarae poetae prae omnibus qui res gestas Christophori Columbi carmine Latino celebraverint palmam dare equidem non dubito.

Karl-Friedrich-Gymnasium, Mannheim;
Germanistisches Seminar der Universität Heidelberg

---

[51] Carrara, op. cit., 6, 146, v. 680 sqq.
[52] Carrara, op. cit., 4, 76, v. 99 sqq.
[53] Op. cit., 4, p. 76, v. 109 sqq.

Vives's De Europae Dissidiis et Bello Turcico, *the Quattrocento Dialogue and "Open" Discourse*

MICHAEL ZAPPALA

In the past, Vives's works most often were read for their philosophical, psychological or pedagogical value.[1] This non-literary parsing was not challenged either by Vives, a frequent critic of imaginative literature, or by the categories established by Mayans in his *Opera Omnia.* Only more recently, with the studies of Coseriu, Norland, or Swift and the first critical edition of Vives's early works has the Valencian begun to be read as an author of highly inventive fiction.[2] While critics of literature have studied *praelectiones* such as "Veritas Fucata" or "Aedes Legum," they have yet to treat Vives's dialogue of the dead, his *De Europae dissidiis et bello*

---

[1] Walter A. Daly, *The Educational Psychology of Juan Luis Vives* (Washington, D.C.: 1924); Carlos Noreña, *Juan Luis Vives* (The Hague: Martinus Nijhoff, 1970); A. Bonilla y San Martín, *Luis Vives y la filosofía del Renacimiento* (Madrid, 1929). Lorenzo Riber, ed. and trans., *Obras completas de Juan Luis Vives* (Madrid: Aguilar, 1947).

[2] For Vives's Neo-Latin fiction, see Abdón Salazar, "Los cinco mitos clásicos de Juan Luis Vives," in *Cuadernos del Sur,* 11 (1972): 37–62. There are also the more recent contributions of Eugenio Coseriu, "Acerca de la teoría del lenguaje de Juan Luis Vives," in *Tradición y novedad en la ciencia del lenguaje: Estudios de historia de la lingüística* (Madrid: Gredos, 1977), 62–85; Louis J. Swift, "*Somnium Vivis* y el *Sueño de Escipión,*" in *VI Congreso de estudios clásicos: Homenaje a Luis Vives* (Madrid: Fundación Universitaria Española, "Seminario Nebrija," 1977), 89–112; Emilio Hidalgo-Serna, "*Ingenium* and Rhetoric in the Work of Vives," in *Philosophy and Rhetoric,* 16 (1983): 228–41; Howard B. Norland, "Vives' Critical View of Drama," in *Humanistica Lovaniensia,* 30 (1981), 93–107. The only critical edition to date of Vives's early fiction is *Early Writings.* intro., crit. ed., trans., and notes C. Matheeussen, C. Fantazzi, and E. George, eds., (New York, Leiden: E. J. Brill, 1987).

turcico, which still awaits a critical edition, a good translation and a literary reading.[3] Marcel Bataillon, for example, only explores this work for the author's ideological positions (Vives as Erasmist, his views on European politics, and Spanish political hegemony),[4] and treats Vives's dialogue much in the same way he treats Alfonso de Valdés's apology of imperial policy, disregarding the clearly different modes of development and argumentation presented in the two apologies.

The literary value of Vives's dialogue on the division of Europe and the Turkish threat can only be recuperated by situating it in the tradition of the *dialogus mortuorum.* The work was written in 1526, a time when Lucian was very much in the Valencian's thoughts.[5] The cast of *De dissidiis* (Minos, Colax, Tiresias, Basilius, Polypragmon, Scipio) is typical of a *dialogus mortuorum.*The presence of the speaker-critic, the underworld setting, the review of souls, the expression of curiosity which motivates the investigation of the political strife of Europe—Minos asks Tiresias what is happening on earth to make so many souls descend, "nam animae huc decidunt tam densae, quam vel grando vehementi aliquo turbine excussa vel folia flante per auctumnum Borea" (453)—recall similar passages in the Charon dialogues of Lucian, Pontano and Erasmus, and anticipate Alfonso de Valdés's *Mercurio y Carón.*[6]

To designate Vives's work as a *dialogus mortuorum,* however, still leaves the critic with the question: which kind of dialogue of the dead? Lucian's literary praxis was not that of his Quattrocento imitators. In fact, some of the contradictions in Vives's development of this work can only be explained by the history of the dialogue form and the transformations it underwent in the hands of the Italian humanists.[7]

---

[3] The old Gregorio Mayans y Siscar *Opera Omnia* (Madrid, 1782–1790), without critical apparatus and an *apparatus fontium,* is, as C. Matheeussen explains (Juan Luis Vives, *Early Writings,* ix), outdated. The translation of Lorenzo Riber does not at all points correspond to the original. Yet in view of the very few editions of *De dissidiis,* the lack of a rigorous edition is less critical than in the case of Vives's more frequently printed works. All Latin quotes from the *De dissidiis* are from *Opera Omnia,* ed. Gregorio Mayans (Valencia, 1783; repr., London: The Gregg Press, 1964), vol. 6, 452–81.

[4] Marcel Bataillon, *Erasmo y España,* trans. A. Alatorre, 2a edición corregida y aumentada (México: Fondo de Cultura Económica, 1966), 615–18.

[5] *Litterae Virorum Eruditorum ad Franciscum Craneveldium 1522–1528,* ed., notes., and commentary, Henry de Vocht (Louvain, 1928), letter of 17 February 1526.

[6] Alfonso de Valdés, *Diálogo de Mercurio y Carón,* ed. José F. Montesinos (Madrid: Espasa-Calpe, 1929), 7–8.

[7] For a history of the Lucianic *dialogus mortuorum* in the Quattrocento, see M.

A hallmark of Lucian's dialogues which sets them apart from the philosophical Ciceronian dialogue or the didactic dialogue of the Middle Ages is the avoidance of "closure" whether ideological or discursive. Definition is normally avoided in Lucian's works by undercutting the authority of the narrator, by interrupting the direction of a line of thought with a dramatic event, or by the use of irony and paradox to suggest that the meaning of the text is contrary to the letter.[8]

The quattrocento humanists (Poggio Bracciolini, Leon Battista Alberti, Aeneas Sylvius Piccolomini, Giovanni Pontano), while they imitate many of the conventions of the Lucianic dialogue, also modify the Syrian's impartial and "open" discourse and place it at the service of a specific agenda. Peace and the need for institutional reform were not, for the majority of humanists, a value-free exploration. The translation of Lucian's Attic Greek into versions marked by a Latin ideal of *gravitas* reinforced this closure.[9] The early Latin renditions of Lucian as well as later imitations are characterized more by demonstration than by the fanciful play of personalities in the satires of Lucian.

The satiric dialogue in the Quattrocento, then, was, from the point of view of discourse, a double tradition: in the Greek original, the discourse was "open." In the Latin translations and imitations, the discourse tended to defend a specific agenda and was, as a result, "closed." For most of the authors of Renaissance *dialogi mortuorum,* it was the Latin Lucian which furnished a model for their discourse.

Vives's *De dissidiis* reflects the contradictions of this double tradition of dialogue discourse. Like the quattrocento reformers, he chose a theme of great political concern–the work was written only three years before the siege of Vienna– a theme treated in the anti-Turkish literature of the period with maximum closure. Yet Vives's treatment is conspicuously "open," and is typical neither of the Lucianic imitations of the quattrocento nor of contemporary chancellery propaganda.

The language of *De dissidiis* is marked by neutralization and inversion

---

Zappala, "Lucian in Italy and Spain (1400–1600)" (Ph.D. diss., Harvard University, 1975).

[8] See *Philopseudes* (29). In the *Musca,* the avoidance of closure is effected by the mock-encomium, and in the *Vitarum Auctio,* the number of contradictory ideologies expounded assures that no single point of view, other than the reductive skepticism of the buyer, will mark the work.

[9] Deborah Shuger, "The Christian Grand Style in Renaissance Rhetoric," in *Viator,* 16 (1985), 337–66. For Lucian and *trattato*-like discourse, see E. Mattioli, *Luciano e l'umanesimo* (Napoli: Istituto italiano per gli studi storici, 1980).

of the polarities of the contemporary political discourse. This reworking of language is, in a sense, not surprising, since all of the Valencian's writing reflect the preoccupation with the relationship between *res* and *verba* logical in a writer who is twice bilingual. In the historical divide between proponents of a "natural" and "conventional" nature of language, Vives falls into the second camp.[10] Words such as "barbarus" (454) and "haeresis" (455) are for Vives culturally relative. Political discourse in particular reveals what he calls the "stulta ambitio nominis sine re" (466), *verba* unrelated to any existing *res.* In *De dissidiis,* he unmasks the manipulators of empty language, whether it is Europeans who band together in "foedus quod sanctum appellarunt" (462), or those who are "Christian" in name only.

In *De dissidiis,* the most important neutralization operates on antitheses expressing cultural antagonisms and their respective moral worlds: Europe/Asia, Christians/Turks, Lutherans/Catholics, and Spaniards/Italians. The author defuses the antithesis Turks/Europeans, for example, by pointing the finger at his own Europe. The origin of the Turkish threat for Vives is largely the fault of Christian insolidarity—"dissidia"—and is, in view of the idea, common in that period, of the weakness of Asia and strength of Europe, an historical anomaly. It is the Christian princes, eager to destroy rather than reform their fellow leaders (455) who are responsible for the Turkish advance.

Vives also neutralizes political polarities by equating Turks and Christians. If a question of Minos—"Quid agunt principes? quid Christiani? quid Turca?" (454)—suggests contrasting groups, Polypragmon's answer identifies the two groups: "Propemodum eadum ista, et bellum ubique, discordiae, odia" (454). The author applies this formula of equation to European affairs as well. Faction-ridden friars are counterbalanced by uncharitable Lutherans (455), and the abuses of the Spanish soldier weighed against those of the Italian soldier (462–63).

Through the reformulation of antitheses—win/lose, triumph/defeat, fame/shame—as identities Vives dismantles conventional discourse and forges a new vocabulary of anti-fame and anti-glory. The Pyrrhic victory is the paradigm of the battle descriptions in the dialogue. One encounter,

---

[10] M. L. Cozad, "A Platonic-Aristotelian Linguistic Controversy of the Spanish Golden Age: Damasio de Frías's *Diálogo de las lenguas (1579),*" in *Florilegium Hispanicum: Medieval and Golden Age Studies presented to Dorothy Clotelle Clarke,* eds. J. S. Geary et alii (Madison: Univ. of Wisconsin Press, 1983). As E. Coseriu has shown ("Acerca de la teoría del lenguaje," 66), Vives does not reject in theory a "lingua perfectissima," but generally treats languages as culturally determined entities.

described as an "ingenti praelio," is "atque ambiguo" (460). A Spanish victory is presented as a lesser defeat—"magna utriusque gentis strage, sed, quod res indicat, Gallorum maiore" (459)—and, in another case, victory is viewed as an ephemeral passage into defeat: "Pugnatum ... ingenti et cruento praelio: Galli quidem victores, sed ita accisi ut coacti sint Italia decedere." Phrases such as "non sine periculo" (458), "in medio fortunae belli" (458) and "gravi bello" (459) neutralize the polarity victory/defeat.

Vives also inverts the civilization/barbarism topic. It is, he claims, Christians who most often use artillery, so that the Turks are forced—"coacti"—to use these new military machines to defend themselves. Related to the inversion of moral antitheses is the reversal of the polarity pagan/Christian. Tiresias exclaims to the nominally Christian Basilius at one point: "Hoc ego scio gentilis, tu ignoras Christianus?" (471). Basilius responds, "Ista Christiana? Audis, Tiresia?" (471).

In the inverted language-world of the *De dissidiis,* agent of destruction and victim are identified. "Suffer" and "inflict," for example, become nearly interchangeable terms in Vives's description of the imperial troops bottled up at Ticino: "maxima fuisset vel accepta ab eis clades, conclusis et fugientibus, vel certe data a desperatis" (461). Likewise, armies "dant damna atrocissima, et accipiunt" (474). This identity of agent and victim ultimately fuses the "other" with the self: "Periculum adit, qui facit" (461), Tiresias states at one point. He later confirms this conflation with the *sententia,* "Qui ad se Martem accersit canem rabidam, fieri secus non potest quin mordeatur" (462). Tiresias, finally, refers to the bands of strife-torn Europe as agents of self-destruction: "Dic uno verbo, hostem esse quemque sibi ipsi" (456).

The openness of the *De dissidiis* is also a function of characterization. Seemingly autonomous speakers guide the development of the dialogue. Often Minos, the impartial judge of the Underworld, directs the dialogue by means of stylistic observations: "Satis es prooemiatus, narra tandem" (453); "dic paucis" (479); "exspecta finem colloquii" (471). The judge, however, does not mandate either during the dialogue or at the end, any single solution, but praises Polypragmon for the impartiality of his narration of European affairs between 1445 and the early sixteenth century (48).

The universalizing viewpoint of the speakers, typical of Lucian's dialogues, serves in *De dissidiis* to satirize the national and dynastic aspirations presented by Polypragmon. The power plays between France, Spain, and Italy are described as child's play. War is referred to as a "brevi comoediae" (458). Vives's reduction of heroic action to fate and his insistence that history is not defined at any point—the incursion of Charles VIII into Italy closes with the king's untimely death and the loss of the conquered territory (458); Navarre is won and then lost (461)–make the strategems of the generals appear ludicrous, and invalidate partisan ambition.

The rhetoric of the *De dissidiis* also reinforces the open discourse of the piece. Questions are answered by questions (452–53). The repetition of the key question of Minos–"Posses ne nobis, Tiresia, dicere, quaemadmodum se se res hominum apud superos habeant?" (452)–serves to collect and qualify a series of answers. Alternative hypotheses are common,[11] declarations are inverted ("sed quid juvat quando non pecuniam regunt reges, sed ipsos pecunia?" [454]), and overly emphatic statements reinterpreted to achieve diminutio. When Polypragmon boasts "Aperuit Alpes Carolus" (457), Tiresias responds: "Hoc est, patefecit aditum spoliationibus, cladibus, miseriae Galliae" (457).

The most striking features of the openness of this dialogue are the contradictory solutions to the Turkish problem presented toward the end of the work, the normal place for closure, by two speakers of great authority, Tiresias and Scipio. The solution of Tiresias the seer, like his refutation of Basilius's praise of military glory, is typical of humanistic irenicism in general as well as of Vives's own *De concordia et discordia* and the late *De pacificatione*,[12] and furnishes what appears to be a closing resume of the conversation and of its corresponding rhetoric up to that point. The dialogue appears to close on affirming a single point of view: the noble Minos and Tiresias present what the reader takes to be the view of the author, and the opposing viewpoint is presented by discredited speakers.

When Vives introduces Scipio, however, the tapestry unravels. Scipio, an exemplar for the renaissance of the civil and military virtues of the Roman Republic,[13] advocates an invasion of Asia for glory and booty, a project which squarely negates the pacificism of Minos and Tiresias. The general's reference to heroes–"Ergo nullus est jam locus, nec honos viris fortibus?" (467) he exclaims when he learns of the invention of the cannon–for example, runs directly counter to Tiresias's description of them as "latrones" (472). Scipio's praise of the "praeclarum decus" and "ingens nomen" (479) as incentives to spur the Christian princes to invade

[11] "Sed quandoquidem te arbitraris hominem, illos deos, aut illos homines, te pecudem . . ." (469); "ut est genus hominum insolens, vel odio quietis atque otii cujus sunt impacientes . . ." (458–59).

[12] Philip Dust, "Luis Vives's Pacifist Sociology in *De pacificacione*," in *Acta Conventus Sanctandreani*, 211–16.

[13] See Giuliana Crevatin, "Scipione e la fortuna di Petrarca nell'umanesimo," in *Rinascimento*, 17 (1977): 3–30; David Cast, "Aurispa, Petrarch and Lucian: an Aspect of Renaissance Translation," in *Renaissance Quarterly*, 27 (1974): 157–73.

Turkish lands contradicts the radical irenicism of the first half of the work. Scipio explicitly criticizes the anti-glory stance of Minos when he notes that "ingens nomen" was something that "meo quidem tempore gloriosum in primis ac praedicandum censebatur" (479).

Though some of Scipio's positions coincide with those of the discredited speakers, his allusion to his own considerable experience, a powerful source of *captatio,* his disinterested pragmatism and the concreteness of his proposals in the face of a pressing problem invite the reader's belief.

The Roman's political agenda creates its own discourse. The antitheses, fused as identities in the speech of Minos and Tiresias, are restored as polarities. Asiatics ("meticulosos homines et bello minime idoneos") and Europeans ("animo ac viribus praestantiores") are presented as clearly distinguished geographical and moral groups (477). Not only are the Asians "worse," they are profoundly "other." Scipio urges the Christians to fight "contra homines alienissimos, procul dissitos, hostes religioni suae ac nominis" (473). The prominent antitheses of Scipio's speech and the use of verbal strategies such as *anteoccupatio* to discount other viewpoints make the general's discourse a notable exception to the discursive "openness" of the rest of the work.

These two world views and their related discourses touch only tangentially in the work. The first half of the dialogue treats only part of the title–*De dissidiis Europae*– and presents through Minos and Tiresias an irenic critique of politics in Christian Europe. Scipio's speech addresses only the second half of the title–*De bello turcico*–and largely parenthesizes the value system of Minos and Tiresias.

Is Vives arguing for an excision of idealism and pragmatism? In view of Scipio's closing remarks, apparently not. The general, having stated the benefits of glory and conquest–and the evangelization of new peoples–expresses a single, critical, doubt which though marking the space between his program and the Christian ideal also provides a point of contact: "Nescio an idem Christo videatur, sed certe hoc tolerabilius malum quam furor ille civilis dissidii" (479).

Tiresias's response to Scipio is surprisingly oblique. He replies only that evangelization should be carried out "non vi aut armis" (479). While Tiresias's comment is not surprising in view of Vives's preoccupation with conversion as member of a *converso* family, it is unusual that the seer should pass over in silence the numerous discrepancies between Scipio's advice and his own. Indeed, only when Minos urges Tiresias to provide his solution to the Turkish problem does the seer furnish a plan which in turn parenthesizes Scipio's proposed invasion. For Tiresias, the only strength of Christians is "Christi ... tutela" (480). Christ's protection is "inexpugnabile" (480), and those under it are "inviolabiles cunctis ... nationibus" (480). In expounding his program of defensive containment, Tiresias exhorts the Christians to pray for peace, and mentions the war against the Turk only as an opportunity for a lesser evil: "aut si regnum liberet augere, alienissimum potius, et pietatis hostem, bello impeterent, quam vicinum, sanguine et mysteriorum initiatione conjunctum" (480). His plan is shorn of Scipio's vision of glory and wealth, nor does it explicitly address the vigorous expansion of the Turks chronicled in the first half of the work.

Even this exposition in the last pages of the dialogue, the appropriate place for closure, is undermined by the seer's own doubts: "non puto esse consiliis locum, nam omnia saevae atque atroces animorum affectiones occuparunt, nec consiliis est ullus aditus" (480). When Minos asks him whether the things he has foreseen will occur, the seer answers "aut facient, aut non facient" (481).

Tiresias's wavering response could as well describe the discourse of *De dissidiis.* At times the language affirms a single value system and at other times denies it. The work, like Tiresias's closing prophecy, is Vives's attempt to frame a dilemma. Different value systems and their corresponding language worlds and courses of action cross only obliquely as unresolved possibilities.

It is instructive to compare the directed, closed discourse of Alfonso de Valdés's *Diálogo de Mercurio y Carón,* an apology of the foreign policy of Charles V, with the language of *De dissidiis.* In the *Diálogo* of Valdés the obligatory defense of imperial policy is reflected in the progressive loss of dialectic tension. Dialogue becomes a monologue voiced by characters defined at times by little more than the rubric on the page. Valdés himself refers to this transformation in discourse in the preface to the reader. While the *dialogus mortuorum,* he writes, had seemed at the outset to suit his purpose, it later became so irksome that he was tempted to destroy the work. Having adopted an "open" form–the dramatic *dialogus mortuorum* in the tradition of Lucian of Samosata–he found it difficult to close.

In the case of Vives, the "open" structure which marks other works of his, in particular the *Exercitationes Linguae Latinae,* was natural to him, since he conceived of the examination of the world around him as a dialogue between object and subject, between objective moral order and the flawed, subjective tools of human investigation. This dialogue of continuous opening and closing, of frequently reversible definition, is inscribed in the discourse of *De dissidiis Europae et bello turcico.*

University of Maryland

Science versus Secular Life: A Central Theme in the Latin Poems of Tycho Brahe

PETER ZEEBERG

The astronomer Tycho Brahe is without doubt the best known character of the Danish renaissance. His international fame is based, not on any single great discovery—like, e.g., Kepler's discovery of the laws of movement in our solar system—but on his being the founder of modern observational astronomy. He was in fact the first one to engage in regular, systematic observation of the stars, and the data he compiled over more than twenty years became the material upon which were based the scientific advances of the following century—and especially Kepler's.

My concern here, though, is not astronomy but his Latin poetry, which in my view is interesting not only for its literary value, but also as a source of knowledge as to his position in the cultural life of Denmark at the time, and as to the atmosphere in which research was carried on at his castle Uraniborg.

But first some biographical facts.[1]

---

[1] The fundamental Tycho Brahe biography is J. L. E. Dreyer, *Tycho Brahe, a Picture of Scientific Life and Work in the Sixteenth Century* (Edinburgh, 1890; repr., New York, 1963). More recently: C. Doris Hellman, "Tycho Brahe," in *Dictionary of Scientific Biography*, ed. C. C. Gillispie, vol. 2 (New York, 1970), 401–16, and Wilhelm Norlind, *Tycho Brahe, En levnadsteckning med nya bidrag belysande hans liv och verk* (Lund, 1970) (in Swedish). – Bibliography: Victor A. Thoren, "Tycho Brahe, Past and Future Research," *History of Science* 11 (1973): 270–82. Tycho's complete works have been published in fifteen volumes: *Opera omnia Tychonis Brahe Dani*, ed. J. L. E. Dreyer, Hans Ræder and Eiler Nystrøm (Copenhagen, 1913–29; repr., Amsterdam: Swets & Zeitlinger, 1972).

He was born in 1546 as the eldest son in a family belonging to the highest aristocracy. He was therefore sent on the usual grand tour of several German universities to study the subjects that would be of use in a career in politics, law in particular. What he learned, though, was astronomy and chemistry. On his return he settled down in his native Scania (then part of Denmark) to pursue these, for a nobleman, quite unsuitable interests.

We have a letter of his from 1576 which gives a clear impression of his situation in this period. Tycho writes to a close friend, a professor at the university of Copenhagen, that he has decided to move to Basle, in order to get the right facilities, and the right milieu, for his studies. He obviously felt that the traditional ideals of the nobility made it impossible to him to pursue his scientific interests seriously. In the letter he complains about having to associate with so many others of his own class, which is utter waste of time, and then goes on: "You know how alien is the behaviour of these noblemen to my way of life—and to philosophy itself. There are exceptions, but I do wish there were more of them."[2] However, his plans came to nothing: in the very same letter he announces that the king, Frederic II, has offered him the island of Hven in the Sound between Copenhagen and Elsinore, and the money to build a castle there. This became one of the most impressive prestige projects Denmark has seen, a scientific academy—named Uraniborg or Uraniburgum after the muse—which Tycho ran for twenty years, supported with huge sums by the crown.

Latin poetry played a great part in life at Uraniborg, at least to Tycho. We have all kinds of poetry from his pen, from impromptu epigrams, over single verse lines dispersed in the prose of his scientific works, to more ambitious poems of several hundred verses. Some belong to private life, others are distinctly official, like the dedications in his printed works, or, in another way, the many inscriptions at Uraniborg. The latter were obviously intended mostly for the many guests that frequented the place, and they were indeed all printed in the official description of the house.[3]

---

[2] Letter to Johannes Pratensis, 14.2.1576 (*Opera omnia*, 7:26): "Cum mei ordinis hominibus, quoniam crebrius mihi agendum est, præsertim Herressuadij, Avunculum, quando apud ipsum dego, convenientibus, aut etiam me ipsum Knudstorpij invisentibus (alias enim quantum possum illorum consortia subterfugio) multum temporis mihi perit, multa alias ingrata audienda et facienda. Nosti enim quam sint nobilium horum mores a meis institutis alieni, quamque ab ipsa philosophia: excipio excipiendos, quos tamen plures esse mallem quam sunt."

[3] Apart from one article by Georg Ellinger ("Tycho de Brahe als lateinischer Dichter," in *Festgabe ... Max Herrmann*, Berlin, 1935) all that has been written about

Among the poems in scientific works the most famous is the "Elegy to Urania", which ends his first published book, the *De nova stella.*[4] This dates from the same period as the letter I cited above, and does in fact deal with the same problem: the noblemen's hostility towards science.

With vague reminiscences of Ovid, *Amores* 3:1, the elegy describes how the muse, Urania, reveals herself to Tycho while he is strolling in the Scanian woods. She reproaches him for doing more work on chemistry than on astronomy, and orders him to devote his life to the restitution (no less) of her own neglected art. As a sign of this vocation she then presents to him the new star.

After this splendid passage (the effect of which is based, as has been pointed out by Karsten Friis-Jensen, on a sort of fusion of the symbolic figure of the muse and the very real star) Tycho gives his own answer to the muse. In a long monologue he describes the choice he has made between aristocratic ideals and a life devoted to science. In this he obviously needs justification. Great parts of the introductory letters (a correspondence between Tycho and a friend who was a professor in Copenhagen) have already been spent on defending the fact that a nobleman is writing a book–here the defence is turned to counterattack.

First the traditional occupations of noblemen are listed in a most polemic manner, starting with warfare, court service, politics and the gathering of riches, all described in terms of bragging, ambition, luxury, etc. Next, without any differentiation, follow drinking, love, gambling, hunting, riding. This, he declares, is what marks a nobleman; it seems, he adds sarcastically, that nobility demands noble deeds:

> Pluraque delectent alios, si plura supersunt,
> More suo ingenuis quæ peragenda viris.

Tycho's latin poetry is in Danish. The topic is treated in several Danish histories of literature, especially in the latest: Karsten Friis-Jensen and Minna Skafte Jensen in *Dansk Litteraturhistorie,* vol. 2 (Copenhagen, 1984), 404–12, but see also: Oluf Friis, *Den danske Litteraturs Historie,* vol. 1 (1938; repr., Copenhagen, 1975): 448–50). – Special studies: Peter Zeeberg, "Kemi og Kærlighed, naturvidenskab i Tycho Brahes latindigtning", in *Litteratur og Lærdom,* ed. Marianne Alenius and Peter Zeeberg. Renæssancestudier, vol. 1 (Copenhagen: Museum Tusculanum Press, 1987), 149–61. This article treats Tycho's Ovidian Heroid "Urania Titani" and contains a list of the known Latin poetry by Tycho Brahe, both extant and lost. Id., "Amor på Hven, Tycho Brahes digt til Erik Lange," *Renæssancen–Dansk, Europæisk, Globalt,* ed. Minna Skafte Jensen and Marianne Pade. Renæssancestudier, vol. 2, (Copenhagen: Museum Tusculanum Press, 1988) 161–181. Id., "Adel og Lærdom hos Tycho Brahe" (forthcoming).

[4] *Tychonis Brahe de nova et nullius ævi memoria prius visa stella* . . . (Hafniæ, 1573) in *Opera omnia*: 1:1–72. (the elegy is on pp. 65–70).

> Scilicet his studiis Virtus generosa probatur,
> Nobile nobilitas forte requirit opus.
>
> (vv. 181-84)

According to Tycho the only good to come from these occupations is the good they do to the body, whereas science—and this is how Tycho presents his own alternative—science is the occupation of the mind, *mens*: "*My mind* burns for greater deeds":

> At mea Mens ausis operum maioribus ardet,
> In quibus excellens cernitur esse labor.
>
> (vv. 197–98)

This pair, body versus mind, announces a comparison between nobility and science in terms of perishable versus eternal. The bodily, and earthly, occupations of his fellow noblemen are compared unfavorably with his own astronomical, that is celestial, pursuits. This is his justification of the choice he has made: a philosophic demonstration, so to speak, that not only has he chosen a better way of life, he has chosen the only one that has any *real* value—as opposed to the vanity of the aristocratic occupations.

As a consequence Tycho becomes able to describe his choice as a mystical experience in the neo-platonic tradition. His emancipation from the aristocratic ideals becomes the emancipation of the mind from the perishable body and its ascension towards the heavens where it belongs.

"Whoever delights in flying through the castles of heavens, and making his genius approach the stars—his interests are different from those of men, and similar to those of the gods. He knows a way to make his mind rise from earth."

> Quisquis enim superas animo volitare per arces,
> Syderaque ingenio gaudet adire suo,
> Dissimiles hominum curas, similesque Deorum,
> Et sua quo terris Mens relevetur, habet.
>
> (vv. 207–10)

Variations on this theme, this description of science, are to be found in several of Tycho's poems—even from later periods when justification towards the aristocratic milieu was no longer the problem at stake.

One example from the time at Hven is the *Parœneticum ad astronomiæ cultores*, which was printed in his *Astronomiæ instauratæ progymnasmata*.[5]

---

[5] Printed posthumously in Prague, 1602, but for the most part written before

This is an address to the young astronomers, calling them to follow the path by now prepared by Tycho.

> Et iam strata via est, multis prius inuia Seclis . . .
> (v. 1)

Here nobility has been substituted by the uncomprehending mob, but they are still characterized by "ambition, money-making, ignorance and luxury" (*ambitio, lucrum, ignorantia, luxus*, v. 48). And the alternative still is to ascend towards the heavens, leaving the ignorant people behind, "not to deprive the mind, which is the divine part of the heavens, of its ancestral good":

> Huc spirate alacres, populo huc post terga relicto
> Tendite, nec Mentem, quæ pars est Enthea Coeli,
> Hoc patrio private bono . . .
> (vv. 16–18)

These as I said are official poems, as opposed to the ones that belong to private life at Hven. Other poems however defy a rigid classification like this. In the winter of 1584–1585, for example, Tycho printed a whole series of at least seven elegies, all dedicated to friends of one kind or another: two are epitaphs for dead friends, the others are formally letters. They were all printed separately. The occasion for this was the inauguration of the Uraniborg printing works–in fact they were written, Tycho says, to give the new printer something to do. These, one would suppose, were not meant for the general public like the ones so far mentioned. They must have been meant to be sent as gifts to specific recipients, presumably both the dedicatees and others. On the other hand they must have circulated quite widely: we happen to know from a letter that a German friend of Tycho's saw one of these poems at the Frankfurt book fair.[6]

This group of dedicatees, and of course the content of those poems that have survived, gives us an excellent impression of what Tycho considered his most important contacts. And very likely Tycho himself meant them to do so. We have here the royal chancellor, who was Tycho's direct connection to the king, and his money. We have the viceroy in Holstein, who was famous as a patron of the arts, as was also the French ambassador who probably got a poem, too. We have several professors at the

---

Tycho left Denmark (See Norlind, op. cit. (n. 1) 144 ff.). I cite it from *Opera omnia*, vol. 2 (the poem is at p. 302–3).

[6] Letter from Christopher Rothmann, 1. Oct. 1587. (*Opera omnia*, 6:117–18).

university, and perhaps also its leader. And then there are three poems adressed to amateur scientists among the Danish nobility. No doubt Tycho was also the centre of a clique of such persons.[7]

In my opinion one of these poems, the one addressed to the alchemist Erik Lange, has very special qualities.[8] It's a love elegy–and this is stressed by the fact that each of its forty-three distichs ends with the word *amor*. Its tone is (as very often with Tycho Brahe) distinctly Ovidian, and the theme is advice to a friend who is hopelessly in love. In spite of all that it's no *genuine* love poem.

The beginning is quite traditional, describing love as an illness that prevents you from occupying yourself with other things–here, according to the recipient (and the sender) of the poem, specified as poetry, chemistry and astronomy.[9] But then Tycho presents a sort of *remedium amoris* which takes us much further. To get rid of this love Erik must replace it by another one. If he is vexed by Venus and by Cupid's arrows, he must substitute them with a love for Pallas. If he can't sleep at night, there's always the love for Urania and her stars. And if it's Cupid's fire that bothers him, the substitute is Vesta's fire, i.e., chemistry. The three arts recur.

Si te blanda Venus per tela Cupidinis urget,
  Palladis egregius substituatur amor.
Si nocturna qvies nimium frustratur amore,
  Urania astriferæ sit tibi noctis amor.
Sive Cupidineo te nox qvoqve conficit igne,
  Sit tibi Vestarum lucidus ignis amor.

(vv. 29–34)

---

[7] To the Royal Chancellor, Niels Kaas: *Opera omnia*, 9:180–87. To Heinrich Rantzau, Viceroy of Holstein: *Opera omnia*, 9:187–90. Epitaphs for two professors at Copenhagen University, Johannes Pratensis and Hans Frandsen: *Opera omnia*, 9:176–77 and 178. To three noblemen: Erik Lange (*Opera omnia*, 15:3–5), Jacob Ulfeldt (*Opera omnia*, 9:179–80) and Falk Gjøe (not extant, see previous note). – The no longer extant poem for the French ambassador, Charles de Dançay, is mentioned among the others in a handwritten list of poems, preserved in the National Library in Vienna (cod. Vindob. 10.686 10 fol. 11a), as is also a poem to "Prof.<?> Nicolaus Laurentius," who may be identified as the leader (*rector*) of the University of Copenhagen for 1585.

[8] This poem is the subject of my article "Amor på Hven, Tycho Brahes digt til Erik Lange" (see note 3), which also contains an edition of the poem which on some points differs from the text in the *Opera omnia*.

[9] A series of items which recurs several times in Tycho's poems, e.g., in two other poems from the same "series": the one to Heinrich Rantzau (*Opera omnia*, 9:189, lines 27–32) and the epitaph for Johannes Pratensis (*Opera omnia*, 9:176, lines 23–8). Also in one of the poems in "De Nova Stella" (*Opera omnia*, 1:14, line 23).

"Thus" he says "one love can become a remedy against another love," and then he adds, with an ingenious rewriting of Virgil's "omnia vincit Amor," that the love that conquers everything should also conquer itself:

> Deniqve qvicqvid erit, leviter qvod nectit amorem,
> Et gravis et melior fac cito pellat amor.
> Sic amor alterius fiet medicamen amoris
> Omnia qui vincit, se quoque vincat amor.
> (vv. 35–38)

Now, this love for science may be found at Uraniborg, where Erik can devote himself to the arts (and again the three arts from above are repeated, in fact they serve as a "leitmotif" throughout the poem). This may be accomplished with the help of Tycho's love for *him*.

What we have here is clearly a remodelling of the theme we met in the first two poems: The choise of science as opposed to the perishable earthly life. But this time it is described in terms of earthly versus heavenly *love*. The latter, which is described as a gift from the gods,[10] is more true, and greater than the first, which is in its turn depicted as very small. Because of his size he can't reach to the stars or penetrate into the bowels of the earth. This "pusillus amor" gets lost in trifles, "perit in minimis." (As you see, some words still refer to the language of elegiac love.)

It would be natural to see this as a reflection of the neo-platonic philosophy of love, which goes back to Marsilio Ficino, but became fashionable through the works of Pietro Bembo and especially through Castiglione's dialogue about "The Courtier": Love as the moving force behind the ascension of the soul towards the divine. Love, that is, as the force behind exactly that movement which Tycho in the elegy to Urania used to describe his scientific urge. And in fact we have passages in other poems where the term of love is used explicitly in this connection.[11]

This also gives us a clue to an understanding of the last distich of our love poem, the epilogue. "If you don't want the true love," he says, "take

---

[10] *Verior et major typis tua pectora nostris*
Musa omnes superos orat ut intret amor. (vv. 69–70)
The mentioning of printing (*typis . . . nostris*) is due to the fact that this poem was the very first text to be printed at the new printing works–a fact which also inspires Tycho to a whole series of puns on the word *premere*.

[11] E.g., *Opera omnia* 2:302 (the Paræneticum) and 6:340 (a poem for Landgraf Wilhelm of Hesse). A poem in the introductory letters in *De nova stella* (*Opera omnia* 1:69) has: "*hæc est ea Diva voluptas / Quæ similes celsis nos facit esse deis.*"

the foolish. From the one will arise the love for the other."

> Si non vis solidum, stolidum secteris amorem,
> In stolido solidi surget amoris AMOR.
>
> (vv. 85–86)

On the surface a complete reversal of the poem's idea, but seen in the light of the philosophy of love a natural consequence: divine love is an urge towards divine beauty, while earthly love is an urge towards the earthly reflections of divine beauty. Therefore divine love can be obtained *through* earthly love.

The change in Tycho's handling of this picture of science from the elegy to Urania to this poem is significant. The first elegy, with its self-righteous tone, reflected the awkward position of a nobleman wanting to be a scientist. The detached, playful poem for Erik Lange, on the other hand, reflects a sophisticated milieu, where the ideal of the literate nobleman has come to be taken very earnestly. A scientific miniature court, where Tycho and his nobleman friends played with fashionable philosophy, and (as we know from other poems and letters)[12] called each other mythological names.

For the study of these aspects of Tycho Brahe and his activities the Latin poems constitute an important, and hitherto largely unused source material.

University of Copenhagen

[12] Erik Lange was called *Titan,* Tycho's sister Sophia was called *Urania* and Tycho himself *Apollo.* These names occur in Tycho's famous heroid about Erik and Sophia, *Urania Titani* (*Opera omnia,* 9:193–207), and in Tycho's description of the sister (*Opera omnia,* 9:324–26), and are used in several letters, e.g., *Opera omnia,* 7:321, 14:157–59, 14:177–82.

SPECIAL SESSION

Nuestro Proyecto de Investigacion sobre los textos Latino-Mexicanos

ROBERTO HEREDIA CORREA

En México el latín se ha estudiado y cultivado sin interrupción desde que fue traído por los españoles en el primer cuarto del siglo XVI, hasta nuestros días. Durante los siglos XVI y XVII y primeros tres cuartos del XVIII el latín fue la lengua de la cultura universitaria y eclesiástica. A partir de las últimas décadas del siglo XVIII su imperio indiscutido fue reduciéndose sin interrupción hasta el presente; sin embargo, en ningún momento de este largo proceso han faltado grupos de estudiosos devotos de la cultura latina y cultores de la lengua.

La historia de nuestras letras neolatinas va, pues, desde el primer cuarto del siglo XVI hasta los días presentes.

§ § §

Todos sabemos en nuestro país que, cuando menos durante los siglos coloniales, se escribieron obras literarias, filosóficas y científicas en latín; los títulos de algunas de ellas han pasado a nuestros manuales de historia de la literatura o de historia de la cultura. Así, por ejemplo, respecto al siglo XVI, todos hemos oído de los *Diálogos* de Francisco Cervantes de Salazar, de las obras filosóficas de fray Alonso de la Vera Cruz, de ciertos escritos jurídicos de fray Bartolomé de las Casas, Vasco de Quiroga y otros misioneros; alguna vez hemos sentido curiosidad por conocer el llamado Códice Badiano, farmacopea compuesta en náhuatl por el indio Martín de la Cruz y traducida al latín por otro indio llamado Juan Badiano; hemos leído también sobre ciertas cartas escritas por indios latinistas formados en el Colegio de Santa Cruz de Tlatelolco. Del siglo XVII se mencionan frecuentemente la *Logica Mexicana* del jesuita Antonio Rubio, el *Regio*

Psalterio escrito en la cárcel por aquel extraño aventurero que se proclamó emperador de México, el irlandés Guillén de Lampart, y algunos pequeños poemas de Sor Juana Inés de la Cruz. Y en el siglo XVIII la lista se alarga: la *Bibliotheca Mexicana* de Juan José de Eguiara y Eguren, la *Rusticatio Mexicana*, bello poema descriptivo de Rafael Landívar, el *De Deo Deoque Homine Heroica*, de Diego José Abad, las obras teológicas, filosóficas, y poéticas de los jesuitas Francisco Xavier Alegre, Francisco Xavier Clavigero y otros; las biografías de jesuitas compuestas por Juan Luis Maneiro y Manuel Fabri, las obras filosóficas de Benito Díaz de Gamarra.

Pero estas obras son apenas una mínima parte, aunque ciertamente selecta, de la bibliografía latino-mexicana. La producción científica, filosófica y literaria novohispana escrita en latín es mucho mayor. Y a estas obras habría que añadir la documentación adminstrativa—por llamarla de algún modo—escrita en esta misma lengua. De los 179 impresos que recoge Joaquín García Icazbalceta en su *Bibliografía Mexicana del siglo XVI*, más de 70 son obras escritas en latín. Al juzgarse esta cifra debe considerarse que durante las primeras décadas del periodo colonial autores e impresores debieron dedicar atención especial a estudios de las lenguas indígenas y a la elaboración de manuales de doctrina christiana y prácticas religiosas. El *Ensayo bibliográfico del siglo XVII*, de Vicente de Paula Andrade, entre las 1228 cédulas que recoge, en las cuales predominan sermones y obras similares, menciona igualmente más de setenta obras escritas en latín, sin contar los numerosos arcos, certámenes, túmulos y festivos aparatos, en los cuales nuestros ingenios lucían sus habilidades en ambas lenguas.

Estos datos se refieren sólo a los libros impresos; el número de escritos que permanecieron inéditos es muchísimo mayor. Una revisión somera de la *Bibliotheca Mexicana* de Juan José de Eguiara y Eguren y de la *Biblioteca Hispanoamericana Septentrional* de José Mariano Beristáin de Souza basta para comprobar la magnitud de la parcela de nuestra cultura escrita en latín. Este hecho es causa de que la gran mayoría de tales obras permanezcan desconocidas y olvidadas en el mejor de los casos, pues son de sobra conocidos los agravios de que han sido objeto los archivos y bibliotecas.

Es importante señalar que, además de adquirirse como instrumento para el estudio de la filosofía, la teología y las ciencias, el latín tuvo muchos cultores devotos que penetraron sus secretos y se sirvieron de ella como del vehículo más idóneo para sus obras de creación literaria. Ya he mencionado a Rafael Landívar y a Diego José Abad, poetas excepcionales sin duda; y no podrían citarse muchos más de semejante altura. Pero pueden ser índice de la profundidad que podía alcanzarse en el conocimiento de la lengua y de la destreza a que podía llegarse en su manejo, los ejemplos siguientes:

1. Don Bernardo de Riofrío, canónigo doctoral de la catedral de Micho-

acán, compuso en 1680 un poema en honor de la Virgen de Guadalupe, intitulado *Centonicum Virgilianum*; la composición está formada "por versos o partes de verso sacados de la obra de Virgilio, que, atormentados en su sentido original, son combinados para que aquí canten las apariciones de la guadalupana." Este tipo de composiciones, como atinadamente comenta Ignacio Osorio, "nos parece absolutamente extravagante . . . , pero a la época barroca le era muy atractivo este tipo de juegos en que el autor no sólo ponía en ejercicio el ingenio sino también ostentaba su conocimiento de los poetas latinos."

2. En 1641 el mercedario Juan de Valencia compuso un singular poema, intitulado *Theressiada*, en honor de Santa Teresa de Jesús, en cerca de 700 hexámetros, todos retrógrados. Envió el poema al cronista de su orden, fray Francisco de Pareja, y actualmente está perdido. Sólo se conoce el siguiente verso que cita el mismo Pareja en su *Crónica de la Provincia de la Vistitación de Nuestra Señora de la Merced redención de cautivos de la Nueva España:* Asseret e Roma nisi lis in amore Teressa.

3. En 1740, a los 23 años de edad, siendo todavía estudiante jesuita, José Mariano Iturriaga compuso el poema conocido con el nombre de *Californiada*. Canta en él, a la manera de las antiguas epopeyas, y en 810 hexámetros, la conquista espiritual de la todavía entonces "isla" de California, realizada por el padre Juan María Salvatierra.

4. Cayetano de Cabrera y Quintero, presbítero secular del arzobispado de México, fue fecundísimo autor de numerosas y variadas obras latinas y castellanas, orador sagrado, historiador, traductor de Horacio y Juvenal, comediógrafo y autor de "artes" de las lenguas hebrea, griega y náhuatl. En la multitud de sus poemas Cabrera hace alarde no sólo de su conocimiento de la lengua y los escritores latinos, clásicos y cristianos, sino de su maestría en el conocimiento y manejo de los distintos metros. "Lo que resulta particularmente fascinante,. . . dice la profesora Lia Coronati, es la increíble variedad de la métrica empleada en el curso de las obras . . . hasta las más complejas y audaces, y a veces inusitadas, composiciones formales de la poesía lírica."

Por otra parte Cabrera tampoco es ajeno a los artificios de ingenio. Pueden servir de ejemplo dos epigramas dedicados a San Juan de la Cruz, en los cuales forma juegos acrósticos no solo iniciales sino medios y finales.

§ § §

El estudio profesional de las Letras Clásicas se inició en nuestro país en 1939, con la creación de un Departamento de Letras Clásicas en la Facultad de Filosofía y Letras de la Universidad Nacional. Para entonces el latín y el griego habían sido confinados en áreas muy reducidas de los ciclos medio y profesional de la enseñanza: el bachillerato de Humanidades y la Facultad de Filosofía y Letras. Durante las dos o tres décadas siguientes continuó el proceso de reducción del estudio de estas lenguas hasta llegar al extremo en que se encuentran actualmente: sendos brevísimos cursos de latín y griego, impartidos a grupos aún más breves de alumnos del bachillerato, y dos cursos de latín que prescribe el plan de estudios de licenciatura de Letras Hispánicas. La situación, con ligeras variantes, es similar en las demás universidades del país.

En extraña paradoja, al tiempo que iba decayendo el estudio de las lenguas clásicas, se iniciaban en la Universidad Nacional proyectos cuya realización requería un número creciente de profesionales de los estudios grecolatinos: en 1938 se fundaba el Instituto Bibliográfico Mexicano; en 1940 nacía el Instituto de Investigaciones Filosóficas; en 1945 se creaba el Instituto de Investigaciones Históricas; en 1967 tomaban forma los Estudios de Posgrado de la Facultad de Filosofía y Letras, etcétera. Y, por otra parte, en torno a 1940 otras instituciones culturales iniciaban proyectos de traducción y publicación de textos clásicos de filosofía, de obras fundamentales de la historiografía y la filología clásicas y de textos latinomexicanos de importancia para nuestra historia.

Hacia 1942 la Universidad Nacional fundó la Bibliotheca Scriptorum Graecorum et Romanorum Mexicana, con el fin de proporcionar a los estudiosos del mundo clásico, y a los lectores en general, las obras de los autores griegos y latinos, en textos autorizados y con traducciones originales y esmeradas. Durante los primeros años vieron la luz un número importante de textos; después el ritmo de publicación decreció. En 1967, con el fin de impulsar este proyecto, se formó el Centro de Traductores de Lenguas Clásicas. Poco tiempo después, en 1973, este grupo de trabajo se convirtió en el actual Centro de Estudios Clásicos, parte integrante del Instituto de Investigaciones Filológicas.

Desde su inicio, los programas de trabajo del Centro de Estudios Clásicos se organizaron en tres áreas:

–Filología griega
–Filología latina
–Textos neolatinos y tradición clásica de México

En relación con la tercera área, tres proyectos principales se encontraban en proceso: La enseñanza del latín en la Nueva España: la vida y la obra del educador y escritor jesuita Bernardino de Llanos (1560-1639); la traducción y publicación de algunos textos neolatinos inéditos.

§ § §

Para entonces la prolongada ausencia de las lenguas clásicas en los planes de estudio del área de Humanidades, aun en la Facultad de Filosofía y Letras, había traído como consecuencia la falta de especialistas en disciplinas para cuyo cultivo son instrumentos indispensables el latín y el griego, como, por ejemplo, la filosofía grecolatina, medieval, renacentista y novohispana, la historia antigua y medieval, las literaturas medievales y renacentistas, el derecho romano e indiano, etcétera.

En 1979 el Departmento de Letra Clásicas, con el propósito de hacer frente al problema, y a partir de conversaciones reiteradas con profesores jóvenes y alumnos de diversos colegios de la Facultad de Filosofía y Letras, estableció sendos cursos optativos de traducción griega y latina, con el fin de que los alumnos de Filosofía, Historia y Letras de nuestra Facultad o cualesquier alumnos de otras facultades, tuvieran la oportunidad de adquirir un manejo competente de estas lenguas.

Por ese mismo tiempo el Centro de Estudios Clásicos emprendió un amplio proyecto de promoción de los estudios neolatinos mexicanos que abarcaba los siguientes pasos:

1. Elaboración de los catálogos de obras latinas impresas en México durante los siglos XVI, XVII y XVIII.
2. Inventario de manuscritos latinos existentes en los principales repositorios de la ciudad de México.
3. Inventario de manuscritos latinos existentes en los principales repositorios del resto del país.
4. Inventario de manuscritos latino-mexicanos referentes a México, existentes en repositorios de otros países, particularmente de España e Italia.
5. Estudio, traducción y publicación de obras y documentos latinos de especial importancia para la historia de nuestra cultura.

Un proyecto de esta naturaleza implicaba, por una parte, la formación de un nutrido grupo de trabajo en nuestro Centro, y por otra, la colaboración de otras instituciones nacionales y extranjeras. Por lo demás, nunca pensamos que pudiera llevarse a cabo con todos los medios necesarios y en las condiciones más ventajosas. Siempre lo consideramos como un quehacer a muy largo plazo, en el cual debían irse insertando programas de trabajo particulares.

En primer lugar, se continuaron y ampliaron los proyectos existentes, y se promovió tanto entre los investiagadores como entre los estudiantes de licenciatura y posgrado, y aun en estudiosos independientes, la traducción y estudio de textos neolatinos. En cuanto a los catálogos de obras impresas, el correspondiente al siglo XVI ya fue publicado, y los relativos a los siglos XVII y XVIII están en preparación. Los inventarios documentales han ido elaborándose muy lentamente y de manera muy parcial. Para la publicación de todos estos trabajos se ha creado recientemente una colección específica, la *Bibliotheca Humanistica Mexicana*, cuyo primer volumen fue editado en 1987, y que comprenderá textos en edición bilingüe, catálogos y estudios.

En el marco de este proyecto de inventario, estudio y traducción de los textos y documentos latinomexicanos, hemos firmado varios convenios de colaboración con otras dependencias de nuestra Universidad (Instituto de Investigaciones Jurídicas e Instituto de Investigationes Filosóficas) y con otras instituciones nacionales y extranjeras (Universidad de Puebla, Universidad de Sonora, El Colegio de Michoacán y Universidad "La Sapienza" de Roma):

1. A partir del convenio firmado con el Instituto de Investigaciones Jurídicas en 1985, se formó un grupo de trabajo de cinco miembros, con el propósito de traducir y estudiar los textos clásicos del derecho romano, medieval e hispano. Con los productos de la investigatión de este grupo se ha iniciado la *Bibliotheca Iuridica Latina Mexicana*, en la cual se han publicado ya dos volúmenes.

2. Según al convenio firmado con el Instituto de Investigaciones Filosóficas, en 1986 se formó un grupo de trabajo de seis miembros, con al propósito de estudiar y traducir la literatura filosófica novohispana. Con los productos de la investigación de este grupo se formará la *Bibliotheca Philosophica Latina Mexicana*, cuyos dos primeros volúmenes están actualmente en prensa.

En 1987, dentro de las actividades de este grupo de trabajo, se realizó en El Colegio de Michoacán un Encuentro Nacional de investigadores de la filosofía novohispana, al cual asistieron 22 profesores. El propósito principal de este coloquio fue el intercambio de información y experiencias y la búsqueda de alguna forma de coordinación. Este año se realizará el II Encuetro; esperamos poder reunir entre treinta y treinta y cinco profesores. Los temas de esta reunión son los siguientes:

- Filosofía social
- Filosofía e identidad nacional
- La enseñanza da le filosifía
- Fray Alonso de la Vera Cruz y la filosofía de su tiempo
- Francisco Xavier Alegre y la filosofía de su tiempo.

3. En 1981 firmamos un convenio con la Universidad "La Sapienza" de Roma, con el fin de colaborar en la búsqueda, inventario y estudio de

textos y documentos latinos referentes a la historia de México. Frutos de este intercambio, hasta ahora, son cuatro catálogos de manuscritos publicados—el quinto a punto de entrar a la imprenta—en nuestra serie *Cuadernos del Centro de Estudios Clásicos*, dos catálogos publicados en la revista *Studi Latini e Italiani*, y algunas otros trabajos.

4. La colaboración con El Colegio de Michoacán ha sido tanto en docencia como en investigación. Fruto de esta labor han sido varios artículos y libros publicados, o en vías de publicarse, por ese Colegio.

5. Los convenios con las universidades de Puebla y Sonora han comprendido diversas actividades: catalogación de fondos bibliográficos antiguos, cursos de latín y asesoría en la búsqueda y estudio de documentación latina.

Finalmente, debo señalar que desde 1983 nuestro Centro cuenta con el anuario *Nova Tellus*, en el cual se recogen trabajos, tanto de los investigadores del propio Centro, como de colaboradores foráneos, referentes a nuestras tres áreas de atención. Actualmente está en prensa el número 5, correspondiente a 1987.

Universidad Nacional Autónoma de México

Latin Works by Some Sixteenth-Century Philosophers From New Spain[*][1]

MAURICIO BEUCHOT

During the sixteenth century some philosophers from New Spain made deliberate attempts to reconcile their own school of thought with the humanistic tendencies currently in vogue. Such attempts are most interesting, since Scholasticism and humanism have been generally regarded not only as incompatible, but even as totally opposed philosophical doctrines. Considering this, any effort, from either side, to reconcile both positions would seem impossible, but, if "Humanism" is understood as the attitude that strives to recover the classical purity of Latin, as well as the ideological outlook that concerns itself more with man's dignity and those affairs that bear directly upon him, in opposition to the abstruse sophistic arguments that proliferated in the scholastic works, it may be feasible to state that some scholastic thinkers allowed themselves to be influenced, even imbued, by the humanistic ideals. This is precisely what some sixteenth-century philosophers attempted.

The works of Alonso de la Vera Cruz and Tomás de Mercado, two scholastic philosophers influenced by humanism, have been chosen to illustrate how this approach took place. These authors are not, by any means, the only ones who made attempts of this nature; other such writers could be mentioned: for example, the Franciscan friar Diego de Valadés, who wrote as part of his philosophical teachings the *Rhetorica christiana*, a treatise in which he endeavours to recover the classical learning while, at

---

* I should like to thank Concepción Abellán and Antonio Corona for their suggestions and translation into English of this paper.

the same time, keeping to the medieval notion of rhetoric as an argumentative rather than a psychagogic doctrine.[1]

Alonso de la Vera Cruz

Alonso was one of the forerunners of the philosophical and, in general terms, intellectual life of the New Spain. He established chairs, schools and libraries, and was one of the first lecturers at the Real y Pontificia Universidad de México.

In 1540 he was the first to teach philosophy at the town of Tiripetío and, after the foundation in 1553 of the Universidad de México, he obtained the chair of Saint Thomas' theology.[2] As a result of his pedagogical experiences here, he wrote a philosophical course; this work, where he deals with minor and major logic as well as physics in the Aristotelian sense, may rightfully be considered as "the first philosophical course" of the New World.[3] The first noticeable humanistic trait in Alonso's work is his polished style, within the limits afforded by the rough scholastic Latin.

A good example of these efforts may be found in the prefaces to his three philosophical treatises: his *Recognitio summularum* (1554), his *Dialectica resolutio* (1554), and his *Physica speculatio* (1557).[4] The complaints against the ergotistic excesses of the decadent scholastics evince even more characteristics of humanism proper. I believe that the criticisms addressed against these writers in Alonso's first work, the *Recognitio summularum*, are of the utmost importance on account of their similarity

---

[1] Fray Diego de Valadés, *Rhetorica christiana* (Perugia: n.p., 1579).

[2] Fray Alonso's biographical data are drawn from D. Basalenque, *Historia de la Provincia de San Nicolás de Tolentino de Michoacán, del orden de N. P. S. Agustín* ([1]Mexico City: Vda. de Bernardo Calderón, 1673); quoted from the 1886 edition published at Mexico City by Ed. de la Voz de México, 192.

[3] It is sure that Alonso's course was the first published in America. See A. Bolaño e Isla, *Ensayo bio-bibliográfico sobre Alonso de la Vera Cruz* (México: Robredo, 1945).

[4] Alonso's works underwent several printings as follows: *Recognitio summularum*: Mexico City: *Ioannes Paulus Brissensis*, 1554; Salamanca: *Ioannes Baptista a Terranoua*, 1562; IDEM, 1569; IDEM, 1573; IDEM, 1579. *Dialectica resolutio*: Mexico City: Ioannes Paulus, 1554; Salamanca: I. B. a Terranova, 1562; IDEM, 1569; IDEM, 1573. *Physica speculatio*: Mexico City: I. Paulus, 1557; Salamanca: I. B. a Terranova, 1562; IDEM, 1569; IDEM, 1573. The printings of the *Recognitio summularum* exhibit several changes and corrections; for more information about the concept of "edition" in Spain during the sixteenth century see J. Moll, "Problemas del libro español en el Siglo de Oro," *Boletín de la Real Academia Española* 59 (1979): 49–107.

to those levelled by other humanistic authors, such as this reprobation found in Luis Vives's *Adversus pseudodialecticos*:

Cur cum ipse [Petrus Hispanus] suppositiones, et expositiones illarum enuntiationum, atque horum similia, quae traduntur in parum logicalibus, nunquam a Boetio acceperit, Aristoteles ipse non praecipiat, tam impudenter illa confinxerit, et praescripserit sensus enuntiationum contra rationem omnem sermonis latini, quem nec primis, ut dicunt labris gustarat, nec summis olfecerat naribus? Cuius profecto leges verae si sunt in Cicerone, Varrone, Quintiliano, Plinio, Boetio, et aliis latinis, latinae orationes innumerae, in Aristotele, Platone, Theophrasto, Carneade, Chrysippo, et ceteris Graecis, graecae, non ex ipsius rei, sed ex istarum suppositionum, ampliationum, expositionum ignorantiae falsae invenientur; nec solum in Aristotelis vel morali, vel naturali philosophia, sed in ipsa quoque dialectica; quid quod nec Petrus quidem ipse Hispanus ad eas quas tulit normas locutus est?[5]

Alonso expressed like thoughts with the following words:

Tradere enim omnia quae ab Enzina, Coeto, Soto, Spinosa, Naverus, Sbarroya, Coronelo et coeteris huius classis viris traduntur, non est visum expediens, cum saeculum jam alio tendat et ex decrepita aetate in istis Summulis et sophismatibus rursus videatur juvenescere et ad sobrietatem sapere circuncidentes penitus amputandae quae opere pretium non sunt.

Qui voluerint perdere tempus, multa legendo de istis, legant librum oppositionum Ezinas et primum suum tractatum et Sbarroyam et magistrum Soto et nobiscum sentient plus justo istis remoratos, ab usui saeculi indulsisse.[6]

and even goes to the extreme of stating that:

Vos vero, loco veritatis, quae simplicissima est, monstra illa, suppositiones, obligationes, exponibilia, insolubilia, calculationes et reliqua terminata et quasi quoddam falsitatis pelagus nobis discenda tradidistis.[7]

---

[5] Luis Vives, *Adversus pseudodialecticos*, ed. Fantazzi (Leiden: Brill, 1979), 67–68.

[6] Alonso de la Vera Cruz, *Recognitio summularum* (Salmanticae: Ioannes Baptista a Terranova, 1579), hereafter referred to as *Recognitio*, fols. 41 and 55.

[7] *Recognitio*, fol. 41.

This author, nevertheless, does not limit himself to these tirades, but also proposes specific innovations: he demonstrates the need to get rid of many of the treatises in question and to substitute for them the authentic teachings of Aristotle, Cicero and Themistius. Besides advocating the return to the classical tradition, Alonso adopts as well some principles from the humanists themselves for his renewal projects, such as Rodolphus Agricola's treatment of the dialectical topics in his *De Inventione Dialectica*; in Alonso's view, Agricola provides the best model to follow.[8]

The high opinion that Agricola merited for his method of dealing with dialectics, among other achievements, is clearly stated by Alonso in his *Recognitio summularum*, where he is praised thus:

> Et post Aristotelem et Ciceronem, vnicus nostris temporibus, Rodolphus Agricola de inuentione, et de locis dialecticis edidit libros eruditissimos, simul et eloquentissimos. Quos consulo legendos ab illis, qui serio in animo habent hanc dialectices partem, quam Topica vocant, adamussim penetrare.[9]

Alonso's admiration for Agricola was such that he admitted that this author had set an example he would desire to follow, since he believed that Agricola could be compared in equal terms with the classical writers:

> Constet Rodolphum doctissimum et antiquis comparandum .$.$. R. Agricola qui pro meritis vix laudari queat, qui in sua De Inventione Dialectica procul a tergo sunt sophismata reliquenda docet.[10]

An examination of Alonso's treatise on dialectic shows that he adopts—right from the first lines—the definition of topic furnished by Agricola, thus setting the pattern for the ulterior development of the subject, thereby confirming the esteem in which he held this author:

> Locus est communis quaedam rei nota, cuius admonitu, quid in quaque reprobabile sit, potest inueniri. Sic Rodolphus. Haec definitio clare ostendit in quem finem loci dialectici sint inuenti, velut quaedam monimenta memoriae, ubi invenitur quod ad rem probandam conducat.[11]

---

[8] R. Agricola, *De inventione dialectica.*

[9] *Recognitio,* fol. 118.

[10] *Recognitio,* fol. 9.

[11] *Recognitio,* fol. 123, col. a.

Agricola's influence upon Alonso can be further traced in the latter's classification of the kinds of topics. Although Alonso already knew the classifications established by Aristotle, Cicero, Themistius, Boethius and Titelman, he complements them, as he himself states, with many of the elements postulated by Agricola, as in the case of internal and external topics.[12] Alonso goes on to explain that Aristotle's exposition of the topics is obscure, and that this fact prompted Cicero, Themistius and Boethius to set upon the task of elucidating them, but that, however, it was not possible to cast any light upon the subject until Agricola condensed all the former systems, endowing them with a new structure, far more simple, useful and adequate to the taste of the contemporary humanists:

> Haec omnia adduxi, vt sicut labor Rodolphi non solum non vanus, sed utilis fuerit in locis tradendis post Aristotelem, Ciceronem, Quintilianum, Boetium, Themistium, eoque claris quam illis hic noster conatus non erit reputandus vanus, quia ad profectum illorum erit, quibus vel non est copia Rodolphi, vel non tantam peritiam habent Romani sermonis, vt eum valeant intelligire.[13]

In Alonso's view, Agricola's classification of the topics is far more suitable to teach this subject, so necessary for the invention and discussion of human affairs, thus approaching the humanistic ideals mentioned before.

The facts enumerated above show that Alonso was fully aware that his philosophical position was leading him towards a humanistic stand; perhaps he did not succeed completely, but it must be remembered that his main concern was to eradicate those shortcomings of the scholastics that had caused the most violent disapproval among the new thinkers of the Renaissance. One of the points in contention was the corruption of Latin, which stemmed from the lack of interest for the language itself, and from the singleminded attention to the straightforward and utilitarian expression of ideas. Alonso was not satisfied with using the language in a haphazard manner, with only just enough clarity to express his thoughts; instead, he strove to avoid the barbarisms that under the cover of technicisms the scholastics introduced into the vocabulary, and from a syntactic standpoint, he endeavoured to recover the classical models within the limits forced upon him by the pedagogical nature of his works. A note-

---

[12] *Recognitio*, fol. 124, col. a.

[13] *Recognitio*, fol. 122, col. b.

worthy proof of Alonso's interest in the return to the classical models is furnished by the abundant quotations of Cicero and Seneca that are found throughout his philosophical writings. Another humanistic trait, or, in other words, another sign of the humanistic influence absorbed by Alonso, manifests itself in his interest in freeing the philosophical doctrine's body from the treatises condemned as abstruse by authors such as Vives and Erasmus.[14] Thus, he eliminates the treatises that deal with logical obligations, insoluble or paradoxical propositions and the calculations, following the criticisms cast upon these scholastic doctrines by the humanistic dialecticians. On the other hand, he strove to integrate the innovations developed by Agricola on the subject of dialectic topics into logic, Alonso's own field of study.

Tomas de Mercado

This Dominican philosopher, theologian and economist was born in Seville and went to México while still an adolescent. There, he entered the Order of Preachers around 1522 and was assigned to the Santo Domingo convent in the capital city. In this convent school he studied philosophy and theology, continuing later his education there, where he obtained the degree of Master in Arts and Theology.[15] Following his ordination, he was appointed in 1558 as lecturer in Arts at the same convent of Santo Domingo, which post he held until 1562, and where he also served as prior for a short period, until he was transferred to Spain. In this country he furthered his studies at Salamanca and later at Seville where he also taught philosophy, moral theology and law, and acted as moral counselor for the merchants. During his stay in Spain Tomás published his works, which, which may be considered as a product of his pedagogical experiences in Mexico, as suggested, among other clues, by the place-names he quotes and the examples he uses, in which things appertaining to the New Spain are mentioned. Tomás' commentary on the *Tractatus* or *Summulae* of logic by Petrus Hispanus, the translation and commentary of part of

[14] Luis Vives, op. cit., 71 ff.

[15] Tomás de Mercado's biographical data are drawn from the *Actas de Capítulos Provinciales*, Archivo Histórico de la Provincia Domincana de Santiago de México, MSS 1 and 2; and A. Dávila Padilla, *Historia de la fundación y discurso de la Provincia de Santiago de México, de la Orden de Predicadores* ([1]Mexico City: 1596; [2]Brussels: 1625), quoted from the facsimile reproduction of the second edition, (Mexico City: Ed. Academia Literaria, 1955), 728.

Aristotle's *Organon* (*Categories* and *Posterior Analytics*), and an *Opusculum* of select arguments about logic proceed from his teachings on Arts. His lectures, discussions and moral counselling may have furnished the material for his theologico-economic work about commercial treatises and contracts, *Suma de tratos y contratos*.[16] After publishing his works and teaching at the Dominican convent in Seville, Tomás set out on the journey back to his province of Santiago de México, but was taken ill on board the ship and finally succumbed to his disease. Tomás de Mercado's burial took place at sea, near the coast of San Juan de Ulúa, Veracruz, in 1575.

In my view, the most interesting facet of Tomás' production, and the one that shows the clearest signs of humanistic influence, or at least, of an attempt at approaching humanistic ideals, is his translation of Aristotle's *Categories* and *Posterior Analytics*, to which Porfirio's *Eisagoge* could be added. Like Alonso de la Vera Cruz, Tomás does not satisfy himself with merely reforming the teaching of logic by eliminating abstruse or useless treatises, nor with just proposing that Aristotle's precepts should find again their proper place in the philosophical text-books, following the humanistic ideal of the return to the classics. Instead, Tomás favours actively this reform and return by rendering Aristotle's major logic in an elegant and polished translation. This text had already been translated by other scholastics, such as William of Moerbecke, but their versions were so inelegant that their very uncouthness prompted Tomás to produce his own. He himself states that one of the reasons why these types of works have become defaced is:

> quod latini Autores e graeco (quo idiomate Aristotiles eam tradidit) sermone rudi, et (vt ita dicam) inciuili transtulerunt.[17]

Tomás also stresses that the difficulties inherent in Aristotle's text have been further compounded by some translators or interpreters who intro-

---

[16] Tomás de Mercado's works also underwent several printings, as follows: *Suma de tratos y contratos*: Salamanca: Matías Guast, 1569; Seville: Fernando Díaz, 1571 and 1578; Italian translation, Brescia: Pietro Maria Marchetti, 1591; modern edition (incomplete) with an introductory study by R. Sierra Bravo, Madrid: Editora Nacional, 1975; modern edition (complete), with an introduction by N. Sánchez Albornoz, Madrid: Clásicos del Pensamiento Económico Español, Instituto de Estudios Fiscales, 1977, 2 vols. *Commentarii lucidissimi in textum Petri Hispani... cum argumentorum selectissimorum opusculo...*: Seville: Fernando Díaz, 1571; *Comentarios lucidísimos al texto de Pedro Hispano*, introduction and translation by M. Beuchot, (Mexico City: Universidad Nacional Autónoma de México, 1985). *In logicam magnam Aristotelis commentarii, cum nova translatione textus ab eodem auctorie:* Seville: Fernando Díaz, 1571.

[17] Tomás de Mercado, *In logicam magnam...*, fols. i–ii.

duced scholastic jargon, and tried to translate literally word by word without caring for correctness, smoothness or elegance. These are the reasons that prompted Tomás to produce a translation:

> que genium sensum, veras rerum notiones, propriam sententiam interpretiones stilo limato, ac leni, verbis selectis, ac idoneis efferet.[18]

For Tomás, the pursuit of a polished and elegant translation does not imply, however, that the Aristotelian sense will be misrepresented, a point on which he insists thus:

> hic textus est ipsius met Aristotelis . . . e graeco in latinum versus (vt Seneca docet) interpraetatus, tam patens, ac lucidus: quam reliqui obscuri, ac inuoluti.[19]

This translation by Mercado was a major contribution to the study of Aristotle, since those available to the scholastics for their commentaries, such as the ones produced by William of Moerbecke, Vatable and Argyropoulos, were most deficient. The poor quality of these versions prompted Tomás to translate the work in order to use it for his own lectures, and to publish it alongside a commentary at Seville in 1571. Bearing in mind all the obstacles, besides geographical distances, that hindered the intellectual exchanges at the time, a strong possibility exists that Tomás may have not known the Latin translation of the *Organum* made by Pacius, published at Frankfurt in 1559; Zabarella's translation and commentary, published at Venice did not appear until 1578, three years after Tomás' death.

Conclusion

In sixteenth-century New Spain, some scholastic philosophers were fully aware of the humanistic ideals and attempted to reconcile this tendency with their own views, adopting some of these ideals and paying heed to the criticisms formulated by the humanists. Both Alonso de la Vera Cruz and Tomás de Mercado endeavoured to render their philosophical and theological works in a more refined Latin than most scholastics; they also cast out from philosophy some treatises and studies that had been criticized by the humanists. Alonso de la Vera Cruz, besides, declares himself

---

[18] Ibid.

[19] Ibid., fol. ii.

a follower or sympathizer of Rodolphus Agricola in what concerns the establishment of a healthy dialectic that would be useful for human affairs. Tomás de Mercado, on the other hand, felt the urge to translate some parts of Aristotle's *Organon* directly from Greek in order to free it from the coarseness introduced by other scholastics in their own translations; with this attitude he shows his concern for the recovery of the classical tradition, a concern that was fully shared by all humanists. Even though Alonso and Tomás are generally recognized as scholastics, the importance they accorded to the elegance of Latin and the depuration of the philosophical corpus, as well as their particular contributions, place them also in the humanistic tendency.

Universidad Nacional Autónoma de México

Las tragedias latinas de Stefano Tucci, especialmente la Iuditha

JOSÉ QUIÑONES MELGOZA

Stefano Tucci o Stephanus Tuccius (1540–97) fue un jesuita italiano nacido en Mesina (Sicilia) que escribió, cuando era profesor del mismo Colegio mesinense donde se educó, además de otras muchas obras, seis tragedias latinas, o mejor dicho, cinco; ya que el *Christus nascens* es solamente una *égloga*. Tres de ellas, las más antiguas, abordan temas del *Antiguo Testamento*. Son: *Nabuchodonosor* (1561), *Goliath* (1562) y *Iuditha* (1563).

Nabuchodonosor, según afirma Benedetto Soldati,[1] posiblemente se ha perdido sin remedio. Debió haber sido una tragedia en cinco actos, y algún éxito debió de haber alcanzado, pues se representó tres veces, según dice Emanuel Aguilera en "Stephanus autem Tuccius dedit tragoediam, quam Nabuchodonosor inscripsit, quae iterum ac tertio, magno civium concursu et voluptate spectata est."[2]

Goliath, tragedia escrita en cinco actos, única de las de Tucci que sigue a Séneca como modelo en cuanto a la métrica (trímetros yámbicos) y a los coros líricos. Fue representada en Mesina en 1563 y parece que fue bien acogida. El mismo Aguilera dice: "IV nonas Octobres scholae renovantur, deditque Stephanus Tuccius tragoediam latinam, quam Goliath appellavit. Spectavit lubentissime Prorex cum principibus Civitatis, et pleraque

---

[1] Benedetto Soldati, *Il Collegio Mamertino e le origini del teatro gesuitico* (Torino, 1908), 72.

[2] Emanuel Aguilera, *Provinciae Siculae Societatis Jesu ortus et res gestae ab anno 1546 ad annum* 1611 (Palermo, 1737), 1:156.

nobilitate."[3] Queda copia de ella en el manuscrito 113 (Fondo Vecchio) de la Biblioteca Universitaria de Mesina.

De la *Iuditha* hablaré después de que me refiera a las otras tres piezas de Tucci, cuyos asuntos tocan el *Nuevo Testamento.* También ellas son tres: *Christus nascens* (1566 o 67), *Christus patiens* (1568) y *Christus iudex* o *De extremo mundi iudicio* (1569). Las dos primeras están sacadas de los *Evangelios*, concretamente de los episodios que ven a la vida de Cristo: en su nacimiento la primera, y en su pasión y muerte la segunda. La tercera y última aborda episodios del *Apocalipsis*, y viene a ser la consecuencia de que Cristo es hijo de Dios y Dios mismo, y por tanto habrá de juzgar a quienes, olvidándolo en la tierra, no creyeron ni en él ni en su doctrina.

Christus nascens, égloga o *diálogo*, escrita en un solo acto, que posiblemente se representó en Mesina. De ella quedan dos copias: una en el manuscrito 113, ya dicho, de la Biblioteca Universitaria de Mesina, y otra en el manuscrito 24 (Fondo Gesuitico) de la Biblioteca Nazionale de Roma.

Christus patiens, tragedia escrita en cinco actos y en versos hexámetros, con un prólogo en dísticos y coros de variados metros. Fue representada en Mesina y luego en Roma, como preludio al éxito singular que alcanzó el *Christus iudex.* De ella quedan también dos copias en la Biblioteca Universitaria de Mesina (Fondo Vecchio), una en el manuscrito 113 y otra (incompleta) en el 237.

Christus iudex, tragedia escrita en cinco actos y en versos hexámetros, con un prólogo en dísticos, que posteriormente le fue cambiado por trímetros yámbicos, y coros de variados metros. Fue representada por primera vez en Mesina, y pronto alcanzó un verdadero éxito teatral. Aguilera dice que "eam deinde tanto plausu excepit orbis terrarum, ut vix ulla sit praeclara Europae civitas, in qua non fuerit exhibita, magno semper fletu atque terrore spectantium."[4] A sus múltiples representaciones siguieron, diez años después, dos traducciones al italiano (1584, 1596), una al ilirio y una más al polaco. Después de un siglo de haber sido compuesta y tantas veces representada, alcanzó, si no más, dos seguras ediciones (Roma, 1673 y Munich, 1698). A su éxito se debe sin duda también que de ella quedan varias copias manuscritas: cinco hasta hoy seguras son conocidas: cuatro en las Bibliotecas de Italia (dos en la Nazionale de Roma–Fondo Gesuitico, manuscritos 80 y 223–una en la Universitaria de Mesina–Fondo Vecchio, manuscrito 113–y otra más en la Ambrosiana de Milán) y una en Francia (París, Archivos de la Provincia).

[3] Ibid., 157.
[4] Ibid., 178.

Paso ahora a ocuparme de la *Iuditha*, tragedia que, después del *Christus iudex*, parece ser la más importante de las escritas por Tucci. Y es importante como lo comprueban los elogios que le otorgan tanto Soldati[5] como Gnerghi[6], quienes dicen que aquélla tiene un grado mayor de excelencia por la belleza de su lenguaje, por la eficaz factura de sus versos y por un no sé qué de sentido y sincero. Y en verdad ella misma conlleva esa importancia, ya que por ser importante llegó a representarse nueve veces (cuatro el mismo año de su estreno, 1564, en Mesina) como asegura Aguilera: "Stephanus interea Tuccius, egregius tragoediarum artifex, redeuntibus Octobri mense studiis, Iuditham spectandam quartum exhibuit, quod novo semper spectandi studio cives reposcerent."[7] Allí mismo en 1565, 1566 y 1579; en Palermo, 1567 y en Roma, 1577; por importante también ha quedado en tres copias manuscritas (manuscrito 24—hojas 95-117r—del Fondo Gesuitico de la Biblioteca Nazionale de Roma, quizá el más antiguo; manuscrito 113—páginas 1-30—del Fondo Vecchio de la Biblioteca Universitaria de Mesina, y manuscrito 1631—hojas 97-117v—del Departamento de Libros Raros y Curiosos de la Biblioteca Nacional de México); por importante tuvo una edición, la cual se basó principalmente en el manuscrito 113, que se conserva en la Biblioteca Universitaria de Mesina,[8] y finalmente por importante también tuvo una traducción al italiano, hecha por Giovanni Scarfi sobre el texto editado (Mesina, 1926).

Especialmente para nosotros los mexicanos, la *Iuditha* adquiere además una doble significación llamémosla cultural o sentimental, pues, como acabo de informar, una de las tres copias conservadas de esta tragedia está guardada en los acervos de nuestra Biblioteca Nacional. Tal llegó acá para ser representada privadamente en alguno de los colegios de la Compañía de Jesús en la capital de la Nueva España. Tal vez fue enviada Vincenzo Lanuchi, coetáneo conterráneo de Tucci, tal vez sólo llegara para servir de modelo a quienes proyectaran componer alguna tragedia latina en México, cosa que hasta hoy, según parece, no se logró concretar.

Debido a todas estas circunstancias y considerando que siempre es bueno en la investigación dejar un tiempo el ámbito nacional y explorar en el exterior para dar a conocer nuestras preseas literarias y también para adquirir los conocimientos que más tarde sean útiles al plantea-

5 Soldati, op. cit., 74.

6 Gualtiero Gnerghi, *Il teatro gesuitico ne' suoi primordi a Roma* (Roma, 1907), 103-4.

7 Aguilera, op. cit., 166.

8 Soldati, op. cit., 122-70.

miento de un nivel standard en las investigaciones nacionales, yo me decidí a estudiar dicha obra, estudio del que quiero dar aquí una breve noticia.

Luego que tuve a mano tanto las copias de los tres manuscritos de la *Iuditha* como la edición de Soldati, la traduccion de Scarfi y demás documentación y bibliografía que recogí en Roma (1983), me di a preparar una edición cuidada del texto latino, confrontando para ello los manuscritos y el impreso. Sobre esta edición efectué mi traducción al español. Adicioné ambas labores con un extenso estudio introductorio, verdadero análisis o disección de la tragedia, que va desde la biografía y bibliografía del autor hasta el examen riguroso de los manuscritos en su integridad, antigüedad y la primacía que ostenta el 24 (por mí signado A) guardado en la Biblioteca Nazionale de Roma.

La introducción, por tanto, aborda principalmente estas cuestiones: hipótesis de cómo, cuándo y para qué llegó el manuscrito de la *Iuditha* a la Nueva España y cuál fue su peregrinaje hasta quedar guardado en nuestra Biblioteca Nacional; el aspecto formal de la tragedia: actos, escenas, personajes y la métrica utilizada, en la cual se encuentran hexámetros, dísticos, adónicos, endecasílabos y estrofas sáficas, trímetros yámbicos y dactílicos, díametros yámbicos y anapésticos, asclepiadeos, endecasílabos alcaicos y glicónicos; la comparación en cuanto al contenido con el libro bíblico "Judith" y el análisis de los motivos humanos de los personajes. Finalmente estudio el léxico y las reminiscencias presentes en la obra.

Si, en medio de la íntima y general mediocridad que Silvio D'Amico[9] y Gnerghi[10] atribuyen al llamado "Teatro jesuítico," la *Iuditha* logró destacar (aunque quizá contenga algunos de los mismos defectos con que se censura a dicho teatro), ciertamente ella debe de tener una verdadera importancia y—¿por qué no?—un verdadero mérito, cualidades que ya antes le atribuí y le concluí por sus multiples representaciones, sus manuscritos existentes y la edición y traducción que precedieron mi esfuerzo. Con todo, como a nadie le gusta hablar sólo de generalidades y quedarse en ellas, desearía pronto poder examinar, y así dar un juicio más objetivo, dos tragedias, compuestas con el nombre de la heroina hebrea, que andan por ahí. Me refiero a *Judith*, obra debida al literato astigiano Federico della Valle, quien floreció a fines del siglo XVI y principios del XVII, y a

---

[9] Silvio d'Amico, *Historia del teatro dramático*, trans. J. R. Wilcock (Buenos Aires, 1954) vol. 2, chap. 11.

[10] Gnerghi, loc. cit.

la *Iudithis tragoedia tertia anno 1585*, de que nos dio noticia el maestro Ignacio Osorio, aquí presente; en "Doce poemas neolatinos de fines del siglo XVI novohispano."[11]

Universidad Nacional Autónoma de México

[11] Ignacio Osorio "Doce poetas neolatinos de fines del siglo XVI novohispano," in *Nova Tellus* 1 (1983): 172, n. 5.

La Enseñanza del Latin a los Indios

IGNACIO OSORIO-ROMERO

La Evangelizacion de los Indios en Latin

La razón fundamental que movilizó al gran número de religiosos que se trasladaron a las regiones recién descubiertas y que justificó a los civiles el apoderamiento, *manu militari*, de los territorios de los indígenas, fue el celo por propagar la doctrina cristiana y lograr la conversión de los indios. Por ello, una vez conquistada Tenochtitlán, Cortés puso tanto empeño en que vinieran a esta tierra frailes que tomaron sobre sus hombros la enorme tarea de la evangelización. Gracias a sus diligencias llegaron el mes de mayo de 1524 los primeros doce franciscanos quienes, al lado de los pocos curas y frailes que habían arribado con anterioridad, se dieron a la tarea de adoctrinar a los indígenas.

Sin embargo, en los principios los frailes "carecían de lenguaje" por no saber la lengua de los indios ni tener intérpretes. No por ello pararon; con la ayuda de Cortés movilizaron a los indios para levantar conventos y junto a ellos capillas, casas y salas donde reunieron a los niños y, en especial, a los hijos de los principales, y en latín les enseñaron el signarse y santiguarse, rezar el *Pater noster*, el *Ave María, Credo* y *Salve Regina*, y para que mejor lo memorizaran acomodaron "todo cantado de un canto muy llano y gracioso."

Posteriormente reunieron a los adultos congregándolos por barrios o parroquias en patios grandes que estaban junto a las casas y ahí les comenzaron a tomar de coro los rudimentos de las cristiandad "haciéndoles decir las oraciones en latín."

Los tropiezos que al principio sufrieron los frailes fueron, sin duda, muchos, pero también se puso a prueba su ingenio.

Recurrieron a muchos métodos mnemotécnicos para que los indígenas conservaran las palabras latinas que les enseñaban. Uno de ellos fue particularmente ingenioso: los indios adecuaron las palabras latinas al sonido más cercano de las palabras nahuas; éstas, a su vez, las trasladaron a la escritura jeroglífica. Escribieron curiosas tiras de papel que, a su modo, representaban los fonemas latinos de la doctrina cristiana.

Otros buscaron otro modo (a mi parecer muy dificultoso, aunque curioso), y era aplicar las palabras que en su lengua conformaran y frisan algo en la pronunciación con las latinas, poníanlas en un papel, por su orden, no las palabras escritas y formados con letras sino el significado de ellas; porque ellos no tenían otras letras, sino pinturas, y así se entendían por caracteres; esto será fácil de entender por ejemplo: El vocablo que ellos tienen que más tira a la pronunciación de *Pater* es *pantli*, que significa una como banderita que significa *pantli* y en ella dicen *Pater.* Para la segunda que dice *Noster,* el vocablo que ellos tienen más parecido a esta pronunciación es *nuchtli,* que es el nombre de lo que los nuestros llaman tuna y en España higo de Indias, pues para acordarse del vocablo *Noster,* pintan consecutivamente tras de la banderita, una tuna, que ellos llaman *nuchtli*; y de esta manera van siguiendo hasta acabar su oración; y por semejante manera hallan otros semejantes caracteres y modos por donde ellos se entendían para hacer memoria de lo que habían de tomar de coro. Y esto lo practicaban dos veces al día, dos horas cada vez y éstas con un intervalo de siete horas.

Sin embargo toda la doctrina así enseñada rindió poco fruto, pues ni los indios entendían lo que decían, ni se apartaban de sus costumbres y ritos, ni, menos, los frailes podían reprenderles por no saber su lengua; vistos estos resultados los frailes pronto dejaron de evangelizar en latín a los indios.

La Enseñanza del Latin a los Indios

Frustrado el primer intento de evangelización y resueltos, en cambio, los problemas de comunicación gracias al celo de los frailes quienes rápidamente aprendieron las lenguas indígenas, el peso del apostolado abrumó prontamente a los pocos misioneros; la necesidad les indujo, pues, a examinar la posibilidad de que los hijos de los principales de la tierra ingresaran a la enseñanza superior e, incluso, accedieran al sacerdocio, con la mira de servirse de ellos para explicar la doctrina en sus comunidades. El Virrey don Antonio de Mendoza escribía sobre esto al Emperador: "si verdadera cristianadad ha de haber en esta gente ésta ha de ser la puerta, y han de aprovechar más que cuantos religiosos hay en la tierra."

La preocupación por las escuelas para los niños indígenas que durante un largo tiempo mantuvo la Orden de San Francisco se refleja constantemente en sus escritos; nada más claro sobre el asunto que la siguiente cita escrita por fray Juan de Zumárraga al Emperador: "la cosa en que mi pensamiento más se ocupa y mi voluntad más se inclina y pelean con mis pocas fuerzas, es que en esta cuidad y en cada obispado haya un colegio de indios muchachos que aprendan gramática a lo menos" y, puesto que en muchas partes no era posible fundar el colegio para la gramática, ésta se enseñaba en los conventos. Por ello en la Real Cédula de 1536 dirigida al Obispo autorizando la fundación del Colegio de Santiago Tlatelolco, el Rey le responde: "Mucho he holgado de lo que decís, que yendo a examinar la inteligencia de los niños hijos de los naturales de esa tierra, *a quienes enseñan gramática en los monasterios*, hallasteís muchos de gran habilidad y viveza de ingenio y memoria aventajada."

El latín que se enseñaba en la mayor parte de estos monasterios era, sin embargo, un latín litúrgico que capacitaba a los alumnos para auxiliar en las funciones religiosas. A su aprendizaje ingresaban los hijos de los principales, pues la educación impartida a los indígenas no era uniforme. Los hijos de los macehuales, esto es, los indios de común, "solamente aprendan la doctrina cristiana y luego en sabiéndola, comiencen desde muchachos a seguir oficios y ejercicios de sus padres para sustentarse a sí mismos y ayudar a su república," los hijos de los principales, en cambio "que se habiliten para el regimiento de sus pueblos y para el servicio de las iglesias."

Es incierto el año en que fray Pedro de Gante fundó el primer colegio para indígenas. Se encontraba ubicado en la capilla de San José detrás de la iglesia del convento de San Francisco de la Ciudad de México. Aquí fray Pedro reunió poco después de 1527 hasta mil niños indígenas de diversas provincias a los que enseñaba a leer y escribir, cantar, tañer instrumentos de iglesia y la doctrina cristiana. Especializaba, igualmente, a los indígenas en diversos oficios. Poco después, añadió el estudio del latín lo cual debió suceder aproximadamente el año de 1530.

En 1533 el Oidor don Sebastían Ramírez de Fuenleal, informa al Emperador que el promovió este estudio: "con los religiosos de la Orden de San Francisco—escribe Fuenleal—he procurado que enseñen gramática, romanzada en lengua mexicana, a los naturales y pareciéndoles bién, nombraron un religioso, para que en ello entendiese, el cual la enseña y muéstranse tan hábiles y capaces que hacen gran ventaja a los españoles."

Su primer profesor fue fray Arnaldo de Bassacio, originario de Aquitania al igual que fray Maturino Gilberti, el autor de la primera gramática latina impresa en Nueva España. La enseñanza de Bassacio se hacía "romanzada en lengua mexicana" y no se detuvo, de acuerdo a los testimonios, en los rudimentos de la gramática sino que, según el proyecto de Fuenleal expresado al Emperador, "sabida alguna gramática y entendiéndola, serán menester personas que les lean buena latinidad y oratoria y por eso bastará que los maestros sean instruidos en la lengua latina aunque no sean frailes naguatatos ni sepan su lengua, pues en latín les han de leer y adoctrinar."

El mismo Fuenleal, para interesar más al Emperador en el proyecto, le señala que los alumnos se mostraban tan hábiles y capaces que hacían gran ventaja a los españoles y que de 1533, fecha de la carta, a 1535 habría cerca de cincuenta indios que sabrían y enseñarían la lengua latina.

El magnífico fruto rendido por esta experiencia movió, a los frailes, al obispo Zumárraga, al Virrey Mendoza y al Oidor Fuenleal a emprender una obra de mayor envergadura y proporciones en cuanto a la enseñanza de los indios se refiere. Así fue como surgió el colegio de Santa Cruz de Tlateloleo a donde pasaron los colegiales más aventajados de San José.

Este centro de educación superior, también llamado el colegio de los gramáticos indios, tuvo por objetivo dotar a los indígenas de un colegio especial donde pudieran ampliar sus estudios y perfeccionarse en la religión, la lectura, la escritura, la gramática latina, la retórica, la filosofía, la música y la medicina mexicana. Los idiomas utilizados para la enseñanza debían ser el latín y el náhuatl.

A los principios, según refiere Torquemada, no fue poco el trabajo que enfrentaron los maestros y discípulos. El caso fue que como la lengua náhuatl no había tratado temas de gramática, y menos de la latina, los frailes no encontraban términos adecuados para explicar los conceptos gramaticales. Tuvieron, pues, tanto frailes como indios, un inicial período de desmayo y desánimo. Sin embargo, pronto encontraron "terminos de nuevo compuestos" con que dieron a entender fácilmente las reglas y se inició un general aprovechamiento.

Muchos testimonios nos quedan tanto de partidarios del proyecto como de opositores sobre el aprovechamiento que los indios hicieron en la lengua latina.

Motolinía dice que "hay muchos de ellos buenos gramáticos y que componen oraciones largas y bien autorizadas y versos hexámetros y pentámetros"; Torquemada escribe que a los "pocos años, salieron tan buenos latinos que hacían y componían versos muy medidos y largas y congruas oraciones, en presencia de los Virreyes y de los prelados eclesiásticos"; en la carta que a favor de los indios dirigió al Papa Paulo III fray Julián Garcés, obispo de Tlaxcala, le decía que los niños indios tenían tanta facilidad de ingenio que comparados los que se dedicaban a la lengua latina con los niños españoles, no sólo no salían menos aprovechados que ellos sino que, incluso, escribían mejor en latín y romance. Uno de los opositores, el escribano Jerónimo López, informa al Emperador que los colegiales "diéronse tanto a ello y con tanta solicitud que había muchachos, y hay de cada día más, que hablan tan elegante latín como Tulio" y que espanta ver cómo escriben en latín cartas y coloquios.

De las generaciones de indios latinistas formadas en el colegio resaltan algunos nombres conservados por los cronistas.

Pablo Nazareo tradujo al náhuatl los evangelios y las epistolas y conservamos, escritas de su propia mano, tres cartas latinas dirigidas al rey en las que defiende sus derechos. La carta tercera tiene la fecha de 1565; las dos primeras son del año 1556. Las tres cartas revelan un manejo fluido de la lengua latina; pero la estructura y giros corresponden al lenguaje cotidianamente usado en la escuela: abundan términos medievales, construcciones hispánicas y uso familiar de la lengua. Es decir, Nazareo escribe el latín escolástico. Estas cartas, por otra parte, son muy atrayentes a causa de los neologismos que del náhuatl incorpora a la lengua latina.

A Francisco de la Cruz y a Juan Badiano, ambos alumnos del colegio de Santa Cruz, debemos uno de los documentos más importantes sobre la medicina y la herbolaria indígena. El primero escribió en náhuatl y el segundo tradujo al latín el tratado *Libellus de medicinalibus indorum herbis*. Su fecha es 1552, año en que Badiano realizó la traducción latina.

El libro permaneció durante varios siglos inédito y custodiado por la Biblioteca Vaticana en Roma, bajo la sigla *Codex Barberini, Latinus 241*, aunque era conocido como el Códice Cruz–Badiano; fue publicado por vez primera el año de 1940. Naturalmente la importancia de esta obra se encuentra en la medicina; pero en la historia de la filología también tiene relevancia.

La razón primera se refiere al elegante estilo latino de Badiano que resalta, especialmente, en el prólogo y en el epílogo.

La segunda razón es el color exótico que produce en el texto el empleo de las palabras náhuas; dos años después en 1554, Francisco Cervantes de Salazar recurrirá al mismo procedimiento para describir los productos nativos de América que se venden en el mercado:

> Semina item, variae quoque virtutis, exposita sunt: qualia sunt *chia, guahtli*; herbarumque et radicum prostrant mille genera, nam *iztacpatli* a phlegmate purgant; *tlalcacaguatl* et *izticpatli* a febri liberant; *culuzizicaztli* capitis gravedinem levat; *ololiuhqui* ulcera et latentia vulnera sanat.

En Cervantes, sin embargo, el empleo de tales palabras no logra adquirir el mestizaje que emana de los textos de Badiano. Véase el inicio del capítulo tercero en que trata de la infección del oído, de la sordera y obstrucción.

> Putrescentibus auribus radix *maçayelli*, herbae *xoxouhquipahtli* semen, aliquot *tlaquilin* folia cum salis mica in aqua calefacta instillata commodant plurimum. Et sub auriculis duarum arbuscularum frondes tritae illinantur. Arbusculae vocantur *toloau* et *tlapahtl.* Lapides pretiosi *tetlahuitl, tlahcalhuatzin, eztetl, xoxouhqui chalchiuitl* cum arboris *tlatlanquaye* frondibus tritis in calefacta aqua attriti instillatique conclusas aures adaperiunt.

Antonio Valeriano leyó gramática latina y náhuatl en el colegio; según fray Juan Bautista, "fue uno de los mejores latinos y retóricos que de él salieron ... y fue tan gran latino que hablaba *ex tempore* (aun en los últimos años de su vejez) con tanta propiedad y elegancia, que parecía un Cicerón o Quintiliano." Torquemada dice que entre otras muchas cosas que le dió de sus muchos trabajos tanto de lengua latina como de traducción mexicana, estuvo un Catón traducido "cosa cierto muy para estimar, el cual (si Dios place) se imprimirá en su nombre." Por desgracia nunca se imprimió. Conservamos, en cambio, una pequeña carta latina de su mano.

Diego Adriano, natural de Tlatelolco, impresor, "fue muy gran latino" que traducía cualquier cosa del latín en mexicano con mucha propiedad; tenía tan buena elección y era tan acertado, que traducía hartos cuadernos sin echar un sólo borrón ni enmendar cosa."

Se siguen muchos otros nombres de los cuales los cronistas nos alaban, de manera parecida, su pericia en la lengua latina. Algunos de estos nombres son Francisco Bautista de Contreras, Esteban Bravo, Juan Gerardo y Hernando de Rivas.

La labor de estos indios, en cuanto a la conservación de las antigüedades mexicanas se refiere, es muy importante porque sin su concurso la labor de evangelización habría sido, por lo menos, mucho más ardua. Fray Bernardino de Sahagún lo constata:

> Si sermones y apostillas y doctrinas se han hecho en la lengua indiana, que pueden parecer y sean limpios de toda heregía, son precisamente los que con ellos se han compuesto, y ellos por ser entendidos en la lengua latina nos dan a entender las propiedades de los vocablos y las propiedades de su manera de hablar y las incongruencias que hablamos en los sermones, o las que decimos en las doctrinas; ellos nos las enmiendan y cualquier cosa que se haya de convertir en su lengua, si no va con ellos examinada, no puede ir

sin defecto, ni escribir congruentemente en la lengua latina, ni en romance, ni en su lengua.

En 1570 Juan de Ovando emite un juicio importante sobre estos indios:

> Aunque en las Artes y Teología no se han mostrado (los indios) más de para aprovecharse a sí mismos, a lo menos salieron tan buenos latinos, que han leído la gramática muchos años, así en el mismo colegio a los indios, como en otras partes a los religiosos de todas las órdenes.

La época en que se formó esta generación, la década de los cuarentas, sin duda fue la mejor del colegio de Santa Cruz de Tlatelolco. El comercio intelectual entre frailes y colegiales fue intenso y fructífero. Los religiosos introducían a los indios a la cultura occidental y estos pagaban especializándoles en las lenguas de la tierra asi como adentrándoles en sus usos, costumbres e historias. Sus mismos detractores se vieron obligados a reconocer la intensa vida intelectual del colegio. No otra cosa se trasluce de cartas como la de Jerónimo López que escribe, alarmado, al Rey:

> Ha venido esto en tanto crecimiento que es cosa de admirar ver los que escriben en latín, cartas, coloquios, y lo que dicen: que habrá ocho días que vino a esta posada un clérigo a decir misa, y me dijo que había ido al colegio a lo ver, e que le cercaron doscientos estudiantes, e que estando platicando con él le hicieron preguntas de la Sagrada Escritura cerca de la fe, que salió admirado y tapado de oídos y dijo, que aquel era el infierno, y los que estaban en él discípulos de Satanás.

Al inicio hemos señalado que hubo diversos pareceres sobre enseñarles lengua latina a los indios; sin embargo, cuando vieron los logros, muchos españoles, seglares y eclesiásticos, se alarmaron; y, todavía más, cuando entendieron que la empresa aventajaba y que los indios iban a más, empezaron, entonces, a contradecirle y combatirle con mayor empeño.

Esta oposición se conjugó con otras circunstancias para destruir al Colegio. Especialmente la peste de 1545 que se abatió sobre los mejores gramáticos del colegio; también, al poco tiempo, los franciscanos abandonaran la dirección a los indios ya formados. Estas circunstancias detuvieron el progreso de este singular experimento.

El hecho causó una honda herida en los indios. En 1584 los pocos colegiales que quedaban protestaron ante el Comisario de los franciscanos, fray Alonso Ponce, satirizando, con dolorosa ironía, los argumentos que el español lanzaba contra ellos.

Un estudiante le dió la bienvenida al fraile en latín y la tradujo en seguida al castellano. En seguida, su "maestro" que debía ser religioso, dijo al Padre Comisario que perdonase a los alumnos que no eran más que papagayos o urracas que decían lo que habían aprendido sin entenderlo. Otro estudiante tomó, entonces, la palabra, en latín primero y luego en castellano y reconoció que muchos en efecto, así los juzgaban, "tanquam picae et psittaci"; que en verdad su habilidad era muy flaca; pero, agregó, que por eso tenían necesidad de ser más ayudados. A esto salió un español y comenzó a decir que la ayuda a los indios era inútil, pues al fin terminaban en borrachos y desagradecidos como los demás. A esto replicó el maestro que los indios eran virtuosos y dados al estudio; pero su mala fama es esparcida por los españoles a quienes sólo interesa explotar el trabajo del indio y combate por tanto cualquier medida que lo arrebate de su servicio.

Con todas estas contradicciones poco a poco fue cesado el primitivo calor y espíritu de los frailes y sus protectores hasta dejar de enseñar latín a los indios.

En la primera década del siglo XVII, el colegio sólo albergaba pocos niños del pueblo de Tlatelolco los cuales sólo aprendían a leer y escribir y las buenas costumbres.

Universidad Nacional Autónoma de Mexico

INDEX NOMINUM

A selective index of the more significant references. Names of modern scholars have not been included.

INDEX RERUM

A selective index of the more significant subject references.

mrts

medieval & renaissance texts & studies
is the publishing program of the
Center for Medieval and Early Renaissance Studies
at the State University of New York at Binghamton.

mrts emphasizes books that are needed —
texts, translations, and major research tools.

mrts aims to publish the highest quality scholarship
in attractive and durable format at modest cost.